HORNGREN'S
COST ACCOUNTING

A MANAGERIAL EMPHASIS

HORNGREN'S

DATAR
Harvard University

RAJAN
Stanford University

BEAUBIEN
Dalhousie University

COST ACCOUNTING

A MANAGERIAL EMPHASIS

8TH CANADIAN EDITION

Pearson

VICE PRESIDENT, EDITORIAL: Anne Williams
ACQUISITION EDITOR: Keara Emmett
MARKETING MANAGER: Spencer Snell
CONTENT MANAGER: Emily Dill
PROJECT MANAGER: Pippa Kennard
CONTENT DEVELOPER: Suzanne Simpson Millar
MEDIA DEVELOPER: Olga Avdyeyeva
PRODUCTION SERVICES: Cenveo® Publisher Services

PERMISSIONS PROJECT MANAGER: Joanne Tang
PHOTO PERMISSIONS RESEARCHER: Integra Publishing Services
TEXT PERMISSIONS RESEARCHER: Integra Publishing Services
INTERIOR DESIGNER: Anthony Leung
COVER DESIGNER: Anthony Leung
COVER IMAGE: © Songquan Deng / Shutterstock
VICE-PRESIDENT, CROSS MEDIA AND PUBLISHING SERVICES: Gary Bennett

Pearson Canada Inc., 26 Prince Andrew Place, North York, Ontario M3C 2H4.

978-0-13-445373-6

10 9 8 7 6 5 4 3

Library and Archives Canada Cataloguing in Publication

Datar, Srikant M., author
        Horngren's Cost accounting : a managerial emphasis
/ Datar (Harvard University), Rajan (Stanford University), Beaubien
(Dalhousie University).—Eighth Canadian edition.

Includes index.
ISBN 978-0-13-445373-6 (hardcover)

        1. Cost accounting—Textbooks. 2. Textbooks. I. Rajan, Madhav
V., author II. Beaubien, Louis A. (Louis Alain), author III. Horngren,
Charles T., 1926- . Cost accounting. IV. Title. V. Title: Cost accounting.

HF5686.C8D38 2018   658.15'11   C2017-903781-1

Brief Contents

Table of Contents

Preface

Cost Accounting

Studying cost accounting is one of the best business investments a student can make. Success in any organization—from the smallest store to the largest multinational corporation—requires the use of cost accounting concepts and practices. Cost accounting provides key data to managers for decision making, planning and controlling, costing products and services, and even managing customer relationships.

This text focuses on how cost accounting helps managers make better decisions, as cost accountants are integral members of an organization's decision-making team. In order to emphasize this prominence in decision making, we focus on basic concepts, analyses, uses, and procedures instead of on procedures alone. It is important to recognize cost accounting as a managerial tool for business strategy and implementation. We also prepare students for the rewards and challenges they will face in professional cost accounting today and tomorrow. For example, we emphasize the development of analytical skills and tools, such as Excel, to leverage available information technology, an evolving approach to sustainability, and the values and behaviours that make cost accountants effective in the workplace.

New to This Edition
Deeper Consideration of Global Issues

Businesses today integrate into an increasingly global ecosystem, including supply chains, product markets, and the market for managerial talent, and have become more international in their outlook. To illustrate this, we incorporate global considerations into many of the chapters. For example, the challenges of budgeting in multinational companies, issues in evaluating the performance of divisions located in different countries, and the importance of transfer pricing in minimizing the tax burden faced by multinational companies are discussions (with new examples) of management accounting applications in companies drawn from international settings.

Greater Emphasis on Sustainability

This edition places significant emphasis on sustainability as one of the critical managerial challenges of the coming decades. Many managers are promoting the development and implementation of strategies to achieve long-term financial, social, and environmental performance as key imperatives. We highlight this early in the text and maintain the focus through chapter "Sustainability in Action" examples that show the impact of effective cost accounting and decision making in organizations today.

Selected Chapter-by-Chapter Content Changes

Thank you for your continued support of Cost Accounting. *In every new edition, we strive to improve this text.*

Chapter 1 includes greater discussion of sustainability and innovation and why these issues have become increasingly critical for managers. We discuss the challenges of planning and control for innovation and sustainability and how companies use these systems to manage these activities. We continue to emphasize the importance of ethics, values, and behaviours in improving the quality of financial reporting.

Chapter 2 has been updated to make it easier for students to understand core cost concepts and to provide a framework for how cost accounting and cost management help managers make decisions. We have added more material on environmental costs to explain how and why these costs may be missed in costing systems.

Chapter 3 now includes greater managerial content, using examples from real companies to illustrate the value of cost–volume–profit analysis in managerial decision making. This aligns with revisions in **Chapter 4** that discuss adjusting normal costs to actual costs using end-of-accounting-year adjustments for different contexts. The chapter also develops the criteria for allocating costs and relates them to real examples to highlight why managers need allocated cost information to make decisions.

Chapter 5 has additional content on product undercosting and overcosting and refining a costing system. We integrate the discussion of behavioural considerations in implementing activity-based costing with the technical material in the chapter.

Chapter 6 presents material on innovation and development costs in the annual budget and the revenues earned in that year. The chapter describes ways to delink innovation from current-year operational performance by developing measures to monitor the success of innovation efforts. We also elaborate on tradeoffs managers must make when choosing different organization structures. This is built upon in both **Chapters 7** and **8** as we develop a revised comprehensive summary of the variances.

Chapter 9 retains the simplified two-period integrated example of capacity choice. There is greater emphasis on linking the impact of the choice of capacity concept to recent changes in financial reporting and tax requirements.

Chapters 10 and **11** are a practical guide to various cost estimation techniques and the determination of the relevance of costs. New content is provided on the costs of quality and the impact of time on the costing and decision-making process. Many revisions are related to the reorganization of the text in the seventh edition.

Chapter 12 focuses on pricing decisions in the long- and short-term contexts, and builds on material in Chapters 10 and 11 to expand understanding of opportunity and relevant costs in how a pricing decision is made.

Chapter 13 is focused on the application in financial, operational, and sustainability decision making. Revisions in this chapter focus on relating concepts to practical examples and other ideas throughout the text.

Chapter 14 has been revised to improve exposition on a variety of concepts in costing, building on changes to **Chapter 15**, which has been updated to reflect the continuing evolution of ASPE/IFRS with regard to joint cost allocations. The chapter provides a discussion of the rationale for joint-cost allocation and the merits and demerits of various joint-cost allocation methods.

Chapter 16 discusses revenue allocation methods and customer profitability. The exhibits for revenue allocation have been summarized to allow for easier comparison of the methods. The discussion around revenue variance analysis is now focused on the contribution margin approach.

Chapters 17 and **18** provide a managerial lens on the estimation of equivalent units and the choice between the FIFO and weighted-average costing methods, both in the chapter content and in new vignettes and real-world examples. The exhibits have been reformatted to make clear how various components are added to get the total costs. **Chapter 18** emphasizes, with illustrative examples, the theme of striving for zero waste and a sustainable environment.

Chapter 19 provides revised content to examine traditional and just-in-time purchasing. The focus remains on developing an effective costing strategy for inventory management.

Chapter 20 focuses on the role of capital budgeting in supporting sustainable long-term projects. The new opening vignette looks at the financing of residential solar panels. The integrated example deals with various examples throughout the chapter and in the new "Concepts in Action" illustrate how companies incorporate sustainability in their capital budgeting decisions.

Chapter 21 has been revised to address the most recent developments in the controversial use of transfer prices for tax minimization by multinational corporations, with several real-world examples. The revision also highlights the changing regulatory environment across the world and provides updated information on the use of tools such as advance pricing agreements.

Chapter 22 updates include the responsibility of executives and boards of directors for corporate governance. This chapter reviews the most recent legislation in Canada, the United States, and the European Union and how it impacts both executive compensation and corporate governance.

Features

- **Learning objectives** are the important concepts in each chapter. Expressed in everyday language, these are also aligned with the CPA Competency Map to ensure the most coverage possible. Learning objectives are mapped throughout the chapter, end-of-chapter material, MyLab Accounting, and instructor resources.
- **Opening vignettes.** Each chapter opens with a vignette on a real company situation. The vignettes engage the reader in a business situation or dilemma, illustrating why and how the concepts in the chapter are relevant in business.
- **CPA Competencies.** We have increased the focus on covering the competencies outlined in the CPA Competency Map and Knowledge Supplement in the eighth edition. Each chapter now includes a list of professional competencies and levels covered in that chapter. These features will allow students and faculty interested in CPA designation to become familiar with the Competency Map and the material covered in the book.
- **Excel exhibits** give students a glimpse into the real-world presentation of accounting, financial statements, and schedules designed to mimic how they would look in Excel.
- **"In Action" boxes.** Found in every chapter are **"Concepts in Action"** boxes that cover real-world cost accounting issues across a variety of industries, including defense contracting, entertainment, manufacturing, retailing, and sports. We also include new **"Sustainability in Action"** boxes to show how cost accountants in real-world situations use sustainability strategies to gain competitive advantage for their organizations.
- **Decision Points** appear at the end of the chapter in a question-and-answer format summarizing the chapter's learning objectives. Each point presents a key question, and the guidelines are the answer to that question.

Practice and Assessment

- **Try It!** Interactive questions are found throughout the chapter and provide students the opportunity to apply the concept they just learned. Solutions to Try It! questions are provided at the end of the chapter. Select **Try It!** questions are available on MyLab Accounting for extra practice.
- **Pulling It All Together** is a problem for self-study appearing at the end of each chapter. A fully worked solution is provided directly after it. This helps students check their understanding of chapter topics.
- **Terms to Learn** provide accounting terms discussed in that chapter, along with a page reference in the chapter where a student can find its definition. Definitions are also provided in the Glossary.

Assignment Material

This includes **Short-Answer Questions, Exercises, Problems, Collaborative Learning Cases,** and **Mini-Cases.**
- **Short-answer questions** test students' understanding of single topics.
- **Exercises, Problems,** and **Cases** provide multitopic questions. All are tagged with the learning objective(s) being tested, and an icon identifies if that exercise is also available in MyLab Accounting.
- In some cases, **Excel templates** are available for an exercise, and these, too, are indicated by an icon.
- Problems also include **Check figures** to allow students to see their progress at a set point during their completion.

Instructor Resources

These instructor supplements are available for download from a password-protected section of Pearson Canada's online catalogue (www.pearson.com). Navigate to your book's catalogue page to view a list of available supplements. Speak to your local Pearson sales representative for details and access.

- **Instructor's Solutions Manual.** The solutions manual provides instructors with a complete set of solutions to all the end-of-chapter material in this text. New to the eighth Canadian edition, an icon now shows which exercises/problems are also available on MyLab Accounting.

- **Computerized Test Bank.** Pearson's computerized test banks allow instructors to filter and select questions to create quizzes, tests, or homework. The more than 2,000 exercises and problems can be filtered by difficulty, taxonomy, Learning Objectives, and CPA competencies. These questions are also available in Microsoft Word format. Instructors can revise questions or add their own.

- **PowerPoint Presentations.** These presentations offer helpful graphics that illustrate key figures and concepts form the text, chapter outlines, and examples.

- **Image Library.** The exhibits and photos from the textbook are available in .jpeg format, for use in customizing your own course material or presentations.

- **Excel Templates.** Excel templates for selected end-of-chapter exercises and problems allow students to use Excel. Exercises and problems in the chapter that have a template online are identified by an icon.

- **Learning Solutions Managers.** Pearson's Learning Solutions Managers work with faculty and campus course designers to ensure that Pearson technology products, assessment tools, and online course materials are tailored to meet your specific needs. This highly qualified team is dedicated to helping schools take full advantage of a wide range of educational resources, by assisting in the integration of a variety of instructional materials and media formats. Your local Pearson Canada sales representative can provide you with more details on this service program.

Acknowledgments

Cost Accounting, eighth Canadian edition, is the product of an ongoing effort to provide an educational and reference resource that will forever be useful to the student and practitioner. I still have a copy of Horngren from a much earlier edition in the 1990s. I aspire to the standard that Chuck Horngren set.

I am indebted to those who provided their time, support, and feedback throughout this process:

Alym Amlani,
Kwantlen Polytechnic University

Dom Cianflone,
York University

Laura Dallas,
Kwantlen Polytechnic University

James Guthrie,
Northern Alberta Institute of Technology

Rhonda Heninger,
Southern Alberta Institute of Technology

Aadil Merali Juma,
McMaster University

Dianne MacDonald,
Conestoga College

Michelle Nicholson,
Okanagan College

John Parkinson,
York University

Daphne Rixon,
Saint Mary's University

Glen Stanger,
Douglas College

I want to thank our colleagues who helped us greatly by accuracy checking the text and supplements. And the people at Pearson Canada for their hard work and dedication, including Megan Farrell, Suzanne Simpson Millar, and Sally Glover. This is a team effort. I am deeply appreciative of their good spirits, humour, and patience to stay calm. Appreciation also goes to the Chartered Professional Accountants of Canada and many other publishers and companies for their generous permission to quote from their publications. I am grateful to the professors who contributed assignment material and to Steve Janz for the development of Excel program material.

Louis Beaubien

About the Authors

SRIKANT M. DATAR—is the Arthur Lowes Dickinson Professor of Business Administration at the Harvard Business School, Faculty Chair of the Harvard University Innovation Labs, and Senior Associate Dean for University Affairs. A graduate with distinction from the University of Bombay, he received gold medals upon graduation from the Indian Institute of Management, Ahmedabad, and the Institute of Cost and Works Accountants of India. A chartered accountant, he holds two master's degrees and a PhD from Stanford University.

Datar has published his research in leading accounting, marketing, and operations management journals, including *The Accounting Review, Contemporary Accounting Research, Journal of Accounting, Auditing and Finance, Journal of Accounting and Economics, Journal of Accounting Research*, and *Management Science*. He has served as an associate editor and on the editorial board of several journals and has presented his research to corporate executives and academic audiences in North America, South America, Asia, Africa, Australia, and Europe. He is a coauthor of two other books: *Managerial Accounting: Making Decisions and Motivating Performance* and *Rethinking the MBA: Business Education at a Crossroads*.

Cited by his students as a dedicated and innovative teacher, Datar received the George Leland Bach Award for Excellence in the Classroom at Carnegie Mellon University and the Distinguished Teaching Award at Stanford University.

Datar is a member of the board of directors of Novartis A.G., ICF International, T-Mobile US, and Stryker Corporation and Senior Strategic Advisor to HCL Technologies. He has worked with many organizations, including Apple Computer, Boeing, DuPont, Ford, General Motors, Morgan Stanley, PepsiCo, Visa, and the World Bank. He is a member of the American Accounting Association and the Institute of Management Accountants.

MADHAV V. RAJAN—is the Robert K. Jaedicke Professor of Accounting at Stanford University's Graduate School of Business. He is also Professor of Law (by courtesy) at Stanford Law School. From 2010 to 2016, he was Senior Associate Dean for Academic Affairs and head of the MBA program at Stanford GSB. In 2017, he will receive the Davis Award for Lifetime Achievement and Service to Stanford GSB.

Rajan received his undergraduate degree in commerce from the University of Madras, India, and his MS in accounting, MBA, and PhD degrees from Carnegie Mellon University. In 1990, his dissertation won the Alexander Henderson Award for Excellence in Economic Theory.

Rajan's research focuses on the economics-based analysis of management accounting issues, especially as they relate to internal control, capital budgeting, supply-chain, and performance systems. He has published his research in a variety of leading journals, including *The Accounting Review, Journal of Accounting and Economics, Journal of Accounting Research, Management Science*, and *Review of Financial Studies*. In 2004, he received the Notable Contribution to Management Accounting Literature award. He is a coauthor of *Managerial Accounting: Making Decisions and Motivating Performance*.

Rajan has served as the Departmental Editor for Accounting at *Management Science* as well as associate editor for both the accounting and operations areas. From 2002 to 2008, Rajan served as an editor of *The Accounting Review*. Rajan has twice been a plenary speaker at the AAA Management Accounting Conference.

Rajan has received several teaching honors at Wharton and Stanford, including the David W. Hauck Award, the highest undergraduate teaching award at Wharton. He teaches in the flagship Stanford Executive Program and is co-director of *Finance and*

Accounting for the Nonfinancial Executive. He has participated in custom programs for many companies, including Genentech, Hewlett-Packard, and nVidia, and is faculty director for the Infosys Global Leadership Program.

Rajan is a director of Cavium, Inc. and iShares, Inc., a trustee of the iShares Trust, and a member of the C.M. Capital Investment Advisory Board

LOUIS BEAUBIEN—Louis Beaubien is a Chartered Professional Accountant and holds a PhD from the Ivey School of Business at the University of Western Ontario. Dr. Beaubien's professional experience includes the financial services, information technology, and healthcare industries. He is an Associate Professor of Accounting at the Rowe School of Business, Dalhousie University, and the Department of Community Health and Epidemiology in the Faculty of Medicine at Dalhousie University. His research is focused on the effective, efficient, and equitable delivery of health care.

The Accountant's Vital Role in Decision Making

1

Alexey Boldin/Shutterstock

▶ Learning Objectives

1. Explain how management accounting data are essential to the process of rational operating and strategic decision making.

2. Explain how business functions help management accountants organize accounting information.

3. Identify the five steps of decision making and the role of relevant accounting information.

4. Describe key guidelines management accountants follow and roles they assume to support management decisions.

5. Distinguish among corporate governance, professional codes of conduct, ethics, and corporate social responsibility.

iTunes Variable Pricing: Downloads Are Down, but Profits Are Up

Can selling less of something be more profitable than selling more of it? Apple developed a pricing structure for songs sold through iTunes as a three-tier price point system of $0.69, $0.99, and $1.29. The top 200 songs in any given week make up more than one-sixth of digital music sales. Apple began charging the highest price ($1.29) for these songs—songs by artists like Adele.

Apple implementation continues to be successful, with the pricing model contributing to sales revenue growth of 19%. Although the number of downloads dropped, the higher prices generated more revenue than the old pricing structure because Apple's iTunes costs—wholesale song costs, network and transaction fees, and other operating costs—do not vary based on the price of each download. Apple has also applied this new pricing structure to movies available through iTunes. To increase profits beyond those created by higher prices, Apple began to manage the costs inherent in iTunes. Transaction costs (what Apple pays credit-card processors like Visa and MasterCard) have decreased, and Apple has reduced the number of people working in the iTunes store.

By studying cost accounting, you will learn how successful managers and accountants run their businesses and prepare yourself for leadership roles in the firms you work for. Many large companies, including Nike and the Toronto Maple Leafs, have senior executives with accounting backgrounds.

▶ CPA Competencies

This chapter covers material outlined in **Section 3: Management Accounting** of the CPA Competency Map. The Learning Objectives in this chapter have been aligned with the CPA Competency Map to ensure the best coverage possible.

3.1.1 Evaluates management information requirements

3.1.2 Evaluates the types of information systems used and the role they play in an organization

3.1.4 Identifies ethical and privacy issues related to information technology

Sources: http://www.apple.com/newsroom/2018/07/apple-reports-third-quarter-results.html; A. Bruno and G. Peoples. 2009. Variable iTunes pricing a moneymaker for artists, *Reuters,* June 21 (http://www.reuters.com/article/idUSTRE55K0DJ20090621; Nekesa Mumbi Moody. 2012).

Accounting Systems: Financial and Management Accounting

▶ **LO 1**

Explain how management accounting data are essential to the process of rational operating and strategic decision making.

Accounting systems are used to record economic events and transactions, such as sales and materials purchases, and process the data into information helpful to managers, sales representatives, production supervisors, and others. Processing any economic transaction means collecting, categorizing, summarizing, and analyzing. For example, costs are collected by category, such as materials, labour, and shipping. These costs are then summarized to determine a firm's total costs by month, quarter, or year. Accountants analyze the results and together with managers evaluate the organization (e.g., cost and revenue changes from one period to the next). Accounting systems also provide the information found in a firm's statement of comprehensive income, statement of financial position, statement of cash flows, and performance reports, such as the cost of serving customers or running an advertising campaign. Managers use this information to make decisions about the activities, businesses, or functional areas they oversee. For example, a report that shows an increase in sales of laptops and iPads at an Apple store may prompt Apple to hire more salespeople at that location. Understanding accounting information is essential for managers in doing their jobs.

Costs and other data are part of the **management information system (MIS)**. The MIS database stores information in a way that allows sales, distribution, and production managers to access the information they need. Many companies build their own comprehensive database, called an **enterprise resource planning (ERP) system**. The ERP software integrates data and provides managers with reports that highlight the interdependence of different business activities.

Cost accounting measures and reports financial and nonfinancial information related to the costs of acquiring and using resources. Cost accounting reports show how costs accumulate as corporations use resources to produce and sell their products and services. Costs are recovered when customers purchase products and services. **Cost management** includes the activities of identifying, reporting, and analyzing all costs of operations. Management decisions range from the quantity and quality of materials used to whether to shut down an entire company. As part of cost management, managers often deliberately incur additional costs in the short run—for example, in advertising and product modifications—to enhance revenues and profits in the long run.

Financial accounting focuses on reporting to external parties such as investors, government agencies, banks, and suppliers. The goal is to present fairly to external parties how the business activities during a specific time period affected the economic health of a company. This is called **economic substance**, which is the financial outcome of all the different types of business transactions that happened. Financial accountants report financial outcomes based on generally accepted accounting principles (GAAP) and standards.[1] Reports formatted in a way similar to statements of financial position, statements of comprehensive income, and statements of cash flows are common to both management accounting and financial accounting.

Management accounting measures, analyzes, and reports financial and nonfinancial information to internal managers. The goal is to use past performance to predict the future. The internal reports should plainly inform managers of the financial results of actual operations. The reports should also show how activities can be changed to affect and improve what will happen in the future. **Management accountants** reorganize and analyze financial and nonfinancial data using rigorous methods. The rigour of management accounting methods is intended to support managers in their efforts to decide on changes that will improve future financial success. The distinction between management accounting and cost accounting is not clear-cut, and we often use these terms interchangeably in the text.

Exhibit 1-1 summarizes the major differences between management accounting and financial accounting. Note, however, that reports such as statements of financial position,

---

[1] Generally accepted accounting principles (i.e., GAAP) is a generic term referring to the practices and rules of accounting consistent with laws and regulations. In Canada, depending on the nature of the organization, GAAP refers to either International Financial Reporting Standards (IFRS) or Accounting Standards for Private Enterprises (ASPE).

	Management Accounting	Financial Accounting
Purpose of information	To help managers make decisions to fulfill an organization's goals	To communicate the organization's financial position to investors, banks, regulators, and other outside parties
Primary users	Managers of the organization	External users such as investors, banks, regulators, and suppliers
Focus and emphasis	Future-oriented (budget for 2018 prepared in 2014)	Past-oriented (reports on 2014 performance prepared in 2018)
Rules of measurement and reporting	Internal measures and reports do not have to follow IFRS/ASPE but are based on cost–benefit analysis	Financial statements must be prepared in accordance with IFRS/ASPE and be attested to by independent auditors
Time span and types of reports	Varies from hourly information to 15 to 20 years, with financial and nonfinancial reports on products, departments, territories, and strategies	Annual and quarterly financial reports, primarily on the company as a whole, and presented as consolidated financial statements
Behavioural implications	Designed to influence the behaviour of managers and other employees	Primarily reports economic events but also influences behaviour because managers' compensation is often based on reported financial results

Exhibit 1-1 Major Differences Between Management Accounting and Financial Accounting

statements of comprehensive income, and statements of cash flows are common to both management accounting and financial accounting.

Business operations are complex sets of activities, and to maximize profit considerable information, analysis, and decision making is required in advance of actual action. Nevertheless, once a plan is implemented most operations run with little intervention from managers. Operating decisions are needed when exceptions arise, such as when supplies of a raw material fail to be delivered, workers go on strike, or machines break down. Decisions are needed when there are real alternatives that managers can choose from to deal with operating problems. Without high-quality information, business could not be conducted.

Strategic Decisions and Management Accounting

Strategy specifies how an organization matches its own capabilities with the opportunities in the marketplace. One of two strategies is available: cost leadership or value leadership by means of product (service) differentiation.[2] Companies such as LG generate growth and profits by providing the right combination of generic product features—quality and low price (cost leadership). Companies such as Apple generate growth and profits by offering unique, innovative products or services (value leadership). Customers who believe the features are valuable will pay a higher price for this type of product. Both LG and Apple understand that their customers are willing to spend their scarce resources on products where there is a value-added component—whether that's low price or innovation (or both). Pursuing the most appropriate strategy sustains competitive advantage for each type of company.

Deciding between these strategies is a critical part of what managers do. Management accountants work closely with managers in formulating strategy by providing information and helping them answer questions such as the following:

■ Who are our most important customers, and how do we deliver value to them?

■ What substitute products exist in the marketplace, and how do we attract customers to purchase our product instead of others?

---

[2] Michael Porter (Harvard University) presented strategy as an interplay of internal and external factors. He distinguished the two generic strategies of differentiation and cost leadership.

■ What are we particularly competent at doing? Innovating? Applying technology? Production? Multiple factors such as price, quality, and timely delivery drive the customer's perception of value. How do we decide to create that value in an affordable way?

■ Will adequate cash be available to fund the strategy? If not, how can we acquire these additional funds?

The best-designed strategies and the best-developed capabilities are of no value unless they are executed well. In the next section, we describe a common framework within which managers take action to create value for their customers and how management accountants help them do it.

Value-Chain and Supply-Chain Analysis and Key Success Factors

▶ **LO 2**

Explain how business functions help management accountants organize accounting information.

Customers demand more than a low price from companies. They expect a useful, quality product or service delivered in a timely way. These factors influence how customers experience their consumption of a product or service and assess its value-in-use. The more positive their experience, the higher is their perceived value added.

Value-Chain Analysis

The **value chain** is the sequence of business functions in which customer usefulness is added to products or services. The flow of costs incurred in a corporation can be classified into the value-adding activities of research and development (R&D), design, production, marketing, distribution, and customer service. From innovation through to verifying customer satisfaction, these costs accumulate and cannot be recovered, plus some reasonable profit, unless customers are willing to pay.

Exhibit 1-2 illustrates these functions using Apple's iPhone division as an example. The business functions are coordinated to make sure that the money being spent on R&D, for example, will provide features of a product that will satisfy customers and for which they will pay. Cost, quality, and the speed with which new products are developed require teamwork among managers across the business functions. For example, it may be worthwhile to increase spending on product design if it saves more on costs related to customer service.

1. **Research and development (R&D)**—Generating and experimenting with ideas related to new products, services, or processes. At Apple, this function includes research on backup systems to ensure reliable access to its communications system.

2. **Design of products, services, or processes**—Detailed planning and engineering of products, services, or processes. Design at Apple includes determining the number of component parts in a smartphone model and the effect of alternative product designs on quality and manufacturing costs.

3. **Production**—Acquiring, coordinating, and assembling resources to produce a product or deliver a service. Production of an iPhone includes the acquisition and assembly of the electronic parts, the handset, and the packaging used for shipping.

Exhibit 1-2 The Value Chain of Business Functions and Costs

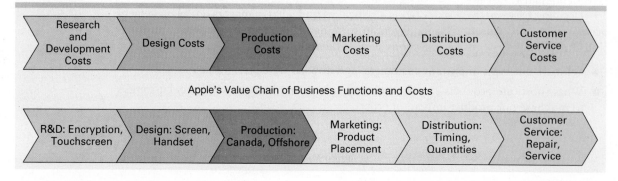

4. **Marketing**—Promoting and selling products or services to customers or prospective customers. Apple markets its iPhones through the internet, trade shows, and advertisements in newspapers and magazines.

5. **Distribution**—Delivering products or services to customers. Apple distribution systems to deliver iPhones include shipping globally to mobile telecommunications providers, governments, retail outlets, and direct sales via the internet.

6. **Customer service**—Providing after-sale support to customers. Apple provides customers both telephone and online help to set up and troubleshoot its smartphones.

Supply-Chain Analysis

Supply-chain analysis is one way companies can implement strategy, cut costs, and create value. The term **supply chain** describes the flow of goods, services, and information from their initial sources to the delivery of products and services to consumers, regardless of whether those activities occur in one or more organizations. Consider Apple. Many companies play a role in bringing its iPhone products to consumers. Exhibit 1-3 presents an overview of Apple's supply chain with various global suppliers.

Cost management emphasizes integrating and coordinating activities across all companies in the supply chain, as well as across each business function in an individual company's value chain, to reduce costs. For example, Apple arranges for frequent delivery of small quantities of expensive materials like microchips directly to the production floor of its assembling companies around the world. This strategy reduces materials-handling costs from inventories held inside the factory.

> **Note** Customer relationship management (CRM) refers to a strategy that integrates people and technology across all business functions and enhances relationships with customers, suppliers, and other stakeholders.

Key Success Factors (KSF)

Customers continue to demand that companies use the value chain and supply chain to deliver ever-improving levels of performance. **Key success factors** are those activities that are essential to successful corporate performance and include the following:

- **Cost and efficiency**—Companies such as IKEA set a target price and operating profit for a product first. Then, working together, managers and management accountants achieve the target cost by minimizing necessary activities and tasks in all value-chain business functions, from R&D through to customer service.

- **Quality**—Customers expect high levels of quality. Total quality management (TQM) directs attention toward simultaneously improving all operations throughout the value chain to deliver products and services that exceed customer expectations. TQM includes the following:
  - Designing products or services to meet the needs and wants of customers.
  - Producing products with zero (or minimal) defects and waste.
  - Maintaining low inventories.

- **Time**—Every value-chain activity takes time. The increasing pace of technological innovation has led to the need for companies to bring new products out faster because of shorter product life cycles. Customer response time continues to increase in importance. Companies compete to meet or exceed customers' expectations of responsiveness in production, delivery, and after-sales service.

Exhibit 1-3 Supply Chain for Apple

| Suppliers of Communications Services | Microchip Manufacturers | Handset Manufacturers | Assembly | Shippers and Distributors | Service Providers and Retailers |

Sustainability in Action | Management Accounting Beyond the Numbers

The interest in sustainability appears to be intensifying among companies. General Electric, Poland Springs (a bottled-water manufacturer), and Hewlett-Packard are among the many companies incorporating sustainability into their decision making. Sustainability is important to these companies for several reasons:

■ More and more investors care about sustainability. These investors make investment decisions based on a company's financial, social, and environmental performance and raise questions about sustainability at shareholder meetings.

■ Companies that emphasize sustainability find that sustainability goals attract and inspire employees.

■ Customers prefer the products of companies with good sustainability records and boycott companies with poor sustainability records.

■ Society and activist nongovernmental organizations, in particular, monitor the sustainability performance of firms and take legal action against those

that violate environmental laws. Countries with fast-growing economies, such as China and India, are now either requiring or encouraging companies to develop and report on their sustainability initiatives.

Management accountants help managers track the key success factors of their firms as well as those of their competitors. Competitive information serves as a *benchmark* managers use to continuously improve their operations. Examples of continuous improvement include WestJet's efforts to increase the number of its flights that arrive on time, eBay's efforts to improve the access its customers have to online auctions, and Lowe's efforts to continuously reduce the cost of its home-improvement products. Sometimes, more fundamental changes and innovations in operations, such as redesigning a manufacturing process to reduce costs, may be necessary. To successfully implement their strategies, firms have to do more than analyze their value chains and supply chains and execute key success factors. They also have to have good decision-making processes.

■ **Innovation**—Constant flows of innovative products in response to customer demand result in ongoing growth and success. Management accountants help managers evaluate alternative investment decisions and R&D decisions.

Management accountants help managers track and compare a company's performance on key success factors relative to their competitors. Tracking what is happening in other companies serves as a benchmark and alerts managers to the changes in the industry. The goal is for a company to continuously improve its critical operations—for example, on-time arrival for WestJet, customer access for online auctions at eBay, and cost reduction at Sumitomo Electric. Sometimes more fundamental changes in operations—such as redesigning a manufacturing process to reduce costs—may be necessary.

Strategy requires careful analyses of information and a decision about the most appropriate alternative to assure long-term success. However, successful strategy implementation requires more than value-chain and supply-chain analysis and execution of key success factors. Central to success is a rigorous decision-making process. Managers can use a well-known framework to assist them in improving the quality of their decisions. The framework encourages objective analyses of evidence in a logical and disciplined process.

Decision Making, Planning, and Control: The Five-Step Decision-Making Process

▶ **LO 3**

Identify the five steps of decision making and the role of relevant accounting information.

We will apply and explain the five-step decision-making process using *Best News*, a fictional national newspaper, as an example. The five-step process is a robust and versatile framework within which to decide the best way to address a wide variety of operating and strategic challenges.

A key challenge for Nicole Simpson, the manager of *Best News*, was to increase revenues. To achieve this goal, Nicole worked through the five-step decision-making process.

1. Identify the problem and uncertainties Nicole's MIS reported a steady decline in revenue, and Nicole and her team agreed that they must increase revenue without a disproportionate increase in costs.

2. Obtain information Decisions cannot be reasonably made without relevant and reliable information to help managers understand the uncertainties. Nicole asked her marketing manager to talk to some representative readers to gauge how they might react to an increase in the newspaper's selling price. She asked her advertising sales manager to talk to current and potential advertisers to get a better understanding of the advertising market. She also reviewed the effect that past price increases had on readership. Ramon Sandoval, the management accountant at *Best News*, provided information about past increases or decreases in advertising rates and the subsequent changes in advertising revenues. He also collected and analyzed information on advertising rates charged by competing media outlets, including other newspapers.

Note What is happening in step 2 is called *benchmarking*.

3. Make predictions about the future On the basis of the information she obtained, Nicole can improve her predictions about the future. Her analysis of the marketing information indicates that readers would be quite upset if she increased prices. One result would be a significant drop in readership volume, which would make Nicole's problem worse, not better. But in contrast, after analyzing the information on advertising rates, it is clear Nicole would not lose any advertisers nor would the pages of advertising space sold decrease if she increased the rates. Ramon's information indicated a likely market-wide increase in all media advertising rates. None of Nicole's predictions are certain, but she is confident enough to decide to raise advertising rates and not subscription prices.

4. Decide on one of the available alternatives Nicole communicated her decision to the sales department to increase advertising rates to $5,200 per page starting March 1, 2018—a 4% increase.

Steps 1 through 4 can be considered planning. **Planning** is a purposeful analysis of information to select and rank in importance the goals of an organization. Rigorous analyses are how managers make reasonable predictions about the best alternative set of actions to take to achieve goals. Management accountants are partners in these planning activities because they can explain and interpret financial and nonfinancial information to team members. Together, the team identifies activities that create value and the key success factors.

The most important planning tool is a budget. A **budget** is the quantitative expression of management's proposed plan of action; it is an aid to coordinating what must be done and when to implement a successful plan.

5. Implement the decision, evaluate performance, and learn Managers at *Best News* take actions to implement the March 2018 budget. Management accountants collect information to follow through on how actual performance compares to planned or budgeted performance (also referred to as scorekeeping). The comparison of actual performance to budgeted performance is the control or post-decision role of information.

When exercising **control**, managers compare actual and targeted nonfinancial measures as well as financial measures and take corrective actions. Performance measures tell managers if subunits are performing as predicted. Rewards linked to achievement motivate managers, and rewards are both intrinsic (self-satisfaction for a job well done) and extrinsic (salary, bonuses, and promotions). A budget serves as both a control and a planning tool since it is a comparison benchmark against actual performance.

Consider performance evaluation at *Best News*. During March 2018, the newspaper sold advertising, issued invoices, and received payments that were all recorded in the accounting system. Exhibit 1-4 shows *Best News*'s performance report of advertising revenues for March 2018. This report indicates that 760 pages of advertising (40 pages fewer

Exhibit 1-4 Performance Report of Advertising Revenues at *Best News* for March 2018

	Actual Result (1)	Budgeted Amount (2)	Difference: (Actual Result – Budgeted Amount) (3) = (1) – (2)	Difference as a Percentage of Budgeted Amount (4) = (3) ÷ (2)
Advertising pages sold	760 pages	800 pages	40 pages Unfavourable	5.0% Unfavourable
Average rate per page	$5,080	$5,200	$120 Unfavourable	2.3% Unfavourable
Advertising revenues	$3,860,800	$4,160,000	$299,200 Unfavourable	7.2% Unfavourable

than the budgeted 800 pages) were sold. The average rate per page was $5,080, compared with the budgeted $5,200 rate, yielding actual advertising revenues of $3,860,800. The actual advertising revenues were $299,200 less than the budgeted $4,160,000. The performance report in Exhibit 1-4 spurs investigation and learning.

The data in this performance report would prompt the management accountant to raise several questions about the implementation of the plan. This is not about laying blame but rather is an opportunity to ask questions and learn.

Management accountants might consider questions such as the following:

■ Is the strategy of differentiating *Best News* from other newspapers attracting more readers?

■ In implementing the new advertising rates, did the marketing and sales department make sufficient efforts to convince advertisers that, even with the higher rate of $5,200 per page, advertising in *Best News* was a good buy?

■ Why was the actual average rate per page $5,080 instead of the budgeted rate of $5,200?

■ Did some sales representatives offer rate discounts?

■ Did economic conditions cause the decline in advertising revenues?

■ Did technological changes create alternative business processes or models, making previous ones less effective?

■ Are revenues falling because editorial and production standards have declined?

Answers to these questions could prompt the newspaper's publisher to take subsequent actions, including, for example, adding more sales personnel or making changes in

Exhibit 1-5 How Accounting Aids Decision Making, Planning, and Control at *Best News*

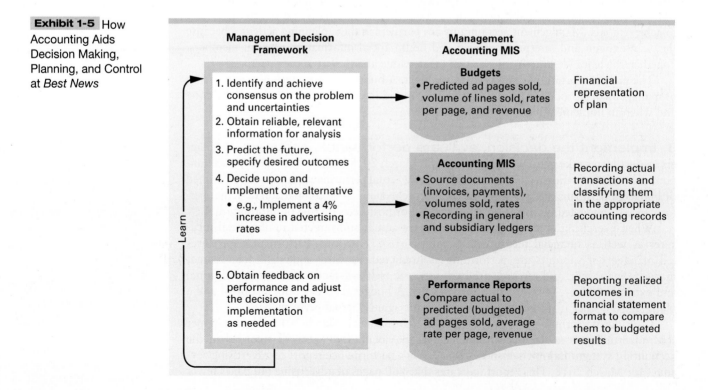

editorial policy. Good implementation requires the marketing, editorial, and production departments to work together and coordinate their actions and develop action plans.

The left side of Exhibit 1-5 provides an overview of the decision-making processes at *Best News*. The right side of the exhibit highlights how the management accounting system aids in decision making.

Action plans often include targets for market share, quality, new-product development, and employee satisfaction, but managers should understand that plans must be flexible because the future and outcomes are always uncertain. Unforeseeable outcomes often arise, and flexibility ensures that managers can seize unforeseen opportunities and remedy unforeseen threats to success. The plan is not a guarantee of any outcome.

Key Management Accounting Guidelines and Organization Structure

Three guidelines help management accountants provide the most value to their companies in strategic and operational decision making:

■ Use a cost–benefit approach.
■ Recognize both behavioural and technical considerations.
■ Use different costs for different purposes.

▶ **LO 4**
Describe key guidelines management accountants follow and roles they assume to support management decisions.

Cost–Benefit Approach

The **cost–benefit approach** (risk/return, downside risk/upside potential) is used to make resource allocations such that the expected benefits exceed the expected costs. The cost–benefit approach should be used to make resource-allocation decisions, such as whether to purchase a new software package or hire a new employee. This approach requires explicit comparisons of the financial costs and benefits of different alternatives. Often good ideas provide too little **upside potential** or benefit for the predicted costs that will be incurred. At other times the upside potential may be quite high, but the **downside risk** of failure is also quite high. When forecasting costs and benefits, managers should take uncertainty into consideration when they combine the two factors of risk and return in calculating the benefits.

Behavioural and Technical Considerations

Consider the human (or behavioural) side of why budgeting is used. **Behavioural considerations** motivate managers and other employees to try to achieve the goals of the organization. Budgets improve decisions within an organization because of better collaboration, planning, and motivation. The **technical considerations** help managers make wise economic decisions. Technical data (e.g., costs in various value-chain categories) in an appropriate format (e.g., actual results versus budgeted amounts) and at the preferred frequency (e.g., weekly versus monthly) improve the quality of information upon which managers make decisions.

Both accountants and managers should always remember that management is not confined exclusively to technical matters. Management is primarily a human activity that should focus on how to help individuals do their jobs better—for example, by helping managers distinguish activities that add value from those that do not. When workers underperform, behavioural considerations suggest that managers should personally discuss with workers ways to improve performance and not just send them a report highlighting their underperformance.

Different Costs for Different Purposes

There are different costs for different purposes—one size does not fit all. A cost concept used for external reporting may not be appropriate for internal, routine reporting to managers.

Consider the advertising costs associated with Apple's launch of a major new product. The product is expected to have a useful life of two years or more. For external reporting to shareholders, television advertising costs for this product are fully expensed in the statement of comprehensive income in the year they are incurred. This is required by IFRS/ASPE for external reporting. In contrast, for internal purposes of evaluating management performance, the television advertising costs could be capitalized and then amortized or written off as expenses over the product's life cycle. Apple could capitalize these advertising costs if it believes doing so results in a more accurate and fairer measure of the performance of the managers who launched the new product.

Corporate Structure and Governance: Accountability, Ethics, and Social Responsibility

Most organizations distinguish between line and staff management. **Line management** is directly responsible for completing or attaining operating goals. These are the core activities that produce the good or service ready for sale. Line managers can hold positions such as production engineers or software architects. By contrast, **staff management** is indirectly responsible for achieving organizational goals through activities that support the organization. This may include management accountants, human resources managers, and information technology staff who provide advice and assistance to line management. Organizations deploy teams that include both line and staff management so that all inputs into a decision are available simultaneously. As a result, the traditional distinctions between line and staff have become less clear-cut than they were a decade ago.

The Chief Financial Officer (CFO)

The **chief financial officer (CFO)**—also called the finance director—is the senior officer empowered to oversee the financial operations of an organization. In Canada the CFO is legally and personally responsible for the quality of financial information publicly reported. Responsibilities encompass the following six areas:

■ **Controllership**—includes providing legal assurance of a high-quality internal control system. Controllers of companies with shares listed on a stock exchange are legally responsible for the design of this system to ensure that bribery, fraud, malfeasance, and misappropriation of assets are reasonably unlikely.

■ **Audit**—ensures internal and external audits are conducted as per the direction of the audit committee.

■ **Treasury**—includes short- and long-term financing and investments, banking, cash management, foreign exchange, and derivatives management.

■ **Taxation**—includes reporting and managing income taxes, sales taxes, and domestic and international tax planning.

■ **Risk management**—includes analysis, evaluation, and minimization of external risks over which management has no control and internal risks over which management has control.

■ **Investor relations**—includes responding to and interacting with shareholders.

The **controller** is responsible for the quality of the information supplied from the accounting department. The controller's line authority extends only over his or her own department. But controllers, through their professional expertise and experience, exercise a broader scope of corporate control. They produce reports and analyses of relevant data that influence and impel management toward improving each step of their decision making. Examples of the functions of the controller's office include financial planning and budgeting, inventory, management of the general ledger, managing accounts payable and receivable, and overseeing subsidiary reporting.

Corporate Governance

Corporate governance comprises activities undertaken to ensure legal compliance and see that accountants fulfill their fiduciary responsibilities. Exhibit 1-6 shows a legally compliant, generic corporate governance structure for a corporation listed on a stock exchange. The **board of directors (BOD)** is responsible for holding the **chief executive officer (CEO)**, chief financial officer (CFO), and **chief operating officer (COO)** accountable for the quality of financial information and organizational outcomes. Legislation now permits people injured as a result of poor corporate governance to conduct lawsuits against alleged perpetrators, which includes not only the corporation but also these executives personally.

The board of directors is led by a chairperson, and its members must be independent from the CEO, COO, and CFO to ensure no conflict of interest. The CEO is legally accountable to the board. The COO is accountable to the CEO for all operating results. In addition to these formal relationships, informal relationships also exist among people throughout the organization. Examples include friendships (professional or personal) among managers and the personal preferences of senior managers for the types of managers they choose to rely on in decision making.

Professional Ethics

At no time has the focus on ethical conduct been sharper than it is today. Corporate scandals at Arthur Andersen (a public accounting firm), Countrywide Financial (a home mortgage company), Enron (an oil and gas company), Lehman Brothers (an investment bank), Olympus (the Japanese optical equipment company), and Bernie Madoff Investment Securities have seriously eroded the public's confidence in corporations. All employees in a

► **LO 5**

Distinguish among corporate governance, professional codes of conduct, ethics, and corporate social responsibility.

Exhibit 1-6 Legal Corporate Governance and Accountability Structure

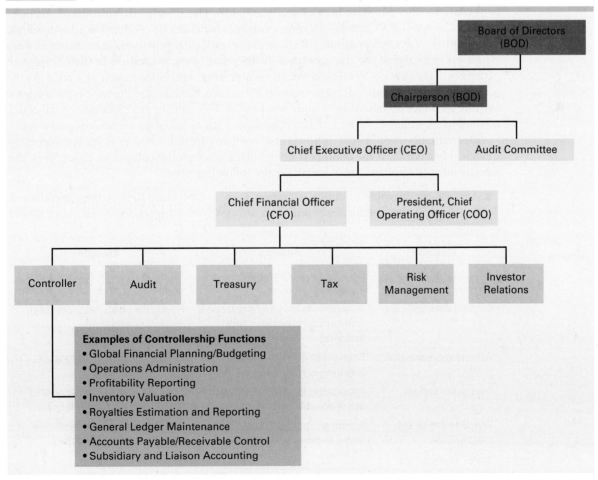

company must comply with the organization's—and more broadly, society's—expectations of ethical standards.

Ethics are the foundation of a well-functioning economy. When ethics are weak, suppliers might bribe executives to win supply contracts rather than invest in improving quality or lowering costs. Because customers would then have very little confidence in the quality of products produced, they can become reluctant to buy them, causing markets to fail. Costs are higher because of higher prices paid to suppliers and fewer products being produced. Investors are unsure about the integrity of financial reports, affecting their ability to make investment decisions, resulting in a reluctance to invest and misallocation of resources. The scandals at Ahold (an international supermarket operator), Tyco International (a diversified global manufacturing company), and others make clear that value is quickly destroyed by unethical behaviour.

Institutional Support

Accountants have special ethical obligations, given that they are responsible for the integrity of the financial information provided to internal and external parties. In Canada, Bill 198C was passed in 2002 in response to a series of large international corporate scandals. In the United States, a parallel legislation (the Sarbanes-Oxley Act) was passed in 2002. Similar legislation was enacted in other countries around the world. These laws focus on improving internal control, corporate governance, monitoring of managers, and financial and nonfinancial disclosure practices of public corporations. The regulations impose tough ethical standards and criminal penalties on managers and accountants who don't meet those standards. The regulations also delineate a process for employees to report violations or illegal and unethical acts (these employees are called whistleblowers).

Professional accounting organizations, which represent management accountants in many countries, offer programs certifying that those who have completed them have management accounting and financial management technical knowledge and expertise. These organizations also advocate high ethical standards. The Chartered Professional Accountants of Canada (CPA Canada) provides guidelines for codes of conduct for all individuals who hold the CPA designation. CPA Canada works with provincial accounting bodies, which are responsible for the regulation of the accounting profession in their respective provinces. This includes the development, maintenance, and enforcement of a code of ethics for chartered professional accountants (CPAs). CPA Canada and the provincial affiliates provide guidance on ethical behaviour (see Exhibit 1-7), which, alongside provincial codes of conduct, is meant to foster important qualities such as integrity, leadership, and trust.

Accountants should first follow their company's established policies for reporting unethical behaviour. If the conflict is not resolved through the company's procedures, the management accountant should consider the following steps:

■ Discuss the possible unethical situation with a supervisor (unless the supervisor is involved in the unethical situation). If so, notify the supervisor at the next higher

Exhibit 1-7 Guidelines for Ethical Behaviour

Guideline	Evidence	Example
Adherence to rules of professional conduct	Compilation of allowed and disallowed behaviours	No ownership interest in an audit client
Enabling competencies	Adherence to laws and professional standards for knowledge and behaviour	Having the requisite knowledge to perform certain tasks
Assessing the situation	Recognition of ethical issues that may arise in work to be performed	Planning and identifying possible conflicts of interest
Integrative analysis	Anticipation of issues and identification of possible alternatives	Scrutinizing ethical constraints to determine the best way forward
Conclude/advise and communicate	A clear and transparent decision based on the ethical analysis	Provide guidance on ethical considerations of a situation

Source: Inspired by CPA.

managerial level. If the immediate supervisor involved is the CEO, notify the audit committee or board of directors.

- Discuss the unethical situation with an objective advisor.
- Consult an attorney regarding legal obligations and rights.

Typical Ethical Challenges

Ethical issues can confront management accountants in many ways. Here are two examples:

- **Case A:** A management accountant knows that reporting a loss for a software division will result in yet another "rightsizing initiative" (a gentler term for "layoffs"). He has concerns about the commercial potential of a software product for which development costs are currently being capitalized as an asset rather than being shown as an expense for internal reporting purposes. The division manager argues that showing development costs as an asset is justified because the new product will generate profits. However, the division manager presents little evidence to support his argument. The last two products from this division have been unsuccessful. The management accountant has many friends in the division and wants to avoid a personal confrontation with the division manager.
- **Case B:** A packaging supplier, bidding for a new contract, offers the management accountant of a purchasing company an all-expenses-paid weekend to Edmonton during the Grey Cup. The supplier does not mention the new contract when giving the offer. The accountant is not a personal friend of the supplier. She knows cost issues are critical in approving the new contract and is concerned that the supplier will ask for details about bids by competing packaging companies.

In each case, the management accountant is faced with an ethical dilemma. Case A involves competence, credibility, and integrity, whereas Case B involves confidentiality and integrity.

Ethical issues are not clear-cut. The management accountant in Case A should request that the division manager provide credible evidence that the new product is commercially viable. If the manager does not provide such evidence, expensing development costs in the current period is appropriate.

In Case B the supplier may have no intention of raising issues associated with the bid. But the appearance of a conflict of interest such as this is sufficient for many companies to prohibit employees from accepting "favours" from suppliers. The accountant in Case B should discuss the invitation with her immediate supervisor. If the visit is approved, the supplier should be informed that the invitation has been officially approved subject to her following corporate policy (which includes the confidentiality of information).

Worldwide, professional accounting organizations issue statements about professional ethics. However, small differences exist and it is the responsibility of CPAs to know the professional code of the jurisdiction in which they work. In the United Kingdom, the Chartered Institute of Management Accountants (CIMA) identifies the four principles of competency, confidentiality, integrity, and objectivity. The Institute of Management Accountants of the United States goes further and provides guidance on how to resolve ethical conflict.

Corporate Social Responsibility (CSR)

Corporate social responsibility (CSR) is the voluntary integration of social and environmental concerns into business decisions.[3] One example is the proactive development of effective social programs that educate and improve the health, safety, and security of workers. Globally active companies have adopted guidelines to measure and achieve CSR goals on a global level, such as fair trade. Many multinational corporations refuse to do business with suppliers who endanger their workers or families. Consumers refuse to purchase

---

[3] D. Silberhorn and R.C. Warren. 2007. Defining Corporate Social Responsibility. *European Business Review.* pp. 352–372.

Exhibit 1-8 The Triple Bottom Line as a Mode of Sustainable Operations

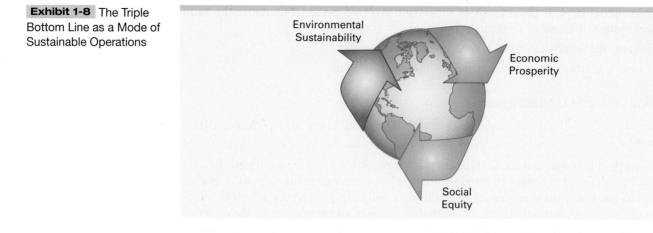

products such as blood diamonds because the proceeds from their sale finance war. Some give away new health products that cure local diseases, while others pay for infrastructure such as roads to improve access for local people to new markets for their work. The overall goal is sustainable management of increasingly scarce or degraded resources.

A number of CSR approaches and initiatives have developed formal approaches. The **triple bottom line** is a term originally coined in 1994 by a British management consultant, John Elkington, and consists of three Ps: profit, people, and planet.[4] The purpose of the TBL approach is not only to draw management's focus to financial prosperity but also to areas of environmental stewardship and protection, as well as the contribution the organization makes to the communities in which it operates and society in general. Exhibit 1-8 depicts Elkington's conception of three strategic goals interacting with one another; he argued that a TBL approach would promote growth and innovation in organizations. For example, a company that works hard to protect the environment may develop new and innovative production processes, which will in turn lead to greater profits. Additionally, by contributing to society in any number of ways (e.g., charitable donations to schools), corporations will be better preparing individuals to join the workforce as creative contributors to the marketplace.

Generally speaking, a TBL organization benefits many stakeholders. By pushing success upstream, a portion of revenues and success make their way back to the original producer of raw material from the final point of sale in the value chain. For instance, if a coffee shop such as Tim Hortons were attempting to be a TBL company, it might buy fair trade coffee so as to provide the most benefit to the supplier stakeholder, rather than exploiting coffee producers in the developing world. And, while TBL organizations strive to maximize value creation in financial terms, they would not do so at the expense of the environment of the community in which they live.

Sustainability Accounting

Sustainability accounting focuses on reporting both financial and nonfinancial information on activities that impact society, the environment, and the financial (or, economic) aspects of an organization's performance to an organization's stakeholders. This is an important area for management and cost accounting as its emphasis is on information and accounting used for internal decision making and strategy development.

The Global Reporting Initiative (GRI) is a nonprofit organization established to develop guidelines so that "reporting on economic, environmental and social performance by all organizations is as routine and comparable as financial reporting."[5] The GRI has developed and supports several frameworks; however, the most common form of sustainability accounting is the TBL, shown in Exhibit 1-9. The trend to sustainability in reporting has emphasized value creation as well as risk mitigation in financial reports and management discussion and analysis of organizations.

---

[4] The Triple Bottom Line. *The Economist*, November 17, 2009.
[5] *GRI Reporting in Government Agencies*, © 2010 GRI. (http://www.globalreporting.org).

Exhibit 1-9 The Triple Bottom-Line Approach

Economic bottom line	Revenue and margin growth
	Resource and capital efficiency
	Shareholder return
	Risk management
Social bottom line	Benefits to stakeholders
	Community outreach and community benefit
	Ethical business practices including employment diversity and good labour relations
	Effective health and safety practices
Environmental bottom line	Clean land, water, and air
	Emission reduction
	Resource-use efficiency
	Sustainable business practices

There are currently no statutory requirements for organizations to produce sustainability reports. However, in efforts to improve credibility and the perception of ethical management practices, many organizations such as the GRI, Organisation for Economic Co-operation and Development (OECD), and United Nations Commission on Sustainable Development (UNCSD) are cooperating to develop policy frameworks to improve adoption of sustainable reporting practices.

Alternative Reporting

Organizations also seek alternative forms of reporting based on their goals and strategies. For example, cooperatives are significant participants in many large economies. Some of the largest cooperatives in North America include Desjardins, Nationwide, Ocean Spray, and Land-o-Lakes. Cooperatives are organized around fulfilling a particular need or around a community and are owned and managed by the people who use their services or those who work at the cooperative. In addition to fulfilling financial objectives, cooperatives follow, seek to fulfill, and report on the seven cooperative principles. Generally, these principles reflect their commitment to the society in which they operate (which includes environmental concern). The cooperative principles are outlined in Exhibit 1-10.

Exhibit 1-10 The Cooperative Principles

1. **Voluntary and Open Membership** Cooperatives are voluntary organizations, open to all people able to use their services and willing to accept the responsibilities of membership, without gender, social, racial, political, or religious discrimination.
2. **Democratic Member Control** Cooperatives are democratic organizations controlled by their members—those who buy the goods or use the services of the cooperative—who actively participate in setting policies and making decisions.
3. **Members' Economic Participation** Members contribute equally to, and democratically control, the capital of the cooperative. This benefits members in proportion to the business they conduct with the cooperative rather than to the capital invested.
4. **Autonomy and Independence** Cooperatives are autonomous, self-help organizations controlled by their members. If the co-op enters into agreements with other organizations or raises capital from external sources, it does so based on terms that ensure democratic control by the members and maintain the cooperative's autonomy.
5. **Education, Training, and Information** Cooperatives provide education and training for members, elected representatives, managers, and employees so they can contribute effectively to the development of their cooperative. Members also inform the general public about the nature and benefits of cooperatives.
6. **Cooperation Among Cooperatives** Cooperatives serve their members most effectively and strengthen the cooperative movement by working together through local, national, regional, and international structures.
7. **Concern for Community** While focusing on member needs, cooperatives work for the sustainable development of communities through policies and programs accepted by the members.

Source: The Co-operative Principles from 2012 International Year of Cooperative. Copyright © 2012. The Co-operative Principles are a product of the International Cooperative Alliance, Reprinted with permission.

Pulling It All Together—Problem for Self-Study

(Try to solve this problem before examining the solution that follows.)

Problem

The Campbell Soup Company incurs the following costs:

a. Purchase of tomatoes by the canning plant for Campbell's tomato soup products.
b. Materials purchased for redesigning Mr. Christie biscuit containers to make biscuits stay fresh longer.
c. Payment to Bates, the advertising agency for the Healthy Request line of soup products.
d. Salaries of food technologists researching feasibility of a Prego pizza sauce that has zero calories.
e. Payment to Sobeys for shelf space to display Campbell's food products.
f. Cost of a toll-free telephone line used for customer inquiries about possible taste problems with Campbell's soups.
g. Cost of gloves used by line operators on the Swanson Fiesta breakfast food production line.
h. Cost of hand-held computers used by Campbell Soup Company delivery staff serving major supermarket accounts.

Required ▶

1. Identify two costs incurred most likely as a result of strategic decisions.
2. Classify each cost item (a) to (h) into a component of the value chain shown in Exhibit 1-2.
3. How would the treatment of (c) by a financial accountant differ from that by a management accountant?
4. How could Campbell Soup Company use corporate social responsibility to brand its products?

Solution

1. Costs incurred for materials for redesign in (b) are likely the result of a strategic decision, as are those from (d).
2. The items should be classified as:
   a. Production
   b. Design of products, services, or processes
   c. Marketing
   d. Research and development
   e. Marketing
   f. Customer service
   g. Production
   h. Distribution
3. Advertising is an expense: a cost that financial accountants must record during the period it is incurred. For internal purposes of management evaluation, advertising costs are likely based on a strategic decision and would be capitalized by management accountants producing a performance report.
4. A strategy of corporate social responsibility would link the attributes of a product to the core values of the customers to whom the product is sold. Campbell's could advertise the wholesome method in which raw materials were produced (e.g., chicken for soup) or its use of organic vegetables. The strategy will only be effective, however, if it is true.

Decision Points

The following question-and-answer format summarizes the chapter's learning objectives. Each point presents a key question, and the guidelines are the answer to that question.

Learning Objectives	Guidelines
1. What information does cost accounting provide?	Cost accounting measures, analyzes, and reports financial and nonfinancial information related to the cost of acquiring or using resources in an organization. Cost accounting provides information for both management and financial accounting. Management accountants contribute to both operating and strategic decisions by providing information about the sources of competitive advantage.
2. How do companies add value?	Companies add value through R&D; design of products, services, or processes; production; marketing; distribution; and customer service. Managers in all business functions of the value chain use management accounting information about the value chain. Customers expect companies to deliver performance through cost, efficiency, quality, timeliness, and innovation.
3. What role does relevant accounting information play in the five steps of decision making?	Planning is undertaken prior to action while control is an evaluation of how well plans have been implemented. Different reports and presentations of the same information are used to identify a problem, gather additional relevant information, predict the future, decide among alternatives, implement the decision, and evaluate results. This information identifies and is used to respond to strategic and operating problems.
4. What guidelines do management accountants use?	Three guidelines that help management accountants increase their value to managers are (a) employ a cost–benefit approach, (b) recognize behavioural as well as technical considerations, and (c) identify different costs for different purposes. Management accounting is an integral part of the controller's function in an organization. In most organizations, the controller reports to the chief financial officer, who is a key member of the top management team.
5. Of what importance for management accountants are corporate governance, codes of conduct, and ethics?	Management accountants must comply with all legislation, civil and criminal. This is a profession that must also comply with well-publicized codes of conduct and ethics. Laws are enforced by the relevant jurisdiction, but professional codes are enforced by the profession itself. Management accountants have ethical responsibilities that are related to competence, confidentiality, integrity, and objectivity.

Terms to Learn

Each chapter includes this section. Like all technical terms, accounting terms have precise meanings. Learn the definitions of new terms when you initially encounter them. The meaning of each of the following terms is given in this chapter and in the Glossary at the end of this book.

behavioural considerations (**p. 9**)
board of directors (BOD) (**p. 11**)
budget (**p. 7**)
chief executive officer (CEO) (**p. 11**)
chief financial officer (CFO) (**p. 10**)
chief operating officer (COO) (**p. 11**)
control (**p. 7**)
controller (**p. 10**)

corporate governance (**p. 11**)
corporate social responsibility (CSR) (**p. 13**)
cost accounting (**p. 2**)
cost–benefit approach (**p. 9**)
cost management (**p. 2**)
customer service (**p. 5**)

design of products, services, or processes (**p. 4**)
distribution (**p. 5**)
downside risk (**p. 9**)
economic substance (**p. 2**)
enterprise resource planning (ERP) system (**p. 2**)
financial accounting (**p. 2**)

key success factors (KSF)
   (**p. 5**)
line management (**p. 10**)
management accountants
   (**p. 2**)
management accounting (**p. 2**)
management information
   system (MIS) (**p. 2**)

marketing (**p. 5**)
planning (**p. 7**)
production (**p. 4**)
research and development
   (R&D) (**p. 4**)
staff management (**p. 10**)
strategy (**p. 3**)
supply chain (**p. 5**)

technical considerations
   (**p. 9**)
triple bottom line (TBL)
   (**p. 14**)
upside potential (**p. 9**)
value chain (**p. 4**)

Assignment Material

MyLab Accounting Make the grade with MyLab Accounting: The Short-Answer Questions, Exercises, and Problems marked with a ⊕ can be found on MyLab Accounting. You can practise them as often as you want, and most feature step-by-step guided instructions to help you find the right answer.

Short-Answer Questions

⊕ **1-1** How does management accounting differ from financial accounting?

⊕ **1-2** "Management accounting should not fit the straitjacket of financial accounting." Explain and give an example.

⊕ **1-3** How can management accountants help formulate strategy?

⊕ **1-4** Describe the business functions in the value chain.

⊕ **1-5** Explain the term *supply chain* and its importance to cost management.

⊕ **1-6** "Management accounting deals only with costs." Do you agree?

⊕ **1-7** How can management accountants help improve quality and achieve timely product deliveries?

⊕ **1-8** Describe the five-step decision-making process.

⊕ **1-9** Distinguish planning decisions from control decisions.

⊕ **1-10** What three guidelines help management accountants provide the most value to managers?

⊕ **1-11** "Knowledge of technical issues such as computer technology is necessary but not sufficient to becoming a successful accountant." Do you agree? Why?

⊕ **1-12** As a new controller, reply to this comment by a plant manager: "As I see it, our accountants may be needed to keep records for shareholders and the Canada Revenue Agency—but I don't want them sticking their noses in my day-to-day operations. I do the best I know how. No pencil-pushing bean counter knows enough about my responsibilities to be of any use to me."

⊕ **1-13** What steps should a management accountant take if established written policies provide insufficient guidance on how to handle an ethical conflict?

Exercises

⊕ **1-14 Terminology.** A number of terms are listed below:

timely	management accounting
ethical guidelines	cost–benefit
technical	control
value chain	reliable
corporate social responsibility	strategy

Required

Select the terms from the above list to complete the following sentences.

1. Management of activities, businesses, or functional areas, which managers oversee and coordinate within the organization, requires _____ and _____ information.

2. The _____ considerations help managers make wise economic decisions by providing them with the desired information in an appropriate format and at the preferred frequency.

3. _____ comprises taking actions that implement the planning decisions, deciding how to evaluate performance, and providing feedback to learn how to improve future decisions.
4. Many professional accounting organizations issue _____ to help their members reason through an appropriate response to an ethical issue.
5. _____ measures, analyzes, and reports financial and nonfinancial information to internal managers who use it to choose, communicate, and implement strategy and operational changes.
6. The _____ approach should be used to make resource-allocation decisions. Resources should be spent if the expected benefits to the company exceed the expected costs.
7. _____ specifies how an organization matches its own capabilities with the opportunities in the marketplace to accomplish its objectives.
8. _____ is the sequence of business functions in which customer usefulness is added to products or services.
9. _____ is the voluntary integration by companies of social and environmental concerns into their business operation.

🌐 **1-15 Cost, management, and financial accounting.** Financial accountants use estimates of financial value differently than either cost or management accountants.　　◀ **LO 1**

Required

1. Identify two differences in use.
2. Identify a similarity among accountants.

🌐 **1-16 Strategy.** Strategy usually includes some formal processes.　　◀ **LO 1**

Required

1. How can managers choose between different strategies?
2. How is strategy different from an operating decision?

🌐 **1-17 Value chain and classification of costs, fast food restaurant.** Burger King, a hamburger fast food restaurant, incurs the following costs:　　◀ **LO 2**

1. Cost of oil for the deep fryer.
2. Wages of the counter help who give customers the food they order.
3. Cost of the costume for the King on the Burger King television commercials.
4. Cost of children's toys given away free with kids' meals.
5. Cost of the posters indicating the special "two cheeseburgers for $2."
6. Costs of frozen onion rings and French fries.
7. Salaries of the food specialists who create new sandwiches for the restaurant chain.
8. Cost of "to-go" bags.

Required

Classify each of the cost items (1–8) as one of the business functions of the value chain shown in Exhibit 1-2.

🌐 **1-18 Value chain and customer expectations.** A Canadian biopharmaceutical company incurs the following costs:　　◀ **LO 2**

1. Cost of redesigning blister packs to make drug containers more tamper-proof.
2. Cost of videos sent to doctors to promote sales of a new drug.
3. Cost of a toll-free telephone line used for customer inquiries about usage, side effects of drugs, and so on.
4. Equipment purchased by a scientist to conduct experiments on drugs awaiting approval by the government.
5. Payment to actors in an infomercial to be shown on television promoting Visudyne, a new treatment for age-related progressive blindness.
6. Labour costs of workers in the packaging area of a production facility.
7. Bonus paid to a salesperson for exceeding monthly sales quota.
8. Cost of the Purolator courier services to deliver drugs to hospitals.

Required

Classify each of the cost items (1–8) as one of the business functions of the value chain shown in Exhibit 1-2.

🌐 **1-19 Planning and control decisions.** Conner Company makes and sells brooms and mops. It takes the following actions, not necessarily in the order given below.　　◀ **LO 3**

Required

For each action (1–5 below), state whether it is a planning decision or a control decision.

1. Conner asks its marketing team to consider ways to get back market share from its newest competitor, Swiffer.
2. Conner calculates market share after introducing its newest product.
3. Conner compares costs it actually incurred with costs it expected to incur for the production of the new product.
4. Conner's design team proposes a new product to compete directly with the Swiffer.
5. Conner estimates the costs it will incur to sell 30,000 units of the new product in the first quarter of the next fiscal year.

LO 3 ▶ ⊕ **1-20 Five-step decision-making role of relevant accounting information.** Honel Foods makes frozen dinners that it sells through grocery stores. Typical products include turkey dinners, pot roast, fried chicken, and meatloaf. The managers at Honel have recently introduced a line of frozen chicken pies. They take the following actions with regard to this decision.

Required

Classify each action (1–7 below) as a step in the five-step decision-making process (identify the problem and uncertainties; obtain information; make predictions about the future; decide on one of the available alternatives; implement the decision, evaluate performance, and learn). The actions below are not listed in the order they are performed.

1. Honel performs a taste test at the local shopping mall to see if consumers like the taste of its proposed new chicken pie product.
2. Honel sales managers estimate they will sell more meat pies in their northern sales territory than in their southern sales territory.
3. Honel managers discuss the possibility of introducing a new product.
4. Honel managers compare actual costs of making chicken pies with their budgeted costs.
5. Costs for making chicken pies are budgeted.
6. Honel decides to make chicken pies.
7. The purchasing manager calls a supplier to check the prices of chicken.

LO 3 ▶ ⊕ **1-21 Five-step decision-making process, service firm.** Brite Exteriors is a firm that provides house painting services. Robert Brite, the owner, is trying to find new ways to increase revenues. Mr. Brite performs the following actions, not in the order listed.

Required

Classify each action below according to its step in the five-step decision-making process (identify the problem and uncertainties; obtain information; make predictions about the future; decide on one of the available alternatives; implement the decision, evaluate performance, and learn).

1. Mr. Brite calls Home Depot to ask the price of paint sprayers.
2. Mr. Brite discusses with his employees the possibility of growing revenues of the firm.
3. One of Mr. Brite's project managers suggests that using paint sprayers instead of hand painting will increase productivity and thus revenues.
4. The workers who are not familiar with paint sprayers take more time to finish a job than they did when painting by hand.
5. Mr. Brite compares the expected cost of buying sprayers to the expected cost of hiring more workers who paint by hand, and estimates profits from both alternatives.
6. The project scheduling manager confirms that demand for house painting services has increased.
7. Mr. Brite decides to buy the paint sprayers rather than hire additional painters.

Problems

LO 3 ▶ ⊕ **1-22 Strategic decisions and management accounting.** A series of independent situations in which a firm is about to make a strategic decision follow.

Decisions

a. Yello Phones is about to decide whether to launch production and sale of a cell phone with standard features.
b. Soft Solutions is trying to decide whether to produce and sell a new home computer software package that includes the ability to interface with a sewing machine and a vacuum cleaner. There is no such software currently on the market.

c. Dot Cosmetics has been asked to provide a "store brand" lip gloss that will be sold at discount retail stores.
d. Buy More Meats is entertaining the idea of developing a special line of gourmet bologna made with sun dried tomatoes, pine nuts, and artichoke hearts.

Required

1. For each decision, state whether the company is following a low price or a differentiated product strategy.
2. For each decision, discuss what information the management accountant can provide about the source of competitive advantage for these firms.

1-23 Planning and control decisions. Softmoc is a shoe retailing company. The majority of its sales are made at its own stores. These stores are often located in shopping malls or in the downtown shopping districts of cities. A small but increasing percentage of sales are made via its internet shopping division.   ◂ **LO 3**

The following five reports were recently prepared by the management accounting group at Softmoc:

a. Annual financial statements included in the annual report sent to its shareholders.
b. Weekly report to the vice-president of operations for each Softmoc store—includes revenue, gross margin, and operating costs.
c. Report to insurance company on losses Softmoc suffered at its new Toronto store resulting from a storm.
d. Weekly report to a new supplier on the sales of that supplier's products both through the Softmoc stores and by the internet division.
e. Study for vice-president of new business development of the expected revenue and expected costs of the Softmoc internet division selling foot-health products (arch supports, heel inserts, etc.) as well as shoes.

Required

For each report, identify how a manager would use it to make both a planning decision and a control decision (either at Softmoc or another company).

1-24 Management accountants' guidelines and roles in a company. Stephen Bergstrom is the new corporate controller of a multinational company that has just overhauled its organizational structure. The company is now decentralized. Each division is under an operating vice-president who, within wide limits, has responsibility and authority to run the division like a separate company.   ◂ **LO 4**

Bergstrom has a number of bright staff members. One of them, Bob Garrett, is in charge of a newly created performance analysis staff. Garrett and staff members prepare monthly division performance reports for the company president. These reports are division statements of comprehensive income, showing budgeted performance and actual results, and they are accompanied by detailed written explanations and appraisals of variances. In the past, each of Garrett's staff members was responsible for analyzing one division; each consulted with division line and staff executives and became generally acquainted with the division's operations.

After a few months, Bill Whisler, vice-president in charge of Division C, stormed into the controller's office. The gist of his complaint follows:

"Your staff is trying to take over part of my responsibility. They come in, snoop around, ask hundreds of questions, and take up plenty of our time. It's up to me, not you and your detectives, to analyze and explain my division's performance to central headquarters. If you don't stop trying to grab my responsibility, I'll raise the whole issue with the president."

Required

1. What events or relationships may have led to Whisler's outburst?
2. As Bergstrom, how would you answer Whisler's contentions?
3. What alternative actions can Bergstrom take to improve future relationships?

1-25 Professional ethics and end-of-year actions. Janet Taylor is the new division controller of the snack-foods division of Gourmet Foods. Gourmet Foods has reported a minimum 15% growth in annual earnings for each of the past five years. The snack-foods division has reported annual earnings growth of more than 20% each year in this same period. During the current year, the economy went into a recession. The corporate controller estimates a 10% annual earnings growth rate for Gourmet Foods this year. One month before the December 31 fiscal year-end of the current year, Taylor estimates the snack-foods division will report an annual earnings growth of only 8%. Warren Ryan, the snack-foods division president, is not happy, but he notes that "the end-of-year actions" still need to be taken.   ◂ **LO 5**

Taylor makes some inquiries and is able to compile the following list of end-of-year actions that were more or less accepted by the previous division controller:

a. Deferring December's routine monthly maintenance on packaging equipment by an independent contractor until January of next year.

b. Extending the close of the current fiscal year beyond December 31 so that some sales of next year are included in the current year.

c. Altering dates of shipping documents of next January's sales to record them as sales in December of the current year.

d. Giving salespeople a double bonus to exceed December sales targets.

e. Deferring the current period's advertising by reducing the number of television spots run in December and running more than planned in January of next year.

f. Deferring the current period's reported advertising costs by having Gourmet Foods's outside advertising agency delay billing December advertisements until January of next year or by having the agency alter invoices to conceal the December date.

g. Persuading carriers to accept merchandise for shipment in December of the current year although they normally would not have done so.

Required

1. Why might the snack-foods division president want to take these end-of-year actions?
2. The division controller is deeply troubled. Classify each of the end-of-year actions (a) to (g) as acceptable or unacceptable.
3. What should Taylor do if Ryan suggests that these end-of-year actions are taken in every division of Gourmet Foods and that she will greatly harm the snack-foods division if she does not cooperate and paint the rosiest picture possible of the division's results?

LO 5 ▶   ⊕   **1-26 Professional ethics and earnings management.** Harvest Day Corporation is a publishing company that produces trade magazines. The company's shareholders are awaiting the announcement of Harvest Day's earnings for the fiscal year, which ends on December 31. Market analysts have predicted earnings to be around $1.34 per share. The CEO of Harvest Day expects earnings to be only $1.20 per share and knows this will cause the price of the stock to drop. The CEO suggests the following ideas to various managers to try to increase reported earnings by the end of the fiscal year:

a. Delaying recording of cancelled subscriptions for December until January.

b. Waiting until the new fiscal year to update the software on office computers.

c. Recognizing unearned subscription revenue (cash received in advance for magazines that will be sent in the future) as revenue when received in the current month (just before fiscal year-end) instead of booking it as a liability.

d. Delaying recording purchases of office supplies on account until after year-end.

e. Booking advertising revenues that relate to January in December.

f. Waiting until after fiscal year-end to do building repairs.

g. Switching from declining balance to straight line depreciation to reduce depreciation expense in the current year.

Required

1. Why would Harvest Day Corporation's CEO want to "manage" earnings?
2. Which of the items in (a) to (g) above are acceptable to Harvest Day's controller? Which are unacceptable?
3. What should the controller do about the CEO's suggestions? What should the controller do if the CEO refuses to change the suggestions?

LO 5 ▶   ⊕   **1-27 Professional ethics and corporate governance.** Janet Segato is division controller and Tom Maloney is division manager of the Sports Shoe Company. Segato has line responsibility to Maloney, but she also has staff responsibility to the company controller.

Maloney is under severe pressure to achieve budgeted division income for the year. He has asked Segato to book $240,000 of sales on December 31. The customers' orders are firm, but the shoes are still in the production process. They will be shipped on or about January 4. Maloney said to Segato, "The key event is getting the sales order, not shipping the shoes. You should support me, not obstruct my reaching division goals."

Required

1. Describe Segato's ethical responsibilities.
2. What should Segato do if Maloney gives her a direct order to book the sales?

🌐 **1-28 Professional ethics and corporate governance.** Jorge Michaels is the Winnipeg-based controller of Sxsw Foods, a rapidly growing manufacturer and marketer of Mexican food products. Michaels is currently considering the purchase of a new cost management package for use by each of its six manufacturing plants and its many marketing personnel. Four major competing products are being considered by Michaels. ◄ **LO 5**

Horizon 1-2-3 is an aggressive software developer. It views Sxsw as a target of opportunity. Every six months Horizon has a three-day users' conference in a Caribbean location. Each conference has substantial time left aside for "rest and recreation." Horizon offers Michaels an all-expenses-paid visit to the upcoming conference in Cancun, Mexico. Michaels accepts the offer, believing that it will be very useful to talk to other users of Horizon software. He is especially looking forward to the visit as he has close relatives in the Cancun area.

Before leaving, Michaels receives a visit from the president of Sxsw. She shows him an anonymous letter sent to her. It argues that Horizon is receiving unfair favourable treatment in the Sxsw software decision-making process. The letter specifically mentions Michaels's upcoming "all-expenses-paid trip to Cancun during Winnipeg's deep winter." Michaels is deeply offended. He says he has made no decision and believes he is very capable of making a software choice on the merits of each product. Sxsw currently does not have a formal written code of ethics.

Required

1. Do you think Michaels faces an ethical problem regarding his forthcoming visit to the Horizon users' group meeting? Explain.
2. Should Sxsw allow executives to attend users' meetings while negotiating with other vendors about a purchase decision? Explain. If yes, what conditions on attending should apply?
3. Would you recommend that Sxsw develop its own code of ethics to handle situations such as this one? What are the pros and cons of having such a written code?

Collaborative Learning Case

1-29 Global company, ethical challenges. In June 2018, the government of Vartan invited bids for the construction of a cellular telephone network. ZenTel, an experienced communications company, was eager to enter the growing field of cellular telephone networks in countries with poor infrastructures for land lines. If ZenTel won a few of these early contracts, it would be sought after for its field experience and expertise. After careful analysis, it prepared a detailed bid for the Communications Ministry of Vartan, building in only half of its usual profit margin and providing a contractual guarantee that the project would be completed in two years or less. The multimillion-dollar bid was submitted before the deadline, and ZenTel received notification that it had reached the Vartan government. Then, despite repeated faxes, emails, and phone calls to the ministry, there was no news on the bids or the project from the Vartan government. ◄ **LO 5**

Steve Cheng, VP of Global Operations for ZenTel, contacted the Canadian commercial attaché in Vartan, who told him that his best chance was to go to Vartan and try to meet the deputy minister of communications in person. Cheng prepared thoroughly for the trip, rereading the proposal and making sure that he understood the details.

At the commercial attaché's office in Vartan's capital, Cheng waited nervously for the deputy minister and his assistant. Cheng had come to Vartan with a clear negotiating strategy to try to win the bid. Soon the deputy minister and his staff arrived, introductions were made, and pleasantries were exchanged. The deputy minister asked a few questions about ZenTel and the bid and then excused himself, leaving his assistant to talk to Cheng. After clearly indicating that many other compelling bids had been made by firms from around the world, the assistant said, "Mr. Cheng, I guarantee that ZenTel's bid will be accepted if you pay a $1 million commission. Of course, your excellent proposal doesn't have to be altered in any way." It was clear to Cheng that the "commission" was, in fact, a bribe. Tactfully, he pointed out that Canadian laws and ZenTel's corporate policy prohibited such a payment. The assistant wished him a good day and a pleasant flight home and left.

Required

1. As a shareholder in ZenTel, would you prefer that ZenTel executives agree to the payment of the "commission"?
2. When Cheng described his experience to his friend Hank Shorn, who managed international business development for another company, Hank said that his own "personal philosophy" was to make such payments if they were typical in the local culture. Do you agree with Hank's point of view? Explain.
3. Why would ZenTel have a corporate policy against such payments?
4. What should Steve Cheng do next?

2

An Introduction to Cost Terms and Purposes

▶ **Learning Objectives**

1. Identify and distinguish between two manufacturing cost classification systems: direct and indirect, prime and conversion.

2. Differentiate fixed from variable cost behaviour, and explain the relationship of cost behaviour to direct and indirect cost classifications.

3. Interpret unitized fixed costs appropriately when making cost management decisions.

4. Apply cost information to produce a GAAP-compliant statement of comprehensive income showing proper cost of goods sold and a statement of financial position showing proper inventory valuation.

5. Explain cost identification, classification, and management systems and their use within the decision framework.

▶ **CPA Competencies**

This chapter covers material outlined in **Section 3: Management Accounting** of the CPA Competency Map. The Learning Objectives in this chapter have been aligned with the CPA Competency Map to ensure the best coverage possible.

3.3.1 Evaluates cost classifications and costing methods for management of ongoing operations

3.1.2 Evaluates and applies cost management techniques appropriate for specific costing decisions

LMspencer/Shutterstock

High Fixed Costs and the Implications for Production

In 2015, surf wear company Quiksilver announced it had filed for Chapter 11 bankruptcy. Its high fixed costs—costs that did not decrease as the number of board shorts and hoodies sold declined—crippled the company.

In the 1990s and early 2000s, Quiksilver rode the wave of young shoppers emulating the cool lifestyle of surfers, skateboarders, and snowboarders to financial success. During this time, the company opened hundreds of retail stores worldwide, many in expensive areas such as Times Square in New York. This expansion saddled the company with a huge amount of debt. In 2017, as sales rapidly declined, the company collapsed under the weight of its high fixed operating costs—like long-term leases and salaries—and crippling debt-servicing payments. After declaring bankruptcy, Quiksilver began rapidly selling off noncore brands and closing many retail stores.

As the story of Quiksilver illustrates, managers must understand their firms' costs and closely manage them. Organizations as varied as the United Way, the Mayo Clinic, and Sony generate reports containing a variety of cost concepts and terms managers need to understand to effectively run their businesses. This chapter discusses cost concepts and terms that are the basis of accounting information used for internal and external reporting.

Sources: Andrew Khouri. 2015. "Wipeout: Quiksilver files for Chapter 11 bankruptcy in U.S.," *Los Angeles Times*, September 9 (http://www.latimes.com/business/la-fi-quiksilver-bankruptcy-20150909-story.html); Deborah Belgum. 2015. "Oaktree Capital Working on Buying Quiksilver," *California Apparel News*, November 3 (https://www.apparelnews.net/news/2015/nov/03/oaktree-capital-working-buying-quiksilver).

Costs and Cost Terminology

Accountants define a **cost** as a resource sacrificed or forgone to achieve a specific objective. A cost (such as direct materials or advertising) is usually measured as the monetary amount that must be paid to acquire goods or services. An **actual cost** is the cost incurred (a historical or past cost), as distinguished from a **budgeted cost**, which is a predicted or forecasted cost (a future cost).

Answering the question "What does it cost?" requires knowing what "it" is and what problem the cost information will be applied to. "It" is anything for which a measurement of costs is desired. Next, managers have to decide if the budgeted cost of a **cost object** or the actual cost or both is desired. Managers often need both when making decisions, since actual or past costs help managers predict future costs in a budget.

A typical cost management information system has two stages: cost accumulation and cost assignment. **Cost accumulation** is the collection (accumulation) of actual cost data in an organized way. Management accountants refer to accumulated costs as **cost pools**. This is not to be confused with what financial accountants collect in general ledger accounts, though on first glance they appear the same. Cost pools can include costs from *different* transactions, whereas costs accumulated in the general ledger are for *similar* transactions only. A cost pool, for example, could include all the material and labour costs for a cost object. At its Woodstock plant, Toyota accumulates actual costs in categories such as raw materials, different types of labour, equipment use, and supervision (see Exhibit 2-1).

Cost assignment systematically links a pool of actual costs to a distinct cost object. For example, managers and management accountants assign accumulated costs to different models of cars (the cost object). Toyota managers use this cost information to help them determine the selling price for that particular model. They also use the information to motivate and influence employees by rewarding actions they take that reduce costs.

Some costs, such as material costs, are easier to assign to a cost object than others, such as supervision costs. One reason is that some costs pay for resources shared in completing many diverse cost objects. Assigning cost pools common to diverse cost objects is not as easy as assigning a cost pool used exclusively to complete a distinct cost object.

Commonly Used Classifications of Manufacturing Costs

Three terms commonly used when describing manufacturing costs are *direct material costs*, *direct manufacturing labour costs*, and *indirect manufacturing costs*.

1. *Direct material costs (DM)* are the acquisition costs of all materials that eventually become part of the cost object (work-in-process and then finished goods) and can be traced to the cost object in an economically feasible way. Acquisition costs of direct materials include freight-in (inward delivery) charges, sales taxes, and customs duties. Examples of direct material costs are the steel and tires used to make the Toyota RAV4, and the computer chips used to make smartphones.

2. *Direct manufacturing labour costs (DML)* include the compensation of all manufacturing labour that can be traced to the cost object (work-in-process and then finished goods) in an economically feasible way. Examples include wages and fringe benefits paid to machine operators and assembly-line workers who convert direct materials purchased into finished goods.

► **LO 1**

Identify and distinguish between two manufacturing cost classification systems: direct and indirect, prime and conversion.

Exhibit 2-1 Examples of Distinct Cost Objects at Toyota

Cost Object	Illustration
Product	A Toyota RAV4 sports activity vehicle
Service	Telephone hotline providing information and assistance to Toyota dealers
Project	R&D project on enhancing the DVD system in Toyota cars
Customer	Herb Chambers Motors, a Toyota dealer that purchases a broad range of Toyota vehicles
Activity	Setting up machines for production or maintaining production equipment
Department	Environmental, Health, and Safety Department

3. *Indirect manufacturing costs*, also referred to as *manufacturing overhead costs (MOH)* or *factory overhead costs*, are all manufacturing costs that are related to the cost object (work-in-process and then finished goods) but cannot be traced to a cost object in an economically feasible way. Examples include depreciation, maintenance supplies, and supervisors' salaries in a specific plant. We use *indirect manufacturing costs* and *manufacturing overhead costs* interchangeably.

Direct Costs and Indirect Costs

We now describe how costs are classified as direct or indirect and the methods used to assign these costs to cost objects.

■ **Direct costs** of a cost object are related to the distinct cost object and can be *traced* to it. For example, the cost of tires can be readily accumulated from invoices, payments, and requisitions from inventory. These documents provide a "paper trail" of costs that can be traced directly to a car model—for example, the Toyota RAV4. The accumulated cost of tires for the Toyota RAV4 is an example of a **direct materials (DM) cost**. Toyota can also electronically trace any individual worker's time spent working on the RAV4 through time sheets. This is an example of a **direct manufacturing labour (DML) cost**. Through its management information system (MIS), Toyota can trace sales commission costs for the RAV4. This is an example of a non-manufacturing **direct labour (DL) cost**.

■ **Indirect costs** of a cost object are necessary but cannot be traced to a specific cost object in a cost-effective way because the benefits from use of the resources are shared among diverse cost objects. The cost of shared resources is common to many cost objects, but often the sharing is unequal. **Cost allocation** is the method used to divide up an indirect cost pool unequally and assign costs to diverse cost objects. Indirect costs may be either manufacturing or non-manufacturing costs.

■ Typical indirect manufacturing costs are often referred to as **manufacturing overhead (MOH)**. Collectively, these indirect costs can represent a far larger proportion of total production costs than total direct costs; some examples of typical MOH costs are

Indirect Materials	Indirect Manufacturing Overhead
Indirect supplies	Security (labour and supplies)
Indirect materials	Cleaning supplies, fittings, and fasteners
Indirect Labour	
All labour fringe benefits	Quality control (labour, equipment, supplies)
Rework of output	Maintenance in the plant (labour, supplies)
Overtime	All statutory fringe benefits (CPP, EI)
Idle time	Plant lease or plant amortization
	Equipment lease or equipment depreciation

Non-manufacturing costs are incurred either before production begins or after production ends. Costs incurred prior to production are often called **upstream costs,** and those incurred after production are called **downstream costs.** Because a company can only be profitable if it recovers its full costs, non-manufacturing costs must be either traced or allocated to cost objects. Salaries for engineers who invent and design a new product are an example of an upstream indirect non-manufacturing cost; sales commission is an example of a downstream direct non-manufacturing cost.

To summarize, *cost assignment* is a general term that encompasses both (1) tracing direct costs to a distinct cost object and (2) allocating indirect costs among diverse cost objects. Exhibit 2-2 depicts upstream, production, and downstream direct and indirect costs with both forms of cost assignment: cost tracing and cost allocation.

Each company determines how to accumulate, trace, allocate, and assign all its costs. Exhibit 2-2 illustrates *one* possible way to assign direct and indirect costs in the value chain using one model Toyota RAV4 as the distinct cost object. The items listed in each

Exhibit 2-2 Cost Assignment of Upstream, Production, and Downstream Business Function Costs

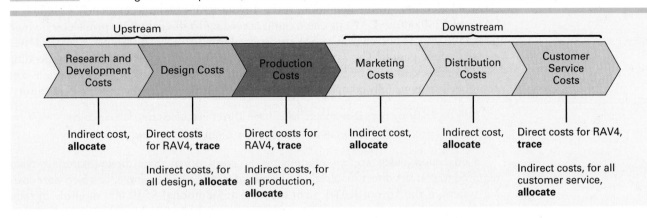

business function would be very different if the cost object was the customer service department or the activity of developing a special Toyota promotion event at the Montreal Grand Prix Formula One Race.

Factors Affecting Direct/Indirect Cost Classifications

Distinguishing direct from indirect costs is not straightforward. Situations differ. Balancing several factors that influence cost classification requires professional judgment:

■ **Selection of the distinct cost object.** Whether a cost pool is classified as direct or indirect will change depending on the cost object. For example, a Toyota assembly-line supervisor's salary can be accumulated in the direct cost pool for the assembly department. This is a distinct cost object that benefits exclusively from the costs of the work done by the supervisor. But if the assembly line produces different models of Toyota vehicles, and some models require more attention than others, then the benefits of the assembly-line supervisor's salary are shared among the various models. More than one model means the cost objects are diverse. The costs cannot be traced but must be allocated.

■ **The materiality or significance of the cost in question.** The smaller the cost, the less likely it is economically feasible to trace that cost to a particular cost object. The cost of the colour of dye added to each plastic interior piece in a Toyota is insignificant—less than a fraction of $0.01—and it costs more than this to trace the dye cost to a distinct model. It is cost effective to accumulate all costs of dye into one MOH account. Models benefiting significantly more (less) from this common resource will be assigned more (less) cost from the MOH cost pool. For financial accountants, *material* refers to the level of materiality, usually a difference of between 5% and 10% of the total dollar value of the cost pool.

■ **Available information-gathering technology.** Integrated cost information systems access cost data electronically through bar codes and radio frequency identification. At Toyota, component parts such as the different computer chips for its on-board computers are identified and can be scanned at every point in the production process. Software makes this cost data accessible to any authorized user in accounts receivable, R&D, customer service, or production.

■ **Design of operations.** It's easier to classify and accumulate direct cost pools when one facility is used exclusively for a specific cost object, such as a specific product, model, activity, or customer.

Prime Costs and Conversion Costs

Two terms describe cost classifications in the production function of the value chain: *prime costs* and *conversion costs*. Cost classification as prime or conversion requires professional judgment because these are not mutually exclusive categories in all situations.

Prime costs are defined as direct manufacturing costs (DM, DML) *but* are not always classified according to the definition. If the Toyota RAV4 plant accumulated $240,000 in DM and $260,000 in DML in one month, according to the definition prime costs would total $500,000. However, prime costs are assigned using an **average cost** per input used over a specific time period. The average cost, also called a **unit cost**, is calculated by dividing the total prime cost pool by physical units consumed. Cost assignment splits the prime cost pools between units fully complete and those remaining in work-in-process (WIP) inventory.

$$\text{Prime costs} = \text{Direct material costs} + \text{Direct manufacturing labour costs}$$
$$= \$240,000 + \$260,000 = \$500,000$$

Conversion costs are all manufacturing costs other than direct materials costs required to convert direct materials into finished goods.[1] For example, in a two-part costing system, if the Toyota RAV4 plant incurred an additional $550,000 monthly in total MOH costs, then total monthly conversion costs would be $810,000 ($260,000 DML + $550,000 total MOH = $810,000).

$$\text{Conversion costs} = \frac{\text{Direct manufacturing}}{\text{labour costs}} + \frac{\text{Manufacturing}}{\text{overhead costs}} = \$260,000 + \$550,000 = \$810,000$$

Cost-Behaviour Patterns: Variable Costs and Fixed Costs

► **LO 2**

Differentiate fixed from variable cost behaviour, and explain the relationship of cost behaviour to direct and indirect cost classifications.

Accounting systems record and accumulate costs of inputs acquired to complete business functions in the value chain over a specific time period. Some total costs change with the quantity of inputs purchased and used to complete outputs. These are variable costs. Other costs remain constant regardless of the quantity of outputs produced within a specified **relevant range**, or band of normal activity level or volume in which there is a specific relationship between the level of activity or volume and the cost in question. These are fixed costs.

Variable Costs

A **variable cost** (VC) changes in proportion to changes in the related level of total activity or volume within a relevant range, because the cost per unit is constant. Relevant range means that between a minimum and a maximum number of units the cost per unit does not change.

For example, at the Toyota Woodstock plant, the relevant range is from 1 to 100 steering wheels. The steering wheel includes all the windshield wiper and Bluetooth controls, directional signals, and audio-visual controllers. Within this range, each steering wheel installed will cost $250 and the total variable cost will equal the variable cost per unit multiplied by the quantity of steering wheels purchased and installed.

Number of RAV4s Produced (1)	Variable Cost per Steering Wheel (2)	Total Variable Cost of Steering Wheels (3) = (1) × (2)
1	$250	$ 250
1,000	250	250,000
3,000	250	750,000

Fixed Costs

In contrast, a **fixed cost** is constant within a relevant range of finished outputs produced. Assume the relevant range at Woodstock is 0 to 100 vehicles. No matter how many Toyota

---

[1] Generally accepted accounting principles (GAAP) guide all financial accounting classifications and reporting to external parties. For Canadian companies listed on a stock exchange, financial disclosure at year-end must be IFRS–GAAP compliant. While standards may differ among countries (the United States does not use IFRS), GAAP remain unchanged.

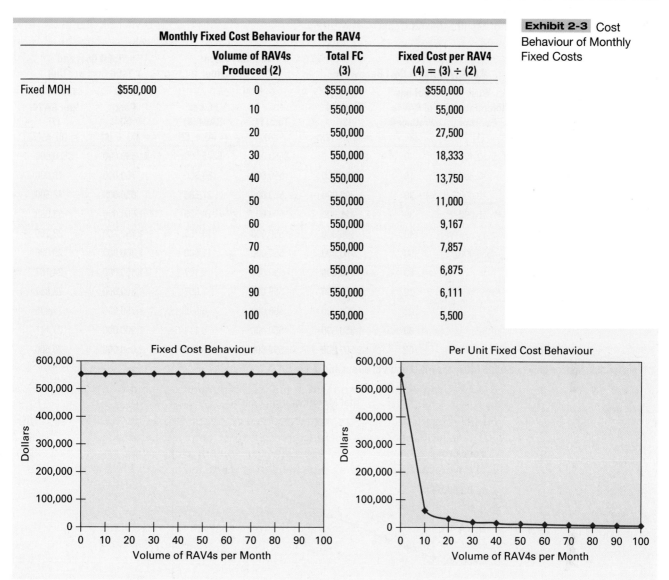

Monthly Fixed Cost Behaviour for the RAV4

		Volume of RAV4s Produced (2)	Total FC (3)	Fixed Cost per RAV4 (4) = (3) ÷ (2)
Fixed MOH	$550,000	0	$550,000	$550,000
		10	550,000	55,000
		20	550,000	27,500
		30	550,000	18,333
		40	550,000	13,750
		50	550,000	11,000
		60	550,000	9,167
		70	550,000	7,857
		80	550,000	6,875
		90	550,000	6,111
		100	550,000	5,500

Exhibit 2-3 Cost Behaviour of Monthly Fixed Costs

RAV4s are produced in one month to a maximum of 100, the fixed cost will remain unchanged. For simplicity, assume the total monthly fixed MOH of the Woodstock plant is $550,000, listed in column (3) of Exhibit 2-3. The monthly fixed cost remains unchanged regardless of the volume of vehicles produced, listed in column (2), from 0 to 100 per month. If managers at Woodstock needed to meet demand of 150 vehicles, then fixed cost would increase because this quantity of output exceeds the relevant range or capacity of the plant. Toyota would have to expand the size of the plant, purchase additional equipment, hire more salaried staff, and so on.

The vehicle per unit fixed cost is calculated as monthly fixed cost divided by the quantity of vehicles produced in the month, as listed in column (4). The per unit fixed cost decreases as the number of vehicles assembled increases.

Exhibit 2-4[2] illustrates the effect on *total* manufacturing costs when the monthly volume of RAV4s produced changes. This is an example of a **mixed cost**. A mixed costs pool comprises both variable and fixed costs. The sloped line originates at $550,000 when 0 vehicles are produced because even if no Toyota RAV4s are produced in a month, the plant will still cost $550,000.

---

[2] The calculations and graph in this example demonstrate that even at zero production, fixed costs must still be paid. However, averaging across zero units is mathematically undefined; therefore, this line begins at 1 unit.

Exhibit 2-4 Cost Behaviour of Monthly Mixed Costs

	Monthly Variable Cost Behaviour			Monthly Fixed Cost Behaviour		Total Cost and Total Cost per Unit	
	Cost Information Per Unit (1)	Volume of RAV4s Produced (2)	Total VC (3) = (1) × (2)*	Total FC (4)	FC per RAV4 (5) = (4) ÷ (2)	Total Cost (6) = (3) + (4)	Total Cost per RAV4 (7) = (6) ÷ (2)
DM VC per steering wheel	$ 2,400	0	$ 0	$550,000	$275,000	$ 550,000	$550,000
DML VC per RAV4	2,600	10	150,000	550,000	55,000	700,000	70,000
Indirect total VC per RAV4	10,000	20	300,000	550,000	27,500	850,000	42,500
Unit VC, direct and indirect	15,000	30	450,000	550,000	18,333	1,000,000	33,333
		40	600,000	550,000	13,750	1,150,000	28,750
Fixed MOH	550,000	50	750,000	550,000	11,000	1,300,000	26,000
		60	900,000	550,000	9,167	1,450,000	24,167
		70	1,050,000	550,000	7,857	1,600,000	22,857
		80	1,200,000	550,000	6,875	1,750,000	21,875
		90	1,350,000	550,000	6,111	1,900,000	21,111
		100	1,500,000	550,000	5,500	2,050,000	20,500

*This formula applies only to the $15,000 in the row "Unit VC, direct and indirect."

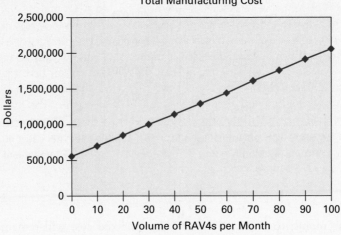

Total Manufacturing Cost

TRY IT! 2.1

Pepsi Corporation uses trucks to transport bottles from the warehouse to different retail outlets. This problem focuses on the cost of operating a truck. Gasoline costs are $0.15 per km driven. Insurance costs are $6,000 per year. Calculate the total costs and the cost per kilometre for gasoline and insurance if the truck is driven (a) 20,000 km per year or (b) 30,000 km per year.

Cost Drivers

A **cost driver** is a variable, such as the level of activity or volume, that causally affects costs over a given time span. For direct costs there is a readily measured cause and effect relationship between the change in either the level of activity (hours of DML) or volume (kilograms of DM used) and a change in the total costs. For other production costs, such as the cost of plant security, which benefits all distinct cost objects, the measure of benefit may be the computer space required to store surveillance records of distinct areas in the plant. The larger the storage space, the higher the assumed benefit for the distinct cost object.

Sustainability in Action | How Enterprise Carshare Reduces Business Transportation Costs

Transforming a fixed to a variable cost for a business is a good cost leadership strategy. AutoShare, now known as Enterprise Carshare, founded by Kevin McLaughlin in 1998, operates in Toronto. It offers a car-sharing service to its members. This form of outsourcing is a pay-on-demand model for periods as short as one hour and as long as one year. Members reserve vehicles online or by phone, then retrieve the vehicle, swipe an electronic card over a sensor that unlocks the vehicle, and drive away. Corporate rates begin at $7.75/hour plus a one-time fee of $125 (to pay for insurance and credit checks) and a deposit of $250, refundable when membership terminates. The cars are picked up from and returned to specified locations.

Car sharing allows companies to convert the fixed costs of owning a company car to variable costs of using a car. If business slows, or a car isn't required to visit a client, AutoShare customers are not saddled with the fixed costs of car ownership. AutoShare's fleet is about 10% hybrid cars, and the company claims its service takes 10 cars off the road for every AutoShare vehicle.

Sources: R. Shahzad. 2016. To own or not to own: Torontonians on why they love car sharing services, CBC News, August 14 (http://www.cbc.ca/news/canada/toronto/car-sharing-toronto-1.3719270); Enterprise Car Share (http://carsharingtoronto.com); How does Zipcar work? (http://www.zipcar.com/how; http://www.thestar.com/business/article/974358-zipcar gears-up-for-ipo; M. Lostracco. 2006. The car sharing shootout: Autoshare vs. Zipcar, *Torontoist*, September 7 (http://torontoist.com/2006/09/the_car_sharing.php).

The cost driver of a variable cost is the level of activity or volume whose change causes proportionate changes in the variable cost. For example, the number of vehicles assembled is the cost driver of the total cost of steering wheels. If setup workers are paid an hourly wage, the number of setup-hours is the cost driver of total (variable) setup costs.

Costs that are fixed in the short run have no cost driver in the short run but may have a cost driver in the long run. Consider the costs of testing, say, 0.1% of the colour printers produced at a Hewlett-Packard plant. These costs consist of equipment and staff costs of the testing department that are difficult to change and, hence, are fixed in the short run with respect to changes in the volume of production. In this case, volume of production is not a cost driver of testing costs in the short run. In the long run, however, Hewlett-Packard will increase or decrease the testing department's equipment and staff to the levels needed to support future production volumes. In the long run, volume of production is a cost driver of testing costs. Costing systems that identify the cost of each activity such as testing, design, or setup are called *activity-based costing systems*.

Total Costs and Unit Costs

The preceding section concentrated on the behaviour patterns of total costs in relation to activity or volume levels. We now consider unit costs.

▶ **LO 3**

Interpret unitized fixed costs appropriately when making cost management decisions.

Unit Costs

Generally, the decision maker should think in terms of relevant costs rather than unit costs. In many decision contexts, however, calculating a unit cost is essential. Consider the booking agent who has to make the decision to book Britney Spears to play at the Rogers Centre. She estimates the cost of the event to be $4,000,000. This knowledge is helpful for the decision, but it is not enough.

Before a decision can be reached, the booking agent also must predict the number of people who will attend. She computes the unit cost of the event by dividing the total cost ($4,000,000) by the expected number of people who will attend. If 50,000 people attend, the unit cost is $80 (= $4,000,000 ÷ 50,000) per person; if 20,000 attend, the unit cost increases to $200 (= $4,000,000 ÷ 20,000).

Unless the total cost is "unitized" (that is, averaged with respect to the level of activity or volume), the $4,000,000 cost is difficult to interpret. The unit cost combines the total cost and the number of people in a handy, communicative way.

Consider the manager of the New Brunswick plant of Acadian Products: Assume the $40,000,000 in costs in 2018 consists of $10,000,000 of fixed costs and $30,000,000 of variable costs (at $60 variable cost per speaker system produced). Suppose the total fixed cost and the variable cost per speaker system in 2019 are expected to be unchanged from 2018. The budgeted costs for 2019 at different production levels, calculated on the basis of total variable costs, total fixed costs, and total costs, are as follows:

Units Produced (1)	Variable Cost per Unit (2)	Total Variable Costs (3) = (1) × (2)	Total Fixed Costs (4)	Total Costs (5) = (3) + (4)	Unit Cost (6) = (5) ÷ (1)
100,000	$60	$ 6,000,000	$10,000,000	$16,000,000	$160.00
200,000	60	12,000,000	10,000,000	22,000,000	110.00
500,000	60	30,000,000	10,000,000	40,000,000	80.00
800,000	60	48,000,000	10,000,000	58,000,000	72.50
1,000,000	60	60,000,000	10,000,000	70,000,000	70.00

A plant manager who uses the 2018 unit cost of $80 per unit will underestimate actual total costs if 2019 output is below the 2018 level of 500,000 units. If actual volume is 200,000 units because of, say, the presence of a new competitor, actual costs would be $22,000,000. The unit cost of $80 × 200,000 units equals $16,000,000, which underestimates the actual total costs by $6,000,000 (= $22,000,000 − $16,000,000). *The unit cost of $80 applies only when 500,000 units are produced.*

An overreliance on *unit* cost in this situation could lead to insufficient cash being available to pay costs if volume declines to 200,000 units. As the table indicates, for making this decision, managers should think in terms of total variable costs, total fixed costs, and total costs rather than unit cost. As a general rule, first calculate total costs, then compute a unit cost, if it is needed for a particular decision.

Cost of Goods Sold and the Statement of Comprehensive Income

▶ **LO 4**

Apply cost information to produce a IFRS/ASPE-compliant statement of comprehensive income showing proper cost of goods sold and a statement of financial position showing proper inventory valuation.

IFRS/ASPE rules on inventory and **cost of goods sold (COGS)** for Canadian companies trading on the Toronto Stock Exchange (TSX) are identical whether finished goods are produced in Canada, the United States, or Europe. For the Toyota RAV4, the COGS is assigned by multiplying the total costs of production by the volume of RAV4s produced and sold. To simplify, assume that the beginning inventory is zero and the manufacturing costs do not change month by month. Next month, the Woodstock plant produces 50 RAV4s. This would mean the Costs of Goods Manufactured would be the total Costs of Goods Available for Sale, as shown in Exhibit 2-5. The per unit total cost as shown below is $26,000. If all 50 vehicles are sold, then the COGS will be $1,300,000 and there will be no

Exhibit 2-5 Finished Goods Ending Inventory Valuation, COGM, and COGS for RAV4s (in $ thousands)

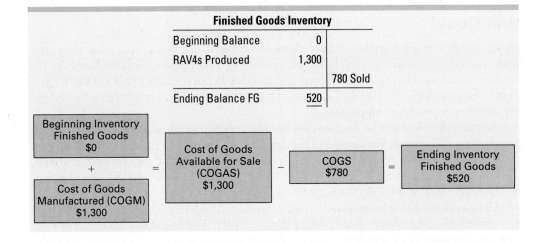

inventory of finished goods at the start of the next month. By contrast, Exhibit 2-5 shows there were 30 vehicles sold, which results in a Cost of Goods Sold (COGS) of $780,000 ($26,000 × 30 vehicles), resulting in an Ending Finished Goods Inventory of $520,000.

The per unit total manufacturing cost depends on the volume of RAV4s produced; therefore, both COGS and **cost of goods manufactured (COGM)** will vary with the volume manufactured each month.

$$\frac{\text{Total manufacturing costs}}{\text{Number of units manufactured}} = \frac{\$1,300,000}{50 \text{ units}} = \$26,000 \text{ per unit}$$

If 30 units are sold at a price of $37,143 each, and 20 units remain in finished goods ending inventory, the per unit cost helps the financial accountant report several important pieces of information. Exhibit 2-5 details how the total cost of goods available for sale (COGAS) is allocated to the COGS, which is matched to all items sold and reported on the statement of comprehensive income; and the remaining amount (in this case, $520,000), which will be designated as ending finished goods inventory and reported on the statement of financial position. Exhibit 2-6 then details how the COGS is used to create a statement of comprehensive income for the sale of RAV4s for the month.

Exhibit 2-7 depicts the flow of transactions through the statement of comprehensive income of Tech1.

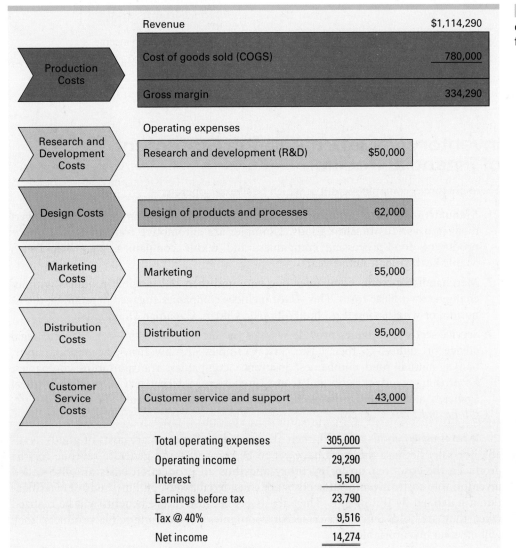

Revenue		$1,114,290
Cost of goods sold (COGS)		780,000
Gross margin		334,290
Operating expenses		
Research and development (R&D)	$50,000	
Design of products and processes	62,000	
Marketing	55,000	
Distribution	95,000	
Customer service and support	43,000	
Total operating expenses	305,000	
Operating income	29,290	
Interest	5,500	
Earnings before tax	23,790	
Tax @ 40%	9,516	
Net income	14,274	

Production Costs
Research and Development Costs
Design Costs
Marketing Costs
Distribution Costs
Customer Service Costs

Exhibit 2-6 Statement of Comprehensive Income for One Month

Exhibit 2-7 Flow of Revenue and Costs for a Manufacturing-Sector Company—Tech1

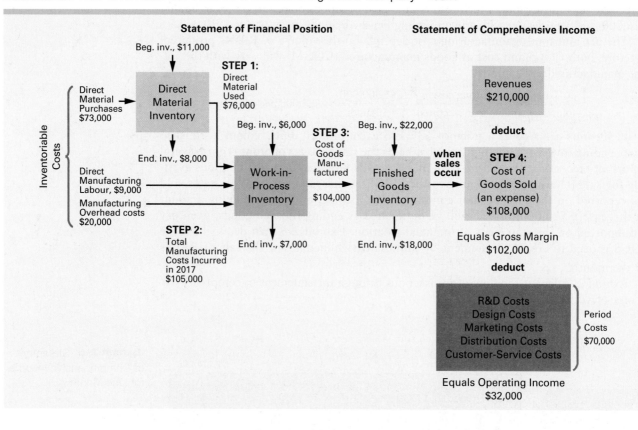

Inventory Valuation and the Statement of Financial Position

There are three economic sectors in which businesses operate:

1. **Manufacturing-sector companies** purchase materials and components and convert them into various finished goods. Examples are automotive companies, cell phone producers, food-processing companies, and textile companies (e.g., BlackBerry, Maple Leaf, Gildan Activewear).

2. **Merchandising-sector companies** purchase and then sell tangible products without changing their basic form. This sector includes companies engaged in retailing, distribution, or wholesaling (e.g., Indigo Books, Gildan, Canadian Diamonds).

3. **Service-sector companies** provide services (intangible products)—for example, legal advice or audits—to their customers. Examples are law firms, accounting firms, banks, mutual fund companies, insurance companies, transportation companies, advertising agencies, radio and television stations, internet service providers, travel agencies, and brokerage firms (e.g., Tory's, Bank of Montreal, Via Rail, Cossette, *Globe and Mail*, Cogeco).

If no finished goods are sold, then all manufacturing costs are costs of goods available for sale. Because the costs have yet to be recovered and generate revenue for the producer, the costs remain in inventory and thus all production costs are also called **inventoriable costs**. Inventoriable costs are considered assets, and methods of classification are defined by IFRS/ASPE. They are assets because future benefits will be realized when they are sold. Since service-sector companies provide intangible products, they will have no inventoriable costs.

When finished goods are sold, their costs move out of cost of goods available for sale and into cost of goods sold (COGS). Nonproduction costs, either upstream or downstream of production, are called period costs (or operating expenses). Not all of the three business sectors generate inventoriable costs.

Types of Inventory

In this section, we describe the different types of inventory that companies hold and some commonly used classifications of manufacturing costs. Manufacturing-sector companies purchase both raw materials and finished components, then convert them into finished goods. These companies typically have the following three types of inventory:

1. **Direct materials inventory (DM)** consists of materials in stock and awaiting use in the manufacturing process, such as computer chips and components needed to manufacture smartphones.

2. **Work-in-process inventory (WIP)** consists of goods partially worked on but not yet completed, such as smartphones at various stages of completion in the manufacturing process. Also called **work in progress.**

3. **Finished goods inventory (FG)** consists of the completed goods that have not been sold yet, such as complete smartphones.

In contrast, merchandising-sector companies purchase finished goods and then sell them without any further conversion to a different form. They hold only finished goods inventory, referred to as *merchandise inventory*. Service-sector companies provide only services, which are intangible and cannot be held in inventory. They have no equivalent to either cost of sales or cost of goods sold.

Inventoriable Costs

Inventoriable costs are all costs of a product that are considered as assets on the statement of financial position when they are incurred. Inventoriable costs become cost of goods sold on the statement of comprehensive income when the product is sold. The cost of goods sold includes all three of the manufacturing costs (direct materials, direct manufacturing labour, and MOH) incurred to produce the goods that are sold. Inventoriable costs arise *only* for companies in the manufacturing sector.

For merchandising-sector companies like The Brick, inventoriable costs are usually called **cost of sales (COS)**. COS includes purchasing costs of the goods (that are eventually sold), incoming freight, insurance, and handling costs. The goods will undergo no further conversion. Service-sector companies provide something that can be experienced, an intangible, which cannot be inventoried. They do not incur any inventoriable costs of production or purchase. Typical costs classified as direct/indirect and variable/fixed for the distinct bank service of mortgage lending would be as follows:

Classification of a Cost for Distinct Cost Object Mortgage Loans

		Direct	Indirect
Cost-Behaviour Pattern	Variable Costs	Appraisal fees to value property	Internet service costs to transmit documents
	Fixed Costs	Mortgage division supervisor's salary	Sponsorship cost of annual charity events

Period Costs

Period costs are all costs in the statement of comprehensive income other than cost of goods sold. They are also referred to as *upstream and downstream costs, non-manufacturing* *costs*, *operating expenses*, and *noninventoriable costs*. Because there is not sufficient evidence to conclude that any future benefit will arise from incurring these costs, they are not considered an asset. Under GAAP, period costs are expensed when incurred.

For merchandising-sector companies, period costs in the statement of comprehensive income are all costs *excluded* from COS. Examples of these period costs are labour costs of sales floor personnel, advertising, distribution, and customer-service costs. For service-sector companies, all costs on the statement of comprehensive income are period costs, because there are neither inventories nor inventoriable costs for these companies. Interest and tax are not operating expenses. They are financing and regulatory costs. They are reported as deductions below the total operating income line.

Illustrating the Flow of Inventoriable Costs: A Manufacturing-Sector Example

We can follow the flow of inventoriable costs through the statement of comprehensive income of a manufacturing company. Exhibit 2-8 shows the GAAP-compliant, audited statement of comprehensive income for Tech1, a technology company. As described earlier, inventoriable costs flow through the statement of financial position accounts as direct materials are converted through work-in-process inventory, where labour and manufacturing overhead are added, and finished goods inventory before entering cost of goods sold in the statement of comprehensive income. This completes all the production transactions required to identify, accumulate, and assign costs of goods manufactured.

Assuming all costs are given for Tech1, the cost assignment to inventory and COGS is described in steps 1 to 4 shown in Exhibit 2-8. The costs to produce finished goods (COGM) are recovered when finished goods are sold and identified as cost of goods sold (COGS) on the statement of comprehensive income. Unsold finished goods inventory is reported on the statement of financial position as one component of total manufacturing inventory.

Step 1: Cost of direct materials used Note how the costs never disappear in Exhibit 2-8 but flow through inventories until they are recovered when finished goods are sold. The correct terminology is *transferred in* when costs accumulate in an account, and *transferred out* when costs flow from one account into another.

Beginning DM inventory value for this year is $11,000. This year's direct material purchases, $73,000, "fill up" the DM inventory as cost of DM available for use. As DM is used, the cost of $76,000 "empties out" inventory, leaving a DM ending inventory value of $8,000 that becomes the beginning inventory value for the next year, as illustrated at the top of Exhibit 2-8.

Beginning inventory of direct materials, January 1	$11,000
+ Purchases of direct materials	73,000
− Ending inventory of direct materials, December 31	8,000
= Direct materials used	$76,000

Step 2: Total manufacturing costs incurred Total manufacturing costs refers to all of Tech1's direct material, labour, and manufacturing overhead costs incurred during conversion this year. Some costs remain in WIP for those goods that were not fully converted to finished foods (FG).

(i) Direct materials used (shaded blue in Exhibit 2-8)	$ 76,000
(ii) Direct manufacturing labour (shaded blue in Exhibit 2-8)	9,000
(iii) Manufacturing overhead costs (shaded blue in Exhibit 2-8)	20,000
Total manufacturing costs incurred	$105,000

Exhibit 2-8 Tech1 Statement of Comprehensive Income

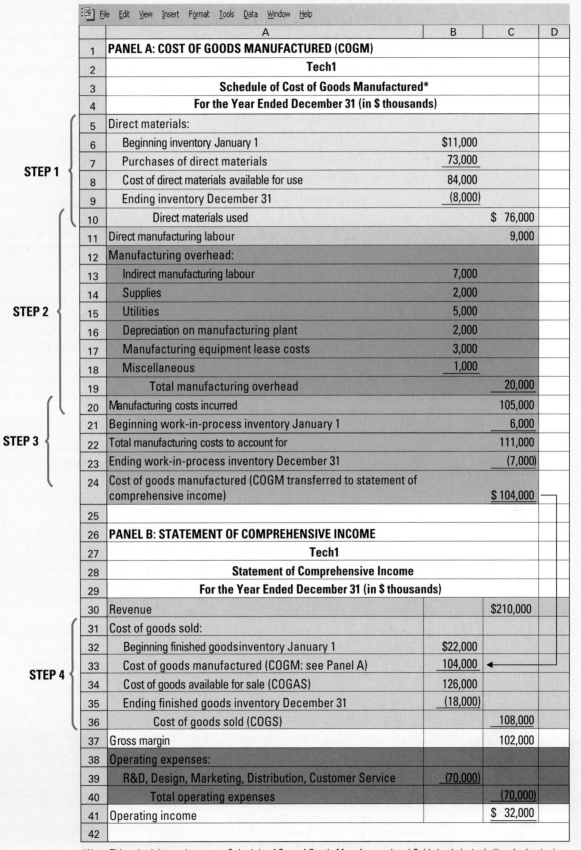

	A	B	C	D
1	**PANEL A: COST OF GOODS MANUFACTURED (COGM)**			
2	**Tech1**			
3	**Schedule of Cost of Goods Manufactured***			
4	**For the Year Ended December 31 (in $ thousands)**			
5	Direct materials:			
6	Beginning inventory January 1	$11,000		
7	Purchases of direct materials	73,000		
8	Cost of direct materials available for use	84,000		
9	Ending inventory December 31	(8,000)		
10	Direct materials used		$ 76,000	
11	Direct manufacturing labour		9,000	
12	Manufacturing overhead:			
13	Indirect manufacturing labour	7,000		
14	Supplies	2,000		
15	Utilities	5,000		
16	Depreciation on manufacturing plant	2,000		
17	Manufacturing equipment lease costs	3,000		
18	Miscellaneous	1,000		
19	Total manufacturing overhead		20,000	
20	Manufacturing costs incurred		105,000	
21	Beginning work-in-process inventory January 1		6,000	
22	Total manufacturing costs to account for		111,000	
23	Ending work-in-process inventory December 31		(7,000)	
24	Cost of goods manufactured (COGM transferred to statement of comprehensive income)		$ 104,000	
25				
26	**PANEL B: STATEMENT OF COMPREHENSIVE INCOME**			
27	**Tech1**			
28	**Statement of Comprehensive Income**			
29	**For the Year Ended December 31 (in $ thousands)**			
30	Revenue		$210,000	
31	Cost of goods sold:			
32	Beginning finished goodsinventory January 1	$22,000		
33	Cost of goods manufactured (COGM: see Panel A)	104,000		
34	Cost of goods available for sale (COGAS)	126,000		
35	Ending finished goods inventory December 31	(18,000)		
36	Cost of goods sold (COGS)		108,000	
37	Gross margin		102,000	
38	Operating expenses:			
39	R&D, Design, Marketing, Distribution, Customer Service	(70,000)		
40	Total operating expenses		(70,000)	
41	Operating income		$ 32,000	
42				

STEP 1 — rows 5–9
STEP 2 — rows 10–19
STEP 3 — rows 20–24
STEP 4 — rows 31–36

Note: This schedule can become a Schedule of Cost of Goods Manufactured and Sold simply by including the beginning and ending finished goods inventory figures in the supporting schedule rather than in the body of the statement of comprehensive income.

Step 3: Cost of goods manufactured

COGM refers to the cost of all goods completely converted from raw materials to finished goods during the year and transferred out to finished goods inventory. Beginning WIP inventory value of $6,000 and total manufacturing costs of $105,000 incurred this year "fill up" the WIP inventory box. Some of the manufacturing costs incurred remain in WIP as the ending work-in-process inventory value of $7,000. This becomes the beginning inventory value for the next year, and the COGM this year of $104,000 "empties out" the WIP inventory value, while "filling up" the finished goods inventory value.

Beginning work-in-process inventory, January 1	$ 6,000
+ Total manufacturing costs incurred	105,000
= Total manufacturing costs to account for	111,000
− Ending work-in-process inventory, December 31	7,000
= Cost of goods manufactured	$104,000

Steps 2 and 3 are combined in the illustration of the flow of costs in Exhibit 2-8 because in combination they lead to the correct value for inventoriable cost assignment to either finished goods or WIP inventory.

Step 4: Cost of goods sold

The COGS is the cost of only the finished goods inventory that has been sold to customers during the current year. The beginning inventory value of finished goods of $22,000 reports unsold inventory from last year. Adding the COGM this year of $104,000 "fills up" the finished goods inventory box. These two accumulated costs are the cost of goods available for sale (COGAS) of $126,000. Subtracting the COGS for this year of $108,000 "empties out" the finished goods inventory value to leave unsold goods of $18,000. COGS matches this year's revenues. Tech1's COGS and ending inventory values are:

Beginning inventory of finished goods, January 1	$ 22,000
+ Cost of goods manufactured	104,000
− Ending inventory of finished goods, December 31	18,000
= Cost of goods sold	$108,000

Newcomers to cost accounting often assume that indirect costs such as utilities, telephone, and depreciation are always costs of the period in which they are incurred. This is not true. The classification depends on the business function where the costs were incurred. If they are incurred specifically in production, then they comprise MOH and, according to GAAP, are inventoriable. When incurred in other non-manufacturing business functions, they are period costs (expenses).

Interest expense is incurred during a specific time period, but it is a financing, not an operating, cost. The value-chain business functions exclude finance decisions. Finance decisions are closely coordinated with strategic and operating decisions, including

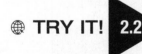 **TRY IT! 2.2**

Diana Corporation provides the following information for 2017.

Beginning inventory of direct materials, 1/1/2017	$12,000
Purchases of direct materials in 2017	$85,000
Ending inventory of direct materials 12/31/2017	$7,000
Direct manufacturing labour costs in 2017	$30,000
Manufacturing overhead costs in 2017	$40,000

Calculate the total manufacturing costs incurred in 2017.

production. Similarly, tax expense is not an operating expense despite being a period cost. It is a regulatory cost of doing business in any country.

Inventoriable Costs and Period Costs for a Merchandising Company

Inventoriable costs and period costs flow through the statement of comprehensive income at a merchandising company similarly to the way costs flow at a manufacturing company. At a merchandising company, however, the flow of costs is much simpler to understand and track because the only inventory is finished goods. Purchased goods are held as merchandise inventory, the cost of which is shown as an asset in the statement of financial position. As the goods are sold, their costs are shown in the statement of comprehensive income as cost of sales.

A merchandising-sector company also has a variety of period costs, such as marketing, distribution, and customer-service costs. In the statement of comprehensive income, period costs are deducted from revenues without ever having been included as part of inventory. In Exhibit 2-9, the top half distinguishes between inventoriable costs and period costs for a retailer or wholesaler who buys goods for resale. The bottom half distinguishes inventoriable and period costs for a manufacturer.

Exhibit 2-9 Merchandising Compared to Manufacturing Ledgers and Statement of Comprehensive Income Terminology

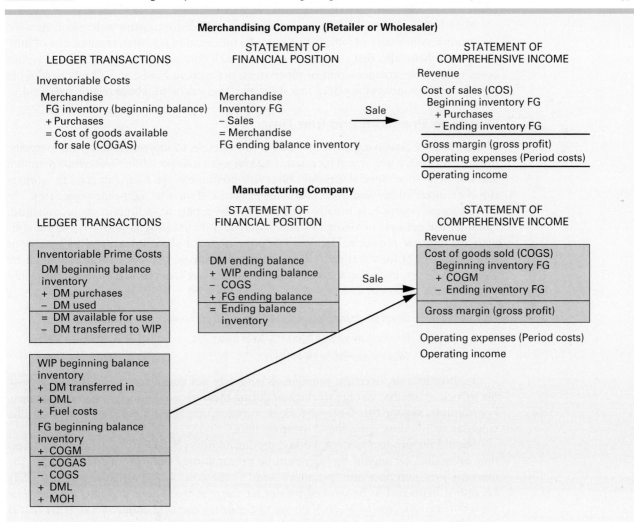

Measuring and Classifying Costs Requires Judgment

▶ **LO 5**

Explain cost identification, classification, and management systems and their use within the decision framework.

Measuring costs requires judgment because costs can be defined and classified in alternative ways. Different companies and even different subunits within the same company may define and classify the same costs differently. Definition and classification of costs depends on the decision that needs to be made, the cost object, and the company. We illustrate this point with respect to labour cost measurement.

Measuring Labour Costs

Although manufacturing labour cost classifications vary among companies, most companies have the following categories:

- Direct labour costs that can be traced to individual products
- Overhead
- Indirect labour compensation for
  - Factory office staff
  - Factory security
- Rework labour (time spent by direct labourers correcting software errors)
- Overtime premium paid to software programmers (explained next)
- Idle time (explained next)
- Managers', department heads', and supervisors' salaries
- Payroll fringe costs—for example, health care premiums and pension costs

Note how *indirect labour costs* are commonly divided into many subclassifications—for example, office staff and idle time—to retain information on different categories of indirect labour. Note also that managers' salaries usually are not classified as indirect labour costs. Instead, the compensation of supervisors, department heads, and all others who are regarded as management is placed in a separate classification of labour-related overhead.

Overtime Premium and Idle Time

The purpose of classifying costs in detail is to associate an individual cost with a specific cause or reason for why it was incurred. Two classes of indirect labour—overtime premium and idle time—need special mention. **Overtime premium** is the wage rate paid to workers (for both direct labour and indirect labour) in *excess* of their straight-time wage rates.

Overtime premium is usually considered to be a part of indirect costs or overhead. Consider the example of George Flexner, a junior software programmer who writes software for multiple products. He is paid $20 per hour for straight-time and $30 per hour (time and a half) for overtime. His overtime premium is $10 per overtime hour. If he worked 44 hours, including 4 overtime hours, in one week, his gross compensation would be classified as follows:

Direct programming labour: 44 hours × $20 per hour	$880
Overtime premium: 4 hours × $10 per hour	40
Total compensation for 44 hours	$920

In this example, overtime premium is generally not considered a direct cost because the particular job that George worked on during the overtime hours is a matter of chance. For example, assume that George worked on two products for 5 hours each on a specific workday of 10 hours, including 2 overtime hours.

Should the product George worked on during hours 9 and 10 be assigned the overtime premium? Or should the premium be prorated over both products? Prorating the overtime premium does not "penalize"—add to the cost of—a particular product solely because it happened to be worked on during the overtime hours. *Instead, the overtime premium is considered to be attributable to the heavy overall volume of work. Its cost is regarded as part of overhead, which is borne by both products.*

Sometimes overtime is not random. For example, a launch deadline for a particular product may clearly be the sole source of overtime. In such instances, the overtime premium is regarded as a direct cost of that product.

Another subclassification of indirect labour is the idle time of both direct and indirect labour. **Idle time** is wages paid for unproductive time caused by lack of orders, machine or computer breakdowns, work delays, poor scheduling, and the like. For example, if George had no work for 3 hours during that week while waiting to receive code from another colleague; George's earnings would be classified as follows:

Direct programming labour: 41 hours $\times$ $20/hour =	$820
Idle time (overhead): 3 hours $\times$ $20/hour =	60
Overtime premium (overhead): 4 hours $\times$ $10/hour =	40
Total earnings for 44 hours =	$920

Clearly, the idle time is not related to a particular product, nor, as we have already discussed, is the overtime premium. Both overtime premium and idle time are considered overhead costs.

Decision Framework and Flexibility of Costing Methods

Many cost terms found in practice have ambiguous meanings. Consider the term *product cost*. A **product cost** is the sum of the costs assigned to a product to make a specific decision. Different decisions often require different measures of product cost, as the brackets on the value chain in Exhibit 2-10 show:

Use the five-step decision-making process to classify costs depending on the decision to be made. IFRS/ASPE limits flexibility in cost classification for external reporting purposes. For internal management decisions, management accountants can provide a customized costing method. This flexibility allows for faithful representation of the economic reality of any business by reporting relevant costs in an orderly way.

1. *Identify the problem and uncertainties.* Decisions to comply with IFRS/ASPE for external reporting differ from those to determine eligibility for government reimbursement or to determine the most profitable product mix. Costing depends on the problem to be solved.

2. *Obtain information.* Identify and classify direct and indirect costs to match the decision that must be made. These data are usually available in the company's MIS, and the higher the data quality, its faithful representation, detail, and timeliness, the more reliable and relevant the information will be. Managers also gather information about the economy, customers, competitors, and prices of substitute products from external sources.

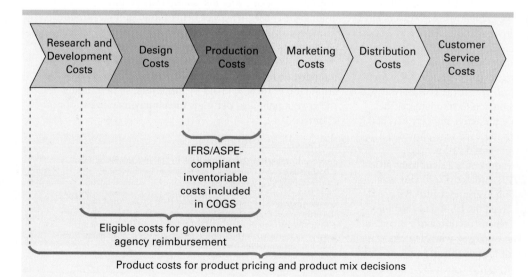

Exhibit 2-10 Different Product Costs for Different Purposes

Different Cost Classification Systems

1. Business function
   a. Research and development
   b. Design of products, services, or processes
   C. Production
   d. Marketing
   e. Distribution
   f. Customer service
2. Assignment to a cost object
   a. Direct cost
   b. Indirect cost

3. Behaviour pattern in relation to the level of activity or volume
   a. Variable cost
   b. Fixed cost
4. Aggregate or average
   a. Total cost
   b. Unit cost
5. Assets or expenses
   a. Inventoriable cost
   b. Period cost

---

3. *Predict the future.* Estimate future costs of the cost object. This requires making predictions about the quantity of outputs that managers expect to sell and understanding fixed and variable cost behaviours as quantities of output change.

4. *Decide among alternatives.* Clarify both the definition and classification systems to more accurately assign costs that identify alternative courses of action, then make a choice.

5. *Implement the decision, evaluate performance, and learn.* Compare actual to predicted cost outcomes to learn from successes and remedy any shortfalls.

The concepts introduced in this chapter are the basis for understanding cost accounting and cost management. The concepts can be applied to many topics, such as strategy evaluation, customer profitability, and investment decisions. We develop and apply these concepts in the remainder of the text.

Concepts in Action   Don't Overcharge the Government

Recently, after a normal audit, the US Pentagon identified in excess of US$1.03 billion billed by Haliburton's subsidiary Kellogg, Brown, and Root (KBR). Two former employees of KBR and a Kuwaiti businessman have been indicted and charged with 10 counts of defrauding the US government of more than $3.5 million. Contracts were awarded by the US military for logistics support to front-line troops during the Iraq war.

But the fraud extended into the US military procurement process itself. Two civilian whistleblowers have testified at special Senate investigations that contracts were awarded without a bidding process. Furthermore, no oversight was extended by those accountable to do so. The logistics contracts awarded exceeded $7 billion, but one KBR employee testified that the government was being overcharged $1 million a month to launder the troops' clothing. And while the active military was being housed at $1.39 per month in leased tents, housing in Kuwait for KBR's employees cost $110 per day.

Defrauding of the government is a significant problem. On November 5, 2010, a different company was fined a total of $69.3 million in criminal and civil penalties. The company overcharged the US Agency for International Development for reconstruction work in Sudan, Iraq, and Afghanistan. The employee who blew the whistle has received a portion of the penalties as a reward for disclosing how the company padded its bills by adding indirect costs unrelated to the contracted projects. Two senior financial officers of the company pleaded guilty to fraud and may spend up to 37 months in jail.

Accounting systems are never intended to provide companies with a way to inflate actual costs or to make up imaginary costs. They are intended to disclose faithfully the costs of what was actually done—the economic reality. For accountants, public disgrace, crippling financial penalties, and loss of the right to practise are among the consequences of being found guilty of fraud. The Code of Professional Ethics states that management accountants must act with responsibility for and fidelity to public needs. This means accounting services are intended to serve both the public and the client. Government contracts are paid by taxpayers, so defrauding the government also defrauds the taxpaying citizens of a country.

Sources: L. Johnston. 2004. New Fuel to Halliburton Fraud Fire, *CBS Evening News*, August 17 (http://www.cbsnews.com/stories/2004/08/17/eveningnews/main636644.shtml); C-Span. 2005. Demotion of Pentagon Whistle Blower, September 16 (http://www.c-spanvideo.org/program/188894-1); J. Risen. 2010. War Reconstruction Fraud Draws Big Fines. *New York Times*, November 5 (http://www.nytimes.com/2010/11/06/world/asia/06contractor.html?_r=1&ref=reconstruction); J. Ryan. 2010. N.J. Company agrees to $69M settlement for overbilling U.S. in Iraq, Afghanistan contacts. *NJ.com*, November 5 (http://www.nj.com/news/index.ssf/2010/11/morristown_company_settles_in.html).

Pulling It All Together—Problem for Self-Study

(Try to solve this problem before examining the solution that follows.)

Problem

A distraught employee, Guy Arson, put a torch to a manufacturing plant on February 26. The resulting blaze completely destroyed the plant and its contents. Fortunately, some accounting records were kept in another building. They revealed the following for the period from January 1 to February 26:

Direct materials (DM) purchased in January	$192,000
Work in process, January 1	40,800
Direct materials (DM), January 1	19,200
Finished goods, January 1	36,000
Indirect manufacturing costs	40% of conversion costs
Revenues	$ 600,000
Direct manufacturing labour (DML)	216,000
Prime costs	352,800
Gross margin percentage based on sales	20%
Cost of goods available for sale	$ 540,000

◄ **Required**

1. Calculate the cost of finished goods inventory, February 26.
2. Calculate the cost of work-in-process inventory, February 26.
3. Calculate the cost of direct materials inventory, February 26.

Solution

1. = $60,000
2. = $33,600
3. = $74,400

This problem is not as easy as it first appears. These answers are obtained by working from the known figures to the unknowns in the schedule below. Use the fact that DML overlaps in both prime and conversion costs. The basic relationships among the categories of costs are:

Prime costs (given)		$352,800
Direct materials used	= $352,800 − Direct manufacturing labour costs	136,800
	= $352,800 − $216,000	
Total conversion costs	= Direct manufacturing labour + Indirect manuf. costs	
0.4 × Conversion costs	= Indirect manufacturing costs	
0.6 × Conversion costs	= Direct manufacturing labour	216,000
Total conversion costs	= $216,000 ÷ 0.6	360,000
Indirect manuf. costs	= 0.40 × $360,000 (or $360,000 − $216,000)	144,000

It may be helpful to follow the key amounts through the work-in-process inventory, finished goods inventory, and cost of goods sold T-accounts. All amounts are in thousands of dollars:

Work-in-Process Inventory			Finished Goods Inventory			Cost of Goods Sold	
BI	40.8		BI	36			
DM used	136.8	COGM 504.0		→ 504	COGS 480		→ 480
DML	216.0						
OH	144.0						
(To account for	537.6)		*(Available for sale*	540)			
EI	33.6		EI	60		COGS	480

Decision Points

The following question-and-answer format summarizes the chapter's learning objectives. Each point presents a key question, and the guidelines are the answer to that question.

Learning Objectives	Guidelines
1. What distinguishes two manufacturing cost classification systems: direct and indirect, prime and conversion?	A direct cost is any cost that can be traced to the cost object in an economically feasible way. All direct costs are defined as prime costs. Indirect costs are related to a specific cost object but cannot be traced in an economically feasible way. All indirect manufacturing costs are conversion costs that may also include direct manufacturing labour. Classification of direct and indirect depends on the cost object.
2. How are variable and fixed costs different from one another, and how do they relate to direct and indirect costs?	A variable cost changes in total in proportion to changes in the related level of total activity or volume. A fixed cost remains unchanged in total for a given time period over a relevant range of volume. A cost may be either direct and variable or direct and fixed. Another cost may be either indirect and variable or indirect and fixed.
3. Why are average costs different from unitized fixed costs?	Analysis requires a focus on total costs, not unit costs. An average cost rate is appropriate only when the quantity of identical units produced is constant. The unitized (or, per unit) cost rate varies as the quantity of distinct units produced varies. The higher the quantity produced, the lower the unitized rate for a fixed cost pool.
4. What distinguishes inventoriable and period costs among manufacturing companies, merchandising companies, and service-sector companies?	Manufacturing-sector companies convert materials into finished goods. These costs are inventoriable under IFRS/ASPE. The three manufacturing inventories depict stages in the conversion process: direct materials, work in process, and finished goods. Non-manufacturing costs are period costs, also called operating expenses. Merchandising-sector companies never convert what they purchase prior to sale. Service-sector companies provide their customers with an intangible experience of a service. Service companies carry no inventory.
5. Explain the usefulness of cost identification, classification, and management systems.	Judgment is needed to distinguish the relevant costs pertaining to each type of decision. Costs from all business functions of the value chain are relevant to pricing and product-mix decisions. Three activities common to all costing systems are (1) calculate the cost of products, services, and other cost objects; (2) obtain information to plan, control, and evaluate performance; (3) analyze relevant information for different types of decisions.

Terms to Learn

This chapter and the Glossary at the end of the book contain definitions of the following important terms:

idle time (**p. 41**)

indirect cost (**p. 26**)

inventoriable costs (**p. 34**)

manufacturing overhead (MOH) (**p. 26**)

manufacturing-sector
   companies (**p. 34**)

merchandising-sector
   companies (**p. 34**)

mixed cost (**p. 29**)

overtime premium (**p. 40**)

period costs (**p. 35**)

prime costs (**p. 28**)

product cost (**p. 41**)

relevant range (**p. 28**)

service-sector companies (**p. 34**)

unit cost (**p. 28**)

upstream costs (**p. 26**)

variable cost (**p. 28**)

work-in-process inventory
   (WIP) (**p. 35**)

work in progress (**p. 35**)

Assignment Material

MyLab Accounting Make the grade with MyLab Accounting: The Short-Answer Questions, Exercises, and Problems marked with a ⊕ can be found on MyLab Accounting. You can practise them as often as you want, and most feature step-by-step guided instructions to help you find the right answer.

Short-Answer Questions

⊕   **2-1** Define *cost object*, and give three examples.

⊕   **2-2** Define *direct costs* and *indirect costs*.

⊕   **2-3** Why do managers consider direct costs to be more accurate than indirect costs?

⊕   **2-4** Name three factors that affect the classification of a cost as direct or indirect.

⊕   **2-5** What is a cost driver? Give one example.

⊕   **2-6** What is the *relevant range*? What role does the relevant-range concept play in explaining how costs behave?

⊕   **2-7** Explain why unit costs must often be interpreted with caution.

⊕   **2-8** Describe how manufacturing-, merchandising-, and service-sector companies differ from each other.

⊕   **2-9** What are three different types of inventory that manufacturing companies hold?

⊕   **2-10** Do service-sector companies have inventoriable costs? Explain.

⊕   **2-11** Describe the overtime-premium and idle-time categories of indirect labour.

⊕   **2-12** Define product cost. Describe three different purposes for computing product costs.

⊕   **2-13** Why do management accountants need to understand financial accounting?

Exercises

⊕   **2-14 Terminology.** A number of terms are listed below:

prime costs	fixed cost
inventoriable costs	period costs
indirect	conversion costs
variable cost	relevant cost

Required

Select the terms from the above list to complete the following sentences.

1. _____ are incurred during the process of transforming direct materials into finished goods ready for sale.

2. A _____ remains unchanged for a given time period, despite wide changes in the related level of total activity or volume of output.

3. _____ are all costs of a product that are considered as assets on the statement of financial position when they are incurred.

4. _____ are all direct manufacturing costs.

5. _____ are all costs in the statement of profit and loss other than cost of goods sold.

6. A _____ changes in proportion to changes in the related level of total activity or volume.
7. _____ costs of a cost object are related to the particular cost object but cannot be traced to it in an economically feasible (cost-effective) way.
8. _____ information is cost information that will change a decision. It is needed to identify and remedy different cost-management problems.

LO 1 ▶ ⊕ **2-15 Inventoriable costs versus period costs.** Each of the following cost items pertains to one of the following companies: Toyota (a manufacturing-sector company), Sobeys (a merchandising-sector company), and Google (a service-sector company):

1. Spring water purchased by Sobeys for sale to its customers.
2. Electricity used to provide lighting for assembly-line workers at a Toyota truck-assembly plant.
3. Depreciation on computer equipment at Google used to update directories of websites.
4. Electricity used to provide lighting for Sobeys store aisles.
5. Depreciation on computer equipment at Toyota used for quality testing of truck components during the assembly process.
6. Salaries of Sobeys marketing personnel planning local newspaper advertising campaigns.
7. Spring water purchased by Google for consumption by its software engineers.
8. Salaries of Google marketing personnel selling banner advertising.

Required

Classify each of the (**1–8**) cost items as an inventoriable cost or a period cost. Explain your answers.

LO 1, 3 ▶ ⊕ **2-16 Classification of costs, service sector.** Buger Research (BR) is a marketing research firm that organizes focus groups for consumer-product companies. Each focus group has eight individuals who are paid $50 per session to provide comments on new products. These focus groups meet in hotels and are led by a trained, independent marketing specialist hired by BR. Each specialist is paid a fixed retainer to conduct a minimum number of sessions and a per session fee of $2,000. A BR staff member attends each session to ensure that all the logistical aspects run smoothly.

Required

Classify each of the following cost items as

a. Direct or indirect (D or I) costs with respect to each individual focus group.
b. Variable or fixed (V or F) costs with respect to how the total costs of BR change as the number of focus groups conducted changes. (If in doubt, select on the basis of whether the total costs will change substantially if there is a large change in the number of groups conducted.)

You will have two answers (D or I; V or F) for each of the following items:

Cost Item	D or I	V or F
A. Payment to individuals in each focus group to provide comments on new products.		
B. Annual subscription of BR to *Consumer Reports* magazine.		
C. Phone calls made by the BR staff member to confirm individuals will attend a focus group session (records of individual calls are not kept).		
D. Retainer paid to the focus group leader to conduct 20 focus groups per year on new medical products.		
E. Meals provided to participants in each focus group.		
F. Lease payment by BR for corporate office.		
G. Cost of tapes used to record comments made by individuals in a focus group session (these tapes are sent to the company whose products are being tested).		
H. Gasoline costs of BR staff for company-owned vehicles (staff members submit monthly bills with no mileage breakdowns).		

LO 1, 3 ▶ ⊕ **2-17 Classification of costs, merchandising sector.** Home Entertainment Centre (HEC) operates a large store in Halifax. The store has both a DVD section and a music section (compact discs, MP3 players, etc.). HEC reports revenues for the DVD section separately from the music section.

Required

Classify each of the following cost items as

a. Direct or indirect (D or I) costs with respect to the DVD section.
b. Variable or fixed (V or F) costs with respect to how the total costs of the DVD section change as the number of DVDs sold changes. (If in doubt, select the cost type based on whether the total costs will change substantially if a large number of DVDs are sold.) You will have two answers (D or I; V or F) for each of the following items:

Cost Item	D or I	V or F

A. Annual retainer paid to a DVD distributor.
B. Electricity costs of HEC store (single bill covers entire store).
C. Costs of DVDs purchased for sale to customers.
D. Subscription to *DVD Trends* magazine.
E. Leasing of computer software used for financial budgeting at HEC store.
F. Cost of popcorn provided free to all HEC customers.
G. Fire insurance policy for HEC store.
H. Freight-in costs of DVDs purchased by HEC.

⊕ 2-18 Classification of costs, manufacturing sector. The Fremont, California, plant of NUMMI (New United Motor Manufacturing, Inc.), a joint venture of General Motors and Toyota, assembles two types of cars (Corollas and Geo Prisms). A separate assembly line is used for each type of car.

◀ **LO 1, 3**

Required

Classify each of the following cost items as

a. Direct or indirect (D or I) costs with respect to the type of car assembled (Corolla or Geo Prism).
b. Variable or fixed (V or F) costs with respect to how the total costs of the plant change as the number of cars assembled changes. (If in doubt, select the cost type based on whether the total costs will change substantially if a large number of cars are assembled.) You will have two answers (D or I, and V or F) for each of the following items:

Cost Item	D or I	V or F

A. Cost of tires used on Geo Prisms.
B. Salary of public relations manager for NUMMI plant.
C. Annual awards dinner for Corolla suppliers.
D. Salary of engineer who monitors design changes on Geo Prism.
E. Freight costs of Corolla engines shipped from Toyota City, Japan, to Fremont, California.
F. Electricity costs for NUMMI plant (single bill covers entire plant).
G. Wages paid to temporary assembly-line workers hired in periods of high production (paid on an hourly basis).
H. Annual fire-insurance policy cost for NUMMI plant.

⊕ 2-19 Variable costs, fixed costs, total costs. Ana Compo is getting ready to open a small restaurant. She is on a tight budget and must choose between the following long-distance phone plans:

◀ **LO 3**

Plan A: Pay 10 cents per minute of long-distance calling.
Plan B: Pay a fixed monthly fee of $16 for up to 300 long-distance minutes, and 5 cents per minute thereafter (if she uses fewer than 300 minutes in any month, she still pays $16 for the month).
Plan C: Pay a fixed monthly fee of $20 for up to 480 long-distance minutes and 4 cents per minute thereafter (if she uses fewer than 480 minutes, she still pays $20 for the month).

Required

Which plan should Compo choose if she expects to make 100 minutes of long-distance calls? 300 minutes? 500 minutes?

⊕ 2-20 Total costs and unit costs. A student association has hired a musical group for a graduation party. The cost will be a fixed amount of $4,800.

◀ **LO 3, 4, 5**
1. Unit cost per person $9.60

Required

1. Suppose 400 people attend the party. What will be the total cost of the musical group; the unit cost per person?
2. Suppose 4,000 people attend. What will be the total cost of the musical group; the unit cost per person?
3. For prediction of total costs, should the manager of the party use the unit cost in requirement 1; the unit cost in requirement 2? What is the major lesson of this problem?

⊕ 2-21 Total and unit costs, decision making. Graham's Glassworks makes glass flanges for scientific use. Materials cost $1 per flange, and the glass blowers are paid a wage rate of $20 per hour. A glass blower blows 10 flanges per hour. Fixed manufacturing costs for flanges are $20,000 per period. Period (non-manufacturing) costs associated with flanges are $10,000 per period and are fixed.

◀ **LO 3, 4, 5**
1. The variable direct manufacturing unit cost, $3/flange

Required

1. Fred's Flasks sells flanges for $8.25 each. Can Graham sell below Fred's price and still make a profit on the flanges? Assume Graham produces and sells 5,000 flanges this period.

2. How would your answer to requirement 2 differ if Graham's Glassworks made and sold 10,000 flanges this period? Why? What does this indicate about the use of unit cost in decision making?

LO 1, 4 ▶
2. Total fixed costs are $20.00

⊕ **2-22 Computing and interpreting manufacturing unit costs.** Maximum Office Products (MOP) produces three different paper products at its Vernon lumber plant—Supreme, Deluxe, and Regular. Each product has its own dedicated production line at the plant. MOP currently uses the following three-part classification for its manufacturing costs: direct materials, direct manufacturing labour, and indirect manufacturing costs. Total indirect manufacturing costs of the plant in May 2018 are $150 million ($20 million of which are fixed). This total amount is allocated to each product line on the basis of direct manufacturing labour costs of each line. Summary data (in millions) for May 2018 are

	Supreme	Deluxe	Regular
Direct materials cost	$ 84	$ 54	$ 62
Direct manufacturing labour costs	14	28	8
Indirect manufacturing costs	42	84	24
Production	90 kilograms	120 kilograms	100 kilograms

Required

1. Compute the total manufacturing cost per kilogram for each product produced in May 2018. Compute the total variable manufacturing cost per kilogram for each product produced in May 2018.
2. Suppose that in June 2018, production was 120 million kilograms of Supreme, 160 million kilograms of Deluxe, and 180 million kilograms of Regular. Why might the May 2018 information on total manufacturing costs per kilogram be misleading when predicting total manufacturing costs in June 2018?

LO 3 ▶
1. Total variable cost per tonne of sand, $130/tonne

⊕ **2-23 Variable costs and fixed costs.** Consolidated Minerals (CM) owns the rights to extract minerals from beach sands on Fraser Island. CM has costs in three areas:

a. Payment to a mining subcontractor who charges $80 per tonne of beach sand mined and returned to the beach (after being processed on the mainland to extract three minerals: ilmenite, rutile, and zircon).
b. Payment of a government mining and environmental tax of $50 per tonne of beach sand mined.
c. Payment to a barge operator. This operator charges $150,000 per month to transport each batch of beach sand—up to 100 tonnes per batch per day—to the mainland and then return to Fraser Island (that is, 0 to 100 tonnes per day = $150,000 per month; 101 to 200 tonnes per day = $300,000 per month, and so on).

Each barge operates 25 days per month. The $150,000 monthly charge must be paid even if fewer than 100 tonnes are transported on any day and even if CM requires fewer than 25 days of barge transportation in that month.

CM is currently mining 180 tonnes of beach sand per day for 25 days per month.

Required

1. What is the variable cost per tonne of beach sand mined? What is the fixed cost to CM per month?
2. Plot a graph of the variable costs and another graph of the fixed costs of CM. Your graphs should be similar to Exhibit 2-3 and Exhibit 2-4. Is the concept of relevant range applicable to your graphs? Explain.
3. What is the unit cost per tonne of beach sand mined (a) if 180 tonnes are mined each day and (b) if 220 tonnes are mined each day? Explain the difference in the unit-cost figures.

LO 3, 4 ▶
1. Annual relevant range of output, 0 to 60,000 jaw-breakers

⊕ **2-24 Variable costs, fixed costs, relevant range.** MegMunchies Ltd. manufactures jaw-breaker candies in a fully automated process. The machine that produces candies was purchased recently and can make 5,000 per month. The machine costs $6,000 and is depreciated using straight-line depreciation over 10 years assuming zero residual value. Rent for the factory space and warehouse, and other fixed manufacturing overhead costs, total $1,000 per month.

The company currently makes and sells 3,000 jaw-breakers per month. MegMunchies buys just enough materials each month to make the jaw-breakers it needs to sell. Materials cost 10 cents per jaw-breaker.

Next year the company expects demand to increase by 100%. At this volume of materials purchased, it will get a 10% discount on price. Rent and other fixed manufacturing overhead costs will remain the same.

Required

1. What is the current annual relevant range of output?
2. What is the current annual fixed manufacturing cost within the relevant range? What is the variable manufacturing cost?
3. What will the relevant range of output be next year? How will total fixed and variable manufacturing costs change next year?

2-25 Using unit costs for making decisions. Rhonda Heninger is a well-known software engineer. Her specialty is writing software code used in maintaining the security of credit card information. Heninger is approached by the Electronic Commerce Group (ECG). It offers to pay her $120,000 for the right to use her code under licence in its eprocurement software package. Heninger rejects this offer because it provides her with no additional benefits if the eprocurement package is a runaway success. Both parties eventually agree to a contract in which ECG pays Heninger a flat fee of $120,000 for the right to use her code in up to 10,000 packages. If eprocurement sells more than 10,000 packages, Heninger receives $9.60 for each package sold beyond the 10,000 level.

◀ LO 4
1. a. $60/package

Required

1. What is the unit cost of ECG for Heninger's software code included in its eprocurement package if it sells (a) 2,000, (b) 6,000, (c) 10,000, and (d) 20,000 packages? Comment on the results.
2. For prediction of ECG's total cost of using Heninger's software code in eprocurement, which unit cost (if any) of (a) to (d) in requirement 1 would you recommend ECG use? Explain.

2-26 Computing cost of goods manufactured and cost of goods sold. The following are account balances relating to 2019 (in thousands):

◀ LO 2, 4
1. Cost of goods manufactured, $252,000

Property tax on plant building	$ 3,800
Marketing, distribution, and customer-service costs	44,400
Finished goods inventory, January 1, 2019	32,400
Plant utilities	20,400
Work-in-process inventory, December 31, 2019	31,200
Depreciation of plant building	10,800
General and administrative costs (nonplant)	51,600
Direct materials used	104,400
Finished goods inventory, December 31, 2019	40,800
Depreciation of plant equipment	13,200
Plant repairs and maintenance	19,200
Work-in-process inventory, January 1, 2019	24,000
Direct manufacturing labour	40,800
Indirect manufacturing labour	27,600
Indirect materials used	13,200
Miscellaneous plant overhead	5,800

Required

Compute cost of goods manufactured and cost of goods sold.

2-27 Statement of comprehensive income and schedule of cost of goods manufactured. The Howell Corporation has the following account balances (in millions):

◀ LO 2, 4
1. Cost of goods manufactured, $774

For Specific Date		For Year 2019	
Direct materials, January 1, 2019	$18	Purchases of direct materials	$ 390
Work in process, January 1, 2019	12	Direct manufacturing labour	120
Finished goods, January 1, 2019	84	Depreciation—plant, building, and equipment	96
Direct materials, December 31, 2019	24	Plant supervisory salaries	6
Work in process, December 31, 2019	6	Miscellaneous plant overhead	42
Finished goods, December 31, 2019	66	Revenues	1,140
		Marketing, distribution, and customer-service costs	288
		Plant supplies used	12
		Plant utilities	36
		Indirect manufacturing labour	72

Required

Prepare a statement of comprehensive income and a supporting schedule of cost of goods manufactured for the year ended December 31, 2019.

🌐 **2-28 Computing cost of goods manufactured and cost of goods sold.** The following are account balances relating to 2019 (in thousands):

Property tax on plant building	$ 4,200
Marketing, distribution, and customer-service costs	44,400
Finished goods inventory, January 1, 2019	37,400
Plant utilities	20,400
Work-in-process inventory, December 31, 2019	32,200
Depreciation of plant building	14,700
General and administrative costs (nonplant)	51,600
Direct materials used	106,800
Finished goods inventory, December 31, 2019	44,800
Depreciation of plant equipment	14,700
Plant repairs and maintenance	19,200
Work-in-process inventory, January 1, 2019	25,000
Direct manufacturing labour	38,400
Indirect manufacturing labour	27,600
Indirect materials used	12,200
Miscellaneous plant overhead	5,200

Required

Compute cost of (a) goods manufactured and (b) cost of goods sold.

🌐 **2-29 Computing cost of goods purchased and cost of sales.** The data below are for Marvin Department Store. The account balances (in thousands) are for 2019.

Marketing, distribution, and customer-service costs	$ 37,000
Merchandise inventory, January 1, 2019	27,000
Utilities	17,000
General and administrative costs	43,000
Merchandise inventory, December 31, 2019	34,000
Purchases	155,000
Miscellaneous costs	4,000
Transportation in	7,000
Purchase returns and allowances	4,000
Purchase discounts	6,000

Required

Compute (a) cost of goods purchased and (b) cost of sales.

🌐 **2-30 Cost drivers and functions.** The list of representative cost drivers in the right column of this table is randomized with respect to the list of functions in the left column. That is, they do not match.

Function	Representative Cost Driver
1. Accounting	A. Number of invoices sent
2. Human resources	B. Number of purchase orders
3. Data processing	C. Number of research scientists
4. Research and development	D. Hours of computer processing unit (CPU)
5. Purchasing	E. Number of employees
6. Distribution	F. Number of transactions processed
7. Billing	G. Number of deliveries made

Required

1. Match each function with its representative cost driver.
2. Give a second example of a cost driver for each function.

Problems

🌐 **2-31 Labour cost, overtime, and idle time.** Len Lippart is a line worker in the assembly department of Maxart Manufacturing. He normally earns $12 per hour but gets time and a half ($18 per hour) for overtime over 40 hours per week. He earns double time if he works holidays even if he has not worked 40 hours that week.

◀ **LO 1**
1. a. $1,941.60

Sometimes the assembly-line equipment goes down and Len has to wait for the mechanics to repair the equipment or there is a scheduling mix-up. Len is paid for this time, and Maxart considers this idle time.

In May, Len worked two 42-hour weeks, one 43-hour week, and the last week he worked 40 hours, but one of those days was a national holiday. During regular hours, the assembly-line equipment was down 4.2 hours in May, and Len had one hour of idle time because of a scheduling mix-up.

Required

1. Calculate (a) direct manufacturing labour, (b) idle time, (c) overtime holiday premium, and (d) total earnings for Len in May.
2. Are idle time and overtime premium direct or indirect costs of the jobs that Len worked on in May? Explain.

2-32 Direct costs versus indirect costs. Gerry, Bonnie, and Juan are sales representatives for Digital Manufacturing Inc. (DMI). DMI specializes in low-volume production orders for the research groups of major companies. Each sales representative receives a base salary plus a bonus based on 20% of the actual profit (gross margin) of each order they sell. Before this year, the bonus was 5% of the revenues of each order they sold. Actual profit in the revised system was defined as actual revenue minus actual manufacturing cost. DMI uses a three-part classification of manufacturing costs—direct materials, direct manufacturing labour, and indirect manufacturing costs. Indirect manufacturing costs are determined as 200% of actual direct manufacturing labour cost.

◀ **LO 5**
1. Gross margin percentage BBC, 6.9%

Benson receives a report on an DMI job for BBC Inc. She is dismayed by the low profit on the BBC job. She prided herself on not discounting the price BBC would pay by convincing BBC of the quality of DMI's work. Gerry discussed the issue with Bonnie and Juan. They share with details of their most recent jobs. Summary data are as follows:

Customer	Westec	La Electricidad	BBC
Sales representative	Juan	Bonnie	Gerry
Revenues	$514	$982	$580
Direct materials	300	492	324
Direct manufacturing labour	48	120	72
Indirect manufacturing	96	240	144
Direct labour-hours	2 hours	5 hours	2 hours

Gerry asks Hilda, DMI's manufacturing manager, to explain the different labour costs charged on the Westec and BBC jobs, given both used two direct labour-hours. She was told the BBC job was done in overtime and the actual rate ($36) was 50% higher than the $24 per hour straight-time rate. Benson noted that she brought the BBC order to EMI one week ago and there was no rush order on the job.

In contrast, the Westec order was a "hot-hot" one with a request it be done by noon the day after the order was received. Brunner said that the "actual cost" he charged to the BBC job was the $24 per hour straight-time rate.

Required

1. Using both the actual straight-time and overtime rates paid for direct labour, what is the actual profit DMI would report on each of the three jobs?
2. Assume that DMI charges each job for direct labour at the $24 straight-time rate (and that the indirect-manufacturing rate of 200% includes an overtime premium). What would be the revised profit DMI would report on each of the three jobs? Comment on any differences from requirement 1.
3. Discuss the pros and cons of charging the BBC job the $36 labour rate per hour.
4. Why might DMI adopt the 20% profit incentive instead of the prior 5% of revenue incentive? How might DMI define *profit* to reduce possible disagreements with its sales representatives?

LO 1, 2, 3 ▶
1. $1,400

🌐 **2-33 Comprehensive problem on unit costs, product costs.** Soo Office Equipment manufactures and sells metal shelving. It began operations on January 1, 2019. Costs incurred for 2019 are as follows (V stands for variable; F stands for fixed):

Direct materials used costs	$140,000 V
Direct manufacturing labour costs	30,000 V
Plant energy costs	5,000 V
Indirect manufacturing labour costs	10,000 V
Indirect manufacturing labour costs	16,000 F
Other indirect manufacturing costs	8,000 V
Other indirect manufacturing costs	24,000 F
Marketing, distribution, and customer-service costs	122,850 V
Marketing, distribution, and customer-service costs	40,000 F
Administrative costs	50,000 F

Variable manufacturing costs are variable with respect to units produced. Variable marketing, distribution, and customer-service costs are variable with respect to units sold.

Inventory data are as follows:

	Beginning, January 1, 2019	Ending, December 31, 2019
Direct materials	0 kilograms	2,000 kilograms
Work in process	0 units	0 units
Finished goods	0 units	? units

Production in 2019 was 100,000 units. Two kilograms of direct materials are used to make one unit of finished product.

Revenues in 2019 were $436,800. The selling price per unit and the purchase price per kilogram of direct materials were stable throughout the year. The company's ending inventory of finished goods is carried at the average unit manufacturing costs for 2019. Finished goods inventory at December 31, 2019, was $20,970.

Required

1. Calculate direct materials inventory, total cost, December 31, 2019.
2. Calculate finished goods inventory, total units, December 31, 2019.
3. Calculate selling price per unit in 2019.
4. Calculate operating income for 2019 (show your computations).

LO 2, 4 ▶
1. 125,000 units

2-34 Budgeted statement of comprehensive income (continuation of 2-33). Assume management predicts that the selling price per unit and variable cost per unit will be the same in 2020 as in 2019. Fixed manufacturing costs and marketing, distribution, and customer-service costs in 2020 are also predicted to be the same as in 2019. Sales in 2020 are forecast to be 122,000 units. The desired ending inventory of finished goods, December 31, 2020, is 12,000 units. Assume zero ending inventories of both direct materials and work in process. The company's ending inventory of finished goods is carried at the average unit manufacturing costs for 2020. The company uses the first-in, first-out inventory method. Management has asked that you prepare a budgeted statement of comprehensive income for 2020. On December 31, 2019, finished goods inventory is 9,000 units.

Required

1. Calculate the units of finished goods produced in 2020.
2. Prepare a budgeted statement of comprehensive income for 2020.

LO 2, 4 ▶
1. COGM $136,000

🌐 **2-35 Cost of goods manufactured.** Consider the following account balances (in thousands) for the Canseco Company:

	Beginning of 2019	End of 2019
Direct materials inventory	$22,000	$26,000
Work-in-process inventory	21,000	20,000
Finished goods inventory	18,000	23,000
Purchases of direct materials		75,000

	Beginning of 2019	End of 2019
Direct manufacturing labour		25,000
Indirect manufacturing labour		15,000
Plant insurance		9,000
Depreciation—plant building and equipment		11,000
Repairs and maintenance—plant		4,000
Marketing, distribution, and customer-service costs		93,000
General and administrative costs		29,000

Required

1. Prepare a schedule of cost of goods manufactured for 2019.
2. Revenues in 2019 were $300 million. Prepare the 2019 statement of comprehensive income.

⊕ **2-36 Flow of inventoriable costs.** Hofstra Plastics Inc.'s selected data for the month of August 2019 are presented below (in millions):

◀ **LO 2**
1. Direct materials inventory, $75

Work-in-process inventory, August 1, 2019	$ 200
Direct materials inventory, August 1, 2019	90
Direct materials purchased	360
Direct materials used	375
Variable manufacturing overhead	250
Total manufacturing overhead	480
Total manufacturing costs incurred during August 2019	1,600
Cost of goods manufactured	1,650
Cost of goods sold	1,700
Finished goods inventory, August 1, 2019	200

Required

Calculate the following costs:

1. Direct materials inventory on August 31, 2019.
2. Fixed manufacturing overhead costs for August.
3. Direct manufacturing labour costs for August.
4. Work-in-process inventory on August 31, 2019.
5. Cost of goods available for sale in August.
6. Finished goods inventory on August 31, 2019.

⊕ **2-37 Statement of comprehensive income and schedule of cost of goods manufactured.** The Powell Corporation has the following account balances (in millions):

◀ **LO 2, 4**
Operating income,
$75 COGM, $762

For Specific Date		For Year 2019	
Direct materials, January 1, 2019	$15	Purchases of direct materials	$ 390
Work in process, January 1, 2019	10	Direct manufacturing labour	120
Finished goods, January 1, 2019	70	Depreciation—plant building and equipment	96
Direct materials, December 31, 2019	20	Plant supervisory salaries	6
Work in process, December 31, 2019	5	Miscellaneous plant overhead	42
Finished goods, December 31, 2019	55	Revenues	1,140
		Marketing, distribution, and customer-service costs	288
		Plant supplies used	12
		Plant utilities	36
		Indirect manufacturing labour	60

Required

Prepare a statement of comprehensive income and a supporting schedule of cost of goods manufactured for the year ended December 31, 2019.

LO 1, 2, 4 ▶
4. Unit cost for direct materials, $385

🌐 **2-38 Interpretation of statements** (continuation of 2-37). Refer to the preceding problem.

Required

1. How would the answer to the preceding problem be modified if you were asked for a schedule of cost of goods manufactured and sold instead of a schedule of cost of goods manufactured? Be specific.
2. Would the sales manager's salary (included in marketing, distribution, and customer-service costs) be accounted for differently if the Powell Corporation were a merchandising company instead of a manufacturing company? Describe how the wages of an assembler in the plant would be accounted for in this manufacturing company.
3. Plant supervisory salaries are usually regarded as indirect manufacturing costs. Under what conditions might some of these costs be regarded as direct manufacturing costs? Give an example.
4. Suppose that both the direct materials used and the plant depreciation were related to the manufacture of 1 million units of product. What is the unit cost for the direct materials assigned to those units? What is the unit cost for plant building and equipment depreciation? Assume that yearly plant depreciation is computed on a straight-line basis.
5. Assume that the historical, actual cost behaviour patterns in requirement 4 persist—that is, direct materials costs behave as a variable cost and depreciation behaves as a fixed cost. Repeat the computations in requirement 4, assuming that the costs are being predicted for the manufacture of 1.2 million units of product. How would the total costs be affected?
6. As a management accountant, explain concisely to the president why the unit costs differed in requirements 4 and 5.

LO 1, 2 ▶
Cost of goods manufactured (to income statement) is $244.80

🌐 **2-39 Prime costs versus conversion costs.** The following items (in millions) pertain to the Chan Corporation:

For Specific Date		For Year 2019	
Work in process, January 1, 2019	$12.00	Plant utilities	$ 6.00
Direct materials, December 31, 2019	6.00	Indirect manufacturing labour	24.00
Finished goods, December 31, 2019	14.40	Depreciation—plant, building, and equipment	10.80
Accounts payable, December 31, 2019	24.00	Revenues	420.00
Accounts receivable, January 1, 2019	60.00	Miscellaneous manufacturing overhead	12.00
Work in process, December 31, 2019	2.40	Marketing, distribution, and customer-service costs	108.00
Finished goods, January 1, 2019	48.00	Purchases of direct materials	96.00
Accounts receivable, December 31, 2019	36.00	Direct manufacturing labour	48.00
Accounts payable, January 1, 2019	48.00	Plant supplies used	7.20
Direct materials, January 1, 2019	36.00	Property taxes on plant	1.20

Chan's manufacturing cost system uses a three-part classification of manufacturing costs. There are two prime costs and one conversion cost: direct materials, direct manufacturing labour, and indirect manufacturing costs.

Required

1. Identify the prime costs. Identify the conversion costs.
2. Prepare a statement of comprehensive income and a supporting schedule of cost of goods manufactured.

2-40 Statement of comprehensive income Beagle-grove Company is a metal- and wood-cutting manufacturer selling products to the home construction market. Consider the following data for the year 2019:

◀ **LO 2, 3, 4**
1. Operating income, $120,000
COGM, $960,000

Sandpaper	$ 2,000
Materials-handling costs	70,000
Lubricants-handling costs	5,000
Miscellaneous indirect manufacturing labour	40,000
Direct manufacturing labour	300,000
Direct materials, January 1, 2019	40,000
Direct materials, December 31, 2019	50,000
Finished goods January 1, 2019	100,000
Finished goods December 31, 2019	150,000
Work in process, January 1, 2019	10,000
Work in process, December 31, 2019	14,000
Plant leasing costs	54,000
Depreciation—plant equipment	36,000
Property taxes on plant equipment	4,000
Fire and casualty insurance on plant equipment	3,000
Direct materials purchased in 2019	460,000
Revenue	1,360,000
Marketing and promotion	60,000
Marketing salaries	100,000
Shipping costs	70,000
Customer-service costs	100,000

Required

1. Prepare a statement of comprehensive income with a separate supporting schedule of cost of goods manufactured. For all manufacturing items, indicate by V or F whether each is basically a variable cost or a fixed cost (where the cost object is a product unit). If in doubt, decide on the basis of whether the total cost will change substantially over a wide range of production output.
2. Suppose that both the direct materials and plant leasing costs are tied to the production of 900,000 units. What is the direct materials cost assigned to each output unit produced? Assume that the plant leasing costs are a fixed cost. What is the unit cost of the plant leasing costs?
3. Repeat the computation in requirement 2 for direct materials and plant leasing costs assuming that the costs are being predicted for the manufacturing of 1 million units next year. Assume no changes in the historical or actual cost behaviour patterns.
4. As a management consultant, explain concisely to the president why the direct materials cost per output unit did not change in requirements 2 and 3 but the plant leasing costs per output unit did change.
5. Calculate what direct manufacturing labour (DML) cost is as a percentage of total cost of goods sold (COGS). In your opinion is this a material cost? Provide your reason(s). Consistent with your opinion, would you classify DML as a prime or a conversion cost?

🌐 **2-41 Inventory decision, opportunity costs.** Lawnox, a manufacturer of lawn mowers, predicts that it will purchase 240,000 spark plugs next year. Lawnox estimates that 20,000 spark plugs will be required each month. A supplier quotes a price of $9 per spark plug. The supplier also offers a special discount option: If all 240,000 spark plugs are purchased at the start of the year, a discount of 4% off the $9 price will be given. Lawnox can invest its cash at 10% per year. It costs Lawnox $200 to place each purchase order.

◀ **LO 5**
1. Opportunity cost, $94,680

Required

1. How much interest income would be forgone from purchasing all 240,000 units at the start of the year instead of in 12 monthly purchases of 20,000 units per order?
2. Would this opportunity cost be recorded in the accounting system? Why?
3. Should Lawnox purchase 240,000 units at the start of the year or 20,000 units each month? Show your calculations.

Collaborative Learning Cases

LO 2 ▶
A = $20,700

2-42 Finding unknown balances. An auditor for Canada Revenue Agency is trying to reconstruct some partially destroyed records of two taxpayers. For each case in the accompanying list, find the unknowns designated by capital letters (figures are in thousands).

	Case 1	Case 2
Accounts receivable, December 31, 2018	$ 6,000	$ 2,100
Cost of goods sold	A	20,000
Accounts payable, January 1, 2018	3,000	1,700
Accounts payable, December 31, 2018	1,800	1,500
Finished goods inventory, December 31, 2018	B	5,300
Gross margin	11,300	C
Work in process, January 1, 2018	0	800
Work in process, December 31, 2018	0	3,000
Finished goods inventory, January 1, 2018	4,000	4,000
Direct materials used	8,000	12,000
Direct manufacturing labour	3,000	5,000
Indirect manufacturing costs	7,000	D
Purchases of direct material	9,000	7,000
Revenues	32,000	31,800
Accounts receivable, January 1, 2018	2,000	1,400

Required

Complete the table by finding the unknowns

LO 5 ▶
Direct manufacturing
labour costs are 16.4%

2-43 Labour-cost ethics, governance. XKY Manufacturing has recently opened a plant in Costa Melon in order to take advantage of certain tax benefits. In order to qualify for these tax benefits, the company's direct manufacturing labour costs must be at least 20% of total manufacturing costs for the period.

XKY Manufacturing normally classifies direct manufacturing labour wages as direct manufacturing labour but classifies fringe benefits, overtime premiums, idle time, and vacation time and sick leave as indirect manufacturing labour.

During the first period of operations in Costa Melon, XKY incurs a total of $2,500,000 in manufacturing costs. Of that, $410,000 is direct manufacturing labour wages, $45,000 is overtime premium, $86,000 is fringe benefits, $20,500 is vacation time and sick leave, and $10,900 is idle time.

Required

1. Will XKY's direct manufacturing labour costs qualify them for the tax benefit?
2. Buyoung Kim, the manager of the new Costa Melon plant, is concerned that she will not get a bonus this year because the plant will not get the tax benefit. What might she ask the plant controller to do to make sure XKY gets the tax benefit? How might these accounting changes be rationalized?
3. Should the plant controller do what the manager has asked in requirement 2? Why or why not?

LO 5 ▶
The variable costs of servicing
each room are $24 a night per
single occupancy

2-44 Classifying costs for managerial decisions. Kamal Diamond is the owner of the Galaxy chain of four-star prestige hotels. These hotels are in Chicago, London, Los Angeles, Montreal, New York, Seattle, Tokyo, and Vancouver. Diamond is currently struggling to set weekend rates for the Vancouver hotel (the Vancouver Galaxy). From Sunday through Thursday, the Galaxy has an average occupancy rate of 90%. On Friday and Saturday nights, however, average occupancy declines to less than 30%. Galaxy's *major customers* are business travellers who stay mainly Sunday through Thursday.

The current room rate at the Galaxy is $180 a night for single occupancy and $216 a night for double occupancy. These rates apply seven nights a week. For many years, Diamond has resisted having rates for Friday and Saturday nights that are different from those for the remainder of the week. Diamond has long believed that price reductions convey a "nonprestige" impression to his guests. The Vancouver Galaxy highly values its reputation for treating its guests as "royalty."

Most room costs at the Galaxy are fixed on a short-stay (per-night) basis. Diamond estimates the variable costs of servicing each room to be $24 a night per single occupancy and $26.40 a night per double occupancy.

Many prestige hotels in Vancouver offer special weekend rate reductions (Friday and/or Saturday) of up to 50% of their Sunday-through-Thursday rates. These weekend rates also include additional items such as a breakfast for two, a bottle of champagne, and discounted theatre tickets.

Required

1. Would you recommend that Diamond reduce room rates at the Vancouver Galaxy on Friday and Saturday nights? What factors to protect the value proposition should be considered in his decision?

2. In six months' time, the Grey Cup is to be held in Vancouver. Diamond observes that several four-star prestige hotels have already advertised a Friday-through-Sunday rate for Grey Cup weekend of $360 a night. Should Diamond charge extra for the Grey Cup weekend? Explain.

2-45 Cost analysis, litigation risk, governance. Sam Nash is the head of new product development of Forever Young (FY). Nash is currently considering Enhance, which would be FY's next major product in its beauty/cosmetics line, and its estimated unit cost is currently $144. Enhance represents a new direction for FY. All FY's current products are cosmetics applied to the skin by the consumer. In contrast, Enhance is inserted via needle into the skin by a nurse after an initial meeting with a doctor. FY planned to sell Enhance at cost plus 20% to physicians. FY used an estimated treatment cost to patients of $432 to provide a financial incentive to physicians. Each treatment will last three months. Enhance is an animal-based product that fills out the skin so that fewer wrinkles are observable.

◀ **LO 5**
With litigation, Physician's margin is $100.80

Nash, however, questions the economics of this product because FY has failed to budget for any litigation costs, which Nash estimated as $132 per unit. At present, the costs recognized are research and development, manufacturing by a third party, marketing, distribution, and a small amount for customer support. Nash's main concern is with recognizing in the current costing proposal potential future litigation costs (such as the costs of lawyers and expert witnesses in defending lawsuits against Enhance). He points to the litigation with breast implants and notes that a settlement of more than $4.8 billion is being discussed in the press. He also notes the tobacco company litigation and those proposed billion-dollar settlements. Elisabeth Savage, the CEO and president of the company, disagrees with Nash. She maintains that she has total confidence in her medical research team and directs Nash not to include any dollar amount for potential litigation cost in his upcoming presentation to the board of directors on the economics and pricing of the Enhance product. Nash was previously controller of FY and has a strong background in finance. His current job represents his first nonfinance position, and he views himself as potential CEO material.

Required

1. What reasons might Savage have for not wanting Nash to record potential future litigation costs on the product in a presentation on Enhance's economics and pricing?

2. Suppose Savage asks Nash to give her an "off-the-record" presentation on the possible magnitude of the potential litigation costs of Enhance. What is the new unit cost including the estimated litigation costs? What should the new selling price to physicians be to maintain the triple-the-cost target? What is the percentage decrease in the margin physicians could expect per unit assuming the cost to the patient cannot be changed?

3. After hearing Nash's presentation (see requirement 2), Savage directs Nash to drop any further discussion of the litigation issue. He is to focus on making Enhance the blockbuster product that field research has suggested it will be. Nash is uneasy with this directive. He tells Savage it is an "ostrich approach" (head-in-the-sand) to a real problem that could potentially bankrupt the company. Savage tells Nash to go and think about her directive. What should Nash do next?

SOLUTIONS

◀ TRY IT!

Try It 2–1

(a) Cost @ 20,000 km / year = $6,000 + (20,000 x $.15/km) = $9,000

(b) Cost @ 30,000 km / year = $6,000 + (30,000 x $.15/km) = $10,500

Try It 2–2

Beginning Inventory DM + Purchases of DM − Ending Inventory DM = DM used

$12,000 + $85,000 − $7,000 = $90,000 DM used

DM + DML + MOH = Manufacturing Costs

$90,000 + $30,000 + $40,000 = $160,000

3

Cost–Volume–Profit Analysis

▶ Learning Objectives

1. Identify the essential elements of cost–volume–profit analysis, and calculate the breakeven point (BEP).

2. Apply the CVP model to calculate a target operating profit before interest and tax.

3. Distinguish among contribution, gross, operating, and net income margins, and apply the CVP model to calculate target net income.

4. Apply the CVP model in decision making, and explain how sensitivity analysis can help managers both identify and manage risk.

5. Analyze the implications of uncertainty on decision models.

6. Interpret the results of CVP analysis in complex strategic, multi-product, and multiple cost driver situations.

▶ CPA Competencies

This chapter covers material outlined in **Section 3: Management Accounting** of the CPA Competency Map. The Learning Objectives in this chapter have been aligned with the CPA Competency Map to ensure the best coverage possible.

3.3.1 Evaluates cost classifications and costing methods for management of ongoing operations

3.3.2 Evaluates and applies cost management techniques appropriate for specific costing decisions

3.4.1 Evaluates sources and drivers of revenue growth

3.5.1 Performs sensitivity analysis

3.5.2 Evaluates sustainable profit maximization and capacity management performance

WENN Ltd/Alamy Stock Photo

How Coachella Tunes Up the Sweet Sound of Profits

Each year, the Coachella music festival in California features more than 150 of the biggest names in rock, hip-hop, and electronic dance music. Putting on this annual music extravaganza is a costly endeavor. Headlining acts such as Drake and Jack White command as much as $4 million to perform, and production costs—including stagehands, insurance, and security—cost up to $12 million before the first note is played. As a result, the festival's financial success depends on recouping its tremendous fixed costs—costs that do not change with the number of fans in the audience.

To cover its high fixed costs and make a profit, Coachella needs to sell a lot of tickets. After struggling for years to turn a profit, Goldenvoice expanded Coachella to two identical editions taking place on consecutive weekends. Same venue, same lineup, and same ticket price. Goldenvoice also launched Stagecoach, a country music festival that occupies the same California venue one week after Coachella. This allowed temporary infrastructure costs such as stages and fencings to be shared across both events. With tickets prices from $375–$889, the 2015 Coachella festival sold a staggering $84 million in tickets, while the follow-on Stagecoach festival grossed more than $21 million in ticket sales. By expanding Coachella's volume, Goldenvoice was able to recover its fixed costs and tune up the sweet sound of profits.

Sources: Chris Parker. 2013. "The Economics of Music Festivals: Who's Getting Rich? Who's Going Broke?" *L.A. Weekly*, April 17 (http://www.laweekly.com/music/the-economics-of-music-festivals-whos-getting-rich-whos-going-broke-4167927); Courtney M. Fowler. 2014. "The Coachella Cash Cow," *Neon Tommy: Annenberg Digital News blog*, University of Southern California Annenberg Media Center, April 8 (http://www.neontommy.com/news/2014/04/coachella-cash-cow-0); Anil Patel. 2015. "Coachella: A Lesson in Strategic Growth," *Anil Patel's blog*, LinkedIn, April 17 (https://www.linkedin.com/pulse/coachella-lesson-strategic-growth-anil-patel); Ray Waddell. 2015. "Coachella Earns Over $84 Million, Breaks Attendance Records" *Billboard*, July 15 (http://www.billboard.com/articles/business/6633636/coachella-2015-earnings-84-million-breaks-attendance-records).

Businesses that have high fixed costs have to pay particular attention to the "what-ifs" behind decisions because making the wrong choices can be disastrous. Examples of well-known companies that have high fixed costs of equipment and facilities are American Airlines and General Motors. When companies have high fixed costs, they need significant revenues just to break even. In the airline industry, for example, companies' fixed costs are so high the profits most airlines make come from the last two to five passengers who board each flight! Consequently, when revenues at American Airlines dropped, it was forced to declare bankruptcy. In this chapter, you will see how cost–volume–profit (CVP) analysis helps managers minimize such risks.

Cost–volume–profit (CVP) analysis is a model to analyze the behaviour of net income in response to changes in total revenue, total costs, or both. In reality, businesses operate in a complex environment; a *model* reduces that complexity by using simplifying assumptions to focus on only the relevant relationships. The most important elements in a model affect one another in a predictable way. In this chapter, when we determine the breakeven point (BEP), we include *all* business function costs in the value chain, not just those of production. The **breakeven point (BEP)** is the point at which total revenue minus total business function costs is $0.

Essentials of CVP Analysis

The CVP model depends on understanding the effects of cost behaviour on profit, and identifies only the relevant relationships. The following assumptions identify relevant information required to complete a CVP analysis:

► **LO 1**

Identify the essential elements of cost–volume–profit analysis, and calculate the breakeven point (BEP).

■ Changes in the sales volume and production (or purchase) volume are identical (purchase volume would apply to a merchandiser). The ending balances in all inventories are zero. Everything purchased is used in production; everything produced is sold. For a merchandiser, the sales volume of finished goods purchased for resale is identical to the sales volume sold.

■ All costs are classified as either fixed (FC) or variable (VC). All mixed costs are broken into their respective fixed and variable components. The fixed costs include *both* manufacturing *and* non-manufacturing fixed costs. The total variable costs include both manufacturing and non-manufacturing variable costs.

■ All cost behaviour is linear (a straight line) within the relevant volume range.

■ The sales price per unit, variable costs per unit, and total fixed costs and sales (or production) volume are known. The management information system (MIS) provides all of this information.

■ Either the product sold or the product mix remains constant, although the volume changes, within the relevant volume range.

■ All revenue and costs can be calculated and compared without considering the time-value of money.

We know that total revenue is the product of total sales volume or quantity (Q) of units sold multiplied by the price per unit. We also know that total variable cost is the product of total Q units produced multiplied by the cost per unit, and together with fixed costs (constant cost regardless of production volume) comprise total costs. Based on the simplifying assumption that Q sold = Q produced, the relationship among relevant elements of the CVP model upon which the BEP can be calculated is:

$$\text{Operating income} = (\text{Unit sales price} \times Q) - (\text{Unit variable cost} \times Q) - (\text{Fixed costs}) \quad (1)$$

At breakeven, operating income is zero. So for the breakeven point, we can rearrange equation (1) above to be:

$$(\text{Unit sales price} \times Q) = (\text{Unit variable cost} \times Q) + (\text{Fixed costs})$$

CVP Analysis: An Example

Decision Framework

We will begin by looking at an example based on known information about operating income (net income before interest and taxes). Then we will determine the required combination of sales volume and unit sales price to break even. In the CVP analysis, only one factor, sales volume (Q), changes.

> **Example:** Wei Shao is considering selling Do-All Software, a home-office software package, at a computer convention in Vancouver. Wei knows she can purchase this software from a computer software wholesaler at $120 per package, with the privilege of returning all unsold packages and receiving a full $120 refund per package. She also knows that she must pay Computer Conventions, Inc. $2,000 for the booth rental at the convention. She will incur no other costs. Should she rent a booth?

Wei faces an uncertain future as she analyzes the information she has at hand. A decision framework can be applied in this situation:

1. *Identify the problem and uncertainties.* Wei has to resolve two important uncertainties—the unit sales price she can charge and the number of packages (Q) she can sell at that price.

2. *Obtain information.* Wei obtains the relevant information on the variable and fixed costs to attend the conference and purchase the software. She uses her own information on sales volume and her previous experience at a similar convention in Seattle four months ago. Wei also gathers published industry information. She realizes that customers may purchase their software from competitors and wants to match her volume and purchase price to customer demand.

3. *Predict the future.* Wei predicts that she can charge $200 for Do-All Software. She is confident of the straight line or linear relationship between volume, price, and total revenue within her relevant range of 30 to 60 units. However, Wei remains uncertain. Have there been important changes in customer demand over the past four months? Her regular sales in the past couple of months have been lower than she expected. Is she too optimistic or biased in her predictions?

4. *Make decisions by choosing among alternatives.* Wei will use the CVP relationship to help her decide among alternatives available for pricing and quantity sold.

5. *Implement the decision, evaluate performance, and learn.* If Wei attends the convention, then she will know her outcome or actual profit. This is important feedback to compare with her predicted profit. Wei can learn from this comparison how to make better decisions in the future.

Cost–Volume–Profit Analysis

Wei knows that the booth-rental cost of $2,000 is a fixed cost because it must be paid even if she sells nothing. Wei's variable cost per Do-All Software package is $120 for quantities between 30 and 60 packages. Wei sorts her data into classifications of revenue and total variable cost, then tests two volumes of sales shown in a spreadsheet:

	Wei Sells 5 Packages	**Wei Sells 40 Packages**
Revenue	$1,000 ($200 per package × 5 packages)	$8,000 ($200 per package × 40 packages)
Total variable cost	600 ($120 per package × 5 packages)	4,800 ($120 per package × 40 packages)
Contribution margin	$ 400	$3,200

The only numbers that change from selling different quantities are total revenues and total variable costs. The difference between total revenues and total variable costs is called the **contribution margin**. That is,

$$\text{Revenue} - \text{Total variable cost} = \text{Contribution margin}$$

What is the *breakeven price* in sales volume Q, where operating income = $0? Wei does not yet know her predicted operating income, nor does she know what her minimum Q must be to cover her costs. By including the fixed cost of $2,000 in her analysis, Wei can calculate how operating income changes as Q changes. If she sells only 5 packages, then she will suffer an operating loss of $1,600 (= $400 − $2,000) and operating income < $0. If she sells 40 packages, then she will enjoy a positive operating income of $1,200 (= $3,200 − $2,000) and operating income > $0.

	Wei Sells 5 Packages	Wei sells 40 Packages
Revenue	$ 1,000 ($200 per package × 5 packages)	$ 8,000 ($200 per package × 40 packages)
Total variable cost	600 ($120 per package × 5 packages)	4,800 ($120 per package × 40 packages)
Contribution margin	$ 400	$ 3,200
Fixed cost	2,000	2,000
Operating income	$(1,600)	$ 1,200

But rather than simply using trial and error, Wei can use the CVP model:

$$Q \text{ sold} = Q \text{ purchased for sale}$$

If Wei assumes that operating income = $0, she can easily calculate the sales volume Q at which she will break even:

$$\$0 = Q \times (\text{Unit price} - \text{Unit variable cost}) - \text{Fixed cost} \qquad (2)$$

Based on the information she has, Wei can substitute the financial values and complete her calculation as follows:

$$\$0 = Q \times (\$200 - \$120) - \$2,000$$
$$\$0 = Q \times (\$80) - \$2,000$$
$$\$2,000 = \$80Q$$
$$\frac{\$2,000}{\$80} = Q$$
$$25 = Q$$

Contribution margin per unit is the difference between selling price and variable cost per unit. In the Do-All Software example, contribution margin per unit is $80 per unit (= $200 price per unit − $120 variable cost per unit). Simplifying her model further,

$$\$0 = Q \times \text{Contribution margin per unit} - \text{Fixed cost} \qquad (3)$$

When the unit sales price is $200, Wei knows that each unit sold covers the variable cost of $120 per unit and provides $80 (= $200 − $120) that can be used to cover her fixed cost of $2,000. By substituting the known amounts into the formula, Wei can calculate the BEP of 25 units (= $2000 ÷ $80):

$$\$0 = Q \times (\$80) - \$2,000$$
$$\$2,000 = \$80Q$$
$$\frac{\$2,000}{\$80} = Q$$
$$25 = Q$$

Exhibit 3-1 shows the result of calculating the BEP in two formats. On the right is the familiar financial statement of comprehensive income format. On the left is a **contribution statement of comprehensive income**, which groups costs as either variable or fixed according to their behaviour. The format of the report does not affect the dollar value of the operating income, since the revenue and total costs are identical. What has changed is the classification system used to report the results.

Exhibit 3-1 Contribution Statement Compared to Financial Statement Format

Quantity Purchased and Sold = 25			
Contribution Format		**Financial Statement of Comprehensive Income Format**	
Revenue ($200 × 25)	$5,000	Revenue ($200 × 25)	$5,000
− Total variable cost ($120 × 25)	3,000	− Total cost of sales (COS)	3,000
Total contribution margin	2,000	Gross margin	2,000
− Fixed costs (always a total)	2,000	− Total period cost	2,000
Operating income	$ 0	Operating income	$ 0

Expressing CVP Relationships

To make good decisions using CVP analysis, we must understand these relationships and the structure of the contribution statement of comprehensive income in Exhibit 3-1. There are three related ways (we will call them methods) to think more deeply about and model CVP relationships:

1. The equation method
2. The contribution margin method
3. The graph method

The equation method and the contribution margin method are most useful when managers want to determine operating income at a few specific levels of sales (for example, in Exhibit 3-2, there are 1, 5, 25, and 40 units sold). The graph method helps managers visualize the relationship between units sold and operating income over a wide range of quantities of units sold. As we shall see later in the chapter, different methods are useful for different decisions.

Equation Method

Each column in Exhibit 3-2 is expressed as an equation.

$$\text{Revenues} - \text{Variable costs} - \text{Fixed costs} = \text{Operating income}$$

How are revenues in each column calculated?

$$\text{Revenues} = \text{Selling price } (SP) \times \text{Quantity of units sold } (Q)$$

How are variable costs in each column calculated?

$$\text{Variable costs} = \text{Variable cost per unit } (VCU) \times \text{Quantity of units sold } (Q)$$

So,

$$\left[\left(\begin{array}{c}\text{Selling} \\ \text{price}\end{array} \times \begin{array}{c}\text{Quantity of} \\ \text{units sold}\end{array} \right) - \left(\begin{array}{c}\text{Variable cost} \\ \text{per unit}\end{array} \times \begin{array}{c}\text{Quantity of} \\ \text{units sold}\end{array} \right) \right] - \begin{array}{c}\text{Fixed} \\ \text{costs}\end{array} = \begin{array}{c}\text{Operating} \\ \text{income}\end{array} \quad (4)$$

Equation 4 becomes the basis for calculating operating income for different quantities of units sold. For example, if you go to cell F7 in Exhibit 3-2, the calculation of operating income when Wei sells 5 packages is

$$(\$200 \times 5) - (\$120 \times 5) - \$2,000 = \$1,000 - \$600 - \$2,000 = -\$1,600$$

Exhibit 3-2 Contribution Statement of Operating Income for Different Quantities of Do-All Software Packages Sold

	A	B	C	D	E	F	G	H
1				**Number of Packages Sold**				
2				0	1	5	25	40
3	Revenues	$ 200	per package	$ 0	$ 200	$ 1,000	$5,000	$8,000
4	Variable costs	120	per package	0	120	600	3,000	4,800
5	Contribution margin	80	per package	0	80	400	2,000	3,200
6	Fixed costs	2,000		2,000	2,000	2,000	2,000	2,000
7	Operating income			$(2,000)	$(1,920)	$(1,600)	$ 0	$1,200

Contribution Margin Method

Rearranging equation 4,

$$\left[\left(\begin{array}{c}\text{Selling} \\ \text{price}\end{array} - \begin{array}{c}\text{Variable cost} \\ \text{per unit}\end{array}\right) \times \left(\begin{array}{c}\text{Quantity of} \\ \text{units sold}\end{array}\right)\right] - \begin{array}{c}\text{Fixed} \\ \text{costs}\end{array} = \begin{array}{c}\text{Operating} \\ \text{income}\end{array}$$

$$\left(\begin{array}{c}\text{Contribution margin} \\ \text{per unit}\end{array} \times \begin{array}{c}\text{Quantity of} \\ \text{units sold}\end{array}\right) - \begin{array}{c}\text{Fixed} \\ \text{costs}\end{array} = \begin{array}{c}\text{Operating} \\ \text{income}\end{array} \qquad (5)$$

In our Do-All Software example, contribution margin per unit is $80 (= $200 − $120), so when Wei sells 5 packages,

$$\text{Operating income} = (\$80 \times 5) - \$2{,}000 = -\$1{,}600$$

Equation 5 expresses the basic idea we described earlier—each unit sold helps Wei recover $80 (in contribution margin) of the $2,000 in fixed costs.

The calculation for the contribution margin method can also be rearranged to show the BEP in relation to fixed costs and the contribution margin per unit.

$$\text{BEP} = \frac{\text{Total fixed costs}}{\text{Contribution margin per unit}}$$

Graph Method

In the graph method, we represent total costs and total revenues graphically. Each is shown as a line on a graph. Exhibit 3-3 illustrates the graph method for Do-All Software sales. Because we have assumed that total costs and total revenues behave in a linear fashion, we need only two points to plot the line representing each of them.

1. **Total costs line.** The total costs line is the sum of fixed costs and variable costs. Fixed costs are $2,000 for all quantities of units sold within the relevant range. To plot the total costs line, use as one point the $2,000 fixed costs at zero units sold (point **A**) because variable costs are $0 when no units are sold. Select a second point by choosing any other convenient output level (say, 40 units sold), and determine the corresponding total costs. Total variable costs at this output level are $4,800 (= 40 units × $120 per unit). Remember, fixed costs are $2,000 at all quantities of units sold within the relevant range, so total costs at 40 units sold equal $6,800 (= $2,000 + $4,800), which is point **B** in Exhibit 3-3. The total costs line is the straight line from point **A** through point **B**.

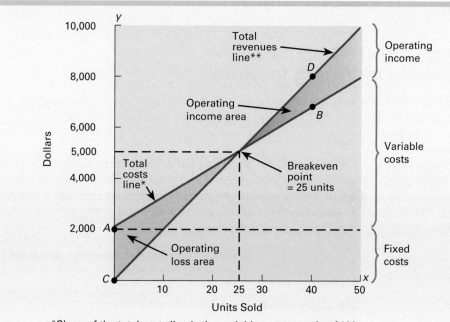

Exhibit 3-3 Cost–Volume–Profit Graph for Do-All Software Sales

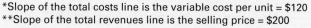

*Slope of the total costs line is the variable cost per unit = $120
**Slope of the total revenues line is the selling price = $200

2. *Total revenues line.* One convenient starting point is $0 revenues at zero units sold, which is **point C** in Exhibit 3-3. Select a second point by choosing any other convenient output level and determining the corresponding total revenues. At 40 units sold, total revenues are $8,000 (= $200 per unit × 40 units), which is point **D** in Exhibit 3-3. The total revenues line is the straight line from point **C** through point **D**.

Profit or loss at any sales level can be determined by the vertical distance between the two lines at that level in Exhibit 3-3. For quantities fewer than 25 units sold, total costs exceed total revenues, and the purple area indicates operating losses. For quantities greater than 25 units sold, total revenues exceed total costs, and the blue-green area indicates operating incomes. At 25 units sold, total revenues equal total costs. Wei will break even by selling 25 packages.

Contribution Margin Percentage: Breakeven Point in Revenue

Instead of expressing contribution margin as a dollar amount per unit, we can also express it as a percentage. **Contribution margin percentage** (also called **contribution margin ratio**) equals the contribution margin per unit divided by the selling price per unit:

$$\text{Contribution margin percentage} = \frac{\$80}{\$200} = 0.40, \text{ or } 40\%$$

The contribution margin percentage tells us how many pennies per $1.00 of revenue contribute to paying fixed costs. For example, a contribution margin percentage of 40% means for each $1.00 a customer pays for Do-All Software, $0.40 contributes to paying fixed costs.

The contribution margin percentage enables us to solve for values with partial data. For example, how do you calculate the breakeven point in revenue when you do not know the sales price per unit? The solution is shown below:

$$\frac{\text{Breakeven}}{\text{revenue}} = \frac{\text{Fixed costs}}{\text{Contribution margin \%}} = \frac{\$2,000}{0.40} = \$5,000$$

Proof: $5,000 ÷ $200 = 25$ units

From previous calculations, we know the BEP in units is 25.

Using CVP to Calculate a Target Operating Income

▶ **LO 2**

Apply the CVP model to calculate a target operating profit before interest and tax.

The BEP can be calculated as either the minimum sales quantity or the minimum revenue required to avoid a loss. However, the point of for-profit business is to earn a profit, not to break even. The CVP model can also be used to calculate a target operating income.

Let's go back to the example of Wei Shao and Do-All Software. Wei can apply her model to determine what her quantity purchased and sold must be to make a positive operating income. Instead of setting operating income = $0, it is set to equal a non-zero amount. The method of calculating this target quantity is identical to the method already described. Wei selects $1,500 as her target operating income.

$$\$1,500 = Q \times (\text{Unit sales price} - \text{Unit variable cost}) - \text{Fixed cost}$$

$$Q \times (\$200 - \$120) - \$2,000 = \$1,500$$

$$\$80 \times Q = \$2,000 + \$1,500$$

$$Q = \$3,500 ÷ \$80 \text{ per unit} = 43.75 \text{ units}$$

Alternatively, Wei knows the contribution margin per unit and can calculate the Q required to achieve a target operating income of $1,500 by starting at the second line of the solution, treating the target operating income as if it were a fixed cost. This is exactly what we have done when adding the $1,500 to the $2,000 to obtain $3,500. The $80 is the contribution margin per unit. Dividing $3,500 by the contribution margin per unit gives the identical answer of $Q = 43.75$ units:

$$\frac{\text{Volume of units}}{\text{required to be sold}} = \frac{\text{Fixed costs} + \text{Target operating income}}{\text{Contribution margin per unit}}$$

$$\frac{\text{Volume of units}}{\text{required to be sold}} = \frac{\$2,000 + \$1,500}{\$80 \text{ per unit}} = 43.75 \text{ units}$$

Proof:

Revenue, $200 per unit × 43.75 units	$8,750
Variable costs, $120 per unit × 43.75 units	5,250
Contribution margin, $80 per unit × 43.75 units	3,500
Fixed costs	2,000
Operating income	$1,500

Of course, Wei cannot sell 75% of one Do-All package. If she rounds down to $Q = 43$ units, she will bring in only $3,440, which is less than the $3,500 she needs to cover her $2,000 fixed cost plus a target operating income of $1,500. Wei must round up to $Q = 44$ units to reach her target.

Finally, Wei can use different information—fixed costs, target operating income, and the contribution margin percentage of 40%—to calculate her target revenue without first calculating her target Q. She will simply divide the sum of fixed costs plus her target operating income by the contribution margin percentage to obtain the target revenue required, as shown:

$$\text{Revenue needed to earn } \$1,500 = \frac{\$2,000 + \$1,500}{0.40} = \frac{\$3,500}{0.40} = \$8,750$$

Contribution Margin, Gross Margin, Operating Margin, and Net Income Margin

The CVP model enables us to clearly distinguish the contribution margin, which provides information for CVP analysis. Recall that there are two formats in which costs can be classified: the contribution and the financial format. Both formats report identical costs, but the costs are classified differently. The difference between contribution and gross margin is shown in the two equations below:

$$\text{Revenue} - \text{Cost of goods sold} = \text{Gross margin}$$

$$\text{Revenue} - \text{Total variable costs} - \text{Contribution margin}$$

Gross margin is a measure of competitiveness—how much a company can charge for its products over and above the cost of either purchasing (cost of sales) or producing them (cost of goods sold). The size of the gross margin depends on the successful competitive strategy of a company. The gross margin can be expressed as a total, as an amount per unit, or as a percentage (called **gross margin percentage**).

Operating margin has the same meaning as operating income. It is the result of deducting all business function costs from revenue. Neither interest nor tax expense is considered a business function cost. The operating margin percentage is simply the operating income divided by revenue. It does not matter what format is used to report costs—because total costs are identical, the reported operating income will be identical. **Net income margin** is an alternative technical term for net income. The nontechnical term that is readily recognized is *net profit margin*. The **net income margin percentage** is calculated by dividing net income by revenue.

▶ **LO 3**

Distinguish among contribution, gross, operating, and net income margins, and apply the CVP model to calculate target net income.

Target Net Income and Income Taxes

So far we have ignored the effect of income taxes when calculating the sales volume required to achieve a target income. The after-tax profit, however, is what matters to any business. Targets are set in terms of net income. In a real situation, managers must gather information on tax. In our example we will assume a corporate tax rate of 40%.

Let's return to the Do-All Software example. Wei's new problem is to calculate the required sales volume Q to earn a *net* income of $960, assuming an income tax rate of 40%. Using the contribution margin format,

$$\text{Target operating income} = \text{Revenue} - \text{Total variable costs} - \text{Fixed costs}$$

Assuming there is no interest expense, a 40% tax rate means the company retains 60% of its operating income. The company's net income = Operating income × (1 − Tax rate), or simply

$$\frac{\text{Net income}}{1 - \text{Tax rate}} = \text{Operating income}$$

It is now straightforward to calculate the number of units that must be sold to achieve a target net income based on a target operating income. First, use the relationship between revenue and total costs, both variable and fixed:

$$\frac{\text{Target net income}}{1 - \text{Tax rate}} = \text{Revenue} - \text{Total variable costs} - \text{Fixed costs}$$

Substitute numbers from our Do-All Software example:

$$\frac{\$960}{1 - 0.40} = (\$200 \times Q) - (\$120 \times Q) - \$2,000$$

$$\$1,600 = (\$200 \times Q) - (\$120 \times Q) - \$2,000$$

$$\$80 \times Q = \$3,600$$

$$Q = \$3,600 \div \$80 \text{ per unit} = 45 \text{ units}$$

Alternatively, we can use the contribution margin and calculate Q as shown:

$$\frac{\text{Target net income}}{1 - \text{Tax rate}} = \text{Target operating income}$$

$$\frac{\text{Fixed costs} + \dfrac{\text{Target net income}}{1 - \text{Tax rate}}}{\text{Contribution margin per unit}} = \text{Volume of units required to be sold}$$

$$\frac{\$2,000 + \dfrac{\$960}{1 - 0.40}}{\$80} = \frac{\$2,000 + \$1,600}{\$80 \text{ per unit}} = 45 \text{ units} = \begin{array}{l}\text{Volume of units} \\ \text{required to be sold}\end{array}$$

Proof:

Revenue, $200 per unit × 45 units	$9,000
Variable costs, $120 per unit × 45 units	5,400
Contribution margin	3,600
Fixed costs	2,000
Operating income	1,600
Income taxes, $1,600 × 0.40	640
Net income	$ 960

Recall that when we needed to calculate Q to achieve a target operating income, we obtained the rounded-up value of $Q = 44$ units. This is not enough, however, to achieve our target net income. But focusing the analysis on target net income instead of target operating income will never change the BEP. This is because, by definition, operating income at the breakeven point is $0, and no income taxes are paid when there is no operating income.

3.1 TRY IT!

Bernard Windows is a small company that installs Chad Windows. Its cost structure is as follows:

Selling price from each window installation	$ 500
Variable cost of each window installation	$ 400
Annual fixed costs	$150,000

Calculate (a) breakeven point in units and revenues and (b) the number of windows Bernard Windows must install and the revenues needed to earn a target operating income of $100,000.

Using CVP Analysis to Make More Complex Decisions

CVP Analysis for Decision Making

CVP analysis is useful for calculating the units that need to be sold to break even, or to achieve a target operating income or target net income. Managers also use CVP analysis to guide other decisions, many of them strategic decisions. Consider a decision about choosing additional features for an existing product. Different choices can affect selling prices, variable cost per unit, fixed costs, units sold, and operating income. CVP analysis helps managers make product decisions by estimating the expected profitability of these choices.

▶ **LO 4**

Apply the CVP model in decision making, and explain how sensitivity analysis can help managers both identify and manage risk.

   Strategic decisions invariably entail risk. CVP analysis can be used to evaluate how operating income will be affected if the original predicted data are not achieved—say, if sales are 10% lower than estimated. Evaluating this risk affects other strategic decisions a company might make. For example, if the probability of a decline in sales seems high, a manager may take actions to change the cost structure to have more variable costs and fewer fixed costs. We return to our earlier example to illustrate how CVP analysis can be used for strategic decisions concerning advertising and selling price.

Decision to Advertise

Wei anticipates she will sell 40 units if she attends the convention. At 40 units, her operating income will be $1,200. However, if Wei pays $500 for an advertisement in the convention brochure, then she anticipates her sales volume will increase to 44 units. Advertising, in this case, is a fixed cost because it must be paid even if Wei sells no units at all. Will her operating profit increase? The following table presents the CVP analysis:

	40 Packages Sold With No Advertising (1)	44 Packages Sold With Advertising (2)	Difference (3) = (2) − (1)
Revenue ($200 × 40; $200 × 44)	$8,000	$8,800	$800
Variable costs ($120 × 40; $120 × 44)	4,800	5,280	480
Contribution margin ($80 × 40; $80 × 44)	3,200	3,520	320
Fixed costs	2,000	2,500	500
Operating income	$1,200	$1,020	$(180)

Operating income decreases from $1,200 to $1,020. Clearly, if the goal is to increase operating income, this is not the correct decision. Notice that this conclusion can be seen in the third column, which predicts the difference with and without advertising. If Wei advertises, then contribution margin will increase by $320 (revenue, $800 − variable costs, $480) *and* fixed costs will increase by $500, resulting in a $180 decrease in operating income (= $320 − $500).

As you become more familiar with CVP analysis, it is more effective to evaluate the financial results of different alternatives based only on those values that differ. It is the differences that affect your decision. Differences are *relevant* information about the consequences of each choice.

Decision to Reduce Selling Price

Wei now wonders if it's a good idea to reduce the selling price to $175 instead of $200. At this price, Wei anticipates she will sell 50 units instead of 40 units. At this higher volume level, the software wholesaler who supplies Do-All Software will sell the packages to Wei for $115 per unit instead of $120. Should Wei reduce the selling price? The following analysis tells Wei the answer is no:

Contribution margin from lowering price to $175: ($175 − $115) per unit × 50 units	$3,000
Contribution margin from maintaining price at $200: ($200 − $120) per unit × 40 units	3,200
Change in contribution margin from lowering price	$ (200)

The contribution margin decreases by $200. The fixed costs of $2,000 will not change under either option; therefore, operating income will decrease by $200.

Wei could also ask, "At what price can I sell 50 units (purchased at $115 per unit) and continue to earn a pre-tax target operating income of $1,200?" The CVP analysis works backward, from the bottom to the top line of the contribution margin statement. Wei simply inserts all the values she knows. The targeted selling price per unit is $179.

	Target operating income	$1,200
	Add fixed costs	2,000
	Target contribution margin	$3,200
	Divided by number of units sold	÷ 50 units
	Target contribution margin per unit	$ 64
	Add variable cost per unit	115
	Target selling price	$ 179
Proof:	Revenue, $179 per unit × 50 units	$8,950
	Variable costs, $115 per unit × 50 units	5,750
	Contribution margin	3,200
	Fixed costs	2,000
	Operating income	$1,200

Given that the target selling price is $179 (in order to earn a target profit of $1,200 at a sales volume of 50 units), Wei will have to assess likelihood of this outcome (her original 50 unit estimate was based on a selling price of $175).

Margin of Safety and Risk

The **margin of safety** is the amount at which either expected or actual revenue exceeds breakeven revenue. Expressed in units, it is calculated as budgeted sales quantity Q minus the breakeven quantity (Q − BEP Q). If the result is zero, then there is no margin of safety. Wei can choose her margin of safety by changing predicted sales quantity. She can use the margin of safety to answer questions such as what the consequences are if revenues decrease below budget and how far they can fall before the breakeven point is reached.

Assume that Wei has fixed costs of $2,000, a selling price of $200, and variable cost per unit of $120. The budgeted revenue is $8,000, budgeted sales volume is 40 units, and the budgeted operating income is $1,200. Wei has already calculated that 25 units is the breakeven point for this set of assumptions and breakeven revenue is $5,000 (= $200 per unit × 25 units). Wei can determine the margin of safety using the following relationship expressed in equation form:

$$\text{Margin of safety} = \frac{\text{Budgeted}}{\text{revenue}} - \frac{\text{Breakeven}}{\text{revenue}} = \$8,000 - \$5,000 = \$3,000$$

$$\frac{\text{Margin of}}{\text{safety (in units)}} = \frac{\text{Budgeted}}{\text{sales (units)}} - \frac{\text{Breakeven}}{\text{sales (units)}} = 40 - 25 = 15 \text{ units}$$

Sometimes margin of safety is expressed as a percentage, and once again the denominator is revenue:

$$\text{Margin of safety percentage} = \frac{\text{Margin of safety in dollars}}{\text{Budgeted (or actual) revenue}}$$

In our example, the margin of safety percentage is 37.5% (= $3,000 ÷ $8,000).

This result means revenue would have to decrease substantially, by 37.5%, to reach breakeven revenue. The high margin of safety gives Wei confidence that she is unlikely to suffer a loss. What if Wei had predicted a sales volume of 30 units? Then, budgeted revenue would be $6,000 and the margin of safety would be as follows:

$$\text{Budgeted revenue} - \text{Breakeven revenue} = \$6,000 - \$5,000 = \$1,000$$

$$\frac{\text{Margin of}}{\text{safety percentage}} = \frac{\text{Margin of safety in dollars}}{\text{Budgeted (or actual) revenue}} = \frac{\$1,000}{\$6,000} = 16.67\%$$

This result means that if revenue decreases by more than 16.67%, Wei would suffer a loss. A lower margin of safety increases the risk of a loss.

Wei has just performed a **sensitivity analysis,** which is a "what-if" technique that managers use to examine how an outcome will change if the original predicted data are not achieved or if an underlying assumption changes. In this case, it reveals how changes to budgeted revenue affect Wei's margin of safety. Sensitivity analysis is a simple approach to recognizing **risk**—the possibility that actual future results will differ from expected results. If Wei does not have the tolerance for this level of risk, she will prefer not to rent a booth at the convention. **Risk tolerance** is the risk of loss measured in percent that a person or team is willing to take. The lower the percentage, the lower the tolerance for risk.

3.2 TRY IT! ⊕

Bernard Windows is a small company that installs Chad Windows. Its cost structure is as follows:

Selling price from each window installation	$ 500
Variable cost of each window installation	$ 400
Annual fixed costs	$150,000

Calculate the margin of safety in units and dollars and the margin of safety percentage if Bernard Windows expects to sell 2,400 windows in the year.

Exhibit 3-4 Profit–Volume Graph for Alternative Rent Contract Options for Do-All Software

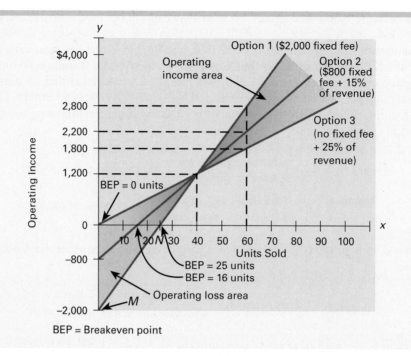

BEP = Breakeven point

Alternative Fixed- and Variable-Cost Structures

Computer Conventions has presented Wei with three booth rental options. Her first option is to rent the booth for the fixed amount of $2,000. Her second option is to pay a fixed amount of $800 and an additional $30 charge (15% of her $200 selling price per unit) for every unit she sells. Her third option is to pay a $50 charge (25% of her $200 selling price per unit) for every unit she sells. The third option does not have a fixed amount. Exhibit 3-4 graphically depicts the profit–volume relationship for each option. The lines represent the relationship between units sold and operating income. We are already familiar with Option 1; this is a fully fixed-costs contract. If Wei fails to sell a single unit, she still must pay $2,000 for the booth.

The line representing Option 2 shows fixed costs of $800 and a contribution margin per unit of $50 (= $200 − $120 − $30). The arithmetic indicates that at 16 units Wei will cover her fixed costs ($800 ÷ $50 = 16 units).

The line representing Option 3 has fixed costs of $0 and a contribution margin per unit of $30 (= $200 − $120 − $50). If Wei sells zero units, it costs her nothing to rent the booth. The graph shows that under each contract, the BEP is either 25, 16, or 0 units. You can read these values where each sloped line crosses the horizontal axis.

Wei's reaction to the different BEPs will depend on how much downside risk she is willing to accept. In the worst case, when she sells nothing, she could lose $2,000, $800, or nothing. The return or upside potential is that if she sells more than the BEP in Option 1, revenue from each unit sold above the BEP goes straight to operating income at the rate of $80 per unit. In Option 2 her BEP is lower, but so too is her upside potential. Revenue from each unit sold above the BEP goes to operating income at the rate of $50 per unit. In Option 3 her BEP is as low as possible. Her upside potential, however, is only $30 per unit sold above that BEP. The risk–return tradeoff across alternative cost structures can be measured as operating leverage.

Operating Leverage

Operating leverage describes the effects that fixed costs have on changes in operating income as changes occur in units sold and contribution margin. Organizations with a high proportion of fixed costs in their cost structures, as is the case under Option 1, have high operating leverage. The line representing Option 1 in Exhibit 3-4 is the steepest of the three lines. Small increases in sales lead to large increases in operating income; small decreases in sales result in relatively large decreases in operating income, leading to a greater risk of operating losses.

$$\text{Degree of operating leverage} = \frac{\text{Contribution margin}}{\text{Operating income}}$$

The following table shows the **degree of operating leverage** at sales of 40 units for the three alternative rent contracts:

	Option 1	Option 2	Option 3	
1. Contribution margin per unit	$ 80	$ 50	$ 30	**Note**
2. Contribution margin (Row 1 × 40 units)	3,200	2,000	1,200	Degree of operating leverage $= \dfrac{\text{Row 2}}{\text{Row 3}}$
3. Operating income (from Exhibit 3-4)	1,200	1,200	1,200	

$$\text{Degree of operating leverage} = \frac{\$3,200}{\$1,200} = 2.67 \quad \frac{\$2,000}{\$1,200} = 1.67 \quad \frac{\$1,200}{\$1,200} = 1.00$$

When sales are 40 units, a 1 percentage change in sales and contribution margin will result in 2.67 times that percentage change in operating income for Option 1. This is why the term *leverage* is used. Under Option 2, for example, the leverage decreases to 1.67 times any 1 percentage change in sales.

Consider, for example, a sales increase of 50% from 40 to 60 units. Contribution margin will increase by 50% under each alternative. However, operating income will increase from $1,200 to $2,800 [(= $1,200) + (2.67 × 50% × $1,200)] in Option 1. In Option 3 operating income will only increase from $1,200 to $1,800 [(= 1,200) + (1.00 × 50% × $1,200)]. The degree of operating leverage at a given level of sales helps managers calculate the effect of fluctuations in sales on operating income.

In general, whenever there are fixed costs, the degree of operating leverage decreases as the level of sales increases beyond the breakeven point. If fixed costs are $0, as in Option 3, contribution margin equals operating income and the degree of operating leverage equals 1.00 at all sales levels.

Cost structure is a long-term decision because fixed costs usually pay for capacity. Companies with a high percentage of fixed costs in their cost structure are often called **capital intensive companies**. Industries such as airlines, mobile communications, and gold mining are very capital intensive. When sales volume exceeds the breakeven point, each additional sale will contribute a large proportion of revenue to operating income. But when sales volumes fail to exceed breakeven, the debt associated with fixed costs must still be repaid, creating financial distress. For example, as the airline and car manufacturing industries accumulated losses from 2001 through 2007, many companies could not sell enough to cover fixed costs and declared bankruptcy.

Managers cannot avoid difficulties arising from a high fixed-costs structure if their industry is capital intensive. High fixed costs simultaneously increase the risk of losses if demand is weak and magnify profit if demand is strong. A high fixed-costs structure requires financing through either debt or equity. Debt carries a mandatory interest payment that shelters profit from tax only as long as there is a profit. If demand drops, the mandatory debt payments increase losses. This is why it is important to carefully evaluate how the level of fixed costs and variable costs will affect the risk–return tradeoff.

Other companies may be labour intensive and reduce costs by transferring manufacturing facilities from Europe and North America to lower-cost countries such as Mexico and China. Companies may also substitute high fixed costs with lower variable costs when they purchase products from lower-cost suppliers instead of manufacturing products themselves. General Electric and Hewlett-Packard recently began offshoring service functions, such as post-sales customer service, to countries like India where costs are lower.

Sustainability in Action

Cost-Volume-Profit Analysis Makes Subway's $5 Foot-Long Sandwiches a Success But Innovation Challenges Loom

Julian Stratenschulte/dpa/picture-alliance/Newscom

Since 2008, the 44,000-location Subway restaurant chain has done big business with the success of its $5 foot-long sandwich deal. Heavily advertised, the promotion lowered the price of many sandwiches, which attracted customers in droves and helped Subway significantly boost profits. Since introducing $5 foot-longs, Subway has sold billions of the sandwiches worldwide.

How did Subway lower prices *and* boost profits, you may ask? Through higher volume and incremental sales of other items. When the price of foot-long sandwiches was lowered to $5, contribution margin per sandwich dropped but customers flocked to Subway and sales skyrocketed, increasing total contribution margin.

At least two-thirds of Subway customers purchase potato chips or a soft drink with their sandwich. Subway's contribution margin on these items is very high, frequently as high as 70%. As the number of customers increased, the total contribution margin from these other items also increased. Fixed costs increased but the increases in contribution margin resulted in big increases in operating income.

But Subway faces challenges going forward. Its rapid sales growth has slowed as customer preferences have changed, and competitors from McDonald's to Firehouse Subs, Jimmy John's and Jersey Mike's have begun offering more-healthy menu options. If Subway is to continue to grow, it needs to get closer to its customers and continue to innovate its product and its marketing.

Sources: Wendy Rotelli. 2013. "How Does Subway Profit From The $5 Foot-Long Deal?" *Restaurant Business* blog, Restaurants.com, April 10 (https://www.restaurants.com/blog/how-does-subway-profit-from-the-5-foot-long-deal); Drew Harwell. 2015. "The Rise and Fall of Subway, the World's Biggest Food Chain," *Washington Post*, May 30 (https://www.washingtonpost.com/business/economy/the-rise-and-fall-of-subway-the-worlds-biggest-food-chain/2015/05/29/0ca0a84a-fa7a-11e4-a13c-193b1241d51a_story.html).

Decision Models and Uncertainty

▶ **LO 5**

Analyze the implications of uncertainty on decision models.

Always distinguish between a good decision and a good outcome. One can exist without the other. Suppose you are offered a one-time-only gamble tossing a coin. You will win $20 if the outcome is heads, but you will lose $1 if the outcome is tails. As a decision maker, you proceed through the logical phases: gathering information, assessing outcomes, and making a choice. You accept the bet. Why? Because the expected value is $9.50 [= 0.5($20) + 0.5(−$1)]. The coin is tossed and the outcome is tails. You lose. From your viewpoint, this was a good decision but a bad outcome.

A decision can be made only on the basis of information that is available at the time of evaluating and making the decision. By definition, uncertainty rules out guaranteeing that the best outcome will always be obtained. As in our example, it is possible that bad luck will produce bad outcomes even when good decisions have been made. A bad outcome does not mean a bad decision was made. The best protection against a bad outcome is a good decision.

Role of a Decision Model

It is important to understand the characteristics of uncertainty, so managers can adopt an approach to make decisions in a world of uncertainty. In the face of uncertainty—the possibility that an actual amount will deviate from an expected amount—managers rely on decision models to help them make the right choices. A decision model is a formal method for making a choice, commonly involving both quantitative and qualitative analyses.

Inputs			
Event, sales volume Q_i		30	60
Probability (p_i)		0.60	0.40
Expected sales volumes		18	24
Total expected sales volumes $(p1) \times (Q1) + (p2) \times (Q2)$	42		
Alternative contracts: fixed cost	$2,000	$ 800	$ –
Alternative contracts: total variable cost as a % of revenues	0%	15%	25%
CVP analysis	**Option a₁**	**Option a₂**	**Option a₃**
Sales price per unit	$ 200	$ 200	$ 200
Variable cost per unit (including rental)	120	150	170
Contribution margin	80	50	30
Expected value analysis			
Expected revenues ($200 × 42)	$8,400	$8,400	$8,400
Expected total variable cost	5,040	6,300	7,140
Expected contribution margin	3,360	2,100	1,260
Fixed cost	2,000	800	–
Expected operating income (outcome x_1, x_2, x_3)	$1,360	$1,300	$1,260

Exhibit 3-5 Decision Table for Do-All Software

Expected Value

The tool best suited to help Wei make a decision is a calculation of expected value. **Expected value** is the sum of the risk-weighted average of the outcomes of each choice. In this example the outcome is the operating income. Assume Wei can say she is 60% sure she will sell 30 units and 40% sure she will sell 60 units at the convention. The 60% and 40% are measures of risk or probability (p_i). The sales volumes are events. Her weighted sales are the most likely events, a combination of $0.60 \times 30 = 18$ units and $0.40 \times 60 = 24$ units, respectively. The notation for 60% is $p_1 = (0.60)$; the notation for 40% is $p_2 = (0.40)$. The mathematical notation for the possible sales volumes are $Q_1 = 30$ and $Q_2 = 60$. The expected or risk-weighted sales volume is calculated as the sum of the risk-weighted volumes:

$$(p_1 \times Q_1) + (p_2 \times Q_2) = \text{Expected sales volume}$$
$$(0.6 \times 30) + (0.4 \times 60) = \text{Expected sales volume}$$
$$= 42 \text{ units}$$

Exhibit 3-5 illustrates how Wei can calculate her expected operating income using the expected sales volume of 42 units.

If Wei is **risk neutral**, she will simply look at the expected operating income under each alternative contract. *Risk neutral* means the decision maker will feel as much pain at losing a dollar as joy at gaining a dollar. Wei will simply select the highest expected operating income. This is Wei's rational choice.

Making a decision is not the end of business planning and control. If Wei makes the decision to attend the convention, she has done so on the basis of predicted outcomes. As a good manager, Wei will conclude by comparing her actual operating income to her expected operating income. Exhibit 3-6 illustrates how the decision framework applies to making a decision using expected values.

Effects of Sales Mix on Income

Sales mix is the quantities of various products (or services) that in sum are the total sales volume of a company. Each product or service is a proportion of the total sales volume measured either as units or revenue.

▶ **LO 6**

Interpret the results of CVP analysis in complex strategic, multi-product, and multiple cost driver situations.

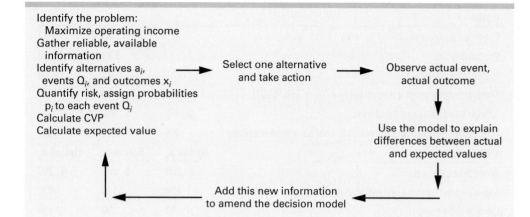

Suppose Wei looks to the future and budgets the following for a conference in Toronto where she expects to sell different quantities of two products, Do-All Software and Superword:

	Do-All	Superword	Total
Expected sales	60	40	100
Revenue, $200 and $100 per unit	$12,000	$4,000	$16,000
Total variable costs ($120 × 60; $70 × 40)	7,200	2,800	10,000
Contribution margin ($80 × 60; $30 × 40)	$ 4,800	$1,200	6,000
Fixed costs			4,500
Operating income			$ 1,500

What is the BEP? The total sales volume to break even in a multi-product company depends on the sales mix—the combination of the number of units of Do-All sold and the number of units of Superword sold. We assume that the budgeted sales mix is 3:2 (60:40), because Wei expects to sell three (60 out of the 100) units of Do-All for every two (40 out of the 100) units she sells of Superword. To simplify her planning, Wei assumes this will not change at different quantities of each product sold. In fact, Wei is selling a bundle composed of three units of Do-All and two units of Superword. The two products are not physically bundled, but for planning purposes (budgeting), it is easier to work with a bundle of five units in total sales volume.

Each bundle yields a contribution margin of $300, calculated as follows:

	Sales Volume per Product in Each Bundle	Contribution Margin per Unit for Do-All and Superword	Contribution Margin of the Bundle
Do-All	3	$80	$240
Superword	2	30	60
Total			$300

With the contribution margin for each bundle, Wei can now calculate the breakeven sales volume in bundles:

$$\text{Breakeven sales volume in bundles} = \frac{\text{Fixed costs}}{\text{Contribution margin per bundle}} = \frac{\$4,500}{\$300 \text{ per bundle}} = 15 \text{ bundles}$$

The breakeven point for each product using the 3:2 ratio is calculated by multiplying the breakeven sales volume of bundles first by three for Do-All, then two for Superword:

Do-All: 15 bundles × 3 units of Do-All per bundle	45 units
Superword: 15 bundles × 2 units of Superword per bundle	30 units
Breakeven sales volume in units	75 units

Breakeven point in dollars for Do-All and Superword is

Do-All: 45 units × $200 per unit	$ 9,000
Superword: 30 units × $100 per unit	3,000
Breakeven revenue	$12,000

We can also calculate the breakeven point in revenue for the multi-products situation as follows:

	Sales Volume in Each Bundle	Sales Price per Unit	Revenue of the Bundle
Do-All	3	$200	$600
Superword	2	100	200
Total			$800

$$\text{Contribution margin percentage for the bundle} = \frac{\text{Contribution margin of the bundle}}{\text{Revenue of the bundle}} = \frac{\$300}{\$800} = 0.375 \text{ or } 37.5\%$$

$$\text{Breakeven revenue} = \frac{\text{Fixed costs}}{\text{Contribution margin \% for the bundle}} = \frac{\$4,500}{0.375} = \$12,000$$

$$\text{Breakeven sales volume in bundles} = \frac{\text{Breakeven revenue}}{\text{Revenue per bundle}} = \frac{\$12,000}{\$800 \text{ per bundle}} = 15 \text{ bundles}$$

Of course, there are many different sales mixes (in units) that result in a contribution margin of $4,500 and cause Wei to break even, as the following table shows:

Sales Mix (Units)		Contribution Margin From		
Do-All (1)	Superword (2)	Do-All (3) = $80 × (1)	Superword (4) = $30 × (2)	Total Contribution Margin (5) = (3) + (4)
48	22	$3,840	$ 660	$4,500
36	54	2,880	1,620	4,500
30	70	2,400	2,100	4,500

If, for example, the sales mix changes from the higher contribution line (Do-All has a 40% contribution margin) to the lower contribution line (Superword has a 30% contribution margin), the total sales volume has to increase to reach breakeven. If the sales mix changes to favour the product line with the lower contribution margin (in this case, Superword), the firm could end up losing money (below breakeven) despite the fact that the breakeven level of total sales was met.

Multiple Cost Drivers

Throughout this chapter, we have assumed that the sales volume Q was exactly the same as the production (or acquisition) volume. This single volume was the only **revenue driver** and the only cost driver. A more complicated problem arises if this assumption is wrong. The CVP analysis can be adapted if there are multiple cost drivers. To simplify, we will examine the situation where there is a single product.

Suppose Wei will incur a variable cost of $10 for preparing documents (including an invoice) for each customer who buys Do-All Software. The cost driver of document-preparation costs is the number of customers who buy Do-All Software. Wei's operating income can then be expressed in terms of revenue and these costs:

$$\text{Operating income} = \text{Revenue} - \left(\begin{array}{c}\text{Variable} \\ \text{cost per} \times \\ \text{unit}\end{array}\begin{array}{c}\text{Quantity of} \\ \text{packages} \\ \text{sold}\end{array}\right) - \left(\begin{array}{c}\text{Variable cost} \\ \text{of documents} \times \\ \text{per customer}\end{array}\begin{array}{c}\text{Quantity of} \\ \text{customers}\end{array}\right) - \text{Fixed costs}$$

If Wei sells 40 units to 15 customers, then operating income is

$$\text{Operating income} = (\$200 \text{ per unit} \times 40 \text{ units}) - (\$120 \text{ per unit} \times 40 \text{ units})$$
$$- (\$10 \text{ per customer} \times 15 \text{ customers}) - \$2,000$$
$$= \$8,000 - \$4,800 - \$150 - \$2,000 = \$1,050$$

If Wei sells 40 units to 40 customers, then operating income is

$$\text{Operating income} = (\$200 \times 40) - (\$120 \times 40) - (\$10 \times 40) - \$2,000$$
$$= \$8,000 - \$4,800 - \$400 - \$2,000 = \$800$$

The number of packages sold is not the only factor that affects Wei's operating income. If sales volume is constant but the quantity of customers increases, then Wei's operating income will decrease. The costs depend on two cost drivers, both the sales volume and the number of customers.

CVP Analysis in Non-Profit and Public Sector Organizations

So far our CVP analysis has focused on a merchandising company. CVP can also be applied to manufacturing, service, non-profit, and public sector organizations. In fact, the key goal of a non-profit company is to break even, not to maximize profit. To apply CVP analysis in service and non-profit organizations, we need to focus on measuring their output. Service and social welfare outputs are measured differently from products sold by manufacturing and merchandising companies. Examples of output measures in various service and non-profit industries are as follows:

Industry	Measure of Output
Airlines	Passenger miles
Hotels/motels	Room-nights occupied
Hospitals	Patient days
Universities	Student credit-hours
Professional associations	Number of memberships

Consider a community care agency that has government support of $900,000 (its revenues) for 2019. This non-profit agency's purpose is to assist differently abled people seeking employment. On average, the agency supplements each individual's annual income by $5,000. The agency's only other costs are fixed costs of rent and administrative salaries equal to $270,000. The agency manager wants to know how many people can be assisted in 2019. We can use CVP analysis here by setting operating income to $0. Let Q be the number of differently abled people to be assisted:

$$\text{Revenue} - \text{Variable costs} - \text{Fixed costs} = \$0$$
$$\$900,000 - \$5,000\,Q - \$270,000 = \$0$$
$$\$5,000\,Q = \$900,000 - \$270,000 = \$630,000$$
$$Q = \$630,000 \div \$5,000 \text{ per person} = 126 \text{ people}$$

Suppose the manager is concerned that the total budget appropriation for 2019 will be reduced by 15% to $765,000 ($900,000 × (1 − 0.15) = $765,000). How many people could be assisted (with $5,000) on this reduced budget?

$$\$765,000 - \$5,000\,Q - \$270,000 = \$0$$
$$\$5,000\,Q = \$765,000 - \$270,000 = \$495,000$$
$$Q = \$495,000 \div \$5,000 \text{ per person} = 99 \text{ people}$$

Note the following two characteristics of the CVP relationships in this non-profit situation:

1. The percentage drop in the number of people assisted, $(126 - 99) \div 126$, or 21.4%, exceeds the 15% reduction in the budget. The reason is that the $270,000 in fixed costs must still be paid. In a lower total budget, less money remains to assist people. The percentage drop in service exceeds the percentage drop in budgeted revenue from the government.

2. Given the reduced revenue of $765,000, the manager can adjust operations to stay within this appropriation in at least one of three basic ways: (a) Reduce the number of people assisted from the current 126; (b) reduce the variable cost of assistance from $5,000 per person; or (c) reduce the total fixed costs from the current $270,000.

Pulling It All Together—Problem for Self-Study

(Try to solve this problem before examining the solution that follows.)

Problem

The following problem illustrates how to use relevant information from both the financial accounting statement of operating income and the contribution statement of operating income to calculate the breakeven point. Wei wants to know how to calculate her breakeven sales volume and her breakeven sales revenue. (R. Lambert, adapted)

Wei has gathered the following information: Operating income for Wei Shao Inc. (WSI) for the year 2019 on production and sales volume (Q) of 200,000 units was summarized in the financial accounting operating statement of income below. Additional accounting information was also provided regarding the inventoriable fixed costs and the period (non-manufacturing, operating expenses) variable costs per unit shown below the operating income:

Wei Shao Inc. Statement of Operating Income Year Ended 2019

Sales revenue	$ 3,120,000
Cost of goods sold (COGS)	1,920,000
Gross margin	1,200,000
Operating expenses	1,380,000
Operating income (loss)	$ (180,000)
Fixed costs (inventoriable)	$ 600,000
Variable cost per unit (non-manufacturing)	$ 6.00

1. Calculate WSI's variable manufacturing costs per unit in 2019. ❶❷ ◄ Required
2. Calculate WSI's fixed marketing and distribution costs in 2019. ❶❷
3. Because WSI's gross margin per unit is $6 (= $1,200,000 ÷ 200,000 units), Wei ❷ believes that if WSI had produced and sold 230,000 units, it would have covered the $1,380,000 of marketing and distribution costs ($1,380,000 ÷ $6 = 230,000) and enabled WSI to break even for the year. Calculate WSI's operating income if production and sales volume had been Q = 230,000 units. Explain briefly why Wei is wrong.
4. Calculate the breakeven point for the year 2019 in both sales volume and revenue. ❶
5. Calculate both the sales volume required to achieve operating income of $100,000 ❸ and the operating profit margin percentage.
6. Calculate total fixed and total variable costs as a proportion of total cost. What is ❹ Wei's cost structure and her risk/return tradeoff?
7. Wei has been following market demand closely and believes there is a 35% proba- ❸❹ bility that sales volume will be 300,000 units in 2019, a 25% probability that sales volume will be 320,000 units, and a 40% probability that sales volume will be 280,000 units. Calculate the risk-weighted expected sales volume in 2019. Can Wei expect to earn her targeted operating income calculated in requirement 5?
8. Calculate Wei's margin of safety in dollars and percentage. How does adding risk as ❹ a factor improve Wei's CVP analysis?
9. If Wei had to pay an additional variable cost of $5 per customer order, calculate her ❹ best alternative to maximize operating income. Alternative 1 is to sell 297,000 units to 15,000 customers. Alternative 2 is to sell 293,334 units to 9,500 customers.

Solution

1. Calculate unit variable cost (inventoriable).

Total inventoriable costs (COGS)	$1,920,000
Fixed costs (inventoriable)	600,000
Total variable cost (inventoriable) = COGS − Fixed costs inventoriable	$1,320,000
Q produced and sold	200,000
Variable cost per unit (inventoriable) = Total variable cost ÷ Q =	$ 6.60

2. Calculate fixed costs (period or non-manufacturing operating expenses).

Total operating expenses	$1,380,000
Total variable cost (Variable cost per unit × Q) = $6.00 × 200,000	1,200,000
Fixed costs (Operating expenses − Total variable non-manufacturing cost) =	$ 180,000

3. Calculate operating income.

Sales price per unit for Q produced and sold = Revenue ÷ Q	200,000	$ 15.60
Contribution margin per unit × (Sales price per unit − Total variable cost per unit)		$ 3.00
Revenue for Q produced and sold =	230,000	$3,588,000
Contribution margin for total Q produced and sold =		690,000
Total fixed costs (inventoriable and non-manufacturing)		780,000
Operating income (Contribution margin − Total fixed costs)		$ (90,000)

Wei has confused gross with total contribution margin. She assumed that the COGS comprised only variable costs and that non-manufacturing costs comprised only fixed costs. Wei does not distinguish that cost behaviour is independent of cost classification. Both manufacturing and non-manufacturing costs comprise both fixed and variable costs.

4. Calculate breakeven point in sales volume Q and revenue.

Breakeven point, Q = (FC ÷ Contribution margin per unit = $780,000 ÷ $3.00)
= 260,000

Breakeven point, Revenue = (Breakeven volume Q × Contribution margin per unit)
= $4,056,000

Alternatively use CM% = Contribution margin per unit ÷ Sales price per unit)
= 19.231%*

Breakeven point, Revenue = (Fixed costs ÷ CM% or $3,120,000 ÷ 0.19231)
= $4,056,000*

*Exactly this percentage can also be obtained from Contribution margin ÷ Revenue using amounts from requirement 3.

5. Calculate a target operating income.

Contribution margin per unit	$ 3.00
Target operating income	$ 100,000
Fixed costs	$ 780,000

$$\text{Sales volume} = \frac{(\text{Fixed costs } + \text{ Target operating income})}{\text{Contribution margin per unit}} = \quad 293,333.3^*$$

Revenue	$ 4,576,011 (rounded)
Operating profit margin percentage	2.2%

Note that Wei cannot make a third of a sale; therefore, her targeted sales volume must be rounded up to 293,334.

6. Calculate total fixed and total variable costs as a proportion of total costs.

	Cost	%
Total fixed costs	$ 780,000	23.6
Total variable costs	2,520,000	76.4
Total costs	$ 3,300,000	

7. Calculate the risk-weighted expected sales volume in 2019.

	Q	Probability	Risk Weighted
Sales volume 1	300,000	0.35	105,000
Sales volume 2	320,000	0.25	80,000
Sales volume 3	280,000	0.40	112,000
Risk-weighted total expected sales volume			297,000

Including risk as a quantitative factor makes it clear to Wei and others if she has a biased view of future demand. Should Wei choose to explain her assumptions, it would be very easy. She can also readily show very pessimistic and very optimistic "what if" expected sales volumes. Based on this model, Wei can also calculate her margin of safety relative to her expected sales volume.

Wei can expect to achieve her targeted operating income of $100,000 because the expected sales volume exceeds the sales volume required to achieve her target.

8. Calculate the margin of safety in dollars and percentage using the expected operating income.

	Expected	Breakeven	Margin of Safety
Margin of safety = Budgeted (expected revenue) = Breakeven revenue	$4,633,200	$4,056,000	$577,200
Margin of safety percentage = Margin of safety ÷ Expected revenue			12.46%

9. Calculate the alternative with the highest operating income.

	Q = Quantity	Sales price	Variable cost		Fixed costs	Operating income
Alternative 1						
Sales in units	297,000	$ 15.60	$ 12.60			
Sales to customers	15,000		5.00			
Totals:			$3,817,200	$4,633,200	$780,000	$ 36,000
Alternative 2						
Sales in units	293,334	$ 15.60	$ 12.60			
Sales to customers	9,500		5.00			
Totals:			$3,743,508	$4,576,011	$780,000	$ 52,502

Wei's operating income is higher under alternative 2, and this is the alternative she would prefer. She has two cost drivers but only one revenue driver. The fewer customer orders, the lower is her total variable cost. Her operating leverage is low and so too is her contribution margin. This information can help Wei market her product to increase the Q or increase the quantity of units per customer order, rather than just focus on increasing Q.

Decision Points

The following question-and-answer format summarizes the chapter's learning objectives. Each point presents a key question, and the guidelines are the answer to that question.

Learning Objectives	Guidelines
1. How can CVP analysis assist managers?	CVP analysis requires managers to distinguish cost behaviour from cost classification in an accurate model of relationships among factors critical to maximize profit. While a statement of comprehensive income provides reliable information, managers use a different contribution margin format for CVP models. The values of relevant cost, volume, and profit factors change among alternatives.
2. How do managers determine the breakeven point or the output needed to achieve a target operating income?	These two analyses differ with respect to one factor: the value assigned to operating income. At the breakeven point, the target operating income = \$0. Any target operating income > \$0 requires a sales volume higher than the breakeven point.
3. How should companies incorporate income taxes into CVP analysis?	Income taxes can be incorporated into CVP analysis by using target net income rather than target operating income. The breakeven point is unaffected by income taxes because no income taxes are paid when operating income = \$0.
4. How should companies cope with risk to explain how cost structure affects decisions?	Expected value uses probability to make the effect of failure on operating income clear. The decision among alternatives requires understanding how cost structure affects both the downside risk and the upside potential effects on operating income.
5. What are the implications of uncertainty on decision models?	Most important decisions are often complex in nature and involve multiple stakeholders, contributing to a high degree of uncertainty. Methodical approaches need to be adopted to collect and analyze data, develop the best answer, and avoid unintended consequences.
6. How can CVP analysis be applied to a company producing multiple products (revenue drivers) and multiple cost drivers?	CVP analysis can be applied to a company producing multiple products by assuming the sales mix of products sold remains constant as the total quantity of units sold changes. The basic concepts of CVP analysis can be applied to multiple cost driver situations, but there is no unique breakeven point.

Terms to Learn

This chapter and the Glossary at the end of the book contain definitions of the following important terms:

breakeven point (BEP) **(p. 59)**
capital intensive companies **(p. 71)**
contribution margin **(p. 60)**
contribution margin
  percentage **(p. 64)**
contribution margin per unit **(p. 61)**
contribution margin ratio **(p. 64)**
contribution statement of
  comprehensive income **(p. 61)**

cost–volume–profit (CVP)
  analysis **(p. 59)**
degree of operating
  leverage **(p. 71)**
expected value **(p. 73)**
gross margin **(p. 65)**
gross margin percentage **(p. 65)**
margin of safety **(p. 68)**
net income margin **(p. 65)**

net income margin percentage **(p. 65)**
operating leverage **(p. 70)**
operating margin **(p. 65)**
revenue driver **(p. 75)**
risk **(p. 69)**
risk neutral **(p. 73)**
risk tolerance **(p. 69)**
sales mix **(p. 73)**
sensitivity analysis **(p. 69)**

Assignment Material

MyLab Accounting Make the grade with MyLab Accounting: The Short-Answer Questions, Exercises, and Problems marked with a ⊕ can be found on MyLab Accounting. You can practise them as often as you want, and most feature step-by-step guided instructions to help you find the right answer.

Short-Answer Questions

⊕ **3-1** Describe the assumptions underlying CVP analysis.

⊕ **3-2** Distinguish between operating income and net income.

⊕ **3-3** "CVP is both simple and simplistic. If you want realistic analysis to underpin your decisions, look beyond CVP." Do you agree? Explain.

⊕ **3-4** How does an increase in the income tax rate affect the breakeven point?

⊕ **3-5** Describe sensitivity analysis. How has spreadsheet software affected its use?

⊕ **3-6** Give an example of how a manager can decrease variable costs while increasing fixed costs.

⊕ **3-7** Give an example of how a manager can increase variable costs while decreasing fixed costs.

⊕ **3-8** What is operating leverage? How is knowing the degree of operating leverage (DOL) helpful to managers?

⊕ **3-9** How can a company with multiple products compute its breakeven point?

Exercises

⊕ **3-10 Terminology.** A number of terms are listed below:

contribution margin	cost–volume–profit analysis
capital intensive	operating leverage
gross margin	sales mix
contribution margin percentage	breakeven point
margin of safety	

Required

Select the terms from the above list to complete the following sentences (use each term only once).

1. A term for a company with a high percentage of fixed costs in its cost structure is _____.
2. _____ is a model to analyze the behaviour of net income in response to change in total revenues, total costs, or both.
3. The _____ in units is the quantity of units sold to attain an operating income of zero.
4. _____ describes the effects that fixed costs have on changes in operating income as changes occur in units sold and contribution margin.
5. The _____ is equal to revenue less variable costs.
6. The _____ equals the contribution margin per unit divided by the selling price per unit.
7. The _____ equals revenues less cost of goods sold.
8. The _____ is the quantities of various products (or services) that in sum are the total sales volume of a company.
9. The _____ is the amount by which expected (or actual) revenues exceed breakeven revenues.

⊕ **3-11 CVP analysis computations.** The following partial information is available. Complete the table by filling in all the blanks. Each case is independent.

◀ **LO 1**

Case a. CM%, 36.50%

Case	Revenues	Variable Costs	Fixed Costs	Total Costs	Operating Income	Contributing Margin Percentage
a	$ 4,000	$ ____	$ 500	$ ____	$1,460	____ %
b	____	7,400	____	8,700	9,800	____
c	10,600	____	3,200	____	____	30
d	9,450	____	2,500	8,170	____	____

LO 1 ▶

Case b. unit selling price, $87

🌐 **3-12 CVP analysis computations.** Fill in the blanks for each of the following independent cases.

Case	Unit Selling Price	Unit Variable Operating Costs	Number of Units Sold	Total Contribution Margin	Total Fixed Costs	Operating Income
a	$ 70	$25	$ _____	$ 900,000	$ _____	$ 200,000
b	—	62	15,000	_____	250,000	125,000
c	250	—	30,000	4,500,000	_____	900,000
d	150	—	24,000	1,728,000	1,500,000	_____

LO 2, 3 ▶

1. a. Total contribution margin, $4,500,000

🌐 **3-13 CVP computations.** Patel Manufacturing sold 300,000 units of its product for $50 per unit. Variable cost per unit is $35, and total fixed costs are $1,800,000.

Required

1. Calculate (a) total contribution margin and (b) operating income.
2. Patel's current manufacturing process is labour intensive. Kate Schoenen, Patel's production manager, has proposed investing in state-of-the-art manufacturing equipment, which will increase the annual fixed costs to $3,400,000. The variable costs are expected to decrease to $23 per unit. Patel expects to maintain the same sales volume and selling price next year. How would acceptance of Schoenen's proposal affect your answers to (a) and (b) in requirement 1?
3. Should Patel accept Schoenen's proposal? Explain.

LO 2, 3 ▶

1. 40 cars

🌐 **3-14 CVP analysis, income taxes.** Diego Motors is a small car dealership. On average it sells a car for $26,000, which it purchases from the manufacturer for $22,000. Each month, Diego Motors pays $60,000 in rent and utilities and $70,000 for salespeople's salaries. In addition to their salaries, salespeople are paid a commission of $500 for each car they sell. Diego Motors also spends $10,000 each month for local advertisements. Its tax rate is 40%.

Required

1. How many cars must Diego Motors sell each month to break even?
2. Diego Motors has a target monthly net income of $63,000. What is its target operating income? How many cars must be sold each month to reach the target monthly net income of $63,000?

LO 2, 3 ▶

🌐 **3-15 CVP analysis, income taxes.** Westover Motors is a small car dealership. On average, it sells a car for $32,000, which it purchases from the manufacturer for $28,000. Each month, Westover Motors pays $53,700 in rent and utilities and $69,000 for salespeople's salaries. In addition to their salaries, salespeople are paid a commission of $400 for each car they sell. Westover Motors also spends $10,500 each month for local advertisements. Its tax rate is 40%.

Required

1. How many cars must Westover Motors sell each month to break even?
2. Westover Motors has a target monthly net income of $69,120. What is its target monthly operating income? How many cars must be sold each month to reach the target monthly net income of $69,120?

LO 2, 3 ▶

1. Revenue, $1,000,000

🌐 **3-16 CVP analysis, income taxes.** The Rapid Meal has two restaurants that are open 24 hours a day. Fixed costs for the two restaurants together total $450,000 per year. Service varies from a cup of coffee to full meals. The average sales bill per customer is $8.00. The average cost of food and other variable costs for each customer is $3.20. The income tax rate is 30%. Target net income is $105,000.

Required

1. Compute the revenue needed to earn the target net income.
2. How many customers are needed to earn net income of $105,000? How many customers are needed to break even?
3. Compute net income if the number of customers is 150,000.

LO 2 ▶

1. Contribution margin, $4,500

🌐 **3-17 Gross margin and contribution margin.** The National Symphony is preparing for its annual appreciation dinner for contributing members. Last year, 500 members attended the dinner. Tickets for the dinner were $20 per attendee. Last year's statement of comprehensive income was as follows:

Ticket sales	$10,000
Cost of dinner	11,000
Gross margin	(1,000)
Invitations and paperwork	3,000
Profit (loss)	$ (4,000)

This year the dinner committee does not want to lose money on the dinner. To help achieve its goal, the committee analyzed last year's costs. Of the $11,000 total cost of the dinner, it was determined that $6,000 were fixed costs and $5,000 were variable costs. Of the $3,000 for invitations and paperwork, $2,500 were fixed and $500 were variable.

Required

1. Prepare last year's profit report using the contribution-margin format.
2. The committee is considering expanding this year's dinner invitation to include volunteer members (in addition to contributing members). If the committee expects attendance to double, calculate the effect this will have on the profitability of the dinner.

🌐 **3-18 CVP, not-for-profit.** Genesee Music Society is a not-for-profit organization that brings guest artists to the community's greater metropolitan area. The music society just bought a small concert hall in the centre of town to house its performances. The lease payments on the concert hall are expected to be $4,000 per month. The organization pays its guest performers $1,800 per concert and anticipates corresponding ticket sales to be $4,500 per concert. The music society also incurs costs of approximately $1,000 per concert for marketing and advertising. The organization pays its artistic director $33,000 per year and expects to receive $30,000 in donations in addition to its ticket sales.

◀ **LO 3**
Net Fixed Costs = $51,000

Required

1. If the Genesee Music Society just breaks even, how many concerts does it hold?
2. In addition to the organization's artistic director, the music society would like to hire a marketing director for $25,500 per year. What is the breakeven point? The music society anticipates that the addition of a marketing director would allow the organization to increase the number of concerts to 41 per year. What is the music society's operating income/(loss) if it hires the new marketing director?
3. The music society expects to receive a grant that would provide the organization with an additional $17,000 toward the payment of the marketing director's salary. What is the breakeven point if the music society hires the marketing director and receives the grant?

🌐 **3-19 CVP analysis, changing revenues and costs.** Sunshine Tours is a travel agency specializing in cruises between Miami and Jamaica. It books passengers on Carib Cruises. Sunshine's fixed costs are $22,000 per month. Carib charges passengers $1,000 per round trip ticket.

◀ **LO 3**
1. a. 489 tickets

Required

Calculate the number of tickets Sunshine must sell each month to (a) break even and (b) make a target operating income of $10,000 per month in each of the following independent cases.

1. Sunshine's variable costs are $35 per ticket, and Carib Cruises pays Sunshine 8% commission on the ticket price.
2. Sunshine's variable costs are $29 per ticket. Carib Cruises pays Sunshine 8% commission on the ticket price.
3. Sunshine's variable costs are $29 per ticket. It receives a $48 commission per ticket from Carib Cruises. Comment on the results.
4. Sunshine's variable costs are $29 per ticket. It receives a $48 commission per ticket from Carib Cruises. It charges customers a delivery fee of $12 per ticket. The cost for Sunshine to deliver the ticket is $2 per ticket. Comment on the result.

🌐 **3-20 Contribution margin, gross margin, and margin of safety.** Mirabel Cosmetics manufactures and sells a face cream to small family-run stores in the greater Montreal area. It presents the monthly operating statement of comprehensive income shown here to François Laval, a potential investor in the business. Help Laval understand Mirabel's cost structure.

◀ **LO 2**
2. CM%, 40%

Mirabel Cosmetics Statement of Operating Income for the Month of June

Units sold		10,000
Revenue		$100,000
Cost of goods sold		
Variable manufacturing costs	$55,000	
Fixed manufacturing costs	20,000	
Total		75,000
Gross margin		25,000
Operating costs		
Variable marketing costs	5,000	
Fixed marketing and administration costs	10,000	
Total operating costs		15,000
Operating income		$ 10,000

Required

1. Recast the statement of operating income in a contribution format.
2. Calculate the contribution margin percentage and breakeven point in units and revenues for June.
3. What is the margin of safety (in units) for June?
4. If sales in June were only 8,000 units and Mirabel's tax rate is 30%, calculate its net income.

LO 2 ▶

1. a. Operating income,
$120,000

3-21 CVP computations. The Chorus Company manufactures and sells pens. Present sales output is 5,000,000 units per year at a selling price of $0.60 per unit. Fixed costs are $1,080,000 per year. Variable costs are $0.36 per unit.

Required

(Consider each case separately.)

1. **a.** What is the present operating income for a year?
   b. What is the present breakeven point in revenue?
2. Compute the new operating income for each of the following independent changes:
   a. A $0.048 per unit increase in variable costs.
   b. A 10% increase in fixed costs and a 10% increase in units sold.
   c. A 20% decrease in fixed costs, a 20% decrease in selling price, a 10% decrease in variable costs per unit, and a 40% increase in units sold.
3. Compute the new breakeven point in units for each of the following changes:
   a. A 10% increase in fixed costs.
   b. A 10% increase in selling price and a $24,000 increase in fixed costs.

LO 4 ▶

1. Breakeven = 12 children

3-22 CVP, target operating income, service firm. Spotted Turtle provides daycare for children Mondays through Fridays. Its monthly variable costs per child are as follows:

Lunch and snacks	$130
Educational supplies	75
Other supplies (paper products, toiletries, etc.)	35
Total	$240

Monthly fixed costs consist of the following:

Rent	$2,100
Utilities	400
Insurance	250
Salaries	1,400
Miscellaneous	650
Total	$4,800

Spotted Turtle charges each parent $640 per child per month.

Required

1. Calculate the breakeven point.
2. Spotted Turtle's target operating income is $10,800 per month. Compute the number of children who must be enrolled to achieve the target operating income.
3. Spotted Turtle lost its lease and had to move to another building. Monthly rent for the new building is $3,500. In addition, at the suggestion of parents, Spotted Turtle plans to take children on field trips. Monthly costs of the field trips are $2,500. By how much should Spotted Turtle increase fees per child to meet the target operating income of $10,800 per month, assuming the same number of children as in requirement 2?

LO 4 ▶

1. Breakeven = 39 carpets

3-23 Operating leverage. Cover Rugs is holding a 2-week carpet sale at Josh's Club, a local warehouse store. Cover Rugs plans to sell carpets for $950 each. The company will purchase the carpets from a local distributor for $760 each, with the privilege of returning any unsold units for a full refund. Josh's Club has offered Cover Rugs two payment alternatives for the use of space.

■ Option 1: A fixed payment of $7,410 for the sale period
■ Option 2: 10% of total revenues earned during the sale period

Assume Cover Rugs will incur no other costs.

Required

1. Calculate the breakeven point in units for (a) Option 1 and (b) Option 2.
2. At what level of revenues will Cover Rugs earn the same operating income under either option?
   a. For what range of unit sales will Cover Rugs prefer Option 1?
   b. For what range of unit sales will Cover Rugs prefer Option 2?
3. Calculate the degree of operating leverage at sales of 65 units for the two rental options.
4. Briefly explain and interpret your answer to requirement 3.

⊕ **3-24 Contribution margin, decision making.** Welch Men's Clothing's revenues and cost data for 2017 are as follows:

◀ **LO 2**
1. CM = $198,000

Revenues		$600,000
Cost of goods sold (all variable costs)		300,000
Gross margin		300,000
Operating costs:		
Salaries fixed	$140,000	
Sales commissions (12% of sales)	72,000	
Depreciation of equipment and fixtures	10,000	
Store rent ($3,500 per month)	42,000	
Other operating costs	45,000	309,000
Operating income (loss)		$ (9,000)

Mr. Welch, the owner of the store, is unhappy with the operating results. An analysis of other operating costs reveals that it includes $30,000 variable costs, which vary with sales volume, and $15,000 (fixed) costs.

Required

1. Compute the contribution margin of Welch Men's Clothing.
2. Compute the contribution margin percentage.
3. Mr. Welch estimates that he can increase units sold, and hence revenues by 25% by incurring additional advertising costs of $8,000. Calculate the impact of the additional advertising costs on operating income.
4. What other actions can Mr. Welch take to improve operating income?

⊕ **3-25 CVP analysis, margin of safety.** Marketing Docs prepares marketing plans for growing businesses. For 2017, budgeted revenues are $1,500,000 based on 500 marketing plans at an average rate per plan of $3,000. The company would like to achieve a margin of safety percentage of at least 45%. The company's current fixed costs are $400,000 and variable costs average $2,000 per marketing plan. (Consider each of the following separately.)

◀ **LO 5**
1. Margin of Safety is 20%

Required

1. Calculate Marketing Docs' breakeven point and margin of safety in units.
2. Which of the following changes would help Marketing Docs achieve its desired margin of safety?
   a. The average revenue per customer increases to $4,000.
   b. The planned number of marketing plans prepared increases by 5%.
   c. Marketing Docs purchases new software that results in a 5% increase to fixed costs but reduces variable costs by 10% per marketing plan.

⊕ **3-26 CVP, international cost structure differences.** Thomas Inc. is considering three countries for the sole manufacturing site of its new product: India, China, and Canada. The product will be sold to retail outlets in Canada at $47.50 per unit. These retail outlets add their own markup when selling to final customers. The three countries differ in their fixed costs and variable costs per product.

◀ **LO 3**
1. a. India unit CM, $20.50

	Annual Fixed Costs	Variable Manufacturing Costs per Unit	Variable Marketing and Distribution Costs per Unit
India	$ 6.4 million	$ 5.20	$21.80
China	4.4 million	9.50	18.40
Canada	10.2 million	19.30	6.20

Required

1. Compute the breakeven point of Thomas Inc. in both (a) units sold and (b) revenues for each of the three countries considered.
2. If Thomas Inc. expects to sell 1,350,000 units this year, what is the budgeted operating income for each of the three countries considered?
3. What level of sales (in units) would be required to produce the same operating income in China and in Canada? What would be the operating income in India at that volume of sales?

LO 5 ▶
1. 6,000 hectares

⊕ **3-27 CVP, not for profit.** The Sunrise Group (SG) is an environmentally conscious organization that buys land with the objective of preserving the natural environment. SG receives private contributions and takes no assistance from the government. Fixed costs of operating the organization are $1,000,000 per year. Variable costs of purchasing the land (including environmental impact reports, title searches, etc.) average $3,000 per hectare. For the next budget year, SG expects to receive private contributions totalling $19,000,000. All contributions in excess of costs will be used to purchase land.

Required

1. How many hectares will SG be able to purchase next year?
2. SG is considering participating in a new government program that will provide $1,000 per hectare to subsidize the purchase of environmentally sensitive land. If SG participates in this program, it estimates the organization will lose $5,000,000 in contributions from supporters who believe that accepting money from the government is not consistent with its mission. If SG does participate in the program, and its forecasts are accurate, how many hectares of land will it be able to purchase? On financial considerations alone, should SG participate in the government program?
3. SG is worried that contributions may decrease by more than the $5,000,000 it has estimated if it takes the subsidy. By how much can contributions decrease for SG to be able to buy the same amount of land if it takes the government subsidy or rejects it? (i.e., What is the point of indifference between the two options?)

LO 5 ▶

⊕ **3-28 CVP exercises.** The Deli-Sub Shop owns and operates six stores in and around Minneapolis. You are given the following corporate budget data for next year:

Revenues	$11,000,000
Fixed costs	$ 3,000,000
Variable costs	$ 7,500,000

Variable costs change based on the number of subs sold.
Compute the budgeted operating income for each of the following deviations from the original budget data. (Consider each case independently.)

Required

1. A 10% increase in contribution margin, holding revenues constant
2. A 10% decrease in contribution margin, holding revenues constant
3. A 5% increase in fixed costs
4. A 5% decrease in fixed costs
5. A 5% increase in units sold
6. A 5% decrease in units sold
7. A 10% increase in fixed costs and a 10% increase in units sold
8. A 5% increase in fixed costs and a 5% decrease in variable costs
9. Which of these alternatives yields the highest budgeted operating income? Explain why this is the case.

LO 3, 4 ▶
1. BEP for assumption
1 is 250 bouquets

⊕ **3-29 Alternative cost structures, uncertainty, and sensitivity analysis.** Edible Bouquets (EB) makes and sells flower bouquets. EB is considering opening a new store in the local mall. The mall has several empty shops, and EB is unsure of the demand for its product. The mall has offered EB two alternative rental agreements. The first is a standard fixed-rent agreement where EB will pay the mall $5,000 per month. The second is a royalty agreement where the mall receives $10 for each bouquet sold. EB estimates that a bouquet will sell for $50 and have a variable cost of $30 to make (including the cost of the flowers and commission for the salesperson).

Required

1. What is the breakeven point in units under each assumption?
2. For what range of sales levels will EB prefer (a) the fixed-rent agreement and (b) the royalty agreement?
3. If EB signs a sales agreement with a local flower stand, it will save $5 in variable costs per bouquet. How would this affect your answer in requirement 2?

4. EB estimates that the store is equally likely to sell 200, 400, 600, 800, or 1,000 arrangements. Using information from the original problem, prepare a table that shows the expected profit at each sales level under each rental agreement. What is the expected value of each rental agreement? Which rental agreement should EB choose?

🌐 **3-30 CVP, alternative cost structures.** Classical Glasses operates a kiosk at the local mall, selling sunglasses for $30 each. Classical Glasses currently pays $1,000 a month to rent the space and pays two full-time employees to each work 160 hours a month at $10 per hour. The store shares a manager with a neighbouring kiosk and pays 50% of the manager's annual salary of $60,000 and benefits of $12,000. The wholesale cost of the sunglasses to the company is $10 a pair.

◀ **LO 6**
1. Breakeven = 360 Sunglasses

Required

1. How many sunglasses does Classical Glasses need to sell each month to break even?
2. If Classical Glasses wants to earn an operating income of $5,300 per month, how many sunglasses does the store need to sell?
3. If the store's hourly employees agreed to a 15% sales-commission-only pay structure, instead of their hourly pay, how many sunglasses would Classical Glasses need to sell to earn an operating income of $5,300?
4. Assume Classical Glasses pays its employees hourly under the original pay structure, but is able to pay the mall 10% of its monthly revenue instead of monthly rent. At what sales levels would Classical Glasses prefer to pay a fixed amount of monthly rent, and at what sales levels would it prefer to pay 10% of its monthly revenue as rent?

🌐 **3-31 Alternate cost structures, uncertainty, and sensitivity analysis.** Corporate Printing Company currently leases its only copy machine for $1,500 a month. The company is considering replacing this leasing agreement with a new contract that is entirely commission based. Under the new agreement, Corporate would pay a commission for its printing at a rate of $20 for every 500 pages printed. The company currently charges $0.20 per page to its customers. The paper used in printing costs the company $0.05 per page and other variable costs, including hourly labour, amount to $0.10 per page.

◀ **LO 4**
CM ratio is 33%

Required

1. What is the company's breakeven point under the current leasing agreement? What is it under the new commission-based agreement?
2. For what range of sales levels will Corporate prefer (a) the fixed lease agreement and (b) the commission agreement?
3. Do this question only if you have covered the chapter appendix in your class. Corporate estimates that the company is equally likely to sell 20,000, 30,000, 40,000, 50,000, or 60,000 pages of print. Using information from the original problem, prepare a table that shows the expected profit at each sales level under the fixed leasing agreement and under the commission-based agreement. What is the expected value of each agreement? Which agreement should Corporate choose?

Problems

🌐 **3-32 Sales mix, new and upgrade customers.** Chartz 1-2-3 is a top-selling electronic spreadsheet product. Chartz is about to release version 5.0. It divides its customers into two groups: new customers and upgrade customers (those who previously purchased Chartz 1-2-3 4.0 or earlier versions). Although the same physical product is provided to each customer group, sizable differences exist in selling prices and variable marketing costs:

◀ **LO 4**
Break even is 150,000 units

	New Customers		Upgrade Customers	
Selling price		$195		$115
Variable costs				
Manufacturing	$15		$15	
Marketing	50	65	20	35
Contribution margin		$130		$ 80

The fixed costs of Chartz 1-2-3 version 5.0 are $16,500,000. The planned sales mix in units is 60% new customers and 40% upgrade customers.

Required

1. What is the Chartz 1-2-3 version 5.0 breakeven point in units, assuming that the planned 60/40 sales mix is attained?

2. If the sales mix is attained, what is the operating income when 170,000 total units are sold?

3. Show how the breakeven point in units changes with the following customer mixes:

   a. New 40% and upgrade 60%

   b. New 80% and upgrade 20%

   c. Comment on the results.

LO 4 ▶ ⊕ **3-33 Uncertainty and expected costs.** Kindmart is an international retail store. Kindmart's managers are considering implementing a new business-to-business (B2B) information system for processing merchandise orders. The current system costs Kindmart $2,000,000 per month and $55 per order. Kindmart has two options, a partially automated B2B and a fully automated B2B system. The partially automated B2B system will have a fixed cost of $6,000,000 per month and a variable cost of $45 per order. The fully automated B2B system has a fixed cost of $14,000,000 per month and a variable cost of $25 per order.

Based on data from the past two years, Kindmart has determined the following distribution on monthly orders:

Monthly Number of Orders	Probability
300,000	0.25
500,000	0.45
700,000	0.30

Required

1. Prepare a table showing the cost of each plan for each quantity of monthly orders.

2. What is the expected cost of each plan?

3. In addition to the information system's costs, what other factors should Kindmart consider before deciding to implement a new B2B system?

LO 3 ▶

Breakeven Revenues is $150,000

⊕ **3-34 Contribution margin, gross margin, and margin of safety.** Juicy Beauty manufactures and sells a face cream to small specialty stores in the greater Los Angeles area. It presents the monthly operating income statement shown here to George Lopez, a potential investor in the business. Help Mr. Lopez understand Juicy Beauty's cost structure.

	Home	Insert	Page Layout	Formulas	Data	Review	View
	A		B		C		D
1			Juicy Beauty				
2			Operating Income Statement June, 2017				
3	Units sold						20,000
4	Revenues						$200,000
5	Cost of goods sold						
6	Variable manufacturing costs				$110,000		
7	Fixed manufacturing costs				40,000		
8	Total cost of goods sold						150,000
9	Gross margin						50,000
10	Operating costs						
11	Variable marketing costs				$ 10,000		
12	Fixed marketing & admin costs				20,000		
13	Total operating costs						30,000
14	Operating income						$ 20,000

Required

1. Recast the income statement to emphasize contribution margin.

2. Calculate the contribution margin percentage and breakeven point in units and revenues for June 2017.

3. What is the margin of safety (in units) for June 2017?

4. If sales in June were only 16,000 units and Juicy Beauty's tax rate is 30%, calculate its net income.

🌐 **3-35 CVP analysis, service firm.** Wildlife Escapes generates average revenues of $9,200 per person on its five-day package tours to wildlife parks in Kenya. The variable costs per person are

◀ LO 3
1. 450 package tours

Airfare	$3,500
Hotel accommodations	1,200
Meals	480
Ground transportation	920
Park tickets and other costs	240

Annual fixed costs total $1,287,000.

Required

1. Calculate the number of package tours that must be sold to break even.
2. Calculate the revenue needed to earn a target operating income of $214,500.
3. If fixed costs increase by $40,500, what decrease in variable costs must be achieved to maintain the breakeven point calculated in requirement 1?

3-36 Multiproduct CVP and decision making. Crystal Clear Products produces two types of water filters. One attaches to the faucet and cleans all water that passes through the faucet. The other is a pitcher/filter that only purifies water meant for drinking.

◀ LO 3
1. Breakeven is 3,000 bundles

The unit that attaches to the faucet is sold for $90 and has variable costs of $25.
The pitcher-cum-filter sells for $110 and has variable costs of $20.

Crystal Clear sells two faucet models for every three pitchers sold. Fixed costs equal $1,200,000.

Required

1. What is the breakeven point in unit sales and dollars for each type of filter at the current sales mix?
2. Crystal Clear is considering buying new production equipment. The new equipment will increase fixed cost by $208,000 per year and will decrease the variable cost of the faucet and the pitcher units by $5 and $10, respectively. Assuming the same sales mix, how many of each type of filter does Crystal Clear need to sell to break even?
3. Assuming the same sales mix, at what total sales level would Crystal Clear be indifferent between using the old equipment and buying the new production equipment? If total sales are expected to be 24,000 units, should Crystal Clear buy the new production equipment?

🌐 **3-37 CVP, target income, service firm.** Teddy Bear Daycare provides daycare for children Mondays through Fridays. Its monthly variable costs per child are

◀ LO 3
1. BEP, 19 children

Lunch and snacks	$ 100
Educational supplies	75
Other supplies (paper products, toiletries, etc.)	25
Total	$ 200

Monthly fixed costs consist of

Rent	$2,000
Utilities	300
Insurance	300
Salaries	2,500
Miscellaneous	500
	$5,600

Teddy Bear charges each parent $500 per child.

Required

1. Calculate the breakeven point.
2. Teddy Bear's target operating income is $10,400 per month. Compute the number of children that must be enrolled to achieve the target operating income.
3. Teddy Bear lost its lease and had to move to another building. Monthly rent for the new building is $3,000. At the suggestion of parents, Teddy Bear plans to take children on field trips. Monthly costs of the field trips are $1,000. By how much should Teddy Bear increase fees per child to meet the target operating income of $10,400 per month, assuming the same number of children as in requirement 2?

LO 4 ▶
1. Q = 1,112

🌐 **3-38 CVP analysis, income taxes, sensitivity.** (CMA, adapted) Thompson Engine Company manufactures and sells diesel engines for use in small farming equipment. For its 2017 budget, Thompson Engine Company estimates the following:

Selling price	$ 7,000
Variable cost per engine	$ 2,000
Annual fixed costs	$5,560,000
Net income	$ 900,000
Income tax rate	40%

The first-quarter income statement, as of March 31, reported that sales were not meeting expectations. During the first quarter, only 300 units had been sold at the current price of $7,000. The income statement showed that variable and fixed costs were as planned, which meant that the 2017 annual net income projection would not be met unless management took action. A management committee was formed and presented the following mutually exclusive alternatives to the president:

  a. Reduce the selling price by 15%. The sales organization forecasts that at this significantly reduced price, 1,400 units can be sold during the remainder of the year. Total fixed costs and variable cost per unit will stay as budgeted.
  b. Lower variable cost per unit by $750 through the use of less-expensive direct materials. The selling price will also be reduced by $800, and sales of 1,130 units are expected for the remainder of the year.
  c. Reduce fixed costs by 5% and lower the selling price by 25%. Variable cost per unit will be unchanged. Sales of 1,500 units are expected for the remainder of the year.

Required

  1. If no changes are made to the selling price or cost structure, determine the number of units that Thompson Engine Company must sell (a) to break even and (b) to achieve its net income objective.
  2. Determine which alternative Thompson Engine Company should select to achieve its net income objective. Show your calculations.

LO 4, 5 ▶
3. Net Income is $108.900

🌐 **3-39 CVP analysis, income taxes.** (CMA, adapted) J.T. Brooks and Company, a manufacturer of quality handmade walnut bowls, has had a steady growth in sales for the past 5 years. However, increased competition has led Mr. Brooks, the president, to believe that an aggressive marketing campaign will be necessary next year to maintain the company's present growth. To prepare for next year's marketing campaign, the company's controller has prepared and presented Mr. Brooks with the following data for the current year, 2017:

Variable cost (per bowl)	
Direct materials	$ 3.00
Direct manufacturing labour	8.00
Variable overhead (manufacturing, marketing, distribution, and customer service)	7.50
Total variable cost per bowl	$ 18.50
Fixed costs	
Manufacturing	$ 20,000
Marketing, distribution, and customer service	194,500
Total fixed costs	$214,500
Selling price	$ 35.00
Expected sales, 22,000 units	$770,000
Income tax rate	40%

Required

  1. What is the projected net income for 2017?
  2. What is the breakeven point in units for 2017?
  3. Mr. Brooks has set the revenue target for 2018 at a level of $875,000 (or 25,000 bowls). He believes an additional marketing cost of $16,500 for advertising in 2018, with all other costs remaining constant, will be necessary to attain the revenue target. What is the net income for 2018 if the additional $16,500 is spent and the revenue target is met?
  4. What is the breakeven point in revenues for 2018 if the additional $16,500 is spent for advertising?

5. If the additional $16,500 is spent, what are the required 2018 revenues for 2018 net income to equal 2017 net income?

6. At a sales level of 25,000 units, what maximum amount can be spent on advertising if a 2018 net income of $108,450 is desired?

3-40 CVP, shoe stores. The Walk Rite Shoe Company operates a chain of shoe stores. The stores sell 10 different styles of inexpensive men's shoes with identical unit costs and selling prices. A unit is defined as a pair of shoes. Each store has a store manager who is paid a fixed salary. Individual salespeople receive a fixed salary and a sales commission. Walk Rite is trying to determine the desirability of opening another store, which is expected to have the following revenue and cost relationships:

Selling price	$ 30.00
Unit variable cost per pair:	
Cost of shoes	19.50
Sales commissions	1.50
Total variable costs	$ 21.00
Annual fixed costs:	
Rent	$ 60,000
Salaries	200,000
Advertising	80,000
Other fixed costs	20,000
Total fixed costs	$360,000

Required

(Consider each question independently.)

1. What is the annual breakeven point in (a) units sold and (b) revenues?
2. If 35,000 units are sold, what will be the store's operating income (loss)?
3. If sales commissions were discontinued for individual salespeople in favour of an $81,000 increase in fixed salaries, what would be the annual breakeven point in (a) units sold and (b) revenues?
4. Refer to the original data. If the store manager were paid $0.30 per unit sold in addition to his current fixed salary, what would be the annual breakeven point in (a) units sold and (b) revenues?
5. Refer to the original data. If the store manager were paid $0.30 per unit commission on each unit sold in excess of the breakeven point, what would be the store's operating income if 50,000 units were sold? (This $0.30 is in addition to both the commission paid to the sales staff and the store manager's fixed salary.)

3-41 CVP, shoe stores (continuation of 3-40). Refer to requirement 3 of 3-40. In this problem assume the role of the owner of Walk Rite.

Required

1. Calculate the number of units sold where the operating income under (a) a fixed-salary plan and (b) a lower fixed-salary-and-commission plan (for salespeople only) would be equal. Above that number of units sold, one plan would be more profitable than the other; below that number of units sold, the reverse would occur.
2. As owner, which sales compensation plan would you choose if forecasted annual sales of the new store were at least 55,000 units? What do you think of the motivation aspects of your chosen compensation plan?
3. Suppose the target operating income is $168,000. How many units must be sold to reach the target under (a) the fixed-salary plan and (b) the lower fixed-salary-and-commission plan?
4. You open the new store on January 1, 2019, with the original salary-plus-commission compensation plan in place. Because you expect the cost of the shoes to rise due to inflation, you place a firm bulk order for 50,000 shoes and lock in the $19.50 per unit price. But, toward the end of the year, only 48,000 pairs of shoes are sold, and you authorize a markdown of the remaining inventory to $18 per unit. Finally all units are sold. Salespeople, as usual, get paid a commission of 5% of revenues. What is the annual operating income for the store?

3-42 Uncertainty and expected costs. Dawmart Corp., an international retail giant, is considering implementing a new business-to-business (B2B) information system for processing purchase orders. The current system costs Dawmart $1,000,000 per month and $40 per order. Dawmart has two options: a partially automated B2B and a fully automated B2B system. The partially automated B2B system will have a fixed

◄ LO 3
1. a. BEP, 40,000 units

◄ LO 3
1. 54,000 units

◄ LO 4
2. Current system expected cost, $20,600,000

cost of $5,000,000 per month and a variable cost of $30 per order. The fully automated B2B system will have fixed costs of $10,000,000 per month and variable costs of $20 per order.

Based on data from the last two years, Dawmart has determined the following distribution on monthly orders:

Monthly Number of Orders	Probability
300,000	0.10
400,000	0.25
500,000	0.40
600,000	0.15
700,000	0.10

Required

1. Prepare a table showing the cost of each plan for each quantity of monthly orders.
2. What is the expected cost of each plan?
3. In addition to the information systems costs, what other factors should Dawmart consider before deciding to implement a new B2B system?

LO 4 ▶   ⊕ **3-43 Gross margin and contribution margin.** The Museum of America is preparing for its annual appreciation dinner for contributing members. Last year, 525 members attended the dinner. Tickets for the dinner were $24 per attendee. The profit report for last year's dinner follows.

Ticket sales	$ 12,600
Cost of dinner	15,300
Gross margin	(2,700)
Invitations and paperwork	2,500
Profit (loss)	$ (5,200)

This year the dinner committee does not want to lose money on the dinner. To help achieve its goal, the committee analyzed last year's costs. Of the $15,300 cost of the dinner, $9,000 were fixed costs and $6,300 were variable costs. Of the $2,500 cost of invitations and paperwork, $1,975 were fixed and $525 were variable.

Required

1. Prepare last year's profit report using the contribution margin format.
2. The committee is considering expanding this year's dinner invitation list to include volunteer members (in addition to contributing members). If the committee expands the dinner invitation list, it expects attendance to double. Calculate the effect this will have on the profitability of the dinner assuming fixed costs will be the same as last year.

LO 5 ▶
1. BEP, 160,000 total units
⊕ **3-44 Revenue mix, two products.** The Goldman Company retails two products, a standard and a deluxe version of a luggage carrier. The budgeted statement of comprehensive income is as follows:

	Standard Carrier	Deluxe Carrier	Total
Units sold	150,000	50,000	200,000
Revenues @ $20 and $30 per unit	$3,000,000	$1,500,000	$4,500,000
Variable costs @ $14 and $18 per unit	2,100,000	900,000	3,000,000
Contribution margins @ $6 and $12 per unit	$ 900,000	$ 600,000	1,500,000
Fixed costs			1,200,000
Operating income			$ 300,000

Required

1. Compute the breakeven point in units, assuming that the planned revenue mix is maintained.
2. Compute the breakeven point in units (a) if only standard carriers are sold and (b) if only deluxe carriers are sold.
3. Suppose 200,000 units are sold, but only 20,000 are deluxe. Compute the operating income. Compute the breakeven point if these relationships persist in the next period. Compare your answers with the original plans and the answer in requirement 1. What is the major lesson of this problem?

3-45 CVP analysis, shoe stores. The HighStep Shoe Company operates a chain of shoe stores that sell 10 different styles of inexpensive men's shoes with identical unit costs and selling prices. A unit is defined as a pair of shoes. Each store has a store manager who is paid a fixed salary. Individual salespeople receive a fixed salary and a sales commission. HighStep is considering opening another store that is expected to have the revenue and cost relationships shown here.

◀ **LO 3**

	Home	Insert	Page Layout	Formulas	Data	Review	View	
	A		B	C		D		E
1	**Unit Variable Data (per pair of shoes)**					**Annual Fixed Costs**		
2	Selling price		$60.00		Rent			$ 30,000
3	Cost of shoes		$37.00		Salaries			100,000
4	Sales commission		3.00		Advertising			40,000
5	Variable cost per unit		$40.00		Other fixed costs			10,000
6					Total fixed costs			$180,000

Consider each question independently.

Required

1. What is the annual breakeven point in (a) units sold and (b) revenues?
2. If 8,000 units are sold, what will be the store's operating income (loss)?
3. If sales commissions are discontinued and fixed salaries are raised by a total of $15,500, what would be the annual breakeven point in (a) units sold and (b) revenues?
4. Refer to the original data. If, in addition to his fixed salary, the store manager is paid a commission of $2.00 per unit sold, what would be the annual breakeven point in (a) units sold and (b) revenues?
5. Refer to the original data. If, in addition to his fixed salary, the store manager is paid a commission of $2.00 *per unit in excess of the breakeven point*, what would be the store's operating income if 12,000 units were sold?

3-46 CVP analysis, shoe stores (continuation of 3-45). Refer to requirement 3 of Problem 3-43. In this problem, assume the role of the owner of HighStep.

◀ **LO 4**

Required

1. As owner, which sales compensation plan would you choose if forecasted annual sales of the new store were at least 10,000 units? What do you think of the motivational aspect of your chosen compensation plan?
2. Suppose the target operating income is $69,000. How many units must be sold to reach the target operating income under (a) the original salary-plus-commissions plan and (b) the higher-fixed-salaries-only plan? Which method would you prefer? Explain briefly.
3. You open the new store on January 1, 2017, with the original salary-plus-commission compensation plan in place. Because you expect the cost of the shoes to rise due to inflation, you place a firm bulk order for 11,000 shoes and lock in the $37 price per unit. But toward the end of the year, only 9,500 shoes are sold, and you authorize a markdown of the remaining inventory to $50 per unit. Finally, all units are sold. Salespeople, as usual, get paid a commission of 5% of revenues. What is the annual operating income for the store?

3-47 Sales mix, two products. The Stackpole Company retails two products: a standard and a deluxe version of a luggage carrier. The budgeted income statement for next period is as follows:

◀ **LO 5**

	Standard Carrier	Deluxe Carrier	Total
Units sold	187,500	62,500	250,000
Revenues at $28 and $50 per unit	$5,250,000	$3,125,000	$8,375,000
Variable costs at $18 and $30 per unit	3,375,000	1,875,000	5,250,000
Contribution margins at $10 and $20 per unit	$1,875,000	$1,250,000	3,125,000
Fixed costs			2,250,000
Operating income			$ 875,000

Required

1. Compute the breakeven point in units, assuming that the company achieves its planned sales mix.
2. Compute the breakeven point in units (a) if only standard carriers are sold and (b) if only deluxe carriers are sold.
3. Suppose 250,000 units are sold but only 50,000 of them are deluxe. Compute the operating income. Compute the breakeven point in units. Compare your answer with the answer to requirement 1. What is the major lesson of this problem?

LO 4 ▶

1. CM% using own sales agents, 37%
CM% using own sales force, 45%

🌐 **3-48 Choosing between compensation plans, operating leverage.** (CMA, adapted) Marston Corporation manufactures pharmaceutical products that are sold through a network of sales agents. The agents are paid a commission of 18% of sales. The statement of income for the year ending December 31, 2019, under two scenarios, is as follows:

Marston Corporation Statement of Income for the Year Ending December 31, 2019

	Using Sales Agents		Using Own Sales Force	
Sales		$26,000,000		$26,000,000
Cost of goods sold				
Variable	$11,700,000		$11,700,000	
Fixed	2,870,000	14,570,000	2,870,000	14,570,000
Gross margin		11,430,000		11,430,000
Marketing costs				
Commissions	4,680,000		2,600,000	
Fixed costs	3,420,000	8,100,000	5,500,000	8,100,000
Operating income		$ 3,330,000		$ 3,330,000

Marston is considering hiring its own sales staff to replace the network of agents. Marston will pay its salespeople a commission of 10% and incur additional fixed costs of $2,080,000.

Required

1. Calculate Marston Corporation's 2019 contribution margin percentage, breakeven revenues, and degree of operating leverage under each of the two scenarios. (You will first have to recast the 2019 statement of income assuming Marston had hired its own sales staff.)
2. Describe the advantages and disadvantages of each type of sales alternative.
3. In 2020, Marston uses its own salespeople, who demand a 15% commission. If all other cost behaviour patterns are unchanged, how much revenue must the salespeople generate in order to earn the same operating income as in 2019?

LO 4 ▶

1. Additional income, $46,000

3-49 Special-order decision. Manitoba Production Corporation (MPC) specializes in the manufacture of one-litre plastic bottles. The plastic moulding machines are capable of producing 100 bottles per hour. The firm estimates that the variable cost of producing a plastic bottle is 25 cents. The bottles are sold for 55 cents each.

Management has been approached by a local toy company that would like the firm to produce a moulded plastic toy for it. The toy company is willing to pay $3.40 per unit for the toy. The unit variable cost to manufacture the toy will be $2.70. In addition, MPC would have to incur a cost of $24,000 to construct the mould required exclusively for this order. Because the toy uses more plastic and is of a more intricate shape than a bottle, a moulding machine can produce only 40 units per hour. The customer wants 100,000 units. Assume that MPC has a total capacity of 10,000 machine hours available during the period in which the toy company wants delivery of the toys. The firm's fixed costs, *excluding* the costs to construct the toy mould, during the same period will be $220,000.

Required

1. Suppose the demand for its bottles is 750,000 units, and the special toy order has to be either taken in full or rejected totally. Should MPC accept the special toy order? Explain your answer.
2. Suppose the demand for its bottles is 850,000 units, and the special toy order has to be either taken in full or rejected totally. Should MPC accept the special toy order? Explain your answer.
3. Suppose the demand for its bottles is 900,000 units, and the special toy order has to be either taken in full or rejected totally. Should MPC accept the special toy order? Explain your answer.

3-50 CVP, sensitivity analysis. Technology of the Past (TOP) produces old-fashioned simple cork-screws. Last year was not a good year for sales, but TOP expects the market to pick up this year. Last year's statement of comprehensive income showed

◄ **LO 4**
1. OI, $5,000

Sales revenues ($4 per corkscrew)	$40,000
Variable cost ($3 per corkscrew)	30,000
Contribution margin	10,000
Fixed costs	6,000
Operating income	$ 4,000

To take advantage of the anticipated growth in the market, TOP is considering various courses of action:

1. Do nothing. If TOP does nothing, it expects sales to increase by 10%.
2. Spend $2,000 on a new advertising campaign that is expected to increase sales by 50%.
3. Raise the price of the corkscrew to $5. This is expected to decrease sales quantities by 20%.
4. Redesign the classic corkscrew and increase the selling price to $6 while increasing the variable costs by $1 per unit. The sales level is not expected to change from last year.

Required

Evaluate each of the alternatives considered by TOP. What should TOP do?

3-51 Non-profit institution. The City of Vancouver makes an $850,000 lump-sum budget appropriation to run a safe injection site for a year. All the appropriation is to be spent. The variable costs average $16 per patient visit. Fixed costs are $500,000 per year.

◄ **LO 4**
1. 21,875 patient visits

Required

1. Compute the number of patient visits that the budget allocation will cover.
2. Suppose the total budget for the following year is reduced by 10%. Fixed costs are to remain the same. The same level of service on each patient visit will be maintained. Compute the number of visits that could be provided in a year.
3. As in requirement 2, assume a budget reduction of 10%. Fixed costs are to remain the same. By how much would variable costs have to decline in order to provide the same number of visits?

3-52 Sales mix, three products. The Ronowski Company has three product lines of belts—A, B, and C—with contribution margins of $3, $2, and $1, respectively. The president foresees sales of 200,000 units in the coming period, consisting of 20,000 units of A, 100,000 units of B, and 80,000 units of C. The company's fixed costs for the period are $255,000.

◄ **LO 3, 4**

Required

1. What is the company's breakeven point in units, assuming that the given sales mix is maintained?
2. If the sales mix is maintained, what is the total contribution margin when 200,000 units are sold? What is the operating income?
3. What would operating income be if 20,000 units of A, 80,000 units of B, and 100,000 units of C were sold? What is the new breakeven point in units if these relationships persist in the next period?

3-53 Ethics, CVP analysis. Megaphone Corporation produces a molded plastic casing, M&M101, for many cell phones currently on the market. Summary data from its 2017 income statement are as follows:

◄ **LO 3**

Revenues	$5,000,000
Variable costs	3,250,000
Fixed costs	1,890,000
Operating income	$ (140,000)

Joshua Kirby, Megaphone's president, is very concerned about Megaphone Corporation's poor profitability. He asks Leroy Gibbs, production manager, and Tony DiNunzo, controller, to see if there are ways to reduce costs.

After 2 weeks, Leroy returns with a proposal to reduce variable costs to 55% of revenues by reducing the costs Megaphone currently incurs for safe disposal of wasted plastic. Tony is concerned that this would expose the company to potential environmental liabilities. He tells Leroy, "We would need to estimate some of these potential environmental costs and include them in our analysis." "You can't do that," Leroy replies. "We are not violating any laws. There is some possibility that we may have to incur environmental costs in the future, but if we bring it up now, this proposal will not go through because our senior management always assumes these costs to be larger than they turn out to be. The market is very tough, and we are in danger of shutting down the company and costing all of us our jobs. The only reason our competitors are making money is because they are doing exactly what I am proposing."

Required

1. Calculate Megaphone Corporation's breakeven revenues for 2017.
2. Calculate Megaphone Corporation's breakeven revenues if variable costs are 55% of revenues.
3. Calculate Megaphone Corporation's operating income for 2017 if variable costs had been 55% of revenues.
4. Given Leroy Gibbs's comments, what should Tony DiNunzo do?

LO 3 ▶

1. a. 632,912 monthly treatments

3-54 Mini-case: Governance, CVP, cost analysis. Ahmed Diba is the relatively new controller of the Body Products Division of World Wide Drugs (WWD). He completed his CPA designation three years earlier (at a major auditing firm in Toronto) and has worked at the Body Products Division for the past six months). The move to Winnipeg was a major decision for Ahmed, but he is getting used to the climate and the new firm.

The Body Products Division (BPD) is located in Winnipeg, which is also the headquarters of WWD. This location gives WWD excellent access to distribution networks across North America while enjoying very low operating costs. (Wages and occupancy costs in Winnipeg are 40–60% lower than metropolitan centres like Vancouver or Toronto.)

At the request of the division's long-time president, Cheryl Kelly, Diba developed a proposal for a new product to be called Vital Hair. This product is a cream to be rubbed on the scalp to restore hair growth. The fixed costs associated with the development, production, and marketing of Vital Hair are $25,000,000. The majority of these costs are associated with the human trials needed to get federal health approval for this type of product. Due to the nature of the product, it has to be monitored by a doctor. Each customer will pay a doctor $98 per monthly treatment, of which $68 is paid to WWD. Diba estimates WWD's variable costs per treatment to be $28.50. Included in this is $9.25 for potential product litigation costs. Diba did some research on this type of product, and while most of the data came from the United States, he noticed that there is an increasing trend in Canada for consumers to take companies to court for the slightest issue with a product.

Cheryl Kelly and Diba are scheduled to make a presentation to the WWD executive committee on the expected profitability of Vital Hair. After reading Diba's report, Kelly called him to her office. Kelly was livid at Diba for including the $9.25 estimate. She argued that it is imperative to get the R&D funds approved (and quickly) and that any number that increases the breakeven point reduces the likelihood of the Vital Hair project being approved. She notes that WWD has had few successful lawsuits against it, in contrast to some recent "horrendous" experiences of competitors with breast implant products. Moreover, she was furious that Diba put the $9.25 amount in writing. "How do we know there will be any litigation problem?" She suggested that Diba redo the report excluding the $9.25 litigation risk cost estimate. "Put it on the whiteboard in the executive committee room, if you insist, but don't put it in the report sent to the committee before the meeting. You can personally raise the issue at the executive committee meeting and have a full and frank discussion."

Diba took Kelly's "advice." He changed the report's variable cost to $19.25 per treatment. Although he felt uneasy about the changes, he was comforted by the fact that he would flag the $9.25 amount to the executive committee in his forthcoming oral presentation.

One month later, Kelly walks into Diba's office. She is in a buoyant mood and announces she has just come back from an executive committee meeting that approved the Vital Hair proposal. Diba asks why he was not invited to the meeting. Kelly says the meeting was held in Toronto, and she decided to save the division money by going alone. She then says to Diba, "It is now time to get behind the new venture and help make it the success the committee and the team members believe it will be."

Required

1. What is the breakeven point (in units of monthly treatments) when WWD's variable costs (a) include the $9.25 estimate and (b) exclude the $9.25 estimate for potential product litigation costs?
2. Should Diba have excluded the $9.25 estimate in his report to the executive committee of WWD? Explain your answer.
3. What should Diba do in response to Kelly's decision to make the Vital Hair presentation on her own? What options does he have? As a CPA, what are his responsibilities to his employer?

3-55 Deciding where to produce. (CMA, adapted) Domestic Engines Company produces the same power generators in two plants, a newly renovated, automated plant in Peona, and an older, less automated plant in Modine. The following data are available for the two plants:

◀ **LO 4**
1. BEP for Peona plant, 73,500 units

	Peona		Modine	
Selling price		$ 150.00		$ 150.00
Variable manufacturing cost per unit	$72.00		$88.00	
Fixed manufacturing cost per unit	30.00		15.00	
Variable marketing and distribution cost per unit	14.00		14.00	
Fixed marketing and distribution cost per unit	19.00		14.50	
Total cost per unit		135.00		131.50
Operating income per unit		$ 15.00		$ 18.50
Production rate per day		400 units		320 units
Normal annual capacity usage		240 days		240 days
Maximum annual capacity		300 days		300 days

All unit fixed costs are calculated based on a normal year of 240 working days. When the number of working days exceeds 240, variable manufacturing costs increase by $3.00 per unit in Peona and $8.00 per unit in Modine.

Domestic Engines is expected to produce and sell 192,000 generators during the coming year. Wanting to maximize the higher unit profit at Modine, Domestic Engines's production manager has decided to manufacture 96,000 units at each plant. This production plan results in Modine operating at capacity (320 units per day 300 days) and Peona operating at its normal volume (400 units per day 240 days).

Required

1. Determine the breakeven point for the Peona and Modine plants in units.
2. Calculate the operating income that would result from the division production manager's plan to produce 96,000 units at each plant.
3. Determine how the production of the 192,000 units should be allocated between Peona and Modine to maximize operating income for Domestic Engines. Show your calculations.

Collaborative Learning Cases

3-56 CVP analysis and revenue mix. Ronowski Company has three product lines of belts, A, B, and C, with contribution margins of $3.60, $2.40, and $1.20, respectively. The president forecasts sales of 200,000 units in the coming period, consisting of 20,000 units of A, 100,000 units of B, and 80,000 units of C. The company's fixed costs for the period are $306,000.

◀ **LO 5**
1. BEP units, 150,000

Required

1. What is the company breakeven point in units, assuming that the given revenue mix is maintained?
2. If the mix is maintained, what is the total contribution margin when 200,000 units are sold? What is the operating income?
3. What would operating income become if 20,000 units of A, 80,000 units of B, and 100,000 units of C were sold? What is the new breakeven point in units if these relationships persist in the next period?

TRY IT! ▶ SOLUTIONS

Try It 3–1

Solution:

(a) Recall the equation method (equation 1):

$$\left[\left(\begin{array}{c}\text{Selling}\\\text{price}\end{array}\times\begin{array}{c}\text{Quantity of}\\\text{units sold}\end{array}\right)-\left(\begin{array}{c}\text{Variable cost}\\\text{per unit}\end{array}\times\begin{array}{c}\text{Quantity of}\\\text{units sold}\end{array}\right)\right]-\begin{array}{c}\text{Fixed}\\\text{costs}\end{array}=\begin{array}{c}\text{Operating}\\\text{income}\end{array}$$

Setting operating income equal to $0 and denoting quantity of output units that must be sold by Q, the breakeven number of units is

$$(\$500 \times Q) - (\$400 \times Q) - \$150,000 = \$0$$
$$\$100 \times Q = \$150,000$$
$$Q = \$150,000 \div \$100 \text{ per unit} = 1,500 \text{ units}$$

Recall the contribution margin method (equation 2):

$$\left(\begin{array}{c}\text{Contribution}\\\text{margin per unit}\end{array}\times\begin{array}{c}\text{Quantity of}\\\text{units sold}\end{array}\right)-\text{Fixed costs}=\text{Operating income}$$

At the breakeven point, operating income is by definition $0, and so,

Contribution margin per unit × Breakeven quantity of units = Fixedcosts (Equation 3)

Rearranging equation 3 and entering the data,

$$\begin{array}{c}\text{Breakeven}\\\text{number of units}\end{array} = \frac{\text{Fixed costs}}{\text{Contribution margin per unit}} = \frac{\$150,000}{\$100 \text{ per unit}} = 1,500 \text{ units}$$

Breakeven revenues = Breakeven number of units × Selling price
$$= 1,500 \text{ units} \times \$500 \text{ per unit} = \$750,000$$

(b) $$\left[\left(\begin{array}{c}\text{Selling}\\\text{price}\end{array}\right)\times\left(\begin{array}{c}\text{Quantity of}\\\text{units sold}\end{array}\right)-\left(\begin{array}{c}\text{Variable cost}\\\text{per unit}\end{array}\right)\times\left(\begin{array}{c}\text{Quantity of}\\\text{units sold}\end{array}\right)\right]-\begin{array}{c}\text{Fixed}\\\text{costs}\end{array}=\begin{array}{c}\text{Operating}\\\text{income}\end{array}$$
(Equation 1)

We denote by Q the unknown quantity of units Emma must sell to earn an operating income of $100,000. Selling price is $500, variable cost per package is $400, fixed costs are $150,000, and target operating income is $100,000. Substituting these values into equation 1, we have

$$(\$500 \times Q) - (\$400 \times Q) - \$150,000 = \$100,000$$
$$\$100 \times Q = \$150,000 + \$100,000 = \$250,000$$
$$Q = \$250,000 \div \$100 \text{ per unit} = 2,500 \text{ units}$$

Alternatively, we could use equation 2:

$$\left(\begin{array}{c}\text{Contribution margin}\\\text{per unit}\end{array}\times\begin{array}{c}\text{Quantity of}\\\text{units sold}\end{array}\right)-\begin{array}{c}\text{Fixed}\\\text{costs}\end{array}=\begin{array}{c}\text{Operating}\\\text{income}\end{array}$$
(Equation 2)

Given a target operating income ($100,000 in this case), we can rearrange terms to get equation 4.

$$\begin{array}{c}\text{Quantity of units}\\\text{required to be sold}\end{array} = \frac{\text{Fixed costs} + \text{Target operating income}}{\text{Contribution margin per unit}}$$
(Equation 4)

$$\begin{array}{c}\text{Quantity of units}\\\text{required to be sold}\end{array} = \frac{\$150,000 + \$100,000}{\$100 \text{ per unit}} = 2,500 \text{ units}$$

Revenues to earn an operating income of $100,000 are

Revenues = Number of units required to be sold × Selling price
$$2,500 \text{ units} \times \$500 = \$1,250,000$$

Try It 3–2

Solution:

$$\text{Margin of safety} = \frac{\text{Budgeted}}{\text{revenues}} - \frac{\text{Breakeven}}{\text{revenues}} = \$1{,}200{,}000 - \$750{,}000 = \$450{,}000$$

$$\frac{\text{Margin of}}{\text{safety (in units)}} = \frac{\text{Budgeted}}{\text{sales (units)}} - \frac{\text{Breakeven}}{\text{sales (units)}} = 2{,}400 - 1{,}500 = 900 \text{ units}$$

The margin of safety indicates that sales would have to decrease by 900 units and revenues by $450,000 before the breakeven point is reached.

Sometimes margin of safety is expressed as a percentage:

$$\text{Margin of safety percentage} = \frac{\text{Margin of safety in dollars}}{\text{Budgeted (or actual) revenues}}$$

In our example, margin of safety percentage $= \dfrac{\$450{,}000}{\$1{,}200{,}000} = 37.5\%$

This result means that revenues would have to decrease substantially, by 37.5%, to reach the breakeven revenues.

The high margin of safety gives management of Bernard Windows confidence that the company is unlikely to suffer a loss.

4

Job Costing

▶ CPA Competencies

This chapter covers material outlined in **Section 3: Management Accounting** of the CPA Competency Map. The Learning Objectives in this chapter have been aligned with the CPA Competency Map to ensure the best coverage possible.

3.3.1 Evaluates cost classifications and costing methods for management of ongoing operations

3.3.2 Evaluates and applies cost management techniques appropriate for specific costing decisions

3.4.1 Evaluates sources and drivers of revenue growth

StockPhotosLV/Shutterstock

What Does It Cost To Do the Job?

Each summer, about 7,500 forest fires burn an average of 450,000 square kilometres of Canadian wilderness. A ferocious force of nature, wildfires cost Canadian taxpayers approximately $500 million per year to suppress. Fires cause evacuations of entire cities, destroy property, create economic hardship, and kill wildlife and people. In May 2016, Fort McMurray in Alberta was destroyed by wildfire. Residents of the entire city and its surrounding areas were evacuated, shutting down the city. The total costs neared $10 billion, and parts of the city remained shut down and declared irretrievable nearly a year after the fire.

The cost to suppress a forest fire depends on how accessible the fire is. Unfortunately, the most inaccessible wildfires can also be the most destructive and expensive to suppress. These fires are fought primarily using aircraft and fire-retardant chemicals. Firefighters are delivered to the site by parachuting in (smoke jumpers) or rappelling in by rope from helicopters. On average, the cost to suppress a Canadian wildfire is approximately $60,000 per fire (although initial cost estimates to fight Fort McMurray are $615 million!). Provincial governments use careful job-costing procedures to refine and improve their cost estimates for fire suppression. Governments need a reliable job-costing system so they can account to the taxpayers when asked how money was spent and to help develop appropriate budgets for future years.

Sources: National Forestry Database. 2016. Forest Fires, 2015 (http://nfdp.ccfm.org/fires/quick_facts_e. php), CBC News. 2016. Fort McMurray fire could cost insurers $9B, BMO predicts, August 19 (http://www.cbc.ca/news/business/fort-mcmurray-insurance-cost-1.3568113); CBC News. 2016. Preliminary cost of Fort McMurray fire estimated at $615 million, August 19 (http://www.cbc.ca/news/canada/edmonton/preliminary-cost-of-fort-mcmurray-fire-estimated-at-615-million-1.3640935).

Building Blocks of Costing Systems

Cost assignment is a general term for assigning costs, whether direct or indirect, to a *cost object*. *Cost tracing* is a specific term for assigning direct costs; *cost allocation* refers to assigning indirect costs. The relationship among these three concepts can be graphically represented as follows:

▶ **LO 1**

Describe the building-block concepts of costing systems.

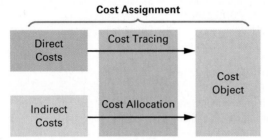

Throughout this chapter, the costs assigned to a cost object—for example, a product such as a Mini Cooper or a service such as an audit of MTV—include both variable costs and costs that are fixed in the short run. Managers cost products and services to guide long-run strategic decisions (for example, what mix of products and services to produce and sell and what prices to charge for them). In the long run, managers want revenues to exceed total costs.

We also need to introduce and explain two more terms before discussing costing systems:

1. *Cost pool.* A cost pool is a grouping of individual indirect cost items. Cost pools can range from broad (such as all manufacturing-plant costs) to narrow (such as the costs of operating metal-cutting machines). Cost pools are often organized in conjunction with cost-allocation bases.

2. *Cost-allocation base.* A cost-allocation base (e.g., number of machine-hours, or number of labour-hours) is a systematic way to link an indirect cost or group of indirect costs to cost objects. For example, if the indirect cost of operating metal-cutting machines is $500,000 based on running these machines for 10,000 hours, the cost allocation rate is $500,000 ÷ 10,000 hours = $50 per machine-hour, where machine-hours are the cost allocation base.

If a product uses 800 machine-hours, it will be allocated $40,000 (= $50 per machine-hour × 800 machine-hours). When the cost object is a job, product, or customer, the cost-allocation base is also called a cost-application base.

These concepts represent the building blocks that we will use to design the costing systems described in this chapter.

Job-Costing and Process-Costing Systems

Management accountants use two basic types of costing systems to assign costs to products or services:

▶ **LO 2**

Distinguish job costing from process costing.

1. *Job-costing system.* In this system, the cost object is a unit or multiple units of a distinct product or service called a job. Each job generally uses different amounts of resources. The product or service is often a single unit, such as a specialized machine made at Samsung, a repair job done at an Audi service centre, or an advertising campaign produced by Saatchi & Saatchi. Each special machine made by Samsung is unique and distinct. An advertising campaign for one client at Saatchi & Saatchi is unique and distinct from advertising campaigns for other clients.

2. *Process-costing system.* In this system, the cost object is masses of identical or similar units of a product or service. For example, Scotiabank provides the same service to all its customers when processing customer deposits. In each period, process-costing systems divide the total costs of producing an identical or similar product or service by the total number of units produced to obtain a per-unit cost. This per-unit cost is the average unit cost that applies to each of the identical or similar units produced in that period.

Exhibit 4-1 Examples of Job Costing and Process Costing in the Service, Merchandising, and Manufacturing Sectors

	Service Sector	Merchandising Sector	Manufacturing Sector
Job Costing Used	• Audit engagements done by PricewaterhouseCoopers • Consulting engagements done by McKinsey & Co. • Advertising-agency campaigns run by DDB Canada • Individual legal cases argued by Borden Ladner Gervais LLP • Computer-repair jobs done by Best Buy • Movies featuring members of the Alliance of Canadian Cinema, Television and Radio Artists (ACTRA)	• Mountain Equipment Co-op sending individual items by mail order • Special promotion of new products by Chapters Indigo	• Assembly of individual aircraft at Bombardier • Construction of automotive components at Linamar Corporation
Process Costing Used	• Bank cheque clearing at TD Canada Trust • Postal delivery (standard items) by Canada Post	• Grain dealing by the Canada Malting Co. Limited • Lumber dealing by Weyerhaeuser	• Oil refining by Irving Oil • Beverage production by Molson Inc.

Exhibit 4-1 presents examples of job costing and process costing in the service, merchandising, and manufacturing sectors.

Job Costing: Evaluation and Implementation

► **LO 3**

Describe the approaches to evaluating and implementing job-costing systems.

Job costing is used at Robinson Company, a company that manufactures and installs specialized machinery for the paper-making industry. In early 2018, Robinson receives a request to bid for the manufacturing and installation of a new paper-making machine for the Western Pulp and Paper Company (WPP). Robinson has never made a machine quite like this one, and its managers wonder what to bid for the job. Robinson's management team works through the five-step decision-making process.

1. *Identify the problems and uncertainties.* The decision of whether and how much to bid for the WPP job depends on how management resolves two critical uncertainties: what it will cost to complete the job, and the prices that its competitors are likely to bid.

2. *Obtain information.* Robinson's managers first evaluate whether doing the WPP job is consistent with the company's strategy. Do they want to do more of these kinds of jobs? Is this an attractive segment of the market? Robinson's managers study the drawings and engineering specifications provided by WPP and decide on technical details of the machine. They compare the specifications of this machine to similar machines they have made in the past, identify competitors who might bid on the job, and gather information on what these bids might be.

3. *Make predictions about the future.* Robinson's managers estimate the cost of direct materials, direct manufacturing labour, and overhead for the WPP job. They also consider qualitative factors and risk factors and think through any biases they might have. For example, do engineers and employees working on the WPP job have the necessary skills and technical competence? How accurate are the cost estimates, and what is the likelihood of cost overruns?

4. *Make decisions by choosing among alternatives.* Robinson bids $15,000 for the WPP job. This bid is based on a manufacturing cost estimate of $10,000 and a markup of 50% over manufacturing cost.

5. *Implement the decision, evaluate performance, and learn.* Robinson wins the bid for the WPP job. As Robinson works on the WPP job, it keeps careful track of all the costs it has incurred (which are detailed later in this chapter). Ultimately, Robinson's

managers compare the predicted amounts against actual costs to evaluate how well they did on the WPP job.

In its job-costing system, Robinson accumulates costs incurred on a job in different parts of the value chain, such as manufacturing, marketing, and customer service. To make a machine, Robinson purchases some components from outside suppliers and makes others itself. Each of Robinson's jobs also has a service element: installing a machine at a customer's site, integrating it with the customer's other machines and processes, and ensuring the machine meets customer expectations.

One form of job-costing system that Robinson can use is *actual costing*. Actual costing is a costing system that traces direct costs to a cost object by using the actual direct-cost rates multiplied by the actual quantities of the direct-cost inputs. It allocates indirect costs based on the actual indirect-cost rates multiplied by the actual quantities of the cost-allocation bases. The actual indirect-cost rate is calculated by dividing actual total indirect costs by the actual total quantity of the cost-allocation base. As its name suggests, an actual costing system calculates the actual costs of a job. Yet, actual costing systems are not commonly found in practice because actual costs cannot be computed in a timely manner.

Actual, Budgeted, and Normal Costing

Normal Costing

The difficulty of calculating actual indirect-cost rates on a weekly or monthly basis means managers cannot calculate the actual costs of jobs as they are completed. However, managers, including those at Robinson, want a close approximation of the costs of various jobs regularly during the year, not just at the end of the fiscal year. Managers want to know manufacturing costs (and other costs, such as marketing costs) for ongoing uses, including pricing jobs, monitoring and managing costs, evaluating the success of the job, learning about what worked and what didn't, bidding on new jobs, and preparing interim financial statements. Because of the need for immediate access to job costs, few companies wait to allocate overhead costs until year-end when the actual manufacturing overhead is finally known. Instead, a *predetermined* or *budgeted indirect-cost rate* is calculated for each cost pool at the beginning of a fiscal year, and overhead costs are allocated to jobs as work progresses. The **budgeted indirect-cost rate** for each cost pool is computed as follows:

► **LO 4**

Distinguish between actual, budgeted, and normal costing.

$$\text{Budgeted indirect cost rate} = \frac{\text{Budgeted annual indirect costs}}{\text{Budgeted annual quantity of the cost allocation base}}$$

Normal costing is a costing system that (1) traces direct costs to a cost object by using the actual direct-cost rates multiplied by the actual quantities of the direct-cost inputs, and (2) allocates indirect costs based on the budgeted indirect-cost rates multiplied by the actual quantities of the cost-allocation bases.

We illustrate normal costing for Robinson Company example using the following steps to assign costs to an individual job.

Step 1: Identify the job that is the chosen cost object. The cost object in the Robinson Company example is Job WPP 298, manufacturing a paper-making machine for Western Pulp and Paper (WPP) in 2018. Robinson's managers and management accountants gather information to cost jobs through source documents. A **source document** is an original record (such as an invoice) that supports journal entries in an accounting system. The main source document for Job WPP 298 is a **job-cost record**. A job-cost record (also called a job-cost sheet) records and accumulates all the costs assigned to a specific job, starting when work begins. Exhibit 4-2 shows the job-cost record for the paper-making machine.

Step 2: Identify the direct costs of the job. Robinson identifies two direct-manufacturing cost categories: direct materials and direct manufacturing labour.

Direct materials: On the basis of the engineering specifications and drawings provided by WPP, a manufacturing engineer orders materials from the storeroom. The order is placed

Exhibit 4-2 Job-Cost Record for the Paper-Making Machine

	A	B	C	D	E	
1				**JOB-COST RECORD**		
2	JOB NO:	WPP 298		CUSTOMER:	Western Pulp and Paper	
3	Date Started:	Feb. 7, 2018		Date Completed	Feb. 28, 2018	
4						
5						
6	**DIRECT MATERIALS**					
7	Date	Materials		Quantity	Unit	Total
8	Received	Requisition No.	Part No.	Used	Cost	Costs
9	Feb. 7, 2018	2011: 198	MB 468-A	8	$14	$112
10	Feb. 7, 2018	2011: 199	TB 267-F	12	63	756
11						●
12						●
13	Total					4,606
14						
15	**DIRECT MANUFACTURING LABOUR**					
16	Period	Labour Time	Employee	Hours	Hourly	Total
17	Covered	Record No.	No.	Used	Rate	Costs
18	Feb. 7-13, 2018	LT 232	551-87-3076	25	$18	$ 450
19	Feb. 7-13, 2018	LT 247	287-31-4671	5	19	95
20						●
21						●
22	Total					1,579
23						
24	**MANUFACTURING OVERHEAD***					
25		Cost Pool		Allocation Base	Allocation-	Total
26	Date	Category	Allocation Base	Quantity Used	Base Rate	Costs
27	Dec. 31, 2018	Manufacturing	Direct Manufacturing	88 hours	$40	$ 3,520
28			Labour-Hours			
29						
30	Total					3,520
31	**TOTAL MANUFACTURING COST OF JOB**					$ 9,705
32						
33						
34	*The Robinson Company uses a single manufacturing-overhead cost pool. The use of multiple overhead cost pools					
35	would mean multiple entries in the "Manufacturing Overhead" section of the job-cost record.					
36						

Note The record specifies the job for which the material is requested (WPP 298), the description of the material (Part Number MB 468-A, metal brackets), the actual quantity (8), the actual unit cost ($14), and the actual total cost ($112). The $112 actual total cost appears on the job-cost record in Exhibit 4-2. If we add the cost of all materials requisitions, the total actual direct materials cost is $4,606, which is shown in the direct materials panel of the job-cost record in Exhibit 4-2.

using a basic source document called a **materials-requisition record,** which contains information about the cost of direct materials used on a specific job and in a specific department. Exhibit 4-3, Panel A, shows a materials-requisition record for Robinson Company.

Direct manufacturing labour: The accounting for direct manufacturing labour is similar to the accounting described for direct materials. The source document for direct manufacturing labour is a **labour-time sheet,** which contains information about the amount of labour time used for a specific job in a specific department.

Exhibit 4-3, Panel B, shows a typical weekly labour-time sheet for a particular employee (G. L. Cook). Each day, Cook records the time spent on individual jobs (in this case WPP 298 and JL 256), as well as the time spent on other tasks, such as maintenance

Exhibit 4-3 Robinson Company Source Documents

PANEL A:

MATERIALS-REQUISITION RECORD				
Materials-Requisition Record No.			2018: 198	
Job No. WPP 298		Date:	FEB. 7, 2018	
Part No.	Part Description	Quantity	Unit Cost	Total Cost
MB 468-A	Metal Brackets	8	$14	$112
Issued By: B. Clyde		Date:	Feb. 7, 2018	
Received By: L. Daley		Date:	Feb. 7, 2018	

PANEL B:

LABOUR-TIME SHEET								
Labour-Time Record No: LT 232								
Employee Name: G. L. Cook Employee No: 551-87-3076								
Employee Classification Code: Grade 3 Machinist								
Hourly Rate: $18								
Week Start: Feb. 7, 2018 Week End: Feb. 13, 2018								
Job. No.	M	T	W	Th	F	S	Su	Total
WPP 298	4	8	3	6	4	0	0	25
JL 256	3	0	4	2	3	0	0	12
Maintenance	1	0	1	0	1	0	0	3
Total	8	8	8	8	8	0	0	40
Supervisor: R. Stuart		Date: Feb. 13, 2018						

of machines or cleaning, that are not related to a specific job. The 25 hours that Cook spent on Job WPP 298 appears on the job-cost record in Exhibit 4-2 at a cost of $450 (= 25 hours × $18 per hour). Similarly, the job-cost record for Job JL 256 will carry a cost of $216 (= 12 hours × $18 per hour).

All costs other than direct materials and direct manufacturing labour are classified as indirect costs.

Step 3: Select the cost-allocation bases to use for allocating indirect costs to the job. Indirect manufacturing costs are costs that are necessary to do a job but that cannot be traced to a specific job. The objective is to allocate the costs of indirect resources in a systematic way to their related jobs. Companies often use multiple cost-allocation bases to allocate indirect costs because different indirect costs have different cost drivers. For example, some indirect costs such as depreciation and repairs of machines are more closely related to machine-hours. Other indirect costs such as supervision and production support are more closely related to direct manufacturing labour-hours. Robinson, however, chooses direct manufacturing labour-hours as the sole allocation base for linking all indirect manufacturing costs to jobs.

In 2018, Robinson budgets 28,000 direct manufacturing labour-hours for the WPP job.

Step 4: Identify the indirect costs associated with each cost-allocation base. Because Robinson believes that a single cost-allocation base—direct manufacturing labour-hours—can be used to allocate indirect manufacturing costs to jobs, Robinson creates a single cost pool called manufacturing overhead costs. This pool represents all indirect costs of the manufacturing department that are difficult to trace directly to individual jobs.

In 2018, budgeted manufacturing overhead costs total $1,120,000.

Step 5: Compute the rate per unit of each cost-allocation base used to allocate indirect costs to the job. For each cost pool, the budgeted indirect-cost rate is calculated by dividing budgeted total indirect costs in the pool (determined in Step 4) by the budgeted total quantity of the cost-allocation base (determined in Step 3). Robinson calculates the allocation rate for its single manufacturing overhead cost pool as follows:

$$\text{Budgeted manufacturing overhead rate} = \frac{\text{Budgeted manufacturing overhead costs}}{\text{Budgeted total quantity of cost allocation base}}$$

$$= \frac{\$1{,}120{,}000}{28{,}000 \text{ direct manufacturing labour hours}}$$

$$= \$40 \text{ per direct manufacturing labour hour}$$

Step 6: Compute the indirect costs allocated to the job. The indirect costs of a job are calculated by multiplying the actual quantity of each different allocation base (one allocation base for each cost pool) associated with the job by the budgeted indirect cost rate of each allocation base (computed in Step 5).

Manufacturing overhead costs allocated to WPP 298 equal $3,520 (= $40 per direct manufacturing labour-hour × 88 hours) and appear in the manufacturing overhead panel of the WPP 298 job-cost record in Exhibit 4-2.

Step 7: Compute the total cost of the job by adding all direct and indirect costs assigned to the job. Exhibit 4-2 shows that the total manufacturing costs of the WPP job are $9,705.

Direct manufacturing costs		
Direct materials	$4,606	
Direct manufacturing labour	1,579	$ 6,185
Manufacturing overhead costs		
($40 per direct manufacturing labour-hour × 88 hours)		3,520
Total manufacturing costs of job WPP 298		$ 9,705

Robinson bid a price of $15,000 for the job. At that revenue, the normal-costing system shows a gross margin of $5,295 (= $15,000 − $9,705) and a gross-margin percentage of 35.3% (= $5,295 ÷ $15,000 = 0.353).

Robinson's manufacturing managers and sales managers can use the gross margin and gross-margin percentage calculations to compare the profitability of different jobs to try to understand why some jobs show low profitability. Have direct materials been wasted? Was direct manufacturing labour too high? Were these jobs simply underpriced? Job-cost analysis provides the information needed for judging the performance of manufacturing and sales managers and for making future improvements.

Exhibit 4-4 is an overview of Robinson Company's job-costing system. This exhibit represents the concepts comprising the five building blocks—cost object, direct costs of a cost object, indirect (overhead) costs of a cost object, indirect-cost pool, and cost allocation base—of job-costing systems that were first introduced at the beginning of this

Exhibit 4-4 Robinson Company Job-Costing System Overview

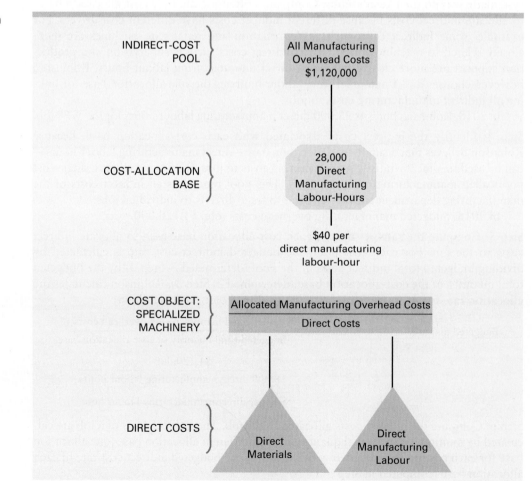

chapter. (The symbols in Exhibit 4-4 are used consistently in the costing-system overviews presented in this text. A triangle always identifies a direct cost, a rectangle represents the indirect-cost pool, and an octagon describes the cost-allocation base.)

Additional Points to Consider When Calculating Job-Cost Allocation Rates

Information technology simplifies the tracing of costs to jobs. If direct manufacturing labour-hours (DMLH) is used as the cost allocation base, very refined systems can trace direct manufacturing labour in minutes or longer intervals to each job. Employees simply scan their identification card and select the job identification code when they begin and again when they end their task. The computer then reports not only the DMLH spent, but also the indirect costs of fringe benefits and rework for each job. For fixed cost allocation, when the cost object is a job it is sensible to collect the fixed costs incurred during the entire time period of the job. There are two reasons for using longer periods, such as a year, to calculate indirect cost rates:

- **Seasonal patterns.** The shorter the period is, the greater is the influence of seasonal patterns on the amount of costs. For example, if indirect cost rates were calculated each month, then heating costs would be charged to production only during the winter months. An annual period incorporates the effects of all four seasons into one annual indirect cost rate.
- **Unitized fixed costs.** Longer periods to produce jobs mean that the unitized fixed cost portion of the machine and other fixed cost pools will be spread out more evenly. Even if output varies from month to month for a single job, the point is to cost the job, not the time period.

Concepts in Action | Job Costing on the Next-Generation Military Fighter Plane

U.S. Air Force photo by Senior Airman Julius Delos Reyes

Northrop Grumman, Inc. is a leading provider of systems and technologies for the US Department of Defense. Competitive bidding processes and increased public and congressional oversight make understanding costs critical in pricing decisions, as well as in winning and retaining government contracts. Each job must be estimated individually because the distinct outputs consume different amounts of Northrop Grumman's resources.

A project team of Northrop Grumman, Lockheed Martin, and BAE Systems was awarded the System Design and Demonstration contract to build the F-35 Lightning II aircraft—also known as the Joint Strike Fighter—in late 2001. This project, worth over $200 billion, will create a family of supersonic, multi-role fighter airplanes designed for the militaries of the United States, the United Kingdom, Italy, the Netherlands, Turkey, Canada, Australia, Denmark, and Norway. In December 2006, the F-35 Lightning II successfully completed its first test flight; yet problems have plagued the jet's development since the testing.

The project team for the F-35 Lightning II uses a job-costing system. There are two direct cost pools, material and manufacturing labour. The remaining costs are accumulated in one overhead cost pool. The cost allocation base is the total budgeted direct materials cost. This job-costing system allows managers to assign costs to processes and projects. Managers use this system to actively manage costs. However, as cost over runs continue, the length of time to complete jobs and the cost associated with individual jobs associated with the overall project continue to mount. Most recently, after spending some months reviewing whether to continue the project, the Government of Canada agreed to contribute an additional $36 million to remain in the ongoing development of the F-35.

Sources: D. Pugliese. 2016. Trudeau government to contribute another $36 million to F-35 fighter jet program, *National Post* November 24 (http://news.nationalpost.com/news/canada/trudeau-government-to-contribute-another-36-million-to-f-35-fighter-jet-program).

For example, an audit firm has a highly seasonal workload. Tax advice accounts for more than 80% of the workload from January through April. Given the following mix of costs for a high-output month such as April and a low-output month such as July, actual indirect cost allocation rates fluctuate by almost 300%. If the low cost allocation rate were charged in April, then clients would be very pleased. If the high cost allocation rate were charged in July, then clients would leave. If costs are allocated and charged at the time they are incurred, then July clients are not paying a fair share of fixed resources for an identical job in April. July clients are penalized for the time of year the resources are consumed. Ultimately the firm could not cover its total annual fixed indirect costs.

	Indirect Costs			Professional Labour-Hours (4)	Allocation Rate per Professional Labour-Hour (5) = (3) ÷ (4)
	Variable (1)	Fixed (2)	Total (3)		
High-output month	$40,000	$60,000	$100,000	3,200	$31.25
Low-output month	10,000	60,000	70,000	800	87.50

 **TRY IT! 4.1**

Donna Corporation manufactures custom cabinets for kitchens. It uses a normal costing system with two direct cost categories—direct materials and direct manufacturing labour—and one indirect cost pool, manufacturing overhead costs. It provides the following information for 2020.

Budgeted manufacturing overhead costs	$960,000
Budgeted direct manufacturing labour-hours	32,000 hours
Actual manufacturing overhead costs	$992,000
Actual direct manufacturing labour-hours	31,000 hours

Required

Calculate the total manufacturing costs of the 32 Berndale Drive job based on the following information:

Actual direct materials costs	$3,500
Actual direct manufacturing labour	160 hours
Actual direct manufacturing labour rate	$ 20 per hour

Actual Costing

How would the cost of Job WPP 298 change if Robinson had used actual costing rather than normal costing? Both actual costing and normal costing trace direct costs to jobs in the same way because source documents identify the actual quantities and actual rates of direct materials and direct manufacturing labour for a job as the work is being done. The only difference between normal costing and actual costing is that normal costing uses budgeted indirect-cost rates, whereas actual costing uses actual indirect-cost rates calculated annually at the end of the year.

	Actual
Total manufacturing overhead costs	$1,215,000
Total direct manufacturing labour-hours	27,000

Steps 1 and 2 are exactly as before: Step 1 identifies WPP 298 as the cost object; Step 2 calculates actual direct material costs of $4,606, and actual direct manufacturing labour costs of $1,579.

Recall from Step 3 that Robinson uses a single cost-allocation base, direct manufacturing labour-hours, to allocate all manufacturing overhead costs to jobs. The actual quantity of direct manufacturing labour-hours for 2018 is 27,000 hours.

In Step 4, Robinson groups all actual indirect manufacturing costs of $1,215,000 into a single manufacturing overhead cost pool.

In Step 5, the actual indirect-cost rate is calculated by dividing actual total indirect costs in the pool (determined in Step 4) by the actual total quantity of the cost-allocation base (determined in Step 3). Robinson calculates the actual manufacturing overhead rate in 2018 for its single manufacturing overhead cost pool as follows:

$$\frac{\text{Actual manufacturing}}{\text{overhead rate}} = \frac{\text{Actual annual manufacturing overhead costs}}{\text{Actual annual quantity of the cost allocation base}}$$

$$= \frac{\$1,215,000}{27,000 \text{ direct manufacturing labour hours}}$$

$$= \$45 \text{ per direct manufacturing labour hour}$$

In Step 6, under an actual-costing system,

$$\frac{\text{Manufacturing overhead costs}}{\text{allocated to WPP 298}} = \frac{\text{Actual manufacturing}}{\text{overhead rate}} \times \frac{\text{Actual quantity of direct}}{\text{manufacturing labour-hours}}$$

$$= \frac{\$45 \text{ per direct manuf.}}{\text{labour-hour}} \times \frac{88 \text{ direct manufacturing}}{\text{labour-hours}}$$

$$= \$3,960$$

Note		
	Actual Costing	**Normal Costing**
Direct Costs	*Actual direct-cost rates* × *actual quantities of direct-cost inputs*	*Actual direct-cost rates* × *actual quantities of direct-cost inputs*
Indirect Costs	*Actual indirect-cost rates* × *actual quantities of cost-allocation bases*	*Budgeted indirect-cost rates* × *actual quantities of cost-allocation bases*

In Step 7, the cost of the job under actual costing is $10,145, calculated as follows:

Direct manufacturing costs		
Direct materials	$4,606	
Direct manufacturing labour	1,579	$ 6,185
Manufacturing overhead costs ($45 per direct manufacturing labour-hour × 88 actual direct manufacturing labour-hours)		3,960
Total manufacturing costs of job		$10,145

A Normal Job-Costing System and Cost Flow

We now explain cost flow for a company with a normal job-costing system, Robinson Company. The following illustration considers events that occurred in February 2018. Exhibit 4-5 illustrates a broad framework for understanding the flow of costs and inventory valuation in job costing.

The upper part of Exhibit 4-5 shows the inventoriable costs from the purchase of materials and other manufacturing inputs, which flow during conversion into work-in-process and finished goods inventory. The sale of the product triggers the transfer of these costs from Cost of Goods Manufactured (COGM) to the Cost of Goods Sold (COGS) account.

Direct materials used and direct manufacturing labour can be easily traced to WPP through the electronic source documents. These costs do not disappear even if they are paid. Rather, these costs are transferred to work-in-process inventory on the statement of financial position. These direct costs are expended to transform or convert raw materials into finished goods inventory. As the goods are converted, value is added, which is why the work-in-process is a current asset.

Robinson also incurs manufacturing overhead costs (MOH), including indirect materials and indirect manufacturing labour. These indirect support costs cannot be readily traced to WPP because the inputs are common and used in different amounts by all of Robinson's jobs. First MOH is accumulated in an MOH ledger account and then allocated and assigned to individual jobs. Once assigned to a job, MOH is transferred to the Work-in-Process Inventory account.

▶ **LO 5**

Analyze the flow of costs from direct and indirect cost pools to inventory accounts, including adjustments for over- and underallocated costs.

Exhibit 4-5 Flow of Costs in Job Costing

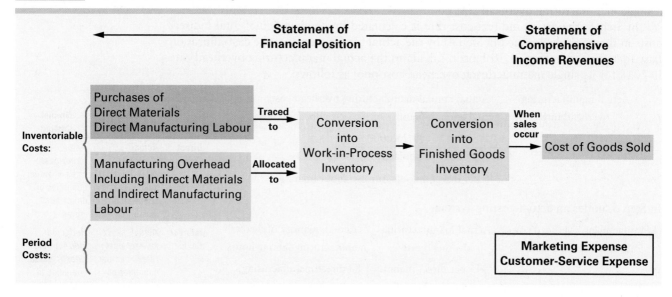

Once complete, all assigned WPP costs are transferred to the Finished Goods Inventory account on the statement of financial position. Only when finished goods are sold is an expense, cost of goods sold, recognized in the statement of comprehensive income and matched against revenue earned from sales.

General Ledger

A summary of the job-cost record is typically found in a subsidiary ledger. The general ledger account Work-in-Process Control presents the total of these separate job-cost records pertaining to all unfinished jobs. The job-cost records and Work-in-Process Control account track job costs from when jobs start until they are complete.

Exhibit 4-6 shows T-accounts for Robinson Company's general ledger. The general ledger gives a "bird's-eye view" of the costing system. The amounts shown in Exhibit 4-6 are based on the transactions and journal entries that follow. As you go through each journal entry, use Exhibit 4-6 to see how the various entries being made come together. General ledger accounts with "Control" in the titles (for example, Materials Control and Accounts Payable Control) have underlying subsidiary ledgers that contain additional details, such as each type of material in inventory and individual suppliers that Robinson must pay.

A general ledger should be viewed as only one of many tools that assist management in planning and control. To control operations, managers rely on not only the source documents used to record amounts in the subsidiary ledgers, but also nonfinancial information such as the percentage of jobs requiring rework.

Explanations of Transactions

We next look at a summary of Robinson Company's transactions for February 2018 and the corresponding journal entries for those transactions.

1. Purchases of materials (direct and indirect) on credit, $89,000.

Materials Control	89,000	
Accounts Payable Control		89,000

2. Usage of direct materials, $81,000, and indirect materials, $4,000.

Work-in-Process Control	81,000	
Manufacturing Overhead Control	4,000	
Materials Control		85,000

Exhibit 4-6 Normal Job Costing for WPP: Diagram of General Ledger Relationships for February 2018

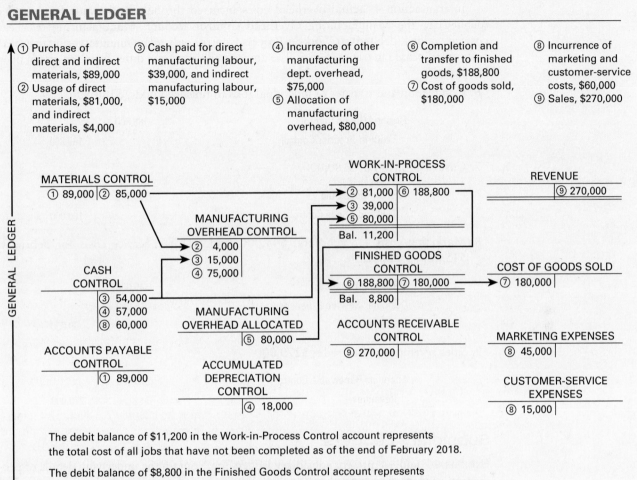

The debit balance of $11,200 in the Work-in-Process Control account represents the total cost of all jobs that have not been completed as of the end of February 2018.

The debit balance of $8,800 in the Finished Goods Control account represents the cost of all jobs that have been completed but not sold as of the end of February 2018.

3. Manufacturing payroll for February: direct labour, $39,000, and indirect labour, $15,000, paid in cash.

Work-in-Process Control	39,000	
Manufacturing Overhead Control	15,000	
Cash Control		54,000

4. Other manufacturing overhead costs incurred during February, $75,000, consisting of supervision and engineering salaries, plant utilities, repairs, insurance, and plant depreciation. The non-cash item, plant depreciation, was $18,000.

Manufacturing Overhead Control	75,000	
Cash Control		57,000
Accumulated Depreciation Control		18,000

5. Allocation of manufacturing overhead to jobs, $80,000.

Work-in-Process Control	80,000	
Manufacturing Overhead Allocated		80,000

Under normal costing, **manufacturing overhead allocated**—also called **manufacturing overhead applied**—is the amount of manufacturing overhead costs allocated to distinct types of jobs based on the budgeted rate multiplied by the actual quantity of the allocation base used.

In transaction 4, actual overhead costs incurred throughout the month are added (debited) to the Manufacturing Overhead Control account. Manufacturing overhead costs are added (debited) to Work-in-Process Control *only when* manufacturing overhead costs are allocated in transaction 5. The amount allocated will differ from the actual overhead costs.

6. Completion and transfer of individual jobs to finished goods, $188,800.

Finished Goods Control	188,800	
Work-in-Process Control		188,800

7. Cost of goods sold, $180,000.

Cost of Goods Sold	180,000	
Finished Goods Control		180,000

8. Marketing costs for February, $45,000, and customer-service costs for February, $15,000, paid in cash.

Marketing Expenses	45,000	
Customer-Service Expenses	15,000	
Cash Control		60,000

9. Sales revenues, all on credit, $270,000.

Accounts Receivable Control	270,000	
Revenues		270,000

Subsidiary Ledgers

Exhibits 4-7 and 4-8 present subsidiary ledgers that contain the underlying details of production, such as each type of materials in inventory and costs accumulated in individual jobs. The sum of all entries in underlying subsidiary ledgers equals the total amount in the corresponding general ledger control accounts.

Material Records by Type of Materials

The subsidiary ledger for materials at Robinson Company—called *Materials Records*—keeps a continuous record of quantity received, quantity issued to jobs, and inventory balances for each type of material. Panel A of Exhibit 4-8 shows the Materials Record for Metal Brackets (Part No. MB 468-A). Source documents supporting the receipt and issue of materials are scanned into a computer. Software programs then automatically update the Materials Records and make all the necessary accounting entries in the subsidiary and general ledgers.

As direct materials are used, they are recorded as issued in the Materials Records. Exhibit 4-7, Panel A shows a record of the metal brackets issued for the WPP machine job. Direct materials are also charged to individual job records, which are the subsidiary ledger accounts for the Work-in-Process Control account in the general ledger. For example, the metal brackets used in the WPP machine job appear as direct material costs of $112 in the subsidiary ledger under the job-cost record for WPP (Exhibit 4-8, Panel A). The cost of direct materials used across all job-cost records for February 2018 is $81,000 (Exhibit 4-8, Panel A).

As indirect materials (for example, lubricants) are used, they are charged to the Manufacturing Department overhead records (Exhibit 4-7, Panel C), which comprise the subsidiary ledger for Manufacturing Overhead Control. The Manufacturing Department overhead records accumulate actual costs in individual overhead categories by each indirect cost pool account in the general ledger. The cost of indirect materials used is not

Exhibit 4-7 Subsidiary Ledger for Materials, Labour, and Manufacturing Department Overhead 2018

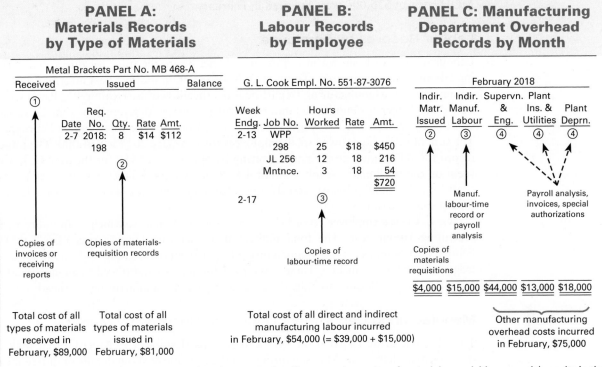

PANEL A: Total cost of all types of materials received in February, $89,000; Total cost of all types of materials issued in February, $81,000

PANEL B: Total cost of all direct and indirect manufacturing labour incurred in February, $54,000 (= $39,000 + $15,000)

PANEL C: Other manufacturing overhead costs incurred in February, $75,000

Note: The arrows show how the supporting documentation (for example, copies of materials-requisition records) results in the journal entry number shown in circles (for example, journal entry number 2) that corresponds to the entries in Exhibit 4-6.

Exhibit 4-8 Subsidiary Ledger for Individual Jobs 2018

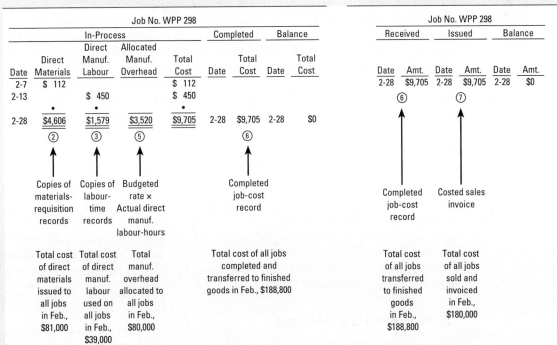

Note: The arrows show how the supporting documentation (for example, copies of materials-requisition records) results in the journal entry number shown in circles (for example, journal entry number 2) that corresponds to the entries in Exhibit 4-6.

added directly to individual job records. Instead, the cost of these indirect materials is allocated to individual job records as a part of manufacturing overhead. Total actual MOH costs of $75,000 were incurred in February.

Labour Records by Employee

Labour-time records shown in Exhibit 4-7, Panel B, are the trace for direct manufacturing labour to individual jobs. These records also contain indirect cost information that is accumulated in Manufacturing Department overhead records (Exhibit 4-7, Panel C). The subsidiary ledger for employee labour records shows the different jobs that G. L. Cook worked on and the $720 of wages owed to G. L. Cook for the week ending February 13. The sum of total wages owed to all employees for February 2018 is $54,000. The job-cost record for WPP shows direct manufacturing labour costs of $450 for the time G. L. Cook spent on the WPP machine job (Exhibit 4-8, Panel A). Total direct manufacturing labour costs recorded in all job-cost records (the subsidiary ledger for Work-in-Process Control) for February 2018 is $39,000.

G. L. Cook's employee record shows $54 for maintenance, which is an indirect manufacturing labour cost. The total indirect manufacturing labour costs of $15,000 for February 2018 appear in the Manufacturing Department overhead records in the subsidiary ledger (Exhibit 4-7, Panel C). These costs, by definition, are not traced to an individual job. Instead, they are allocated to individual jobs as a part of manufacturing overhead.

Manufacturing Department Overhead Records by Month

The Manufacturing Department overhead records (Exhibit 4-7, Panel C) that make up the subsidiary ledger for Manufacturing Overhead Control show details of different categories of overhead costs such as indirect materials, indirect manufacturing labour, supervision and engineering, plant insurance and utilities, and plant depreciation. The source documents for these entries include invoices (for example, a utility bill) and special schedules (for example, a depreciation schedule) from the responsible accounting officer.

Work-in-Process Inventory Records by Jobs

The job-cost record for each individual job in the subsidiary ledger will be debited by the cost of direct materials and direct manufacturing labour used by individual jobs. The job-cost record for each individual job in the subsidiary ledger will also be debited for manufacturing overhead allocated for the actual direct manufacturing labour-hours used in that job. For example, the job-cost record for Job WPP (Exhibit 4-8, Panel A) shows Manufacturing Overhead Allocated of $3,520 (budgeted rate of $40 per labour-hour × 88 actual direct manufacturing labour-hours used). We assume 2,000 actual direct manufacturing labour-hours were used for all jobs in February 2018, resulting in a total manufacturing overhead allocation of $40 per labour-hour × 2,000 direct manufacturing labour-hours = $80,000.

Finished Goods Inventory Records by Jobs

Exhibit 4-8, Panel A, shows that Job WPP was completed at a cost of $9,705. Job WPP also simultaneously appears in the finished goods records of the subsidiary ledger. Given Robinson's use of normal costing, cost of goods completed consists of actual direct materials, actual direct manufacturing labour, and manufacturing overhead allocated to each job based on the budgeted manufacturing overhead rate multiplied by the actual direct manufacturing labour-hours. Exhibit 4-8, Panel B, indicates that Job WPP was sold and delivered to the customer on February 28, 2018.

Other Subsidiary Records

Robinson maintains employee labour records in subsidiary ledgers for marketing and customer-service payroll as well as records for different types of advertising costs (print, television, and radio). An accounts receivable subsidiary ledger is also used to record the

February 2018 amounts due from each customer, including the $15,000 due from the sale of Job WPP.

Non-Manufacturing Costs and Job Costing

Product costs reported as inventoriable costs to shareholders may differ from product costs reported for government contracting and may also differ from product costs reported to managers for guiding pricing and product-mix decisions. Even though marketing and customer-service costs are expensed when incurred for financial accounting purposes, companies often trace or allocate these costs to individual jobs for pricing, product-mix, and cost-management decisions.

Budgeted Indirect Costs and End-of-Accounting-Year Adjustments

Using budgeted indirect cost rates and normal costing instead of actual costing has the advantage that indirect costs can be assigned to individual jobs on an ongoing and timely basis, rather than only at the end of the fiscal year when actual costs are known. However, budgeted rates are unlikely to equal actual rates because they are based on estimates made up to 12 months before actual costs are incurred. We now consider adjustments that are needed when, at the end of the fiscal year, indirect costs allocated differ from actual indirect costs incurred.

Underallocated indirect costs occur when the allocated amount of indirect costs in an accounting period is less than the actual amount. **Overallocated indirect costs** occur when the allocated amount of indirect costs in an accounting period is greater than the actual amount.

Underallocated (overallocated) indirect costs = Actual indirect costs incurred − Indirect costs allocated

Consider the manufacturing overhead indirect cost pool at Robinson Company. There are two indirect cost accounts in the general ledger that have to do with manufacturing overhead:

1. Manufacturing Overhead Control, the record of the actual costs in all the individual overhead categories (such as indirect materials, indirect manufacturing labour, supervision, engineering, utilities, and plant depreciation).
2. Manufacturing Overhead Allocated, the record of the manufacturing overhead allocated to individual jobs on the basis of the budgeted rate multiplied by actual direct manufacturing labour-hours.

Assume the following annual data for Robinson Company:

Manufacturing Overhead Control		Manufacturing Overhead Allocated	
Bal. Dec. 31, 2018 1,215,000		Bal. Dec. 31, 2018 1,080,000	

The $1,080,000 credit balance in Manufacturing Overhead Allocated results from multiplying the 27,000 actual direct manufacturing labour-hours worked on all jobs in 2018 by the budgeted rate of $40 per direct manufacturing labour-hour.

The $135,000 difference (a net debit) is an underallocated amount because actual manufacturing overhead costs are greater than the allocated amount. This difference arises from two reasons related to the computation of the $40 budgeted hourly rate:

1. Numerator reason (indirect cost pool). Actual manufacturing overhead costs of $1,215,000 are greater than the budgeted amount of $1,120,000.
2. Denominator reason (quantity of allocation base). Actual direct manufacturing labour-hours of 27,000 are fewer than the budgeted 28,000 hours.

There are three main approaches to account for the $135,000 underallocated manufacturing overhead amount: (1) adjusted allocation-rate approach, (2) proration approach, and (3) write-off to cost of goods sold approach.

● **TRY IT!** **4.2**

Donna Corporation manufactures custom cabinets for kitchens. It uses a normal costing system with two direct cost categories—direct materials and direct manufacturing labour—and one indirect cost pool, manufacturing overhead costs. It provides the following information about manufacturing overhead costs for April 2020.

Actual direct materials used	$60,000
Actual direct manufacturing labour costs paid in cash	54,000
Indirect materials used	$3,000
Supervision and engineering salaries paid in cash	$50,000
Plant utilities and repairs paid in cash	10,000
Plant depreciation	$16,000
Actual direct manufacturing labour-hours	2,700
Cost of individual jobs completed and transferred to finished goods	$180,000
Cost of goods sold	$175,000
The following information is also available for 2020:	
Budgeted manufacturing overhead costs for 2020	$960,000
Direct manufacturing labour-hours for 2020	32,000 hours

Required

Present journal entries for (a) usage of direct and indirect materials, (b) manufacturing labour incurred, (c) manufacturing overhead costs incurred, (d) allocation of manufacturing overhead costs to jobs, (e) cost of jobs completed and transferred to finished goods, and (f) cost of goods sold.

Adjusted Allocation-Rate Approach

The **adjusted allocation-rate approach** restates all overhead entries in the general ledger and subsidiary ledgers using actual cost rates rather than budgeted cost rates. First, the actual manufacturing overhead rate is computed at the end of the fiscal year. Then, the manufacturing overhead costs allocated to every job during the year are recomputed using the actual manufacturing overhead rate (rather than the budgeted manufacturing overhead rate). Finally, end-of-year closing entries are made. The result is that at year-end, every job-cost record and finished goods record—as well as the ending Work-in-Process Control, Finished Goods Control, and Cost of Goods Sold accounts—represent actual manufacturing overhead costs incurred.

The widespread adoption of computerized accounting systems has greatly reduced the cost of using the adjusted allocation-rate approach. Consider the Robinson example. The actual manufacturing overhead ($1,215,000) exceeds the manufacturing overhead allocated ($1,080,000) by 12.5% [(= $1,215,000 − $1,080,000) ÷ $1,080,000]. At year-end, Robinson could increase the manufacturing overhead allocated to each job in 2018 by 12.5% using a single software command. The command would adjust both the subsidiary ledgers and the general ledger.

Consider the Western Pulp and Paper machine job, WPP. Under normal costing, the manufacturing overhead allocated to the job is $3,520 (the budgeted rate of $40 per direct manufacturing labour-hour × 88 hours). Increasing the manufacturing overhead allocated by 12.5%, or $440 (= $3,520 × 0.125), means the adjusted amount of manufacturing overhead allocated to Job WPP equals $3,960 (= $3,520 + $440). Note that, using actual costing, manufacturing overhead allocated to this job is also $3,960 (the actual rate of $45 per direct manufacturing labour-hour × 88 hours). Making this adjustment under normal costing for each job in the subsidiary ledgers ensures that all $1,215,000 of manufacturing overhead is allocated to jobs.

The adjusted allocation-rate approach yields the benefits of both the *timeliness and convenience of normal costing during the year and the allocation of actual manufacturing overhead costs at year-end*. Each individual job-cost record and the end-of-year account balances for inventories and cost of goods sold are adjusted to actual costs. After-the-fact analysis of actual profitability of individual jobs provides managers with accurate and useful insights for future decisions about job pricing, which jobs to emphasize, and ways to manage job costs.

Proration Approach

Proration spreads underallocated overhead or overallocated overhead among ending work-in-process inventory, finished goods inventory, and cost of goods sold. Materials inventory is not included in this proration because no manufacturing overhead costs have been allocated to it. In our Robinson example, end-of-year proration is made to the ending balances in Work-in-Process Control, Finished Goods Control, and Cost of Goods Sold. Assume the following actual results for Robinson Company in 2018:

	A	B	C
1	Account	Account Balance (Before Proration)	Allocated Manufacturing Overhead Included in Each Account Balance (Before Proration)
2	Work-in-Process Control	$ 50,000	$ 16,200
3	Finished Goods Control	75,000	31,320
4	Cost of Goods Sold	2,375,000	1,032,480
5		$2,500,000	$1,080,000

Robinson prorates the underallocated amount of $135,000 at the end of 2018. The $135,000 underallocated overhead is prorated over the three affected accounts in proportion to the total amount of manufacturing overhead allocated (before proration) in column 2 of the following table, resulting in the ending balances (after proration) in column 5 at actual costs.

	A	B	C	D	E	F	G
10		Account Balance (Before Proration)	Allocated Manufacturing Overhead Included in Each Account Balance (Before Proration)	Allocated Manufacturing Overhead Included in Each Account Balance as a Percent of Total	Proration of $135,000 of Underallocated Manufacturing Overhead		Account Balance (After Proration)
11	Account	(1)	(2)	(3) = (2) / $1,080,000	(4) = (3) x $135,000		(5) = (1) + (4)
12	Work-in-Process Control	$ 50,000	$ 16,200	1.5%	0.015 x $135,000 =	$ 2,025	$ 52,025
13	Finished Goods Control	75,000	31,320	2.9	0.029 x 135,000 =	3,915	78,915
14	Cost of Goods Sold	2,375,000	1,032,480	95.6	0.956 x 135,000 =	129,060	2,504,060
15	Total	$2,500,000	$1,080,000	100.0%		$135,000	$2,635,000

Prorating on the basis of the manufacturing overhead allocated (before proration) results in allocating manufacturing overhead based on actual manufacturing overhead costs. Recall that the actual manufacturing overhead ($1,215,000) in 2018 exceeds the manufacturing overhead allocated ($1,080,000) in 2018 by 12.5%. The proration amounts in column 4 can also be derived by multiplying the balances in column 2 by 0.125. For example, the $3,915 proration to Finished Goods is 0.125 × $31,320. Adding these amounts effectively means allocating manufacturing overhead at 112.5% of what had been allocated before.

The journal entry to record this proration is:

Work-in-Process Control	2,025	
Finished Goods Control	3,915	
Cost of Goods Sold	129,060	
Manufacturing Overhead Allocated	1,080,000	
Manufacturing Overhead Control		1,215,000

If manufacturing overhead had been overallocated, the Work-in-Process Control, Finished Goods Control, and Cost of Goods Sold accounts would be decreased (credited) instead of increased (debited).

This journal entry closes (brings to zero) the manufacturing overhead-related accounts and restates the 2018 ending balances for Work-in-Process Control, Finished Goods Control, and Cost of Goods Sold to what they would have been if actual manufacturing overhead rates had been used rather than budgeted manufacturing overhead rates. This method reports the same 2018 ending balances in the general ledger as the adjusted allocation-rate approach.

Write-off to Cost of Goods Sold Approach

Under this approach, the total under- or overallocated manufacturing overhead is included in this year's Cost of Goods Sold. For Robinson, the journal entry would be:

Cost of Goods Sold	135,000	
Manufacturing Overhead Allocated	1,080,000	
Manufacturing Overhead Control		1,215,000

Robinson's two Manufacturing Overhead accounts are closed with the difference between them included in cost of goods sold. The Cost of Goods Sold account after the write-off equals $2,510,000, the balance before the write-off of $2,375,000 *plus the underallocated manufacturing overhead amount* of $135,000.

Choice Among Approaches

The write-off to Cost of Goods Sold is the simplest approach for dealing with under- or overallocated overhead. If the amount of under- or overallocated overhead is insignificant relative to total operating income or some other measure of materiality, then a write-off yields a good approximation to the more complex approaches. Managers must be guided by cost/benefit. Companies have become more stringent in inventory control and work to minimize inventory quantities. As a result, cost of goods sold tends to be higher in relation to the dollar amount of work-in-process and finished goods inventories. Also, the inventory balances of job-costing companies are usually small because goods are often made in response to customer orders. Consequently, writing off, instead of prorating, under- or overallocated overhead will usually not cause a material misstatement in the financial statements.

Regardless of which of the three approaches is used, the underallocated overhead is not carried in the overhead accounts beyond the end of the fiscal year. The reason is that ending balances in Manufacturing Overhead Control and Manufacturing Overhead Allocated are closed to zero when transferred to Work-in-Process Control, Finished Goods Control, and Cost of Goods Sold at year-end.

Variations from Normal Costing—Budgeted Costing: A Service-Sector Example

Job costing is also very useful in service organizations such as accounting and consulting firms, advertising agencies, auto repair shops, and hospitals. In an accounting firm, each audit is a job. The costs of each audit are accumulated in a job-cost record, much like the document used by Robinson Company, based on the seven-step approach described earlier. On the basis of labour-time sheets, direct labour costs of the professional staff—audit partners, audit managers, and audit staff—are traced to individual jobs. Other direct costs, such as travel, out-of-town meals and lodging, phone, fax, and copying, are also traced to jobs. The costs of administrative support, office staff, rent, and depreciation of furniture and equipment are indirect costs because these costs cannot be traced to jobs in an economically feasible way. Indirect costs are allocated to jobs, for example, using a cost-allocation base such as number of professional labour-hours.

In some service organizations, a variation from normal costing is helpful because actual direct-labour costs, the largest component of total costs, can be difficult to trace to jobs as they are completed. For example, the actual direct-labour costs of an audit may include bonuses that become known only at the end of the year (a numerator reason). Also, the hours worked each period might vary significantly depending on the number of working days each month and the demand for services (a denominator reason) while the direct-labour costs remain largely fixed. It would be inappropriate to charge a job with higher actual direct labour costs simply because a month had fewer working days or demand for services was low in that month. Using budgeted rates gives a better picture of the direct labour cost per hour that the company had planned when it hired the workers. In situations like these, a company needing timely information during the progress of an audit will use budgeted rates for some direct costs and budgeted rates for other indirect costs. All budgeted rates are calculated at the start of the fiscal year. In contrast, normal costing uses actual cost rates for all direct costs and budgeted cost rates only for indirect costs.

The mechanics of using budgeted rates for direct costs are similar to the methods employed when using budgeted rates for indirect costs in normal costing. We illustrate this for Donahue and Associates, a public accounting firm. For 2020, Donahue budgets total direct-labour costs of $14,400,000, total indirect costs of $12,960,000, and total direct (professional) labour-hours of 288,000. In this case,

$$\frac{\text{Budgeted direct-labour}}{\text{cost rate}} = \frac{\text{Budgeted total direct-labour costs}}{\text{Budgeted total direct-labour hours}}$$

$$= \frac{\$14,400,000}{288,000 \text{ direct labour-hours}} = \$50 \text{ per direct labour-hour}$$

Assuming only one indirect-cost pool and total direct-labour costs as the cost-allocation base,

$$\frac{\text{Budgeted indirect}}{\text{cost rate}} = \frac{\text{Budgeted total costs in indirect cost pool}}{\text{Budgeted total quantity of cost-allocation base (direct-labour costs)}}$$

$$= \frac{\$12,960,000}{\$14,400,000} = 0.90, \text{ or } 90\% \text{ of direct-labour costs}$$

Suppose that in March 2020, an audit of Hanley Transport, a client of Donahue, uses 800 direct labour-hours. Donahue calculates the direct-labour costs of the audit by multiplying the budgeted direct-labour cost rate, $50 per direct labour-hour, by 800, the actual quantity of direct labour-hours. The indirect costs allocated to the Hanley Transport audit are determined by multiplying the budgeted indirect-cost rate (90%) by the direct-labour costs assigned to the job ($40,000). Assuming no other direct costs for travel and the like, the cost of the Hanley Transport audit is as follows:

Direct-labour costs, $50 × 800	$ 40,000
Indirect costs allocated, 90% × $40,000	36,000
Total	$76,000

At the end of the fiscal year, the direct costs traced to jobs using budgeted rates will generally not equal actual direct costs because the actual rate and the budgeted rate are developed at different times using different information. End-of-year adjustments for under- or overallocated direct costs would need to be made in the same way that adjustments are made for under- or overallocated indirect costs.

The Donahue and Associates example illustrates that all costing systems do not exactly match either the actual-costing system or the normal-costing system described earlier in the chapter. As another example, engineering consulting firms, such as Tata Consulting Engineers in India and Terracon Consulting Engineers in the United States, often use budgeted rates to allocate indirect costs (such as engineering and office-support costs) as well as some direct costs (such as professional labour-hours) and trace some actual direct costs (such as the cost of making blueprints and fees paid to outside experts). Users of costing systems should be aware of the different systems that they may encounter.

Pulling it all Together—Problem for Self-Study

(Try to solve this problem before examining the solution that follows.)

Problem

You are asked to bring the following incomplete accounts of Endeavour Printing, Inc., up to date through January 31, 2018. Consider the data that appear in the T-accounts as well as the following information in items (a) through (j).

Endeavour's normal costing system has two direct cost categories (direct material costs and direct manufacturing labour costs) and one indirect cost pool (manufacturing overhead costs, which are allocated using direct manufacturing labour costs).

Materials Control	Wages Payable Control
12-31-2017 Bal. 15,000	1-31-2018 Bal. 3,000

Work-in-Process Control	Manufacturing Overhead Control
	1-31-2018 Bal. 57,000

Finished Goods Control	Costs of Goods Sold
12-31-2017 Bal. 20,000	

Additional Information

a. Manufacturing overhead is allocated using a budgeted rate that is set every December. Management forecasts next year's manufacturing overhead costs and next year's direct manufacturing labour costs. The budget for 2018 is $600,000 for manufacturing overhead costs and $400,000 for direct manufacturing labour costs.
b. The only job unfinished on January 31, 2018, is No. 419, on which direct manufacturing labour costs are $2,000 (125 direct manufacturing labour-hours) and direct material costs are $8,000.
c. Total direct materials issued to production during January 2018 are $90,000.
d. Cost of goods completed during January is $180,000.
e. Materials inventory as of January 31, 2018, is $20,000.
f. Finished goods inventory as of January 31, 2018, is $15,000.
g. All plant workers earn the same wage rate. Direct manufacturing labour-hours used for January total 2,500 hours. Other labour costs total $10,000.
h. The gross plant payroll paid in January equals $52,000. Ignore withholdings.
i. All "actual" manufacturing overhead incurred during January has already been posted.
j. All materials are direct materials.

Required ▶

Calculate the following:
1. Materials purchased during January.
2. Cost of Goods Sold during January.
3. Direct manufacturing labour costs incurred during January.
4. Manufacturing Overhead Allocated during January.

5. Balance, Wages Payable Control, December 31, 2017.
6. Balance, Work-in-Process Control, January 31, 2018.
7. Balance, Work-in-Process Control, December 31, 2017.
8. Manufacturing Overhead Underallocated or Overallocated for January 2018. ⑤

Solution

Letters alongside entries and in T-accounts correspond to letters in the preceding additional information. Numbers alongside entries in T-accounts correspond to numbers in the requirements above. Amounts from the T-accounts are labelled "(T)."

1. From Materials Control T-account, Materials Purchased: $90,000 (c) + $20,000 (e) − $15,000 (T) = $95,000
2. From Finished Goods Control T-account, Cost of Goods Sold: $20,000 (T) + $180,000 (d) − $15,000 (f) = $185,000
3. Direct manufacturing wage rate: $2,000 (b) ÷ 125 direct manufacturing labour-hours (b) = $16 per direct manufacturing labour-hour
   Direct manufacturing labour costs: 2,500 direct manufacturing labour-hours (g) × $16 per hour = $40,000
4. Manufacturing overhead rate: $600,000 (a) ÷ $400,000 (a) = 150% Manufacturing Overhead Allocated: 150% of $40,000 = 1.50 × $40,000 (see 3) = $60,000
5. From Wages Payable Control T-account, Wages Payable Control, December 31, 2017: $52,000 (h) + $3,000 (T) − $40,000 (see 3) − $10,000 (g) = $5,000
6. Work-in-Process Control, January 31, 2018: $8,000 (b) + $2,000 (b) + 150% of $2,000 (b) = $13,000 (This answer is used in item 7.)
7. From Work-in-Process Control T-account, Work-in-Process Control, December 31, 2017: $180,000 (d) + $13,000 (see 6) − $90,000 (c) − $40,000 (see 3) − $60,000 (see 4) = $3,000
8. Manufacturing overhead overallocated: $60,000 (see 4) − $57,000 (T) = $3,000

Materials Control

December 31, 2017 Bal.	(given)	15,000		
	(1)	95,000*	(c) 90,000	
January 31, 2018 Bal.	(e)	20,000		

Work-in-Process Control

December 31, 2017 Bal.	(7)	3,000	(d) 180,000	
Direct materials	(c)	90,000		
Direct manufacturing labour	(b) (g) (3)	40,000		
Manufacturing overhead allocated	(3) (a) (4)	60,000		
January 31, 2018 Bal.	(b) (6)	13,000		

Finished Goods Control

December 31, 2017 Bal.	(given)	20,000	(2) 185,000	
	(d)	180,000		
January 31, 2018 Bal.	(f)	15,000		

Wages Payable Control

	(h)	52,000	December 31, 2017 Bal.	(5) 5,000
				(g) (3) 40,000
				(g) 10,000
			January 31, 2018	(given) 3,000

Manufacturing Overhead Control

Total January charges	(given) 57,000	

Manufacturing Overhead Allocated

| | (3) (a) (4) 60,000 |

Cost of Goods Sold

| (d) (f) (2) 185,000 | |

*Can be computed only after all other postings in the account have been found.

Decision Points

The following question-and-answer format summarizes the chapter's learning objectives. Each point presents a key question, and the guidelines are the answer to that question.

Learning Objectives	Guidelines
1. What are the building-block concepts of costing systems?	The building-block concepts of a costing system are a cost object, direct costs of a cost object, indirect costs of a cost object, cost pool, and cost-allocation base. Costing-system overview diagrams represent these concepts in a systematic way. Costing systems aim to report cost numbers that reflect the way cost objects (such as products or services) use the resources of an organization.
2. What is the difference between job costing and process costing?	Job-costing systems assign costs to distinct units of a product or service. Process-costing systems assign costs to masses of identical or similar units and compute unit costs on an average basis. These two costing systems represent opposite ends of a continuum. The costing systems of many companies combine some elements of both job costing and process costing.
3. What are the approaches to evaluating and implementing job costing systems?	A general approach to implementing costing systems requires identifying the job and the actual direct costs, the budgeted cost-allocation bases, the budgeted indirect-cost pools, the budgeted cost-allocation rates, and the allocated indirect costs (budgeted rates multiplied by actual quantities of an input) to establish the total direct and indirect costs of a job.

4. What are the differences between actual, budgeted, and normal costing?

Actual costing and normal costing differ in the type of indirect-cost rates used:

	Actual Costing	Normal Costing
Direct-cost rates	Actual rates	Actual rates
Indirect-cost rates	Actual rates	Budgeted rates

Both systems use actual quantities of inputs for tracing direct costs and actual quantities of the allocation bases for allocating indirect costs.

5. How do we show the flow of costs from direct and indirect cost pools to inventory accounts, including adjustments for over- and underallocated costs?

The two standard approaches to disposing of under- or overallocated manufacturing overhead costs at the end of the accounting year for the purposes of the statement of financial position and the statement of comprehensive income amounts at actual costs are (1) to adjust the allocation rate and (2) to prorate on the basis of the total amount of the allocated manufacturing overhead cost in the ending balances of Work-in-Process Control, Finished Goods Control, and Cost of Goods Sold accounts. Many companies, however, simply write off amounts of under- or overallocated manufacturing overhead to Cost of Goods Sold when amounts are immaterial.

Terms to Learn

This chapter and the Glossary at the end of the book contain definitions of the following important terms:

adjusted allocation-rate approach **(p. 116)**

budgeted indirect-cost rate **(p. 103)**

job-cost record **(p. 103)**

labour-time sheet **(p. 104)**

materials-requisition record **(p. 104)**

manufacturing overhead allocated **(p. 111)**

manufacturing overhead applied **(p. 111)**

overallocated indirect costs **(p. 115)**

proration **(p. 117)**

source document **(p. 103)**

underallocated indirect costs **(p. 115)**

Assignment Material

MyLab Accounting Make the grade with MyLab Accounting: The Short-Answer Questions, Exercises, and Problems marked with a ⊕ can be found on MyLab Accounting. You can practise them as often as you want, and most feature step-by-step guided instructions to help you find the right answer.

Short-Answer Questions

4-1 How does a job-costing system differ from a process-costing system?

4-2 What is the benefit of creating more than one manufacturing overhead cost pool?

4-3 Why might an advertising agency use job costing for an advertising campaign by Pepsi, whereas a bank might use process costing to determine the cost of chequing account deposits?

4-4 Describe the seven steps in job costing.

4-5 What are the two major types of organizational elements that managers focus on in companies using job costing?

4-6 Describe the three major source documents used in job-costing systems.

4-7 What is the main concern about source documents used to prepare job-cost records?

4-8 Give two reasons why most organizations use an annual period rather than a weekly or monthly period to compute budgeted indirect cost allocation rates.

4-9 How does actual costing differ from normal costing?

4-10 Describe two ways in which a house-construction company may use job-cost information.

4-11 Comment on the following statement: "In a normal costing system, the amounts in the Manufacturing Overhead Control account will always equal the amounts in the Manufacturing Overhead Allocated account."

4-12 Describe three different debit entries in the Work-in-Process Control general ledger T-account.

4-13 Describe three alternative ways to dispose of underallocated or overallocated indirect costs.

4-14 When might a company use budgeted costs rather than actual costs to compute direct labour rates?

4-15 Describe briefly why modern technology such as Electronic Data Interchange (EDI) is helpful to managers.

Exercises

4-16 Terminology. A number of terms are listed below:

source document	actual
cost tracing	cost allocation rate
proration	opportunity cost
cost pool	

Required

Select the terms from the above list to complete the following sentences. Use each term only once.

1. _____ spreads underallocated overhead or overallocated overhead among ending work-in-process inventory, finished goods inventory, and cost of goods sold.
2. The benefits of using a(n) _____ cost system is that your costing information is very accurate.
3. The _____ is the result of dividing the indirect cost pool by the cost allocation base.
4. A _____ is an original record that supports journal entries in an accounting system.
5. A(n) _____ is the contribution to income lost or forgone by not using a limited resource in its next-best alternative use.
6. _____ is the assigning of direct costs to the chosen cost object.
7. A _____ is a grouping of individual cost items.

LO 1 ▶   ⊕ **4-17 Job costing, process costing.** In each of the following situations, determine whether job costing or process costing would be more appropriate.

a. A public accounting firm
b. An oil refinery
c. A custom furniture manufacturer
d. A tire manufacturer
e. A textbook publisher
f. A pharmaceutical company
g. An advertising agency
h. An apparel manufacturing factory
i. A flour mill
j. A paint manufacturer
k. A medical care facility
l. A landscaping company
m. A cola-drink-concentrate producer
n. A movie studio
o. A law firm
p. A commercial aircraft manufacturer
q. A management consulting firm
r. A breakfast cereal company
s. A catering service
t. A paper mill
u. An auto repair garage

LO 3, 4, 5 ▶
1. Budget is 85% of direct labour-costs.

⊕ **4-18 Actual costing, normal costing, manufacturing overhead.** Destin Products uses a job-costing system with two direct cost categories (direct materials and direct manufacturing labour) and one manufacturing overhead cost pool. Destin allocates manufacturing overhead costs using direct manufacturing labour costs. Destin provides the following information:

	Budget for Year 2018	Actuals for Year 2018
Direct manufacturing labour costs	$2,600,000	$2,540,000
Direct manufacturing overhead costs	2,210,000	2,311,400
Direct materials costs	1,800,000	1,740,000

Required

1. Compute the actual and budgeted manufacturing overhead rates for 2018.
2. During March, the cost record for Job 626 contained the following:

Direct materials used	$48,000
Direct manufacturing labour costs	27,000

Compute the cost of Job 626 using (a) an actual costing system and (b) a normal costing system.
3. At the end of 2018, compute the underallocated or overallocated manufacturing overhead under Destin's normal costing system. Why is there no underallocated or overallocated overhead under Destin's actual costing system?
4. Comment briefly on the advantages and disadvantages of actual costing systems and normal costing systems.

LO 3, 4 ▶
1a. Direct cost rate, $58 per professional labour-hour; Indirect cost rate, $48 per professional labour-hour

⊕ **4-19 Job costing; actual, normal, and variation of normal costing.** Chirac & Partners is a Quebec-based public accounting partnership specializing in audit services. Its job-costing system has a single direct cost category (professional labour) and a single indirect cost pool (audit support, which contains all the costs in the Audit Support Department). Audit support costs are allocated to individual jobs using actual professional labour-hours. Chirac & Partners employs 10 professionals who are involved in their auditing services.

Budgeted and actual amounts for 2018 are as follows:

Budget for 2018

Professional labour compensation	$ 960,000
Audit support department costs	$ 720,000
Professional labour-hours billed to clients	16,000 hours

Actual results for 2018

Audit support department costs	$ 744,000
Professional labour-hours billed to clients	15,500 hours
Actual professional labour cost rate	$58 per hour

Required

1. Identify the direct cost rate per professional labour-hour and the indirect cost rate per professional labour-hour for 2018 under (a) actual costing, (b) normal costing, and (c) variation of normal costing that uses budgeted rates for direct costs.
2. The audit of Pierre & Company done in 2018 was budgeted to take 110 hours of professional labour time. The actual professional labour time on the audit was 120 hours. Compute the 2018 job cost using (a) actual costing, (b) normal costing, and (c) variation of normal costing that uses budgeted rates for direct costs. Explain any differences in the job cost.

⊕ **4-20 Job costing; actual, normal, and budgeted costing.** Michael and Gabitel (MG) is a law firm that specializes in writing wills. Its job-costing system has one direct cost pool, professional labour, and a single indirect cost pool that includes all supporting costs of running the law office. The support costs are allocated to clients on the basis of professional labour-hours. In addition to the two senior partners at MG, there are six associates who work directly with clients. Each of the eight lawyers is expected to work for approximately 2,500 hours per year.

◄ **LO 2, 4**
1a. Direct cost rate, $60 per professional labour-hour; Indirect cost rate, $109.09 per professional labour-hour

Budgeted and actual costs for 2019 were

Budgeted professional labour costs	$1,100,000
Budgeted support costs	2,000,000
Actual professional labour costs	1,320,000
Actual support costs	2,400,000
Actual total professional hours	22,000 hours

Required

1. Compute the direct cost rate and the indirect cost rate per professional labour-hour under
   a. Actual costing.
   b. Normal costing.
   c. Budgeted costing.
2. The will for a rich tycoon, Ari Roos, was very complex and took four lawyers at the firm 500 hours each to prepare. What would be the cost of writing this will under each of the costing methods in requirement 1?

⊕ **4-21 Job costing, normal, and actual costing.** Anderson Construction assembles residential homes. It uses a job-costing system with two direct cost categories (direct materials and direct labour) and one indirect cost pool (assembly support). The allocation base for assembly support costs is direct labour-hours. In December 2018, Anderson budgets 2019 assembly support costs to be $7,200,000 and 2019 direct labour-hours to be 150,000.

◄ **LO 3, 4, 5**
1a. $48 per direct labour-hour;
b. $44 per direct labour-hour

At the end of 2019, Anderson is comparing the costs of several jobs that were started and completed in 2019. Information for a couple of jobs follows.

Construction Period	Laguna Model February–June 2019	Mission Model May–October 2019
Direct materials	$106,450	$127,604
Direct labour	$ 35,275	$ 40,320
Direct labour-hours	850	960

Direct materials and direct labour are paid for on a contract basis. The costs of each are known when direct materials are used or direct labour-hours are worked. The 2019 actual assembly support costs were $6,888,000, while the actual direct labour-hours were 164,000.

Required

1. Compute the (a) budgeted and (b) actual indirect cost rate. Why do they differ?
2. What is the job cost of the Laguna Model and the Mission Model using (a) normal costing and (b) actual costing?
3. Why might Anderson Construction prefer normal costing over actual costing?

LO 4, 5 ▶
Actual Indirect cost rate is $42/hr

🌐 **4-22 Job costing, normal and actual costing.** Atkinson Construction assembles residential houses. It uses a job-costing system with two direct-cost categories (direct materials and direct labour) and one indirect-cost pool (assembly support). Direct labour-hours is the allocation base for assembly support costs. In December 2016, Atkinson budgets 2017 assembly-support costs to be $8,800,000 and 2017 direct labour-hours to be 220,000.

At the end of 2017, Atkinson is comparing the costs of several jobs that were started and completed in 2017.

	Laguna Model	Mission Model
Construction period	Feb–June 2017	May–Oct 2017
Direct material costs	$106,550	$127,450
Direct labour costs	$ 36,250	$ 41,130
Direct labour-hours	970	1,000

Direct materials and direct labour are paid for on a contract basis. The costs of each are known when direct materials are used or when direct labour-hours are worked. The 2017 actual assembly-support costs were $8,400,000, and the actual direct labour-hours were 200,000.

Required

1. Compute the (a) budgeted indirect-cost rate and (b) actual indirect-cost rate. Why do they differ?
2. What are the job costs of the Laguna Model and the Mission Model using (a) normal costing and (b) actual costing?
3. Why might Atkinson Construction prefer normal costing over actual costing?

LO 3, 4, 5 ▶
1. Total MOH allocated to Job 494, $99,000

🌐 **4-23 Job costing, accounting for manufacturing overhead, budgeted rates.** Lynn Company uses a job-costing system at its Mississauga plant. The plant has a Machining Department and an Assembly Department. Its job-costing system has two direct cost categories (direct materials and direct manufacturing labour) and two manufacturing overhead cost pools (the Machining Department, allocated using actual MH, and the Assembly Department, allocated using actual direct manufacturing labour cost). The 2019 budget for the plant is as follows:

	Machining Department	Assembly Department
Manufacturing overhead (MOH)	$1,800,000	$3,600,000
Direct manufacturing labour cost	$1,400,000	$2,000,000
Direct manufacturing labour-hours (DMLH)	100,000	200,000
Machine-hours (MH)	50,000	200,000

The company uses a budgeted overhead rate for allocating overhead to production orders on a machine-hour basis in Machining and on a direct-manufacturing-labour-cost basis in Assembly.

Required

1. During February, the cost record for Job 494 contained the following:

	Machining Department	Assembly Department
Direct materials used	$45,000	$70,000
Direct manufacturing labour cost	$14,000	$15,000
Direct manufacturing labour-hours (DMLH)	1,000	1,500
Machine-hours (MH)	2,000	1,000

Compute the total manufacturing overhead costs of Job 494.

2. At the end of 2019, the actual manufacturing overhead costs were $1,900,000 in Machining and $4,000,000 in Assembly. Assume that 55,000 actual machine-hours were used in Machining and that actual direct manufacturing labour costs in Assembly were $2,200,000. Compute the overallocated or underallocated manufacturing overhead for each department.

🌐 **4-24 Job costing, accounting for manufacturing overhead, budgeted rates.** The Matthew Company uses a normal job-costing system at its Minneapolis plant. The plant has a machining department and an assembly department. Its job-costing system has two direct-cost categories (direct materials and direct manufacturing labour) and two manufacturing overhead cost pools (the machining department overhead, allocated to jobs based on actual machine-hours, and the assembly department overhead, allocated to jobs based on actual direct manufacturing labour costs). The 2017 budget for the plant is as follows:

◀ **LO 3, 4, 5**
Machining Department Overhead is $50/hr

	Machining Department	Assembly Department
Manufacturing overhead	$1,500,000	$5,100,000
Direct manufacturing labour costs	$1,600,000	$3,000,000
Direct manufacturing labour-hours	120,000	280,000
Machine-hours	30,000	270,000

Required

1. Present an overview diagram of Matthew's job-costing system. Compute the budgeted manufacturing overhead rate for each department.

2. During February, the job-cost record for Job 494 contained the following:

	Machining Department	Assembly Department
Direct materials used	$42,000	$78,000
Direct manufacturing labour costs	$15,000	$19,000
Direct manufacturing labour-hours	1,100	1,300
Machine-hours	2,800	1,100

Compute the total manufacturing overhead costs allocated to Job 494.

3. At the end of 2017, the actual manufacturing overhead costs were $1,800,000 in machining and $5,300,000 in assembly. Assume that 33,000 actual machine-hours were used in machining and that actual direct manufacturing labour costs in assembly were $3,200,000. Compute the over- or underallocated manufacturing overhead for each department.

🌐 **4-25 Job costing, consulting firm.** Frontier Partners, a management consulting firm, has the following condensed budget for 2017:

◀ **LO 2**
Total Budgeted Costs are $35,550

Revenues		$50,000,000
Total costs:		
Direct costs		
Professional Labour	$ 20,000,000	
Indirect costs		
Client support	25,000,000	45,000,000
Operating income		$ 5,000,000

Frontier has a single direct-cost category (professional labour) and a single indirect-cost pool (client support). Indirect costs are allocated to jobs on the basis of professional labour costs.

Required

1. Prepare an overview diagram of the job-costing system. Calculate the 2017 budgeted indirect-cost rate for Frontier Partners.

2. The markup rate for pricing jobs is intended to produce operating income equal to 10% of revenues. Calculate the markup rate as a percentage of professional labour costs.

3. Frontier is bidding on a consulting job for Sentinel Communications, a wireless communications company. The budgeted breakdown of professional labour on the job is as follows:

Professional Labour Category	Budgeted Rate per Hour	Budgeted Hours
Director	$200	9
Partner	100	24
Associate	50	100
Assistant	30	220

Calculate the budgeted cost of the Sentinel Communications job. How much will Frontier bid for the job if it is to earn its target operating income of 10% of revenues?

LO 3, 5 ▶
1. Overallocation, $130

⊕ **4-26 Job costing, journal entries.** The University of Toronto Press is wholly owned by the university. It performs the bulk of its work for other university departments, which pay as though the Press were an outside business enterprise. The Press also publishes and maintains a stock of books for general sale. A job-costing system is used to cost each job. There are two direct cost categories (direct materials and direct manufacturing labour) and one indirect cost pool (manufacturing overhead, allocated based on direct labour costs).

The following data (in thousands) pertain to 2019:

Direct materials and supplies purchased on account	$ 800
Direct materials used	710
Indirect materials issued to various production departments	100
Direct manufacturing labour	1,300
Indirect manufacturing labour incurred by various departments	900
Depreciation on building and manufacturing equipment	400
Miscellaneous manufacturing overhead* incurred by various departments (ordinarily would be detailed as repairs, photocopying, utilities, etc.)	650
Manufacturing overhead allocated at 160% of direct manufacturing labour costs	?
Cost of goods manufactured	4,120
Revenues	8,000
Cost of goods sold	4,020
Inventories, December 31, 2018:	
Materials control	100
Work-in-process control	60
Finished goods control	500

*The term *manufacturing overhead* is not used uniformly. Other terms that are often encountered in printing companies include *job overhead* and *shop overhead.*

Required

1. Prepare general journal entries to summarize 2019 transactions. As your final entry, dispose of the year-end overallocated or underallocated manufacturing overhead as a direct write-off to Cost of Goods Sold. Number your entries. Explanations for each entry may be omitted.
2. Show posted T-accounts for all inventories, Cost of Goods Sold, Manufacturing Overhead Control, and Manufacturing Overhead Allocated.

LO 3, 5 ▶
1. WIP ending balance, $17.40

⊕ **4-27 Job costing, journal entries.** Duchess Ltd. manufactures and installs kitchen cabinetry. It uses normal job costing with two direct cost categories (direct materials and direct manufacturing labour) and one indirect cost pool for MOH, applied on the basis of MH. At the beginning of the year, the company estimated that it would work 980,000 MH and had budgeted $73,500,000 for MOH. The following data (in $ millions) pertain to operations for the year 2019:

Materials control (beginning balance), December 31, 2018	$ 6.0
Work-in-process control (beginning balance), December 31, 2018	1.8
Finished goods control (beginning balance), December 31, 2018	7.2
Materials and supplies purchased on account	238
Direct materials used	194
Indirect materials (supplies) issued to various production departments	27
Direct manufacturing labour	123
Indirect manufacturing labour incurred by various departments	19
Depreciation on plant and manufacturing equipment	21
Miscellaneous manufacturing overhead incurred (credit Various Liabilities; ordinarily would be detailed as repairs, utilities, etc.)	9
Manufacturing overhead allocated (972,000 actual MH)	?
Cost of goods manufactured	374.3
Revenues	512
Cost of goods sold	368.4

Required

1. Prepare general journal entries. Post to T-accounts. What is the ending balance of Work-in-Process Control?
2. Show the journal entry for disposing of over- or underallocated manufacturing overhead directly as a year-end write-off to Cost of Goods Sold. Post the entry to T-accounts.

4-28 Job costing, unit cost, ending work in process. Rowan Company produces pipes for concert-quality organs. Each job is unique. In April 2016, it completed all outstanding orders, and then, in May 2016, it worked on only two jobs, M1 and M2:

◀ **LO 3, 5**
Cost per pipe is $370

	Home	Insert	Page Layout	Formulas	Data
		A		B	C
1	**Rowan Company, May 2016**			**Job M1**	**Job M2**
2	Direct materials			$ 75,000	$ 56,000
3	Direct manufacturing labour			275,000	209,000

Direct manufacturing labour is paid at the rate of $25 per hour. Manufacturing overhead costs are allocated at a budgeted rate of $22 per direct manufacturing labour-hour. Only Job M1 was completed in May.

Required

1. Calculate the total cost for Job M1.
2. 1,600 pipes were produced for Job M1. Calculate the cost per pipe.
3. Prepare the journal entry transferring Job M1 to finished goods.
4. What is the ending balance in the Work-in-Process Control account?

4-29 Job costing; actual, normal, and variation from normal costing. Cheney & Partners, a Quebec-based public accounting partnership, specializes in audit services. Its job-costing system has a single direct-cost category (professional labour) and a single indirect-cost pool (audit support, which contains all costs of the Audit Support Department). Audit support costs are allocated to individual jobs using actual professional labour-hours. Cheney & Partners employs 10 professionals to perform audit services.

◀ **LO 3, 5**
Budgeted Indirect Cost rate is $45 per professional labour hour

Budgeted and actual amounts for 2017 are as follows:

	A	B	C
1	**Cheney & Partners**		
2	**Budget for 2017**		
3	Professional labour compensation	$960,000	
4	Audit support department costs	720,000	
5	Professional labour-hours billed to clients	16,000	hours
6			
7	**Actual results for 2017**		
8	Audit support department costs	$744,000	
9	Professional labour-hours billed to clients	15,500	hours
10	Actual professional labour cost rate	$ 53	per hour

Required

1. Compute the direct-cost rate and the indirect-cost rate per professional labour-hour for 2017 under (a) actual costing, (b) normal costing, and (c) the variation from normal costing that uses budgeted rates for direct costs.
2. Which job-costing system would you recommend Cheney & Partners use? Explain.
3. Cheney's 2017 audit of Pierre & Co. was budgeted to take 170 hours of professional labour time. The actual professional labour time spent on the audit was 185 hours. Compute the cost of the Pierre & Co. audit using (a) actual costing, (b) normal costing, and (c) the variation from normal costing that uses budgeted rates for direct costs. Explain any differences in the job cost.

LO 3, 5 ▶

2. Overallocation, $16,000

🌐 **4-30 Job costing, journal entries, T-accounts, source documents.** Production Company produces gadgets for the coveted small appliance market. The following data reflect activity for the most recent year, 2019:

Costs incurred

Purchases of direct materials (net) on account	$124,000
Direct manufacturing labour cost	80,000
Indirect labour	54,500
Depreciation, factory equipment	30,000
Depreciation, office equipment	7,000
Maintenance, factory equipment	20,000
Miscellaneous factory overhead	9,500
Rent, factory building	70,000
Advertising expense	90,000
Sales commissions	30,000

Beginning and ending inventories for the year were as follows:

	January 1, 2019	December 31, 2019
Direct materials	$ 9,000	$11,000
Work-in-process	6,000	21,000
Finished goods	69,000	24,000

Production Company uses a normal job-costing system and allocates overhead to work-in-process at a rate of $2.50 per direct manufacturing labour dollar. Indirect materials are insignificant, so there is no inventory account for indirect materials.

Required

1. Prepare journal entries to record the 2019 transactions including an entry to close out over- or under-allocated overhead to cost of goods sold. For each journal entry, indicate the source document that would be used to authorize each entry. Also note which subsidiary ledger, if any, should be referenced as backup for the entry.
2. Post the journal entries to T-accounts for all of the inventories, Cost of Goods Sold, Manufacturing Overhead Control, and Manufacturing Overhead Allocated accounts.

⊕ **4-31 Job costing; variation on actual, normal, and variation from normal costing.** Creative Solutions designs Web pages for clients in the education sector. The company's job-costing system has a single direct cost category (Web-designing labour) and a single indirect cost pool composed of all overhead costs. Overhead costs are allocated to individual jobs based on direct labour-hours. The company employs six Web designers. Budgeted and actual information regarding Creative Solutions follows:

◄ **LO 3, 5**
Budgeted Indirect Cost rate is $15 per direct labour hour

Budget for 2017:	
Direct labour costs	$273,000
Direct labour-hours	10,500
Overhead costs	$157,500
Actual results for 2017:	
Direct labour costs	$285,000
Direct labour-hours	11,400
Overhead costs	$159,600

Required

1. Compute the direct-cost rate and the indirect-cost rate per Web-designing labour-hour for 2017 under (a) actual costing, (b) normal costing, and (c) the variation from normal costing that uses budgeted rates for direct costs.
2. Which method would you suggest Creative Solutions use? Explain.
3. Creative Solutions' Web design for Greenville Day School was budgeted to take 86 direct labour-hours. The actual time spent on the project was 79 hours. Compute the cost of the Greenville Day School job using (a) actual costing, (b) normal costing, and (c) the variation from normal costing that uses budgeted rates for direct costs.

⊕ **4-32 Proration of overhead.** The Ride-On-Water (ROW) Company produces a line of non-motorized boats. ROW uses a normal job-costing system and allocates manufacturing overhead costs using direct manufacturing labour cost. The following data are available for 2019:

◄ **LO 3, 5**
1. 50% of direct manufacturing labour-costs

Budgeted manufacturing overhead costs	$100,000
Budgeted direct manufacturing labour cost	200,000
Actual manufacturing overhead costs	106,000
Actual direct manufacturing labour cost	220,000

Inventory balances on December 31, 2019, were

Account	Ending Balance	2019 Direct Manufacturing Labour Cost in Ending Balance
Work-in-Process	$ 50,000	$ 20,000
Finished Goods	240,000	60,000
Cost of Goods Sold	560,000	140,000

Required

1. Calculate the budgeted manufacturing overhead rate.
2. Calculate the amount of under- or overallocated manufacturing overhead.
3. Calculate the ending balances in Work-in-Process, Finished Goods, and Cost of Goods Sold if under- or overallocated overhead is:
   a. Written off to Cost of Goods Sold
   b. Prorated based on ending balances (before proration) in each of the three accounts
   c. Prorated based on the overhead allocated in 2019 in the ending balances, before proration, in each of the three accounts
4. Which disposition method do you prefer in requirement 3? Explain.

Problems

LO 5 ▶

🌐 **4-33 Job costing, journal entries.** The University of Chicago Press is wholly owned by the university. It performs the bulk of its work for other university departments, which pay as though the press were an outside business enterprise. The press also publishes and maintains a stock of books for general sale. The press uses normal costing to cost each job. Its job-costing system has two direct-cost categories (direct materials and direct manufacturing labour) and one indirect-cost pool (manufacturing overhead, allocated on the basis of direct manufacturing labour costs).

The following data (in thousands) pertain to 2017:

Direct materials and supplies purchased on credit	$ 800
Direct materials used	710
Indirect materials issued to various production departments	100
Direct manufacturing labour	1,300
Indirect manufacturing labour incurred by various production departments	900
Depreciation on building and manufacturing equipment	400
Miscellaneous manufacturing overhead* incurred by various production departments (ordinarily would be detailed as repairs, photocopying, utilities, etc.)	550
Manufacturing overhead allocated at 160% of direct manufacturing labour costs	?
Cost of goods manufactured	4,120
Revenues	8,000
Cost of goods sold (before adjustment for under- or overallocated manufacturing overhead)	4,020
Inventories, December 31, 2016 (not 2017):	
Materials Control	100
Work-in-Process Control	60
Finished Goods Control	500

* The term *manufacturing overhead* is not used uniformly. Other terms that are often encountered in printing companies include *job overhead* and *shop overhead*.

Required

1. Prepare an overview diagram of the job-costing system at the University of Chicago Press.
2. Prepare journal entries to summarize the 2017 transactions. As your final entry, dispose of the year-end under- or overallocated manufacturing overhead as a write-off to Cost of Goods Sold. Number your entries. Explanations for each entry may be omitted.
3. Show posted T-accounts for all inventories, Cost of Goods Sold, Manufacturing Overhead Control, and Manufacturing Overhead Allocated.
4. How did the University of Chicago Press perform in 2017?

LO 2, 4 ▶
1. $65 per professional labour-hour

🌐 **4-34 Job costing, law firm.** Keating & Partners is a law firm specializing in labour relations and employee-related work. It employs 25 professionals (5 partners and 20 managers) who work directly with its clients. The average budgeted total compensation per professional for 2019 is $104,000. Each professional is budgeted to have 1,600 billable hours to clients in 2019. Keating is a highly respected firm, and all professionals work for clients to their maximum 1,600 billable hours available. All professional labour costs are included in a single direct cost category and are traced to jobs on a per-hour basis.

All costs of Keating & Partners other than professional labour costs are included in a single indirect cost pool (legal support) and are allocated to jobs using professional labour-hours as the allocation base. The budgeted level of indirect costs in 2019 is $2.2 million.

Required

1. Compute the 2019 budgeted professional labour-hour direct cost rate.
2. Compute the 2019 budgeted indirect cost rate per hour of professional labour.
3. Keating & Partners is considering bidding on two jobs:
   a. Litigation work for Richardson Inc. that requires 100 budgeted hours of professional labour.
   b. Labour contract work for Punch Inc. that requires 150 budgeted hours of professional labour.

Prepare a cost estimate for each job.

LO 2, 4 ▶
1a. $125 per hour
b. $50 per hour

🌐 **4-35 Job costing with two direct cost and two indirect cost categories, law firm** (continuation of 4-34). Keating has just completed a review of its job-costing system. This review included a detailed analysis of how past jobs used the firm's resources and interviews with personnel about what factors drive the level of indirect costs. Management concluded that a system with two direct cost categories (professional partner labour and professional manager labour) and two indirect cost categories (general support and administration support) would yield more accurate job costs. Budgeted information for 2019 related to the two direct cost categories is as follows:

	Professional Partner Labour	Professional Manager Labour
Number of professionals	5	20
Hours of billable time per professional	1,600 per year	1,600 per year
Total compensation (average per professional)	$200,000	$80,000

Budgeted information for 2019 relating to the two indirect cost categories is

	General Support	Administration Support
Total costs	$1,800,000	$400,000
Cost allocation base	Professional labour-hours	Partner labour-hours

Required

1. Compute the 2019 budgeted direct cost rates for (a) professional partners and (b) professional managers.
2. Compute the 2019 budgeted indirect cost rates for (a) general support and (b) administration support.
3. Compute the budgeted job costs for the Richardson and Punch jobs, given the following information:

	Richardson Inc.	Punch Inc.
Professional partners	60 hours	30 hours
Professional managers	40 hours	120 hours

4. Comment on the results in requirement 3. Why are the job costs different from those computed in Problem 4-34?

🌐 **4-36 Normal costing, overhead allocation, working backward.** Gardi Manufacturing uses normal costing for its job-costing system, which has two direct-cost categories (direct materials and direct manufacturing labour) and one indirect-cost category (manufacturing overhead). The following information is obtained for 2017:

◀ **LO 4**

- Total manufacturing costs, $8,300,000
- Manufacturing overhead allocated, $4,100,000 (allocated at a rate of 250% of direct manufacturing labour costs)
- Work-in-process inventory on January 1, 2017, $420,000
- Cost of finished goods manufactured, $8,100,000

Required

1. Use information in the first two bullet points to calculate (a) direct manufacturing labour costs in 2017 and (b) cost of direct materials used in 2017.
2. Calculate the ending work-in-process inventory on December 31, 2017.

🌐 **4-37 Disposition of overhead overallocation or underallocation, two indirect cost pools.** Glavine Corporation manufactures precision equipment made to order for the semiconductor industry. Glavine uses two manufacturing overhead cost pools—one for the overhead costs incurred in its highly automated Machining Department and another for overhead costs incurred in its labour-based Assembly Department. Glavine uses a normal costing system. It allocates Machining Department overhead costs to jobs based on actual machine-hours using a budgeted machine-hour overhead rate. It allocates Assembly Department overhead costs to jobs based on actual direct manufacturing labour-hours using a budgeted direct manufacturing labour-hour rate.

The following data are for the year 2019:

◀ **LO 2, 4, 5**
2. Machining Department: Overallocation, $510,000; Assembly Department: Underallocation, $170,000

	Machining Department	Assembly Department
Budgeted overhead	$5,850,000	$7,812,000
Budgeted machine-hours (MH)	90,000	0
Budgeted direct manufacturing labour-hours (DMLH)	0	124,000
Actual manufacturing overhead costs	$5,470,000	$8,234,000

Machine-hours and direct manufacturing labour-hours and the ending balances (before proration of underallocated overhead) are as follows:

	Actual Machine-Hours	Actual Direct Manufacturing Labour-Hours	Balance before Proration, December 31, 2019
Cost of Goods Sold	69,000	83,200	$21,600,000
Finished Goods	6,900	12,800	2,800,000
Work-in-Process	16,100	32,000	7,600,000

Required

1. Compute the budgeted overhead rates for the year in the Machining and Assembly departments.
2. Compute the under- or overallocated overhead in *each* department for the year. Dispose of the under- or overallocated amount in *each* department using:
   a. Immediate write-off to Cost of Goods Sold.
   b. Proration based on ending balances (before proration) in Cost of Goods Sold, Finished Goods, and Work-in-Process.
   c. Proration based on the allocated overhead amount (before proration) in the ending balances of Cost of Goods Sold, Finished Goods, and Work-in-Process.
3. Which disposition method do you prefer in requirement 2? Explain.

LO 3, 4, 5 ▶ 🌐 **4-38 Journal entries, T-accounts, and source documents.** Visual Company produces gadgets for the coveted small appliance market. The following data reflect activity for the year 2017:

Costs incurred:

Purchases of direct materials (net) on credit	$121,000
Direct manufacturing labour cost	87,000
Indirect labour	54,400
Depreciation, factory equipment	53,000
Depreciation, office equipment	7,700
Maintenance, factory equipment	46,000
Miscellaneous factory overhead	9,100
Rent, factory building	99,000
Advertising expense	97,000
Sales commissions	39,000

Inventories:

	January 1, 2017	December 31, 2017
Direct materials	$ 9,400	$18,000
Work in process	6,500	26,000
Finished goods	60,000	31,000

Visual Co. uses a normal-costing system and allocates overhead to work in process at a rate of $3.10 per direct manufacturing labour dollar. Indirect materials are insignificant so there is no inventory account for indirect materials.

Required

1. Prepare journal entries to record the transactions for 2017 including an entry to close out over- or underallocated overhead to cost of goods sold. For each journal entry indicate the source document that would be used to authorize each entry. Also note which subsidiary ledger, if any, should be referenced as backup for the entry.
2. Post the journal entries to T-accounts for all of the inventories, Cost of Goods Sold, the Manufacturing Overhead Control Account, and the Manufacturing Overhead Allocated Account.

LO 4 ▶ 🌐 **4-39** (25–30 min.) **Job costing, ethics.** Joseph Underwood joined Anderson Enterprises as controller in October 2016. Anderson Enterprises manufactures and installs home greenhouses. The company uses a normal-costing system with two direct-cost pools, direct materials and direct manufacturing labour, and one indirect-cost pool, manufacturing overhead. In 2016, manufacturing overhead was allocated to jobs at 150% of direct manufacturing labour cost. At the end of 2016, an immaterial amount of underallocated overhead was closed out to cost of goods sold, and the company showed a small loss.

Underwood is eager to impress his new employer, and he knows that in 2017, Anderson's upper management is under pressure to show a profit in a challenging competitive environment because they are hoping to be acquired by a large private equity firm sometime in 2018. At the end of 2016, Underwood decides to adjust the manufacturing overhead rate to 160% of direct labour cost. He explains to the company president that, because overhead was underallocated in 2016, this adjustment is necessary. Cost information for 2017 follows:

Direct materials control, 1/1/2017	25,000
Direct materials purchased, 2017	650,000
Direct materials added to production, 2017	630,000
Work in process control, 1/1/2017	280,000
Direct manufacturing labour, 2017	880,000
Cost of goods manufactured, 2017	2,900,000
Finished goods control, 1/1/2017	320,000
Finished goods control, 12/31/2017	290,000
Manufacturing overhead costs, 2017	1,300,000

Anderson's revenue for 2017 was $5,550,000, and the company's selling and administrative expenses were $2,720,000.

Required

1. Insert the given information in the T-accounts below. Calculate the following amounts to complete the T-accounts:
   a. Direct materials control, 12/31/2017
   b. Manufacturing overhead allocated, 2017
   c. Cost of goods sold, 2017

Direct Materials Control	**Work-in-Process Control**	**Finished Goods Control**

Manufacturing OH Control	**Manufacturing OH Allocated**	**Cost of Goods Sold**

2. Calculate the amount of under- or overallocated manufacturing overhead.
3. Calculate Anderson's net operating income under the following:
   a. Under- or overallocated manufacturing overhead is written off to cost of goods sold.
   b. Under- or overallocated manufacturing overhead is prorated based on the ending balances in work in process, finished goods, and cost of goods sold.
4. Underwood chooses option 3a above, stating that the amount is immaterial. Comment on the ethical implications of his choice. Do you think that there were any ethical issues when he established the manufacturing overhead rate for 2017 back in late 2016? Refer to the IMA Statement of Ethical Professional Practice.

⊕ **4-40 Service industry, job costing, two direct- and two indirect-cost categories, law firm.** Kidman has just completed a review of its job-costing system. This review included a detailed analysis of how past jobs used the firm's resources and interviews with personnel about what factors drive the level of indirect costs. Management concluded that a system with two direct-cost categories (professional partner labour and professional associate labour) and two indirect-cost categories (general support and secretarial support) would yield more accurate job costs. Budgeted information for 2017 related to the two direct-cost categories is as follows: ◀ LO 5

	Professional Partner Labour	Professional Associate Labour
Number of professionals	5	25
Hours of billable time per professional	1,500 per year	1,500 per year
Total compensation (average per professional)	$210,000	$75,000

Budgeted information for 2017 relating to the two indirect-cost categories is as follows:

	General Support	Secretarial Support
Total costs	$2,025,000	$450,000
Cost-allocation base	Professional labour-hours	Partner labour-hours

Required

1. Compute the 2017 budgeted direct-cost rates for (a) professional partners and (b) professional associates.
2. Compute the 2017 budgeted indirect-cost rates for (a) general support and (b) secretarial support.
3. Compute the budgeted costs for the Richardson and Punch jobs, given the following information:

	Richardson, Inc.	Punch, Inc.
Professional partners	48 hours	32 hours
Professional associates	72 hours	128 hours

4. Comment on the results in requirement 3. Why are the job costs different from those computed in Problem 4-37?
5. Would you recommend Kidman & Associates use the job-costing system in Problem 4-37 or the job-costing system in this problem? Explain.

LO 3, 5 ▶   ⊕   **4-41 General ledger relationships, under- and overallocation.** (S. Sridhar, adapted) Keezel Company uses normal costing in its job-costing system. Partially completed T-accounts and additional information for Keezel for 2017 are as follows:

Direct Materials Control		
1-1-2017	42,000	148,000
	135,000	

Work-in-Process Control		
1-1-2017	82,000	
Dir. manuf.		
labour	285,000	

Finished Goods Control		
1-1-2017	105,000	700,000
	705,000	

Manufacturing Overhead Control	
425,000	

Manufacturing Overhead Allocated	

Cost of Goods Sold	

Additional information follows:

a. Direct manufacturing labour wage rate was $15 per hour.
b. Manufacturing overhead was allocated at $20 per direct manufacturing labour-hour.
c. During the year, sales revenues were $1,550,000, and marketing and distribution costs were $810,000.

Required

1. What was the amount of direct materials issued to production during 2017?
2. What was the amount of manufacturing overhead allocated to jobs during 2017?
3. What was the total cost of jobs completed during 2017?
4. What was the balance of work-in-process inventory on December 31, 2017?
5. What was the cost of goods sold before proration of under- or overallocated overhead?
6. What was the under- or overallocated manufacturing overhead in 2017?
7. Dispose of the under- or overallocated manufacturing overhead using the following:
   a. Write-off to Cost of Goods Sold
   b. Proration based on ending balances (before proration) in Work-in-Process Control, Finished Goods Control, and Cost of Goods Sold
8. Using each of the approaches in requirement 7, calculate Keezel's operating income for 2017.
9. Which approach in requirement 7 do you recommend Keezel use? Explain your answer briefly.

LO 3, 4 ▶   ⊕   **4-42 Proration of overhead with two indirect cost pools.** Adventure Designs makes custom backyard play structures that it sells to dealers across the Midwest. The play structures are produced in two departments, fabrication (a mostly automated department) and custom finishing (a mostly manual department). The company uses a normal-costing system in which overhead in the fabrication department is allocated to jobs on the basis of machine-hours and overhead in the finishing department is allocated to jobs based on direct manufacturing labour-hours. During May, Adventure Designs reported actual overhead of $42,600 in the fabrication department and $39,800 in the finishing department. Additional information follows:

Manufacturing overhead rate (fabrication department)	$12 per machine-hour
Manufacturing overhead rate (finishing department)	$20 per direct manuf. labour-hour
Machine-hours (fabrication department) for May	3,200 machine-hours
Direct manuf. labour-hours (finishing department) for May	1,800 labour-hours
Work-in-process inventory, May 31	$60,000
Finished-goods inventory, May 31	$180,000
Cost of goods sold, May	$360,000

Adventure Designs prorates under- and overallocated overhead monthly to work in process, finished goods, and cost of goods sold based on the ending balance in each account.

Required

1. Calculate the amount of overhead allocated in the fabrication department and the finishing department in May.
2. Calculate the amount of under- or overallocated overhead in each department and in total.
3. How much of the under- or overallocated overhead will be prorated to (a) work-in-process inventory, (b) finished-goods inventory, and (c) cost of goods sold based on the ending balance (before proration) in each of the three accounts? What will be the balance in work-in-process, finished-goods, and cost of goods sold after proration?
4. What would be the effect of writing off under- and overallocated overhead to cost of goods sold? Would it be reasonable for Adventure Designs to change to this simpler method?

⊕ **4-43 Disposition of underallocated or overallocated overhead—Advanced.** (Z. Iqbal, adapted) Naf Radiator Company uses a normal costing system with a single MOH cost pool and MH as the cost allocation base. The following data are for 2019:

◀ **LO 3, 4, 5**
1. $60 per machine hour

Budgeted manufacturing overhead (MOH)	$4,800,000
Overhead allocation base	machine-hours (MH)
Budgeted machine-hours (MH)	80,000
Manufacturing overhead (MOH) incurred	$4,900,000
Actual machine-hours (MH)	75,000

Machine-hours data and the ending balances (before proration of under- or overallocated overhead) are as follows:

	Actual Machine-Hours (MH)	2019 End-of-Year Balance
Cost of Goods Sold	60,000	$8,000,000
Finished Goods Control	11,000	1,250,000
Work-in-Process Control	4,000	750,000

Required

1. Compute the budgeted manufacturing overhead rate for 2019.
2. Compute the under- or overallocated manufacturing overhead of Naf Radiator in 2019. Dispose of this under- or overallocated amount using:
   a. Write-off to Cost of Goods Sold.
   b. Proration based on ending balances (before proration) in Work-in-Process Control, Finished Goods Control, and Cost of Goods Sold.
   c. Proration based on the allocated overhead amount (before proration) in the ending balances of Work-in-Process Control, Finished Goods Control, and Cost of Goods Sold.
3. Which method do you prefer in requirement 2? Explain.

Collaborative Learning Cases

4-44 Normal job costing, unit costs. (J. Watson) Pearson Ltd. uses a normal job-costing system and applies overhead on the basis of direct labour-hours. At the beginning of the year, the company estimated

◀ **LO 2, 4**
1. $12 per direct labour-hour

that total overhead costs for the year would be $180,000, and it budgeted total labour-hours of 15,000. Actual labour-hours worked for the period January 1 to November 30 were 13,750.

On December 1, the company had three jobs in process:

Work-in-Process at December 1

Job Number	815	817	822
Direct Materials (DM)	$1,400	$2,500	$1,700
Direct Labour (DL)	1,200	2,400	600
Overhead (OH)	600	1,350	450
Total	3,200	6,250	2,750

During the month of December the following costs were incurred by job:

Job #	815	817	822	823	824
DM	$500	$ 700	$1,300	$1,250	$1,500
DL	$900	$1,440	$3,060	$3,960	$5,940
DL hours	50 hours	80 hours	170 hours	220 hours	330 hours

In addition, the company incurred the following costs during the month of December (these costs have not yet been recorded in the books):

DM purchases	$7,800	Advertising expense	$5,200
Plant depreciation	2,490	Factory repairs and maintenance	1,500
Factory utilities	1,800	Factory supplies	1,800
Production supervisor salary	2,200	Sales personnel salaries	9,700
Administrative salaries	3,450	Interest expense	1,400

Additional Information

1. The balance in the Overhead Control account on December 1 was $195,010.
2. There were no jobs in Finished Goods as of December 1.
3. Jobs 815, 822, 823, and 824 were completed during December.
4. Job 824 is the only job in Finished Goods as of December 31.
5. The company's pricing policy is 200% of total manufacturing cost.

Required

1. Calculate the budgeted overhead rate used by Pearson.
2. Calculate the unit cost of ending work-in-process inventory assuming that the number of units in the job(s) total 250 units.
3. Calculate the cost of goods manufactured and the unadjusted gross margin for the month of December.
4. Calculate the amount of over- or underallocated overhead for the year.

LO 2, 4 ▶

1. Irok GIP $2,770

4-45 Job costing—service industry. Jordan Brady schedules gigs for local bands and creates CDs and T-shirts to sell at each gig. Brady uses a normal-costing system with two direct-cost pools, labour and materials, and one indirect-cost pool, general overhead. General overhead is allocated to each gig based on 120% of direct labour cost. Actual overhead equaled allocated overhead as of March 2019. Actual overhead in April was $1,980. All costs incurred during the planning stage for a gig and during the gig are gathered in a balance sheet account called "Gigs in Progress (GIP)." When a gig is completed, the costs are transferred to an income statement account called "Cost of Completed Gigs (CCG)." Following is cost information for April 2019:

Band	From Beginning GIP		Incurred in April	
	Materials	Labour	Materials	Labour
Irok	$570	$750	$110	$200
Freke Out	700	550	140	100
Bottom Rung	250	475	310	250
Dish Towel	—	—	540	450
Rail Ride	—	—	225	250

As of April 1, there were three gigs in progress: *Irok, Freke Out,* and *Bottom Rung.* The gigs for *Dish Towel* and *Rail Ride* were started during April. The gigs for *Freke Out* and *Dish Towel* were completed during April.

Required

1. Calculate GIP at the end of April.
2. Calculate CCG for April.

3. Calculate under- or overallocated overhead at the end of April.
4. Calculate the ending balances in GIP and CCG if the under- or overallocated overhead amount is as follows:
   a. Written off to CCG.
   b. Prorated based on the ending balances (before proration) in GIP and CCG.
   c. Prorated based on the overhead allocated in April in the ending balances of GIP and CCG (before proration).
5. Which method would you choose? Explain. Would your choice depend on whether overhead cost is underallocated or overallocated? Explain.

SOLUTIONS

TRY IT!

Try It 4–1

$$\frac{\text{Budgeted indirect}}{\text{cost rate}} = \frac{\text{Budgeted manufacturing overhead costs}}{\text{Budgeted annual quantity of the cost-allocation base}}$$

$$\frac{\text{Budgeted indirect}}{\text{cost rate}} = \frac{\$960,000}{32,000 \text{ hours}} = \$30 \text{ per direct manufacturing labour-hour}$$

Total manufacturing costs of the 32 Berndale Drive job equals

Direct manufacturing costs

Direct materials	$3,500	
Direct manufacturing labour ($20 per direct manufacturing labour-hour × 160 direct manufacturing labour-hours)	3,200	$ 6,700
Manufacturing overhead costs		
($30 per direct manufacturing labour-hour × 160 hours)		4,800
Total manufacturing costs of job 32 Berndale Drive job		$11,500

Try It 4–2

$$\frac{\text{Budgeted indirect}}{\text{cost rate}} = \frac{\text{Budgeted manufacturing overhead costs}}{\text{Budgeted annual quantity of the cost-allocation base}}$$

$$\frac{\text{Budgeted indirect}}{\text{cost rate}} = \frac{\$960,000}{32,000 \text{ hours}} = \$30 \text{ per direct manufacturing labour-hour}$$

(a) Usage of direct materials, $60,000, and indirect materials, $3,000 during April

Work-in-Process Control	60,000	
Manufacturing Overhead Control	3,000	
Materials Control		63,000

(b) Manufacturing payroll for April: direct labour, $54,000 paid in cash

Work-in-Process Control	54,000	
Cash Control		54,000

(c) Other manufacturing overhead costs incurred during April, $76,000, consisting of
   ■ supervision and engineering salaries, $50,000 (paid in cash);
   ■ plant utilities and repairs $10,000 (paid in cash); and
   ■ plant depreciation, $16,000

Manufacturing Overhead Control	76,000	
Cash Control		60,000
Accumulated Depreciation Control		16,000

(d) Allocation of manufacturing overhead to jobs = Budgeted manufacturing overhead rate × Actual direct manufacturing labour-hours = $30 × 2,700 = $81,000

Work-in-Process Control	81,000	
Manufacturing Overhead Allocated		81,000

(e) The sum of all individual jobs completed and transferred to finished goods in April 2017 is $180,000

Finished Goods Control	180,000	
Work-in-Process Control		180,000

(f) Cost of goods sold in April 2017, $175,000

Cost of Goods Sold	175,000	
Finished Goods Control		175,000

5

Activity-Based Costing and Management

▶ CPA Competencies

This chapter covers material outlined in **Section 3: Management Accounting** of the CPA Competency Map. The Learning Objectives in this chapter have been aligned with the CPA Competency Map to ensure the best coverage possible.

3.3.1 Evaluates cost classifications and costing methods for management of ongoing operations

3.3.2 Evaluates and applies cost management techniques appropriate for specific costing decisions

3.4.1 Evaluates sources and drivers of revenue growth

marilyna/iStock/Getty Images Plus/Getty Images

Accurate Assignment = Better Profit

How much does a large double-double from Tim Hortons cost to produce? What about a venti latte from Starbucks? Both companies sell hundreds of millions of cups of coffee, beverages, mugs, and food products each year. As customers, we know the price. Managers must know the costs. Coffee beans (the raw materials) cost little compared to the indirect and overhead costs of converting them into products to sell at a price where customers will buy. In the extremely competitive world of coffee, the more accurate the assignment of indirect costs, the more likely organizations will remain profitable.

Improving indirect cost assignment requires classifying the scope of the cost effects of activities. An *activity* is an event or task, or series of related tasks, that provides a measurable benefit in the completion of goods or services ready for sale. Some activities transform inputs to a single unit of output, such as brewing and pouring a venti mocha latte. Some activities transform many similar inputs to larger quantities of similar outputs called a batch, such as mixing, baking, and glazing 10 dozen double-chocolate doughnuts. Some activities transform inputs for an entire product, such as manufacturing Tim Hortons thermal mugs. The indirect costs of an activity become a cost pool that supports production at the unit, batch, or product level. A focus on the scope of the effects of support activities results in an activity-based costing (ABC) system.

Product Costing: Overcosting and Undercosting

Using simple costing systems to allocate costs broadly is an easy, inexpensive, and reasonably accurate approach to calculating average costs required to provide a product or service. However, as product and service diversity and indirect costs increase, broad averaging results in inaccurate information, which can lead to bad decisions. For example, the use of a single plantwide manufacturing overhead rate to allocate costs to products often produces unreliable cost data. The term **peanut-butter costing** describes a particular costing approach that uses broad averages for assigning (or spreading, as in spreading peanut butter) the cost of resources uniformly to cost. Broad averaging can lead to undercosting or overcosting of products or services:

- **Product undercosting**—a product consumes a high level of resources but is reported to have a low cost per unit.

- **Product overcosting**—a product consumes a low level of resources but is reported to have a high cost per unit.

► **LO 1**

Identify the basic elements of activity-based costing (ABC) systems as distinguished from traditional systems, and explain how preventable undercosting and overcosting of products and services affects profitability.

Undercosting and Overcosting

The following example illustrates how averaging can result in inaccurate and misleading cost data. Consider the cost of a restaurant bill for four colleagues who meet monthly to discuss business developments. Each diner orders separate entrees, desserts, and drinks. The restaurant bill for the most recent meeting is as follows:

	Emma	James	Jessica	Matthew	Total	Average
Entree	$11	$20	$15	$14	$ 60	$15
Dessert	0	8	4	4	16	4
Drinks	4	14	8	6	32	8
Total	$15	$42	$27	$24	$108	$27

If the $108 total restaurant bill is divided evenly, $27 is the average cost per diner. This cost-averaging approach treats each diner the same. Emma would probably object to paying $27 because her actual cost is only $15; she ordered the lowest-cost entree, had no dessert, and had the lowest-cost drink. When costs are averaged across all four diners, both Emma and Matthew are overcosted, James is undercosted, and Jessica is (by coincidence) accurately costed.

The strategic consequences of product undercosting and overcosting can lead to mistakes in pricing decisions. In such cases, undercosted products will be underpriced and may even lead to sales that actually result in losses—sales bring in less revenue than the cost of resources they use. Overcosted products lead to overpricing, causing these products to lose market share to competitors producing similar products. Worse still, product undercosting and overcosting causes managers to focus on the wrong products, drawing attention to overcosted products whose costs may in fact be perfectly reasonable, and ignoring undercosted products that in fact consume large amounts of resources.

Product-Cost Cross-Subsidization

Product-cost cross-subsidization means that if a company undercosts one of its products, it will overcost at least one of its other products. Similarly, if a company overcosts one of its products, it will undercost at least one of its other products. Product-cost cross-subsidization is very common in situations in which a cost is uniformly spread—meaning it is broadly averaged—across multiple products without recognizing the amount of resources consumed by each product.

In the restaurant-bill example, the amount of cost cross-subsidization of each diner can be readily computed *because all cost items can be traced as direct costs to each diner*. If all diners pay $27, Emma is paying $12 more than her actual cost of $15. She is cross-subsidizing James, who is paying $15 less than his actual cost of $42. Calculating the amount of cost cross-subsidization takes more work when there are indirect costs to be considered.

Because resources represented by indirect costs are used by two or more diners, the restaurant needs to find a way to allocate costs to each diner. Consider, for example, a $40 bottle of wine whose cost is shared equally. Each diner would pay $10 (= $40 ÷ 4). Suppose Matthew drinks two glasses of wine while Emma, James, and Jessica drink one glass each for a total of five glasses. Allocating the cost of the bottle of wine on the basis of the glasses of wine that each diner drinks would result in Matthew paying $16 (= $40 × 2/5).

Simple Costing System at Plastim Corporation

▶ **LO 2**

Identify and explain the problem of preventable over- and undercosting.

Plastim Corporation manufactures lenses for the rear taillights of automobiles. A lens—made from black, red, orange, or white plastic—is the part of the lamp visible on the automobile's exterior. Lenses are made by injecting molten plastic into a mould to give the lamp its desired shape. The mould is cooled to allow the molten plastic to solidify, and the lens is removed.

Under its contract with Giovanni Motors, a major automobile manufacturer, Plastim makes two types of lenses: a complex lens (CL5), and a simple lens (S3). The complex lens is a large lens with special features, such as multicolour moulding (when more than one colour is injected into the mould) and a complex shape that wraps around the corner of the car. Manufacturing CL5 lenses is more complex because various parts in the mould must align and fit precisely. The S3 lens is simpler to make because it has a single colour and few special features.

Design, Manufacturing, and Distribution Processes

The sequence of steps to design, produce, and distribute lenses, whether simple or complex, is as follows:

1. *Design products and processes.* Each year Giovanni Motors specifies some modifications to the simple and complex lenses. Plastim's design department designs the moulds from which the lenses will be made and specifies the processes needed (that is, details of the manufacturing operations).

2. *Manufacture lenses.* The lenses are moulded, finished, cleaned, and inspected.

3. *Distribute lenses.* Finished lenses are packed and sent to Giovanni Motors.

Plastim is operating at capacity and incurs very low marketing costs. Because of its high-quality products, Plastim has minimal customer-service costs. Plastim's business environment is very competitive with respect to simple lenses. At a recent meeting, Giovanni's purchasing manager indicated that a new supplier, Bandix, which makes only simple lenses, is offering to supply the S3 lens to Giovanni at a price of $53, well below the $63 price that Plastim is currently projecting and budgeting for 2019. Unless Plastim can lower its selling price, it will lose the Giovanni business for the simple lens for the upcoming model year. Fortunately, the same competitive pressures do not exist for the complex lens, which Plastim currently sells to Giovanni at $137 per lens.

Plastim's management has two primary options:

■ Plastim can give up the Giovanni business in simple lenses if selling simple lenses is unprofitable. Bandix makes only simple lenses and perhaps, therefore, uses simpler technology and processes than Plastim. The simpler operations may give Bandix a cost advantage that Plastim cannot match. If so, it is better for Plastim not to supply the S3 lens to Giovanni.

■ Plastim can reduce the price of the simple lens and either accept a lower margin or aggressively seek to reduce costs.

To make these long-run strategic decisions, management needs first to understand the costs to design, make, and distribute the S3 and CL5 lenses.

While Bandix makes only simple lenses and can fairly accurately calculate the cost of a lens by dividing total costs by units produced, Plastim's costing environment is more challenging. The processes to make both simple and complex lenses are more complicated than the processes required to make only simple lenses. Plastim needs to find a way to allocate costs to each type of lens.

Overview of Plastim's Simple Costing System

In computing costs, Plastim assigns both variable costs and costs that are fixed in the short run to the S3 and CL5 lenses. Managers cost products and services to guide long-run strategic decisions (for example, what mix of products and services to produce and sell and what prices to charge for them). In the long run, managers want revenues to exceed total costs (variable and fixed) to design, make, and distribute the lenses.

To guide their pricing and cost-management decisions, Plastim's managers assign all costs, both manufacturing and non-manufacturing, to the S3 and CL5 lenses. Plastim has historically had a simple costing system that allocates indirect costs using a single indirect-cost rate. The budgeted costs for each type of lens in 2019 using Plastim's simple costing system are described in Exhibit 5-1.

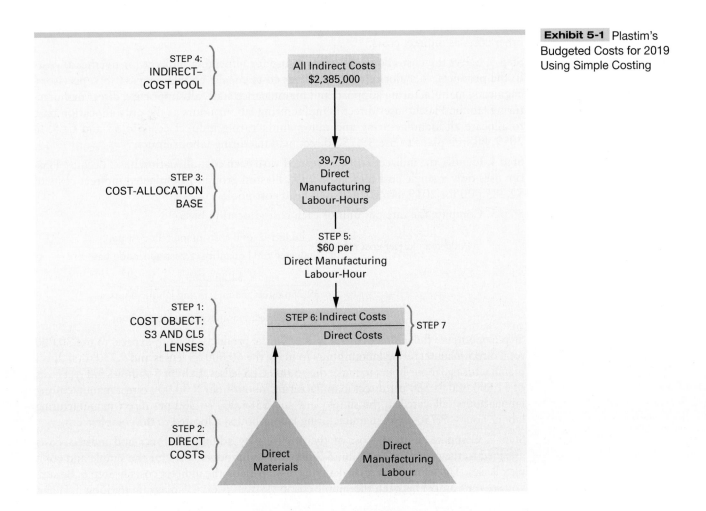

Exhibit 5-1 Plastim's Budgeted Costs for 2019 Using Simple Costing

Exhibit 5-2 Plastim's Product Costs Using the Simple Costing System

	A	B	C	D	E	F	G
1		60,000			15,000		
2		Simple Lenses (S3)			Complex Lenses (CL5)		
3		Total	per Unit		Total	per Unit	Total
4		(1)	(2) = (1) ÷ 60,000		(3)	(4) = (3) ÷ 15,000	(5) = (1) + (3)
5	Direct materials	$1,125,000	$18.75		$ 675,000	$45.00	$1,800,000
6	Direct manufacturing labour	600,000	10.00		195,000	13.00	795,000
7	Total direct costs (Step 2)	1,725,000	28.75		870,000	58.00	2,595,000
8	Indirect costs allocated (Step 6)	1,800,000	30.00		585,000	39.00	2,385,000
9	Total costs (Step 7)	$3,525,000	$58.75		$1,455,000	$97.00	$4,980,000
10							

Note: Numbers reference the calculation steps shown in Exhibit 5-1.

The process of cost allocation can be described as follows:

Step 1. Identify the products that are the chosen cost objects. The cost objects are the 60,000 simple S3 lenses and the 15,000 complex CL5 lenses that Plastim will produce in 2019. Plastim's goal is to calculate first the total costs and then the unit cost of designing, manufacturing, and distributing these lenses.

Step 2. Identify the direct costs of the products. Plastim identifies the direct costs—direct materials and direct manufacturing labour—of the lenses. Exhibit 5-2 shows the direct and indirect costs for the S3 and the CL5 lenses using the simple costing system. The direct cost calculations appear on lines 5, 6, and 7 of Exhibit 5-2. Plastim classifies all other costs as indirect costs.

Step 3. Select the cost-allocation bases to use for allocating indirect (or overhead) costs to the products. A majority of the indirect costs consist of salaries paid to supervisors, engineers, manufacturing support, and maintenance staff, all supporting direct manufacturing labour. Plastim uses direct manufacturing labour-hours as the only allocation base to allocate all manufacturing and non-manufacturing indirect costs to S3 and CL5. In 2019, Plastim plans to use 39,750 direct manufacturing labour-hours.

Step 4. Identify the indirect costs associated with each cost-allocation base. Because Plastim uses only a single cost-allocation base, Plastim groups all budgeted indirect costs of $2,385,000 for 2019 into a single overhead cost pool.

Step 5. Compute the rate per unit of each cost-allocation base.

$$\text{Budgeted indirect-cost rate} = \frac{\text{Budgeted total costs in indirect-cost pool}}{\text{Budgeted total quantity of cost-allocation base}}$$

$$= \frac{\$2,385,000}{39,750 \text{ direct manufacturing labour-hours}}$$

$$= \$60 \text{ per direct manufacturing labour-hour}$$

Step 6. Compute the indirect costs allocated to the products. Plastim expects to use 30,000 total direct manufacturing labour-hours to make the 60,000 S3 lenses and 9,750 total direct manufacturing labour-hours to make the 15,000 CL5 lenses. Exhibit 5-2 shows indirect costs of $1,800,000 (= $60 per direct manufacturing labour-hour × 30,000 direct manufacturing labour-hours) allocated to the simple lens and $585,000 (= $60 per direct manufacturing labour-hour × 9,750 direct manufacturing labour-hours) allocated to the complex lens.

Step 7. Compute the total cost of the products by adding all direct and indirect costs assigned to the products. Exhibit 5-2 presents the product costs for the simple and complex lenses. The direct costs are calculated in Step 2 and the indirect costs in Step 6. Be sure you see the parallel between the simple costing system overview diagram (Exhibit 5-1) and

5.1 TRY IT! ⊕

Amherst Metal Works produces two types of metal lamps. Amherst manufactures 20,000 basic lamps and 5,000 designer lamps. Its simple costing system uses a single indirect-cost pool and allocates costs to the two lamps on the basis of direct manufacturing labour-hours. It provides the following budgeted cost information:

	Basic Lamps	Designer Lamps	Total
Direct materials per lamp	$8	$15	
Direct manufacturing labour per lamp	0.5 hours	0.6 hours	
Direct manufacturing labour rate per hour	$20	$20	
Indirect manufacturing costs			$234,000

Required

Calculate the total budgeted costs of the basic and designer lamps using Amherst's simple costing system.

the costs calculated in Step 7. Exhibit 5-1 shows two direct-cost categories and one indirect-cost category. Hence, the budgeted cost of each type of lens in Step 7 (Exhibit 5-2) has three line items: two for direct costs and one for allocated indirect costs. The budgeted cost per S3 lens is $58.75, well above the $53 selling price quoted by Bandix. The budgeted cost per CL5 lens is $97.

Applying the Five-Step Decision-Making Process at Plastim

To decide how it should respond to the threat that Bandix poses to its S3 lens business, Plastim's management works through the five-step decision-making process.

Step 1. Identify the problem and uncertainties. The problem is clear: If Plastim wants to retain the Giovanni business for S3 lenses and make a profit, it must find a way to reduce the price and costs of the S3 lens. The two major uncertainties Plastim faces are (1) whether Plastim's technology and processes for the S3 lens are competitive with Bandix's and (2) whether the S3 lens is overcosted by the simple costing system.

Step 2. Obtain information. Management asks a team of its design and process engineers to analyze and evaluate the design, manufacturing, and distribution operations for the S3 lens. The team is very confident that the technology and processes for the S3 lens are not inferior to those of Bandix and other competitors because Plastim has many years of experience in manufacturing and distributing the S3 with a history and culture of continuous process improvements. If anything, the team is less certain about Plastim's capabilities in manufacturing and distributing complex lenses, because it only recently started making this type of lens. Given these doubts, management is happy that Giovanni Motors considers the price of the CL5 lens to be competitive. It is somewhat of a puzzle, though, how at the currently budgeted prices, Plastim is expected to earn a very large profit margin percentage (operating income divided by revenues) on the CL5 lenses and a small profit margin on the S3 lenses:

	60,000 Simple Lenses (S3)		15,000 Complex Lenses (CL5)		Total
	Total (1)	per Unit (2) = (1) ÷ 60,000	Total (3)	per Unit (4) = (3) ÷ 15,000	Total (5) = (1) + (3)
Revenues	$3,780,000	$63.00	$2,055,000	$137.00	$5,835,000
Total costs	3,525,000	58.75	1,455,000	97.00	4,980,000
Operating income	$ 255,000	$ 4.25	$ 600,000	$ 40.00	$ 855,000
Profit margin percentage		6.75%		29.20%	

As it continues to gather information, Plastim's management begins to ponder why the profit margins (and process) are under so much pressure for the S3 lens, where the company has strong capabilities, but high on the newer, less-established CL5 lens. Plastim is not deliberately charging a low price for S3, so management starts to believe that perhaps the problem lies with its costing system. Plastim's simple costing system may be overcosting the simple S3 lens (assigning too much cost to it) and undercosting the complex CL5 lens (assigning too little cost to it).

Step 3. Make predictions about the future. Plastim's key challenge is to get a better estimate of what it will cost to design, make, and distribute the S3 and CL5 lenses. Management is fairly confident about the direct material and direct manufacturing labour costs of each lens because these costs are easily traced to the lenses. But management is quite concerned about how accurately the simple costing system measures the indirect resources used by each type of lens. It believes it can do much better.

At the same time, management wants to ensure that no biases enter its thinking. In particular, it wants to be careful that the desire to be competitive on the S3 lens should not lead to assumptions that bias in favour of lowering costs of the S3 lens.

Step 4. Make decisions by choosing among alternatives. On the basis of predicted costs, and taking into account how Bandix might respond, Plastim's managers must decide whether they should bid for Giovanni Motors's S3 lens business, and if they do bid, what price they should offer.

Step 5. Implement the decision, evaluate performance, and learn. If Plastim bids and wins Giovanni's S3 lens business, it must compare actual costs, as it makes and ships S3 lenses, to predicted costs and learn why actual costs deviate from predicted costs. Such evaluation and learning form the basis for future improvements.

Guidelines for Refining a Costing System

There are three main guidelines for refining a costing system. In the following sections, we delve more deeply into each in the context of the Plastim example.

1. *Direct-cost tracing.* Identify as many direct costs as is economically feasible. This guideline aims to reduce the amount of costs classified as indirect, thereby minimizing the extent to which costs have to be allocated, rather than traced.

2. *Indirect-cost pools.* Expand the number of indirect-cost pools until each pool is more homogeneous. All costs in a homogeneous cost pool have the same or a similar cause-and-effect (or benefits-received) relationship with a single cost driver that is used as the cost-allocation base. Consider, for example, a single indirect-cost pool containing both indirect machining costs and indirect distribution costs that are allocated to products using machine-hours. This pool is not homogeneous because machine-hours are a cost driver of machining costs but not of distribution costs, which has a different cost driver, number of shipments. If, instead, machining costs and distribution costs are separated into two indirect-cost pools (with machine-hours as the cost-allocation base for the machining cost pool and number of shipments as the cost-allocation base for the distribution cost pool), each indirect-cost pool would become homogeneous.

3. *Cost-allocation bases.* As we describe later in the chapter, whenever possible, use the cost driver (the cause of indirect costs) as the cost-allocation base for each homogenous indirect-cost pool (the effect).

Activity-Based Costing Systems

► **LO 3**

Apply the cost hierarchy to develop an activity-based costing (ABC) system.

One of the best tools for refining a costing system is activity-based costing. **Activity-based costing (ABC)** refines a costing system by identifying individual activities as the fundamental cost objects. An activity is an event, task, or unit of work with a specified purpose—for example, designing products, setting up machines, operating machines, and distributing products. To help make strategic decisions, ABC systems identify activities in all functions of the value chain, calculate costs of individual activities, and assign costs to cost objects such as products and services on the basis of the mix of activities needed to produce each product or service. Structuring activity cost pools with cost drivers for each activity leads to more accurate costing of activities. Additionally, allocating these costs to products by measuring the cost-allocation bases of different activities used by different products leads to more accurate product costs.

Plastim's ABC System

After reviewing its simple costing system and the potential misrepresentation of product costs, Plastim decides to implement an ABC system. Direct materials costs and direct manufacturing labour costs can be traced to products easily, so the ABC system focuses on refining the assignment of indirect costs to departments, processes, products, or other cost objects. Plastim's ABC system identifies various activities that help explain why Plastim incurs the costs it currently classifies as indirect in its simple costing system. In other words, it breaks up the current indirect cost pool into finer pools of costs related to various activities. To identify these activities, Plastim organizes a team of managers from design, manufacturing, distribution, accounting, and administration.

Defining activities is not a simple matter. The team evaluates hundreds of tasks performed at Plastim before choosing the activities that form the basis of its ABC system. For example, it decides if maintenance of moulding machines, operations of moulding machines, and process control should each be regarded as a separate activity or should be combined into a single activity. An ABC system with many activities becomes overly detailed and unwieldy to operate. An ABC system with too few activities may not be refined enough to measure cause-and-effect relationships between cost drivers and various indirect costs. Plastim's team focuses on activities that account for a sizable fraction of indirect costs and combines activities that have the same cost driver into a single activity. For example, the team decides to combine maintenance of moulding machines, operations of moulding machines, and process control into a single activity—moulding machine operations—because all these activities have the same cost driver: moulding machine-hours.

The team identifies the following seven activities by developing a flowchart of all the steps and processes needed to design, manufacture, and distribute S3 and CL5 lenses:

a. Design products and processes.

b. Set up moulding machines to ensure that the moulds are properly held in place and parts are properly aligned before manufacturing starts.

c. Operate moulding machines to manufacture lenses.

d. Clean and maintain the moulds after lenses are manufactured.

e. Prepare batches of finished lenses for shipment.

f. Distribute lenses to customers.

g. Administer and manage all processes at Plastim.

These activity descriptions form the basis of the ABC system—this is sometimes called an activity list or activity dictionary. Compiling the list of tasks is, however, only the first step in implementing ABC systems. Plastim must also identify the cost of each activity and the related cost driver. To do so, Plastim uses the three guidelines for refining a costing system:

1. **Direct-cost tracing.** Plastim's ABC system subdivides the single indirect cost pool into seven smaller cost pools related to the different activities. The costs in the cleaning and maintenance activity cost pool (item (d)) consist of salaries and wages paid to

workers who clean the mould. These costs are direct costs, because they can be economically traced to a specific mould and lens.

2. *Indirect-cost pools.* The remaining six activity cost pools are indirect cost pools. Unlike the single indirect cost pool of Plastim's simple costing system, each of the activity-related cost pools is homogeneous. That is, each activity cost pool includes only those costs that have the same cost driver. For example, the distribution cost pool includes only those costs (such as wages of truck drivers) that, over time, increase as the cost driver of distribution costs, volume of packages delivered, increases.

3. *Cost-allocation bases.* For each activity cost pool, the cost driver is used (whenever possible) as the cost-allocation base. To identify cost drivers, Plastim's managers consider various alternatives and use their knowledge of operations to choose among them. For example, Plastim's managers choose setup-hours rather than the number of setups as the cost driver of setup costs, because Plastim's managers believe that more complex setups take more time and are more costly. Over time, Plastim's managers can use data to test their beliefs.

Setting up moulding machines frequently entails trial runs, fine-tuning, and adjustments. Improper setups cause quality problems such as scratches on the surface of the lens. The resources needed for each setup depend on the complexity of the manufacturing operation. Complex lenses require more setup resources (setup-hours) per setup than simple lenses. Furthermore, complex lenses can be produced only in small batches because the moulds for complex lenses need to be cleaned more often than moulds for simple lenses. Thus, relative to simple lenses, complex lenses not only use more setup-hours per setup, but they also require more frequent setups.

Setup data for the simple S3 lens and the complex CL5 lens are as follows:

		Simple S3 Lens	Complex CL5 Lens	Total
1	Quantity of lenses produced	60,000	15,000	
2	Number of lenses produced per batch	240	50	
3 = (1) ÷ (2)	Number of batches	250	300	
4	Setup time per batch	2 hours	5 hours	
5 = (3) × (4)	Total setup-hours	500 hours	1,500 hours	2,000 hours

Of the $2,385,000 in the total indirect-cost pool, Plastim identifies the total costs of setups (consisting mainly of depreciation on setup equipment and allocated costs of process engineers, quality engineers, and supervisors) to be $300,000. Recall that in its simple costing system, Plastim uses direct manufacturing labour-hours to allocate all indirect costs to products. The following table compares how setup costs allocated to simple and complex lenses will be different if Plastim allocates setup costs to lenses based on setup-hours rather than direct manufacturing labour-hours. Of the $60 total rate per direct manufacturing labour-hour, the setup cost per direct manufacturing labour-hour amounts to $7.54717 (= $300,000 ÷ 39,750 total direct manufacturing labour-hours). The setup cost per setup-hour equals $150 (= $300,000 ÷ 2,000 total setup-hours).

	Simple S3 Lens	Complex CL5 Lens	Total
Setup cost allocated using direct manufacturing labour-hours: $7.54717 × 30,000; $7.54717 × 9,750	$226,415	$ 73,585	$300,000
Setup cost allocated using setup-hours: $150 × 500; $150 × 1,500	$ 75,000	$225,000	$300,000

Setup-hours, not direct manufacturing labour-hours, are the cost driver of setup costs. The CL5 lens uses substantially more setup-hours than the S3 lens (1,500 hours ÷ 2,000 hours = 75% of the total setup-hours) because the CL5 requires a greater number of setups (batches) and each setup is more challenging and requires more setup-hours.

The ABC system therefore allocates substantially more setup costs to CL5 than to S3. When direct manufacturing labour-hours rather than setup-hours are used to allocate setup costs in the simple costing system, it is the S3 lens that is allocated a very large share of the setup costs because the S3 lens uses a larger proportion of direct manufacturing labour-hours ($30{,}000 \div 39{,}750 = 75.47\%$). As a result, the simple costing system overcosts the S3 lens with regard to setup costs.

> Note that setup-hours are related to batches (or groups) of lenses made, not the number of individual lenses. ABC attempts to identify the most relevant cause-and-effect relationship for each activity pool, without restricting the cost driver to only units of output or variables related to units of output (such as direct manufacturing labour-hours). Limiting cost-allocation bases in this manner weakens the cause-and-effect relationship between the cost-allocation base and the costs in a cost pool.

Cost Hierarchies

A **cost hierarchy** categorizes various activity cost pools on the basis of the different types of cost drivers, or cost-allocation bases, or different degrees of difficulty in determining cause-and-effect (or benefits-received) relationships. ABC systems commonly use a cost hierarchy with four levels—output unit-level costs, batch-level costs, product-sustaining costs, and facility-sustaining costs—to identify cost-allocation bases that are cost drivers of the activity cost pools.

Output unit-level costs are the costs of activities performed on each individual unit of a product or service. Machine operations costs (such as the cost of energy, machine depreciation, and repair) related to the activity of running the automated moulding machines are output unit-level costs. They are output unit-level costs because, over time, the cost of this activity increases with additional units of output produced (or machine-hours used). Plastim's ABC system uses moulding machine-hours—an output unit-level cost-allocation base—to allocate machine operations costs to products.

Batch-level costs are the costs of activities related to a group of units of a product or service rather than each individual unit of product or service. In the Plastim example, setup costs are batch-level costs because, over time, the cost of this setup activity increases with setup-hours needed to produce batches (groups) of lenses.

- The S3 lens requires 500 setup-hours (2 setup-hours per batch × 250 batches).
- The CL5 lens requires 1,500 setup-hours (5 setup-hours per batch × 300 batches).

The total setup costs allocated to S3 and CL5 depend on the total setup-hours required by each type of lens, not on the number of units of S3 and CL5 produced. (Setup costs, being a batch-level cost, cannot be avoided by producing one unit fewer of S3 or CL5.) Plastim's ABC system uses setup-hours—a batch-level cost-allocation base—to allocate setup costs to products. Other examples of batch-level costs are materials-handling and quality-inspection costs associated with batches (not the quantities) of products produced, and costs of placing purchase orders, receiving materials, and paying invoices related to the number of purchase orders placed rather than the quantity or value of materials purchased.

Product-sustaining costs (**service-sustaining costs**) are the costs of activities undertaken to support individual products or services regardless of the number of units or batches in which the units are produced. In the Plastim example, design costs are product-sustaining costs. Over time, design costs depend largely on the time designers spend designing and modifying the product, the mould, and the process. These design costs are a function of the complexity of the mould, measured by the number of parts in the mould multiplied by the area (in square feet) over which the molten plastic must flow (12 parts × 2.5 square feet, or 30 parts-square feet for the S3 lens, and 14 parts × 5 square feet, or 70 parts-square feet for the CL5 lens). As a result, the total design costs allocated to S3 and CL5 depend on the complexity of the mould, regardless of the number of units or batches of production. Design costs cannot be avoided by producing fewer units or running fewer batches. Plastim's ABC system uses parts-square feet—a product-sustaining cost-allocation base—to allocate design costs to products. Other examples of product-sustaining costs are product research and development costs, costs of making engineering changes, and marketing costs to launch new products.

Facility-sustaining costs are the costs of activities that cannot be traced to individual products or services but that support the organization as a whole. In the Plastim

⊕ **TRY IT!** **5.2**

Amherst Metal Works produces two types of metal lamps. Amherst manufactures 20,000 basic lamps and 5,000 designer lamps. Its ABC system uses two indirect-cost pools. One cost pool is for setup costs and the other for general manufacturing overhead. Amherst allocates setup costs to the two lamps based on setup labour-hours and general manufacturing overhead costs on the basis of direct manufacturing labour-hours. It provides the following budgeted cost information:

	Basic Lamps	Designer Lamps	Total
Direct materials per lamp	$ 8	$15	
Direct manufacturing labour-hours per lamp	0.5 hours	0.6 hours	
Direct manufacturing labour rate per hour	$20	$20	
Setup costs			$114,000
Lamps produced per batch	250	50	
Setup hours per batch	1 hour	3 hours	
General manufacturing overhead costs			$120,000

Required

Calculate the total budgeted costs of the basic and designer lamps using Amherst's ABC system.

example, the general administration costs (including top management compensation, rent, and building security) are facility-sustaining costs. It is usually difficult to find a good cause-and-effect relationship between these costs and the cost-allocation base. This lack of a cause-and-effect relationship causes some companies not to allocate these costs to products and instead to deduct them as a separate lump-sum amount from operating income. Other companies, such as Plastim, allocate facility-sustaining costs to products on some basis—for example, direct manufacturing labour-hours—because management believes all costs should be allocated to products. Allocating all costs to products or services becomes important when management wants to set selling prices on the basis of an amount of cost that includes all costs.

Implementing Activity-Based Costing

▶ **LO 4**

Assign costs using activity-based costing (ABC).

Exhibit 5-3 shows an overview of Plastim's ABC system, which is developed through the following process.

Step 1. Identify the products that are the chosen cost objects. The cost objects are the 60,000 S3 and the 15,000 CL5 lenses that Plastim will produce in 2019. Plastim's goal is to calculate first the total costs and then the per-unit cost of designing, manufacturing, and distributing these lenses.

Step 2. Identify the direct costs of the products. Because these costs can be economically traced to a specific lens or mould, Plastim identifies as direct costs of the lenses: direct materials costs, direct manufacturing labour costs, and mould cleaning and maintenance costs. Exhibit 5-5 shows the direct and indirect costs for the S3 and CL5 lenses using the ABC system. The direct costs calculations appear on lines 6, 7, 8, and 9 of Exhibit 5-5. Plastim classifies all other costs as indirect costs.

Step 3. Select the activities and cost-allocation bases to use for allocating indirect costs to the products. Plastim identifies six activities—(a) design, (b) moulding machine setups, (c) machine operations, (d) shipment setup, (e) distribution, and (f) administration—for allocating indirect costs to products. Exhibit 5-4, column 2, shows the cost hierarchy category, and column 4 shows the cost-allocation base and the budgeted quantity of the

Exhibit 5-3 Overview of Plastim's Activity-Based Costing System

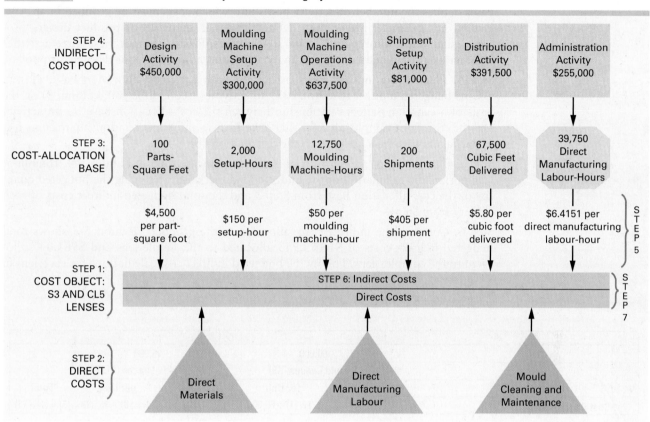

Exhibit 5-4 Activity-Cost Rates for Indirect-Cost Pools

	A	B	C	D	E	F	G	H
1			(Step 4)	(Step 3)		(Step 5		
2	**Activity**	**Cost Hierarchy Category**	**Total Budgeted Indirect Costs**	**Budgeted Quantity of Cost-Allocation Base**		**Budgeted Indirect Cost Rate**		**Cause-and-Effect Relationship Between Allocation Base and Activity Cost**
3	(1)	(2)	(3)	(4)		(5) = (3) ÷ (4)		(6)
4	Design	Product-sustaining	$450,000	100	parts-square feet	$ 4,500	per part-square foot	Design Department indirect costs increase with more complex moulds (more parts, larger surface area).
5	Setup moulding machines	Batch-level	$300,000	2,000	setup-hours	$ 150	per setup-hour	Indirect setup costs increase with setup-hours.
6	Machine operations	Output unit-level	$637,500	12,750	moulding machine-hours	$ 50	per moulding machine-hour	Indirect costs of operating moulding machines increases with moulding machine-hours.
7	Shipment setup	Batch-level	$81,000	200	shipments	$ 405	per shipment	Shipping costs incurred to prepare batches for shipment increase with the number of shipments.
8	Distribution	Output unit-level	$391,500	67,500	cubic feet delivered	$ 5.80	per cubic foot delivered	Distribution costs increase with the cubic feet of packages delivered.
9	Administration	Facility sustaining	$255,000	39,750	direct manuf. labour-hours	$6.4151	per direct manuf. labour-hour	The demand for administrative resources increases with direct manufacturing labour-hours.

cost-allocation base for each activity described in column 1. Identifying the cost-allocation bases defines the number of activity pools into which costs must be grouped in an ABC system. For example, rather than define the design activities of product design, process design, and prototyping as separate activities, Plastim defines these three activities together as a combined "design" activity and forms a homogeneous design cost pool.

Step 4. Identify the indirect costs associated with each cost-allocation base. Plastim assigns budgeted indirect costs for 2019 to activities (see Exhibit 5-4, column 3) on the basis of a cause-and-effect relationship between the cost-allocation base for an activity and the cost. For example, all costs that have a cause-and-effect relationship to cubic feet of packages moved are assigned to the distribution cost pool.

Step 5. Compute the rate per unit of each cost-allocation base. Exhibit 5-4, column 5, summarizes the calculation of the budgeted indirect cost rates using the budgeted quantity of the cost-allocation base from Step 3 and the total budgeted indirect costs of each activity from Step 4.

Step 6. Compute the indirect costs allocated to the products. Exhibit 5-5 shows total budgeted indirect costs of $1,153,953 allocated to the simple lens and $961,047 allocated to the complex lens. Follow the budgeted indirect cost calculations for each lens in

Exhibit 5-5 Plastim's Product Costs Using Activity-Based Costing System

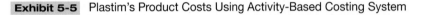

	A	B	C	D	E	F	G
1		60,000			15,000		
2		Simple Lenses (S3)			Complex Lenses (CL5)		
3		Total	per Unit		Total	per Unit	Total
4	Cost Description	(1)	(2) = (1) ÷ 60,000		(3)	(4) = (3) ÷ 15,000	(5) = (1) + (3)
5	Direct costs						
6	Direct materials	$1,125,000	$18.75		$ 675,000	$ 45.00	$1,800,000
7	Direct manufacturing labour	600,000	10.00		195,000	13.00	795,000
8	Direct mould cleaning and maintenance costs	120,000	2.00		150,000	10.00	270,000
9	Total direct costs (Step 2)	1,845,000	30.75		1,020,000	68.00	2,865,000
10	Indirect Costs of Activities						
11	Design						
12	S3, 30 parts-sq.ft. × $4,500	135,000	2.25				} 450,000
13	CL5, 70 parts-sq.ft. × $4,500				315,000	21.00	
14	Setup of moulding machines						
15	S3, 500 setup-hours × $150	75,000	1.25				} 300,000
16	CL5, 1,500 setup-hours × $150				225,000	15.00	
17	Machine operations						
18	S3, 9,000 moulding machine-hours × $50	450,000	7.50				} 637,500
19	CL5, 3,750 moulding machine-hours × $50				187,500	12.50	
20	Shipment setup						
21	S3, 100 shipments × $405	40,500	0.67				} 81,000
22	CL5, 100 shipments × $405				40,500	2.70	
23	Distribution						
24	S3, 45,000 cubic feet delivered × $5.80	261,000	4.35				} 391,500
25	CL5, 22,500 cubic feet delivered × $5.80				130,500	8.70	
26	Administration						
27	S3, 30,000 dir. manuf. labour-hours × $6.4151	192,453	3.21				} 255,000
28	CL5, 9,750 dir. manuf. labour-hours × $6.4151				62,547	4.17	
29	Total indirect costs allocated (Step 6)	1,153,953	19.23		961,047	64.07	2,115,000
30	Total Costs (Step 7)	$2,998,953	$49.98		$1,981,047	$132.07	$4,980,000
31							

Exhibit 5-5. For each activity, Plastim's operations personnel indicate the total quantity of the cost-allocation base that will be used by each type of lens.

For example, lines 15 and 16 of Exhibit 5-5 show that of the 2,000 total setup-hours, the S3 lens is budgeted to use 500 hours and the CL5 lens 1,500 hours. The budgeted indirect cost rate is $150 per setup-hour (Exhibit 5-4, column 5, line 5). Therefore, the total budgeted cost of the setup activity allocated to the S3 lens is $75,000 (= 500 setup-hours × $150 per setup-hour) and to the CL5 lens is $225,000 (= 1,500 setup-hours × $150 per setup-hour). Budgeted setup cost per unit equals $1.25 (= $75,000 ÷ 60,000 units) for the S3 lens and $15 (= $225,000 ÷ 15,000 units) for the CL5 lens.

Step 7. Compute the total cost of the products by adding all direct and indirect costs assigned to the products. Exhibit 5-5 presents the product costs for the simple and complex lenses. The direct costs are calculated in Step 2, and the indirect costs are calculated in Step 6. The ABC system overview in Exhibit 5-3 shows three direct-cost categories and six indirect-cost categories. The budgeted cost of each lens type in Exhibit 5-5 has nine line items, with three for direct costs and six for indirect costs. The differences between the ABC product costs of S3 and CL5 calculated in Exhibit 5-5 highlight how each of these products uses different amounts of direct and indirect costs in each activity area.

Comparing Alternative Costing Systems

Exhibit 5-6 compares the simple costing system using a single indirect-cost pool (Exhibit 5-1 and Exhibit 5-2) Plastim had been using and the ABC system (Exhibit 5-3 and Exhibit 5-5). Note three points in Exhibit 5-6, consistent with the guidelines for refining a costing

Exhibit 5-6 Comparing Alternative Costing Systems

	Simple Costing System Using a Single Indirect-Cost Pool (1)	ABC System (2)	Difference (3) = (2) – (1)
Direct-cost categories	2	3	1
	Direct materials	Direct materials	
	Direct manufacturing labour	Direct manufacturing labour	
		Direct mould cleaning and maintenance labour	
Total direct costs	$2,595,000	$2,865,000	$270,000
Indirect-cost pools	1	6	5
	Single indirect-cost pool allocated using direct manufacturing labour-hours	Design (parts-square feet)[1] Moulding machine setup (setup-hours) Machine operations (moulding machine-hours) Shipment setup (number of shipments) Distribution (cubic feet delivered) Administration (direct manufacturing labour-hours)	
Total indirect costs	$2,385,000	$2,115,000	($270,000)
Total costs assigned to simple (S3) lens	$3,525,000	$2,998,953	($526,047)
Cost per unit of simple (S3) lens	$58.75	$49.98	($8.77)
Total costs assigned to complex (CL5) lens	$1,455,000	$1,981,047	$526,047
Cost per unit of complex (CL5) lens	$97.00	$132.07	$35.07

[1]Cost drivers for the various indirect-cost pools are shown in parentheses.

system: (1) ABC systems trace more costs as direct costs; (2) ABC systems create homogeneous cost pools linked to different activities; and (3) for each activity-cost pool, ABC systems seek a cost-allocation base that has a cause-and-effect relationship with costs in the cost pool.

The homogeneous cost pools and the choice of cost-allocation bases, tied to the cost hierarchy, give Plastim's managers greater confidence in the activity and product cost numbers from the ABC system. The bottom part of Exhibit 5-6 shows that allocating costs to lenses using only an output unit-level allocation base—direct manufacturing labour-hours, as in the single indirect-cost pool system used prior to ABC—overcosts the simple S3 lens by $8.77 per unit and undercosts the complex CL5 lens by $35.07 per unit. The CL5 lens uses a disproportionately larger amount of output unit-level, batch-level, and product-sustaining costs than is represented by the direct manufacturing labour-hour cost-allocation base. The S3 lens uses a disproportionately smaller amount of these costs.

The benefit of an ABC system is that it provides information to make better decisions. But this benefit must be weighed against the measurement and implementation costs of an ABC system.

Considerations in Implementing Activity-Based-Costing Systems

When a company decides to implement ABC, it must make important choices about the level of detail to use. Should it choose many finely specified activities, cost drivers, and cost pools, or would a few suffice? For example, Plastim could identify a different moulding machine-hour rate for each different type of moulding machine. In making such choices, managers weigh the benefits against the costs and limitations of implementing a more detailed costing system. Managers choose the level of detail to use in a costing system by evaluating the expected costs of the system against the expected benefits that result from better decisions. Signs of when an ABC system is likely to provide the most benefits include the following:

- Significant amounts of indirect costs are allocated using only one or two cost pools.

- All or most indirect costs are identified as output unit-level costs (few indirect costs are described as batch-level costs, product-sustaining costs, or facility-sustaining costs).

- Products make diverse demands on resources because of differences in volume, process steps, batch size, or complexity.

- Products that a company is well-suited to make and sell show small profits; whereas products that a company is less suited to produce and sell show large profits.

- Operations staff has substantial disagreement with the reported costs of manufacturing and marketing products and services.

The main costs and limitations of an ABC system are the measurements necessary to implement it. ABC systems require management to estimate costs of activity pools and to identify and measure cost drivers for these pools to serve as cost-allocation bases. Even basic ABC systems require many calculations to determine costs of products and services. These measurements are costly. Activity cost rates also need to be updated regularly.

As ABC systems get very detailed and more cost pools are created, more allocations are necessary to calculate activity costs for each cost pool. This increases the chances of misidentifying the costs of different activity cost pools. For example, supervisors are more likely to incorrectly identify the time they spent on different activities if they have to allocate their time over five activities rather than only two activities.

▶ **LO 5**

Explain the benefits of activity-based costing (ABC) systems for activity-based management (ABM).

ABC: The Foundation of ABM

Using ABC information to guide management decisions is referred to as **activity-based management (ABM)**. ABM is a strategic approach to cost control that avoids impairing the activities of customization for which customers are willing to pay. An ABC system is one building block of ABM. The second building block is the ability of managers to understand that the demand for output is central to profitability. In the earlier example, Plastim must produce lenses that are desirable to its customers at a desirable price. In principle, all activities should not only add cost but also add value to outputs.

Value added is always considered from the customers' perspective. The outcome of **value-added activities** is that the costs plus some predictable profit will be fully recovered when the output is sold. Customers pay for features they perceive as desirable. In contrast, **non-value-added activities** add costs that fail to improve desirability and for which customers will not pay. ABM focuses cost control on reducing non-value-added activities. The management accountant's role is to apply the ABC system and distinguish value from non-value-added activities. Effective ABM will

- Reduce costs and improve processes.
- Improve selection of process activities in pricing and product mix decisions.
- Assist in making design decisions.
- Achieve planned growth.

Pricing and Product-Mix Decisions

An ABC system gives managers information about the costs of making and selling diverse products. With this information, managers can make pricing and product-mix decisions. For example, the ABC system indicates that Plastim can match its competitor's price of $53 for the S3 lens and still make a profit because the ABC cost of S3 is $49.98 (see Exhibit 5-5).

Plastim's managers offer Giovanni Motors a price of $52 for the S3 lens. Plastim's managers are confident that they can use the deeper understanding of costs that the ABC system provides to improve efficiency and further reduce the cost of the S3 lens. Without information from the ABC system, Plastim's managers might have erroneously concluded that they would incur an operating loss on the S3 lens at a price of $53. This incorrect conclusion would probably have caused Plastim to reduce its business in simple lenses and focus instead on complex lenses, where its single indirect-cost-pool system indicated it is very profitable.

Focusing on complex lenses would have been a mistake. The ABC system indicates that the cost of making the complex lens is much higher—$132.07 versus $97 indicated by the direct manufacturing labour-hour–based costing system Plastim had been using. As Plastim's operations staff had thought all along, Plastim has no competitive advantage in making CL5 lenses. At a price of $137 per lens for CL5, the profit margin is very small ($137.00 − $132.07 = $4.93). As Plastim reduced its prices on simple lenses, it would need to negotiate a higher price for complex lenses with Giovanni Motors.

Cost Reduction and Process Improvement Decisions

Manufacturing and distribution personnel use ABC systems to focus on how and where to reduce costs. Managers set cost reduction targets in terms of reducing the cost per unit of the cost-allocation base in different activity areas. For example, the supervisor of the distribution activity area at Plastim could have a performance target of decreasing distribution cost per cubic foot of products delivered from $5.80 to $5.40 by reducing distribution labour and warehouse rental costs. The goal is to reduce these costs by improving the way work is done without compromising customer service or the actual or perceived value (usefulness) customers obtain from the product or service. That is, Plastim will attempt to take out only those costs that are non-value-added. Controlling physical cost drivers, such as setup-hours or cubic feet delivered, is another fundamental way that operating personnel manage costs. For example, Plastim can decrease distribution costs by packing the lenses in a way that reduces the bulkiness of the packages delivered.

The following table shows the reduction in distribution costs of the S3 and CL5 lenses as a result of actions that lower cost per cubic foot delivered.

	60,000 (S3) Lenses		15,000 (CL5) Lenses	
	Total (1)	per Unit (2) = (1) ÷ 60,000	Total (3)	per Unit (4) = (3) ÷ 15,000
Distribution costs (from Exhibit 5-5) S3, 45,000 cubic feet × $5.80/cubic foot	$261,000	$4.35		
CL5, 22,500 cubic feet × $5.80/cubic foot			$130,500	$8.70
Distribution costs as a result of process improvements S3, 40,000 cubic feet × $5.40/cubic foot	216,000	3.60		
CL5, 20,000 cubic feet × $5.40/cubic foot			108,000	7.20
Savings in distribution costs from process improvements	$ 45,000	$0.75	$ 22,500	$1.50

In the long run, total distribution costs will decrease from $391,500 (= $261,000 + $130,500) to $324,000 (= $216,000 + $108,000). In the short run, however, distribution costs may be fixed and may not decrease. Suppose all $391,500 of distribution costs are fixed costs in the short run. ABC systems distinguish costs incurred from resources used to design, manufacture, and deliver products and services. For the distribution activity, after process improvements

Costs incurred = $391,500
Resources used = $216,000 (for S3 lens) + $108,000 (for CL5 lens) = $324,000

On the basis of the resources used by each product, Plastim's ABC system allocates $216,000 to S3 and $108,000 to CL5 for a total of $324,000. The difference of $67,500 (= $391,500 − $324,000) is shown as costs of unused but available distribution capacity. Plastim's ABC system does not allocate the costs of unused capacity to products so as not to burden the product costs of S3 and CL5 with the cost of resources not used by these products. Instead, the system highlights the amount of unused capacity as a separate line item to signal to managers the need to reduce these costs, such as by redeploying labour to other uses or laying off workers.

Design Decisions

Management can evaluate how its current product and process designs affect activities and costs as a way of identifying new designs to reduce costs. For example, design decisions that decrease complexity of the mould reduce costs of design, materials, labour, machine setups, machine operations, and mould cleaning and maintenance. Plastim's customers may be willing to give up some features of the lens in exchange for a lower price. Note that Plastim's previous costing system, which used direct manufacturing labour-hours as the cost-allocation base for all indirect costs, would have mistakenly signaled that Plastim should choose those designs that most reduce direct manufacturing labour-hours when, in fact, there is a weak cause-and-effect relationship between direct manufacturing labour-hours and indirect costs.

We close this section with a note of caution: Do not assume that because department costing systems require the creation of multiple indirect cost pools, they properly recognize the drivers of costs within departments as well as how resources are used by products. As we have indicated, in many situations, department costing systems can be refined using ABC. Emphasizing activities leads to more-focused and homogeneous cost pools, aids in identifying cost-allocation bases for activities that have a better cause-and-effect relationship with the costs in activity cost pools, and leads to better design and process decisions. But these benefits of an ABC system would need to be balanced against its costs and limitations.

The ABC system itself, augmented by ABM, will improve the value added of management activities. The team will make better decisions on how to coordinate different business function activities, identify and reduce costs of non-value-added activities, improve effectiveness of process activities, match the company's resources to customer demand, and achieve planned growth.

Sustainability in Action

Mayo Clinic Uses Time-Driven Activity-Based Costing to Reduce Costs and Improve Care

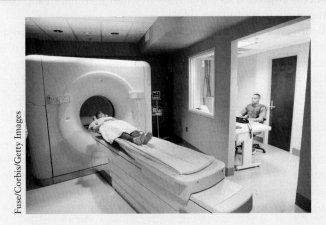

Fuse/Corbis/Getty Images

By 2024, $1 of every $5 spent in the United States will be on health care. Several medical centres, such as the Mayo Clinic in Rochester, Minnesota, are using time-driven activity-based costing (TDABC) to help bring accurate cost and value measurement practices into the health care delivery system.

TDABC assigns all of the organization's resource costs to cost objects using a framework that requires two sets of estimates. TDABC first calculates the cost of supplying resource capacity, such as a doctor's time. The total cost of resources—including personnel, supervision, insurance, space occupancy, technology, and supplies—is divided by the available capacity—the time available for doctors to do their work—to obtain the capacity cost rate. Next, TDABC uses the capacity cost rate to drive resource costs to cost objects, such as the number of patients seen, by estimating the demand for resource capacity (time) that the cost object requires.

Medical centres implementing TDABC have succeeded in reducing costs. For orthopaedic procedures at the Mayo Clinic, the TDABC-modified process resulted in shorter stays for patients, a 24% decrease in patients discharged to expensive skilled nursing facilities, and a 15% decrease in cost. Follow-on improvements have included obtaining patient-reported outcomes from tablets and smartphones and eliminating major variations in the cost of prostheses and other supplies.

More broadly, health care providers implementing TDABC have found that better outcomes for patients often go hand in hand with lower total costs. For example, spending more on early detection and better diagnosis of disease reduces patient suffering and often leads to less-complex and less-expensive care. With the insights from TDABC, health care providers can utilize medical staff, equipment, facilities, and administrative resources far more efficiently; streamline the path of patients through the system; and select treatment approaches that improve outcomes while eliminating services that do not.

Sources: Derek A. Haas, Richard A. Helmers, March Rucci, Meredith Brady, and Robert S. Kaplan. 2015. The Mayo Clinic Model for Running a Value-Improvement Program, HBR.org, October 22 (https://hbr.org/2015/10/the-mayo-clinic-model-for-running-a-value-improvement-program); Dan Mangan. 2015. $1 of Every $5 Spent in US Will Be on Health Care, CNBC, July 28 (http://www.cnbc.com/2015/07/28/1-of-every-5-spent-in-us-will-be-on-health-care.html); Robert S. Kaplan and Michael E. Porter. 2011. How to Solve the Cost Crisis in Health Care, *Harvard Business Review*, September (https://hbr.org/2011/09/how-to-solve-the-cost-crisis-in-health-care); Robert S. Kaplan and Steven R. Anderson. 2007. The Innovation of Time-Driven Activity-Based Costing, *Journal of Cost Management* 21, no. 2 (March–April): 5–15; Robert S. Kaplan and Steven R. Anderson. 2007. *Time-Driven Activity-Based Costing* (Boston: Harvard Business School Press).

ABC in Service and Merchandising Companies

Although many of the early examples of ABC originated in manufacturing, ABC has many applications in service and merchandising companies. In addition to manufacturing activities, the Plastim example includes the application of ABC to a service activity—design—and to a merchandising activity—distribution. Companies such as the Cooperative Bank, Braintree Hospital, TELUS in the telecommunications industry, and Union Pacific in the railroad industry have implemented some form of ABC system to identify profitable product mixes, improve efficiency, and satisfy customers. Similarly, many retail and wholesale companies—for example, Supervalu, a retailer and distributor of grocery store products, and Owens and Minor, a medical supplies distributor—have used ABC systems. Finally, as we describe in Chapter 14, a large number of financial services companies (as well as other companies) employ variations of ABC systems to analyze and improve the profitability of their customer interactions.

The widespread use of ABC systems in service and merchandising companies reinforces the idea that ABC systems are used by managers for strategic decisions rather than for inventory valuation. (Inventory valuation is fairly straightforward in merchandising companies and not needed in service companies.) Service companies, in particular, find great value from ABC because a vast majority of their cost structure comprises indirect costs. After all, there are few direct costs when a bank makes a loan or when a representative answers a phone call at a call centre. As we have seen, a major benefit of ABC is its ability to assign indirect costs to cost objects by identifying activities and cost drivers. As a result, ABC systems provide greater insight than traditional systems into the management of these indirect costs. The general approach to ABC in service and merchandising companies is similar to the ABC approach in manufacturing.

The Cooperative Bank followed the approach described in this chapter when it implemented ABC in its retail banking operations. It calculated the costs of various activities, such as performing ATM transactions, opening and closing accounts, administering mortgages, and processing Visa transactions. It then used the activity cost rates to calculate costs of various products, such as chequing accounts, mortgages, and Visa cards and the costs of supporting different customers. ABC information helped the Cooperative Bank to improve its processes and to identify profitable products and customer segments.

ABC raises some interesting issues when it is applied to a public service institution such as Canada Post. The costs of delivering mail to remote locations are far greater than the costs of delivering mail within urban areas. However, for fairness and community-building reasons, Canada Post cannot charge higher prices to customers in remote areas. In this case, ABC is valuable for understanding, managing, and reducing costs but not for pricing decisions.

Pulling It All Together—Problem for Self-Study

(Try to solve this problem before examining the solution that follows.)

Problem

Family Supermarkets (FS) has decided to increase the size of its St. John's store. It wants information about the profitability of individual product lines: soft drinks, fresh produce, and packaged food.

Operating personnel at FS provide the following data for each product line:

	Soft Drinks	Fresh Produce	Packaged Food
Revenue	$317,400	$840,240	$483,960
Cost of goods sold	$240,000	$600,000	$360,000
Cost of bottles returned	$ 4,800	$ 0	$ 0
Number of purchase orders placed	144	336	144
Number of deliveries received	120	876	264
Hours of shelf-stocking time	216	2,160	1,080
Items sold	50,400	441,600	122,400

FS also provides the following information for the year 2019:

Activity (1)	Description of Activity (2)	Total Costs (3)	Cost Allocation Base (4)		
Bottle returns	Returning empty bottles to store	$ 4,800	Direct tracing to soft-drink line		
Ordering	Placing orders for purchases	62,400	purchase orders	=	624
Delivery	Physical delivery and receiving of merchandise	100,800	deliveries	=	1,260
Shelf-stocking	Stocking and restocking merchandise	69,120	hours stocking	=	3,456
Customer support	Assistance provided for customers	122,880	items sold	=	614,400
Total		360,000			

1. FS currently allocates store support costs (all costs other than cost of goods sold) to product lines based on the cost of goods sold of each product line. Calculate the operating income and operating income as a percentage of revenues for each product line.

2. If FS allocates store support costs (all costs other than cost of goods sold) to product lines using an ABC system, calculate the operating income and operating income as a percentage of revenues for each product line.

3. Comment on your answers to requirements 1 and 2.

◄ **Required**

❶

❷ ❸ ❹

❺

Solution

1. The following table shows the operating income and operating margin (operating income as a percentage of revenues). All store support costs (that is, costs other than cost of goods sold) are allocated to product lines using cost of goods sold of each product line as the cost allocation base. Total store support costs equal $360,000 (= Cost of bottles returned, $4,800 + Cost of purchase orders, $62,400 + Cost of deliveries, $100,800 + Cost of shelf-stocking, $69,120 + Cost of customer support, $122,880). If cost of goods sold is the cost allocation base, the allocation rate for store support costs = $360,000 ÷ $1,200,000 = $0.30 per dollar of cost of goods sold. To allocate support costs to each product line, FS multiplies the cost of goods sold of each product line by 0.30. Operating income for each product line is as follows:

	Soft Drinks	Fresh Produce	Packaged Food	Total
Revenue	$317,400	$840,240	$483,960	$1,641,600
Cost of goods sold	240,000	600,000	360,000	1,200,000
Store support cost ($240,000; $600,000; $360,000 × 0.30)	72,000	180,000	108,000	360,000
Total costs	312,000	780,000	468,000	1,560,000
Operating income	$ 5,400	$ 60,240	$ 15,960	$ 81,600
Operating margin (Operating income ÷ Revenue)	1.70%	7.17%	3.30%	4.97%

2. Under an ABC system, FS identifies bottle return costs as a direct cost since these costs can be traced easily to the soft drink product line. FS then calculates cost allocation rates for each activity area. The activity rates are as follows:

Activity (1)	Cost Hierarchy (2)	Total Costs (3)	Quantity of Cost Allocation Base (4)	Overhead Allocation Rate (5) = (3) ÷ (4)
Ordering	Batch level	$ 62,400	624 purchase orders	$ 100 per purchase order
Delivery	Batch level	100,800	1,260 deliveries	80 per delivery
Shelf-stocking	Unit level	69,120	3,456 hours stocking	20 per hour stocking
Customer support	Unit level	122,880	614,400 items sold	0.20 per item sold

Store support costs for each product line by activity are obtained by multiplying the total quantity of the cost allocation base for each product line by the activity cost rate. Operating income for each product line is as follows:

	Soft Drinks	Fresh Produce	Packaged Food	Total
Revenue	$317,400	$840,240	$ 483,960	$1,641,600
Cost of goods sold	240,000	600,000	360,000	1,200,000
Bottle-return costs	4,800	–	–	4,800
Ordering costs (144; 336; 144) PO × $100	14,400	33,600	14,400	62,400
Delivery costs (120; 876; 264) del. × $80	9,600	70,080	21,120	100,800
Shelf-stocking costs (216; 2,160; 1,080) hr × $20	4,320	43,200	21,600	69,120
Customer support costs (50,400; 441,600; 122,400) items × $0.20	10,080	88,320	24,480	122,880
Total costs	283,200	835,200	441,600	1,560,000
Operating income	$ 34,200	$ 5,040	$ 42,360	$ 81,600
Operating margin (Operating income ÷ Revenue)	10.78%	0.60%	8.75%	4.97%

3. Managers believe the ABC system is more credible than the previous costing system. It distinguishes the different types of activities at FS more precisely. It also tracks more accurately how individual product lines use their resources. Rankings of relative profitability (the percentage of operating income to revenues) of the three product lines under the previous costing system and under the ABC system are as follows:

Simple Costing System		ABC System	
1. Fresh produce	7.17%	1. Soft drinks	10.78%
2. Packaged food	3.30	2. Packaged food	8.75
3. Soft drinks	1.70	3. Fresh produce	0.60

The percentage of revenues, cost of goods sold, and activity costs for each product line are as follows:

	Soft Drinks	Fresh Produce	Packaged Food
Revenue	19.335%	51.184%	29.481%
Cost of goods sold	20.000	50.000	30.000
Bottle-return costs	100.000	0.000	0.000
Ordering costs	23.077	53.846	23.077
Delivery costs	9.524	69.524	20.952
Shelf-stocking costs	6.250	62.500	31.250
Customer support costs	8.203	71.875	19.922

Soft drinks consume less of all resources. Soft drinks have fewer deliveries and require less shelf-stocking than does either fresh produce or packaged food. Most major soft-drink suppliers deliver merchandise to the store shelves and stock the shelves themselves. In contrast, the fresh produce area has the most deliveries and consumes a large percentage of shelf-stocking time. It also has the highest number of individual sales items. The previous costing system assumed that each product line used the resources in each activity area in the same ratio as their respective individual cost of goods sold to total cost of goods sold ratio. Clearly, this assumption was inappropriate. The previous costing system was a classic example of broad averaging via cost smoothing.

FS managers can use the ABC information to guide decisions on how to allocate the planned increase in floor space. An increase in the percentage of space allocated to soft drinks is warranted. Note, however, that ABC information should be but one input into decisions about shelf space allocation. FS may have minimum limits on the shelf space allocated to fresh produce because of shoppers' expectations that supermarkets will carry merchandise from this product line.

Pricing decisions can also be made in a more informed way with the ABC information. For example, suppose a competitor announces a 5% reduction in soft-drink prices. Given the 10.78% margin FS currently earns on its soft-drink product line, it has flexibility to reduce prices and still make a profit on this product line. In contrast, the previous costing system erroneously implied that soft drinks only had a 1.70% margin, leaving little room to counter a competitor's pricing initiatives.

Decision Points

The following question-and-answer format summarizes the chapter's learning objectives. Each point presents a key question, and the guidelines are the answer to that question.

Learning Objectives	Guidelines
1. When does product undercosting or product overcosting occur?	Product undercosting (overcosting) occurs when a product or service consumes a high (low) level of shared support activities but is reported to have a low (high) cost. Traditional, or peanut butter, costing is a common cause of under- or overcosting. This method uniformly assigns costs based on a simple average for all products. It is not effective when products obtain unequal benefit from unequal use of shared inputs common to complete distinct types of products. Product cost cross-subsidization exists when one undercosted (overcosted) product results in at least one other product being overcosted (undercosted).
2. How does traditional cost assignment differ from the activities cost hierarchy?	The activities cost hierarchy separates a single total indirect cost pool into as many as four "chunks" according to the scope of benefits from the activity. From smallest scope of activity to largest, the units are output level, batch level, product level, and facilities level. Traditional costing separates costs into manufacturing and non-manufacturing cost pools without regard to the scope of benefits.
3. How are cost assignment systems refined using ABC?	The refinement of cost assignment systems should only be undertaken when shared inputs give rise to indirect costs that are both significant relative to total costs and not used equally to complete a distinct type of output unit. Managers identify activities and their scope of benefits, and identify a measure of benefit from the activity common throughout its scope. The measure is called an *activity cost driver*. It reliably explains how the total activity cost pool changes when the quantity of the cost driver changes.
4. How are costs assigned using ABC?	Once the indirect activity cost pools and measures of the activity cost drivers are identified, an activity cost driver rate can be calculated. For activity cost pools at the batch, product, and facilities levels, calculating the activity cost driver rates is an intermediate step that allows costs to be assigned per batch or product or facility. The final step is to assign costs per batch, product, or facility to each unit of a distinct output.
5. How can ABC systems be used to manage better?	ABM describes management decisions based on ABC information to satisfy customers and improve profits. ABC systems are used for such management decisions as pricing, product-mix, cost reduction, process improvement, product and process redesign, and planning and managing activities.

Terms to Learn

This chapter and the Glossary at the end of the book contain definitions of the following important terms:

activity **(p. 141)**

activity-based costing (ABC) **(p. 146)**

activity-based management (ABM)
  (p. 154)

batch-level costs **(p. 149)**

cost hierarchy **(p. 149)**

facility-sustaining cost **(p. 149)**

non-value-added activities **(p. 155)**

output unit-level cost **(p. 149)**

peanut butter costing **(p. 141)**

product-cost cross-subsidization
  (p. 142)

product overcosting **(p. 141)**

product undercosting **(p. 141)**

product-sustaining cost **(p. 149)**

service-sustaining cost **(p. 149)**

value-added activities **(p. 155)**

Assignment Material

MyLab Accounting Make the grade with MyLab Accounting: The Short-Answer Questions, Exercises, and Problems marked with a ⊕ can be found on MyLab Accounting. You can practise them as often as you want, and most feature step-by-step guided instructions to help you find the right answer.

Short-Answer Questions

⊕ **5-1** Define cost smoothing, and describe the consequences it can have on costs.

⊕ **5-2** Why should managers worry about product overcosting or undercosting?

⊕ **5-3** What is costing system refinement? Describe three guidelines for such refinement.

⊕ **5-4** What is an activity-based approach to refining a cost assignment system?

⊕ **5-5** Describe four levels of a cost hierarchy.

⊕ **5-6** Why is it important to classify costs into a cost hierarchy?

⊕ **5-7** What are the key reasons for product cost differences between traditional costing systems and ABC systems?

⊕ **5-8** Describe four decisions for which ABC information is useful.

⊕ **5-9** "Department indirect cost rates are never activity cost rates." Do you agree? Explain.

⊕ **5-10** Describe four ways that help indicate when ABC systems are likely to provide the most benefits.

⊕ **5-11** What are the main costs and limitations of implementing ABC systems?

⊕ **5-12** "ABC systems apply only to manufacturing companies." Do you agree? Explain.

⊕ **5-13** "ABC is the wave of the present and the future. All companies should adopt it." Do you agree? Explain.

⊕ **5-14** "Increasing the number of indirect cost pools is guaranteed to sizably increase the accuracy of product or service costs." Do you agree? Why?

⊕ **5-15** The controller of a retailer has just had a $50,000 request to implement an ABC system quickly turned down. A senior vice-president involved in rejecting the request noted, "Given a choice, I will always prefer a $50,000 investment in improving things a customer sees or experiences, such as our shelves or our store layout. How does a customer benefit by our spending $50,000 on a supposedly better accounting system?" How should the controller respond?

Exercises

⊕ **5-16 Terminology.**

activity-based costing (ABC) system	batch	activity cost driver
activity cost pools	output	cross-subsidization
non-value-added activity	peanut butter	product (or service)
refinement	value-added activity	facility sustaining
activity-based management (ABM)	cost plus	

Required

Select the terms from the above list to complete the following sentences.

One common _____ to a traditional or _____ costing system is called an _____. The single manufacturing overhead cost pool is separated into different _____ distinguished from one another by their measure of benefits provided, or the _____. Benefits provided unequally to distinct types of outputs provide value added to customers, for which customers are willing to pay. This is the basic concept that guides the approach to cost reduction and control called _____. The management team identifies and eliminates _____ and its costs and reorganizes the _____ to minimize costs. There are four levels of activities in a cost hierarchy. From narrowest to broadest in scope they are _____, _____, _____ (or _____), and _____ cost.

When a management team fails to develop a cost management system that reports faithfully the unequal benefits (and costs) of value-added activities, there is a high risk of mispricing distinct types of outputs. If managers use _____ pricing, an overcosted output will be priced too high and an undercosted product will be priced too low relative to the economic value added. The result is preventable of _____ costs of the lower-priced by the higher-priced product.

⊕ **5-17 Cost hierarchy.** Teledor Inc. manufactures boomboxes (music systems with radio, MP3, and compact disc players) for different well-known companies. The boomboxes differ significantly in their complexity and the batch sizes in which they are manufactured. The following costs were incurred in 2018: ◀ LO 2, 3

a. Indirect manufacturing labour costs such as supervision that supports direct manufacturing labour, $1,500,000.
b. Procurement costs of placing purchase orders, receiving materials, and paying suppliers that are related to the number of purchase orders placed, $800,000.
c. Cost of indirect materials, $450,000.
d. Costs incurred to set up machines each time a different product needs to be manufactured, $900,000.
e. Designing processes, drawing process charts, making engineering process changes for products, $900,000.
f. Machine-related overhead costs such as depreciation, maintenance, production engineering, $1,200,000. These resources are related to the activity of running the machines.
g. Plant management, plant rent, and insurance, $950,000.

Required

1. Classify each of the preceding costs as output unit-level, batch-level, product-sustaining, or facility-sustaining. Explain your answers.
2. Consider two boomboxes made by Teledor Inc. One boombox is complex to make and is made in many small batches. The other boombox is simple to make and is made in a few large batches. Suppose that Teledor needs the same number of machine-hours to make either boombox. If Teledor allocated all overhead costs using machine-hours as the only allocation base, how, if at all, would the boomboxes be miscosted? Briefly explain why.
3. How is the cost hierarchy helpful to Teledor in managing its business?

⊕ **5-18 Plant-wide, department, and activity-cost rates.** Acclaim Inc. makes two styles of trophies, basic and deluxe, and operates at capacity. Acclaim does large custom orders. Acclaim budgets to produce 10,000 basic trophies and 5,000 deluxe trophies. Manufacturing takes place in two production departments: forming and assembly. In the forming department, indirect manufacturing costs are accumulated in two cost pools, setup and general overhead. In the assembly department, all indirect manufacturing costs are accumulated in one general overhead cost pool. The basic trophies are formed in batches of 200 but because of the more intricate detail of the deluxe trophies, they are formed in batches of 50. ◀ LO 2, 3
Budgeted general overhead rate = $1 per direct manuf. Labour dollar

The controller has asked you to compare plant-wide, department, and activity-based cost allocation.

Acclaim Budgeted Information for the Year Ended November 30, 2017

Forming Department	Basic	Deluxe	Total
Direct materials	$60,000	$35,000	$95,000
Direct manufacturing labour	30,000	20,000	50,000
Overhead costs			
Setup			48,000
General overhead			32,000

Assembly Department	Basic	Deluxe	Total
Direct materials	$5,000	$10,000	$15,000
Direct manufacturing labour	15,000	25,000	40,000
Overhead costs			
General overhead			40,000

Required

1. Calculate the budgeted unit cost of basic and deluxe trophies based on a single plant-wide overhead rate, if total overhead is allocated based on total direct costs. (Don't forget to include direct material and direct manufacturing labour cost in your unit cost calculation.)

2. Calculate the budgeted unit cost of basic and deluxe trophies based on departmental overhead rates, where forming department overhead costs are allocated based on direct manufacturing labour costs of the forming department and assembly department overhead costs are allocated based on total direct manufacturing labour costs of the assembly department.

3. Calculate the budgeted unit cost of basic and deluxe trophies if Acclaim allocates overhead costs in each department using activity-based costing, where setup costs are allocated based on number of batches and general overhead costs for each department are allocated based on direct manufacturing labour costs of each department.

4. Explain briefly why plant-wide, department, and activity-based costing systems show different costs for the basic and deluxe trophies. Which system would you recommend and why?

LO 3 ▶

1. $6 per machine hour

🌐 **5-19 Apply the logic of an ABC cost hierarchy.** Huey Parker produces mathematical and financial calculators. Data related to the two products are presented below.

	Mathematical	Financial
Annual production in units	50,000	100,000
Direct materials costs	$180,000	$360,000
Direct manufacturing labour costs	$60,000	$150,000
Direct manufacturing labour-hours	2,500	5,000
Machine-hours	35,000	40,000
Number of production runs	50	50
Inspection hours	1,000	500

Both products pass through Department 1 and Department 2. The departments' combined manufacturing overhead costs are

Costs	Total
Machining	$450,000
Setup	144,000
Inspection	126,000

Required

1. Compute the manufacturing overhead cost for each product.
2. Compute the manufacturing cost for each product.

LO 2, 3 ▶

2. Total variable MOH, $308,600

🌐 **5-20 Plantwide indirect cost rates.** Car Parts (CP) designs, manufactures, and sells automotive parts. Actual variable manufacturing overhead costs for 2018 were $308,600. CP's simple costing system allocates variable manufacturing overhead to its three customers based on machine-hours and prices its contracts based on full costs. One of its customers has regularly complained of being charged noncompetitive prices, so CP's controller, Devon Smith, realizes that it is time to examine the consumption of resources more closely. CP has three main operating departments: design, engineering, and production.

- Design—the design of parts, using state-of-the-art, computer-aided design (CAD) equipment
- Engineering—the prototyping of parts and testing of their specifications
- Production—the manufacture of parts

Interviews with the department personnel and examination of time records yield the following detailed information:

Department	Cost Driver	Variable MOH in 2018	Use of Cost Drivers by Customer		
			United Motors	Holden Motors	Leland Motors
Design	CAD design-hours	$ 39,000	110	200	80
Engineering	Engineering-hours	29,600	70	60	240
Production	Machine-hours	240,000	120	2,800	1,080
Total		$308,600			

Required

1. Using the simple costing system, compute the plantwide variable manufacturing overhead rate for 2018 and the variable manufacturing overhead allocated to each contract in 2018.
2. Compute the variable manufacturing overhead rate for 2018 and the variable manufacturing overhead allocated to each contract in 2018 using department-based variable overhead rates.
3. Comment on your answers in requirements 1 and 2. Which customer do you think was complaining about being overcharged in the simple system? If the new department-based rates are used to price contracts, which customer(s) will be unhappy? How would you respond to these concerns?
4. How else might CP use the information available from its department-by-department analysis of variable manufacturing overhead costs?
5. CP's managers are wondering if they should further refine the department-by-department costing system into an ABC system by identifying different activities within each department. Under what conditions would it not be worthwhile to further refine the department costing system into an ABC system?

⊕ **5-21 ABC, process costing.** Sander Company produces mathematical and financial calculators and operates at capacity. Data related to the two products are presented here:

◀ **LO 4**
Inspection costs $65 per inspection hour

	Mathematical	Financial
Annual production in units	45,000	90,000
Direct material costs	$180,000	$360,000
Direct manufacturing labour costs	$ 90,000	$180,000
Direct manufacturing labour-hours	4,500	9,000
Machine-hours	30,000	60,000
Number of production runs	45	45
Inspection hours	1,200	600

Total manufacturing overhead costs are as follows:

	Total
Machining costs	$360,000
Setup costs	108,000
Inspection costs	117,000

Required

1. Choose a cost driver for each overhead cost pool and calculate the manufacturing overhead cost per unit for each product.
2. Compute the manufacturing cost per unit for each product.
3. How might Sander's managers use the new cost information from its activity-based costing system to better manage its business?

⊕ **5-22 Explain undercosting and overcosting of services.** The Wolfson Group (WG) provides tax advice to multinational firms. WG charges clients for (a) direct professional time (at an hourly rate) and (b) support services (at 30% of the direct professional costs billed). The three professionals in WG and their rates per professional hour are as follows:

◀ **LO 1**
1. WG amount billed to Tokyo Enterprises, $7,322

Professional	Billing Rate per Hour
Myron Wolfson	$800
Naomi Ku	144
John Anderson	96

WG has just prepared the May 2018 bills for two clients. The hours of professional time spent on each client are as follows:

	Hours per Client	
Professional	**Winnipeg Dominion**	**Tokyo Enterprises**
Wolfson	15	2
Ku	3	8
Anderson	22	30
Total	40	40

Required

1. What amounts did WG bill to Winnipeg Dominion and Tokyo Enterprises for May 2018?
2. Suppose support services were billed at $60 per professional labour-hour (instead of 30% of professional labour costs). How would this change affect the amounts WG billed to the two clients for May 2018? Comment on the differences between the amounts billed in requirements 1 and 2.
3. How would you determine whether professional labour costs or professional labour-hours are the more appropriate allocation base for WG's support services?

LO 2 ▷

Costs of designing tests = $60 / hour

⊕ **5-23 ABC, cost hierarchy, service.** (CMA, adapted) Vineyard Test Laboratories does heat testing (HT) and stress testing (ST) on materials and operates at capacity. Under its current simple costing system, Vineyard aggregates all operating costs of $1,190,000 into a single overhead cost pool. Vineyard calculates a rate per test-hour of $17 ($1,190,000 ÷ 70,000 total test-hours). HT uses 40,000 test-hours, and ST uses 30,000 test-hours. Gary Celeste, Vineyard's controller, believes that there is enough variation in test procedures and cost structures to establish separate costing and billing rates for HT and ST. The market for test services is becoming competitive. Without this information, any miscosting and mispricing of its services could cause Vineyard to lose business. Celeste divides Vineyard's costs into four activity-cost categories.

a. Direct-labour costs, $146,000. These costs can be directly traced to HT, $100,000, and ST, $46,000.
b. Equipment-related costs (rent, maintenance, energy, and so on), $350,000. These costs are allocated to HT and ST on the basis of test-hours.
c. Setup costs, $430,000. These costs are allocated to HT and ST on the basis of the number of setup-hours required. HT requires 13,600 setup-hours, and ST requires 3,600 setup-hours.
d. Costs of designing tests, $264,000. These costs are allocated to HT and ST on the basis of the time required for designing the tests. HT requires 3,000 hours, and ST requires 1,400 hours.

Required

1. Classify each activity cost as output unit–level, batch-level, product- or service-sustaining, or facility-sustaining. Explain each answer.
2. Calculate the cost per test-hour for HT and ST. Explain briefly the reasons why these numbers differ from the $17 per test-hour that Vineyard calculated using its simple costing system.
3. Explain the accuracy of the product costs calculated using the simple costing system and the ABC system. How might Vineyard's management use the cost hierarchy and ABC information to better manage its business?

LO 4, 5 ▷

1. Overall cost, $15,600 per student

⊕ **5-24 Allocation of costs to activities, unused capacity.** Heights Academy, a private school, serves 500 students: 200 in the middle school (Grades 6 to 8) and 300 in the high school (Grades 9 to 12). Each school group has its own assistant principal, and there is one principal, Brian Smith, for the academy. For any single student, almost all of Heights's costs are indirect. Heights currently has five indirect cost categories, which are listed in the following table. Smith wants to develop an ABC system for the school. He identifies four activities—academic instruction, administration, sports training, and community relationships—related to the educational enterprise.

Smith and his team identify the number of students as the cost driver of academic instruction and administration costs, and the number of team sports offered by the school as the driver of sports training costs. The cost of maintaining community relationships—dealing with the town council and participating in local activities—is a facility-sustaining cost that the school has to incur each year. The table shows the percentage of costs in each line item used by each activity.

Percentage of Costs Used by Each Activity

Indirect Cost	Academic Instruction	Administration	Sports Training	Community Relationships	2018 Expenditures
Teachers' salaries/benefits	60%	20%	8%	12%	$4,000,000
Principals' salaries and benefits	10	60	5	25	400,000
Facilities	35	15	45	5	2,600,000
Office staff salaries and benefits	5	60	10	25	300,000
Sports program staff salaries and benefits	35	10	45	10	500,000

Required

1. What is the overall cost of educating each student? Of this cost, what percentage is the cost of academic instruction? Of administration?

2. Smith is dismayed at the high cost of sports training. Further examination reveals that $300,000 of those costs are for ice hockey, a sport pursued by a total of 40 students. What would be the overall cost of educating each student if the ice hockey program is eliminated and its cost saved?

3. For the 2019 school year, Heights charges an annual fee of $1,000 for any student who wants to play ice hockey. As a result, 10 of the less-motivated students drop the sport. Assuming the costs of the school in 2019 are the same as in 2018, what is the overall cost of educating each student in 2019?

4. Consider the costs of the academic instruction activity, and assume they are fixed in the short run. At these costs, Heights could serve 600 students. What is the cost of the academic instruction resources used by Heights's current 500 students? What is the cost of unused academic instruction capacity? What actions can Smith take to reduce the cost of academic instruction per student in the short run? In the long run?

🌐 **5-25 Special order, activity-based costing.** (CMA, adapted) The Medal Plus Company manufactures medals for winners of athletic events and other contests. Its manufacturing plant has the capacity to produce 12,000 medals each month; current production and sales are 9,000 medals per month. The company normally charges $200 per medal. Cost information for the current activity level is as follows:

◀ **LO 5**
1. Operating income increase, $190,000

Variable costs (vary with units produced):	
Direct materials	$ 360,000
Direct labour	405,000
Variable costs (vary with number of batches): Setups, materials handling, quality control	126,000*
Fixed manufacturing costs	325,000
Fixed marketing costs	224,000
Total costs	$1,440.000

*Costs of $126,000 are based on 180 batches at $700 per batch.

Medal Plus has just received a special one-time-only order for 2,500 medals at $168 per medal. Accepting the special order would not affect the company's regular business. Medal Plus makes medals for its existing customers in batch sizes of 50 medals (180 batches × 50 medals per batch = 9,000 medals). The special order requires Medal Plus to make the medals in 25 batches of 100 each.

Required

1. Should Medal Plus accept this special order? Explain briefly.

2. Suppose plant capacity was only 10,000 medals instead of 12,000 medals each month. The special order must either be taken in full or rejected totally. Should Medal Plus accept the special order?

3. As in requirement 1, assume that monthly capacity is 12,000 medals. Medal Plus is concerned that if it accepts the special order, its existing customers will immediately demand a price discount of $11 in the month in which the special order is being filled. They would argue that Medal Plus's capacity costs are now being spread over more units and that existing customers should get the benefit of these lower costs. Should Medal Plus accept the special order under these conditions? Show all calculations.

🌐 **5-26 ABC, wholesale, customer profitability.** Veritek Wholesalers operates at capacity and sells furniture items to four department-store chains (customers). Mr. Veritek commented, "We apply ABC to determine product-line profitability. The same ideas apply to customer profitability, and we should find out our customer profitability as well." Veritek Wholesalers sends catalogs to corporate purchasing departments on a monthly basis. The customers are entitled to return unsold merchandise within a six-month

◀ **LO 4**
Customer 1 profitability is 8.2%

period from the purchase date and receive a full purchase price refund. The following data were collected from last year's operations:

	Customer			
	1	**2**	**3**	**4**
Gross sales	$40,000	$20,000	$110,000	$95,000
Sales returns:				
Number of items	96	24	64	32
Amount	$ 8,000	$ 3,000	$ 7,700	$ 9,000
Number of orders:				
Regular	30	140	55	100
Rush	8	46	12	45

Veritek has calculated the following activity rates:

Activity	Cost-Driver Rate
Regular order processing	$30 per regular order
Rush order processing	$150 per rush order
Returned items processing	$15 per item
Catalogs and customer support	$1,200 per customer

Required
Customers pay the transportation costs. The cost of goods sold averages 75% of sales.
Determine the contribution to profit from each customer last year. Comment on your solution.

LO 4 ▶
Chain 1 contribution to profit,
$3,200

⊕ **5-27 ABC, wholesale, customer profitability.** Ames Wholesalers sells furniture items to four department-store chains. Sharon Ames commented, "We apply ABC to determine profit line profitability. The same ideas apply to customer profitability, and we should find out our customer profitability as well." Ames Wholesalers sends catalogues to the corporate purchasing departments on a monthly basis. The customers are entitled to return unsold merchandise within a six-month period from the purchase date and receive a full purchase-price refund. The following data were collected from last year's operations:

	Chain 1	**Chain 2**	**Chain 3**	**Chain 4**
Gross sales	$50,000	$30,000	$100,000	$70,000
Sales returns:				
Number of items	100	26	60	40
Amount	$10,000	$ 5,000	$ 7,000	$ 6,000
Number of orders:				
Regular	40	150	50	70
Rush	10	50	10	30

Ames has calculated the following activity rates:

Activity	Cost Driver Rate
Regular order processing	$ 20 per regular order
Rush order processing	100 per rush order
Returned items processing	20 per item
Catalogues and customer support	1,000 per customer

Required
Determine the contribution to profit from each chain last year. Cost of goods sold is 70% of net sales. Comment on your solution.

🌐 **5-28 ABC, retail product-line profitability.** Fitzgerald Supermarkets (FS) operates at capacity and decides to apply ABC analysis to three product lines: baked goods, milk and fruit juice, and frozen foods. It identifies four activities and their activity cost rates as follows:

◀ LO 4
1. Baked Goods Operating Income is $6,700

Ordering	$95 per purchase order
Delivery and receipt of merchandise	$76 per delivery
Shelf-stocking	$19 per hour
Customer support and assistance	$ 0.15 per item sold

The revenues, cost of goods sold, store support costs, activities that account for the store support costs, and activity-area usage of the three product lines are as follows:

	Baked Goods	Milk and Fruit Juice	Frozen Products
Financial data			
Revenues	$60,000	$66,500	$50,500
Cost of goods sold	$41,000	$51,000	$32,000
Store support	$12,300	$15,300	$ 9,600
Activity-area usage (cost-allocation base)			
Ordering (purchase orders)	44	24	14
Delivery (deliveries)	120	60	36
Shelf-stocking (hours)	170	150	20
Customer support (items sold)	15,400	20,200	7,960

Under its simple costing system, FS allocated support costs to products at the rate of 30% of cost of goods sold.

Required

1. Use the simple costing system to prepare a product-line profitability report for FS.
2. Use the ABC system to prepare a product-line profitability report for FS.
3. What new insights does the ABC system in requirement 2 provide to FS managers?

🌐 **5-29 ABC, product costing at banks, cross-subsidization.** International Trust (IT) is examining the profitability of its Premier Account, a combined savings and chequing account. Depositors receive a 6% annual interest rate on their average deposit. IT earns an interest rate spread of 2.5% (the difference between the rate at which it lends money and the rate it pays depositors) by lending money for residential home loan purposes at 8.5%. Thus, IT would gain $250 on the interest spread if a depositor had an average Premier Account balance of $10,000 in 2018 ($10,000 × 2.5% = $250).

◀ LO 4, 5
1. 2018 profitability of Robinson account, $321.90 operating loss

The Premier Account allows depositors unlimited use of services such as deposits, withdrawals, chequing account, and foreign currency drafts. Depositors with Premier Account balances of $2,500 or more receive unlimited free use of services. Depositors with minimum balances of less than $2,500 pay a $35 monthly service fee for their Premier Account.

IT recently conducted an ABC study of its services. It assessed the following costs for six individual services. The use of these services in 2018 by three Premier Account customers is as follows:

	ABC Cost per Transaction	Account Usage		
		Robinson	Skerrett	Farrel
Deposits/withdrawals with teller	$ 4.00	45	55	10
Deposits/withdrawals at ATM	1.20	12	24	18
Prearranged monthly deposit/withdrawal	0.80	0	15	60
Cheques written	11.25	10	5	4
Foreign currency drafts	12.50	4	1	7
Account balance inquiries	2.50	12	20	11
Average cash balance		$2,600	$1,200	$40,000

Assume Robinson and Farrel always maintain a balance above $2,500 while Skerrett always has a balance below $2,500 in 2018.

Required

1. Compute the 2018 profitability of the Robinson, Skerrett, and Farrell Premier Accounts at IT.
2. What evidence is there of cross-subsidization across Premier Accounts? Why might IT worry about this cross-subsidization if the Premier Account product offering is profitable as a whole?
3. What changes at IT would you recommend for its Premier Account?

LO 3 ▶
Shipping Costs are
$365 per batch

5-30 Choosing cost drivers, activity-based costing, activity-based management. Pastel Bags (PB) is a designer of high-quality backpacks and purses. Each design is made in small batches. Each spring, PB comes out with new designs for the backpack and for the purse. The company uses these designs for a year and then moves on to the next trend. The bags are all made on the same fabrication equipment that is expected to operate at capacity. The equipment must be switched over to a new design and set up to prepare for the production of each new batch of products. When completed, each batch of products is immediately shipped to a wholesaler. Shipping costs vary with the number of shipments. Budgeted information for the year is as follows:

Pastel Bags
Budget for Costs and Activities
For the Year Ended February 28, 2017

Direct materials—purses	$ 319,155
Direct materials—backpacks	454,995
Direct manufacturing labour—purses	99,000
Direct manufacturing labour—backpacks	113,000
Setup	64,000
Shipping	73,000
Design	169,000
Plant utilities and administration	221,000
Total	$1,513,150

Other budget information follows:

	Backpacks	Purses	Total
Number of bags	6,175	3,075	9,250
Hours of production	1,665	2,585	4,250
Number of batches	120	80	200
Number of designs	2	2	4

Required

1. Identify the cost hierarchy level for each cost category.
2. Identify the most appropriate cost driver for each cost category. Explain briefly your choice of cost driver.
3. Calculate the budgeted cost per unit of cost driver for each cost category.
4. Calculate the budgeted total costs and cost per unit for each product line.
5. Explain how you could use the information in requirement 4 to reduce costs.

Problems

LO 3 ▶
2. Widnes Coal costs, $18,200

5-31 Job costing with single direct-cost category, single indirect-cost pool, law firm. Marc and Associates is a recently formed law partnership. The managing partner of Marc and Associates has just finished a tense phone call with the president of Widnes Coal, who complained about the price charged for some legal work done for Widnes Coal. At the same time, a different client call (St. Helen's Glass) confirmed the client was very pleased with both the quality of the work and the price charged on its most recent case.

Marc and Associates operates at capacity and uses a cost-based approach to pricing (billing) each job. Currently it uses a single direct-cost category (for professional labour-hours) and a single indirect-cost pool (general support). Indirect costs are allocated to cases on the basis of professional labour-hours per case. The case files show the following:

	Widnes Coal	St. Helen's Glass
Professional labour	104 hours	96 hours

Professional labour costs at Marc and Associates are $70 an hour. Indirect costs are allocated to cases at $105 an hour. Total indirect costs in the most recent period were $21,000.

Required

1. Why is it important for Marc and Associates to understand the costs associated with individual cases?
2. Compute the costs of the Widnes Coal and St. Helen's Glass cases using Marc and Associates' simple costing system.

🌐 **5-32 Job costing with multiple direct-cost categories, single indirect-cost pool, law firm** (continuation of 5-31). Hanley asks his assistant to collect details on those costs included in the $21,000 indirect-cost pool that can be traced to each individual case. After further analysis, Marc and Associates is able to reclassify $14,000 of the $21,000 as direct costs:

◀ **LO 4**

1. Revised indirect cost: allocation rate, $35 per professional labour-hour

Other Direct Costs	Widnes Coal	St. Helen's Glass
Research support labour	$1,600	$ 3,400
Computer time	500	1,300
Travel and allowances	600	4,400
Telephones/faxes	200	1,000
Photocopying	250	750
Total	$3,150	$10,850

Hanley decides to calculate the costs of each case had Marc and Associates used six direct-cost pools and a single indirect-cost pool. The single indirect-cost pool would have $7,000 of costs and would be allocated to each case using the professional labour-hours base.

Required

1. What is the revised indirect cost allocation rate per professional labour-hour for Marc and Associates when total indirect costs are $7,000?
2. Compute the costs of the Widnes and St. Helen's cases if Marc and Associates had used its refined costing system with multiple direct-cost categories and one indirect-cost pool.
3. Compare the costs of the Widnes and St. Helen's cases in requirement 2 with those in requirement 2 of Problem 5-31. Comment on the results.

🌐 **5-33 Job costing with multiple direct-cost categories, multiple indirect-cost pools, law firm** (continuation of 5-31 and 5-32). Marc and Associates has two classifications of professional staff—partners and managers. Hanley asks his assistant to examine the relative use of partners and managers on the recent Widnes Coal and St. Helen's cases. The Widnes case used 24 partner-hours and 80 manager-hours. The St. Helen's case used 56 partner-hours and 40 manager-hours.

◀ **LO 5**

Widnes Coal costs to be billed, $12,530

Hanley decides to examine how the use of separate direct-cost and indirect-cost pools for partners and managers would have affected the costs of the Widnes and St. Helen's cases. Indirect costs in each cost pool would be allocated based on total hours of that category of professional labour.

The rates per category of professional labour are as follows:

Category of Professional Labour	Direct Cost per Hour	Calculation	Indirect Cost per Hour
Partner	$100.00	$4,600/80 hours	$57.50
Manager	$ 50.00	$2,400/120 hours	$20.00

Required

Compute the costs of the Widnes and St. Helen's cases with Marc and Associates further refined system, with multiple direct-cost categories and multiple indirect-cost pools.

🌐 **5-34 Contrast the logic of two cost assignment systems.** Halifax Test Laboratories does heat testing (HT) and stress testing (ST) on materials. Under its current costing system, Halifax aggregates all operating costs of $1,440,000 into a single overhead cost pool. Halifax calculates a rate per test-hour of $18 (= $1,440,000 ÷ 80,000 total test-hours). HT uses 50,000 test-hours and ST uses 30,000 test-hours. Gary Celeste, Halifax's controller, believes that there is enough variation in test procedures and cost structures to establish separate costing and billing rates. The market for test services is very competitive, and without this information, any miscosting and mispricing could cause Halifax to lose business. Celeste breaks down Halifax's costs into four activity-cost categories.

◀ **LO 2**

2. Cost of heat testing, $20.16 per hour

1. Direct labour costs, $288,000. These costs can be directly traced to HT, $216,000, and ST, $72,000.
2. Equipment-related costs (rent, maintenance, energy, and so on), $480,000. These costs are allocated to HT and ST based on test-hours.

3. Setup costs, $420,000. These costs are allocated to HT and ST based on the number of setup-hours required. HT requires 13,500 setup-hours and ST requires 4,000 setup-hours.
4. Costs of designing tests, $252,000. These costs are allocated to HT and ST based on the time required to design the tests. HT requires 2,800 hours and ST requires 1,400 hours.

Required

1. Classify each of the activity costs as output unit-level, batch-level, product- or service-sustaining, or facility-sustaining. Explain your answers.
2. Calculate the cost per test-hour for HT and ST using ABC. Explain briefly the reasons why these numbers differ from the $18 per test-hour that Halifax had calculated using its existing costing system.
3. Explain the cost differences and the accuracy of the product costs calculated using the existing and the ABC systems. How might Halifax's management use the cost hierarchy and ABC information to manage its business better?

LO 5 ▶

1. Operating margin percentage for baked goods, 13.33%

⊕ **5-35 Use ABC systems for ABM.** Family Supermarkets (FS) found that its ABC analysis (see the Pulling It All Together problem in this chapter) provided important insights. FS extends the analysis to cover three more product lines: baked goods, milk and fruit juice, and frozen products. It identifies four activities and activity cost rates for each activity as

Ordering	$120 per purchase order
Delivery and receipt of merchandise	96 per delivery
Shelf-stocking	24 per hour
Customer support and assistance	0.24 per item sold

The revenues, cost of goods sold, store support costs, and activity area usage of the three product lines are as follows:

	Baked Goods	Milk and Fruit Juice	Frozen Products
Financial data:			
Revenues	$78,400	$85,600	$72,400
Cost of goods sold	45,600	56,400	42,000
Store support	13,680	16,920	12,600
Activity area usage (cost driver):			
Ordering (purchase orders)	30	25	13
Delivery (deliveries)	98	36	28
Shelf-stocking (hours)	183	166	24
Customer support (items sold)	15,500	20,500	7,900

There are no bottle returns for any of these three product lines.

Required

1. Use the previous costing system (support costs allocated to products at the rate of 30% of cost of goods sold) to compute a product line profitability report for FS.
2. Use the ABC system (ordering at $120 per purchase order, delivery at $96 per delivery, shelf-stocking at $24 per hour, and customer support at $0.24 per item sold) to compute a product line profitability report for FS.
3. What new insights does the ABC system in requirement 2 provide to FS managers?

LO 4, 5 ▶

1. Budgeted cost for service, $56.16 per X-ray

⊕ **5-36 Department and activity cost rates, service sector.** Radhika's Radiology Centre (RRC) performs X-rays, ultrasounds, CT scans, and MRIs. RRC has developed a reputation as a top radiology centre in the area. RRC has achieved this status because it constantly re-examines its processes and procedures. RRC has been using a single, facility-wide overhead allocation rate. The VP of Finance believes that RRC can make better process improvements if it uses more disaggregated cost information. She says, "We have state-of-the-art medical imaging technology. Can't we have state-of-the-art accounting technology?"

The following budgeted information is available:

Radhika's Radiology Centre
Budgeted Information
For the Year Ending May 30, 2019

	X-Rays	Ultrasound	CT Scan	MRI	Total
Technician labour	$ 61,440	$105,600	$ 96,000	$ 105,000	$ 368,040
Depreciation	32,240	268,000	439,000	897,500	1,636,740
Materials	22,080	16,500	24,000	31,250	93,830
Administration					20,610
Maintenance					247,320
Sanitation					196,180
Utilities					134,350
Totals	$115,760	$390,100	$559,000	$1,033,750	$2,697,070
Number of procedures	3,840	4,400	3,000	2,500	
Minutes to clean after each procedure	5	5	15	35	
Minutes for each procedure	5	15	20	45	

RRC operates at capacity. The proposed allocation bases for overhead are as follows:

Administration	Number of procedures
Maintenance (including parts)	Capital cost of equipment (depreciation)
Sanitation	Total cleaning minutes
Utilities	Total procedure minutes

Required

1. Calculate the budgeted cost per service for X-rays, ultrasounds, CT scans, and MRIs using the direct technician labour as the cost allocation base.
2. Calculate the budgeted cost per service for X-rays, ultrasounds, CT scans, and MRIs if RRC allocated overhead costs using ABC.
3. Explain how the disaggregation of information could be helpful to RRC's intention to continuously improve its services.

⊕ **5-37 Activity-based costing, merchandising.** Pharmacare Inc. specializes in the distribution of pharmaceutical products. Pharmacare operates at capacity and has three main market segments:

◀ LO 5

1. General supermarket chains gross margin percentage, 2.91%

a. General supermarket chains
b. Drugstore chains
c. "Mom and Pop" single-store pharmacies

Rick Flair, the new controller of Pharmacare, reported the following data for August 2018:

	General Supermarket Chains	Drugstore Chains	"Mom and Pop" Single Stores	Total
Revenues	$3,708,000	$3,150,000	$1,980,000	$8,838,000
Cost of goods sold	3,600,000	3,000,000	1,800,000	8,400,000
Gross margin	$ 108,000	$ 150,000	$ 180,000	438,000
Other operating costs				301,080
Operating income				$ 136,920

For many years, Pharmacare has used gross margin percentage [(Revenue − Cost of goods sold) ÷ Revenue] to evaluate the relative profitability of its different groupings of customers (distribution outlets).

Flair recently attended a seminar on ABC and decides to consider using it at Pharmacare. Flair meets with all the key managers and many staff members. People generally agree that there are five key activity areas at Pharmacare:

Activity Area	Cost Driver
Order processing	Number of customer purchase orders
Line-item processing	Number of line items ordered by customers
Delivering to stores	Number of store deliveries
Cartons shipped to store	Number of cartons shipped
Stocking of customer store shelves	Hours of shelf-stocking

Each customer order consists of one or more line items. A line item represents a single product (such as Extra-Strength Tylenol Tablets). Each product line item is delivered in one or more separate cartons. Each store delivery entails the delivery of one or more cartons of products to a customer. Pharmacare's staff stacks cartons directly onto display shelves in customers' stores. Currently, there is no additional charge to the customer for shelf-stocking, and not all customers use Pharmacare for this activity. The level of each activity in the three market segments and the total cost incurred for each activity in 2018 are shown below:

Activity	General Supermarket Chains	Drugstore Chains	"Mom and Pop" Single Stores	Total Cost of Activity in 2018
Number of orders processed	140	360	1,500	$80,000
Number of line items ordered	1,960	4,320	15,000	63,840
Number of store deliveries made	120	360	1,000	71,000
Number of cartons shipped to stores	36,000	24,000	16,000	76,000
Shelf stocking (hours)	360	180	100	10,240

Required

1. Compute the August 2018 gross margin percentage for each of Pharmacare's three market segments.
2. Compute the August 2018 per-unit cost driver rate for each of the five activity areas.
3. Use the ABC information to allocate the $301,080 of "other operating costs" to each of the market segments. Compute the operating income for each market segment.
4. Comment on the results. What new insights are available with the activity-based information?

LO 4 ▶ ⊕ **5-38 Unused capacity, activity-based costing, activity-based management.** Archer Pro manufactures two models of sport bows, Basic and Deluxe, using a combination of machining and hand finishing. Machine setup costs are driven by the number of setups. Indirect manufacturing labour costs increase with direct manufacturing labour costs. Equipment and maintenance costs increase with the number of machine-hours, and facility rent is paid per square foot. Capacity of the facility is 10,000 square feet, and Archer Pro is using only 75% of this capacity. Archer Pro records the cost of unused capacity as a separate line item and not as a product cost. For the current year, Archer Pro has budgeted the following:

**Archer Pro Budgeted
Costs and Activities for the
Year Ended December 31, 2017**

Direct materials—Basic bows	$ 450,000
Direct materials—Deluxe bows	320,000
Direct manufacturing labour—Basic bows	155,000
Direct manufacturing labour—Deluxe bows	195,000
Indirect manufacturing labour costs	105,000
Machine setup costs	60,000
Equipment and maintenance costs	264,000
Facility rent	250,000
Total	$1799,000

Other budget information follows:

	Basic	Deluxe
Number of bows	10,000	5,000
Machine-hours	15,000	18,000
Number of setups	500	300
Square footage of production space used	4,000	3,500

Required

1. Calculate the cost per unit of each cost-allocation base.
2. What is the budgeted cost of unused capacity?
3. Calculate the budgeted total cost and the cost per unit for each model.
4. Why might excess capacity be beneficial for Archer Pro? What are some of the issues Archer Pro should consider before increasing production to use the space?

⊕ **5-39 Choosing cost drivers, activity-based costing, activity-based management.** Pumpkin Bags (PB) is a designer of high-quality backpacks and purses. Each design is made in small batches. Each spring, PB comes out with new designs for the backpack and for the purse. They use these designs for one year and then move on to the next trend. The bags are all made on the same fabrication equipment that is expected to operate at capacity. The equipment must be switched over to a new design and set up to prepare for the production of each new batch of products. When completed, each batch of products is immediately shipped to a wholesaler. Shipping costs vary with the number of shipments. Budgeted information for the year is as follows:

◄ **LO 4, 5**

3. Cost for setup, $320 per batch

Pumpkin Bags
Budgeted Costs and Activities
for the Year Ending February 28, 2019

Direct materials—purses	$ 362,000
Direct materials—backpacks	427,000
Direct labour—purses	98,000
Direct labour—backpacks	115,597
Setup	64,960
Shipping	72,065
Design	167,000
Plant utilities and administration	225,000
Total	$1,531,622

Other information:

	Backpacks	Purses	Total
Number of bags	6,000	3,150	9,150
Hours of production	1,560	2,600	4,160
Number of batches	133	70	203
Number of designs	3	2	5

Required

1. Identify the cost hierarchy level for each cost category.
2. Identify the most appropriate cost driver for each cost category. Explain briefly your choice of cost driver.
3. Calculate the cost per unit of cost driver for each cost category.
4. Calculate the total costs and cost per unit for each product line.
5. Explain how you could use the information in requirement 4 to reduce costs.

⊕ **5-40 Unused capacity, activity-based costing, activity-based management.** Zarson's Netballs is a manufacturer of high-quality basketballs and volleyballs. Setup costs are driven by the number of setups. Equipment and maintenance costs increase with the number of machine-hours, and lease rent

◄ **LO 5**

is paid per square foot. Capacity of the facility is 14,000 square feet, and Zarson is using only 80% of this capacity. Zarson records the cost of unused capacity as a separate line item and not as a product cost. The following is the budgeted information for Zarson:

Zarson's Netballs
Budgeted Costs and Activities
For the Year Ended December 31, 2017

Direct materials—basketballs	$ 168,100
Direct materials—volleyballs	303,280
Direct manufacturing labour—basketballs	111,800
Direct manufacturing labour—volleyballs	100,820
Setup	157,500
Equipment and maintenance costs	115,200
Lease rent	210,000
Total	$1,166,700

Other budget information follows:

	Basketballs	Volleyballs
Number of balls	58,000	85,000
Machine-hours	13,500	10,500
Number of setups	450	300
Square footage of production space used	3,200	8,000

Required

1. Calculate the budgeted cost per unit of cost driver for each indirect cost pool.
2. What is the budgeted cost of unused capacity?
3. What is the budgeted total cost and the cost per unit of resources used to produce (a) basketballs and (b) volleyballs?
4. Why might excess capacity be beneficial for Zarson? What are some of the issues Zarson should consider before increasing production to use the space?

LO 5 ▶   ⊕   **5-41 ABC, implementation, ethics.** (CMA, adapted) Plum Electronics, a division of Berry Corporation, manufactures two large-screen television models: the Mammoth, which has been produced since 2013 and sells for $990, and the Maximum, a newer model introduced in early 2015 that sells for $1,254. Based on the following income statement for the year ended November 30, 2017, senior management at Berry have decided to concentrate Plum's marketing resources on the Maximum model and to begin to phase out the Mammoth model because Maximum generates a much bigger operating income per unit.

Plum Electronics
Income Statement for the
Fiscal Year Ended November 30, 2017

	Mammoth	Maximum	Total
Revenues	$21,780,000	$5,016,000	$26,796,000
Cost of goods sold	13,794,000	3,511,200	17,305,200
Gross margin	7,986,000	1,504,800	9,490,800
Selling and administrative expense	6,413,000	1,075,800	7,488,800
Operating income	$ 1,573,000	$ 429,000	$ 2,002,000
Units produced and sold	22,000	4,000	
Operating income per unit sold	$71.50	$107.25	

Details for cost of goods sold for Mammoth and Maximum are as follows:

	Mammoth		Maximum	
	Total	**Per Unit**	**Total**	**Per Unit**
Direct materials	$ 5,033,600	$ 228.80	$2,569,600	$642.40
Direct manufacturing labour[a]	435,600	19.80	184,800	46.20
Machine costs[b]	3,484,800	158.40	316,800	79.20
Total direct costs	$ 8,954,000	$ 407.00	$3,071,200	$767.80
Manufacturing overhead costs[c]	$ 4,840,000	$ 220.00	$ 440,000	$110.00
Total cost of goods sold	$13,794,000	$ 627.00	$3,511,200	$877.80

[a] Mammoth requires 1.5 hours per unit and Maximum requires 3.5 hours per unit. The direct manufacturing labour cost is $13.20 per hour.
[b] Machine costs include lease costs of the machine, repairs, and maintenance. Mammoth requires 8 machine-hours per unit and Maximum requires 4 machine-hours per unit. The machine-hour rate is $19.80 per hour.
[c] Manufacturing overhead costs are allocated to products based on machine-hours at the rate of $27.50 per hour.

Plum's controller, Steve Jacobs, is advocating the use of activity-based costing and activity-based management and has gathered the following information about the company's manufacturing overhead costs for the year ended November 30, 2017.

		Units of the Cost-Allocation Base		
Activity Centre (Cost-Allocation Base)	**Total Activity Costs**	**Mammoth**	**Maximum**	**Total**
Soldering (number of solder points)	$1,036,200	1,185,000	385,000	1,570,000
Shipments (number of shipments)	946,000	16,200	3,800	20,000
Quality control (number of inspections)	1,364,000	56,200	21,300	77,500
Purchase orders (number of orders)	1,045,440	80,100	109,980	190,080
Machine power (machine-hours)	63,360	176,000	16,000	192,000
Machine setups (number of setups)	825,000	16,000	14,000	30,000
Total manufacturing overhead	$5,280,000			

After completing his analysis, Jacobs shows the results to Charles Clark, the Plum division president. Clark does not like what he sees. "If you show headquarters this analysis, they are going to ask us to phase out the Maximum line, which we have just introduced. This whole costing stuff has been a major problem for us. First Mammoth was not profitable and now Maximum."

"Looking at the ABC analysis, I see two problems. First, we do many more activities than the ones you have listed. If you had included all activities, maybe your conclusions would be different. Second, you used number of setups and number of inspections as allocation bases. The numbers would be different had you used setup-hours and inspection-hours instead. I know that measurement problems precluded you from using these other cost-allocation bases, but I believe you ought to make some adjustments to our current numbers to compensate for these issues. I know you can do better. We can't afford to phase out either product."

Jacobs knows that his numbers are fairly accurate. As a quick check, he calculates the profitability of Maximum and Mammoth using more and different allocation bases. The set of activities and activity rates he had used results in numbers that closely approximate those based on more detailed analyses. He is confident that headquarters, knowing that Maximum was introduced only recently, will not ask Plum to phase it out. He is also aware that a sizable portion of Clark's bonus is based on division revenues. Phasing out either product would adversely affect his bonus. Still, he feels some pressure from Clark to do something.

Required

1. Using activity-based costing, calculate the gross margin per unit of the Maximum and Mammoth models.
2. Explain briefly why these numbers differ from the gross margin per unit of the Maximum and Mammoth models calculated using Plum's existing simple costing system.
3. Comment on Clark's concerns about the accuracy and limitations of ABC.
4. How might Plum find the ABC information helpful in managing its business?
5. What should Steve Jacobs do in response to Clark's comments?

Mini-Case

LO 5 ▶

2. COGS Impulse $11,400,000

5-42 Using ABC for activity-based management (ABM). Jenny Chen is in charge of marketing at General Mills. Jenny reports to Mark Hamin, vice-president of product development. Mark has tasked Jenny with analyzing the different channels used to market its Colombo frozen yogurt products to find the best path to profitability.

Jenny has decided to take an ABC/ABM approach to analyzing the operations at General Mills. Currently, General Mills charged the same prices and provided the same promotions—$3 per case—to its customers, whether the customer was in the grocery channel (food purchased for later consumption or preparation at home) or the food-service (outside of home, immediate consumption) channel. Jenny quickly noticed there were two segments within food service: destination yogurt shops or restaurants and impulse locations, located in business cafeterias and on school campuses and military bases. She also noticed that sales dollars for frozen yogurt products were relatively constant, but profits were declining. Jenny sensed that destination yogurt shops might be more profitable than impulse locations, but the company didn't have the information about profit differences to make changes. The case sales data and income statements for last year, by segment, looked like this:

Category	Impulse Location	Yogurt Shops	Total
Sales in cases	1,200,000	300,000	1,500,000
Sales revenue	$23,880,000	$5,970,000	$29,850,000
Less: Promotions	3,600,000	900,000	4,500,000
Net sales	20,280,000	5,070,000	25,350,000
Cost of goods sold	13,800,000	3,450,000	17,250,000
Gross margin	6,480,000	1,620,000	8,100,000
Less: Merchandising	1,380,000	345,000	1,725,000
Less: Selling, general, and admin. expenses	948,000	237,000	1,185,000
Net income	$ 4,152,000	$1,038,000	$ 5,190,000

Additional cost data: Cost of goods sold includes $14,250,000 for ingredients, packaging, and storage, and $3,000,000 for picking, packing, and shipping. The product is the same across segments, so cost to produce is the same. However, picking, packing, and shipping costs vary if the order is for a full pallet. Full pallets cost $75 to pick and ship, where individual orders cost $2.25 per case. There are 75 cases in a pallet, with pallet and case usage by segment shown here:

	Segment		
	Impulse Location	Yogurt Shops	Total
Cases in full pallets	60,000	240,000	300,000
Individual cases	1,140,000	60,000	1,200,000
Total cases	1,200,000	300,000	1,500,000

Sales and merchandising kits sell for $500 each. A total of 3,450 kits were delivered in the period, 90 of them to yogurt shops. For selling, general, and administration, costs were allocated to products based on gross sales dollars.

Jenny investigated and found when a random sample of the sales force was asked to keep diaries for 60 days, the resulting data revealed they spent much more time per sales dollar on yogurt sales than other General Mills products. Jenny found when selling, general, and administration costs were allocated based on time, the total allocation to yogurt products jumped from $1,185,000 to $3,900,000. Of the total time spent on selling Colombo frozen yogurt, only 1% of that time was spent in shops.

Required

1. How do the two segments identified by Jenny for Colombo frozen yogurt sales differ from each other?
2. Using ABC analysis, restate the income statements above to show new net income (*Hint:* add a line item for shipping). What is "per case" net income?
3. Based on your analysis in requirement 2, what changes should General Mills make?

(IMA adapted; Colombo Frozen Yogurt by Jon Guy from *Cases from Management Accounting Practice* by Wayne Bremser. Copyright © 2000. Used by permission of Institute of Management Accountants.)

SOLUTIONS

Try It 5–1

We first calculate the budgeted indirect cost rate for the overhead cost pool.

$$\text{Total budgeted direct manufacturing labour-hours} = 0.5 \text{ hrs.} \times 20{,}000 + 0.6 \text{ hrs.} \times 5{,}000$$
$$= 13{,}000 \text{ hours}$$

$$\text{Budgeted indirect-cost rate} = \frac{\text{Budgeted total costs in indirect-cost pool}}{\text{Budgeted total quantity of cost-allocation base}}$$

$$= \frac{\$234{,}000}{13{,}000 \text{ direct manufacturing labour-hours}}$$

$$= \$18 \text{ per direct manufacturing labour-hour}$$

		20,000		**5,000**		
		Basic Lamps		**Designer Lamps**		
		per Unit			**per Unit**	**Total**
	Total (1)	**(2) = (1) ÷ 20,000**	**Total (3)**		**(4) = (3) ÷ 5,000**	**(5) = (1) + (3)**
Direct materials	$160,000	$8	$ 75,000		$15.00	$235,000
Direct manufacturing labour	200,000	10	60,000		12.00	260,000
($20 × 0.5 hrs. × 20,000; $20 × 0.6 hrs. × 5,000)						
Total direct costs (Step 2)	360,000	18	135,000		27.00	495,000
Indirect costs allocated (Step 6) $18 × 10,000 hours; $18 × 3,000 hours	180,000	9	54,000		10.80	234,000
Total costs	$540,000	$27	$189,000		$37.80	$729,000

Try It 5–2

We first calculate the overhead rates for each indirect cost pool.

	Basic Lamps	**Designer Lamps**	**Total**
1 Quantity of lamps produced	20,000 lamps	5,000 lamps	
2 Number of lamps produced per batch	250 lamps per batch	50 lamps per batch	
3 = (1) ÷ (2) Number of batches	80 batches	100 batches	
4 Setup time per batch	1 hour per batch	3 hours per batch	$114,000
5 = (3) × (4) Total setup-hours	80 setup-hours	300 setup-hours	380 setup-hours
6 General manufacturing over head costs			$120,000
7 Direct manufacturing labour-hours per lamp	0.5 hours	0.6 hours	
8 = (1) × (7) Total direct manufacturing labour-hours	10,000 hours	3,000 hours	13,000 hours

$$\text{Budgeted indirect-cost rate} = \frac{\text{Budgeted total costs in indirect-cost pool}}{\text{Budgeted total quantity of cost-allocation base}}$$

$$= \frac{\$114{,}000}{380 \text{ setup labour-hours}}$$

$$= \$300 \text{ per setup labour-hour}$$

(Continued)

$$\text{Budgeted indirect-cost rate} = \frac{\text{Budgeted total costs in indirect-cost pool}}{\text{Budgeted total quantity of cost-allocation base}}$$

$$= \frac{\$120,000}{13,000 \text{ direct manufacturing labour-hours}}$$

$$= \$9.2308 \text{ per direct manufacturing labour-hour}$$

	20,000 Basic Lamps		5,000 Designer Lamps		
	Total (1)	per Unit (2) = (1) ÷ 20,000	Total (3)	per Unit (4) = (3) ÷ 5,000	Total (5) = (1) + (3)
Direct materials	$160,000	$ 8.00	$ 75,000	$15.00	$235,000
Direct manufacturing labour ($20 × 0.5 hrs. × 20,000; $20 × 0.6 hrs. × 5,000)	200,000	10.00	60,000	12.00	260,000
Total direct costs (Step 2)	360,000	18.00	135,000	27.00	495,000
Indirect costs of activities					
Setup of machines Basic: $300 × 80 setup-hours Designer: $300 × 300 setup-hours	24,000	1.20	90,000	18.00	114,000
General manufacturing overhead Basic: $9.2308 × 10,000 labour-hrs. Designer: $9.2308 × 3,000 labour-hrs.	92,308	4.62	27,692	5.54	120,000
Indirect costs allocated (Step 6)	116,308	5.82	117,692	23.54	234,000
Total costs	$476,308	$23.82	$252,692	$50.54	$729,000

Master Budget and Responsibility Accounting

6

Jonathan Weiss/Shutterstock

► **Learning Objectives**

1. Distinguish the long-term from the short-term benefits of budgets (pro forma financial statements).

2. Prepare a master operating budget and all supporting budgets or schedules.

3. Prepare a cash budget.

4. Contrast responsibility and controllability.

5. Appendix 6A: Distinguish among sensitivity analysis, Kaizen budgeting, and activity-based budgeting.

Budgets Communicate Choices

Fiat Chrysler's budget forecasts how changes in the business and economic environment are likely to affect Fiat Chrysler's financial health. Fiat Chrysler has limited resources, and its budgets represent choices about where those resources will be used, based on both experience from the past and assumptions about the future. A budget reports pro forma, or expected, financial results in standard financial statement format. The pro forma financial reports are performance targets that Fiat Chrysler's managers have committed to achieving. In part, it is budgeting that enabled Fiat Chrysler, North America's third-largest auto-maker, to return to profitability faster than expected after the world financial crisis in 2008. In 2015, Chrysler reported a US$410 million profit.

► **CPA Competencies**

This chapter covers material outlined in **Section 3: Management Accounting** of the CPA Competency Map. The Learning Objectives in this chapter have been aligned with the CPA Competency Map to ensure the best coverage possible.

3.2.1 Develops or evaluates information inputs for operational plans, budgets, and forecasts

3.2.2 Prepares, analyzes, or evaluates operational plans, budgets, and forecasts

3.2.3 Computes, analyzes, or assesses implications of variances

3.4.1 Evaluates sources and drivers of revenue growth

3.6.2 Evaluates performance of responsibility centres

Financial budgets such as pro forma income statements, statements of cash flow, and balance sheets report expected results in ASPE/IFRS-compliant formats. **Nonfinancial budgets** report on both the timing and quantity of resources required to achieve predicted financial results. The key purpose of nonfinancial budgets is coordination of all business functions in the value chain. With coordination comes control. Once in place, the predicted outcomes can be compared against actual outcomes with the goal of improving on any unfavourable actual performance relative to what was expected in the budget. As one observer has said, "Few businesses plan to fail, but many of those that flop failed to plan."[1]

Budgets help managers:

1. Communicate directions and goals to different departments of a company to help them coordinate the actions they must pursue to satisfy customers and succeed in the marketplace.

2. Judge performance by measuring financial results against planned objectives, activities, and time lines and learn about potential problems.

3. Motivate employees to achieve their goals.

This chapter presents the budgeting process used to create an operating budget (reported as a pro forma income statement), a cash budget, and a pro forma balance sheet. These pro forma statements are predictions, not historical outcomes; therefore, they are never audited.

The Decision Framework and Budgets

► **LO 1**

Distinguish the long-term from the short-term benefits of budgets (pro forma financial statements).

A **budget** is a quantitative expression of a proposed (future) plan of action by management for a set time period. It is because resources are constrained that choices must be made to obtain the maximum benefit of the resources available for use. The **budget constraints** describe the combination of limitations on nonfinancial and financial resources within a company's management control.

The **master budget** summarizes all the financial and nonfinancial plans into a single document. The financial predictions are reported according to ASPE/IFRS standards and are supported by nonfinancial schedules. The term *master* in master budget means it is a comprehensive, coordinated, organization-wide set of schedules and a budget.

The terminology used to describe budgets varies among organizations. For example, budgeted financial statements are sometimes called **pro forma statements** (or *forecasted or estimated statements*). Some organizations refer to budgeting as targeting. Indeed, to give a more positive thrust to budgeting, many organizations—for example, Nissan Canada and Bombardier—describe the budget as a *profit plan*.

Budgets are the result of a simultaneous set of complex *decision processes*.

Step 1: Identify the Problem and Uncertainties All organizations must both plan and control their activities and costs to meet their budget resource constraints. The problem is how to maximize profit and thrive in the long term. Like all well-disciplined team decision making, the process begins with discussion to identify and understand any control and planning issues. Once key issues are identified and ordered in priority, the management team can begin the budget process as a coordinated response to the issues. The issue identification and prioritization will, to a large extent, be driven by the organization's strategy.

Step 2: Obtain Information Evidence to justify various opinions must be gathered both internally from the MIS and externally from the political, economic, social, technological, environmental, and legal context (commonly known as a PESTEL analysis) and the industrial context. There will be detailed gathering of information upon which to create the various schedules that will justify the final budget. Throughout the process, however, many decisions will be made about resource allocation to support the core production process or service provision activities of a company.

Step 3: Make Predictions About the Future Budgets themselves are predictions about the future that represent choices among alternative uses of available resources. Intelligent

---

[1] This is a paraphrase of similar quotes attributed to Sir Winston Churchill, Alan Lakein, and Ben Franklin.

assumptions, based on the management team's understanding of its own strengths and weaknesses as well as the external opportunities and threats, are central to budgets.

Step 4: Decide On and Implement One of the Available Alternatives Implementation in well-managed organizations usually follows four steps in the **budgeting cycle:**

1. Plan the performance of organizational sub-units and coordinate into a whole. The entire management team must agree with what is expected and commit to achieving the budget targets.

2. Provide a frame of reference—a set of specific expectations against which actual results can be compared. Budget targets are not discretionary but mandatory achievements. If one sub-unit fails, then failure may cascade through the rest of the units.

3. Investigate variations from the original budget. If necessary, corrective action follows investigation so the budget will be met in the future.

4. Plan again, based on feedback from changed conditions and actual performance.

The prevalence of budgets in companies of all sizes is evidence that the benefits of budgeting processes outweigh their costs. Executive support is especially critical for obtaining active line participation in the formulation of budgets and for successful administration of budgets. The "garbage in, garbage out" maxim applies to budgets. At all levels in a company, managers must understand and support both the budget and the control it imposes on their decision making.

Budgets need to be somewhat flexible, because changing conditions call for changes in plans. A manager may commit to the budget, but opportunities often develop where some unexpected repairs or a special advertising program would better serve the interests of the organization. Deferring the repairs or the advertising to meet the budget is foolish if it will hurt the organization in the long run. Attaining the budget should never be an end in itself.

Often, but not always, budgeted amounts are also standards. A **standard** is a carefully predetermined price, cost, or quantity used for judging performance (see Chapter 7, Appendix 7A). The term is frequently used to refer to amounts estimated from either engineering or time-motion studies. Standard amounts are usually expressed on a per-unit basis (e.g., per hour, per square metre, per task, per output, etc.). Not all budgeted costs, however, are standard costs. Many budgeted costs are based on historical data and the assumption that they can be used to predict the future. Managers can use time series linear regression, but this approach fails to examine whether history represents the best or even good performance levels in any competitive situation.

There is a danger when companies rely entirely on internal data to set standards. Their more successful competitors clearly have achieved higher standards. To improve their own performance, companies need to look outside the firm. This type of standard is often referred to as a **benchmark**. It arises from a broader scope of information sought outside the company. Benchmarks encourage the setting of **stretch goals**, those that challenge managers to achieve excellent performance rather than maintain the status quo.

Step 5: Implement the Decision, Evaluate Performance, and Learn Probably the most disliked application, but at the same time the most important, is the evaluation of actual results against predicted or budgeted performance. Actual outcome that falls short of expectations may indicate a problem with the original budget (e.g., it was unrealistic), a problem with implementation of the budget, or changing external factors that weren't considered or anticipated in the original budget. Often managers are paid bonuses for exceeding, not for failing to meet, expectations. Without feedback, however, there is no basis upon which to analyze how the failure occurred and remedy it.

Advantages of Budgets

Budgets are a major feature of most management-control systems. When administered intelligently, budgets

- Compel planning and monitoring of the implementation of plans.
- Provide reliable performance assessment criteria.
- Promote communication and coordination within the organization.

Budgeting is most useful when it is part of a company's strategic analysis.[2] **Strategic analysis** is the evaluation of how well the organization has matched its own capabilities with the relevant features of the competitive environment to progress toward its future success. For the strategy to succeed, the company also needs to match its activities to the strategy in a reliable way.

Approaches to Budgeting

There are many different approaches to budgeting. The following is a list of selected examples:

■ *Traditional (historic) incremental/decremental approach.* This is the classic "every department gets a 4% (or whatever amount) increase (or decrease) next year." While easier to implement than other, more effective approaches to budgeting, it is fundamentally flawed because it starts from the basic assumptions that the organization is currently healthy and resources are allocated effectively. Therefore, any increase or decrease in resources should be shared equally. While this makes the budget process simple for senior management (if anyone complains about not getting enough new resources or, alternatively, losing resources, senior management can simply say that everyone is in the same boat and being treated equally), it can be tremendously damaging. Unless the "across the board" increase/decrease is just a one-time event, it means that ineffective parts of the organization will continue to be given new resources, while effective parts of the organization are being (comparatively) starved for resources. Or even worse, in a budget cut scenario, profitable/growing departments will be cut by the same amount that unprofitable/shrinking departments are cut. This approach is often referred to as the "death of a thousand cuts."

■ *Priority approach.* This type of budgeting is in direct contrast to the traditional approach discussed above. In priority-based budgeting, the organization uses its strategic plan to establish the priorities for allocating new resources or areas that need to be protected if resources have to be cut. While this approach may require some difficult decisions to be made (it may result in entire activities/products/regions being cut), it is considered to be much more effective in helping the organization reach its strategic goals. The examples in this chapter assume that a priority-based approach is being used to make the budgeting decisions.

■ *Zero-based budgeting.* Zero-based budgeting involves all areas of the organization building their budgets from the "ground up" or from a starting point of zero. Essentially, every expense and revenue has to be justified as essential to the organization's operations. Frequently this type of budgeting exercise can identify significant cost savings and/or opportunities to reallocate existing resources. Unfortunately, zero-based budgeting is very time consuming, anxiety provoking, and process intensive. Organizations have to make sure that the items to be cut are, indeed, not needed. For zero-based budgeting to be successful, management typically needs to be trained in zero-based methodology, budget time lines need to be extended (to ensure that changes are adequately evaluated), and senior management must commit to minimizing any impact on the current workforce (albeit with possible reallocation or retraining). Without these steps, zero-based budgeting often does not achieve any significant savings or fails entirely due to organizational resistance. Also, zero-based budgeting should not be used continuously; instead it might be an approach that an organization uses periodically but infrequently (e.g., once every five years).

■ *Activity-based budgeting.* This is an extension of the concepts introduced in Chapter 5 around activity-based costing. **Activity-based budgeting** (ABB) develops budgets based on the level of the various activities needed to fulfill the organizational goals. Instead of the number of units of product or hours of service being the basis for the budget, activity costs are calculated based on the level of activity needed to meet

---

[2] See J. Hope and R. Fraser, *Beyond Budgeting* (Boston, MA: Harvard Business School Press, 2003) for several examples.

forecasted demand. This approach helps management to focus on the activities and costs needed to achieve the organization's goals. (For a more detailed discussion, see Appendix 6A.)

■ *Kaizen budgeting.* This approach to budgeting is related to (and supports) the concept of continuous improvement and lean manufacturing. It establishes steadily decreasing budget numbers or targets (for costs) as a way to motivate less waste and more efficiency. Rather than sudden, annual decreases in resources (typified by traditional approaches to budget reductions), Kaizen budgeting builds small decreases into every monthly/quarterly/yearly budget. (For a more detailed discussion, see Appendix 6A.)

Operating and Strategic Performance Assessment

Budgeted performance measures need to overcome two key limitations of using past performance as a basis for judging actual results. For example, past results incorporate past mistakes and substandard performance. There is clearly a problem if past sales records are used when the departed employees selling the product did not understand their customers. Using the sales records of those departed employees would set the performance bar for knowledgeable salespeople far too low.

Another limitation of past performance is that the anticipated future may be very different from the past. Looking at the following data, what would have been an appropriate 2019 revenue growth target for this company?

	2018 Actual	2019 Forecasts	2019 Actual
Company revenue growth	10%	?	20%
Industry revenue growth	N/A	40%	50%

If the company had used the 2018 actual performance as a basis for setting 2019 targets, then the 2019 actual of 20% would probably have looked very good. On the other hand, if the 2019 industry forecast of 40% had been used as a basis for the 2019 company target, then the 20% actual would probably be considered disappointing.

Exhibit 6-1 illustrates the strategic analysis and planning processes. The dual-directional arrows indicate the interdependence among these activities and outcomes. The cycle of planning and budgeting is continuous as actual results provide feedback regarding how well managers forecast future results. When the feedback is negative, it is sensible for managers to reassess their long-run and short-run plans to determine where changes can be made to improve the achievement of their financial and nonfinancial goals.

Coordination and Communication

Coordination is the meshing and balancing of all factors of production or service and of all the departments and business functions so that the company can meet its objectives. *Communication* is getting those objectives understood and accepted by all employees.

Coordination forces executives to think of relationships and interdependencies among individual operations, departments, and the company as a whole. Purchasing officers make

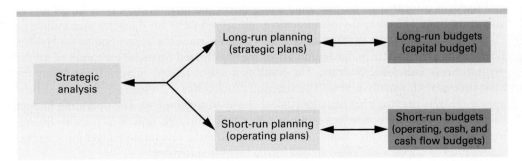

Exhibit 6-1 Strategic Analysis in the Formulation of Long-Run and Short-Run Budgets

material purchase plans based on either production, service, or merchandising requirements. Reduction in purchasing costs can improve profitability in other value-chain functions because of interdependence. In a manufacturing setting, after marketing managers forecast future demand, production managers plan personnel and machinery needs to produce the number of products necessary to meet revenue forecasts.

How does a budget lead to coordination? Consider Snapple Beverage Corporation. Production managers, who are evaluated on maximizing output while keeping unit costs per bottle low, would prefer long production runs with very few changeovers of flavours. But if the output cannot be sold, Snapple may find itself awash in a costly inventory buildup of an unpopular flavour. The budget achieves coordination by constraining production managers to produce only what marketing forecasts.

Communication is key to coordination. Production managers must know the sales plan, purchasing managers must know the production plans, and so on. A formal document, such as the budget, is an effective means of communicating a consistent set of plans to the organization as a whole.

The Master Operating Budget

Time Coverage

► **LO 2**

Prepare a master operating budget and all supporting budgets or schedules.

The purpose(s) for budgeting should guide the time period chosen for the budget. Consider budgeting for a new Harley-Davidson motorcycle. If the purpose is to budget for the total profitability of this new model, a five-year period (or more) may be appropriate because it covers design, manufacture, sales, and after-sales support. In contrast, consider budgeting for a school Christmas play. If the purpose is to estimate all cash outlays, a six-month period from the planning to staging of the play may be adequate.

The most frequently used budget period is one year. The annual budget is often subdivided by months for the first quarter and by quarters for the remainder of the year. The budgeted data for a year are frequently revised as the year unfolds. For example, at the end of the first quarter, the budget for the next three quarters is changed in light of new information gathered from actual experience.

Businesses increasingly use rolling budgets. A **rolling budget** is a budget or plan that is always available for a specified future period by adding a month, quarter, or year in the future as the current month, quarter, or year is completed. Thus, a 12-month rolling continuous budget for the March 2018 to February 2019 period becomes a 12-month rolling budget for the April 2018 to March 2019 period the next month, and so on. This way there is always a 12-month budget in place. Rolling budgets motivate managers to look forward 12 months, regardless of the month at hand.

Steps in Developing an Operating Budget

Budgeting, like swimming, is best learned by doing. We will move through the development of an actual master budget because it provides a comprehensive picture of the entire budgeting process. Our example is a mid-size, owner-managed manufacturer of aircraft replacement parts, Halifax Engineering. Its job-costing system for manufacturing costs has two direct cost categories, direct materials and direct manufacturing labour, as well as one indirect cost pool, manufacturing overhead. Manufacturing overhead (both variable and fixed) is allocated to output units using direct manufacturing labour-hours as the allocation base. The company manufactures specialized parts for the aerospace industry.

Exhibit 6-2 illustrates the flow among the various parts of the master budget for Halifax Engineering. The master budget summarizes the anticipated financial outcomes of all the organization's individual budgets. The result is a set of related financial statements for a set time period, usually a year. The schedules in Exhibit 6-2 illustrate the logical flow among budgets that together are often called the *operating budget*. The **operating budget** presents the results of operations in many value-chain business functions prior to financing and taxes. Later in this chapter you will learn how the remaining budget information is produced to create a budgeted or pro forma income statement.

Exhibit 6-2 Overview of the Master Budget for Halifax Engineering

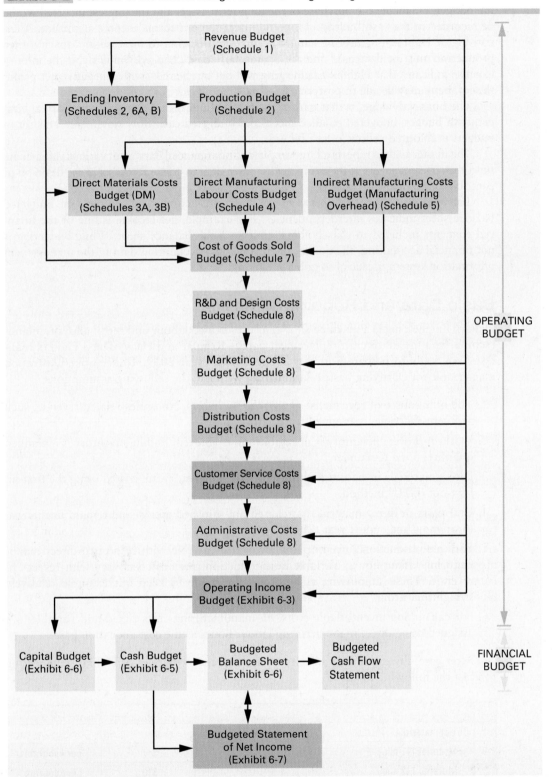

The operating budget and budgeted income statement, new elements introduced in this chapter, are coloured green, as is the arrow indicating all the schedules required to produce the operating budget.

The dual-direction arrows in Exhibit 6-2 indicate interdependencies among elements. For example, the operating budget will be amended to include added depreciation if the demand forecast indicates that a permanent increase in production is required. A permanent increase in production means the purchase of long-term assets would be added to the capital budget. Financing the purchase of the long-term assets and the interest incurred would be recorded in the cash budget and would affect the pro forma income statement. Alternatively, if Halifax Engineering cannot access the financing to increase its capacity, then production must be decreased and the operating budget changed. Similarly, if the interest expense indicates that Halifax Engineering will be "in the red" with a negative net profit, the company may decide to postpone its expansion plans.

The financial budget is that part of the master budget that comprises the capital budget, cash budget, budgeted balance sheet, and budgeted cash flow statement. This set of budgets is coloured yellow in Exhibit 6-2.

The master budget reports a large amount of nonfinancial data from various value-chain functions. The managers at the company use these data to create forecasts of the drain on or contribution to financial resources.

The dual-direction arrow between the budgeted income statement and the budgeted balance sheet indicates interdependencies. For example, net income is one of the financial elements included in shareholders' equity on the balance sheet. While budgeting is not financial accounting, the quality of the financial-accounting data in the management information system is crucial to good budgeting.

Basic Data and Requirements

Halifax Engineering is a machine shop that uses skilled labour and metal alloys to manufacture two types of aircraft replacement parts—Regular and Heavy-Duty. Halifax managers are ready to prepare a master budget for the year 2019. To keep our illustration manageable for clarifying basic relationships, we make the following assumptions:

1. The only source of revenue is sales of the two parts. Non-sales-related revenue, such as interest income, is assumed to be zero.

2. Work-in-process inventory is negligible and is ignored. Ending inventory is a planned quantity, not a remainder.

3. Direct materials inventory and finished goods inventory are costed using the first-in, first-out (FIFO) method.

4. Unit costs of direct materials purchased and finished goods sold remain unchanged throughout the budget year (2019).

5. Variable production (inventoriable) costs are variable with respect to direct manufacturing labour-hours. Variable nonproduction (period) costs vary with respect to revenue. These simplifying assumptions are made to keep our example relatively straightforward.

6. For calculating inventoriable costs, *all* manufacturing costs (fixed and variable) are assigned using direct manufacturing labour-hours as the cost allocation base.

After carefully examining all relevant factors, the executives of Halifax Engineering forecast the following for 2019:

	A	B	C
1	Direct materials:		
2	Material 111 alloy	$ 7	per kilogram
3	Material 112 alloy	$10	per kilogram
4	Direct manufacturing labour	$20	per hour
5			
6	**Content of Each Product Unit**	**Regular**	**Heavy-Duty**
7	Direct materials 111 alloy—kilograms	12	12
8	Direct materials 112 alloy—kilograms	6	8
9	Direct manufacturing labour-hours (DMLH)	4	6

All direct manufacturing costs are variable with respect to the units of output produced. Additional information regarding the year 2019 is as follows:

A	B	C
1		**Product**	
2		**Regular**	**Heavy-Duty**
3 Expected sales in units	5,000	1,000
4 Selling price per unit	$ 600	$ 800
5 Target ending inventory in units*	1,100	50
6 Beginning inventory in units	100	50
7 Beginning inventory value in dollars	$35,800	$24,200
8		
9		**Direct Materials**	
10		**111 Alloy**	**112 Alloy**
11 Beginning inventory in kilograms	7,000 kg	6,000 kg
12 Target ending inventory in kilograms*	8,000 kg	2,000 kg
13		
14 *Target inventories depend on expected sales, expected variation in demand for products, and management philosophies such as just-in-time (JIT) inventory management.		

At the anticipated output levels for the Regular and Heavy-Duty aircraft parts, management believes the manufacturing overhead costs will be incurred as shown below. Notice that depreciation of the manufacturing plant and equipment is included in the cost of goods sold (COGS). To keep this example simple, it is assumed that there is no depreciation expense reported in the non-inventoriable (period cost) schedule.

A	B	C
1 **Manufacturing Overhead Costs**		
2 Variable:		
3 Supplies	$ 90,000	
4 Indirect manufacturing labour	190,000	
5 Direct and indirect manufacturing labour fringe costs @ 15.4% (rounded)	121,689	
6 Power	120,000	
7 Maintenance	60,000	$ 581,689
8 Fixed:		
9 Depreciation	220,000	
10 Property taxes	50,000	
11 Property insurance	10,000	
12 Supervision (includes fringe costs)	100,000	
13 Power	22,000	
14 Maintenance	18,000	420,000
15 Total		$1,001,689

The period or nonproduction overhead costs are

	A	B	C
1	**Other (Non-manufacturing or Period) Costs**		
2	Variable:		
3	R&D/product design	$ 56,000	
4	Marketing	92,600	
5	Distribution	66,500	
6	Customer service	47,600	
7	Administrative	78,000	$340,700
8	Fixed:		
9	R&D/product design	45,000	
10	Marketing	35,000	
11	Distribution	28,000	
12	Customer service	16,870	
13	Administrative	100,000	224,870
14	Total		$565,570

Our task at hand is to prepare a budgeted income statement for the year 2019. As shown in Exhibit 6-2, this is one component of Halifax's master budget. Other components of the master budget—the budgeted balance sheet and the cash budget—are discussed in the next section of this chapter.

The following supporting budget schedules will be prepared when developing Halifax's budgeted income statement:

1. Revenue budget.
2. Production budget (in units).
3. Direct materials usage budget and direct materials purchases budget.
4. Direct manufacturing labour budget.
5. Manufacturing overhead budget (which includes manufacturing plant and equipment depreciation, an expense that is also included in the cost of goods sold budget).
6. Ending inventory budget.
7. Cost of goods sold (COGS) budget.
8. Other (nonproduction) costs budget.

While specific budget details differ among organizations, the sequence of events outlined below is common for developing a budgeted income statement. Beginning with the revenue budget, each budget is developed in logical fashion. In most cases, computer software speeds the budget calculations.

Preparing a Master Operating Budget

■ **Schedule 1:** *Revenue budget.* The revenue budget (Schedule 1) is the usual starting point for budgeting. The reason is that production (and hence costs) and inventory levels generally depend on the forecasted level of revenue.

	A	B	C	D
1		**Schedule 1: Revenue Budget**		
2		**For the Year Ended December 31, 2019**		
3			Selling	Total
4		Units	Price	Revenues
5	Regular	5,000	$600	$3,000,000
6	Heavy-Duty	1,000	800	800,000
7	Total			$3,800,000

The $3.8 million is the amount of revenue in the budgeted income statement. The revenue budget results from elaborate information gathering and intense discussions among sales managers and field sales representatives.

Pressures can exist for budgeted revenue to be either overestimates or underestimates of the expected amounts. Pressure for employees to underestimate budgeted revenue can occur when a company uses the difference between actual and budget amounts to evaluate managers. These managers may respond by giving highly conservative forecasts. **Padding** the budget or introducing **budgetary slack** refers to underestimating budgeted revenue (or overestimating budgeted costs) to make budgeted targets easier to achieve. From the marketing manager's standpoint, budgetary slack hedges against unexpected downturns in demand. Similarly, managers can build in slack or pad the budget when it comes to expenses. If expenses are overestimated, it is that much easier for the actual expenses to come in below budget, thus making the company more likely to reach any operating income goals that might have been established as part of the budget process.

One way to address this potential for budgetary slack is to use external data (e.g., standards, benchmarks, peer companies, or industry data) to establish budget targets. This will help to offset the temptation for managers to "game" the budget system (and their performance bonuses) by setting easily achievable targets.[3] However, their superiors know this game and, in turn, they set more challenging targets. Negotiating then begins among the levels of the organization's managers to decide what the budget will be. General Electric's former CEO Jack Welch maintained that demanding, yet achievable, goals created anxiety for managers but improved corporate performance. He perceived these "stretch" goals as a means of motivating creative change.

Occasionally, revenue is limited by available production capacity. For example, unusually heavy market demand, shortages of labour or resources, or strikes may cause a company to exhaust its finished goods inventory completely. Additional sales cannot be made because no stock of the product is available. In such cases, the production capacity—the factor that limits revenue—is the starting point for preparing the revenue budget.

■ **Schedule 2:** *Production budget (in units).* After revenue is budgeted, the production budget (Schedule 2) can be prepared. The total finished goods units to be produced depends on planned sales and expected changes in inventory levels:

$$
\begin{array}{ccccccc}
\text{Budgeted} & & \text{Budgeted} & & \text{Target ending} & & \text{Beginning} \\
\text{production} & = & \text{sales} & + & \text{finished goods} & - & \text{finished goods} \\
\text{(units)} & & \text{(units)} & & \text{inventory} & & \text{inventory} \\
& & & & \text{(units)} & & \text{(units)}
\end{array}
$$

	A	B	C
1	**Schedule 2: Production Budget**		
2	**For the Year Ended December 31, 2019**		
3		**Product**	
4		**Regular**	**Heavy-Duty**
5	Budgeted sales (Schedule 1)	5,000	1,000
6	Add: Target ending finished goods inventory	1,100	50
7	Total requirements	6,100	1,050
8	Deduct: Beginning finished goods inventory	(100)	(50)
9	Units to be produced	6,000	1,000

When unit sales are not stable throughout the year, managers must decide whether (1) to adjust production levels periodically to minimize inventory held or (2) to maintain constant production levels and let inventory rise and fall. Increasingly, managers are choosing to adjust production in order to minimize inventory levels.

---

[3] For a more detailed discussion, see R. Varnick, G. Wu, and C. Heath, "Raising the Bar on Goals," *Graduate School of Business Publication*, University of Chicago, Spring, 1999.

⊕ TRY IT! 6.1

Jimenez Corporation manufactures and sells two types of decorative lamps, Knox and Ayer. The following data are available for the year 2017.

	Product	
	Knox	Ayer
Expected sales in units	21,000	10,000
Selling price	$ 25	$ 40
Target ending inventory in units	2,000	1,000
Beginning inventory in units	3,000	1,000

Calculate the revenues budget (label it Schedule 1) and the production budget in units (label it Schedule 2) for year ending December 31, 2017.

■ **Schedule 3:** *Direct materials usage budget and direct materials purchases budget.* The decision on the quantity of each type of output unit produced (Schedule 2) provides the data required to calculate the quantities of direct materials used. Information from purchasing will provide the cost data to produce Schedule 3A.

	A	B	C	D	E
1	**Schedule 3A: Direct Materials Usage Budget in Kilograms and Dollars**				
2	**For the Year Ended December 31, 2019**				
3		**Materials**			
4		**111 Alloy**	**112 Alloy**	**Total**	
5	Direct materials to be used in production of Regular parts (6,000 units) × 12 and 6 kilograms	72,000 kg	36,000 kg		see Schedule 2
6	Direct materials to be used in production of Heavy-Duty (1,000 units) × 12 and 8 kilograms	12,000 kg	8,000 kg		see Schedule 2
7	Total direct materials to be used	84,000 kg	44,000 kg		
8	Direct materials to be used from beginning inventory (assume FIFO cost flow)	7,000 kg	6,000 kg		
9	Multiply by: Cost per kilogram of beginning inventory	$ × 7	$ × 10		
10	Cost of direct materials to be used from beginning inventory (a)	$ 49,000	$ 60,000	$ 109,000	
11	Direct materials to be used from purchases (84,000 kg − 7,000 kg; 44,000 kg − 6,000 kg)	77,000 kg	38,000 kg		
12	Multiply by: Cost per kilogram of purchased materials	$ × 7	$ × 10		
13	Cost of direct materials to be used from purchases (b)	$539,000	$380,000	$ 919,000	
14	Total costs of direct materials to be used (a) + (b)	$588,000	$440,000	$1,028,000	

■ **Schedule 3B** computes the budget for direct materials purchases, which depends on the budgeted direct materials to be used, the beginning inventory of direct materials, and the target ending inventory of direct materials:

$$
\begin{array}{c}
\text{Purchases} \\
\text{of direct} \\
\text{materials}
\end{array}
=
\begin{array}{c}
\text{Usage} \\
\text{of direct} \\
\text{materials}
\end{array}
+
\begin{array}{c}
\text{Target ending} \\
\text{inventory of} \\
\text{direct materials}
\end{array}
-
\begin{array}{c}
\text{Beginning} \\
\text{inventory of} \\
\text{direct materials}
\end{array}
$$

	A	B	C	D
1	**Schedule 3B: Direct Materials Purchases Budget in Kilograms and Dollars**			
2	**For the Year Ended December 31, 2019**			
3		**Materials**		
4		**111 Alloy**	**112 Alloy**	**Total**
5	Direct materials to be used in production	84,000 kg	44,000 kg	
6	Add: Target ending direct materials inventory	8,000 kg	2,000 kg	
7	Total requirements	92,000 kg	46,000 kg	
8	Deduct: Beginning direct materials inventory	(7,000) kg	(6,000) kg	
9	Direct materials to be purchased	85,000 kg	40,000 kg	
10	Multiply by: Cost per kilogram of purchased materials	$ × 7	$ × 10	
11	Total direct materials purchase costs	$ 595,000	$ 400,000	$995,000

■ **Schedule 4:** *Direct manufacturing labour budget.* These costs depend on wage rates, production methods, and hiring plans. The computations of budgeted direct manufacturing labour costs appear in Schedule 4.

	A	B	C	D	E	F
1	**Schedule 4: Direct Manufacturing Labour Budget**					
2	**For the Year Ended December 31, 2019**					
3		**Output**	**Direct**			
4		**Units**	**Manufacturing**		**Hourly**	
5		**Produced**	**Labour-Hours**	**Total**	**Wage**	
6		**(Schedule 2)**	**per Unit**	**Hours**	**Rate**	**Total**
7	Regular	6,000	4	24,000	$20	$480,000
8	Heavy-Duty	1,000	6	6,000	$20	120,000
9	Total			30,000		$600,000

■ **Schedule 5:** *Manufacturing overhead budget.* The total of these costs depends on how individual overhead costs vary with the assumed cost allocation base, direct manufacturing labour-hours. The calculations of budgeted manufacturing overhead costs appear in Schedule 5. Notice that manufacturing equipment and plant depreciation has been transferred from the schedule of Manufacturing Overhead Costs and included in this budget. This means some depreciation expense is included in the Cost of Goods Sold (COGS) budget and is allocated to each unit of output. The remaining depreciation, if any, of nonproduction long-term assets is included in fixed non-inventoriable or period costs, a separate schedule.

	A	B	C	D
1	**Schedule 5: Manufacturing Overhead Budget***			
2	**For the Year Ended December 31, 2019**			
3		**At Budgeted Level of 30,000 Direct**		
4		**Manufacturing Labour-Hours**		
5	Variable manufacturing overhead costs:			
6	Supplies	$ 90,000		
7	Indirect manufacturing labour	190,000		
8	Direct and indirect manufacturing labour fringe costs @ 15.4% (rounded)	121,689		
9	Power	120,000		
10	Maintenance	60,000	$ 581,689	
11	Fixed:			
12	Depreciation*	220,000		
13	Property taxes	50,000		
14	Property insurance	10,000		
15	Supervision (includes fringe costs)	100,000		
16	Power	22,000		
17	Maintenance	18,000	420,000	
18	Total		$1,001,689	
19				
20	*The annual depreciation expense becomes part of COGS (Schedule 7).			

⊕ TRY IT! 6.2

Jimenez Corporation manufactures and sells two types of decorative lamps, Knox and Ayer. It expects to manufacture 20,000 Knox lamps and 10,000 Ayer lamps in 2017. The following data are available for the year 2017.

Direct materials	
Metal	$3 per kilogram (same as in 2016)
Fabric	$4 per metre (same as in 2016)
Direct manufacturing labour	$20 per hour

Content of Each Product Unit

	Product	
	Knox	**Ayer**
Metal	2 kilograms	3 kilograms
Fabric	1 metres	1.5 metres
Direct manufacturing labour	0.15 hours	0.2 hours

	Direct Materials	
	Metal	**Fabric**
Beginning inventory	12,000 kilograms	7,000 metres
Target ending inventory	10,000 kilograms	5,000 metres

Calculate (a) the direct materials usage budget in quantity and dollars (label it Schedule 3A), (b) the direct materials purchase budget in quantity and dollars (label it Schedule 3B), and (c) the direct manufacturing labour costs budget (label it Schedule 4) for the year ending December 31, 2017.

Schedule 5 reports two costs, power and maintenance, as both variable and fixed costs. This suggests that most of these two manufacturing overhead cost pools vary with some common input measure. Managers at Halifax Engineering have decided that the $22,000 of fixed power costs and $18,000 of fixed maintenance costs are material and should be reported separately as a fixed manufacturing overhead cost pool. Halifax treats all MOH as inventoriable costs and does not separate variable from fixed in this cost pool.[4]

- **Schedule 6:** *Ending inventory budget.* Schedule 6A shows the computation of unit costs for the two products. These unit costs are used to calculate the costs of target ending inventories of direct materials and finished goods in Schedule 6B.

	A	B	C	D	E	F
1	**Schedule 6A: Computation of Units Costs of Manufacturing**					
2			**Product**			
3			**Regular**		**Heavy-Duty**	
4		**Cost per Unit**				
5		**of Input***	**Inputs***	**Amount**	**Inputs***	**Amount**
6	Material 111 alloy	$ 7	12	$ 84	12	$ 84
7	Material 112 alloy	$10	6	60	8	80
8	Direct manufacturing labour	$20†	4	80	6	120
9	Manufacturing overhead	$33.39‡	4	134	6	200
10	Total			$358**		$484**
11						
12	*In kilograms or hours. ** total unit costs rounded.					
13	†Data are from p. 193.					
14	‡Direct manufacturing labour-hours is the sole allocation base for manufacturing overhead (both variable and fixed). The budgeted manufacturing overhead rate per direct manufacturing labour-hour is $33.39 (= $1,001,689 ÷ 30,000 budgeted DMLH).					

	A	B	C	D	E
1	**Schedule 6B: Ending Inventory Budget**				
2	**For the Year Ended December 31, 2019**				
3			**Cost per**		
4		**Kilograms**	**Kilogram**		**Total**
5	Direct materials				
6	111 alloy	8,000*	$ 7	$ 56,000	
7	112 alloy	2,000*	$10	20,000	$ 76,000
8			**Cost per**		
9		**Units**	**Unit**		
10	Finished goods				
11	Regular	1,100†	$358‡	$393,314	
12	Heavy-Duty	50†	$484‡	24,217	417,531
13	Total Ending Inventory				$493,531
14					
15	*Data are from p. 193.				
16	†Data are from pp. 193–194.				
17	‡From Schedule 6A: This is based on 2019 costs of manufacturing finished goods because, under the FIFO costing method, the units in finished goods ending inventory consist of units that are produced during 2019.				

---

[4] This inventory costing method is termed *full absorption costing* because the costs of production, including fixed manufacturing overhead, are recorded in COGS and recovered in the price of the outputs sold.

⊕ **TRY IT!** 6.3

Jimenez Corporation manufactures and sells two types of decorative lamps, Knox and Ayer. The following data are available for the year 2017. Machine setup-hours is the only driver of manufacturing overhead costs. Jimenez has a setup capacity of 1,100 hours.

	Knox	Ayer
1. Quantity of lamps to be produced	20,000 lamps	10,000 lamps
2. Number of lamps to be produced per batch	100 lamps/batch	80 lamps/batch
3. Setup time per batch	3 hours/batch	4 hours/batch

Variable cost = $60 per setup-hour
Fixed cost = $77,000

Calculate the manufacturing overhead costs budget (label it Schedule 5).

■ **Schedule 7:** *Cost of goods sold budget.* The information from Schedules 1 to 6 leads to Schedule 7:

	A	B	C	D
1	**Schedule 7: Cost of Goods Sold Budget**			
2	**For the Year Ended December 31, 2019**			
3		**From Schedule**		**Total**
4	Beginning finished goods inventory, January 1, 2019	Given		$ 60,000
5	Direct materials used	3A	$1,028,000	
6	Direct manufacturing labour	4	600,000	
7	Manufacturing overhead	5	1,001,689	
8	Cost of goods manufactured			2,629,689
9	Cost of goods available for sale			2,689,689
10	Deduct: Ending finished goods inventory,			
11	December 31, 2019	6B		(417,531)
12	Cost of goods sold			$2,272,158
13				
14	*Note:* The annual depreciation expense has been included in manufacturing overhead and therefore is part of COGS.			

Note that the following holds:

$$\text{Cost of goods sold} = \text{Beginning finished goods inventory} + \text{Cost of goods manufactured} - \text{Ending finished goods inventory}$$

⊕ **TRY IT!** 6.4

Jimenez Corporation manufactures and sells two types of decorative lamps, Knox and Ayer. The following data are available for the year 2017.

	Product	
	Knox	Ayer
Target ending inventory in units	2,000	1,000

Direct materials

Metal	$ 3 per kilogram (same as in 2016)
Fabric	$ 4 per kilogram (same as in 2016)
Direct manufacturing labour	$ 20 per hour
Machine setup overhead	$130 per hour

Content of Each Product Unit

	Product	
	Knox	Ayer
Metal	2 kilograms	3 kilograms
Fabric	1 metre	1.5 metres
Direct manufacturing labour	0.15 hours	0.2 hours
Machine setup overhead	0.03 hours	0.05 hours

	Direct Materials	
	Metal	Fabric
Target ending inventory	10,000 kilograms	5,000 metres

Calculate (1) the budgeted unit costs of ending finished goods inventory on December 31, 2017 (label it Schedule 6A), and (2) the ending inventories budget on December 31, 2017 (label it Schedule 6B).

■ **Schedule 8:** *Other (nonproduction) costs budget.* Schedules 2 to 7 cover budgeting for Halifax's production area of the value chain. For brevity, other areas of the value chain are combined into a single schedule.

	A	B	C	D	E
1	Schedule 8: Other (Nonproduction) Costs Budget				
2	For the Year Ended December 31, 2019				
3					
4	Variable costs:				
5	R&D/product design	$ 56,000			
6	Marketing	92,600			
7	Distribution	66,500			
8	Customer service	47,600			
9	General and administrative	78,000	$340,700		
10	Fixed costs:				
11	R&D/product design	45,000			
12	Marketing	35,000			
13	Distribution	28,000			
14	Customer service	16,870			
15	General and administrative	100,000	224,870		
16	Total other costs		$565,570		

■ **Schedule 9:** *Budgeted income statement.* Schedules 1, 7, and 8 provide the necessary information to complete the budgeted operating income statement, shown in Exhibit 6-3. Of course, more details could be included in the income statement and then fewer supporting schedules would be prepared.

Exhibit 6-3 Budgeted
Income Statement for
Halifax Engineering for the
Year Ended December 31,
2019

	A	B	C	D
1	**Budgeted Operating Income Statement for Halifax Engineering**			
2	**For the Year Ended December 31, 2019**			
3	Revenue	Schedule 1		$3,800,000
4	Costs:			
5	Cost of goods sold	Schedule 7		2,272,158
6	Gross margin			1,527,842
7	Operating (period) costs			
8	R&D/product design costs	Schedule 8	$101,000	
9	Marketing costs	Schedule 8	127,600	
10	Distribution costs	Schedule 8	94,500	
11	Customer service costs	Schedule 8	64,470	
12	Administrative costs	Schedule 8	178,000	565,570
13	Operating income			$ 962,272

Remember that a budget is a forecast of anticipated future performance—it can be changed. Exhibit 6-3 illustrates a pro forma operating income statement. Almost all companies own long-term assets that generate depreciation, or depletion, which is reported on the income statement. But Halifax Engineering reports no depreciation expense under its period costs. The reason is clear if you refer to the Manufacturing Overhead Costs and the Other (Non-manufacturing) Costs data, which are reported as Schedule 5 and Schedule 8, respectively. In order to keep the example simple, all depreciation expenses for Halifax Engineering, a machine shop, are assumed to be related to the manufacturing plant and equipment. This non-cash cost has been correctly reported, in full ASPE/IFRS compliance, as an inventoriable cost and included in the COGS amount in Exhibit 6-3. This is why there is no depreciation expense reported in the Operating (Period) Cost section.

Top management's strategies for achieving revenue and operating income goals influence the costs planned for the different business functions of the value chain. In particular, all direct variable costs will change as volumes change, while all indirect variable costs will change as the quantities of common inputs consumed change. If a large expansion is planned, then the depreciation expense as well as fixed costs, such as insurance and taxes, may also change. The actual financial results will be compared to budgeted results. Management can then evaluate whether the operating plan has been successful and change the future plan if necessary.

Preparing the Cash Budget

► LO 3

Prepare a cash budget.

So far this chapter has featured the operating budget, which reports the expected inventoriable and period costs for Halifax Engineering but does not report the interest expense, tax expense, or net income. Without these estimates, the company will not be able to complete any of its financial budgets. In this section we focus on developing the cash budget. The **cash budget** is a schedule of *expected* cash receipts and disbursements, and is essential for forecasting any expected interest expense as a result of borrowing. Once interest expense has been estimated, Halifax Engineering can prepare a pro forma income statement in proper financial format.

Typically, all cash flows from operations shown in a cash budget will differ from the revenue, COGS, and operating expenses in the supporting schedules. This is because there is a time lag between when sales are made and when accounts are paid by purchasers.

Concepts in Action

Web-Enabled Budgeting and Hendrick Motorsports

In recent years, an increasing number of companies have implemented comprehensive software packages that manage budgeting and forecasting functions across the organization. One such option is Microsoft Forecaster, which was originally designed by FRx Software for businesses looking to gain control over their budgeting and forecasting process within a fully integrated web-based environment.

Among the more unusual companies implementing web-enabled budgeting is Hendrick Motorsports. Featuring champion drivers Jeff Gordon and Jimmie Johnson, Hendrick is the premier NASCAR Sprint Cup stock car racing organization. According to *Forbes* magazine, Hendrick is NASCAR's most valuable team, with an estimated value of US$350 million. Headquartered on a 12 building, 600,000-square-foot campus near Charlotte, North Carolina, Hendrick operates four full-time teams in the Sprint Cup series, which runs annually from February through November and features 36 races at 22 speedways across the United States. The Hendrick organization has annual revenues of close to US$195 million and more than 500 employees, with tasks ranging from accounting and marketing to engine building and racecar driving. Such an environment features multiple functional areas and units, varied worksites, and ever-changing circumstances. Patrick Perkins, director of marketing, noted, "Racing is a fast business. It's just as fast off the track as it is on it. With the work that we put into development of our teams and technologies, and having to respond to change as well as anticipate change, I like to think of us in this business as change experts."

Microsoft Forecaster, Hendrick's web-enabled budgeting package, has allowed Hendrick's financial managers to seamlessly manage the planning and budgeting process. Authorized users from each functional area or team sign on to the application through the corporate intranet. Security on the system is tight: Access is limited to only the accounts that a manager is authorized to budget. (For example, Jeff Gordon's crew chief is not able to see what Jimmie Johnson's team members are doing.) Forecaster also allows users at the racetrack to access the application remotely, which allows managers to receive or update real-time "actuals" from the system. This way, team managers know their allotted expenses for each race. Forecaster also provides users with additional features, including seamless links with general ledger accounts and the option to perform what-if (sensitivity) analyses. Scott Lampe, chief financial officer, said, "Forecaster allows us to change our forecasts to respond to changes, either rule changes [such as changes in the series' points system] or technology changes [such as pilot testing NASCAR's new, safer "Car of Tomorrow"] throughout the racing season."

Hendrick's web-enabled budgeting system frees the finance department so it can work on strategy, analysis, and decision making. It also allows Hendrick to complete its annual budgeting process in only six weeks, a 50% reduction in the time spent budgeting and planning, which is critical given NASCAR's extremely short off-season. Patrick Pearson from Hendrick Motorsports believes the system gives the organization a competitive advantage: "In racing, the team that wins is not only the team with the fastest car, but the team that is the most disciplined and prepared week in and week out. Forecaster allows us to respond to that changing landscape."

Sources: J. Gage. 2009. Nascar's most valuable teams. Forbes.com, June 3 http://www.forbes.com/2009/06/03/nascar-most-valuable-teams-businesssports-nascar.html; J. Goff. 2004. In the fast lane. *CFO Magazine*, December 1; Hendrick Motorsports. 2010. About Hendrick Motorsports. Hendrick Motorsports website, May 28. www.hendrickmotorsports.com; S. Lampe. 2003. "NASCAR racing team stays on track with FRx Software's comprehensive budget planning solution." *DM Review*, July 1; Microsoft Corporation. 2009. Microsoft Forecaster: Hendrick Motorsports customer video. October 8. http://www.microsoft.com/BusinessSolutions/frx_hendrick_video.mspx; R. Nate. 2006. "Hendrick empire strikes back with three contenders in chase for the Nextel Cup." *USA Today*, September 17.

At year-end, there is always some revenue that has not been realized as a cash payment by customers. There is also a time lag between when companies are invoiced and when they pay the invoice. At the end of the year, some bills owing have not been paid in cash. Accrual accounting in compliance with ASPE/IFRS results in these timing differences between when a benefit or obligation must be reported for financial accounting purposes and when the cash inflow or outflow actually occurs.

The following table shows the anticipated cash receipts and disbursements for each quarter of the 2019 budget year. These are generated from quarterly versions of the preceding schedules (i.e., Schedules 1 to 8) with adjustments for the timing of the cash flows. In some instances, even more detailed schedules may be required. For example, see Exhibit 6-8 on page 205 for details of how Quarter 3's cash collection of $950,000 is calculated.

| | **Quarters** | | | | |
	(1)	(2)	(3)	(4)	Total
Collections from customers	$800,000	$700,000	$950,000	$918,400	$3,368,400
Disbursements:					
Direct materials	350,000	230,000	200,000	230,000	1,010,000
Payroll	312,000	242,000	226,000	231,689	1,011,689
Other costs	246,000	233,000	227,000	229,570	935,570
Income taxes	50,000	47,912	47,912	47,912	193,736
Office equipment purchase				35,080	35,080

Note: These cash receipts and disbursements are used in Exhibit 6-5.

We have included disbursements for income taxes in the table above, however, a discussion of corporate income tax installments is beyond the scope of this text. It is sufficient to assume that the budgeted quarterly tax payments are based on the previous year's actual tax expense. This is the typical approach taken by businesses that are required to make installment payments for the current year before the actual net income (for the entire year) is known. The Quarter 1 payment of $50,000 is equal to the income taxes payable shown on the 2018 balance sheet (Exhibit 6-4). The remaining quarterly payments are one-third of the remaining balance of the 2018 income tax expense of $193,736 (assumed for this budget).

Exhibit 6-4 Balance Sheet for Halifax Engineering as of December 31, 2018 (Actual)

	A	B	C
1	**Assets**		
2	Current Assets		
3	Cash	$ 30,000	
4	Accounts receivable	100,000	
5	Direct materials*	109,000	
6	Finished goods*	60,000	$ 299,000
7	Property, plant, and equipment		
8	Land	100,000	
9	Building and equipment	6,200,000	
10	Accumulated depreciation	(3,100,000)	3,200,000
11	Total Assets		$3,499,000
12			
13	**Liabilities and Shareholders' Equity**		
14	Current Liabilities		
15	Accounts payable	$ 50,000	
16	Income taxes payable	50,000	$ 100,000
17	Shareholders' Equity:		
18	Common shares, no par value 25,000 I/OS	2,150,000	
19	Retained earnings	1,249,000	3,399,000
20	Total Liabilities and Shareholders' Equity		$3,499,000
21	*These inventory balances are the same as the balances used in Schedules 3A and 7.		

The actual balance sheet for Halifax Engineering for the year ended December 31, 2018, is reported in Exhibit 6-4; these will be the opening balances for the 2019 cash budget. The cash budget for 2019 will affect all the amounts on the balance sheet except those reported for land and common shares. The capital budget is necessary for the preparation of the pro forma balance sheet ; this is addressed in Chapter 21.

Halifax Engineering budgets for a $35,000 minimum cash balance at the end of each quarter. The company can borrow or repay exactly the amount required at an annual interest rate of 6%. The terms of the agreement with the bank call for the company to pay interest at the end of each borrowing period (in this case, quarters) and as much of the principal outstanding as possible. Interest each quarter is at a quarterly rate of 1.5% (= 0.06 ÷ 4 quarters = 0.015 or 1.5% per quarter). Assume that any *borrowing* of principal happens *at the beginning* of the quarter in question and any *repayment* of principal occurs *at the end* of that quarter. For simplicity's sake, assume that *interest payments* on any outstanding balances are made in the *following quarter*.

Interest is calculated to the nearest dollar. Tax expense has been rounded to the nearest dollar, using a 40% tax rate.

There are three facts to remember when preparing cash budgets:

■ The ending balance (EB) of the previous quarter must be the beginning balance (BB) of the next quarter, *except*.

■ The "Year as a Whole" column reports the total cash receipts and disbursements for four quarters. This is because the BB for 2019 quarter 1 is the *year-end* balance for 2018, which becomes the BB for the *year* 2019. The EB for this "Year as a Whole" column must be the same as the EB for Quarter 4 because there is no further activity in cash inflow or outflow.

■ Depreciation is not a cash disbursement and is therefore not reported in the cash budget. A sophisticated approach would be to use the actual capital cost allowance (CCA) and estimated taxes. These refinements are presented in Chapter 21.

The company must now prepare the cash budget in a logical flow:

1. Prepare a statement of cash receipts and disbursements by quarters, including details of borrowing, repayment, and interest expense.

2. Prepare a budgeted balance sheet.

3. Prepare a budgeted income statement, including the effects of interest expense and income taxes. Assume that income tax expense for 2019 is at a rate of 40%.

Preparation of the Cash Budget

1. The cash budget (Exhibit 6-5) details expected cash receipts and disbursements quarter by quarter. It predicts the effects on the cash position at a given level of operations. Each quarter, this budget clearly shows the impact of cash-flow timing on bank loans and their repayment. In practice, monthly—and sometimes weekly—cash budgets are helpful for cash planning and control, depending on the company's needs. Cash budgets help avoid unnecessary idle cash and unexpected cash deficiencies. Ordinarily, the cash budget has the following main sections:

   a. The *beginning cash balance* plus cash receipts equals the total cash available for needs. Cash receipts depend on collections of accounts receivable, cash sales, and miscellaneous recurring sources such as rental or royalty receipts. Information on the prospective collectibility of accounts receivable is needed for accurate predictions. Key factors include bad debt (uncollectible accounts) experience and average time lag between sales and collections.

   b. *Cash disbursements* include the following items:

      i. Direct materials purchases, which depend on credit terms extended by suppliers and bill-paying patterns of the buyer.

      ii. Direct labour and other wage and salary outlays, which depend on payroll dates.

Exhibit 6-5 Cash Budget for Halifax Engineering for the Year Ended December 31, 2019

	A	B	C	D	E	F
1		Quarters				Total
2		(1)	(2)	(3)	(4)	for the Year
3	Cash balance, beginning	$ 30,000	$ 35,000	$ 35,000	$ 62,456	$ 30,000
4	Add: Receipts					
5	Collections from customers	800,000	700,000	950,000	918,400	3,368,400
6	Total cash available for needs: (a)	830,000	735,000	985,000	980,856	3,398,400
7	Deduct: Disbursements					
8	Direct materials	350,000	230,000	200,000	230,000	1,010,000
9	Payroll	312,000	242,000	226,000	231,689	1,011,689
10	Other costs	246,000	233,000	227,000	229,570	935,570
11	Income taxes	50,000	47,912	47,912	47,912	193,736
12	Machinery purchase	—	—	—	35,080	35,080
13	Total disbursements (b)	958,000	752,912	700,912	774,251	3,186,075
14	Cash balance before borrowing (a) − (b) = (c)	(128,000)	(17,912)	284,088	206,605	
15	Minimum cash balance desired (d)	35,000	35,000	35,000	35,000	
16	Additional cash available/(needed) (c) − (d) = (e)	(163,000)	(52,912)	249,088	171,605	
17	Interest payment (1.5% interest per quarter, based on previous quarter's loan balance) (f)	—	2,445	3,275	—	5,720
18	Loan borrowing/(repayment) (e) + (f)	163,000	55,357	(218,357)	—	
19	Cash balance, ending	$ 35,000	$ 35,000	$ 62,456	$206,605	$ 206,605
20	Financing					
21	Loan balance, beginning of period	—	$163,000	$218,357	$ —	
22	Borrowing (at beginning of each quarter)	163,000	55,357	—	—	
23	Repayment (at end of each quarter)	—	—	(218,357)	—	
24	Loan balance, end of period	$163,000	$218,357	$ —	$ —	

    iii. Other costs that depend on timing and credit terms. Depreciation is *not* a cash outlay.

    iv. Other disbursements are cash outlays for property, plant, and equipment, as well as long-term investments.

  c. *Financing requirements* depend on how the cash balance before borrowing, keyed as (a) − (b) in Exhibit 6-5, line 14, compares with the minimum cash balance desired, keyed as (d), line 15. The financing plans will depend on the relationship between the cash balance before borrowing and the minimum cash balance desired. If there is excess cash, loans may be repaid or temporary investments made. The outlays for interest expense (f) are usually shown in this section of the cash budget. Interest payment calculations present an interesting "Alice through the looking glass" problem for cash flow budgets. Assume that in a given quarter the budget shows a need to borrow $100,000. If the interest payment for borrowing the $100,000 (for that quarter) is added to *that quarter's* budget, your required borrowing will now be more than $100,000 (due to the interest payment). That, in turn, will increase the interest payment, which will increase the required borrowing, and so on! While this type of situation can be solved in a computer spreadsheet formatted budget (because it can calculate all the required iterations), it would be prohibitively time consuming to do this manually. A common approach to this problem is to assume that while the borrowing takes place in one period (e.g., t_1), the interest payment happens in the following period (e.g., t_2), and, as a result, the borrowing requirements (in t_1) will not change.

d. *Ending cash balance* reports the net effect of the financing decisions on the cash budget. When the cash balance before financing (c) is negative as it is at the end of the first quarter $(128,000)$, the company must borrow enough to cover this shortfall plus $35,000 to achieve its desired ending balance for the quarter. From the cash budget, Halifax managers can forecast their annual interest payment and proceed to calculate pretax income and estimate tax at 40% on their budgeted income statement for 2019.

The cash budget in Exhibit 6-5 shows the short-term *self-liquidating cycle* of cash loans. Seasonal peak load on production or sales often results in heavy cash disbursements for purchases, payroll, and other operating outlays as the products are produced and sold. Cash receipts from customers typically lag behind sales. The loan is self-liquidating in the sense that the borrowed money is used to acquire resources that are combined for sale, and the proceeds from sales are used to repay the loan. This **self-liquidating cycle**—sometimes called the **working capital cycle**, **cash cycle**, or **operating cycle**—is the movement of cash from producing inventories to receivables (from sales) and back to cash (from collections).

2. The budgeted balance sheet is presented in Exhibit 6-6. Each item is projected in light of the details of the business plan as expressed in all the previous budget schedules. The beginning balances for this pro forma balance sheet for 2019 were, of course, the ending balances for the actual balance sheet for 2018.

3. The budgeted income statement is presented in Exhibit 6-7. It is merely the budgeted operating income statement in Exhibit 6-3 expanded to include interest expense and income taxes. It would have been impossible to forecast the interest expense without the cash budget, and without that estimate Halifax could not calculate its pretax income. Once the cash budget is complete, Halifax can forecast its net income and calculate retained earnings for the budgeted year 2019. The managers begin with the actual ending balance in retained earnings in 2018 and add the forecast income for 2019 to obtain the forecast 2019 retained earnings.

Depreciation of the new office equipment is reported as a period cost in Exhibit 6-7. Because the expected acquisition of a long-term asset is not manufacturing plant or equipment, the depreciation is reported as a period cost and there has been no change in the total COGS reported.

For simplicity, the cash receipts and disbursements were given explicitly in this illustration of a cash budget. Frequently, there are lags between the items reported on the accrual basis of accounting in an income statement and their related cash receipts and disbursements.

The cash collection budget (Exhibit 6-8) requires detailed analysis of the different ways that customers can pay for their purchases. Halifax managers have assumed (based on past experience) that 10% of monthly sales will be paid in cash. They assume that the remaining 90% will be on credit with a 30-day payment term. However, past experience tells them that only 50% of the credit sales are collected in the month following the sale, while the remaining 50% are collected two months after the month of sale. Therefore, the remainder of May's sales will be collected in July.

Of course, such schedules of cash collections depend on credit terms, collection histories, and expected bad debts. Similar monthly schedules can be prepared for operating costs and their related cash disbursements.

Exhibit 6-6 Halifax Engineering: Budgeted Balance Sheet as of December 31, 2019

	A	B	C	D
1	**Assets**			
2	Current Assets			
3	Cash (from Exhibit 6-5)	$ 206,605		
4	Accounts receivable (1)	531,600		
5	Direct materials (2)	76,000		
6	Finished goods (2)	417,531		$1,231,736
7	Property, plant, and equipment			
8	Land (3)		$ 100,000	
9	Building and equipment (4)	6,235,080		
10	Accumulated depreciation (5)	(3,321,754)	2,913,326	3,013,326
11	Total Assets			$4,245,062
12				
13	**Liabilities and Shareholders' Equity**			
14	Current Liabilities			
15	Accounts payable (6)		$ 35,000	
16	Income taxes payable (7)		238,183	$ 273,183
17	Shareholders' Equity			
18	Common shares, no par value 25,000 I/OS (8)		2,150,000	
19	Retained earnings (9)		1,821,879	3,971,879
20	Total Liabilities and Shareholders' Equity			$4,245,062
21				
22	*Notes:*			
23	Beginning balances from Exhibit 6-4 are used as the starting point for most of the following computations:			
24	(1) $100,000 + $3,800,000 revenue − $3,368,400 receipts (Exhibit 6-5) = $531,600.			
25	(2) From Schedule 6B.			
26	(3) From beginning balance sheet (Exhibit 6-4).			
27	(4) $6,200,000 + $35,080 purchases = $6,235,080.			
28	(5) $3,100,000 + $220,000 (Schedule 5) plus incremental depreciation of $1,754 Exhibit 6-7.			
29	(6) $50,000 + $995,000 (Schedule 3B) − $1,010,000 (Exhibit 6-5) = $35,000.			
30	(7) $50,000 + $381,919 − $193,736 = $238,183.			
31	(8) From beginning balance sheet (Exhibit 6-4).			
32	(9) $1,249,000 + $572,879 net income (Exhibit 6-7) = $1,821,879.			

	A	B	C	D
1	Revenue	Schedule 1		$3,800,000
2	Costs:			
3	Cost of goods sold	Schedule 7		2,272,158
4	Gross margin			1,527,842
5	Period costs:			
6	R&D and product design costs	Schedule 8	$101,000	
7	Marketing costs	Schedule 8	127,600	
8	Distribution	Schedule 8	94,500	
9	Customer service	Schedule 8	64,470	
10	Administration costs	Schedule 8	178,000	
11	Depreciation on new purchase*		1,754	567,324
12	Operating income			960,518
13	Interest expense			5,720
14	Income before tax			954,798
15	Income tax at 40%			381,919
16	Net income			$ 572,879
17				
18	*Depreciation on the new purchase was excluded from the initial estimate of manufacturing overhead and COGS. Incremental expense has been calculated by applying the half-year rule, assuming a useful life of 10 years and no residual value.			

Exhibit 6-7 Budgeted Income Statement for Halifax Engineering for the Year Ended December 31, 2019

Exhibit 6-8 Projected Quarter 3 2019 Cash Collections for Halifax Engineering

	A	B	C	D	E	F	G
1							Cash Collections in Quarter 3 as a Whole
2		Quarter 2		Quarter 3			
3		May	June	July	August	September	
4	Monthly cash budget for Halifax assumes the following revenue flows:						
5	Credit sales, 90%	$255,164	$300,000	$285,000	$285,000	$284,084	
6	Cash sales, 10%	52,516	30,000	31,691	31,662	31,565	
7	Total Sales (***or revenues)	$307,680	$330,000	$316,691	$316,662	$315,649	
8	Cash collections from:						
9	Cash sales from this month			$ 31,691	$ 31,662	$ 31,565	
10	Credit sales from last month			150,000	142,500	142,500	
11	Credit sales from two months ago			127,582	150,000	142,500	
12	Total collection			$309,273	$324,162	$316,565	$950,000
13							
14	Assume credits are 90% of all sales.						
15	Collection is 50% of credit sales the month after the sale and the remaining 50% two months after the sale.						
16	July credit sales collections from June; 50% × $300,000 = $150,000						
17	July credit sales collection from May; 50% × $255,164 = $127,582						

Responsibility Versus Controllability

Organizational Structure and Responsibility

▶ **LO 4**

Contrast responsibility and controllability.

Organizational structure is the arrangement of centres of responsibility within an entity. A company like Petro-Canada may be organized primarily by business function: exploration, refining, and marketing. Another company like Procter & Gamble, a household-products giant, may be organized by product or brand line.

Managers and executives are assigned responsibility and held accountable for achieving specific financial and nonfinancial performance targets. A **responsibility centre** is a part, segment, or sub-unit of an organization whose manager is accountable for a specified set of activities. The higher the manager's level, the broader the responsibility centre he or she manages and, generally, the larger the number of subordinates who report to him or her. **Responsibility accounting** is a system that measures the plans (by budgets) and actions (by actual results) of each responsibility centre. The complexity of the processes in a company often requires decentralizing both authority and responsibility. Four major types of responsibility centres are as follows:

1. **Cost centre.** The manager is accountable for costs only, not revenue. Some managers may have authority over subordinate managers responsible for the outcomes of quantity, price, and scheduling decisions; others may not. The scope of authority, and therefore the amount of decentralization, will depend on the organizational structure.

2. **Revenue centre.** The manager is accountable for revenue only, not costs incurred to generate the revenue. Some managers of revenue centres may have authority over subordinate managers responsible for the outcomes of quantity and unit price decisions; others may not.

3. **Profit centre.** The manager is accountable for revenue and costs and has some authority over others who decide upon key factors affecting both revenue and cost. A profit-centre manager can coordinate among those responsible for either costs or revenue; however, this increases centralization.

4. **Investment centre.** The manager is accountable for investments, revenue, and costs.

The maintenance department of a Delta hotel is a cost centre if the maintenance manager is responsible only for costs; the budget would also emphasize costs. The sales department of the hotel is a revenue centre if the sales manager is responsible only for revenue, and the budget would emphasize revenue. The hotel manager might be considered as a profit centre if he or she is accountable for both revenue and costs, and the budget would then emphasize both. The regional manager responsible for investments in new hotel projects and for revenue and costs generated by those investments could be in charge of an investment centre; revenue, costs, and the investment base would be emphasized in the budget for this manager.

Responsibility accounting affects behaviour. Consider the following incident:

> The sales department requests a rush production run. The plant scheduler argues that it will disrupt production and will cost a substantial, though not clearly determined, amount of money. The answer coming from sales is, "Do you want to take responsibility for losing X Company as a customer?" Of course, the production scheduler does not want to take such a responsibility and gives up, but not before a heavy exchange of arguments and the accumulation of a substantial backlog of ill feeling.
>
> The controller proposes an innovative solution. He analyzes the payroll in the assembly department to determine the costs involved in getting out rush orders. This information eliminates the cause for argument. Henceforth, any rush order is accepted by the production scheduler, "no questions asked." The extra costs are duly recorded and charged to the sales department.
>
> As a result, the tension created by rush orders disappears, and the number of rush orders requested by the sales department is progressively reduced to an insignificant level.[5]

---

[5] R. Villers, "Control and Freedom in a Decentralized Company," *Harvard Business Review*, 32.2: 95.

Responsibility accounting assigns accountability to

- The individual who has the best knowledge about why the costs arose.
- The individual undertaking the activity that caused the costs.

In this incident, the cause was the sales activity, and the resulting costs were charged to the sales department. If rush orders occur regularly, the sales department might have a budget for such costs, and the department's actual performance would then be compared against the budget.

Feedback

When applied to budgets, responsibility accounting provides feedback to top management about the performance of different responsibility-centre managers relative to the budget. Differences between actual results and budgeted amounts—also called variances (see Chapter 7)—if properly used, can be helpful in three ways:

1. *Early warning.* Variances alert managers early to events neither easily nor immediately evident. Managers can then take corrective actions or exploit the available opportunities.

2. *Performance evaluation.* Variances inform managers about how well the company has performed in implementing its strategies. Were materials and labour used efficiently? Was R&D spending increased as planned? Did product warranty costs decrease as planned?

3. *Evaluating strategy.* Variances sometimes signal to managers that their strategies are ineffective. For example, a company seeking to compete by reducing cost and improving quality may find that it is achieving these goals but with little effect on sales and profits. Top management may then want to reevaluate the strategy.

Definition of Controllability

Controllability is the degree of authority that a specific manager has over costs, revenue, or other items in question. A **controllable cost** is any cost that is primarily subject to the authorization of a specific manager of a specific responsibility centre for a specific time span. A responsibility accounting system could either exclude all uncontrollable costs from a manager's performance report or segregate such costs from the controllable costs. It is a widely accepted organizational behaviour theory that if an individual is held responsible for something they cannot control, the likely result is frustration and reduced motivation (to achieve the stated organizational goals).

Recall the separation of variable from fixed costs of manufacturing overhead. Fixed costs comprised items such as insurance, property taxes, lease costs, depreciation, and management salaries. These costs are rarely controllable. Insurance companies set premiums with executives of corporations rather than plant managers; and cities, provinces, and countries set tax policies independent of corporations (not to mention individuals). While some negotiation of insurance premiums may be possible from year to year, governments do not negotiate tax increases. Other examples include foreign currency exchange rates, commodity prices, and interest rates. All are important factors over which individual companies and managers have no control.

Within a corporation, for example, a machining supervisor's performance report might be confined to quantities (not costs) of direct materials, direct manufacturing labour, power, and supplies. Unless the machining supervisor has the authority to set the price at which materials are procured, this approach is fair to the supervisor. Assume the purchasing manager has the authority to decide at what price materials will be purchased. The problem of cost control arises because the supervisor may order a lower quantity than required, or incur more than the expected level of waste in a time period. To meet customer demand, the supervisor will request a rush order. The purchasing manager has no authority to refuse and knows the cost of a rush order is higher than orders with a normal delivery time. Who is responsible for any cost overrun: the supervisor who needs the materials or the purchasing manager who negotiates prices with suppliers?

In practice, controllability is difficult to pinpoint:

1. Few costs are clearly under the sole influence of one manager. For example, costs of direct materials may be influenced by a purchasing manager, but such costs also depend on market conditions beyond the manager's control. Quantities used may be influenced by a production manager but also depend on the quality of materials purchased. Moreover, managers often work in teams. How can individual responsibility be evaluated in a team decision?

2. With a long enough time span, all costs will come under somebody's control. However, most performance reports focus on periods of a year or less. A current manager may have inherited problems and inefficiencies from his or her predecessor. For example, current managers may have to work under undesirable contracts with suppliers or labour unions that were negotiated by their predecessors. How can we separate what the current manager actually controls from the results of decisions made by others? Exactly what is the current manager accountable for?

Emphasis on Information and Behaviour

Responsibility accounting focuses on information and knowledge, not control. To succeed, however, other incentive systems must be aligned to the goal of free exchange of accurate information.

Performance reports for responsibility centres may also include uncontrollable items because this approach could change behaviour for the better. For example, some companies have changed cost centres to profit centres to motivate a change in managers' decisions and actions. A cost centre manager may emphasize production efficiency and deemphasize the pleas of sales personnel for faster service and rush orders. In a profit centre, the manager is responsible for both costs and revenue. Although the manager still has no control over sales personnel, the manager will now more likely weigh the impact of his or her decisions on costs *and* revenue rather than solely on costs.

Human Aspects of Budgeting

Why did we cover three major topics—master budgets, cash budgets, and responsibility accounting—in the same chapter? Primarily to emphasize that human factors are crucial aspects of budgeting. The budgeting techniques themselves are free of emotion; however, their administration requires education, persuasion, and intelligent interpretation. To be effective, budgeting requires honest communication about the business from subordinates and lower-level managers to their bosses. But budgeting also generates human responses that senior management must be prepared for. Some examples (and possible solutions) are

- Subordinates may be tempted to "pad" or build in budgetary slack. Here are several things that top management can do to obtain accurate budget forecasts from lower-level managers:
  - Obtain independent standards or benchmarks to compare to the firm's forecasts. Managers would be expected (as part of the regular budgeting process) to explain any material differences.[6]
  - Senior managers should regularly involve themselves in understanding the operational activities happening within their span of control. Regular interactions with subordinates allow managers to become knowledgeable about operations and diminish the ability of subordinates to create slack in their budgets.
  - Senior managers should create core values and norms that discourage budgetary slack. An important part of this is senior managers' being seen to set reasonable budgets for their own areas (and to achieve them).

---

[6] For an excellent discussion of these issues, see Chapter 14 ("Formal Models in Budgeting and Incentive Contracts") of R.S. Kaplan and A.A. Atkinson, *Advanced Management Accounting*, 3rd ed. (Upper Saddle River, NJ): Prentice Hall, 1998.

Sustainability in Action | 24 Hour Fitness and Internet-Based Budgeting

24 Hour Fitness is one of the largest fitness-club chains in the United States, with nearly 4 million members, more than 450 clubs in 16 states, and $1.5 billion in annual revenues. The company uses Longview, an internet-based software platform, to manage its planning and budgeting process.

Using detailed operational statistics including number of members, number of workouts, and hours worked by each category of staff, accounting and finance managers sign on to the platform and develop budgets for each club. Using Longview at 24 Hour Fitness has resulted in more accurate budgets and forecasts being developed in less time. Managers can also conduct "what if" budget scenario analysis. Advertising costs are allocated to each club based on the size, age, and traffic of each club.

The platform also allows each club manager to track very-detailed revenue and expense data covering individual aspects of club activity, including juice bars, personal training sessions, product sales, and credit card membership dues and to take corrective action. It also enables staff to better support senior management

B Christopher/Alamy Stock Photo

decision making by responding more quickly to information requests. Mike Patano, Senior Director of Financial Planning & Analysis, summarized, "Day to day, it's about being able to thoroughly understand our business, benchmark the performance of our clubs, and understand our business drivers much better and quicker."

Sources: Longview Solutions. 2014. Longview Case Study: 24 Hour Fitness (http://info.longview.com/CaseStudy-24HourFitness.html); 24 Hour Fitness. 2019. About Us (http://www.24hourfitness.com/company/about_us).

- Some firms, like IBM, have designed performance evaluation measures that reward managers based on the subsequent accuracy of the forecasts used in preparing budgets.

- Subordinates may regard budgets negatively. Frequently, budgets are viewed as processes by which departments may lose staff, operating budgets, or capital items (or all three!). Top management must convince them that budgets are a tool that can be used to justify operating levels and can help them to set and reach goals.

- Budget systems often appear to reward bad performance and penalize good performance. Take the example of the department that goes over-budget (in regards to expenditures) one year, only to use that performance to justify asking for a larger budget in the next budget cycle. Conversely, consider the department that manages, through careful expenditures and creative solutions, to come in under budget, only to find that in the next budget cycle it gets a smaller budget (since the employees apparently didn't need the budget they had!).

  - Organizations can set incentives and consequences for budget performance. Some firms have moved to budget models that require (over a number of periods) repayments (from the future budget amounts) of any over expenditures. For units that don't use all of their current budget, organizations make some portion of the savings available for use in future budget cycles.

Budgeting: A Process in Transition

Many areas of management accounting are subject to ongoing debate. Budgeting is no exception. Advocates of new proposals invariably include criticisms of so-called "traditional budgeting." Exhibit 6-9 summarizes six proposals designed to address some of the shortcomings of traditional budgeting systems. Earlier sections of this chapter have mentioned the importance of avoiding many of these problems.

Exhibit 6-9 Criticisms of Traditional Budgeting and Proposals for Change

Criticism of Traditional Budgeting	Proposal for Change
Consumes large amounts of management time	Budget by major groups/programs/departments rather than a line-by-line approach. This type of aggregated budgeting allows managers to keep the "big picture" in view.
Based on old data	Adopt rolling quarterly budgets instead of annual budgets. Rolling budgets are prepared more frequently, but with more current data. This makes them more relevant and useful.
Doesn't motivate desired behaviours	Use relative targets (e.g., sales per employee) or benchmarked targets instead of absolute targets (e.g., $10 million sales for the department). This allows for changes in the environment that a fixed budget does not.
Doesn't promote strategic direction of the firm	Make sure that the budgeting process starts with the strategic intent of the firm. The Balanced Scorecard is an excellent tool for this.
	Ensure that nonfinancial objectives/targets are developed (in addition to the traditional financial targets) as part of the budgeting process.
	Look at *processes* as the base for the budgeting activity instead of units or departments. This encourages cross-department planning and cooperation.

Source: Adapted from Prof. Peter Horvath "Why Budgeting Fails: One Management System Is Not Enough."

Pulling It All Together—Problem for Self-Study

(Try to solve this problem before examining the solution that follows.)

Problem

Consider the Halifax Engineering example described in this chapter. Suppose Halifax Engineering managers wanted to know how the budgets would be impacted by a 10% price increase in material 112 alloy from $10 to $11; a 12% increase in the variable supplies cost; a 22% increase in power costs to account for an unexpected jump in oil prices; and a corresponding 22% increase in distribution costs to account for ground and air transportation cost increases together with an oil-price increase.

Required ▶ ❶ 1. What are the benefits of budgeting for these specific changes now?

❷ 2. Before preparing a budgeted income statement, identify the supporting budget schedules that will *not* change as a result of this sensitivity analysis.

❷ 3. Prepare the budgeted operating income statement, including all necessary supporting schedules.

❹ 4. Discuss the results. Focus on any important changes that can be planned should the increases happen.

❺ 5. Discuss how responsibility and controllability will affect Halifax Engineering's response to the events noted in the sensitivity analysis.

Solution

1. In the short term, the budget constraints for Halifax have changed. Only by recalculating the affected schedules can the company's managers understand what remedies may be available to reduce the effects of these cost increases. The team can agree in advance what responses may be made to sustain operating profits. The managers are already anticipating how to protect the company from external threats over which the company itself has no control.

5. Appendix 6A: How do the strategies of sensitivity analysis, Kaizen budgeting, and ABB differ?

Sensitivity analysis is a way to alter the assumptions of the master budget. This analysis permits managers to establish plans in advance of possible adverse events. Kaizen budgeting is incremental cost reduction through elimination of waste in various business processes. ABB is the reduction of non-value-added activities that fail to contribute to the customers' value proposition. They are all long-term strategies to reduce costs.

Terms to Learn

This chapter and the Glossary at the end of the book contain definitions of the following important terms:

activity-based budgeting (ABB) **(p. 184)**

benchmark **(p. 183)**

budget **(p. 182)**

budget constraints **(p. 182)**

budgetary slack **(p. 191)**

budgeting cycle **(p. 183)**

cash budget **(p. 198)**

cash cycle **(p. 203)**

controllability **(p. 207)**

controllable cost **(p. 207)**

cost centre **(p. 206)**

financial budgets **(p. 182)**

investment centre **(p. 206)**

Kaizen budgeting **(p. 216)**

master budget **(p. 182)**

nonfinancial budgets **(p. 182)**

operating budget **(p. 186)**

operating cycle **(p. 203)**

organizational structure **(p. 206)**

padding **(p. 191)**

profit centre **(p. 206)**

pro forma statements **(p. 182)**

responsibility accounting **(p. 206)**

responsibility centre **(p. 206)**

revenue centre **(p. 206)**

rolling budget **(p. 186)**

self-liquidating cycle **(p. 203)**

standard **(p. 183)**

strategic analysis **(p. 184)**

stretch goals **(p. 183)**

working capital cycle **(p. 203)**

Assignment Material

MyLab Accounting Make the grade with MyLab Accounting: The Short-Answer Questions, Exercises, and Problems marked with a ⊕ can be found on MyLab Accounting. You can practise them as often as you want, and most feature step-by-step guided instructions to help you find the right answer.

Short-Answer Questions

⊕ **6-1** What are the four elements of the budgeting cycle?

⊕ **6-2** Define *master budget*.

⊕ **6-3** If actual results do not match the budget, what should managers do?

⊕ **6-4** "Strategy, plans, and budgets are unrelated to one another." Do you agree? Explain.

⊕ **6-5** "Budgeted performance is a better criterion than past performance for judging managers." Do you agree? Explain.

⊕ **6-6** How might a company benefit by sharing its own internal budget information with other companies?

⊕ **6-7** Define *rolling budget*. Give an example.

⊕ **6-8** Outline the steps in preparing an operating budget.

⊕ **6-9** "The revenue budget is the cornerstone for budgeting." Why?

⊕ **6-10** How can the use of sensitivity analysis increase the benefits of budgeting?

⊕ **6-11** Explain "padding" and why managers might be motivated to employ this negative budget behaviour. What are some of senior management's options to address this behaviour?

⊕ **6-12** Describe how non-output-based cost drivers can be incorporated into budgeting.

6-13 Explain how the choice of the responsibility centre type (cost, revenue; profit, or investment) affects budgeting.

6-14 When governments reduce their funding to hospitals and universities, often the executives respond with a demand for an equal percentage reduction in costs by all business functions. Is this the best strategic approach?

Exercises

6-15 Terminology. A number of terms are listed below:

budget constraint(s)	budgetary slack
cash cycle	controllable cost
investment budget	operating cycle
rolling budget	self-liquidating cycle

Required

Select the terms from the above list to complete the following sentences.

A _____, also known as an _____, is the movement of cash arising from business functions to inventories, to receivables, and back to cash when outputs are sold. It is a _____ where all costs of a corporation are recovered when output is sold. _____ is the practice of underestimating revenue and overestimating costs to make the _____ less challenging. Once the corporate budget is produced, all managers make a commitment to reach budget targets. They are responsible for _____ that must be at or below the budget constraint during each reporting time period. Some companies produce a _____ that adds a reporting time period as one is completed. An _____ affects the inflow and outflow of cash either to make the investment or to pay to finance it.

LO 5 ▶

6-16 Responsibility and controllability. Consider each of the following independent situations:

1. A very successful salesperson at Amcorp Computers regularly ignores the published sales catalogue and offers lowered prices to customers in order to close sales. The VP of sales notices that revenue is substantially lower than budgeted.
2. Every "special deal" offered to a customer by any salesperson at Amcorp Computers has to be cleared by the VP of sales. Revenue for the second quarter has been lower than budgeted.
3. The shipping department of Amcorp has limited capacity, and sales orders are being cancelled by customers because of delays in delivery. Revenue for the past month has been lower than budgeted.
4. At Planetel Corp., a manufacturer of telecommunications equipment, the production supervisor notices that a significantly larger number of direct manufacturing labour-hours were used than had been budgeted. Investigation revealed that it was due to a decline in educational standards required by the human resources department when it interviewed applicants for hourly production jobs six months earlier.
5. At Planetel Corp., a relatively new production supervisor finds that more direct manufacturing labour-hours were used than had been budgeted. Interviews revealed that workers were unhappy with the supervisor's management style and were intentionally working slowly and inefficiently.
6. At Planetel Corp., the production supervisor traces the excessive consumption of direct materials (relative to the budget) to the fact that waste was high on machines that had not been properly maintained.

Required

For each situation described, determine where (that is, with whom) (a) responsibility and (b) controllability lie. Suggest what might be done to solve the problem or to improve the situation.

LO 3 ▶

1. Wool direct materials used this period, $6,017,450

6-17 Budgeting; direct material usage, manufacturing cost, and gross margin. Covered Manufacturing Company manufactures blue rugs, using wool and dye as direct materials. All other materials are indirect. At the beginning of the year Covered has an inventory of 349,000 skeins of wool at a cost of $715,450 and 5,000 litres of dye at a cost of $24,850. Target ending inventory of wool and dye is zero. Covered uses the FIFO inventory cost flow method.

One blue rug is budgeted to use 30 skeins of wool at a cost of $2 per skein and 0.5 litres of dye at a cost of $5 per litre.

Covered blue rugs are very popular and demand is high, but because of capacity constraints the firm will produce only 100,000 blue rugs per year. The budgeted selling price is $2,000 each. There are no rugs in beginning inventory. Target ending inventory of rugs is also zero.

Covered makes rugs by hand, but uses a machine to dye the wool. Thus, overhead costs are accumulated in two cost pools—one for weaving and the other for dyeing. Weaving overhead is allocated to product based on direct manufacturing labour-hours (DMLH). Dyeing overhead is allocated to product based on machine-hours (MH).

There is no direct manufacturing labour cost for dyeing Covered budgets 56 direct manufacturing labour-hours to weave a rug at a budgeted rate of $15 per hour. It budgets 0.15 machine-hours to dye each skein in the dyeing process.

The following table presents the budgeted overhead costs for the dyeing and weaving cost pools:

	Dyeing (based on 450,000 MH)	Weaving (based on 5,600,000 DMLH)
Variable costs		
Indirect materials	$ 0	$11,200,000
Maintenance	4,950,000	2,240,000
Utilities	5,400,000	1,680,000
Fixed costs		
Indirect labour	239,000	1,300,000
Depreciation	1,900,000	52,000
Other	320,000	2,380,000
Total budgeted costs	$12,809,000	$18,852,000

Required

1. Prepare a direct material usage budget in both units and dollars.
2. Calculate the budgeted overhead allocation rates for weaving and dyeing.
3. Calculate the budgeted unit cost of a blue rug for the year.
4. Prepare a revenue budget for blue rugs for the year, assuming Covered sells (a) 100,000 or (b) 95,000 blue rugs (that is, at two different sales levels).
5. Calculate the budgeted cost of goods sold for blue rugs under each sales assumption.
6. Find the budgeted gross margin for blue rugs under each sales assumption.

🌐 **6-18 Sales budget, service setting.** In 2018, McGrath & Sons, a small environmental-testing firm, performed 11,000 radon tests for $250 each and 15,200 lead tests for $200 each. Because newer homes are being built with lead-free pipes, lead-testing volume is expected to decrease by 10% next year. However, awareness of radon-related health hazards is expected to result in a 10% increase in radon-test volume each year in the near future. Jim McGrath feels that if he lowers his price for lead testing to $190 per test, he will have to face only a 5% decline in lead-test sales in 2019.

◀ **LO 2**
1. Total revenue, $5,623,500

Required

1. Prepare a 2019 sales budget for McGrath & Sons assuming that McGrath holds prices at 2018 levels.
2. Prepare a 2019 sales budget for McGrath & Sons assuming that McGrath lowers the price of a lead test to $190. Should McGrath lower the price of a lead test in 2019 if its goal is to maximize sales revenue?

🌐 **6-19 Sales and production budget.** The Russell Company expects 2019 sales of 135,000 units of serving trays. Russell's beginning inventory for 2019 is 9,700 trays; target ending inventory: 16,300 trays.

◀ **LO 2**
Total requirements, 141,600

Required

Compute the number of trays budgeted for production in 2019.

🌐 **6-20 Direct materials budget.** The wine-producing company Lebeau Vineyard expects to produce 2.1 million 3-litre bottles of Chablis in 2019. Lebeau purchases empty glass bottles from a reliable supplier. The target ending inventory of such bottles is 55,000; the beginning inventory is 23,700. For simplicity, ignore loss due to breakage.

◀ **LO 3**
Total requirements (bottles), 2,131,300

Required

Compute the number of bottles to be purchased in 2019.

🌐 **6-21 Budgeting material purchases.** In the preparation of the sales budget for the next three-month period, the Westing Company determined that 52,250 finished units would be needed to fulfill sales obligations. The company has an inventory of 27,300 units of finished goods on hand at December 31 and has a target finished goods inventory of 29,400 units at the end of the succeeding quarter.

It takes three litres of direct materials to make one unit of finished product. The company has an inventory of 117,350 litres of direct materials at December 31 and has a target ending inventory of 110,000 litres.

◀ **LO 2**
54,350 production units

Required

How many litres of direct materials should be ordered for delivery during the three months ending March 31?

LO 2 ▶
2. Units to be produced
5,680,000

🌐 **6-22 Revenues and production budget.** Saphire, Inc., bottles and distributes mineral water from the company's natural springs in northern Oregon. Saphire markets two products: 12-ounce disposable plastic bottles and 1-gallon reusable plastic containers.

Required

1. For 2018, Saphire marketing managers project monthly sales of 500,000 12-ounce bottles and 130,000 1-gallon containers. Average selling prices are estimated at $0.30 per 12-ounce bottle and $1.60 per 1-gallon container. Prepare a revenues budget for Saphire, Inc., for the year ending December 31, 2018.
2. Saphire begins 2018 with 980,000 12-ounce bottles in inventory. The vice president of operations requests that 12-ounce bottles ending inventory on December 31, 2018, be no less than 660,000 bottles. Based on sales projections as budgeted previously, what is the minimum number of 12-ounce bottles Saphire must produce during 2018?
3. The VP of operations requests that ending inventory of 1-gallon containers on December 31, 2018, be 300,000 units. If the production budget calls for Saphire to produce 1,200,000 1-gallon containers during 2018, what is the beginning inventory of 1-gallon containers on January 1, 2018?

LO 2 ▶
3. Total Budgeted per unit cost
of Blue Rug is $1,127.30

🌐 **6-23 Budgeting; direct material usage, manufacturing cost, and gross margin.** Xander Manufacturing Company manufactures blue rugs, using wool and dye as direct materials. One rug is budgeted to use 36 skeins of wool at a cost of $2 per skein and 0.8 gallons of dye at a cost of $6 per gallon. All other materials are indirect. At the beginning of the year Xander has an inventory of 458,000 skeins of wool at a cost of $961,800 and 4,000 gallons of dye at a cost of $23,680. Target ending inventory of wool and dye is zero. Xander uses the FIFO inventory cost-flow method.

Xander blue rugs are very popular and demand is high, but because of capacity constraints the firm will produce only 200,000 blue rugs per year. The budgeted selling price is $2,000 each. There are no rugs in beginning inventory. Target ending inventory of rugs is also zero.

Xander makes rugs by hand, but uses a machine to dye the wool. Thus, overhead costs are accumulated in two cost pools—one for weaving and the other for dyeing. Weaving overhead is allocated to products based on direct manufacturing labour-hours (DMLH). Dyeing overhead is allocated to products based on machine-hours (MH).

There is no direct manufacturing labour cost for dyeing. Xander budgets 62 direct manufacturing labour-hours to weave a rug at a budgeted rate of $13 per hour. It budgets 0.2 machine-hours to dye each skein in the dyeing process.

The following table presents the budgeted overhead costs for the dyeing and weaving cost pools:

	Dyeing (based on 1,440,000 MH)	Weaving (based on 12,400,000 DMLH)
Variable costs		
Indirect materials	$ 0	$15,400,000
Maintenance	6,560,000	5,540,000
Utilities	7,550,000	2,890,000
Fixed costs		
Indirect labour	347,000	1,700,000
Depreciation	2,100,000	274,000
Other	723,000	5,816,000
Total budgeted costs	$17,280,000	$31,620,000

Required

1. Prepare a direct materials usage budget in both units and dollars.
2. Calculate the budgeted overhead allocation rates for weaving and dyeing.
3. Calculate the budgeted unit cost of a blue rug for the year.
4. Prepare a revenues budget for blue rugs for the year, assuming Xander sells (a) 200,000 or (b) 185,000 blue rugs (that is, at two different sales levels).
5. Calculate the budgeted cost of goods sold for blue rugs under each sales assumption.
6. Find the budgeted gross margin for blue rugs under each sales assumption.
7. What actions might you take as a manager to improve profitability if sales drop to 185,000 blue rugs?
8. How might top management at Xander use the budget developed in requirements 1–6 to better manage the company?

⊕ 6-24 Revenue, production, and purchases budget. The Suzuki Company in Japan has a division that manufactures two-wheel motorcycles. Its budgeted sales for Model G in 2019 are 985,000 units. Suzuki's target ending inventory is 115,000 units, and its beginning inventory is 152,000 units. The company's budgeted selling price to its distributors and dealers is 505,000 yen (¥) per motorcycle.

◄ **LO 2**
2. Total production, 948,000 units

Suzuki buys all its wheels from an outside supplier. No defective wheels are accepted. (Suzuki's needs for extra wheels for replacement parts are ordered by a separate division of the company.) The company's target ending inventory is 28,000 wheels, and its beginning inventory is 19,000 wheels. The budgeted purchase price is ¥21,300 per wheel.

Required

1. Compute the budgeted revenue in yen.
2. Compute the number of motorcycles to be produced.
3. Compute the budgeted purchases of wheels in units and in yen.

⊕ 6-25 Budgets for production and direct manufacturing labour. (CMA, adapted) The All Frame Company makes and sells artistic frames for pictures of weddings, graduations, and other special events. Martin Flack, the company controller, is responsible for preparing the master budget and has accumulated the following information for 2019:

◄ **LO 2**
$595,900 Total DL cost

	2019				
	January	**February**	**March**	**April**	**May**
Estimated sales in units	10,000	12,000	8,000	9,000	9,000
Selling price	$54.00	$51.50	$51.50	$51.50	$51.50
Direct manufacturing labour-hours per unit	2.0	2.0	1.5	1.5	1.5
Wage per direct manufacturing labour-hour	$10.00	$10.00	$10.00	$11.00	$11.00

Direct manufacturing labour-related costs include pension contributions of $0.50 per hour, workers' compensation insurance of $0.15 per hour, employee medical insurance of $0.40 per hour, and employment insurance, in addition to wages. Assume that as of January 1, 2019, the employment insurance rates are 7.5% of wages for employers and 7.5% of wages for employees. The cost of employee benefits paid by All Frame for its employees is treated as a direct manufacturing labour cost.

All Frame has an employee labour contract that calls for a wage increase to $11.00 per hour on April 1, 2019. New labour-saving machinery has been installed and will be fully operational by March 1, 2019.

The controller has been informed that the company expects to have 16,000 frames on hand on December 31, 2018, and has a policy of carrying an end-of-month inventory of 100% of the following month's sales plus 50% of the second following month's sales.

Required

Prepare a production budget and a direct manufacturing labour budget for the All Frame Company by month and for the first quarter of 2019. The direct manufacturing labour budget should include labour-hours and show the details for each labour cost category.

⊕ 6-26 Cash flow analysis. (CMA, adapted) TabComp Inc. is a retail distributor for MZB-33 computer hardware and related software and support services. TabComp prepares annual sales forecasts of which the first six months for 2019 are presented here. Cash sales account for 25% of TabComp's total sales, 30% of the total sales are paid by bank credit card, and the remaining 45% are on open account (TabComp's own charge accounts). The cash sales and cash from bank credit-card sales are received in the month of the sale. Bank credit-card sales are subject to a 4% discount deducted at the time of the daily deposit. The cash receipts for sales on open account are 70% in the month following the sale and 28% in the second month after the sale. The remaining accounts receivable are estimated to be uncollectible.

◄ **LO 3**
1. $429,400

TabComp's month-end inventory requirements for computer hardware units are 30% of the next month's sales. A one-month lead time is required for delivery from the manufacturer. Thus, orders for computer hardware units are placed on the 25th of each month to assure that they will be in the store by the first day of the month needed. The computer hardware units are purchased under terms of n/45 (payment in full within 45 days of invoice), measured from the time the units are delivered to TabComp. TabComp's purchase price for the computer units is 70% of the selling price.

TabComp Inc.
Sales Forecast for First Six Months of 2019

| | Hardware Sales | | Software Sales | |
	Units	Dollars	and Support	Total Revenues
January	130	$ 390,000	$160,000	$ 550,000
February	120	360,000	140,000	500,000
March	110	330,000	150,000	480,000
April	90	270,000	130,000	400,000
May	100	300,000	125,000	425,000
June	125	375,000	225,000	600,000
Total	$675	$2,025,000	$930,000	$2,955,000

Required

1. Calculate the cash that TabComp Inc. can expect to collect during April 2019. Be sure to show all of your calculations.
2. TabComp Inc. is determining how many MZB-33 computer hardware units to order on January 25, 2019.
   a. Determine the projected number of computer hardware units that will be ordered.
   b. Calculate the dollar amount of the order that TabComp will place for these computer hardware units.
3. As part of the annual budget process, TabComp prepares a cash budget by month for the entire year. Explain why a company such as TabComp would do this.

LO 5 ▶
1. Total budgeted indirect cost, $27,147

🌐 **6-27 Activity-based budgeting.** The Parksville location of Your Mart (YM), a chain of small neighbourhood grocery stores, is preparing its activity-based budget for January 2019. YM has three product categories: soft drinks, fresh produce, and packaged food. The following table shows the four activities that consume indirect resources at the Parksville store, the cost drivers and their rates, and the cost driver amount budgeted to be consumed by each activity in January 2019.

| | | January 2019 Budgeted Cost Driver Rate | January 2019 Budgeted Amount of Cost Driver Used | | |
Activity	Cost Driver		Soft Drinks	Fresh Produce	Packaged Food
Ordering	Number of purchase orders	$90.00	14	24	14
Delivery	Number of deliveries	82.00	12	62	19
Shelf-stocking	Hours of stocking time	21.00	16	172	94
Customer support	Number of items sold	0.18	4,600	34,200	10,750

Required

1. What is the total budgeted indirect cost at the Parksville store in January 2019? What is the total budgeted cost of each activity at the Parksville store for January 2019? What is the budgeted indirect cost of each product category for January 2019?
2. Which product category has the largest fraction of total budgeted indirect costs?
3. Given your answer in requirement 2, what advantage does YM gain by using an activity-based approach to budgeting over, say, allocating indirect costs to products based on cost of goods sold?

LO 5 ▶
1. Total budgeted indirect cost for March 2019, $27,025

🌐 **6-28 Kaizen approach to activity-based budgeting.** Your Mart (YM) has a Kaizen (continuous improvement) approach to budgeting activity area costs for each month of 2019. Each successive month, the budgeted cost driver rate decreases by 0.2% relative to the preceding month (so, for example, February's budgeted cost driver rate is 0.998 times January's budgeted cost driver rate, and March's budgeted cost driver rate is 0.998 times the budgeted February 2019 rate). YM assumes that the budgeted amount of cost driver usage remains the same each month.

Required

1. What is the total budgeted cost for each activity and the total budgeted indirect cost for March 2019?
2. What are the benefits of using a Kaizen approach to budgeting? What are the limitations of this approach, and how might YM management overcome them?

Problems

🌐 **6-29 Revenue and production budgets.** (CPA, adapted) Two products are manufactured by the Fraser Corporation: Widgets and Thingamajigs. In July 2018, the controller of Fraser, upon instructions from senior management, had the budgeting department gather the following data in order to prepare budgets for 2019:

◀ LO 2
2. Production: Widgets,
65,000 units
Thingamajigs, 41,000 units

2019 Projected Sales

Product	Units	Price
Widget	60,000	$198
Thingamajig	40,000	$300

2019 Inventories in Units

Product	Expected January 1, 2019	Target December 31, 2019
Widget	22,000	27,000
Thingamajig	10,000	11,000

The following direct materials are used to produce one unit of Widget and Thingamajig:

		Amount Used per Unit	
Direct Material	Unit	Widget	Thingamajig
A	Kilograms	4	5
B	Kilograms	2	3
C	Each	0	1

Projected data for 2019 with respect to direct materials are as follows:

Direct Material	Anticipated Purchase Price	Expected Inventories, January 1, 2019	Target Inventories, December 31, 2019
A	$14	32,000 kilograms	36,000 kilograms
B	$ 7	29,000 kilograms	32,000 kilograms
C	$ 5	6,000 units	7,000 units

Projected direct manufacturing labour requirements and rates for 2019 are as follows:

Product	Hours per Unit	Rate per Hour
Widget	2	$15
Thingamajig	3	19

Manufacturing overhead is allocated at the rate of $24 per direct manufacturing labour-hour.

Required

Based on the preceding projections and budget requirements for Widgets and Thingamajigs, prepare the following budgets for 2019:

1. Revenue budget (in dollars).
2. Production budget (in units).
3. Direct materials purchases budget (in quantities).
4. Direct materials purchases budget (in dollars).
5. Direct manufacturing labour budget (in dollars).
6. Budgeted finished goods inventory at December 31, 2019 (in dollars).

🌐 **6-30 Budgeted income statement.** (CMA, adapted) Easecom Company is a manufacturer of video-conferencing products. Regular units are manufactured to meet marketing projections, and specialized units are made after an order is received. Maintaining the video-conferencing equipment is an important area of customer satisfaction. With the recent downturn in the computer industry, the video-conferencing equipment segment has suffered, leading to a decline in Easecom's financial performance. The following income statement shows results for 2018.

◀ LO 2
Operating income, $843

Easecom Company
Income Statement
For the Year Ended December 31, 2018 (in $ thousands)

Revenues:		
Equipment	$6,000	
Maintenance contracts	1,800	
Total revenues		$7,800
Cost of goods sold		4,600
Gross margin		3,200
Operating costs:		
Marketing	600	
Distribution	150	
Customer maintenance	1,000	
Administration	900	
Total operating costs		2,650
Operating income		$ 550

1. Selling prices of equipment are expected to increase by 15% as the economic recovery begins. The selling price of each maintenance contract is expected to remain unchanged from 2018.
2. Equipment sales in units are expected to increase by 6%, with a corresponding 6% growth in units of maintenance contracts.
3. Cost of each unit sold is expected to increase by 3% to pay for the necessary technology and quality improvements.
4. Marketing costs are expected to increase by $250,000, but administration costs are expected to remain at 2018 levels.
5. Distribution costs vary in proportion to the number of units of equipment sold.
6. Two maintenance technicians are to be hired at a total cost of $130,000, which covers wages and related travel costs. The objective is to improve customer service and shorten response time.
7. There is no beginning or ending inventory of equipment.

Required

Prepare a budgeted income statement for the year ending December 31, 2019.

LO 2 ▶ ⊕ **6-31 Budget schedules for a manufacturer.** Hale Specialties manufactures, among other things, woolen blankets for the athletic teams of the two local high schools. The company sews the blankets from fabric and sews on a logo patch purchased from the licensed logo store site. The teams are as follows:

- Broncos, with red blankets and the Broncos logo
- Rams, with black blankets and the Rams logo

Also, the black blankets are slightly larger than the red blankets.
The budgeted direct-cost inputs for each product in 2017 are as follows:

	Broncos Blanket	Rams Blanket
Red wool fabric	5 yards	0 yards
Black wool fabric	0	6
Broncos logo patches	1	0
Rams logo patches	0	1
Direct manufacturing labour	4 hours	5 hours

Unit data pertaining to the direct materials for March 2017 are as follows:

Actual Beginning Direct Materials Inventory (3/1/2017)

	Broncos Blanket	Rams Blanket
Red wool fabric	40 yards	0 yards
Black wool fabric	0	20
Broncos logo patches	50	0
Rams logo patches	0	65

Target Ending Direct Materials Inventory (3/31/2017)

	Broncos Blanket	Rams Blanket
Red wool fabric	30 yards	0 yards
Black wool fabric	0	20
Broncos logo patches	30	0
Rams logo patches	0	30

Unit cost data for direct-cost inputs pertaining to February 2017 and March 2017 are as follows:

	February 2017 (actual)	March 2017 (budgeted)
Red wool fabric (per yard)	$10	$11
Black wool fabric (per yard)	14	13
Broncos logo patches (per patch)	8	8
Rams logo patches (per patch)	7	9
Manufacturing labour cost per hour	27	28

Manufacturing overhead (both variable and fixed) is allocated to each blanket on the basis of budgeted direct manufacturing labour-hours per blanket. The budgeted variable manufacturing overhead rate for March 2017 is $17 per direct manufacturing labour-hour. The budgeted fixed manufacturing overhead for March 2017 is $14,625. Both variable and fixed manufacturing overhead costs are allocated to each unit of finished goods.

Data relating to finished-goods inventory for March 2017 are as follows:

	Broncos Blankets	Rams Blankets
Beginning inventory in units	14	19
Beginning inventory in dollars (cost)	$1,960	$2,945
Target ending inventory in units	24	29

Budgeted sales for March 2017 are 140 units of the Broncos blankets and 195 units of the Rams blankets. The budgeted selling prices per unit in March 2017 are $305 for the Broncos blankets and $378 for the Rams blankets. Assume the following in your answer:

- Work-in-process inventories are negligible and ignored.
- Direct materials inventory and finished-goods inventory are costed using the FIFO method.
- Unit costs of direct materials purchased and finished goods are constant in March 2017.

Required

1. Prepare the following budgets for March 2017:
   a. Revenues budget
   b. Production budget in units
   c. Direct material usage budget and direct materials purchases budget
   d. Direct manufacturing labour costs budget
   e. Manufacturing overhead costs budget
   f. Ending inventories budget (direct materials and finished goods)
   g. Cost of goods sold budget
2. Suppose Hale Specialties decides to incorporate continuous improvement into its budgeting process. Describe two areas where it could incorporate continuous improvement into the budget schedules in requirement 1.

🌐 **6-32 Revenue and production budgets.** (CPA, adapted) The Chen Corporation manufactures and sells two products: Thingone and Thingtwo. In July 2016, Chen's budget department gathered the following data to prepare budgets for 2017:   ◀ LO 2

2017 Projected Sales

Product	Units	Price
Thingone	69,000	$160
Thingtwo	44,000	$258

2017 Inventories in Units

	Expected Target	
Product	January 1, 2017	December 31, 2017
Thingone	24,000	29,000
Thingtwo	7,000	8,000

The following direct materials are used in the two products:

	Amount Used per Unit		
Direct Material	Unit	Thingone	Thingtwo
A	pound	6	7
B	pound	4	5
C	each	0	3

Projected data for 2017 for direct materials are:

Direct Material	Anticipated Purchase Price	Expected Inventories January 1, 2017	Target Inventories December 31, 2017
A	$13	36,000 lb.	38,000 lb.
B	8	31,000 lb.	34,000 lb.
C	7	9,000 units	12,000 units

Projected direct manufacturing labour requirements and rates for 2017 are:

Product	Hours per Unit	Rate per Hour
Thingone	4	$13
Thingtwo	5	18

Manufacturing overhead is allocated at the rate of $24 per direct manufacturing labour-hour.

Required

Based on the preceding projections and budget requirements for Thingone and Thingtwo, prepare the following budgets for 2017:

1. Revenues budget (in dollars)
2. What questions might the CEO ask the marketing manager when reviewing the revenues budget? Explain briefly.
3. Production budget (in units)
4. Direct material purchases budget (in quantities)
5. Direct material purchases budget (in dollars)
6. Direct manufacturing labour budget (in dollars)
7. Budgeted finished-goods inventory at December 31, 2017 (in dollars)
8. What questions might the CEO ask the production manager when reviewing the production, direct materials, and direct manufacturing labour budgets?
9. How does preparing a budget help Chen Corporation's top management better manage the company?

LO 3 ▶ ⊕ **6-33 Comprehensive operating budget.** Skulas, Inc., manufactures and sells snowboards. Skulas manufactures a single model, the Pipex. In late 2017, Skulas's management accountant gathered the following data to prepare budgets for January 2018:

Materials and Labour Requirements

Direct materials	
Wood	9 board feet (b.f.) per snowboard
Fiberglass	10 yards per snowboard
Direct manufacturing labour	5 hours per snowboard

Skulas's CEO expects to sell 2,900 snowboards during January 2018 at an estimated retail price of $650 per board. Further, the CEO expects 2018 beginning inventory of 500 snowboards and would like to end January 2018 with 200 snowboards in stock.

Direct Materials Inventories

	Beginning Inventory 1/1/2018	Ending Inventory 1/31/2018
Wood	2,040 b.f.	1,540 b.f.
Fiberglass	1,040 yards	2,040 yards

Variable manufacturing overhead is $7 per direct manufacturing labour-hour. There are also $81,000 in fixed manufacturing overhead costs budgeted for January 2018. Skulas combines both variable and fixed manufacturing overhead into a single rate based on direct manufacturing labour-hours. Variable marketing costs are allocated at the rate of $250 per sales visit. The marketing plan calls for 38 sales visits during January 2018. Finally, there are $35,000 in fixed nonmanufacturing costs budgeted for January 2018.

Other data include:

	2017 Unit Price	2018 Unit Price
Wood	$32.00 per b.f.	$34.00 per b.f.
Fiberglass	$ 8.00 per yard	$ 9.00 per yard
Direct manufacturing labour	$28.00 per hour	$29.00 per hour

The inventoriable unit cost for ending finished-goods inventory on December 31, 2017, is $374.80. Assume Skulas uses a FIFO inventory method for both direct materials and finished goods. Ignore work in process in your calculations.

Required

1. Prepare the January 2018 revenues budget (in dollars).
2. Prepare the January 2018 production budget (in units).
3. Prepare the direct material usage and purchases budgets for January 2018.
4. Prepare a direct manufacturing labour costs budget for January 2018.
5. Prepare a manufacturing overhead costs budget for January 2018.
6. What is the budgeted manufacturing overhead rate for January 2018?
7. What is the budgeted manufacturing overhead cost per output unit in January 2018?
8. Calculate the cost of a snowboard manufactured in January 2018.
9. Prepare an ending inventory budget for both direct materials and finished goods for January 2018.
10. Prepare a cost of goods sold budget for January 2018.
11. Prepare the budgeted income statement for Skulas, Inc., for January 2018.
12. What questions might the CEO ask the management team when reviewing the budget? Should the CEO set stretch targets? Explain briefly.
13. How does preparing the budget help Skulas's management team better manage the company?

⊕ **6-34 Cash budgeting, budgeted balance sheet.** Refer to the information in Problem 6-33.   ◂ **LO 5**
Budgeted balances at January 31, 2018 are as follows:

Cash	?
Accounts receivable	?
Inventory	?
Property, plant and equipment (net)	$1,175,600
Accounts payable	?
Long-term liabilities	182,000
Stockholders' equity	?

Selected budget information for December 2017 follows:

Cash balance, December 31, 2017	$ 124,000
Budgeted sales	1,650,000
Budgeted materials purchases	820,000

Customer invoices are payable within 30 days. From past experience, Skulas's accountant projects 40% of invoices will be collected in the month invoiced, and 60% will be collected in the following month.

Accounts payable relates only to the purchase of direct materials. Direct materials are purchased on credit with 50% of direct materials purchases paid during the month of the purchase, and 50% paid in the month following purchase.

Fixed manufacturing overhead costs include $64,000 of depreciation costs and fixed nonmanufacturing overhead costs include $10,000 of depreciation costs. Direct manufacturing labour and the remaining manufacturing and nonmanufacturing overhead costs are paid monthly.

All property, plant, and equipment acquired during January 2018 were purchased on credit and did not entail any outflow of cash.

There were no borrowings or repayments with respect to long-term liabilities in January 2018.

On December 15, 2017, Skulas's board of directors voted to pay a $160,000 dividend to stockholders on January 31, 2018.

Required

1. Prepare a cash budget for January 2018. Show supporting schedules for the calculation of collection of receivables and payments of accounts payable, and for disbursements for fixed manufacturing and nonmanufacturing overhead.

2. Skulas is interested in maintaining a minimum cash balance of $120,000 at the end of each month. Will Skulas be in a position to pay the $160,000 dividend on January 31?

3. Why do Skulas's managers prepare a cash budget in addition to the revenue, expenses, and operating income budget?

4. Prepare a budgeted balance sheet for January 31, 2018 by calculating the January 31, 2018 balances in (a) cash (b) accounts receivable (c) inventory (d) accounts payable and (e) plugging in the balance for stockholders' equity.

LO 5 ▶

2. Production units: Cat-allac, 520 Dog-eriffic, 285

🌐 **6-35 Comprehensive problem with ABC costing.** Pet Transport Company makes two pet carriers, the Cat-allac and the Dog-eriffic. They are both made of plastic with metal doors, but the Cat-allac is smaller. Information for the two products for the month of April is given in the following tables:

Input prices

Direct materials	
Plastic	$ 4 per kilogram
Metal	$ 3 per kilogram
Direct manufacturing labour	$10 per direct manufacturing labour-hour

Input quantities per unit of output

	Cat-allac	Dog-eriffic
Direct materials		
Plastic	4 kilograms	6 kilograms
Metal	0.5 kilograms	1 kilogram
Direct manufacturing labour-hours (DMLH)	3 hours	5 hours
Machine-hours (MH)	10 MH	18 MH

Inventory information, direct materials

	Plastic	Metal
Beginning inventory	250 kilograms	60 kilograms
Target ending inventory	380 kilograms	55 kilograms
Cost of beginning inventory	$950	$180

Pet Transport accounts for direct materials using a FIFO cost flow assumption.

Sales and inventory information, finished goods

	Cat-allac	Dog-eriffic
Expected sales	500 units	300 units
Selling price	$ 160	$ 250
Target ending inventory	35 units	15 units
Beginning inventory	15 units	30 units
Beginning inventory value	$ 1,500	$ 5,580

Pet Transport uses a FIFO cost flow assumption for finished goods inventory.

Pet Transport uses an activity-based costing system and classifies overhead into three activity pools: Setup, Processing, and Inspection. Activity rates for these activities are $100 per setup-hour, $5 per machine-hour, and $16 per inspection-hour. Other information follows:

Cost driver information

	Cat-allac	Dog-eriffic
Number of units per batch	20	15
Setup time per batch	1.5 hours	1.75 hours
Inspection time per batch	0.5 hour	0.6 hour

Nonproduction fixed costs for March equal $36,000, of which half are salaries. Salaries are expected to increase by 5% in April. The only variable nonproduction cost is sales commission, equal to 1% of sales revenue.

Required

Prepare the following for April:

1. Revenue budget.
2. Production budget in units.
3. Direct material usage budget and direct material purchases budget.
4. Direct manufacturing labour cost budget.
5. Manufacturing overhead cost budgets for each of the three activities.
6. Budgeted unit cost of ending finished goods inventory and ending inventories budget.
7. Cost of goods sold budget.
8. Non-manufacturing costs budget.
9. Budgeted income statement (ignore income taxes).

🌐 **6-36 Cash budget** (continuation of 6-35). Assume the following: Pet Transport (PT) does not make any sales on credit. PT sells only to the public, and accepts cash and credit cards. Of its sales, 90% are to customers using credit cards, for which PT gets the cash right away, less a 3% transaction fee.

◀ **LO 3**
Ending cash balance, $20,740

Purchases of materials are on account. PT pays for half the purchases in the period of the purchase and the other half in the following period. At the end of March, PT owes suppliers $8,500. PT plans to replace a machine in April at a net cash cost of $13,700. Labour, other production costs, and nonproduction costs are paid in cash in the month incurred except, of course, depreciation, which is not a cash flow. For April, $20,000 of the production cost and $10,000 of the nonproduction cost is depreciation.

PT currently has a $2,000 loan at an annual interest rate of 12%. The interest is paid at the end of each month. If PT has more than $10,000 cash at the end of April, it will pay back the loan. PT owes $5,000 in income taxes that need to be remitted in April. PT has cash of $5,360 on hand at the end of March.

Required

Prepare a cash budget for April for Pet Transport.

🌐 **6-37 Responsibility and controllability.** Sylvain Durier is the purchasing agent for Food Manufacturing Company. Marge Belvedere is head of the production planning and control department. Every six months, Belvedere gives Durier a general purchasing program. Durier gets specifications from the engineering department. He then selects suppliers and negotiates prices. When he took this job, Durier was informed very clearly that he bore responsibility for meeting the general purchasing program once he accepted it from Belvedere.

◀ **LO 4**

During week 24, Durier was advised that Part No. 1234—a critical part—would be needed for assembly on Tuesday morning of week 32. He found that the regular supplier could not deliver. He called everywhere and finally found a supplier across the country and accepted the commitment.

He followed up by mail. Yes, the supplier assured him, the part would be ready. The matter was so important that on Thursday of week 31, Durier checked by phone. Yes, the shipment had left on time. Durier was reassured and did not check further. But on Tuesday of week 32, the part had not arrived. Inquiry revealed that the shipment had been misdirected by the railroad and was stuck in Winnipeg.

Required

Which department should bear the costs of time lost in the plant? Why? As a purchasing agent, do you think it fair that such costs be charged to your department?

🌐 **6-38 Budgeting and governance.** Duncan Company manufactures a variety of products in a variety of departments, and evaluates departments and departmental managers by comparing actual costs and outputs relative to their budgets. Departmental managers help create the budgets and usually provide information about input quantities for materials, labour, and overhead costs. Sheryl Maki is the manager of the department that produces Product Z. Maki has estimated these inputs for Product Z:

◀ **LO 4**

Input	Budget Quantity per Unit of Output
Direct materials	3 kilograms
Direct manufacturing labour	20 minutes
Machine time	10 minutes

The department produces about 100 units of Product Z each day. Maki's department always gets excellent evaluations, sometimes exceeding budgeted production quantities. Each 100 units of Product Z uses, on average, about 32 hours of direct manufacturing labour (four people working eight hours each), 295 kilograms of materials, and 16.5 machine-hours.

Top management of Duncan Company has decided to implement budget standards that will challenge the workers in each department, and it has asked Maki to design more challenging input standards for Product Z. Maki provides top management with the following input quantities:

Input	Budget Quantity per Unit of Output
Direct materials	2.95 kilograms
Direct manufacturing labour	19.2 minutes
Machine time	9.9 minutes

Required

Discuss the following:

1. Are these challenging standards for Maki's department?
2. Why do you suppose Maki picked these particular standards?
3. What steps can Duncan Company top management take to make sure Maki's standards really meet the goals of the firm?

LO 2 ▶ ⊕ **6-39 Comprehensive problem with ABC costing.** Animal Gear Company makes two pet carriers, the Cat-allac and the Dog-eriffic. They are both made of plastic with metal doors, but the Cat-allac is smaller. Information for the two products for the month of April is given in the following tables:

Input Prices

Direct materials

Plastic	$ 5 per pound
Metal	$ 4 per pound
Direct manufacturing labour	$10 per direct manufacturing labour-hour

Input Quantities per Unit of Output

	Cat-allac	Dog-eriffic
Direct materials		
Plastic	4 pounds	6 pounds
Metal	0.5 pounds	1 pound
Direct manufacturing labour-hours	3 hours	5 hours
Machine-hours (MH)	11 MH	19 MH

Inventory Information, Direct Materials

	Plastic	Metal
Beginning inventory	290 pounds	70 pounds
Target ending inventory	410 pounds	65 pounds
Cost of beginning inventory	$1,102	$217

Animal Gear accounts for direct materials using a FIFO cost-flow assumption.

Sales and Inventory Information, Finished Goods

	Cat-allac	Dog-eriffic
Expected sales in units	530	225
Selling price	$ 205	$ 310
Target ending inventory in units	30	10
Beginning inventory in units	10	19
Beginning inventory in dollars	$1,000	$4,650

Animal Gear uses a FIFO cost-flow assumption for finished-goods inventory.

Animal Gear uses an activity-based costing system and classifies overhead into three activity pools: Setup, Processing, and Inspection. Activity rates for these activities are $105 per setup-hour, $10 per machine-hour, and $15 per inspection-hour, respectively. Other information follows:

Cost-Driver Information

	Cat-allac	Dog-eriffic
Number of units per batch	25	9
Setup time per batch	1.50 hours	1.75 hours
Inspection time per batch	0.5 hour	0.7 hour

If necessary, round up to calculate number of batches.

Nonmanufacturing fixed costs for March equal $32,000, half of which are salaries. Salaries are expected to increase 5% in April. Other nonmanufacturing fixed costs will remain the same. The only variable nonmanufacturing cost is sales commission, equal to 1% of sales revenue.

Required

Prepare the following for April:

1. Revenues budget
2. Production budget in units
3. Direct material usage budget and direct material purchases budget
4. Direct manufacturing labour cost budget
5. Manufacturing overhead cost budgets for each of the three activities
6. Budgeted unit cost of ending finished-goods inventory and ending inventories budget
7. Cost of goods sold budget
8. Nonmanufacturing costs budget
9. Budgeted income statement (ignore income taxes)
10. How does preparing the budget help Animal Gear's management team better manage the company?

⊕ **6-40 Cash budget** (continuation of 6-39). ◄ LO 3

Assume the following: Animal Gear (AG) does not make any sales on credit. AG sells only to the public and accepts cash and credit cards; 90% of its sales are to customers using credit cards, for which AG gets the cash right away, less a 2% transaction fee.

Purchases of materials are on account. AG pays for half the purchases in the period of the purchase and the other half in the following period. At the end of March, AG owes suppliers $8,000.

AG plans to replace a machine in April at a net cash cost of $13,000.

Labour, other manufacturing costs, and nonmanufacturing costs are paid in cash in the month incurred except of course depreciation, which is not a cash flow. Depreciation is $25,000 of the manufacturing cost and $10,000 of the nonmanufacturing cost for April.

AG currently has a $2,000 loan at an annual interest rate of 12%. The interest is paid at the end of each month. If AG has more than $7,000 cash at the end of April it will pay back the loan. AG owes $5,000 in income taxes that need to be remitted in April. AG has cash of $5,900 on hand at the end of March.

Required

1. Prepare a cash budget for April for Animal Gear.
2. Why do Animal Gear's managers prepare a cash budget in addition to the revenue, expenses, and operating income budget?

6-41 Comprehensive budgeting problem; activity-based costing, operating and financial budgets. Tyva makes a very popular undyed cloth sandal in one style, but in Regular and Deluxe. The Regular sandals have cloth soles and the Deluxe sandals have cloth-covered wooden soles. Tyva is preparing its budget for June 2018 and has estimated sales based on past experience. ◄ LO 4

Other information for the month of June follows:

Input Prices

Direct materials

Cloth	$5.25 per yard
Wood	$7.50 per board foot
Direct manufacturing labour	$15 per direct manufacturing labour-hour

Input Quantities per Unit of Output (per pair of sandals)

	Regular	Deluxe
Direct materials		
Cloth	1.3 yards	1.5 yards
Wood	0	2 b.f.
Direct manufacturing labour-hours (DMLH)	5 hours	7 hours
Setup-hours per batch	2 hours	3 hours

Inventory Information, Direct Materials

	Cloth	Wood
Beginning inventory	610 yards	800 b.f.
Target ending inventory	386 yards	295 b.f.
Cost of beginning inventory	$3,219	$6,060

Tyva accounts for direct materials using a FIFO cost-flow assumption.

Sales and Inventory Information, Finished Goods

	Regular	Deluxe
Expected sales in units (pairs of sandals)	2,000	3,000
Selling price	$ 120	$ 195
Target ending inventory in units	400	600
Beginning inventory in units	250	650
Beginning inventory in dollars	$23,250	$92,625

Tyva uses a FIFO cost-flow assumption for finished-goods inventory.

All the sandals are made in batches of 50 pairs of sandals. Tyva incurs manufacturing overhead costs, marketing and general administration, and shipping costs. Besides materials and labour, manufacturing costs include setup, processing, and inspection costs. Tyva ships 40 pairs of sandals per shipment. Tyva uses activity-based costing and has classified all overhead costs for the month of June as shown in the following chart:

Cost Type	Denominator Activity	Rate
Manufacturing		
Setup	Setup-hours	$ 18 per setup-hour
Processing	Direct manufacturing labour-hours (DMLH)	$1.80 per DMLH
Inspection	Number of pairs of sandals	$1.35 per pair
Nonmanufacturing		
Marketing and general administration	Sales revenue	8%
Shipping	Number of shipments	$ 15 per shipment

Required

1. Prepare each of the following for June:
   a. Revenues budget
   b. Production budget in units
   c. Direct material usage budget and direct material purchases budget in both units and dollars; round to dollars
   d. Direct manufacturing labour cost budget
   e. Manufacturing overhead cost budgets for setup, processing, and inspection activities
   f. Budgeted unit cost of ending finished-goods inventory and ending inventories budget
   g. Cost of goods sold budget
   h. Marketing and general administration and shipping costs budget
2. Tyva's balance sheet for May 31 follows.

Tyva Balance Sheet as of May 31

Assets		
Cash		$ 9,435
Accounts receivable	$324,000	
Less: Allowance for bad debts	16,200	307,800
Inventories		
Direct materials		9,279
Finished goods		115,875
Fixed assets	$870,000	
Less: Accumulated depreciation	36,335	733,665
Total assets		$1,176,054

Liabilities and Equity

Accounts payable	$ 15,600
Taxes payable	10,800
Interest payable	750
Long-term debt	150,000
Common stock	300,000
Retained earnings	698,904
Total liabilities and equity	$1,176,054

Use the balance sheet and the following information to prepare a cash budget for Tyva for June. Round to dollars.

- All sales are on account; 60% are collected in the month of the sale, 38% are collected the following month, and 2% are never collected and written off as bad debts.

- All purchases of materials are on account. Tyva pays for 80% of purchases in the month of purchase and 20% in the following month.

- All other costs are paid in the month incurred, including the declaration and payment of a $15,000 cash dividend in June.

- Tyva is making monthly interest payments of 0.5% (6% per year) on a $150,000 long-term loan.

- Tyva plans to pay the $10,800 of taxes owed as of May 31 in the month of June. Income tax expense for June is zero.

- 30% of processing, setup, and inspection costs and 10% of marketing and general administration and shipping costs are depreciation.

3. Prepare a budgeted income statement for June and a budgeted balance sheet for Tyva as of June 30, 2018.

Mini-Case

6-42 Comprehensive budgeting problem; activity-based costing, operating and financial budgets. Grant Shew is the product manager at Yummi-Lik. Yummi-Lik sells really big lollipops in two sizes, large and giant lollipops to convenience stores, at fairs, and to schools for fundraisers, as well as a bulk channel on the internet. The lollipops are handmade, mostly out of sugar, and attached to wooden sticks Grant is preparing the sales budget for the summer, knowing a successful sales season will have a big impact on his performance review. Expected sales are based on past experience.

◀ LO 1, 2, 3, 5
3. Budgeted net income, $998

Other information for the month of June follows:

Input prices

Direct materials

Sugar	$0.50 per kilogram (lb)
Sticks	$0.30 each
Direct manufacturing labour	0.008 per direct manufacturing labour-hour

Input quantities per unit of output

	Large	Giant
Direct materials		
Sugar	0.25 lb	0.50 lb
Sticks	1	1
Direct manufacturing labour-hours (DMLH)	0.20 hours	0.25 hours
Setup-hours per batch	0.08 hours	0.09 hours

Inventory information, direct materials

	Sugar	Sticks
Beginning inventory	125 lb	350
Target ending inventory	240 lb	480
Cost of beginning inventory	$64	$105

Yummi-Lik accounts for direct materials using a FIFO cost flow assumption.

Sales and inventory information, finished goods

	Large	Giant
Expected sales in units	3,000	1,800
Selling price	$ 3	$ 4
Target ending inventory in units	300	180
Beginning inventory in units	200	150
Beginning inventory in dollars	$ 500	$ 474

Yummi-Lik uses a FIFO cost flow assumption for finished goods inventory.

All the lollipops are made in batches of 10. Yummi-Lik incurs manufacturing overhead costs, and marketing and general administration costs, but customers pay for shipping. Other than manufacturing labour costs, monthly processing costs are very low. Yummy-Lik uses ABC and has classified all overhead costs for the month of June as shown in the following chart:

Cost Type	Denominator Activity	Rate
Manufacturing:		
Setup	Setup-hours	$20 per setup-hour
Processing	Direct manufacturing labour-hours (DMLH)	$1.70 per DMLH
Non-manufacturing:		
Marketing and general administration	Sales revenue	10%

Required

1. Grant needs to prepare a full set of budgets for June:
   a. Revenue budget.
   b. Production budget in units.
   c. Direct material usage budget and direct material purchases budget.
   d. Direct manufacturing labour cost budget.
   e. Manufacturing overhead cost budgets for processing and setup activities.
   f. Budgeted unit cost of ending finished goods inventory and ending inventories budget.
   g. Cost of goods sold budget.
   h. Marketing and general administration costs budget.

Grant knows that 80% of sales are on account, of which half are collected in the month of the sale, 49% are collected the following month, and 1% are never collected and written off as bad debts, which has an impact on net revenues. In addition to this, all purchases of materials are on account. Yummi-Lik pays for 70% of purchases in the month of purchase and 30% in the following month. However, all other costs are paid in the month incurred. Knowing this, Grant has to create

2. A cash budget for Yummi-Lik for June.
3. A budgeted income statement for June and a budgeted balance sheet for Yummi-Lik as of June 30.

The following information is necessary:

i. Yummi-Lik's balance sheet for May 31 follows. Use it and the following information to prepare a cash budget for Yummi-Lik for June.
ii. Yummi-Lik is making monthly interest payments of 1% (12% per year) on a $20,000 long-term loan.
iii. Yummi-Lik plans to pay the $500 of taxes owed as of May 31 in the month of June. Income tax expense for June is zero.
iv. 40% of processing and setup costs, and 30% of marketing and general administration costs, are depreciation.

Yummi-Lik
Balance Sheet
May 31

Assets

Cash		$ 587
Accounts receivable	$ 4,800	
Less: Allowance for bad debts	96	4,704
Inventories:		
Direct materials		169
Finished goods		974
Fixed assets	190,000	
Less: Accumulated depreciation	55,759	134,241
Total assets		$140,675

Liabilities and Equity

Accounts payable		$ 696
Taxes payable		500
Interest payable		200
Long-term debt		20,000
Common shares		10,000
Retained earnings		109,279
Total liabilities and equity		$140,675

6-43 University department, budget revision options. David Tax is the athletics director of Maritime University (MU). He has been director for more than 10 years. MU is a men's football and basketball powerhouse. The women's athletics program, however, has had less success. Last year, the women's basketball team finally had more wins than losses.

◄ LO 3

Tax has just had a meeting with Laura Medley, the newly appointed president of MU. It did not go well. Medley and Tax discussed what she called "Draft I" of the 2019 athletics department budget. He had believed it was the final draft. Medley expressed four grave concerns about Draft I in particular and about the MU athletics program in general:

■ **Concern 1.** The athletics department was budgeting a loss of more than $3.6 million in 2019. Given the tight fiscal position of the university, this was unacceptable. A budgeted loss of $1.2 million was the most she would tolerate for 2019. Draft II of the 2019 budget was due in two weeks' time. By 2017, the athletics department had to operate with a balanced budget. She told Tax this was nonnegotiable.

■ **Concern 2.** There was very little money allocated to the women's athletics program. *Frontline*, a tabloid television show, recently ran a program titled "It's a Man's World at the Maritime University Athletics Program." Medley said Tax was treating female athletes as "third-class citizens."

■ **Concern 3.** The men's football athletes, many of whom had full scholarships, had poor academic performance. Medley noted that the local TV news recently ran an interview with three football team students, none of whom "exemplified the high academic credentials she wanted Maritime to showcase to the world." She called one student "incoherent" and another "incapable of stringing sentences together."

■ **Concern 4.** The salary paid to Bill Madden, the football coach, was outrageous. Medley noted it was twice that of the highest-paid academic on campus, a Nobel Prize winner! Moreover, Madden received other payments from his "Football the Atlantic Way" summer program for high-school students.

The following exhibit is a summary of the Draft I athletics department budget for 2019.

Maritime University 2019 Athletics Department Budget (in $ millions)

Revenues:		
Men's athletics programs	$12.420	
Women's athletics programs	0.936	
Other (endowment income, gifts)	4.080	$ 17.436
Costs:		
Men's athletics programs	13.248	
Women's athletics programs	3.360	
Other (not assigned to programs)	4.440	21.048
Operating income		$ (3.612)

Men's Athletics Programs

	Football	Basketball	Swimming	Other	Total
Revenues	$10.320	$1.800	$0.120	$0.180	$12.420
Costs	8.880	3.240	0.360	0.768	13.248
Full student scholarships	37	21	6	4	68

Women's Athletic Programs

	Basketball	Swimming	Other	Total
Revenues	$0.720	$0.096	$0.120	$0.936
Costs	2.160	0.240	0.960	3.360
Full student scholarships	11	4	2	17

Instructions

Form groups of two or more students to complete the following requirement.

Required

Your group should discuss the concerns noted both from quantitative and qualitative perspectives. What should be addressed in preparing Draft II of the athletics department's 2019 budget? This draft will form the basis of a half-day meeting Tax will have with key officials of the athletics department.

TRY IT! ▶ **SOLUTIONS**

Try It 6–1

Schedule 1: Revenues Budget
for the Year Ending December 31, 2017

	Units	Selling Price	Total Revenues
Knox	21,000	$25	$525,000
Ayer	10,000	40	400,000
Total			$925,000

Schedule 2: Production Budget (in Units)
for the Year Ending December 31, 2017

	Product	
	Knox	Ayer
Budgeted sales in units (Schedule 1)	21,000	10,000
Add target ending finished goods inventory	2,000	1,000
Total required units	23,000	11,000
Deduct beginning finished goods inventory	3,000	1,000
Units of finished goods to be produced	20,000	10,000

Try It 6–2

Schedule 3A: Direct Material Usage Budget in Quantity and Dollars
for the Year Ending December 31, 2017

	Material		
	Metal	**Fabric**	**Total**
Physical Units Budget			
Direct materials required for Knox lamps (20,000 units × 2 kilograms and 1 metres)	40,000 kilograms	20,000 metres	
Direct materials required for Ayer lamps (10,000 units × 3 kilograms and 1.5 metres)	30,000 kilograms	15,000 metres	
Total quantity of direct materials to be used	70,000 kilograms	35,000 metres	
Cost Budget			
Available from beginning direct materials inventory (under a FIFO cost-flow assumption) (Given)			
Metal: 12,000 kilograms × $3 per kilograms	$ 36,000		
Fabric: 7,000 metres × $4 per metre		$ 28,000	
To be purchased and used this period			
Metal: (70,000 − 12,000) kilograms ×$3 per kilograms	174,000		
Fabric: (35,000 − 7,000) metres ×$4 per metres		112,000	
Direct materials to be used this period	$210,000	$140,000	$350,000

Schedule 3B: Direct Material Purchases Budget
for the Year Ending December 31, 2017

	Material		
	Metal	**Fabric**	**Total**
Physical Units Budget			
To be used in production (from Schedule 3A)	70,000 kilograms	35,000 metres	
Add target ending inventory	10,000 kilograms	5,000 metres	
Total requirements	80,000 kilograms	40,000 metres	
Deduct beginning inventory	12,000 kilograms	7,000 metres	
Purchases to be made	68,000 kilograms	33,000 metres	
Cost Budget			
Metal: 68,000 kilograms × $3 per kilogram	$204,000		
Fabric: 33,000 metres × $4 per metre		$132,000	
Direct materials to be purchased this period	$204,000	$132,000	$336,000

(Continued)

**Schedule 4: Direct Manufacturing Labour Costs Budget
for the Year Ending December 31, 2017**

	Output Units Produced (Schedule 2)	Direct Manufacturing Labour-Hours per Unit	Total Hours	Hourly Wage Rate	Total
Knox	20,000	0.15	3,000	$20	$ 60,000
Ayer	10,000	0.2	2,000	20	40,000
Total			5,000		$100,000

Try It 6–3

	Knox	Ayer
1. Quantity of lamps to be produced	20,000 lamps	10,000 lamps
2. Number of lamps to be produced per batch	100 lamps/batch	80 lamps/batch
3. Number of batches (1) ÷ (2)	200 batches	125 batches
4. Setup time per batch	3 hours/batch	4 hours/batch
5. Total setup-hours (3) × (4)	600 hours	500 hours

**Schedule 5: Manufacturing Overhead Costs Budget
for the Year Ending December 31, 2017
Machine Setup Overhead Costs**

Variable costs ($60 per setup-hour × 1,100 setup-hours)	$ 66,000
Fixed costs (to support capacity of 1,100 setup-hours)	77,000
Total machine setup overhead costs	$143,000
Total manufacturing overhead costs	$143,000

Try It 6–4

**Schedule 6A: Budgeted Unit Costs of Ending Finished
Goods Inventory December 31, 2017**

		Product			
		Knox		Ayer	
	Cost per Unit of Input	Input per Unit of Output	Total	Input per Unit of Output	Total
Metal	$ 3	2 kilograms	$ 6.00	3 kilograms	$ 9.00
Fabric	4	1 metre	4.00	1.5 metres	6.00
Direct manufacturing labour	20	0.15 hrs.	3.00	0.2 hrs.	4.00
Machine setup overhead	130	0.03 hrs.	3.90	0.05 hrs.	6.50
Total			$16.90		$25.50

Under the FIFO method, managers use this unit cost to calculate the cost of target ending inventories of finished goods in Schedule 6B.

Schedule 6B: Ending Inventories Budget December 31, 2017

	Quantity	Cost per Unit		Total
Direct materials				
Metal	10,000	$ 3.00	$30,000	
Fabric	5,000	4.00	20,000	$ 50,000
Finished goods				
Knox	2,000	$16.90	$33,800	
Ayer	1,000	25.50	25,500	59,300
Total ending inventory				$109,300

Flexible Budgets, Variances, and Management Control: I

7

Juanmonino/iStock/Getty Images Plus/Getty Images

Keeping It Real

At McDonald's, "Would you like fries with that?" is *cross-selling*. If diners say yes, then the larger sale contributes to the restaurant's sales targets and profitability. Managers track both actual sales and costs. Budgeted food and labour costs are compared to actual restaurant performance. Any significant differences between the budgeted and actual results must be explained. If the differences are unfavourable, variance analysis helps managers find the appropriate remedies and then implement them quickly.

▶ Learning Objectives

1. Distinguish between a static budget and a flexible budget.

2. Develop Level 2 flexible budgets, and calculate flexible-budget and sales-volume variances.

3. Develop Level 3 rate and efficiency variances for direct manufacturing costs.

4. Undertake variance analysis in activity-based costing systems.

5. Describe how managers use variance analysis.

6. Appendix 7A: Distinguish among standards, budgets, and benchmarks.

7. Appendix 7B: Distinguish between Levels 3 and 4 variance analysis for substitutable inputs, and calculate Level 4 direct mix and yield variances.

▶ CPA Competencies

This chapter covers material outlined in **Section 3: Management Accounting** of the CPA Competency Map. The Learning Objectives in this chapter have been aligned with the CPA Competency Map to ensure the best coverage possible.

3.2.1 Develops or evaluates information inputs for operational plans, budgets, and forecasts

3.2.2 Prepares, analyzes, or evaluates operational plans, budgets, and forecasts

3.2.3 Computes, analyzes, or assesses implications of variances

3.4.1 Evaluates sources and drivers of revenue growth

Managers quantify their operating and strategic plans for the future in the form of budgets, which summarize a series of complex decisions. A **variance** is the difference between the budgeted (predicted) results and the actual results. **Variance analysis** is a management control tool that enables **management by exception**, the practice of focusing management attention on areas where performance fails to meet expectations. By analyzing the exceptions, managers can examine why actual results failed to meet expectations.

Variances are often referred to as favourable or unfavourable. A **favourable (F) variance** will result in an actual operating income that **exceeds** the budgeted amount. An **unfavourable (U) variance** will result in an actual operating income that is **less** than the budgeted amount. The logic of variance analysis is clear. All other things being equal, unfavourable variances are when either actual revenue is less than expected or actual expenses are more than projected.

The 5 DM Framework and Variance Analysis

Step 1: Identify the Problem and Uncertainties The first step in any decision process is to identify or frame the problem. Management can use flexible budgets and variance analysis to help identify problem areas. Usually the results of variance analysis focus on failure, but a management team can also learn from success and then intentionally repeat it.

Step 2: Obtain Information Variance analysis depends on the availability and communication of timely, reliable financial accounting information reported in good form. The management information system (MIS) supplies the basic budgeted and actual data, then managers analyze it to produce a variance report. These reports are feedback on how well the organization achieved its predicted targets.

Step 3: Make Predictions About the Future Because the future is uncertain, the one sure thing about budgeted values is that they will be wrong. The question is whether or not the inaccuracies are tolerable. Are they so large or critical that they threaten the economic health of the organization?

Step 4: Decide On and Implement One of the Available Alternatives If the variances are likely to harm the organization, the managers must identify what caused the failures and find remedies. Unfavourable variances indicate that actual results failed to meet what was budgeted. In some cases, the remedy is to change expectations and revise the budget. Usually, however, an unfavourable variance indicates the need to regain control of costs by changing operations.

Step 5: Implement the Decision, Evaluate Performance, and Learn Quick identification of the cause of unfavourable variances improves results and allows the management team to learn from its past mistakes. Future budgets may incorporate the results of current variance analysis through changed standards (expectations) or through changed practices (management of the organization). Causes of variances should be documented so that they are available for future analyses.

Static and Flexible Budgets

► **LO 1**

Distinguish between a static budget and a flexible budget.

A **static budget** is a budget that is based on one level of output. It is not adjusted or altered after it is set. It usually represents the original plan (budget) or expectations for a period of time (e.g., month, quarter, or year). A static-budget *variance* is the difference between the actual results and the static-budget numbers. Unfortunately, the static-budget variance analysis has limited use. For example, if the volume of sales is higher than expected, all other things being equal the operating income variance will be favourable. However, this can be deceptive. Some costs vary directly with the quantity produced and sold (i.e., variable costs). As a result, actual direct material costs, for example, will be greater than the budgeted because an increased quantity produced and sold. Higher variable costs are caused by the higher sales volume, not by some inefficiency in the purchase and use of direct materials (which is what variance analysis is meant to predict). In a static-budget analysis, this cost variance would be reported as unfavourable (because it causes operating income to decrease), even though it is predictable as a result of the higher-than-expected sales volume.

To avoid wasting time investigating predictable variances, the **flexible budget** is more effective than the static-budget analysis. After each time period (e.g., month, quarter, or year), the budgeted variable costs and budgeted revenue amounts will be adjusted according to the actual quantity produced and sold. So, the flexible budget is the *hypothetical* budget that an organization would have prepared at the start of the budget period if it had correctly forecast the actual output. A flexible budget enables managers to calculate a more informative set of variances in order to provide more useful feedback.

Budgets, both static and flexible, can differ in their level of detail. In this text, the term *Level* followed by a number denotes the amount of detail indicated by the variance(s) isolated. Level 0 reports the least detail; Levels 1, 2, 3, and 4 offer progressively more detailed information. Detail is also referred to as **fineness** in financial accounting. Fineness is a characteristic of reliable information that identifies cause with effect and cost with benefit. The finer the detail and the clearer the cause–effect and cost–benefit relationships, the more readily costs can be controlled.

The Costing System at Webb Company

We will use information from Webb Company's costing system to illustrate static and flexible budgets. Webb manufactures and sells a single product, a distinctive jacket, which is wholesaled to independent clothing stores and retail chains. Production of the finished goods requires different raw materials, tailoring, and hand and machine operations. Webb's costing system classifies the direct and indirect costs of manufacturing into four cost pools as shown. The non-manufacturing costs are represented by the three downstream cost pools for marketing; one is direct and two are indirect.

	Direct Costs	**Indirect Costs**
Manufacturing	Direct materials	Variable manufacturing overhead
	Direct manufacturing labour	Fixed manufacturing overhead
Marketing	Direct marketing labour	Variable marketing overhead
		Fixed marketing overhead

Webb's marketing division has estimated budgeted revenue (budgeted selling price × budgeted units sold) for the year and per month. Other operating division managers have estimated budgeted costs for the year and per month based on the sales estimates. Once a budget is developed, this provides Webb's management team with all the relevant information required to do a very fine (detailed) level of variance analysis.

Before starting our discussion about budgeting, we will make four simplifying assumptions:

1. The monthly estimates are 1/12 of the annual amounts.
2. Each jacket requires identical amounts of both labour and machine time.
3. The quantity (Q) produced equals the quantity sold or, in other words, there is zero finished goods inventory at the end of each month.
4. The variable direct costs and revenues have an identical driver (Q).

It is important to note that many firms use *standard costs* as the basis for many of their budgeted cost figures. A *standard* is a carefully predetermined amount based on investigation of external performance achieved by similar processes. A standard is usually expressed on a per-unit basis and communicates an average amount indicating what *should* be achieved by any similar process each time period that performance measures are taken. A more complete discussion of standards is found in Appendix 7A.

The variable manufacturing overhead costs (VMOH) are allocated using direct machine-hours (DMH) as the cost driver, while the variable period or non-manufacturing overhead costs (VPOH) are allocated using the cost driver direct marketing labour-hours (DLH). Exhibit 7-1 reports data available in Webb's costing MIS.

Period costs include downstream marketing costs, which are traced to each jacket. The downstream distribution, customer service, and advertising costs form the variable

Exhibit 7-1 Webb Company's Accounting System Data

The traceable costs per jacket are direct materials (DM) purchased *and* used (there will be zero DM ending inventory). The DM are purchased in square metres (m²).

The direct manufacturing labour-hours (DMLH) and direct marketing labour-hours (DLH) are traced to each jacket produced and sold.

The direct machine-hours (DMH) are not traced but are used in fixed cost allocation and indirect variance analysis.

	Budgeted	Actual
Unit sales price per jacket	$180.00	$185.00
Q = Relevant range of jackets produced and sold	8,000–16,000	10,000

Cost Category per Jacket	**Budgeted Cost Driver**	**Budgeted Q Cost Driver per Jacket**	**Budgeted Cost per Input Unit**	**Budgeted Cost per Jacket**
Direct materials (DM) measured in square metres (m²)	m²	2.000	$30.00	$60.00
Direct manufacturing labour (DMLH)	DMLH	0.800	20.00	16.00
Variable manufacturing overhead (VMOH*)	DMH	0.400	30.00	12.00
Total budgeted variable manufacturing costs per jacket				88.00
Direct marketing labour downstream (DLH)	DLH	0.250	24.00	6.00
Variable marketing overhead downstream (VPOH**)	DLH	0.125	40.00	5.00
Total budgeted variable period costs per jacket				11.00
Total budgeted variable costs per unit				$99.00
Fixed costs of production (FMOH*)	$276,000			
Fixed period costs (FPOH**)	434,000			
Total budgeted fixed costs	$710,000			

*VMOH and FMOH refer to manufacturing overhead for variable and fixed costs.
**VPOH and FPOH refer to period overhead for variable and fixed non-manufacturing overhead costs.

period overhead cost pool and are allocated costs. The relevant range for both the manufacturing and period cost drivers is from 8,000 to 16,000 units.

Static-Budget Variances

Webb's actual results and the *static*-budget amounts for operating income in April 2018, in operating income format, are as follows:

	LEVEL 0 Variance Analysis		
	Actual	**Static-Budget Variance**	**Static-Budget Amount**
Operating income	$25,000	$(237,000) U	$262,000

Interpretation of Level 0 Results

Webb's managers receive limited useful feedback from a Level 0 variance analysis report. While it is clear is that the actual performance failed to meet the budget, there is no indication as to why. The *static-budget variance* of $(237,000) U is based on the actual result of $25,000 less the operating income of $262,000 that was forecast. Level 0 variance analysis provides a signal but no insight to the management team about how the large unfavourable variance arose.

Webb can improve the quality of feedback by using a contribution margin format as shown in Exhibit 7-2. This format encourages a line-by-line variance analysis that provides the management team with insight about the budget shortfall. This is a Level 1 variance analysis. The Level 0 and 1 variance analysis are compared in Exhibit 7-2.

The table in Exhibit 7-2 provides a number of insights:

■ An unfavourable revenue variance of $310,000 (row 5) resulted from Webb's failure to sell the predicted volume of Q = 12,000 jackets

LEVEL 0 Variance Analysis

	Actual Results	Static-Budget Variance	Static-Budget Amount
Operating income	$25,000	$(237,000) U	$262,000

LEVEL 1 Variance Analysis

	A	B	C	D
1		**Actual**	**Static-Budget**	**Static-Budget**
2		**Results**	**Variance**	**Amount**
3		**(1)**	**(2)**	**(3)**
4	Jackets Q sold	10,000	(2,000) U	12,000
5	Total revenue	$1,850,000	$(310,000) U	$2,160,000
6	Total variable costs	1,120,000	(68,000) F	1,188,000
7	Contribution margin	730,000	(242,000) U	972,000
8	Fixed costs	705,000	(5,000) F	710,000
9	Operating income	$ 25,000	**$(237,000) U**	$ 262,000
10		↑		↑
11			$(237,000) U	
12		Total static-budget variance		
13				
14	*F = favourable effect on operating income; U = unfavourable effect on operating income.			

- A favourable total variable cost variance of $68,000 occurred because Webb produced and sold only 10,000 jackets instead of the original (static-budget) amount of 12,000 jackets.

- As production was within the relevant range, the fixed cost variance may have been due to an unpredictable change in period costs (e.g., a decrease in insurance premiums).

- The total actual variable costs (row 6) are less than the predicted variable costs by $(68,000). Webb's actual costs are under budget. All other things equal, the result is good news because less will be paid out for materials, labour, and machine use.

- The actual contribution margin (row 7) is less than the predicted contribution margin by $(242,000). Webb's actual contribution margin is under budget. All other things equal, the result is bad news because there is less contribution from operations available to pay fixed costs.

Note: A variance is either favourable (F) or unfavourable (U) based on the **impact on operating income**, not on whether it is a positive or negative number in the above table.

> **Note** For the rest of the exhibits and examples in this chapter (and the remainder of the text), brackets *will not* be used with variances. In keeping with commonly accepted variance reporting practice, unfavourable variances are signified with a U and favourable variances with an F.

Interpretation of Level 1 Results

At Level 1, the variance analysis in Exhibit 7-2 reveals additional interesting information. The actual unit sales price per jacket was $185 (= $1,850,000 ÷ 10,000 jackets), not the budgeted $180 per jacket shown in Exhibit 7-1. The total variable costs were actually $112 per jacket (= $1,120,000 ÷ 10,000 jackets), not the budgeted $99 per jacket shown in Exhibit 7-1. On a per jacket-basis, the revenue was $5 favourable and the variable cost was $13 unfavourable.

Exhibit 7-3 Relationship Between Cost Variance Analysis Levels 0 and 1

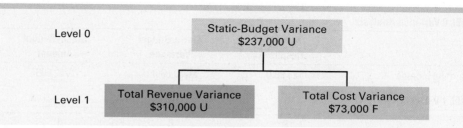

The budgeted contribution margin percentage of 45.0% (= $972,000 ÷ $2,160,000) decreases to 39.5% (= $730,000 ÷ $1,850,000) for the actual results. This is, in fact, the most important information provided—it answers the question of what effect the net change of actual performance had on operating income. Unfortunately, it does not tell management what caused a significant unfavourable variance. To do so requires more data and the creation of a more dynamic budget, the flexible budget. The reconciliation of the Level 0 and Level 1 variance analysis is illustrated in Exhibit 7-3. The two values in Level 1 add to the value in Level 0.

TRY IT! 7.1

Steve-A-Rena's coffee shop at the Farmer's Market makes fruit salads as a refreshing and healthy snack for its customers. Each fruit salad requires ½ kilogram of fruit, which costs $8/kg. Steve pays his staff $20/hr. Each salad requires 6 minutes of variable overhead time at a cost of $0.60 per salad. Calculate the standard cost for direct materials, direct labour, and variable overhead for the fruit salad operation.

Developing a Flexible Budget From Cost Data

LO 2

Develop Level 2 flexible budgets, and calculate flexible-budget and sales-volume variances.

Webb's MIS report in Exhibit 7-1 summarizes relevant data from the budget schedules. Exhibit 7-4 demonstrates how, by using more of the data available, the management team can develop a *flexible budget* and improve the feedback to a finer or more detailed Level 2 variance analysis. Flexible budgets give management an approximate idea of the various outcomes (i.e., revenues, costs, and operating incomes) that might result from different levels of activity using the same assumptions about selling prices, costs, and productivity that were used to create the static budget. In a manner of speaking, they represent a type of sensitivity analysis. Of particular interest is the flexible budget that reflects the activity level that is the same as the *actual* activity level achieved in the budget year. This specific flexible budget is, in effect, what the static budget would have looked like if management could have been 100% accurate with regard to the quantity (Q) that was produced and sold.

For example, to generate three different flexible budgets, instead of multiplying by Q = 12,000 produced and sold, the price per jacket and each variable cost per jacket are multiplied by three different Q. Keep in mind that any variable cost amounts will change as Q changes, but fixed costs will not. The three Q are within the relevant range of 8,000 to 16,000 jackets produced and sold. The results of Q = 10,000 are reported in column (3), Q = 12,000 in column (4), and Q = 16,000 in column (5). *Actual* results are reported in column (6).

Having developed the flexible-budget amounts and included the actual results, the management team will focus on the differences between them. This begins the Level 2 analysis.

Flexible-Budget Variances and Sales-Volume Variances

The Level 2 flexible-budget variance analysis will help Webb Company identify where the unfavourable difference of $237,000 arose. The Level 2 results are compared to the Level 0 static-budget variance analysis in Exhibit 7-5. Only the lines in the contribution format of the statement of comprehensive income have been analyzed.

Exhibit 7-4 Flexible-Budget Data for Webb Company for April 2018

	A	B	C	D	E	F
1		Budgeted	Flexible-Budget Amounts for			Actual
2		Amount	Alternative Levels of Output Units Sold			Results for
3	Line Item	per Unit	10,000	12,000	16,000	10,000 Units
4	(1)	(2)	(3)	(4)	(5)	(6)
5						
6	Revenue	$180	$1,800,000	$2,160,000	$2,880,000	$1,850,000
7	Variable costs					
8	Direct materials	60	600,000	720,000	960,000	688,200
9	Direct manufacturing labour	16	160,000	192,000	256,000	198,000
10	Direct marketing labour	6	60,000	72,000	96,000	57,600
11	Variable manufacturing overhead	12	120,000	144,000	192,000	130,500
12	Variable marketing overhead	5	50,000	60,000	80,000	45,700
13	Total variable costs	99	990,000	1,188,000	1,584,000	1,120,000
14	Contribution margin	$ 81	810,000	972,000	1,296,000	730,000
15	Fixed costs					
16	Manufacturing overhead		276,000	276,000	276,000	285,000
17	Marketing overhead		434,000	434,000	434,000	420,000
18	Total fixed costs		710,000	710,000	710,000	705,000
19	Total costs		1,700,000	1,898,000	2,294,000	1,825,000
20	Operating income		$ 100,000	$ 262,000	$ 586,000	$ 25,000

The total Level 0 unfavourable static-budget variance has two sources:

- The first is the **flexible-budget variance**, which is the total of the differences between the *actual results* and the flexible-budget amounts. In Exhibit 7-4, subtracting the last amount in column (3) from the last amount in column (6) equals the flexible-budget variance. This variance arose because the *actual* revenues and *actual* costs for the 10,000 jackets produced and sold were different from the *forecasted* flexible-budget amounts for 10,000 jackets:

$$\text{Flexible-budget variance} = \text{Actual results} - \text{Flexible} - \text{budget amount}$$
$$= \$25,000 - \$100,000$$
$$= \$75,000 \text{ U}$$

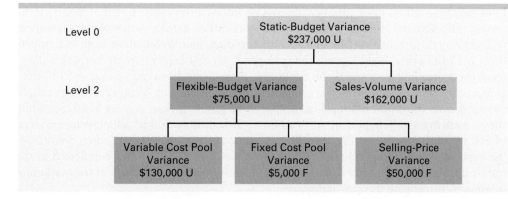

Exhibit 7-5 Relationship Between Cost Variance Analysis Levels 0 and 2

Level 0 — Static-Budget Variance $237,000 U

Level 2 — Flexible-Budget Variance $75,000 U — Sales-Volume Variance $162,000 U

Variable Cost Pool Variance $130,000 U — Fixed Cost Pool Variance $5,000 F — Selling-Price Variance $50,000 F

■ The second source of static-budget variance is the **sales-volume variance**. The sales-volume variance is the difference between the flexible-budget and *static-budget amounts*. These variances arise because the actual number of units *sold*, Q = 10,000, was lower than the static-budget quantity of Q = 12,000:

$$\text{Sales-volume variance} = \text{Flexible} - \text{budget amount} - \text{Static} - \text{budget amount}$$
$$= \$100,000 - \$262,000$$
$$= \$162,000 \text{ U}$$

Using contribution margin information available at Level 2, the third line in Exhibit 7-5 indicates that there are three sources of flexible-budget variance of $75,000 U. The first is the difference between actual and flexible-budget revenue arising from the difference in selling price:

$$\begin{array}{l} \text{Selling-price} \\ \text{variance} \end{array} = \left(\begin{array}{c} \text{Actual selling} \\ \text{price} \end{array} - \begin{array}{c} \text{Budgeted} \\ \text{selling price} \end{array}\right) \times \begin{array}{c} \text{Actual units} \\ \text{sold} \end{array}$$
$$= (\$185 - \$180) \times 10,000$$
$$= \$50,000 \text{ F}$$

The second and third sources contributing to the total flexible-budget variance are the variable and fixed cost pool variances. In Exhibit 7-4 the total actual variable cost is $1,120,000 (column 6) and the total flexible-budget variable cost is $990,000 (column 3). The difference is

$$\text{Variable cost variance} = \text{Actual variable cost} - \text{Flexible-budget variable cost}$$
$$= \$1,120,000 - \$990,000$$
$$= \$130,000 \text{ U}$$

For the fixed costs, the difference between the total actual fixed costs of $705,000 and the flexible-budget fixed costs of $710,000 is

$$\text{Fixed cost variance} = \text{Actual fixed cost} - \text{Flexible-budget fixed cost}$$
$$= \$705,000 - \$710,000$$
$$= \$5,000 \text{ F}$$

The two sets of variance calculations are in column (2) of Exhibit 7-6. The actual results are in column (1). In column (3), all the flexible-budgeted values are reported as if managers could tell the future perfectly and budget for Q = 10,000 jackets produced and sold in April. The values indicate what Webb should have paid to produce the jackets, what it should have recovered when the jackets were sold, and what it should have earned if the team had achieved its budget.

The difference reported in column (2) is the difference between what did happen and what should have happened at the actual Q produced and sold. In column (2) the reasons for the variable and fixed cost variances are found by investigating the direct and indirect factors of production for the 10,000 jackets. The reasons for the sales-volume variance (column 4) are found by investigating why there was a difference between expected and actual consumer demand for jackets. This is covered in Chapter 16.

Interpretation of Level 2 Results

Looking at the selling-price variance, there is no information suggesting that Webb's jackets are differentiated from others by especially desirable attributes for which customers will pay more. Customers set the price for the product, and Webb, along with its competitors, is a price taker. Webb's profitability depends on cost leadership. By keeping a sharp focus on controlling its costs, Webb could earn more profit from each jacket at $180 than competitors with a lessor focus on cost control. It is possible that Webb's customers simply switched from the jacket costing $185 to purchase similar jackets costing $180. So, while the increase in the selling price results in a favourable flexible-budget selling-price variance of $50,000 F, it may have also caused the reduction in the quantity of jackets sold (from the expected static-budget Q = 12,000 to the actual Q = 10,000). This is reflected in the unfavourable sales-volume revenue variance of $360,000 U. It is the task of the marketing division to investigate this possibility.

Exhibit 7-6 Flexible-Budget-Based Level 2 Variance Analysis for Webb Company for April 2018

LEVEL 2 Variance Analysis

	A	B	C	D	E	F
		Actual	**Flexible-Budget**	**Flexible**	**Sales-Volume**	**Static**
2		**Results**	**Variances**	**Budget**	**Variances**	**Budget**
3		(1)	(2) = (1) − (3)	(3)	(4) = (3) − (5)	(5)
4	Units sold	10,000	—	10,000	2,000 U	12,000
5	Revenue	$1,850,000	$ 50,000 F	$1,800,000	$360,000 U	$2,160,000
6	Variable costs	1,120,000	130,000 U	990,000	198,000 F	1,188,000
7	Contribution margin	730,000	80,000 U	$ 810,000	162,000 U	972,000
8	Fixed costs	705,000	5,000 F	710,000	—	710,000
9	Operating income	$ 25,000	$ 75,000 U	$ 100,000	$162,000 U	$ 262,000
10		↑			↑	↑
11			$75,000 U		$162,000 U	
12		Total flexible-budget variance			Total sales-volume variance	
13		↑				↑
14				$237,000 U		
15				Total static-budget variance		
	Note: Pay careful attention because the variances in columns (2) and (4) depend on how the variance affects operating income.					

It is interesting that Webb's actual fixed costs were less than the flexible-budget amount. It may be because insurance premiums or perhaps property taxes decreased unexpectedly. This change is likely to persist, and the budget should be revised. Alternatively, perhaps a salaried manager resigned in April. In this case, the unexpected change is temporary until a replacement is hired, and no change should be made to the budget.

Webb also exceeded its flexible-budgeted variable costs by approximately 13% (= $130,000 ÷ $990,000), which might be considered a significant amount of variance. Depending on the industry and situation, different levels of variances for different types of costs might be considered acceptable or not acceptable. Some firms set guidelines that consider both monetary (dollar) and relative (percentage) amounts. For example, a firm might have a policy that any variance exceeding $5,000 or 5% of the budgeted cost (whichever is lower) should be investigated. The Level 2 analysis has helped clarify how the overall $237,000 U static-budget variance came about. Additional information is needed to identify what changes happened to the quantities and unit rates generating the variable costs. Webb must use more of the information already reported in its MIS. Important non-financial data are also reported in Exhibit 7-1 on the budgeted quantities of different inputs purchased and used as well as cost allocation bases for the indirect costs. The level of detail in the existing MIS is fine enough to isolate the effect of changes in quantities from changes in cost per input and provide feedback sufficient to do a Level 3 analysis.

Direct Variable Rate and Efficiency Variances

The added value of a Level 3 analysis is to direct attention to specific elements of production that are outside of the expected parameters. Conventional terms may be somewhat confusing at first. We can refer to the cost per unit of input as its rate (i.e., dollar amount), input rate, or rate per unit. A **rate variance** is the difference between the actual rate and the budgeted rate multiplied by the actual quantity of input in question (such as direct materials purchased or used). This is sometimes also referred to as an **input price variance**.

▶ **LO 3**

Develop Level 3 rate and efficiency variances for direct manufacturing costs.

Exhibit 7-7 Detailed Variable-Cost Sources of Variance

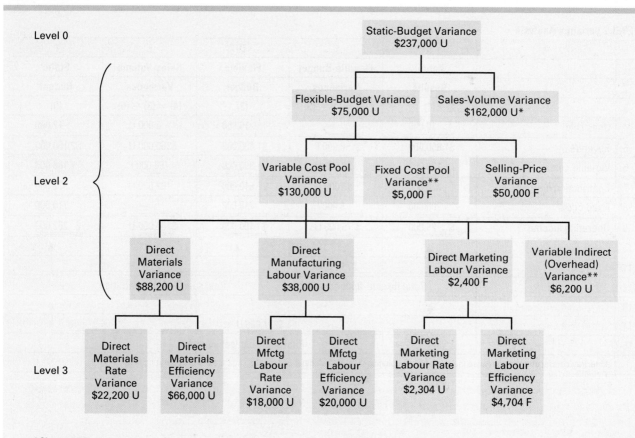

*Chapter 16
**Fixed $5,000 F and variable overhead $6,200 U analyses are in Chapter 8.

An **efficiency variance** is the difference between the actual quantity of input used (such as metres of cloth in direct materials) and the budgeted quantity of input that should have been used, multiplied by the budgeted rate to obtain the flexible-budget value. *Efficiency variances* are sometimes also called **input-efficiency variances** or **usage variances**.

The relationship of these two direct variable-cost variances is shown in Exhibit 7-7. The manufacturing costs are in the boxes shaded blue, the colour of the production business function. The non-manufacturing costs are shaded yellow, the colour of the marketing function in the value chain. Indirect variances (variable and fixed) are analyzed in Chapter 8.

In reality, managers are responsible for controlling efficiency variances and have the authority to do so. This is not usually the case with rate variances. Unless the company is a very large consumer (a monopsony) of direct materials or direct labour it has little power to affect the cost per unit of those items. This is especially true if there is only one supplier (a monopoly). The company depends on astute negotiation with the supplier or the union to obtain the lowest possible rate per unit at the right quality level and at the right time. Managers remain responsible for explaining rate variance but have little control over it.

An Illustration of Rate and Efficiency Variances for Inputs

Consider Webb's three direct-cost categories of materials, manufacturing labour, and marketing labour. For simplicity, assume that direct materials used is equal to direct materials purchased; therefore, there will be no ending inventory. At this point in our analysis, we

Exhibit 7-8 Detailed Variable-Cost Sources of Variance

LEVEL 2 ANALYSIS

	A	B	C	D	E	F	G	H
1		Budgeted				Actual		
2	Unit sales price per jacket	$ 180.00				$ 185.00		
3	Q = Relevant range of jackets produced and sold							
4	Cost Category per Jacket	Budgeted Cost Driver (0)	Q Cost Driver per Jacket (1)	Budgeted Cost per Input Unit (2)	Budgeted Cost per Jacket (1) × (2)	Actual Q Cost Driver per Jacket (3)	Actual Cost per Input Unit (4)	Actual Cost per Jacket (3) × (4)
5	Direct material (DM) measured in square metres (m²) m²	2.000		$ 30	$60	2.2200	$ 31.00	$ 68.82
6	Direct manufacturing labour (DMLH) DMLH	0.800		20	16	0.9000	22.00	19.80
7	Variable manufacturing overhead (VMOH)* DMH	0.400		30	12	0.4500	29.00	13.05
8	Total variable manufacturing costs per jacket				88			101.67
9	Direct marketing labour (DLH) DLH	0.250		24.00	6	0.2304	25.00	5.76
10	Variable marketing overhead (VPOH)† DLH	0.125		40.00	5	0.1828	25.00	4.57
11	Total variable period costs per jacket				11			10.33
12	Total variable costs per unit				$99		$112.00	
13	Fixed costs of production (FMOH)	$276,000				$285,000		
14	Fixed period costs (FPOH)	434,000				420,000		
15	Total fixed costs	$710,000				$705,000		
16	*Budgeted VMOH is $12/jacket or $144,000 ÷ 12,000 jackets. The standard of 0.40 DMH/jacket at a rate of $30/DMH is derived in Chapter 8. †Non-manufacturing cost allocation is discussed in Chapter 14.							

do not want to complicate the variance analysis with questions of inventory valuation. (See "Impact of Inventories" at the end of the chapter, which addresses inventory issues, direct materials, and direct material variances.) By expanding the data in Exhibit 7-1 to include actual results, Exhibit 7-8 shows the basis for a Level 3 analysis.

We can summarize the data for all direct inputs that are the first stage of a Level 2 analysis as follows:

	Actual Results (1)	Flexible-Budget Variances (2) = (1) − (3)	Flexible Budget (3)	
Direct materials (22,200 × $31/m²)	$688,200	$ 88,200 U	$600,000	(20,000 × $30/m²)
Direct manufacturing labour (9,000 × $22/DMLH)	198,000	38,000 U	160,000	(8,000 × $20/DMLH)
Direct marketing labour (2,304 × $25/DLH)	57,600	2,400 F	60,000	(2,500 × $24/DLH)
Total	$943,800	$123,800 U	$820,000	

But this tells us only how the flexible-budget variances are distributed among the three direct inputs; we do not know what caused the variances. Was it rates, efficiency, or a combination of both? The data summarized in Exhibit 7-8 are sufficient to more sharply focus the attention of Webb's management team on what items require the most immediate attention to bring their costs back under control, the costs per unit or the quantities used.

Rate Variances

The formula for computing a rate variance is

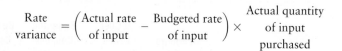

$$\begin{array}{c}\text{Rate}\\\text{variance}\end{array} = \left(\begin{array}{c}\text{Actual rate}\\\text{of input}\end{array} - \begin{array}{c}\text{Budgeted rate}\\\text{of input}\end{array}\right) \times \begin{array}{c}\text{Actual quantity}\\\text{of input}\\\text{purchased}\end{array}$$

Based on the formula, the rate variances for each of Webb's three direct cost categories are as follows:

	Actual Less Budgeted Rate per Unit (1)	**Actual Quantity of Input Units Purchased (2)**	**=**	**Input Rate Variance (1) × (2)**
Direct materials ($31/m² − $30/m²) × 22,200 m²	$1.00	22,200	=	$22,200 U
Direct manufacturing labour ($22/DMLH − $20/DMLH) × 9,000 DMLH	2.00	9,000	=	18,000 U
Direct marketing labour ($25/DLH − $24/DLH) × 2,304 DLH	1.00	2,304	=	2,304 U
				$42,504 U

All three rate variances are unfavourable (they reduce operating income) because the actual direct rate per input unit exceeds the budgeted rate. In total, Webb incurred more direct cost per input unit than was budgeted.

Interpretation of Level 3 Result of Rate Variance Analysis Generally speaking, the management team's attention will be directed to the largest U variance, in this case, the direct materials rate variance. But more investigation is needed because there are many potential reasons for the rate variance:

■ Budgeted purchase rates for Webb's materials were set without careful analysis of its suppliers.

■ Webb's purchasing manager negotiated less skillfully than was committed to in the budget.

■ Webb's purchasing manager bought in smaller lot sizes than budgeted, even though quantity discounts were available for the larger lot sizes.

■ Materials rates unexpectedly increased because of unanticipated increases in market demand or unanticipated increases in costs of transportation from the supplier to Webb.

■ The specified quality of materials required was discontinued by suppliers. Quality of the replacement materials purchased exceeded the production specifications, leading to higher rates.

The first step is to identify the cause, which will affect the remedy. If Webb identifies the reason as poor negotiating by its purchasing officer, then the remedy may be to invest more in training this officer in negotiation. Alternatively, Webb may decide to hire a more skillful purchasing officer. Another alternative is to negotiate long-term fixed rate contracts to ensure no future unfavourable rate variance for the life of the contract.

Efficiency Variances

For any actual level of output, the efficiency variance is the difference between the actual and budgeted quantity of inputs multiplied by the budgeted rate per input. An organization is inefficient if it uses more inputs than budgeted for the actual output units achieved, and it is efficient if it uses fewer inputs than budgeted for the actual output units achieved. Holding the rate constant isolates the effect of variance in quantity purchased and used from any change in rate:

$$\frac{\text{Efficiency}}{\text{variance}} = \left(\begin{array}{cc}\text{Actual quantity} & \text{Budgeted quantity of input allowed} \\ \text{of input used} & \text{for actual output units achieved}\end{array}\right) \times \frac{\text{Budgeted rate}}{\text{of input}}$$

The efficiency variances for each of Webb's direct cost categories are as follows:

	Actual Less Budgeted Quantity per Input Unit (1)	×	Budgeted Rate per Unit Purchased (2)	=	Input Efficiency Variance (1) × (2)
Direct materials [22,200 m² − (10,000 units of output × 2 m²)] × $30/m²	2,200	×	$30	=	$66,000 U
Direct manufacturing labour [9,000 − (10,000 units of output × 0.80)] × $20/DMLH	1,000	×	20	=	20,000 U
Direct marketing labour [2,304 − (10,000 units of output × 0.25)] × $24/DLH	196	×	24	=	4,704 F
Total					$81,296 U

The two manufacturing-efficiency variances (direct materials and direct manufacturing labour) are both unfavourable because more input was used than was budgeted, resulting in a decrease in operating income. The marketing-efficiency variance is favourable because less input was used than was budgeted, resulting in an increase in operating income.

Interpretation of Level 3 Result of Efficiency Variance Analysis

Like the rate variance, the largest efficiency variance also arises from direct materials. But the management team must consider a range of intertwined reasons for efficiency variances. The direct materials variance could be influenced by the unfavourable direct manufacturing labour variance. Webb's unfavourable direct manufacturing labour variance could be due to one or more of the following reasons:

■ Budgeted time standards were set without careful analysis of the operating conditions and employees' skills.

■ Webb's human resources manager hired underskilled workers, or their training was inadequate.

■ Webb's production process was reorganized or a new machine was installed, creating additional direct manufacturing labour time per jacket as workers learn the new process.

■ Webb's production scheduler inefficiently scheduled work, resulting in more direct manufacturing labour time per jacket.

■ Webb's marketing department promised early deliveries to clients, which created too many rush-order interruptions that led to overtime.

■ Webb's maintenance department did not properly maintain machines, resulting in additional direct manufacturing labour time per jacket to avoid damage done by the machines.

The first step is to identify the cause of the unfavourable variance. If the cause was poor machine maintenance, then one reasonable response is to create a team consisting of plant machine engineers and machine operators who will develop a new maintenance schedule so that there will be less materials spoilage. Another alternative is to remove any incentives in the marketing area to place rush orders. Additionally, it may be time for Webb to replace obsolete machines to reduce spoilage and maintenance hours.

Presentation of Rate and Efficiency Variances for Inputs

Note how the sum of the direct cost rate variance and the efficiency variance equals the direct cost flexible-budget variance as reported in the fourth row of Exhibit 7-7:

	Input Rate Variances	Input Efficiency Variances	Flexible-Budget Variance
Direct materials	$22,200 U	$66,000 U	$ 88,200 U
Direct manufacturing labour	18,000 U	20,000 U	38,000 U
Direct marketing labour	2,304 U	4,704 F	2,400 F
Total	$42,504 U	$81,296 U	$123,800 U

	Input Rate Variances	Input Efficiency Variances	Flexible-Budget Variance
Direct materials	17.93% U	53.31% U	71.24% U
Direct manufacturing labour	14.54 U	16.16 U	30.70 U
Direct marketing labour	1.86 U	3.80 F	1.94 F
Total	34.33% U	65.67% U	100.00% U

Exhibit 7-9 integrates the actual and budgeted input information used to compute the rate and efficiency variances for direct materials and direct manufacturing labour.

Exhibit 7-9 Columnar Presentation of Direct Materials and Direct Manufacturing Labour Variance Analysis for Webb Company for April 2018

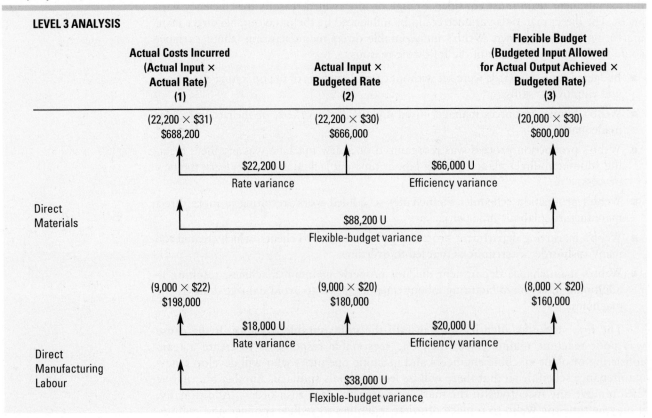

A comparison of the fineness among three levels of variance analysis is reported. Notice that as the fineness increases, the insight with respect to what has caused the variance becomes clearer. But Webb's value-added activities in its chain of business functions are not separate but rather interdependent on one another. What explains one variance may explain several.

LEVEL 0 Variance Analysis

	Actual	Static-Budget Variance	Static Budget
Operating income	$25,000	$237,000 U	$262,000

LEVEL 1 Variance Analysis

	Actual	Static-Budget Variance	Static Budget
Jackets Q sold	10,000	2,000 U	12,000
Total revenue	$1,850,000	$310,000 U	$2,160,000
Total variable costs	1,120,000	68,000 F	1,188,000
Contribution margin	730,000	242,000 U	972,000
Fixed costs	705,000	5,000 F	710,000
Operating income	$ 25,000	$237,000 U	$ 262,000

$237,000 U

Total static-budget variance

LEVEL 2 Variance Analysis*

	Actual Results (1)	Flexible-Budget Variances (2) = (1) − (3)	Flexible Budget (3)	Sales-Volume Variances (4) = (3) − (5)	Static Budget (5)
Units sold	10,000	—	10,000	2,000 U	12,000
Revenue	$1,850,000	$ 50,000 F	$1,800,000	$360,000 U	$2,160,000
Variable costs	1,120,000	130,000 U	990,000	198,000 F	1,188,000
Contribution margin	730,000	80,000 U	810,000	162,000 U	972,000
Fixed costs	705,000	5,000 F	710,000	—	710,000
Operating income	$ 25,000	$ 75,000 U	$ 100,000	$162,000 U	$ 262,000

$ 75,000 U $162,000 U

Total flexible-budget variance   Total sales-volume variance

$237,000 U

Total static-budget variance

*Pay careful attention because the variances reported in columns (2) and (4) show how the variance affects operating income.

LEVEL 2 Variance Analysis—More Detail

	Actual Results (1)	Flexible-Budget Variances (2) = (1) − (3)	Flexible Budget (3)	Sales-Volume Variances (4) = (3) − (5)	Static Budget (5)
Units sold	10,000	—	10,000	2,000 U	12,000
Revenue	$1,850,000	$ 50,000 F	$1,800,000	$360,000 U	$2,160,000
Variable costs		—		—	
Direct materials	688,200	88,200 U	600,000	120,000 U	720,000
Direct manufacturing labour	198,000	38,000 U	160,000	32,000 F	192,000
Direct marketing labour	57,600	2,400 F	60,000	12,000 F	72,000
Variable manufacturing overhead*	130,500	10,500 U	120,000	24,000 F	144,000
Variable marketing overhead*	45,700	4,300 F	50,000	10,000 F	60,000
Total variable costs	1,120,000	130,000 U	990,000	198,000 F	1,188,000
Contribution margin	730,000	80,000 U	810,000	162,000 F	972,000
Fixed manufacturing costs	285,000	9,000 U	276,000	—	276,000
Fixed marketing costs	420,000	14,000 F	434,000	—	434,000
Operating income	$ 25,000	$ 75,000 U	$ 100,000	$162,000 U	$ 262,000

*Total flexible-budget variable overhead variance is $6,200 U ($4,300 F − $10,500 U).

Flexible Budgeting and Activity-Based Costing

▶ **LO 4**

Undertake variance analysis in activity-based costing systems.

Activity-based costing (ABC) systems focus on individual activities that occur throughout the value-chain functions. ABC systems classify the costs of various activities into a cost hierarchy—output unit-level costs, batch-level costs, product-sustaining costs, and facility-sustaining costs. The two common direct cost categories—direct materials costs and direct manufacturing labour costs—are examples of output unit-level costs. In this section, we focus on batch-level costs to show how the basic principles and concepts of flexible budgets and variance analysis can be applied to other levels of the cost hierarchy. Batch-level costs are the costs of activities related to a group of units of products or services rather than to each individual unit of product or service.

Relating Batch Costs to Product Output

Consider Lyco Brass Works, which manufactures Jacutaps, a line of decorative brass faucets for home spas. Lyco produces Jacutaps in batches. For each product line, Lyco dedicates material-handling labour to bring materials to the manufacturing area, transport work in process from one work centre to the next, and take the finished product to the shipping area. Hence, material-handling labour costs are direct costs of Jacutaps. Because the materials for a batch are moved together, material-handling labour costs vary with the number of batches rather than with the number of units in a batch. Material-handling labour costs are variable direct batch-level costs.

Information regarding Jacutaps for 2018 is as follows:

	Static-Budget Amounts	Actual Amounts
1. Units of Jacutaps produced and sold	180,000	151,200
2. Batch size (units per batch)	150	140
3. Number of batches (Line 1 ÷ Line 2)	1,200	1,080
4. Material-handling labour-hours per batch	5	5.25
5. Total material-handling labour-hours (Line 3 × Line 4)	6,000	5,670
6. Cost per material-handling labour-hour	$ 14.00	$ 14.50
7. Total material-handling labour costs	$84,000	$82,215

To prepare the flexible budget for material-handling labour costs, Lyco starts with the actual units of output produced, 151,200 units, and proceeds as follows:

■ *Using budgeted batch size, calculate the number of batches that should have been used to produce the actual output.* At the budgeted batch size of 150 units per batch, Lyco should have produced the 151,200 units of output in 1,008 batches (= 151,200 units ÷ 150 units per batch).

■ *Using budgeted material-handling labour-hours per batch, calculate the number of material-handling labour-hours that should have been used.* At the budgeted quantity of 5 hours per batch, 1,008 batches should have required 5,040 material-handling labour-hours (= 1,008 batches × 5 hours per batch).

■ *Using budgeted cost per material-handling labour-hour, calculate the flexible-budget amount for material-handling labour-hours.* The flexible-budget amount is 5,040 material-handling labour-hours × $14 budgeted cost per material-handling labour-hour = $70,560.

Note how the flexible-budget calculations for material-handling costs focus on batch-level quantities (material-handling labour-hours) rather than on output unit-level amounts (such as material-handling labour-hours per unit of output). The flexible-budget variance for material-handling costs can then be calculated as

Flexible-budget variance = Actual costs − Flexible-budget costs
= (5,670 hours × $14.50 per hour) − (5,040 hours × $14 per hour)
= $82,215 − $70,560 = $11,655, or $11,655 U

The unfavourable variance indicates that material-handling labour costs were $11,655 higher than the flexible-budget target.

Rate and Efficiency Variances

We develop insight into the possible reasons for this $11,655 unfavourable variance by examining the rate and efficiency components of the flexible-budget variance:

$$\frac{\text{Rate}}{\text{variance}} = \left(\begin{array}{c}\text{Actual rate} \\ \text{of input}\end{array} - \begin{array}{c}\text{Budgeted rate} \\ \text{of input}\end{array}\right) \times \begin{array}{c}\text{Actual quantity} \\ \text{of input}\end{array}$$

= ($14.50 per hour − $14 per hour) × 5,670 hours
= $0.50 per hour × 5,670 hours
= $2,835, or $2,835 U

The $14.50 actual cost per material-handling labour-hour exceeds the $14.00 budgeted cost, indicating an unfavourable rate variance for material-handling labour. This variance could be due to (1) Lyco's human resources manager negotiating less skillfully than was planned in the budget or (2) unexpected wage rate increases due to scarcity of labour.

There is also an unfavourable efficiency variance:

$$\frac{\text{Efficiency}}{\text{variance}} = \left(\begin{array}{c}\text{Actual quantity} \\ \text{of input used}\end{array} - \begin{array}{c}\text{Budgeted quantity of input} \\ \text{allowed for actual output}\end{array}\right) \times \begin{array}{c}\text{Budgeted rate} \\ \text{of input}\end{array}$$

= (5,670 hours − 5,040 hours) × $14 per hour
= 630 hours × $14 per hour
= $8,820, or $8,820 U

The 5,670 actual material-handling labour-hours exceeded the 5,040 material-handling labour-hours that Lyco should have used for the number of batches it produced, indicating an unfavourable efficiency variance. Two reasons for the unfavourable efficiency variance are

■ Smaller actual batch sizes of 140 units, instead of the budgeted batch sizes of 150 units, resulting in Lyco producing the 151,200 units in 1,080 batches instead of 1,008 (= 151,200 ÷ 150) batches.

- Higher actual material-handling labour-hours per batch of 5.25 hours instead of budgeted material-handling labour-hours of 5 hours.

Reasons for smaller-than-budgeted batch sizes could include

- Quality problems if batch sizes exceed 140 faucets.
- High costs of carrying inventory.

Reasons for higher actual material-handling labour-hours per batch could include

- Inefficient layout of the Jacutap production line relative to the layout proposed in the budget.
- Material-handling labour having to wait at work centres before picking up or delivering materials.
- Unmotivated, inexperienced, or underskilled employees.
- Standards for material-handling time that are too tight.

Identifying the reasons for the efficiency variance will help Lyco's managers develop a plan for improving material-handling labour efficiency.

Focus on Hierarchy

The greatest improvement in control will arise if managers focus the flexible-budget quantity computations at the appropriate level of the cost hierarchy. For example, because material handling is a batch-level cost, the flexible-budget quantity calculations are made at the batch level—the quantity of material-handling labour-hours that Lyco should have used based on the number of batches it should have taken to produce the actual quantity of 151,200 units. If a cost had been a product-sustaining cost—such as product design—the flexible-budget quantity computations would focus on the product-sustaining level, for example, by evaluating the actual complexity of product design relative to the budget.

Managerial Uses of Variance Analysis

Performance Evaluation

▶ **LO 5**

Describe how managers use variance analysis.

The increased access to organizational data from information systems and market data from a variety of data streams and "Big Data" sources has increased the ability for management to perform deeper levels of analysis on the operations of an organization, most commonly seen in performance evaluations and performance metrics. A key use of variance analysis is in performance evaluation. Two attributes of performance are commonly measured:

- **Effectiveness:** The degree to which a predetermined objective or target is met.
- **Efficiency:** The relative amount of inputs used to achieve a given level of output.

To illustrate the difference, consider that killing a fly with a sledgehammer will be effective (if you hit the fly), but not efficient, since you will expend a lot of extra energy. Killing a fly with a fly swatter is both effective and efficient.

Managers must be careful to understand the cause(s) of a variance before using it as a performance measure. Assume that a Webb purchasing manager has just negotiated a deal resulting in a favourable rate variance for materials. The deal could have achieved a favourable variance for any or all of three reasons:

- The purchasing manager bargained effectively with suppliers.
- The purchasing manager accepted lower-quality materials at a lower rate.
- The purchasing manager secured a discount for buying in bulk. However, he or she bought higher quantities than necessary for the short run, which resulted in excessive inventories.

If the purchasing manager's performance is evaluated solely on materials rate variances, only the first reason will be considered acceptable, and the evaluation will be positive. The second and third reasons will be considered unacceptable and will likely cause the company to incur additional costs, such as higher inventory storage costs, higher quality inspection costs, higher costs to repair or replace defects, and higher materials scrap costs. *Managers should not automatically interpret a favourable variance as "good" news.*

Financial and Nonfinancial Performance Measures

Almost all organizations use a combination of financial and nonfinancial performance measures rather than relying exclusively on either type. Control is often exercised by focusing on nonfinancial measures like combining the least expensive quantities in a product mix. But overall cost leadership is not a simple matter. Managers are evaluated on financial measures of results. This introduces conflict of interest. Depending on the level of the cost hierarchy of an activity, cutting a volume of input to the benefit of one business function may increase costs throughout the entire value chain.

Performance measures should focus managers' attention on reducing the total costs incurred by the entire company. When a single performance measure (e.g., a direct materials variance) receives excessive emphasis, managers tend to make decisions that will maximize their own reported performance based on favourable direct materials variance. A focus on cost control for functions at a high level in the hierarchy will motivate decisions to benefit the entire company.

Ironically, long-term profitability and cost control often mean more costs in the short run to achieve long-run benefit. A new machine might result in unfavourable efficiency variances in the short run as workers are not familiar with the new equipment (learning curve effect). But in the longer run, the new equipment might result in increased efficiency (less labour input per unit) and possibly increased quality. This, in turn, might give the

Sustainability in Action   Sustainability and Variance Analysis

Warren Price Photography/Shutterstock

Companies are able to use the massive amounts of data collected in the MIS to better understand how products are produced and ultimately supplied to their customers.

In efforts to manage both costs and goals for more sustainable operations, a number of organizations are re-engineering their operations using fine-tuned analysis of production and sales variances to understand where changes can most effectively be made. Since 2010 Kraft has been experimenting with reductions in the amount of plastics used in their bottles and bottle-caps, creating thinner but more resilient packaging. Similarly, McDonald's[1] has been piloting different approaches to beef farming to better understand how quality can be maintained while costs might be reduced and more sustainable approaches to industrial farming can be achieved.

Such initiatives require organizations to re-examine how they source direct material in terms of quantity, quality, and the physical distance of the supply chain (distance often equates to less sustainable models); as well as price standards. Re-engineering these processes will also result in changes to manufacturing overhead, with new equipment, changes in transportation timing, and cost (lighter products are cheaper to ship). Organizations are also creating standards for the management of waste and pollution to create a more sustainable business environment.

Adapted from K. Welshans. 2016. McDonald's concludes sustainable beef pilot project. *Feedstuffs*, August 10 (http://feedstuffs.com/story-mcdonalds-concludes-sustainable-beef-pilot-project-45-145136).

Exhibit 7-10 Flexible-Budget Variable Direct Variances, Levels 0, 1, 2, 3, and 4

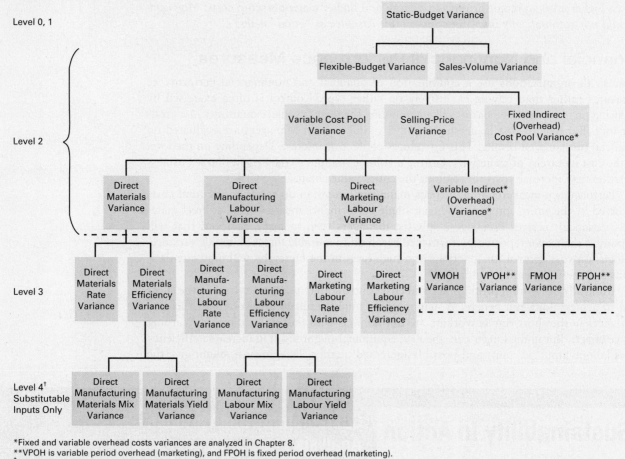

*Fixed and variable overhead costs variances are analyzed in Chapter 8.
**VPOH is variable period overhead (marketing), and FPOH is fixed period overhead (marketing).
†See Appendix 7B for a discussion of Level 4 yield and mix variances.

firm a competitive advantage that would allow it to sell more units and/or raise its price. Additional cost reductions may also result if there are fewer returns.

When to Investigate Variances

Exhibit 7-10 illustrates all four levels of variance analysis possible within a very simple costing system for products with substitutable inputs. This type of production process is most recognizable in industrial food processing and resource refining. It seems almost inevitable that for any specific time period there will be an unfavourable variance somewhere. When to use expensive and scarce management time to investigate and explain variances depends on the situation. Usually this feedback directs attention to the largest U variance first.

For critical items, however, a small variance may prompt follow-up. For other items, a minimum dollar variance or a specific percentage of variance from budget may prompt investigations. Of course, a 4% variance in direct materials costs of $1,000,000 may deserve more attention than a 20% variance in repair costs of $10,000. Therefore, rules such as "investigate all variances exceeding $5,000 or 5% of budgeted costs, whichever is lower" are common.

Continuous Improvement

The most important task in variance analysis is to interpret and learn from variance analysis. At each opportunity for feedback, small improvements can be made to control variances. **Continuous improvement** is a budgeted cost that is successively reduced over succeeding time periods. Improvement opportunities can be easier to identify at the initial

Concepts in Action

Starbucks Reduces Direct-Cost Variances to Brew a Turnaround

Along with coffee, Starbucks brewed profitable growth for many years. From Seattle to Singapore, customers lined up to buy $4 lattes and Frappuccinos. Walking around with a coffee drink from Starbucks became an affordable-luxury status symbol. But when consumers tightened their purse strings amid the recession, the company was in serious trouble. With customers cutting back and lower-priced competition—from Dunkin' Donuts and McDonald's among others—increasing, Starbucks's profit margins were under attack.

For Starbucks, profitability depends on making each high-quality beverage at the lowest possible costs. As a result, an intricate understanding of direct costs is critical. Variance analysis helps managers assess and maintain profitability at desired levels. In each Starbucks store, the two key direct costs are materials and labour.

Materials costs at Starbucks include coffee beans, milk, flavouring syrups, pastries, paper cups, and lids. To reduce budgeted costs for materials, Starbucks focused on two key inputs: coffee and milk. For coffee, Starbucks sought to avoid waste and spoilage by no longer brewing decaffeinated and darker coffee blends in the afternoon and evening, when store traffic is slower. Instead, baristas were instructed to brew a pot only when a customer ordered it. With milk prices rising (and making up around 10% of Starbucks's cost of sales), the company switched to 2% milk, which is healthier and costs less, and redoubled efforts to reduce milk-related spoilage.

Labour costs at Starbucks, which cost 24% of company revenue annually, were another area of variance focus. Many stores employed fewer baristas. In other stores, Starbucks adopted many "lean" production techniques. With 30% of baristas' time involved in walking around behind the counter, reaching for items, and blending drinks, Starbucks sought to make its drink-making processes more efficient. While the changes seem small—keeping bins of coffee beans on top of the counter so baristas don't have to bend over, moving bottles of flavoured syrups closer to where drinks are made, and using coloured tape to quickly differentiate between pitchers of soy, nonfat, and low-fat milk—some stores experienced a 10% increase in transactions using the same number of workers or fewer.

The company took additional steps to align labour costs with its pricing. Starbucks cut prices on easier-to-make drinks like drip coffee, while lifting prices by as much as 30 cents for larger and more complex drinks, such as a venti caramel macchiato.

Starbucks's focus on reducing year-over-year variances paid off. In fiscal year 2009, the company reduced its store operating expenses by $320 million, or 8.5%. Continued focus on direct-cost variances will be critical to the company's future success in any economic climate.

Sources: J. Adamy. 2009. Starbucks brews up new cost cuts by putting lid on afternoon decaf. *Wall Street Journal*, January 28; J. Adamy. 2008. New Starbucks brew attracts customers, flak. *Wall Street Journal*, July 1; C. Harris. 2007. Starbucks slips; lattes rise. *Seattle Post Intelligencer*, July 23; J. Jargon. 2010. Starbucks growth revives, perked by Via. *Wall Street Journal*, January 21; J. Jargon. 2009. Latest Starbucks buzzword: 'Lean' Japanese techniques. *Wall Street Journal*, August 4; D. Kesmodel. 2009. Starbucks sees demand stirring again. *Wall Street Journal*, November 6.

stages of production, but for mature internal processes this becomes more difficult. Some companies use Kaizen budgeting to target explicit amounts of reductions in budgeted costs over successive periods.

For example, the budgeted direct materials cost for each jacket that Webb Company manufactured in April 2018 is $60 per unit. The budgeted cost for variance analysis for subsequent periods could be based on a targeted 1% reduction each period:

Month	Prior Month's Amount	Reduction in Budgeted Amount	Revised Budgeted Amount
April 2018	—	—	$60.00
May 2018	$60.00	$0.600 (= 0.01 × $60.00)	59.40
June 2018	59.40	0.594 (= 0.01 × 59.40)	58.81
July 2018	58.81	0.588 (= 0.01 × 58.81)	58.22

The source of the 1% reduction in budgeted direct materials costs could be efficiency improvements or rate reductions. By using continuous improvement budgeted costs, an organization signals the importance of constantly seeking ways to reduce total costs. For example, managers could avoid unfavourable materials efficiency variances by continuously reducing materials waste.

Impact of Inventories

Our Webb Company illustration assumed the following:

■ All units are manufactured and sold in the same accounting period. There was no work-in-process or finished goods inventory at either the beginning or the end of the accounting period.

■ All direct materials were purchased and used in the same accounting period. There was no direct materials inventory at either the beginning or the end of the period.

Both assumptions can be relaxed without changing the key concepts introduced in this chapter. However, changes in the computation or interpretation of variances would be required when beginning or ending inventories exist. Suppose direct materials are purchased some time before their use and the beginning direct materials inventories are almost always non-zero. The direct materials purchased do not equal the direct materials used. Managers typically want to pinpoint variances at the earliest possible time to regain control over costs quickly.

For *direct materials rate variances with inventories*, the purchase date will almost always be the earliest possible time to isolate a variance. As a result, many organizations calculate direct materials rate variances using the quantities *purchased* in an accounting period. In contrast, the direct materials efficiency variance is calculated using the amount of inputs that were *used* in the accounting period (as opposed to the amount purchased). This method of calculating direct material variances is sometimes referred to as the *"4-peg analysis."* This method is illustrated below in the Problem for Self-Study, which shows how to calculate the direct materials variances when the materials purchased and the materials used are two different amounts.

Pulling It All Together—Problem for Self-Study

Try to solve this problem before examining the solution that follows. Note: In this situation, the amount of direct materials purchased *does not* match the amount of direct materials used. This results in a slightly different approach to calculating the rate variance (where the amount of materials *purchased* is used in the calculation) and the efficiency variance (where the amount of materials *used* is the basis for the calculation.) This type of variance analysis is sometimes referred to as a "4-peg analysis."

Problem

O'Shea Company manufactures ceramic vases. It uses its standard costing system when developing its flexible-budget amounts. In April 2018, 2,000 finished units were produced. The following information is related to its two direct manufacturing cost categories of direct materials and direct manufacturing labour.

Direct materials *used* were 4,400 kilograms. The standard direct materials input allowed for one output unit is 2 kilograms at $15 per kilogram, and 5,000 kilograms of materials were *purchased* at $16.50 per kilogram, for a total of $82,500.

Actual direct manufacturing labour-hours were 3,250 at a total cost of $66,300. Standard manufacturing labour time allowed is 1.5 hours per output unit, and the standard direct manufacturing labour cost is $20 per hour.

Required ▶

❶ 1. Calculate the direct materials rate and efficiency variances and the direct manufacturing labour rate and efficiency variances. The direct materials rate variance will be based on a flexible budget for *actual quantities purchased*, but the efficiency variance will be based on a flexible budget for *actual quantities used*.

❷ 2. Prepare journal entries for a standard-costing system that isolates variances as early as feasible.

Exhibit 7-11 Columnar Presentation of Variance Analysis: Direct Materials and Direct Manufacturing Labour

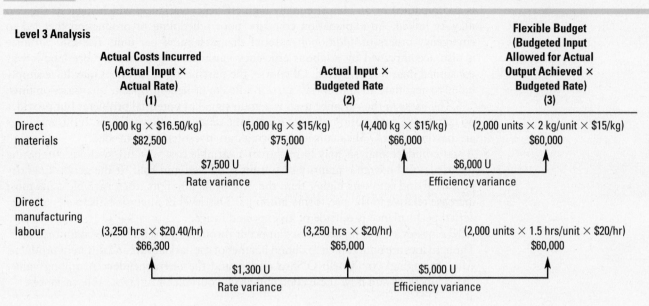

3. Based on these results, list in order from most to least important the variances you ⑤ would investigate. Explain briefly what you considered in your ranking.
4. Give three alternative explanations for the most important variance. ⑤
5. Give reasons why the flexible-budget variance analysis is more helpful than a ❶ static-budget variance analysis for O'Shea.
6. O'Shea likely produces vases in a variety of shapes and colours. What advantages ❹ might arise from using the strategy of ABC budgeting and variance analysis?

Solution

1. Exhibit 7-11 shows how the columnar presentation of variances introduced in Exhibit 7-9 can be adjusted for the difference in timing between the purchase and use of materials. In particular, note the two sets of computations in column 2 for direct materials. The $75,000 pertains to the direct materials purchased; the $66,000 pertains to the direct materials used.

2.

Materials Control (5,000 kilograms × $15/kg)	$75,000	
Direct Materials Rate Variance (5,000 kilograms × $1.50/kg)	7,500	
Accounts Payable Control (5,000 kilograms × $16.50/kg)		$82,500
Work-in-Process Control (2,000 units × 2 kg/unit × $15/kg)	60,000	
Direct Materials Efficiency Variance (400 kilograms × $15/kg)	6,000	
Materials Control (4,400 kilograms × $15/kg)		66,000
Work-in-Process Control (2,000 units × 1.5 hrs/unit × $20/hr)	60,000	
Direct Manufacturing Labour Rate Variance (3,250 hours × $0.40/hr)	1,300	
Direct Manufacturing Labour Efficiency Variance (250 hours × $20/hr)	5,000	
Wages Payable Control (3,250 hours × $20.40/hr)		66,300

3. In order, the most important variances from most to least important are direct materials rate variance of $7,500 U; direct materials efficiency variance of $6,000 U; direct manufacturing labour efficiency variance of $5,000 U; and direct manufacturing labour rate variance of $1,300 U. No guidelines are provided; therefore, the only reason for this ranking is the level of materiality—the highest unfavourable variance first followed by the lower unfavourable variances, in order.

4. The direct materials rate variance could have several explanations. The rate variance is accompanied by an almost equally high efficiency variance, which suggests the two may be linked. An explanation could be poor scheduling of production that led to emergency orders of additional material that cost more per unit. The rate variance is also accompanied by a labour efficiency variance, which means more labour was consumed than was budgeted. Of course, the purchasing department may have simply failed to negotiate an appropriate rate or failed to order appropriate quantities on time.

   The value of the variance itself is a good signal of potential problems but provides no conclusive explanation of what caused the unfavourable variances. If the variances are beyond what O'Shea considers normal, an investigation is needed.

5. A static-budget analysis may have shown a variable cost variance without comparing the actual to budgeted quantity of output produced and sold. If the actual quantity produced and sold was higher than the pro forma amounts, then variable costs must increase relative to the pro forma amounts. This level of analysis fails to signal when actual performance is outside of an expected range.

6. ABC requires a focus on activities that occur throughout a set of value-chain functions. The activities are undertaken to obtain batches of similar outputs and different products. ABC budgeting would help O'Shea understand the interdependencies among value-chain functions and how these contribute to favourable or unfavourable variances.

Appendix 7A

Budgets, Benchmarks, and Standards

▶ **LO 6**

Distinguish among standards, budgets, and benchmarks.

In our analyses we referred to the static- and flexible-budget data. Webb's budget data were the result of careful planning. The management team used its experience to examine all the amounts used to create the budget schedules.

Budgeted amounts are often predictions based on past actual input rates and quantities. Past data are available at a relatively low cost from the company's MIS. The limitations of using this source are (1) past data include past inefficiencies and (2) past data do not incorporate any planned changes that are expected to occur in the budget period.

Benchmarking

An ideal rather than average performance may be chosen as the budgeted threshold. A **benchmark** typically reflects the best possible performance achieved anywhere in any industry using a similar process. Unless, however, external and internal conditions match those in the benchmarked company, this standard cannot be achieved. Using a benchmark requires commitment to internal change. If this is absent then, inevitably, Webb would report unfavourable variances and part of the explanation would always be that ideal conditions did not prevail.

Benchmarking reports are based on the costs of other companies and may be developed for many activities and products. For example, Webb Company could estimate (possibly with the aid of consultants) the materials cost of the jackets manufactured by its competitors. The materials cost estimate of the lowest-cost competitor could be used as the budgeted amounts in its variance computations. However, Webb needs to be careful in choosing the firms that it looks at when it develops its benchmarks. Very large firms may experience economies of scale and/or scope (and therefore, lower unit costs) than smaller firms in the same industry. Obviously, it would serve little purpose to select a benchmark that is unreasonably low (or high) and, in fact, could result in demotivating managers trying to achieve the budget targets. An unfavourable materials-efficiency variance would signal that Webb has a higher materials cost than "best cost practice" in its industry. The magnitude of the cost difference would be of great interest to Webb. It could prompt Webb to do an extensive search into how to bring its own cost structure in line with that of the lowest in the industry.

Standards

A **standard** is a carefully predetermined amount based on investigation of external performance achieved by similar processes. A standard is usually expressed on a per-unit basis and communicates an average amount indicating what *should* be achieved by any similar process in each time period that performance measures are taken. Once a standard is set, it remains unchanged over time. Standards differ from budget amounts because budget amounts change from one time period to the next. Standards differ from benchmarks because they are average, not ideal, amounts.

Assume Webb uses industry time-and-motion and engineering studies to determine its standard amounts. Each task involved in making a jacket, for example, is assigned a standard amount of time based on work by an experienced operator using equipment operating in an efficient manner.

Webb has developed standard inputs and standard costs per unit for each of its variable cost items. A **standard input** is a predetermined average quantity of inputs (such as kilograms of materials or hours of labour time) required for one unit of output. A **standard cost** method is based on either a predetermined average cost per input or a predetermined average total input cost per unit of output. Webb's budgeted cost for each variable cost item is calculated using the following formula:

Standard inputs allowed for one output unit × Standard cost per input unit

And the variable cost items are

- *Direct materials:* a standard of 2 square metres (m²) of cloth input allowed per output unit (jacket) manufactured, at $30 standard cost per square metre:

Standard cost = 2 × $30 = $60 per output unit manufactured

- *Direct manufacturing labour:* 0.80 manufacturing labour-hours of input allowed per output unit manufactured, at $20 standard cost per hour:

Standard cost = 0.80 × $20 = $16 per output unit manufactured

- *Direct marketing labour:* 0.25 marketing labour-hours of input allowed per output unit sold, at $24 standard cost per hour:

Standard cost = 0.25 × $24 = $6 per output unit sold

- *Variable manufacturing overhead:* Allocated based on 0.40 machine-hours per output unit manufactured at $30 standard cost per machine-hour:

Standard cost = 0.40 × $30 = $12 per output unit manufactured

- *Variable marketing overhead:* Allocated based on 0.125 direct marketing labour-hours per output unit sold at $40 standard rate per hour:

Standard cost = 0.125 × $40 = $5 per output unit sold

These standard cost calculations reconcile to Exhibit 7-8.

Standard Costing and Information Technology

Modern information technology greatly facilitates the use of standard costing systems for product costing and control. The company's MIS can readily store barcode scanner or radio frequency identification (RFID) information to record the receipt of materials, immediately costing each material using its stored standard rate. The receipt of materials is matched with the purchase order to record accounts payable and to isolate the direct materials rate variance.

As output is completed, the standard quantity of direct materials that should have been used is computed and compared with the actual quantity requested for direct materials that was input into the MIS by an operator on the production floor. This difference is multiplied by the standard direct material rate to obtain the direct materials efficiency variance. Labour variances are calculated as employees log into production floor terminals and punch in their employee numbers, start and end times, and the quantity of the product they helped produce. Managers use this instantaneous feedback on variances to initiate immediate corrective action, as needed.

Control Feature of Standard Costs

We will now illustrate journal entries when standard costs are used. For illustrative purposes, we will focus on direct materials and direct manufacturing labour and continue with the data from the Webb Company illustration with one exception. Assume that during April 2018, Webb purchases 25,000 m^2 of materials. The actual quantity used is 22,200 m^2, and the standard quantity allowed for the actual output achieved is 20,000 m^2. The actual purchase cost was $31/$m^2$, while the standard rate was $30/$m^2$. In fact, *contrary* to the budget assumption, Webb had a DM ending inventory of 2,800 m^2.

If Webb's managers were well-informed when they generated the budget, the performance in April generated unnecessary expense in two ways. First, actual cost exceeded budget, although we do not know why. Second, the quantity of DM purchased was 25% more than expected ((25,000 m^2 − 20,000 m^2) ÷ 20,000 m^2), and 11% more was used than expected ((22,200 m^2 − 20,000 m^2) ÷ 20,000 m^2). Note that in each of the following entries, unfavourable cost variances are always debits because they decrease operating income. Favourable cost variances are always credits because they increase operating income.

- **Entry 1(a).** Isolate the direct materials rate variance at the time of purchase by debiting Materials Control at standard rates. This is the earliest date possible to isolate this variance.

  1. a. Materials Control
     ($25,000 m^2 \times \$30/m^2$) 750,000
        Direct Materials Rate Variance
        ($25,000 m^2 \times \$1/m^2$) 25,000
             Accounts Payable Control 775,000
     To record direct materials purchased.

- **Entry 1(b).** Isolate the direct materials efficiency variance at the time of usage by debiting Work-in-Process Control at standard input quantities allowed for actual output units achieved at standard input rates. This approach is consistent with Chapter 4, where, under the actual and normal cost methods, the direct costs are calculated using actual unit costs.

  1. b. Work-in-Process Control
     ($20,000 m^2 \times \$30/m^2$) 600,000
     Direct Materials Efficiency Variance 66,000
     ($2,200 m^2 \times \$30/m^2$)
             Materials Control 666,000
             ($22,200 m^2 \times \$30/m^2$)
     To record direct materials used.

- **Entry 2.** Isolate the direct manufacturing labour rate and efficiency variances at the time this labour is used by debiting Work-in-Process Control at standard quantities allowed for actual output units achieved at standard input rates. Note that Wages Payable Control measures the payroll liability and hence is always at actual wage rates. Because direct manufacturing labour can never be inventoried, there is only one journal entry for both the purchase and use of direct manufacturing labour.

  2. Work-in-Process Control
     ($8,000 hours \times \$20/hr$) 160,000
     Direct Manufacturing Labour Rate Variance ($9,000 hours \times \$2/hr$) 18,000
     Direct Manufacturing Labour Efficiency Variance ($1,000 hours \times \$20/hr$) 20,000
             Wages Payable Control ($9,000 hours \times \$22/hr$) 198,000
     To record liability for direct manufacturing labour costs.

A major advantage of this standard costing system is its emphasis on the control feature of standard costs. All variances are isolated at the earliest possible time, when managers can make informed decisions based on those variances.

End-of-Period Adjustments

There are three approaches to recognizing the underallocated or overallocated manufacturing overhead at the end of a period:

- The adjusted allocation rate approach, which adjusts every job cost record for the difference between the allocated and actual indirect cost amounts.
- The direct write-off approach, which adjusts the cost of goods sold by the amount of the variances. This method is particularly appropriate when the amounts are not material (i.e., they are small in size).
- The proration approach, which makes adjustments to one or more of the following end-of-period account balances: materials, work-in-process, finished goods, and cost of goods sold.

Rate and efficiency variances can also be disposed of using these same three approaches.

Benchmarking and Variance Analysis

If a benchmark is the best possible performance, then theoretically a favourable variance will be impossible. Competitive benchmarking, as it is now known, is only one form of strategic management accounting.

Benchmarking is also a useful way to set internal performance standards, especially for large multinational companies. Companies also benchmark key competencies, quality, product or service attributes, customer profitability, intellectual capital, and environmental sustainability.[1] Benchmarking involves continuous change within a company in an effort to match or exceed the best performance in some domain. Changes in the outputs offered, design processes, speed of innovation, target markets, and customers served are often needed to achieve or exceed a benchmark. Management's choice to benchmark can either support an existing corporate mission and strategy, or signal a change. The answer to whether or not benchmarking is the best remedy depends on careful reconsideration of existing strategic choices.

The benchmarking team may discover that the most important data are only available from competitors. The problem is that sharing some competitive information is illegal if it leads to price fixing or discourages competition in a market. If, legally, the data cannot be shared, then the company must analyze any available information as best it can.

In Canada, an important source of benchmarking data is available through Industry Canada (the federal government department responsible for promoting and supporting Canadian industry). The small and medium enterprise (SME) benchmarking tool[2] allows firms to compare key business activities across similar-size enterprises.

Not-for-Profit Benchmarking

Benchmarking key activities can be even more important in not-for-profit/non-profit (NFP) organizations. Without a clear profit objective (and in fact, most NFPs are not allowed to generate profits by virtue of the regulations governing NFP entities), it can be difficult to measure performance. Instead, they need to rely on measures of efficiency with regard to their service delivery mandate (most NFP organizations are involved in service delivery). These measures could range from cost per student per course for a university to wait times for emergency room patients for a hospital.

---

[1] W.P. Wong and K.Y. Wong, "A Review on Benchmarking of Supply Chain Performance Measures," *Benchmarking: An International Journal*, 15.1 (2008): 25–51.

[2] Government of Canada. 2015. Financial Performance Data (http://www.ic.gc.ca/eic/site/pp-pp.nsf/eng/home).

For NFP benchmarks to be useful, they should have the following characteristics:

■ Be based on a similar sized organization.
■ Be from a similar regulatory environment (e.g., similar laws, labour codes, legal requirements, etc.).
■ Be in a similar labour environment (union vs. non-union).
■ Have a similar physical environment, if relevant (there's little point in comparing the costs of delivering meals to seniors in an urban setting to the costs of delivery in a rural setting).
■ Have a similar physical plant (e.g., buildings, equipment, vehicles, etc.).

The cost differences in the above-mentioned characteristics can be used by NFPs for a variety of purposes. For example, an organization could use the difference in the benchmark costs for new physical plants vs. the benchmark costs for old physical plants as support for updating an aging physical plant.

In contrast to firms in the for-profit sector, NFPs often find it easier to collect data from other, similar organizations. This is due to the fact that most NFPs do not see themselves in competition with each other. So, for example, a women's shelter in Toronto may be able to get cost and performance data from a similar shelter in Vancouver. Some NFP sectors have very effective associations that collect data from individual members and then publish that data in aggregate form. In other sectors, the sheer size of the sector means that for-profit organizations have developed benchmarking services on a fee-for-service basis. For example, in the United States, healthcare benchmarking for hospitals and health maintenance organizations (HMOs) has become a big business. Numerous types of reports and analyses are available (for a fee) to help hospitals compare their operating costs, wait times, and surgical outcomes (to name just a few) to other similar-size hospitals. In Canada, the Canadian Institute for Health Information (CIHI), an organization formed by the federal and provincial governments, provides similar services on a not-for-profit basis.[3]

In the case of a hospital, the type of benchmark information could take a variety of forms. For example, it could rank one hospital against other hospitals of a similar size and similar function. To make this type of benchmark comparison, a common approach is to create a standard "product/service" that can be compared across various organizations. In the hospital NFP sector, this standard is called a "case mix group."

In Exhibit 7A-1, Panel A, a hypothetical ranking of a group of hospitals is shown using this case mix group approach. This benchmarking methodology is used by hospitals around the world to evaluate performance and costs.[4] The typical report ranks hospitals of a similar size and with similar caseloads/medical procedures against each other. In Panel A, some hospitals are below the average, while others are above the average (in this type of statistical reporting, the median figure is often used as the average measure since it is not as influenced by data that are extremely high or low compared with the majority of data). Another type of data that is commonly benchmarked is performance with regards to specific service activities. In the case of hospital reporting, it is also common to report on activities like readmission rates, infection rates, length of stay, etc. Panel B reflects this type of report. With these types of benchmarks, a hospital can identify how its performance compares to the range of performance achieved by similar hospitals for the same procedure/activity.

Cost reports like Exhibit 7A-1 provide an external benchmark that forces hospital administrators, boards of directors, and funding agencies to ask why cost and performance levels differ between hospitals and how best practices can be transferred from the more efficient to the less efficient hospitals. While this level of analysis is easy to understand in the case of hospitals, due to the financial implications (for either private or publicly funded healthcare) and the quality of healthcare, similar benchmarking practices can be (and are being) taken in many other NFP sectors.

---

[3] Canadian Institute for Health Information website (http://www.cihi.ca/CIHI-ext-portal/internet/EN/Home/home/cihi000001).
[4] Ministry of Health. 2010. *DHB Hospital Benchmark Information. Report for the Quarter January–March 2010.* Wellington: Ministry of Health (http://www.moh.govt.nz/notebook/nbbooks.nsf/0/fc0590e749aa6f93cc25734e006d039c/$FILE/dhb-hospital-benchmark-information-mar2010.pdf).

Exhibit 7A-1 Benchmark Reporting for Hospitals

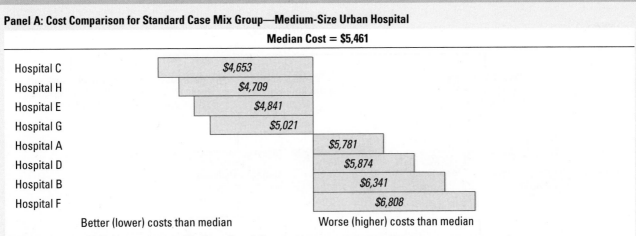

Panel A: Cost Comparison for Standard Case Mix Group—Medium-Size Urban Hospital

Median Cost = $5,461

Hospital C	$4,653
Hospital H	$4,709
Hospital E	$4,841
Hospital G	$5,021
Hospital A	$5,781
Hospital D	$5,874
Hospital B	$6,341
Hospital F	$6,808

Better (lower) costs than median   Worse (higher) costs than median

Reflects cost per CMG (case mix group) in Canadian dollars.

Panel B: Examples of Common Hospital Performance Benchmarks

1. Heart attack readmission rate*		2. Pneumonia 30-day mortality rate*	
(Based on 5,219 hospitals)		(Based on 5,212 hospitals)	
25th percentile:	15.9	25th percentile:	12.5
Median:	17.4	Median:	14.1
Average (mean)	17.6	Average (mean)	14.0
75th percentile	19.1	75th percentile	15.2

The costs and performance benchmarks are hypothetical figures and should not be taken as indicators of actual costs or performance rates.
*This is the rate per 1,000 patients.

Appendix 7B

Mix and Yield Level 4 Variances for Substitutable Inputs

For most mass production manufacturing processes—for example, refining oil—the barrel of oil from one Hibernia well is the same as the barrel of oil from a different Hibernia well. These are called **substitutable inputs** because the manufacturer can readily replace one with the other. Substitutability enables a more detailed analysis of the direct materials efficiency variance. Both materials and labour inputs may be substitutable in manufacturing, merchandising, or service industries.

But sometimes the output is distinguished by its taste—for example, wine or ketchup. The taste difference is due to the **input mix**, which is the determination of the *standard* combination and proportion of very similar direct material inputs that may be substituted for one another (see Appendix 7A for a discussion of standards). For ketchup, a combination of different tomatoes leads to the distinctive taste that distinguishes one brand from another. Small differences in the input mix that do not affect taste can reduce costs. The managers are given some discretion about the proportions of different tomatoes used to give them the flexibility necessary to exercise good cost leadership.

In changing the input mix, however, managers must ensure that the quantity of output is unchanged. It is only by selling the finished ketchup that all the costs of inputs can be recovered. The **yield** is the proportion of output obtained from a specified quantity of input. It is measured in the same units as inputs. Yield is calculated as the total quantity of output units divided by the total quantity of input units. **Mix variance** measures the variance of actual from expected input mix. The **yield variance** measures the variance of

▶ **LO 7**

Distinguish between Levels 3 and 4 variance analysis for substitutable inputs, and calculate Level 4 direct mix and yield variances.

Exhibit 7B-1 Detailed Direct Cost Sources of Materials and Labour Efficiency Variances: Substitutable Inputs

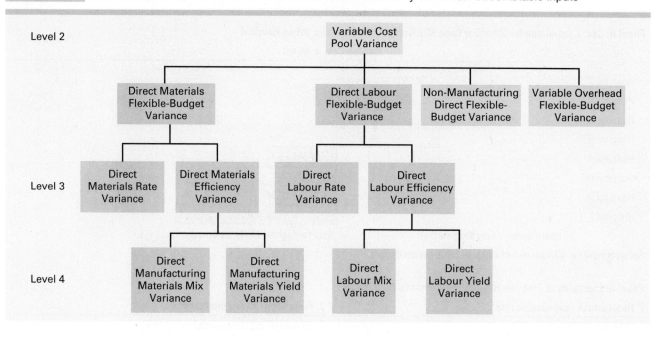

the actual from expected yield of outputs obtained from expected quantity of inputs. The relationship among the variance components of the direct materials and labour mix and yield variances is shown in Exhibit 7B-1.

Substitutable Direct Materials Inputs

To illustrate mix and yield variances, let's examine Delpino Corporation, which makes tomato ketchup. Our example focuses on direct material inputs and substitution among three of these inputs, but the same approach can be used to examine substitutable direct labour inputs. To produce ketchup of the desired consistency, colour, and taste, Delpino mixes three types of tomatoes grown in three different regions—Latin American tomatoes (Latoms), California tomatoes (Caltoms), and Florida tomatoes (Flotoms). Delpino's production standards require 1.60 tonnes of tomatoes to produce 1 tonne of ketchup, with 50% of the tomatoes being Latoms, 30% Caltoms, and 20% Flotoms. The direct materials input standards to produce 1 tonne of ketchup are

0.80 (= 50% of 1.6) tonne of Latoms at $70 per tonne	$ 56.00
0.48 (= 30% of 1.6) tonne of Caltoms at $80 per tonne	38.40
0.32 (= 20% of 1.6) tonne of Flotoms at $90 per tonne	28.80
Total standard cost of 1.6 tonnes of tomatoes	$123.20

Budgeted average cost per tonne of tomatoes is $123.20 ÷ 1.60 tonnes = $77.00 per tonne. The total quantity of inputs is 1.60 tonnes regardless of the type of tomato.

Because Delpino uses fresh tomatoes to make ketchup, no inventories of tomatoes are kept. Purchases are made as needed. All rate variances relate to tomatoes purchased and used. Actual results for June 2018 show that a total of 6,500 tonnes of tomatoes were used to produce 4,000 tonnes of ketchup:

3,250 tonnes of Latoms at actual cost of $70 per tonne	$ 227,500
2,275 tonnes of Caltoms at actual cost of $82 per tonne	186,550
975 tonnes of Flotoms at actual cost of $96 per tonne	93,600
6,500 tonnes of tomatoes	507,650
Standard cost of 4,000 tonnes of ketchup at $123.20 per tonne	492,800
Total variance to be explained	$ 14,850 U

Given the standard ratio of 1.60 tonnes of tomatoes to 1 tonne of ketchup, 6,400 tonnes of tomatoes should be used to produce 4,000 tonnes of ketchup. At the standard mix, the quantities of each type of tomato required are as follows:

Latoms	$0.50 \times 6{,}400 = 3{,}200$ tonnes
Caltoms	$0.30 \times 6{,}400 = 1{,}920$ tonnes
Flotoms	$0.20 \times 6{,}400 = 1{,}280$ tonnes

Direct Materials Rate and Efficiency Variances

The direct materials rate and efficiency variances are calculated separately for each input material and then added together. The variance analysis prompts Delpino to investigate the unfavourable rate and efficiency variances—why did they pay more for the tomatoes and use greater quantities than they should have? Causes could include a higher market rate for tomatoes or poor negotiation by the purchasing department. One is uncontrollable; the other is controllable. Inefficiency could also have been due to poor-quality tomatoes with too much water content or issues with the processing. To calculate the rate and efficiency variances,

Rate variance = (Actual rate of input − Budgeted rate of input) × Actual quantity of input used

$$\text{Efficiency variance} = \left(\begin{array}{c} \text{Actual quantity} \\ \text{of input used} \end{array} - \begin{array}{c} \text{Budgeted quantity of input allowed for actual} \\ \text{output units achieved} \end{array} \right) \times \begin{array}{c} \text{Budgeted rate} \\ \text{of input} \end{array}$$

The results are shown in Exhibit 7B-2. The management team will focus on how to explain the $4,450 U efficiency variance in terms of input mix or yield variance since the rate (price of tomatoes) variance is probably beyond management's control.

Direct Materials Mix and Direct Materials Yield Variances

Managers sometimes have discretion to substitute one material for another. For example, the manager of Delpino's ketchup plant has some leeway in combining Latoms, Caltoms, and Flotoms without affecting quality. We will assume that to maintain quality, the mix percentages of each type of tomato can vary only up to 5% from the standard mix. For example, the percentage of Caltoms in the mix can vary between 25% and 35% (= 30% ± 5%).

When inputs are substitutable, direct materials efficiency improvements relative to budgeted costs can come from two sources: (1) using a cheaper mix to produce a given

Exhibit 7B-2 Direct Materials Rate and Efficiency Variances for the Delpino Corporation for June 2018

	Actual Cost Incurred (Actual Input × Actual Rate) (1)	Actual Input × Budgeted Rate (2)	Flexible Budget (Budgeted Input Allowed for Actual Output × Budgeted Rate) (3)
Latoms	$3{,}250 \times \$70 = \$227{,}500$	$3{,}250 \times \$70 = \$227{,}500$	$3{,}200 \times \$70 = \$224{,}000$
Caltoms	$2{,}275 \times 82 = 186{,}550$	$2{,}275 \times 80 = 182{,}000$	$1{,}920 \times 80 = 153{,}600$
Flotoms	$975 \times 96 = \underline{93{,}600}$	$975 \times 90 = \underline{87{,}750}$	$1{,}280 \times 90 = \underline{115{,}200}$
	$\$507{,}650$	$\$497{,}250$	$\$492{,}800$

Level 3	$10,400 U Total rate variance		$4,450 U Total efficiency variance

| Level 2 | | $14,850 U Total flexible-budget variance | |

Exhibit 7B-3 Total Direct Materials Mix and Yield Variances for the Delpino Corporation for June 2018

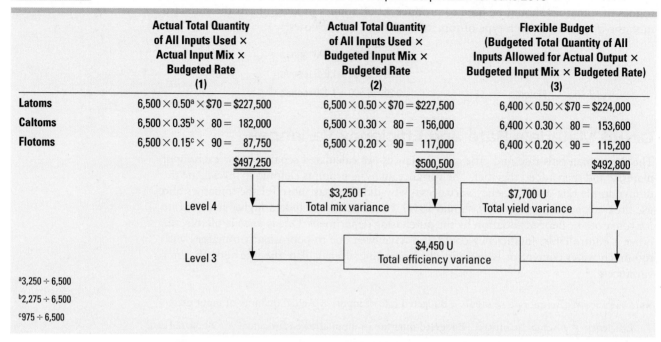

	Actual Total Quantity of All Inputs Used × Actual Input Mix × Budgeted Rate (1)	Actual Total Quantity of All Inputs Used × Budgeted Input Mix × Budgeted Rate (2)	Flexible Budget (Budgeted Total Quantity of All Inputs Allowed for Actual Output × Budgeted Input Mix × Budgeted Rate) (3)
Latoms	$6,500 \times 0.50^a \times \$70 = \$227,500$	$6,500 \times 0.50 \times \$70 = \$227,500$	$6,400 \times 0.50 \times \$70 = \$224,000$
Caltoms	$6,500 \times 0.35^b \times\ \ 80 =\ \ 182,000$	$6,500 \times 0.30 \times\ \ 80 =\ \ 156,000$	$6,400 \times 0.30 \times\ \ 80 =\ \ 153,600$
Flotoms	$6,500 \times 0.15^c \times\ \ 90 =\ \ \ \ 87,750$	$6,500 \times 0.20 \times\ \ 90 =\ \ 117,000$	$6,400 \times 0.20 \times\ \ 90 =\ \ 115,200$
	$497,250	$500,500	$492,800

Level 4 → $3,250 F Total mix variance → $7,700 U Total yield variance →

Level 3 → $4,450 U Total efficiency variance →

$^a 3,250 \div 6,500$

$^b 2,275 \div 6,500$

$^c 975 \div 6,500$

quantity of output or (2) using less input to achieve a given quantity of output. The direct materials mix and yield variances divide the efficiency variance into two variances: the mix variance focuses on how the multiple types of substitutable materials or labour are combined, and the yield variance focuses on how much of those inputs are used.

Holding constant the actual total quantity of all direct materials inputs used, the total **direct materials mix variance** is the difference between two amounts: (1) the budgeted cost for the actual mix of the total quantity of direct materials used, and (2) the budgeted cost of the budgeted mix of the actual total quantity of direct materials used. Signify each input as x_i and calculate the variance as

$$\text{Direct materials mix variance} = \sum\nolimits_{i=1}^{n}(\text{Actual} - \text{Budgeted input mix } x_i) \times \text{Budgeted rate } x_i$$

Please note that $\sum$ is the Greek letter sigma. In an equation, it means that you need to add up (or sum) the various iterations from 1 to n that can be calculated for that formula. In this situation, it is the combinations of the three different types of tomatoes that can be used to make the ketchup. The details of the calculation are shown in column format in Exhibit 7B-3.

Holding the budgeted input mix constant, the **direct materials yield variance** is the difference between two amounts: (1) the budgeted cost of direct materials based on the actual total quantity of all direct materials inputs used, and (2) the flexible-budget cost of direct materials based on the budgeted total quantity of direct materials inputs for the actual output. Again, with each input signified as x_i, the variance is calculated as

$$\text{Direct yield variance} = \sum\nolimits_{i=1}^{n}(\text{Actual } x_i \times [\text{Actual} - \text{Budgeted input mix \% } x_i] \times \text{Budgeted rate } x_i)$$

Exhibit 7B-3 presents the calculation of total direct materials mix and yield variances for the Delpino Corporation.

Interpretation of Direct Materials Mix Variance

Compare columns 1 and 2 in Exhibit 7B-3. Both columns calculate cost using the actual total quantity of all inputs used (6,500 tonnes) and budgeted input rates (Latoms, $70; Caltoms, $80; and Flotoms, $90). The *only* difference is that column 1 uses *actual input mix* (Latoms, 50%; Caltoms, 35%; Flotoms, 15%), and column 2 uses *budgeted input mix* (Latoms, 50%; Caltoms, 30%; and Flotoms, 20%). The difference in costs between the two columns is the total direct materials mix variance, attributable solely to differences in the mix of inputs used. The total direct materials mix variance is the sum of the direct materials mix variances for each input:

Latoms	$(0.50 - 0.50) \times 6{,}500 \times \$70 = 0.00 \times 6{,}500 \times \$70 =$	\$ 0
Caltoms	$(0.35 - 0.30) \times 6{,}500 \times \$80 = 0.05 \times 6{,}500 \times \$80 =$	26,000 U
Flotoms	$(0.15 - 0.20) \times 6{,}500 \times \$90 = 0.05 \times 6{,}500 \times \$90 =$	29,250 F
Total direct materials mix variance		$ 3,250 F

Interpretation of Level 4 Direct Materials Yield Variance

Compare columns 2 and 3 of Exhibit 7B-3. Column 2 calculates costs using the budgeted input mix and the budgeted rates. Column 3 calculates the flexible-budget cost based on the budgeted cost of the total quantity of all inputs used (6,400 tonnes of tomatoes) for the actual output achieved (4,000 tonnes of ketchup) times the budgeted input mix (Latoms, 50%; Caltoms, 30%; Flotoms, 20%).

The only difference in the two columns is that column 2 uses the actual total quantity of all inputs used (6,500 tonnes), while column 3 uses the budgeted total quantity of all inputs used (6,400 tonnes). Hence, the difference in costs between the two columns is the total direct materials yield variance, due solely to differences in actual and budgeted total input quantity used. The total direct materials yield variance is the sum of the direct materials yield variances for each input:

Latoms	$(6{,}500 - 6{,}400) \times 0.50 \times \$70 = 100 \times 0.50 \times \$70 =$	\$3,500 U
Caltoms	$(6{,}500 - 6{,}400) \times 0.30 \times \$80 = 100 \times 0.30 \times \$80 =$	2,400 U
Flotoms	$(6{,}500 - 6{,}400) \times 0.20 \times \$90 = 100 \times 0.20 \times \$90 =$	1,800 U
Total direct materials yield variance		$7,700 U

The total direct materials yield variance is unfavourable because Delpino used 6,500 tonnes of tomatoes rather than the 6,400 tonnes it should have used to produce 4,000 tonnes of ketchup. Holding the budgeted mix and budgeted rates of tomatoes constant, the budgeted cost per tonne of tomatoes in the budgeted mix is \$77 per tonne. The unfavourable yield variance represents the budgeted cost of using 100 more tonnes of tomatoes: $(6{,}500 - 6{,}400) \times \$77 = \$7{,}700$ U. The direct materials variances can be summarized as shown in Exhibit 7B-4.

Exhibit 7B-4 Delpino Corporation's Flexible-Budget Variable Direct Variances, Levels 2, 3, and 4

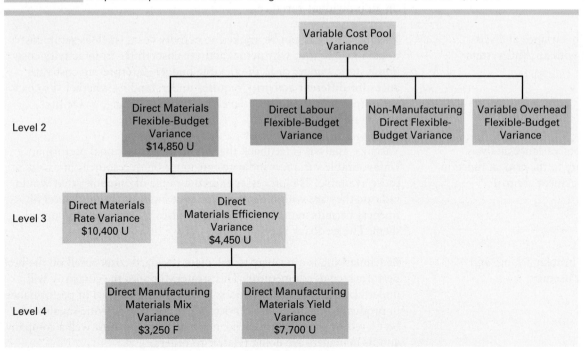

The Level 4 direct materials variance analysis of mix and yield extends efficiency and effective analysis to substitutable inputs. For perishable food processing such as ketchup, olive oil, and imperishable processing of ethanol from corn, an inescapable economic fact is that the higher the yield, the lower the costs of finished goods. This is because the finished goods are also substitutable. All other things equal, people will find one litre of ketchup the same as another.

Decision Points

The following question-and-answer format summarizes the chapter's learning objectives. Each point presents a key question, and the guidelines are the answer to that question.

Learning Objectives	Guidelines
1. How do flexible budgets differ from static budgets, and why should companies use flexible budgets?	A static budget is based on the level of output planned at the start of the budget period. A flexible budget is adjusted (flexed) to recognize the actual output level of the budget period. Flexible budgets help managers gain more insight into the causes of variances.
2. How can you develop a Level 2 flexible budget and calculate flexible-budget and sales-volume variances?	The static-budget variance can be subdivided into a flexible-budget variance (the difference between the actual result and the corresponding flexible-budget amount) and a sales-volume variance (the difference between the flexible-budget amount and the corresponding static-budget amount).
3. How can you develop Level 3 rate and efficiency variances for direct manufacturing costs?	The computation of efficiency variances helps managers gain insight into two different—but not independent—aspects of performance. The efficiency variance focuses on the difference between the actual quantity of input and the budgeted quantity of input allowed for actual output. When using variances for these purposes, managers should consider several variances together rather than focusing only on an individual variance.
4. How can variance analysis be used with an ABC system?	Variance analysis can be applied to activity costs (such as setup costs) to gain insight into why actual activity costs differ from activity costs in the static budget or in the flexible budget. Interpreting cost variances for different activities requires understanding whether the costs are output unit-level, batch-level, product-sustaining, or facility-sustaining costs.
5. What does variance analysis contribute to the critical function of management control?	Variance analysis is feedback that highlights exceptional performance. Unfavourable variances indicate consumption of resources in excess of those available. The processes exceed a range of outcomes that would indicate they are within control. Variance analysis at a high level of fineness permits managers to identify causes of variance and control them. The feedback is essential to improve decisions.
6. What is benchmarking, and why is it useful?	Benchmarking is a strategy to calculate standard costs based on the best performance of competitors. This strategy implies the company will undertake the continuous process of comparing its level of performance in producing products and services and executing activities against the best levels of performance. Benchmarking measures how well a company and its managers are doing relative to others.

7. What is a substitutable product, and how do input mix and yield variances improve control?

Continuous processes such as ketchup manufacturing use different varieties of tomatoes that are almost identical. Varieties are substitutable one for the other. The mix of varieties is specified. A significant departure from the mix affects both cost and yield. Yield variance is the difference between actual quantity of finished goods obtained and predicted quantity that should have been obtained.

Terms to Learn

This chapter and the Glossary at the end of the book contain definitions of the following important terms:

benchmark **(p. 264)**
benchmarking reports **(p. 264)**
continuous improvement **(p. 260)**
direct materials mix variance **(p. 272)**
direct materials yield variance **(p. 272)**
effectiveness **(p. 258)**
efficiency **(p. 258)**
efficiency variance **(p. 250)**
favourable (F) variance **(p. 242)**
fineness **(p. 243)**

flexible budget **(p. 243)**
flexible-budget variance **(p. 247)**
input mix **(p. 269)**
input price variance **(p. 249)**
input-efficiency variance **(p. 250)**
management by exception **(p. 242)**
mix variance **(p. 269)**
rate variance **(p. 249)**
sales-volume variance **(p. 248)**
standard **(p. 265)**

standard cost **(p. 265)**
standard input **(p. 265)**
static budget **(p. 242)**
substitutable inputs **(p. 269)**
unfavourable (U) variance **(p. 242)**
usage variance **(p. 250)**
variance **(p. 242)**
variance analysis **(p. 242)**
yield **(p. 269)**
yield variance **(p. 269)**

Assignment Material

MyLab Accounting Make the grade with MyLab Accounting: The Short-Answer Questions, Exercises, and Problems marked with a ⊕ can be found on MyLab Accounting. You can practise them as often as you want, and most feature step-by-step guided instructions to help you find the right answer.

Short-Answer Questions

7-1 How does static-budget variance analysis mislead those assessing actual performance against pro forma performance indicators?

7-2 What is the relationship between *management by exception* and *variance analysis*?

7-3 Distinguish between a *favourable variance* and an *unfavourable variance*.

7-4 What is the key difference between a *static budget* and a *flexible budget*?

7-5 Describe the steps in developing a flexible budget.

7-6 List four reasons for using standard costs.

7-7 List three causes of a favourable materials rate variance.

7-8 Describe why direct materials rate variance and direct materials efficiency variance may be computed with reference to different points in time.

7-9 Describe three reasons for an unfavourable direct manufacturing labour efficiency variance.

7-10 Distinguish between processes where the inputs are nonsubstitutable and where they are substitutable.

7-11 Explain how the direct materials mix and direct materials yield variances provide additional information about the direct materials efficiency variance.

7-12 How does variance analysis help in continuous improvement?

7-13 Why might an analyst examining variances in the production area look beyond that business function for explanations of those variances?

7-14 Comment on the following statement made by a plant supervisor: "Meetings with my plant accountant are frustrating. All he wants to do is pin the blame for the many variances he reports."

Exercises

⊕ 7-15 Terminology. A number of terms are listed below:

direct materials mix variance	fineness	management by exception
favourable (F) variance	input mix	input rate variance
flexible-budget variance	sales-volume variance	efficiency variance
rate variance	unfavourable (U) variance	flexible budget
substitutable inputs	yield variance	mix variance
yield	variance analysis	static budget
direct materials yield variance	static budget variance	variance

Required

Select the terms from the above list to complete the following sentences.

The question is whether or not the actual results met expectations, exceeded expectations, or failed to meet expectations and a _____ will respond to this question. A _____ is the result of subtracting the budgeted or predicted outcome from the actual outcome. A _____ means the effect of the variance is to increase operating income. An _____ means the effect of the variance is to decrease operating income. A _____ simply fails to reflect the routine effect of changes in quantity produced and sold on the revenue and the variable costs. A _____ does reflect the routine changes to be expected when the quantity produced and sold fluctuates from what was predicted. The _____ permits more _____ in the report of non-routine variances and _____. The _____ plus the _____ equals the _____.

When quantities of direct materials purchased and used differ from budget, the variance can be the result of either a _____ _____ arising in an unexpected difference in the cost/unit or an *efficiency variance* arising from an unexpected difference in the quantity of the input used, or a combination of both. When a direct materials _____ has _____, both the _____ and the _____ become important. These elements of a Level 4 analysis permit the managers to assess how changes from what was expected affected the _____.

LO 2 ▶
1. Total sales-volume variance, $7,200 U

⊕ 7-16 Flexible budget. Brabham Enterprises manufactures tires for the Formula I motor racing circuit. For August 2018, it budgeted to manufacture and sell 3,000 tires at a variable cost of $74 per tire and total fixed costs of $54,000. The budgeted selling price was $110 per tire. Actual results in August 2018 were 2,800 tires manufactured and sold at a selling price of $115 per tire. The actual total variable costs were $229,600, and the actual total fixed costs were $50,000.

Required

1. Prepare a performance report (akin to Exhibit 7-6) that uses a flexible budget and a static budget.
2. Comment on the results in requirement 1.

LO 2 ▶
Flexible-budget variance, $24,000 U

⊕ 7-17 Flexible budget. Connor Company's budgeted prices for direct materials, direct manufacturing labour, and direct marketing (distribution) labour per attaché case are $40, $8, and $12, respectively. The president is pleased with the following performance report:

	Actual Costs	Static Budget	Variance
Direct materials	$364,000	$400,000	$36,000 F
Direct manufacturing labour	78,000	80,000	2,000 F
Direct marketing (distribution) labour	110,000	120,000	10,000 F

Actual output was 8,800 attaché cases. Assume all three direct cost items above are variable costs.

Required

Is the president's pleasure justified? Prepare a revised performance report that uses a flexible budget and a static budget.

LO 2 ▶
Direct manufacturing labour efficiency variance, $6,000 U

⊕ 7-18 Materials and manufacturing-labour variances. Consider the following data collected for Blakes Construction Trailers:

	Direct Materials	Direct Manufacturing Labour
Costs incurred: Actual inputs × actual rates	$200,000	$90,000
Actual inputs × standard rates	214,000	86,000
Standard inputs allowed for actual outputs × standard rates	225,000	80,000

Required

Compute the rate, efficiency, and flexible-budget variances for direct materials and direct manufacturing labour.

⊕ **7-19 Rate and efficiency variances.** Doux Dulce manufactures kale salads. For January 2018, it budgeted to purchase and use 16,000 kilograms of kale at $1.11 per kilogram; budgeted output was 60,000 salads. Actual purchases and use for January 2018 were 17,000 kilograms at 0.99 per kilogram; actual output was 60,800 salads.

◀ **LO 2**
2. Rate variance, $2,040 F

Required

1. Calculate the flexible-budget variance.
2. Calculate the price and efficiency variances.
3. Comment on the results in requirements 1 and 2.

⊕ **7-20 Flexible budget.** Bryant Company's budgeted prices for direct materials, direct manufacturing labour, and direct marketing (distribution) labour per attaché case are $43, $6, and $13, respectively. The president is pleased with the following performance report:

◀ **LO 2**
Actual Direct Marketing Labour
$13.35

	Actual Costs	Static Budget	Variance
Direct materials	$438,000	$473,000	$35,000 F
Direct manufacturing labour	63,600	66,000	2,400 F
Direct marketing (distribution) labour	133,500	143,000	9,500 F

Required

Actual output was 10,000 attaché cases. Assume all three direct-cost items shown are variable costs.

Is the president's pleasure justified? Prepare a revised performance report that uses a flexible budget and a static budget.

⊕ **7-21 Flexible-budget and sales volume variances.** Cascade, Inc., produces the basic fillings used in many popular frozen desserts and treats—vanilla and chocolate ice creams, puddings, meringues, and fudge. Cascade uses standard costing and carries over no inventory from one month to the next. The ice-cream product group's results for June 2017 were as follows:

◀ **LO 2, 5**
Static Budget Variance $52,900

	Home	Insert	Page Layout	Formulas	Data
	A		B	C	

	A	B	C
1	**Performance Report, June 2017**		
2		**Actual Results**	**Static Budget**
3	Units (pounds)	460,000	447,000
4	Revenues	$2,626,600	$2,592,600
5	Variable manufacturing costs	1,651,400	1,564,500
6	Contribution margin	$ 975,200	$1,028,100

Jeff Geller, the business manager for ice-cream products, is pleased that more pounds of ice cream were sold than budgeted and that revenues were up. Unfortunately, variable manufacturing costs went up, too. The bottom line is that contribution margin declined by $52,900, which is just over 2% of the budgeted revenues of $2,592,600. Overall, Geller feels that the business is running fine.

Required

1. Calculate the static-budget variance in units, revenues, variable manufacturing costs, and contribution margin. What percentage is each static-budget variance relative to its static-budget amount?
2. Break down each static-budget variance into a flexible-budget variance and a sales-volume variance.
3. Calculate the selling-price variance.
4. Assume the role of management accountant at Cascade. How would you present the results to Jeff Geller? Should he be more concerned? If so, why?

LO 2 ▶
2. Total flexible-budget variance, $19,000 F

7-22 Flexible-budget preparation and analysis. Trustex Printers Inc. produces luxury chequebooks with three cheques and stubs per page. Each chequebook is designed for an individual customer and is ordered through the customer's bank. The company's operating budget for September 2018 included these data:

Number of chequebooks	15,000
Selling price per book	$ 20
Variable costs per book	$ 8
Total fixed costs for the month	$145,000

The actual results for September 2018 were

Number of chequebooks produced and sold	10,000
Average selling price per book	$ 25.20
Variable costs per book	$ 7
Total fixed costs for the month	$150,000

The executive vice-president of the company observed that the operating income for September was much less than anticipated, despite a higher-than-budgeted selling price and a lower-than-budgeted variable cost per unit. You have been asked to provide explanations for the disappointing September results.

Trustex develops its flexible-budget-based budgeted revenue per output unit and variable costs per output unit without a detailed analysis of budgeted inputs.

Required

1. Prepare a Level 1 analysis of the September performance.
2. Prepare a Level 2 analysis of the September performance.
3. Why might Trustex find the Level 2 analysis more informative than the Level 1 analysis? Explain your answer.

LO 2 ▶
Total Static Budget
Variance = $0

7-23 Flexible budget, working backward. The Clarkson Company produces engine parts for car manufacturers. A new accountant intern at Clarkson has accidentally deleted the company's variance analysis calculations for the year ended December 31, 2017. The following table is what remains of the data.

	Home	Insert	Page Layout	Formulas	Data	Review	View	
	A		B	C	D	E		F
1			Performance Report, Year Ended December 31, 2017					
2								
3			Actual Results	Flexible-Budget Variances	Flexible Budget	Sales-Volume Variances		Static Budget
4	Units sold		130,000					120,000
5	Revenues (sales)		$715,000					$420,000
6	Variable costs		515,000					240,000
7	Contribution margin		200,000					180,000
8	Fixed costs		140,000					120,000
9	Operating income		$ 60,000					$ 60,000

Required

1. Calculate all the required variances. (If your work is accurate, you will find that the total static-budget variance is $0.)
2. What are the actual and budgeted selling prices? What are the actual and budgeted variable costs per unit?
3. Review the variances you have calculated and discuss possible causes and potential problems. What is the important lesson learned here?

LO 2 ▶
2. Flexible Budget Variance is $16F

7-24 Price and efficiency variances. Sunshine Foods manufactures pumpkin scones. For January 2017, it budgeted to purchase and use 14,750 kilograms of pumpkin at $0.92 a kilogram. Actual purchases and usage for January 2017 were 16,000 kilograms at $0.85 a kilogram. Sunshine budgeted for 59,000 pumpkin scones. Actual output was 59,200 pumpkin scones.

Required

1. Compute the flexible-budget variance.
2. Compute the price and efficiency variances.
3. Comment on the results for requirements 1 and 2 and provide a possible explanation for them.

🌐 **7-25 Materials and manufacturing labour variances, standard costs with inventory.** Keats Inc. is a privately held furniture manufacturer. For August 2018, the company had the following standards for one of its products, a wicker chair:

◀ **LO 2**
1. Direct materials price variance, $370 U

	Standards per Chair
Direct materials	2 square metres of input at $5 per square metre
Direct manufacturing labour	0.5 hours of input at $10 per hour

The following data were compiled regarding actual performance: actual output units (chairs) produced, 2,000; square metres of input purchased and used, 3,700; price per square metre, $5.10; direct manufacturing labour costs, $8,820; actual hours of input, 900; labour price per hour, $9.80.

Required

1. Show your computations on the rate and efficiency variances for direct materials and for direct manufacturing labour. Give a plausible explanation of why the variances occurred.
2. Suppose 6,000 square metres of materials were purchased (at $5.10 per square metre) even though only 3,700 square metres were used. Suppose further that variances are identified with their most likely control point; accordingly, direct materials price variances are isolated and traced to the purchasing department rather than to the production department. Compute the rate and efficiency variances under this approach.

🌐 **7-26 Journal entries and T-accounts** (continuation of 7-25). Prepare journal entries and post them to T-accounts for all transactions in Exercise 7-25, including requirement 2. Summarize how these journal entries differ from normal costing entries.

◀ **LO 2**

🌐 **7-27 Materials and manufacturing labour variances.** Consider the following data collected for Great Homes, Inc.:

◀ **LO 2**
Flexible Budget Variance is $10,000 U

	Direct Materials	Direct Manufacturing Labour
Cost incurred: Actual inputs × actual prices	$200,000	$90,000
Actual inputs × standard prices	214,000	86,000
Standard inputs allowed for actual output × standard prices	225,000	80,000

Required

Compute the price, efficiency, and flexible-budget variances for direct materials and direct manufacturing labour.

🌐 **7-28 Direct materials and direct manufacturing labour variances.** Rugged Life, Inc., designs and manufactures fleece quarter-zip jackets. It sells its jackets to brand-name outdoor outfitters in lots of one dozen. Rugged Life's May 2017 static budget and actual results for direct inputs are as follows:

◀ **LO 3**
Total Efficiency Variance is $2,210

Static Budget	
Number of jacket lots (1 lot = 1 dozen)	300

Per Lot of Jackets:	
Direct materials	18 metres at $4.65 per metre = $83.70
Direct manufacturing labour	2.4 hours at $12.50 per hour = $30.00

Actual Results	
Number of jacket lots sold	325

Total Direct Inputs:	
Direct materials	6,500 metres at $4.85 per metre = $31,525
Direct manufacturing labour	715 hours at $12.60 = $9,009

Rugged Life has a policy of analyzing all input variances when they add up to more than 8% of the total cost of materials and labour in the flexible budget, and this is true in May 2017. The production manager discusses the sources of the variances: "A new type of material was purchased in May. This led to faster cutting and sewing, but the workers used more material than usual as they learned to work with it. For now, the standards are fine."

Required

1. Calculate the direct materials and direct manufacturing labour price and efficiency variances in May 2017. What is the total flexible-budget variance for both inputs (direct materials and direct manufacturing labour) combined? What percentage is this variance of the total cost of direct materials and direct manufacturing labour in the flexible budget?
2. Comment on the May 2017 results. Would you continue the "experiment" of using the new material?

 LO 3 ▶

7-29 Price and efficiency variances, journal entries. The Schuyler Corporation manufactures lamps. It has set up the following standards per finished unit for direct materials and direct manufacturing labour:

Direct materials: 10 kg at $4.50 per kg	$45.00
Direct manufacturing labour: 0.5 hour at $30 per hour	15.00

The number of finished units budgeted for January 2017 was 10,000; 9,850 units were actually produced. Actual results in January 2017 were as follows:

Direct materials: 98,055 kg used	
Direct manufacturing labour: 4,900 hours	$154,350

Assume that there was no beginning inventory of either direct materials or finished units.

During the month, materials purchased amounted to 100,000 kg, at a total cost of $465,000. Input price variances are isolated upon purchase. Input-efficiency variances are isolated at the time of usage.

Required

1. Compute the January 2017 price and efficiency variances of direct materials and direct manufacturing labour.
2. Prepare journal entries to record the variances in requirement 1.
3. Comment on the January 2017 price and efficiency variances of Schuyler Corporation.
4. Why might Schuyler calculate direct materials price variances and direct materials efficiency variances with reference to different points in time?

Problems

LO 5 ▶

2. Flexible-budget variance for labour, $300 F

7-30 Variance analysis, non-manufacturing setting. Stevie McQueen has run Lightning Car Detailing for the past 10 years. His static-budget and actual results for June 2018 are provided below. Stevie has one employee who has been with him for all 10 years that he has been in business. He has not been as lucky with his second and third employees. Stevie is hiring new employees in those positions almost every second month. It usually takes 2 hours to detail a vehicle. It takes as long for the seasoned employee as for the new ones, as the former tends to put more into the job. Stevie pays his long-term employee $20 per hour and the other two employees $10 per hour. Stevie pays all employees for 2 hours of work on each car, regardless of how long the work actually takes them. There were no wage increases in June.

Lightning Car Detailing
Actual and Budgeted Statement of Comprehensive Income
For the Month Ending June 30, 2018

	Budget	Actual
Cars detailed	200	225
Revenue	$30,000	$39,375
Variable costs:		
Costs of supplies	1,500	2,250
Labour	5,600	6,000
Total variable costs	7,100	8,250
Contribution margin	22,900	31,125
Fixed costs	9,500	9,500
Operating income	$13,400	$21,625

Required

1. Prepare a statement of the static-budget variances that Stevie would be interested in.
2. Compute any flexible-budget variances that you believe would be appropriate.
3. What information, in addition to that provided in the statements of comprehensive income, would you want Stevie to gather if you wanted to improve operational efficiency?
4. How many cars, on average, did Stevie budget for each employee? How many cars did they actually detail?
5. What advice would you give Stevie about motivating his employees?

🌐 **7-31 Materials and manufacturing labour variances, standard costs.** Dawson, Inc., is a privately held furniture manufacturer. For August 2017, Dawson had the following standards for one of its products, a wicker chair:

◀ **LO 4**

Standards per Chair	
Direct materials	3 square metres of input at $5.50 per square metre
Direct manufacturing labour	0.5 hour of input at $10.50 per hour

The following data were compiled regarding *actual performance*: actual output units (chairs) produced, 2,200; square metres of input purchased and used, 6,200; price per square metre, $5.70; direct manufacturing labour costs, $9,844; actual hours of input, 920; labour price per hour, $10.70.

1. Show computations of price and efficiency variances for direct materials and direct manufacturing labour. Give a plausible explanation of why each variance occurred.
2. Suppose 8,700 square metres of materials were purchased (at $5.70 per square metre), even though only 6,200 square metres were used. Suppose further that variances are identified at their most timely control point; accordingly, direct materials price variances are isolated and traced at the time of purchase to the purchasing department rather than to the production department. Compute the price and efficiency variances under this approach.

🌐 **7-32 Variance procedures; price and efficiency variances, journal entries.** Grant Electric Inc. manufactures lamps. It has set up the following standards per finished unit for direct materials and direct manufacturing labour:

◀ **LO 2**
1. Direct materials efficiency variance, $2,002 F

Direct materials: 10 kg at $4.50/kg	$45.00
Direct manufacturing labour: 0.5 hour at $30 per hour	15.00

The number of finished units budgeted for January 2018 was 10,000; 9,850 units were actually produced.

Actual results in January 2018 were

Direct materials: 98,055 kg used	
Direct manufacturing labour: 4,900 hours	$154,350

Assume that there was no beginning inventory of either direct materials or finished units.

During the month, materials purchases amounted to 100,000 kg, at a total cost of $465,000. Input rate variances are isolated upon purchase. Input-efficiency variances are isolated at the time of usage.

Required

1. Compute the January 2018 rate and efficiency variances of direct materials and direct manufacturing labour.
2. Prepare journal entries to record the variances in requirement 1.
3. Comment on the January 2018 rate and efficiency variances of Grant Electric.
4. Why might Grant calculate direct materials rate variances and direct materials efficiency variances with reference to different points in time?

LO 2 ▶

1. Standard DMLH for actual output achieved, 2,000 hours

🌐 **7-33 Direct materials and manufacturing labour variances, solving unknowns.** (CPA, adapted) On May 1, 2018, Terra Company began the manufacture of a new internet paging device known as Flare. The company installed a standard costing system to account for manufacturing costs. The standard costs for a unit of Flare are as follows:

Direct materials (3 kg at $5/kg)	$15.00
Direct manufacturing labour (0.5 hours at $20 per hour)	10.00
Manufacturing overhead (75% of direct manufacturing labour costs)	7.50
	$32.50

The following data were obtained from Terra's records for the month of May:

	Debit	Credit
Revenues		$125,000
Accounts payable control (for May's purchases of direct materials)		68,250
Direct materials rate variance	$3,250	
Direct materials efficiency variance	2,500	
Direct manufacturing labour rate variance	1,900	
Direct manufacturing labour efficiency variance		2,000

Actual production in May was 4,000 units of Flare, and actual sales in May were 2,500 units. The amount shown for direct materials price variance applies to materials purchased during May. There was no beginning inventory of materials on May 1, 2018.

Required

Compute each of the following items for Terra for the month of May. Show your computations.

1. Standard direct manufacturing labour-hours (DMLH) allowed for actual output achieved.
2. Actual direct manufacturing labour-hours (DMLH) worked.
3. Actual direct manufacturing labour wage rate.
4. Standard quantity of direct materials allowed (in kilograms).
5. Actual quantity of direct materials used (in kilograms).
6. Actual quantity of direct materials purchased (in kilograms).
7. Actual direct materials rate per kilograms.

LO 2 ▶

1. Direct manufacturing labour rate variance, $16,000 F

🌐 **7-34 Direct manufacturing labour and direct materials variances, missing data.** (CMA, adapted) Hang9 manufactures fibreglass paddlebaords. The standard cost of direct materials and direct manufacturing labour is $100 per board. This includes 20 kilograms of direct materials, at the budgeted price of $2 per kilogram, and 5 hours of direct manufacturing labour, at the budgeted rate of $12 per hour. Following are additional data for the month of July:

Units completed	6,000 units
Direct material purchases	150,000 kilograms
Cost of direct material purchases	$292,500
Actual direct manufacturing labour-hours	32,000 hours
Actual direct-labour cost	$368,000
Direct materials efficiency variance	$ 12,500 U

There were no beginning inventories.

Required

1. Compute direct manufacturing labour variances for July.
2. Compute the actual number of kilograms of direct materials used in production in July.
3. Calculate the actual price per kilograms of direct materials purchased.
4. Calculate the direct materials rate variance.

LO 2 ▶

🌐 **7-35 Journal entries and T-accounts** (continuation of 7-31). Prepare journal entries and post them to T-accounts for all transactions in Exercise 7-31, including requirement 2. Summarize how these journal entries differ from the normal-costing entries described in Chapter 4, pages 120–123.

7-36 Direct materials and manufacturing labour variances, solving unknowns. (CPA, adapted) On May 1, 2017, Bovar Company began the manufacture of a new paging machine known as Dandy. The company installed a standard costing system to account for manufacturing costs. The standard costs for a unit of Dandy follow:

◀ **LO 2, 5**

Direct materials (3 kg at $4 per kg)	$12.00
Direct manufacturing labour (1/2 hour at $20 per hour)	10.00
Manufacturing overhead (75% of direct manufacturing labour costs)	7.50
	$29.50

The following data were obtained from Bovar's records for the month of May:

	Debit	Credit
Revenues		$125,000
Accounts payable control (for May's purchases of direct materials)		55,000
Direct materials price variance	$3,500	
Direct materials efficiency variance	2,400	
Direct manufacturing labour price variance	1,890	
Direct manufacturing labour efficiency variance		2,200

Actual production in May was 4,000 units of Dandy, and actual sales in May were 2,500 units.

The amount shown for direct materials price variance applies to materials purchased during May. There was no beginning inventory of materials on May 1, 2017.

Compute each of the following items for Bovar for the month of May. Show your computations.

Required

1. Standard direct manufacturing labour-hours allowed for actual output produced
2. Actual direct manufacturing labour-hours worked
3. Actual direct manufacturing labour wage rate
4. Standard quantity of direct materials allowed (in kilograms)
5. Actual quantity of direct materials used (in kilograms)
6. Actual quantity of direct materials purchased (in kilograms)
7. Actual direct materials price per kilogram

7-37 Flexible budget, direct materials, and direct manufacturing labour variances. Emerald Statuary manufactures bust statues of famous historical figures. All statues are the same size. Each unit requires the same amount of resources. The following information is from the static budget for 2017:

◀ **LO 5**

Expected production and sales	7,000 units
Expected selling price per unit	$ 680
Total fixed costs	$1,400,000

Standard quantities, standard prices, and standard unit costs follow for direct materials and direct manufacturing labour:

	Standard Quantity	Standard Price	Standard Unit Cost
Direct materials	10 kilograms	$ 8 per kilogram	$ 80
Direct manufacturing labour	3.7 hours	$50 per hour	$185

During 2017, actual number of units produced and sold was 4,800, at an average selling price of $720. Actual cost of direct materials used was $392,700, based on 66,000 kilograms purchased at $5.95 per kilogram. Direct manufacturing labour-hours actually used were 18,300, at the rate of $48 per hour. As a result, actual direct manufacturing labour costs were $878,400. Actual fixed costs were $1,170,000. There were no beginning or ending inventories.

Required

1. Calculate the sales-volume variance and flexible-budget variance for operating income.
2. Compute price and efficiency variances for direct materials and direct manufacturing labour.

LO 2 ▶   🌐 **7-38 Variance analysis, nonmanufacturing setting.** Joyce Brown has run Medical Maids, a specialty cleaning service for medical and dental offices, for the past 10 years. Her static budget and actual results for April 2017 are shown below. Joyce has one employee who has been with her for all 10 years that she has been in business. In addition, at any given time she also employs two other less-experienced workers. It usually takes each employee 2 hours to clean an office, regardless of his or her experience. Brown pays her experienced employee $30 per office and the other two employees $15 per office. There were no wage increases in April.

Medical Maids Actual and Budgeted Income Statements For the Month Ended April 30, 2017

	Budget	Actual
Offices cleaned	140	160
Revenue	$26,600	$36,000
Variable costs:		
Costs of supplies	630	680
Labour	3,360	4,200
Total variable costs	3,990	4,880
Contribution margin	22,610	31,120
Fixed costs	4,900	4,900
Operating income	$17,710	$26,220

Required

1. How many offices, on average, did Brown budget for each employee? How many offices did each employee actually clean?
2. Prepare a flexible budget for April 2017.
3. Compute the sales price variance and the labour efficiency variance for each labour type.
4. What information, in addition to that provided in the income statements, would you want Brown to gather, if you wanted to improve operational efficiency?

LO 3 ▶   🌐 **7-39 Variances in the service sector.** Derek Wilson operates Clean Ride Enterprises, an auto detailing company with 20 employees. Jamal Jackson has recently been hired by Wilson as a controller. Clean Ride's previous accountant had done very little in the area of variance analysis, but Jackson believes that the company could benefit from a greater understanding of his business processes. Because of the labour-intensive nature of the business, he decides to focus on calculating labour variances.

Jackson examines past accounting records, and establishes some standards for the price and quantity of labour. While Clean Ride's employees earn a range of hourly wages, they fall into two general categories: skilled labour, with an average wage of $20 per hour, and unskilled labour, with an average wage of $10 per hour. One standard 5-hour detailing job typically requires a combination of 3 skilled hours and 2 unskilled hours.

Actual data from last month, when 600 detailing jobs were completed, are as follows:

Skilled (2,006 hours)	$ 39,117
Unskilled (944 hours)	9,292
Total actual direct labour cost	$ 48,409

Looking over last month's data, Jackson determines that Clean Ride's labour price variance was $1,151 favourable, but the labour efficiency variance was $1,560 unfavourable. When Jackson presents his findings to Wilson, the latter is furious. "Do you mean to tell me that my employees wasted $1,560 worth of time last month? I've had enough. They had better shape up, or else!" Jackson tries to calm him down, saying that in this case the efficiency variance doesn't necessarily mean that employees were wasting time. Jackson tells him that he is going to perform a more detailed analysis, and will get back to him with more information soon.

Required

1. What is the budgeted cost of direct labour for 600 detailing jobs?
2. How were the $1,151 favourable price variance and the $1,560 unfavourable labour efficiency variance calculated? What was the company's flexible-budget variance?

3. What do you think Jackson meant when said that "in this case the efficiency variance doesn't necessarily mean that employees were wasting time"?

4. For the 600 detailing jobs performed last month, what is the actual direct labour input mix percentage? What was the standard mix for labour?

5. Calculate the total direct labour mix and yield variances.

6. How could these variances be interpreted? Did the employees waste time? Upon further investigation, you discover that there were some unfilled vacancies last month in the unskilled labour positions that have recently been filled. How will this new information likely impact the variances going forward?

🌐 **7-40 Direct manufacturing labour variances: price, efficiency, mix, and yield.** Elena Martinez employs two workers in her wedding cake bakery. The first worker, Gabrielle, has been making wedding cakes for 20 years and is paid $25 per hour. The second worker, Joseph, is less experienced and is paid $15 per hour. One wedding cake requires, on average, 6 hours of labour. The budgeted direct manufacturing labour quantities for one cake are as follows: ◀ **LO 3**

	Quantity
Gabrielle	3 hours
Joseph	3 hours
Total	6 hours

That is, each cake is budgeted to require 6 hours of direct manufacturing labour, composed of 50% of Gabrielle's labour and 50% of Joseph's, although sometimes Gabrielle works more hours on a particular cake and Joseph less, or vice versa, with no obvious change in the quality of the cake.

During the month of May, the bakery produces 50 cakes. Actual direct manufacturing labour costs are as follows:

Gabrielle (140 hours)	$ 3,500
Joseph (165 hours)	2,475
Total actual direct labour cost	$ 5,975

Required

1. What is the budgeted cost of direct manufacturing labour for 50 cakes?

2. Calculate the total direct manufacturing labour price and efficiency variances.

3. For the 50 cakes, what is the total actual amount of direct manufacturing labour used? What is the actual direct manufacturing labour input mix percentage? What is the budgeted amount of Gabrielle's and Joseph's labour that should have been used for the 50 cakes?

4. Calculate the total direct manufacturing labour mix and yield variances. How do these numbers relate to the total direct manufacturing labour efficiency variance? What do these variances tell you?

🌐 **7-41 Use of materials and manufacturing labour variances for benchmarking.** You are a new junior accountant at In Focus Corporation, maker of lenses for eyeglasses. Your company sells generic-quality lenses for a moderate price. Your boss, the controller, has given you the latest month's report for the lens trade association. This report includes information related to operations for your firm and three of your competitors within the trade association. The report also includes information related to the industry benchmark for each line item in the report. You do not know which firm is which, except that you know you are Firm A. ◀ **LO 4**

Unit Variable Costs Member Firms
for the Month Ended September 30, 2017

	Firm A	Firm B	Firm C	Firm D	Industry	Benchmark
Materials input	2.15	2.00	2.20	2.60	2.15	oz. of glass
Materials price	$ 5.00	$ 5.25	$ 5.10	$ 4.50	$ 5.10	per oz.
Labour-hours used	0.75	1.00	0.65	0.70	0.70	hours
Wage rate	$14.50	$14.00	$14.25	$15.25	$12.50	per DLH
Variable overhead rate	$ 9.25	$14.00	$ 7.75	$11.75	$12.25	per DLH

Required

1. Calculate the total variable cost per unit for each firm in the trade association. Compute the percent of total for the material, labour, and variable overhead components.
2. Using the trade association's industry benchmark, calculate direct materials and direct manufacturing labour price and efficiency variances for the four firms. Calculate the percent over standard for each firm and each variance.
3. Write a brief memo to your boss outlining the advantages and disadvantages of belonging to this trade association for benchmarking purposes. Include a few ideas to improve productivity that you want your boss to take to the department heads' meeting.

LO 4 ▶   ⊕ **7-42 Direct-cost and selling price variances.** MicroDisk is the market leader in the Secure Digital (SD) card industry and sells memory cards for use in portable devices such as mobile phones, tablets, and digital cameras. Its most popular card is the Mini SD, which it sells through outlets such as Target and Walmart for an average selling price of $8. MicroDisk has a standard monthly production level of 420,000 Mini SDs in its Taiwan facility. The standard input quantities and prices for direct-cost inputs are as follows:

	Home	Insert	Page Layout	Formulas	Data	Review	View
	A		B	C	D		E
1			**Quantity per**		**Standard**		
2	**Cost Item**		**Mini SD card**		**Unit Costs**		
3	Direct materials:						
4	Specialty polymer		17	mm	$0.05		/mm
5	Connector pins		10	units	0.10		/unit
6	Wi-Fi transreceiver		1	unit	0.50		/unit
7							
8	Direct manufacturing labour:						
9	Setup		1	min.	24.00		/hr.
10	Fabrication		2	min.	30.00		/hr.

Phoebe King, the CEO, is disappointed with the results for June 2017, especially in comparison to her expectations based on the standard cost data.

	Home	Insert	Page Layout	Formulas	Data	Review	View	
13			**Performance Report, June 2017**					
14		**Actual**		**Budget**		**Variance**		
15	Output units	462,000		420,000		42,000		F
16	Revenues	$3,626,700		$3,360,000		$266,700		F
17	Direct materials	1,200,000		987,000		213,000		U
18	Direct manufacturing labour	628,400		588,000		40,400		U

King observes that despite the significant increase in the output of Mini SDs in June, the product's contribution to the company's profitability has been lower than expected. She gathers the following information to help analyze the situation:

	Home	Insert	Page Layout	Formulas	Data	Review	View

21	**Input Usage Report, June 2017**				
22	**Cost Item**	**Quantity**		**Actual Cost**	
23	Direct materials:				
24	Specialty polymer	8,300,000	mm	$415,000	
25	Connector pins	5,000,000	units	550,000	
26	Wi-Fi transreceiver	470,000	units	235,000	
27					
28	Direct manufacturing labour:				
29	Setup	455,000	min.	182,000	
30	Fabrication	864,000	min.	446,400	

Calculate the following variances. Comment on the variances and provide potential reasons why they might have arisen, with particular attention to the variances that may be related to one another:

Required

1. Selling-price variance
2. Direct materials price variance, for each category of materials
3. Direct materials efficiency variance, for each category of materials
4. Direct manufacturing labour price variance, for setup and fabrication
5. Direct manufacturing labour efficiency variance, for setup and fabrication

7-43 Price and efficiency variances, benchmarking. Nantucket Enterprises manufactures insulated cold beverage cups printed with college and corporate logos, which it distributes nationally in lots of 12 dozen cups. In June 2017, Nantucket produced 5,000 lots of its most popular line of cups, the 24-ounce lidded tumbler, at each of its two plants, which are located in Providence and Amherst. The production manager, Shannon Bryant, asks her assistant, Joel Hudson, to find out the precise per-unit budgeted variable costs at the two plants and the variable costs of a competitor, Beverage Mate, who offers similar-quality tumblers at cheaper prices. Hudson pulls together the following information for each lot:

◀ **LO 5**

Per lot	Providence Plant	Amherst Plant	Beverage Mate
Direct materials	74 lbs. @ $3.20 per lb.	76.5 lbs. @ $3.10 per lb.	70 lbs. @ $2.90 per lb.
Direct manufacturing labour	2.5 hrs. @ $12.00 per hr.	2.4 hrs. @ $12.20 per hr.	2.4 hrs. @ $10.50 per hr.
Variable overhead	$20 per lot	$22 per lot	$20 per lot

Required

1. What is the budgeted variable cost per lot at the Providence Plant, the Amherst Plant, and at Beverage Mate?
2. Using the Beverage Mate data as the standard, calculate the direct materials and direct manufacturing labour price and efficiency variances for the Providence and Amherst plants.
3. What advantage does Nantucket get by using Beverage Mate's benchmark data as standards in calculating its variances? Identify two issues that Bryant should keep in mind in using the Beverage Mate data as the standards.

Mini Cases

7-44 Procurement costs, variance analysis, governance. Rashid Daley is the manager of the athletic shoe division of Raider Products. Raider is a European-based company that has just purchased Fastfoot, a leading European shoe company. Fastfoot has long-term production contracts with suppliers in two East European countries: Hergonia and Tanista. Daley receives a request from Karen Neal, president of Raider Products. Daley and his controller, Brooke Mullins, are to make a presentation to the next board of directors' meeting on the cost competitiveness of its Fastfoot subsidiary. This should include budgeted and actual procurement costs for 2018 at its Hergonia and Tanista supply sources.

◀ **LO 5**
1. Hergonia rate $400,000 U

Mullins decides to visit the two supply operations. The budgeted average procurement cost for 2018 was $14 per pair of shoes. This includes payments to the shoe manufacturer and all other payments to conduct business in each country. Mullins reports the following to Daley:

■ **Hergonia.** Total 2018 procurement costs for 250,000 pairs of shoes were $3,900,000. Payment to the shoe manufacturer was $3,108,000. Very few receipts exist for the remaining $792,000. Kickback payments are viewed as common in Hergonia.

■ **Tanista.** Total 2018 procurement costs for 900,000 pairs of shoes were $12,300,000. Payment to the shoe manufacturer was $10,136,000. Receipts exist for $827,000 of the other costs, but Mullins is skeptical of their validity. Kickback payments are a "way of business" in Tanista.

At both the Hergonia and Tanista plants, Mullins is disturbed by the employment of young children (many of them under 15 years). She is told that all major shoe-producing companies have similar low-cost employment practices in both countries.

Daley is uncomfortable about the upcoming presentation to the board of directors. He was a leading advocate of the acquisition. A recent business magazine reported that the Fastfoot acquisition would make Raider Products the global low-cost producer in its market lines. The stock price of Raider Products jumped 21% the day the Fastfoot acquisition was announced. Mullins, likewise, is widely identified as a proponent of the acquisition. She is seen as a rising star due for promotion to a division management post in the near future.

Required

1. What summary procurement cost variances could be reported to the board of directors of Raider Shoes?
2. What ethical issues do (a) Daley and (b) Mullins face when preparing and making a report to the board of directors?
3. How should Mullins address the issues you identify in requirement 2?

LO 2, 5 ▶
1. Direct-materials rate variance
$306 F

7-45 Rate and efficiency variances, problems in standard-setting, benchmarking. New Fashions Inc. manufactures shirts for retail chains. Andy Jorgenson, the controller, is becoming increasingly disenchanted with New Fashions's standard costing system. The budgeted and actual amounts for direct materials and direct manufacturing labour for June 2018 were as follows:

	Budgeted Amounts	Actual Amounts
Shirts manufactured	6,000	6,732
Direct material costs	$30,000	$30,294
Direct material units (rolls of cloth)	600	612
Direct manufacturing labour costs	$27,000	$27,693
Direct manufacturing labour-hours (DMLH)	1,500	1,530

There were no beginning or ending inventories of materials.

Standard costs are based on a study of the operations conducted by an independent consultant six months earlier. Jorgenson observes that, since that study, he has rarely seen an unfavourable variance of any magnitude. He notes that even at their current output levels, the workers seem to have a lot of time for sitting around and gossiping. Jorgenson is concerned that the production manager, Charlie Fenton, is aware of this but does not want to tighten up the standards because the lax standards make his performance look good.

Required

1. Compute the rate and efficiency variances of New Fashions for direct materials and direct manufacturing labour in June 2018.
2. Describe the types of actions the employees at New Fashions may have taken to reduce the accuracy of the standards set by the independent consultant. Why would employees take those actions? Is this behaviour ethical?
3. If Jorgenson does nothing about the standard costs, will his behaviour violate any ethical conduct guidelines?
4. What actions should Jorgenson take?
5. Jorgenson can obtain benchmarking information about the estimated costs of New Fashions's major competitors from Benchmarking Clearing House (BCH). Discuss the pros and cons of using the BCH information to compute the variances in requirement 1.

SOLUTION

Try It 7–1

Direct Materials = Standard Q × Standard rate

= .5 kg × \$8/kg

= \$4 per salad

Direct Labour = Standard Q of labour × Standard labour rate

= \$20 × (6 minutes per salad/60 minutes per hour)

= \$2 per salad

Standard Variable overhead

= Standard Q × Standard rate

= \$6 minutes × \$.10 per minute

= \$.60

8

Flexible Budgets, Variances, and Management Control: II

▶ Learning Objectives

1. Assign manufacturing overhead (MOH) fixed costs, then calculate and analyze flexible-budget variances.

2. Establish variable overhead cost allocation rates; calculate and analyze flexible-budget variances.

3. Calculate activity-based cost (ABC) overhead variances.

4. Integrate the fixed and variable overhead cost variance analyses to reconcile the actual overhead incurred with overhead allocated.

5. Analyze non-manufacturing variances.

▶ CPA Competencies

This chapter covers material outlined in **Section 3: Management Accounting** of the CPA Competency Map. The Learning Objectives in this chapter have been aligned with the CPA Competency Map to ensure the best coverage possible.

3.2.1 Develops or evaluates information inputs for operational plans, budgets, and forecasts

3.2.2 Prepares, analyzes, or evaluates operational plans, budgets, and forecasts

3.2.3 Computes, analyzes, or assesses implications of variances

3.4.1 Evaluates sources and drivers of revenue growth

Barrick Gold Corporation

Tracking Performance

Manufacturing and non-manufacturing overhead comprise a large proportion of total costs. For extraction industries such as oil, gold, and iron ore, the costs of exploration, development, and refining are in the hundreds of millions. For service industries like airline transportation, one new aircraft, such as a Boeing 787 that seats 300 people, can cost over US$250 million. These long-term assets are used for many years.

Barrick Gold Corporation, a Canadian company and the largest gold producer in the world, explores for, refines, and produces gold, all of which are capital intensive activities. In Barrick's 2015 annual report, its property, plant, and equipment were valued at more than $20 billion. Barrick's long-term profit depends on recovering the costs of both its fixed assets and annual costs of operation as it sells each ounce of gold. Barrick cannot control the gold price, but it can control costs as long as it knows the fixed and variable overhead costs per ounce produced.

Sources: M. Grady. 2015. Step inside the custom interior of this Boeing 787-9 Dreamliner private jet. *Robb Report*, November 13. (http://robbreport.com/aviation/step-inside-custom-interior-boeing-787-9-dreamliner-private-jet-video); Barrick Gold Corporation. Annual Report 2015 (http://www.barrick.com/files/annual-report/Barrick-Annual-Report-2015.pdf).

This chapter completes the Level 3 flexible-budget variance for both fixed and variable manufacturing overhead. Fixed manufacturing overhead (FMOH) costs include property taxes, depreciation, lease expenses, insurance, and salaries. Some fixed costs are locked in by legal contracts for terms as short as one year, such as salaries and insurance. Others are locked in by long-term contracts to purchase or lease plant and equipment. These FMOH costs are assigned to each unit of output because companies have only one way to recover the costs—charge a reasonable price when they sell output.

Variable manufacturing overhead (VMOH) costs also contribute to overhead. These VMOH costs of shared resources are assigned to each unit of output in proportion to the benefit received. VMOH costs can only be recovered in the price charged when output is sold, which is why both FMOH and VMOH costs are assigned to units of output.

Flexible-Budget MOH Cost Variances

Continuing our analysis of Webb Company begun in Chapter 7, we simplify the example by examining only inventoriable costs or manufacturing overhead costs (MOH). MOH costs are defined by ASPE/IFRS and used to estimate both cost of goods sold (COGS) and inventory values. Referring back to Exhibit 7-4, this discussion includes only the VMOH of $120,000 budgeted for the 10,000-jackets level of output and FMOH of $276,000 budgeted for the relevant range including 10,000 jackets. The task is to explain the FMOH cost pool variance of $9,000 U (= $276,000 − $285,000) and the VMOH cost pool variance of $10,500 U (= $120,000 − $130,500).

▶ **LO 1**

Assign MOH fixed costs, then calculate and analyze flexible-budget variances.

Note Inventoriable product costs are initially recorded on the balance sheet as an asset. When the product is sold, the costs move from the balance sheet to the income statement and appear as COGS.[1]

Webb's cost structure illustrates the importance of management planning and control of manufacturing overhead costs. The following percentages of total static-budget costs of $1,898,000 (column (4) of Exhibit 7-4) are based on Webb's static budget for 12,000 jackets for April:

	Variable Overhead Costs	Fixed Overhead Costs	Total Overhead Costs
Manufacturing[2]	7.59%	14.54%	22.13%
Marketing	3.16	22.87	26.03
Total	10.75%	37.41%	48.16%

Total overhead costs are significant and amount to almost half (48.16%) of Webb's total budgeted costs at 12,000 output units per month (= $914,000 ÷ $1,898,000). The remainder of the costs (51.86% of the budgeted 12,000 units) are direct costs. Based on fixed costs as a percentage of total costs of approximately 37.41% (= $710,000 ÷ $1,898,000), Webb may be classified as having a high degree of operating leverage (see Chapter 3). As a result, fluctuations in revenues are likely to result in large changes in profits. Variable costs for Webb consume $0.55 (or 55%) of every revenue dollar earned ($1,188,000 ÷ $2,160,000). In other words, $0.45 (or 45%) of every dollar of revenue earned contributes toward paying for fixed costs. After breakeven is reached, this proportion contributes to operating income.

Given Webb's fixed costs projected in the static budget, the breakeven point, **BEP in revenue**, is approximately $1,577,778:

$$\frac{\$710,000}{0.45} = \$1,577,778 \text{ (rounded)}$$

In terms of **BEP in units**, this is equal to 8,766 jackets produced and sold ($1,577,778 ÷ $180 SP = 8,765.43 rounded up to 8,766).

---

[1] IAS2—Inventories. Deloitte (http://www.iasplus.com/en/standards/ias/ias2).

[2] VMOH as a percentage of total costs is $144,000 ÷ $1,898,000 = 7.59%, and FMOH is $276,000 ÷ 1,898,000 = 14.54%. Total manufacturing overhead is $420,000 ÷ $1,898,000 = 22.13%. Similar calculations will result in the percentages shown for marketing overhead costs. The total variable marketing and manufacturing overhead costs as a percentage of total costs is ($144,000 + $60,000) ÷ $1,898,000 = 10.75%.

If Webb achieves its *static* budget sales, its operating income will be approximately $262,000 (= 12,000 jackets − 8,766 BEP jackets = 3,234 jackets × $180 × 0.45). When Webb only sold 10,000 jackets (or a 17% decrease in sales), its *flexible*-budget operating income was approximately $100,000 (= 10,000 jackets − 8,766 BEP jackets = 1,234 jackets × $180 × 0.45). This represents a 62% decrease in operating income [($262,000 − $100,000) / $262,000 = 0.6183].

While there was a relatively small decline in sales (17%), Webb's higher degree of operation leverage (amount of fixed costs relative to total costs) resulted in a relatively large decrease in operating income (62%).

This analysis serves to remind us that fixed costs can have a significant impact on a firm's profitability and its ability to withstand unexpected fluctuations. Webb's recovery of overhead and its profits depend on meeting its budget.

TRY IT! 8.1

Steve-A-Rena owns a coffee shop at the Farmer's Market. The budgeted fixed overhead costs to rent his booth space are $2,000, advertising is $500, and equipment and other expenses are $410. His actual expenses in fixed costs for the month were $3,200. Steve had planned on selling 9,600 coffees per month but actually sold 10,000 this month. What is the fixed overhead budget for the month?

Planning for Overhead Costs

Effective planning of fixed overhead costs is basically a capacity planning issue. **Capacity** refers to the quantity of outputs that can be produced from long-term resources available to the company, and it is acquired through the purchase or lease of long-term assets. This means decisions about capacity are *strategic* decisions. Decisions would include consideration of current capacity, forecasted future demand and risks, potential alternative uses of idle capacity, and ease of disposal of excess capacity.

The fixed overhead issue is that either the lease or acquisition cost of capacity must be recovered through the sale of outputs (goods or services). But Webb is a price-taker; consumers have set the price they are willing to pay for a jacket at $180. If the management team leased or purchased too many machines relative to demand for the jackets, Webb would have unutilized or idle capacity. This unutilized capacity cost must be paid for, but Webb cannot simply increase its price to cover idle capacity cost per jacket. Competitors may not have any or as much idle capacity and, all other things being equal, will achieve higher profitability per jacket at $180 than Webb. This means Webb needs to be right when it forecasts consumer demand and invests in capacity.

Capacity cost is a FMOH cost. Webb's cost system is not an ABC system and, as a result, the company collects all FMOH into a single indirect cost pool. While this chapter focuses on inventoriable capacity costs, period capacity costs also exist. It is often more readily apparent in manufacturing than in service industries what is the most informative grouping of capacity costs into overhead cost pools.

Idle capacity occurs even in well-managed and well-planned companies when machines require maintenance to repair the wear and tear arising from normal use. Without scheduled idle or down time for maintenance, the machines would break down. Good capacity management utilizes excess capacity to make up for output forgone during both scheduled maintenance and unexpected breakdowns. See Chapter 9 for a more complete discussion of capacity.

In service industries, period overhead costs arise when the same building houses both those whose activities generate revenue as well as those who engage in all service-support activities. Capacity is related to the people and their intangible skills rather than to tangible equipment and property. These intangible skills may be referred to as *human capital*. The labour expense can be recorded, but the benefit is shared throughout the business.

Exhibit 8-1 FMOH Cost Assignment

		Flexible- and Static-Budgeted Amounts for the Year			
FMOH* (1)	DMH/Year (2)	Rate per DMH (3) = (1) ÷ (2)	Q Jackets/Year (4)	DMH/Jacket (5) = (2) ÷ (4)	Rate per Jacket (6) = (3) × (5)
$3,312,000	57,600	$57.50	144,000	0.40	$23.00

*Annual FMOH = $276,000 × 12

ASPE/IFRS prohibits accounting for costs of this type in inventory. Period support costs, however, must still be recovered when the service is provided or the product is sold. Management accountants may use one of five methods (see Chapter 14) to assign period costs to distinct output units based on the proportion of benefit to the unit.

Assigning Fixed Manufacturing Overhead at Webb

The data in Exhibit 8-1 are available from Webb's MIS. The FMOH cost allocation rate and cost assigned per jacket can be readily calculated as shown in the exhibit.

The fixed cost pools do not change when the volume of output changes; therefore, the static budget is also the flexible budget. The assignment of budgeted, unitized FMOH costs to units of output depends on the quantity of output in the denominator. But first the FMOH cost pool is allocated in Webb's traditional system using direct machine-hours (DMH) as the cost allocation base. This allocation base is sensible if a significant portion of the FMOH is due to the amount of machinery used in the production process. The economic reality should be that the more DMH used for a distinct type of jacket, the higher the cost per jacket and the higher the value added or benefit to the customer. But a **production denominator level** (or **volume**) that will be divided into the FMOH cost pool to calculate the rate per jacket is a measure of capacity *available*, not *actual* customer demand or capacity *used*. From four potential choices, Webb's management team has chosen the amount that is ASPE/IFRS-compliant. The alternative denominators are discussed in detail in Chapter 9.

The equipment *input* capacity budgeted for the year is 57,600 DMH, and the total volume of output for the year is budgeted at 144,000 jackets. On a per unit basis, the rate of use is 0.40 DMH/jacket (= 57,600 DMH ÷ 144,000 jackets). The budget for one month of output is 4,800 DMH/month (= 0.40 DMH × 12,000 jackets). The fixed MOH cost pool is budgeted at $276,000/month, so the budgeted FMOH rate will be $57.50/DMH (= $276,000 ÷ 4,800 DMH).

$$\begin{aligned}\text{Budgeted fixed overhead rate} \atop \text{per unit of allocation base} &= \frac{\text{Budgeted fixed overhead costs}}{\text{Budgeted quantity of allocation base units}}\\ &= \$276,000 \div 4,800 \text{ DMH}\\ &= \$57.50 \text{ per DMH}\end{aligned}$$

Fixed Overhead Cost Variance Calculation and Analysis

The actual results for FMOH are shown in Exhibit 7-4. The *static-budget* amount for FMOH is based on 12,000 output units. The *Level 1 static-budget variance* for Webb's FMOH is $9,000 U:

$$\begin{aligned}\text{FMOH static-budget variance} &= \text{Actual results} - \text{Static-budget amount}\\ &= \$285,000 - \$276,000\\ &= \$9,000 \text{ U}\end{aligned}$$

Given that this static-budget amount is for a fixed cost, $276,000 would also be the FMOH budgeted amount *for all output levels in the relevant range*. There is no "flexing" of fixed costs. Therefore, the *flexible-budget* amount for FMOH at Q = 10,000 (actual output) is $276,000, or the same as the static-budget amount. Thus, the *Level 2 flexible-budget variance* is also $9,000 U:

$$\text{FMOH flexible-budget variance} = \text{Actual results} - \text{Flexible-budget amount}$$
$$= \$285,000 - \$276,000$$
$$= \$9,000 \ U$$

Budgeted fixed costs are, by definition, unaffected by changes in the sales-volume. Within the relevant range (in this case, 8,000 to 16,000 jackets), there will never be a sales-volume variance because sales-volume variances only arise for items affected by changes in the volume of sales (i.e., revenues, variable costs, contribution margins, and operating income).

> **Note** Alternatively, the arithmetic also proves that there is no variance (Flexible budget $276,000 – Static budget $276,000 = Sales-volume variance $0). Therefore, the *Level 2 sales-volume variance* is never a variance.

For a *Level 3* analysis (deconstructing the flexible-budget variance into its rate and efficiency components), the entire FMOH flexible-budget variance is attributed to *rate variance* because efficiency does not affect FMOH. The quantity of DMH in the cost allocation base remains unchanged over the relevant range of output produced. Unless the actual quantity produced is outside the relevant range, any difference in DMH consumed compared to the quantity in the cost-allocation base is irrelevant. Exceeding the relevant range implies (for example) that new equipment must be acquired (or leased), which is a strategic decision with long-term implications. The *Level 3 rate variance* is $9,000 U:

$$\text{FMOH rate variance} = \text{Actual results} - \text{Amount allowed for relevant range}$$
$$\text{(same as static and flexible amount)}$$
$$= \$285,000 - \$276,000$$
$$= \$9,000 \ U$$

The *Level 3 efficiency variance* is never a variance:

$$\text{FMOH efficiency variance} = \text{Never a variance}$$

Interpretation of Fixed Manufacturing Overhead Rate Variance

The math involved here is simple: The value of FMOH variance analysis arises from finding the cause or causes of the variance. Reasons for the unfavourable FMOH rate variance could include

■ Poor/unrealistic FMOH projections in the original budget process
■ An unplanned salary increase to retain the plant manager
■ Increased equipment lease or depreciation rates
■ Increased insurance premiums on the production assets
■ Increased property taxes on the production facilities

Assume Webb investigated and determined that there was a $9,000 per month unexpected increase in its equipment leasing costs. However, management concluded the new lease rates were competitive with lease rates available elsewhere. If the rate had not been competitive, then the management team could have looked elsewhere to lease equipment from other suppliers. The increase was not controllable by individual managers, and it is a permanent increase in FMOH. The appropriate response is to change the FMOH budgeted cost pool. Unfortunately, there is no value added to a customer when it costs more to run the same equipment, and it is very unlikely that Webb can increase the cost per jacket without losing sales. To achieve the budgeted gross margin, the management team must find ways to reduce other controllable costs.

Exhibit 8-2 shows a summary of the Levels 1, 2, and 3 variance analyses for Webb's FMOH in April.

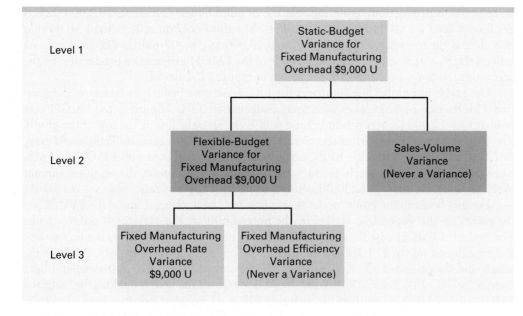

Exhibit 8-2 Levels 1, 2, and 3 Fixed Manufacturing Overhead Variances

Production-Volume Variance Calculation and Analysis

FMOH variance analysis requires the calculation of one new variance: the production-volume variance. The **production-volume variance** (PVV) arises because of a misallocation of FMOH from using the method of normal costing in a traditional system. Normal cost assignment for overhead costs multiplies actual quantities by budgeted rates. The PVV is the difference between budgeted fixed overhead ($276,000) and the fixed overhead that the accounting system assigned for the *actual* quantity of outputs. The rate is constant, but the multiplier changes. Other terms for this variance are **denominator-level variance** and **output-level overhead variance**. The management team can now analyze the PVV to identify how the difference of $55,000 arose between the actual FMOH incurred in the month and the FMOH assigned to production by the accounting system.

The PVV analysis applies what you learned about unitized fixed cost behaviour, as illustrated in Exhibit 8-3. The first column in Exhibit 8-3 shows the possible (relevant) range of output for Webb. The second column shows the amount of FMOH that would

Exhibit 8-3 Production-Volume Assigned Total Cost Behaviour

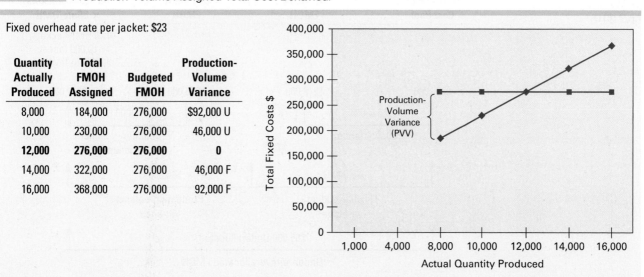

Fixed overhead rate per jacket: $23

Quantity Actually Produced	Total FMOH Assigned	Budgeted FMOH	Production-Volume Variance
8,000	184,000	276,000	$92,000 U
10,000	230,000	276,000	46,000 U
12,000	**276,000**	**276,000**	**0**
14,000	322,000	276,000	46,000 F
16,000	368,000	276,000	92,000 F

be assigned to production, assuming that the original budget anticipated 12,000 jackets per month (and a FMOH rate of $23/jacket). The third column reflects the FMOH that is budgeted for the relevant range of output (8,000 to 16,000 units). The final column reflects the PVV that would exist (as a result of the FMOH assigned to production by the accounting system), depending on the actual output level achieved.

The graph in Exhibit 8-3 compares the total fixed cost behaviour based on the unitized FMOH rate of $23/jacket with total budgeted FMOH. The budgeted FMOH cost pool at Q = 12,000 jackets produced and sold is the straight line at the top of the graph. The sloped line indicates what the total FMOH *would* have been if Webb could have matched its capacity available to the actual Q produced and sold and FMOH was able to be varied with output levels. At Q = 10,000 produced and sold, the assigned amount Webb *should* have spent is $230,000/month using the budgeted rate.

The gap between the point on the sloped line and the horizontal line is the PVV. When the points on the sloped line are below the horizontal line, the variance is unfavourable. The budgeted FMOH cost for the actual output is more than what the accounting system assigned (based on the FMOH rate of $23 per jacket) for that level of output. Where the actual and the budgeted Q are equal (i.e., 12,000 units), the sloped and horizontal lines intersect and the PVV is zero. Where the sloped line exceeds the horizontal line, the budgeted FMOH of $276,000 is less than the amount of FMOH assigned (for that level of output) by the accounting system and the PVV is favourable. The calculation of PVV is as follows:

$$\text{Production-volume variance} = \begin{pmatrix} \text{Budgeted} \\ \text{fixed} \\ \text{overhead} \end{pmatrix} - \begin{pmatrix} \text{Total fixed} \\ \text{overhead assigned} \times \begin{pmatrix} \text{Budgeted fixed} \\ \text{overhead rate} \end{pmatrix} \\ \text{for actual output} \end{pmatrix}$$

$$= \$276,000 - (10.000 \text{ jackets} \times 0.40 \text{ DMH per jacket} \times \$57.50 \text{ per DMH})$$

$$= \$276,000 - (4,000 \text{ DMH} \times \$57.50 \text{ per DMH})$$

$$= \$276,000 - \$230,000$$

$$= \$46,000 \text{ U}$$

Interpretation of Production-Volume Variance

Exhibit 8-4 shows the Level 3 FMOH variance analysis for Webb Company for the month of April. Inevitably, there will almost always be a PVV reported. The capacity level used to calculate the fixed overhead rate is the budgeted value selected during the budget process.

Exhibit 8-4 Level 3 FMOH Variance Analysis for Webb Company for April 2018

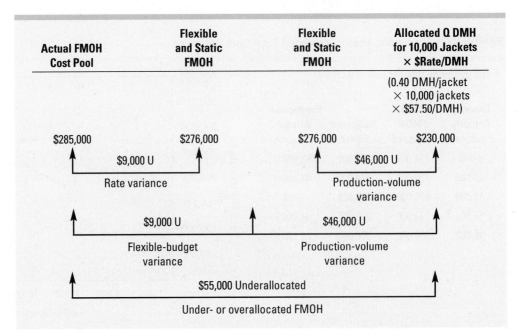

Actual FMOH Cost Pool		Flexible and Static FMOH		Flexible and Static FMOH		Allocated Q DMH for 10,000 Jackets × $Rate/DMH
						(0.40 DMH/jacket × 10,000 jackets × $57.50/DMH)
$285,000		$276,000		$276,000		$230,000
	$9,000 U				$46,000 U	
	Rate variance				Production-volume variance	
	$9,000 U			$46,000 U		
	Flexible-budget variance			Production-volume variance		
			$55,000 Underallocated			
			Under- or overallocated FMOH			

The FMOH rate is the FMOH cost pool divided by the expected (static) budgeted quantity of output (Q), assumed in this example to be Q = 12,000 jackets. PVV can be thought of as an opportunity cost. Webb paid for the opportunity, the benefit from producing and selling 12,000 jackets in April, but only produced and sold Q = 10,000.

Webb's management team must determine why this occurred. Perhaps the sales price of $185/jacket instead of $180/jacket affected demand and that is why the amount produced and sold was less than what the management team committed to in the budget. Webb's cost of equipment is a sunk cost, and the investment was made in anticipation of meeting monthly consumer demand with capacity to produce 12,000 jackets. Overpricing may cause a persistent shortfall in profit.

Perhaps the reduction in Q was due to an unexpected equipment malfunction that caused both idle time while repairs were made and overtime to make up volume when equipment was operational again. We already know there was an unfavourable rate and efficiency variance for direct labour, and equipment malfunction could explain all three variances. This is temporary, and the management team would have less cause for concern. It may be that Webb's management team increased the price per jacket in the hope it would minimize impairment to operating income. In this case the team may have made a good decision, and the profit from an extra $5/jacket could persist.

Journal Entries for Fixed Overhead Costs and Variances

The journal entries are illustrated below for the month of April using the Fixed Overhead Control and the contra account Fixed Manufacturing Overhead (FMOH) Allocated. These data are identical to those in Exhibit 8-11 Panel B. The FMOH variances are the same as those shown in Exhibit 8-4. The reconciliation of the two data sets will be explained by the variable cost variances in the next section.

1. FMOH Control	285,000	
Salaries, lease, tax, insurance payable		285,000
To record actual fixed overhead costs incurred		
2. WIP Control	230,000	
FMOH Allocated		230,000
To record fixed overhead costs allocated (0.40 DMH/jacket × 10,000 jackets × $57.50/DMH)		

The costs accumulated in WIP Control are transferred to Finished Goods Control when production is completed and into Cost of Goods Sold Control when the goods are sold (Chapter 4).

3. FMOH Allocated	230,000	
FMOH Rate Variance	9,000	
FMOH PVV	46,000	
FMOH Control		285,000
Records variances for the accounting period		

The FMOH rate variance and PVV reconcile to the $55,000 (= $285,000 − $230,000) of FMOH costs that were incurred but not allocated to the jackets produced. These are the underallocated FMOH costs from normal costing.

How the FMOH variance is treated at the end of the fiscal year depends on its materiality. If it is immaterial, it may be either written off to COGS or prorated among the Work-In-Process Control, Finished Goods Control, and COGS accounts on the basis of the fixed overhead allocated to these accounts. Obviously, writing off the amount to COGS is the easiest approach. If the amounts are material, some companies combine the write-off and proration methods. They write off the portion of variance arising from inefficiency that could have been avoided, and then prorate the portion that was unavoidable. For example, if the balance in the Fixed Overhead Rate Variance account at the end of April is also the year-end balance in December and is deemed to be immaterial, then the following journal entry records the write-off to COGS:

| Cost of Goods Sold | 9,000 | |
| FMOH Rate Variance | | 9,000 |

Also assume that the balance in the Fixed Overhead Production-Volume Variance account at the end of April remains unchanged and is the year-end balance in December. Assume there is some WIP and finished goods inventory at December 31. There is some argument about the appropriate treatment of an unfavourable PVV. Some accountants contend that the $46,000 U measures the cost of resources expended in anticipation of 2,000 jackets that were not produced ($23/jacket × 2,000 jackets = $46,000). Prorating would inappropriately allocate fixed overhead costs incurred for jackets not produced to those that were produced. In principle, the jackets produced already bear their fair share (i.e., $23 per jacket) of the burden of FMOH incurred during the year. This interpretation favours charging the unfavourable PVV against the year's revenue to ensure that the fixed costs of unused capacity are not carried in the WIP and finished goods inventories. This avoids an understatement of COGS from an overstated inventory valuation.

This approach is also consistent with ASPE/IFRS requirements for external reporting. These standards (IAS 2 and ASPE 3031) state that "unallocated overheads are recognized as an expense in the period in which they are incurred." It should be noted that these standards assume that *normal* capacity is used as the allocation base for the overhead (see Chapter 9 for a more complete discussion about capacity-level decisions). They also specify that "the amount of fixed overhead allocated to each unit [should] not be increased as a consequence of low production or idle plant." This indicates that an unfavourable PVV (a result of lower-than-budgeted output) should be expensed (to COGS) in the period it arises (since the other two methods of allocating PVV would increase the amount of MOH allocated to units).

On the other hand, the standards also specify that "in periods of abnormally high production, the amount of fixed overhead allocated to each unit of production *is* decreased so that inventories are not measured above cost. [emphasis added]" This indicates that a favourable PVV, if it is the result of a *usual* fluctuation in production output, should be credited to COGS in the period that it arises. Alternatively, if the PVV is the result of *abnormally* high production output, the implication is that the FMOH allocation rate should be recalculated (using the higher actual output) and the inventory unit costs reduced.

FMOH Variance	Actual Output *Less* Than Expected	Actual Output *More* Than Expected (But Still Considered a *Usual* Fluctuation)	Actual Output *More* Than Expected and *Abnormally High*
Production-volume variance	• Unfavourable variance • Expense to COGS	• Favourable variance • Expense to COGS	• Favourable variance • Recalculate allocation rate and apply to inventories

Alternatively, some accountants look at the choice of a denominator level as merely an estimate of the fixed capacity needed to produce jackets. Unforeseen events happen randomly, which can cause the actual available capacity to differ from the denominator level. Such random events in April led to the production of 10,000 jackets rather than the planned 12,000. We know this because there is no systematic and repeated unfavourable PVV in months leading to year-end. The budgeted $276,000 supported the cost of manufacturing the 10,000 jackets. Therefore, it is appropriate to also prorate this fixed overhead cost to the remaining WIP and finished goods inventories.

Concepts in Action | Cost Allocation Base Denominator Decision: There Is a Right Way

A lower capacity level avoids unfavourable variances that reduce operating income. If Webb's management team had chosen 48,000 instead of 57,600 direct machine-hours, then the FMOH cost allocation rate would have been applied to 10,000 jackets per month, not 12,000. But equipment capacity is a fact, not a choice. To be relevant, data such as FMOH rates need to be unbiased or the managers' decisions will be biased.

Favourable PVV could also arise. Assume Webb had manufactured and sold 13,800 jackets in April:

$$\begin{aligned} \text{Production-} \\ \text{volume variance} \end{aligned} = \begin{aligned} \text{Budgeted} \\ \text{fixed} \\ \text{overhead} \end{aligned} - \begin{aligned} \text{Fixed overhead allocated using} \\ \text{the budgeted cost per output unit overhead} \\ \text{allowed for the actual output produced} \end{aligned}$$

$$= \$276,000 - (\$23/\text{jacket} \times 13,800 \text{ jackets})$$

$$= \$276,000 - \$317,400$$

$$= \$41,400 \text{ F}$$

The fixed overhead costs of $276,000 in this situation supported the production of all 13,800 jackets and must be allocated to the actual production volume. The more conservative approach is to prorate the favourable PVV of $41,400 to WIP inventory, COGS, and finished goods inventory as opposed to simply crediting the entire amount to COGS. The prorating approach is more conservative because the amount credited to COGS is less than if the entire amount was credited to COGS (which would result in a higher reported operating income). That being said, if Webb wrote off the favourable PVV to COGS (as would be consistent with ASPE/IFRS for non-abnormal variances), the journal entry would be

FMOH Production-Volume Variance	41,400	
Cost of Goods Sold		41,400

Recall that the process of setting standards used for a budget is complex, and if variances were written off only to COGS, there would be temptation for managers to set standards to affect financial reports rather than to improve operating and strategic management decisions. The denominator level could be chosen to increase (for financial-reporting purposes) or decrease (for tax purposes) the reported operating income. Webb could generate a favourable (or unfavourable) PVV by setting the denominator level to allocate fixed overhead costs either low (or high) to either increase (or decrease) reported operating income.

Sustainable Overhead

The recent years of tough economic conditions and recession have highlighted the importance organizations place on optimizing overhead costs. Reactive efforts focused on economic activity often result in short-term measures (e.g., cutting the operating budgets). This does little to improve structural functions and overhead in the organization typically captured as sales and administration expenses.

Attenuation to variance analyses can directed insight primary functions (e.g., finance, human resources) and reveal specific adjustments that can be made to cost structures and processes in manufacturing and service overhead. Understanding of the internal relationships between functional areas enables management to determine how individual operations can be more effective, beyond mere efficiencies, to creating sustainable value. For example, monitoring how maintenance activities relate to the actual production operations (and the associated costs) may highlight the need to acquire more specific targeted maintenance programs to better serve the processes at play in the organization, rather than simply finding a cheaper rate to perform the same maintenance procedures.

Flexible-Budget Variable Overhead Variances

► LO 2

Establish variable overhead cost allocation rates; calculate and analyze flexible-budget variances.

Among Webb's VMOH costs are energy, machine maintenance, engineering support, indirect materials, and indirect manufacturing labour.

Webb's management team uses direct machine-hours as the cost allocation base and a single VMOH cost pool budgeted at $1,728,000 for the year. Monthly VMOH has been budgeted at $144,000, given the same budgeted Q = 12,000 jackets produced and sold.

Variable Overhead Cost Variance Calculations and Analyses

The Webb Company summary information for April is as shown:

Overhead Category	Actual Results	Flexible-Budget Amount (for 10,000 Output Units)	Static-Budget Amount (for 12,000 Output Units)
Variable manufacturing overhead	$130,500	$120,000	$144,000
Variable marketing overhead	45,700	50,000	60,000

The VMOH cost per input unit is $30/DMH (= $1,728,000 ÷ 57,600 DMH). Webb's cost per output is $12/jacket (at $30/DMH × 0.40 DMH/jacket). This rate will be used in both the static budget and the monthly performance reports:

Flexible- and Static-Budgeted Amounts for the Year

VMOH* (1)	DMH/Year (2)	Rate per DMH (3) = (1) ÷ (2)	Q Jackets/ Year (4)	DMH/ Jacket (5) = (2) ÷ (4)	Rate per Jacket (6) = (3) × (5)
$ 1,728,000	57,600	$ 30.00	144,000	0.40	$ 12.00

*Annual VMOH = $144,000 × 12.

The budgeted VMOH and the actual rate per jacket in April has been reported as

Item	Actual Results	Flexible-Budget Amount (for 10,000 output units)	Static-Budget Amount (for 12,000 output units)
1. Variable overhead costs	$130,500	$120,000	$144,000
2. DMH	4,500	4,000	4,800
3. Output, jackets	10,000	10,000	12,000
4. DMH/jacket (Line 2 ÷ Line 3)	0.45	0.40	0.40
5. VMOH/DMH (Line 1 ÷ Line 2)	$ 29.00	$ 30.00	$ 30.00
6. Variable overhead rate/jacket (Line 4 × Line 5)	$ 13.05	$ 12.00	$ 12.00

The discussion of VMOH begins with the Level 1 static-budget variance, which is $13,500 F:

$$\frac{\text{Variable overhead}}{\text{static-budget variance}} = \frac{\text{Actual}}{\text{results}} - \frac{\text{Static-budget}}{\text{amount}}$$
$$= \$130,500 - \$144,000$$
$$= \$13,500 \text{ F}$$

Unfortunately, the result of a simple subtraction provides no insight into what caused the variance. More insight is gained by analyzing the relationships among the Levels 2 and 3 variances, as illustrated in Exhibit 8-5.

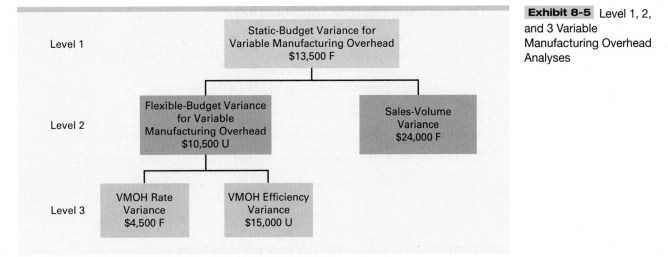

Exhibit 8-5 Level 1, 2, and 3 Variable Manufacturing Overhead Analyses

Level 2 Variable Manufacturing Overhead Variance Analysis

The Level 2 flexible-budget analysis will get the attention of the management team. The April flexible budget for VMOH is $120,000 (= 0.4 × 10,000 × $30). This is the amount Webb should have incurred to produce and sell Q = 10,000 jackets, as shown in Exhibit 8-6.

Exhibit 8-6 Static-Budget and Flexible-Budget Analysis of Variable Manufacturing Overhead Costs

LEVEL 1 ANALYSIS

	Actual Results (1)	Static-Budget Variance (2) = (1) – (3)	Static Budget (3)
Cost driver: Number of units manufactured	10,000	2,000 U	12,000
Variable manufacturing overhead	$130,500		(0.40 × 12,000 × $30) $144,000

$13,500 F
Static-budget variance

LEVEL 2 ANALYSIS

	Actual Results (1)	Flexible-Budget Variance (2) = (1) – (3)	Flexible Budget (3)	Sales-Volume Variance (4) = (3) – (5)	Static Budget (5)
Cost driver: Number of units manufactured	10,000	—	10,000	2,000 U	12,000
Variable manufacturing overhead	$130,500		(0.40 × 10,000 × $30) $120,000		(0.40 × 12,000 × $30) $144,000

$10,500 U
Flexible-budget variance

$24,000 F
Sales-volume variance

$13,500 F
Static-budget variance

The actual amount spent on VMOH was higher:

Variable manufacturing
overhead flexible-budget = Actual result − Flexible − budget amount
variance

= \$130,500 − \$120,000

= \$10,500 U

Variable manufacturing
overhead sales-volume = Flexible-budget amount − Static-budget amount
variance

= \$120,000 − \$144,000

= \$24,000 F

Interpretation of the Level 2 Variance Analysis

The VMOH flexible-budget variance reflects that the consumption of common resources per jacket exceeded what it *should* have by \$10,500. Either the rate per DMH or the amount of DMH per jacket exceeded what managers had committed to spend.

The favourable sales-volume variance of \$24,000 includes only that variance arising from lowered shared consumption of the VMOH items as a result of only producing and selling Q = 10,000 jackets instead of the originally budgeted Q = 12,000 jackets. This is part of the unfavourable total sales-volume variance of \$162,000 illustrated in Exhibit 7-5. For simplicity, we have excluded discussion of the \$50,000 of variable marketing (period cost) overhead and the \$434,000 of fixed marketing (period cost) overhead.

Webb's management team now knows that the operations in April produced poor results. A Level 3 analysis will give managers insight into why they failed.

Level 3 Variable Manufacturing Overhead Rate and Efficiency Variances

At Level 3, Webb's management team will isolate the VMOH variance arising from using too many DMH per jacket from the variance arising from paying too high a rate per DMH. Recall that overall this company fell short of budget by a total of \$237,000, only \$162,000 of which can be explained by the lower output level, and of that, \$24,000 or about 15% in savings came from VMOH (\$24,000 ÷ \$162,000). Of the remaining \$75,000 (= \$237,000 − \$162,000) unfavourable flexible-budget variance, approximately 14% (= \$10,500 ÷ \$75,000) can be attributed to the VMOH variance. It is a significant source of unfavourable variance.

The **variable overhead rate variance** measures the effectiveness of purchasing variable overhead and controlling the use of the variable overhead driver (since using less driver will result in less variable overhead being generated, if it is truly variable and the driver is appropriate to the cost pool). It is the difference between actual cost per unit for the DMH and budgeted rate per unit of \$30/DMH (allocation base), or what *should* have been used. The result of the subtraction is then multiplied by the actual quantity of DMH used to produce actual output:

$$\text{Variable overhead rate variance} = \left(\begin{array}{c}\text{Actual variable overhead cost per unit of cost allocation base}\end{array} - \begin{array}{c}\text{Budgeted variable overhead rate per unit of cost allocation base}\end{array}\right) \times \begin{array}{c}\text{Actual quantity of variable overhead rate allocation base used for actual output units achieved}\end{array}$$

= (\$29 per DMH − \$30 per DMH) × 4,500 DMH

= +1 per DMH × 4,500 DMH

= \$4,500 F

The **variable overhead efficiency variance** measures the efficiency with which the DMH have been used to produce jackets. It is a way to measure yield. It is the difference between the actual amount of DMH used and the budgeted input of 0.40 DMH/jacket for the actual amount of output (10,000 jackets). The result of the subtraction is then multiplied by the budgeted rate for the input (DMH):

$$
\begin{pmatrix} \text{Variable overhead} \\ \text{efficiency variance} \end{pmatrix} = \begin{pmatrix} \text{Actual units of} & \text{Budgeted units of} \\ \text{variable overhead} & \text{variable overhead} \\ \text{cost allocation base} & - & \text{cost allocation base} \\ \text{used for actual output} & \text{allowed for actual} \\ \text{units achieved} & \text{output units achieved} \end{pmatrix} \times \begin{pmatrix} \text{Budgeted} \\ \text{variable overhead} \\ \text{allocation rate} \end{pmatrix}
$$

$$= [4{,}500 \text{ DMH} - (10{,}000 \text{ units} \times 0.40 \text{ DMH/unit})] \times \$30 \text{ per DMH}$$

$$= (4{,}500 \text{ DMH} - 4{,}000 \text{ DMH}) \times \$30 \text{ per DMH}$$

$$= 500 \text{ DMH} \times \$30 \text{ per DMH}$$

$$= \$15{,}000 \text{ U}$$

It is important to remember that although the Level 3 direct and indirect variances are called the same, the VMOH is not caused by nor is it explained by the DMH consumed. The VMOH inputs include janitorial labour and supplies, maintenance labour and supplies, and fringe benefits. These inputs are shared throughout the production of all jackets. The measure of benefit provided to all jackets is a decision made by Webb's managers. They have decided that the best measure of benefit is direct machine-hours, DMH.

As the DMH/jacket changes, the total VMOH cost pool assigned to each jacket will change because of the arithmetic relationship between cost and benefit created by the managers. In their judgment this is the best measure of economic reality at Webb. There is no *direct* relationship between the DMH cost driver and the total amount in the VMOH cost pool. The relationship is not causal but rather one of cost and benefit. In columnar format, Exhibit 8-7 reconciles the Levels 2 and 3 variance analyses.

Interpretation of the Level 3 Variance Analysis

Webb's unfavourable efficiency variance of $15,000 means that actual DMH used per jacket exceeded budget. The yield or quantity of jackets produced was too low for the DMH used. In fact, at 0.4 DMH/jacket, Webb should have produced 11,250 jackets for sale (= 4,500 DMH ÷ 0.4 DMH). Possible causes for the deterioration in the relationship between shared input and shared benefit are as varied as the resource costs accumulated in

Exhibit 8-7 Columnar Presentation of Variance Analysis: Variable Manufacturing Overhead for Webb Company

LEVEL 3 ANALYSIS

Actual Costs Incurred (1)		Actual Input × Budgeted Rate (2)		Flexible Budget: Budgeted Input Allowed for Actual Output Achieved × Budgeted Rate (3)
(4,500 × $29) $130,500		(4,500 × $30) $135,000		(0.40 × 10,000 × $30) $120,000
	↑ $4,500 F	↑	$15,000 U	↑
	Rate variance		Efficiency variance	
↑		$10,500 U		↑
		Flexible-budget variance		

this single VMOH cost pool. For example, the efficiency variance may have arisen because of any of the following reasons:

- Machine malfunction because of poor maintenance resulting in more time per jacket than 0.40 DMH.
- Poor production scheduling resulting in too much idle time waiting for the materials to be cut and moved to the sewing area.
- Poor coordination between sales and production resulting in displacement of normal batches by rush orders and excessive setup times.
- Poor quality of materials resulting in downtime to clean the machines of debris when the materials disintegrated during sewing.

In the analysis of the PVV, the difference in the capacity purchased and the capacity used could be explained in part by neglecting machine maintenance. If this was the case, then it is reasonable to expect that DMH actually used per jacket would be unfavourably affected by downtime. In fact, what the four potential causes have in common is that they interrupt access to the benefits provided by well-working machinery.

The favourable rate variance may arise from the manufacturing labour portion of VMOH, any variable utilities costs, or reduction in quantities of supplies purchased and used. For example,

- Probationary workers receive no paid leave for idle time and no other discretionary benefits resulting in lower fringe benefit costs.
- Statutory holidays resulting in lower custodial costs from fewer cleaning hours paid and lower quantity of cleaning supplies used.
- Statutory holidays resulting in lower consumption of utilities.
- Change in classification of an input from an indirect to a direct cost.

The actual costs of individual items included in VMOH cost pools, for example, security or cleaning supplies, could have been lower than expected in April. The favourable rates could be the result of skillful negotiation on the part of the purchasing manager or oversupply in the market.

The use of patch labels on jackets illustrates the difference between the efficiency variance for direct cost inputs and the efficiency variance for variable overhead cost categories. If Webb classifies garment patch labels as a direct cost item, the direct materials efficiency will indicate whether more or fewer patch labels per jacket were used (than was budgeted for the actual output achieved). If Webb classifies patch labels as an indirect cost, then the number of patch labels used will not affect the VMOH *efficiency* variance (because it is determined by the number of direct machine-hours used). In this case, any variance in the number of patch labels used would be reflected in the VMOH *rate* variance (because the cost of patch labels used is part of the VMOH actual cost pool).

Based on their analysis of the situation, the key cause of Webb's unfavourable flexible-budget manufacturing overhead variance is that the actual use of machine-hours is higher than budgeted. Exhibit 8-8 excludes all direct costs and non-manufacturing overhead variances.[3]

Webb's costing system distinguished between variable and FMOH cost pools. Some companies do not segregate their overhead costs this way. For these companies, all overhead costs are assumed to be fixed when conducting variance analyses. Any interpretation of the variance analysis for these companies will be limited because of the selection of this type of cost system.

Journal Entries for Variable Overhead Costs and Variances

Variable Manufacturing Overhead VMOH Control and the contra account VMOH Allocated are used for the journal entries for April (Exhibit 8-6):

---

[3] Reconciling with Chapter 7, Exhibit 7-7, from data in Exhibit 7-4, non-manufacturing fixed overhead is $14,000 F (= $420,000 − $434,000), while the FMOH is $9,000 U for net total fixed cost variance of $5,000 F. Variable non-manufacturing overhead is $4,300 F (= $45,700 − $50,000), while the VMOH is $10,500 U for a net total variable overhead cost variance of $6,200 U (= $4,300 − $10,500).

Exhibit 8-8 Static-Budget and Flexible-Budget Analysis of Fixed and Variable Manufacturing Overhead Costs

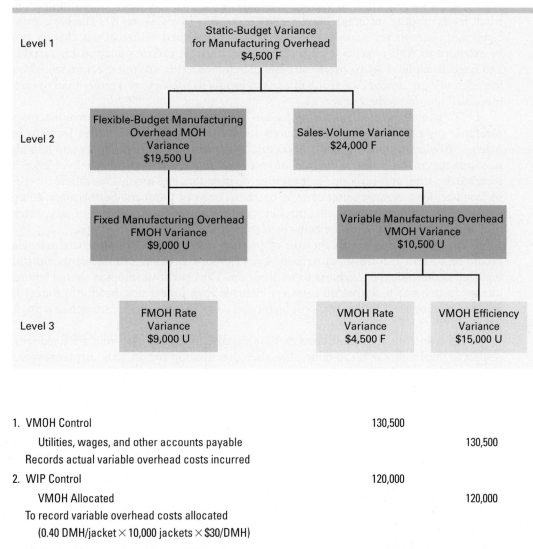

1. VMOH Control   130,500

    Utilities, wages, and other accounts payable   130,500

    Records actual variable overhead costs incurred

2. WIP Control   120,000

    VMOH Allocated   120,000

    To record variable overhead costs allocated

    (0.40 DMH/jacket × 10,000 jackets × $30/DMH)

The costs accumulated in WIP control are transferred to Finished Goods Control when production is completed and into Cost of Goods Sold Control when the goods are sold (Ch. 4).

3. VMOH Allocated   120,000

    VMOH Efficiency Variance   15,000

        VMOH Control   130,500

        VMOH Rate Variance   4,500

    Records variances for the accounting period

The variances arise because of under- or overallocated VMOH costs. At the end of the fiscal year, the treatment of a variance depends on whether it is significant. If the variances are not significant, then the variance accounts are written off to COGS. If the variances are significant, then they are prorated among WIP Control, Finished Goods Control, and COGS accounts on the basis of the VMOH allocated to these accounts. Assume that the April variances are also those at the end of the fiscal year and are not significant. The following journal entry records the write-off of the variance accounts to COGS:

        Cost of Goods Sold   10,500

        VMOH Rate Variance   4,500

            VMOH Efficiency Variance   15,000

Activity-Based Costing and Variance Analysis

▶ **LO 3**

Calculate ABC overhead variances.

ABC systems classify costs of various activities into a cost hierarchy: output-unit level, batch level, product sustaining, and facility sustaining (see Chapter 5). The basic principles and concepts for variable and FMOH costs presented earlier in this chapter can be extended to ABC systems. In this section, we illustrate variance analysis for variable and fixed batch-level setup overhead costs. Batch-level costs are resources sacrificed on activities that are related to a group of units of product(s) or service(s) rather than to each individual unit of product or service.

Let's continue our example from Chapter 7 of Lyco Brass Works, which manufactures Jacutaps, a line of decorative brass faucets for Jacuzzis. Lyco manufactures Jacutaps in batches. To manufacture a batch of Jacutaps, Lyco must set up the machines and moulds to ensure the correct colour is injected into each batch. Setup is a skilled activity. Hence, a separate department is responsible for setting up machines and moulds for different types of Jacutaps. Lyco regards setup costs as overhead costs of products. Furthermore, setup requires that the machines be idle; machines cannot be set up for batches of, say, black taps at the same time as they are being used to produce batches of white taps.

Lyco wants to ensure that the cost of productive capacity is appropriately assigned according to benefit for distinct outputs. Lyco cannot run batches of different coloured taps unless they idle the machines to set them up. The benefit of setups is shared among all taps in that batch, and setup costs are incurred each time a new batch of product is going to be produced. In the ABC cost hierarchy, setup cost is a batch rather than a product cost.

Setup costs consist of some costs that are variable and some costs that are fixed with respect to the number of setup-hours. Variable costs of setup consist of hourly wages paid to setup labour and indirect support labour, costs of maintenance of setup equipment, and costs of indirect materials and energy used during setups. Fixed setup costs consist of salary costs of engineers, supervisors, and setup equipment leases.

Information regarding Jacutaps for 2018 follows:

	Static-Budget Amounts	Actual Amounts
1. Units of Jacutaps produced and sold	180,000	151,200
2. Batch size (units/batch)	150	140
3. Number of batches (Line 1 ÷ Line 2)	1,200	1,080
4. Setup-hours per batch	6	6.25
5. Total setup-hours (Line 3 × Line 4)	7,200	6,750
6. Variable overhead rate per setup-hour	$ 20	$ 21
7. Variable setup overhead costs (Line 5 × Line 6)	$144,000	$141,750
8. Total fixed setup overhead costs	$216,000	$220,000

ABC Variance Analyses

To prepare the flexible budget for variable setup overhead costs, Lyco starts with the actual units of output produced (151,200 units), then undertakes a series of interdependent processes. Development of ABC systems is a complex process. The management team at Lyco has carefully considered and chosen the best cost driver or measure of benefit for its batches of taps. The batch size (number of coloured taps) has also been selected as well as what variable and fixed costs will accumulate in the batch cost pool.

Now Lyco's managers can calculate the budgeted variable overhead setup cost driver rate per setup-hour. They can also calculate how many batches are required to produce an actual quantity of output units (e.g., blue taps) during a specified time period.

Lyco should have manufactured the 151,200 units of output in 1,008 batches (= 151,200 ÷ 150). Based on the quantity of setups, Lyco's managers calculate the quantity of setup-hours (cost driver) that should have been consumed for the actual number of batches during a specified time period. At the budgeted quantity of 6 setup-hours per batch, 1,008 batches should have required 6,048 setup-hours (1,008 batches × 6 setup-hours/batch). Notice that this is a flexible-budgeting approach to establishing variable overhead cost variances. What has changed is that the unit of measure is a different level in the cost hierarchy.

At this stage in the process, it is relatively straightforward to multiply the variable overhead setup cost driver rate by the budgeted (standard or benchmark) flexible quantity of setup-hours for the actual output produced. The flexible-budget amount is 6,048 setup-hours × \$20/setup-hour = \$120,960.

$$\text{Flexible-budget variance for variable setup overhead costs} = \text{Actual costs} - \text{Flexible-budget costs}$$

$$= \left\{ \begin{matrix} 6{,}750 \text{ setup-hours} \\ \times \ \$21/\text{setup-hour} \end{matrix} \right\} - \left\{ \begin{matrix} 6{,}048 \text{ setup-hours} \\ \times \ \$20/\text{setup-hour} \end{matrix} \right\}$$

$$= \$141{,}750 - \$120{,}960$$

$$= \$20{,}790 \text{ U}$$

Exhibit 8-9 presents the variances for variable setup overhead costs in columnar form.

The flexible-budget variance for variable setup overhead costs can be subdivided into rate and efficiency variances.

$$\text{Variable setup overhead rate variance} = \left(\begin{matrix} \text{Actual variable} \\ \text{overhead cost} \\ \text{per unit of cost} \\ \text{allocation base} \end{matrix} - \begin{matrix} \text{Budgeted variable} \\ \text{overhead cost per} \\ \text{unit of cost} \\ \text{allocation base} \end{matrix} \right) \times \begin{matrix} \text{Actual units of variable} \\ \text{overhead cost allocation} \\ \text{base used for actual output} \end{matrix}$$

$$= (\$21/\text{setup-hour} - \$20/\text{setup-hour}) \times 6{,}750 \text{ setup-hours}$$

$$= \$1/\text{setup-hour} \times 6{,}750 \text{ setup-hours}$$

$$= \$6{,}750 \text{ U}$$

Interpretation of Variable Setup Overhead Rate Variance

The unfavourable rate variance indicates that Lyco operated in 2018 with higher-than-budgeted variable overhead costs per setup-hour. Two main reasons that could contribute to the unfavourable rate variance are (1) the actual prices of individual items included in variable overhead, such as setup labour, indirect support labour, or energy, are higher than the budgeted prices, and (2) the actual quantity usage of individual items such as

Exhibit 8-9 Columnar Presentation of Variable Setup Overhead Variance Analysis for Lyco Brass Works for 2018

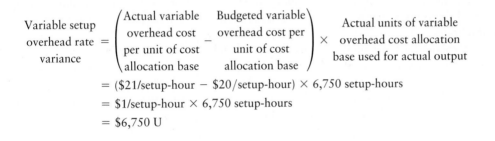

Actual Costs Incurred (1)		Actual Input × Budgeted Rate (2)		Flexible Budget: Budgeted Input Allowed for Actual Output Achieved × Budgeted Rate (3)
(6,750 × \$21) \$141,750		(6,750 × \$20) \$135,000		(6,048 × \$20) \$120,960
	\$6,750 U		\$14,040 U	
	Rate variance		Efficiency variance	
		\$20,790 U		
		Flexible-budget variance		

energy increases more than the increase in setup-hours, due perhaps to setups becoming more complex because of equipment problems. Thus, equipment problems could lead to an unfavourable efficiency variance because setup-hours increase, but they could also lead to an unfavourable rate variance because each setup-hour requires more resources from the setup-cost pool than the budgeted amounts. Identifying the reason for the variances is important because it helps managers plan for and take action to regain control.

$$\begin{array}{l} \text{Variable setup} \\ \text{overhead rate} \\ \text{variance} \end{array} = \left(\begin{array}{c} \text{Actual units of} \\ \text{variable overhead} \\ \text{cost allocation base} \\ \text{used for actual output} \end{array} - \begin{array}{c} \text{Budgeted units of} \\ \text{variable overhead cost} \\ \text{allocation base allowed} \\ \text{for actual output} \end{array} \right) \times \begin{array}{c} \text{Budgeted} \\ \text{variable} \\ \text{overhead rate} \end{array}$$

$$= (\$6,750 \text{ setup-hours} - 6,048 \text{ setup-hours}) \times \$20/\text{setup-hour}$$

$$= 702 \text{ setup-hours} \times \$20/\text{setup-hour}$$

$$= \$14,040 \text{ U}$$

Interpretation of Variable Setup Overhead Efficiency Variance

The unfavourable variable setup overhead efficiency variance of $14,040 arises because the actual number of setup-hours (6,750) exceeds the number of setup-hours that Lyco should have used (6,048) for the number of units it produced.

Two possible reasons for the unfavourable efficiency variance are (1) smaller actual batch sizes of 140 units instead of budgeted batch sizes of 150 units, which results in Lyco producing the 151,200 units in 1,080 batches instead of 1,008 batches, and (2) higher actual setup-hours per batch of 6.25 hours instead of the budgeted setup-hours per batch of 6 hours.

Explanations for smaller-than-budgeted batch sizes could include (1) quality problems if batch sizes exceed 140 faucets or (2) high costs of carrying inventory. Explanations for longer actual setup-hours per batch could include (1) problems with equipment, (2) unmotivated or inexperienced employees, or (3) inappropriate setup-time standards. Now let's consider fixed setup overhead costs.

ABC Variance Analysis for Fixed Manufacturing Overhead Cost

For fixed setup overhead costs, the flexible-budget amount equals the static-budget amount of $216,000; there is no "flexing" of fixed costs over a relevant range of production.

$$\begin{array}{l} \text{Fixed setup overhead} \\ \text{flexible-budget variance} \end{array} = \begin{array}{c} \text{Actual} \\ \text{costs} \end{array} - \begin{array}{c} \text{Flexible-budget} \\ \text{costs} \end{array}$$

$$= \$220,000 - \$216,000$$

$$= \$4,000 \text{ U}$$

The fixed setup overhead rate variance is also the same amount as the fixed overhead flexible-budget variance (because fixed overhead costs have no efficiency variance).

$$\begin{array}{l} \text{Fixed setup overhead} \\ \text{rate variance} \end{array} = \begin{array}{c} \text{Actual} \\ \text{costs} \end{array} - \begin{array}{c} \text{Flexible-budget} \\ \text{costs} \end{array}$$

$$= \$220,000 - \$216,000$$

$$= \$4,000 \text{ U}$$

Interpretation of Fixed Setup Overhead Rate Variance

The unfavourable fixed setup overhead rate variance could be due to lease costs of new setup equipment or higher salaries paid to engineers and supervisors. Lyco may have incurred these costs to alleviate some of the difficulties it was having in setting up machines.

Next Lyco will calculate its PVV. The budgeted cost allocation rate for fixed overhead setup costs for the year used MIS data. The annual budgeted setup-hours are 7,200.

Exhibit 8-10 Columnar Presentation of Fixed Setup Overhead Variance Analysis

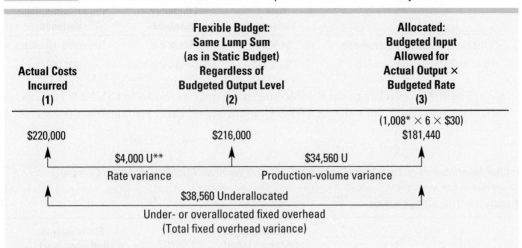

*1,008 batches = 151,200 units ÷ 150 units per batch.

**Recall that for FMOH, a rate variance equals the flexible-budget variance which equals the static-budget variance.

The budgeted fixed overhead cost pool for setups is $216,000. The fixed overhead rate is $30/setup-hour ($216,000 ÷ 7,200 setup-hours).

$$\frac{\text{Budgeted fixed setup}}{\text{overhead rate}} = \frac{\text{Budgeted total costs in overhead cost pool}}{\text{Budgeted total quantity of cost allocation base}} = \frac{\$216,000}{7,200 \text{ setup-hours}}$$

During 2018, Lyco planned to produce 180,000 units of Jacutaps but actually produced only 151,200 units. The unfavourable PVV measures the amount of extra fixed setup costs that Lyco incurred for setup capacity it planned to use but did not.

$$\begin{aligned}
\text{Production-volume} & \quad \text{Budgeted fixed} & \text{Fixed setup overhead allocated} \\
\text{variance for fixed} &= \text{setup overhead} - \text{using budgeted input allowed for} \\
\text{setup overhead costs} & \quad \text{costs} & \text{actual output units produced}
\end{aligned}$$

$$= \$216,000 - (1,008 \text{ batches} \times 6 \text{ hours per batch} \times \$30/\text{setup-hour})$$

$$= \$216,000 - (6,048 \text{ setup-hours} \times \$30/\text{setup-hour})$$

$$= \$216,000 - \$181,440$$

$$= \$34,560 \text{ U}$$

Exhibit 8-10 presents and reconciles the ABC variance analyses of fixed setup overhead in columnar form.

Interpretation of Production-Volume Variance

One interpretation is that the unfavourable $34,560 PVV represents inefficient utilization of setup capacity. However, Lyco may have earned higher operating income by selling 151,200 units at a higher price than what it would have earned by selling 180,000 units at a lower price. The PVV should be interpreted cautiously based on full information.

Summary of All Overhead Cost Variances

All of these variances can be summarized in a simple table that eliminates unnecessary overhead variances from the model. A VMOH cost pool can never incur a PVV. A FMOH cost pool can never incur an efficiency variance. This simplifies Webb's presentation considerably. In total, the overhead manufacturing cost variance is $65,500 U, of which the majority is opportunity cost arising from underuse of capacity.

► **LO 4**

Integrate the fixed and variable overhead cost variance analyses to reconcile the actual overhead incurred with overhead allocated.

Four-Variance Analysis

	Rate Variance	Efficiency Variance	Production-Volume Variance
Variable manufacturing overhead	$4,500 F	$15,000 U	(Never a variance)
Fixed manufacturing overhead	$9,000 U	(Never a variance)	$46,000 U

The variances relate to the flexible-budget variance as shown in Exhibit 8-11: Panel A summarizes relationships among VMOH variances, and Panel B summarizes those among

Exhibit 8-11 Columnar Presentation of Total Manufacturing Overhead Variance Analyses at Webb Company

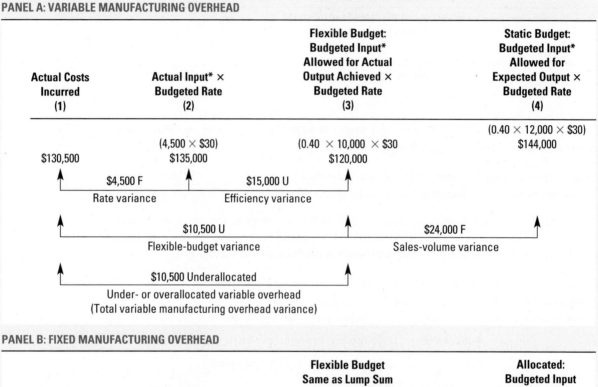

PANEL A: VARIABLE MANUFACTURING OVERHEAD

| Actual Costs Incurred (1) | Actual Input* × Budgeted Rate (2) | Flexible Budget: Budgeted Input* Allowed for Actual Output Achieved × Budgeted Rate (3) | Static Budget: Budgeted Input* Allowed for Expected Output × Budgeted Rate (4) |

$130,500   (4,500 × $30) $135,000   (0.40 × 10,000 × $30) $120,000   (0.40 × 12,000 × $30) $144,000

$4,500 F Rate variance $15,000 U Efficiency variance

$10,500 U Flexible-budget variance $24,000 F Sales-volume variance

$10,500 Underallocated
Under- or overallocated variable overhead
(Total variable manufacturing overhead variance)

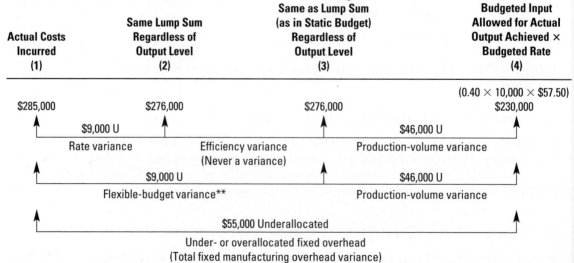

PANEL B: FIXED MANUFACTURING OVERHEAD

| Actual Costs Incurred (1) | Same Lump Sum Regardless of Output Level (2) | Flexible Budget Same as Lump Sum (as in Static Budget) Regardless of Output Level (3) | Allocated: Budgeted Input Allowed for Actual Output Achieved × Budgeted Rate (4) |

$285,000 $276,000 $276,000   (0.40 × 10,000 × $57.50) $230,000

$9,000 U Rate variance   Efficiency variance (Never a variance) $46,000 U Production-volume variance

$9,000 U Flexible-budget variance** $46,000 U Production-volume variance

$55,000 Underallocated
Under- or overallocated fixed overhead
(Total fixed manufacturing overhead variance)

*For overhead costs, *input* refers to units of cost-allocation base.
**Since fixed costs don't change with sales volume, there is no sales-volume variance for fixed costs.

FMOH cost variances. In total, the total variance (between actual and allocated) for overhead costs is $65,500 U, the sum of the $10,500 U variable overhead variance and the $55,000 U fixed overhead variance.

Reporting overhead variances at this level of detail assists managers in large and complex businesses to focus attention on where actual or realized results did not meet expectations. In smaller and less complex businesses, managers might choose not to distinguish the variable from fixed overhead because they are very familiar with the causes of cost overruns.

The $65,500 unfavourable total manufacturing overhead variance for Webb Company in April 2018 is largely the result of the $46,000 unfavourable production-volume variance. Using the four-variance analysis presentation, the next-largest amount is the $15,000 unfavourable variable overhead efficiency variance. This variance arises from the additional 500 direct machine-hours used in April above the 4,000 direct machine-hours allowed to manufacture the 10,000 jackets. The two rate variances ($4,500 F and $9,000 U) partially offset each other. At this point the management team simply knows that some combination of changes to expected variable inputs included in the variable cost pool was favourable. The unexpected changes to fixed cost were, on balance, unfavourable during April.

In the next table, the two *rate* variances from the four-variance analysis have been combined to produce a three-variance analysis in the table. The only loss of information in the three-variance analysis is in the overhead rate variance area—only one rate variance is reported instead of separate variable and fixed overhead rate variances. Three-variance analysis is sometimes called **combined-variance analysis** because it combines variable-cost and fixed-cost variances when reporting overhead cost variances. Mixed costs have both a fixed and a variable component. In some cases, it may not be worthwhile to separate the components of these semivariable or semifixed costs, so combining them is sensible.

Three-Variance Analysis

	Rate Variance	Efficiency Variance	Production-Volume Variance
Total manufacturing overhead	$4,500 U	$15,000 U	$46,000 U

The table below combines the rate and efficiency variances from the three-variance analysis into a two-variance analysis. The first cost pool includes the variable overhead rate and efficiency variances as well as the fixed overhead rate variance. In constructing these variances, it is not necessary to know the actual machine-hours because no efficiency variance is calculated.

Two-Variance Analysis

	Flexible-Budget Variance	Production-Volume Variance
Total manufacturing overhead	$19,500 U	$46,000 U

The single variance of $65,500 U in one-variance analysis is the sum of the flexible-budget variance and the PVV under two-variance analysis. This simply reports the variance between the $415,500 (= $130,500 + $285,000) total manufacturing overhead actually realized in April and the $350,000 (= $120,000 + $230,000) budgeted manufacturing overhead allocated to produce 10,000 jackets (actual output) during that month.

One-Variance Analysis

	Total Overhead Variance
Total manufacturing overhead	$65,500 U

Concepts in Action | Interdependencies and Shared Benefits

Webb's attention has, so far, been directed by the most significant unfavourable variance. Yes, direct machine-hours is certainly a measurable and required resource, but in the value chain there are business functions beyond production. The team must be aware of a broader scope of effects than simply maximizing jackets produced per direct machine-hour.

The reason Webb is successful is beyond its corporate boundaries. It succeeds because it meets its customers' expectations of value in use from the jacket. Customer cost management views Webb's business function value chain through the eyes of the customer. Webb's team may also look out to those who do similar tasks best and replace a "do the best we can" with "do the best that can be done" cost management policy. These approaches to strategic cost management require an external perspective.

Non-manufacturing Variance Analysis

► LO 5

Analyze non-manufacturing variances.

The overhead variances discussed in this chapter have been examples of *financial* performance measures. Services ranging from passenger air transportation to recuperative health care to management accounting are also provided by for-profit companies. A customer's **value proposition** is the satisfaction or value added the customer expects to receive from purchasing the product or service. Value propositions change quickly for service providers. To retain customers and remain profitable, service providers must respond quickly and appropriately to changes in both what their customers value and attributes for which they will pay.

A **value-added cost** is one that, if eliminated, would reduce the value customers obtain from using the product or service. A **non-value-added cost** is one that, if eliminated, would not reduce the value customers obtain from using the product or service. For example, to offset problems that arise if suppliers fail to meet their delivery schedule, Webb inventories rolls of cloth in its warehouse. To the customer, a jacket sewn from cloth stored in a warehouse is no different from a jacket sewn from cloth delivered by a supplier directly to the production floor. Therefore, the activity of storing cloth is non-value-added for the customer, and managers view the manufacturing overhead costs associated with warehousing as non-value-added costs. There is a continuum between value-added costs and non-value-added costs. Many overhead cost items are in a grey, uncertain area between value-adding and non-value-adding costs.

As Webb's management team works through a plan to bring costs back under control, the focus should be on eliminating non-value-added costs first. This is a strategic cost management approach to ensuring that most of Webb's costs are value-added and therefore may be recovered when the jacket is sold.

Nonfinancial Performance Measures

Nonfinancial performance measures include market share, on-time delivery performance (e.g., Purolator), customer acquisition rate, customer retention rate, and order time to completion. These measures will vary from one service industry to another. In the hospitality industry, a hotel would track nonfinancial measures of satisfaction with hotel location; room availability and reservations; check-in; room security, quietness, cleanliness, and amenities; restaurant and bar services; spa services; entertainment; and concierge services.[4] While the core services of a hotel are lodging and food, other ancillary services contribute to the customer's positive experience and satisfaction.

---

[4] A. Cuigini, A. Carù, and F. Zerbini, "The Cost of Customer Satisfaction: A Framework for Strategic Cost Management in Service Industries," *European Accounting Review*, 16.3 (2007): 499–530.

Effective and efficient customer response or **agility** implies a process of service design, implementation, and delivery with flexible performance indicators. It seems that at least four standards are required—quality, timeliness, customization, and cost—to capture measures of agility. The agile service company has the ability to excel simultaneously in quality, delivery time, customization, and cost in a coordinated way.[5]

Crucial for a profitable service provider is the customer's satisfaction. Where the value proposition is the customer's view of cost and benefit, what brings the customer back is satisfaction, a nonfinancial measure of value. Management accountants have applied cost estimation techniques to identify and measure nonfinancial factors contributing most to customers' satisfaction. Within the service sector, the selection of standards is difficult to reconcile with the need for agility. Standards make for straightforward comparisons between customer segments, but they are, by definition, constant. Ironically, agility requires solutions to problems that were not imagined when the standards were chosen. The challenge for management accountants is to provide excellent measures of a service company's economic reality that reflect a dynamic value proposition.

Strategically, service companies often must both customize their service and exercise cost leadership strategies to maintain profitability. Service companies may respond by segmenting their services based on types of customers. Satisfaction may arise from flexible responses by the provider to purchasing preference (rush orders, standing contracts), delivery (face-to-face, electronic), range of services (core, facilitating, peripheral), service provision (the vice-president, managers), and after-sale support. Overall, service companies can also examine a value chain beginning with the business acquisition and marketing, development of relationships, customer account maintenance, and customer account administration overhead. Non-manufacturing overhead or backroom operations would include contract management, billing, collections, and general administration such as technical and legal support.

Starbucks, for example, lost its place as first in customer loyalty in 2007 to Dunkin' Donuts. After analysis of the competition, Starbucks decided that its strategic approach had been inappropriate. The company had removed the roasting process and had automated espresso and cappuccino delivery, which reduced the time customers spent chatting with baristas. The relentless focus on controlling costs by changing internal processes did not conform to the value proposition of customers: Starbucks customers wanted the coffee "experience" rather than fast-food delivery.[6] Starbucks had improved the time and cost of service delivery, but the quality of its service from the customers' point of view had deteriorated. One analytical approach is shown below:

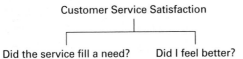

The two dimensions of satisfaction include a thoughtful or cognitive dimension and an emotional or affective dimension. For a Starbucks customer, a cognitive response to satisfaction could be that a beverage quenched thirst in the anticipated way. The affective response could be delight, happiness, or contentment from being pampered at an affordable price. The chairman of Revlon once said, "We don't sell cosmetics; we sell hope," in an attempt to characterize the difference between the cognitive and affective dimensions of Revlon's products.

Service attributes such as timeliness appeal to cognitive satisfaction, while those such as quality and customization appeal to affective satisfaction. The smell of roasting and fresh ground coffee delighted the Starbucks customers who left to quench their thirst elsewhere when this perk was eliminated. More careful analysis of the multidimensional

[5] L.J. Menor, A.V. Roth, and C.H. Mason, "Agility in Retail Banking: A Numerical Taxonomy of Strategic Service Groups," *Manufacturing and Service Operations Management*, 3.4 (Fall 2001): 273–292.

[6] http://www.forbes.com/sites/genemarcial/2016/07/31/why-starbucks-stock-remains-appetizing/#7354fa644cd0.

nature of what a cup of Starbucks meant to customers could have given managers information relevant to their decision, which changed the experience and meaning of purchasing a cup of Starbucks coffee.

Even in manufacturing environments, nonfinancial measures have proven value as indicators of benefit. Webb Company identified the following:

- Actual indirect materials usage in metres per machine-hour, compared with budgeted indirect materials usage in metres per machine-hour.

- Actual energy usage per machine-hour, compared with budgeted energy usage per machine-hour.

- Actual number of spoiled jackets, compared to budgeted spoilage.

A service company such as an airline would likely analyze nonfinancial measures of satisfaction with the personal space per seat, seat comfort, food, and baggage handling, as well as flight availability, on-time take-off and arrival, and convenient connections with other flights. Few costs can be traced to these outputs in a cost-effective way. The majority of airline costs are fixed overhead costs (for example, costs of equipment, buildings, and staff). Using capacity effectively is the key to profitability, and fixed overhead variances can help managers in this task. For airlines, the nonfinancial capacity measure is available seat miles (ASM) while the financial measures are revenue per ASM (RASM) and costs per ASM (CASM).

Consider the following data for WestJet from 2006 to 2012. Available seat miles (ASM) are the actual seats in a plane multiplied by the distance travelled. One measure of capacity management is the operating income per ASM (= RASM − CASM), which tells managers what WestJet's annual operating income has been, given its total capacity of ASM.

WestJet Annual Reports 2006–2012

Year	Total ASM (billions) (1)	Revenue per ASM (2)	Cost per ASM (3)	Operating Income per ASM (4) = (2) − (3)
2012	22.064	$0.1553	$0.1383	$0.0170
2011	21.186	0.1450	0.1329	0.0121
2010	19.535	0.1335	0.1237	0.0098
2009	17.588	0.1297	0.1177	0.0120
2008	17.139	0.1488	0.1317	0.0171
2007	14.139	0.1462	0.1236	0.0226
2006	12.524	0.1398	0.1210	0.0188

The global recession hit in 2008, yet despite a dramatic drop in demand for air travel in 2008–2010, WestJet managed to survive. In part this resulted from negotiating flexible delivery dates for aircraft. The company also increased the distance travelled per flight. Relative to the cost of keeping the aircraft aloft, takeoffs and landings comprise almost all the operating costs per flight (especially fuel). By lengthening the distances per flight, the costs of takeoff and landing were spread over more ASM. WestJet kept its CASM almost constant while RASM increased slightly. It could charge slightly more because it was flying passengers farther, a feature for which they were willing to pay. The financial result was a large increase in operating income per ASM from 2010 to 2012.

In an industry as equipment intensive as an airline, cost management extends to the fourth decimal place. Once committed to lease and purchasing contracts, the company cannot change the fixed cost per ASM. The $0.1383/ASM capacity cost in 2012 is a sunk cost that will not change. That is why WestJet enjoys great benefit from either a very small increase in RASM or decrease in CASM relative to budgeted values. Fractions of a cent will generate a large favourable variance in operating income. The management team has also kept most of its fleet to a single aircraft type (Boeing 737) to reduce maintenance expenses and cabin and flight crew training costs and to retain a negotiating advantage with its supplier. WestJet implements its cost leadership strategy through a relentless focus on controlling or reducing its cost of capacity use.

Pulling It All Together—Problem for Self-Study

(Try to solve this problem before examining the solution that follows.)

Dawn Smith is the newly appointed president of Laser Products. She is examining the May 2018 results for the Aerospace Products division. This division manufactures exterior panels for satellites. Smith's current concern is with manufacturing overhead costs at the aerospace products division. Both variable and FMOH costs are allocated to the panels based on laser-cutting-hours. The budgeted cost rates are VMOH of $200 per hour and FMOH of $240 per hour. The budgeted laser-cutting time per panel is 1.50 hours. Budgeted production and sales for 2018 are 5,000 panels. Budgeted FMOH costs for May 2018 are $1,800,000.

Exterior panels produced and sold	4,800 units
Laser-cutting-hours used	8,400 hours
Variable manufacturing overhead costs	$1,478,400
Fixed manufacturing overhead costs	$1,832,200

1. Calculate the rate variance and the efficiency variance for VMOH.   ❶ ◄ **Required**
2. Calculate the rate variance and the production variance for fixed manufacturing ❷ overhead.
3. Give explanations for the variances in requirements 1 and 2 to illustrate how fixed ❹ and variable overhead cost variances provide integrated relevant information.
4. What nonfinancial variables could Laser Products use as performance measures? ❺
5. What customer-satisfaction measures would be important to Laser Products? ❺

Solution

1. and 2. See Exhibit 8-12.
3. a. VMOH variance ($201,600 F). One possible reason is that the actual prices of individual items included in variable overhead (such as utilities cost) are lower than the budgeted prices. A second possible reason is that the percentage increase in the actual quantity usage of individual items in the variable overhead cost pool is less than the percentage increase in machine-hours compared to the flexible budget.
   b. VMOH efficiency variance ($240,000 U). One possible reason is inadequate maintenance of laser machines, causing them to take more laser time per panel. A second possible reason is use of less-trained workers with the laser-cutting machines, resulting in longer laser time per panel.
   c. FMOH rate variance ($32,200 U). One possible reason is that the actual prices of individual items in the fixed-cost pool unexpectedly increased from those budgeted (such as an unexpected increase in the manager's salary). Overhead also includes maintenance supplies and labour, inspection labour, taxes, and insurance costs. It could be that an unanticipated increase in taxes or inspection time caused the rate variance for the month.
   d. Production-volume variance ($72,000 U). Actual production of panels is 4,800 units compared with the 5,000 units budgeted. One possible reason is demand factors,

Exhibit 8-12 Columnar Presentation of Integrated Variance Analysis: Laser Products

PANEL A: VARIABLE MANUFACTURING OVERHEAD

Actual Costs Incurred (1)	Actual Inputs × Budgeted Rate (2)	Flexible Budget: Budgeted Input Allowed for Actual Output × Budgeted Rate (3)	Allocated: Budgeted Input Allowed for Actual Output × Budgeted Rate (4)
(8,400 × $176)	(8,400 × $200)	(4,800 × 1.5 × $200) (7,200 × $200) $1,440,000	(4,800 × 1.5 × $200) (7,200 × $200) $1,440,000
$1,478,400	$1,680,000		

$201,600 F
Rate variance

$240,000 U
Efficiency variance

Production-volume variance
(Never a variance)

$38,400 U
Flexible-budget variance

Production-volume variance
(Never a variance)

PANEL B: FIXED MANUFACTURING OVERHEAD

Actual Costs Incurred (1)	Same Lump Sum (as in Static Budget) Regardless of Budgeted Output Level (2)	Flexible Budget: Same Lump Sum (as in Static Budget) Regardless of Budgeted Output Level (3)	Allocated: Budgeted Input Allowed for Actual Output × Budgeted Rate (4)
			(4,800 × 1.5 × $240) (7,200 × $240) $1,728,000
$1,832,200	$1,800,000	$1,800,000	

$32,200 U
Rate variance

Efficiency variance
(Never a variance)

$72,000 U
Production-volume variance

$32,200 U
Flexible-budget variance

$72,000 U
Production-volume variance

such as a decline in the aerospace program that led to a decline in the demand for panels. What is known with certainty is that the use of the laser time exceeded what would have been budgeted for 4,800 panels. An actual inefficiency may have caused this increased consumption of laser-hours or the company could have chosen an inappropriate denominator level. The increased use of laser-hours could have several causes, from ill-trained operators who took more time and caused waste to an improperly functioning machine. It may also have been a smart decision by the company not to produce 5,000 panels if quality control was an issue or if demand had fallen.

4. Laser Products is already measuring nonfinancial variables when it measures the actual quantity consumed of the cost allocation base. Other nonfinancial variables that could be important would depend upon the competitive environment. If, for example, the environment is becoming increasingly competitive, Laser Products may

want to plan ways of becoming more agile. For a manufacturing company, this could involve cross-training equipment operators, and some measure of hours of training would be needed. As those purchasing Laser Products parts become more demanding and request more customization, the company may choose to analyze the types of customers it may be able to serve according to the attributes of the products they demand such as physical size, fragility, complexity, and so on.

5. Customers for exterior panels are unlikely to have an affective response to receiving these products. They are focused on how useful the product is, how well it meets engineering specifications, and if it is delivered on time within the costs stated in the contract. These are cognitive measures of customer satisfaction appropriate to this manufacturing setting.

Decision Points

The following question-and-answer format summarizes the chapter's learning objectives. Each point presents a key question, and the guidelines are the answer to that question.

Learning Objectives	Guidelines
1. How do managers budget pro forma fixed overhead cost rates and analyze fixed overhead variances?	Managers combine internal experience and external information about competitors to set a budgeted cost rate per unit of equipment input. They estimate the quantity of input needed to produce a single output unit to calculate an overhead cost rate per output unit. Fixed cost variances can arise from unforeseen changes in items such as taxes or salaries of production supervisors. The former is persistent and uncontrollable; the latter is usually temporary and controllable. Production volume variance is an opportunity cost of poor capacity management that reports a misallocation of overhead fixed costs to output units actually made.
2. How do managers analyze and interpret variable overhead variances?	Variable overhead variances reflect a difference in the actual compared to the pro forma relationship between variable costs of shared resources and the benefits to distinctive outputs from sharing resources. Either the budgeted cost per unit of shared resource or the quantity of benefit to the output unit, or both, differed from actual amounts.
3. Can the flexible-budget variance approach for analyzing overhead costs be used in activity-based costing?	Flexible budgeting in ABC systems gives insight into why actual overhead activity costs differ from budgeted overhead activity costs. The relationship remains one between the cost for shared activities and a measure of benefit to the output unit.
4. How does increasing detail of variance analyses help reconcile actual with budgeted overhead costs?	A four-variance analysis presents rate and efficiency variances for variable overhead costs, as well as rate and production-volume variances for fixed overhead costs. By analyzing these variances together, managers can reconcile the actual overhead costs with the amount of overhead allocated to output produced during a period.
	Indirect cost pools can also be separated by either business function or department, and separate cost allocation bases selected. These are two alternatives to using ABC to refine costing systems.
5. Of what use are nonfinancial and non-manufacturing performance measures?	Increasingly, companies must simultaneously manage costs, quality, customization, and timely delivery. The separation of cost from value leadership by differentiating either products or outputs will not accomplish this goal. Nonfinancial measures of customer satisfaction and comparisons to some pro forma amounts are relevant to important management decisions that will affect revenue.

Terms to Learn

This chapter and the Glossary at the end of the book contain definitions of the following important terms:

agility **(p. 313)**

BEP in revenue **(p. 291)**

BEP in units **(p. 291)**

capacity **(p. 292)**

capacity cost **(p. 292)**

combined-variance analysis **(p. 311)**

denominator-level variance **(p. 295)**

non-value-added cost **(p. 312)**

output-level overhead variance
 (p. 295)

production denominator level **(p. 293)**

production-volume variance **(p. 295)**

value-added cost **(p. 312)**

value proposition **(p. 312)**

variable overhead efficiency
 variance **(p. 302)**

variable overhead rate variance **(p. 302)**

volume **(p. 293)**

Assignment Material

MyLab Accounting Make the grade with MyLab Accounting: The Short-Answer Questions, Exercises, and Problems marked with a ⊕ can be found on MyLab Accounting. You can practise them as often as you want, and most feature step-by-step guided instructions to help you find the right answer.

Short-Answer Questions

⊕ **8-1** How do managers plan for variable overhead costs?

⊕ **8-2** How does the planning of fixed overhead costs differ from the planning of variable overhead costs?

⊕ **8-3** How do standard and actual costing differ?

⊕ **8-4** What are the steps in developing a budgeted variable overhead cost allocation rate?

⊕ **8-5** The rate variance for VMOH is affected by several factors. Explain.

⊕ **8-6** Assume VMOH is allocated using machine-hours. Give three possible reasons for a $30,000 favourable variable overhead efficiency variance.

⊕ **8-7** Describe the difference between a direct materials efficiency variance and a VMOH efficiency variance.

⊕ **8-8** What are the steps in developing a budgeted fixed overhead rate?

⊕ **8-9** Why is the flexible-budget variance the same amount as the rate variance for FMOH?

⊕ **8-10** Explain how the analysis of fixed overhead costs differs for (a) planning and control on the one hand and (b) inventory costing for financial reporting on the other.

⊕ **8-11** Provide one caution that will affect whether a production-volume variance is a good measure of the economic cost of unused capacity.

⊕ **8-12** The production-volume variance should always be written off to "Cost of Goods Sold." Do you agree? Explain.

⊕ **8-13** Explain how four-variance analysis differs from one-, two-, and three-variance analysis.

⊕ **8-14** "Overhead variances should be viewed as interdependent rather than independent." Give an example.

Exercises

⊕ **8-15 Terminology.** A number of terms are listed below:

agility	value-added cost
capacity	capacity cost
non-value-added cost	denominator-level variance
fixed overhead rate variance	production-volume variance
variable overhead efficiency variance	variable overhead rate variance

Required

Select the terms from the above list to complete the following sentences.

Interpretation of variances strategically means management teams must place their internal performance relative to their competitors and to what their customers value. Decisions about _____ incur _____ of ownership and maintenance for the long term. To the customer, however, the cost of unused capacity is a _____ for which they will not pay. This cost arises because the quantity produced is less than the capacity available. The cost is fixed; therefore, the burden assigned to each actual unit produced is higher than it should be. This unfavourable outcome is a _____. It is also referred to as the _____ and is an underallocation of capacity costs that will persist until consumer demand, actual production, and available capacity intersect. But fixed costs also include contractual costs such as salaries and regulatory costs of taxes. These costs can change unexpectedly and will result in a _____. Equipment also requires maintenance that, along with custodial and security costs, are required and shared resources that benefit all outputs. When the actual measure of benefit provided exceeds the budget, what arises is an unfavourable _____. When the actual cost per unit of benefit provided exceeds budget, there arises an unfavourable _____. Both are underallocations of variable overhead cost.

🌐 **8-16 Variable manufacturing overhead, variance analysis.** Young Clothing is a manufacturer of designer suits. The cost of each suit is the sum of three variable costs (direct materials costs, direct manufacturing labour costs, and manufacturing overhead costs) and one fixed-cost category (manufacturing overhead costs). VMOH cost is allocated to each suit based on budgeted direct manufacturing labour-hours (DMLH) per suit. For June 2018, each suit is budgeted to take 4 labour-hours. Budgeted VMOH costs per labour-hour are $12.00. The budgeted number of suits to be manufactured in June 2018 is 1,040.

Actual VMOH costs in June 2018 were $53,298 for 1,080 suits started and completed. There was no beginning or ending inventory of suits. Actual DMLH for June were 4,536.

◀ **LO 2**
1. Flexible-budget variance, $324 U

Required

1. Calculate the flexible-budget variance, the rate variance, and the efficiency variance for VMOH.
2. Comment on the results.

🌐 **8-17 Fixed manufacturing overhead variance analysis** (continuation of 8-16). Young Clothing allocates FMOH to each suit using budgeted DMLH per suit. Data pertaining to FMOH costs for June 2018 are $62,400 budgeted and $63,916 actual.

◀ **LO 1**
1. Rate variance, $1,516 U

Required

1. Calculate the rate variance for FMOH. Comment on these results.
2. Calculate the production-volume variance for June 2018. What inferences can Young Clothing draw from this variance?
3. Calculate the over- or underallocated FMOH. What does this tell the management about June's performance?

🌐 **8-18 Variable manufacturing overhead, variance analysis.** Esquire Clothing is a manufacturer of designer suits. The cost of each suit is the sum of three variable costs (direct material costs, direct manufacturing labour costs, and manufacturing overhead costs) and one fixed-cost category (manufacturing overhead costs). Variable manufacturing overhead cost is allocated to each suit on the basis of budgeted direct manufacturing labour-hours per suit. For June 2017, each suit is budgeted to take 4 labour-hours. Budgeted variable manufacturing overhead cost per labour-hour is $12. The budgeted number of suits to be manufactured in June 2017 is 1,040.

Actual variable manufacturing costs in June 2017 were $52,164 for 1,080 suits started and completed. There were no beginning or ending inventories of suits. Actual direct manufacturing labour-hours for June were 4,536.

◀ **LO 1, 2**
Flexible Budget Variance $324 U

Required

1. Compute the flexible-budget variance, the spending variance, and the efficiency variance for variable manufacturing overhead.
2. Comment on the results.

🌐 **8-19 Fixed manufacturing overhead variance analysis.** The Lebanese Bakery Inc. also allocates FMOH to products on the basis of standard direct manufacturing labour-hours. For 2018, FMOH was budgeted at $4.00 per DMLH. Actual FMOH incurred during the year was $272,000.

Baguettes are baked in batches of 100 loaves. Following are some pertinent data for Lebanese Bakery Inc.:

◀ **LO 1**
1. Rate variance, $35,200 F

Direct manufacturing labour use	2.00 DMLH per batch
Fixed manufacturing overhead	$4.00 per DMLH

Lebanese Bakery Inc. recorded the following additional data for the year ended December 31,2018:

Planned (budgeted) output	3,840,000 baguettes
Actual production	3,360,000 baguettes
Direct manufacturing labour	50,400 DMLH
Actual fixed MOH	$272,000

Required

1. Prepare a variance analysis of FMOH costs.
2. Is fixed overhead under- or overallocated? By how much?
3. Comment on your results. Discuss the various variances, and explain what may be driving them.

LO 1, 2 ▶

1. Variable MOH rate variance
= $90 U

🌐 **8-20 Manufacturing overhead, variance analysis.** G-Force Corporation is a manufacturer of centrifuges. Fixed and VMOH cost pools are allocated to each centrifuge using budgeted assembly-hours. Budgeted assembly time is two hours per unit. The following table shows the budgeted amounts and actual results related to overhead for June 2018.

G-Force Corporation (June 2018)	Actual Results	Static Budget
Number of centrifuges assembled and sold	216	200
Hours of assembly time	411	
Variable manufacturing overhead cost per hour of assembly time		$ 30.00
Variable manufacturing overhead costs	$12,420	
Fixed manufacturing overhead costs	$20,560	$19,200

Required

1. Prepare an analysis of all VMOH and FMOH variances using the columnar approach in Exhibit 8-11.
2. Prepare journal entries for G-Force's June 2018 variable and FMOH costs and variances; write off these variances to COGS for the quarter ended June 30, 2018.
3. How does the planning and control of VMOH costs differ from the planning and control of FMOH costs?

LO 1, 2 ▶

1. Variable MOH rate variance,
$4,200 U

🌐 **8-21 Four-variance analysis, fill in the blanks.** Pandom Inc. produces chemicals for large biotech companies. It has the following data for manufacturing overhead costs during August 2018:

	Variable	Fixed
Actual costs incurred	$35,700	$18,000
Costs allocated to products	27,000	14,400
Flexible budget: Budgeted input allowed for actual output produced × budgeted rate	27,000	15,000
Actual input × budgeted rate	31,500	15,000

Required

Fill in the variances in the table below. Use F for favourable and U for unfavourable.

	Variable	Fixed
1. Rate variance	$_____	$_____
2. Efficiency variance	$_____	$_____
3. Production-volume variance	$_____	$_____
4. Flexible-budget variance	$_____	$_____
5. Underallocated (overallocated) manufacturing overhead	$_____	$_____

LO 4 ▶

1. Variable MOH rate variance,
$17,800 U

🌐 **8-22 Straightforward four-variance overhead analysis.** Singh Company uses a standard cost system in its manufacturing plant for auto parts. The standard cost of a particular auto part, based on a denominator level of 4,000 output units per year, included 6 machine-hours of VMOH at $8 per hour and 6 machine-hours of FMOH at $15 per hour. Actual output achieved was 4,400 units. VMOH incurred was $245,000. FMOH incurred was $373,000. Actual incurred machine-hours were 28,400.

Required

1. Prepare an analysis of all VMOH and FMOH variances, using the four-variance analysis in Exhibit 8-11.
2. Prepare journal entries using the four-variance analysis.
3. Describe how individual VMOH items are controlled from day to day. Also, describe how individual FMOH items are controlled.

8-23 Straightforward coverage of manufacturing overhead, standard cost system. The Singapore division of a Canadian telecommunications company uses a standard cost system for its machine-based production of telephone equipment. Data regarding production during June are as follows:

◀ LO 4
1. Variable MOH rate variance, $43,704 F

Variable manufacturing overhead costs incurred	$186,120
Variable manufacturing overhead costs allocated (per standard machine-hour allowed for actual output achieved)	$ 14.40
Fixed manufacturing overhead costs incurred	$481,200
Fixed manufacturing overhead budgeted	$468,000
Denominator level in machine-hours	15,600
Standard machine-hours allowed per unit of output	0.30
Units of output	49,200
Actual machine-hours used	15,960
Ending work-in-process inventory	0

Required

1. Prepare an analysis of all manufacturing overhead variances. Use the four-variance analysis framework illustrated in Exhibit 8-11.
2. Prepare journal entries for manufacturing overhead without explanations.
3. Describe how individual VMOH items are controlled from day to day. Also, describe how individual FMOH items are controlled.

8-24 Overhead variances, service sector. Meals on Wheels (MOW) operates a meal home-delivery service. It has agreements with 20 restaurants to pick up and deliver meals to customers who phone or fax orders to MOW. MOW allocates variable and fixed overhead costs on the basis of delivery time. MOW's owner, Josh Carter, obtains the following information for May 2018 overhead costs:

◀ LO 1, 2
1. Variable MOH rate variance, $1,716 U

Meals on Wheels (May 2018)	Actual Results	Static Budget
Output units (number of deliveries)	8,800	10,000
Hours per delivery		0.70
Hours of delivery time	5,720	
Variable overhead cost per hour of delivery time		$ 1.50
Variable overhead costs	$10,296	
Fixed overhead costs	$38,600	$35,000

Required

1. Calculate rate and efficiency variances for MOW's variable overhead in May 2018.
2. Calculate the rate variance and production-volume variance for MOW's fixed overhead in May 2018.
3. Comment on MOW's overhead variances, and suggest how Josh Carter might manage MOW's variable overhead differently from its fixed overhead costs.

8-25 Manufacturing overhead, variance analysis. The Rotations Corporation is a manufacturer of centrifuges. Fixed and variable manufacturing overheads are allocated to each centrifuge using budgeted assembly-hours. Budgeted assembly time is 2 hours per unit. The following table shows the budgeted amounts and actual results related to overhead for June 2017.

◀ LO 4
Static Budget Fixed mfg. overhead costs per hour of assembly time = $47.00

	A	B	C	D	E	F Actual Results	G Static Budget
1	The Rotations Corporation (June 2017)					Actual Results	Static Budget
2	Number of centrifuges assembled and sold					220	150
3	Hours of assembly time					396	
4	Variable manufacturing overhead cost per hour of assembly time						$ 31.00
5	Variable manufacturing overhead costs					$12,693	
6	Fixed manufacturing overhead costs					$15,510	$14,100

Required

1. Prepare an analysis of all variable manufacturing overhead and fixed manufacturing overhead variances using the columnar approach in Exhibit 8-4 (page 296).
2. Prepare journal entries for Rotations' June 2017 variable and fixed manufacturing overhead costs and variances; write off these variances to Cost of Goods Sold for the quarter ending June 30, 2017.
3. How does the planning and control of variable manufacturing overhead costs differ from the planning and control of fixed manufacturing overhead costs?

LO 4 ▶
1. Variable MOH rate (spending) variance, $375

⊕ **8-26 4-variance analysis, fill in the blanks.** ProChem, Inc., produces chemicals for large biotech companies. It has the following data for manufacturing overhead costs during August 2017:

	Variable	Fixed
Actual costs incurred	$35,000	$16,500
Costs allocated to products	36,000	15,200
Flexible budget	_____	16,000
Actual input × budgeted rate	31,500	_____

Required

Fill in the blanks. Use F for favourable and U for unfavourable:

	Variable	Fixed
(1) Spending variance	$_____	$_____
(2) Efficiency variance	_____	_____
(3) Production-volume variance	_____	_____
(4) Flexible-budget variance	_____	_____
(5) Underallocated (overallocated) manufacturing overhead	_____	_____

LO 4 ▶
First scenario: Variable overhead rate variance, cannot be determined

⊕ **8-27 Identifying favourable and unfavourable variances.** Purdue Inc. manufactures tires for large auto companies. It uses standard costing and allocates variable and FMOH based on machine-hours.

Required

For each independent scenario given, indicate whether each of the manufacturing variances will be favourable or unfavourable or, in case of insufficient information, indicate "cannot be determined."

Scenario	Variable Overhead Rate Variance	Variable Overhead Efficiency Variance	Fixed Overhead Rate Variance	Fixed Overhead Production-Volume Variance
Production output is 5% more than budgeted, and actual FMOH costs are 6% more than budgeted				
Production output is 10% more than budgeted; actual machine-hours are 5% less than budgeted				
Production output is 8% less than budgeted				
Actual machine-hours are 15% greater than flexible-budget machine-hours				
Relative to the flexible budget, actual machine-hours are 10% greater, and actual variable manufacturing overhead costs are 15% greater				

LO 4 ▶
Fixed Manufacturing Overhead Spending Variance = $500 U

⊕ **8-28 Flexible-budget variances, review of Chapters 7 and 8.** Eric Williams is a cost accountant and business analyst for Diamond Design Company (DDC), which manufactures expensive brass doorknobs. DDC uses two direct-cost categories: direct materials and direct manufacturing labour. Williams feels that manufacturing overhead is most closely related to material usage. Therefore, DDC allocates manufacturing overhead to production based upon kilograms of materials used.

At the beginning of 2017, DDC budgeted annual production of 420,000 doorknobs and adopted the following standards for each doorknob:

	Input	Cost/Doorknob
Direct materials (brass)	0.3 kg @ $10/kg	$ 3.00
Direct manufacturing labour	1.2 hours @ $17/hour	20.40
Manufacturing overhead:		
Variable	$5/kg × 0.3 kg	1.50
Fixed	$15/kg × 0.3 kg	4.50
Standard cost per doorknob		$29.40

Actual results for April 2017 were as follows:

Production	29,000 doorknobs
Direct materials purchased	12,400 kg at $11/kg
Direct materials used	8,500 kg
Direct manufacturing labour	29,200 hours for $671,600
Variable manufacturing overhead	$ 65,100
Fixed manufacturing overhead	$158,000

Required

1. For the month of April, compute the following variances, indicating whether each is favourable (F) or unfavourable (U):
   a. Direct materials price variance (based on purchases)
   b. Direct materials efficiency variance
   c. Direct manufacturing labour price variance
   d. Direct manufacturing labour efficiency variance
   e. Variable manufacturing overhead spending variance
   f. Variable manufacturing overhead efficiency variance
   g. Production-volume variance
   h. Fixed manufacturing overhead spending variance
2. Can Williams use any of the variances to help explain any of the other variances? Give examples.

Problems

⊕ **8-29 Comprehensive variance analysis.** Magic Dice manufactures premium food processors. The following is some manufacturing overhead data for Magic Dice for the year ended December 31, 2018.

◀ **LO 4**
1. Budgeted DMH, 1,776

Manufacturing Overhead	Actual Results	Flexible Budget	Amount Allocated
Variable	$ 76,608	$ 76,800	$ 76,800
Fixed	350,208	348,096	376,320

Budgeted number of output units: 888
Planned allocation rate: 3 machine-hours per unit
Actual number of machine-hours used: 1,824
Static-budget variable manufacturing overhead costs: $71,040

Required

Calculate the following quantities (you should be able to do so in the prescribed order):

1. Budgeted number of machine-hours planned.
2. Budgeted FMOH costs per machine-hour.
3. Budgeted VMOH costs per machine-hour.
4. Budgeted number of machine-hours allowed for actual output achieved.
5. Actual number of output units.
6. Actual number of machine-hours used per output unit.

LO 1, 2, 4 ▶   ⊕ **8-30 Journal entries** (continuation of 8-29). Refer to Problem 8-29.

Required

1. Prepare journal entries for VMOH and FMOH (you will need to calculate the various variances to accomplish this).
2. Overhead variances are written off to the COGS account at the end of the fiscal year. Show how COGS is adjusted through journal entries.

LO 1, 2 ▶

2. Variable MOH rate variance, $475,000 U

⊕ **8-31 Graphs and overhead variances.** Fresh Inc. is a manufacturer of vacuums and uses standard costing. Manufacturing overhead (both variable and fixed) is allocated to products on the basis of budgeted machine-hours. In 2018, budgeted FMOH cost was $18,000,000. Budgeted VMOH was $9 per machine-hour. The denominator level was 1,000,000 machine-hours.

Required

1. Prepare a graph for FMOH. The graph should display how Fresh Inc.'s FMOH costs will be depicted for the purposes of (a) planning and control and (b) inventory costing.
2. Suppose that 875,000 machine-hours were allowed for actual output produced in 2018, but 950,000 actual machine-hours were used. Actual manufacturing overhead was $9,025,000, variable, and $18,050,000, fixed. Calculate (a) the VMOH rate and efficiency variances and (b) the FMOH rate and production-volume variances. Use the columnar presentation illustrated in Exhibit 8-11.
3. What is the amount of the under- or overallocated VMOH and the under- or overallocated FMOH? Why are the flexible-budget variance and the under- or overallocated overhead amount always the same for VMOH but rarely the same for FMOH?
4. Suppose the denominator level were 750,000 rather than 1,000,000 machine-hours. What variances in requirement 2 would be affected? Recalculate them.

LO 1 ▶   ⊕ **8-32 Variable manufacturing overhead variance analysis.** The Sourdough Bread Company bakes baguettes for distribution to upscale grocery stores. The company has two direct-cost categories: direct materials and direct manufacturing labour. Variable manufacturing overhead is allocated to products on the basis of standard direct manufacturing labour-hours. Following is some budget data for the Sourdough Bread Company:

Direct manufacturing labour use	0.02 hours per baguette
Variable manufacturing overhead	$10.00 per direct manufacturing labour-hour

The Sourdough Bread Company provides the following additional data for the year ended December 31, 2017:

Planned (budgeted) output	3,100,000 baguettes
Actual production	2,600,000 baguettes
Direct manufacturing labour	46,800 hours
Actual variable manufacturing overhead	$617,760

Required

1. What is the denominator level used for allocating variable manufacturing overhead? (That is, for how many direct manufacturing labour-hours is Sourdough Bread budgeting?)
2. Prepare a variance analysis of variable manufacturing overhead. Use Exhibit 8-4 (page 296) for reference.
3. Discuss the variances you have calculated and give possible explanations for them.

LO 1 ▶   ⊕ **8-33 Fixed manufacturing overhead variance analysis** (continuation of 8-32). The Sourdough Bread Company also allocates fixed manufacturing overhead to products on the basis of standard direct manufacturing labour-hours. For 2017, fixed manufacturing overhead was budgeted at $3.00 per direct manufacturing labour-hour. Actual fixed manufacturing overhead incurred during the year was $294,000.

Required

1. Prepare a variance analysis of fixed manufacturing overhead cost. Use Exhibit 8-4 (page 296) as a guide.
2. Is fixed overhead underallocated or overallocated? By what amount?
3. Comment on your results. Discuss the variances and explain what may be driving them.

LO 2 ▶   ⊕ **8-34 Overhead variances, service sector.** Meals Made Easy (MME) operates a meal home-delivery service. It has agreements with 20 restaurants to pick up and deliver meals to customers who place orders

Meals Made Easy (May 2017)	Actual Results	Static Budget
Output units (number of deliveries)	8,750	13,000
Hours per delivery		0.70
Hours of delivery time	5,600	
Variable overhead cost per hour of delivery time		$1.60
Variable overhead costs	$10,640	
Fixed overhead costs	$39,200	$36,400

(Excel spreadsheet: Home, Insert, Page Layout, Formulas, Data, Review; columns A, B, C; rows 1–7)

on MME's website. MME allocates variable and fixed overhead costs on the basis of delivery time. MME's owner, Thomas Stewart, obtains the following information for May 2017 overhead costs:

Required

1. Compute spending and efficiency variances for MME's variable overhead in May 2017.
2. Compute the spending variance and production-volume variance for MME's fixed overhead in May 2017.
3. Comment on MME's overhead variances and suggest how Thomas Stewart might manage MME's variable overhead differently from its fixed overhead costs.

8-35 Identifying favourable and unfavourable variances. Tred-America, Inc., manufactures tires for large auto companies. It uses standard costing and allocates variable and fixed manufacturing overhead based on machine-hours. For each independent scenario given, indicate whether each of the manufacturing variances will be favourable or unfavourable or, in case of insufficient information, indicate "CBD" (cannot be determined).

◀ LO 1, 2

Scenario	Variable Overhead Spending Variance	Variable Overhead Efficiency Variance	Fixed Overhead Spending Variance	Fixed Overhead Production-Volume Variance
Production output is 8% more than budgeted, and actual fixed manufacturing overhead costs are 7% less than budgeted				
Production output is 11% more than budgeted; actual machine-hours are 5% less than budgeted				
Production output is 15% less than budgeted				
Actual machine-hours are 18% greater than flexible-budget machine-hours				
Relative to the flexible budget, actual machine-hours are 10% greater, and actual variable manufacturing overhead costs are 15% less				

8-36 Activity-based costing, batch-level variance analysis. Amir's Fleet Feet Inc. produces dance shoes for stores all over the world. While the pairs of shoes are boxed individually, they are crated and shipped in batches. The shipping department records both variable and fixed overhead costs. The following information pertains to shipping costs for 2018.

◀ LO 3

1. Static-budget number of crates, 20,000

	Static-Budget Amounts	Actual Results
Pairs of shoes shipped	240,000	180,000
Average number of pairs of shoes per crate	12	10
Packing hours per crate	1.2 hours	1 hours
Variable overhead cost per hour	$ 20	$ 21
Fixed overhead cost	$60,000	$55,000

Required

1. What is the static-budget number of crates for 2018?
2. What is the flexible-budget number of crates for 2018?
3. What is the actual number of crates shipped in 2018?
4. Assuming fixed overhead is allocated using crate-packing hours, what is the predetermined fixed overhead allocation rate?
5. For variable overhead costs, calculate the rate and efficiency variances.
6. For fixed overhead costs, calculate the rate and the production-volume variances.

LO 3 ▶

1. Static-budget number of setups, 400

● **8-37 Activity-based costing, batch-level variance analysis.** Jo Nathan Publishing Company specializes in printing specialty textbooks for a small but profitable college market. Due to the high setup costs for each batch printed, Jo Nathan holds the book requests until demand for a book is approximately 500. At that point Jo Nathan will schedule the setup and production of the book. For rush orders, Jo Nathan will produce smaller batches for an additional charge of $700 per setup.

Budgeted and actual costs for the printing process for 2018 were

	Static-Budget Amounts	Actual Results
Number of books produced	200,000	216,000
Average number of books per setup	500	480
Hours to set up printers	6 hours	6.5 hours
Variable overhead cost per setup-hour	$ 100	$ 90
Total fixed setup overhead costs	$72,000	$79,000

Required

1. What is the static-budget number of setups for 2018?
2. What is the flexible-budget number of setups for 2018?
3. What is the actual number of setups in 2018?
4. Assuming fixed setup overhead costs are allocated using setup-hours, what is the predetermined fixed setup overhead allocation rate?
5. Does Jo Nathan's charge of $700 cover the budgeted variable overhead cost of an order? The budgeted total overhead cost?
6. For variable setup overhead costs, calculate the rate and efficiency variances.
7. For fixed setup overhead costs, calculate the rate and the production-volume variances.
8. What qualitative factors should Jo Nathan consider before accepting or rejecting a special order?

LO 4 ▶

● **8-38 Production-volume variance analysis and sales-volume variance.** Chart Hills Company makes customized golf shirts for sale to golf courses. Each shirt requires 3 hours to produce because of the customized logo for each golf course. Chart Hills uses direct labour-hours to allocate the overhead cost to production. Fixed overhead costs, including rent, depreciation, supervisory salaries, and other production expenses, are budgeted at $28,500 per month. The facility currently used is large enough to produce 5,000 shirts per month.

During March, Chart Hills produced 4,200 shirts and actual fixed costs were $28,000.

Required

1. Calculate the fixed overhead spending variance and indicate whether it is favourable (F) or unfavourable (U).
2. If Chart Hills uses direct labour-hours available at capacity to calculate the budgeted fixed overhead rate, what is the production-volume variance? Indicate whether it is favourable (F) or unfavourable (U).
3. An unfavourable production-volume variance could be interpreted as the economic cost of unused capacity. Why would Chart Hills be willing to incur this cost?
4. Chart Hills' budgeted variable cost per unit is $18, and it expects to sell its shirts for $35 apiece. Compute the sales-volume variance and reconcile it with the production-volume variance calculated in requirement 2. What does each concept measure?

LO 4 ▶

● **8-39 Flexible budgets, 4-variance analysis.** (CMA, adapted) Wilson Products uses standard costing. It allocates manufacturing overhead (both variable and fixed) to products on the basis of standard direct manufacturing labour-hours (DLH). Wilson Products develops its manufacturing overhead rate from the current annual budget. The manufacturing overhead budget for 2017 is based on budgeted output of 672,000 units, requiring 3,360,000 DLH. The company is able to schedule production uniformly throughout the year.

A total of 72,000 output units requiring 321,000 DLH was produced during May 2017. Manufacturing overhead (MOH) costs incurred for May amounted to $355,800. The actual costs, compared with the annual budget and 1/12 of the annual budget, are as follows:

Annual Manufacturing Overhead Budget 2017

	Total Amount	Per Output Unit	Per DLH Input Unit	Monthly MOH Budget May 2017	Actual MOH Costs for May 2017
Variable MOH					
Indirect manufacturing labour	$1,008,000	$1.50	$0.30	$ 84,000	$ 84,000
Supplies	672,000	1.00	0.20	56,000	117,000
Fixed MOH					
Supervision	571,200	0.85	0.17	47,600	41,000
Utilities	369,600	0.55	0.11	30,800	55,000
Depreciation	705,600	1.05	0.21	58,800	58,800
Total	$3,326,400	$4.95	$0.99	$277,200	$355,800

Calculate the following amounts for Wilson Products for May 2017:

Required

1. Total manufacturing overhead costs allocated
2. Variable manufacturing overhead spending variance
3. Fixed manufacturing overhead spending variance
4. Variable manufacturing overhead efficiency variance
5. Production-volume variance

Be sure to identify each variance as favourable (F) or unfavourable (U).

⊕ **8-40 Review of Chapters 7 and 8, three-variance analysis.** (CPA, adapted) Beal Manufacturing Company's costing system has two direct cost categories: direct materials and direct manufacturing labour. Manufacturing overhead (both variable and fixed) is allocated to products on the basis of standard DMLH. At the beginning of 2018, Beal adopted the following standards for its manufacturing costs:

◀ LO 4
2. a. Direct materials rate variance, $5,000 U

	Input	Cost per Output Unit
Direct materials	3 kg at $5 per kg	$ 15
Direct manufacturing labour	5 hours at $15 per hour	75
Manufacturing overhead:		
Variable	$6 per DMLH	30
Fixed	$8 per DMLH	40
Standard manufacturing cost per output unit		$160

The denominator level for total manufacturing overhead per month in 2018 is 40,000 DMLH. Beal's flexible budget for January 2018 was based on this denominator level. The records for January indicate the following:

Direct materials purchased	25,000 kg at $5.20/kg
Direct materials used	23,100 kg
Direct manufacturing labour	40,100 hours at $14.60/hour
Total actual manufacturing overhead (variable and fixed)	$600,000
Actual production	7,800 output units

Required

1. Prepare a schedule of total standard manufacturing costs for the 7,800 output units in January 2018.
2. For January 2018, calculate the following variances, indicating whether each is favourable (F) or unfavourable (U):
   a. Direct materials rate variance, based on purchases.
   b. Direct materials efficiency variance.

    c. Direct manufacturing labour rate variance.
    d. Direct manufacturing labour efficiency variance.
    e. Total manufacturing overhead rate variance.
    f. VMOH efficiency variance.
    g. Production-volume variance

LO 5 ▶
1. Efficiency Variance, 10 hrs U

⊕ **8-41 Nonfinancial and non-manufacturing variances.** Belle's Treats produces high-quality dog food distributed only through veterinary offices. To ensure that the food is of the highest quality and has taste appeal, Belle has a rigorous inspection process. For quality-control purposes, Belle has a standard based on the number of kilograms inspected per hour and the number of kilograms that pass or fail the inspection.

Belle expects that for every 10,000 kilograms of food produced, 1,000 kilograms of food will be inspected. Inspection of 1,000 kilograms of dog food should take 1 hour. Belle also expects that 2% of the food inspected will fail the inspection. During the month of May, Belle produced 2,250,000 kilograms of food and inspected 200,000 kilograms of food in 210 hours. Of the 200,000 kilograms of food inspected, 3,500 kilograms of food failed to pass the inspection.

Required

1. Calculate two variances that help determine whether the time spent on inspections was more or less than expected. (Follow a format similar to the one used for the variable overhead rate and efficiency variances, but without prices.)
2. Calculate two variances that can be used to evaluate the percentage of the food that fails the inspection.

LO 5 ▶

⊕ **8-42 Nonfinancial variances.** Kathy's Kettle Potato Chips produces gourmet chips distributed to chain sub shops throughout California. To ensure that their chips are of the highest quality and have taste appeal, Kathy has a rigorous inspection process. For quality control purposes, Kathy has a standard based on the number of kilograms of chips inspected per hour and the number of kilograms that pass or fail the inspection.

Kathy expects that for every 1,000 kilograms of chips produced, 200 kilograms of chips will be inspected. Inspection of 200 kilograms of chips should take 1 hour. Kathy also expects that 1% of the chips inspected will fail the inspection. During the month of May, Kathy produced 113,000 kilograms of chips and inspected 22,300 kilograms of chips in 120 hours. Of the 22,300 kilograms of chips inspected, 215 kilograms of chips failed to pass the inspection.

Required

1. Compute two variances that help determine whether the time spent on inspections was more or less than expected. (Follow a format similar to the one used for the variable overhead spending and efficiency variances, but without prices.)
2. Compute two variances that can be used to evaluate the percentage of the chips that fails the inspection.

LO 2 ▶
1. a. Budgeted fixed overhead,
$6,250,000

⊕ **8-43 Overhead variances, governance.** Levie Company uses standard costing. The company prepared its static budget for 2018 at 2,500,000 machine-hours for the year. Total budgeted overhead cost is $31,250,000. The variable overhead rate is $11 per machine-hour ($22 per unit). Actual results for 2018 follow:

Machine-hours	2,400,000 hours
Output	1,245,000 units
Variable overhead	$25,200,000
Fixed overhead rate variance	$ 1,500,000 U

Required

1. Calculate for the fixed overhead:
    a. Budgeted amount.
    b. Budgeted cost per machine-hour.
    c. Actual cost.
    d. Production-volume variance.
2. Calculate the variable overhead rate variance and the variable overhead efficiency variance.
3. Angela Remich, the controller, prepares the variance analysis. It is common knowledge in the company that she and Ronald Monroe, the production manager, are not on the best of terms. In a recent executive committee meeting, Monroe had complained about the lack of usefulness of the accounting reports he receives. To get back at him, Remich manipulated the actual fixed overhead amount by assigning a greater-than-normal share of allocated costs to the production area. And, she decided to amortize all of the newly acquired production equipment using the double-declining-balance method rather than the straight-line method, contrary to company practice. As a result, there was a sizable unfavourable fixed overhead rate variance. She boasted to one of her confidants, "I am just returning the favour." Discuss Remich's actions and their ramifications.

8-44 Activity-based costing, batch-level variance analysis. The Saluki Company specializes in making ◄ **LO 3**
fraternity and sorority T-shirts for the college market. Due to the high setup costs for each batch printed,
Saluki holds the T-shirt requests until demand is approximately 100 shirts. At that point Saluki will schedule
the setup and production of the shirts. For rush orders, Saluki will produce smaller batches for an additional
charge of $175 per setup.

Budgeted and actual costs for the production process for 2017 were as follows:

	Static-Budget Amounts	Actual Results
Number of shirts produced	125,000	114,000
Average number of shirts per setup	100	95
Hours to set up machines	5	5.20
Direct variable cost per setup-hour	$ 30	$ 32
Total fixed setup overhead costs	$56,250	$56,000

Required

1. What is the static budget number of setups for 2017?
2. What is the flexible-budget number of setups for 2017?
3. What is the actual number of setups in 2017?
4. Assuming fixed setup overhead costs are allocated using setup-hours, what is the predetermined fixed setup overhead allocation rate?
5. Does Saluki's charge of $175 cover the budgeted direct variable cost of an order? The budgeted total cost?
6. For direct variable setup costs, compute the price and efficiency variances.
7. For fixed setup overhead costs, compute the spending and the production-volume variances.
8. What qualitative factors should Saluki consider before accepting or rejecting a special order?

8-45 Activity-based costing, batch-level variance analysis. Audrina's Fleet Feet, Inc., produces dance ◄ **LO 3**
shoes for stores all over the world. While the pairs of shoes are boxed individually, they are crated and
shipped in batches. The shipping department records both variable direct batch-level costs and fixed batch-
level overhead costs. The following information pertains to shipping department costs for 2017.

	Static-Budget Amounts	Actual Results
Pairs of shoes shipped	225,000	180,000
Average number of pairs of shoes per crate	15	10
Packing hours per crate	0.9 hours	1.1 hour
Variable direct cost per hour	$ 18	$ 16
Fixed overhead cost	$54,000	$56,500

Required

1. What is the static budget number of crates for 2017?
2. What is the flexible budget number of crates for 2017?
3. What is the actual number of crates shipped in 2017?
4. Assuming fixed overhead is allocated using crate-packing hours, what is the predetermined fixed over-head allocation rate?
5. For variable direct batch-level costs, compute the price and efficiency variances.
6. For fixed overhead costs, compute the spending and the production-volume variances.

8-46 Overhead variance, missing information. Consider the following two situations—cases A and B—inde- ◄ **LO 4**
pendently. Data refer to operations for April 2017. For each situation, assume standard costing. Also assume
the use of a flexible budget for control of variable and fixed manufacturing overhead based on machine-hours.

		Cases	
		A	B
(1)	Fixed manufacturing overhead incurred	$27,000	$132,900
(2)	Variable manufacturing overhead incurred	$10,511	—
(3)	Denominator level in machine-hours	—	45,000
(4)	Standard machine-hours allowed for actual output achieved	4,700	—
(5)	Fixed manufacturing overhead (per standard machine-hour)	—	—

Flexible-Budget Data:

(6)	Variable manufacturing overhead (per standard machine-hour)	—	$ 2.10
(7)	Budgeted fixed manufacturing overhead	$23,375	$130,500
(8)	Budgeted variable manufacturing overhead[a]	—	—
(9)	Total budgeted manufacturing overhead[a]	—	—

Additional Data:

(10)	Standard variable manufacturing overhead allocated	$10,340	—
(11)	Standard fixed manufacturing overhead allocated	$19,975	—
(12)	Production-volume variance	—	$ 580 F
(13)	Variable manufacturing overhead spending variance	$ 457 U	$ 1,490 F
(14)	Variable manufacturing overhead efficiency variance	—	$ 1,680 F
(15)	Fixed manufacturing overhead spending variance	—	—
(16)	Actual machine-hours used	—	—

[a]For standard machine-hours allowed for actual output produced.

Required

Fill in the blanks under each case. [*Hint*: Prepare a worksheet similar to that in Exhibit 8-4 (page 296). Fill in the knowns and then solve for the unknowns.]

LO 4 ▶

⊕ **8-47 Graphs and overhead variances.** Best Around, Inc., is a manufacturer of vacuums and uses standard costing. Manufacturing overhead (both variable and fixed) is allocated to products on the basis of budgeted machine-hours. In 2017, budgeted fixed manufacturing overhead cost was $17,000,000. Budgeted variable manufacturing overhead was $10 per machine-hour. The denominator level was 1,000,000 machine-hours.

Required

1. Prepare a graph for fixed manufacturing overhead. The graph should display how Best Around, Inc.'s fixed manufacturing overhead costs will be depicted for the purposes of (a) planning and control and (b) inventory costing.
2. Suppose that 1,125,000 machine-hours were allowed for actual output produced in 2017, but 1,200,000 actual machine-hours were used. Actual manufacturing overhead was $12,075,000, variable, and $17,100,000, fixed. Compute (a) the variable manufacturing overhead spending and efficiency variances and (b) the fixed manufacturing overhead spending and production-volume variances. Use the columnar presentation illustrated in Exhibit 8-4 (page 296).
3. What is the amount of the under- or overallocated variable manufacturing overhead and the under- or overallocated fixed manufacturing overhead? Why are the flexible-budget variance and the under- or overallocated overhead amount always the same for variable manufacturing overhead but rarely the same for fixed manufacturing overhead?
4. Suppose the denominator level was 1,700,000 rather than 1,000,000 machine-hours. What variances in requirement 2 would be affected? Recompute them.

LO 1, 2 ▶

8-48 Overhead variances, ethics. Carpenter Company uses standard costing. The company has a manufacturing plant in Georgia. Standard labour-hours per unit are 0.50, and the variable overhead rate for the Georgia plant is $3.50 per direct labour-hour. Fixed overhead for the Georgia plant is budgeted at $1,800,000 for the year. Firm management has always used variance analysis as a performance measure for the plant.

Tom Saban has just been hired as a new controller for Carpenter Company. Tom is good friends with the Georgia plant manager and wants him to get a favourable review. Tom decides to underestimate production, and budgets annual output of 1,200,000 units. His explanation for this is that the economy is slowing and sales are likely to decrease.

At the end of the year, the plant reported the following actual results: output of 1,500,000 using 760,000 labour-hours in total, at a cost of $2,700,000 in variable overhead and $1,850,000 in fixed overhead.

Required

1. Compute the budgeted fixed cost per labour-hour for the fixed overhead.
2. Compute the variable overhead spending variance and the variable overhead efficiency variance.
3. Compute the fixed overhead spending and volume variances.
4. Compute the budgeted fixed cost per labour-hour for the fixed overhead if Tom Saban had estimated production more realistically at the expected sales level of 1,500,000 units.
5. Summarize the fixed overhead variance based on both the projected level of production of 1,200,000 units and 1,500,000 units.

6. Did Tom Saban's attempt to make his friend, the plant manager, look better work? Why or why not?
7. What do you think of Tom Saban's behaviour overall?

Mini-Case

8-49 Standard setting, benchmarking, governance. Ira Stone, is the president of General Hospital, a large metropolitan health-care complex that has had difficulty controlling its accounts receivable. Ira has a meeting with the Medical Economics Group (MEG). MEG is a consulting firm in the health services sector. It reports that General's costs currently available from the information system are inaccurate and have led to gross errors in reports to the various government funding agencies, which have indicated that the hospital appears to be operating at a deficit. In addition, billing operations are grossly inefficient. Its standard costing per bill is above 90% of the 130 hospitals MEG tracks in its benchmark.

◀ **LO 4**
1. 1,600 hours

The accountant of General Hospital provides Ira and MEG with the following for April 2018:

Variable overhead costs, allowance per standard hour	$ 12
Fixed overhead flexible budget variance	$ 240 F
Total budgeted overhead costs for the bills prepared	$ 27,000
Production-volume variance	$ 1,080 F
Variable cost rate variance	$ 2,400 U
Variable cost efficiency variance	$ 2,400 F
Standard hours allowed for the bills prepared	1,800 labour-hours

Ira suspects the billing group deliberately "padded" its standard costs and standard amounts. Despite large investment in new information systems, the standards for 2018 were not below actual results for 2014. He does not want to institute a witch hunt, but he does want to eliminate the excess in General's cost structure.

Required

1. Ira asks to have Meg calculate: Actual hours of input used; Fixed overhead budget; Fixed overhead allocated; Budgeted fixed overhead rate per hour; Denominator level in hours.
2. How might General's billing operations group have "padded" its standard costs and standard amounts? Why might they do this padding?
3. What steps should Stone take to "reduce the excess" in the overhead costs of the billing operations at General Hospital?

SOLUTION ◀ TRY IT!

Try It 8–1
The fixed overhead budget for the month is $3,200 (actual) − $2,910 (budgeted) = $290. It is an unfavourable variance as it will decrease operating income.

9

Income Effects of Denominator Level on Inventory Valuation

▶ Learning Objectives

1. Identify the factors important to choosing the denominator level used to calculate fixed overhead allocation rates.

2. Explain how the choice of denominator affects capacity management, costing, pricing, and performance evaluation.

3. Distinguish absorption costing from variable costing; prepare and explain the differences in operating income under each costing policy.

4. Appendix 9A: Distinguish throughput costing from variable costing and absorption costing, and explain differences in operating income under each costing policy.

5. Appendix 9B: Explain breakeven under each of the two costing policies.

▶ CPA Competencies

This chapter covers material outlined in **Section 3: Management Accounting** of the CPA Competency Map. The Learning Objectives in this chapter have been aligned with the CPA Competency Map to ensure the best coverage possible.

3.2.2 Prepares, analyzes, or evaluates operational plans, budgets, and forecasts

3.3.1 Evaluates cost classifications and costing methods for management of ongoing operations

3.3.2 Evaluates and applies cost management techniques appropriate for specific costing decisions

Capacity-Level Choices

Intel is a high-operating-leverage company. When it operates at full capacity, the higher the production output, the lower the fixed-cost rate per unit. There is, however, a limit or constraint on just how many chips Intel can produce without purchasing more capacity.

The cost of goods sold includes only the fixed costs of units sold, not units produced, and the difference remains in the valuation of work-in-process and finished goods inventory. The decision about what capacity will be in the denominator level used to calculate the fixed-cost manufacturing overhead rate affects the reported operating income because it affects both the inventory values and cost of goods sold.

In this chapter we examine the capacity choices available to managers who decide on the denominator level used to calculate fixed overhead rates. Managers' capacity choice is called the denominator level. This decision affects product costing and pricing, capacity management, governance (compliance with external reporting regulations), and performance evaluation. This is one of the most strategically important and complex decisions managers face.

The decision to acquire too much capacity relative to demand will incur idle, unproductive capacity costs that often cannot be recovered. Too little capacity relative to demand means companies will incur the opportunity cost of lost market share as competitors serve their customers, who may never return.

Denominator Levels: A Complex Decision with Complex Effects

There are four choices for the denominator-level decision. The first two choices define the denominator based on the firm's ability to supply output.

> ▶ **LO 1**
>
> Identify the factors important to choosing the denominator level used to calculate fixed overhead allocation rates.

- **Theoretical capacity** is the amount of output theoretically possible if there were never any delays or interruptions in production—a 24/7/365 quantity.
- **Practical capacity** is the amount of output practically possible after taking into account required idle time for maintenance, safety inspections, holidays, and other relevant factors.

Theoretical capacity must always be greater than practical capacity because practical capacity excludes any volume lost through idle time.

The following two denominator-level choices define output based on the existing demand level for the output:

- **Normal capacity** is the level of output that will satisfy average customer demand over a specified time period and complies with ASPE/IFRS.
- **Master-budget capacity** is the level of output that will satisfy customer demand for a single budget cycle and complies with Canada Revenue Agency (CRA) for tax purposes.

Exhibit 9-1 illustrates the four potential choices of capacity and the implications of using each capacity option as the denominator level. The decision process itself is in purple, and there are two pairs of denominator-level choices: The pair of choices based on production capacity is illustrated in blue, and the pair based on demand factors is in gold.

The issues arising from the selection of the denominator level based on either a supply or demand measure of capacity affect both the statement of financial position and the statement of comprehensive income. Although high-operating-leverage companies rely more heavily on machines (or capital) than labour in the production process, the capacity level will also entail changes to labour supply.

Assume that managers have good business intelligence about the level of demand (market size) in the industry and how well their competitors perform (market share). The first decision is whether to acquire all the forecast capacity required to supply growth in the company's market share or to make acquisitions as the need arises. Bear in mind that most capacity is purchased in large increments (such as the addition of a new production line, plant, division, etc.) on the basis that it will provide net cash inflow from sales of output. This will sum to a return on investment over the useful life of the capacity. This means, for acquisition purposes, that capacity costs are semifixed. The demand, however, is usually a continuous growth curve that peaks, then tapers off as the life cycle of the product ends. There is no perfect capacity choice to ensure a perfect denominator level because the behaviours of fixed costs, demand, and inventory values differ.

Managers have two sets of objectives to consider—capacity management and performance evaluation—and four different capacity measures to choose from—theoretical, practical, normal, and master-budget capacity. Bushells Company produces labelled bottles of iced tea for Tazo. The company uses absorption costing (discussed below) for

Exhibit 9-1 Stage in the Denominator Level Choice Process

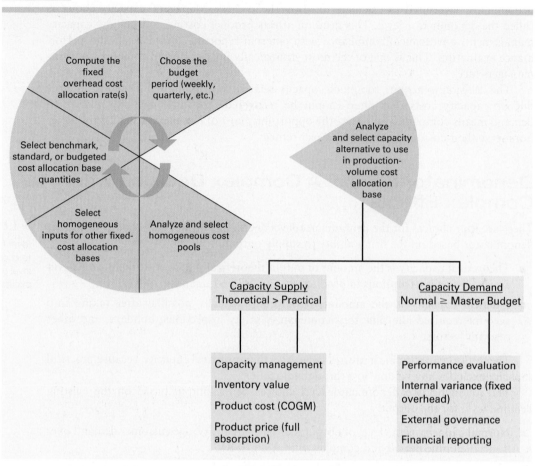

monthly internal reporting and for financial reporting to shareholders. Capacity is measured as bottles of iced tea. The management team determines that for external reporting purposes there is no choice. The denominator required by CRA when fixed costs are allocated to cost of goods sold and inventory is the denominator used for financial accounting purposes. Income tax rules effectively prohibit using either theoretical capacity or practical capacity denominator levels. Both would typically result in companies taking write-offs of fixed manufacturing overhead as tax deductions more quickly than desired by the CRA. On the other hand, both ASPE and IFRS[1] require that *normal* capacity must be the denominator used.

Notice that two of the choices are measures of supply of capacity and two are measures of demand by customers. The quantity demanded by customers will influence the amount of unused capacity. Exhibit 9-2 illustrates this. The blue dashed line is a stepped or discontinuous capacity. The curved gold line is the demand assumed over time for the product life cycle. The different patterns make it unlikely that the lines will intersect. This means that corporations will almost always have a production-volume variance. For internal management purposes, the dollar value of that production-volume variance will depend on the capacity measure—the denominator level—chosen by managers.

Notice in Exhibit 9-2 that the distance between the demand curve and the semifixed capacity visually represents the presence of production-volume variance. This relationship implies that the company has decided the cost of excess capacity is preferable to the opportunity cost of being unable to meet demand.

---

[1] ASPE 3031.14 and IAS 2.13 state that "allocation of fixed production overheads ... is based on the normal capacity of the production facilities." The authors thank Alison Parker of Camosun College, Victoria, BC, for her insight into this area of financial accounting standards.

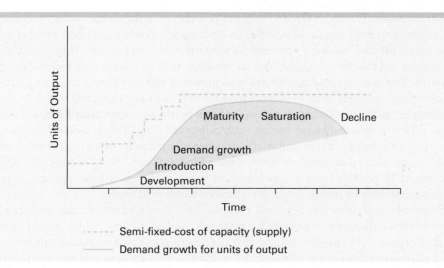

Exhibit 9-2 The Product Life Cycle, Capacity Planning, and Production-Volume Variance

Source: Based on P. Kotler and G. Armstrong, *Principles of Marketing*, 13th ed. (Toronto: Prentice Hall, 2010), p. 397.

The Decision Framework and Denominator Choice

Step 1: Identify the Problem and Uncertainties At Bushells, top management identifies the issue as needing to decide on an appropriate denominator level for pricing and *internal* performance evaluation (since the denominator level for *external* ASPE/IFRS reporting is *normal* capacity).

Step 2: Obtain Information Through gathering information, Bushells knows that the variable manufacturing costs of each bottle are $0.35. The fixed monthly costs of manufacturing at the bottling plant are $50,000. Bushells can produce 2,400 bottles per hour when the line operates at full speed. The labour union has negotiated a maximum of two eight-hour shifts per day. The constraint on use of direct manufacturing labour-hours reduces the potential output for the plant.

Supply Measures: Theoretical Capacity or Practical Capacity?

Theoretical capacity is theoretical in the sense that it does not allow for any plant maintenance or interruptions from bottle breakages on the filling lines or a host of other factors. Although it is a rare plant that is able to operate at theoretical capacity, it can represent a goal or target level of usage. The strategic tradeoff here is that scheduled idle time for maintenance can lengthen the useful life of equipment and the long-term total output, or it can improve short-term cost savings. Bushells's theoretical monthly capacity for a 30-day month is

$$2,400 \text{ bottles per hour} \times 16 \text{ hours per day} \times 30 \text{ days} = 1,152,000 \text{ bottles}$$

Assume that the financial-accounting reporting method is used to estimate cost of goods manufactured and sold, which includes fixed overhead costs as well as variable manufacturing costs. This is called **absorption costing** or **full absorption costing**. No idle time results in the highest possible supply-side denominator level, the lowest fixed overhead cost rate, and the lowest inventory valuation. Since actual production is less than theoretical capacity (as it must be), there will be a production-volume variance that indicates the opportunity cost of idle productive capacity. This is a non-value-added cost to the customer for which a customer will not pay.

Practical capacity reduces theoretical capacity for unavoidable operating interruptions such as scheduled maintenance time, shutdowns for holidays, safety inspections, and so on.[2] This type of scheduled idle capacity is often called **off-limits idle capacity**. Strategically, companies might schedule off-limits idle capacity to comply with regulations and safety legislation.

---

[2] P.R. Sopariwala, "Capacity Utilization: Using the CAM-I Capacity Model in a Multi-Hierarchical Manufacturing Environment," *Management Accounting Quarterly*, 7.2 (Winter 2006): pp. 17–34.

For example, Transport Canada requires companies in the airline industry to comply with numerous safety regulations. After an aircraft has flown a specified number of air miles, taken off and landed a specified number of times, and so on, Transport Canada requires the aircraft be grounded, and its systems, such as wiring and hydraulics, must be rebuilt. The goal of these procedures is to minimize risk to passengers. This illustrates why companies in some industries must plan for off-limits idle capacity.

Another cause of downtime is setups, and at a bottling company like Bushells customers use different size and shape bottles with different labels. This is **non-productive idle capacity**. This type of capacity is not off limits because it can be minimized with excellent scheduling or used to accomplish other value-added activities. Bushells may also acquire idle capacity to provide some excess resources required if there are unexpected delays in obtaining materials or unscheduled interruptions to fill rush orders.

Practical capacity is not constant over the life of equipment. Process redesign can improve labour efficiency, wait time for materials, and scheduling, which would increase practical capacity. At Bushells, assume that the practical hourly production rate including non-productive and off-limits idle capacity is 2,000 bottles an hour and that the plant can operate 25 days a month. The practical monthly capacity is

$$2,000 \text{ bottles per hour} \times 16 \text{ hours} \times 25 \text{ days} = 800,000 \text{ bottles}$$

Corporations cannot purchase long-term capacity in small increments. Investment in capacity to meet long-term anticipated normal demand is often made well in advance of actually reaching this level. But investments are made to retain and expand market share, understanding the risk that normal demand may never match the practical capacity.

Sustainability in Action   Sustainability Flying High

Antony Nettle/Alamy Stock Photo

After years of record sales, Boeing had an eight-year backlog of orders for its 737, 777, and 787 Dreamliner commercial aircraft. By 2014, the company's $489 billion order book was larger than the GDP of Belgium, the world's 36th largest economy. Facing production snags, parts shortages, and mandatory overtime for workers as it tried to catch up on back work, Boeing embraced lean manufacturing, which focuses on systematically reducing waste within the company's manufacturing processes.

The sustainability processes of lean manufacturing were intensified to speed up delivery of its 5,700-plane backlog. The company continually reconfigured old manufacturing processes to be more efficient. As a result,

- 777 airplanes are now completed 31% more quickly, while 737 airplanes are now delivered 55% more quickly.
- The 787 Dreamliner now requires 20% fewer worker hours for assembly.
- Production quality has improved 35–55% on all new manufactured airplanes, reducing rework, waste, and repair.

These efficiency gains reduced Boeing's inventory costs while increasing the company's operating margin from 2.7% in 2009 to 7.9% in 2014. The drive at Boeing was not only to build more planes but to do so sustainably and efficiently. Boeing CEO Jim McNerney summarized: "We must not leave any part of our work unexamined in our drive to continually improve the productivity of our enterprise."

Sources: S. Wilhelm. 2015. Boeing has a lot of work to do as it drives to cash in on $489B backlog. *Puget Sound Business Journal*, August 12; S. Wilhelm. 2015. Boeing's cost-cutting success is beyond belief as 737, 787, 777 drive revenue gains. *Puget Sound Business* Journal, May 13; The Boeing Company, 2014 Annual Report (Chicago, The Boeing Company, 2015).

Demand Measures: Normal Capacity or Master-Budget Capacity?

Normal capacity utilization and master-budget capacity utilization measure the denominator level in terms of demand for the output. In many cases, demand is well below the capacity or supply available, as was illustrated in Exhibit 9-2. Bushells's senior management believes that over the next one to three years the normal monthly production level will be 500,000 bottles. This also explains the distance between the demand and semifixed cost lines in Exhibit 9-2. External reporting requires the use of normal capacity in the denominator, taking into account off-limits idle capacity. Unallocated overhead (variance) is recognized in the time period incurred. ASPE/IFRS also permit the use of actual production level if it is not materially different from normal capacity.

Strategically, Bushells's managers may have concluded that the excess non-productive capacity can be used in other revenue-generating ways until demand growth accelerates. Increased demand by customers may not only be for product but also for services customized to their needs. Bushells may also have made this decision as an agility-response strategy; that is, the managers may have seen the ability to provide faster delivery (using idle capacity) as a competitive advantage in acquiring new customers and considered the benefit greater than the cost of excess capacity.

Normal capacity utilization is based on the level of capacity utilization that satisfies average customer demand over a period (say, of two to three years) that includes seasonal, cyclical, or other trend factors. *Master-budget capacity* utilization is based on the anticipated level of capacity utilization for the next operating budget period of a month, a quarter, or a year. The key difference is the *time period* under consideration, whether the term is long (normal) or short (master). These two denominator levels will differ when an industry has cyclical periods of high and low demand or when management believes that the budgeted production for the coming period is unrepresentative of "long-term" demand.

Consider our Bushells example. Assume the master budget for 2018 is based on production of 400,000 bottles per month. Hence, the master budget denominator level is 400,000 bottles, which is a short-term estimate of market share for the year 2018.

Effects on Reporting, Costing, Pricing, and Evaluation

Step 3: Make Predictions About the Future Bushells has budgeted fixed manufacturing costs of $50,000 per month. Assume the actual costs are also $50,000. To keep this example simple, we assume all fixed manufacturing costs are indirect. Bushells's top management team must now forecast the outcomes from using the different capacity alternatives in the denominator.

▶ **LO 2**

Explain how the choice of denominator affects capacity management, costing, pricing, and performance evaluation.

Bushells's budgeted fixed manufacturing overhead rates in May 2018 for the four alternative capacity denominator levels are as follows:

Capacity Concept (1)	Budgeted Fixed Manufacturing Overhead per Month (2)	Budgeted Capacity Level (in Bottles) (3)	Budgeted Manufacturing Overhead Cost Rate (4) = (2) ÷ (3)
Theoretical capacity	$50,000	1,152,000	$0.0434
Practical capacity	50,000	800,000	0.0625
Normal capacity utilization	50,000	500,000	0.1000
Master-budget capacity utilization	50,000	400,000	0.1250

The budgeted fixed manufacturing overhead rate based on master-budget capacity utilization ($0.1250) represents an increase of more than 188% from the rate based on theoretical capacity ($0.0434). The fixed-cost pool is $50,000 over the relevant range of 400,000 to 1,152,000 bottles.

Exhibit 9-3 Fixed-Cost Overhead Rate per Bottle at Bushells

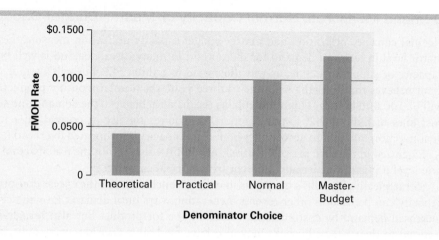

Exhibit 9-3 illustrates the four possible fixed overhead cost rates per bottle as the denominator-level choice changes. If the managers decide to use only one system for both internal management and external financial reporting purposes, then they will choose 500,000 (normal capacity) as the denominator level. The company will be consistent with ASPE/IFRS and will use full absorption costing to estimate inventory value and cost of goods sold. This will lead to applying the full cost of all idle capacity of 752,000 bottles (= 1,152,000 − 400,000 bottles) when pricing each of the 400,000 bottles expected to be sold.

Step 4: Decide On and Implement One of the Available Alternatives Deciding on the denominator level requires more quantitative input about how the choices will affect performance assessment. Assume now that Bushells's actual production in May 2018 is 460,000 bottles. Actual sales are 420,000 bottles. Also assume no beginning inventory on May 1, 2018, and no rate or efficiency variances for May 2018. The manufacturing plant sells the bottles of iced tea to another division for $0.50 per bottle. Its only costs are variable manufacturing costs of $0.35 per bottle and $50,000 per month for fixed manufacturing overhead. Bushells writes off all variances to cost of goods sold each month.

The budgeted manufacturing costs per bottle of iced tea for each capacity concept are the sum of $0.35 in variable manufacturing costs and the budgeted fixed manufacturing overhead costs (shown from the preceding table):

Capacity Concept (1)	Variable Manufacturing Costs (2)	Fixed Manufacturing Overhead Cost Rate (3)	Total Manufacturing Costs (4) = (2) + (3)
Theoretical capacity	$0.3500	$0.0434	$0.3934
Practical capacity	0.3500	0.0625	0.4125
Normal capacity utilization	0.3500	0.1000	0.4500
Master-budget capacity utilization	0.3500	0.1250	0.4750

Each capacity concept will result in a different production-volume variance:

$$\text{Production-volume variance} = \left(\begin{array}{c}\text{Denominator}\\ \text{level in}\\ \text{output units}\end{array} - \begin{array}{c}\text{Actual}\\ \text{output units}\end{array}\right) \times \begin{array}{c}\text{Budgeted fixed}\\ \text{manufacturing overhead}\\ \text{rate per output unit}\end{array}$$

$$\text{Theoretical capacity} = (1,152,000 - 460,000) \times \$0.0434$$

$$= \$30,033 \text{ U}$$

$$\text{Practical capacity} = (800,000 - 460,000) \times \$0.0625$$
$$= \$21,250 \text{ U}$$
$$\text{Normal capacity utilization} = (500,000 - 460,000) \times \$0.1000$$
$$= \$4,000 \text{ U}$$
$$\text{Master-budget capacity utilization} = (400,000 - 460,000) \times \$0.1250$$
$$= \$7,500 \text{ F}$$

Exhibit 9-4 shows how the choice of a denominator affects Bushells's operating income for May 2018. Using the master-budget denominator will mean assigning the highest amount of fixed manufacturing overhead costs per bottle to the 40,000 bottles in ending inventory. Accordingly, operating income is highest using the master-budget capacity utilization denominator. Recall that Bushells had no beginning inventory on

Exhibit 9-4 Bushells Company Statement of Comprehensive Income Effects of Alternative Denominator Levels for May 2018

Actual sales volume (bottles)	420,000			
Actual output (bottles)	460,000			
Variable manufacturing overhead rate	$0.3500			
	Denominator-Level Alternatives			
	Theoretical	**Practical**	**Normal**	**Master-Budget**
Capacity alternative (denominator level)	1,152,000	800,000	500,000	400,000
Fixed overhead cost rate	$ 0.0434	$ 0.0625	$ 0.1000	$ 0.1250
Sales, $0.50 × 420,000	$ 210,000	$210,000	$210,000	$210,000
Cost of goods sold (COGS)				
Beginning inventory	0	0	0	0
Variable manufacturing costs*	161,000	161,000	161,000	161,000
Fixed manufacturing overhead costs[†]	19,964	28,750	46,000	57,500
Cost of goods available for sale	180,964	189,750	207,000	218,500
Ending inventory[‡]	15,736	16,500	18,000	19,000
Total COGS (at standard)	165,228	173,250	189,000	199,500
Adjustments for variances[§]	30,033 U	21,250 U	4,000 U	(7,500) F
Total COGS	195,261	194,500	193,000	192,000
Gross margin	14,739	15,500	17,000	18,000
Marketing, other expenses	10,000	10,000	10,000	10,000
Operating income	$ 4,739	$ 5,500	$ 7,000	$ 8,000

*$0.35 × 460,000 = $161,000
[†]Fixed manufacturing overhead costs

Production	460,000	460,000	460,000	460,000
× Rate	× $0.0434	× $0.0625	× $0.1000	× $0.1250
FMOH costs	$19,964	$28,750	$46,000	$57,500

[‡]Ending inventory costs

Variable cost	$0.3500	$0.3500	$0.3500	$0.3500
+ Fixed costs	0.0434	0.0625	0.1000	0.1250
= Unit cost	$0.3944	$0.4125	$0.4500	$0.4750
× Units in ending inventory	× 40,000	× 40,000	× 40,000	× 40,000
= Ending inventory value	$15,736	$16,500	$18,000	$19,000

[§]The production-volume variance is calculated elsewhere. It is the only variance Bushells incurred in May, 2018.

May 1, 2018, production in May of 460,000 bottles, and sales in May of 420,000 bottles. Hence, the ending inventory on May 31 is 40,000 bottles. The differences between the operating incomes for the four denominator-level concepts in Exhibit 9-4 are due to different amounts of fixed manufacturing overhead costs being inventoried:

Fixed Manufacturing Overhead in the May 31, 2018, Inventory Valuation

Denominator Level (1)	Pro Forma Quantity (2)	Fixed Overhead Rate (3)	Pro Forma Inventory (4) = (2) × (3)
Theoretical	40,000	$0.0434	$1,736
Practical	40,000	0.0625	2,500
Normal	40,000	0.1000	4,000
Master-budget	40,000	0.1250	5,000

Thus, in Exhibit 9-4 the difference in operating income between the *master-budget* capacity utilization concept and the *normal* capacity utilization concept of $1,000 (= $8,000 − $7,000) is due to the difference in the amount of fixed manufacturing overhead being inventoried ($5,000 − $4,000 = $1,000).

Product Costing

Cost data from a standard-costing system are often used in pricing or product-mix decisions. As the Bushells example illustrates, the different denominator choices present different issues:

■ The use of *theoretical* capacity results in an unachievably small fixed manufacturing overhead cost per bottle because it is based on an unattainable level of capacity utilization. Theoretical capacity is rarely used as the denominator because it departs significantly from the real capacity available to a company.

■ Many companies favour *practical* capacity as the denominator to calculate the budgeted fixed manufacturing cost per bottle. Practical capacity in the Bushells example represents the maximum number of bottles that Bushells could produce per year. If Bushells had consistently planned to produce fewer bottles of iced tea, it would have built a smaller plant and incurred lower costs. The drawback is that neither ASPE/IFRS nor CRA accept this denominator for external reporting purposes. But, for internal performance measurement and product pricing, this denominator level is superior to the others at predicting recoverable costs. It is also appropriate to assess production managers' performances. It is not, however, appropriate to assess the marketing function because marketing managers have no control over production functions.

Bushells budgets $0.0625 in fixed manufacturing overhead cost per bottle based on the $50,000 it costs to acquire the practical capacity to produce 800,000 bottles. This plant capacity is acquired well before Bushells uses the capacity and even before Bushells knows how much of the capacity it will actually use. That is, the budgeted fixed manufacturing cost of $0.0625 per bottle measures the *cost per bottle of supplying the capacity*.

Demand for Bushells's iced tea bottles in 2018 is expected to be 400,000 bottles lower than practical capacity. The cost of *supplying* the capacity needed to make bottles is still $0.0625 per bottle. That's because capacity is acquired in "lumpy" amounts (i.e., there is a step fixed cost), and it costs $50,000 per month to acquire the capacity to make 800,000 bottles. The capacity and its cost are fixed in the *short run*; the capacity supplied cannot be reduced to match the capacity needed in 2018. As a result, not all of the capacity supplied at $0.0625 per bottle will be needed or used in 2018.

Using practical capacity reflects the cost of idle capacity in the fixed overhead cost rate. For Bushells, the cost of unused capacity is $25,000 per month (practical capacity of 800,000 bottles less master-budget capacity of 400,000 bottles = 400,000 bottles of unused capacity × FMOH rate of $0.0625/bottle [practical capacity FMOH rate] = $25,000/month). Highlighting the cost of capacity acquired but not used directs managers' attention to managing unused capacity, perhaps by designing new products to fill unused capacity or leasing out unused capacity to others.

■ In contrast, using either of the capacity levels based on the demand for Bushells's iced tea bottles—*master-budget* capacity utilization or **normal capacity** utilization—hides the amount of unused capacity in the FMOH rate.

If Bushells had used the master-budget capacity utilization as the capacity level, it would have calculated the budgeted fixed manufacturing cost per bottle as $0.1250 (= $50,000 ÷ 400,000 bottles). This calculation does not use data about practical capacity, so it does not separately identify the cost of unused capacity. Note, however, that the cost of $0.1250 per bottle includes a charge for unused capacity—the $0.0625 fixed manufacturing resource that would be used to produce each bottle at practical capacity plus the cost of unused capacity allocated to each bottle, $0.0625 per bottle.

The next section illustrates how the use of normal capacity utilization or master-budget capacity utilization results in setting selling prices that are not competitive.

Product Pricing: the Downward Demand Spiral

The easiest way to understand the downward demand spiral is by an example. The **downward demand spiral** is a progressive reduction in capacity use, which leads to an increase in the fixed overhead rate. As sales decrease, the actual capacity used also decreases to control the amount in ending inventory. This means that the realized quantity in the master-budget denominator of any fixed overhead cost rate decreases, but the fixed-cost pool remains constant.

The master-budget fixed overhead rate increases each time the master-budget denominator decreases. This does not mean, however, that the increased unitized fixed cost can be recovered by increasing the price. A decreased quantity of forecast sales must bear higher costs per unit—which leads to an increased unit sales price to cover full costs. In a competitive market, all else being equal, this will further decrease sales. This is a drawback of using master-budget capacity as the denominator level. The downward demand spiral (also sometimes called the "death spiral") is demonstrated in the following situation:

■ **Iteration 1** Assume Bushells uses master-budget capacity utilization of 400,000 bottles for full product costing in 2018. The resulting manufacturing cost is $0.4750 (= $0.35 + $0.125) per bottle. Assume in December 2018 that a competitor, Lipton Iced Tea, offers to supply a major customer of Bushells at $0.45 per bottle. Bushells's forecast of sales to this customer was 100,000 bottles in 2018. The Bushells manager, not wanting to show a loss on the account of $0.025 per bottle (= $0.45 SP − $0.475 full cost) and wanting to recoup all costs in the long run, does not match the competitor's price, and the account is lost. The lost account means budgeted fixed manufacturing costs of $50,000 will be spread over the remaining master-budget volume of 300,000 bottles. This means the unitized rate will increase to $0.167 (= $50,000 ÷ 300,000 bottles) from $0.125 (= $50,000 ÷ 400,000). The variable MOH rate remains at $0.35. The new full absorption cost, all other things being equal, will be $0.517 per bottle ($0.35 + $0.167 = $0.517).

■ **Iteration 2** Suppose then, another customer of Bushells—also accounting for 100,000 bottles of budgeted volume—receives a bid from a competitor priced at $0.45. The Bushells manager compares this bid with his revised unit cost of $0.517, declines to match the competition, and the account is lost. The planned output would shrink further to 200,000 units. The budgeted fixed manufacturing cost per unit for the remaining 200,000 now would be $0.25 (= $50,000 ÷ 200,000 bottles). With the variable costs remaining at $0.35, the new full absorption cost will be $0.60.

At the extreme, if Bushells only sold one bottle, its share of the fixed overhead cost would be $50,000! The use of practical capacity as the denominator to calculate the

Concepts in Action

Denominator-Level Choice Reflects Recoverable Costs in Strategic Pricing

If Bushells has adequate business intelligence data to benchmark its fixed overhead to become at least as good as or better than its competitors, the $0.0625 rate is more aggressive than the $0.1250 master-budget rate yet remains possible to achieve, while the $0.0434 theoretical rate is not. Practical capacity focuses on the supply constraint on production and does not include any non-productive idle capacity cost. It is, by definition, a long-term estimate of what Bushells will need in the long run to meet demand. But often corporations anticipate growth by purchasing capacity before master-budget demand requires it.

In a competitive market where gross margins are very slim, the cost of idle capacity is non-value-added to the customer, who expects Bushells to either manage its capacity or bear the costs of ineffectiveness. Customers are very sensitive to price, and if Bushells tries to recover non-value-added expenditures from customers, they will simply purchase a less expensive product from a competitor. In the long run, Bushells must recover all costs in its sales price if it is to be profitable. Until actual capacity use reaches practical capacity, the difference in cost per unit that cannot be recovered will erode gross margin.

budgeted fixed manufacturing cost per bottle avoids the recalculation of unit costs when expected demand levels change. This is an example of standard rates used in budgeting and variance analysis. The fixed-cost rate is calculated based on the standard or practical capacity available rather than the capacity used to meet demand. Managers who use reported unit costs in a mechanical way to set prices are less likely to promote a downward demand spiral when they use practical capacity concepts because this quantity remains unchanged regardless of demand. Use of either normal capacity or master-budget capacity utilization can promote the downward demand spiral as capacity used decreases.

Performance Evaluation

Step 5: Implement the Decision, Evaluate Performance, and Learn   Consider how the choice between normal capacity utilization, master-budget capacity utilization, and practical capacity affects how a marketing manager is evaluated. Normal capacity utilization is often used as a basis for long-term plans. The normal capacity utilization depends on the time span selected and the forecasts made for each year. However, *normal capacity utilization is an average that provides no meaningful feedback to the marketing manager for a particular year*. Using normal capacity utilization as a reference for judging current performance of a marketing manager is an example of misusing a long-run measure for a short-run purpose.

Obtaining feedback after implementation is also something that Bushells needs to consider. None of the denominator levels is suitable to all purposes. The *master-budget capacity utilization*, rather than normal capacity utilization or practical capacity, is what should be used for evaluating a marketing manager's performance in the current year. This is because the master budget is the principal short-run planning and control tool. Managers feel more obligated to reach the levels specified in the master budget, which should have been carefully set in relation to the maximum opportunities for sales in the current year.

When large differences exist between practical capacity and master-budget capacity utilization, companies routinely classify part of the large difference as *planned unused capacity*. One reason they do so is performance evaluation. At Bushells, for example, the managers in charge of capacity planning usually do not make pricing decisions. Top management decided to build an iced-tea plant with 800,000 bottles of practical capacity, focusing on demand over the next five years. Bushells's marketing managers, who are mid-level managers, make the pricing decisions. This group believes it should be held accountable only for the manufacturing overhead costs related to the potential customer base in 2018. The master-budget capacity utilization suggests a customer base in 2018 of 400,000 bottles. Using responsibility accounting principles, part of the budgeted total fixed manufacturing costs would be attributed to the fixed capacity costs of meeting 2018 demand. The remaining costs would be separately shown as the capacity cost of meeting long-run demand increases expected to occur beyond 2018.

Capacity Decisions and Denominator-Level Issues

The choice of any denominator level introduces rigidity into the budgeting and costing system. Standard cost systems do not recognize fluctuations and uncertainty. The managers must make a choice despite their knowledge that they will almost certainly be wrong. ASPE/IFRS require frequent updating because standards may change quickly over time. Managers know that both supply of and demand for capacity is uncertain, if only because of random events. Bushells's plant has an estimated practical capacity of 800,000 bottles. The estimated master-budget capacity utilization for 2018 is 400,000 bottles. These estimates are uncertain. To deal with uncertainty, Bushells more than likely built its current plant with an 800,000-bottle practical capacity in part to provide the capability to meet unexpected surges in growth in demand.

Capacity cost issues are also prominent in many service-sector companies, such as airlines, hospitals, railroads, and banks, even though these companies carry no inventory and have no inventory-costing issues. For example, in calculating the fixed overhead cost per patient-day in its obstetrics and gynecology department, a hospital must decide what denominator to use—practical capacity, normal utilization, or master-budget utilization. Its decision may have implications for capacity management as well as performance evaluation.

Inventory Valuation: Variable and Absorption Costing

The two most common methods of costing inventories in manufacturing companies are *variable costing* and *absorption costing*. We describe each in this section and then discuss them in detail, using a hypothetical telescope-manufacturing company as an example.

▶ **LO 3**

Distinguish absorption costing from variable costing; prepare and explain the differences in operating income under each costing policy.

Variable Costing

Variable costing is a method of inventory costing in which all variable manufacturing costs (direct and indirect) are included as inventoriable costs. All fixed manufacturing costs are excluded from inventoriable costs and are instead treated as costs of the period in which they are incurred. Note that *variable costing* is an imprecise term to describe this inventory-costing method because only variable manufacturing costs are inventoried; variable non-manufacturing costs are still treated as period costs and are expensed. Another common term used to describe this method is **direct costing**. This term is also imprecise because variable costing considers variable manufacturing overhead (an indirect cost) as inventoriable, while excluding direct marketing costs, for example.

Absorption Costing

Absorption costing is a method of inventory costing in which all variable manufacturing costs and all fixed manufacturing costs are included as inventoriable costs. That is, inventory "absorbs" all manufacturing costs. The job costing system you studied in Chapter 4 is an example of absorption costing.

Under both variable costing and absorption costing, all variable manufacturing costs are inventoriable costs and all non-manufacturing costs in the value chain (such as research and development and marketing), whether variable or fixed, are period costs and are recorded as expenses when incurred.

Comparing Variable and Absorption Costing

The easiest way to understand the difference between variable costing and absorption costing is with an example. In this chapter, we will study Stassen Company, an optical consumer-products manufacturer, and focus on its product line of high-end telescopes.

Stassen uses standard costing:

- Direct costs are traced to products using standard prices and standard inputs allowed for actual outputs produced.

- Indirect (overhead) manufacturing costs are allocated using standard indirect rates times standard inputs allowed for actual outputs produced.

Stassen's management wants to prepare an income statement for 2018 (the fiscal year just ended) to evaluate the performance of the telescope product line. The operating information for the year is as follows:

	A	B
1		**Units**
2	Beginning Inventory	0
3	Production	8,000
4	Sales	6,000
5	Ending Inventory	2,000

Actual price and cost data for 2018 are as follows:

10	Selling price	$ 1,000
11	Variable manufacturing cost per unit	
12	Direct material cost per unit	$ 110
13	Direct manufacturing labour cost per unit	40
14	Manufacturing overhead cost per unit	50
15	Total variable manufacturing cost per unit	$ 200
16	Variable marketing cost per unit sold	$ 185
17	Fixed manufacturing costs (all indirect)	$1,080,000
18	Fixed marketing costs (all indirect)	$1,380,000

For simplicity and to focus on the main ideas, we assume the following about Stassen:

- Stassen incurs manufacturing and marketing costs only. The cost driver for all variable manufacturing costs is units produced; the cost driver for variable marketing costs is units sold. There are no batch-level costs and no product-sustaining costs.

- There are no price variances, efficiency variances, or spending variances. Therefore, the *budgeted* (standard) price and cost data for 2018 are the same as the *actual* price and cost data.

- Work-in-process inventory is zero.

- Stassen budgeted production of 8,000 units for 2018. This was used to calculate the budgeted fixed manufacturing cost per unit of $135 ($1,080,000/8,000 units).[3]

- Stassen budgeted sales of 6,000 units for 2018, which is the same as the actual sales for 2018.

- The actual production for 2018 is 8,000 units. As a result, there is no production-volume variance for manufacturing costs in 2018. A later example, based on data for 2018, does include production-volume variances. However, even in that case, the income statement contains no variances other than the production-volume variance.

- Variances are written off to cost of goods sold in the period (year) in which they occur.

---

[3] Throughout this section, we use budgeted output as the basis for calculating the fixed manufacturing cost per unit for ease of exposition. In the latter half of this chapter, we consider the relative merits of alternative denominator-level choices for calculating this unit cost.

Based on the preceding information, Stassen's inventoriable costs per unit produced in 2018 under the two inventory costing methods are as follows:

	Variable Costing		Absorption Costing	
Variable manufacturing cost per unit produced:				
Direct materials	$110		$110	
Direct manufacturing labour	40		40	
Manufacturing overhead	50	$200	50	$200
Fixed manufacturing cost per unit produced		—		135
Total inventoriable cost per unit produced		$200		$335

To summarize, the main difference between variable costing and absorption costing is the accounting for fixed manufacturing costs:

■ Under variable costing, fixed manufacturing costs are not inventoried; they are treated as an expense of the period.

■ Under absorption costing, fixed manufacturing costs are inventoriable costs. In our example, the standard fixed manufacturing cost is $135 per unit ($1,080,000 ÷ 8,000 units) produced.

9.1 TRY IT! ⊕

Achilles Auto makes and sells batteries. In 2017, it made 100,000 batteries and sold 75,000 of them, at an average selling price of $60 per unit. The following additional information relates to Achilles Auto for 2017:

Direct materials	$ 20.00 per unit
Direct manufacturing labour	$ 4.00 per unit
Variable manufacturing costs	$ 1.00 per unit
Sales commissions	$ 6.00 per part
Fixed manufacturing costs	$ 750,000 per year
Administrative expenses, all fixed	$ 270,000 per year

What is Achilles Auto's inventoriable cost per unit using (a) variable costing and (b) absorption costing?

Variable vs. Absorption Costing: Operating Income and Income Statements

When comparing variable and absorption costing, we must also take into account whether we are looking at short- or long-term numbers. How does the data for a one-year period differ from that of a two-year period under variable and absorption costing?

Comparing Income Statements for One Year

What will Stassen's operating income be if it uses variable costing or absorption costing? The differences between these methods are apparent in Exhibit 9-5. Panel A shows the variable costing income statement and Panel B the absorption-costing income statement for Stassen's telescope product line for 2018. The variable-costing income statement uses the contribution-margin format (introduced in Chapter 3). The absorption-costing income

Exhibit 9-5 Comparison of Variable Costing and Absorption Costing for Stassen Company: Telescope Product-Line Income Statements for 2018

	A	B	C	D	E	F	G
	Home Insert Page Layout Formulas Data Review View						
1	**Panel A: VARIABLE COSTING**				**Panel B: ABSORPTION COSTING**		
2	Revenues: $1,000 × 6,000 units		$6,000,000		Revenues: $1,000 × 6,000 units		$6,000,000
3	Variable cost of goods sold:				Cost of goods sold:		
4	Beginning inventory	$ 0			Beginning inventory	$ 0	
5	Variable manufacturing costs: $200 × 8,000 units	1,600,000			Variable manufacturing costs: $200 × 8,000 units	1,600,000	
6					Allocated fixed manufacturing costs: $135 × 8,000 units	1,080,000	
7	Cost of goods available for sale	1,600,000			Cost of goods available for sale	2,680,000	
8	Deduct ending inventory: $200 × 2,000 units	(400,000)			Deduct ending inventory: $335 × 2,000 units	(670,000)	
9	Variable cost of goods sold		1,200,000		Cost of goods sold		2,010,000
10	Variable marketing costs: $185 × 6,000 units sold		1,110,000				
11	Contribution margin		3,690,000		Gross Margin		3,990,000
12	Fixed manufacturing costs		1,080,000		Variable marketing costs: $185 × 6,000 units sold		1,110,000
13	Fixed marketing costs		1,380,000		Fixed marketing costs		1,380,000
14	Operating income		$1,230,000		Operating Income		$1,500,000
15							
16	Manufacturing costs expensed in Panel A:				Manufacturing costs expensed in Panel B:		
17	Variable cost of goods sold		$1,200,000				
18	Fixed manufacturing costs		1,080,000				
19	Total		$2,280,000		Cost of goods sold		$2,010,000

Source: Courtesy of Microsoft Corporation.

statement uses the gross-margin format (introduced in Chapter 2). Why these different formats? The distinction between variable costs and fixed costs is central to variable costing, and it is highlighted by the contribution-margin format. Similarly, the distinction between manufacturing and non-manufacturing costs is central to absorption costing, and it is highlighted by the gross-margin format.

Absorption-costing income statements do not need to differentiate between variable and fixed costs. However, we will make this distinction between variable and fixed costs in the Stassen example to show how individual line items are classified differently under variable costing and absorption costing. In Exhibit 9-5, Panel B, note that inventoriable cost is $335 per unit under absorption costing: allocated fixed manufacturing costs of $135 per unit plus variable manufacturing costs of $200 per unit.

Notice how the fixed manufacturing costs of $1,080,000 are accounted for under variable costing and absorption costing in Exhibit 9-5. The income statement under variable costing deducts the $1,080,000 lump sum as an expense for 2018. In contrast, under absorption costing, the $1,080,000 ($135 per unit × 8,000 units) is initially treated as an inventoriable cost in 2018. Of this $1,080,000, $810,000 ($135 per unit × 6,000 units) subsequently becomes a part of cost of goods sold in 2018, and $270,000 ($135 per unit × 2,000 units) remains an asset—part of ending finished goods inventory on December 31, 2018.

Operating income is $270,000 higher under absorption costing compared with variable costing because only $810,000 of fixed manufacturing costs are expensed under absorption costing, whereas all $1,080,000 of fixed manufacturing costs are expensed under variable costing. Note that the variable manufacturing cost of $200 per unit is accounted for the same way in both income statements in Exhibit 9-5.

These points can be summarized as follows:

	Variable Costing	Absorption Costing
Variable manufacturing costs: $200 per telescope produced	Inventoriable	Inventoriable
Fixed manufacturing costs: $1,080,000 per year	Deducted as an expense of the period	Inventoriable at $135 per telescope produced using budgeted denominator level of 8,000 units produced per year ($1,080,000 ÷ 8,000 units = $135 per unit)

The basis of the difference between variable costing and absorption costing is how fixed manufacturing costs are accounted for. If inventory levels change, operating income will differ between the two methods because of the difference in accounting for fixed manufacturing costs. To see this difference, let's compare telescope sales of 6,000, 7,000, and 8,000 units by Stassen in 2018, when 8,000 units were produced. Of the $1,080,000 total fixed manufacturing costs, the amount expensed in the 2018 income statement under each of these scenarios would be as follows:

	A	B	C	D	E	F	G
1			Variable Costing			Absorption Costing	
2						Fixed Manufacturing Costs	
3	Units	Ending	Fixed Manufacturing Costs			Included in Inventory	Amount Expensed
4	Sold	Inventory	Included in Inventory	Amount Expensed		= $135 × Ending Inv.	= $135 × Units Sold
5	6,000	2,000	$0	$1,080,000		$270,000	$ 810,000
6	7,000	1,000	$0	$1,080,000		$135.000	$ 945,000
7	8,000	0	$0	$1,080,000		$ 0	$1,080,000

In the last scenario, where 8,000 units are produced and sold, both variable and absorption costing report the same net income because inventory levels are unchanged. This chapter's appendix describes how the choice of variable costing or absorption costing affects the breakeven quantity of sales when inventory levels are allowed to vary.

9.2 TRY IT! ⊕

ZB Toys started 2017 with no inventories. During the year, its expected and actual production was 30,000 units, of which it sold 24,000 units at $50 each. Cost data for the year is as follows:

Manufacturing costs incurred:

Variable:	$525,000
Fixed:	$372,000

Marketing costs incurred:

Variable:	$144,800
Fixed:	$ 77,400

Calculate ZB Toys's operating income under (a) variable costing and (b) absorption costing. Explain why operating income differs under the two approaches.

Comparing Income Statements for Multiple Years

To get a more comprehensive view of the effects of variable costing and absorption costing, Stassen's management accountants prepare income statements for two years of operations, starting with 2018. The data are given in units in the following table:

E	F	G
	2018	2019
Budgeted production	8,000	8,000
Beginning inventory	0	2,000
Actual Production	8,000	5,000
Sales	6,000	6,500
Ending inventory	2,000	500

All other 2018 data given earlier for Stassen also apply for 2019.

In 2018, Stassen has a production-volume variance because actual telescope production differs from the budgeted level of production of 8,000 units per year used to calculate the budgeted fixed manufacturing cost per unit. The actual quantity sold for 2018 is 6,500 units, which is the same as the sales quantity budgeted for that year.

Exhibit 9-6 presents the income statement under variable costing in Panel A and the income statement under absorption costing in Panel B for 2018 and 2019. As you study Exhibit 9-6, note that the 2018 columns in both Panels A and B show the same figures as Exhibit 9-5. The 2019 column is similar to 2018 *except for the production-volume variance line item under absorption costing in Panel B*. Keep in mind the following points about absorption costing as you study Panel B of Exhibit 9-6:

1. The $135 fixed manufacturing cost rate is based on the budgeted denominator capacity level of 8,000 units in 2018 and 2019 ($1,080,000 ÷ 8,000 units = $135 per unit). Whenever production (the quantity produced, not the quantity sold) deviates from

Exhibit 9-6 Comparison of Variable Costing and Absorption Costing for Stassen Company: Telescope Product-Line Income Statements for 2018 and 2019

	A	B	C	D	E
	Home Insert Page Layout Formulas Data Review View				
1	**Panel A: VARIABLE COSTING**				
2			2018		2019
3	Revenues: $1,000 × 6,000; 6,500 units		$6,000,000		$6,500,000
4	Variable cost of goods sold:				
5	Beginning inventory: $200 × 0; 2,000 units	$ 0		$ 400,000	
6	Variable manufacturing costs: $200 × 8,000; 5,000 units	1,600,000		1,000,000	
7	Cost of goods available for sale	1,600,000		1,400,000	
8	Deduct ending inventory: $200 × 2,000; 500 units	(400,000)		(100,000)	
9	Variable cost of goods sold		1,200,000		1,300,000
10	Variable marketing costs: $185 × 6,000; 6,500 units		1,110,000		1,202,500
11	Contribution margin		3,690,000		3,997,500
12	Fixed manufacturing costs		1,080,000		1,080,000
13	Fixed marketing costs		1,380,000		1,380,000
14	Operating income		$1,230,000		$1,537,500
15					
16	**Panel B: ABSORPTION COSTING**				
17			2018		2019
18	Revenues: $1,000 × 6,000; 6,500 units		$6,000,000		$6,500,000
19	Cost of goods sold:				
20	Beginning inventory: $335 × 0; 2,000 units	0		670,000	
21	Variable manufacturing costs: $200 × 8,000; 5,000 units	1,600,000		1,000,000	
22	Allocated fixed manufacturing costs: $135 × 8,000; 5,000 units	1,080,000		675,000	
23	Cost of goods available for sale	2,680,000		2,345,000	
24	Deduct ending inventory: $335 × 2,000; 500 units	(670,000)		(167,500)	
25	Adjustment for production-volume variance[a]	$ 0		$ 405,000	U
26	Cost of goods sold		2,010,000		2,582,500
27	Gross Margin		3,990,000		3,917,500
28	Variable marketing costs: $185 × 6,000; 6,500 units		1,110,000		1,202,500
29	Fixed marketing costs		1,380,000		1,380,000
30	Operating Income		$1,500,000		$1,335,000
31					
32	[a]Production-volume variance = Budgeted fixed manufacturing costs – Fixed manufacturing overhead allocated using budgeted cost per output unit allowed for actual output produced (Panel B, line 22)				
33	2018: $1,080,000 – ($135 × 8,000) = $1,080,000 – $1,080,000 = $0				
34	2019: $1,080,000 – ($135 × 5,000) = $1,080,000 – $675,000 = $405,000 U				
35					
36	Production-volume variance can also be calculated as follows:				
37	Fixed manufacturing cost per unit × (Denominator level – Actual output units produced)				
38	2018: $135 × (8,000 – 8,000) units = $135 × 0 = $0				
39	2019: $135 × (8,000 – 5,000) units = $135 × 3,000 = $405,000 U				

Source: Courtesy of Microsoft Corporation.

Concepts in Action Capacity at Nissan

Capacity decisions are, in many industries, long-run strategic decisions. Rapid changes in the environment can be difficult to anticipate and may result in costly stock-outs (opportunity cost) and negative publicity. In addition, these capacity decisions can have negative "ripple" effects throughout the supply chain.

For example, in 2010 Nissan Motors had to halt production unexpectedly at four of its five domestic (Japan) assembly plants because of shortages of engine control units (ECU), which are a key electronic component in today's cars. One of Nissan's major suppliers, Hitachi, had not been able to secure an adequate supply of the electronic chips that are an essential part of the ECU. The three-day halt in production resulted in an estimated loss of productive capacity of approximately 15,000 cars. This represents an opportunity cost (lost output) and a potential marketing dilemma as customers may choose a competitor if the Nissan model they want is not available.

The lack of ECU inventory is a result of demand outstripping capacity in the supply chain. Part of this may be due to the recovery in automotive demand after the 2008–2009 world financial crisis. As chip manufacturing capacity is expensive to increase, it is suspected that production may have lagged behind the automotive recovery. Nissan's shutdown may also have been aggravated by the Japanese auto industry's well-known practice of "just-in-time" (Kanban) inventory management.

Sources: J. Yoshida. 2010. Nissan abrupt production halt, *EETimes*, July 13 (http://www.eetimes.com/document.asp?doc_id=1256835); B. Huang. 2010. Supply chain hitch puts brakes on Nissan production, GlobalSCM.net, July 21 (http://www.globalscm.net/share.php?ac=view&id=402&uid=64); D. Wakabayashi. 2010. Update: Hitachi Engine Part Delay Caused By STMicroelectronics—Source, London South East, July 14 (http://www.lse.co.uk/sharecast-news-article.asp?ArticleCode=3571920&ArticleHeadline=UPDATE_Hitachi_Engine_Part_Delay_Caused_By_STMicroelectronics_Source).

the denominator level, there will be a production-volume variance. The amount of Stassen's production-volume variance is determined by multiplying $135 per unit by the difference between the actual level of production and the denominator level.

Recall how standard costing works under absorption costing. Each time a unit is manufactured, $135 of fixed manufacturing costs is included in the cost of goods manufactured and available for sale. In 2018, when 5,000 units are manufactured, $675,000 ($135 per unit × 5,000 units) of fixed manufacturing costs is included in the cost of goods available for sale (see Exhibit 9-6, Panel B, line 22). Total fixed manufacturing costs for 2018 are $1,080,000. The production-volume variance of $405,000 U equals the difference between $1,080,000 and $675,000. In Panel B, note how, for each year, the fixed manufacturing costs included in the cost of goods available for sale plus the production-volume variance always equals $1,080,000.

2. As a result of the production-volume variance, note that the absorption costing income is lower in 2019 than in 2018 even though Stassen sold 500 more units. We explore the impact of production levels on income under absorption costing in greater detail later in this chapter.

3. The production-volume variance, which relates only to fixed manufacturing overhead, exists under absorption costing but not under variable costing. Under variable costing, fixed manufacturing costs of $1,080,000 are always treated as an expense of the period, regardless of the level of production (and sales).

Here's a summary (using information from Exhibit 9-6) of the operating-income differences for Stassen Company during 2018 and 2019:

	2018	2019
1. Absorption-costing operating income	$1,500,000	$1,335,000
2. Variable-costing operating income	$1,230,000	$1,537,500
3. Difference: (1) – (2)	$ 270,000	$ (202,500)

The sizable differences in the preceding table illustrate why managers whose performance is measured by reported income are concerned about the choice between variable costing and absorption costing.

Why do variable costing and absorption costing report different operating income numbers? In general, if inventory increases during an accounting period, less operating income will be reported under variable costing than absorption costing. Conversely, if inventory decreases, more operating income will be reported under variable costing than absorption costing. The difference in reported operating income is due solely to (a) moving fixed manufacturing costs into inventories as inventories increase and (b) moving fixed manufacturing costs out of inventories as inventories decrease under absorption costing.

The difference between operating income under absorption costing and variable costing can be computed by formula 1, which focuses on fixed manufacturing costs in beginning inventory and ending inventory:

	A	B	C	D	E	F	G	H
1	Formula 1							
2						Fixed manufacturing		Fixed manufacturing
3		Absorption-costing	–	Variable-costing	=	costs in ending inventory	–	costs in beginning inventory
4		operating income		operating income		under absorption costing		under absorption costing
5	2018	$1,500,000	–	$1,230,000	=	($135 × 2,000 units)	–	($135 × 0 units)
6		$270,000			=	$270,000		
7								
8	2019	$1,335,000	–	$1,537,500	=	($135 × 500 units)	–	($135 × 2,000 units)
9		($202,500)			=	($202,500)		

Fixed manufacturing costs in ending inventory are deferred to a future period under absorption costing. For example, $270,000 of fixed manufacturing overhead is deferred to 2019 at December 31, 2018. Under variable costing, all $1,080,000 of fixed manufacturing costs are treated as an expense of 2018.

Recall that

$$\text{Beginning inventory} + \text{Cost of goods manufactured} = \text{Cost of goods sold} + \text{Ending inventory}$$

Therefore, instead of focusing on fixed manufacturing costs in ending and beginning inventory (as in formula 1), we could alternatively look at fixed manufacturing costs in units produced and units sold. The latter approach (see formula 2) highlights how fixed manufacturing costs move between units produced and units sold during the fiscal year.

12	Formula 2							
13						Fixed manufacturing costs		Fixed manufacturing costs
14		Absorption-costing	–	Variable-costing	=	inventoried in units produced	–	in cost of goods sold
15		operating income		operating income		under absorption costing		under absorption costing
16	2018	$1,500,000	–	$1,230,000	=	($135 × 8,000 units)	–	($135 × 6,000 units)
17		$270,000			=	$270,000		
18								
19	2019	$1,335,000	–	$1,537,500	=	($135 × 5,000 units)	–	($135 × 6,500 units)
20		($202,500)			=	($202,500)		

Managers face increasing pressure to reduce inventory levels. Some companies are achieving steep reductions in inventory levels using policies such as just-in-time production—a production system under which products are manufactured only when needed. Formula 1 illustrates that, as Stassen reduces its inventory levels, operating income differences between absorption costing and variable costing become immaterial. Consider, for example, the formula for 2018. If instead of 2,000 units in ending inventory, Stassen had only 2 units in ending inventory, the difference between absorption-costing operating income and variable-costing operating income would drop from $270,000 to just $270.

Variable Costing and the Effect of Sales and Production on Operating Income

Given a constant contribution margin per unit and constant fixed costs, the period-to-period change in operating income under variable costing is *driven solely by changes in the quantity of units actually sold*. Consider the variable-costing operating income of Stassen in 2019 versus 2018. Recall the following:

$$\frac{\text{Contribution}}{\text{margin per unit}} = \text{Selling price} - \frac{\text{Variable manufacturing}}{\text{cost per unit}} - \frac{\text{Variable marketing}}{\text{cost per unit}}$$

$$= \$1,000 \text{ per unit} - \$200 \text{ per unit} - \$185 \text{ per unit}$$

$$= \$615 \text{ per unit}$$

$$\frac{\text{Change in}}{\text{variable-costing}} = \frac{\text{Contribution}}{\text{margin}} \times \frac{\text{Change in quantity}}{\text{of units sold}}$$
$$\text{operating income} \quad \text{per unit}$$

2019 vs. 2018: $\$1,537,500 - \$1,230,000 = \$615$ per unit $\times$ (6,500 units $-$ 6,000 units)

$$\$307,500 = \$307,500$$

Under variable costing, Stassen managers cannot increase operating income by "producing for inventory." Why not? Because, as you can see from the preceding computations, when using variable costing, only the quantity of units sold drives operating income. We'll explain later in this chapter that absorption costing enables managers to increase operating income by increasing the unit level of sales, as well as by producing more units. Before you proceed to the next section, make sure that you examine Exhibit 9-7 for a detailed comparison of the differences between variable costing and absorption costing.

Exhibit 9-7 Comparative Income Effects of Variable Costing and Absorption Costing

Question	Variable Costing	Absorption Costing	Comment
Are fixed manufacturing costs inventoried?	No	Yes	Basic theoretical question of when these costs should be expensed
Is there a production-volume variance?	No	Yes	Choice of denominator level affects measurement of operating income under absorption costing only
Are classifications between variable and fixed costs routinely made?	Yes	Infrequently	Absorption costing can be easily modified to obtain subclassifications for variable and fixed costs, if desired (for example, see Exhibit 9-1, Panel B)
How do changes in unit inventory levels affect operating income?[a]			Differences are attributable to the timing of when fixed manufacturing costs are expensed
Production = sales	Equal	Equal	
Production > sales	Lower[b]	Higher[c]	
Production < sales	Higher	Lower	
What are the effects on cost-volume-profit relationship (for a given level of fixed costs and a given contribution margin per unit)?	Driven by unit level of sales	Driven by (a) unit level of sales, (b) unit level of production, and (c) chosen denominator level	Management control benefit: Effects of changes in production level on operating income are easier to understand under variable costing

[a]Assuming that all manufacturing variances are written off as period costs, that no change occurs in work-in-process inventory, and no change occurs in the budgeted fixed manufacturing cost rate between accounting periods.

[b]That is, lower operating income than under absorption costing.

[c]That is, higher operating income than under variable costing.

Explaining Differences in Operating Income

If the inventory level increases during an accounting period, the value of total ending inventory increases more under the absorption than variable valuation policy. The period cost, however, will be lower under the absorption than variable valuation policy. The difference between operating income under absorption costing and variable costing can be computed by Formula 1, which is illustrated with Exhibit 9-6 data:[4]

Formula 1

$$\begin{pmatrix} \text{Absorption costing} \\ \text{operating} \\ \text{income} \end{pmatrix} - \begin{pmatrix} \text{Variable costing} \\ \text{operating} \\ \text{income} \end{pmatrix} = \begin{pmatrix} \text{Fixed manufacturing} \\ \text{costs in} \\ \text{ending inventory} \end{pmatrix} - \begin{pmatrix} \text{Fixed manufacturing} \\ \text{costs in} \\ \text{ending beginning inventory} \end{pmatrix}$$

January $\$4,000 - \$800 = (200 \times \$16) - (0 \times \$16)$
$$\$3,200 = \$3,200$$

February $\$20,200 - \$21,800 = (100 \times \$16) - (200 \times \$16)$
$$-\$1,600 = -\$1,600$$

Fixed manufacturing costs in ending inventory are a current-period expense under variable costing that absorption costing defers to future periods.

Two alternative formulas can be used if we assume that all manufacturing variances are written off as period costs, that no change occurs in work-in-process inventory, and that no change occurs in the budgeted fixed manufacturing overhead rate between accounting periods:

Formula 2

$$\begin{pmatrix} \text{Absorption costing} \\ \text{operating} \\ \text{income} \end{pmatrix} - \begin{pmatrix} \text{Variable costing} \\ \text{operating} \\ \text{income} \end{pmatrix} = \begin{pmatrix} \text{Units} \\ \text{produced} - \text{Units} \\ \text{sold} \end{pmatrix} \times \begin{pmatrix} \text{Budgeted fixed} \\ \text{manufacturing} \\ \text{cost rate} \end{pmatrix}$$

January $\$4,000 - \$800 = (600 - 400) \times \$16$
$$\$3,200 = \$3,200$$

February $\$20,200 - \$21,800 = (650 - 750) \times \$16$
$$-\$1,600 = -\$1,600$$

Formula 3

$$\begin{pmatrix} \text{Absorption costing} \\ \text{operating} \\ \text{income} \end{pmatrix} - \begin{pmatrix} \text{Variable costing} \\ \text{operating} \\ \text{income} \end{pmatrix} = \begin{pmatrix} \text{Ending} \\ \text{inventory} - \text{Beginning} \\ \text{in units} - \text{inventory} \\ \text{in units} \end{pmatrix} \times \begin{pmatrix} \text{Budgeted fixed} \\ \text{manufacturing} \\ \text{cost rate} \end{pmatrix}$$

January $\$4,000 - \$800 = (200 - 0) \times \$16$
$$\$3,200 = \$3,200$$

February $\$20,200 - \$21,800 = (100 - 200) \times \$16$
$$-\$1,600 = -\$1,600$$

Effect of Sales and Production on Operating Income

The period-to-period change in operating income under variable costing is driven solely by changes in the unit level of sales, given a constant contribution margin per unit. Consider for Stassen the variable costing operating income in February 2018 versus that in January 2018:

$$\frac{\text{Change in}}{\text{operating income}} = \frac{\text{Contribution}}{\text{margin}} \times \frac{\text{Change in unit}}{\text{sales level}}$$

$$\$21,800 - \$800 = (\$99 - \$39) \times (750 - 400)$$
$$\$21,000 = \$60 \times 350$$
$$\$21,000 = \$21,000$$

---

[4] This formula assumes that the amounts used for beginning and ending inventory are after proration of manufacturing overhead variances.

Note that under variable costing, Stassen managers cannot increase operating income (and hence their bonuses) by producing to increase inventory.

Under absorption costing, however, period-to-period change in operating income is driven by variations in *both* the unit level of sales and the unit level of production. Exhibit 9-7 illustrates this point by showing how absorption costing operating income for February 2018 changes as the production level in February 2018 changes. This exhibit assumes that all variances (including the production-volume variance) are written off to cost of goods sold at the end of each accounting period. The beginning inventory in February 2018 of 200 units and the February sales of 750 units are unchanged. Exhibit 9-7 shows that production of only 550 units meets February 2018 sales of 750. Operating income at this production level (column 1) is $18,600. By producing more than 550 units in February 2018, Stassen increases absorption costing operating income.

Each extra unit in February 2018 ending inventory will increase February operating income by $16. For example, if 800 units are produced, ending inventory will be 250 units and operating income will be $22,600. This amount is $4,000 more than what operating income is with zero ending inventory (250 units × $16 = $4,000) at the end of the month. Recall that Stassen's managers receive a bonus based on monthly operating income. Absorption costing enables them to increase operating income (and hence their bonuses) by producing to increase inventory.

Exhibit 9-8 Stassen Company: Effect on Absorption Costing Operating Income of Different Production Levels Holding the Unit Sales Level Constant—Data for February 2018 with Sales of 750 Units

	February 2018 Production Level				
	550	650	700	800	850
Unit data:					
Beginning inventory	200	200	200	200	200
Production	550	650	700	800	850
Goods available for sale	750	850	900	1,000	1,050
Sales	750	750	750	750	750
Ending inventory	0	100	150	250	300
Statement of Comprehensive Income					
Revenues	$74,250	$74,250	$74,250	$74,250	$74,250
Beginning inventory ($36/unit)	7,200	7,200	7,200	7,200	7,200
Variable manufacturing (production) costs*	11,000	13,000	14,000	16,000	17,000
Fixed manufacturing costs†	8,800	10,400	11,200	12,800	13,600
Cost of goods available for sale	27,000	30,600	32,400	36,000	37,800
Ending inventory‡	0	3,600	5,400	9,000	10,800
Cost of goods sold (at standard cost)	27,000	27,000	27,000	27,000	27,000
Adjustment for manufacturing variances§	4,000 U	2,400 U	1,600 U	0	800 F
Total cost of goods sold	31,000	29,400	28,600	27,000	26,200
Gross margin	43,250	44,850	45,650	47,250	48,050
Total marketing and administrative costs	24,650	24,650	24,650	24,650	24,650
Operating income	$18,600	$20,200	$21,000	$22,600	$23,400

*$20 per unit.

†Assigned at $16 per unit.

‡$36 per unit.

§(Production in units − 800) × $16. All written off to cost of goods sold at end of the accounting period.

Managers whose performance evaluation and compensation are based on absorption costing income have incentives to increase production solely to increase reported income. But this will increase the costs of doing business (increased inventory costs, product obsolescence, etc.) without an attendant increase in revenue obtained from additional sales. Each additional unit produced absorbs fixed manufacturing costs that would otherwise have been written off as a cost of the period.

Performance Evaluation: Undesirable Buildup of Inventories

Absorption costing is the required inventory valuation method for external reporting in Canada, and to avoid any internal confusion that could arise by using a different valuation method for internal planning and control, most companies use one method for both internal and external purposes. Using the same method for valuation and performance evaluation helps avoid situations wherein managers take action that enhances their individual evaluation but harms overall corporate performance.

Unfortunately, absorption costing can lead managers to increase operating income in the short run by increasing the production schedule independent of customer demand. In practice this is a well-known possibility and can be controlled either by monitoring the inventory levels or choosing a variable cost method for internal performance evaluation based on the efficiency and effectiveness of manufacturing activities. The added advantage of variable costing is to reveal the cost–volume–profit relationships that improve the quality of information upon which managers make short-run decisions. Exhibit 9-8 compares the key differences between variable and absorption costing.

Exhibit 9-9 Comparative Income Effects of Variable Costing and Absorption Costing

Question	Variable Costing	Absorption Costing	Comment
Are fixed manufacturing costs inventoried?	No	Yes	Basic theoretical question of when these costs should be expensed as period costs.
Is there a production-volume variance?	No	Yes	Choice of denominator level affects measurement of operating income under absorption costing only.
How are the other variances treated?	Same	Same	Highlights that the basic difference is the accounting for fixed manufacturing costs, not the accounting for any variable manufacturing costs.
Are classifications between variable and fixed costs routinely made?	Yes	Not always	Absorption costing can be easily modified to obtain subclassifications for variable and fixed costs, if desired (for example, see Exhibit 9-5, Panel B).
How do changes in unit inventory levels affect operating income?			
Production = sales	Equal	Equal	Differences are attributable to the timing of when fixed manufacturing costs become period costs.
Production > sales	Lower*	Higher†	
Production < sales	Higher	Lower	
What are the effects on cost-volume-profit relationships?	Driven by unit sales level	Driven by unit sales level and unit production level	Management control benefit: Effects of changes in production level on operating income are easier to understand with variable costing.

*That is, lower operating income than under absorption costing.

†That is, higher operating income than under variable costing.

The undesirable effects of an increase in production to increase operating income in the short run may be sizable, and they can arise in several ways, as the following examples show:

■ A plant manager may switch production to those orders that absorb the highest amount of fixed manufacturing costs, regardless of the customer demand for these products (called "cherry picking" the production line).

■ A plant manager may accept a particular order to increase production, even though another plant in the same company is better suited to handle that order.

■ To meet increased production, a manager may defer maintenance beyond the current accounting period. Although operating income may increase now, future operating income will probably decrease because of increased repairs and less-efficient equipment.

Early criticisms of absorption costing concentrated on whether fixed manufacturing overhead qualified as an asset under ASPE/IFRS. However, current criticisms of absorption costing have increasingly emphasized its potentially undesirable incentives for managers. Indeed, one critic labels absorption costing as "one of the black holes of cost accounting," in part because it may induce managers to make decisions against the long-run interests of the company.

Proposals for Revising Performance Evaluation

Critics of absorption costing have made a variety of proposals for revising how managers are evaluated:

1. *Change the accounting system.* As discussed previously and will be shown later in this chapter, both variable and throughput costing reduce the incentives of managers to build up inventory.

2. *Use careful budgeting and inventory planning* to reduce management's freedom to build up excess inventory. For example, the budgeted monthly statement of financial position has estimates of the dollar amount of inventories. If actual inventories exceed these dollar amounts, top management can investigate the inventory buildups.

3. *Incorporate a carrying charge for inventory* in the internal accounting system. For example, an inventory carrying charge of 1% per month could be assessed for the investment tied up in inventory and for spoilage and obsolescence when evaluating a manager's performance.

4. *Change the time period used to evaluate performance.* Critics of absorption costing give examples where managers take actions that maximize quarterly or annual income at the potential expense of long-run income. By evaluating performance over a three- to five-year period, the incentive to take short-run actions that reduce long-term income is reduced.

5. *Include nonfinancial as well as financial variables in the measures used to evaluate performance.* Companies currently are using nonfinancial variables, such as the following, drawn from the Stassen data:

a. $\dfrac{\text{Ending inventory in units February 2018}}{\text{Begining inventory in units February 2018}} = \dfrac{100}{200} = 0.5$

b. $\dfrac{\text{Units produced in February 2018}}{\text{Units sold in February 2018}} = \dfrac{650}{750} = 0.867$

A good report of manufacturing performance would show not only stable inventory ratios of outputs over time for each product, but also a production to sales-volume ratio very close to 1 to indicate all production and inventory was sold during the period it was produced. Of course, these nonfinancial ratios would also be interpreted in light of, for example, fluctuations due to seasonal demand, perishability, and other factors appropriate to a specific manufacturing situation.

Pulling It All Together—Problem for Self-Study

(Try to solve this problem before examining the solution that follows.)

Problem

Suppose that Bushells Company from our chapter example is computing the operating income for May 2019. This month is identical to May 2018, the results of which are in Exhibit 9-4, except that master-budget capacity utilization for 2019 is 600,000 bottles per month instead of 400,000 bottles. There was no beginning inventory on May 1, 2019, and no variances other than the production-volume variance. Bushells writes off this variance to cost of goods sold each month.

Required ▶

❶ 1. Identify the four potential denominator levels, and calculate each fixed overhead rate.

❶ 2. Calculate the new production-volume variance for the new master-budget denominator level, and explain the CRA effect of the production-volume variance.

❷ 3. How would the financial results in Exhibit 9-4 for Bushells Company be different if the month were May 2019 rather than May 2018? Show your computations.

❷ 4. Explain what the higher master-budget denominator level means.

❸ 5. What changes would adopting a variable inventory valuation method mean to the internal reports of cost of goods sold (COGS) and period expense?

❹ 6. What change would adopting a throughput inventory valuation method mean to the internal reports of COGS and period expense?

❺ 7. Calculate a breakeven for Bushells (there is no unique solution).

Solution

1. The four possible levels are theoretical, practical, normal, and master budget. The rates are calculated by dividing $50,000 by 1,152,000, 800,000, 500,000, and 600,000. All but the master-budget rate are in Exhibit 9-4. The rates are $0.0434, $0.0625, $0.1000, and $0.0833.

$$\frac{\$50,000}{600,000 \text{ bottles}} = \$0.0833 \text{ per bottle}$$

2. The manufacturing cost per bottle becomes $0.4333 (= $0.3500 + $0.0833). In turn, the production volume variance for May 2019 becomes:

$$(600,000 - 460,000) \times (0.0833) = 11,662 \text{ U}$$

The master-budget level conforms with CRA regulations. The unfavourable production-volume variance must be prorated over the inventory remaining in finished goods. The unfavourable variance increases the finished goods inventory value, which is subtracted from COGS. A lower COGS will be reported for tax purposes and therefore a higher taxable income.

3. The statement of comprehensive income for May 2019 is now

Revenue	$210,000
Cost of goods sold:	
Beginning inventory	0
Variable manufacturing costs:	
$0.35 × 460,000	161,000
Fixed manufacturing costs:	
$0.0833 × 460,000	38,318
Cost of goods available for sale	199,318
Ending inventory:	
$0.4333 × (460,000 − 420,000)	17,332
Total cost of goods sold (at standard costs)	181,986
Adjustment for variances	11,662 U
Total cost of goods sold	193,648
Gross margin	16,352
Marketing, other expenses	10,000
Operating income	$ 6,352

4. The higher denominator level in the 2019 master budget means that a temporary set of circumstances has led Bushells to expect a higher than normal denominator level of sales and production in 2019. The normal denominator level is based on a longer-term expected average demand.

5. For purposes of external reporting, the use of variable inventory valuation does not comply either with ASPE/IFRS or with CRA, which both require absorption inventory valuation. Variable inventory valuation collects all manufacturing and non-manufacturing costs incurred during a production time period and allocates this total variable cost pool to each unit remaining in finished goods inventory. All fixed manufacturing and non-manufacturing costs are deducted as period expenses. This method will make it easier for Bushells to calculate a breakeven volume.

6. Throughput inventory valuation collects only the direct materials costs during a production time period, and these are traced to each unit of output remaining in finished goods inventory. All other costs are treated as period costs. Very likely, the immediate recognition of all variable and fixed-cost pools during the period they were incurred will reduce the internally reported operating income.

7. There is no *unique* solution—the answer will depend on assumptions made.

Decision Points

The following question-and-answer format summarizes the chapter's learning objectives. Each decision presents a key question related to a learning objective.

Decision	Guidelines
1. How does variable costing differ from absorption costing?	Variable costing and absorption costing differ in only one respect: how to account for fixed manufacturing costs. Under variable costing, fixed manufacturing costs are excluded from inventoriable costs and are a cost of the period in which they are incurred. Under absorption costing, fixed manufacturing costs are inventoriable and become a part of COGS sold in the period when sales occur.

2. How does income differ under variable and absorption costing?

The variable-costing income statement is based on the contribution-margin format. Under it, operating income is driven by the unit level of sales. Under absorption costing, the income statement follows the gross-margin format. Operating income is driven by the unit level of production, the unit level of sales, and the denominator level used for assigning fixed costs.

3. Why might managers build up finished goods inventory if they use absorption costing?

When absorption costing is used, managers can increase current operating income by producing more units for inventory. Producing for inventory absorbs more fixed manufacturing costs into inventory and reduces costs expensed in the period. Critics of absorption costing label this manipulation of income as the major negative consequence of treating fixed manufacturing costs as inventoriable costs.

4. How does throughput costing differ from variable costing and absorption costing?

Throughput costing treats all costs except direct materials as costs of the period in which they are incurred. Throughput costing results in a lower amount of manufacturing costs being inventoried than either variable or absorption costing.

5. What are the various capacity levels a company can use to compute the budgeted fixed manufacturing cost rate?

Capacity levels can be measured in terms of capacity supplied—theoretical capacity or practical capacity. Capacity can also be measured in terms of output demanded—normal capacity utilization or master-budget capacity utilization.

6. What are the major factors managers consider in choosing the capacity level to compute the budgeted fixed manufacturing cost rate?

The major factors managers consider in choosing the capacity level to compute the budgeted fixed manufacturing cost rate are (a) effect on product costing and capacity management, (b) effect on pricing decisions, (c) effect on performance evaluation, (d) effect on financial statements, and (e) regulatory requirements.

7. What issues must managers take into account when planning capacity levels and for assigning capacity costs?

Critical factors when planning capacity levels and for assigning capacity costs include the uncertainty about the expected spending on capacity costs and the demand for the installed capacity; the role of capacity-related issues in non-manufacturing areas; and the possible use of activity-based costing techniques in allocating capacity costs.

Appendix 9A

Throughput: Super-Variable Costing

▶ **LO 4**

Distinguish throughput costing from variable costing and absorption costing, and explain differences in operating income under each costing policy.

Some managers believe that even variable costing promotes an excessive amount of costs being inventoried. They argue that only direct materials, such as the lenses, casing, scope, and mount in the case of Stassen's telescopes, are "truly variable" in output. **Throughput costing**, which is also called **super-variable costing**, is an extreme form of variable costing in which only direct material costs are included as inventoriable costs. All other costs are costs of the period in which they are incurred. In particular, variable direct manufacturing labour costs and variable manufacturing overhead costs are regarded as period costs and are deducted as expenses of the period.

Exhibit 9A-1 is the throughput-costing income statement for Stassen Company for 2018 and 2019. *Throughput margin* equals revenues minus all direct material cost of the goods sold. Compare the operating income amounts reported in Exhibit 9-5 with those for absorption costing and variable costing:

	2018	2019
Absorption-costing operating income	$1,500,000	$1,335,000
Variable-costing operating income	$1,230,000	$1,537,500
Throughput-costing operating income	$1,050,000	$1,672,500

Only the $110 direct material cost per unit is inventoriable under throughput costing, compared with $335 per unit for absorption costing and $200 per unit for variable costing.

	A	B	C
		2018	**2019**
1			
2	Revenues: $1,000 × 6,000; 6,500 units	$6,000,000	$6,500,000
3	Direct material cost of goods sold		
4	Beginning inventory: $110 × 0; 2,000 units	0	220,000
5	Direct materials: $110 × 8,000; 5,000 units	880,000	550,000
6	Cost of goods available for sale	880,000	770,000
7	Deduct ending inventory: $110 × 2,000; 500 units	(220,000)	(55,000)
8	Direct material cost of goods sold	660,000	71,500
9	Throughput margin[a]	5,340,000	5,785,000
10	Manufacturing costs (other than direct materials)[b]	1,800,000	1,530,000
11	Marketing costs[c]	2,490,000	2,582,500
12	Operating income	$1,050,000	$1,672,500
13			
14	[a]Throughput margin equals revenues minus all direct material cost of goods sold		
15	[b]Fixed manuf. costs + [(variable manuf. labour cost per unit + variable manuf. overhead cost per		
16	unit) × units produced]; $1,080,000 + [($40 + $50) × 8,000; 5,000 units]		
17	[c]Fixed marketing costs + [(variable marketing cost per unit × units sold)]		

Exhibit 9A-1 Throughput Costing for Stassen Company: Telescope Product-Line Income Statements for 2018 and 2019

When the production quantity exceeds sales, as in 2018, throughput costing results in the largest amount of expenses in the current period's income statement. Advocates of throughput costing say it provides managers less incentive to produce for inventory than either variable costing or, especially, absorption costing. Throughput costing is a more recent phenomenon in comparison with variable costing and absorption costing and has avid supporters, but so far it has not been widely adopted.[5]

9.3 TRY IT! ⊕

Potter Replica produces a specialty statue for sale to collectors. In 2017, Potter's expected and actual output was 12,000 statues. Potter sold 10,000 statues at an average selling price of $425. Other information for Potter for 2017 is given below:

Direct material costs	$87.50 per unit
Variable manufacturing costs	$50.00 per unit
Fixed manufacturing costs	$62.50 per unit
Variable administrative costs	$25.00 per unit

Calculate Potter Replica's cost per statue under (a) absorption costing, (b) variable costing, and (c) throughput costing. What is Potter's throughput margin for 2017?

A Comparison of Alternative Inventory-Costing Methods

Variable costing and absorption costing may be combined with actual, normal, or standard costing. Exhibit 9A-1 compares product costing under these six alternative inventory-costing systems.

---

[5] See E. Goldratt, *The Theory of Constraints* (New York: North River Press, 1990); E. Noreen, D. Smith, and J. Mackey, *The Theory of Constraints and Its Implications for Management Accounting* (New York: North River Press, 1995).

Variable costing has been controversial among accountants because of how it affects *external reporting*, not because of disagreement about the need to delineate between variable and fixed costs for internal planning and control. Accountants who favour variable costing for external reporting maintain that the fixed portion of manufacturing costs is more closely related to the capacity to produce than to the actual production of specific units. Fixed costs should therefore be expensed, not inventoried.

Accountants who support absorption costing for *external reporting* maintain that inventories should carry a fixed-manufacturing-cost component because both variable manufacturing costs and fixed manufacturing costs are necessary to produce goods. Therefore, both types of costs should be inventoried in order to match all manufacturing costs to revenues, regardless of their different behaviour patterns. For external reporting to shareholders, companies around the globe tend to follow the generally accepted accounting principle that all manufacturing costs are inventoriable. This also eases the burden on firms and auditors to attempt to disentangle fixed and variable costs of production, a distinction that is not always clear-cut in practice.

Similarly, for tax reporting in the Canada, managers must take direct production costs, as well as fixed and variable indirect production costs, into account in the computation of inventoriable costs in accordance with the "full absorption" method of inventory costing. Indirect production costs include items such as rent, utilities, maintenance, repair expenses, indirect materials, and indirect labour. For other indirect cost categories (including depreciation, insurance, taxes, officers' salaries, factory administrative expenses, and strike-related costs), the portion of the cost that is "incident to and necessary for production or manufacturing operations or processes" is inventoriable for tax purposes *only* if it is treated as inventoriable for the purposes of financial reporting. Accordingly, managers must often allocate costs between those portions related to manufacturing activities and those not related to manufacturing.[6]

Exhibit 9A-1 Comparison of Alternative Inventory-Costing Systems

			Actual Costing	Normal Costing	Standard Costing
Absorption Costing	**Variable Costing**	**Variable Direct Manufacturing Cost**	Actual prices × Actual quantity of inputs used	Actual prices × Actual quantity of inputs used	Standard prices × Standard quantity of inputs allowed for actual output achieved
		Variable Manufacturing Overhead Costs	Actual variable overhead rates × Actual quantity of cost-allocation bases used	Budgeted variable overhead rates × Actual quantity of cost-allocation bases used	Standard variable overhead rates × Standard quantity of cost-allocation bases allowed for actual output achieved
		Fixed Direct Manufacturing Costs	Actual prices × Actual quantity of inputs used	Actual prices × Actual quantity of inputs used	Standard prices × Standard quantity of inputs allowed for actual output achieved
		Fixed Manufacturing Overhead Costs	Actual fixed overhead rates × Actual quantity of cost-allocation bases used	Budgeted fixed overhead rates × Actual quantity of cost-allocation bases used	Standard fixed overhead rates × Standard quantity of cost-allocation bases allowed for actual output achieved

[6] Details regarding tax rules can be found in the Income Tax Act (ITA) of Canada (http://laws-lois.justice.gc.ca/eng/acts/I-3.3/index.html).

Appendix 9B

Breakeven Under Two Costing Policies

If variable costing is used, the breakeven point (operating income of $0) is computed in the usual manner. There is only one breakeven point in this case, and it is a function of

► LO 5

Explain breakeven under each of the two costing policies.

- fixed costs,
- contribution margin per unit, and
- unit level of sales.

Holding fixed cost and unit contribution margin constant, operating income rises as the level of sales rises. The formula for computing the breakeven point with variable costing is a special case of the more general target operating income formula:

$$Q = \frac{\text{Total fixed costs } + \text{ Target operating income}}{\text{Contribution margin per unit}}$$

$$= \text{Number of units sold to earn the target operating income}$$

Breakeven occurs when the target operating income is $0. In our Stassen illustration for 2018:[7]

$$Q = \frac{(\$12,800 + \$10,400) + \$0}{\$99 - (\$20 + \$19)} = \frac{\$23,200}{\$60}$$

$$= 387 \text{ units (rounded)}$$

If absorption costing is used, the required number of units sold to achieve a specific target operating income is not unique because of the number of variables involved. The following formula highlights the factors that will affect the target operating income under absorption costing:

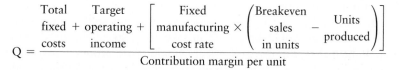

$$Q = \frac{\begin{array}{c}\text{Total} \\ \text{fixed} \\ \text{costs}\end{array} + \begin{array}{c}\text{Target} \\ \text{operating} \\ \text{income}\end{array} + \left[\begin{array}{c}\text{Fixed} \\ \text{manufacturing} \\ \text{cost rate}\end{array} \times \left(\begin{array}{c}\text{Breakeven} \\ \text{sales} \\ \text{in units}\end{array} - \begin{array}{c}\text{Units} \\ \text{produced}\end{array}\right)\right]}{\text{Contribution margin per unit}}$$

This formula has three terms in the numerator compared with two terms in the numerator of the variable-costing formula stated earlier. In this formula, total fixed costs include all manufacturing and non-manufacturing fixed costs. The extra term added to the numerator under absorption costing is as follows:

$$\left[\begin{array}{c}\text{Fixed manufacturing} \\ \text{cost rate}\end{array} \times \left(\begin{array}{c}\text{Breakeven sales} \\ \text{in units}\end{array} - \begin{array}{c}\text{Units} \\ \text{produced}\end{array}\right)\right]$$

This term captures the additional amount of target operating income in the numerator caused by absorption costing, which moves fixed manufacturing costs to inventory from cost of goods sold for all units produced that exceed the breakeven sales quantity. This formula shows that under absorption costing, there is still a unique breakeven point for each quantity of units produced.

There is also an inverse relationship (as one goes up, the other goes down) between the quantity of units produced and the required quantity of units sold to break even. The higher

---

[7] Operating income is not $0 because the breakeven number of units is rounded up to 387 from 386.67.

Proof of breakeven point:

Revenues, $99 × 387	$38,313
Variable costs, $39 × 387	15,093
Contribution margin, $60 × 387	23,220
Fixed costs	23,200
Operating income	$ 20

the quantity of units produced, the higher the level of fixed manufacturing overhead costs absorbed into finished goods inventory and the higher the COGS. The period costs remain unchanged; therefore, the quantity of units that must be sold to cover these costs too (and break even) will decrease.

Consider Stassen Company in 2018. One breakeven point under absorption costing for production of 500 units is as follows:

$$Q = \frac{(\$12,800 + \$10,400) + \$0 + [\$16(Q - 500)]}{\$99 - (\$20 + \$19)}$$

$$= \frac{\$23,200 + \$16Q - \$8,000}{\$60}$$

$$\$60Q = \$15,200 + \$16Q$$

$$\$44Q = \$15,200$$

$$Q = 346 \text{ (rounded)}$$

The breakeven point under absorption costing depends on the

- fixed costs,
- contribution margin per unit,
- unit level of sales,
- unit level of production, and
- overhead cost rate.

For Stassen in 2018, a combination of 346 units sold, 500 units produced, and an 800-unit denominator level would result in an operating income of $0.[8] Note, however, that there are many combinations of these five factors that would give an operating income of $0. For example, a combination of 291 units sold, 650 units produced, and an 800-unit denominator level also results in an operating income of $0 under absorption costing.

Suppose in our illustration that actual production in 2018 were equal to the denominator level, 800 units. Also suppose that there were no units sold and no fixed operating costs. All the production would be placed in inventory, so all the fixed manufacturing overhead would be included in inventory; there would be no production-volume variance. Thus, the company would break even with no sales whatsoever! In contrast, under variable costing the operating loss would be equal to the fixed manufacturing costs of $12,800.

---

[8] Operating income is not exactly $0 because the breakeven number of units is rounded up to 346 from 345.45.

Terms to Learn

This chapter and the Glossary at the end of the book contain definitions of the following important terms:

absorption costing **(p. 335)**	non-productive idle capacity **(p. 336)**	theoretical capacity **(p. 333)**
direct costing **(p. 343)**	normal capacity **(p. 333)**	throughput costing **(p. 358)**
downward demand spiral **(p. 341)**	off-limits idle capacity **(p. 335)**	variable costing **(p. 343)**
full absorption costing **(p. 335)**	practical capacity **(p. 333)**	
master-budget capacity **(p. 333)**	super-variable costing **(p. 358)**	

Assignment Material

MyLab Accounting Make the grade with MyLab Accounting: The Short-Answer Questions, Exercises, and Problems marked with a ⊕ can be found on MyLab Accounting. You can practise them as often as you want, and most feature step-by-step guided instructions to help you find the right answer.

Short-Answer Questions

9-1 "Differences in operating income between variable and absorption costing are due solely to accounting for fixed costs." Do you agree? Explain.

9-2 Why is the term *direct costing* a misnomer for variable costing?

9-3 Do companies in either the service sector or the merchandising sector make choices about absorption costing versus variable costing?

9-4 Explain the main conceptual issue under variable and absorption costing regarding the proper timing for the release of fixed manufacturing overhead as expense.

9-5 "Companies that make no variable-cost/fixed-cost distinctions must use absorption costing, and those that do make variable-cost/fixed-cost distinctions must use variable costing." Do you agree? Explain.

9-6 "The main trouble with variable costing is that it ignores the increasing importance of fixed costs in modern manufacturing." Do you agree? Why?

9-7 Give an example of how, under absorption costing, operating income could fall even though the unit sales level rises.

9-8 What are the factors that affect the breakeven point under (a) variable costing and (b) absorption costing?

9-9 Critics of absorption costing have increasingly emphasized its potential for promoting undesirable incentives for managers. Give an example.

9-10 What are two ways of reducing the negative aspects associated with using absorption costing to evaluate the performance of a plant manager?

9-11 Describe the downward demand spiral and its implications for pricing decisions.

9-12 Will the financial statements of a company always differ when different choices at the start of the period are made regarding the denominator-level capacity concept?

9-13 Which denominator-level concepts emphasize what a plant can supply? Which denominator-level concepts emphasize what customers demand for products produced by a plant?

9-14 "The difference between practical capacity and master-budget capacity utilization is the best measure of management's ability to balance the costs of having too much capacity and having too little capacity." Do you agree? Explain.

Exercises

9-15 Terminology. A number of terms are listed below:

absorption costing	super-variable costing
theoretical capacity	practical capacity
normal capacity	master budget capacity
non-productive idle capacity	off-limits idle capacity

Required

Select the terms from the above list to complete the following sentences.

When the full costs of production are included, this is called _____, but it is sometimes more appropriate to use either variable costing or to include only direct materials called throughput or _____. The two types of demand capacity that can be used in the denominator to calculate a unitized fixed-cost rate are long-term demand _____ or short-term demand called _____. The only acceptable measure for CRA is _____, while the only ASPE/IFRS compliant measure to value inventory and COGS is _____. The two supply-side measures that may be used in the denominator to calculate a unitized fixed-cost rate are long-term measures. The first is unrealistic and excludes any allowance for _____. It is a 24/7/365 measure called _____. The second includes allowance for scheduled maintenance but not for _____. It is called _____.

9-16 Variable and absorption costing; explaining operating-income differences. TC Motors assembles and sells motor vehicles, and uses standard costing. Actual data relating to April and May 2018 are

◄ **LO 3**
1. a. Operating income, April 2018, $1,250,000

	April	May
Unit data:		
Beginning inventory	0	150
Production	500	400
Sales	350	520
Variable costs:		
Manufacturing cost per unit produced	$ 10,000	$ 10,000
Operating (marketing) cost per unit sold	$ 3,000	$ 3,000
Fixed costs:		
Manufacturing costs	$2,000,000	$2,000,000
Operating (marketing) costs	$ 600,000	$ 600,000

The selling price per vehicle is $26,000. The budgeted level of production used to calculate the budgeted fixed manufacturing cost per unit is 500 units. There are no price, efficiency, or rate variances. Any production-volume variance is written off to COGS in the month in which it occurs.

Required

1. Prepare April and May 2018 statements of comprehensive income for TC Motors under (a) variable costing and (b) absorption costing.
2. Prepare a numerical reconciliation and explanation of the difference between operating income for each month under variable costing and absorption costing.

LO 4 ▶

1. Operating income, April 2018, $755,000

⊕ **9-17 Throughput costing** (continuation of 9-16). The variable manufacturing costs per unit of TC Motors are

	April	May
Direct material cost per unit	$6,700	$6,700
Direct manufacturing labour cost per unit	1,500	1,500
Manufacturing overhead cost per unit	1,800	1,800

Required

1. Prepare operating statements of comprehensive income for TC Motors in April and May of 2018 under throughput costing.
2. Contrast the results in requirement 1 with those in requirement 1 of Exercise 9-16.
3. Give one motivation for TC Motors to adopt throughput costing.

LO 3 ▶

1. a. Operating income, January $510,000

⊕ **9-18 Variable and absorption costing, explaining operating-income differences.** 4KPlay Inc. manufactures and sells 50-inch television sets and uses standard costing. Actual data relating to January, February, and March of 2018 are

	January	February	March
Unit data:			
Beginning inventory	0	300	300
Production	1,000	800	1,250
Sales	700	800	1,500
Variable costs:			
Manufacturing cost per unit produced	$ 900	$ 900	$ 900
Operating (marketing) cost per unit sold	$ 600	$ 600	$ 600
Fixed costs:			
Manufacturing costs	$400,000	$400,000	$400,000
Operating (marketing) costs	$140,000	$140,000	$140,000

The selling price per unit is $3,000.

Required

1. Present statements of comprehensive income for January, February, and March of 2018 under (a) variable costing and (b) absorption costing.
2. Explain the difference in operating income for January, February, and March under variable costing and absorption costing.

🌐 **9-19 Throughput costing** (continuation of 9-18). The variable manufacturing costs per unit of 4KPlay Inc. are

◀ LO 4
1. Operating income, January 2018, $390,000

	January	February	March
Direct material cost per unit	$500	$500	$500
Direct manufacturing labour cost per unit	100	100	100
Manufacturing overhead cost per unit	300	300	300
	$900	$900	$900

Required

1. Prepare operating statements of comprehensive income for January, February, and March of 2018 under throughput costing.
2. Contrast the results in requirement 1 with those in requirement 1 of Exercise 9-18.
3. Give one motivation to adopt throughput costing.

🌐 **9-20 Absorption and variable costing.** Osawa Inc. planned and actually manufactured 200,000 units of its single product in 2018, its first year of operation. Variable manufacturing cost was $20 per unit produced. Variable operating (non-manufacturing) cost was $10 per unit sold. Planned and actual fixed manufacturing costs were $600,000. Planned and actual fixed operating (non-manufacturing) costs totalled $400,000. Osawa sold 120,000 units of product at $40 per unit.

◀ LO 3
1. Absorption costing operating income, $440,000

Required

1. Osawa's 2018 operating income using absorption costing is (a) $440,000, (b) $200,000, (c) $600,000, (d) $840,000, or (e) none of these. Show supporting calculations.
2. Osawa's 2018 operating income using variable costing is (a) $800,000, (b) $440,000, (c) $200,000, (d) $600,000, or (e) none of these. Show supporting calculations.

🌐 **9-21 Variable and absorption costing, explaining operating-income differences.** Nascar Motors assembles and sells motor vehicles and uses standard costing. Actual data relating to April and May 2017 are as follows:

◀ LO 3
May 2017 Operating Income is $3,120,000

	Home	Insert	Page Layout	Formulas	Data	Review	
	A				B	C	D
1					**April**		**May**
2	Unit data:						
3	Beginning inventory				0		150
4	Production				500		400
5	Sales				350		520
6	Variable costs:						
7	Manufacturing cost per unit produced				$ 10,000		$ 10,000
8	Operating (marketing) cost per unit sold				3,000		3,000
9	Fixed costs:						
10	Manufacturing costs				$2,000,000		$2,000,000
11	Operating (marketing) costs				600,000		600,000

The selling price per vehicle is $24,000. The budgeted level of production used to calculate the budgeted fixed manufacturing cost per unit is 500 units. There are no price, efficiency, or spending variances. Any production-volume variance is written off to cost of goods sold in the month in which it occurs.

Required

1. Prepare April and May 2017 income statements for Nascar Motors under (a) variable costing and (b) absorption costing.
2. Prepare a numerical reconciliation and explanation of the difference between operating income for each month under variable costing and absorption costing.

LO 3 ▶

1. Operating income, $2,531,520

⊕ **9-22 Absorption versus variable costing.** Electron Inc. is a semiconductor company based in Winnipeg. In 2018, it produced a new router system for its corporate clients. The average wholesale selling price of the system is $1,200 each. For 2018, Electron estimates that it will sell 10,000 router systems and so produces 10,000 units. Actual 2018 sales are 8,960 units. Electron's actual 2018 costs are:

Variable costs per unit:	
Manufacturing cost per unit produced	
Direct materials	$ 55
Direct manufacturing labour	45
Manufacturing overhead	120
Marketing cost per unit sold	75
Fixed costs:	
Manufacturing costs	1,471,680
R&D	981,120
Marketing	3,124,480

Required

1. Calculate the operating income under variable costing.
2. Each router unit produced is allocated $165 in fixed manufacturing costs. If the production-volume variance is written off to cost of goods sold, and there are no price, rate, or efficiency variances, calculate the operating income under absorption costing.
3. Explain the differences in operating incomes obtained in requirement 1 and requirement 2.
4. Electron's management is considering implementing a bonus for the supervisors based on gross margin under absorption costing. What incentives will this create for the supervisors? Do you think this new bonus plan is a good idea? Explain briefly.

LO 1, 2 ▶

1. a, b

⊕ **9-23 Capacity management, denominator-level capacity concepts.**

Required

Match each of the following numbered items with one or more of the denominator-level capacity concepts by putting the appropriate letter(s) by each item:

a. Theoretical capacity
b. Practical capacity
c. Normal capacity utilization
d. Master-budget capacity utilization

1. Measures the denominator level in terms of what a plant can supply
2. Is based on producing at full efficiency all the time
3. Represents the expected level of capacity utilization for the next budget period
4. Measures the denominator level in terms of demand for the output of the plant
5. Takes into account seasonal, cyclical, and trend factors
6. Should be used for performance evaluation
7. Represents the "ideal" benchmark
8. Highlights the cost of capacity acquired but not used
9. Should be used for long-term pricing purposes
10. Hides the cost of capacity acquired but not used
11. If used as the denominator-level concept, would avoid the restatement of unit costs when expected demand levels change

LO 4 ▶

1. Variable Costing Operating income, $2,577,320

⊕ **9-24 Variable vs. absorption costing.** The Zwatch Company manufactures trendy, high-quality moderately priced watches. As Zwatch's senior financial analyst, you are asked to recommend a method of inventory costing. The CFO will use your recommendation to prepare Zwatch's 2018 statement of comprehensive income. The following data are for the year ended December 31, 2018:

Beginning inventory, January 1, 2018	85,000 units
Ending inventory, December 31, 2018	34,500 units
2018 sales	345,400 units
Selling price (to distributor)	$22.00 per unit
Variable manufacturing cost per unit, including direct materials	$5.10 per unit
Variable operating (marketing) cost per unit sold	$1.10 per unit sold
Fixed manufacturing costs	$1,440,000
Denominator-level machine-hours	6,000
Standard production rate	50 units per machine-hour
Fixed operating (marketing) costs	$1,440,000

Assume standard costs per unit are the same for units in beginning inventory and units produced during the year. Also, assume no price, rate, or efficiency variances. Any production-volume variance is written off to COGS in the month in which it occurs.

Required

1. Prepare statements of comprehensive income under variable and absorption costing for the year ended December 31, 2018.
2. What is Zwatch's operating income as a percentage of revenues under each costing method?
3. Explain the difference in operating income between the two methods.
4. Which costing method would you recommend to the CFO? Why?

Problems

🌐 **9-25 Variable and absorption costing and breakeven points.** Camino, a leading firm in the sports industry, produces basketballs for the consumer market. For the year ended December 31, 2017, Camino sold 400,000 basketballs at an average selling price of $12 per unit. The following information also relates to 2017 (assume constant unit costs and no variances of any kind):

◀ **LO 2**

Inventory, January 1, 2017:	0 basketballs
Inventory, December 31, 2017:	20,000 basketballs
Fixed manufacturing costs:	$380,000
Fixed administrative costs:	$660,000
Direct materials costs:	$ 3 per basketball
Direct labour costs:	$ 4 per basketball

Required

1. Calculate the breakeven point (in basketballs sold) in 2017 under:
   a. Variable costing
   b. Absorption costing
2. Suppose direct materials costs were $4 per basketball instead. Assuming all other data are the same, calculate the minimum number of basketballs Camino must have sold in 2017 to attain a target operating income of $120,000 under:
   a. Variable costing
   b. Absorption costing

🌐 **9-26 Absorption costing and production-volume variance—alternative capacity bases.** Earth Light First (ELF), a producer of energy-efficient light bulbs, expects that demand will increase markedly over the next decade. Due to the high fixed costs involved in the business, ELF has decided to evaluate its financial performance using absorption costing income. The production-volume variance is written off to COGS. The variable cost of production is $2.50 per bulb. Fixed manufacturing costs are $1,000,000 per year.

◀ **LO 1, 2, 3**
1. Theoretical inventoriable cost per unit, $3.75

Variable and fixed selling and administrative expenses are $0.25 per bulb sold and $250,000, respectively. Because its light bulbs are currently popular with environmentally conscious customers, ELF can sell the bulbs for $9 each.

ELF is deciding whether to use, when calculating the cost of each unit produced,

Theoretical capacity	800,000 bulbs
Practical capacity	500,000 bulbs
Normal capacity	250,000 bulbs (average production for the next three years)
Master-budget capacity	200,000 bulbs produced this year

Required

1. Calculate the inventoriable cost per unit using each level of capacity to compute fixed manufacturing cost per unit.
2. Calculate the production-volume variance using each level of capacity to compute the fixed manufacturing overhead allocation rate and this year's production of 220,000 bulbs.
3. Assuming ELF has no beginning inventory, calculate operating income for ELF using each type of capacity to compute fixed manufacturing cost per unit and this year's sales of 200,000 bulbs.

LO 3 ▶   ⊕ **9-27 Variable costing versus absorption costing.** The Garvis Company uses an absorption-costing system based on standard costs. Variable manufacturing cost consists of direct material cost of $4.50 per unit and other variable manufacturing costs of $1.50 per unit. The standard production rate is 20 units per machine-hour. Total budgeted and actual fixed manufacturing overhead costs are $840,000. Fixed manufacturing overhead is allocated at $14 per machine-hour based on fixed manufacturing costs of $840,000 ÷ 60,000 machine-hours, which is the level Garvis uses as its denominator level.

The selling price is $10 per unit. Variable operating (nonmanufacturing) cost, which is driven by units sold, is $2 per unit. Fixed operating (nonmanufacturing) costs are $240,000. Beginning inventory in 2017 is 60,000 units; ending inventory is 80,000 units. Sales in 2017 are 1,080,000 units.

The same standard unit costs persisted throughout 2016 and 2017. For simplicity, assume that there are no price, spending, or efficiency variances.

Required

1. Prepare an income statement for 2017 assuming that the production-volume variance is written off at year-end as an adjustment to cost of goods sold.
2. The president has heard about variable costing. She asks you to recast the 2017 statement as it would appear under variable costing.
3. Explain the difference in operating income as calculated in requirements 1 and 2.
4. Graph how fixed manufacturing overhead is accounted for under absorption costing. That is, there will be two lines: one for the budgeted fixed manufacturing overhead (which is equal to the actual fixed manufacturing overhead in this case) and one for the fixed manufacturing overhead allocated. Show the production-volume variance in the graph.
5. Critics have claimed that a widely used accounting system has led to undesirable buildups of inventory levels. (a) Is variable costing or absorption costing more likely to lead to such buildups? Why? (b) What can managers do to counteract undesirable inventory buildups?

LO 4 ▶   ⊕ **9-28 Throughput Costing** (continuation of 9-27)

Required

1. Prepare an income statement under throughput costing for the year ended December 31, 2017 for Garvis Company.
2. Reconcile the difference between the contribution margin and throughput margin for Garvis in 2017. Then reconcile the operating income between variable costing and throughput costing for Garvis in 2017.
3. Advocates of throughput costing say it provides managers less incentive to produce for inventory than either variable costing or, especially, absorption costing. Do you agree? Why or why not? Under what circumstances might you recommend that Garvis use throughput costing?

9-29 Denominator-level choices, changes in inventory levels, effect on operating income.
Yates Corporation is a manufacturer of computer accessories. It uses absorption costing based on standard costs and reports the following data for 2018:

◀ LO 1, 2, 3
4. Reconciliation, $16,000

	A	B	C
1	Theoretical capacity	144,000	units
2	Practical capacity	120,000	units
3	Normal capacity utilization	96,000	units
4	Selling price	$ 30	per unit
5	Beginning inventory	10,000	units
6	Production	104,000	units
7	Sales volume	112,000	units
8	Variable budgeted manufacturing cost	$ 3	per unit
9	Total budgeted fixed manufacturing costs	$1,440,000	
10	Total budgeted operating (non-manuf.) costs (all fixed)	$ 400,000	

There are no rate or efficiency variances. Actual operating costs equal budgeted operating costs. The production-volume variance is written off to COGS. For each choice of denominator level, the budgeted production cost per unit is also the cost per unit of beginning inventory.

Required

1. What is the production-volume variance in 2018 when the denominator level is (a) theoretical capacity, (b) practical capacity, and (c) normal capacity utilization?
2. Prepare absorption costing-based statements of comprehensive income for Yates Corporation using theoretical capacity, practical capacity, and normal capacity utilization as the denominator levels.
3. Why is the operating income under normal capacity utilization lower than the other two scenarios?
4. Reconcile the difference in operating income based on theoretical capacity and practical capacity with the difference in fixed manufacturing overhead included in inventory.

9-30 Variable and absorption costing, sales, and operating-income changes. Headsmart, a three-year-old company, has been producing and selling a single type of bicycle helmet. Headsmart uses standard costing. After reviewing the statements of comprehensive income for the first three years, Stuart Weil, president of Headsmart, commented, "I was told by our accountants—and in fact, I have memorized—that our breakeven volume is 50,000 units. I was happy that we reached that sales goal in each of our first two years. But, here's the strange thing: In our first year, we sold 50,000 units and indeed we broke even. Then, in our second year we sold the same volume and had a positive operating income. I didn't complain, of course ... but here's the bad part. In our third year, we sold 20% more helmets, but our operating income fell by more than 80% relative to the second year! We didn't change our selling price or cost structure over the past three years and have no price, efficiency, or rate variances ... so what's going on?!"

◀ LO 2, 3
3. Operating income for 2017,
2018 = $0

Absorption Costing	2017	2018	2019
Sales (units)	50,000	50,000	60,000
Revenues	$2,100,000	$2,100,000	$2,520,000
Cost of goods sold:			
Beginning inventory	0	0	380,000
Production	1,900,000	2,280,000	1,900,000
Available for sale	1,900,000	2,280,000	2,280,000
Deduct ending inventory	0	(380,000)	0
Adjustment for production-volume variance	0	(240,000)	0
Cost of goods sold	1,900,000	1,660,000	2,280,000
Gross margin	200,000	440,000	240,000
Selling and administrative expenses (all fixed)	200,000	200,000	200,000
Operating income	$ 0	$ 240,000	$ 40,000
Beginning inventory	0	0	10,000
Production (units)	50,000	60,000	50,000
Sales (units)	50,000	50,000	60,000
Ending inventory	0	10,000	0
Variable manufacturing cost per unit	$ 14	$ 14	$ 14
Fixed manufacturing overhead costs	$1,200,000	$1,200,000	$1,200,000
Fixed manufacturing costs allocated per unit produced	$ 24	$ 24	$ 24

Required

1. What denominator level is Headsmart using to allocate fixed manufacturing costs to the bicycle helmets? How is Headsmart disposing of any favourable or unfavourable production-volume variance at the end of the year? Explain your answer briefly.
2. How did Headsmart's accountants arrive at the breakeven volume of 50,000 units?
3. Prepare a variable-costing-based statements of comprehensive income for each year. Explain the variation in variable costing operating income for each year based on contribution margin per unit and sales volume.
4. Reconcile the operating incomes under variable costing and absorption costing for each year, and use this information to explain to Stuart Weil the positive operating income in 2018 and the drop in operating income in 2019.

LO 1, 2 ▶
1. Theoretical budgeted fixed manufacturing overhead cost rate, $1,388.89

🌐 **9-31 Denominator-level problem.** AJG Inc. is a manufacturer of the very popular G36 motorcycles. The management at AJG has recently adopted absorption costing and is debating which denominator level concept to use. The G36 motorcycles sell for an average price of $8,500. Budgeted fixed manufacturing overhead costs for 2018 are estimated at $4,000,000. AJG Inc. uses subassembly operators that provide component parts. The following are the denominator-level options that management has been considering:

a. Theoretical capacity—based on two shifts, completion of four motorcycles per shift, and a 360-day year—$2 \times 4 \times 360 = 2,880$.
b. Practical capacity—theoretical capacity adjusted for unavoidable interruptions, breakdowns, and so forth—$2 \times 3 \times 320 = 1,920$.
c. Normal capacity utilization—estimated at 1,200 units.
d. Master-budget capacity utilization—the growing popularity of motorcycles has prompted the marketing department to issue an estimate for 2018 of 1,500 units.

Required

1. Calculate the budgeted fixed manufacturing overhead cost rates under the four denominator-level concepts.
2. What are the benefits to AJG Inc. of using either theoretical capacity or practical capacity?
3. Under a cost-based pricing system, what are the negative aspects of a master-budget denominator level? What are the positive aspects?

LO 2 ▶
2. Budgeted cost per meal, $6.25

🌐 **9-32 Cost allocation, downward demand spiral.** Deli One operates a chain of 10 retirement homes in the Toronto area. Its central food-catering facility, Deliman, prepares and delivers meals to the retirement homes. It has the capacity to deliver up to 1,460,000 meals a year. In 2018, based on estimates from each retirement home controller, Deliman budgeted for 1,022,000 meals a year. Budgeted fixed costs in 2018 were $1,533,000. Each retirement home was charged $7.00 per meal—$5.50 variable costs plus $1.50 allocated budgeted fixed cost.

Recently, the retirement homes have been complaining about the quality of Deliman's meals and their rising costs. In mid-2018, Deli One's president announces that all Deli One retirement homes and support facilities will be run as profit centres. Retirement homes will be free to purchase quality-certified services from outside the system. Ron Smith, Deliman's controller, is preparing the 2019 budget. He hears that three retirement homes have decided to use outside suppliers for their meals; this will reduce the 2019 estimated demand to 876,000 meals. No change in variable cost per meal or total fixed costs is expected in 2019.

Required

1. How did Smith calculate the budgeted fixed cost per meal of $1.50 in 2018?
2. Using the same approach to calculating budgeted fixed cost per meal and pricing as in 2018, how much would retirement homes be charged for each Deliman meal in 2019? What would their reaction be?
3. Suggest an alternative cost-based price per meal that Smith might propose and that might be more acceptable to the retirement homes. What can Deliman and Smith do to make this price profitable in the long run?

LO 2, 3 ▶

🌐 **9-33 Effects of differing production levels on absorption costing income: Metrics to minimize inventory buildups.** Mountain Press produces textbooks for high school accounting courses. The company recently hired a new editor, Jan Green, to handle production and sales of books for an introductory accounting course. Jan's compensation depends on the gross margin associated with sales of this book. Jan needs to decide how many copies of the books to produce. The following information is available for the fall semester of 2017:

Estimated sales	50,000 books
Beginning inventory	0 books
Average selling price	$ 160 per book
Variable production costs	$ 100 per book
Fixed production costs	$750,000 per semester

The fixed-cost allocation rate is based on expected sales and is therefore equal to $750,000/50,000 books = $15 per book.

Jan has decided to produce either 50,000, 65,000, or 70,000 books.

Required

1. Calculate expected gross margin if Jan produces 50,000, 65,000, or 70,000 books. (Make sure you include the production-volume variance as part of cost of goods sold.)
2. Calculate ending inventory in units and in dollars for each production level.
3. Managers who are paid a bonus that is a function of gross margin may be inspired to produce a product in excess of demand to maximize their own bonus. The chapter suggested metrics to discourage managers from producing products in excess of demand. Do you think the following metrics will accomplish this objective? Show your work.
   a. Incorporate a charge of 10% of the cost of the ending inventory as an expense for evaluating the manager.
   b. Include nonfinancial measures (such as the ones recommended on page 341) when evaluating management and rewarding performance.

⊕ **9-34 Variable costing and absorption costing, the Z-Var Corporation.** (R. Marple, adapted) It ◀ **LO 3** is the end of 2017. Z-Var Corporation began operations in January 2016. The company is so named because it has no variable costs (Zero VARiable). All its costs are fixed; they do not vary with output.

Z-Var Corp. is located on the bank of a river and has its own hydroelectric plant to supply power, light, and heat. The company manufactures a synthetic fertilizer from air and river water and sells its product at a price that is not expected to change. It has a small staff of employees, all paid fixed annual salaries. The output of the plant can be increased or decreased by pressing a few buttons on a keyboard.

The following budgeted and actual data are for the operations of Z-Var. The company uses budgeted production as the denominator level and writes off any production-volume variance to cost of goods sold.

	2016	2017[a]
Sales	30,000 tons	30,000 tons
Production	60,000 tons	0 tons
Selling price	$ 90 per ton	$ 90 per ton
Costs (all fixed):		
Manufacturing	$2,580,000	$2,580,000
Operating (nonmanufacturing)	$ 102,000	$ 102,000

[a]Management adopted the policy, effective January 1, 2017, of producing only as much product as needed to fill sales orders. During 2017, sales were the same as for 2016 and were filled entirely from inventory at the start of 2017.

Required

1. Prepare income statements with one column for 2016, one column for 2017, and one column for the two years together using (a) variable costing and (b) absorption costing.
2. What is the breakeven point under (a) variable costing and (b) absorption costing?
3. What inventory costs would be carried in the balance sheet on December 31, 2016 and 2017 under each method?
4. Assume that the performance of the top manager of Z-Var is evaluated and rewarded largely on the basis of reported operating income. Which costing method would the manager prefer? Why?

⊕ **9-35 Variable and absorption costing, and breakeven points.** Shasta Hills, a winery in British ◀ **LO 5** Columbia, manufactures a premium white cabernet and sells primarily to distributors. Wine is sold in cases 3. b. operating Q = 252,647 of one dozen bottles. In the year ended December 31, 2018, Shasta Hills sold 242,400 cases at an aver- (rounded up) age selling price of $112.80 per case. The following additional data are for Shasta Hills for the year ended December 31, 2018 (assume constant unit costs and no price, rate, or efficiency variances):

Beginning inventory, January 1, 2018	32,600 cases
Ending inventory, December 31, 2018	24,800 cases
Fixed manufacturing overhead	$4,504,320
Fixed operating costs	$7,882,560
Variable costs per case:	
Direct materials	
Grapes	$ 19.20 per case
Bottles, corks, and crates	$ 12.00 per case
Direct labour	
Bottling	$ 7.20 per case
Winemaking	$ 16.80 per case
Aging	$ 2.40 per case

On December 31, 2018, the unit costs per case for closing inventory are $57.60 for variable costing and $76.80 for absorption costing.

Required

1. Calculate cases of production for Shasta Hills in 2018.
2. Find the breakeven point (number of cases) in 2018:
   a. Under variable costing.
   b. Under absorption costing.
3. Grape prices are expected to increase 25% in 2019. Assuming all other data remain constant, what is the minimum number of cases Shasta Hills must sell in 2019 to break even? Calculate the breakeven point:
   a. Under variable costing.
   b. Under absorption costing.
4. Assume the owners of Shasta Hills want to increase 2019 operating income 10% over 2018 levels. Using the same data as in requirement 3, recalculate the target quantity of cases under variable and absorption costing. Use approximation method for absorption costing.

LO 4 ▶   ⊕ **9-36 Comparison of variable costing and absorption costing.** Gammaro Company uses standard costing. Tim Sweeney, the new president of Gammaro Company, is presented with the following data for 2017:

		Home	Insert	Page Layout	Formulas	Data	Review	View	
		A					B	C	
1			Gammaro Company						
2			Income Statements for the Year Ended December 31, 2017						
3							Variable	Absorption	
4							Costing	Costing	
5	Revenues						$9,350,000	$9,350,000	
6	Cost of goods sold (at standard costs)						4,695,000	5,855,000	
7	Fixed manufacturing overhead (budgeted)						1,350,000	—	
8	Fixed manufacturing overhead variances (all unfavourable):								
9	Spending						125,000	125,000	
10	Production volume						—	405,000	
11	Total marketing and administrative costs (all fixed)						1,570,000	1,570,000	
12	Total costs						7,740,000	7,955,000	
13	Operating income						$1,610,000	$1,395,000	
14									
15	Inventories (at standard costs)								
16	December 31, 2016						$1,345,000	$1,730,000	
17	December 31, 2017						45,000	215,000	

Required

1. At what percentage of denominator level was the plant operating during 2017?
2. How much fixed manufacturing overhead was included in the 2016 and the 2017 ending inventory under absorption costing?
3. Reconcile and explain the difference in 2017 operating incomes under variable and absorption costing.
4. Tim Sweeney is concerned: He notes that despite an increase in sales over 2016, 2017 operating income has actually declined under absorption costing. Explain how this occurred.

LO 2, 3, 4 ▶   ⊕ **9-37 Denominator-level choices, changes in inventory levels, effect on operating income.** Me is a manufacturer of magic kits. It uses absorption costing based on standard costs and reports the following data for 2017:

	A	B	C
	Home Insert Page Layout Formulas Data Review		
1	Theoretical capacity	300,000	units
2	Practical capacity	279,070	units
3	Normal capacity utilization	232,558	units
4	Selling price	$ 50	per unit
5	Beginning inventory	40,000	units
6	Production	240,000	units
7	Sales volume	260,000	units
8	Variable budgeted manufacturing cost	$ 10	per unit
9	Total budgeted fixed manufacturing costs	$3,000,000	
10	Total budgeted operating (non-manuf.) costs (all fixed)	$ 500,000	

There are no price, spending, or efficiency variances. Actual operating costs equal budgeted operating costs. The production-volume variance is written off to cost of goods sold. For each choice of denominator level, the budgeted production cost per unit is also the cost per unit of beginning inventory.

Required

1. What is the production-volume variance in 2017 when the denominator level is (a) theoretical capacity, (b) practical capacity, and (c) normal capacity utilization?
2. Prepare absorption costing–based income statements for Magic Me Corporation using theoretical capacity, practical capacity, and normal capacity utilization as the denominator levels.
3. Why is the operating income under normal capacity utilization lower than the other two scenarios?
4. Reconcile the difference in operating income based on theoretical capacity and practical capacity with the difference in fixed manufacturing overhead included in inventory.

⊕ **9-38 Alternative denominator-level capacity concepts, effect on operating income.** Castle Lager has just purchased the Jacksonville Brewery. The brewery is two years old and uses absorption costing. It will "sell" its product to Castle Lager at $47 per barrel. Peter Bryant, Castle Lager's controller, obtains the following information about Jacksonville Brewery's capacity and budgeted fixed manufacturing costs for 2017: ◀ LO 1, 2

	A	B	C	D	E
	Home Insert Page Layout Formulas Data Review View				
1		**Budgeted Fixed**	**Days of**	**Hours of**	
2	**Denominator-Level**	**Manufacturing**	**Production**	**Production**	**Barrels**
3	**Capacity Concept**	**Overhead per Period**	**per Period**	**per Day**	**per Hour**
4	Theoretical capacity	$27,900,000	358	22	545
5	Practical capacity	$27,900,000	348	20	510
6	Normal capacity utilization	$27,900,000	348	20	410
7	Master-budget capacity utilization for each half year:				
8	(a) January–June 2017	$13,950,000	174	20	315
9	(b) July–December 2017	$13,950,000	174	20	505

Required

1. Compute the budgeted fixed manufacturing overhead rate per barrel for each of the denominator-level capacity concepts. Explain why they are different.
2. In 2017, the Jacksonville Brewery reported these production results:

	A	B
	Home Insert Page Layout Formulas Data	
12	Beginning inventory in barrels, 1-1-2017	0
13	Production in barrels	2,670,000
14	Ending inventory in barrels, 12-31-2017	210,000
15	Actual variable manufacturing costs	$80,634,000
16	Actual fixed manufacturing overhead costs	$26,700,000

There are no variable cost variances. Fixed manufacturing overhead cost variances are written off to cost of goods sold in the period in which they occur. Compute the Jacksonville Brewery's operating income when the denominator-level capacity is (a) theoretical capacity, (b) practical capacity, and (c) normal capacity utilization.

LO 2 ▶
1. Production volume variance,
$121,030 U

⊕ **9-39 Cost allocation, responsibility accounting, ethics** (continuation of 9-32). In 2019, only 806,840 Deliman meals were produced and sold to the retirement homes. Smith suspects that retirement home controllers had systematically inflated their 2019 meal estimates.

Required

1. Recall that Deliman uses the master-budget capacity utilization to allocate fixed costs and to price meals. What was the effect of production-volume variance on Deliman's operating income in 2019?
2. Why might retirement home controllers deliberately overestimate their future meal counts?
3. What other evidence should Deli One's controller seek to investigate Smith's concerns?
4. Suggest two specific steps that Deli One's controller might take to reduce retirement home controllers' incentives to inflate their estimated meal counts.

LO 5 ▶
1. a. Operating income, $10,000

⊕ **9-40 Variable and absorption costing, and breakeven points.** Tammy Cat Tree Co. (TCTC) builds luxury cat trees and sells them through the internet to cat owners who want to provide their cats with a more natural environment. At the start of 2018, TCTC carried no inventory. During the year, it produced 1,000 cat trees and sold 800 cat trees for $300 each. Fixed production costs were $100,000, and variable production costs were $75 per cat tree. Fixed advertising, website, and other general and administrative expenses were $50,000, and variable shipping costs were $25 per tree.

Required

1. Prepare an operating statement of comprehensive income assuming TCTC uses
   a. Variable costing.
   b. Absorption costing.
2. Compute the breakeven point in units assuming TCTC uses
   a. Variable costing.
   b. Absorption costing.
3. Due to recent changes in local conservation laws, the price of the wood used in the cat trees is expected to increase by $25 for each tree. What effect would this have on the breakeven points calculated above?
4. Using the original data in the problem and the breakeven/target income formulas, show that it would be necessary to sell 800 cat trees to earn the income calculated in requirements 1a and 1b above.

Collaborative Learning Cases

LO 3, 4 ▶
1. Operating income for April,
$75,000

9-41 Absorption, variable, and throughput costing. EnRG Inc. produces trail mix packaged for sale in convenience stores across Canada. At the beginning of April 2018, EnRG has no inventory of trail mix. Demand for the next three months is expected to remain constant at 50,000 bags per month. EnRG plans to produce 50,000 bags in April. However, many of the employees take vacation in June, so EnRG plans to produce 70,000 bags in May and only 30,000 bags in June.

Costs for the three months are expected to remain unchanged. The costs and revenues for April, May, and June are expected to be

Sales revenue	$6.00 per bag
Direct material cost	$0.80 per bag
Direct manufacturing labour cost	$0.45 per bag
Variable manufacturing overhead cost	$0.30 per bag
Variable selling cost	$0.15 per bag
Fixed manufacturing overhead cost	$105,000 per month
Fixed administrative costs	$ 35,000 per month

Suppose the actual costs, market demand, and levels of production for April, May, and June are as expected.

Required

1. Compute operating income for April, May, and June under variable costing.
2. Compute operating income for April, May, and June under absorption costing. Assume that the denominator level for each month is that month's expected level of output.

3. Compute operating income for April, May, and June under throughput costing.
4. Discuss the benefits and problems associated with using throughput costing.

Mini-Case

9-42 Capacity-level (denominator) choices. Sooke Ale recently purchased a brewing plant from a bankrupt company. It was constructed only two years ago. The plant has budgeted fixed manufacturing overhead of $50 million per year ($4.167 million each month) in 2018. Paul Vautin, the controller of the brewery, must decide on the denominator-level concept to use in its absorption costing system for 2018. The options available to him are:

◄ **LO 1, 2**
1. Theoretical budgeted fixed manufacturing overhead rate per barrel, $9.51

a. Theoretical capacity: 600 barrels an hour for 24 hours a day for 365 days = 5,256,000 barrels
b. Practical capacity: 500 barrels an hour for 20 hours a day for 350 days = 3,500,000 barrels
c. Normal capacity utilization for 2018: 400 barrels an hour for 20 hours a day for 350 days = 2,800,000 barrels
d. Master-budget capacity utilization for 2018 (separate rates computed for each half-year):

■ January to June 2018 budget—320 barrels an hour for 20 hours a day for 175 days = 1,120,000 barrels
■ July to December 2018 budget—480 barrels an hour for 20 hours a day for 175 days = 1,680,000 barrels

Variable standard manufacturing costs per barrel are $51.40 (variable direct materials, $38.40; variable manufacturing labour, $6.00; and variable manufacturing overhead, $7.00). The brewery "sells" its output to the sales division of Sooke Ale at a budgeted price of $82.00 per barrel.

In 2018, the brewery of Sooke Ale showed these results:

Unit data in barrels:

Beginning inventory, January 1, 2018	0
Production	2,600,000
Ending inventory, December 31, 2018	200,000

The brewery had actual costs of

Cost data:

Variable manufacturing	$144,456,000
Fixed manufacturing overhead	48,758,400

The sales division of Sooke Ale purchased 2,400,000 barrels in 2018 at the $82 per barrel rate. All manufacturing variances are written off to COGS in the period in which they are incurred.

Required

1. Compute the budgeted fixed manufacturing overhead rate using each of the four *denominator-level* concepts for (a) beer produced in March 2018 and (b) beer produced in September 2018. Explain why any differences arise.
2. Explain why the theoretical capacity and practical capacity concepts are different.
3. Which denominator-level concept would the plant manager of the brewery prefer when senior management of Sooke Ale is judging plant manager performance during 2018? Explain.
4. Compute the operating income of the brewery using the following: (a) theoretical capacity, (b) practical capacity, and (c) normal capacity utilization denominator-level capacity concepts. Explain any differences between (a), (b), and (c).
5. What denominator-level concept would Sooke Ale prefer for income tax reporting? Explain.
6. Explain the ways in which the CRA might restrict the flexibility of a company like Sooke Ale, which uses absorption costing to reduce its reported taxable income.

TRY IT! ▶ SOLUTIONS

Try It 9–1

(a) Under variable costing, all variable manufacturing costs are inventoriable costs. This includes direct materials, direct manufacturing labour, and variable overhead. Therefore, the inventoriable cost per unit under variable costing is $20 + $4 + $1 = $25.

(b) Absorption costing considers all variable manufacturing costs and all fixed manufacturing costs as inventoriable costs. Therefore, the inventoriable cost per unit under absorption costing is $20 + $4 + $1 + ($750,000 ÷ 100,000 units) = $32.50.

Try It 9–2

(a) Variable costing

Revenues: 24,000 × $50	$1,200,000
Variable cost of goods sold: $525,000 × (24,000/30,000)	420,000
Variable marketing costs:	144,800
Contribution margin	635,200
Fixed manufacturing costs	372,000
Fixed marketing costs	77,400
Operating income	$ 185,800

(b) Absorption costing

Revenues: 24,000 × $50	$1,200,000
Cost of goods sold: ($525,000 + $372,000) × (24,000/30,000)	717,600
Gross margin	482,400
Variable marketing costs	144,800
Fixed marketing costs	77,400
Operating income	$ 260,200

Absorption costing treats fixed manufacturing cost as a product cost, while variable costing treats it as a period cost. ZB Toys has 6,000 units in ending inventory. Under absorption costing, these units have a fixed manufacturing cost of $12.40 per unit ($372,000/30,000). So, the total fixed manufacturing cost in ending inventory under absorption costing is $74,400 (6,000 units × $12.40). Since these costs are inventoried under absorption costing, and not expensed as they would be under variable costing, operating income is higher under absorption costing by $74,400 ($260,200 − $185,800).

Try It 9–3

(a) Absorption costing: $87.50 + $50.00 + $62.50 = $200

(b) Variable costing: $87.50 + $50.00 = $137.50

(c) Throughput costing: $87.50

(d) Throughput margin = 10,000 × ($425 − $87.50) = $3,375,000

Analysis of Cost Behaviour

Cisco Understands Its Costs While Helping the Environment

Can understanding how costs behave contribute to environmental sustainability? At Cisco Systems, an in-depth understanding of the company's costs and operations led to reduced costs while also helping the environment. Cisco, makers of computer networking equipment including routers and wireless switches, traditionally regarded the used equipment it received back from its business customers as scrap and recycled it at a cost of about $8 million a year. In 2005, Cisco began trying to find uses for the equipment, mainly because 80% of the returns were in working condition.

A value recovery team at Cisco identified groups within the company that could use the returned equipment. These included its customer service group, which supports warranty claims and service contracts, and the labs that provide technical support, training, and product demonstrations. Based on the initial success of the value recovery team, Cisco designated its recycling group as a company business unit, set clear objectives for it, and assigned the group its own income statement. As a result, the value of the reuse of equipment rose to $365 million in 2018, up 5% from the previous year. Beyond recycling, Cisco now reduces costs by cutting energy consumption in its labs and using renewable sources to generate 71.9% of its global energy consumption.

As the Cisco example illustrates, managers must understand how costs behave to make strategic and operating decisions that have a positive environmental impact. Consider several other examples. Managers at FedEx decided to replace old planes with new Boeing 757s that reduced fuel consumption by 36% while increasing capacity by 20%. At Clorox, managers created a new line of nonsynthetic cleaning products that were better for the environment and helped create a new category of "green" cleaning products worth about $200 million annually.

In each situation, knowing how costs behave was essential to answer key managerial questions. This chapter will focus on how managers determine cost-behaviour patterns—that is, how costs change in relation to changes in activity levels, in the quantity of products produced, and so on.

Sources: Cisco Systems, Inc. 2016. *2015 corporate social responsibility report.* San Jose, CA: Cisco Systems, Inc.; R. Nidumolu, C. Prahalad, and M. Rangaswami. 2009. Why sustainability is now the key driver of innovation. *Harvard Business Review,* September.

10

▶ Learning Objectives

1. Describe linear cost functions and their behaviour.

2. Explain the importance of causality in estimating cost functions.

3. Understand various methods of cost estimation.

4. Outline the steps in estimating a cost function using quantitative analysis.

5. Explain nonlinear cost functions, in particular those arising from learning curve effects.

6. Describe the impact of time as a cost driver.

7. Describe quality control and its implications as a cost driver.

8. Understand issues of data collection and quality.

9. Appendix 10A: Discuss the interpretation of regression models.

10. Appendix 10B: Describe a learning curve model.

▶ CPA Competencies

This chapter covers material outlined in **Section 3: Management Accounting** of the CPA Competency Map. The Learning Objectives in this chapter have been aligned with the CPA Competency Map to ensure the best coverage possible.

3.3.1 Evaluates cost classifications and costing methods for management of ongoing operations

3.3.2 Evaluates and applies cost management techniques appropriate for specific costing decisions

3.4.1 Evaluates sources and drivers of revenue growth

3.5.2 Evaluates sustainable profit maximization and capacity management performance

Basic Assumptions and Examples of Cost Functions

Managers are able to understand cost behaviour through cost functions. A **cost function** is a mathematical description of how a cost changes with changes in the level of an activity relating to that cost. For example, total variable costs will change in relation to increased activity, and fixed costs will not change.

Cost functions can be plotted on a graph by measuring the level of an activity, such as number of batches produced or number of machine-hours used, on the horizontal axis (called the x-axis) and the amount of total costs corresponding to—or, preferably, dependent on—the levels of that activity on the vertical axis (called the y-axis).

Basic Assumptions

► **LO 1**

Describe linear cost functions and their behaviour.

Managers often estimate cost functions based on two assumptions:

1. Variations in the level of a single activity (the cost driver) explain the variations in the related total costs.

2. Cost behaviour is approximated by a linear cost function within the relevant range. A relevant range is the range of the activity in which there is a relationship between total cost and the level of activity. For a linear cost function represented graphically, total cost versus the level of a single activity related to that cost is a straight line within the relevant range.

These two assumptions are used throughout most, but not all, of this chapter. Not all cost functions are linear and can be explained by a single activity. Later sections will discuss cost functions that do not rely on these assumptions.

Linear Cost Functions

To understand three basic types of linear cost functions and to see the role of cost functions in business decisions, consider the negotiations between Kannon Services and World Wide Communications (WWC) for exclusive use of a videoconferencing line between New York and Paris.

■ *Alternative 1:* $5 per minute used. Total cost to Kannon changes in proportion to the number of minutes used. The number of minutes used is the only factor whose change causes a change in total cost.

Panel A in Exhibit 10-1 presents this *variable cost* for Kannon Services. Under alternative 1, there is no fixed cost. The cost function in Panel A of Exhibit 10-1 is

$$y = \$5x$$

where x measures the number of minutes used (on the x-axis), and y measures the total cost of the minutes used (on the y-axis) calculated using the cost function. The slope represents a $5 change in cost for every one-minute change in activity.

Exhibit 10-1 Kannon Services's Mixed Costs

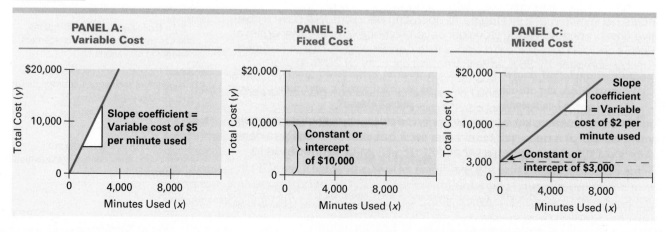

- *Alternative 2:* Total cost will be fixed at $10,000 per month, regardless of the number of minutes used. (We use the same activity measure, number of minutes used, to compare cost-behaviour patterns under the three alternatives.) Panel B in Exhibit 10-1 presents this *fixed cost* for Kannon Services as

$$y = \$10,000$$

The fixed cost of $10,000 is called a **constant**; it is the component of total cost that does not vary with changes in the level of the activity. Under alternative 2, the constant accounts for all the cost because there is no variable cost.

- *Alternative 3:* $3,000 per month plus $2 per minute used. This is an example of a mixed cost. A **mixed cost**—also called a **semi-variable cost**—has both fixed and variable elements. Panel C in Exhibit 10-1 presents this *mixed cost* for Kannon Services as

$$y = \$3,000 + \$2x$$

Unlike the graphs for alternatives 1 and 2, Panel C has both a constant, or intercept, value of $3,000 and a slope coefficient of $2. In the case of a mixed cost, total cost in the relevant range increases as the number of minutes used increases. Note that total cost does not vary strictly in proportion to the number of minutes used within the relevant range. For example, with 4,000 minutes of usage, the total cost is $11,000 [= $3,000 + ($2 per minute × 4,000 minutes)], but when 8,000 minutes are used, total cost is $19,000 [= $3,000 + ($2 per minute × 8,000 minutes)]. Although the usage in terms of minutes has doubled, total cost has increased by only about 73% [= ($19,000 − $11,000) ÷ $11,000].

Suppose Kannon expects to do at least 4,000 minutes of videoconferencing per month. Its cost for 4,000 minutes under the three alternatives would be as follows:

- *Alternative 1:* $20,000 (= $5 per minute × 4,000 minutes)
- *Alternative 2:* $10,000
- *Alternative 3:* $11,000 [= $3,000 + ($2 per minute × 4,000 minutes)]

Note that the graphs in Exhibit 10-1 are linear. That is, they appear as straight lines. We simply need to know the constant, or intercept, the amount (commonly designated *a*), and the slope coefficient (commonly designated *b*). For any linear cost function based on a single activity (recall our two assumptions discussed at the start of the chapter), knowing *a* and *b* is sufficient to describe and graphically plot all the values within the relevant range of number of minutes used. The general form of this linear cost function is

$$y = a + bx$$

Cost Classification: Choice of Cost Object

A particular cost item could be variable with respect to one cost object and fixed with respect to another cost object. Consider Super Shuttle, an airport transportation company. If the fleet of vans it owns is the cost object, then the annual van registration and licence costs would be variable costs with respect to the number of vans owned. But if a particular van is the cost object, then the registration and licence costs for that van are fixed costs with respect to the distance driven during a year.

Time Horizon

Whether a cost is variable or fixed with respect to a particular activity depends on the time horizon being considered. The longer the time horizon, all other things being equal, the more likely it is that the cost will be variable. For example, inspection costs at Boeing Company are typically fixed in the short run with respect to inspection-hours used because inspectors earn a fixed salary in a given year regardless of the number of inspection-hours of work done. But, in the long run, Boeing's total inspection costs will vary with the inspection-hours required: More inspectors will be hired if more

Exhibit 10-2 Relationship of Labour Costs and Snowboards Produced

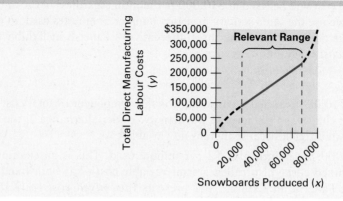

inspection-hours are needed, and some inspectors will be reassigned to other tasks or laid off if fewer inspection-hours are needed.

Relevant Range

Managers should never forget that variable and fixed cost-behaviour patterns are valid for linear cost functions only within a given relevant range. Outside the relevant range, variable and fixed cost-behaviour patterns change, causing costs to become unpredictable. For example, Exhibit 10-2 plots the relationship (over several years) between total direct manufacturing labour costs and the number of snowboards produced each year by Ski Authority at its British Columbia plant. In this case, the costs outside the relevant range occur because of labour costs and possible inefficiencies (first because workers are learning to produce snowboards and later because capacity limits are being stretched). Knowing the relevant range is essential to properly classifying costs.

The Cause-and-Effect Criterion

▶ **LO 2**

Explain the importance of causality in estimating cost functions.

The most important issue in estimating a cost function is determining whether a cause-and-effect relationship exists between the level of an activity and the costs related to that level of activity. Without a cause-and-effect relationship, managers will be less confident about their ability to estimate or predict costs. When a cause-and-effect relationship exists between a change in the level of an activity and a change in the level of total costs, the activity measure is known as a *cost driver*. The terms *level of activity* and *level of cost driver* are used interchangeably when estimating cost functions.

Understanding the drivers of costs is crucially important for managing costs. The cause-and-effect relationship might arise as a result of the following:

- *A physical relationship between the level of activity and costs.* For example, when units of production are used as the activity that affects direct material costs, producing more units requires more direct materials, which results in higher total direct materials costs.

- *A contractual arrangement.* In alternative 1 of the Kannon Services example described earlier, number of minutes used is specified in the contract as the level of activity that affects the videoconferencing line costs.

- *Knowledge of operations.* For example, when number of parts is used as the activity measure of ordering costs, a product with many parts will incur higher ordering costs than a product with few parts.

Managers must be careful not to interpret a high correlation, or connection, in the relationship between two variables to mean that either variable causes the other. Consider direct materials costs and labour costs. For a given product mix, producing more units generally results in higher materials costs and higher labour costs. Materials costs and labour costs are highly correlated, but neither causes the other. Using labour costs to predict materials costs is problematic.

Some products require more labour costs relative to materials costs, while other products require more materials costs relative to labour costs. If the product mix changes toward more labour-intensive products, then labour costs will increase relative to materials costs as a percentage of the total cost. Labour costs are a poor predictor of materials costs. By contrast, factors that drive materials costs—such as product mix, product designs, and manufacturing processes—would have more accurately predicted the changes in materials costs.

Only a cause-and-effect relationship—not merely correlation—establishes an economically plausible relationship between the level of an activity and its costs. Economic plausibility is critical because it gives analysts and managers confidence that the estimated relationship will appear again and again in other sets of data from the same situation. Identifying cost drivers also gives managers insights into ways to reduce costs, and confidence that reducing the quantity of the cost drivers will lead to a decrease in costs.

Cost Drivers and the Decision-Making Process

Consider Elegant Rugs, which uses state-of-the-art automated weaving machines to produce carpets for homes and offices. Management has made many changes in manufacturing processes and wants to introduce new styles of carpets. Using the five-step decision-making process, it would like to evaluate how these changes have affected costs and what styles of carpets it should introduce.

Step 1: Identify the problem and uncertainties. Examine the changes in the manufacturing process specifically targeted at reducing indirect manufacturing labour costs.

Step 2: Obtain information. Gather information about potential cost drivers—factors such as machine-hours or direct manufacturing labour-hours that cause indirect manufacturing labour costs to be incurred. Consider different techniques (such as the industrial engineering method, the conference method, the account analysis method, the high–low method, and the regression method) for estimating the magnitude of the effect of the cost driver on indirect manufacturing labour costs.

Step 3: Make predictions about the future. Use past data to estimate the relationship between cost drivers and costs used in the relationship to predict future costs.

Step 4: Make decisions by choosing among alternatives. As described later, Elegant Rugs chose machine-hours as the cost driver of indirect manufacturing labour costs. Using the regression analysis estimate of indirect manufacturing labour cost per machine-hour, managers estimated the costs of alternative styles of carpets and chose to introduce the most profitable styles.

Step 5: Implement the decision, evaluate performance, and learn. After the managers at Elegant Rugs introduced the new carpet styles, they focused on evaluating the results of their decision. Comparing predicted to actual costs helped managers to learn how accurate the estimates were, to set targets for continuous improvement, and to constantly seek ways to improve efficiency and effectiveness.

Cost Estimation Methods

The four methods of cost estimation—the industrial engineering method, the conference method, the account analysis method, and the quantitative analysis method (which takes different forms)—differ with respect to their implementation cost, assumptions, and the information they provide about the accuracy of the estimated cost function. They are not mutually exclusive, and many organizations use a combination of these methods.

▶ **LO 3**

Understand various methods of cost estimation.

Industrial Engineering Method

The **industrial engineering method**, also called the **work-measurement method**, estimates cost functions by analyzing the relationship between inputs and outputs in physical terms. Consider Elegant Rugs. It uses inputs of cotton, wool, dyes, direct manufacturing labour, machine time, and power. Production output is square metres of carpet.

Time-and-motion studies analyze the time required to perform the various operations to produce the carpet.

For example, a time-and-motion study may conclude that to produce 10 square metres of carpet requires one hour of direct manufacturing labour. Standards and budgets transform these physical input measures into costs. The result is an estimated cost function relating direct manufacturing labour costs to the cost driver, square metres of carpet produced.

The industrial engineering method is a very thorough and detailed way to estimate a cost function when there is a physical relationship between inputs and outputs, but it can be very time consuming. Some government contracts mandate its use. Many organizations, such as Bose and Nokia, use it to estimate direct manufacturing costs but find it too costly or impractical for analyzing their entire cost structure. For example, physical relationships between inputs and outputs are difficult to specify for some items, such as indirect manufacturing costs, R&D costs, and advertising costs.

Conference Method

The **conference method** estimates cost functions on the basis of analysis and opinions about costs and their drivers gathered from various departments of a company (purchasing, process engineering, manufacturing, employee relations, etc.). The Cooperative Bank in the United Kingdom has a cost-estimating department that develops cost functions for its retail banking products (chequing accounts, VISA cards, mortgages, and so on) based on the consensus of estimates from personnel of the particular departments. Elegant Rugs gathers opinions from supervisors and production engineers about how indirect manufacturing labour costs vary with machine-hours and direct manufacturing labour-hours.

The conference method encourages interdepartmental cooperation. The pooling of expert knowledge from different business functions of the value chain gives the conference method credibility. Because the conference method does not require detailed analysis of data, cost functions and cost estimates can be developed quickly. However, the emphasis on opinions rather than systematic estimation means that the accuracy of the cost estimates depends largely on the care and skill of the people providing the inputs.

Account Analysis Method

The **account analysis method** estimates cost functions by classifying various cost accounts as variable, fixed, or mixed with respect to the identified level of activity. Typically, managers use qualitative rather than quantitative analysis when making these cost-classification decisions. The account analysis approach is widely used because it is reasonably accurate, cost-effective, and easy to use.

Consider indirect manufacturing labour costs for a small production area (or cell) at Elegant Rugs. Indirect manufacturing labour costs include wages paid for supervision, maintenance, quality control, and setups. During the most recent 12-week period, Elegant Rugs ran the machines in the cell for a total of 862 hours and incurred total indirect manufacturing labour costs of $12,501. Using qualitative analysis, the manager and the cost analyst determine that over this 12-week period, indirect manufacturing labour costs are mixed costs with only one cost driver—machine-hours. As machine-hours vary, one component of the cost (such as supervision cost) is fixed, whereas another component (such as maintenance cost) is variable. The goal is to use account analysis to estimate a linear cost function for indirect manufacturing labour costs with number of machine-hours as the cost driver. The cost analyst uses experience and judgment to separate total indirect manufacturing labour costs ($12,501) into fixed costs ($2,157, based on 950 hours of machine capacity for the cell over a 12-week period) and variable costs ($10,344) with respect to the number of machine-hours used. Variable cost per machine-hour is $10,344 ÷ 862 machine-hours = $12 per machine-hour. The linear cost equation, $y = a + bx$, in this example is as follows:

$$\text{Indirect manufacturing labour costs} = \$2,157 + (\$12 \text{ per machine-hour} \times \text{Number of machine-hours})$$

Exhibit 10-3 Historical Data and Cost Functions

	A	B	C
1	**Week**	**Cost Driver: Machine-Hours**	**Indirect Manufacturing Labour Costs**
2		*(x)*	*(y)*
3	1	68	$ 1,190
4	2	88	1,211
5	3	62	1,004
6	4	72	917
7	5	60	770
8	6	96	1,456
9	7	78	1,180
10	8	46	710
11	9	82	1,316
12	10	94	1,032
13	11	68	752
14	12	48	963
15	Total	862	$12,501
16			

Management at Elegant Rugs can use the cost function to estimate the indirect manufacturing labour costs of using, say, 950 machine-hours to produce carpet in the next 12-week period. Estimated costs are $13,557 (= $2,157 + (950 machine-hours × $12 per machine-hour)).

To obtain reliable estimates of the fixed and variable components of cost, organizations must take care to ensure that individuals thoroughly knowledgeable about the operations make the cost-classification decisions. Supplementing the account analysis method with the conference method improves credibility.

Quantitative Analysis Method

Quantitative analysis uses a formal mathematical method to fit cost functions to past data observations. Spreadsheet software such as Microsoft Excel is a useful tool for performing quantitative analysis. Columns B and C of Exhibit 10-3 show the breakdown of Elegant Rugs's total machine-hours (862) and total indirect manufacturing labour costs ($12,501) into weekly data for the most recent 12-week period. Note that the data are paired; for each week, there is data for the number of machine-hours and corresponding indirect manufacturing labour costs. For example, week 12 shows 48 machine-hours and indirect manufacturing labour costs of $963. The next section uses the data in Exhibit 10-3 to illustrate how to estimate a cost function using quantitative analysis. We examine two techniques—the relatively simple high–low method and regression analysis, the quantitative tool more commonly used to examine and understand data.

Steps in Estimating a Cost Function Using Quantitative Analysis

Step 1: Choose the dependent variable. Choice of the **dependent variable** (the cost to be predicted and managed) will depend on the cost function being estimated. In the Elegant Rugs example, the dependent variable is indirect manufacturing labour costs.

Step 2: Identify the independent variable, or cost driver. The **independent variable** (level of activity or cost driver) is the factor used to predict the dependent variable (costs). When the cost is an indirect cost, as it is with Elegant Rugs, the independent variable is

▶ **LO 4**

Outline the steps in estimating a cost function using quantitative analysis.

also called a cost-allocation base. Although these terms are sometimes used interchangeably, we use the term *cost driver* to describe the independent variable.

As an example, consider several types of fringe benefits paid to employees and the cost drivers of the benefits:

Fringe Benefit	Cost Driver
Health benefits	Number of employees
Cafeteria meals	Number of employees
Pension benefits	Salaries of employees
Life insurance	Salaries of employees

The costs of health benefits and cafeteria meals can be combined into one homogenous cost pool because they have the same cost driver—the number of employees. Pension benefits and life insurance costs have a different cost driver—the salaries of employees—and, therefore, should not be combined with health benefits and cafeteria meals. Instead, pension benefits and life insurance costs should be combined into a separate homogenous cost pool. The cost pool comprising pension benefits and life insurance costs can be estimated using salaries of employees receiving these benefits as the cost driver.

Step 3: Collect data on the dependent variable and the cost driver. This is usually the most difficult step in cost analysis. Cost analysts obtain data from company documents, from interviews with managers, and through special studies. These data may be time-series data or cross-sectional data.

Time-series data pertain to the same entity (organization, plant, activity, and so on) over successive past periods. Weekly observations of indirect manufacturing labour costs and number of machine-hours at Elegant Rugs are examples of time-series data. The ideal time-series database would contain numerous observations for a company whose operations have not been affected by economic or technological change. A stable economy and technology ensure that data collected during the estimation period represent the same underlying relationship between the cost driver and the dependent variable. Moreover, the periods used to measure the dependent variable and the cost driver should be consistent throughout the observations.

Cross-sectional data pertain to different entities during the same period. For example, studies of loans processed and the related personnel costs at 50 individual, yet similar, branches of a bank during March would produce cross-sectional data for that month. The cross-sectional data should be drawn from entities that, within each entity, have a similar relationship between the cost driver and costs. Later in this chapter, we describe the problems that arise in data collection.

Step 4: Plot the data. The general relationship between the cost driver and costs can be readily observed in a graphical representation of the data, which is commonly called a plot of the data. The plot provides insight into the relevant range of the cost function and reveals whether the relationship between the driver and costs is approximately linear.

Exhibit 10-4 is a plot of the weekly data from columns B and C of the spreadsheet in Exhibit 10-3. This graph provides strong visual evidence of a positive linear relationship between number of machine-hours and indirect manufacturing labour costs (that is, when machine-hours go up, so do indirect manufacturing labour costs). There do not appear to be any extreme observations in Exhibit 10-4. The relevant range is from 46 to 96 machine-hours per week (weeks 8 and 6, respectively).

Step 5: Estimate the cost function, and evaluate the cost driver of the estimated cost function. The high–low method and regression analysis are the two most frequently described forms of quantitative analysis. The widespread availability of computer packages such as Excel makes regression analysis much more easy to use. However, use the high–low method to provide some basic intuition for the idea of drawing a line to "fit" a number of data points.

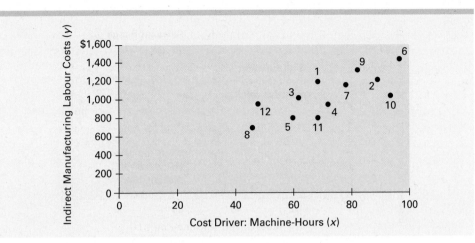

Exhibit 10-4 Relationship Between Machine Hours and Labour Costs

The High–Low Method Compared to Regression Analysis

The simplest form of quantitative analysis to "fit" a line to data points is the **high–low method**. It uses only the highest and lowest observed values of the cost driver within the relevant range and their respective costs to estimate the slope coefficient and the constant of the cost function. It is the first attempt at understanding the relationship between a cost driver and costs.

	Cost Driver: Machine-Hours (x)	Indirect Manufacturing Labour Costs (y)
Highest observation of cost driver (week 6)	96	$1,456
Lowest observation of cost driver (week 8)	46	710
Difference	50	$ 746

The slope coefficient, b, is calculated as follows:

$$\text{Slope coefficient} = \frac{\text{Difference between costs associated with highest and lowest observations of the cost driver}}{\text{Difference between highest and lowest observations of the cost driver}}$$

$$= \$746 \div 50 \text{ machine-hours} = \$14.92 \text{ per machine-hour}$$

To compute the constant, we can use either the highest or the lowest observation of the cost driver. Both calculations yield the same answer because the solution technique solves two linear equations with two unknowns, the slope coefficient and the constant. Because

$$y = a + bx$$

the constant, a, is calculated as

$$a = y - bx$$

At the highest observation of the cost driver,

Constant = $1,456 − ($14.92 per machine-hour × 96 machine-hours) = $23.68

And at the lowest observation of the cost driver,

Constant = $710 − ($14.92 per machine-hour × 46 machine-hours) = $23.68

Thus, the high–low estimate of the cost function is as follows:

$$y = a + bx$$
$$y = \$23.68 + (\$14.92 \text{ per machine-hour} \times \text{Number of machine-hours})$$

The advantage of the high–low method is that it is simple to compute and easy to understand; it gives a quick, initial insight into how the cost driver, number of machine-hours, affects indirect manufacturing labour costs (see Exhibit 10-5). The disadvantage is that it ignores information from all but two observations when estimating the cost function.

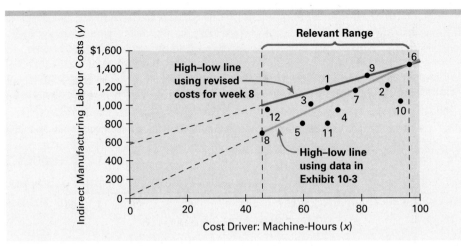

Regression analysis is a statistical method that measures the average amount of change in the dependent variable associated with a unit change in one or more independent variables. In the Elegant Rugs example, the dependent variable is total indirect manufacturing labour costs. The independent variable, or cost driver, is number of machine-hours. **Simple regression** analysis estimates the relationship between the dependent variable and *one* independent variable. **Multiple regression** analysis estimates the relationship between the dependent variable and *two or more* independent variables. Multiple regression analysis for Elegant Rugs might use as the independent variables, or cost drivers, number of machine-hours and number of batches. Appendix 10A will explore simple regression and multiple regression in more detail.

The regression line in Exhibit 10-6 is derived using the least-squares technique. The least-squares technique determines the regression line by minimizing the sum of the squared vertical differences from the data points (the various points in the graph) to the regression line. The vertical difference, called the **residual term**, measures the distance between actual cost and estimated cost for each observation of the cost driver. Exhibit 10-6 shows the residual term for the week 1 data. The line from the observation to the regression line is drawn perpendicular to the horizontal axis, or *x*-axis. The smaller the residual terms, the better the fit between actual cost observations and estimated costs. *Goodness of fit* indicates the strength of the relationship between the cost driver and costs. The regression line in Exhibit 10-6 rises from left to right. The positive slope of this line and small residual terms indicate that, on average, indirect manufacturing labour costs increase as the number of machine-hours increases. The vertical dashed lines in Exhibit 10-6 indicate the relevant range, the range within which the cost function applies.

The estimate of the slope coefficient, *b*, indicates that indirect manufacturing labour costs vary at the average amount of $10.31 for every machine-hour used within the relevant range. Management can use the regression equation when budgeting for future

Exhibit 10-6 Application of a Cost Function in the Relevant Range

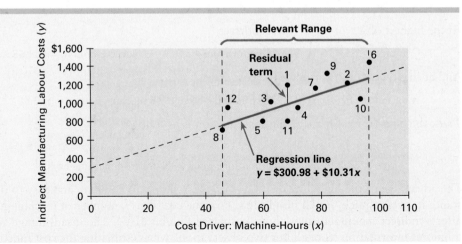

indirect manufacturing labour costs. For instance, if 90 machine-hours are budgeted for the coming week, the predicted indirect manufacturing labour costs would be

$$y = \$300.98 + (\$10.31 \text{ per machine-hour} \times 90 \text{ machine-hours}) = \$1,228.88$$

The regression method is more accurate than the high–low method because the regression equation estimates costs using information from all observations, whereas the high–low equation uses information from only two observations. The inaccuracies of the high–low method can mislead managers. Consider the high–low method equation in the preceding section:

$$y = \$23.68 + (\$14.92 \text{ per machine-hour} \times \text{Number of machine-hours})$$

For 90 machine-hours, the predicted weekly cost based on the high–low method equation is $1,366.48 (= $23.68 + ($14.92 per machine-hour × 90 machine-hours)). Suppose that for 7 weeks over the next 12-week period, Elegant Rugs runs its machines for 90 hours each week. Assume average indirect manufacturing labour costs for those 7 weeks are $1,300. Based on the high–low method prediction of $1,366.48, Elegant Rugs would conclude it has performed well because actual costs are less than predicted costs. But comparing the $1,300 performance with the more-accurate $1,228.88 prediction of the regression model tells a much different story and would probably prompt Elegant Rugs to search for ways to improve its cost performance.

Nonlinear Cost Functions

In practice, cost functions are not always linear. A **nonlinear cost function** is a cost function for which the graph of total costs (based on the level of a single activity) is not a straight line within the relevant range. To see what a nonlinear cost function looks like, return to Exhibit 10-2, where the relevant range is currently set at 20,000 to 65,000 snowboards. If we extend the relevant range to encompass the region from 0 to 80,000 snowboards produced, it is evident that the cost function over this expanded range is graphically represented by a line that is not straight.

Consider another example. Economies of scale in advertising may enable an advertising agency to produce double the number of advertisements for less than double the costs. Even direct material costs are not always linear variable costs because of quantity discounts on direct material purchases. As shown in Exhibit 10-7, Panel A, total direct material costs rise

▶ **LO 5**

Explain nonlinear cost functions, in particular those arising from learning curve effects.

Exhibit 10-7 Forms of Cost Functions

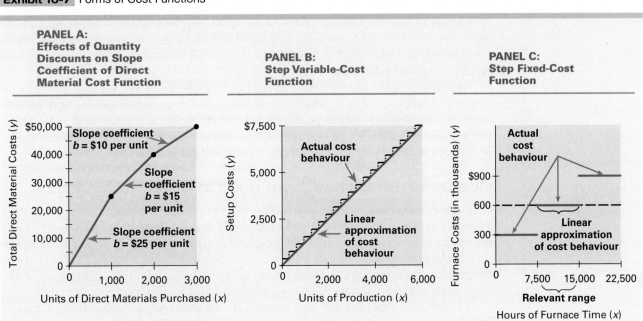

as the units of direct materials purchased increase. But, because of quantity discounts, these costs rise more slowly (as indicated by the slope coefficient) as the units of direct materials purchased increase. This cost function has $b = \$25$ per unit for 1–1,000 units purchased, $b = \$15$ per unit for 1,001–2,000 units purchased, and $b = \$10$ per unit for 2,001–3,000 units purchased. The direct material cost per unit falls at each price break—that is, the cost per unit decreases with larger purchase orders. If managers are interested in understanding cost behaviour over the relevant range of 1–3,000 units, the cost function is nonlinear—not a straight line. If, however, managers are only interested in understanding cost behaviour over a more narrow relevant range (for example, of 1–1,000 units), the cost function is linear.

Step cost functions are also examples of nonlinear cost functions. In a **step cost function**, the cost remains the same over various ranges of the level of activity, but the cost increases by discrete amounts—that is, increases in steps—as the level of activity increases from one range to the next. Panel B in Exhibit 10-7 shows a *step variable-cost function*, a step cost function in which cost remains the same over *narrow* ranges of the level of activity in each relevant range. Panel B presents the relationship between units of production and setup costs. If the relevant range is considered to be 0–6,000 production units, the cost function is nonlinear. However, as shown by the blue line in Panel B, managers often approximate step variable costs with a continuously variable cost function. This type of step cost pattern also occurs when production inputs such as materials-handling labour, supervision, and process engineering labour are acquired in discrete quantities but used in fractional quantities.

Panel C in Exhibit 10-7 shows a *step fixed-cost function* for Crofton Steel, a company that operates large heat-treatment furnaces to harden steel parts. Looking at Panel C and Panel B, you can see that the main difference between a step variable-cost function and a step fixed-cost function is that the cost in a step fixed-cost function remains the same over *wide* ranges of the activity in each relevant range. The ranges indicate the number of furnaces being used (each furnace costs $300,000). The cost increases from one range to the next higher range when the hours of furnace time needed require the use of another furnace. The relevant range of 7,500–15,000 hours of furnace time indicates that the company expects to operate with two furnaces at a cost of $600,000. Management considers the cost of operating furnaces as a fixed cost within this relevant range of operation. However, if the relevant range is considered to be 0–22,500 hours, the cost function is nonlinear: The graph in Panel C is not a single straight line; it is three broken lines.

Time as a Competitive Tool

▶ **LO 6**

Describe the impact of time as a cost driver.

Companies increasingly view time as a driver of strategy. For example, Capital One has increased the business on its website by promising home-loan approval decisions in 30 minutes or less. Companies such as General Electric and Walmart attribute not only higher revenues but also lower costs to doing things faster and on time. These firms claim, for example, that they need to carry fewer inventories because they are able to respond rapidly to customer demands.

Managers need to measure time to manage it properly. In this section, we focus on two *operational measures of time: customer-response time*, which reveals how quickly companies respond to customers' demands for their products and services, and *on-time performance*, which indicates how reliably companies meet their scheduled delivery dates. We also show how managers measure the causes and costs of delays.

Customer-Response Time and On-Time Performance

Customer-response time is how long it takes from the time a customer places an order for a product or service to the time the product or service is delivered to the customer. Quickly responding to customers is strategically important in many industries, including the construction, banking, car-rental, and fast-food industries. Some companies, such as Airbus, have to pay penalties to compensate their customers (airline companies) for lost revenues and profits (from being unable to operate flights) as a result of delays in delivering aircraft to them.

Exhibit 10-8 describes the components of customer-response time. **Receipt time** is how long it takes the marketing department to specify to the manufacturing department the exact requirements of the customer's order. **Manufacturing cycle time** (also called

Exhibit 10-8 Components of Customer-Response Time

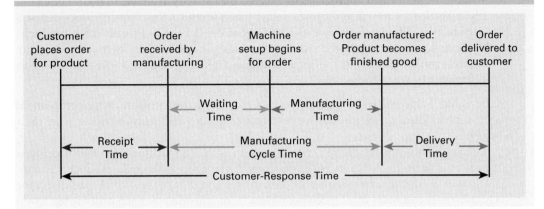

manufacturing lead time) is how long it takes from the time an order is received by manufacturing to the time a finished good is produced. Manufacturing cycle time is the sum of waiting time and manufacturing time for an order. For example, an aircraft order received by Airbus's manufacturing department may need to wait for components before the plane can be assembled. **Delivery time** is how long it takes to deliver a completed order to a customer.

Some companies evaluate their response time improvement efforts using a measure called **manufacturing cycle efficiency (MCE):**

MCE = (Value-added manufacturing time ÷ Manufacturing cycle time)

Value-added manufacturing activities (see Chapter 13) are activities that customers perceive as adding value or utility to a product. The time spent efficiently assembling the product is value-added manufacturing time. The rest of the manufacturing cycle time, such as the time a product spends waiting for parts or for the next stage in the production process or being repaired, is non-value-added manufacturing time. Identifying and minimizing the sources of non-value-added manufacturing time increases a firm's responsiveness to its customers and reduces its costs.

Similar measures apply to service-sector companies. Consider a 40-minute doctor's office visit. Suppose a patient spends 9 of those minutes on administrative tasks such as filling out forms, 20 minutes waiting in the reception area and examination room, and 11 minutes with a nurse or doctor. The service cycle efficiency for this visit equals 11 ÷ 40, or 0.275. In other words, only 27.5% of the 40 minutes added value to the patient/customer. Minimizing their non-value-added service times has allowed hospitals such as Alle-Kiski Medical Center in Pennsylvania to treat more patients in less time.

On-time performance is the delivery of a product or service by the time it is scheduled to be delivered. Consider FedEx, which specifies a price per package and a next-day delivery time of 10:30 a.m. for its overnight courier service. FedEx measures the on-time performance of the service based on how often the firm meets that standard. Commercial airlines gain loyal passengers as a result of consistent on-time service. But there is a tradeoff between a customer's desire for a shorter response time and better on-time performance. Scheduling longer customer-response times, such as airlines lengthening scheduled arrival times, displeases customers on the one hand but increases customer satisfaction on the other hand by improving the airline's on-time performance.

Bottlenecks and Time Drivers

Managing customer-response time and on-time performance requires managers to understand the causes and costs of delays, for example, at a machine in a manufacturing plant or at a checkout counter in a store. A **time driver** is any factor that causes a change in the speed of an activity when the factor changes. Two time drivers are

1. *Uncertainty about when customers will order products or services.* For example, the more randomly Airbus receives orders for its airplanes, the more likely queues will form and delays will occur.

2. *Bottlenecks due to limited capacity.* A **bottleneck** occurs in an operation when the work to be performed approaches or exceeds the capacity available to do it. For example, a bottleneck results and causes delays when products that must be processed at a particular machine arrive while the machine is being used to process other products. Bottlenecks also occur on the internet, for example, when many users try to operate wireless mobile devices at the same time (see Concepts in Action: Netflix Works to Overcome Internet Bottlenecks).

Many banks, such as Bank of China; grocery stores, such as Kroger; and entertainment parks, such as Disneyland, actively work to reduce queues and delays to better serve their customers.

Consider Photon Corporation, which uses one turning machine to convert steel bars into a special fuser roller for its copier machines. The roller is the only product the company makes on the turning machine. Photon makes and sells the rollers as spare parts for its photocopier machines after receiving orders from wholesalers. Each order is for 1,000 fuser rollers.

Photon's managers are examining opportunities to produce and sell other products to increase the firm's profits without sacrificing its short customer-response times. The managers examine these opportunities using the five-step decision-making process introduced in Chapter 1.

Step 1: Identify the problem and uncertainties. Photon's managers are considering introducing a second product, a fuser gear, which will use the same turning machine currently used to make fuser rollers. The primary uncertainty is how the introduction of a second product will affect the manufacturing cycle times for rollers. (We focus on Photon's manufacturing cycle time because the receipt time and delivery time for the rollers and gears are minimal.)

Step 2: Obtain information. Managers gather data on the number of past orders for rollers, the time it takes to manufacture them, the available capacity, and their average manufacturing cycle time. Photon typically receives 30 orders for rollers each year, but it could receive 10, 30, or 50 orders. Each order is for 750 units and takes 100 hours of manufacturing time (8 hours of setup time to clean and prepare the machine that makes the rollers and 92 hours of processing time). The annual capacity of the machine is 4,000 hours.

Step 3: Make predictions about the future. If Photon only makes rollers in 2017, it expects to receive 30 orders of 750 units each requiring 100 hours of manufacturing time. The total amount of manufacturing time required on the machine is 3,000 hours (100 hours per order × 30 orders), which is less than the available machine capacity of 4,000 hours. Queues and delays will still occur because wholesalers can place their orders at any time, while the machine is processing an earlier order.

Average waiting time, the average amount of time that an order waits in line before the machine is set up and the order is processed, equals[1]

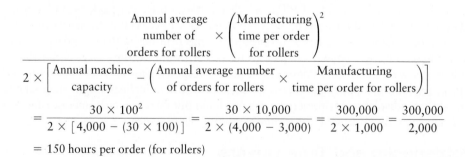

$$= \frac{30 \times 100^2}{2 \times [4,000 - (30 \times 100)]} = \frac{30 \times 10,000}{2 \times (4,000 - 3,000)} = \frac{300,000}{2 \times 1,000} = \frac{300,000}{2,000}$$

$$= 150 \text{ hours per order (for rollers)}$$

---

[1] The technical assumptions are (1) that customer orders for the product follow a Poisson distribution with a mean equal to the expected number of orders (30 in our example) and (2) that orders are processed on a first-in, first-out (FIFO) basis. The Poisson arrival pattern for customer orders has been found to be reasonable in many real-world settings. The FIFO assumption can be modified. Under the modified assumptions, the basic queuing and delay effects will still occur, but the precise formulas will be different.

Therefore, the average manufacturing cycle time for an order is 250 hours (150 hours of average waiting time + 100 hours of manufacturing time). Note that manufacturing time per order is a squared term in the numerator. The squared term indicates the disproportionately large impact the manufacturing time has on the waiting time. As the manufacturing time lengthens, there is a much greater chance that the machine will be in use when an order arrives, leading to longer delays. The denominator in this formula is a measure of the unused capacity, or cushion. As the unused capacity becomes smaller, the chance that the machine is processing an earlier order becomes more likely, leading to greater delays.

The formula describes only the *average* waiting time. A particular order might arrive when the machine is free, in which case manufacturing will start immediately. In another situation, Photon may receive an order while two other orders are waiting to be processed, which means the delay will be longer than 150 hours.

If Photon makes rollers and gears in 2017, it expects to receive the following:

Rollers: 30 orders of 750 units each requiring 100 hours of manufacturing time.

Gears: 10 orders for gears of 800 units each requiring 50 hours of manufacturing time, composed of 3 hours for setup and 47 hours of processing.

The expected demand for rollers will be unaffected by whether Photon produces and sells gears.

If Photon makes both rollers and gears, the average waiting time *before* the machine setup begins is expected to be as follows (the formula is an extension of the preceding formula for the single-product case):

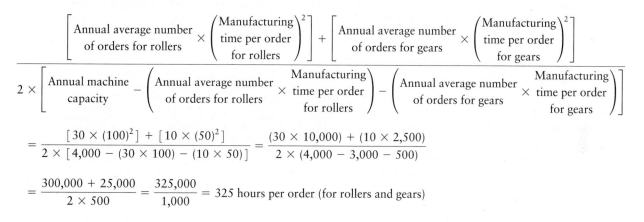

$$= \frac{[30 \times (100)^2] + [10 \times (50)^2]}{2 \times [4,000 - (30 \times 100) - (10 \times 50)]} = \frac{(30 \times 10,000) + (10 \times 2,500)}{2 \times (4,000 - 3,000 - 500)}$$

$$= \frac{300,000 + 25,000}{2 \times 500} = \frac{325,000}{1,000} = 325 \text{ hours per order (for rollers and gears)}$$

Producing gears will cause the average waiting time for an order to more than double, from 150 hours to 325 hours. The waiting time increases because the production of gears will cause the machine's unused capacity to shrink, increasing the probability that new orders will arrive while current orders are being manufactured or waiting to be manufactured. The average waiting time is very sensitive to the shrinking of unused capacity.

If Photon's managers decide to make gears as well as rollers, the average manufacturing cycle time will be 425 hours for a roller order (325 hours of average waiting time + 100 hours of manufacturing time) and 375 hours for a gear order (325 hours of average waiting time + 50 hours of manufacturing time). A roller order will spend 76.5% (325 hours ÷ 425 hours) of its manufacturing cycle time just waiting for its manufacturing to start!

Step 4: Make decisions by choosing among alternatives. Should Photon produce gears given how much it would slow down the manufacturing cycle time for rollers? To help the company's managers make a decision, the management accountant identifies and analyzes the relevant revenues and relevant costs of producing gears and, in particular, the cost of delays on all products. The next section focuses on this step.

Concepts in Action

Netflix Works to Overcome Internet Bottlenecks

Netflix is the world's largest provider of streaming movies and television shows. More than 80 million Netflix subscribers in over 190 countries watch more than 125 million hours of video per day. As a result, Netflix consumes a large amount of internet bandwidth. In North America, the company accounts for 37% of all downstream traffic in the evening, when the most people are in front of their televisions watching feature films and original shows such as *House of Cards*.

Aware of its bandwidth consumption, Netflix actively works behind the scenes to alleviate data bottlenecks that can slow the delivery of its content. The company's subscribers expect smooth streaming of movies and television shows, and they can become quickly dissatisfied by buffering delays and poor-quality video.

In recent years, Netflix has deployed two new strategies to overcome internet data bottlenecks that can affect videostream speed and quality:

- In 2014, Netflix began paying some large US internet service providers (ISPs), including Verizon and Comcast, to place its servers at locations that have direct access to the ISP's networks. This helps the company bypass bottlenecks caused at the heavily congested points where Netflix's data enters the ISP's network at the same time as all other internet data.

- In late 2015, Netflix began deploying movies and television shows that were re-encoded using a new bandwidth-saving technology that produces higher-quality video while using up to 20% less data. This helps alleviate bottlenecks by reducing the amount of data that passes through the internet's backbone, which is

IanDagnall Computing/Alamy Stock Photo

particularly critical in areas with slower wired internet speeds or mobile-first regions such as India, Africa, and the Middle East.

As Netflix continues to grow rapidly across the globe, and consume more internet bandwidth, these efforts to reduce data bottlenecks will ensure smoother operations for the company and more satisfied subscribers.

Sources: J. Roettgers. 2015. Inside Netflix's Plan to Boost Streaming Quality and Unclog the Internet, *Variety*, December 14 (http://variety.com/2015/digital/news/netflix-better-streaming-quality-1201661116); C. MacDonald. 2015. America Really Does Love to Netflix and Chill: Site Now Accounts for 37% of All US Broadband Traffic and Video Takes 70% Overall, *The Daily Mail* (UK), December 8 (http://www.dailymail.co.uk/sciencetech/article-3351849/America-really-DOES-love-Netflix-chill-Site-accounts-37-broadband-traffic-video-takes-70-overall.html); Netflix, Inc., "About Netflix" (https://media.netflix.com/en/about-netflix).

Relevant Revenues and Costs of Delays

To determine the relevant revenues and costs of producing gears under Step 4, the management accountant prepares the following additional information:

Product	Annual Average Number of Orders	Average Selling Price per Order If the Average Manufacturing Cycle Time per Order Is		Direct Materials Cost per Order	Inventory Carrying Cost per Order per Hour
		Less Than 300 Hours	More Than 300 Hours		
Rollers	30	$22,000	$21,500	$16,000	$1.00
Gears	10	10,000	9,600	8,000	0.50

Manufacturing cycle times affect both revenues and costs. Revenues are affected because customers are willing to pay a higher price for faster delivery. On the cost side, direct materials costs and inventory carrying costs are the only relevant costs of introducing gears (all other costs are unaffected and therefore irrelevant). Inventory

Exhibit 10-9 Determining Expected Relevant Revenues and Relevant Costs for Photon's Decision to Introduce Gears

Relevant Items	Alternative 1: Introduce Gears (1)	Alternative 2: Do Not Introduce Gears (2)	Difference (3) = (1) − (2)
Expected revenues	$741,000[a]	$660,000[b]	$ 81,000
Expected variable costs	560,000[c]	480,000[d]	80,000
Expected inventory carrying costs	14,625[e]	7,500[f]	7,125
Expected total costs	574,625	487,500	87,125
Expected revenues minus expected costs	$166,375	$172,500	$ (6,125)

[a]($21,500 × 30) + ($9,600 × 10) = $741,000; average manufacturing cycle time will be more than 300 hours.

[b]($22,000 × 30) = $660,000; average manufacturing cycle time will be less than 300 hours.

[c]($16,000 × 30) + ($8,000 × 10) = $560,000.

[d]$16,000 × 30 = $480,000.

[e](Average manufacturing cycle time for rollers × Carrying cost per order per hour for rollers × Expected number of orders for rollers) + (Average manufacturing cycle time for gears × Carrying cost per order per hour for gears × Expected number of orders for gears) = (425 × $1.00 × 30) + (375 × $0.50 × 10) = $12,750 + $1,875 = $14,625.

[f]Average manufacturing cycle time for rollers × Carrying cost per order per hour for rollers × Expected number of orders for rollers = 250 × $1.00 × 30 = $7,500.

carrying costs equal the opportunity costs of the investment tied up in inventory and the relevant costs of storage, such as space rental, spoilage, deterioration, and materials handling. Usually, companies calculate inventory carrying costs on a per-unit, per-year basis. To simplify the calculations, the management accountant calculates inventory carrying costs on a per-order, per-hour basis. Also, Photon acquires direct materials at the time the order is received by manufacturing and, therefore, calculates inventory carrying costs for the duration of the manufacturing cycle time.

Exhibit 10-9 presents relevant revenues and relevant costs for the "introduce gears" and "do not introduce gears" alternatives. Based on the analysis, Photon's managers decide not to introduce gears, even though they have a positive contribution margin of $1,600 ($9,600 − $8,000) per order and Photon has the capacity to make them. If it produces gears, Photon will, on average, use only 3,500 (Rollers: 100 hours per order × 30 orders + Gears: 50 hours per order × 10 orders) of the available 4,000 machine-hours. So why is Photon better off not introducing gears? *Because of the negative effects that producing them will have on the existing product, rollers.* The following table presents the *costs of time*, the expected loss in revenues and expected increase in carrying costs as a result of the delays caused by manufacturing gears.

Product	Effect of Increasing Average Manufacturing Cycle Time		Expected Loss in Revenues Plus Expected Increase in Carrying Costs of Introducing Gears (3) = (1) + (2)
	Expected Loss in Revenues for Rollers (1)	Expected Increase in Carrying Costs for All Products (2)	
Rollers	$15,000[a]	$5,250[b]	$20,250
Gears	—	1,875[c]	1,875
Total	$15,000	$7,125	$22,125

[a]($22,000 − $21,500) per order × 30 expected orders = $15,000.

[b](425 − 250) hours per order × $1.00 per hour × 30 expected orders = $5,250.

[c](375 − 0) hours per order × $0.50 per hour × 10 expected orders = $1,875.

Introducing gears will cause the average manufacturing cycle time of rollers to increase from 250 hours to 425 hours. Longer manufacturing cycle times will increase the inventory carrying costs of rollers and decrease roller revenues (the average manufacturing cycle time for rollers will exceed 300 hours, so the average selling price per order will decrease from $22,000 to $21,500). Together with the inventory carrying cost of the gears, the expected cost of introducing the gears, $22,125, will exceed the expected contribution margin of $16,000 ($1,600 per order × 10 expected orders) from selling gears by $6,125 (the difference calculated in Exhibit 10-9).

This example illustrates that when demand uncertainty is high, some unused capacity is desirable.[2] Increasing the capacity of a bottleneck resource reduces manufacturing cycle times and delays. One way to increase capacity is to reduce the time it takes for setups and processing. Another way to increase capacity is to invest in new equipment, such as flexible manufacturing systems that can be programmed to switch quickly from producing one product to producing another. Delays can also be reduced by carefully scheduling production, such as by batching similar jobs together for processing.

Companies such as Unilever, FedEx, and TiVo use nonfinancial measures to manage quality. The first step is to look at quality through the eyes of customers. Managers then turn their attention inward toward their organizations to develop processes that help improve quality and corporate cultures that help sustain it.

Photon's managers track the following measures of customer satisfaction:

- Market research information on customer preferences for and customer satisfaction with specific product features (as measures of design quality)
- Market share
- Percentage of highly satisfied customers
- Number of defective units shipped to customers as a percentage of total units shipped
- Number of customer complaints (Companies estimate that for every customer who actually complains, there are 10 to 20 others who have had bad experiences with the product or service but did not complain.)
- Percentage of products that fail soon after they have been delivered to customers
- Average delivery delays (difference between the scheduled delivery date and the date requested by the customer)
- On-time delivery rate (percentage of shipments delivered on or before the scheduled delivery date)

Balanced Scorecard and Time-Based Measures

In this section, we focus on the final step of the five-step decision-making process—**implement the decision, evaluate performance, and learn**—by tracking changes in time-based measures, evaluating and learning whether these changes affect financial performance, and modifying decisions and plans to achieve the company's goals. We use the structure of the balanced scorecard perspectives—financial, customer, internal business processes, and learning and growth—to summarize how financial and nonfinancial measures of time relate to one another, reduce delays, and increase the output of bottleneck operations.

---

[2] Other complexities, such as analyzing a network of machines, priority scheduling, and allowing for uncertainty in processing times, are beyond the scope of this text. In these cases, the basic queuing and delay effects persist, but the precise formulas are more complex.

Financial measures

Revenue gains or price increases from fewer delays

Carrying cost of inventories

Customer measures

Customer-response time (the time it takes to fulfill a customer order)

On-time performance (delivering a product or service by the scheduled time)

Internal-business-process measures

Average manufacturing time for key products

Manufacturing cycle efficiency for key processes

Defective units produced at bottleneck operations

Average reduction in setup time and processing time at bottleneck operations

Learning-and-growth measures

Employee satisfaction

Number of employees trained to manage bottlenecks

To see the cause-and-effect linkages across these balanced scorecard perspectives, consider the example of the Bell Group, a designer and manufacturer of equipment for the jewelry industry. A key financial measure is to achieve a higher profit margin on a specific product line. In the customer-measure category, the company sets a goal of a 2-day turnaround time on all orders for the product. To achieve this goal, an internal-business-process measure requires a bottleneck machine to be operated 22 hours per day, 6 days a week. Finally, in the learning-and-growth measures category, the company trains new employees to carry out nonbottleneck operations to free experienced employees to operate the bottleneck machine. The Bell Group's emphasis on time-related measures in its balanced scorecard has allowed the company to substantially increase manufacturing throughput and decrease customer-response times, leading to higher revenues and increased profits.

Managers use both financial and nonfinancial measures to manage the performance of their firms along the time dimension. Nonfinancial measures help managers evaluate how well they have done on goals such as improving manufacturing cycle times and customer-response times. Revenue and cost measures help managers evaluate the financial effects of increases or decreases in nonfinancial measures, such as manufacturing cycle time and customer-response times.

▲ **10.1** **TRY IT!**

The Seawall Corporation uses an injection molding machine to make a plastic product, Z39, after receiving firm orders from its customers. Seawall estimates that it will receive 50 orders for Z39 during the coming year. Each order of Z39 will take 80 hours of machine time. The annual machine capacity is 5,000 hours.

Required

1. Calculate (a) the average amount of time that an order for Z39 will wait in line before it is processed and (b) the average manufacturing cycle time per order for Z39.

2. Seawall is considering introducing a new product, Y28. The company expects it will receive 25 orders of Y28 in the coming year. Each order of Y28 will take 20 hours of machine time. Assuming the demand for Z39 will not be affected by the introduction of Y28, calculate (a) the average waiting time for an order received and (b) the average manufacturing cycle time per order for each product, if Seawall introduces Y28.

(continued)

3. Seawall is debating whether it should introduce Y28. The following table provides information on selling prices, variable costs, and inventory carrying costs for Z39 and Y28:

| Product | Annual Average Number of Orders | Selling Price per Order If Average Manufacturing Cycle Time per Order Is | | Variable Cost per Order | Inventory Carrying Cost per Order per Hour |
		Less Than 320 Hours	More Than 320 Hours		
Z39	50	$27,000	$26,500	$15,000	$0.75
Y28	25	6,400	6,000	5,000	0.25

Using the average manufacturing cycle times calculated in requirement 2, should Seawall manufacture and sell Y28?

Quality as an Element of Cost

► **LO 7**

Describe quality control and its implications as a cost driver.

Measures of organizational success and effectiveness—such as revenue growth, operating income, and other financial measures—are impacted by quality. The most direct financial measure of quality, however, is *costs of quality*. **Costs of quality** (COQ) are the costs incurred to prevent, or the costs arising as a result of, the production of a low quality product. Costs of quality are classified into four categories; examples for each category are listed in Exhibit 10-10.

- **Prevention costs** are incurred to preclude the production of products that do not conform to specifications.

- **Appraisal costs** are incurred to detect which of the individual units of products do not conform to specifications.

- **Internal failure costs** are incurred on defective products *before* they are shipped to customers.

- **External failure costs** are incurred on defective products *after* they have been shipped to customers.

An important role for management accountants is preparing COQ reports for managers. Photon Corporation determines the COQ of its photocopying machines by using the 5DM method.

Step 1: Identify the chosen cost object. The cost object is the quality of the photocopying machine that Photon made and sold in 2018. Photon's goal is to calculate the total costs of quality of these 20,000 machines.

Exhibit 10-10 Examples of Costs of Quality

Prevention Costs	Appraisal Costs	Internal Failure Costs	External Failure Costs
Design engineering	Inspection	Spoilage	Customer support
Process engineering	Online product	Rework	Manufacturing/
Supplier evaluations	manufacturing	Scrap	process
Preventive equipment	and process	Machine repairs	engineering
maintenance	inspection	Manufacturing/	for external
Quality training	Product testing	process	failures
Testing of new		engineering on	Warranty repair
materials		internal failures	costs
			Liability claims

Step 2: Identify the direct costs of quality of the product. The photocopying machines have no direct costs of quality because there are no resources such as inspection or repair workers dedicated to managing the quality of the photocopying machines.

Step 3: Select the activities and cost-allocation bases to use for allocating indirect costs of quality to the product. Column 1 of Exhibit 10-11, Panel A, classifies the activities that result in prevention, appraisal, and internal and external failure costs of quality at Photon Corporation and the business functions of the value chain in which these costs occur. For example, the quality-inspection activity results in appraisal costs and occurs in the manufacturing function. Photon identifies the total number of inspection-hours (across all products) as the cost-allocation base for the inspection activity. (To avoid details not needed to explain the concepts here, we do not show the total quantities of each cost-allocation base.)

Exhibit 10-11 Cost of Quality Report

	A	B	C	D	E	F	G
1	**PANEL A: ACCOUNTING COQ REPORT**						**Percentage of**
2		**Cost Allocation**		**Quantity of Cost**		**Total**	**Revenues**
3	**Cost of Quality and Value-Chain Category**	**Rate**[a]		**Allocation Base**		**Costs**	**(5) = (4) ÷**
4	**(1)**	**(2)**		**(3)**		**(4) = (2) x (3)**	**$300,000,000**
5	*Prevention costs*						
6	Design engineering (R&D/Design)	$ 80	per hour	40,000	hours	$ 3,200,000	1.1%
7	Process engineering (R&D/Design)	60	per hour	45,000	hours	2,700,000	0.9
8	Total prevention costs					5,900,000	2.0
9	*Appraisal costs*						
10	Inspection (Manufacturing)	40	per hour	240,000	hours	9,600,000	3.2
11	Total appraisal costs					9,600,000	3.2
12	*Internal failure costs*						
13	Rework (Manufacturing)	100	per hour	100,000	hours	10,000,000	3.3
14	Total internal failure costs					10,000,000	3.3
15	*External failure costs*						
16	Customer support (Marketing)	50	per hour	12,000	hours	600,000	0.2
17	Transportation (Distribution)	240	per load	3,000	loads	720,000	0.2
18	Warranty repair (Customer service)	110	per hour	120,000	hours	13,200,000	4.4
19	Total external failure costs					14,520,000	4.8
20	Total costs of quality					$40,020,000	13.3%
21							
22	[a]Calculations not shown.						
23							
24	**PANEL B: OPPORTUNITY COST ANALYSIS**						
25						**Total Estimated**	**Percentage**
26						**Contribution**	**of Revenues**
27	**Cost of Quality Category**					**Margin Lost**	**(3) = (2) ÷**
28	**(1)**					**(2)**	**$300,000,000**
29	*External failure costs*						
30	Estimated forgone contribution margin						
31	and income on lost sales					$12,000,000[b]	4.0%
32	Total external failure costs					$12,000,000	4.0%
33							
34	[b]Calculated as total revenues minus all variable costs (whether output-unit, batch, product-sustaining, or facility-sustaining) on						
35	lost sales in 2018. If poor quality causes Photon to lose sales in subsequent years as well, the opportunity costs will be						
36	even greater.						

Step 4: Identify the indirect costs of quality associated with each cost-allocation base. These are the total costs (variable and fixed) incurred for each of the costs-of-quality activities, such as inspections, across all of Photon's products. (To avoid details not needed to understand the points described here, we do not present these total costs.)

Step 5: Compute the rate per unit of each cost-allocation base. For each activity, total costs (identified in step 4) are divided by total quantity of the cost-allocation base (calculated in step 3) to compute the rate per unit of each cost-allocation base. Column 2 of Exhibit 10-11, Panel A, shows these rates (without supporting calculations).

The indirect costs of quality of the photocopying machines (shown in Exhibit 10-11, Panel A, column 4) equal the cost-allocation rate from step 5 (column 2) multiplied by the total quantity of the cost-allocation base used by the photocopying machines for each activity (column 3). For example, inspection costs for assuring the quality of the photocopying machines are $9,600,000 (= $40 per hour × 240,000 inspection-hours). Photon's total costs of quality in the COQ report for photocopying machines are $40.02 million (Exhibit 10-11, Panel A, column 4), or 13.3% of current revenues (column 5).

Analyzing Quality: Nonfinancial Measures

Nonfinancial measures are an important aspect of measuring and analyzing quality as a driver of cost. Some of these measures include

- Market research information on customer preferences for and customer satisfaction with specific product features (to measure design quality)
- Market share
- Percentage of highly satisfied customers
- Number of defective units shipped to customers as a percentage of total units shipped
- Number of customer complaints (companies estimate that for every customer who actually complains, there are 10 to 20 others who have had bad experiences with the product or service but did not complain)
- Percentage of products that fail soon after delivery
- Average delivery delays (difference between the scheduled delivery date and the date requested by the customer)
- On-time delivery rate (percentage of shipments made on or before the scheduled delivery date)

A number of techniques can be applied to analyzing quality that take into account such nonfinancial measures. Three of the most prominent analytical tools are control charts, Pareto diagrams, and cause-and-effect diagrams.

TRY IT! 10.2

Baldwin Company makes tables for the outdoors. The company has been working on improving quality over the past year and wants to evaluate how well it has done on costs of quality (COQ) measures. Here are the results:

Annual COQ Report, Baldwin Company

	2017	2018
Process engineering	$ 10,000	$ 10,200
Scrap	$ 15,000	$ 12,800
Warranty repair costs	$ 19,960	$ 17,520
Design engineering	$ 8,950	$ 12,950
Inspection	$ 7,000	$ 9,200
Rework	$ 17,960	$ 12,400
Total COQ	$ 78,870	$ 75,070
Total Revenue	$1,000,000	$1,150,000

Required

1. Identify costs of quality category (prevention, appraisal, internal failure, and external failure) for each of these costs.
2. Prepare a COQ report by calculating the COQ for each category and the ratio of each COQ category to revenues and total quality costs.

Control Charts

Statistical quality control (SQC), also called statistical process control (SPC), is a formal means of distinguishing between random and nonrandom variations in an operating process. Random variations occur, for example, when chance fluctuations in the speed of equipment cause defective products to be produced such as copiers that produce fuzzy and unclear copies or copies that are too light or too dark. Nonrandom variations occur when defective products are produced as a result of a systematic problem such as an incorrect speed setting, a flawed part design, or mishandling of a component part. A **control chart**, an important tool in SQC, is a graph of a series of successive observations of a particular step, procedure, or operation taken at regular intervals of time.

Each observation is plotted relative to specified ranges that represent the limits within which observations are expected to fall. Only those observations outside the control limits are ordinarily regarded as nonrandom and worth investigating. Exhibit 10-12 presents control charts for the daily defect rates (defective copiers divided by the total number of copiers produced) observed at Photon's three photocopying machine production lines. Defect rates in the prior 60 days for each production line were assumed to provide a good basis from which to calculate the distribution of daily defect rates. The two parameters of the distribution that are used in the control charts in Exhibit 10-12 are the arithmetic mean (μ, read as *mu*) and standard deviation (σ, read as *sigma*, representing how much an observation deviates from the mean). On the basis of experience, the company decides that any observation outside the $\mu \pm 2\sigma$ range should be investigated.

For production line A, all observations are within the range of $\mu \pm 2\sigma$, so management believes no investigation is necessary. For production line B, the last two observations signal that a much higher percentage of copiers are not performing as they should, indicating that the problem is probably because of a nonrandom, out-of-control occurrence such as an incorrect speed setting or mishandling of a component part. Given the $\pm 2\sigma$ rule, both observations would be investigated. Production line C illustrates a process that would not prompt an investigation under the $\pm 2\sigma$ rule but that may well be out of control, because the last eight observations show a clear direction, and over the last six days, the percentage of defective copiers is increasing and getting further away from the mean. The pattern of observations moving away from the mean could be due, for example, to the tooling on a machine beginning to wear out, resulting in poorly machined parts. As the tooling deteriorates further, the trend in producing defective copiers is likely to persist until the production

Exhibit 10-12 Observation Range and the Cost of Quality

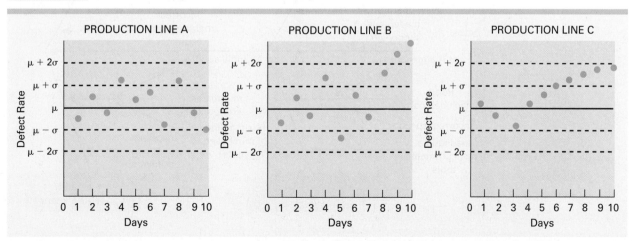

Exhibit 10-13 Quality Problems in Copier Quality

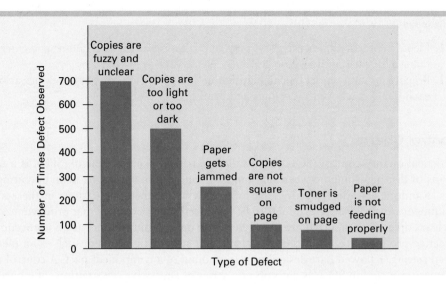

line is no longer in statistical control. Statistical procedures have been developed using the trend as well as the variation to evaluate whether a process is out of control.

Pareto Diagrams

Observations outside control limits serve as inputs for Pareto diagrams. A **Pareto diagram** is a chart that indicates how frequently each type of defect occurs, ordered from the most frequent to the least frequent. Exhibit 10-13 presents a Pareto diagram of quality problems for all observations outside the control limits at the final inspection point in 2018. Fuzzy and unclear copies are the most frequently recurring problem. Fuzzy and unclear copies result in high rework costs. Sometimes fuzzy and unclear copies occur at customer sites and result in high warranty and repair costs and low customer satisfaction.

Cause-and-Effect Diagrams

The most frequently recurring and costly problems identified by the Pareto diagram are analyzed using cause-and-effect diagrams. A **cause-and-effect diagram** identifies potential causes of defects using a diagram that resembles the bone structure of a fish (hence, cause-and-effect diagrams are also called *fishbone diagrams*). Exhibit 10-14 presents the cause-and-effect diagram describing potential reasons for fuzzy and unclear copies.

Exhibit 10-14 Cause and Effect Diagram of Quality Problems

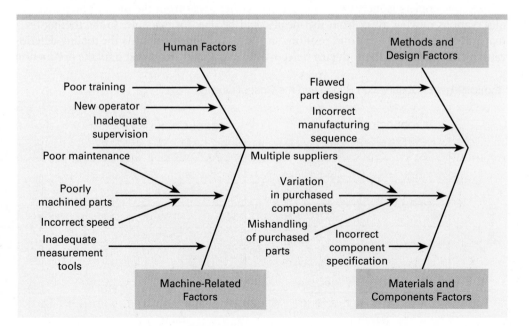

Concepts in Action

What Does It Cost to Send a Text Message?

In 2016, customers sent an estimated 8.3 *trillion* text messages, according to Pew Research Center from mobile phones worldwide. Text messaging is a very lucrative business. How, you ask? After understanding how text messaging costs behave, you learn that it is very inexpensive for wireless carriers to provide this wildly popular service.

Text messaging does not require a wireless company like TELUS or Rogers to add any additional infrastructure, equipment, or wireless spectrum. A text message travels wirelessly from a phone to the closest base tower station and is then transferred through wired links to the digital pipes of the telephone network. Then, near its destination, it is converted back into a wireless signal to traverse the final leg, from tower to the recipient's phone. Text messages do not require extra spectrum. Generally limited to 160 characters, small text messaging files are "free riders" tucked into what's called a control channel, or the space reserved for operation of the wireless network.

Other text messaging costs are semi-variable and minimal. For billing, each text message triggers a control message back to the wireless company's billing system with the identity of the sender and the receiver so their monthly bills can be updated. If a text message cannot be delivered, it must be stored until the recipient is available. TELUS, Bell, or Rogers would pay for its message storage system based on capacity: the higher the capacity, the greater the cost, though data storage is fairly inexpensive.

So what does it cost a wireless to send a text message? University of Waterloo professor Srinivasan Keshav has calculated the cost: $0.003 cent. That's right, three-tenths of one cent! Dr. Keshav found that wireless channels contribute about a tenth of a cent to the carrier's cost, that accounting charges are twice that, and that, due to volume, the other costs basically round to zero because texting requires so little infrastructure. As you can see, the text messaging business is incredibly profitable.

- The "backbone" of the diagram represents the problem being examined.
- The large "bones" coming off the backbone represent the main categories of potential causes of failure. The exhibit identifies four of these: human factors, methods and design factors, machine-related factors, and materials and components factors. Photon's engineers identify the materials and components factor as an important reason for the fuzzy and unclear copies.
- Additional arrows or bones are added to provide more-detailed reasons for each higher-level cause.

For example, the engineers determine that two potential causes of materials and components problems are variation in purchased components and incorrect component specification. They quickly settle on variation in purchased components as the likely cause and focus on the use of multiple suppliers and mishandling of purchased parts as the root causes of variation in purchased components. Further analysis leads them to conclude that mishandling of the steel frame that holds in place various components of the copier such as drums, mirrors, and lenses results in the misalignment of these components, causing fuzzy and unclear copies.

The analysis of quality problems is aided by automated equipment and computers that record the number and types of defects and the operating conditions that existed at the time the defects occurred. Using these inputs, computer programs simultaneously and iteratively prepare control charts, Pareto diagrams, and cause-and-effect diagrams with the goal of continuously reducing the mean defect rate, μ, and the standard deviation, σ.

Data Collection and Adjustment Issues

The ideal database for estimating cost functions quantitatively has two characteristics:

1. The database should contain numerous reliably measured observations of the cost driver (the independent variable) and the related costs (the dependent variable). Errors in measuring costs can result in inaccurate estimates of the effect of the cost driver on costs.

▶ **LO 8**

Understand issues of data collection and quality.

2. The database should consider many values spanning a wide range for the cost driver. Using only a few values of the cost driver that are grouped closely considers too small a segment of the relevant range and reduces the confidence in the estimates obtained.

Unfortunately, cost analysts typically do not have the advantage of working with a database having both characteristics. This section outlines some frequently encountered data problems and steps the cost analyst can take to overcome these problems.

1. The time period for measuring the dependent variable (for example, machine-lubricant costs) does not properly match the period for measuring the cost driver. This problem often arises when accounting records are not kept on the accrual basis.

2. Fixed costs are allocated as if they were variable. For example, costs such as depreciation, insurance, or rent may be allocated to products to calculate cost per unit of output. To avoid this problem, the analyst should carefully distinguish fixed costs from variable costs and not treat allocated fixed cost per unit as a variable cost.

3. Data are either not available for all observations or are not uniformly reliable. Additionally, recording data manually rather than electronically tends to result in a higher percentage of missing observations and erroneously entered observations. Errors also arise when data on cost drivers originate outside the internal accounting system. For example, the accounting department may obtain data on testing-hours for medical instruments from the manufacturer.

4. Extreme values of observations occur from errors in recording costs (for example, a misplaced decimal point), from nonrepresentative periods (for example, from a period in which a major machine breakdown occurred, or from a period in which a delay in delivery of materials from an international supplier curtailed production).

5. There is no homogeneous relationship between the cost driver and the individual cost items in the dependent variable-cost pool. A homogeneous relationship exists when each activity whose costs are included in the dependent variable has the same cost driver. In this case, a single cost function can be estimated.

6. The relationship between the cost driver and the cost is not stationary. That is, the underlying process that generated the observations has not remained stable over time. For example, the relationship between number of machine-hours and manufacturing overhead costs is unlikely to be stationary when the data cover a period in which new technology was introduced.

7. Inflation has affected costs, the cost driver, or both. For example, inflation may cause costs to change even when there is no change in the level of the cost driver. To study the underlying cause-and-effect relationship between the level of the cost driver and costs, the analyst should remove purely inflationary price effects from the data by dividing each cost by the price index on the date the cost was incurred.

In many cases, a cost analyst must expend considerable effort to reduce the effect of these problems before estimating a cost function on the basis of past data.

Pulling it all Together—Problem for Self-Study

(Try to solve this problem before examining the solution that follows.)

Problem

Dan Wong is examining customer service costs in the Southern Region of Capitol Products. Capitol Products has over 200 separate electrical products that are sold with a six-month guarantee of full repair or replacement with a new product. When a product is returned by a customer, a service report is made. This service report includes details of the problem and the time and cost of resolving the problem.

Each product manager shares the services of the customer service department, a separate business function in the company. The total costs of this support service are all pooled in one traditional overhead cost pool. The management team wants to determine what the cost per service request is and to predict future values of the cost pool without refining the entire cost system.

In the following table of data pairs for the most recent 16-week period, X is the quantity of customer service requests and Y is the actual service support cost for the customer service department in each week. Notice that there is a shutdown in week 11 for audit purposes when no requests were received.

Week	Customer Service Department Costs	Customer Service Requests
1	$ 16,614	201
2	24,750	276
3	15,530	122
4	22,142	386
5	17,810	274
6	26,268	436
7	20,198	321
8	25,715	328
9	21,920	243
10	20,198	161
11	6,500	—
12	15,325	185
13	19,522	300
14	17,120	250
15	19,300	300
16	20,050	315
Total	$308,962	

1. Plot the relationship between the number of service reports and customer service costs. Is the relationship economically plausible? ③ ◀ **Required**
2. What variables, in addition to number of service reports, might be cost drivers of monthly service costs of Capitol Products? ① ④
3. Use the high–low method to compute (predict) the value of the customer service indirect cost pool when the number of service reports X = 436. ⑨
4. Using the statistical results from the Excel Ordinary Least Squares (OLS) simple linear regression, calculate (predict) the value of the customer service indirect cost pool when the number of customer service reports X = 436. ⑩
5. Dan predicts that, 11 weeks in the future, the number of service reports will equal 425. Estimate the customer service costs of 425 service reports using the results of the calculation of the high–low and regression cost functions. ②
6. Why is the OLS simple linear regression analysis cost function usually the more accurate cost function? ① ⑨
7. What is the importance of a sufficient *quality* of actual data? ⑥ ⑦ ⑧
8. What is the importance of a sufficient *quantity* of historical data? ⑥ ⑦ ⑧

Solution

1. There is a positive relationship between the number of service reports and the customer service department costs. This relationship is economically plausible because as quantity of defective output changes, so, too, will the requests to return the product. Ultimately the defective output will be either scrapped or reworked. Thus, the cost to process customer returns is a support cost of production that

must be recovered in the price. If it is not recovered in the price, then the company must bear the cost itself and profit will decrease.

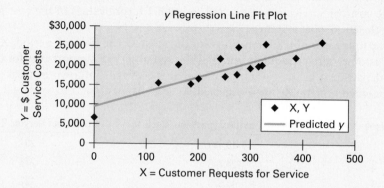

2. Other possible cost drivers of customer service department costs are
   a. Number of products replaced with a new product (and the dollar value of the new products charged to the customer service department).
   b. Number of products repaired and the time and cost of repairs.
3. The predicted value of the indirect customer service cost pool at X = 436 is

High–Low Method	High	Low	Difference			
Y = Service costs	$26,268	$ 6,500	$19,768			
X = Customer requests	436	—	436			
Rate of change (slope) b	$45.339	$ 45.339	per request			
High constant a	$26,268	−	($45.339	×	436)	=	$ 6,500
Low constant a	$ 6,500	−	($45.339	−	−)	=	6,500
y = a + bX where X =	$ 6,500	+	($45.339	×	436)	=	26,268

4. Using the Excel report (rounded), the value of the indirect customer service cost pool is

Regression Statistics	Service Requests	Std Error	t-Stat	P-value
R Square	0.7061			
Observations	16.0			
Degrees of freedom (df)	15.0			
Intercept a	$9,549.909	1,812.1184	5.2700	0.0001
Slope b	$38.107	6.5701	5.8001	0.0000

The prediction of the future value of the customer service overhead cost pool is expressed as a linear cost function:

$$y = \$9,549.909 + \$38.107(436) = \$26,164.561$$

5. High–Low Estimate = $6,500 + $45.339(425) = $25,769.075
   Regression Estimate = $9,549.909 + $38.107(425) = $25,745.384
6. The regression equation uses information from all observations, whereas the high–low method relies only on the observations that have the highest and lowest values of the cost driver. These high and low observations are generally not representative of all the data. Therefore, the regression equation is usually the more accurate cost function.

7. Of course the data must be reported accurately and must reliably reflect the actual, economically plausible relationship between changes in a cost driver and changes in the MOH cost pool. The relationship needs to be stationary or have a constant slope over the time period for which these data were reported. Finally, where there are either missing or extreme data points (outliers), the management team must make a hard decision about whether to adjust or exclude these data. If the reason(s) for the extreme values is highly unlikely to recur, then the team is more justified in adjusting or excluding these data.

8. The quantity of X, Y actual data pairs is important because the management team must be reasonably sure the data set represents the normal economic reality of what happens in the company. A single year of monthly observations might be a special year, either extremely cost-efficient or extremely resource wasteful, or any combination of the two. The management team wants to predict a routine future MOH cost, and to do that needs a data set that has enough observations to report a routine past. The regression line is mathematically the most likely future, but the actual outcome will almost certainly differ, though not by too much, from the predicted point on the regression line.

Appendix 10A

Regression Analysis

This appendix describes estimation of the regression equation, several commonly used regression statistics, and how to choose among cost functions that have been estimated by regression analysis. We use the data for Elegant Rugs presented in Exhibit 10-3 and displayed here again for easy reference.

► **LO 9**

Discuss the interpretation of regression models.

Week	Cost Driver: Machine-Hours (X)	Indirect Manufacturing Labour Costs (Y)
1	68	$ 1,190
2	88	1,211
3	62	1,004
4	72	917
5	60	770
6	96	1,456
7	78	1,180
8	46	710
9	82	1,316
10	94	1,032
11	68	752
12	48	963
Total	862	$ 12,501

Estimating the Regression Line

The least-squares technique for estimating the regression line minimizes the sum of the squares of the vertical deviations from the data points to the estimated regression line (also called *residual term*). The objective is to find the values of a and b in the linear cost function $y = a + bX$, where y is the *predicted* cost value as distinguished from the *observed* cost value, which we denote by Y. We wish to find the numerical values of a and b that minimize $\sum(Y - y)^2$, the sum of the squares of the vertical deviations between Y and y.

Generally, these computations are done using software packages such as Excel. For the data in our example,[3] $a = \$300.98$ and $b = \$10.31$, so that the equation of the regression line is $y = \$300.98 + \$10.31X$.

Goodness of Fit

Goodness of fit measures how well the predicted values, y, based on the cost driver, X, match actual cost observations, Y. The regression analysis method computes a measure of goodness of fit, called the **coefficient of determination** (r^2), that measures the percentage of variation in Y explained by X (the independent variable). It is more convenient to express the coefficient of determination as 1 minus the proportion of total variance that is *not* explained by the independent variable—that is, 1 minus the ratio of unexplained variation to total variation. The unexplained variance arises because of differences between the actual values, Y, and the predicted values, y, which in the Elegant Rugs example is given by[4]

$$r^2 = 1 - \frac{\text{Unexplained variation}}{\text{Total variation}} = 1 - \frac{\Sigma(Y - y)^2}{\Sigma(Y - \overline{Y})^2} = 1 - \frac{290,824}{607,699} = 0.52$$

The calculations indicate that r^2 increases as the predicted values, y, more closely approximate the actual observations, Y. The range of r^2 is from 0 (implying no explanatory power) to 1 (implying perfect explanatory power). Generally, an r^2 of 0.30 or higher passes the goodness-of-fit test. However, do not rely exclusively on goodness of fit. It can lead to the indiscriminate inclusion of independent variables that increase r^2 but have no economic plausibility as cost drivers. *Goodness of fit has meaning only if the relationship between the cost drivers and costs is economically plausible.*

An alternative and related way to evaluate goodness of fit is to calculate the *standard error of the regression*. The **standard error of the regression** is the variance of the residuals. It is equal to

$$S = \sqrt{\frac{\Sigma(Y - y)^2}{\text{Degrees of freedom}}} = \sqrt{\frac{\Sigma(Y - y)^2}{n - 2}} = \sqrt{\frac{290,824}{12 - 2}} = \$170.54$$

Degrees of freedom equal the number of observations, 12, *minus* the number of coefficients estimated in the regression (in this case two, a and b). On average, actual Y and the predicted value, y, differ by \$170.54. For comparison, $\overline{Y}$, the average value of Y, is \$1,041.75. The smaller the standard error of the regression, the better the fit and the better the predictions for different values of X.

---

[3] The formulae for a and b are as follows:

$$a = \frac{(\Sigma Y)(\Sigma X^2) - (\Sigma X)(\Sigma XY)}{n(\Sigma X^2) - (\Sigma X)(\Sigma X)} \text{ and } b = \frac{n(\Sigma XY) - (\Sigma X)(\Sigma Y)}{n(\Sigma X^2) - (\Sigma X)(\Sigma X)}$$

where for the Elegant Rugs data in Exhibit 10-3,

$n =$ number of data points $= 12$

$\Sigma X =$ sum of the given X values $= 68 + 88 + \ldots + 48 = 862$

$\Sigma X^2 =$ sum of squares of the X values $= (68)^2 + (88)^2 + \ldots + (48)^2 + 4,624 + 7,744 + \ldots + 2,304 = 64,900$

$\Sigma Y =$ sum of given Y values $= 1,190 + 1,211 + \ldots + 963 = 12,501$

$\Sigma XY =$ sum of the amounts obtained by multiplying each of the given X values by the associated observed

Y value $= (68)(1,190) + (88)(1,211) + \ldots + (48)(963)$

$= 80,920 + 106,568 + \ldots + 46,224 = 928,716$

$$a = \frac{(12,501)(64,900) - (862)(928,716)}{12(64,900) - (862)(862)} = \$300.98$$

$$b = \frac{12(928,716) - (862)(12,501)}{12(64,900) - (862)(862)} = \$10.31$$

[4] From footnote 3, $\Sigma Y = 12,501$ and $\overline{Y} = 12,501 \div 12 = 1,041.75$

$$\Sigma(Y - \overline{Y})^2 = (1,190 - 1,041.75)^2 + (1,211 - 1,041.75)^2 + \ldots + (963 - 1,041.75)^2 = 607,699$$

Each value of X generates a predicted value of y. For example, in week 1, $y = \$300.98 + (\$10.31 \times 68) = \$1002.06$; in week 2, $y = \$300.98 + (\$10.31 \times 88) = \$1,208.26$; and in week 12, $y = \$300.98 + (\$10.31 \times 48) = \$795.86$. Comparing the predicted and actual values,

$$\Sigma(Y - y)^2 = (1,190 - 1,002.06)^2 + (1,211 - 1208.26)^2 + \ldots + (963 - 795.86)^2 = 290,824.$$

Significance of Independent Variables

Do changes in the economically plausible independent variable result in significant changes in the dependent variable? Or, alternatively stated, is the slope coefficient, $b = \$10.31$, of the regression line statistically significant (that is, different from \$0)? Recall, for example, that in the regression of number of machine-hours and indirect manufacturing labour costs in the Elegant Rugs illustration, b is estimated from a sample of 12 weekly observations. The estimate, b, is subject to random factors, as are all sample statistics. That is, a different sample of 12 data points would undoubtedly give a different estimate of b. The **standard error of the estimated coefficient** indicates how much the estimated value, b, is likely to be affected by random factors. The t-value of the b coefficient measures how large the value of the estimated coefficient is relative to its standard error.

The cutoff t-value for making inferences about the b coefficient is a function of the number of degrees of freedom, the significance level, and whether it is a one-sided or two-sided test. A 5% level of significance indicates that there is less than a 5% probability that random factors could have affected the coefficient b. A two-sided test assumes that random factors could have caused the coefficient to be either greater than \$10.31 or less than \$10.31 with equal probability. At a 5% level of significance, this means that there is less than a 2.5% ($= 5\% \div 2$) probability that random factors could have caused the coefficient to be greater than \$10.31 and less than 2.5% probability that random factors could have caused the coefficient to be less than \$10.31. Under the expectation that the coefficient of b is positive, a one-sided test at the 5% level of significance assumes that there is less than 5% probability that random factors would have caused the coefficient to be less than \$10.31. The cutoff t-value at the 5% significance level and 10 degrees of freedom for a two-sided test is 2.228. If there were more observations and 60 degrees of freedom, the cutoff t-value would be 2.00 at a 5% significance level for a two-sided test.

The t-value (called t Stat in the Excel output) for the slope coefficient b is the value of the estimated coefficient, \$10.31 ÷ the standard error of the estimated coefficient \$3.12 $= 3.30$, which exceeds the cutoff t-value of 2.228. In other words, a relationship exists between the independent variable, machine-hours, and the dependent variable that cannot be attributed to random chance alone. Exhibit 10A-1 shows a convenient format (in Excel) for summarizing the regression results for number of machine-hours and indirect manufacturing labour costs.

An alternative way to test that the coefficient b is significantly different from zero is in terms of a *confidence interval*: There is less than a 5% chance that the true value of the machine-hours coefficient lies outside the range \$10.31 ± (2.228 × \$3.12), or \$10.31 ± \$6.95, or from \$3.36 to \$17.26. Because 0 does not appear in the confidence interval, we can conclude that changes in the number of machine-hours do affect indirect manufacturing labour costs. Similarly, using data from Exhibit 10A-1, the t-value for the constant

Exhibit 10A-1 Simple Regression Results with Indirect Manufacturing Labour Costs as Dependent Variable and Machine-Hours as Independent Variable (Cost Driver) for Elegant Rugs

	A	B	C	D	E	F
1		**Coefficients**	**Standard Error**	**t Stat**		**= Coefficient/Standard Error**
2		**(1)**	**(2)**	**(3) = (1) ÷ (2)**		= B3/C3
3	Intercept	$300.98	$ 229.75	1.31 ——————▶		= 300.98/229.75
4	Independent Variable: Machine-Hours (X)	$ 10.31	$ 3.12	3.30		
5						
6	**Regression Statistics**					
7	R Square	0.52				
8	Durbin-Watson Statistic	2.05				

term *a* is $300.98 ÷ $229.75 = 1.31, which is less than 2.228. This *t*-value indicates that, within the relevant range, the constant term is *not* significantly different from zero. The Durbin-Watson statistic in Exhibit 10A-1 will be discussed in the following section.

Specification Analysis of Estimation Assumptions

Specification analysis is the testing of the assumptions of regression analysis. If the assumptions of (1) linearity within the relevant range, (2) constant variance of residuals, (3) independence of residuals, and (4) normality of residuals all hold, then the simple regression procedures give reliable estimates of coefficient values. This section provides a brief overview of specification analysis. When these assumptions are not satisfied, more-complex regression procedures are necessary to obtain the best estimates.[5]

1. *Linearity within the relevant range.* A common assumption—and one that appears to be reasonable in many business applications—is that a linear relationship exists between the independent variable *X* and the dependent variable *Y* within the relevant range. If a linear regression model is used to estimate a nonlinear relationship, however, the coefficient estimates obtained will be inaccurate.

   When there is only one independent variable, the easiest way to check for linearity is to study the data plotted in a scatter diagram, a step that often is unwisely skipped. Exhibit 10-4 presents a scatter diagram for the indirect manufacturing labour costs and machine-hours variables of Elegant Rugs shown in Exhibit 10-3. The scatter diagram reveals that linearity appears to be a reasonable assumption for these data.

   The learning-curve models discussed in Appendix 10B are examples of nonlinear cost functions. Costs increase when the level of production increases, but by lesser amounts than would occur with a linear cost function. In this case, the analyst should estimate a nonlinear cost function that incorporates learning effects.

2. *Constant variance of residuals.* The vertical deviation of the observed value *Y* from the regression line estimate *y* is called the *residual term, disturbance term*, or *error term*, $u = Y - y$. The assumption of constant variance implies that the residual terms are unaffected by the level of the cost driver. The assumption also implies that there is a uniform scatter, or dispersion, of the data points about the regression line as in Exhibit 10A-2, Panel A. This assumption is likely to be violated, for example, in

Exhibit 10A-2 Constant Variance of Residuals Assumption

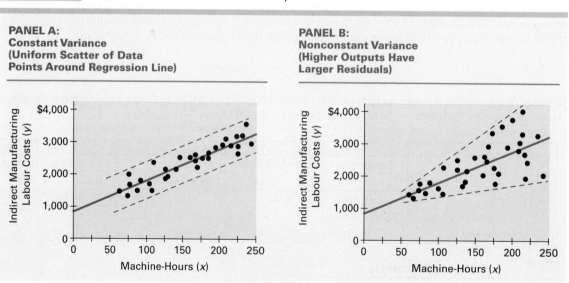

PANEL A:
Constant Variance
(Uniform Scatter of Data
Points Around Regression Line)

PANEL B:
Nonconstant Variance
(Higher Outputs Have
Larger Residuals)

---

[5] For details see, for example, W.H. Greene, *Econometric Analysis*, 6th ed. (Upper Saddle River, NJ: Prentice Hall, 2007).

cross-sectional estimation of costs in operations of different sizes. For example, suppose Elegant Rugs has production areas of varying sizes. The company collects data from these different production areas to estimate the relationship between machine-hours and indirect manufacturing labour costs. It is very possible that the residual terms in this regression will be larger for the larger production areas that have higher machine-hours and higher indirect manufacturing labour costs. There would not be a uniform scatter of data points about the regression line (see Exhibit 10A-2, Panel B). Constant variance is also known as *homoscedasticity*. Violation of this assumption is called *heteroscedasticity*.

Heterosc*edasticity* does not affect the accuracy of the regression estimates *a* and *b*. It does, however, reduce the reliability of the estimates of the standard errors and thus affects the precision with which inferences about the population parameters can be drawn from the regression estimates.

3. *Independence of residuals.* The assumption of independence of residuals is that the residual term for any one observation is not related to the residual term for any other observation. The problem of *serial correlation* (also called *autocorrelation*) in the residuals arises when there is a systematic pattern in the sequence of residuals such that the residual in observation *n* conveys information about the residuals in observations *n* + 1, *n* + 2, and so on. Consider another production cell at Elegant Rugs that has, over a 20-week period, seen an increase in production and hence machine-hours. Exhibit 10A-3 Panel B, is a scatter diagram of machine-hours and indirect manufacturing labour costs. Observe the systematic pattern of the residuals in Panel B—positive residuals for extreme (high and low) quantities of machine-hours and negative residuals for moderate quantities of machine-hours. One reason for this observed pattern at low values of the cost driver is the "stickiness" of costs. When machine-hours are below 50 hours, indirect manufacturing labour costs do not decline. When machine-hours increase over time as production is ramped up, indirect manufacturing labour costs increase more as managers at Elegant Rugs struggle to manage the higher volume. How would the plot of residuals look if there were no auto-correlation? Like the plot in Exhibit 10A-3, Panel A, that shows no pattern in the residuals.

Like nonconstant variance of residuals, serial correlation does not affect the accuracy of the regression estimates *a* and *b*. It does, however, affect the standard errors of the coefficients, which in turn affect the precision with which inferences about the population parameters can be drawn from the regression estimates.

Exhibit 10A-3 Independence of Residuals Assumption

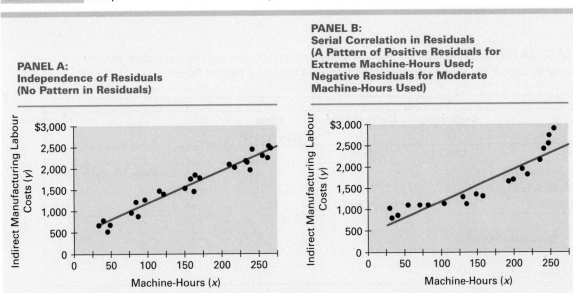

PANEL A:
Independence of Residuals
(No Pattern in Residuals)

PANEL B:
Serial Correlation in Residuals
(A Pattern of Positive Residuals for
Extreme Machine-Hours Used;
Negative Residuals for Moderate
Machine-Hours Used)

The Durbin-Watson statistic is one measure of serial correlation in the estimated residuals. For samples of 10 to 20 observations, a Durbin-Watson statistic in the 1.10–2.90 range indicates that the residuals are independent. The Durbin-Watson statistic for the regression results of Elegant Rugs in Exhibit 10A-1 is 2.05. Therefore, an assumption of independence in the estimated residuals is reasonable for this regression model.

4. *Normality of residuals.* The normality of residuals assumption means that the residuals are distributed normally around the regression line. The normality of residuals assumption is frequently satisfied when using regression analysis on real cost data. Even when the assumption does not hold, accountants can still generate accurate estimates based on the regression equation, but the resulting confidence interval around these estimates is likely to be inaccurate.

Using Regression Output to Choose Cost Drivers of Cost Functions

Consider the two choices of cost drivers we described earlier in this chapter for indirect manufacturing labour costs (*y*):

$$y = a + (b \times \text{Number of machine-hours})$$
$$y = a + (b \times \text{Number of direct manufacturing labour-hours})$$

Exhibit 10-6 shows a plot of the data for the regression of number of machine-hours. Exhibit 10A-1 reports regression results for the cost function using number of machine-hours as the independent variable. Exhibit 10A-4 presents comparable regression results (in Excel) for the cost function using number of direct manufacturing labour-hours as the independent variable.

On the basis of the material presented in Appendix 10A, which regression is better? Exhibit 10A-5 compares these two cost functions in a systematic way. For several criteria, the cost function based on machine-hours is preferable to the cost function based on direct manufacturing labour-hours. The economic plausibility criterion is especially important.

Do not always assume that any one cost function will perfectly satisfy all the criteria in Exhibit 10A-5. A cost analyst must often make a choice among "imperfect" cost functions, in the sense that the data of any particular cost function will not perfectly meet one or more of the assumptions underlying regression analysis. For example, both of the cost functions in Exhibit 10A-5 are imperfect because, as stated in the section on specification analysis of estimation assumptions, inferences drawn from only 12 observations are not reliable.

Exhibit 10A-4 Simple Regression Results with Indirect Manufacturing Labour Costs as Dependent Variable and Direct Manufacturing Labour-Hours as Independent Variable (Cost Driver) for Elegant Rugs

	A	B	C	D	E	F	G	H
		Coefficients	**Standard Error**	***t* Stat**				
1		(1)	(2)	(3) = (1) ÷ (2)				
2								
3	Intercept	$744.67	$217.61	3.42				
4	Independent Variable: Direct Manufacturing Labour-Hours (*X*)	$ 7.72	$ 5.40	1.43		= Coefficient/Standard Error = B4/C4 = 7.72/5.40		
5								
6	**Regression Statistics**							
7	R Square	0.17						
8	Durbin-Watson Statistic	2.26						

Exhibit 10A-5 Comparison of Alternative Cost Functions for Indirect Manufacturing Labour Costs Estimated with Simple Regression for Elegant Rugs

Criterion	Cost Function 1: Machine-Hours as Independent Variable	Cost Function 2: Direct Manufacturing Labour-Hours as Independent Variable
Economic plausibility	A positive relationship between indirect manufacturing labour costs (technical support labour) and machine-hours is economically plausible in Elegant Rugs' highly automated plant.	A positive relationship between indirect manufacturing labour costs and direct manufacturing labour-hours is economically plausible, but less so than machine-hours in Elegant Rugs' highly automated plant on a week-to-week basis.
Goodness of fit*	$r^2 = 0.52$; standard error of regression = $170.50. Excellent goodness of fit.	$r^2 = 0.17$; standard error of regression = $224.60. Poor goodness of fit.
Significance of independent variable(s)	The t-value of 3.30 is significant at the 0.05 level.	The t-value of 1.43 is not significant at the 0.05 level.
Specification analysis of estimation assumptions	Plot of the data indicates that assumptions of linearity, constant variance, independence of residuals (Durbin-Watson statistic = 2.05), and normality of residuals hold, but inferences drawn from only 12 observations are not reliable.	Plot of the data indicates that assumptions of linearity, constant variance, independence of residuals (Durbin-Watson statistic = 2.26), and normality of residuals hold, but inferences drawn from only 12 observations are not reliable.

*If the number of observations available to estimate the machine-hours regression differs from the number of observations available to estimate the direct manufacturing labour-hours regression, an *adjusted* r^2 can be calculated to take this difference (in degrees of freedom) into account. Programs such as Excel calculate and present *adjusted* r^2.

Multiple Regression and Cost Hierarchies

In some cases, a satisfactory estimation of a cost function may be based on only one independent variable, such as number of machine-hours. In many cases, however, basing the estimation on more than one independent variable (that is, *multiple regression*) is more economically plausible and improves accuracy. The most widely used equations to express relationships between two or more independent variables and a dependent variable are linear in the form

$$y = a + b_1X_1 + b_2X_2 + \ldots + u$$

where,

y = Cost to be predicted

$X_1, X_2, \ldots$ = Independent variables on which the prediction is to be based

$a, b_1, b_2, \ldots$ = Estimated coefficients of the regression model

u = Residual term that includes the net effect of other factors not in the model as well as measurement errors in the dependent and independent variables

Example: Consider the Elegant Rugs data in Exhibit 10A-6. The company's ABC analysis indicates that indirect manufacturing labour costs include large amounts incurred for setup and changeover costs when a new batch of carpets is started. Management believes that in addition to number of machine-hours (an output unit-level cost driver), indirect manufacturing labour costs are also affected by the number of batches of carpet produced during each week (a batch-level driver). Elegant Rugs estimates the relationship between two independent variables, number of machine-hours and number of production batches of carpet manufactured during the week, and indirect manufacturing labour costs.

Exhibit 10A-6 Weekly Indirect Manufacturing Labour Costs, Machine-Hours, Direct Manufacturing Labour-Hours, and Number of Production Batches for Elegant Rugs

	A	B	C	D	E
1	Week	Machine-Hours (X_1)	Number of Production Batches (X_2)	Direct Manufacturing Labour-Hours	Indirect Manufacturing Labour Costs (Y)
2	1	68	12	30	$ 1,190
3	2	88	15	35	1,211
4	3	62	13	36	1,004
5	4	72	11	20	917
6	5	60	10	47	770
7	6	96	12	45	1,456
8	7	78	17	44	1,180
9	8	46	7	38	710
10	9	82	14	70	1,316
11	10	94	12	30	1,032
12	11	68	7	29	752
13	12	48	14	38	963
14	Total	862	144	462	$12,501
15					

Exhibit 10A-7 presents results (in Excel) for the following multiple regression model, using data in columns B, C, and E of Exhibit 10A-6:

$$y = \$42.58 + \$7.60X_1 + \$37.77X_2$$

where X_1 is the number of machine-hours and X_2 is the number of production batches. It is economically plausible that both number of machine-hours and number of production batches would help explain variations in indirect manufacturing labour costs at Elegant Rugs. The r^2 of 0.52 for the simple regression using number of machine-hours (Exhibit 10A-1) increases to 0.72 with the multiple regression in Exhibit 10A-7. The t-values suggest that the independent variable coefficients of both number of machine-hours ($7.60) and number of production batches ($37.77) are significantly different from zero ($t = 2.74$ is the t-value for number of machine-hours, and $t = 2.48$ is the t-value for number of production batches compared to the cut-off t-value of 2.26). The multiple

Exhibit 10A-7 Multiple Regression Results with Indirect Manufacturing Labour Costs and Two Independent Variables of Cost Drivers (Machine-Hours and Production Batches) for Elegant Rugs

	A	B	C	D	E	F
1		Coefficients	Standard Error	t Stat		
2		(1)	(2)	(3) = (1) ÷ (2)		
3	Intercept	$42.58	$213.91	0.20		
4	Independent Variable 1: Machine-Hours (X_1)	$ 7.60	$ 2.77	2.74 ⟶		= Coefficient/Standard Error = B4/C4 = 7.60/2.77
5	Independent Variable 2: Number of Production Batches (X_2)	$37.77	$ 15.25	2.48		
6						
7	**Regression Statistics**					
8	R Square	0.72				
9	Durbin-Watson Statistic	2.49				

regression model in Exhibit 10A-7 satisfies both economic plausibility and statistical criteria, and it explains much greater variation (that is, r^2 of 0.72 versus r^2 of 0.52) in indirect manufacturing labour costs than the simple regression model using only number of machine-hours as the independent variable.[6] The standard error of the regression equation that includes number of batches as an independent variable is

$$\sqrt{\frac{\Sigma(Y - y)^2}{n - 3}} = \sqrt{\frac{170,156}{9}} = \$137.50$$

which is lower than the standard error of the regression with only machine-hours as the independent variable, \$170.50. That is, even though adding a variable reduces the degrees of freedom in the denominator, it substantially improves fit so that the numerator, $\Sigma(Y - y)^2$, decreases even more. Number of machine-hours and number of production batches are both important cost drivers of indirect manufacturing labour costs at Elegant Rugs.

In Exhibit 10A-7, the slope coefficients—\$7.60 for number of machine-hours and \$37.77 for number of production batches—measure the change in indirect manufacturing labour costs associated with a unit change in an independent variable (assuming that the other independent variable is held constant). For example, indirect manufacturing labour costs increase by \$37.77 when one more production batch is added, assuming that the number of machine-hours is held constant.

An alternative approach would create two separate cost pools for indirect manufacturing labour costs: one for costs related to number of machine-hours and another for costs related to number of production batches. Elegant Rugs would then estimate the relationship between the cost driver and the costs in each cost pool. The difficult task under this approach is to properly subdivide the indirect manufacturing labour costs into the two cost pools.

Multicollinearity

A major concern that arises with multiple regression is multicollinearity. **Multicollinearity** exists when two or more independent variables are highly correlated with each other. Generally, users of regression analysis believe that a *coefficient of correlation* between independent variables greater than 0.70 indicates multicollinearity. Multicollinearity increases the standard errors of the coefficients of the individual variables. That is, variables that are economically and statistically significant will appear not to be significantly different from zero.

The matrix of correlation coefficients of the different variables described in Exhibit 10A-6 are as follows:

	Indirect Manufacturing Labour Costs	Machine-Hours	Number of Production Batches	Direct Manufacturing Labour-Hours
Indirect manufacturing labour costs	1			
Machine-hours	0.72	1		
Number of production batches	0.69	0.4	1	
Direct manufacturing labour-hours	0.41	0.12	0.31	1

---

[6] Adding another variable always increases r^2. The question is whether adding another variable increases r^2 sufficiently. One way to get insight into this question is to calculate an adjusted r^2 as follows:

Adjusted $r^2 = 1 - (1 - r^2)\dfrac{n - 1}{n - p - 1}$, where n is the number of observations and p is the number of coefficients estimated. In the model with only machine-hours as the independent variable, adjusted $r^2 = 1 - (1 - 0.52)\dfrac{12 - 1}{12 - 2 - 1} = 0.41$. In the model with both machine-hours and number of batches as independent variables, adjusted $r^2 = 1 - (1 - 0.72)\dfrac{12 - 1}{12 - 3 - 1} = 0.62$.

Adjusted r^2 does not have the same interpretation as r^2 but the increase in adjusted r^2 when number of batches is added as an independent variable suggests that adding this variable significantly improves the fit of the model in a way that more than compensates for the degree of freedom lost by estimating another coefficient.

These results indicate that multiple regressions using any pair of the independent variables in Exhibit 10A-6 are not likely to encounter multicollinearity problems.

When multicollinearity exists, try to obtain new data that do not suffer from multi-collinearity problems. Do not drop an independent variable (cost driver) that should be included in a model because it is correlated with another independent variable. Omitting such a variable will cause the estimated coefficient of the independent variable included in the model to be biased away from its true value.

Appendix 10B

▶ **LO 10**

Describe a learning curve model.

Learning Curves

Nonlinear cost functions also result from learning curves. A learning curve is a function that measures how labour-hours per unit decline as units of production increase because workers are learning and becoming better at their jobs. Managers use learning curves to predict how labour-hours, or labour costs, will increase as more units are produced.

The aircraft-assembly industry first documented the effect that learning has on efficiency. In general, as workers become more familiar with their tasks, their efficiency improves. Managers learn how to improve the scheduling of work shifts and how to operate the plant more efficiently. As a result of improved efficiency, unit costs decrease as productivity increases, and the unit-cost function behaves nonlinearly. These nonlinearities must be considered when estimating and predicting unit costs.

Managers have extended the learning-curve notion to other business functions in the value chain, such as marketing, distribution, and customer service, and to costs other than labour costs. The term *experience curve* describes this broader application of the learning curve. An experience curve is a function that measures the decline in cost per unit in various business functions of the value chain—marketing, distribution, and so on—as the amount of these activities increases. For companies such as Dell, Walmart, and McDonald's, learning curves and experience curves are key elements of their strategies. These companies use learning curves and experience curves to reduce costs and increase customer satisfaction, market share, and profitability.

Cumulative Average-Time Learning Model

In the **cumulative average-time learning model**, cumulative average time per unit declines by a constant percentage each time the cumulative quantity of units produced doubles. Consider Rayburn Corporation, a radar systems manufacturer. Rayburn has an 80% learning curve. The 80% means that when the quantity of units produced is doubled from X to 2X, cumulative average time *per unit* for 2X units is 80% of cumulative average time *per unit* for X units. Average time per unit has dropped by 20% (= 100% − 80%).

Exhibit 10B-1 is an Excel spreadsheet showing the calculations for the cumulative average-time learning model for Rayburn Corporation. Note that as the number of units produced doubles from 1 to 2 in column A, cumulative average time per unit declines from 100 hours to 80% of 100 hours (0.80 × 100 hours = 80 hours) in column B. As the number of units doubles from 2 to 4, cumulative average time per unit declines to 80% of 80 hours = 64 hours, and so on. To obtain the cumulative total time in column D, multiply cumulative average time per unit by the cumulative number of units produced. For example, to produce 4 cumulative units would require 256 labour-hours (= 4 units × 64 cumulative average labour-hours per unit).

Incremental Unit-Time Learning Model

In the **incremental unit-time learning model**, incremental time needed to produce the last unit declines by a constant percentage each time the cumulative quantity of units produced doubles. Again, consider Rayburn Corporation and an 80% learning curve. The 80% here means that when the quantity of units produced is doubled from X to 2X, the time needed to produce the last unit when 2X total units are produced is 80% of the time needed to produce the last unit when X total units are produced. Exhibit 10B-2

Exhibit 10B-1 Cumulative Average-Time Learning Model

	A	B	C	D	E	F	G	H	I
1	Cumulative Average-Time Learning Model for Rayburn Corporation								
2									
3		80% Learning Curve							
4									
5	Cumulative	Cumulative		Cumulative	Individual Unit				
6	Number	Average Time		Total Time:	Time for *X*th				
7	of Units (*X*)	per Unit (*y*)*: Labour-Hours		Labour-Hours	Unit: Labour-Hours				
8									
9				D = Col A × Col B					
10							E13 = D13 – D12		
11	1	100.00		100.00	100.00		= 210.63 – 160.00		
12	2	80.00	= (100 × 0.8)	160.00	60.00				
13	3	70.21		210.63	50.63				
14	4	64.00	= (80 × 0.8)	256.00	45.37				
15	5	59.56		297.82	41.82				
16	6	56.17		337.01	39.19				
17	7	53.45		374.14	37.13				
18	8	51.20	= (64 × 0.8)	409.60	35.46				
19	9	49.29		443.65	34.05				
20	10	47.65		476.51	32.86				
21	11	46.21		508.32	31.81				
22	12	44.93		539.22	30.89				
23	13	43.79		569.29	30.07				
24	14	42.76		598.63	29.34				
25	15	41.82		627.30	28.67				
26	16	40.96	= (51.2 × 0.8)	655.36	28.06				
27									

*The mathematical relationship underlying the cumulative average-time learning model is as follows:

$$y = aX^b$$

where y = Cumulative average time (labour-hours) per unit
  X = Cumulative number of units produced
  a = Time (labour-hours) required to produce the first unit
  b = Factor used to calculate cumulative average time to produce units

The value of b is calculated as

$$\frac{\ln (\text{learning-curve } \% \text{ in decimal form})}{\ln 2}$$

For an 80% learning curve, $b = \ln 0.8/\ln 2 = -0.2231/0.6931 = -0.3219$
For example, when $X = 3$, $a = 100$, $b = -0.3219$,
  $y = 100 \times 3^{-0.3219} = 70.21$ labour-hours
The cumulative total time when $X = 3$ is $70.21 \times 3 = 210.63$ labour-hours.
Numbers in table may not be exact because of rounding.

Exhibit 10B-2 Incremental Unit-Time Learning Model

	A	B	C	D	E	F	G	H	I
1	Incremental Unit-Time Learning Model for Rayburn Corporation								
2									
3		80% Learning Curve							
4									
5	Cumulative	Individual Unit Time		Cumulative	Cumulative				
6	Number	for Xth Unit (*y*)*:		Total Time:	Average Time				
7	of Units (*X*)	Labour-Hours		Labour-Hours	per Unit:				
8					Labour-Hours				
9									
10					E = Col D ÷ Col A				
11									
12	1	100.00		100.00	100.00		D14 = D13 + B14		
13	2	80.00	= (100 × 0.8)	180.00	90.00		= 180.00 + 70.21		
14	3	70.21		250.21	83.40				
15	4	64.00	= (80 × 0.8)	314.21	78.55				
16	5	59.56		373.77	74.75				
17	6	56.17		429.94	71.66				
18	7	53.45		483.39	69.06				
19	8	51.20	= (64 × 0.8)	534.59	66.82				
20	9	49.29		583.89	64.88				
21	10	47.65		631.54	63.15				
22	11	46.21		677.75	61.61				
23	12	44.93		722.68	60.22				
24	13	43.79		766.47	58.96				
25	14	42.76		809.23	57.80				
26	15	41.82		851.05	56.74				
27	16	40.96	= (51.2 × 0.8)	892.01	55.75				
28									

*The mathematical relationship underlying the incremental unit-time learning model is as follows:

$$y = aX^b$$

where y = Time (labour-hours) taken to produce the last single unit
  X = Cumulative number of units produced
  a = Time (labour-hours) required to produce the first unit
  b = Factor used to calculate incremental unit time to produce units
   $= \dfrac{\ln (\text{learning-curve } \% \text{ in decimal form})}{\ln 2}$

For an 80% learning curve, $b = \ln 0.8 \div \ln 2 = -0.2231 \div 0.6931 = -0.3219$
For example, when $X = 3$, $a = 100$, $b = -0.3219$,
  $y = 100 \times 3^{-0.3219} = 70.21$ labour-hours
The cumulative total time when $X = 3$ is $100 + 80 + 70.21 = 250.21$ labour-hours.
Numbers in the table may not be exact because of rounding.

Exhibit 10B-3 Plotting the Learning Curve Model

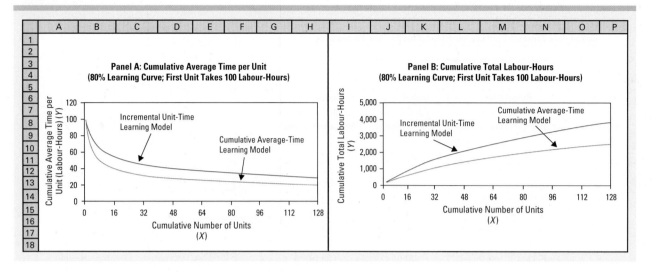

is a spreadsheet showing the calculations for the incremental unit-time learning model for Rayburn Corporation based on an 80% learning curve. Note how when units produced double from 2 to 4 in column A, the time to produce unit 4 (the last unit when 4 units are produced) is 64 hours in column B, which is 80% of the 80 hours needed to produce unit 2 (the last unit when 2 units are produced). We obtain the cumulative total time in column D by summing individual unit times in column B. For example, to produce 4 cumulative units would require 314.21 labour-hours (= 100.00 + 80.00 + 70.21 + 64.00).

Exhibit 10B-3 presents graphs using Excel for the cumulative average-time learning model (using data from Exhibit 10B-1) and the incremental unit-time learning model (using data from Exhibit 10B-2). Panel A graphically illustrates cumulative average time per unit as a function of cumulative units produced for each model (column A in Exhibit 10B-1 or Exhibit 10B-2). The curve for the cumulative average-time learning model is plotted using the data from Exhibit 10B-1, column B, while the curve for the incremental unit-time learning model is plotted using the data from Exhibit 10B-2, column E. Panel B graphically illustrates cumulative total labour-hours, again as a function of cumulative units produced for each model. The curve for the cumulative average-time learning model is plotted using the data from Exhibit 10B-1, column D, while that for the incremental unit-time learning model is plotted using the data from Exhibit 10B-2, column D.

The incremental unit-time learning model predicts a higher cumulative total time to produce 2 or more units than the cumulative average-time learning model, assuming the same learning rate for both models. That is, in Exhibit 10B-3, Panel B, the graph for the 80% incremental unit-time learning model lies above the graph for the 80% cumulative average time learning model. If we compare the results in Exhibit 10B-1 (column D) with the results in Exhibit 10B-2 (column D), to produce 4 cumulative units, the 80% incremental unit-time learning model predicts 314.21 labour-hours versus 256.00 labour-hours predicted by the 80% cumulative average-time learning model. That's because under the cumulative average-time learning model *average labour-hours needed to produce all 4 units* is 64 hours; the labour-hour amount needed to produce unit 4 is much less than 64 hours—it is 45.37 hours (see Exhibit 10B-1). Under the incremental unit-time learning model, the labour-hour amount needed to produce unit 4 is 64 hours, and the labour-hours needed to produce the first 3 units are more than 64 hours, so average time needed to produce all 4 units is more than 64 hours.

It is important to recognize that managers make choices about which model and what percent learning curve to use on a case-by-case basis. For example, if the behaviour

	A	B	C	D	E	F
1		**Cumulative**				
2	**Cumulative**	**Average Time**	**Cumulative**		**Cumulative Costs**	**Additions to**
3	**Number of**	**per Unit:**	**Total Time:**		**at $50 per**	**Cumulative**
4	**Units**	**Labour-Hours**[a]	**Labour-Hours**[a]		**Labour-Hour**	**Costs**
5	1	100.00	100.00	$ 5,000	(100.00 × $50)	$ 5,000
6	2	80.00	160.00	8,000	(160.00 × 50)	3,000
7	4	64.00	256.00	12,800	(256.00 × 50)	4,800
8	8	51.20	409.60	20,480	(409.60 × 50)	7,680
9	16	40.96	655.36	32,768	(655.36 × 50)	12,288
10						
11	[a] Based on the cumulative average-time learning model. See Exhibit 10B-1 for the computations of these amounts.					
12						

Exhibit 10B-4 Application of Cost Prediction Using the Learning Curve Model

of manufacturing labour-hour usage as production levels increase follows a pattern like the one predicted by the 80% learning curve cumulative average-time learning model, then the 80% learning curve cumulative average-time learning model should be used. Engineers, plant managers, and workers are good sources of information on the amount and type of learning actually occurring as production increases. Plotting this information and estimating the model that best fits the data is helpful in selecting the appropriate model.

Incorporating Learning-Curve Effects Into Prices and Standards

Consider the data in Exhibit 10B-1 for the cumulative average-time learning model at Rayburn Corporation. Suppose variable costs subject to learning effects consist of direct manufacturing labour, at $20 per hour, and related overhead, at $30 per direct manufacturing labour-hour. Managers should predict the costs shown in Exhibit 10B-4. These data show that the effects of the learning curve could have a major influence on decisions. For example, managers at Rayburn Corporation might set an extremely low selling price on its radar systems to generate high demand. As its production increases to meet this growing demand, cost per unit drops. Rayburn "rides the product down the learning curve" as it establishes a larger market share.

Although it may have earned little operating income on its first unit sold—it may actually have lost money on that unit—Rayburn earns more operating income per unit as output increases. Alternatively, subject to legal and other considerations, Rayburn's managers might set a low price on just the final 8 units. After all, the total labour and related overhead costs per unit for these final 8 units are predicted to be only $12,288 (= $32,768 − $20,480). On these final 8 units, the $1,536 cost per unit (= $12,288 ÷ 8 units) is much lower than the $5,000 cost per unit of the first unit produced.

Many companies, such as Pizza Hut and Home Depot, incorporate learning-curve effects when evaluating performance. The Nissan Motor Company expects its workers to learn and improve on the job and evaluates performance accordingly. It sets assembly labour efficiency standards for new models of cars after taking into account the learning that will occur as more units are produced.

The learning-curve models examined in Exhibits 10B-1 to 10B-4 assume that learning is driven by a single variable (production output). Other models of learning have been developed (by companies such as Analog Devices and Hewlett-Packard) that focus on how quality—rather than manufacturing labour-hours—will change over time, regardless of whether more units are produced. Studies indicate that factors other than production output, such as job rotation and organizing workers into teams, contribute to learning that improves quality.

Decision Points

The following question-and-answer format summarizes the chapter's learning objectives. Each point presents a key question, and the guidelines are the answer to that question.

Learning Objectives	Guidelines
1. What are linear cost functions, and how do they behave?	A linear cost function is a cost function in which, within the relevant range, the graph of total costs based on the level of a single activity is a straight line. Linear cost functions can be described by a constant, *a*, which represents the estimate of the total cost component that, within the relevant range, does not vary with changes in the level of the activity; and a slope coefficient, *b*, which represents the estimate of the amount by which total costs change for each unit change in the level of the activity within the relevant range. Three types of linear cost functions are variable, fixed, and mixed (or semi-variable).
2. Why is causality important in estimating cost functions?	The most important issue in estimating a cost function is determining whether a cause-and-effect relationship exists between the level of an activity and the costs related to it. Only a cause-and-effect relationship—not merely correlation—establishes an economically plausible relationship between the level of an activity and its costs.
3. What are various methods of cost estimation?	Four methods for estimating cost functions are the industrial engineering method, the conference method, the account analysis method, and the quantitative analysis method (which includes the high–low method and the regression analysis method). If possible, the cost analyst should use more than one method. Each method is a check on the others.
4. What are the steps in estimating a cost function using quantitative analysis?	Six steps need to be taken to estimate a cost function using quantitative analysis: (1) Choose the dependent variable; (2) identify the cost driver; (3) collect data on the dependent variable and the cost driver; (4) plot the data; (5) estimate the cost function; and (6) evaluate the cost driver of the estimated cost function. In most situations, working closely with operations managers, the cost analyst will cycle through these steps several times before identifying an acceptable cost function.
5. What are nonlinear cost functions, in particular those arising from learning curve effects?	A nonlinear cost function is one in which the graph of total costs based on the level of a single activity is not a straight line within the relevant range. Nonlinear costs can arise because of quantity discounts, step cost functions, and learning-curve effects. Due to learning curves, labour-hours per unit decline as units of production increase. With the cumulative average-time learning model, the cumulative average-time per unit declines by a constant percentage each time the cumulative quantity of units produced doubles. With the incremental unit-time learning model, the time needed to produce the last unit declines by a constant percentage each time the cumulative quantity of units produced doubles.
6. What is the impact of time as a cost driver?	The relevant costs of time are the expected incremental costs to implement a program. The relevant benefits are the cost savings and the estimated increase in contribution margin from the higher revenues expected from improvements.

7. What is quality control, and how does it act as a cost driver?

Costs of quality programs are prevention costs (costs incurred to prevent the production of products that do not conform to specifications), appraisal costs (costs incurred to detect which of the individual units of products do not conform to specifications), internal failure costs (costs incurred on defective products before they are shipped to customers), and external failure costs (costs incurred on defective products after they are shipped to customers).

8. What issues of data collection and quality must be noted?

Data for quality measures managers can use include customer satisfaction measures such as the number of customer complaints and percentage of defective units shipped to customers; internal-business-process measures such as the percentage of defective and reworked products; and learning-and-growth measures such as the percentage of employees trained in and empowered to use quality principles.

Three methods to identify quality problems and to improve quality are (1) control charts to distinguish random from nonrandom variations in an operating process, (2) Pareto diagrams to indicate how frequently each type of failure occurs, and (3) cause-and-effect diagrams to identify and respond to potential causes of failure.

9. How are regression models interpreted?

A regression analysis is a function used to describe the relationship between one or more independent variables and the dependent variable. An independent variable that has a low P-value is likely a useful component of a cost function because changes in the independent variable's value are related to changes in the dependent variable.

10. What is a learning curve model?

A learning curve is a function that measures how labour-hours per unit decline as units of production increase because workers are learning and becoming better at their jobs. Managers use learning curves to predict how labour-hours, or labour costs, will increase as more units are produced.

Terms to Learn

This chapter and the Glossary at the end of the book contain definitions of the following important terms:

account analysis method (**p. 382**)

appraisal costs (**p. 396**)

average waiting time (**p. 390**)

bottleneck (**p. 390**)

cause-and-effect diagram (**p. 400**)

coefficient of determination (**p. 406**)

conference method (**p. 382**)

constant (**p. 379**)

control chart (**p. 399**)

cost function (**p. 378**)

costs of quality (**p. 396**)

cross-sectional data (**p. 384**)

cumulative average-time learning
    model (**p. 414**)

customer-response time (**p. 388**)

delivery time (**p. 389**)

dependent variable (**p. 383**)

external failure costs (**p. 396**)

high–low method (**p. 385**)

incremental unit-time learning
    model (**p. 414**)

internal failure costs (**p. 396**)

independent variable (**p. 383**)

industrial engineering method (**p. 381**)

manufacturing cycle efficiency (**p. 389**)

manufacturing cycle time (**p. 388**)

manufacturing lead time (**p. 389**)

mixed cost (**p. 379**)

multicollinearity (**p. 413**)

multiple regression (**p. 386**)

nonlinear cost function (**p. 387**)

on-time performance (**p. 389**)

Pareto diagram (**p. 400**)

prevention costs (**p. 396**)

receipt time (**p. 388**)

regression analysis (**p. 386**)

residual term (**p. 386**)

semi-variable cost (**p. 379**)

simple regression (**p. 386**)

specification analysis (**p. 408**)

standard error of the estimated
    coefficient (**p. 407**)

standard error of the
    regression (**p. 406**)

step cost function (**p. 388**)

time driver (**p. 389**)

work-measurement
    method (**p. 381**)

Assignment Material

MyLab Accounting Make the grade with MyLab Accounting: The Short-Answer Questions, Exercises, and Problems marked with a ⊕ can be found on MyLab Accounting. You can practise them as often as you want, and most feature step-by-step guided instructions to help you find the right answer.

Short-Answer Questions

10-1 What two assumptions are frequently made when estimating a linear cost function?

10-2 What is a linear cost function? Describe three alternative linear cost functions.

10-3 What is the first step in any statistical analysis?

10-4 "High correlation between two variables means that one is the cause and the other is the effect." Do you agree? Explain.

10-5 What is a discontinuous linear cost function? What types of analyses can be done to improve cost control when the data sets indicate a discontinuous linear cost function?

10-6 Name four approaches to estimating a cost function.

10-7 Discuss the conference method for estimating a cost function. What are advantages of this method?

10-8 When using the high–low method, should you base the high and low observations on the outcome variable or on the predictor variable?

10-9 What is the goal of an ordinary least squares (OLS) linear regression?

10-10 Describe three criteria for evaluating cost functions and choosing cost drivers.

10-11 What is the difference between the coefficient of determination, r^2, and the goodness of fit?

10-12 "All independent variables in a cost function estimated with regression analysis are cost drivers." Do you agree?

10-13 Discuss four frequently encountered problems when collecting cost data on variables included in a cost function.

10-14 Describe two benefits of improving quality.

10-15 How does conformance quality differ from design quality? Explain.

10-16 Name two items classified as prevention costs.

10-17 Distinguish between internal failure costs and external failure costs.

Exercises

10-18 Terminology. A number of terms are listed below:

account analysis method	conference method	correlation
economic plausibility	explanatory power	goodness of fit
high–low method	industrial engineering method	linear cost function
ordinary least squares (OLS)	simple linear regression	outcome variable
predictor variable	method	r^2
t-Stat	P-value	time series

Required

Select the terms from the above list to complete the following sentences.

A management team can use several methods of quantitative analysis to predict the value of a single over-head cost pool in a traditional costing system. The methods are _____, _____, _____, _____, and _____. There are different criteria to consider when choosing a method of analysis: affordability, understandability, data availability and quality, _____, and _____. The relationship between cost of unequally shared resources used in production and their benefit to distinct types of cost objects must be economically plausible. The change in quantity of resources used must be a good measure of change in benefit. The relationship must be a _____ if OLS simple linear regression analysis is to be used. Ideally, the OLS will be based on at least 25 data points observed and reported in the past as a _____. If insufficient data are available, then the other methods of analysis will help the management team predict the value of the indirect cost pool. When true, the orderly change in the quantity of resource used will explain a large proportion of the change in the indirect cost pool. This is called _____. A high explanatory power indicates a high _____ between the change in the measure of benefit or the _____ variable, X, and the change in the predicted indirect cost pool, or _____, y. You can observe this in the _____ between the predicted (X, y) line and the actual data points (X, Y) from which the prediction was made. The measure of goodness of fit is called _____. Other important statistics that assess the reliability of the predicted regression line are the _____ and _____. While the OLS is a very rigorous analysis and can predict future values at a specific _____, it is not appropriate for all situations.

🌐 **10-19 Estimating a cost function.** The controller of the Ijiri Company wants you to estimate a cost ◀ **LO 1** function from the following two observations in a general ledger account called Maintenance:

Month	Machine-Hours	Maintenance Costs Incurred
January	5,000	$4,000
February	10,000	5,400

Required

1. Estimate the cost function for maintenance.
2. Can the constant in the cost function be used as an estimate of fixed maintenance cost per month? Explain.

🌐 **10-20 Discontinuous linear cost functions.** Select the graph that matches the numbered manufacturing cost data. Indicate by letter which of the graphs best fits each of the situations or items described.

The vertical axes of the graphs represent total dollars of cost, and the horizontal axes represent production output during a calendar year. In each case, the zero point of dollars and production is at the intersection of the two axes. The graphs may be used more than once.

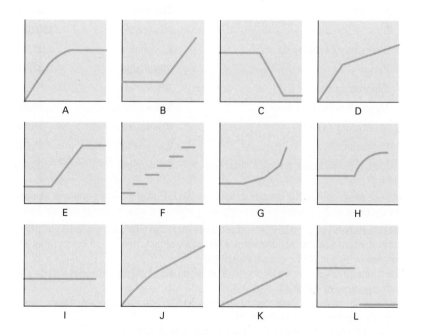

1. Annual depreciation of equipment, where the amount of depreciation charged is computed by the machine-hours method.
2. Electricity bill—a flat fixed charge, plus a variable cost after a certain number of kilowatt-hours are used, where the quantity of kilowatt-hours used varies proportionately with quantity of production output.

3. City water bill, which is computed as follows:

First 1,000,000 litres or less	$1,000 flat fee
Next 10,000 litres	$0.003 per litre used
Next 10,000 litres	$0.006 per litre used
Next 10,000 litres	$0.009 per litre used
And so on	And so on

The litres of water used vary proportionately with the quantity of production output.

4. Cost of lubricant for machines, where cost per unit decreases with each kilogram of lubricant used (for example, if one kilogram is used, the cost is $10; if two kilograms are used, the cost is $19.98; if three kilograms are used, the cost is $29.94) with a minimum cost per kilogram of $9.20.

5. Annual depreciation of equipment, where the amount is computed by the straight-line method. When the depreciation rate was established, it was anticipated that the obsolescence factor would be greater than the wear-and-tear factor.

6. Rent on a manufacturing plant donated by the city, where the agreement calls for a fixed fee payment unless 200,000 labour-hours are worked, in which case no rent need be paid.

7. Salaries of repair personnel, where one person is needed for every 1,000 machine-hours or less (that is, 0 to 1,000 hours requires one person, 1,001 to 2,000 hours requires two people, etc.).

8. Cost of direct materials used (assume no quantity discounts).

9. Rent on a manufacturing plant donated by the county, where the agreement calls for rent of $100,000 reduced by $1 for each direct manufacturing labour-hour worked in excess of 200,000 hours, but a minimum rental fee of $20,000 must be paid.

LO 1, 2 ▶
Total Variable Cost per unit = $8.45

⊕ **10-21 Account analysis method.** Gower, Inc., a manufacturer of plastic products, reports the following manufacturing costs and account analysis classification for the year ended December 31, 2017.

Account	Classification	Amount
Direct materials	All variable	$300,000
Direct manufacturing labour	All variable	225,000
Power	All variable	37,500
Supervision labour	20% variable	56,250
Materials-handling labour	50% variable	60,000
Maintenance labour	40% variable	75,000
Depreciation	0% variable	95,000
Rent, property taxes, and administration	0% variable	100,000

Gower, Inc., produced 75,000 units of product in 2017. Gower's management is estimating costs for 2018 on the basis of 2017 numbers. The following additional information is available for 2018.

a. Direct materials prices in 2018 are expected to increase by 5% compared with 2017.

b. Under the terms of the labour contract, direct manufacturing labour wage rates are expected to increase by 10% in 2018 compared with 2017.

c. Power rates and wage rates for supervision, materials handling, and maintenance are not expected to change from 2017 to 2018.

d. Depreciation costs are expected to increase by 5%, and rent, property taxes, and administration costs are expected to increase by 7%.

e. Gower expects to manufacture and sell 80,000 units in 2018.

Required

1. Prepare a schedule of variable, fixed, and total manufacturing costs for each account category in 2018. Estimate total manufacturing costs for 2018.

2. Calculate Gower's total manufacturing cost per unit in 2017, and estimate total manufacturing cost per unit in 2018.

3. How can you obtain better estimates of fixed and variable costs? Why would these better estimates be useful to Gower?

🌐 10-22 Linear cost approximation. Bailey Nickles, managing director of the Vancouver Consulting Group, is examining how overhead costs behave with changes in monthly professional labour-hours billed to clients. Assume the following historical data:

◀ **LO 1, 2**
1. Slope coefficient is $43.00
2. a. At 5,000 hours, costs overstated by $8,000

Total Overhead Costs	Professional Labour-Hours Billed to Clients
$340,000	3,000
400,000	4,000
435,000	5,000
477,000	6,000
529,000	7,000
587,000	8,000

Required

1. Compute the linear cost function, relating total overhead cost to professional labour-hours, using the representative observations of 4,000 and 7,000 hours. Plot the linear cost function. Does the constant component of the cost function represent the fixed overhead costs? Why?
2. What would be the predicted total overhead costs for (a) 5,000 hours and (b) 8,000 hours using the cost function estimated in requirement 1? Plot the predicted costs and actual costs for 5,000 and 8,000 hours.
3. Nickles had a chance to accept a special job that would have boosted professional labour-hours from 4,000 to 5,000 hours. Suppose Nickles, guided by the linear cost function, rejected this job because it would have brought a total increase in contribution margin of $38,000, before deducting the predicted increase in total overhead cost, $43,000. What is the actual total contribution margin forgone?

🌐 10-23 Cost–volume–profit and regression analysis. Garvin Corporation manufactures a children's bicycle, model CT8. Garvin currently manufactures the bicycle frame. During 2019, Garvin made 30,000 frames at a total cost of $900,000. Ryan Corporation has offered to supply as many frames as Garvin wants at a cost of $28.50 per frame. Garvin anticipates needing 36,000 frames each year for the next few years.

◀ **LO 1, 2**
1. a. Average cost per frame, $30

Required

1. **a.** What is the average cost of manufacturing a bicycle frame in 2019? How does it compare to Ryan's offer?
   b. Can Garvin use the answer in requirement 1a to determine the cost of manufacturing 36,000 bicycle frames? Explain.
2. Garvin's cost analyst uses annual data from past years to estimate the following regression equation with total manufacturing costs of the bicycle frame as the dependent variable and bicycle frames produced as the independent variable:

$$y = \$432,000 + \$15X$$

During the years used to estimate the regression equation, the production of bicycle frames varied from 28,000 to 36,000. Using this equation, estimate how much it would cost Garvin to manufacture 36,000 bicycle frames. How much more or less costly is it to manufacture the frames rather than to acquire them from Ryan?
3. What other information would you need to be confident that the equation in requirement 2 accurately predicts the cost of manufacturing bicycle frames?

🌐 10-24 Regression analysis, service company. (CMA, adapted) Linda Olson owns a professional character business in a large metropolitan area. She hires local college students to play these characters at children's parties and other events. Linda provides balloons, cupcakes, and punch. For a standard party the cost on a per-person basis is as follows:

◀ **LO 4, 5**
2. Total Variable Cost per person is $15.67

Balloons, cupcakes, and punch	$ 7
Labour (0.25 hour × $20 per hour)	5
Overhead (0.25 hour × $40 per hour)	10
Total cost per person	$22

Linda is quite certain about the estimates of the materials and labour costs, but is not as comfortable with the overhead estimate. The overhead estimate was based on the actual data for the past 9 months, which are presented here. These data indicate that overhead costs vary with the direct labour-hours used. The $40 estimate was determined by dividing total overhead costs for the 9 months by total labour-hours.

Month	Labour-Hours	Overhead Costs
April	1,400	$ 65,000
May	1,800	71,000
June	2,100	73,000
July	2,200	76,000
August	1,650	67,000
September	1,725	68,000
October	1,500	66,500
November	1,200	60,000
December	1,900	72,500
Total	15,475	$619,000

Linda has recently become aware of regression analysis. She estimated the following regression equation with overhead costs as the dependent variable and labour-hours as the independent variable:

$$y = \$43,563 + \$14.66X$$

Required

1. Plot the relationship between overhead costs and labour-hours. Draw the regression line and evaluate it using the criteria of economic plausibility, goodness of fit, and slope of the regression line.
2. Using data from the regression analysis, what is the variable cost per person for a standard party?
3. Linda Olson has been asked to prepare a bid for a 20-child birthday party to be given next month. Determine the minimum bid price that Linda would be willing to submit to recoup variable costs.

LO 4, 5 ▶
Slope coefficient per service
report is $30.00 per service report

⊕ **10-25 Estimating a cost function, high-low method.** Lacy Dallas is examining customer-service costs in the southern region of Camilla Products. Camilla Products has more than 200 separate electrical products that are sold with a 6-month guarantee of full repair or replacement with a new product. When a product is returned by a customer, a service report is prepared. This service report includes details of the problem and the time and cost of resolving the problem. Weekly data for the most recent 8-week period are as follows:

Week	Customer-Service Department Costs	Number of Service Reports
1	$13,300	185
2	20,500	285
3	12,000	120
4	18,500	360
5	14,900	275
6	21,600	440
7	16,500	350
8	21,300	315

Required

1. Plot the relationship between customer-service costs and number of service reports. Is the relationship economically plausible?
2. Use the high-low method to compute the cost function relating customer-service costs to the number of service reports.
3. What variables, in addition to number of service reports, might be cost drivers of weekly customer-service costs of Camilla Products?

Problems

🌐 **10-26 High-low, regression.** May Blackwell is the new manager of the materials storeroom for Clayton Manufacturing. May has been asked to estimate future monthly purchase costs for part #696, used in two of Clayton's products. May has purchase cost and quantity data for the past 9 months as follows:

◄ LO 3, 4

Month	Cost of Purchase	Quantity Purchased
January	$12,675	2,710 parts
February	13,000	2,810
March	17,653	4,153
April	15,825	3,756
May	13,125	2,912
June	13,814	3,387
July	15,300	3,622
August	10,233	2,298
September	14,950	3,562

Estimated monthly purchases for this part based on expected demand of the two products for the rest of the year are as follows:

Month	Purchase Quantity Expected
October	3,340 parts
November	3,710
December	3,040

Required

1. The computer in May's office is down, and May has been asked to immediately provide an equation to estimate the future purchase cost for part #696. May grabs a calculator and uses the high-low method to estimate a cost equation. What equation does she get?
2. Using the equation from requirement 1, calculate the future expected purchase costs for each of the last 3 months of the year.
3. After a few hours May's computer is fixed. May uses the first 9 months of data and regression analysis to estimate the relationship between the quantity purchased and purchase costs of part #696. The regression line May obtains is as follows:

$$y = \$2,582.6 + 3.54X$$

Evaluate the regression line using the criteria of economic plausibility, goodness of fit, and significance of the independent variable. Compare the regression equation to the equation based on the high-low method. Which is a better fit? Why?
4. Use the regression results to calculate the expected purchase costs for October, November, and December. Compare the expected purchase costs to the expected purchase costs calculated using the high-low method in requirement 2. Comment on your results.

🌐 **10-27 High-low method.** Wayne Mueller, financial analyst at CELL Corporation, is examining the behaviour of quarterly utility costs for budgeting purposes. Mueller collects the following data on machine-hours worked and utility costs for the past 8 quarters:

◄ LO 3, 4, 5

Quarter	Machine-Hours	Utility Costs
1	120,000	$215,000
2	75,000	150,000
3	110,000	200,000
4	150,000	270,000
5	90,000	170,000
6	140,000	250,000
7	130,000	225,000
8	100,000	195,000

Required

1. Estimate the cost function for the quarterly data using the high-low method.
2. Plot and comment on the estimated cost function.
3. Mueller anticipates that CELL will operate machines for 125,000 hours in quarter 9. Calculate the predicted utility costs in quarter 9 using the cost function estimated in requirement 1.

LO 3 ▶ ⊕ **10-28 Interpreting regression results.** Spirit Freightways is a leader in transporting agricultural products in the western provinces of Canada. Reese Brown, a financial analyst at Spirit Freightways, is studying the behaviour of transportation costs for budgeting purposes. Transportation costs at Spirit are of two types: (a) operating costs (such as labour and fuel) and (b) maintenance costs (primarily overhaul of vehicles).

Brown gathers monthly data on each type of cost, as well as the total freight miles traveled by Spirit vehicles in each month. The data collected are shown below (all in thousands):

Month	Operating Costs	Maintenance Costs	Freight Miles
January	$ 942	$ 974	1,710
February	1,008	776	2,655
March	1,218	686	2,705
April	1,380	694	4,220
May	1,484	588	4,660
June	1,548	422	4,455
July	1,568	352	4,435
August	1,972	420	4,990
September	1,190	564	2,990
October	1,302	788	2,610
November	962	762	2,240
December	772	1,028	1,490

Required

1. Conduct a regression using the monthly data of operating costs on freight miles. You should obtain the following result:
   Regression: Operating costs $= a + (b \times$ Number of freight miles)

Variable	Coefficient	Standard Error	t-Value
Constant	$445.76	$112.97	3.95
Independent variable: No. of freight miles	$ 0.26	$ 0.03	7.83

$r^2 = 0.86$; Durbin-Watson statistic $= 2.18$

2. Plot the data and regression line for the above estimation. Evaluate the regression using the criteria of economic plausibility, goodness of fit, and slope of the regression line.
3. Brown expects Spirit to generate, on average, 3,600 freight miles each month next year. How much in operating costs should Brown budget for next year?
4. Name three variables, other than freight miles, that Brown might expect to be important cost drivers for Spirit's operating costs.
5. Brown next conducts a regression using the monthly data of maintenance costs on freight miles. Verify that she obtained the following result:
   Regression: Maintenance costs $= a + (b \times$ Number of freight miles)

Variable	Coefficient	Standard Error	t-Value
Constant	$1,170.57	$91.07	12.85
Independent variable: No. of freight miles	$ −0.15	$ 0.03	−5.83

$r^2 = 0.77$; Durbin-Watson statistic $= 1.94$

6. Provide a reasoned explanation for the observed sign on the cost driver variable in the maintenance cost regression. What alternative data or alternative regression specifications would you like to use to better capture the above relationship?

🌐 **10-29 Cost estimation, cumulative average-time learning curve.** The Pacific Boat Company, which is under contract to the U.S. Navy, assembles troop deployment boats. As part of its research program, it completes the assembly of the first of a new model (PT109) of deployment boats. The Navy is impressed with the PT109. It requests that Pacific Boat submit a proposal on the cost of producing another six PT109s.

◀ **LO 5**

Pacific Boat reports the following cost information for the first PT109 assembled and uses a 90% cumulative average-time learning model as a basis for forecasting direct manufacturing labour-hours for the next six PT109s. (A 90% learning curve means b = −0.152004.)

	A	B	C
1	Direct material cost	$199,000	
2	Direct manufacturing labour time for first boat	14,700	labour hours
3	Direct manufacturing labour rate	$ 42	per direct manufacturing labour-hour
4	Variable manufacturing overhead cost	$ 26	per direct manufacturing labour-hour
5	Other manufacturing overhead	20%	of direct manufacturing labour costs
6	Tooling costs[a]	$279,000	
7	Learning curve for manufacturing labour time per boat	90%	cumulative average time[b]
8			
9	[a]Tooling can be reused at no extra cost because all of its cost has been assigned to the first deployment boat.		
10			
11	[b]Using the formula (Appendix 10B) for a 90% learning curve, $b = \dfrac{\ln 0.9}{\ln 2} = \dfrac{-0.105361}{0.693147} = -0.152004$		

Required

1. Calculate predicted total costs of producing the six PT109s for the Navy. (Pacific Boat will keep the first deployment boat assembled, costed at $1,477,600, as a demonstration model for potential customers.)
2. What is the dollar amount of the difference between (a) the predicted total costs for producing the six PT109s in requirement 1 and (b) the predicted total costs for producing the six PT109s, assuming that there is no learning curve for direct manufacturing labour? That is, for (b) assume a linear function for units produced and direct manufacturing labour-hours.

🌐 **10-30 Costs of quality analysis.** Safe Travel produces car seats for children from newborn to 2 years old. The company is worried because one of its competitors has recently come under public scrutiny because of product failure. Historically, Safe Travel's only problem with its car seats was stitching in the straps. The problem can usually be detected and repaired during an internal inspection. The cost of the inspection is $5.00 per car seat, and the repair cost is $1.00 per car seat. All 200,000 car seats were inspected last year, and 5% were found to have problems with the stitching in the straps during the internal inspection. Another 1% of the 200,000 car seats had problems with the stitching, but the internal inspection did not discover them. Defective units that were sold and shipped to customers needed to be shipped back to Safe Travel and repaired. Shipping costs are $8.00 per car seat, and repair costs are $1.00 per car seat. However, the out-of-pocket costs (shipping and repair) are not the only costs of defects not discovered in the internal inspection. Negative publicity will result in a loss of future contribution margin of $100 for each external failure.

◀ **LO 7,8**

Required

1. Calculate appraisal cost.
2. Calculate internal failure cost.
3. Calculate out-of-pocket external failure cost.
4. Determine the opportunity cost associated with the external failures.
5. What are the total costs of quality?
6. Safe Travel is concerned with the high up-front cost of inspecting all 200,000 units. It is considering an alternative internal inspection plan that will cost only $3.00 per car seat inspected. During the internal inspection, the alternative technique will detect only 3.5% of the 200,000 car seats that have stitching problems. The other 2.5% will be detected after the car seats are sold and shipped. What are the total costs of quality for the alternative technique?
7. What factors other than cost should Safe Travel consider before changing inspection techniques?

LO 7,8 ▶ 🌐 **10-31 Costs of quality, ethical considerations.** Refer to information in Exercise 10-30 in answering this question. Safe Travel has discovered a more serious problem with the plastic core of its car seats. An accident can cause the plastic in some of the seats to crack and break, resulting in serious injuries to the occupant. It is estimated that this problem will affect about 200 car seats in the next year. This problem could be corrected by using a higher quality of plastic that would increase the cost of every car seat produced by $10. If this problem is not corrected, Safe Travel estimates that out of the 200 car seats affected, customers will realize that the problem is due to a defect in the seats in only three cases. Safe Travel's legal team has estimated that each of these three cases would result in a lawsuit that could be settled for about $500,000. All lawsuits settled would include a confidentiality clause, so Safe Travel's reputation would not be affected.

1. Assuming that Safe Travel expects to sell 200,000 car seats next year, what would be the cost of increasing the quality of all 200,000 car seats?
2. What will be the total cost of the lawsuits next year if the problem is not corrected?
3. Suppose Safe Travel has decided not to increase the quality of the plastic because the cost of increasing the quality exceeds the benefits (saving the cost of lawsuits). What do you think of this decision? (*Note:* Because of the confidentiality clause, the decision will have no effect on Safe Travel's reputation.)
4. Are there any other costs or benefits that Safe Travel should consider?

LO 7 ▶ 🌐 **10-32 Costs of quality, quality improvement.** Cell Design produces cell phone covers for all makes and models of cell phones. Cell Design sells 1,050,000 units each year at a price of $10 per unit and a contribution margin of 40%.

A survey of Cell Design customers over the past 12 months indicates that customers were very satisfied with the products, but a disturbing number of customers were disappointed because the products they purchased did not fit their phones. They then had to hassle with returns and replacements.

Cell Design's managers want to modify their production processes to develop products that more closely match Cell Design's specifications because the quality control in place to prevent ill-fitting products from reaching customers is not working very well.

The current costs of quality are as follows:

Prevention costs	$210,000
Appraisal costs	$100,000
Internal failure costs	
Rework	$420,000
Scrap	$ 21,000
External failure costs	
Product replacements	$315,000
Lost sales from customer returns	$787,500
The QC manager and controller have forecast the following additional costs to modify the production process.	
CAD design improvement	$150,000
Improve machine calibration to specifications	$137,500

Required

1. Which cost of quality category are managers focusing on? Why?
2. If the improvements result in a 60% decrease in customer replacement cost and a 70% decrease in customer returns, what is the impact on the overall COQ and the company's operating income? What should Cell Design do? Explain.
3. Calculate prevention, appraisal, internal failure, and external failure costs as a percentage of total quality costs and as a percentage of sales before and after the change in the production process. Comment briefly on your results.

⊕ **10-33 Quality improvement, relevant costs, relevant revenues.** SpeedPrint manufactures and sells 18,000 high-technology printing presses each year. The variable and fixed costs of rework and repair are as follows:

◄ **LO 7, 8**

	Variable Cost	Fixed Cost	Total Cost
Rework cost per hour	$ 79	$115	$194
Repair costs			
Customer support cost per hour	35	55	90
Transportation cost per load	350	115	465
Warranty repair cost per hour	89	150	239

SpeedPrint's current presses have a quality problem that causes variations in the shade of some colours. Its engineers suggest changing a key component in each press. The new component will cost $70 more than the old one. In the next year, however, SpeedPrint expects that with the new component it will (1) save 14,000 hours of rework, (2) save 850 hours of customer support, (3) move 225 fewer loads, (4) save 8,000 hours of warranty repairs, and (5) sell an additional 140 printing presses, for a total contribution margin of $1,680,000. SpeedPrint believes that even as it improves quality, it will not be able to save any of the fixed costs of rework or repair. SpeedPrint uses a 1-year time horizon for this decision because it plans to introduce a new press at the end of the year.

Required

1. Should SpeedPrint change to the new component? Show your calculations.
2. Suppose the estimate of 140 additional printing presses sold is uncertain. What is the minimum number of additional printing presses that SpeedPrint needs to sell to justify adopting the new component?
3. What other factors should managers at SpeedPrint consider when making their decision about changing to a new component?

10-34 Quality improvement, relevant costs, relevant revenues. Keswick Conference Center and Catering is a conference centre and restaurant facility that hosts more than 300 national and international events each year attended by 50,000 professionals. Due to increased competition and soaring customer expectations, the company has been forced to revisit its quality standards. In the company's 25-year history, customer demand has never been greater for high-quality products and services. Keswick has the following budgeted fixed and variable costs for 2013:

◄ **LO 7, 8**

	Total Conference Centre Fixed Costs	Variable Cost per Conference Attendee
Building and facilities	$4,320,000	
Management salaries	$1,680,000	
Customer support and service personnel		$ 66
Food and drink		$120
Conference materials		$ 42
Incidental products and services		$ 18

The company's budgeted operating income is $4,200,000.

After conducting a survey of 3,000 conference attendees, the company has learned that its customers would most like to see the following changes in the quality of the company's products and services: (1) more menu options and faster service; (2) more incidental products and services (wireless access in all meeting rooms, computer stations for internet use, free local calling, and so on); and (3) upscale and cleaner meeting facilities. To satisfy these customer demands, the company would be required to increase fixed costs by 50% per year and increase variable costs by $12 per attendee as follows:

Customer support and service personnel	$4
Food and drink	$5
Conference materials	$0
Incidental products and services	$3

Keswick believes that the preceding improvements in product and service quality would increase overall conference attendance by 40%.

Required

1. What is the budgeted revenue per conference attendee?
2. Assuming budgeted revenue per conference attendee is unchanged, should Keswick implement the proposed changes?
3. Assuming budgeted revenue per conference attendee is unchanged, what is the variable cost per conference attendee at which Keswick would be indifferent between implementing and not implementing the proposed changes?

LO 6 ▶ 🌐 **10-35 Waiting time.** Kitty Wonderland (KW) makes toys for cats and kittens. KW's managers have recently learned that they can calculate the average waiting time for an order from the time an order is received and the time it is manufactured. They have asked for your help and have provided the following information.

> Expected number of orders for the product: 2,000
> Manufacturing time per order: 4 hours
> Annual machine capacity in hours: 10,000

1. Calculate the average waiting time per order.
2. After learning about the average waiting time, KW's managers are confused. They do not understand why, if annual machine capacity is greater than the average number of orders for the product, there would be any waiting time at all. Write a memo to clarify the situation.
3. The managers have asked for your suggestions on what they can do to minimize or eliminate waiting time. How would you respond?
4. Management is expecting sales to increase. Will average waiting time increase or decrease? Explain briefly.

LO 6 ▶ 🌐 **10-36 Waiting time, service industry.** The registration advisors at Small Western University (SWU) help 4,200 students develop their class schedules and register for classes each semester. Each advisor works for 10 hours a day during the registration period. SWU currently has 10 advisors. While advising an individual student can take anywhere from 2 to 30 minutes, it takes an average of 12 minutes per student. During the registration period, the 10 advisors see an average of 300 students a day on a first-come, first-served basis.

Required

1. Using the formula in Appendix 10B, calculate how long the average student will have to wait in the advisor's office before being advised.
2. The head of the registration advisors would like to increase the number of students seen each day because at 300 students a day it would take 14 working days to see all of the students. This is a problem because the registration period lasts for only 2 weeks (10 working days). If the advisors could advise 420 students a day, it would take only 2 weeks (10 days). However, the head advisor wants to make sure that the waiting time is not excessive. What would be the average waiting time if 420 students were seen each day?
3. SWU wants to know the effect of reducing the average advising time on the average wait time. If SWU can reduce the average advising time to 10 minutes, what would be the average waiting time if 420 students were seen each day?

LO 6 ▶ **10-37 Waiting time, cost considerations, customer satisfaction.** Refer to the information presented in Exercise 10-36. The head of the registration advisors at SWU has decided that the advisors must finish their advising in 2 weeks and therefore must advise 420 students a day. However, the average waiting time given a 12-minute advising period will result in student complaints, as will reducing the average advising time to 10 minutes. SWU is considering two alternatives:

a. Hire two more advisors for the 2-week (10-working day) advising period. This will increase the available number of advisors to 12 and therefore lower the average waiting time.
b. Increase the number of days that the advisors will work during the 2-week registration period to 6 days a week. If SWU increases the number of days worked to 6 per week, then the 10 advisors need only see 350 students a day to advise all of the students in 2 weeks.

Required

1. What would the average wait time be under alternative A and under alternative B?
2. If advisors earn $100 per day, which alternative would be cheaper for SWU (assume that if advisors work 6 days in a given work week, they will be paid time and a half for the sixth day)?
3. From a student satisfaction point of view, which of the two alternatives would be preferred? Why?

Collaborative Learning Cases

10-38 Cost estimation, incremental unit-time learning model. Assume the same information for the Pacific Boat Company as in Problem 10-29 with one exception. This exception is that Pacific Boat uses a 90% incremental unit-time learning model as a basis for predicting direct manufacturing labour-hours in its assembling operations. (A 90% learning curve means $b = -0.152004$.)

◄ LO 1, 2, 3, 4

Required

1. Prepare a prediction of the total costs for producing the six PT109s for the Navy.
2. If you solved requirement 1 of Problem 10-29, compare your cost prediction there with the one you made here. Why are the predictions different? How should Pacific Boat decide which model it should use?

10-39 Evaluating alternative simple regression models, not-for-profit. (Appendixes 10A and 10B) Kathy Hanks, executive assistant to the president of Eastern University, is concerned about the overhead costs at her university. Cost pressures are severe, so controlling and reducing overhead is very important. Hanks believes overhead costs incurred are generally a function of the number of different academic programs (including different specializations, degrees, and majors) that the university has and the number of enrolled students. Both have grown significantly over the years. She collects the following data:

◄ LO 5

Year	Overhead Costs (in thousands)	Number of Programs	Enrolled Students
1	$16,200	29	3,400
2	23,040	36	5,000
3	20,160	49	2,600
4	24,120	53	4,700
5	23,400	54	3,900
6	27,720	58	4,900
7	28,440	88	5,700
8	24,120	72	3,900
9	27,360	83	3,500
10	35,640	73	3,700
11	37,440	101	5,600
12	45,720	103	7,600

■ **Regression 1.** Overhead costs $= a + (b \times$ number of academic programs)

Variable	Coefficient	Standard Error	t-Value
Constant	$8,553.30	$4,002.41	2.14
Independent variable 1: number of academic programs	$ 288.76	$ 56.80	5.08

$r^2 = 0.72$; Durbin-Watson statistic $= 1.81$
The adjusted $r^2 = 0.693$

■ **Regression 2.** Overhead costs $= a + (b \times$ number of enrolled students)

Variable	Coefficient	Standard Error	t-Value
Constant	$7,190.10	$6,081.45	1.18
Independent variable 1: number of enrolled students	$ 4.53	$ 1.29	3.52

$r^2 = 0.55$; Durbin-Watson statistic $= 0.7694$
The adjusted $r^2 = 0.509$

Instructions

Form groups of two or more students to complete the following requirements:

Required

1. Plot the relationship between overhead costs and each of the following variables: (a) number of academic programs and (b) number of enrolled students.
2. Compare and evaluate the two simple regression models estimated by Hanks. Use the comparison format.
3. What insights do the analyses provide about controlling and reducing overhead costs at the university?
4. What are two important issues that would suggest the predictions are unreliable?

LO 5 ▶ **10-40 Interpreting regression results, matching time periods.** Nandita Summers works at Modus, a store that caters to fashion for young adults. Nandita is responsible for the store's online advertising and promotion budget. For the past year, she has studied search engine optimization and has been purchasing keywords and display advertising on Google, Facebook, and Twitter. In order to analyze the effectiveness of her efforts and to decide whether to continue online advertising or move her advertising dollars back to traditional print media, Nandita collects the following data:

	A	B	C
	Home	Insert	Page Layout	Formulas
1	**Month**	**Online Advertising Expense**	**Sales Revenue**
2	September	$5,125	$44,875
3	October	5,472	42,480
4	November	3,942	53,106
5	December	1,440	64,560
6	January	4,919	34,517
7	February	4,142	59,438
8	March	1,290	51,840
9	April	5,722	36,720
10	May	5,730	62,564
11	June	2,214	59,568
12	July	1,716	35,450
13	August	1,875	36,211

Required

1. Nandita performs a regression analysis, comparing each month's online advertising expense with that month's revenue. Verify that she obtains the following result:

$$\text{Revenue} = \$51,999.64 - (0.98 \times \text{Online advertising expense})$$

Variable	Coefficient	Standard Error	t-Value
Constant	$51,999.64	7,988.68	6.51
Independent variable: Online advertising expense	−0.98	1.99	−0.49

$r^2 = 0.02$; Durbin-Watson statistic $= 2.14$

2. Plot the preceding data on a graph and draw the regression line. What does the cost formula indicate about the relationship between monthly online advertising expense and monthly revenues? Is the relationship economically plausible?

3. After further thought, Nandita realizes there may have been a flaw in her approach. In particular, there may be a lag between the time customers click through to the Modus website and peruse its social media content (which is when the online ad expense is incurred) and the time they actually shop in the physical store. Nandita modifies her analysis by comparing each month's sales revenue to the advertising expense in the *prior* month. After discarding September revenue and August advertising expense, show that the modified regression yields the following:

$$\text{Revenue} = \$28,361.37 + (5.38 \times \text{Online advertising expense})$$

Variable	Coefficient	Standard Error	t-Value
Constant	$28,361.37	5,428.69	5.22
Independent variable: Previous month's online advertising expense	5.38	1.31	4.12

$r^2 = 0.65$; Durbin-Watson statistic $= 1.71$

4. What does the revised formula indicate? Plot the revised data on a graph. Is this relationship economically plausible?

5. Can Nandita conclude that there is a cause-and-effect relationship between online advertising expense and sales revenue? Why or why not?

10-41 Purchasing department cost drivers, activity-based costing, simple regression analysis. Perfect Fit operates a chain of 10 retail department stores. Each department store makes its own purchasing decisions. Carl Hart, assistant to the president of Perfect Fit, is interested in better understanding the drivers of purchasing department costs. For many years, Perfect Fit has allocated purchasing department costs to products on the basis of the dollar value of merchandise purchased. A $100 item is allocated 10 times as many overhead costs associated with the purchasing department as a $10 item.

◀ LO 5, 7, 8

Hart recently attended a seminar titled "Cost Drivers in the Retail Industry." In a presentation at the seminar, Kaliko Fabrics, a leading competitor that has implemented activity-based costing, reported number of purchase orders and number of suppliers to be the two most important cost drivers of purchasing department costs. The dollar value of merchandise purchased in each purchase order was not found to be a significant cost driver. Hart interviewed several members of the purchasing department at the Perfect Fit store in Miami. They believed that Kaliko Fabrics' conclusions also applied to their purchasing department.

Hart collects the following data for the most recent year for Perfect Fit's 10 retail department stores:

	A	B	C	D	E
	Home	Insert	Page Layout	Formulas Data	Review View
1	**Department Store**	**Purchasing Department Costs (PDC)**	**Dollar Value of Merchandise Purchased (MP$)**	**Number of Purchase Orders (No. of POs)**	**Number of Suppliers (No. of Ss)**
2	Baltimore	$1,522,000	$ 68,307,000	4,345	125
3	Chicago	1,095,000	33,463,000	2,548	230
4	Los Angeles	542,000	121,800,000	1,420	8
5	Miami	2,053,000	119,450,000	5,935	188
6	New York	1,068,000	33,575,000	2,786	21
7	Phoenix	517,000	29,836,000	1,334	29
8	Seattle	1,544,000	102,840,000	7,581	101
9	St. Louis	1,761,000	38,725,000	3,623	127
10	Toronto	1,605,000	139,300,000	1,712	202
11	Vancouver	1,263,000	130,110,000	4,736	196

Hart decides to use simple regression analysis to examine whether one or more of three variables (the last three columns in the table) are cost drivers of purchasing department costs. Summary results for these regressions are as follows:

Regression 1: PDC = $a + (b \times$ MP$)

Variable	Coefficient	Standard Error	t-Value
Constant	$1,041,421	$346,709	3.00
Independent variable 1: MP$	0.0031	0.0038	0.83

$r^2 = 0.08$; Durbin-Watson statistic = 2.41

Regression 2: PDC = $a + (b \times$ No. of POs)

Variable	Coefficient	Standard Error	t-Value
Constant	$722,538	$265,835	2.72
Independent variable 1: No. of POs	$ 159.48	$ 64.84	2.46

$r^2 = 0.43$; Durbin-Watson statistic = 1.97

Regression 3: PDC $= a + (b \times$ No. of Ss)

Variable	Coefficient	Standard Error	t-Value
Constant	$828,814	$246,571	3.36
Independent variable 1: No. of Ss	$ 3,816	$ 1,698	2.25

$r^2 = 0.39$; Durbin-Watson statistic $= 2.01$

1. Compare and evaluate the three simple regression models estimated by Hart. Graph each one.
2. Do the regression results support the Kaliko Fabrics' presentation about the purchasing department's cost drivers? Which of these cost drivers would you recommend in designing an ABC system?
3. How might Hart gain additional evidence on drivers of purchasing department costs at each of Perfect Fit's stores?

LO 5, 7, 8 ▶ **10-42 Purchasing department cost drivers, multiple regression analysis** (continuation of 10-41). Carl Hart decides that the simple regression analysis used in Problem 10-41 could be extended to a multiple regression analysis. He finds the following results for two multiple regression analyses:

Regression 4: PDC $= a + (b_1 \times$ No. of POs$) + (b_2 \times$ No. of Ss)

Variable	Coefficient	Standard Error	t-Value
Constant	$484,522	$256,684	1.89
Independent variable 1: No. of POs	$ 126.66	$ 57.80	2.19
Independent variable 2: No. of Ss	$ 2,903	$ 1,459	1.99

$r^2 = 0.64$; Durbin-Watson statistic $= 1.91$

Regression 5: PDC $= a + (b_1 \times$ No. of POs$) + (b_2 \times$ No. of Ss$) + (b_3 \times$ MP\$)

Variable	Coefficient	Standard Error	t-Value
Constant	$483,560	$312,554	1.55
Independent variable 1: No. of POs	$ 126.58	$ 63.75	1.99
Independent variable 2: No. of Ss	$ 2,901	$ 1,622	1.79
Independent variable 3: MP$	0.00002	0.0029	0.01

$r^2 = 0.64$; Durbin-Watson statistic $= 1.91$

The coefficients of correlation between combinations of pairs of the variables are as follows:

	PDC	MP$	No. of POs
MP$	0.28		
No. of POs	0.66	0.27	
No. of Ss	0.62	0.30	0.29

Required

1. Evaluate regression 4 using the criteria of economic plausibility, goodness of fit, significance of independent variables, and specification analysis. Compare regression 4 with regressions 2 and 3 in Problem 10-41. Which one of these models would you recommend that Hart use? Why?
2. Compare regression 5 with regression 4. Which one of these models would you recommend that Hart use? Why?
3. Hart estimates the following data for the Baltimore store for next year: dollar value of merchandise purchased, $78,500,000; number of purchase orders, 4,100; number of suppliers, 110. How much should Hart budget for purchasing department costs for the Baltimore store for next year?
4. What difficulties do not arise in simple regression analysis that may arise in multiple regression analysis? Is there evidence of such difficulties in either of the multiple regressions presented in this problem? Explain.
5. Give two examples of decisions in which the regression results reported here (and in Problem 10-41) could be informative.

SOLUTIONS

TRY IT!

Try It 10–1

1a. Average waiting time for an order of Z39

$$\frac{\left(\begin{array}{c}\text{Annual average number}\\\text{of orders of Z39}\end{array}\right) \times \left(\begin{array}{c}\text{Manufacturing time}\\\text{per order of Z39}\end{array}\right)^2}{2 \times \left[\begin{array}{c}\text{Annual machine}\\\text{capacity}\end{array} - \left(\begin{array}{c}\text{Annual average number}\\\text{of orders of Z39}\end{array} \times \begin{array}{c}\text{Manufacturing time}\\\text{per order of Z39}\end{array}\right)\right]}$$

$$= \frac{\left[50 \times (80)^2\right]}{2 \times \left[5{,}000 - (50 \times 80)\right]} = \frac{(50 \times 6{,}400)}{2 \times (5{,}000 - 4{,}000)} = \frac{320{,}000}{(2 \times 1{,}000)} = 160 \text{ hours per order}$$

1b.

$$\begin{array}{c}\text{Average manufacturing}\\\text{cycle time per order for Z39}\end{array} = \begin{array}{c}\text{Average order}\\\text{waiting time}\end{array} + \begin{array}{c}\text{Order manufacturing}\\\text{time for Z39}\end{array}$$

$$= 160 \text{ hours} + 80 \text{ hours} = 240 \text{ hours per order}$$

2a. Average waiting time for Z39 and Y28

$$\frac{\left[\left[\left(\begin{array}{c}\text{Annual average}\\\text{number of}\\\text{orders of Z39}\end{array}\right) \times \left(\begin{array}{c}\text{Manufacturing}\\\text{time per order}\\\text{of Z39}\end{array}\right)^2\right] \times \left[\left(\begin{array}{c}\text{Annual average}\\\text{number of}\\\text{orders of Y28}\end{array}\right) \times \left(\begin{array}{c}\text{Manufacturing}\\\text{time per order}\\\text{of Y28}\end{array}\right)^2\right]\right]}{2 \times \left[\begin{array}{c}\text{Annual}\\\text{machine}\\\text{capacity}\end{array} - \left[\left(\begin{array}{c}\text{Annual average}\\\text{number of}\\\text{orders of Z39}\end{array}\right) \times \left(\begin{array}{c}\text{Manufacturing}\\\text{time per order}\\\text{of Z39}\end{array}\right)\right] - \left[\left(\begin{array}{c}\text{Annual average}\\\text{number of}\\\text{orders of Y28}\end{array}\right) \times \left(\begin{array}{c}\text{Manufacturing}\\\text{time per order}\\\text{of Y28}\end{array}\right)\right]\right]}$$

$$= \frac{\left[50 \times (80)^2\right] + \left[25 \times (20)^2\right]}{2 \times \left[5{,}000 - (50 \times 80) - (25 \times 20)\right]} = \frac{\left[(50 \times 6{,}400) + (25 \times 400)\right]}{2 \times \left[5{,}000 - 4{,}000 - 500\right]} = \frac{(320{,}000 + 10{,}000)}{2 \times 500}$$

$$= \frac{330{,}000}{1{,}000} = 330 \text{ hours}$$

2b.

$$\begin{array}{c}\text{Average manufacturing}\\\text{cycle time for Z39}\end{array} = \begin{array}{c}\text{Average order}\\\text{waiting time}\end{array} + \begin{array}{c}\text{Order manufacturing}\\\text{time for Z39}\end{array}$$

$$= 330 \text{ hours} + 80 \text{ hours} = 410 \text{ hours}$$

$$\begin{array}{c}\text{Average manufacturing}\\\text{cycle time for Y28}\end{array} = \begin{array}{c}\text{Average order}\\\text{waiting time}\end{array} + \begin{array}{c}\text{Order manufacturing}\\\text{time for Y28}\end{array}$$

$$= 330 \text{ hours} + 20 \text{ hours} = 350 \text{ hours}$$

3.

Selling price per order of Y28, which has an average manufacturing lead time of more than 320 hours	$ 6,000
Variable cost per order	5,000
Additional contribution per order of Y28	$ 1,000
Multiply by expected number of orders	× 25
Increase in expected contribution from Y28	$25,000

Expected loss in revenues and increase in costs from introducing Y28:

Product (1)	Expected Loss in Revenues from Increasing Average Manufacturing Cycle Times for All Products (2)	Expected Increase in Carrying Costs from Increasing Average Manufacturing Cycle Times for All Products (3)	Expected Loss in Revenues Plus Expected Increases in Carrying Costs of Introducing Y28 (4) = (2) + (3)
Z39	$25,000.00[a]	$6,375.00[b]	$31,375.00
Y28	–	2,187.50[c]	2,187.50
Total	$25,000.00	$8,562.50	$33,562.50

[a]50 orders × ($27,000 − $26,500)
[b](410 hours − 240 hours) × $0.75 × 50 orders
[c](350 hours − 0) × $0.25 × 25

(Continued)

Increase in expected contribution from Y28 of $25,000 is less than increase in expected costs of $33,562.50 by $8,562.50. Therefore, Seawall should not introduce Y28.

Alternative calculations of incremental revenues and incremental costs of introducing Y28:

	Alternative 1: Introduce Y28 (1)	Alternative 2: Do Not Introduce Y28 (2)	Relevant Revenues and Relevant Costs (3) = (1) – (2)
Expected revenues	$1,475,000.00[a]	$1,350,000.00[b]	$125,000.00
Expected variable costs	875,000.00[c]	750,000.00[d]	125,000.00
Expected inv. carrying costs	17,562.50[e]	9,000.00[f]	8,562.50
Expected total costs	892,562.50	759,000.00	133,562.50
Expected revenues minus expected costs	$ 582,437.50	$ 591,000.00	$ (8562.50)

[a](50 × $26,500) + (25 × $6,000) [b]50 × $27,000
[c](50 × $15,000) + (25 × $5,000) [d]50 × $15,000
[e](50 × $0.75 × 410) + (25 × $0.25 × 350) [f]50 × $0.75 × 240

Try It 10–2

1. Prevention Costs: Design engineering, Process engineering
   Appraisal Costs: Inspection
   Internal Failure Costs: Rework, Scrap
   External Failure Costs: Warranty repair costs

2.

	2017	2017 % of Total COQ	2017 % of Revenue	2018	2018 % of Total COQ	2018 % of Revenue
Prevention costs:						
Design engineering	$ 8,950			$12,950		
Process engineering	10,000			10,200		
Total prevention costs	18,950	24.0%	1.9%	23,150	30.8%	2.0%
Appraisal costs (Inspection)	7,000	8.9%	0.7%	9,200	12.3%	0.8%
Internal failure costs						
Rework	17,960			12,400		
Scrap	15,000			12,800		
Total internal failure costs	32,960	41.8%	3.3%	25,200	33.6%	2.2%
External failure costs (Warranty repair costs)	19,960	25.3%	2.0%	17,520	23.3%	1.5%
Total costs of quality	$78,870	100.0%	7.9%	$75,070	100.0%	6.5%

Decision Making and Relevant Information

Lester Balajadia/Shutterstock

▶ Learning Objectives

1. Distinguish relevant from irrelevant information in decision situations.

2. Identify the differences among relevant costs for short-term and long-term production output decisions.

3. Contrast relevant and irrelevant costs and revenue as well as quantitative and qualitative information influencing decisions.

4. Explain the opportunity-cost concept and why it is used in decision making.

5. Explain the theory of constraints and how to manage "bottlenecks."

6. Explain why book value of equipment is irrelevant in equipment replacement decisions.

Relevant Costs, Porter, and Twitter

What does it cost Porter to fly a customer from Niagara on the Lake to Toronto? The incremental cost is very small, because the other costs (the plane, pilots, ticket agents, fuel, airport landing fees, and baggage handlers) are fixed. Because most costs are fixed, would it be worthwhile for Porter to fill a seat provided it earns at least $5 for that seat? The answer depends on whether the flight is full.

Suppose Porter normally charges $344 for this round-trip ticket. If the flight is full, Porter would not sell the ticket for anything less than $344 because there are still customers willing to pay this fare for the flight. But what if there are empty seats? Selling a ticket for something more than $5 is better than leaving the seat empty and earning nothing.

If a customer uses the internet to purchase the ticket a month in advance, Porter will likely quote $344 because it expects the flight to be full. If, on the Monday before the scheduled Friday departure, Porter finds that the plane will not be full, the airline may be willing to lower its prices dramatically in hopes of attracting more customers and earning a profit on the unfilled seats.

Just like at Porter, managers in corporations around the world use a decision process. Managers at Scotiabank gather information about financial markets, consumer preferences, and economic trends before determining whether to offer new services to customers. Managers at the Bay examine all the relevant information related to domestic and international clothing manufacturing before selecting vendors. Managers at VW gather cost information to decide whether to manufacture a component part or purchase it from a supplier. The decision process may not always be easy, but as Peter Drucker said, "Wherever you see a successful business, someone once made a courageous decision."

▶ CPA Competencies

This chapter covers material outlined in **Section 3: Management Accounting** of the CPA Competency Map. The Learning Objectives in this chapter have been aligned with the CPA Competency Map to ensure the best coverage possible.

3.3.1 Evaluates cost classifications and costing methods for management of ongoing operations

3.3.2 Evaluates and applies cost management techniques appropriate for specific costing decisions

3.4.1 Evaluates sources and drivers of revenue growth

Source: K. Owram. 2016. From Niagara-on-the-Lake to Toronto in 8 minutes: Region pitches Porter Airlines on commuter flight to Toronto. *Financial Post*, May 20.

Accountants serve as technical experts, gathering and analyzing data, forecasting future outcomes, and recommending the best possible course of action or alternative. Reliable and relevant information is essential to good decision making, but it does not guarantee good decisions. The ability to distinguish relevant from irrelevant data and analyze relationships in an organizational system is a fundamental skill needed for making reasonable business decisions. It is important to recognize the limitations of data quality or analytic techniques, and not to ignore recommendations or take impulsive actions. With objective use of high-quality data and readily used techniques of analyses, managers will make informed assumptions to predict future outcomes.

Forecasting outcomes is the heart of a decision, but it is quite normal that the most relevant information is missing. There will almost always be a gap between what was expected and what is actually realized because the future cannot be predicted with accuracy. A good decision process includes a post-implementation assessment and explanation of the key causes of differences between expected and actual outcomes. This is how managers learn from their experiences.

Relevant Information and Decision Making

▶ **LO 1**

Distinguish relevant from irrelevant information in decision situations.

Managers usually follow a *decision model* for choosing among different courses of action. A **decision model** is a formal method of making a choice that often involves both quantitative and qualitative analyses. Management accountants analyze and present relevant data to guide managers' decisions. The five-step decision-making process presented in Exhibit 11-1 can be used to assist in making such a decision.

Consider a strategic decision facing management at Precision Sporting Goods, a manufacturer of golf clubs: Should it reorganize its manufacturing operations to reduce manufacturing labour costs? Precision Sporting Goods has only two alternatives: (1) do not reorganize or (2) reorganize. Reorganization will eliminate all manual handling of materials. Current manufacturing labour consists of 20 workers—15 workers operate machines and 5 workers handle materials. The 5 materials-handling workers have been hired on contracts that permit layoffs without additional payments. Each worker works 2,000 hours annually.

Reorganization is predicted to cost $90,000 each year (mostly for new equipment leases). Production output of 25,000 units as well as the selling price of $250, the direct material cost per unit of $50, manufacturing overhead of $750,000, and marketing costs of $2,000,000 will be unaffected by the reorganization.

The Concept of Relevance

▶ **LO 2**

Identify the differences among relevant costs for short-term and long-term production output decisions.

Much of this chapter focuses on Step 4 in Exhibit 11-1 and on the concepts of relevant costs and relevant revenues when choosing among alternatives.

Relevant Costs and Relevant Revenues

Relevant costs are *expected future costs,* and **relevant revenues** are *expected future revenues.* Revenues and costs that are not relevant are said to be irrelevant. It is important to recognize that to be relevant costs and relevant revenues, they *must*

- *Occur in the future*—every decision deals with selecting a course of action based on its expected future results.
- *Differ among the alternative courses of action*—costs and revenues that do not differ will not matter and, hence, will have no bearing on the decision being made.

The question is always, "What difference will an action make?"

Exhibit 11-2 presents the financial data underlying the choice between the "do-not-reorganize" and "reorganize" alternatives for Precision Sporting Goods. There are two methods to analyze the data. The first considers *all revenues and costs,* while the second considers only *relevant revenues and costs.*

Exhibit 11-1 The Five-Step Decision Model

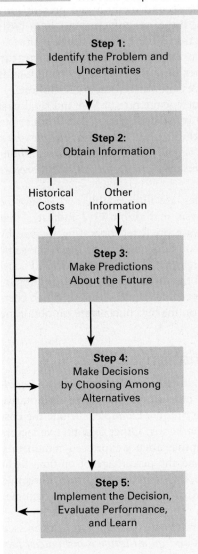

Step 1:
Identify the Problem and Uncertainties

Should Precision Sporting Goods reorganize its manufacturing operations to reduce manufacturing labour costs? An important uncertainty is how the reorganization will affect employee morale.

Step 2:
Obtain Information

Historical Costs

Other Information

Historical hourly wage rates are $14 per hour. However, a recently negotiated increase in employee benefits of $2 per hour will increase wages to $16 per hour. The reorganization of manufacturing operations is expected to reduce the number of workers from 20 to 15 by eliminating all 5 workers who handle materials. The reorganization is likely to have negative effects on employee morale.

Step 3:
Make Predictions About the Future

Managers use information from Step 2 as a basis for predicting future manufacturing labour costs. Under the existing do-not-reorganize alternative, costs are predicted to be $640,000 (= 20 workers × 2,000 hours per worker per year × $16 per hour), and under the reorganize alternative, costs are predicted to be $480,000 (= 15 workers × 2,000 hours per worker per year × $16 per hour). Recall, the reorganization is predicted to cost $90,000 per year.

Step 4:
Make Decisions by Choosing Among Alternatives

Managers compare the predicted benefits calculated in Step 3 ($640,000 − $480,000 = $160,000—that is, savings from eliminating materials-handling labour costs, 5 workers × 2,000 hours per worker per year × $16 per hour = $160,000) against the cost of the reorganization ($90,000) along with other considerations (such as likely negative effects on employee morale). Management chooses the reorganize alternative because the financial benefits are significant and the effects on employee morale are expected to be temporary and relatively small.

Step 5:
Implement the Decision, Evaluate Performance, and Learn

Evaluating performance after the decision is implemented provides critical feedback for managers, and the five-step sequence is then repeated in whole or in part. Managers learn from actual results that the new manufacturing labour costs are $540,000, rather than the predicted $480,000, because of lower-than-expected manufacturing labour productivity. This (now) historical information can help managers make better subsequent predictions that allow for more learning time. Alternatively, managers may improve implementation via employee training and better supervision.

Exhibit 11-2 Financial Data Underlying Alternatives for Precision Sporting Goods

	All Revenues and Costs		**Relevant Revenues and Costs**	
	Alternative 1: Do Not Reorganize	**Alternative 2: Reorganize**	**Alternative 1: Do Not Reorganize**	**Alternative 2: Reorganize**
Revenues[a]	$6,250,000	$6,250,000	—	—
Costs:				
Direct materials[b]	1,250,000	1,250,000	—	—
Manufacturing labour	640,000[c]	480,000[d]	$ 640,000[c]	$480,000[d]
Manufacturing overhead	750,000	750,000	—	—
Marketing	2,000,000	2,000,000	—	—
Reorganization costs	—	90,000	—	90,000
Total costs	4,640,000	4,570,000	640,000	570,000
Operating income	$1,610,000	$1,680,000	$(640,000)	$(570,000)
	$70,000 Difference		$70,000 Difference	

[a]25,000 units × $250 per unit = $6,250,000
[b]25,000 units × $50 per unit = $1,250,000
[c]20 workers × 2,000 hours per worker × $16 per hour = $640,000
[d]15 workers × 2,000 hours per worker × $16 per hour = $480,000

The first two columns of Exhibit 11-2 describe the first method and present *all cost and revenue data*. The last two columns describe the second method and present *only relevant costs*—the $640,000 and $480,000 expected future manufacturing labour costs and the $90,000 expected future reorganization costs that differ between the two alternatives. The revenues, direct materials, manufacturing overhead, and marketing items can be ignored because they will remain the same whether or not Precision Sporting Goods reorganizes. They do not differ between the alternatives and, therefore, are irrelevant.

Note that the past (historical) manufacturing hourly wage rate of $14 and total past (historical) manufacturing labour costs of $560,000 (= 20 workers × 2,000 hours per worker per year × $14 per hour) do not appear in Exhibit 11-2. *Although they may be a useful basis for making informed predictions of the expected future manufacturing labour costs of $640,000 and $480,000, historical costs themselves are past costs that therefore are irrelevant to decision making.*

Past costs are also called **sunk costs** because they are unavoidable and cannot be changed no matter what action is taken. The analysis in Exhibit 11-2 indicates that reorganizing the manufacturing operations will increase predicted operating income by $70,000 each year. Note that the managers at Precision Sporting Goods reach the same conclusion whether they use all data or include only relevant data in the analysis. Focusing on the relevant data is especially helpful when all the information needed to prepare a detailed statement of comprehensive income is unavailable. Understanding which costs are relevant and which are irrelevant helps the decision maker concentrate on obtaining only the pertinent data and is more efficient.

Quantitative and Qualitative Information

▶ **LO 3**

Contrast relevant and irrelevant costs and revenue as well as quantitative and qualitative information influencing decisions.

Managers divide the outcomes of decisions into two broad categories: *quantitative* and *qualitative*. **Quantitative factors** are outcomes measured in numerical terms. Some quantitative factors are financial; they can be expressed in monetary terms. Examples include the cost of direct materials, direct manufacturing labour, and marketing. Other quantitative factors are nonfinancial; they can be measured numerically, but they are not expressed in monetary terms. Reduction in new product-development time and the percentage of on-time flight arrivals are examples of quantitative nonfinancial factors. **Qualitative factors** are outcomes that are difficult to measure accurately in numerical terms. Employee morale and customer loyalty are some examples.

Relevant-cost analysis generally emphasizes quantitative factors that can be expressed in financial terms. *But just because qualitative factors and quantitative nonfinancial factors cannot be measured easily in financial terms does not make them unimportant.* In fact, managers must wisely weigh these factors. In the Precision Sporting Goods example, managers carefully considered the negative effect on employee morale of laying off materials handling workers, a qualitative factor, before choosing the reorganize alternative. Comparing and trading off nonfinancial and financial considerations is seldom easy. Exhibit 11-3 summarizes the key features of relevant information.

Some factors, such as health and safety, are not always calculated as part of a cost–benefit analysis. Responsible management teams will go to experts outside their enterprise to help them more clearly understand the risks a particular decision may pose to their employees, customers, and other stakeholders without assessing financial value. The idea of putting a price or a cost on safety and health is often enough to make the decision team aware that it will not sacrifice safety, regardless of the financial benefits of doing so.

Exhibit 11-3 Key Features of Relevant Information

- Past (historical) costs may be helpful as a basis for making *predictions*. However, past costs, what are commonly also called *sunk costs*, themselves are always irrelevant when making *decisions*.
- Different alternatives can be compared by examining differences in expected total future revenues and expected total future costs.
- Not all expected future revenues and expected future costs are relevant. Expected future revenues and expected future costs that do not differ among alternatives are irrelevant and, hence, can be eliminated from the analysis. The key question is always, "What difference will an action make?"
- Appropriate weight must be given to qualitative factors and quantitative nonfinancial factors.

Output Level Changes: Short- and Long-Term Decisions

Production output decisions involve identifying differences among relevant costs, but some decisions are short-term and some are long-term in nature. Short-term production output decisions have no capacity-management effects, such as accepting or rejecting one-time-only special orders when there is idle production capacity and when the order has no long-run implications. Consider the following example of Surf Gear, a company that produces towels. To simplify this short-term decision process and the identification of relevant costs, assume

- All costs can be classified as either variable with respect to a single driver (units of output) or fixed.
- No variable marketing costs are incurred to obtain the special one-time order.
- All outcome data have already been weighted by their respective probabilities (risks).

Under these assumptions, fixed costs are irrelevant. They must be paid whether the special order is accepted or not. Full absorption costing is inappropriate to the pricing of the finished goods. Only the incremental variable costs are relevant, and those costs must be recovered plus some profit. Variable (and in some cases, throughput) costing is appropriate to pricing the finished goods. When there is idle capacity, the effect of a special order on operating income depends on the customer accepting the contract, not on full absorption cost recovery.

Any increase in output will reduce the average unit fixed cost. But total fixed costs must be paid even if production or sales, or both, is zero. As long as there is capacity available, there are no opportunity costs. As long as all variable costs plus some profit are recovered, the special order will be an additional contribution to cover fixed costs. There is no other opportunity available; therefore, accepting the special order is the best use of available excess resources.

A Special Order Example

Surf Gear manufactures quality beach towels at its highly automated plant. The plant has a production capacity of 48,000 towels each month. Current monthly production is 30,000 towels. Retail department stores account for all existing sales. Expected results for the coming month (August) are shown in Exhibit 11-4. (These amounts are predictions based on past costs.) We assume all costs can be classified as either fixed or variable with respect to a single cost driver (units of output).

As a result of a strike at its existing towel supplier, Azelia, a luxury hotel chain, has offered to buy 5,000 towels from Surf Gear in August at $11 per towel. No subsequent sales to Azelia are anticipated. Fixed manufacturing costs are based on the 48,000-towel production capacity. That is, fixed manufacturing costs relate to the production capacity available and not the actual capacity used. If Surf Gear accepts the special order, it will use existing idle capacity to produce the 5,000 towels, and fixed manufacturing costs will not change. No marketing costs will be necessary for the 5,000-unit one-time-only special order. Accepting this special order is not expected to affect the selling price or the quantity of towels sold to regular customers. Should Surf Gear accept Azelia's offer?

Exhibit 11-4 presents data for this example on an absorption-costing basis (that is, both variable and fixed manufacturing costs are included in inventory costs and cost of goods sold). In this exhibit, the manufacturing cost of $12 per unit and the marketing cost of $7 per unit include both variable and fixed costs. The sum of all costs (variable and fixed) in a particular business function of the value chain, such as manufacturing costs or marketing costs, is called **business function costs**. **Full product costs**—in this case, $19 per unit—are the sum of all variable and fixed costs in all business functions of the value chain (R&D, design, production, marketing, distribution, and customer service). For Surf Gear, full costs of the product consist of costs in manufacturing and marketing because these are the only business functions. No marketing costs are necessary for the special order, so the manager of Surf Gear will focus only on manufacturing costs. Based on the manufacturing cost per unit of $12—which is greater than the $11-per-unit price offered by Azelia—the manager might decide to reject the offer.

Exhibit 11-4 Surf Gear
Expected Results for
Augusta

	A	B	C	D
1		**Total**	**Per Unit**	
2	Units sold	30,000		
3				
4	Revenues	$600,000	$20.00	
5	Cost of goods sold (manufacturing costs)			
6	Variable manufacturing costs	225,000	7.50[b]	
7	Fixed manufacturing costs	135,000	4.50[c]	
8	Total cost of goods sold	360,000	12.00	
9	Marketing costs			
10	Variable marketing costs	150,000	5.00	
11	Fixed marketing costs	60,000	2.00	
12	Total marketing costs	210,000	7.00	
13	Full costs of the product	570,000	19.00	
14	Operating income	$ 30,000	$ 1.00	
15				
16	[a]Surf Gear incurs no R&D, product-design, distribution, or customer-service costs			
17	[b]$\text{Variable manufacturing cost per unit} = \text{Direct material cost per unit} + \text{Variable direct manufacturing labour cost per unit} + \text{Variable manufacturing overhead cost per unit}$ $= \$6.00 + \$0.50 + \$1.00 = \$7.50$			
18	[c]$\text{Fixed manufacturing cost per unit} = \text{Fixed direct manufacturing labour cost per unit} + \text{Fixed manufacturing overhead cost per unit}$ $= \$1.50 + \$3.00 = \$4.50$			

Exhibit 11-5 separates manufacturing and marketing costs into their variable- and fixed-cost components and presents data in the format of a contribution statement of comprehensive income. The relevant revenues and costs are the expected future revenues and costs that differ as a result of accepting the special offer—revenues of $55,000 (= $11 per unit × 5,000 units) and variable manufacturing costs of $37,500 (= $7.50 per unit × 5,000 units). The fixed manufacturing costs and all marketing costs (*including variable marketing costs*) are irrelevant in this case because these costs will not change in total whether the special order is accepted or rejected. Surf Gear would gain an additional $17,500 (= Relevant revenues of $55,000 − Relevant costs of $37,500) in operating income by accepting the special order. In this example, comparing total amounts for 30,000 units versus 35,000 units, or focusing only on the relevant amounts in the difference column in Exhibit 11-5, avoids a misleading implication—the implication that would result from comparing the $11-per-unit selling price against the manufacturing cost per unit of $12 (Exhibit 11-4), which includes both variable and fixed manufacturing costs.

The assumption of no long-run or strategic implications is crucial to management's analysis of the one-time-only special-order decision. Suppose Surf Gear concludes that the retail department stores (its regular customers) will demand a lower price if it sells towels at $11 apiece to Azelia. In this case, revenues from regular customers will be relevant.

Why? Because the future revenues from regular customers will differ depending on whether the special order is accepted or rejected. The relevant-revenue and relevant-cost analysis of the Azelia order would have to be modified to consider both the short-run benefits from accepting the order and the long-run consequences on profitability if prices were lowered to all regular customers.

Outsourcing—Make or Buy—and Idle Facilities

Another type of output-level decision is long-term in nature. This is the decision either to expand existing capacity to **insource**, and produce more output in-house, or to **outsource** the additional production externally. Another term to describe this decision

Exhibit 11-5 Surf Gear Contribution Format Presentation of Manufacturing and Marketing Costs

	A	B	C	D	E	F	G	H
1				Without the Special Order		With the Special Order		Difference: Relevant Amounts
2				30,000		35,000		for the
3				Units to Be Sold		Units to Be Sold		5,000
4		Per Unit		Total		Total		Units Special Order
5		(1)		(2) = (1) ×30,000		(3)		(4) = (3) − (2)
6	Revenues	$20.00		$600,000		$655,000		$55,000[a]
7	Variable costs:							
8	Manufacturing	7.50		225,000		262,500		37,500[b]
9	Marketing	5.00		150,000		150,000		0[c]
10	Total variable costs	12.50		375,000		412,500		37,500
11	Contribution margin	7.50		225,000		242,500		17,500
12	Fixed costs:							
13	Manufacturing	4.50		135,000		135,000		0[d]
14	Marketing	2.00		60,000		60,000		0[d]
15	Total fixed costs	6.50		195,000		195,000		0
16	Operating income	$ 1.00		$ 30,000		$ 47,500		$17,500
17								
18	[a]5,000 units × $11.00 per unit = $55,000.							
19	[b]5,000 units × $7.50 per unit = $37,500.							
20	[c]No variable marketing costs would be incurred for the 5,000-unit one-time-only special order.							
21	[d]Fixed manufacturing costs and fixed marketing costs would be unaffected by the special order.							

is a **make/buy decision**. For example, Apple Computer outsources microchip production (formerly an in-house operation) to Intel.

Insourcing implies a strategy of **vertical integration**, which means a company grows by including as much of the production function as possible within itself, from direct materials to finished goods. The oil and gas industry is made up of the very different activities of oil and gas exploration, extraction, refining, and retailing. Suncor, for example, is a vertically integrated company that controls all of these various activities. It explores for new raw materials, extracts them, and transports them to its own refineries where the direct materials are inputs for gasoline, home heating oil, and other petroleum products. It sells gasoline and other automotive products at its Sunoco stations.

Sometimes a company decides to protect its competitive advantage by protecting the secure supply of key inputs. For other companies, making the product in-house allows retention of control of the product and technology. For example, to safeguard Coca-Cola's formula, the company does not outsource the manufacture of its concentrate. What are the most important factors in the make/buy decision? Surveys of company practices indicate they are quality, dependability of supplies, and cost.

An Outsourcing Decision Example

The Soho Company manufactures a two-in-one video system consisting of a DVD player and a digital media receiver (that streams movies and video from internet sites such as Netflix). Columns 1 and 2 of the following table show the expected total and per-unit costs for manufacturing the DVD player of the video system. Soho plans to manufacture the 250,000 units in 2,000 batches of 125 units each. Variable batch-level costs of $625 per batch vary with the number of batches, not the total number of units produced.

	Expected Total Costs of Producing 250,000 Units in 2,000 Batches Next Year (1)	Expected Cost per Unit (2) = (1) ÷ 250,000
Direct materials ($36 per unit × 250,000 units)	$ 9,000,000	$36
Direct manufacturing labour ($10 per unit × 250,000 units)	2,500,000	10
Variable manufacturing overhead costs of power and utilities ($6 per unit × 250,000 units)	1,500,000	6
Mixed (variable and fixed) batch-level manufacturing overhead costs of materials handling and setup [$750,000 + ($625 per batch × 2,000 batches)]	2,000,000	8
Fixed manufacturing overhead costs of plant lease, insurance, and administration	3,000,000	12
Total manufacturing cost	$18,000,000	$72

Broadfield Inc., a manufacturer of DVD players, offers to sell Soho 250,000 DVD players next year for $64 per unit on Soho's preferred delivery schedule. Assume that financial factors will be the basis of this make-or-buy decision. Should Soho make or buy the DVD player?

Columns 1 and 2 of the preceding table indicate the expected total costs and expected cost per unit of producing 250,000 DVD players next year. The expected manufacturing cost per unit for next year is $72. At first glance, it appears that the company should buy DVD players because the expected $72-per-unit cost of making the DVD player is more than the $64 per unit to buy it. But a make-or-buy decision is rarely obvious. To make a decision, management needs to answer the question, "What is the difference in relevant costs between the alternatives?"

For the moment, suppose (a) the capacity now used to make the DVD players will become idle next year if the DVD players are purchased, and (b) the $3,000,000 of fixed manufacturing overhead will continue to be incurred next year regardless of the decision made. Assume the $750,000 in fixed salaries to support materials handling and setup will not be incurred if the manufacture of DVD players is completely shut down.

Exhibit 11-6 presents the relevant-cost computations. Note that Soho will *save* $1,000,000 by making DVD players rather than buying them from Broadfield. Making DVD players is the preferred alternative. Note how the key concepts of relevance apply here.

■ Past costs are always irrelevant when making decisions. We should only consider differences in expected total future revenues and expected total future costs.

Exhibit 11-6 Soho Company's Relevant Cost Computations

Relevant Items	Total Relevant Costs		Relevant Cost Per Unit	
	Make	Buy	Make	Buy
Outside purchase of parts ($64 × 250,000 units)		$16,000,000		$64
Direct materials	$ 9,000,000		$36	
Direct manufacturing labour	2,500,000		10	
Variable manufacturing overhead	1,500,000		6	
Mixed (variable and fixed) materials-handling and setup overhead	2,000,000		8	
Total relevant costs[a]	$15,000,000	$16,000,000	$60	$64
Difference in favour of making DVD players	$1,000,000		$4	

[a]The $3,000,000 of plant-lease, plant-insurance, and plant-administration costs could be included under both alternatives. Conceptually, they do not belong in a listing of relevant costs because these costs are irrelevant to the decision. Practically, some managers may want to include them in order to list all costs that will be incurred under each alternative.

- The $1,000,000 in Exhibit 11-6 represents future costs that differ between the alternatives, which are relevant to the make-or-buy decision. Buying DVD players and not manufacturing them will save $1,000,000 in future variable costs per batch and avoidable fixed costs.

- The $3,000,000 of plant-lease, insurance, and administration costs are the same under both alternatives. Because these future costs will not differ between the alternatives, they are irrelevant.

A common term in decision making is *incremental cost*. An **incremental cost** is the additional total cost incurred for an activity. In Exhibit 11-6, the incremental cost of making DVD players is the additional total cost of $15,000,000 that Soho will incur if it decides to make DVD players. The $3,000,000 of fixed manufacturing overhead is not an incremental cost because Soho will incur this cost whether or not it makes DVD players. Similarly, the incremental cost of buying DVD players from Broadfield is the additional total cost of $16,000,000 that Soho will incur if it decides to buy DVD players. A **differential cost** is the difference in total cost between two alternatives. In Exhibit 11-6, the differential cost between the make-DVD-players and buy-DVD-players alternatives is $1,000,000 (= $16,000,000 − $15,000,000).

Note that *incremental cost* and *differential cost* are sometimes used interchangeably in practice. When faced with these terms, always be sure to clarify what they mean. We define *incremental revenue* and *differential revenue* similarly to incremental cost and differential cost. **Incremental revenue** is the additional total revenue from an activity. **Differential revenue** is the difference in total revenue between two alternatives.

The Rainier Company provides landscaping services to corporations and businesses. All its landscaping work requires Rainier to use landscaping equipment. Its landscaping equipment has the capacity to do 10,000 hours of landscaping work. It is currently utilizing 9,000 hours of equipment time. Rainier charges $80 per hour for landscaping work. Cost information for the current activity level is as follows:

Revenues ($80 × 9,000 hours)	$720,000
Variable landscaping costs (including materials and labour), which vary with the number of hours worked ($50 per hour × 9,000 hours)	450,000
Fixed landscaping costs	108,000
Variable marketing costs (5% of revenues)	36,000
Fixed marketing costs	72,000
Total costs	666,000
Operating income	$ 54,000

Rainier has just received a one-time only special order for landscaping work from Lasell Corporation at $60 per hour that would require 1,000 hours of equipment time. Should Rainier accept the offer even though revenue per hour is less than Rainier's landscaping cost of $62 per hour [($450,000 + $108,000) ÷ 9,000 hours]? No marketing costs will be necessary for the one-time only special order.

Potential Problems in Relevant-Cost Analysis

Managers should avoid two potential problems in relevant-cost analysis. First, they must watch for incorrect general assumptions, such as "All variable costs are relevant and all fixed costs are irrelevant." In the Surf Gear example, the variable marketing cost of $5 per unit is irrelevant because Surf Gear will incur no extra marketing costs by accepting the special order. But fixed manufacturing costs could be relevant. The extra production of 5,000 towels per month does not affect fixed manufacturing costs because we assumed that the relevant range is from 30,000 to 48,000 towels per month. In some cases, however, producing the extra 5,000 towels might increase fixed manufacturing costs.

Suppose Surf Gear would need to run three shifts of 16,000 towels per shift to achieve full capacity of 48,000 towels per month. Increasing the monthly production from 30,000 to 35,000 would require a partial third shift because two shifts could produce only 32,000 towels. The extra shift would increase fixed manufacturing costs, thereby making these additional fixed manufacturing costs relevant for this decision.

Second, unit-cost data can potentially mislead decision makers in two ways:

1. *When irrelevant costs are included.* Consider the $4.50 of fixed manufacturing cost per unit (direct manufacturing labour, $1.50 per unit, plus manufacturing overhead, $3 per unit) included in the $12-per-unit manufacturing cost in the one-time-only special-order decision (see Exhibits 11-4 and 11-5). This $4.50-per-unit cost is irrelevant, given the assumptions in our example, so it should be excluded.

2. *When the same unit costs are used at different output levels.* Generally, managers use total costs rather than unit costs because total costs are easier to work with and reduce the chance for erroneous conclusions. Then, if desired, the total costs can be unitized. In the Surf Gear example, total fixed manufacturing costs remain at $135,000 even if Surf Gear accepts the special order and produces 35,000 towels. Including the fixed manufacturing cost per unit of $4.50 as a cost of the special order would lead to the incorrect conclusion that total fixed manufacturing costs would increase to $157,500 (= $4.50 per towel × 35,000 towels).

The best way for managers to avoid these two potential problems is to base decisions on (1) total revenues and total costs (rather than unit revenue and unit cost) and (2) the relevance concept. Managers should always require all items included in an analysis to be expected total future revenues and expected total future costs that differ among the alternatives.

Sustainability in Action   Starbucks Sustains

Andrew Winning/Reuters/Alamy Stock Photo

After years of outsourcing production to lower-cost countries around the world, many American-based companies are relocating their manufacturing activities within the United States. Starbucks, the world's largest coffee chain, is a leader in the domestic outsourcing movement. In 2012, the company began sourcing its coffee mugs from American Mug and Stein, a reopened ceramics factory in northeastern Ohio. Starbucks also "re-shored" some of its own production back to the United States. For example, the company built a new $172 million facility in Georgia to produce its ready-brew VIA coffee and the coffee base for its Frappuccino blended beverages.

While labour costs at the Ohio and Georgia plants are higher than in many offshore locations, Stephen Lovejoy, senior vice president of global supply chain at Starbucks, identified several cost-savings benefits from domestic production. These include

- Access to highly-skilled labour, which helps with production efficiency

- Reduced transportation and warehousing costs, since more than 50% of Starbucks's retail stores are in the United States

- Greater speed to market, which cuts lead time and inventory carrying costs

While many companies continue to benefit from the global supply chain, Starbucks is among many United States-based companies, including American Apparel and Ralph Lauren, who have benefited from having domestic manufacturing and outsourcing as part of their production mix.

Sources: Z. Hines. 2015. "Case Study: Starbucks' New Manufacturing in the USA," University of San Diego Reshoring Institute (San Diego: University of San Diego), (http://www.reshoringinstitute.org/wp-content/uploads/2015/05/Starbucks-Casestudy.pdf); S. Li, T. Hsu, and A. Chang. 2014. American Apparel, others try to profit from domestic production, *Los Angeles Times*, August 10 (http://www.latimes.com/business/la-fi-american-apparel-made-in-usa-20140810-story.html); A. Selko. 2012. Starbucks Chooses Domestic Production, *Industry Week*, July 13 (http://www.industryweek.com/expansion-management/starbucks-chooses-domestic-production).

Opportunity Costs and Outsourcing

In the make-or-buy decision in Exhibit 11-6, we assumed that the capacity currently used to make DVD players would remain idle if Soho purchased the parts from Broadfield. Often, however, the unused capacity can be used for other, profitable purposes. In this case, the choice Soho's managers are faced with is not whether to make or buy, but rather how best to use available production capacity.

Suppose that if Soho decides to buy DVD players for its video systems from Broadfield, then Soho's best use of the capacity that becomes available is to produce 100,000 units of the Digitek, a portable, stand-alone DVD player. From a manufacturing standpoint, Digiteks are similar to DVD players made for the video system. With help from operating managers, Soho's management accountant estimates the following future revenues and costs if Soho decides to manufacture and sell Digiteks:

Incremental future revenues		$8,000,000
Incremental future costs		
Direct materials	$3,400,000	
Direct manufacturing labour	1,000,000	
Variable overhead (such as power, utilities)	600,000	
Materials-handling and setup overheads	500,000	
Total incremental future costs		5,500,000
Incremental future operating income		$2,500,000

Because of capacity constraints, Soho can make either DVD players for its video-system unit or Digiteks, but not both. Which of the following two alternatives should Soho choose?

1. Make video-system DVD players and do not make Digiteks.
2. Buy video-system DVD players and make Digiteks.

The "Total-Alternatives" Approach

Exhibit 11-7, Panel A, summarizes alternative 1 (the "total-alternatives" approach)—the future costs and revenues for *all* products. Alternative 2, buying video-system DVD players and using the available capacity to make and sell Digiteks, is the preferred alternative. The future incremental costs of buying video-system DVD players from an outside supplier ($16,000,000) exceed the future incremental costs of making video-system DVD players in-house ($15,000,000). Soho can use the capacity freed up by buying video-system DVD players to gain $2,500,000 in operating income (incremental future revenues of $8,000,000 minus total incremental future costs of $5,500,000) by making and selling Digiteks. The *net relevant* costs of buying video-system DVD players and making and selling Digiteks are $16,000,000 − $2,500,000 = $13,500,000.

The Opportunity-Cost Approach

Deciding to use a resource for a particular purpose causes a manager to forgo the opportunity to use the resource in alternative ways. This lost opportunity is a cost that the manager must consider when making a decision. **Opportunity cost** is the contribution to operating income that is lost by not using a limited resource in its next-best alternative use.

For example, the (relevant) cost of going to school for an MBA degree is not only the cost of tuition, books, lodging, and food, but also the income sacrificed (opportunity cost) by not working. Presumably, the estimated future benefits of obtaining an MBA (for example, a higher-paying career) will exceed these costs.

Exhibit 11-7, Panel B, displays the opportunity-cost approach for analyzing the alternatives faced by Soho. *Note that the alternatives are defined differently under the two approaches.*

► **LO 4**

Explain the opportunity-cost concept and why it is used in decision making.

Exhibit 11-7 Soho Company's Production Alternatives

Relevant Items	Alternatives for Soho	
	1. Make Video-System DVD Players and Do Not Make Digitek	**2. Buy Video-System DVD Players and Make Digitek**
PANEL A Total-Alternatives Approach to Make-or-Buy Decisions		
Total incremental future costs of making/buying video-system DVD players (from Exhibit 11-6)	$15,000,000	$16,000,000
Deduct excess of future revenues over future costs from Digitek	0	(2,500,000)
Total relevant costs under total-alternatives approach	$15,000,000	$13,500,000
	1. Make Video-System DVD Players	**2. Buy Video-System DVD Players**
PANEL B Opportunity-Cost Approach to Make-or-Buy Decisions		
Total incremental future costs of making/buying video-system DVD players (from Exhibit 11-6)	$15,000,000	$16,000,000
Opportunity cost: Profit contribution forgone because capacity will not be used to make Digitek, the next-best alternative	2,500,000	0
Total relevant costs under opportunity-cost approach	$17,500,000	$16,000,000

Note that the differences in costs across the columns in Panels A and B are the same: The cost of alternative 3 is $1,500,000 less than the cost of alternative 1, and $2,500,000 less than the cost of alternative 2.

Total-Alternatives Approach		Opportunity-Cost Approach	
(1) Make video-system DVD players and do not make Digiteks	(2) Buy video-system DVD players and make Digiteks.	(1) Make video-system DVD players (with no reference to Digiteks).	(2) Buy video-system DVD players (with no reference to Digiteks).

Under the opportunity-cost approach, the cost of each alternative includes (1) the incremental costs and (2) the opportunity cost, the profit forgone from not making Digiteks. This opportunity cost arises because Digitek is excluded from formal consideration in the alternatives.

Consider the opportunity-cost approach's alternative 1, to make video-system DVD players. What are all the costs of making video-system DVD players? Certainly Soho will incur $15,000,000 of incremental costs to make video-system DVD players, but is this the entire cost? No, because by deciding to use limited manufacturing resources to make video-system DVD players, Soho will give up the opportunity to earn $2,500,000 by not using these resources to make Digiteks. Therefore, the relevant costs of making video-system DVD players are the incremental costs of $15,000,000 plus the opportunity cost of $2,500,000. Next, consider alternative 2, to buy video-system DVD players. The incremental cost of buying video-system DVD players will be $16,000,000. The opportunity cost is zero, because by choosing this alternative, Soho will not forgo the profit it can earn from making and selling Digiteks.

Panel B leads management to the same conclusion as Panel A: Buying video-system DVD players and making Digiteks is the preferred alternative.

Opportunity costs are not recorded in financial accounting systems because historical recordkeeping is limited to transactions involving alternatives that were *actually selected*, rather than alternatives that were rejected. Rejected alternatives do not produce transactions and so they are not recorded. If Soho makes video-system DVD players, it will not make Digiteks, and it will not record any accounting entries for Digiteks. Yet the opportunity cost of making video-system DVD players, which equals the operating income that Soho forgoes by not making Digiteks, is a crucial input into the make-or-buy decision.

Besides quantitative considerations, the make-or-buy decision should also consider strategic and qualitative factors. If Soho decides to buy video-system DVD players from an outside supplier, it should consider factors such as the supplier's reputation for quality and timely delivery. Soho would also want to consider the strategic consequences of selling Digiteks. For example, will selling Digiteks take Soho's focus away from its video-system business?

The Rainier Company provides landscaping services to corporations and businesses. All its landscaping work requires Rainier to use landscaping equipment. Its landscaping equipment has the capacity to do 10,000 hours of landscaping work. It currently anticipates getting orders that would utilize 9,000 hours of equipment time from existing customers. Rainier charges $80 per hour for landscaping work. Cost information for the current expected activity level is as follows:

Revenues ($80 × 9,000 hours)	$720,000
Variable landscaping costs (including materials and labour), which vary with the number of hours worked ($50 per hour × 9,000 hours)	450,000
Fixed landscaping costs	108,000
Variable marketing costs (5% of revenue)	36,000
Fixed marketing costs	72,000
Total costs	666,000
Operating income	$ 54,000

Rainier has received an order for landscaping work from Victoria Corporation at $60 per hour that would require 2,000 hours of equipment time. Variable landscaping costs for the Victoria Corporation order are $50 per hour and variable marketing costs are 5% of revenues. Rainier can either accept the Victoria offer in whole or reject it. Should Rainier accept the offer?

The Carrying Costs of Inventory

Under the opportunity cost approach, the relevant cost of any alternative is (1) the incremental cost of the alternative plus (2) the opportunity cost of the profit forgone from choosing that alternative. The opportunity cost of holding inventory is the income forgone by tying up money in inventory and not investing it elsewhere. The cost associated with inventory encompasses more than the cost of the physical materials, and includes elements such as insurance, warehouse rental space, security, janitorial staff, theft, obsolescence, and other storage costs. The opportunity cost would not be recorded in the accounting system because, once the money is invested in inventory, there is no money available to invest elsewhere, and hence no return related to this investment to record.

Consider the following data for Soho, and determine which alternative is best:

Annual estimated video-system DVD player requirements for next year	250,000 units
Cost per unit when each purchase is equal to 2,500 units	$64
Cost per unit when each purchase is equal to or greater than 125,000 units; $64 minus 1% discount	$63.36
Cost of a purchase order	$500

Alternatives under consideration:

A. Make 100 purchases of 2,500 units each during next year

B. Make 2 purchases of 125,000 units during the year

Average investment in inventory:

A. (2,500 units × $64 per unit) ÷ 2[a]	$80,000
B. (125,000 units × $63.36 per unit) ÷ 2[a]	$3,960,000
Annual rate of return if cash is invested elsewhere (for example, bonds or stocks at the same level of risk as investment in inventory)	9%

[a] The example assumes that video-system-DVD-player purchases will be used uniformly throughout the year. The average investment in inventory during the year is the cost of the inventory when a purchase is received plus the cost of inventory just before the next purchase is delivered (in our example, zero) divided by 2.

The following table presents the analysis using the total-alternatives approach, recognizing that Soho has, on average, $3,960,000 of cash available to invest. If Soho invests only $80,000 in inventory as in alternative A, it will have $3,880,000 (= $3,960,000 − $80,000) of cash available to invest elsewhere, which at a 9% rate of return will yield a total return of $349,200. This income is subtracted from the ordering and purchasing costs incurred under alternative A. If Soho invests all $3,960,000 in inventory as in alternative B, it will have $0 (= $3,960,000 − $3,960,000) available to invest elsewhere and will earn no return on the cash.

	Alternative A: Make 100 Purchases of 2,500 Units Each During the Year and Invest Any Excess Cash (1)	Alternative B: Make 2 Purchases of 125,000 Units Each During the Year and Invest Any Excess Cash (2)	Difference (3) = (1) − (2)
Annual purchase-order costs (100 purch. orders × $500/purch. order; 2 purch. orders × $500/purch. order)	$ 50,000	$ 1,000	$ 49,000
Annual purchase costs (250,000 units × $64/unit; 250,000 units × $63.36/unit)	16,000,000	15,840,000	160,000
Deduct annual rate of return earned by investing cash not tied up in inventory elsewhere at the same level of risk [0.09 × ($3,960,000 − $80,000); 0.09 × ($3,960,000 − $3,960,000)]	(349,200)	0	(349,200)
Relevant costs	$15,700,800	$15,841,000	$(140,200)

Now look at the alternatives using the opportunity-cost approach. Each alternative is defined only in terms of the two purchasing choices with no explicit reference to investing the excess cash, as follows:

	Alternative A: Make 100 Purchases of 2,500 Units Each During the Year (1)	Alternative B: Make 2 Purchases of 125,000 Units Each During the Year (2)	Difference (3) = (1) − (2)
Annual purchase-order costs (100 purch. orders × $500/purch. order; 2 purch. orders × $500/purch. order)	$ 50,000	$ 1,000	$ 49,000
Annual purchase costs (250,000 units × $64/unit; 250,000 units × $63.36/unit)	16,000,000	15,840,000	160,000
Opportunity cost: Annual rate of return that could be earned if investment in inventory were invested elsewhere at the same level of risk (0.09 × $80,000; 0.09 × $3,960,000)	7,200	356,400	(349,200)
Relevant costs	$16,057,200	$16,197,400	$(140,200)

Both approaches show that, consistent with the trends toward holding smaller inventories, purchasing smaller quantities of 2,500 units 100 times a year is preferred to purchasing 125,000 units twice a year by $140,200.

Product Mix Decisions

The concept of relevance also applies to product-mix decisions—the decisions made by a company about which products to sell and in what quantities. These decisions usually have only a short-run focus, because they typically arise in the context of capacity constraints that can be relaxed in the long run. In the short run, for example, BMW, the German car manufacturer, continually adapts the mix of its different models of cars (for example, 325i, 525i, and 740i) to fluctuations in selling prices and demand.

To determine product mix, a company maximizes operating income, subject to constraints such as capacity and demand. Throughout this section, we assume that as short-run changes in product mix occur, the only costs that change are costs that are variable with respect to the number of units produced (and sold). Under this assumption, the analysis of individual product contribution margins provides insight into the product mix that maximizes operating income.

Let us consider the example of Power Recreation, a company whose plant assembles two engines: a snowmobile engine and a boat engine.

	Snowmobile Engine	Boat Engine
Selling price	$800	$1,000
Variable cost per unit	560	625
Contribution margin per unit	$240	$ 375
Contribution margin percentage ($240 ÷ $800; $375 ÷ $1,000)	30%	37.5%

Assume that only 600 machine-hours are available daily for assembling engines. Additional capacity cannot be obtained in the short run. Power Recreation can sell as many engines as it produces. The constraining resource, then, is machine-hours. It takes two machine-hours to produce one snowmobile engine and five machine-hours to produce one boat engine. What product mix should Power Recreation's managers choose to maximize its operating income?

In terms of contribution margin per unit and contribution margin percentage, boat engines are more profitable than snowmobile engines. The product that Power Recreation should produce and sell, however, is not necessarily the product with the higher individual contribution margin per unit or contribution margin percentage. Managers should choose the product with *the highest contribution margin per unit of the constraining resource (factor)*. That is the resource that restricts or limits the production or sale of products.

	Snowmobile Engine	Boat Engine
Contribution margin per unit	$240	$375
Machine-hours required to produce one unit	2 machine-hours	5 machine-hours
Contribution margin per machine-hour		
$240 per unit ÷ 2 machine-hours/unit	$120/machine-hour	
$375 per unit ÷ 5 machine-hours/unit		$75/machine-hour
Total contribution margin for 600 machine-hours		
$120/machine-hour × 600 machine-hours	$72,000	
$75/machine-hour × 600 machine-hours		$45,000

The number of machine-hours is the constraining resource in this example, and snowmobile engines earn more contribution margin per machine-hour ($120/machine-hour) compared to boat engines ($75/machine-hour). Therefore, choosing to produce and sell snowmobile engines maximizes *total* contribution margin ($72,000 versus

$45,000 from producing and selling boat engines) and operating income. Other constraints in manufacturing settings can be the availability of direct materials, components, or skilled labour, as well as financial and sales factors. In a retail department store, the constraining resource may be display space. Regardless of the specific constraining resource, managers should always focus on maximizing *total* contribution margin by choosing products that give the highest contribution margin per unit of the constraining resource.

⊕ **TRY IT!** **11.3** ▶

> The Rainier Company provides landscaping services to corporations and businesses. All its landscaping work requires Rainier to use landscaping equipment. Its landscaping equipment has the capacity to do 10,000 hours of landscaping work. It currently anticipates getting orders that would utilize 9,000 hours of equipment time. Rainier charges $80 per hour for landscaping work. Cost information for the current expected activity level is as follows:
>
> | | |
> |---|---:|
> | Revenues ($80 × 9,000 hours) | $720,000 |
> | Variable landscaping costs (including materials and labour), which vary with the number of hours worked ($50 per hour × 9,000 hours) | 450,000 |
> | Fixed landscaping costs | 108,000 |
> | Variable marketing costs (5% of revenue) | 36,000 |
> | Fixed marketing costs | 72,000 |
> | Total costs | 666,000 |
> | Operating income | $ 54,000 |
>
> In order to fill its available capacity, Rainier's salespersons are trying to find new business. Hudson Corporation wants Rainier to do 4,000 hours of landscaping work for $70 per hour. Variable servicing costs for the Hudson Corporation order are $45 per hour, and variable marketing costs are 5% of revenues. Rainier can accept as much or as little of the 4,000 hours of Hudson's landscaping work. What should Rainier Corporation do?

The Theory of Constraints

▶ **LO 5**

Explain the theory of constraints and how to manage "bottlenecks."

The **theory of constraints** (**TOC**) describes methods to maximize operating income (or, "throughput") when faced with operations that because of limited capacity form a **constraint**, or "bottleneck." The most important aspect of the TOC is to establish the organizational goals in terms of income, and also in terms of quality of output, legal and regulatory compliance, and other matters. The TOC suggests organizations can be measured and controlled by variations in three factors: throughput, operational expense, and investments.

The steps of the TOC focuses on managing bottleneck operations as explained in the following steps:

Step 1: Recognize that the bottleneck operation determines throughput margin of the entire system.

Step 2: Identify the bottleneck operation by identifying operations with large quantities of inventory waiting to be worked on.

Step 3: Keep the bottleneck operation busy, and subordinate all non-bottleneck operations to the bottleneck operation. That is, the needs of the bottleneck operation determine the production schedule of the non-bottleneck operations.

Step 4: Increase bottleneck efficiency and capacity.

A process of continuous evaluation must also be adopted, as resolving one bottleneck will often highlight other weaknesses in the organizational system. For example, consider Cardinal Industries (CI), which manufactures car doors in two operations—stamping and pressing—as described in the table below.

	Stamping	Pressing
Capacity per hour	20 units	15 units
Annual capacity (6,000 hours of capacity available in each operation) (6,000 hours × 20 units/hour; 6,000 hours × 15 units/hour)	120,000 units	90,000 units
Annual production and sales	90,000 units	90,000 units
Other fixed operating costs (excluding direct materials)	$720,000	$1,080,000
Other fixed operating costs per unit produced ($720,000 ÷ 90,000 units; $1,080,000 ÷ 90,000 units)	$8 per unit	$12 per unit

Each door sells for $100 and has a direct materials cost of $40. Variable costs in other functions of the value chain—design of products and processes, marketing, distribution, and customer service—are negligible. CI's output is constrained by the capacity of 90,000 units in the pressing operation.

What can CI do to relieve the bottleneck constraint of the pressing operation? Desirable actions include the following:

1. *Eliminate idle time at the bottleneck operation (time when the pressing machine is neither being set up to process products nor actually processing products).* CI's manager is evaluating permanently positioning two workers at the pressing operation to unload finished units as soon as one batch of units is processed and to set up the machine to begin processing the next batch. This action will cost $48,000, and bottleneck output will increase by 1,000 doors per year. Should CI incur the additional costs? Yes, because CI's throughput margin will increase by $60,000 [= (Selling price per door of $100 − Direct materials cost per door of $40) × 1,000 doors], which is greater than the incremental cost of $48,000. All other costs are irrelevant.

2. *Process only those parts or products that increase throughput margin, not parts or products that will be placed in finished goods or spare parts inventories.* Making products that remain in inventory will not increase throughput margin.

3. *Shift products that do not have to be made on the bottleneck machine to non-bottleneck machines or to outside processing facilities.* Suppose Spartan Corporation, an outside contractor, offers to press 1,500 doors at $15 per door from stamped parts that CI supplies. Spartan's quoted price is greater than CI's own operating costs in the pressing department of $12 per door. Should CI accept the offer? Yes, because pressing is the bottleneck operation. Getting additional doors pressed by Spartan will increase throughput margin by $90,000 [= ($100 − $40) per door × 1,500 doors], while the relevant cost of increasing capacity will be $22,500 (= $15 per door × 1,500 doors). The fact that CI's unit cost is less than Spartan's quoted price is irrelevant.

   Suppose Gemini Industries, another outside contractor, offers to stamp 2,000 doors from direct materials that CI supplies at $6 per door. Gemini's price is lower than CI's operating cost of $8 per door in the stamping department. Should CI accept the offer? No, because other operating costs are fixed costs. CI will not save any costs by subcontracting the stamping operations. Instead, its costs will increase by $12,000 (= $6 per door × 2,000 doors) with no increase in throughput margin, which is constrained by pressing capacity.

4. *Reduce setup time and processing time at bottleneck operations (for example, by simplifying the design or reducing the number of parts in the product).* Suppose CI can press 2,500 more doors at a cost of $55,000 a year by reducing setup time at the pressing operation. Should CI incur this cost? Yes, because throughput margin will

increase by \$150,000 [= (\$100 − \$40) per door × 2,500 doors], which is greater than the incremental costs of \$55,000. CI will not find it worthwhile to incur costs to reduce machining time at the non-bottleneck stamping operation, as other operating costs will increase while throughput margin will remain unchanged because bottleneck capacity of the pressing operation will not increase.

5. *Improve the quality of parts or products manufactured at the bottleneck operation.* Poor quality is more costly at a bottleneck operation than at a non-bottleneck operation. The cost of poor quality at a non-bottleneck operation is the cost of materials wasted. If CI produces 1,000 defective doors at the stamping operation, the cost of poor quality is \$40,000 (= Direct materials cost of \$40 per door × 1,000 doors). No throughput margin is forgone because stamping has unused capacity. Despite the defective production, stamping can produce and transfer 90,000 good-quality doors to the pressing operation.

At an operational bottleneck, the cost of poor quality is the cost of materials wasted *plus* the opportunity cost of lost throughput. If CI produces 1,000 defective units at the pressing operation, the cost of poor quality is the lost revenue of \$100,000 or, alternatively stated, direct materials costs of \$40,000 (= Direct materials cost of \$40 per door × 1,000 doors) plus forgone throughput margin of \$60,000 [= (\$100 − \$40) per door × 1,000 doors].

The high cost of poor quality at the bottleneck operation means that bottleneck time should not be wasted processing units that are defective. That is, parts should be inspected before the bottleneck operation to ensure that only good-quality parts are processed at the bottleneck operation. Furthermore, quality-improvement programs should place special emphasis on minimizing defects at bottleneck machines.

If successful, the actions in Step 4 will increase the capacity of the pressing operation until it eventually exceeds the capacity of the stamping operation. The bottleneck will then shift to the stamping operation. CI would then focus continuous-improvement actions on increasing stamping efficiency and capacity. For example, the contract with Gemini Industries to stamp 2,000 doors at \$6 per door from direct materials supplied by CI will become attractive because throughput margin will increase by \$120,000 (= \$100 − \$40 per door × 2,000 doors), which is greater than the incremental costs of \$12,000 (= \$6 per door × 2,000 doors).

The theory of constraints emphasizes management of bottleneck operations as the key to improving performance of production operations as a whole. It focuses on short-run maximization of throughput margin, revenues minus direct materials costs of goods sold. Because TOC regards operating costs as difficult to change in the short run, it does not identify individual activities and drivers of costs. TOC is, therefore, less useful for the long-run management of costs. In contrast, activity-based costing (ABC) systems take a long-run perspective and focus on improving processes by eliminating non-value-added activities and reducing the costs of performing value-added activities. ABC systems, therefore, are more useful for long-run pricing, cost control, and capacity management. The short-run TOC emphasis on maximizing throughput margin by managing bottlenecks complements the long-run strategic-cost-management focus of ABC.

Irrelevance of Past Costs and Equipment Replacement Decisions

▶ **LO 6**

Explain why book value of equipment is irrelevant in equipment replacement decisions.

At several points in this chapter, when discussing the concept of relevance, we reasoned that past (historical or sunk) costs are irrelevant to decision making because a decision cannot change something that has already happened. We now apply this concept to decisions about replacing equipment. We stress the idea that **book value**—original cost minus accumulated depreciation—of existing equipment is a past cost that is irrelevant.

Toledo Company, a manufacturer of aircraft components, is considering replacing a metal-cutting machine with a newer model. The new machine is more efficient than the old machine, but it has a shorter life. Revenues from aircraft parts (\$1.1 million per year) will be unaffected by the replacement decision. Here are the data the management accountant prepares for the existing (old) machine and the replacement (new) machine:

	Old Machine	New Machine
Original cost	$1,000,000	$600,000
Useful life	5 years	2 years
Current age	3 years	0 years
Remaining useful life	2 years	2 years
Accumulated depreciation	$600,000	Not acquired yet
Book value	$400,000	Not acquired yet
Current disposal value (in cash)	$40,000	Not acquired yet
Terminal disposal value (in cash 2 years from now)	$0	$0
Annual operating costs (maintenance, energy, repairs, coolants, and so on)	$800,000	$460,000

Toledo Company uses straight-line depreciation (time-value of money and taxes are ignored in this example).

Exhibit 11-8 presents a cost comparison of the two machines. Consider why each of the four items in Toledo's equipment replacement decision is relevant or irrelevant:

1. *Book value of old machine, $400,000:* Irrelevant, because it is a past or sunk cost. Nothing can change what has already been spent or what has already happened.

2. *Current disposal value of old machine, $40,000:* Relevant, because it is an expected future benefit that will only occur if the machine is replaced.

3. *Loss on disposal, $360,000:* This is the difference between amounts in items (1) and (2). It is a meaningless combination blurring the distinction between the irrelevant book value and the relevant disposal value. Each should be considered separately.

4. *Cost of new machine, $600,000:* Relevant, because it is an expected future cost that will only occur if the machine is purchased.

Exhibit 11-8 should clarify these four assertions. Column 3 in Exhibit 11-8 shows that the book value of the old machine does not differ between the alternatives and could be ignored for decision-making purposes. No matter what the timing of the

Exhibit 11-8 Toledo Company Cost Comparison of Two Machines

	Two Years Together		
	Keep (1)	Replace (2)	Difference (3) = (1) − (2)
Revenues	$2,200,000	$2,200,000	—
Operating costs			
Cash operating costs ($800,000/yr. × 2 years; $460,000/yr. × 2 years)	1,600,000	920,000	$ 680,000
Book value of old machine			
Periodic write-off as depreciation or	400,000	—	—
Lump-sum write-off	—	400,000[a]	
Current disposal value of old machine	—	(40,000)[a]	40,000
New machine cost, written off periodically as depreciation	—	600,000	(600,000)
Total operating costs	2,000,000	1,880,000	120,000
Operating income	$ 200,000	$ 320,000	$(120,000)

[a]In a formal statement of comprehensive income, these two items would be combined as "loss on disposal of machine" of $360,000.

Exhibit 11-9 Toledo Company Relevant Items in Cost Comparison

	Two Years Together		
	Keep **(1)**	**Replace** **(2)**	**Difference** **(3) = (1) − (2)**
Cash operating costs	$1,600,000	$920,000	$680,000
Current disposal value of old machine	—	(40,000)	40,000
New machine, written off periodically as depreciation	—	600,000	(600,000)
Total relevant costs	$1,600,000	$1,480,000	$120,000

write-off—whether a lump-sum charge in the current year, or depreciation charges over the next two years—the total amount is still $400,000 because it is a past (historical) cost.

By contrast, the $600,000 cost of the new machine and the current disposal value of $40,000 for the old machine are relevant because they would not arise if Toledo's managers decided not to replace the machine. Note that the operating income from replacing is $120,000 higher for the two years together.

Exhibit 11-9 concentrates only on relevant items. Note that the same answer—higher operating income as a result of lower costs of $120,000 by replacing the machine—is obtained even though the book value is omitted from the calculations. The only relevant items are the cash operating costs, the disposal value of the old machine, and the cost of the new machine that is represented as depreciation.

Decisions and Performance Evaluation

The decision model analysis (Step 4) for Toledo Company, which is presented in Exhibits 11-8 and 11-9, dictates replacing the machine rather than keeping it. In the real world, however, would the manager replace it? An important factor in replacement decisions is the manager's perception of whether the decision model is consistent with how the manager's performance will be judged after the decision is implemented (the performance-evaluation model in Step 5).

From the perspective of their own careers, it is no surprise that managers tend to favour the alternative that makes their performance look better. If the performance evaluation model conflicts with the decision model, the performance-evaluation model often prevails in influencing managers' decisions. For example, if the promotion or bonus of the manager at Toledo hinges on his or her first year's operating income performance under accrual accounting, the manager's temptation *not* to replace will be overwhelming. Why? Because the accrual accounting model for measuring performance will show a higher first-year operating income if the old machine is kept rather than replaced (as the following table shows).

First-Year Results: Accrual Accounting	**Keep**	**Replace**
Revenues	$1,100,000	$1,100,000
Operating costs		
Cash-operating costs	$800,000	$460,000
Depreciation	200,000	300,000
Loss on disposal	—	360,000
Total operating costs	1,000,000	1,120,000
Operating income (loss)	$ 100,000	$ (20,000)

Resolving the conflict between the decision model and the performance-evaluation model is frequently a baffling problem in practice. In theory, resolving the difficulty seems obvious: Design models that are consistent. Consider our replacement example.

Year-by-year effects on operating income of replacement can be budgeted for the two-year planning horizon. The manager then would be evaluated on the expectation that the first year would be poor and the next year would be much better. Doing this for every decision, however, makes the performance-evaluation model very cumbersome. As a result of these practical difficulties, accounting systems rarely track each decision separately.

Performance evaluation focuses on responsibility centres for a specific period, not on projects or individual items of equipment over their useful lives. Thus, the impacts of many different decisions are combined in a single performance report and evaluation measure (for example, operating income). Lower-level managers make decisions to maximize operating income, and top management—through the reporting system—is rarely aware of particular desirable alternatives that were *not* chosen by lower-level managers because of conflicts between the decision and performance-evaluation models.

Appendix 11A

Linear Programming

Linear programming (LP) is an optimization technique used to maximize total contribution margin (the objective function) given multiple constraints. **Optimization techniques** are ways to find the best answer using a mathematical model. LP models typically assume that all costs can be classified as either variable or fixed with respect to a single driver (units of output). LP models also require particular assumptions to hold. When these assumptions fail, other decision models should be considered.[1]

Consider again the example of Power Engines. Suppose that both the snowmobile and boat engines must be tested on a very expensive machine before they are shipped to customers. The available testing machine time is limited. Production data are as follows:

Department	Available Daily Capacity in Hours	Use of Capacity in Hours per Unit of Product		Daily Maximum Production in Units	
		Snowmobile Engine	Boat Engine	Snowmobile Engine	Boat Engine
Assembly	600 machine-hours	2.0	5.0	300*	120
Testing	120 testing-hours	1.0	0.5	120	240

*For example, 600 machine-hours ÷ 2.0 machine-hours per snowmobile engine = 300, the maximum number of snowmobile engines that the assembly department can make if it works exclusively on snowmobile engines.

Exhibit 11A-1 summarizes these and other relevant data. Note that snowmobile engines have a contribution margin of $240 and that boat engines have a contribution margin of $375. Material shortages for boat engines will limit production to 110 boat engines per day. How many engines of each type should be produced daily to maximize operating income?

Product	Department Capacity (per Day) in Product Units		Selling Price	Variable Cost per Unit	Contribution Margin per Unit
	Assembly	Testing			
Only snowmobile engines	300	120	$ 800	$560	$240
Only boat engines	120	240	1,000	625	375

Exhibit 11A-1 Operating Data for Power Engines

[1] Other decision models are described in G. Eppen, F. Gould, and C. Schmidt, *Quantitative Concepts for Management* (Englewood Cliffs, N.J.: Prentice-Hall, 1991) and S. Nahmias, *Production and Operations Analysis* (Homewood, Ill.: Irwin, 1993).

Steps in Solving an LP Problem

We use the data in Exhibit 11A-1 to illustrate the three steps in solving an LP problem. Throughout this discussion, S equals the number of units of snowmobiles produced, and B equals the number of units of boat engines produced.

Step 1: *Determine the objective.* The **objective function** of a linear program expresses the objective or goal to be maximized (for example, operating income) or minimized (for example, operating costs). In our example, the objective is to find the combination of products that maximizes total contribution margin in the short run. Fixed costs remain the same regardless of the product mix chosen and are therefore irrelevant. The linear function expressing the objective for the total contribution margin (TCM) is

$$\text{TCM} = \$240S + \$375B$$

Step 2: *Specify the constraints.* A **constraint** is a mathematical inequality or equality that must be satisfied by the variables in a mathematical model. The following linear inequalities depict the relationships in our example:

Assembly department constraint	$2S + 5B \leq 600$
Testing department constraint	$1S + 0.5B \leq 120$
Material shortage constraint for boat engines	$B \leq 110$
Negative production is impossible	$S \geq 0$ and $B \geq 0$

The three solid lines on the graph in Exhibit 11A-2 show the existing constraints for assembly and testing and the material shortage constraint.[2] A line means the constraint never appears with an exponent or square root. If it did, then the line would curve and the relationship would be curvilinear. In Exhibit 11A-2, all the constraints are labelled and appear as straight lines. The coefficients of the constraints are often called *technical coefficients*. For example, in the assembly department, the technical coefficient is 2 machine-hours for snowmobile engines and 5 machine-hours for boat engines.

The feasible alternatives are those combinations of quantities of snowmobile engines and boat engines that satisfy all the constraining factors. The shaded "Area of feasible solutions" in Exhibit 11A-2 shows the boundaries of those product combinations that are feasible, or technically possible.

Exhibit 11A-2 Linear Programming—Graphic Solution for Power Engines

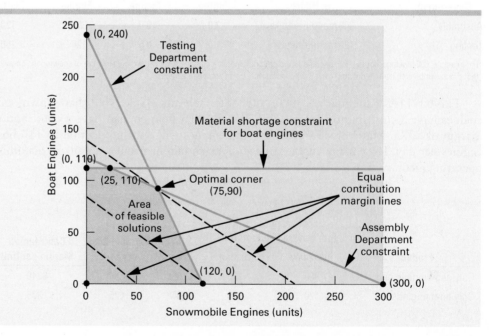

---

[2] For an example of how the lines are plotted in Exhibit 11A-2, use equal signs instead of inequality signs and assume for the assembly department that $B = 0$; then $S = 300$ (= 600 machine-hours ÷ 2 machine-hours per snowmobile engine). Assume that $S = 0$; then $B = 120$ (= 600 machine-hours ÷ 5 machine-hours per boat engine). Connect those two points with a straight line.

Step 3: *Compute the optimal solution.*   In most real-world LP applications, however, managers use computer software packages to calculate the optimal solution. One common approach is the "trial-and-error" approach, and another is the graphic approach.

Trial-and-Error Approach

Under this method, the optimal solution can be found by working with the coordinates of the corners of the area of feasible solutions. The approach is simple. First, select any set of corner points and compute the total contribution margin. Five corner points appear in Exhibit 11A-2. It is helpful to use simultaneous equations to obtain the exact graph coordinates. For instance, the graphical point $(S = 75, B = 90)$ can be derived by solving the two pertinent constraint inequalities as simultaneous equations.[3]

$$2S + 5B = 600 \qquad\qquad (1)$$
$$1S + 0.5B = 120 \qquad\qquad (2)$$

Multiplying (2) by 2.0, we get $2S + 1B = 240 \qquad\qquad (3)$

Subtracting (3) from (1) $\qquad\quad 4B = 360$

Therefore $\qquad\qquad\qquad\quad B = 360 \div 4 = 90$

Substituting B in (2) $\quad 1S + 0.5(90) = 120$

$$S = 120 - 45 = 75$$

Given $S = 75$ and $B = 90$, TCM = \$240(75) + \$375(90) = \$51,750.

Second, move from corner point to corner point, computing the total contribution margin at each corner point:

Trial	Corner Point (S, B)	Snowmobile Engines (S)	Boat Engines (B)	Total Contribution Margin		
1	(0, 0)	0	0	$240(0)	+ $375(0)	= $ 0
2	(0, 110)	0	110	$240(0)	+ $375(110)	= 41,250
3	(25, 110)	25	110	$240(25)	+ $375(110)	= 47,250
4	(75, 90)	75	90	$240(75)	+ $375(90)	= 51,750*
5	(120, 0)	120	0	$240(120)	+ $375(0)	= 28,800

*Indicates the optimal solution

The optimal product mix is the mix that yields the highest total contribution—75 snowmobile engines and 90 boat engines.

Graphic Approach

Consider all possible combinations that will produce an equal total contribution margin of, say, \$12,000. That is,

$$\$240S + \$375B = \$12,000$$

The solution will not change so long as the contribution margin of the snowmobile engine does not fall below \$150. *Big changes in the contribution margin per unit of snowmobile engines have no effect on the optimal solution.*

What happens if the contribution margin falls below \$150? The optimal solution will then shift to the corner $(S = 25, B = 110)$. Snowmobile engines now generate so little contribution margin per unit that Power Engines will choose to shift its mix in favour of boat engines.

---

[3] Although the trial-and-error and graphic approaches can be useful for two or possibly three variables, they are impractical when many variables exist. One alternative is to use the Solver function in Excel. Please refer to the online tutorial for a full presentation of how to input data into the Solver menus to minimize cost.

Appendix 11B

Using Excel Solver

In Appendix 11A, linear programming is explained and solved through the trial-and-error approach and the graphic approach. However, a more powerful and faster method of solving a linear programming problem exists. The add-in tool Solver, which works in Microsoft Excel, will allow you to solve very advanced linear programming problems (© Pearson Education).

Steps in Solving a Linear Programming Problem Using Solver

We will use the data in Appendix 11A to illustrate the steps in solving a linear programming problem using Solver. A review of the data follows.

Power Engines assembles two engines, a snowmobile engine and a boat engine. Information on these two products is as follows:

	Snowmobile Engine	Boat Engine
Selling price	$800	$1,000
Variable costs per unit	$560	$ 625
Contribution margin per unit	$240	$ 375

Assume that only 600 machine-hours are available daily for assembling engines. It takes 2 machine-hours to assemble 1 snowmobile engine. It takes 5 machine-hours to assemble 1 boat engine.

Assume that both the snowmobile and boat engines must be tested on a very expensive machine before they are shipped to customers. Only 120 testing machine-hours are available daily for testing the engines. It takes 1 hour (60 minutes) to test each snowmobile engine. It takes half an hour (30 minutes) to test each boat engine.

Assume that material shortages for boat engines will limit Power Engines to 110 boat engines per day.

Step 1: Determine the Objective

Use Solver to determine the solution to two types of linear programming problems. The first type of problem is to determine the optimum volume of product to be produced that will *maximize* total contribution margin. The second type of problem is to determine the optimum volume of product to be produced that will *minimize* costs.

In the case of Power Engines, we are looking to determine the optimum volume to be produced that will maximize total contribution margin. The linear function expressing this objective is

$$\text{TCM (total contribution margin)} = \$240S + \$375B$$

Where:

S: Represents the number of snowmobile engines assembled per day.

B: Represents the number of boat engines assembled per day.

The "where" items (S & B) represent volume variables. We are looking to determine the assembly volumes of each of these that will maximize total contribution margin.

Step 2: Specify the Constraints

Everyone (personally and in business) faces constraints. For example, you can't work 25 hours in a day, because there are only 24 hours in a day. Constraints also apply to Power Engines, and these constraints must be taken into consideration:

Assumption 1: Assume only 600 machine-hours are available daily for assembling engines. It takes 2 machine-hours to produce 1 snowmobile engine. It takes 5 machine-hours to produce 1 boat engine.

The assembly constraint is $2S + 5B <= 600$

Assumption 2: Assume that both the snowmobile and boat engines must be tested on a very expensive machine before they are shipped to customers. Only 120 testing machine-hours are available daily for testing the engines. It takes 1 hour (60 minutes) to test each snowmobile engine. It takes half an hour (30 minutes) to test each boat engine.

The testing constraint is $1S + 0.5B <= 120$

Assumption 3: Assume that material shortages for boat engines will limit Power Engines to 110 boat engines per day.

The boating constraint is $B <= 110$

Assumption #4: Use Solver to solve the maximum daily contribution margin. In order to do so, *always* add a non-negativity constraint for each of the where variables. It is impossible for Power Engines to produce negative units of B or S, for example.

The non-negativity constraint is $S >= 0$ and $B >= 0$

This can be shortened to $S, B >= 0$

Step 3: Creating the Solver Worksheet

In the Power Engines example, managers need to solve two volume variables: how many snowmobiles engines to assemble (S) and how many boat engines to assemble (B). The easiest way to solve the problem is to build a worksheet with the first column of information representing line descriptions, the next columns representing volume variables (in this case, there are two, S and B), and the last two columns representing total and constraints, respectively.

	A	B	C	D	E
1	Descriptions	S	B	Total	Constraints
2					

The next step is to add the volume and total contribution margin descriptions. At the bottom of the page, the second to last row will always say *volume*. Remember, this is what you are trying to solve. *Most* of the formulas you build within your worksheet tie into volume. The last row will say *total contribution margin* or *total costs*, depending on whether you are maximize total contribution margin or minimize costs. In the case of Power Engines, you are maximizing total contribution margin.

	A	B	C	D	E
1	Descriptions	S	B	Total	Constraints
2					
3					
4					
5					
6					
7					
8					
9					
10	Volume				
11	Total Contribution Margin				

You'll notice there are a lot of blank rows. We'll fill those in next.

The next step is to add the descriptions.

	A	B	C	D	E
1	Descriptions	S̲	B̲	Total	Constraints
2					
3	Contribution Margin				
4	Data & Constraints:				
5	Assembly Data				
6	Assembly Constraint				
7	Testing				
8	Testing Constraint				
9	Boat Constraint				
10	Volume				
11	Total Contribution Margin				

Now you need to build in the data and formulas. The first constraint is assembly. Assume that it takes 2 hours to assemble 1 snowmobile engine, 5 hours to assemble 1 boat engine, and Power Engines has 600 assembly hours available each day.

	A	B	C	D	E
1	Descriptions	S̲	B̲	Total	Constraints
2					
3	Contribution Margin				
4	Data & Constraints:				
5	Assembly Data	2	5		
6	Assembly Constraint	0	0	0	600
7	Testing				
8	Testing Constraint				
9	Boat Constraint				
10	Volume				
11	Total Contribution Margin				

The 0 values you see in cells B6, C6, and D6 represent assembly formulas. The formula in cell B6 is =B5*B10. The formula is cell C6 is =C5*C10. These values will be determined once you run solver and the optimum volume is determined. The formula in D6 is =SUM(B6:C6). This value determines the total of assembly-hours for snowmobile and boat engines. You will compare this value (in Solver) to your constraint of 600 (cell E6).

The second constraint is testing. Assume that it takes 1 hour to test 1 snowmobile engine, half an hour to test 1 boat engine, and Power Engines has 120 testing-hours available each day.

	A	B	C	D	E
1	Descriptions	S̲	B̲	Total	Constraints
2					
3	Contribution Margin				
4	Data & Constraints:				
5	Assembly Data	2	5		
6	Assembly Constraint	0	0	0	600
7	Testing	1	0.5		
8	Testing Constraint	0	0	0	120
9	Boat Constraint				
10	Volume				
11	Total Contribution Margin				

The 0 values in cells B8, C8, and D8 represent testing formulas (very similar to assembly formulas). The formula in cell B8 is =B7*B10. The formula is cell C8 is =C7*C10. These values will be determined once you run Solver and the optimum volume is determined.

The formula in D8 is =SUM(B8:C8). This value determines the total testing-hours for snowmobile and boat engines. You will compare this value (in Solver) to your constraint of 120 (cell E8).

The third constraint is a material shortage constraint for boat engines. Power Engines is limited to 110 boat engines per day.

	A	B	C	D	E
1	Descriptions	S	B	Total	Constraints
2					
3	Contribution Margin				
4	Data & Constraints:				
5	Assembly Data	2	5		
6	Assembly Constraint	0	0	0	600
7	Testing	1	0.5		
8	Testing Constraint	0	0	0	120
9	Boat Constraint			0	110
10	Volume				
11	Total Contribution Margin				

The formula in cell D9 is =C10. C10 represents the volume of boat engines that will be assembled each day. You will compare the D12 value (in Solver) to your constraint of 110 (cell E9).

The last constraint, non-negativity, will be entered in the Solver Parameters worksheet. You don't need to worry about that in this worksheet.

The last set of formulas will determine total contribution margin. Note: You are adding data on line 3.

	A	B	C	D	E
1	Descriptions	S	B	Total	Constraints
2					
3	Contribution Margin	240	375		
4	Data & Constraints:				
5	Assembly Data	2	5		
6	Assembly Constraint	0	0	0	600
7	Testing	1	0.5		
8	Testing Constraint	0	0	0	120
9	Boat Constraint			0	110
10	Volume				
11	Total Contribution Margin	0	0	0	

The 0 values in cells B11, C11, and D11 represent contribution margin formulas. The formula in cell B11 is =B3*B10. The formula is cell C11 is =C3*C10. These values will be determined once you run Solver and the optimum volume is determined. The formula in D11 is =SUM(B11:C11). This value determines the total contribution margin (what you are looking to maximize).

Step 4: Installing Solver

You may have to install Solver into your Excel package. The steps are as follows:

a. Open Excel

b. Select Blank workbook

c. Click on File (top left)

d. Click Options (left side)

e. Select Add-Ins (left side)

f. Select Solver Add-in

g. Click Go

h. Click Solver Add-In (Add-Ins window)

i. Click OK

j. Click Data (menu bar of your worksheet)

k. At the right-hand side, you should see Solver. Click Solver (Analysis). The Solver Parameters worksheet should be shown.

Step 5: Completing the Solver Parameters Section

Open Solver <u>Note: It is important that you have your cursor located in the area you want to change or add information.</u>

Set Objective: Select cell D11 of the worksheet. Select the cell that is the total contribution margin cell (maximization problem).

To: Select Max (for maximization problems).

By Changing Variable Cells: Move your cursor into the first volume cell of the worksheet, and drag it to the right to the last volume cell. The formula should look like $B$10:$C$10.

Subject to the Constraints: Click the Add button. This will allow you to enter in your constraint information.

The first constraint is the 600-hour assembly constraint. Within the Cell Reference section (make sure your cursor is in there), click cell D6 of the worksheet. The <= symbol is the default. In the Constraint section (make sure your cursor is in there), click cell E6. You are finished with this constraint. Click Add.

The second constraint is the 120-hour testing constraint. Within the Cell Reference section (make sure your cursor is in there), click cell D8 of the worksheet. The <= symbol is the default. In the Constraint section (make sure your cursor is in there), click cell E8. You are finished with this constraint. Click Add.

The third constraint is the 110 boat constraint. Within the Cell Reference section (make sure your cursor is in there), click cell D9 of the worksheet. The <= symbol is the default. In the Constraint section (make sure your cursor is in there), click cell E9. You are finished with this constraint. Click Add.

The last two constraints are the non-negativity constraints. Ensure that "Make Unconstrained Variables Non-Negative" is checked off.

Click Solve, and your worksheet should look like this:

	A	B	C	D	E
1	Descriptions	<u>S</u>	<u>B</u>	Total	Constraints
2					
3	Contribution Margin	240	375		
4	Data & Constraints:				
5	Assembly Data	2	5		
6	Assembly Constraint	150	450	600	600
7	Testing	1	0.5		
8	Testing Constraint	75	45	120	120
9	Boat Constraint			90	110
10	Volume	75	90		
11	Total Contribution Margin	<u>18,000</u>	<u>33,750</u>	<u>51,750</u>	

Visit MyLab Accounting to access five problems to practice using Excel solver.

You will want to print the Answer Report to help you interpret areas of slack. Select Answer in the Reports section, and click OK. You will see the Answer Report in a new tab at the bottom of the Excel page.

A major advantage of using Solver over many other approaches is if one of your conditions changes, you simply have to make an adjustment to your worksheet, re-run Solver, and, within seconds, you will have new volume requirements and a recalculated total contribution margin answer.

Pulling it all Together—Problem for Self-Study

(Try to solve this problem before examining the solution that follows.)

Problem

Wally Lewis is manager of the engineering development division of Mainland Products. Lewis has just received a proposal signed by all 10 of his engineers to replace the office computers (PCs) with newer models. Lewis is not enthusiastic about the proposal.

	Old PCs	New PCs
Original cost	$300,000	$135,000
Useful life	5 years	3 years
Current age	2 years	0 years
Remaining useful life	3 years	3 years
Accumulated depreciation	$120,000	Not acquired yet
Current book value	$180,000	Not acquired yet
Current disposal value (in cash)	$95,000	Not acquired yet
Terminal disposal value (in cash 3 years from now)	$0	$0
Annual computer-related cash operating costs	$40,000	$10,000
Annual revenue	$1,000,000	$1,000,000
Annual non-computer-related operating costs	$880,000	$880,000

Lewis's annual bonus includes a component based on division operating income. He has a promotion possibility next year that would make him a group vice-president of Mainland Products.

◀ **Required**

1. Compare the costs of the old PCs and new PCs options. Consider the cumulative results for the three years together, ignoring the time value of money. What is the best alternative?
2. What are some important interdependencies that should be considered?
3. Explain how this is either a short-term or a long-term decision.
4. Explain how the table indicates how book value should be considered in this replacement decision.
5. Why might Lewis be reluctant to purchase the 10 new computers?

Solution

1. The following table considers all cost items when comparing future costs of the old and new PCs options:

All Items	Three Years Together		
	Old PCs	New PCs	Difference
Revenues	$3,000,000	$3,000,000	—
Operating costs:			
Non-computer-related operating costs	2,640,000	2,640,000	—
Computer-related cash operating costs	120,000	30,000	$ 90,000
Old PC book value:			
Periodic writeoff as depreciation	180,000	— ⎫	
or Lump sum writeoff	—	180,000 ⎭	
Current disposal price of PCs	—	(95,000)	95,000
New PCs, written off periodically as depreciation	—	135,000	(135,000)
Total operating costs	2,940,000	2,890,000	50,000
Operating income	$ 60,000	$ 110,000	$ 50,000

Alternatively, the analysis could focus on only those items in the preceding table that differ across the alternatives.

| Relevant Items | Three Years Together | | |
	Old PCs	New PCs	Difference
Computer-related cash operating costs	$120,000	$ 30,000	$ 90,000
Current disposal price of old PCs	—	(95,000)	95,000
New PCs, written off periodically as depreciation	—	135,000	(135,000)
Total relevant costs	$120,000	$ 70,000	$ 50,000

The conclusion from this analysis is that operating income would be strengthened by $50,000 if the old PCs were replaced with new PCs.

2. This is a system management decision about how engineers can best gather and communicate various types of engineering nonfinancial data. Systems management affects areas of capacity management, process improvement, and overall financial performance. This manager should not be making this decision on his own, but as part of a team that includes the managers of these other areas.

3. One reason this is a long-term decision is that the useful life of the PCs is longer than one year, although likely less than three years for an engineer whose productivity improves when the best equipment and software is available.

4. In the table, the old PC book value appears as $180,000 in both alternatives; one is a line below the other. Book value is irrelevant because the acquisition cost of the old PCs is a historical cost and will remain unchanged irrespective of this decision. The book value of the old machines is not an element of difference between alternatives and could be completely ignored for decision-making purposes.

5. The accrual accounting operating incomes for the first year under the "keep old PCs" versus the "buy new PCs" alternatives are as follows:

	Keep Old PCs		Buy New PCs	
Revenue		$1,000,000		$1,000,000
Operating costs:				
Non-computer-related operating costs	$880,000		$880,000	
Computer-related operating costs	40,000		10,000	
Amortization	60,000		45,000	
Loss on disposal of old PCs	—		85,000*	
Total operating costs		980,000		1,020,000
Operating income		$ 20,000		$ (20,000)

*$85,000 = Book value of old PCs, $180,000 − Current disposal price, $95,000.

Lewis would probably react negatively to the expected operating loss of $20,000 if the old PCs are replaced as compared to an operating income of $20,000 if the old PCs are kept. The decision would eliminate the component of his bonus based on operating income. He might also perceive the $20,000 operating loss as reducing his chances of being promoted to group vice-president. This, however, is not in the best interests of Mainland Products because the obsolete PCs are slowing down the production of his engineers.

Engineers represent capacity—labour capacity—and their time is constrained. The extra time they spend on projects because they have no access to modern equipment is also a waste of money for Mainland. Fewer projects can be undertaken and completed, which affects the top line, incoming revenue, of the company. If engineering salaries are fixed, then any incremental revenue that could be gained if the engineers could work more effectively would go straight to operating income. Wally needs an accountant to point out important relevant information that remains unconsidered in this decision.

Decision Points

The following question-and-answer format summarizes the chapter's learning objectives. Each point presents a key question, and the guidelines are the answer to that question.

Learning Objective	Guideline
1. How are relevant and irrelevant information distinguished in decision situations?	Only costs and revenues that are expected to occur in the future and differ among alternative courses of action are relevant.
2. What are the differences among relevant costs for short-term and long-term production output decisions?	Long-term production costs must consider strategic elements and have lasting impact on the financial structure of the organization. Short-term decisions are typically related to individual projects and terminate.
3. How do relevant and irrelevant costs and revenue differ, and how do quantitative and qualitative information differ?	Relevant information is the sets of data that should be included in the decision-making process. These data can be made of financial and other numerical data (quantitative) as well as contextual and descriptive data (qualitative).
4. What is the opportunity-cost concept, and why is it used in decision making?	In all decisions, it is important to consider the contribution to income forgone by choosing a particular alternative and rejecting others.
5. Explain the theory of constraints and how to manage bottlenecks.	Select the product with the highest contribution margin per unit of the limiting resource, and keep bottlenecks busy and increase their efficiency and capacity by increasing throughput (contribution) margin.
6. Why is book value of equipment irrelevant in equipment replacement decisions?	It is a past cost and should not be considered in present decisions.

Terms to Learn

This chapter and the Glossary at the end of the book contain definitions of the following important terms:

book value (**p. 454**)
business function costs (**p. 441**)
constraint (as a limiting factor) (**p. 452**)
constraint (of an LP problem) (**p. 458**)
decision model (**p. 438**)
differential cost (**p. 445**)
differential revenue (**p. 445**)
full product costs (**p. 441**)

incremental cost (**p. 445**)
incremental revenue (**p. 445**)
insource (**p. 442**)
linear programming (LP) (**p. 457**)
make/buy decision (**p. 443**)
objective function (**p. 458**)
opportunity cost (**p. 447**)
optimization techniques (**p. 457**)

outsource (**p. 442**)
qualitative factors (**p. 440**)
quantitative factors (**p. 440**)
relevant costs (**p. 438**)
relevant revenues (**p. 438**)
sunk costs (**p. 440**)
theory of constraints (TOC) (**p. 452**)
vertical integration (**p. 443**)

Assignment Material

MyLab Accounting Make the grade with MyLab Accounting: The Short-Answer Questions, Exercises, and Problems marked with a ⊕ can be found on MyLab Accounting. You can practise them as often as you want, and most feature step-by-step guided instructions to help you find the right answer.

Short-Answer Questions

⊕ **11-1** Provide examples of interdependencies, and relate them to the decision framework.

⊕ **11-2** Define *relevant cost*. Why are historical costs irrelevant?

⊕ **11-3** Distinguish between *quantitative* and *qualitative* factors in decision making.

⊕ **11-4** Describe two potential problems that should be avoided in relevant-cost analysis.

⊕ **11-5** Define *opportunity cost*.

⊕ **11-6** "A component part should be purchased whenever the purchase price is less than its total manufacturing cost per unit." Do you agree? Explain briefly.

⊕ **11-7** "Management should always maximize sales of the product with the highest contribution margin per unit." Do you agree? Explain briefly.

⊕ **11-8** "Managers should always buy inventory in quantities that result in the lowest purchase cost per unit." Do you agree? Explain briefly.

⊕ **11-9** "A branch office or business segment that shows negative operating income should be shut down." Do you agree? Explain briefly.

⊕ **11-10** "Cost written off as depreciation on equipment already purchased is always irrelevant." Do you agree? Explain briefly.

⊕ **11-11** "Managers will always choose the alternative that maximizes operating income or minimizes costs in the decision model." Do you agree? Explain briefly.

⊕ **11-12** "All future costs are relevant." Do you agree? Explain briefly.

⊕ **11-13** Describe the four key steps in managing bottleneck resources.

Exercises

⊕ **11-14 Terminology.** A number of terms are listed below:

cost minimization	opportunity cost
differential cost	optimization technique
full product costs	out-of-pocket costs
incremental costs	outlay cost
incremental revenue	sunk costs
objective function	profit maximization

Required

Select the terms from the above list to complete the following sentences.

A full absorption cost refers to all manufacturing costs including manufacturing overhead costs, whereas _____ refers to all period or non-manufacturing costs as well as all manufacturing costs to bring the product to point of sale. The _____ is the value lost because a different alternative was not chosen. The _____ and _____ are the unique inflows and outflows arising from a specific alternative, should it be chosen. Similarly, a(n) _____ arises from implementation of a specific alternative. In comparison, a differential cost is the savings or added costs that arise when comparing alternatives to the current state. There are some costs that are always irrelevant, and one category is _____ that have already been spent and cannot be recovered by making a different decision. One way to select an alternative is to use a(n) _____ called linear programming. Optimization under specific constraints on resources may target either _____ or _____. The technical name to calculate what will be optimized is the _____.

LO 6 ▶
1. Difference in favour of not machining, $400

⊕ **11-15 Disposal of assets.** Answer the following questions.

1. A company has an inventory of 1,000 assorted parts for a line of missiles that has been discontinued. The inventory cost is $88,000. The parts can be either (a) remachined at total additional costs of $33,000 and then sold for $37,000 or (b) sold as scrap for $4,400. Which action is more profitable? Show your calculations.

2. A truck, costing $110,000 and uninsured, is wrecked on its first day in use. It can be either (a) disposed of for $11,000 cash and replaced with a similar truck costing $112,200 or (b) rebuilt for $93,500, and thus be brand-new as far as operating characteristics and looks are concerned. Which action is less costly? Show your calculations.

⊕ **11-16 Inventory decision, opportunity costs.** Lawnox, a manufacturer of lawn mowers, predicts that it will purchase 240,000 spark plugs next year. Lawnox estimates that 20,000 spark plugs will be required each month. A supplier quotes a price of $9 per spark plug. The supplier also offers a special discount option: If all 240,000 spark plugs are purchased at the start of the year, a discount of 4% off the $9 price will be given. Lawnox can invest its cash at 10% per year. It costs Lawnox $200 to place each purchase order.

◀ **LO 4**
1. Opportunity cost of interest forgone, $94,680

Required

1. What is the opportunity cost of interest forgone from purchasing all 240,000 units at the start of the year instead of in 12 monthly purchases of 20,000 units per order?
2. Would this opportunity cost be recorded in the accounting system? Why?
3. Should Lawnox purchase 240,000 units at the start of the year or 20,000 units each month? Show your calculations.

⊕ **11-17 Relevant and irrelevant costs.** Answer the following questions.

◀ **LO 1**
1. Unit relevant cost, $200

Required

1. Ewing Computers makes 5,000 units of a circuit board, CB76, at a cost of $230 each. Variable cost per unit is $180, and fixed cost per unit is $50. HT Electronics offers to supply 5,000 units of CB76 for $210. If Ewing buys from HT, it will be able to save $20 per unit of fixed costs but continues to incur the remaining $30 per unit. Should Ewing accept HT's offer? Explain.
2. AP Manufacturing is deciding whether to keep or replace an old machine. It obtains the following information:

	Old Machine	New Machine
Original cost	$10,000	$8,000
Useful life	10 years	4 years
Current age	6 years	0 years
Remaining useful life	4 years	4 years
Accumulated depreciation	$6,000	Not acquired yet
Book value	$4,000	Not acquired yet
Current disposal value (in cash)	$2,500	Not acquired yet
Terminal disposal value (4 years from now)	$0	$0
Annual cash operating costs	$20,000	$12,000

AP Manufacturing uses straight-line depreciation. Ignore the time value of money and income taxes. Should AP replace the old machine? Explain.

⊕ **11-18 The careening personal computer.** An employee in the accounting department of a certain business was moving a personal computer from one room to another. As he came alongside an open stairway, he slipped and let the computer get away from him. It went careening down the stairs with a great racket and wound up at the bottom, completely wrecked. Hearing the crash, the office manager came rushing out and turned rather pale when he saw what had happened. "Someone tell me quickly," the manager yelled, "if that is one of our fully depreciated items." A check of the accounting records showed that the smashed computer was, indeed, one of those items that had been written off. "Thank God!" said the manager.

◀ **LO 1, 6**

Required

Explain and comment on the point of this anecdote.

⊕ **11-19 Keep or drop a business segment.** Lees Corp. is deciding whether to keep or drop a small segment of its business. Key information regarding the segment includes:

◀ **LO 3**

Contribution margin: 35,000
Avoidable fixed costs: 30,000
Unavoidable fixed costs: 25,000

Given the information above, Lees should:

a. Drop the segment because the contribution margin is less than total fixed costs.
b. Drop the segment because avoidable fixed costs exceed unavoidable fixed costs.
c. Keep the segment because the contribution margin exceeds avoidable fixed costs.
d. Keep the segment because the contribution margin exceeds unavoidable fixed costs.

LO 3, 6 ▶

🌐 **11-20 Relevant costs.** Ace Cleaning Service is considering expanding into one or more new market areas. Which costs are relevant to Ace's decision on whether to expand?

	Sunk Costs	Variable Costs	Opportunity Costs
a.	No	Yes	Yes
b.	Yes	Yes	Yes
c.	No	Yes	No
d.	Yes	No	Yes

LO 5 ▶
1. Lost Operating Income is $212,000

🌐 **11-21 Dropping a product line, selling more tours.** Nelson River Tours, a division of Old World Travel, offers two types of guided fishing tours, Beginner and Advanced. Operating income for each tour type in 2017 is as follows:

	Beginner	Advanced
Revenues (1,000 × $900; 800 × $1,650)	$900,000	$1,320,000
Operating costs		
Administrative salaries	240,000	200,000
Guide wages	260,000	760,000
Supplies	100,000	200,000
Depreciation of equipment	50,000	120,000
Vehicle fuel	60,000	48,000
Allocated corporate overhead	90,000	132,000
Total operating costs	800,000	1,460,000
Operating income (loss)	$100,000	$ (140,000)

The equipment has a zero disposal value. Guide wages, supplies, and vehicle fuel are variable costs with respect to the number of tours. Administrative salaries are fixed costs with respect to the number of tours. Dennis Baldwin, Nelson River Tours' president, is concerned about the losses incurred on the Advanced tours. He is considering dropping the Advanced tour and offering only the Beginner tour.

Required

1. If the Advanced tours are discontinued, one administrative position could be eliminated, saving the company $100,000. Assuming no change in the sales of Beginner tours, what effect would dropping the Advanced tour have on the company's operating income?
2. Refer back to the original data. If Nelson River Tours drops the Advanced tours, Baldwin estimates that sales of Beginner tours would increase by 50%. He believes that he could still eliminate the $100,000 administrative position. Equipment currently used for the Advanced tours would be used by the additional Beginner tours. Should Baldwin drop the Advanced tour? Explain.
3. What additional factors should Baldwin consider before dropping the Advanced tours?

LO 5 ▶
1. Increase in Operating Income is $11,000

🌐 **11-22 Theory of constraints, throughput margin, relevant costs.** The Denver Corporation manufactures filing cabinets in two operations: machining and finishing. It provides the following information:

	Machining	Finishing
Annual capacity	120,000 units	100,000 units
Annual production	100,000 units	100,000 units
Fixed operating costs (excluding direct materials)	$600,000	$300,000
Fixed operating costs per unit produced ($600,000 ÷ 100,000; $300,000 ÷ 100,000)	$6 per unit	$3 per unit

Each cabinet sells for $75 and has direct material costs of $35 incurred at the start of the machining operation. Denver has no other variable costs. Denver can sell whatever output it produces. The following requirements refer only to the preceding data. There is no connection between the requirements.

Required

1. Denver is considering using some modern jigs and tools in the finishing operation that would increase annual finishing output by 1,150 units. The annual cost of these jigs and tools is $35,000. Should Denver acquire these tools? Show your calculations.
2. The production manager of the Machining Department has submitted a proposal to do faster setups that would increase the annual capacity of the Machining Department by 9,000 units and would cost $20,000 per year. Should Denver implement the change? Show your calculations.
3. An outside contractor offers to do the finishing operation for 10,000 units at $9 per unit, triple the $3 per unit that it costs Denver to do the finishing in-house. Should Denver accept the subcontractor's offer? Show your calculations.
4. The Hammond Corporation offers to machine 5,000 units at $3 per unit, half the $6 per unit that it costs Denver to do the machining in-house. Should Denver accept Hammond's offer? Show your calculations.
5. Denver produces 2,000 defective units at the machining operation. What is the cost to Denver of the defective items produced? Explain your answer briefly.
6. Denver produces 2,000 defective units at the finishing operation. What is the cost to Denver of the defective items produced? Explain your answer briefly.

11-23 Sell or process further. Xylon Processing Limited is a chemical manufacturer. Two chemicals, Aardyn and Gargaton, are produced from the common chemical xylon. The joint process requires 15,000 litres of xylon to be processed at a cost of $21,500 (including the cost of the chemical itself). From these 15,000 litres, the company produces 9,600 litres of Aardyn and 5,400 litres of Gargaton. The joint costs of $21,500 are allocated $13,760 to Aardyn and $7,740 to Gargaton. The company can sell the Aardyn and the Gargaton at the split-off point for $15,360 and $8,748, respectively. Alternatively, the company can process the Aardyn further to produce 9,600 litres of Anardyn. The Anardyn sells for $2.38 per litre, and additional processing costs are $6,945.

◀ **LO 3**
Incremental revenue from further processing, $22,848

Required

Should Xylon sell Aardyn, or should it process it further to produce Anardyn?

11-24 Special order, activity-based costing. (CMA, adapted) The Reward One Company manufactures windows. Its manufacturing plant has the capacity to produce 12,000 windows each month. Current production and sales are 10,000 windows per month. The company normally charges $250 per window. Cost information for the current activity level is as follows:

◀ **LO 2**
Variable cost per batch is $1,500

Variable costs that vary with number of units produced	
Direct materials	$ 600,000
Direct manufacturing labour	700,000
Variable costs (for setups, materials handling, quality control, and so on) that vary with number of batches, 100 batches × $1,500 per batch	150,000
Fixed manufacturing costs	250,000
Fixed marketing costs	400,000
Total costs	$2,100,000

Reward One has just received a special one-time-only order for 2,000 windows at $225 per window. Accepting the special order would not affect the company's regular business or its fixed costs. Reward One makes windows for its existing customers in batch sizes of 100 windows (100 batches × 100 windows per batch = 10,000 windows). The special order requires Reward One to make the windows in 25 batches of 80 windows.

Required

1. Should Reward One accept this special order? Show your calculations.
2. Suppose plant capacity were only 11,000 windows instead of 12,000 windows each month. The special order must either be taken in full or be rejected completely. Should Reward One accept the special order? Show your calculations.
3. As in requirement 1, assume that monthly capacity is 12,000 windows. Reward One is concerned that if it accepts the special order, its existing customers will immediately demand a price discount of $20 in the month in which the special order is being filled. They would argue that Reward One's capacity costs are now being spread over more units and that existing customers should

get the benefit of these lower costs. Should Reward One accept the special order under these conditions? Show your calculations.

LO 1, 2, 3 ▶
Per unit costs, it is more favourable to MAKE by $41 / unit

🌐 **11-25 Make versus buy, activity-based costing.** The Svenson Corporation manufactures cellular modems. It manufactures its own cellular modem circuit boards (CMCB), an important part of the cellular modem. It reports the following cost information about the costs of making CMCBs in 2017 and the expected costs in 2018:

	Current Costs in 2017	Expected Costs in 2018
Variable manufacturing costs		
Direct material cost per CMCB	$ 180	$ 170
Direct manufacturing labour cost per CMCB	50	45
Variable manufacturing cost per batch for setups, materials handling, and quality control	1,600	1,500
Fixed manufacturing cost		
Fixed manufacturing overhead costs that can be avoided if CMCBs are not made	320,000	320,000
Fixed manufacturing overhead costs of plant depreciation, insurance, and administration that cannot be avoided even if CMCBs are not made	800,000	800,000

Svenson manufactured 8,000 CMCBs in 2017 in 40 batches of 200 each. In 2018, Svenson anticipates needing 10,000 CMCBs. The CMCBs would be produced in 80 batches of 125 each.

The Minton Corporation has approached Svenson about supplying CMCBs to Svenson in 2018 at $300 per CMCB on whatever delivery schedule Svenson wants.

Required

1. Calculate the total expected manufacturing cost per unit of making CMCBs in 2018.
2. Suppose the capacity currently used to make CMCBs will become idle if Svenson purchases CMCBs from Minton. On the basis of financial considerations alone, should Svenson make CMCBs or buy them from Minton? Show your calculations.
3. Now suppose that if Svenson purchases CMCBs from Minton, its best alternative use of the capacity currently used for CMCBs is to make and sell special circuit boards (CB3s) to the Essex Corporation. Svenson estimates the following incremental revenues and costs from CB3s:

Total expected incremental future revenues	$2,000,000
Total expected incremental future costs	$2,150,000

On the basis of financial considerations alone, should Svenson make CMCBs or buy them from Minton? Show your calculations.

LO 2, 5 ▶
Direct material cost per pound that Wechsler can pay without contribution margin becoming negative is $30

🌐 **11-26 Product mix, constrained resource.** Wechsler Company produces three products: A130, B324, and C587. All three products use the same direct material, Brac. Unit data for the three products are:

	Product		
	A130	B324	C587
Selling price	$252	$168	$210
Variable costs			
Direct materials	$ 72	$ 45	$ 27
Labour and other costs	$ 84	$ 81	$ 120
Quantity of Brac per unit	8 lb.	5 lb.	3 lb.

The demand for the products far exceeds the direct materials available to produce the products. Brac costs $9 per pound, and a maximum of 5,000 pounds is available each month. Wechsler must produce a minimum of 200 units of each product.

Required

1. How many units of product A130, B324, and C587 should Wechsler produce?
2. What is the maximum amount Wechsler would be willing to pay for another 1,200 pounds of Brac?

🌐 **11-27 Theory of constraints, throughput margin, and relevant costs.** Washington Industries manufactures electronic testing equipment. Washington also installs the equipment at customers' sites and ensures that it functions smoothly. Additional information on the manufacturing and installation departments is as follows (capacities are expressed in terms of the number of units of electronic testing equipment):

◀ **LO 5**
2. Increase in Operating Income is $305,000

	Equipment Manufactured	Equipment Installed
Annual capacity	285 units per year	250 units per year
Equipment manufactured and installed	250 units per year	250 units per year

Washington manufactures only 250 units per year because the installation department has only enough capacity to install 250 units. The equipment sells for $55,000 per unit (installed) and has direct material costs of $30,000. All costs other than direct material costs are fixed. The following requirements refer only to the preceding data. There is no connection between the requirements.

Required

1. Washington's engineers have found a way to reduce equipment manufacturing time. The new method would cost an additional $500 per unit and would allow Washington to manufacture 30 additional units a year. Should Washington implement the new method? Show your calculations.
2. Washington's designers have proposed a change in direct materials that would increase direct material costs by $2,000 per unit. This change would enable Washington to install 285 units of equipment each year. If Washington makes the change, it will implement the new design on all equipment sold. Should Washington use the new design? Show your calculations.
3. A new installation technique has been developed that will enable Washington's engineers to install 7 additional units of equipment a year. The new method will increase installation costs by $145,000 each year. Should Washington implement the new technique? Show your calculations.
4. Washington is considering how to motivate workers to improve their productivity (output per hour). One proposal is to evaluate and compensate workers in the manufacturing and installation departments on the basis of their productivities. Do you think the new proposal is a good idea? Explain briefly.

🌐 **11-28 Selection of most profitable product.** Body Image, Inc., produces two basic types of weight-lifting equipment, Model 9 and Model 14. Pertinent data are as follows:

◀ **LO 2, 5**
Contribution margin per machine hour for Model 9 is $40

		Per Unit	
	A	B Model 9	C Model 14
3	Selling Price	$150.00	$85.00
4	Costs		
5	Direct material	23.00	13.00
6	Variable direct manufacturing labour	16.00	19.00
7	Variable manufacturing overhead	18.00	9.00
8	Fixed manufacturing overhead*	9.00	4.50
9	Marketing (all variable)	13.00	15.00
10	Total costs	79.00	60.50
11	Operating income	$ 71.00	$24.50
12			
13	*Allocated on the basis of machine-hours		

The weight-lifting craze suggests that Body Image can sell enough of either Model 9 or Model 14 to keep the plant operating at full capacity. Both products are processed through the same production departments.

Required

Which product should the company produce? Briefly explain your answer.

Problems

LO 1, 2 ▶   🌐 **11-29 Multiple choice.** (CPA) Choose the best answer.

1. The Cozy Company manufactures slippers and sells them at $10 a pair. Variable manufacturing cost is $5.75 a pair, and allocated fixed manufacturing cost is $1.75 a pair. It has enough idle capacity available to accept a one-time-only special order of 25,000 pairs of slippers at $7.50 a pair. Cozy will not incur any marketing costs as a result of the special order. What would the effect on operating income be if the special order could be accepted without affecting normal sales: (a) $0, (b) $43,750 increase, (c) $143,750 increase, or (d) $187,500 increase? Show your calculations.

2. The Manchester Company manufactures Part No. 498 for use in its production line. The manufacturing cost per unit for 10,000 units of Part No. 498 is as follows:

Direct materials	$ 3
Variable direct manufacturing labour	40
Variable manufacturing overhead	10
Fixed manufacturing overhead allocated	21
Total manufacturing cost per unit	$74

The Remnant Company has offered to sell 10,000 units of Part No. 498 to Manchester for $71 per unit. Manchester will make the decision to buy the part from Remnant if there is an overall savings of at least $45,000 for Manchester. If Manchester accepts Remnant's offer, $11 per unit of the fixed overhead allocated would be eliminated. Furthermore, Manchester has determined that the released facilities could be used to save relevant costs in the manufacture of Part No. 575. For Manchester to achieve an overall savings of $45,000, the amount of relevant costs that would have to be saved by using the released facilities in the manufacture of Part No. 575 would be which of the following: (a) $30,000, (b) $115,000, (c) $125,000, or (d) $100,000? Show your calculations. What other factors might Manchester consider before outsourcing to Remnant?

LO 1, 2, 3 ▶   🌐 **11-30 Relevant costs, contribution margin, product emphasis.** The Beach Comber is a take-out food store at a popular beach resort. Sara Miller, owner of the Beach Comber, is deciding how much refrigerator space to devote to four different drinks. Pertinent data on these four drinks are as follows:

	Cola	Lemonade	Punch	Natural Orange Juice
Selling price per case	$19.10	$20.25	$27.10	$39.50
Variable cost per case	$14.40	$15.90	$21.50	$29.80
Cases sold per foot of shelf space per day	10	24	25	22

Miller has a maximum front shelf space of 12 feet to devote to the four drinks. She wants a minimum of 1 foot and a maximum of 6 feet of front shelf space for each drink.

Required

1. Calculate the contribution margin per case of each type of drink.
2. A coworker of Miller's recommends that she maximize the shelf space devoted to those drinks with the highest contribution margin per case. Do you agree with this recommendation? Explain briefly.
3. What shelf-space allocation for the four drinks would you recommend for the Beach Comber? Show your calculations.

LO 1, 3 ▶
1. Contribution margin per case of orange juice, $9.00

🌐 **11-31 Relevant costs, contribution margin, product emphasis.** The Beach Comber is a take-out food store at a popular beach resort. Susan Sexton, owner of the Beach Comber, is deciding how much refrigerator space to devote to four different drinks. Pertinent data on these four drinks are as follows:

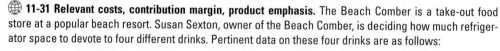

	Cola	Lemonade	Punch	Natural Orange Juice
Selling price per case	$18.80	$20.00	$27.10	$39.20
Variable cost per case	$14.20	$16.10	$20.70	$30.20
Cases sold per foot of shelf space per day	25	24	4	5

Sexton has a maximum front shelf space of 12 feet to devote to the four drinks. She wants a minimum of 1 foot and a maximum of 6 feet of front shelf space for each drink.

Required

1. Compute the contribution margin per case of each type of drink.

2. A coworker of Sexton's recommends that she maximize the shelf space devoted to those drinks with the highest contribution margin per case. Evaluate this recommendation.

3. What shelf-space allocation for the four drinks would you recommend for the Beach Comber? Show your calculations.

🌐 **11-32 Opportunity cost.** Wolverine Corporation is working at full production capacity producing 10,000 units of a unique product, Rosebo. Manufacturing costs per unit for Rosebo are as follows:

◀ **LO 4**
1. Variable costs per unit, $11

Direct materials	$ 2
Direct manufacturing labour	$ 3
Manufacturing overhead	$ 5
Total manufacturing cost	$10

The unit manufacturing overhead cost is based on a variable cost per unit of $2 and fixed costs of $30,000 (at full capacity of 10,000 units). The selling costs, all variable, are $4 per unit, and the selling price is $20 per unit.

A customer, the Miami Company, has asked Wolverine to produce 2,000 units of Orangebo, a modification of Rosebo. Orangebo would require the same manufacturing processes as Rosebo. Miami Company has offered to pay Wolverine $15 for a unit of Orangebo and half the selling costs per unit.

Required

1. What is the opportunity cost to Wolverine of producing the 2,000 units of Orangebo? (Assume that no overtime is worked.)

2. Buckeye Corporation has offered to produce 2,000 units of Rosebo for Wolverine so that Wolverine may accept the Miami offer. That is, if Wolverine accepts the Buckeye offer, Wolverine would manufacture 8,000 units of Rosebo and 2,000 units of Orangebo and purchase 2,000 units of Rosebo from Buckeye. Buckeye would charge Wolverine $14 per unit to manufacture Rosebo. Should Wolverine accept the Buckeye offer? (Support your conclusions with specific analysis.)

3. Suppose Wolverine had been working at less than full capacity, producing 8,000 units of Rosebo at the time the Orangebo offer was made. What is the minimum price Wolverine should accept for Orangebo under these conditions? (Ignore the previous $15 selling price.)

🌐 **11-33 Optimal product mix.** (CMA adapted) Della Simpson, Inc., sells two popular brands of cookies: Della's Delight and Bonny's Bourbon. Della's Delight goes through the Mixing and Baking departments, and Bonny's Bourbon, a filled cookie, goes through the Mixing, Filling, and Baking departments.

◀ **LO 3**

Michael Shirra, vice president for sales, believes that at the current price, Della Simpson can sell all of its daily production of Della's Delight and Bonny's Bourbon. Both cookies are made in batches of 3,000. In each department, the time required per batch and the total time available each day are as follows:

A	B	C	D
	Department Minutes		
	Mixing	**Filling**	**Baking**
3 Della's Delight	30	0	10
4 Bonny's Bourbon	15	15	15
5 Total available per day	660	270	300

Revenue and cost data for each type of cookie are as follows:

A	B	C
	Della's	**Bonny's**
	Delight	**Bourbon**
9 Revenue per batch	$ 475	$ 375
10 Variable cost per batch	175	125
11 Contribution margin per batch	$ 300	$ 250
12 Monthly fixed costs		
13 (allocated to each product)	$18,650	$22,350

Required

1. Using *D* to represent the batches of Della's Delight and *B* to represent the batches of Bonny's Bourbon made and sold each day, formulate Shirra's decision as an LP model.
2. Compute the optimal number of batches of each type of cookie that Della Simpson, Inc., should make and sell each day to maximize operating income.

LO 2, 3, 5 ▶
Maximize $300D + $250 B
where D = Della's Delight and
B = Bonnie's Bourbon

⊕ **11-34 Optimal production mix.** Della Simpson Inc. sells two popular brands of cookies, Della's Delight and Bonnie's Bourbon. Della's Delight goes through the Mixing and Baking Departments, and Bonnie's Bourbon, a filled cookie, goes through the Mixing, Filling, and Baking departments.

Michael Shirra, vice-president of sales, believes that at the current price, Della Simpson can sell all of its daily production of Della's Delight and Bonnie's Bourbon. Both cookies are made in batches of 3,000 cookies. The batch times (in minutes) for producing each type of cookie and the minutes available per day are as follows:

	Department Minutes		
	Mixing	**Filling**	**Baking**
Della's Delight	30	0	10
Bonnie's Bourbon	15	15	15
Minutes available per day	660	270	300

Revenue and cost data for each type of cookie are:

	Della's Delight	**Bonnie's Bourbon**
Revenue per batch	$ 475	$ 375
Variable cost per batch	175	125
Contribution margin per batch	300	250
Monthly fixed costs (allocated to each product)	18,650	22,350

Required

1. Using D to represent the batches of Della's Delight and B to represent the batches of Bonnie's Bourbon made and sold each day, formulate Shirra's decision as a linear programming model.
2. Compute the optimal number of batches of each type of cookie that Della Simpson Inc. should make and sell each day to maximize operating income.

LO 4 ▶
1. Net relevant OI on
Easyspread 1.0, $165

⊕ **11-35 Opportunity costs.** (H. Schaefer, adapted) The Wild Orchid Corporation is working at full production capacity producing 13,000 units of a unique product, Everlast. Manufacturing cost per unit for Everlast is:

Direct materials	$10
Variable direct manufacturing labour	2
Manufacturing overhead	14
Total manufacturing cost	$26

Manufacturing overhead cost per unit is based on variable cost per unit of $8 and fixed costs of $78,000 (at full capacity of 13,000 units). Marketing cost per unit, all variable, is $4, and the selling price is $52.

A customer, the Apex Company, has asked Wild Orchid to produce 3,500 units of Stronglast, a modification of Everlast. Stronglast would require the same manufacturing processes as Everlast. Apex has offered to pay Wild Orchid $40 for a unit of Stronglast and share half of the marketing cost per unit.

Required

1. What is the opportunity cost to Wild Orchid of producing the 3,500 units of Stronglast? (Assume that no overtime is worked.)
2. The Chesapeake Corporation has offered to produce 3,500 units of Everlast for Wild Orchid so that Wild Orchid may accept the Apex offer. That is, if Wild Orchid accepts the Chesapeake offer, Wild Orchid would manufacture 9,500 units of Everlast and 3,500 units of Stronglast and purchase 3,500 units of Everlast from Chesapeake. Chesapeake would charge Wild Orchid $36 per unit to manufacture Everlast. On the basis of financial considerations alone, should Wild Orchid accept the Chesapeake offer? Show your calculations.
3. Suppose Wild Orchid had been working at less than full capacity, producing 9,500 units of Everlast, at the time the Apex offer was made. Calculate the minimum price Wild Orchid should accept for Stronglast under these conditions. (Ignore the previous $40 selling price.)

⊕ **11-36 Choosing customers.** Newbury Printers operates a printing press with a monthly capacity of 3,200 machine-hours. Newbury has two main customers: Wallace Corporation and Kimberly Corporation. Data on each customer for January are:

◀ **LO 3**

	Wallace Corporation	Kimberly Corporation	Total
Revenues	$240,000	$160,000	$400,000
Variable costs	129,600	112,000	241,600
Contribution margin	110,400	48,000	158,400
Fixed costs (allocated)	75,000	50,000	125,000
Operating income	$ 35,400	$ (2,000)	$ 33,400
Machine-hours required	2,400 hours	800 hours	3,200 hours

Kimberly Corporation indicates that it wants Newbury to do an *additional* $160,000 worth of printing jobs during February. These jobs are identical to the existing business Newbury did for Kimberly in January in terms of variable costs and machine-hours required. Newbury anticipates that the business from Wallace Corporation in February will be the same as that in January. Newbury can choose to accept as much of the Wallace and Kimberly business for February as its capacity allows. Assume that total machine-hours and fixed costs for February will be the same as in January.

Required

What action should Newbury take to maximize its operating income? Show your calculations. What other factors should Newbury consider before making a decision?

11-37 Reduce conflict. Make or buy, unknown level of volume. Denver Engineering manufactures small engines that it sells to manufacturers who install them in products such as lawn mowers. The company currently manufactures all the parts used in these engines but is considering a proposal from an external supplier who wishes to supply the starter assemblies used in these engines.

◀ **LO 3**

The starter assemblies are currently manufactured in Division 3 of Denver Engineering. The costs relating to the starter assemblies for the past 12 months were as follows:

Direct materials	$ 400,000
Variable direct manufacturing labour	300,000
Manufacturing overhead	800,000
Total	$1,500,000

Over the past year, Division 3 manufactured 150,000 starter assemblies. The average cost for each starter assembly is $10 ($1,500,000 ÷ 150,000).

Further analysis of manufacturing overhead revealed the following information. Of the total manufacturing overhead, only 25% is considered variable. Of the fixed portion, $300,000 is an allocation of general overhead that will remain unchanged for the company as a whole if production of the starter assemblies is discontinued. A further $200,000 of the fixed overhead is avoidable if production of the starter assemblies is discontinued. The balance of the current fixed overhead, $100,000, is the division manager's salary. If Denver Engineering discontinues production of the starter assemblies, the manager of Division 3 will be transferred to Division 2 at the same salary. This move will allow the company to save the $80,000 salary that would otherwise be paid to attract an outsider to this position.

Required

1. Tutwiler Electronics, a reliable supplier, has offered to supply starter-assembly units at $8 per unit. Because this price is less than the current average cost of $10 per unit, the vice president of manufacturing is eager to accept this offer. On the basis of financial considerations alone, should Denver Engineering accept the outside offer? Show your calculations. (*Hint:* Production output in the coming year may be different from production output in the past year.)
2. How, if at all, would your response to requirement 1 change if the company could use the vacated plant space for storage and, in so doing, avoid $100,000 of outside storage charges currently incurred? Why is this information relevant or irrelevant?

LO 3, 6 ▶

1. Total relevant cost to replace, $5,040,000

11-38 Equipment upgrade versus replacement. The TechMech Company produces and sells 6,000 modular computer desks per year at a selling price of $500 each. Its current production equipment, purchased for $1,500,000 and with a five-year useful life, is only two years old. It has a terminal disposal value of $0 and is depreciated on a straight-line basis. The equipment has a current disposal price of $600,000. However, the emergence of a new moulding technology has led TechMech to consider either upgrading or replacing the production equipment. The following table presents data for the two alternatives:

	A	B	C
1		**Upgrade**	**Replace**
2	One-time equipment costs	$2,700,000	$4,200,000
3	Variable manufacturing cost per desk	$ 140	$ 80
4	Remaining useful life of equipment (years)	3	3
5	Terminal disposal value of equipment	$ 0	$ 0

All equipment costs will continue to be depreciated on a straight-line basis. For simplicity, ignore income taxes and the time value of money.

Required

1. Should TechMech upgrade its production line or replace it? Show your calculations.
2. Now suppose the one-time equipment cost to replace the production equipment is somewhat negotiable. All other data are as given previously. What is the maximum one-time equipment cost that TechMech would be willing to pay to replace the old equipment rather than upgrade it?
3. Assume that the capital expenditures to replace and upgrade the production equipment are as given in the original exercise, but that the production and sales quantity is not known. For what production and sales quantity would TechMech (a) upgrade the equipment or (b) replace the equipment?
4. Assume that all data are as given in the original exercise. Dan Doria is TechMech's manager, and his bonus is based on operating income. Because he is likely to relocate after about a year, his current bonus is his primary concern. Which alternative would Doria choose? Explain.

LO 1, 3, 5 ▶

11-39 Product mix, special order. (N. Melumad, adapted) Gormley Precision Tools makes cutting tools for metalworking operations. It makes two types of tools: A6, a regular cutting tool, and EX4, a high-precision cutting tool. A6 is manufactured on a regular machine, but EX4 must be manufactured on both the regular machine and a high-precision machine. The following information is available:

	A6	EX4
Selling price	$ 180	$ 280
Variable manufacturing cost per unit	$ 110	$ 190
Variable marketing cost per unit	$ 20	$ 60
Budgeted total fixed overhead costs	$700,000	$1,100,000
Hours required to produce one unit on the regular machine	1.0	0.5

Additional information includes the following:

a. Gormley faces a capacity constraint on the regular machine of 50,000 hours per year.
b. The capacity of the high-precision machine is not a constraint.
c. Of the $1,100,000 budgeted fixed overhead costs of EX4, $600,000 are lease payments for the high-precision machine. This cost is charged entirely to EX4 because Gormley uses the machine exclusively to produce EX4. The company can cancel the lease agreement for the high-precision machine at any time without penalties.
d. All other overhead costs are fixed and cannot be changed.

Required

1. What product mix—that is, how many units of A6 and EX4—will maximize Gormley's operating income? Show your calculations.
2. Suppose Gormley can increase the annual capacity of its regular machines by 15,000 machine-hours at a cost of $300,000. Should Gormley increase the capacity of the regular machines by 15,000 machine-hours? By how much will Gormley's operating income increase or decrease? Show your calculations.
3. Suppose that the capacity of the regular machines has been increased to 65,000 hours. Gormley has been approached by Clark Corporation to supply 20,000 units of another cutting tool, V2, for $240 per

unit. Gormley must either accept the order for all 20,000 units or reject it totally. V2 is exactly like A6 except that its variable manufacturing cost is $130 per unit. (It takes 1 hour to produce one unit of V2 on the regular machine, and variable marketing cost equals $20 per unit.) What product mix should Gormley choose to maximize operating income? Show your calculations.

⊕ **11-40 Relevant costs, opportunity costs.** Gavin Martin, the general manager of Oregano Software, must decide when to release the new version of Oregano's spreadsheet package, Easyspread 2.0. Development of Easyspread 2.0 is complete; however, the diskettes, compact discs, and user manuals have not yet been produced. The product can be shipped starting July 1, 2017. ◀ LO 3

The major problem is that Oregano has overstocked the previous version of its spreadsheet package, Easyspread 1.0. Martin knows that once Easyspread 2.0 is introduced, Oregano will not be able to sell any more units of Easyspread 1.0. Rather than just throwing away the inventory of Easyspread 1.0, Martin is wondering if it might be better to continue to sell Easyspread 1.0 for the next three months and introduce Easyspread 2.0 on October 1, 2017, when the inventory of Easyspread 1.0 will be sold out.

The following information is available:

	Easyspread 1.0	Easyspread 2.0
Selling price	$165	$215
Variable cost per unit of diskettes, compact discs, user manuals	24	38
Development cost per unit	60	95
Marketing and administrative cost per unit	31	41
Total cost per unit	115	174
Operating income per unit	$ 50	$ 41

Development cost per unit for each product equals the total costs of developing the software product divided by the anticipated unit sales over the life of the product. Marketing and administrative costs are fixed costs in 2017, incurred to support all marketing and administrative activities of Oregano Software. Marketing and administrative costs are allocated to products on the basis of the budgeted revenues of each product. The preceding unit costs assume Easyspread 2.0 will be introduced on October 1, 2017.

Required

1. On the basis of financial considerations alone, should Martin introduce Easyspread 2.0 on July 1, 2017, or wait until October 1, 2017? Show your calculations, clearly identifying relevant and irrelevant revenues and costs.
2. What other factors might Gavin Martin consider in making a decision?

11-41 Product mix. Short-run pricing, capacity constraints. Fashion Fabrics makes pants from a special material. The fabric is special because of the way it fits many body types. The pants sell for $142. A well-known retail establishment has asked Fashion Fabrics to produce 3,000 shorts from the same fabric. The factory has unused capacity, so Barbara Brooks, the owner of Fashion Fabrics, calculates the cost of making a pair of shorts from the fabric. Costs for the pants and shorts are as follows: ◀ LO 1, 2, 3

	Pants	Shorts
Fabric (6 yds. × $12; 3 yds. × $12)	$ 72	36
Variable direct manufacturing labour	20	10
Variable manufacturing overhead	8	4
Fixed manufacturing cost allocated	15	9
Total manufacturing cost	$115	$59

Required

1. Suppose Fashion Fabrics can acquire all the fabric that it needs. What is the minimum price the company should charge for the shorts?
2. Now suppose that the fabric is in short supply. Every yard of fabric Fashion Fabrics uses to make shorts will reduce the pants that it can make and sell. What is the minimum price the company should charge for the shorts?

LO 1, 2, 3 ▶ ⊕ **11-42 Special order, short-run pricing.** Diamond Corporation produces baseball bats for kids that it sells for $37 each. At capacity, the company can produce 54,000 bats a year. The costs of producing and selling 54,000 bats are as follows:

	Cost per Bat	Total Costs
Direct materials	$14	$ 756,000
Variable direct manufacturing labour	4	216,000
Variable manufacturing overhead	2	108,000
Fixed manufacturing overhead	5	270,000
Variable selling expenses	2	108,000
Fixed selling expenses	3	162,000
Total costs	$30	$1,620,000

Required

1. Suppose Diamond is currently producing and selling 44,000 bats. At this level of production and sales, its fixed costs are the same as given in the preceding table. Home Run Corporation wants to place a one-time special order for 10,000 bats at $21 each. Diamond will incur no variable selling costs for this special order. Should Diamond accept this one-time special order? Show your calculations.
2. Now suppose Diamond is currently producing and selling 54,000 bats. If Diamond accepts Home Run's offer, it will have to sell 10,000 fewer bats to its regular customers. (a) On financial considerations alone, should Diamond accept this one-time special order? Show your calculations. (b) On financial considerations alone, at what price would Diamond be indifferent between accepting the special order and continuing to sell to its regular customers at $37 per bat. (c) What other factors should Diamond consider in deciding whether to accept the one-time special order?

Collaborative Learning Case

LO 1, 2, 3 ▶
1. Hardt forecast to make
32,000 units, $714,840

11-43 Make versus buy, governance. Lynn Hardt, a management accountant with the Paibec Corporation, is evaluating whether a component, MTR-2000, should continue to be manufactured by Paibec or purchased from Marley Company, an outside supplier. Marley has submitted a bid to manufacture and supply the 32,000 units of MTR-2000 that Paibec will need for 2019 at a unit price of $17.30, to be delivered according to Paibec's production specifications and needs. While the contract price of $17.30 is only applicable in 2019, Marley is interested in entering into a long-term arrangement beyond 2019.

From plant records and interviews with John Porter, the plant manager, Hardt gathered the following information regarding Paibec's costs to manufacture 30,000 units of MTR-2000 in 2018:

	A	B
1		**Costs for**
2		**30,000**
3		**Units in 2018**
4	Direct materials	$195,000
5	Direct manufacturing labour	120,000
6	Plant space rental	84,000
7	Equipment leasing	36,000
8	Other manufacturing overhead	225,000
9	Total manufacturing costs	$660,000

Hardt has collected the following additional information related to manufacturing MTR-2000:

■ Variable costs per unit in 2019 for the MTR-2000 are expected to be the same as variable costs per unit in 2018.

■ Plant rental and equipment lease are annual contracts that are going to be expensive to wiggle out of. Porter estimates it will cost $10,000 to terminate the plant rental contract and $5,000 to terminate the equipment-lease contract.

- 40% of the other manufacturing overhead is variable, proportionate to the direct manufacturing labour costs. The fixed component of other manufacturing overhead is expected to remain the same whether MTR-2000 is manufactured by Paibec or outsourced to Marley.
- Paibec's just-in-time policy means inventory is negligible.

Hardt is aware that cost studies can be threatening to current employees because the findings may lead to reorganizations and layoffs. She knows that Porter is concerned that outsourcing MTR-2000 will result in some of his close friends being laid off. Therefore, she performs her own independent analysis of competitive and other economic data, which reveals that

- Prices of direct materials are likely to increase by 8% in 2019 compared to 2018.
- Direct manufacturing labour rates are likely to be higher by 5% in 2019 compared to 2018.
- The plant rental contract can, in fact be terminated by paying $10,000. Paibec will not have any need for this space if MTR-2000 is outsourced.
- The equipment lease can be terminated by paying $3,000.

Hardt shows Porter her analysis. Porter argues that Hardt is ignoring the amazing continuous improvement that is occurring at the plant and that the increases in direct material prices and direct manufacturing labour rates assumed by Hardt will not occur. But Hardt is very confident about the accuracy of the information she has collected.

Required

1. Based on the information Hardt has obtained, should Paibec make MTR-2000 or buy it? Show all calculations.
2. What other factors should Paibec consider before making a decision?
3. What should Lynn Hardt do in response to John Porter's comments?

11-44 Relevance, short-term. Hernandez Corporation is bidding on a new construction contract, here called Contract No. 1. If the bid is accepted, work will begin in a few days, on January 1, 2019. Contract No. 1 requires a special cement. Hernandez has already purchased 10,000 kilograms of the special cement for $20,000. The current purchase cost of the cement is $2.40 per kilogram. The company could sell the cement now for $1.60 per kilogram after all selling costs. Hernandez will also bid on Contract No. 2 one month from now. If Contract No. 1 is not landed, the special cement will be available for Contract No. 2. If Contract No. 1 is landed, Hernandez will need to buy 10,000 kilograms of another grade of cement for $2.50 per kilogram to fulfill Contract No. 2.

⬩ **LO 1, 2, 3**
1. Relevant cost, $25,000

If it is not used in either of these two ways, the special cement would be of no use to the company and would be sold a little more than a month from now for $1.50 per kilogram after all selling costs.

The president of Hernandez, Julio Gomez, is puzzled about the appropriate total cost of the special cement to be used in bidding on Contract No. 1. Competition is intense and markups are very thin, so determining the relevant material costs when bidding on Contract No. 1 is crucial.

Required

1. Suppose Gomez is certain that Hernandez will land Contract No. 2; what (relevant) cost figure should Gomez use for the special cement when bidding on Contract No. 1?
2. This part requires knowledge of the material on decision making under uncertainty, which was covered in Chapter 3. Suppose Gomez estimates a probability of 0.7 that Hernandez will land Contract No. 2. What (relevant) cost figure should Gomez use for the special cement when bidding on Contract No. 1?
3. Suppose Hernandez could sell the special cement now for $2.30 per kilogram after all selling costs (instead of $1.60 per kilogram as described in paragraph 1). Suppose Gomez is certain that Hernandez will land Contract No. 2. What (relevant) cost figure should Gomez use for the special cement when preparing a bid on Contract No. 1?

TRY IT! ▶ SOLUTIONS

Try It 11–1

The relevant revenues and costs are the expected future revenues and costs that differ as a result of Rainier accepting the special offer:

Revenues ($60 per hour × 1,000 hours)	$60,000
Variable landscaping costs ($50 per hour × 1,000 hours)	50,000
Increase in operating income by accepting the one-time special order	$10,000

The fixed landscaping costs and all marketing costs (*including variable marketing costs*) are irrelevant in this case because these costs will not change in total whether the special order is accepted or rejected. In this example, by focusing only on the relevant amounts, the manager avoids a misleading implication: to reject the special order because the $60-per-hour selling price is lower than the landscaping cost per hour of $62, which includes both relevant variable landscaping costs and irrelevant fixed landscaping costs.

Try It 11–2

Rainier could use either the Total Alternatives Approach or the Opportunity-Cost Approach to make a decision.

Total Alternatives Approach

The two options available to Rainier are

1. Do 8,000 hours of landscaping work for its current customers and 2,000 hours of work for Victoria
2. Do 9,000 hours of landscaping work for its current customers

The table below presents the relevant revenues and relevant costs, those future revenues and costs that differ between the alternatives. It shows that Rainier is better off rejecting Victoria's offer because it reduces operating income by $12,000.

	Current customers: 8,000 hours Victoria: 2,000 hours	Current customers: 9,000 hours
Relevant revenues ($80 × 8,000 + $60 × 2,000) ($80 × 9,000)	$760,000	$720,000
Relevant costs Variable landscaping costs ($50 × 10,000) ($50 × 9,000)	500,000	450,000
Variable marketing costs (5% × $760,000) (5% × $720,000)	38,000	36,000
Total relevant costs	538,000	486,000
Relevant operating income	222,000	234,000

The Opportunity Cost Approach

In the opportunity cost approach, the options are defined as follows:

1. Accept Victoria's offer for 2,000 hours of landscaping work.
2. Reject Victoria's offer.

The analysis focuses only on the Victoria offer.

We first calculate the opportunity cost of accepting Victoria's offer.

There is no opportunity cost for the first 1,000 hours of equipment time since Rainier has 10,000 hours of equipment time and its current customers require only 9,000 hours.

For using the next 1,000 hours of equipment time on the Victoria offer, Rainier will have to forgo contribution margin on the 1,000 hours of services it would have sold to its existing customers.

Revenue from 1,000 hours of landscaping for existing customers ($80 × 1,000 hours)	$80,000
Variable costs of landscaping ($50 × 1,000 hours)	50,000
Variable marketing costs (5% × $80,000)	4,000
Contribution margin from 1,000 hours of landscaping from serving existing customers	$26,000

The opportunity cost of accepting Victoria's offer is $26,000.

We next focus only on Victoria's offer and the effect on operating income from accepting it.

	Accept Victoria's offer	Reject Victoria's offer
Incremental future revenues	$120,000 ($60 × 2,000 hours)	$0
Incremental future costs		
Variable landscaping costs	100,000 ($50 × 1,000 hours)	0
Variable marketing costs	6,000 (5%×$120,000)	0
Opportunity cost of using 1,000 hours of equipment for the Victoria offer and forgoing the profit contribution on existing customers	26,000	0
Total relevant costs	132,000	0
Effect on operating income of accepting Victoria's offer	$ (12,000)	$0

The opportunity cost approach yields the same conclusions as the total alternatives approach. Rainier's operating income decreases by $12,000 if it accepts Victoria's offer. Note that by considering only the incremental revenues and incremental costs, it would appear that Rainier should accept Victoria's offer because incremental revenues exceed incremental costs of the Victoria offer by $14,000 ($120,000 − $106,000). But there is an opportunity cost of $26,000 by using the equipment for Victoria's business because the next-best use of this equipment by Rainier would result in an increase in operating income of $26,000. Unless the contract with Victoria results in more than $26,000 in operating income, Rainier should reject the offer.

Try It 11–3

This problem is one of making product- (or customer-) mix decisions with capacity constraints.

Rainier's managers should choose the product with *the highest contribution margin per unit of the constraining resource (equipment-hours)*. That's the resource that restricts or limits the sale of Rainier's services.

Contribution margin from regular customers:

Revenues ($80 × 9,000 hours)	$720,000
Variable landscaping costs (including materials and labour), which vary with the number of hours worked ($50 per hour × 9,000 hours)	450,000
Variable marketing costs (5% of revenue)	36,000
Total variable costs	486,000
Contribution margin	$234,000
Contribution margin per hour of equipment time from regular customers ($234,000 ÷ 9,000 hours)	$26 per hour

Contribution margin from Hudson Corporation:

Revenues ($70 × 4,000 hours)	$280,000
Variable landscaping costs (including materials and labour), which vary with the number of hours worked ($45 per hour × 4,000 hours)	180,000
Variable marketing costs (5% of revenue)	14,000
Total variable costs	194,000
Contribution margin	$ 86,000
Contribution margin per hour of equipment time from Hudson Corporation ($86,000 ÷ 4,000 hours)	$21.50 per hour

To maximize operating income, Rainier should allocate as much of its capacity to customers who generate the most contribution margin per unit of the constraining resource (equipment). That is, Rainier should first allocate equipment capacity to existing customers ($26 per hour) and only the balance to Hudson Corporation ($21.50 per hour). Rainier maximizes total contribution margin by allocating 9,000 hours of equipment capacity to existing customers yielding contribution margin of $234,000 ($26 per hour × 9,000 hours) and only the balance 1,000 hours to Hudson Corporation yielding contribution margin of $21,500 ($21.50 per hour × 1,000 hours) for a total contribution margin of $255,500 ($234,000 + $21,500).

Pricing Decisions: Profitability and Cost Management

Allen Creative/Steve Allen/Alamy Stock Photo

▶ Learning Objectives

1. Discuss the three major influences on pricing decisions.

2. Understand how companies make short-run pricing decisions.

3. Understand how companies make long-run pricing decisions.

4. Price products using the target-costing approach.

5. Price products using the cost-plus approach.

6. Use life-cycle budgeting and costing when making pricing decisions.

▶ CPA Competencies

This chapter covers material outlined in **Section 3: Management Accounting** of the CPA Competency Map. The Learning Objectives in this chapter have been aligned with the CPA Competency Map to ensure the best coverage possible.

3.3.1 Evaluates cost classifications and costing methods for management of ongoing operations

3.3.2 Evaluates and applies cost management techniques appropriate for specific costing decisions

3.4.1 Evaluates sources and drivers of revenue growth

Extreme Pricing and Cost Management at IKEA

IKEA is a global furniture retailing industry phenomenon. Known for products named after Swedish towns, modern design, flat packaging, and do-it-yourself instructions, IKEA has grown into the world's largest furniture retailer with 343 stores worldwide. The company has a strong Canadian presence, continuing its expansion in Canada with a new store in Halifax, NS.

IKEA's success is a combination of successful strategies around local markets in which they operate and effective approaches to pricing and cost management. When IKEA selects a site for a store, primary characteristics include the size and density of the population and its disposable income, brand awareness, and ease of access to media. Considerations such as having a developed transportation infrastructure (e.g., a port) also play a role. When IKEA decides to create a new product, product developers survey competitors to determine how much they charge for similar items and then select a target price that is 30% to 50% lower than competitors' prices. With a product and price established, IKEA determines the materials to be used and selects one of its 1,800 suppliers to manufacture the item through a competitive-bidding process. It also identifies cost efficiencies throughout design and production. All IKEA products are shipped unassembled in flat packages, because shipping costs are at least six times higher than shipping assembled product. IKEA applies the same cost management techniques to existing products. For example, one of IKEA's best-selling products, the Lack bedside table, has retailed for the same low price since 1981 despite increases in raw materials prices and wage rates. Since hitting store shelves, more than 100 technical development projects have been performed on the Lack table to reduce product and

Sources: IKEA.com. 2016. IKEA Canada announces full size store in Halifax (January 22) (http://www.ikea.com/ca/en/about_ikea/newsitem/2016_ikea_canada_halifax); L. Margonelli. 2002. How IKEA designs its sexy price tags, *Business 2.0* (October); D. Terdiman. 2008. Anatomy of an IKEA product, CNET News.com, April 19 (http://news.cnet.com/8301-13772_3-9923315-52.html); and A. Ringstrom. 2013. IKEA Founder to Leave Board, *The New York Times* (June 5); IKEA Annual Report, 2015.

distribution costs and maintain profitability. As founder Ingvar Kamprad once summarized, "Waste of resources is a mortal sin at IKEA. Expensive solutions are a sign of mediocrity, and an idea without a price tag is never acceptable."

Like IKEA, managers at many companies, such as Microsoft, Unilever, and Walmart, are strategic in their pricing decisions. This chapter describes how managers evaluate demand at different prices and manage customers and costs across the value chain and over a product's life cycle to achieve profitability.

This chapter describes how managers integrate relevant information about consumer demand at different prices to manage costs, influence supply, and earn a predicted profit. Managers make pricing decisions about the products and services their companies deliver in a highly competitive environment. There is no universal principle of relevant cost selection for product pricing when different customers demand different value propositions from different products.

Major Influences on Pricing

▶ **LO 1**

Discuss the three major influences on pricing decisions.

Three pricing strategies are discussed in this chapter:

1. **Target pricing**, where the price is based on what customers are willing to pay.
2. **Cost-plus pricing**, where a flat rate target profit percentage is added to the full product cost.
3. **Life-cycle pricing** (cradle to grave), which includes the environmental costs of production, reclamation, recycling, and reuse of materials.

Customers, costs, and competitors all influence which of the above three strategies is most appropriate. Pricing decisions also depend on the time horizon—relevant information in the short run will differ from relevant information for the long-run pricing decision. Some factors can be controlled by managers of a company, while others, such as the nature of the competition, are uncontrollable. Three major influences on pricing decisions are as follows:

■ *Customers* Customers influence price through their effect on the demand for a product or service, based on factors such as the features of a product and its quality. Companies must always examine pricing decisions through the eyes of their customers and then manage costs to earn a profit.

■ *Competitors* No business operates in a vacuum. Companies must always be aware of the actions of their competitors. At one extreme, alternative or substitute products of competitors hurt demand and force a company to lower prices. At the other extreme, a company without a competitor is free to set higher prices. When there are competitors, companies try to learn about competitors' technologies, plant capacities, and operating strategies to estimate competitors' costs—valuable information when setting prices. Because competition spans international borders, fluctuations in exchange rates between different countries' currencies affect costs and pricing decisions. For example, if the yen weakens against the US dollar, Japanese products become cheaper for American consumers and, consequently, more competitive in US markets.

■ *Costs* Costs influence prices because they affect supply. The lower the cost of producing a product, the greater the quantity of product the company is willing to supply. Generally, as companies increase supply, the cost of producing an additional unit initially declines but eventually increases. Companies supply products as long as the revenue from selling additional units exceeds the cost of producing them. Managers who understand the cost of producing products set prices that make the products attractive to customers while maximizing operating income.

Corporations weigh the importance of the influence of customers, competitors, and costs differently. Companies selling commodity products such as steel, wheat, and rice have many competitors, each offering identical products or substitute products. The customers in the market set the price, but cost data can help sellers decide on the output levels that best meet a company's particular profit objective. In less competitive markets where products can be distinguished or differentiated by their desirable features (e.g., luxury automobiles), the pricing decision depends on three factors:

1. How much customers value and will pay for the attributes of the product.
2. The costs of producing, selling, distributing, and after-sale service of a product.
3. The pricing strategies of any competitors.

Managers of a company who know about its rival's technology, plant capacity, and operating policies can estimate a rival's costs, which is valuable information in setting competitive prices. For multinational corporations with excess production capacity, there are opportunities to sell the same product at different prices in different countries.

Costing and Pricing for the Short Run

▶ **LO 2**

Understand how companies make short-run pricing decisions.

Short-run pricing decisions typically have a time horizon of less than a year and include decisions such as (a) pricing a *one-time-only special order* with no long-run implications and (b) adjusting product mix and output volume in a competitive market. By contrast, long-run pricing decisions have a time horizon of a year or longer and include pricing a product in a market where there is some leeway in setting price.

Consider a short-run pricing decision facing the management team at Astel Computers. Astel manufactures two brands of personal computers (PCs): Deskpoint, Astel's top-of-the-line product; and Provalue, a less-powerful alternative. Datatech Corporation has asked Astel to bid on supplying 5,000 Provalue computers over the last three months of 2018. After this three-month period, Datatech is unlikely to place any future sales orders with Astel. Datatech will sell Provalue computers under its own brand name in regions and markets where Astel does not sell Provalue. Whether Astel accepts or rejects this order will not affect Astel's revenues—neither the units sold nor the selling price—from existing sales channels.

Relevant Costs for Short-Run Pricing Decisions

Before Astel can bid on Datatech's offer, Astel's managers must estimate how much it will cost to supply the 5,000 computers. Astel's managers must include all direct and indirect costs throughout the value chain that will change in total by accepting the one-time-only special order from Datatech. Astel's managers outline the relevant costs as follows:

Direct materials ($460 per computer × 5,000 computers)	$2,300,000
Direct manufacturing labour ($64 per computer × 5,000 computers)	320,000
Fixed costs of additional capacity to manufacture Provalue	250,000
Total costs	$2,870,000*

*No additional costs will be required for R&D, design, marketing, distribution, or customer service.

The relevant cost per computer is $574 (= $2,870,000 ÷ 5,000). Therefore, any selling price above $574 will improve Astel's profitability in the short run. What price should Astel's managers bid for the 5,000-computer order?

Strategic and Other Factors in Short-Run Pricing

Based on its market intelligence, Astel believes that competing bids will be between $600 and $625 per computer, so Astel makes a bid of $610 per computer. If it wins this bid, operating income will increase by $180,000 (relevant revenues, $610 × 5,000 = $3,050,000 minus relevant costs, $2,870,000). In light of the extra capacity and strong competition, management's strategy is to bid as high above $574 as possible while remaining lower than competitors' bids.

What if Astel were the only supplier and Datatech could undercut Astel's selling price in Astel's current markets? The relevant cost of the bidding decision would then include the contribution margin lost on sales to existing customers. What if there were many parties eager to bid and win the Datatech contract? In this case, the contribution margin lost on sales to existing customers would be irrelevant to the decision because the existing business would be undercut by Datatech regardless of whether Astel wins the contract.

In contrast to the Astel case, in some short-run situations, a company may experience strong demand for its products or have limited capacity. In these circumstances, a company will strategically increase prices in the short run to as much as the market will bear. This results in high short-run prices in the case of new products or new models of older products, such as microprocessors, computer chips, cell phones, and software.

Effect of Time Horizon on Short-Run Pricing Decisions

Two key factors affect short-run pricing:

1. *Many costs are irrelevant in short-run pricing decisions.* In the Astel example, most of Astel's costs in R&D, design, manufacturing, marketing, distribution, and customer service are irrelevant for the short-run pricing decision, because these costs will not change whether Astel wins or does not win the Datatech business. These costs will change in the long run and therefore will be relevant.

2. *Short-run pricing is opportunistic.* Prices are decreased when demand is weak and competition is strong and increased when demand is strong and competition is weak. As we will see, long-run prices need to be set to earn a reasonable return on investment.

Costing and Pricing for the Long Run

▶ **LO 3**

Understand how companies make long-run pricing decisions.

Long-run pricing is a strategic decision designed to build long-run relationships with customers based on stable and predictable prices. A stable price reduces the need for continuous monitoring of prices, improves planning, and builds long-run buyer–seller relationships. But to charge a stable price and earn the target long-run return, a company must, over the long run, know and manage its costs of supplying products to customers. Accordingly, relevant costs for long-run pricing decisions include *all* future fixed and variable costs.

Calculating Product Costs for Long-Run Pricing Decisions

In the Astel example, the company has no beginning or ending inventory of Provalue and manufactures and sells 150,000 units during the year. Astel uses activity-based costing (ABC) to calculate the manufacturing cost of Provalue. Astel has three direct manufacturing costs (direct materials, direct manufacturing labour, and direct machining costs), and three manufacturing overhead cost pools (ordering and receiving components, testing and inspection of final products, and rework [correcting and fixing errors and defects]) in its accounting system. Astel treats machining costs as a direct cost of Provalue because Provalue is manufactured on machines that only make Provalue.[1]

Astel uses a long-run time horizon to price Provalue. Over this horizon, Astel's managers observe the following:

- Direct materials costs vary with number of units of Provalue produced.
- Direct manufacturing labour costs vary with number of direct manufacturing labour-hours used.

---

[1] Astel makes two types of PCs: Deskpoint and Provalue. If Deskpoint and Provalue had shared the same machines, Astel would have allocated machining costs on the basis of the budgeted machine-hours used to manufacture the two products and would have treated these costs as fixed overhead costs.

Exhibit 12-1 Provalue Manufacturing Costs, 2018

	A	B	C	D	E	F	G	H
1			**Manufacturing Cost Information**					
2			**to Produce 150,000 Units of Provalue**					
3	**Cost Category**	**Cost Driver**	**Details of Cost Driver Quantities**				**Total Quantity of Cost Driver**	**Cost per Unit of Cost Driver**
4	(1)	(2)	(3)		(4)		(5) = (3) × (4)	(6)
5	**Direct Manufacturing Costs**							
6	Direct materials	No. of kits	1	kit per unit	150,000	units	150,000	$460
7	Direct manufacturing labour (DML)	DML hours	3.2	DML hours per unit	150,000	units	480,000	$ 20
8	Direct machining (fixed)	Machine-hours					300,000	$ 38
9	**Manufacturing Overhead Costs**							
10	Ordering and receiving	No. of orders	50	orders per component	450	components	22,500	$ 80
11	Testing and inspection	Testing-hours	30	testing-hours per unit	150,000	units	4,500,000	$ 2
12	Rework				8%	defect rate		
13		Rework-hours	2.5	rework-hours per defective unit	12,000[a]	defective units	30,000	$ 40
14								
15	[a]8% defect rate × 150,000 units = 12,000 defective units							

- Direct machining costs are fixed costs of leasing 300,000 machine-hours of capacity over multiple years. These costs do not vary with the number of machine-hours used each year. Each unit of Provalue requires 2 machine-hours. In 2018, Astel uses the entire machining capacity to manufacture Provalue (2 machine-hours per unit × 150,000 units = 300,000 machine-hours).

- Ordering and receiving, testing and inspection, and rework costs vary with the quantity of their respective cost drivers. For example, ordering and receiving costs vary with the number of orders. In the long run, staff members responsible for placing orders can be reassigned or laid off if fewer orders need to be placed, or increased if more orders need to be processed.

Exhibit 12-1 summarizes manufacturing cost information to produce 150,000 units of Provalue in 2018.

Exhibit 12-2 indicates that the total cost of manufacturing Provalue in 2018 is $102 million, and the manufacturing cost per unit is $680. Manufacturing is just one business function in the value chain, however. To set long-run prices, Astel's managers must calculate the *full cost* of producing and selling Provalue.

For each non-manufacturing business function, Astel's managers trace direct costs to products and allocate indirect costs using cost pools and cost drivers that measure cause-and-effect relationships (supporting calculations not shown). Exhibit 12-3 summarizes Provalue's 2018 operating income and shows that Astel earned $15 million from Provalue, or $100 per unit sold in 2018.

Companies operating in *competitive* markets (for example, commodities such as steel, oil, and natural gas) use the market-based approach. The items produced or services

Exhibit 12-2 Manufacturing Costs of Provalue for 2018 Using Activity-Based Costing

	A	B	C
		Total Manufacturing	
1			
2		Costs for	Manufacturing
3		150,000 Units	Cost per Unit
4		(1)	(2) = (1) ÷ 150,000
5	Direct manufacturing costs		
6	Direct material costs		
7	(150,000 kits × $460 per kit)	$ 69,000,000	$460
8	Direct manufacturing labour costs		
9	(480,000 DML-hours × $20 per hour)	9,600,000	64
10	Direct machining costs		
11	(300,000 machine-hours × $38 per machine-hour)	11,400,000	76
12	Direct manufacturing costs	90,000,000	600
13			
14	Manufacturing overhead costs		
15	Ordering and receiving costs		
16	(22,500 orders × $80 per order)	1,800,000	12
17	Testing and inspection costs		
18	(4,500,000 testing-hours × $2 per hour)	9,000,000	60
19	Rework costs		
20	(30,000 rework-hours × $40 per hour)	1,200,000	8
21	Manufacturing overhead cost	12,000,000	80
22	Total manufacturing costs	$102,000,000	$680

Exhibit 12-3 Product Profitability of Provalue for 2018 Using Value-Chain Activity-Based Costing

	A	B	C
1		Total Amounts	
2		for 150,000 Units	Per Unit
3		(1)	(2) = (1) ÷ 150,000
4	Revenues	$150,000,000	$1,000
5	Costs of goods sold[a] (from Exhibit 12-2)	102,000,000	680
6	Operating costs[b]		
7	R&D costs	5,400,000	36
8	Design cost of product and process	6,000,000	40
9	Marketing costs	15,000,000	100
10	Distribution costs	3,600,000	24
11	Customer-service costs	3,000,000	20
12	Operating costs	33,000,000	220
13	Full cost of the product	135,000,000	900
14	Operating income	$ 15,000,000	$ 100
15			
16	[a]Cost of goods sold = Total manufacturing costs because there is no beginning or ending		
17	inventory of Provalue in 2018		
18	[b]Numbers for operating cost line-items are assumed without supporting calculations		

provided by one company are very similar to items produced or services provided by others. Companies in these markets must accept the prices set by the market. Companies operating in *less competitive* markets offer products or services that differ from each other (for example, automobiles, computers, management consulting, and legal services) can use either the market-based or cost-based approach as the starting point for pricing decisions.

It is common for an organization to look first at costs because cost information is more easily available and then consider customers or competitors (the cost-based approach). Others start by considering customers and competitors and then look at costs (the market-based approach). Both approaches consider customers, competitors, and costs; only their starting points differ. Management must always keep market forces in mind, regardless of which pricing approach they use. For example, building contractors often bid on a cost-plus basis but then reduce their prices during negotiations to respond to other lower-cost bids.

Companies operating in markets that are *not competitive* favour cost-based approaches because these companies do not need to respond or react to competitors' prices. The margin they add to costs to determine price depends on the value customers place on the product or service.

Target Costing for Target Pricing

Market-based pricing starts with a **target price**—the estimated price for a product or service that potential customers are willing to pay. This estimate is based on an understanding of customers' perceived value for a product or service and how competitors will price competing products or services. This understanding of customers and competitors is becoming increasingly important for three reasons:

► **LO 4**

Price products using the target-costing approach.

1. Competition from lower-cost producers is continually restraining prices.
2. Products are on the market for shorter periods of time, leaving less time and opportunity to recover from pricing mistakes, loss of market share, and loss of profitability.
3. Customers are becoming more knowledgeable and incessantly demanding products of higher and higher quality at lower and lower prices.

Understanding Customers' Perceived Value

A company's sales and marketing organization, through close contact and interaction with customers, identifies customer needs and perceptions of product value. Companies such as Samsung also conduct market research on features that customers want and the prices they are willing to pay for those features for products such as the Galaxy brand phones and tablets.

Competitor Analysis

To gauge how competitors might react to a prospective price, a company must understand competitors' technologies, products or services, costs, and financial conditions. In general, the more distinctive its product or service, the higher the price a company can charge. Where do companies like Ford Motor Company or PPG Industries obtain information about their competitors? Usually from former customers, suppliers, and employees of competitors. Another source of information is *reverse engineering*—that is, disassembling and analyzing competitors' products to determine product designs and materials and to become acquainted with the technologies competitors use. At no time should a company resort to illegal or unethical means to obtain information about competitors. For example, a company should never pay off a competitor's current employees or pose as a supplier or customer in order to obtain competitor information.

Sustainability in Action | **H&M Uses Target Pricing to Bring Fast Fashion to Stores Worldwide**

Doug Houghton/Alamy Stock Photo

H&M is the worldwide leader in fast fashion, bringing trendy, affordable clothes from the runway to stores in a matter of weeks. Famous for offering Alexander Wang–designed dresses for $4.95 and trench coats for $20, the Swedish-based company is now the world's second-largest clothing retailer, with more than 3,900 stores across 61 countries and $25.3 billion in 2015 sales. How did this happen? Aggressive target pricing, coupled with "cost-consciousness" across the company.

When H&M decides to produce an item, its 160 in-house designers set out to strike the right balance between fashion, quality, and price. Concept teams of designers, buyers, pattern makers, and a controller work together to set a target price. H&M outsources to suppliers throughout Europe and Asia to manufacture the item. High-volume items such as basics and children's wear are ordered far in advance to ensure volume-based cost efficiencies. Trendy items in small quantities are produced at shorter notice. Once produced, the items are shipped to H&M's logistics centres for distribution to stores. H&M stores carry no backup stocks. Stores are replenished directly from the logistic centres, allowing stores to be restocked quickly with only the best-selling products.

H&M has incorporated sustainability into its target pricing and cost management practices. Around 90% of H&M's products are transported from suppliers to distribution centres via sea or rail to avoid fossil fuel-intensive air and road shipping. Additionally, certified organic cotton and environmentally-conscious materials, such as organic hemp and recycled wool, make up 14% of the company's total material use.

Sources: A. Hoffman et al., "H&M's Global Supply Chain Management Sustainability: Factories and Fast Fashion," University of Michigan Erb Institute No. 1-429-373 (Ann Arbor, MI: University of Michigan, 2014); "Sales development in 2015," H&M AB press release (Stockholm, Sweden, December 15, 2015, http://about.hm.com/en/news/newsroom/news.html/en/financial-reports/2015/12/2065879.html); H&M AB, "From Idea to Store," http://about.hm.com/en/About/Facts-About-HM/Idea-to-Store; C. Lu. 2014. Behind H&M's fashion forward retail inventory control, *TradeGecko* blog, August 12 (https://www.tradegecko.com/blog/hm-retail-inventory-control).

Implementing Target Pricing and Target Costing

There are five steps in developing target prices and target costs. We illustrate these steps using the Provalue example.

Step 1: Develop a product that satisfies the needs of potential customers. Customer requirements and competitors' products dictate the product features and design modifications for Provalue for 2019. Astel's market research indicates that customers do not value Provalue's extra features, such as special audio features and designs that accommodate upgrades to make the PC run faster. They want Astel to redesign Provalue into a no-frills but reliable PC and to sell it at a much lower price.

Step 2: Choose a target price. Astel expects its competitors to lower the prices of PCs that compete with Provalue to $850. Astel's management wants to respond aggressively, reducing Provalue's price by 20%, from $1,000 to $800 per unit. At this lower price, Astel's marketing manager forecasts an increase in annual sales from 150,000 to 200,000 units.

Step 3: Derive a target cost per unit by subtracting target operating income per unit from the target price. Target cost per unit is really just that—a target—something the company must commit to achieve. To attain the target return on the capital invested in the business, Astel's management needs to earn 10% target operating income on target revenues. (**Target operating income per unit** is the operating income that a company aims to earn per unit of a product or service sold. **Target cost per unit** is the estimated long-run cost per unit of a product or service that enables the company to achieve its target operating income per unit when selling at the target price.)

Note	
Total target revenues	= $800 per unit × 200,000 units = $160,000,000
Total target operating income	= 10% × $160,000,000 = $16,000,000
Target operating income per unit	= $16,000,000 ÷ 200,000 units = $80 per unit
Target cost per unit = Target price − Target operating income per unit	= $800 per unit − $80 per unit = $720 per unit
Total current full costs of Provalue	= $135,000,000 (from Exhibit 12-3)
Current full cost per unit of Provalue	= $135,000,000 ÷ 150,000 units = $900 per unit

Step 4: Perform cost analysis. This step analyzes the specific aspects of a product or service to target for cost reduction. Astel's managers focus on the following elements of Provalue:

- The functions performed by, and the current costs, of different component parts.
- The importance that customers place on different product features. For example, Provalue's customers value reliability more than video quality.
- The relationship and tradeoffs across product features and component parts. For example, choosing a simpler motherboard enhances reliability but is unable to support the top-of-the-line video card.

Step 5: Perform value engineering to achieve target cost. This systematic evaluation of all aspects of the value chain focuses on reducing costs and achieving a quality level that satisfies customers.

Value-Analysis and Cross-Functional Teams

Usually a value-analysis team consists of top management experts in marketing, product design and engineering, process improvement, supply-chain management,

 12.1 TRY IT! ⊕

Gonzalo Inc. is a small distributor of mechanical pencils. Gonzalo identifies its three major activities and cost pools as ordering, receiving and storage, and shipping, and it reports the following details for 2016:

Activity	Cost Driver	Quantity of Cost Driver	Cost per Unit of Cost Driver
1. Placing and paying for orders of pencil packs	Number of orders	500	$100 per order
2. Receiving and storage	Loads moved	4,000	$60 per load
3. Shipping of pencil packs to retailers	Number of shipments	1,500	$80 per shipment

For 2016, Gonzalo buys 250,000 pencil packs at an average cost of $6 per pack and sells them to retailers at an average price of $8 per pack. Assume Gonzalo has no fixed costs and no inventories. For 2017, retailers are demanding a 5% discount off the 2016 price. Gonzalo's suppliers are only willing to give a 4% discount. Gonzalo expects to sell the same quantity of pencil packs in 2017 as it did in 2016.

Required

If all other costs and cost-driver information remain the same, by how much must Gonzalo reduce its total cost and cost per unit if it is to earn the same target operating income in 2017 as it earned in 2016 (and thereby earn its required rate of return on investment)?

distribution, customer service, and management accounting. The team evaluates the impact of design innovations and modifications on all business functions of the value chain. They choose modifications that have the greatest value to their customers relative to the costs required to provide those features. Here are some of the team's ideas for Astel:

- Use a simpler, more reliable motherboard without complex features.
- Design Provalue so that various parts snap-fit together rather than solder together to decrease direct manufacturing labour-hours and the related costs.
- Simplify the Provalue design and use fewer components to decrease ordering and receiving costs and also decrease testing and inspection costs.
- Design Provalue to be lighter and smaller to reduce distribution and packaging costs.
- Design Provalue to reduce repair costs at customer sites to lower customer-service costs.

Key concepts in value analysis are cost incurrence and locked-in costs. **Cost incurrence** arises when a resource is sacrificed or consumed. Financial reporting systems recognize and record costs only when costs are incurred, and this transactions logic assures reliability. Astel's costing system, for example, recognizes the direct materials costs of Provalue as each unit of Provalue is assembled and sold. But Provalue's direct materials costs per unit are determined much earlier when designers finalize the components that will go into Provalue. Direct materials costs per unit of Provalue are locked in (or designed in) at the product design stage. **Locked-in costs** (or **designed-in costs**) are those costs that have not yet been incurred but that will be incurred in the future on the basis of decisions that have already been made.

Locked-in costs become unavoidable. For example, rework costs incurred during manufacturing could be locked in by a faulty design. Similarly, in the software industry, costs of producing software are often locked in at the design and analysis stage. Costly and difficult-to-fix errors that appear during coding and testing are frequently locked in by bad designs.

It is important to note that costs are not always locked in at the design stage. In some industries (such as bulk chemical manufacturing, legal services, and consulting) costs are locked in and incurred at the same time. If costs are not locked in early, cost reduction can be achieved right up to the time when costs are incurred. In such cases, costs are lowered through improved operating efficiency and productivity (for example, reducing the time it takes to do a task) rather than better design.

Management accountants use their understanding of the technical and business aspects of the entire value chain to quickly estimate cost savings and to explain the cost implications of alternative design choices to the team. These cost estimates are based on elements required by the new design or operating process.

Having finished the value analysis, Astel's management team feels it has two alternatives: respond less aggressively to its competitors or replace Provalue with a newly designed computer that has fewer complex features and is therefore less costly to make. Astel decides to go with the second alternative.

Exhibit 12-4 illustrates how the locked-in cost curve and the cost-incurrence curve might appear in the case of Provalue. (The numbers underlying the graph are assumed.) The bottom curve plots the cumulative costs per unit incurred in different business functions. The top curve plots the cumulative costs locked in. Both curves deal with the same total cumulative costs per unit. The graph emphasizes the wide divergence between the time when costs are locked in and the time when those costs are incurred. In our example, once the product and processes are designed, nearly 87% (say, $780 ÷ $900) of the unit costs of Provalue are locked in when only about 8% (say, $76 ÷ $900) of the unit costs are actually incurred. For example, at the end of the design stage, costs such as direct materials, direct manufacturing labour, direct machining, and many manufacturing, marketing, distribution, and customer-service overheads are all locked in. To reduce total costs, Astel must act to modify the design before costs get locked in.

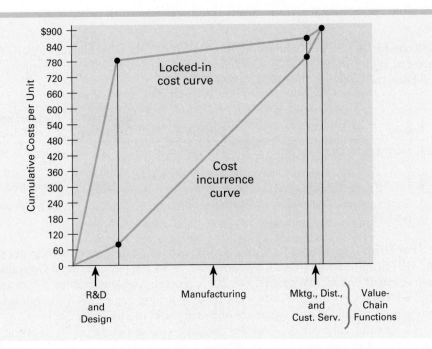

In the Provalue example, direct materials, direct manufacturing labour, and machining costs are value-added costs; ordering and testing costs fall in the grey area (customers perceive some portion of but not all of these costs as necessary for adding value); and rework costs are non-value-added costs. Astel's goal is to reduce and if possible eliminate non-value-added costs such as ordering, quality control, and rework costs by reducing the defect rate.

Reducing costs requires reducing unit input costs, which may be achieved by good negotiation or changing suppliers or quantity of the input consumed. Other factors such as appropriate training, production scheduling, and maintenance also contribute to reduced direct labour costs. The variable direct and indirect costs throughout the value chain are interdependent. For example, replacing the motherboard with a simpler, less expensive component will reduce direct materials costs per unit but may require a more complex assembly that will increase variable manufacturing labour costs. This is an example of how one outcome, driven externally by customer preference, affects two other outcomes driven internally by the consumption of labour in a more complex process.

Value engineering is a systematic evaluation of all aspects of the value chain. The purpose is to reduce costs but retain both product attributes and quality the customer desires and will pay for. Both value engineering and target costing have some undesirable effects if these processes are mismanaged:

■ Decreased morale if employees fail to attain performance targets.

■ A poorly designed product as the cross-functional team compromises on the various customer attributes.

■ A protracted development cycle causing a missed market opportunity.

■ Conflict among business functions, as the goal is to remove non-value-added costs wherever they arise, but the burden of cost reduction will be unequal.

Strong employee participation in the new project and realistic expectations regarding the difficulties of manufacturing of new products using new processes will encourage employees. Retaining focus on the customer's priorities among the attributes will reduce the problem of compromises within the pricing team. Disciplined progress toward the goal of a timely introduction of a new product will reduce the problem of paralysis by analysis, in which managers decide to wait and wait for more information, with the danger that the opportunity to actually remedy problems can disappear faster than relevant information can appear.

⊕ **TRY IT!** **12.2**

Gonzalo Inc. is a small distributor of mechanical pencils. Gonzalo identifies its three major activities and cost pools as ordering, receiving and storage, and shipping, and it reports the following details for 2016:

Activity	Cost Driver	Quantity of Cost Driver	Cost per Unit of Cost Driver
1. Placing and paying for orders of pencil packs	Number of orders	500	$100 per order
2. Receiving and storage	Loads moved	4,000	$60 per load
3. Shipping of pencil packs to retailers	Number of shipments	1,500	$80 per shipment

For 2016, Gonzalo buys 250,000 pencil packs at an average cost of $6 per pack and sells them to retailers at an average price of $8 per pack. Assume Gonzalo has no fixed costs and no inventories. For 2017, retailers are demanding a 5% discount off the 2016 price. Gonzalo's suppliers are only willing to give a 4% discount. Gonzalo expects to sell the same quantity of pencil packs in 2017 as it did in 2016.

Using value engineering, Gonzalo decides to make changes in its ordering and receiving-and-storing practices. By placing long-run orders with its key suppliers, Gonzalo expects to reduce the number of orders to 400 and the cost per order to $75 per order. By redesigning the layout of the warehouse and reconfiguring the crates in which the pencil packs are moved, Gonzalo expects to reduce the number of loads moved to 3,500 and the cost per load moved to $50.

Required

Will Gonzalo achieve its target operating income of $90,000 and its target operating income per unit of $0.36 per pencil pack in 2017? Show your calculations.

Cost-Plus Pricing

► **LO 5**

Price products using the cost-plus approach.

In the previous section, Astel used an external market-based approach in its long-run pricing decisions. One alternative strategy has an internal focus to determine a cost-based price. This is the cost-plus pricing strategy. Managers can turn to numerous pricing formulas based on cost. The starting point is relevant information about costs, not relevant information about attributes and price. The general formula for setting a price adds a markup to the cost base:

Cost base	$ X
Markup component	Y
Prospective selling price	$X + Y

Consider a cost-based pricing formula that Astel could use for the redesigned Provalue. Assume that Astel's engineers have successfully redesigned the Provalue—the Provalue II—and that Astel uses a 12% markup on the full product cost per unit in developing the prospective selling price.

Cost base (full product cost per unit, from Exhibit 12-5)	$720.00
Markup component (12% × $720)	86.40
Prospective selling price	$806.40

The markup was obtained by first estimating the **target rate of return on investment (ROI)**. The target ROI is the target operating income that an organization must earn divided by **invested capital**. Invested capital to redesign the Provalue is defined as total assets (long-term or fixed assets plus current assets), in total $96 million. Companies usually

Concepts in Action

Operating Income Analysis Reveals Strategic Challenges at Best Buy

Best Buy is a leader of electronics retailing initially based on a successful strategy of aggressive "big box" store expansion. From 2008 to 2012, Best Buy added 532 stores across the United States, increasing capacity by 49% and growing annual revenue by $10.6 billion.

However, by 2013, an analysis of the company's operating income revealed strategic challenges. Revenue had declined 105 from the year before to $45 billion, and net EBITDA was $1.98 billion (down approximately 35% from the previous year). While the company pursued strategic differentiation through customer experience and add-on services, many consumers were drawn to the low prices of Amazon and other online retailers. To respond to this challenge, Best Buy ramped

up spending on advertising and its e-commerce capabilities, and adopted an aggressive price and cost management strategy. This approached was effective; by fiscal year-end 2015, Best Buy had been able to manage the economic environment of falling prices (revenues were $40 billion, down 11% from 2013, and down 20% from 2012). However, despite this lessor revenue base, the efficient management of resources and the ability to more effectively get products into customers' hands net EBITDA rose to $2.1 billion, up 10% from 2013 and on target to return to 2012 levels.

Sources: Best Buy, Inc. Annual Report 2015.

specify their target ROI. Suppose Astel's (pretax) target ROI is 18%. The target operating income that Astel must earn from Provalue II can then be calculated as follows:

Invested capital	$96,000,000
Target rate of return on investment	18%
Total target operating income (18% × $96,000,000)	$17,280,000
Target operating income per unit of Provalue II ($17,280,000 ÷ 200,000 units)	$ 86.40

The calculation indicates that Astel needs to earn a target operating income of $86.40 on each unit of Provalue II. The $86.40 expressed as a percentage of the full product cost per unit of $720 equals 12% ($86.40 ÷ $720).

The ROI cost-plus pricing method is often used when prices are regulated. In Canada, examples include milk,

Note Do not confuse the 18% target ROI with the 12% operating income markup percentage. The 18% target rate of return on investment expresses Astel's expected operating income as a percentage of investment. The 12% markup expresses operating income per unit as a percentage *of the full product cost* per unit.

hydroelectric power, and telecommunications. Government regulators examine the full product costs of the supplier and negotiate a target ROI. The new price is established on this cost-plus basis for a specified time period with periodic, regulated increases. Suppliers may not charge consumers a rate higher than the contracted rate.

Alternative Cost-Plus Methods

We illustrate these alternatives using the Astel example. Exhibit 12-5 separates the cost per unit for each value-chain business function into its variable and fixed components (without providing details of the calculations). The following table illustrates some alternative cost bases and markup percentages:

Cost Base	Estimated Cost per Unit of Provalue II (1)	Markup Percentage (2)	Markup Component for Provalue II (3) = (1) × (2)	Forecast Selling-Price For Provalue II (4) = (1) + (3)
Variable manufacturing cost	$483.00	65%	$313.95	$796.95
Variable product cost	547.00	45	246.15	793.15
Manufacturing cost (COGS)	540.00	50	270.00	810.00
Absorption cost	720.00	12	86.40	806.40

Exhibit 12-5 Estimated Cost Structure of Provalue II for 2019

Business Function	Estimated Variable Cost per Unit	Estimated Fixed Cost per Unit[a]	Business-Function Cost per Unit
R&D	$ 8	$ 12	$ 20
Design of product/process	10	20	30
Manufacturing	483	57	540
Marketing	25	65	90
Distribution	13	9	22
Customer service	8	10	18
Total	$547	$173	$720
	↑	↑	↑
	Per-unit variable cost of the product	Per-unit fixed cost of the product	Per-unit full cost of the product

[a]Based on budgeted annual capacity of 200,000 units.

The different cost bases and markup percentages that are used in the table give prospective selling prices that are relatively close to one another. In practice, a company will choose a cost base that it regards as reliable, and a markup percentage on the basis of its experience in pricing products and to recover its costs and earn a desired return on investment. For example, a company may choose a full product cost base if it is unsure about variable and fixed cost distinctions.

The markup percentages in the table vary a great deal, from a high of 65% on variable manufacturing costs to a low of 12% on absorption costs. To set a price high enough to cover both total period costs and cost of goods sold (COGS) requires that a higher percentage of variable costs be added. The markup percentage on full product costs is much lower because this cost already includes all period costs and COGS. The markup percentage on variable costs is higher as fixed costs are reflected in variable costs, but still must be covered in the final price. The desired markup percentage may need to be adjusted depending on the competitiveness of the product market. Markups and profit margins tend to be lower in more competitive markets.

Surveys indicate that most managers use full product costing and include unitized fixed costs from COGS and period costs per unit as well as variable costs per unit from both COGS and period costs in the cost base when making their pricing decisions. The advantages cited for including unitized fixed costs for pricing decisions include the following:

■ *Full product cost recovery.* For long-run pricing decisions, absorption costing informs managers of the bare minimum costs they need to recover to continue in business rather than shut down. Using variable costs as a base does not give managers this information. There is then a temptation to engage in excessive long-run price cutting as long as prices give a positive contribution margin. Long-run price cutting, however, may result in long-run revenue being less than long-run full product costs, resulting in the company going out of business.

■ *Price stability.* Managers believe that a full product cost policy for pricing promotes price stability, because it limits the ability of managers to cut prices. Managers prefer price stability because it facilitates planning.

■ *Simplicity.* A full product cost policy does not require a detailed analysis of cost behaviour patterns to separate costs into fixed and variable components for each product. Calculating variable costs for each product is expensive and prone to errors. For these reasons, many managers believe that full product cost pricing meets the cost–benefit test.

Including unit fixed costs when pricing is not without its problems. Allocating fixed costs to products can be somewhat arbitrary. Calculating fixed cost per unit requires an estimate of expected future sales quantities. If actual sales fall short of this estimate, the actual full product cost per unit could exceed the selling price per unit.

Cost-Plus Pricing Contrasted Against Target Pricing

The selling prices calculated under cost-plus pricing are prospective or forecast prices. For example, suppose Astel's initial product design results in a $750 cost for the redesigned Provalue II. Assuming a 12% markup, Astel sets a prospective price of $840 [=$750 + (12% × $750)]. Since the computer market is extremely competitive, customer and competitor reactions to this price may force Astel to reduce the markup percentage and reduce the price to $800. Alternatively, Astel may redesign Provalue again to reduce cost to $720 per unit, as in our example, and achieve a markup of $80 per unit. The eventual design and cost-plus price balance the conflicting tensions among costs, markup, and customer reactions.

The target-pricing approach eliminates the need to go back and forth among cost-plus prospective prices, customer reactions, and design and cost modifications. Instead, the target-pricing approach first determines product characteristics and price on the basis of customer preferences and competitor responses. Professional service firms also consider a multiyear client perspective when choosing prices. Chartered accountants, for example, may charge a client a low price initially and higher prices later, a practice referred to as "penetration pricing."

Refined cost driver identification and cost information play an important role in both cost-plus pricing and target costing and pricing. Service companies such as home repair, automobile repair, and architectural firms often use a cost-plus pricing method called the time and materials method. Individual jobs are priced based on materials and labour time. The price charged for materials equals the cost of materials plus a markup. The price charged for labour represents the cost of labour, allocated overhead, and a markup. Therefore, the price charged for each cost item includes its own markup.

Fixed and Variable Cost Coverage

Assume that the full cost of a product is $50, of which $20 is fixed and avoidable if the product is discontinued and $30 is a variable cost per unit. Also assume that the fixed cost rate is based on sales of 1,000 units. Avoidable costs are those that will not be incurred if a company stops the activity that causes the cost. At a unit sales price of $35. there will still be a positive contribution margin of $5 per unit ($35 unit sales price − $30 unit variable cost = $5 unit contribution margin). The total contribution margin will be $5,000 if the sales volume is 1,000 units ($5 unit contribution margin × 1,000 units = $5,000 total contribution margin). The remaining avoidable costs are incurred and total $20,000 ($20 avoidable per unit × 1,000 units = $20,000) because the product has not been discontinued. There will be an unrecovered cost of $15,000 using full product costing ($20,000 − $5,000 = $15,000). This company will have to sell a minimum of 4,000 units to cover the fixed cost of $20,000 ($5 unit contribution margin × 4,000 units sold = $20,000) and be profitable in the long-run.

Life-Cycle Costing and Relevant Qualitative Factors in Pricing

The meaning of a **product life cycle** is viewed differently by different stakeholders. From the internal view of the company, the product life cycle spans the time from initial R&D to the time at which support to customers is withdrawn. If the company is purchasing an asset, then its life cycle begins with the acquisition through maintenance to disposal. **Life-cycle budgeting** requires that managers estimate full product costs across the entire value chain of business functions. This view is evolving, however, to include recycling, reuse, and reclamation costs of disposing of obsolete finished products.

Customer life-cycle costing focuses on the external customer's costs to acquire, maintain, and dispose of the product or services.

Life-cycle costing tracks and accumulates the actual costs attributable to each product from start to finish. The terms *cradle-to-grave costing* and *womb-to-tomb costing* convey the sense of fully capturing all costs associated with the product. Clearly, in this long-term approach the past, current, and expected cost, behaviour for a specific product will change as technology and other factors affect the product's usefulness. Throughout its life cycle, improvements need to be made to the product simply to keep costs and price

▶ **LO 6**

Use life-cycle budgeting and costing when making pricing decisions.

within a competitive range. This is particularly important if the company has focused on a strategy of agility and customization to differentiate the product.

Life-cycle budgeted costs can provide important information for pricing decisions. For some products, the development period is relatively long and many costs are incurred before manufacturing. Consider Insight, Inc., a computer software company developing a new accounting package, General Ledger. Assume the following budgeted amounts for General Ledger over a six-year product life cycle:

Years 1 and 2	
R&D costs	$240,000
Design costs	160,000

Years 3 to 6		
	Total Fixed Costs	Variable Unit Costs
Production costs	$100,000	$25
Marketing costs	70,000	24
Distribution costs	50,000	16
Customer-service costs	80,000	30

Insight's strategic goals require the company to generate revenue to cover costs in all six business functions. A product life-cycle budget highlights the importance of setting prices and budgeting revenue to recover costs in all the value-chain business functions rather than costs in only some of the functions (such as production). The life-cycle budget also indicates the costs to be incurred over the life of the product. Exhibit 12-6 presents the life-cycle budget for General Ledger. The sensitivity analysis reports on three sets of assumptions about selling price and sales quantity combinations. These alternatives reflect the general economic principle that, in a competitive market, as the price of a commodity increases the demand or quantity sold decreases.

Exhibit 12-6 Budgeted Life-Cycle Revenue and Costs for the General Ledger Software Package[a]

	Alternative Selling Price/ Sales Quantity Combinations		
	1	2	3
Selling price per package	$ 400	$ 480	$ 600
Sales quantity in units	5,000	4,000	2,500
Life-cycle revenues ($400 × 5,000; $480 × 4,000; $600 × 2,500)	$2,000,000	$1,920,000	$1,500,000
Life-cycle costs:			
R&D costs	240,000	240,000	240,000
Design costs of product/process	160,000	160,000	160,000
Production costs:			
$100,000 + ($25 × 5,000); $100,000 + ($25 × 4,000); $100,000 + ($25 × 2,500)	225,000	200,000	162,500
Marketing costs:			
$70,000 + ($24 × 5,000); $70,000 + ($24 × 4,000); $70,000 + ($24 × 2,500)	190,000	166,000	130,000
Distribution costs:			
$50,000 + ($16 × 5,000); $50,000 + ($16 × 4,000); $50,000 + ($16 × 2,500)	130,000	114,000	90,000
Customer-service costs:			
$80,000 + ($30 × 5,000); $80,000 + ($30 × 4,000); $80,000 + ($30 × 2,500)	230,000	200,000	155,000
Total life cycle costs	1,175,000	1,080,000	937,500
Life-cycle operating income	$ 825,000	$ 840,000	$ 562,500

[a]This exhibit does not take into consideration the time value of money when computing life-cycle revenues or life-cycle costs.

A sensitivity analysis of three combinations of both prospective selling price per package and demand are shown in Exhibit 12-6. For example, R&D and product design costs constitute more than 30% of total costs for each of the three combinations of selling price and predicted sales quantity. At 5,000 units in sales, the costs in years 1 and 2 are 34% of total life cycle costs ($400,000 ÷ $1,175,000 = 0.34 or 34%), and at 2,500 units in sales, this increases to 42.7%.

Developing Life-Cycle Reports

Most accounting systems emphasize reporting on a calendar basis—monthly, quarterly, and annually. In contrast, product life-cycle reporting does not have this calendar-based focus. Consider the life spans of four Insight products shown below, where each product spans more than one calendar year:

	Year 1	Year 2	Year 3	Year 4	Year 5	Year 6
General Ledger package						
Law package						
Payroll package						
Engineering package						

Developing life-cycle reports for each product requires tracking costs and revenue on a product-by-product basis over several calendar periods. For example, the R&D costs included in a product life-cycle cost report are often incurred in different calendar years. When R&D costs are tracked over the entire life cycle, the total magnitude of these costs for each individual product can be computed and analyzed.

A product life-cycle reporting format offers at least three important benefits:

1. The full set of revenue and costs associated with each product becomes visible. Manufacturing costs are highly visible in most accounting systems, but the costs associated with upstream areas (for example, R&D) and downstream areas (for example, customer service) are frequently less visible on a product-by-product basis.

2. Differences in when the bulk of product costs are incurred are highlighted on a product-by-product basis. For example, the largest contribution to the total cost of Product A is design, and the largest contribution to the total cost of Product B is customer service.

3. Interrelationships among business functions are highlighted. For example, companies that cut back their R&D and product design costs may experience major increases in customer-service costs in subsequent years. Those costs arise because products fail to meet promised quality-performance levels.

Life-cycle costs further reinforce the importance of locked-in costs, target costing, and value engineering in pricing and cost management. For products with long life cycles, a very small fraction of the total life-cycle costs is actually incurred at the time when costs are locked in. But locked-in costs will determine how actual costs will be incurred later. For example, poor product design can lock in very costly rework and quality-control activities at the production stage.

Conducting Fair Business and Pricing Decisions

The *Competition Act* in Canada is the legislation enacted to "protect the specific public interest in free competition."[2] Each of the pricing practices discussed below is a criminal offence

---

[2] See *Weidman v. Schragge* (1912), 20 C.C.C. 177 at 147 where the Supreme Court of Canada first considered the rationale to regulate trades and industries.

for contravening the Act.[3] For example, under section 50(1) of the Act, companies cannot engage in **price discrimination** between two customers with the intent to reduce or obstruct competition among customers. There are four key elements of the price discrimination laws:

1. They apply to manufacturers, not service providers.

2. Different pricing to different customers is not an offence unless there is intent to obstruct competition among the customers.

3. Different pricing to different customers on the basis of different costs of production is not an offence.

4. Illegality hinges on the intent to obstruct or destroy competition when a manufacturer engages in price discrimination.[4]

Consider the prices airlines charged for a round-trip flight from Toronto to Beijing during the 2008 Summer Olympics. Booking prior to the opening day of the Olympics, a direct Air Canada one-week return flight in economy-class was listed on Expedia.ca as $1,772. Booking the opening day of the Olympics and returning one week later cost $2,809, and during the last week of the Olympics the flight would have cost you $2,799. Can the price differences be explained by the difference in the cost to Air Canada of these round-trip flights? No, it cost the airline the same amount of money to transport the passenger from Toronto to Beijing and back regardless of whether the passenger flew August 1, 8, or 18, 2008.

In the airline example, the demand for airline tickets comes from two main sources: business travellers and pleasure travellers. Business travellers generally travel to their destinations and return home within the same week. These aspects make business travellers' demand for air travel relatively insensitive to prices. The insensitivity of demand to price changes is called demand inelasticity. Airlines can charge business travellers higher fares because the higher fares have little effect on demand and earn higher operating income for the airlines.

It is also illegal under section 50(1)(c) of the Act to engage in **predatory pricing**, which occurs when manufacturers sell products at lower than cost with the intent to reduce competition. It is difficult to say with any certainty what the legal thresholds are because few cases have been tried.[5] To clarify matters, the Director of Investigation and Research at Consumer and Corporate Affairs Canada released the *Predatory Pricing and Enforcement Guidelines* (the *Guidelines*) on May 21, 1992. In these Guidelines the Director defined predatory pricing as a "situation where a dominant firm charges low prices over a long enough period of time so as to drive a competitor from the market or deter others from entering and raises prices to recoup its losses."[6] According to these Guidelines, the predator must account for more than 35% of the market and be able to sustain a pricing increase for more than two years after the period of low pricing for its actions to be considered predatory pricing.

In determining whether pricing is "unreasonably low," the courts draw a distinction between pricing a product above average variable cost and below. It is likely that as long as a product is sold above average variable cost (even when the price is below average total product cost), and it cannot be established that the accused would have made a greater total contribution to overhead by raising prices, a court will not find the price "unreasonably low." In economic terms, the court is aware of the effect of price inelasticity of demand.

There are only limited circumstances when pricing below average variable costs will be tolerated by the courts. In *R. v. Hoffmann-La Roche Ltd.*[7] the Ontario Court of Appeal affirmed the trial judge's decision of an "unreasonably low" price. In this trial, it was held that the pharmaceutical firm that chose to combat new competition in the hospital market by giving away Valium was "selling" its products at an unreasonably low price. The

---

[3] Although a "practice" is not specifically defined, more than one sale is likely required to establish this as a corporate practice. The practice of price discrimination does not actually have to result in any observable adverse effect on competition for companies to contravene the Act.

[4] This section is provided with assistance from Russell Hoffman, LLB., MBA.

[5] Although the Supreme Court of Canada has never considered a case under this section, *R. v. Hoffmann-La Roche Ltd.* (1980), 28 O.R. (2d) 164, was affirmed by the Ontario Court of Appeal in 1981, 125 D.L.R. (3d) 607 (C.A.).

[6] Director of Investigation and Research, "Executive Summary," *Predatory Pricing Enforcement Guidelines* (Ottawa: Consumer and Corporate Affairs Canada, 1992).

[7] See n. 5 *supra*.

year-long Valium giveaways were in response to a new competitor's price reductions of 25% to 50% of the Hoffmann-La Roche Ltd. price.

The Court stated that in determining the reasonableness or unreasonableness of a particular price, it will "take into account all the economic costs, which include the direct production costs as well as any potential future savings or benefits."[8] This includes looking at benefits that derive to related markets or future markets. The trial judge continued, stating that the Court should look into four general considerations to determine if the price was unreasonably low:

1. The magnitude of difference between the average variable cost and the sales price is important, and the greater the unrecovered average variable cost, the greater the probability the price will be seen as unreasonable.

2. The greater the duration of sales at less than average variable cost, the more likely the price will be declared unreasonable.

3. The circumstances of the situation need to be taken into account, because a price cut to defend against a competitor may be justifiable.

4. Any accrual of external or long-term benefits to the seller arising from selling at a price below average variable cost is considered, and the higher the estimated long-term benefit, the more likely the price will be seen as unreasonable.[9]

This highlights documenting the decision process as it can provide a defence against the accusation that the intent of the price cut was to obstruct or destroy competition.

Dumping is closely related to predatory pricing and occurs when a non-Canadian company:

1. sells goods in Canada at a price below the market value in the home country;

2. receives a government subsidy; and,

3. the action materially injures or threatens to materially injure an industry in Canada.

If dumping is proven under section 42(1)(c)(ii) of the *Special Import Measures Act* (SIMA), the Canadian International Trade Tribunal has the power to impose a countervailing duty, sometimes called a tax or tariff, on the goods to prevent the recurrence of the material injury. Cases related to dumping have occurred in the agricultural and automotive industries and more recently in the softwood lumber industry.[10]

Collusive pricing is also a violation of the *Competition Act*. Collusive pricing occurs when companies in an industry conspire in their pricing and output decisions to achieve a price above the competitive price. Section 45 of the Act makes it a criminal offence to conspire, agree, or combine with another person to prevent, lessen, or unduly restrain competition. Collusive pricing violates the Act because an agreement on pricing and output levels prevents competition among the companies in an industry. Recently, suspicions have been voiced regarding alleged collusive pricing among retail gasoline companies, but no one has filed a lawsuit.

In addition to price discrimination, pricing decisions also consider other noncost considerations such as capacity constraints. **Peak-load pricing** is the practice of charging a higher price for the same product or service when demand approaches physical capacity limits. That is, the prices charged during busy periods (when loads on the system are high) are greater than the prices charged when slack or excess capacity is available. Peak-load pricing can be found in the telephone, telecommunication, hotel, car rental, and electric utility industries. The following are the daily rental rates charged by Discount Car Rental for compact cars rented at its Yonge and Bloor Toronto location at 8:00 a.m. and returned by noon the next day:

Weekdays (Monday–Thursday)	$39 per day
Weekends (Friday–Sunday)	$32 per day

Discount's incremental costs of renting a car are the same whether the car is rented on a weekday or a weekend. So what explains the difference in prices? We offer two separate

---

[8] *R. v. Hoffmann-La Roche Ltd.*, p. 199.

[9] *R. v. Hoffmann-La Roche Ltd.*, pp. 200–204.

[10] See *American Farm Bureau Federation v. Canadian Import Tribunal* (1990), 74 D.L.R. (4th) 449.

but related explanations. One explanation is that there is a greater demand for cars during weekdays because of business activity. Faced with capacity limits, Discount raises rental rates to levels that the market will bear. A second explanation is that the rental rates are a form of price discrimination. During weekdays, the demand for cars comes largely from business travellers who need to rent cars to conduct their business and who are relatively insensitive to prices. Charging higher rental rates during weekdays is profitable because it has little effect on demand. In contrast, the demand for weekend rentals comes largely from nonbusiness or pleasure travellers who are more price-sensitive. Lower rates stimulate demand from these individuals and increase Discount's operating income. Under either explanation, the pricing decision is not driven by cost considerations.

Managing Environmental and Sustainability Costs

Environmental sustainability and *life-cycle costing* touch on the increasing social concern about what constitutes the end of a product's life cycle.

Managing environmental costs is another example of life-cycle costing and value engineering. Environmental laws like the US Clean Air Act and the US Superfund Amendment and Reauthorization Act have introduced tougher environmental standards, imposed stringent cleanup requirements, and introduced severe penalties for polluting the air and contaminating subsurface soil and groundwater. In some countries, such as Sweden, the government levies a carbon tax, a fee or surcharge on carbon-based fuels and other sources of pollution. A carbon tax puts a monetary price on greenhouse gas emissions. Other regions such as the European Union use a cap-and-trade system, where the government puts a limit or cap on the overall level of carbon pollution and conducts a market auction for pollution quotas. Companies pay for the right to pollute and can then either sell (or buy) these rights to (or from) other companies if they pollute less (or more) than their quotas.

Environmental costs that are incurred over several years of the product's life cycle are often locked in at the product- and process-design stage. To avoid environmental liabilities, reduce carbon taxes, or reduce the cost of buying pollution quotas, managers in industries such as oil refining, chemical processing, and automobile manufacturing value engineer and design products and processes to prevent and reduce pollution over the product's life cycle. For example, laptop computer manufacturers like Hewlett-Packard and Apple have introduced recycling programs to ensure that chemicals from nickel-cadmium batteries do not leak hazardous chemicals into the soil. The carbon tax has spurred innovation in the design of energy-efficient products and clean energy solutions, such as solar and wind power.[11]

What is the effect of sustainability investments on overall financial performance in subsequent periods? A new organization, the Sustainability Accounting Standards Board (SASB), has begun defining standards for environmental, social, and governance (ESG) performance for different industries. The relevant (or material) ESG standards vary across industries based on financial impact and interest of user groups. For example, the relevant ESG standards in the oil and gas industry include greenhouse gas emissions and water and wastewater management, while the relevant ESG standards in the technology and communications industries include life-cycle impacts of products and services and energy management. When measured over multiple periods, companies that have higher relevant ESG ratings have higher future profitability and financial performance, perhaps because of customer loyalty and satisfaction, employee engagement, or brand and reputation.

Manufacturers can reclaim the 1.36 billion kilograms of high-value plastic used in casings for laptops, smartphones, and HDTV converters by recycling the casings back into a high-value plastic supply chain. In one reporting year, TELUS recycled 17,024 tonnes of materials of which 6% arose from electronic products. At a disposal cost of $70 per tonne, TELUS estimated it avoided approximately $2 million in landfill fees. Used, recycled, and surplus equipment produced $4.8 million revenue that would not have otherwise been realized.[12]

---

[11] Although Sweden has one of the highest carbon taxes at $140 per tonne of carbon pollution, its economy has continued to grow strongly since the tax was introduced in 1991.

[12] TELUS, *Leading the Telecommunications Sector in CSR* at http://www.nrcan-rncan.gc.ca/sd-dd/pubs/csr-rse/pdf/cas/telus_e.pdf.

The enactment of strict environmental laws for resource extraction and refining industries has introduced tougher environmental standards and increased the penalties and fines for polluting the air and contaminating subsurface soil and groundwater. The goal is to include ecological responsibility as a *value-added cost* engineered in at the design phase.[13] It is difficult to forget watching millions of litres of oil gushing into the Gulf of Mexico from a BP offshore deep water well in 2010. Environmental costs are often locked in at the product and process design phase, but some arise from negligence, bad decision-making, or simply bad luck.

One example is gold. Over 90% of gold production is direct material for the jewellery industry. Reclamation of even very small amounts of gold from obsolete finished products carries with it a far smaller potential environmental cost than refining. The demand for gold, however, exceeds the supply available from recycled gold. As little as approximately 16.5 grams of gold per tonne of ore can be profitable at September 2017's price of $1,280 per ounce.

Some companies adopt proactive strategies to remedy the environmental effects of production. Others adopt a reactive strategy of minimal compliance with health, safety, and environmental regulations. Still others ignore the problems they create until confronted with them in court. Their legal costs, including fines, comprise part of the life-cycle costing of the risks of environmental degradation, being caught, and being successfully prosecuted. For yet other companies, excellent environmental practices can generate revenue through the sale of emissions credits on global exchanges in Chicago and Montreal. Those unable or unwilling to adopt benchmark practices can incorporate the purchase of emissions credits into their environmental sustainability strategy.[14]

---

[13] E. Westkämper, J. Niemann, and A. Dauensteiner, "Economic and Ecological Aspects in Product Life Cycle Evaluation," *Proceedings of the Institute of Mechanical Engineers* 215. B (2001): 673–681.

[14] Much of this section was based on information from S. Fields, "Tarnishing the Earth: Gold Mining's Dirty Secret," *Environmental Health Perspectives* 109.10 (2001): A474–481 at http://www.jstor.org/sici?sici=0091-6765(200110)109:10%3CA474: TTEGMD%3E2.0.CO;2-4; I.M. Kiss, "The Bond Is Dead," *Central Europe Review* 2.7 (2000) at http://www.ce-review. org/00/7/kiss7.html; S.G. Vick, "Failure of the Omai Tailings Dam," *Geotechnical News*, September (1996): 34–40 at http://www.infomine.com/publications/docs/Vick1996.pdf; N. Langerman, "Cyanide Spill," *Chemical Health and Safety*, 7.3 May–June (2000): 41–42 at http://www.sciencedirect.com/science?_ob=HomePageURL&_method=userHomePage&_ btn=Y&_acct=C000050221&_version=1&_urlVersion=0&_userid=10&md5=6b8f8a0bb11c4ebe676f09e6d7da52c8; and L. Loopnarine, "Wounding Guyana: Gold Mining and Environmental Degradation," *Revista Europea de Estudios Latinoamericanos y del Caribe*, 73 October (2002): 83–90 at http://www.cedla.uva.nl/60_publications/PDF_files_ publications/73RevistaEuropea/73Loopnarine.pdf.

Pulling it all Together—Problem for Self-Study

(Try to solve this problem before examining the solution that follows.)

Problem

Reconsider the Astel Computer example. Astel's marketing manager realizes that a further reduction in prices is necessary to sell 200,000 units of the redesigned Provalue. To maintain a target profitability of $16 million, or $80 per unit, Astel will need to reduce costs of Provalue by $6 million, or $30 per unit. Astel targets a reduction of $4 million, or $20 per unit, in manufacturing costs, and $2 million, or $10 per unit, in marketing, distribution, and customer-service costs. The cross-functional team assigned to this task proposes the following changes to manufacture a different version of Provalue, called Provalue II:

1. Reduce direct materials and ordering costs by purchasing subassembled components rather than individual components.
2. Reengineer ordering and receiving. Reduce ordering and receiving costs per order.
3. Reduce testing time and the labour and power required per hour of testing.
4. Develop new rework procedures to reduce rework costs per hour.

No changes are proposed in direct manufacturing labour costs per unit and in total machining costs. Exhibit 12-7 summarizes the revised cost-driver quantities and the revised cost per unit of each cost driver.

Exhibit 12-7 Provalue II Manufacturing Cost Data

PROVALUE MANUFACTURING COST DATA

Output Level: 200,000

	Cost Driver (1)	Quantity (2)	Unit of Measure	Quantity (3)	Unit of Measure	Total Quantity of Cost Driver (4)=(2)×(3)	Input Cost Driver Rate
Direct Costs							
Direct materials	No. of kits	1.0	kit per output unit	200,000	output units	200,000	$385
Direct manufacturing labour (DMLH)	DMLH	2.65	DMLH per output unit	200,000	output units	530,000	$ 20
Direct machining-fixed (DMH)	DMH hours	1.5	DMH per output unit	200,000	output units	300,000	$ 38
Overhead Costs							
Ordering and receiving	No. of orders	50.0	orders per component	425	components	21,250	$ 80
Testing and inspection (TH)	Testing hours	15.0	TH per output unit	200,000	output units	3,000,000	$ 2
Rework (RMH)	Rework hours	2.5	RMH per defective unit*	13,000	defective units	32,500	$ 40
Defect rate				6.5%	defect rate		

*6.5% defect rate × 200,000 output units = 13,000 defective units.

PROVALUE II MANUFACTURING COST DATA

Output Level: 200,000

	Cost Driver (1)	Quantity (2)	Unit of Measure	Quantity (3)	Unit of Measure	Total Quantity of Cost Driver (4)=(2)×(3)	Input Cost Driver Rate
Direct Costs							
Direct materials	No. of kits	1.0	kit per output unit	200,000	output units	200,000	$ 375
Direct manufacturing labour (DMLH)	DMLH	2.65	DMLH per output unit	200,000	output units	530,000	$ 20
Direct machining-fixed (DMH)	DMH hours	1.5	DMH per output unit	200,000	output units	300,000	$ 38
Overhead Costs							
Ordering and receiving	No. of orders	50.0	orders per component	400	components	20,000	$ 60
Testing and inspection (TH)	Testing hours	14.0	TH per output unit	200,000	output units	2,800,000	$1.70
Rework (RMH)	Rework hours	2.5	RMH per defective unit*	13,000	defective units	32,500	$ 32
Defect rate				6.5%	defect rate		

1. What long-term factors are relevant in target pricing?

2. Will the proposed changes achieve the target cost of $20 per output unit and for a total cost reduction of $4 million to manufacture Provalue III? Show your calculations.

3. As a producer of electronics, what environmental factors should Astel consider?

4. Explain the importance of locked-in costs.

5. If Astel decided upon life-cycle pricing, justify a management choice between the value-chain focus and the customer life-cycle focus.

❶ ◀ Required
❷
❸
❹
❺

Solution

1. Astel must consider fixed as well as variable costs and use absorption costing to ensure the target price will cover all costs of production including period costs.

2. Exhibit 12-8 presents the manufacturing costs for Provalue III based on the proposed changes. Manufacturing costs will decline from $108 million, or $540 per unit, to $104 million, or $522 per unit, and will achieve the target reduction of $4 million, or $20 per unit.

3. Electronics producers can recycle the high-value plastic covers and other components for recycling. Recycling is more environmentally sustainable than new plastics production, can avoid disposal costs, and can improve revenue. These recycling costs and benefits can be locked in at the design stage of Provalue II. In addition, Astel could consider price discrimination if it has a global customer base. The ability to pay could determine that a lower price would be charged to customers in developing countries than in developed. Astel views its product life cycle from an internal perspective without considering the needs of groups other than its customers. In fact, if Astel were producing in Europe, the life cycle of Provalue II would extend to disposal of the obsolete product.

4. Locked-in costs become unavoidable. Astel is planning to invest $96 million in the redesign and wants to avoid a situation where rework costs incurred during manufacturing are locked in by a faulty design. Design decisions influence direct materials costs through the choices of printed circuit boards and add-on features used in Provalue. Better designs also reduce both product failures in the plant and the time it takes to rework defective products. Ease in assembly decreases direct manufacturing labour costs. Fewer components reduces ordering and materials-handling costs and decreases the time required for testing and inspection. Finally, designing Provalue to reduce the need for repairs as well as the time it takes to service and repair Provalue at customer sites reduces customer service costs.

5. This is a highly competitive environment with a short product life cycle. These two factors justify a customer life-cycle pricing policy wherein the customer sets the price target. Astel must then determine the full product costs such that the operating income meets a targeted percentage of full product costs.

Exhibit 12-8 Target Manufacturing Costs of Provalue III for 2019 Based on Proposed Changes

Output Level: 200,000 Units	Provalue III	
	Total Manufacturing Costs (1)	Manufacturing Cost per Output Unit (2) = (1) ÷ 200,000
Direct manufacturing costs:		
Direct materials costs	$ 75,000,000	$375.00
Direct manufacturing labour costs	10,600,000	53.00
Direct machining costs (fixed)	11,400,000	38.00
Direct manufacturing costs	97,000,000	433.00
Manufacturing overhead costs:		
Ordering and receiving	1,200,000	60.00
Testing and inspection	4,760,000	23.80
Rework	1,040,000	5.20
Manufacturing overhead costs	7,000,000	89.00
Total manufacturing costs	$104,000,000	$522.00

Decision Points

The following question-and-answer format summarizes the chapter's learning objectives. Each point presents a key question, and the guidelines are the answer to that question.

Learning Objectives	Guidelines
1. What are the three major influences on pricing decisions?	Customers, competitors, and costs influence prices through their effects on demand and supply—customers and competitors affect demand, and costs affect supply. These factors will differ depending on the time horizon of the pricing decision. The time horizon affects the set of costs that are relevant to assure profitability.
2. How do companies implement either target pricing or cost-plus pricing to achieve short-term profitability?	Target pricing is one response to a decision with a long-term time horizon. Target price is driven by the customer in the marketplace. It is the estimated price that potential customers are willing to pay for a product or service. Given the GM%, the target cost is [(1 − GM%) × Target price]. In comparison, the cost-plus approach to pricing adds a markup component to a cost base, usually the full product cost, as the starting point for pricing decisions. Prices are then modified on the basis of customers' reactions and competitors' responses. Therefore, the size of the "plus" is determined by the market.
3. How do companies make long-run pricing decisions?	Managers and accountants should consider all future variable and fixed costs and earn a target return on investment.
4. How do companies price products using target costing?	Target cost per unit is the estimated long-run cost of a product or service that, when sold, enables the company to achieve target operating income per unit. The challenge for the organization is to make the necessary cost improvements through value analysis and value-engineering methods to achieve the target cost.
5. How do companies implement target and cost-plus pricing for long-term profitability?	Over the long term, the target ROI determines the target of operating income divided by total product costs required. In a competitive environment, the customer determines the target price. Given the target price, the target ROI will determine the full product target cost that is divided into the operating income.
6. How do companies choose between customer life-cycle and life-cycle pricing?	In a highly competitive environment, companies must respond to the value-in-use for which customers will pay throughout their acquisition, maintenance, and disposal of the product. Failure to do so will impair profit because customers can purchase a substitute. This is customer life-cycle costing. The corporation must then set its target costs to achieve a long-term return on their investment in the product. Life-cycle pricing is an internal focus on ensuring all the corporation's value-chain costs for all business functions, including recycling, reuse, and reclamation of the product on disposal, are included.

Terms to Learn

This chapter and the Glossary at the end of the book contain definitions of the following important terms:

collusive pricing (p. 503)
cost incurrence (p. 494)
cost-plus pricing (p. 486)
customer life-cycle costing (p. 499)
designed-in costs (p. 494)
dumping (p. 503)
invested capital (p. 496)
life-cycle budgeting (p. 499)

life-cycle costing (p. 499)
life-cycle pricing (p. 486)
locked-in costs (p. 494)
peak-load pricing (p. 503)
predatory pricing (p. 502)
price discrimination (p. 502)
product life cycle (p. 499)
target cost per unit (p. 493)

target operating income
 per unit (p. 492)
target price (p. 491)
target pricing (p. 486)
target rate of return on investment
 (ROI) (p. 496)
value engineering (p. 495)

Assignment Material

MyLab Accounting Make the grade with MyLab Accounting: The Short-Answer Questions, Exercises, and Problems marked with a ⊕ can be found on MyLab Accounting. You can practise them as often as you want, and most feature step-by-step guided instructions to help you find the right answer.

Short-Answer Questions

⊕ **12-1** What are the three major influences on pricing decisions?

⊕ **12-2** When might a company price below full cost?

⊕ **12-3** Give two examples of pricing decisions with a short-run focus.

⊕ **12-4** How is ABC useful for pricing decisions?

⊕ **12-5** Describe two alternative approaches to long-run pricing decisions.

⊕ **12-6** What does *product life cycle* mean?

⊕ **12-7** How does collusive pricing differ from predatory pricing?

⊕ **12-8** What is life-cycle budgeting?

⊕ **12-9** "It is not important for a firm to distinguish between cost incurrence and locked-in costs." Do you agree? Explain.

⊕ **12-10** What are three benefits of using a product life-cycle reporting format?

⊕ **12-11** Describe three alternative cost-plus methods.

⊕ **12-12** Give two examples where the difference in the costs of two products or services is much smaller than the difference in their prices.

Exercises

⊕ **12-13 Terminology.** A number of terms are listed below:

target pricing	target cost per unit
value engineering	value analysis
price discrimination	peak-load pricing
life-cycle pricing	customer life-cycle pricing
invested capital	target return on investment

Required

Select the terms from the above list to complete the following sentences.

_____ is a policy well suited to a highly competitive environment where many substitutes are available that may provide customers with the same valuable attributes at lower cost. _____ is set after the price and target margin are determined. This target margin may be in percent or dollars at either the gross or operating margin level.

In a highly competitive environment, _____ refers to the total cost of ownership of a product, including purchase, operating costs, maintenance, and disposal. In comparison, _____ refers to the total cost to the seller of the product from cradle to grave.

The _____ refers in this chapter to total assets. The _____ is the target operating income divided by the invested capital.

_____ is illegal because the manufacturer's intent is to obstruct or destroy competition. In contrast, _____ is the practice of charging the highest rate to provide a service when demand for the service is highest. It is common practice and not illegal.

_____ is the evaluation by a top management team of any innovations and modifications to any business function that customers would value most highly. In comparison, _____ is a process to retain both quality and all attributes that customers value while reducing costs.

LO 1, 5 ▶

🌐 **12-14 Noncost factors.** Examples of prices charged by Phones-R-Us for long-distance telephone calls within Canada at different times of the day and week are as follows:

Peak period (8:00 a.m. to 6:00 p.m., Monday through Friday)	Basic rate
Evenings (6:00 p.m. to 11:00 p.m., Monday through Friday)	35% savings
Nights and weekends	60% savings

Required

Are there differences in incremental or outlay costs per minute for Phones-R-Us for telephone calls made during peak hours compared with telephone calls made at other times of the day?

LO 5 ▶
1. Selling price is $9.36

🌐 **12-15 Cost-plus, target pricing, working backward.** The new CEO of Rusty Manufacturing has asked for information about the operations of the firm from last year. The CEO is given the following information, but with some data missing:

Total sales revenue	?
Number of units produced and sold	500,000 units
Selling price	?
Operating income	$180,000
Total investment in assets	$2,250,000
Variable cost per unit	$4.00
Fixed costs for the year	$2,500,000

Required

1. Find (a) total sales revenue, (b) selling price, (c) rate of return on investment, and (d) markup percentage on full cost for this product.
2. The new CEO has a plan to reduce fixed costs by $225,000 and variable costs by $0.30 per unit while continuing to produce and sell 500,000 units. Using the same markup percentage as in requirement 1, calculate the new selling price.
3. Assume the CEO institutes the changes in requirement 2 including the new selling price. However, the reduction in variable cost has resulted in lower product quality resulting in 5% fewer units being sold compared with before the change. Calculate operating income (loss).
4. What concerns, if any, other than the quality problem described in requirement 3, do you see in implementing the CEO's plan? Explain briefly.

LO 5 ▶
1. Target contribution per room-night, $38

🌐 **12-16 Cost-plus target return on investment pricing.** John Beck is the managing partner of a business that has just finished building a 60-room motel. Beck anticipates that he will rent these rooms for 16,000 nights next year (or 16,000 room-nights). All rooms are similar and will rent for the same price. Beck estimates the following operating costs for next year:

Variable operating costs	$8 per room-night
Fixed costs	
Salaries and wages	$177,000
Maintenance of building and pool	50,000
Other operating and administration costs	141,000
Total fixed costs	$368,000

The capital invested in the motel is $1,000,000. The partnership's target return on investment is 25%. Beck expects demand for rooms to be uniform throughout the year. He plans to price the rooms at full cost plus a markup on full cost to earn the target return on investment.

Required

1. What price should Beck charge for a room-night? What is the markup as a percentage of the full cost of a room-night?

2. Beck's market research indicates that if the price of a room-night determined in requirement 1 is reduced by 10%, the expected number of room-nights Beck could rent would increase by 10%. Should Beck reduce prices by 10%? Show your calculations.

🌐 **12-17 Short-run pricing, capacity constraints.** Manitoba Dairy, maker of specialty cheeses, produces a soft cheese from the milk of Holstein cows raised on a special corn-based diet. One kilogram of soft cheese, which has a contribution margin of $8, requires 4 litres of milk. A well-known gourmet restaurant has asked Manitoba Dairy to produce 2,000 kilograms of a hard cheese from the same milk of Holstein cows. Knowing that the dairy has sufficient unused capacity, Elise Princiotti, owner of Manitoba Dairy, calculates the costs of making one kilogram of the desired hard cheese:

◀ **LO 2**
1. Variable cost per kg,
$15 + 5 + 5 = $25

Milk (10 litres × $1.50 per litre)	$15
Variable direct manufacturing labour	5
Variable manufacturing overhead	5
Fixed manufacturing cost allocated	6
Total manufacturing cost	$31

Required

1. Suppose Manitoba Dairy can acquire all the Holstein milk that it needs. What is the minimum price per kilogram it should charge for the hard cheese?
2. Now suppose that the Holstein milk is in short supply. Every kilogram of hard cheese produced by Manitoba Dairy will reduce the quantity of soft cheese that it can make and sell. What is the minimum price per kilogram it should charge to produce the hard cheese?

🌐 **12-18 Target costs, effect of product-design changes on product costs.** Medical Instruments uses a manufacturing costing system with one direct cost category (direct materials) and three indirect cost categories:

◀ **LO 4**
1. Total manufacturing cost per unit HJ6 in 2017, $1,738

a. Setup, production order, and materials-handling costs that vary with the number of batches.
b. Manufacturing operations costs that vary with machine-hours.
c. Costs of engineering changes that vary with the number of engineering changes made.

In response to competitive pressures at the end of 2017, Medical Instruments used value-engineering techniques to reduce manufacturing costs. Actual information for 2017 and 2018 is

	2017	2018
Setup, production order, and materials-handling costs per batch	$8,000	$7,500
Total manufacturing-operations cost per machine-hour	55	50
Cost per engineering change	12,000	10,000

The management of Medical Instruments wants to evaluate whether value engineering has succeeded in reducing the target manufacturing cost per unit of one of its products, HJ6, by 10%.
Actual results for 2017 and 2018 for HJ6 are

	Actual Results for 2017	Actual Results for 2018
Units of HJ6 produced	3,500	4,000
Direct material cost per unit of HJ6	$1,200	$1,100
Total number of batches required to produce HJ6	70	80
Total machine-hours required to produce HJ6	21,000	22,000
Number of engineering changes made	14	10

Required

1. Calculate the manufacturing cost per unit of HJ6 in 2017.
2. Calculate the manufacturing cost per unit of HJ6 in 2018.
3. Did Medical Instruments achieve the target manufacturing cost per unit for HJ6 in 2018? Explain.
4. Explain how Medical Instruments reduced the manufacturing cost per unit of HJ6 in 2018.

LO 6 ▶

2. Total costs are $1,510,000

⊕ **12-19 Value-added, non-value-added costs.** The Magill Repair Shop repairs and services machine tools. A summary of its costs (by activity) for 2017 is as follows:

a.	Materials and labour for servicing machine tools	$1,100,000
b.	Rework costs	90,000
c.	Expediting costs caused by work delays	65,000
d.	Materials-handling costs	80,000
e.	Materials-procurement and inspection costs	45,000
f.	Preventive maintenance of equipment	55,000
g.	Breakdown maintenance of equipment	75,000

Required

1. Classify each cost as value-added, non-value-added, or in the gray area between.
2. For any cost classified in the gray area, assume 60% is value-added and 40% is non-value-added. How much of the total of all seven costs is value-added and how much is non-value-added?
3. Magill is considering the following changes: (a) introducing quality-improvement programs whose net effect will be to reduce rework and expediting costs by 40% and materials and labour costs for servicing machine tools by 5%; (b) working with suppliers to reduce materials-procurement and inspection costs by 20% and materials-handling costs by 30%; and (c) increasing preventive-maintenance costs by 70% to reduce breakdown-maintenance costs by 50%. Calculate the effect of programs (a), (b), and (c) on value-added costs, non-value-added costs, and total costs. Comment briefly.

LO 6 ▶

1. BEP in units, 714,840

⊕ **12-20 Life-cycle product costing.** Digital Arts Inc. manufactures game systems. Digital Arts has decided to create and market a new system with wireless controls and excellent video graphics. Digital Arts's managers are thinking of calling this system the Yew. Based on past experience they expect the total life cycle of the Yew to be four years, with the design phase taking about a year. They budget the following costs for the Yew:

		Total Fixed Costs over Four Years	Variable Cost per Unit
Year 1	R&D costs	$ 6,590,000	—
	Design costs	1,450,000	—
Years 2–4	Production	19,560,000	$50 per unit
	Marketing and distribution	5,242,000	10 per unit
	Customer service	2,900,000	—

Required

1. Suppose the managers at Digital Arts price the Yew game system at $110 per unit. How many units do they need to sell to break even?
2. The managers at Digital Arts are thinking of two alternative pricing strategies.
   a. Sell the Yew at $110 each from the outset. At this price, they expect to sell 1,500,000 units over its life cycle.
   b. Boost the selling price of the Yew in year 2 when it first comes out to $200 per unit. At this price they expect to sell 100,000 units in year 2. In years 3 and 4 drop the price to $110 per unit. The managers expect to sell 1,200,000 units in years 3 and 4.

   Which pricing strategy would you recommend? Explain.
3. What other factors should Digital Arts consider in choosing its pricing strategy?

LO 4 ▶

1. Per unit operating income is $.18

⊕ **12-21 Target prices, target costs, activity-based costing.** Snappy Tiles is a small distributor of marble tiles. Snappy identifies its three major activities and cost pools as ordering, receiving and storage, and shipping, and it reports the following details for 2016:

Activity	Cost Driver	Quantity of Cost Driver	Cost per Unit of Cost Driver
1. Placing and paying for orders of marble tiles	Number of orders	500	$50 per order
2. Receiving and storage	Loads moved	4,000	$30 per load
3. Shipping of marble tiles to retailers	Number of shipments	1,500	$40 per shipment

For 2016, Snappy buys 250,000 marble tiles at an average cost of $3 per tile and sells them to retailers at an average price of $4 per tile. Assume Snappy has no fixed costs and no inventories.

Required

1. Calculate Snappy's operating income for 2016.
2. For 2017, retailers are demanding a 5% discount off the 2016 price. Snappy's suppliers are only willing to give a 4% discount. Snappy expects to sell the same quantity of marble tiles in 2017 as in 2016. If all other costs and cost-driver information remain the same, calculate Snappy's operating income for 2017.
3. Suppose further that Snappy decides to make changes in its ordering and receiving-and-storing practices. By placing long-run orders with its key suppliers, Snappy expects to reduce the number of orders to 200 and the cost per order to $25 per order. By redesigning the layout of the warehouse and reconfiguring the crates in which the marble tiles are moved, Snappy expects to reduce the number of loads moved to 3,125 and the cost per load moved to $28. Will Snappy achieve its target operating income of $0.30 per tile in 2017? Show your calculations.

🌐 **12-22 Target service costs, value engineering, activity-based costing.** Lagoon is an amusement park that offers family-friendly entertainment and attractions. The park boasts more than 25 acres of fun. The admission price to enter the park, which includes access to all attractions, is $35. To earn the required rate of return on investment, Lagoon's target operating income is 35% of total revenues. Lagoon's managers have identified the major activities that drive the cost of operating the park. The activity cost pools, the cost driver for each activity, and the cost per unit of the cost driver for each pool are:

◄ **LO 1**
1. Operating Profit $685,150

Activity	Description of Activity	Cost Driver	Cost per Unit of Cost Driver
1. Ticket sales and verification	Selling and verifying tickets for entry into the park	Number of tickets sold	$3.35 per ticket sold
2. Operating attractions	Loading, monitoring, off-loading patrons on attraction	Number of runs	$90 per run
3. Litter patrol	Roaming the park and cleaning up waste as necessary	Number of litter patrol hours	$20 per hour

The following information describes the existing operations:

a. The average number of patrons per week is 55,000.
b. The total number of runs across all attractions is 11,340 runs each week.
c. It requires 1,750 hours of litter patrol hours to keep the park clean.

In response to competitive pressures and to continue to attract 55,000 patrons per week, Lagoon has decided to lower ticket prices to $33 per patron. To maintain the same level of profits as before, Lagoon is looking to make the following changes to reduce operating costs:

a. Reduce the cost of selling and verifying tickets by $0.35 per ticket sold.
b. Reduce the total number of runs across all attractions by 1,000 runs by reducing the operating hours of some of the attractions that are not very popular.
c. Increase the number of refuse containers in the park at an additional cost of $250 per week. This will decrease the litter patrol hours by 20%.

The cost per unit of cost driver for all other activities will remain the same.

Required

1. Will Lagoon achieve its target operating income of 35% of revenues at ticket prices of $35 per ticket before any operating changes?
2. After Lagoon reduces ticket prices and makes the changes and improvements described above, will Lagoon achieve its target operating income in dollars calculated in requirement 1? Show your calculations.
3. What challenges might managers at Lagoon encounter in achieving the target cost? How might they overcome these challenges?
4. A new carbon tax of $3 per run is proposed to be levied on the energy consumed to operate the attractions. Will Lagoon achieve its target operating income calculated in requirement 1? If not, by how much will Lagoon have to reduce its costs through value engineering to achieve the target operating income calculated in requirement 1?

LO 2 ▶

3. Operating Income $208,890

🌐 **12-23 Target operating income, value-added costs, service company.** Calvert Associates prepares architectural drawings to conform to local structural-safety codes. Its income statement for 2017 is as follows:

Revenues	$701,250
Salaries of professional staff (7,500 hours × $52 per hour)	390,000
Travel	15,000
Administrative and support costs	171,600
Total costs	576,600
Operating income	$124,650

The percentage of time spent by professional staff on various activities follows:

Making calculations and preparing drawings for clients	77%
Checking calculations and drawings	3
Correcting errors found in drawings (not billed to clients)	8
Making changes in response to client requests (billed to clients)	5
Correcting own errors regarding building codes (not billed to clients)	7
Total	100%

Assume administrative and support costs vary with professional-labour costs. Consider each requirement independently.

Required

1. How much of the total costs in 2017 are value-added, non-value-added, or in the gray area between? Explain your answers briefly. What actions can Calvert take to reduce its costs?
2. What are the consequences of misclassifying a non-value-added cost as a value-added cost? When in doubt, would you classify a cost as a value-added or non-value-added cost? Explain briefly.
3. Suppose Calvert could eliminate all errors so that it did not need to spend any time making corrections and, as a result, could proportionately reduce professional-labour costs. Calculate Calvert's operating income for 2017.
4. Now suppose Calvert could take on as much business as it could complete, but it could not add more professional staff. Assume Calvert could eliminate all errors so that it does not need to spend any time correcting errors. Assume Calvert could use the time saved to increase revenues proportionately. Assume travel costs will remain at $15,000. Calculate Calvert's operating income for 2017.

LO 4 ▶

1. Price per room-night is $50

🌐 **12-24 Cost-plus target return on investment pricing.** Jason Brady is the managing partner of a business that has just finished building a 60-room motel. Brady anticipates that he will rent these rooms for 15,000 nights next year (or 15,000 room-nights). All rooms are similar and will rent for the same price. Brady estimates the following operating costs for next year:

Variable operating costs	$3 per room-night
Fixed costs	
Salaries and wages	$177,000
Maintenance of building and pool	38,000
Other operating and administration costs	190,000
Total fixed costs	$405,000

The capital invested in the motel is $1,500,000. The partnership's target return on investment is 20%. Brady expects demand for rooms to be uniform throughout the year. He plans to price the rooms at full cost plus a markup on full cost to earn the target return on investment.

Required

1. What price should Brady charge for a room-night? What is the markup as a percentage of the full cost of a room-night?
2. Brady's market research indicates that if the price of a room-night determined in requirement 1 is reduced by 10%, the expected number of room-nights Brady could rent would increase by 10%. Should Brady reduce prices by 10%? Show your calculations.

12-25 Cost-plus, target return on investment pricing. Sweet Tastings makes candy bars for vending machines and sells them to vendors in cases of 30 bars. Although Sweet Tastings makes a variety of candy, the cost differences are insignificant, and the cases all sell for the same price.

◀ LO 1, 2
2. Selling price is $12 /case

Sweet Tastings has a total capital investment of $10,000,000. It expects to produce and sell 400,000 cases of candy next year. Sweet Tastings requires a 12% target return on investment.

Expected costs for next year are:

Variable production costs	$3.00 per case
Variable marketing and distribution costs	$2.00 per case
Fixed production costs	$400,000
Fixed marketing and distribution costs	$700,000
Other fixed costs	$500,000

Sweet Tastings prices the cases of candy at full cost plus markup to generate profits equal to the target return on capital.

Required

1. What is the target operating income?
2. What is the selling price Sweet Tastings needs to charge to earn the target operating income? Calculate the markup percentage on full cost.
3. Sweet Tastings is considering increasing its selling price to $13 per case. Assuming production and sales decrease by 10%, calculate Sweet Tastings' return on investment. Is increasing the selling price a good idea?

12-26 Target operating income, value-added costs, service company. Carson Associates prepares architectural drawings to conform to local structural-safety codes. Its statement of comprehensive income for 2018 is

◀ LO 4
1. Total value-added costs, $471,600

Revenue	$680,000
Salaries of professional staff (8,000 hours × $50 per hour)	400,000
Travel	18,000
Administrative and support costs	160,000
Total costs	578,000
Operating income	$102,000

Following is the percentage of time spent by professional staff on various activities:

Making calculations and preparing drawings for clients	75%
Checking calculations and drawings	4
Correcting errors found in drawings (not billed to clients)	7
Making changes in response to client requests (billed to clients)	6
Correcting own errors regarding building codes (not billed to clients)	8
Total	100%

Assume administrative and support costs vary with professional-labour costs.

Required

Consider each requirement independently.

1. How much of the total costs in 2018 are value-added, non-value-added, or in the grey area in between? Explain your answers briefly. What actions can Carson take to reduce its costs?
2. Suppose Carson could eliminate all errors so that it did not need to spend any time making corrections and, as a result, could proportionately reduce professional-labour costs. Calculate Carson's operating income for 2018.
3. Now suppose Carson could take on as much business as it could complete, but it could not add more professional staff. Assume Carson could eliminate all errors so that it does not need to spend any time correcting errors. Assume Carson could use the time saved to increase revenue proportionately. Assume travel costs will remain at $18,000. Calculate Carson's operating income for 2018.

Problems

LO 5 ▶

12-27 Cost-plus, time and materials, ethics. C & S Mechanical sells and services plumbing, heating, and air-conditioning systems. C & S's cost accounting system tracks two cost categories: direct labour and direct materials. C & S uses a time-and-materials pricing system, with direct labour marked up 90% and direct materials marked up 40% to recover indirect costs of support staff, support materials, and shared equipment and tools and to earn a profit.

During a hot summer day, the central air-conditioning in Brooke Lee's home stops working. C & S technician John Anderson arrives at Lee's home and inspects the air conditioner. He considers two options: replace the compressor or repair it. The cost information available to Anderson follows:

	Labour	**Materials**
Repair option	5 hours	$140
Replace option	2 hours	$240
Labour rate	$30 per hour	

Required

1. If Anderson presents Lee with the replace or repair options, what price would he quote for each?
2. If the two options were equally effective for the 3 years that Lee intends to live in the home, which option would she choose?
3. If Anderson's objective is to maximize profits, which option would he recommend to Lee? What would be the ethical course of action?

LO 5 ▶

12-28 Cost-plus, target pricing, working backward. The new CEO of Roile Manufacturing has asked for a variety of information about the operations of the firm from last year. The CEO is given the following information, but with some data missing:

Total sales revenue	?
Number of units produced and sold	500,000 units
Selling price	?
Operating income	$225,000
Total investment in assets	$2,500,000
Variable cost per unit	$2.50
Fixed costs for the year	$3,250,000

Required

1. Find (a) total sales revenue, (b) selling price, (c) rate of return on investment, and (d) markup percentage on full cost for this product.
2. The new CEO has a plan to reduce fixed costs by $250,000 and variable costs by $0.50 per unit. Using the same markup percentage as in requirement 1, calculate the new selling price.
3. Assume the CEO institutes the changes in requirement 2 including the new selling price, expecting to sell more units of product because of the lower price. However, the reduction in variable cost has resulted in lower product quality, leading to 10% fewer units being sold compared to before the change. Calculate operating income (loss).

LO 4 ▶

12-29 Value engineering, target pricing, and target costs. Westerly Cosmetics manufactures and sells a variety of makeup and beauty products. The company has developed its own patented formula for a new anti-aging cream The company president wants to make sure the product is priced competitively because its purchase will also likely increase sales of other products. The company anticipates that it will sell 400,000 units of the product in the first year with the following estimated costs:

Product design and licensing	$1,700,000
Direct materials	4,000,000
Direct manufacturing labour	1,600,000
Variable manufacturing overhead	400,000
Fixed manufacturing overhead	2,500,000
Fixed marketing	3,000,000

Required

1. The company believes that it can successfully sell the product for $45 a bottle. The company's target operating income is 30% of revenue. Calculate the target full cost of producing the 400,000 units. Does the cost estimate meet the company's requirements? Is value engineering needed?
2. A component of the direct materials cost requires the nectar of a specific plant in South America. If the company could eliminate this special ingredient, the materials cost would decrease by 25%. However, this would require design changes of $300,000 to engineer a chemical equivalent of the ingredient. Will this design change allow the product to meet its target cost?
3. The company president does not believe that the formula should be altered for fear it will tarnish the company's brand. She prefers that the company become more efficient in manufacturing the product. If fixed manufacturing costs can be reduced by $250,000 and variable direct manufacturing labour costs are reduced by $1 per unit, will Westerly achieve its target cost?
4. Would you recommend the company follow the proposed solution in requirement 2 or requirement 3?

⊕ 12-30 Relevant-cost approach to pricing decisions. Stardom Inc. cans peaches for sale to food distributors. All costs are classified as either manufacturing or marketing. Stardom prepares monthly budgets. The March 2018 budgeted absorption-costing statement of comprehensive income is as follows:

◄ **LO 1**
1. Normal markup, 85.19%

Revenue (1,000 crates × $100 a crate)	$100,000
Cost of goods sold	60,000
Gross margin	40,000
Marketing costs	30,000
Operating income	$ 10,000

Normal markup percentage: $40,000 ÷ $60,000 = 66.7% of absorption cost

Monthly costs are classified as fixed or variable (with respect to the number of crates produced for manufacturing costs and with respect to the number of crates sold for marketing costs):

	Fixed	Variable
Manufacturing	$20,000	$40,000
Marketing	16,000	14,000

Stardom has the capacity to can 1,500 crates per month. The relevant range in which monthly fixed manufacturing costs will be "fixed" is from 500 to 1,500 crates per month.

Required

1. Calculate the markup percentage based on total variable costs.
2. Assume that a new customer approaches Stardom to buy 200 crates at $55 per crate for cash. The customer does not require any marketing effort. Additional manufacturing costs of $4,000 (for special packaging) will be required. Stardom believes that this is a one-time-only special order because the customer is discontinuing business in six weeks' time. Stardom is reluctant to accept this 200-crate special order because the $55-per-crate price is below the $60-per-crate absorption cost. Do you agree with this reasoning? Explain.
3. Assume that the new customer decides to remain in business. How would this longevity affect your willingness to accept the $55-per-crate offer? Explain.

⊕ 12-31 Cost-plus and market-based pricing. Georgia Temps, a large labour contractor, supplies contract labour to building-construction companies. For 2017, Georgia Temps has budgeted to supply 84,000 hours of contract labour. Its variable costs are $13 per hour, and its fixed costs are $168,000. Roger Mason, the general manager, has proposed a cost-plus approach for pricing labour at full cost plus 20%.

◄ **LO 5**

Required

1. Calculate the price per hour that Georgia Temps should charge based on Mason's proposal.
2. The marketing manager supplies the following information on demand levels at different prices:

Price per Hour	Demand (Hours)
$16	124,000
17	104,000
18	84,000
19	74,000
20	61,000

Georgia Temps can meet any of these demand levels. Fixed costs will remain unchanged for all the demand levels. On the basis of this additional information, calculate the price per hour that Georgia Temps should charge to maximize operating income.

3. Comment on your answers to requirements 1 and 2. Why are they the same or different?

LO 5 ▶
1. Price per hour at full cost plus 20%, $15 × 1.20 = $18 per hour

🌐 **12-32 Cost-plus and market-based pricing.** Time Temps, a large labour contractor, supplies contract labour to building-construction companies. For 2018, Time Temps has budgeted to supply 80,000 hours of contract labour. Its variable costs are $12 per hour, and its fixed costs are $240,000. Roger Mason, the general manager, has proposed a cost-plus approach for pricing labour at full cost plus 20%.

Required

1. Calculate the price per hour that Time Temps should charge based on Mason's proposal.
2. The marketing manager supplies the following information on demand levels at different prices:

Price per Hour	Demand (Hours)
$16	120,000
17	100,000
18	80,000
19	70,000
20	60,000

Time Temps can meet any of these demand levels. Fixed costs will remain unchanged for all the demand levels. On the basis of this additional information, calculate the price per hour that the company should charge to maximize operating income.

3. Comment on your answers to requirements 1 and 2. Why are they the same or different?

LO 3 ▶
1. Net benefit, $128,000

12-33 Pricing of a special order. Fane Industries Ltd. has been approached by a customer who wishes to purchase 50,000 units of its product at $52 per unit. The customer requires delivery within one month. The company has capacity to produce 350,000 units per month and has 5,000 units currently in stock. Sales to Fane's regular customers are forecast at 325,000 units for the upcoming month. The sales manager has indicated that if the company accepts the special order, it would be able to recover 30% of the sales lost to regular customers. Units sold through normal distribution channels have a selling price of $70 per unit, and the gross margin earned on each unit is $24. Selling and administration costs total $16 per unit.

A further analysis determined that the variable manufacturing costs of the regular units are $35 per unit with variable selling costs of $12 per unit. Because of the nature of the special order, the selling costs will be reduced to $8.00 per unit.

Required

1. Should Fane accept the offer from the customer?
2. What is the minimum price Fane should charge for this order?
3. What factors should be considered in pricing special orders?

LO 6 ▶
1. Budgeted life-cycle operating income per desk, $3,970,400

🌐 **12-34 Life-cycle costing.** Fearless Furniture Manufacturing (FFM) has been manufacturing furniture for the home for over 30 years. George Fearless, the owner, has decided he would like to manufacture an executive desk that contains space for not only a laptop dock but also an MP3 player dock. Based on his experience with furniture, he believes the desk will be a popular item for four years, and then will be obsolete because technology will have changed again.

FFM expects the design phase to be very short; maybe four months. There is no R&D cost because the idea came from George, without any real research. Also, fixed production costs will not be high because FFM has excess capacity in the factory. The FFM accountants have developed the following budget for the new executive desk:

		Fixed	Variable
Months 1–4	Design costs	$700,000	—
Months 5–36	Production	9,000	$225 per desk
	Marketing	3,000	—
	Distribution	2,000	20 per desk
Months 37–52	Production	9,000	225 per desk
	Marketing	1,000	—
	Distribution	1,000	22 per desk

The design cost is for the total period of four months. The fixed costs of production, marketing, and distribution are the expected costs per month. Ignore time value of money.

Required

1. Assume FFM expects to make and sell 16,000 units in the first 32 months (months 5–36) of production (500 units per month), and 4,800 units (300 per month) in the last 16 months (months 37–52) of production. If FFM prices the desks at $500 each, how much profit will FFM make in total and on average per desk?

2. Suppose FFM is wrong about the demand for these executive desks, and after the first 36 months it stops making them altogether. It sells 16,000 desks for $400 each with the costs described for months 5–36, and then incurs no additional costs and generates no additional revenue. Will this have been a profitable venture for FFM?

3. Will your answer to requirement 2 change if FFM still must incur the estimated fixed production costs for the whole period through month 52, even if FFM stops making executive desks at the end of 36 months?

🌐 **12-35 Airline pricing, considerations other than cost in pricing.** Snowbound Air is about to introduce a daily round-trip flight from Edmonton to Winnipeg and is determining how it should price its round-trip tickets.

◀ **LO 1, 6**
1. Contribution margin at a price of $500, $420 × 100 passengers = $42,000

The market research group at Snowbound Air segments the market into business and pleasure travellers. It provides the following information on the effects of two different prices on the number of seats expected to be sold and the variable cost per ticket, including the commission paid to travel agents:

Price Charged	Variable Cost per Ticket	Number of Seats Expected to Be Sold	
		Business	Pleasure
$ 500	$ 80	200	100
2,000	180	190	20

Pleasure travellers start their travel during one week, spend at least one weekend at their destination, and return the following week or thereafter. Business travellers usually start and complete their travel within the same work week. They do not stay over weekends.

Assume that round-trip fuel costs are fixed costs of $24,000 and that fixed costs allocated to the round-trip flight for airplane-lease costs, ground services, and flight-crew salaries total $188,000.

Required

1. If you could charge different prices to business travellers and pleasure travellers, would you? Show your computations.
2. Explain the key factor (or factors) for your answer in requirement 1.
3. How might Snowbound Air implement price discrimination? That is, what plan could the airline formulate so that business travellers and pleasure travellers each pay the price desired by the airline?

🌐 **12-36 Ethics and pricing.** Instyle Interior Designs has been requested to prepare a bid to decorate four model homes for a new development. Winning the bid would be a big boost for sales representative Jim Doogan, who works entirely on commission. Sara Groom, the cost accountant for Instyle, prepares the bid based on the following cost information:

◀ **LO 1, 6**
1. Bid amount, $88,000

Direct costs		
Design costs		$ 20,000
Furniture and artwork		70,000
Direct labour		10,000
Delivery and installation		20,000
Overhead costs		
Design software	5,200	
Furniture handling	4,800	
General and administration	8,000	
Total overhead costs		18,000
Full product costs		$138,000

Based on the company policy of pricing at 120% of full cost, Groom gives Doogan a figure of $165,600 to submit for the job. Doogan is very concerned. He tells Groom that at that price, Instyle has no chance of winning the job. He confides in her that he spent $600 of company funds to take the developer to a basketball playoff game where the developer disclosed that a bid of $156,000 would win the job. He hadn't planned to tell Groom because he was confident that the bid she developed would be below that amount. Doogan reasons that the $600 he spent will be wasted if Instyle doesn't capitalize on this valuable information. In any case, the company will still make money if it wins the bid at $156,000 because it is higher than the full cost of $138,000.

Required

1. Is the $600 spent on the basketball tickets relevant to the bid decision? Why or why not?
2. Groom suggests that if Doogan is willing to use cheaper furniture and artwork, he can achieve a bid of $156,000. The designs have already been reviewed and accepted and cannot be changed without additional cost, so the entire amount of reduction in cost will need to come from furniture and artwork. What is the target cost of furniture and artwork that will allow Doogan to submit a bid of $156,000 assuming a target markup of 20% of full cost?
3. Evaluate whether Groom's suggestion to Doogan to use the developer's tip is unethical. Would it be unethical for Doogan to reduce the cost of furniture and artwork to arrive at a lower bid? What steps should Doogan and Groom take to resolve this situation?

Collaborative Learning Case

LO 3, 4 ▶
1. Tvez total ABC overhead allocation, $545,000

12-37 Target prices, target costs, value engineering. Avery, Inc. manufactures two component parts for the television industry:

- Tvez: Annual production and sales of 50,000 units at a selling price of $52.50 per unit.
- Premia: Annual production and sales of 25,000 units at a selling price of $72 per unit.

Avery includes all R&D and design costs in engineering costs. Assume that Avery has no marketing, distribution, or customer-service costs.

The direct and overhead costs incurred by Avery on Tvez and Premia are described as follows:

	Tvez	Premia	Total
Direct materials costs (variable)	$1,020,000	$720,000	$1,740,000
Direct manufacturing labour costs (variable)	360,000	240,000	600,000
Direct machining costs (fixed)	180,000	120,000	300,000
Manufacturing overhead costs:			
Machine setup costs		112,500	
Testing costs		600,000	
Engineering costs		480,000	
Manufacturing overhead costs			1,192,500
Total costs			$3,832,500

Avery's management identifies the following activity cost pools, cost drivers for each activity, and the costs per unit of cost driver for each overhead cost pool:

Activity	Description	Cost Driver	Cost per Unit of Cost Driver
Setup	Preparing machine to manufacture a new batch of products	Setup-hours	$30 per setup-hour
Testing	Testing components and final product (each unit is tested individually)	Testing-hours	$2.40 per testing-hour
Engineering	Designing products and processes and ensuring their smooth functioning	Complexity of product and process	Costs assigned to products by special study

Over a long-run time horizon, Avery's management views direct materials costs and direct manufacturing labour costs as variable with respect to the units of Tvez and Premia produced. Direct machining costs for each product do not vary over this time horizon and are fixed long-run costs. Overhead costs vary with respect to their chosen cost drivers. For example, setup costs vary with the number of setup-hours. Additional information is as follows:

	Tvez	Premia
Production batch size	500 units	200 units
Setup time per batch	15 hours	18 hours
Testing and inspection time per unit of product produced	2.5 hours	5 hours
Engineering costs incurred on each product	$200,000	$280,000

Avery is facing competitive pressure to reduce the price of Tvez and has set a target price of $48, well below its current price of $52.50. The challenge for Avery is to reduce the cost of Tvez. Avery's engineers have proposed a new product design and process improvements for the "New Tvez" to replace Tvez. The new design would improve product quality, and reduce scrap and waste. The reduction in prices will not enable Avery to increase its current sales. (However, if Avery does not reduce prices, it will lose sales.)

The expected effects of the new design relative to Tvez are as follows:

1. Direct materials costs for New Tvez are expected to decrease by $2.50 per unit.
2. Direct manufacturing labour costs for New Tvez are expected to decrease by $0.70 per unit.
3. Time required for testing each unit of New Tvez is expected to be reduced by 0.5 hours.
4. Machining time required to make New Tvez is expected to decrease by 20 minutes. It currently takes 1 hour to manufacture 1 unit of Tvez. The machines are dedicated to the production of New Tvez.
5. New Tvez will take 7 setup-hours for each setup.
6. Engineering costs are unchanged.

Assume that the batch sizes are the same for New Tvez as for Tvez. If Avery requires additional resources to implement the new design, it can acquire these additional resources in the quantities needed. Further assume the costs per unit of cost driver for the New Tvez are the same as those described for Tvez.

Instructions

Form groups of two students to complete the following requirements.

Required

1. Develop full product costs per unit for Tvez and Premia, using an activity-based product costing approach.
2. What is the markup on the full product cost per unit for Tvez?
3. What is Avery's target cost per unit for New Tvez if it is to maintain the same markup percentage on the full product cost per unit as it had for Tvez?
4. Will the New Tvez design achieve the cost reduction targets that Avery has set?
5. What price would Avery charge for New Tvez if it used the same markup percentage on the full product cost per unit for New Tvez as it did for Tvez?
6. What price should Avery charge for New Tvez, and what next steps should Avery take regarding New Tvez?

SOLUTIONS

 TRY IT!

Try It 12–1

Price to retailers in 2017 is 95% of 2016 price = 0.95 × $8 = $7.60
Cost per pack in 2017 is 96% of 2016 cost = 0.96 × $6 = $5.76

Gonzalo's operating income in 2017 is as follows:

	Total for 250,000 Packs (1)	Per Unit (2) = (1) ÷ 250,000
Revenues ($7.60 × 250,000)	$1,900,000	$7.60
Purchase cost of packs ($5.76 × 250,000)	1,440,000	5.76
Ordering costs ($100 × 500)	50,000	0.20
Receiving and storage ($60 × 4,000)	240,000	0.96
Shipping ($80 × 1,500)	120,000	0.48
Total costs	1,850,000	7.40
Operating income	$ 50,000	$0.20

Gonzalo's operating income in 2016 is $90,000. Gonzalo will need to reduce its total costs by $40,000 ($90,000 − $50,000) or $0.16 ($40,000 ÷ 250,000) per unit if it is to achieve its target operating income in 2017.

Try It 12–2

Gonzalo's operating income in 2017, if it makes changes in ordering and receiving and storage, will be as follows:

	Total for 250,000 Packs (1)	Per Unit (2) = (1) ÷ 250,000
Revenues ($7.60 × 250,000)	$1,900,000	$7.60
Purchase cost of packs ($5.76 × 250,000)	1,440,000	5.76
Ordering costs ($75 × 400)	30,000	0.12
Receiving and storage ($50 × 3,500)	175,000	0.70
Shipping ($80 × 1,500)	120,000	0.48
Total costs	1,765,000	7.06
Operating income	$ 135,000	$0.54

Through value engineering that reduces the quantity of the activity and the cost-driver rate, Gonzalo exceeds its target operating income of $90,000 and $0.36 per pencil pack despite the fact that its revenue per pencil pack has decreased by $0.40 ($8.00 − $7.60), while its purchase cost per pencil pack has decreased by only $0.24 ($6.00 − $5.76).

Strategy, the Balanced Scorecard, and Profitability Analysis

13

Matthew Horwood/Alamy Stock Photo

Barclays Turns to the Balanced Scorecard

The reputation of Barclays, the British multinational bank, took a beating in 2012 when company traders rigged a key interest rate called LIBOR, a benchmark rate that helps set global borrowing costs. When new CEO Antony Jenkins was tasked with turning the company around, he turned to the balanced scorecard to change the company's performance goals and incentive structure.

Introduced in 2014, Barclays's balanced scorecard set out specific goals and metrics across each of the company's "5Cs": customer and client, colleague, citizenship, conduct, and company. With a five-year goal of becoming the world's "go to" bank, the balanced scorecard became the instrument to ensuring Barclays was "helping people achieve their ambitions—in the right way."

Rather than focusing solely on short-term financial results, Barclays's balanced scorecard aligned the company's 5Cs with the broader perspectives of the balanced scorecard. Most notably, the learning and growth perspective incorporated Barclays's conduct and citizenship goals, which included new purpose and value statements for the company. Jenkins even took the extraordinary step of tying the performance bonuses of managers to Barclays's corporate ethics and citizenship goals, rather than just quarterly profits and stock price gains.

By the end of 2018, Barclays was already seeing progress toward its balanced scorecard goals. Company profitability increased, as did long-term capital strengthening, employee engagement, corporate citizenship goals, and the percentage of women in senior leadership at the bank. The company's recent balanced scorecard report noted, "The balanced scorecard is the final crucial piece of our plan—alongside our purpose, values, and behaviours—to embed the right culture in our business and become the bank of choice."

Sources: Barclays PLC, "Barclays' Balanced Scorecard," https://www.home.barclays/about-barclays/balanced-scorecard.html; Barclays PLC, 2015 Annual Report (London, Barclays PLC, 2016) https://www.home.barclays/content/dam/barclayspublic/docs/InvestorRelations/ResultAnnouncements/2015FYResults/20190301_Barclays_Bank_PLC_2015_Annual_Report.pdf; J. Horowitz. 2012. New Barclays chief ties executive compensation to societal goals, Reuters, September 24 (http://www.reuters.com/article/us-barclays-jenkins-idUSBRE88N0YY20120924); A. Brownsell. 2014. Barclays reveals '5Cs' values scorecard in drive for brand transformation, *Marketing*, November 2 (http://www.marketingmagazine.co.uk/article/1230626/barclays-reveals-5cs-values-scorecard-drive-brand-transformation).

This chapter focuses on how management accounting information helps companies such as Barclays, Infosys, Merck, Verizon, and Volkswagen implement and evaluate their strategies. Strategy drives the operations of a company and guides managers' short-run and long-run decisions. We describe the balanced scorecard approach to implementing strategy and methods to analyze operating income to evaluate the success of a strategy. We also show how management accounting information helps strategic initiatives, such as productivity improvement, reengineering, and downsizing.

Strategy specifies how an organization can create value for its customers while differentiating itself from its competitors. Strategy is both open and flexible, but strategic outcomes arise from a deliberate, rational, reflective process. This chapter discusses an important tool to measure the success of competitive corporate strategy—the balanced scorecard (BSC).[1] The BSC translates a corporation's strategy into a comprehensive set of performance measures to assess how well the strategy is implemented through changes to how a corporation operates.

Application of the BSC will be explored using Chipset Inc., a manufacturer of linear integrated circuit devices (LICDs) used in communication networks. Chipset has one specialized model, LCX1. Chipset consulted extensively with its customers and designed this chip to meet their needs. Important features of the LCX1 are its versatility in many integrated circuits used in different devices, and the scaleability of the chips. **Scaleability** means one chip can be added to another in a single circuit to increase the speed and power of the device.

Chipset currently has 10 customers demanding approximately equal volumes of the LCX1, and has the practical capacity to meet normal demand growth. The efficiency and yield from the production process is due to the engineering talent of Chipset's product and process designers. The company follows a target pricing policy because similar products are readily available to its customers. The company has set its return on investment (ROI) and operating income margin percentage, which will determine the target cost of the LCX1.

Industry analysts anticipate an annual growth rate of 10% in market size from which Chipset will benefit because it already has the capacity to match this growth. Chipset can increase production readily because it has some older and fully depreciated production equipment that can provide excess capacity when required. Managers continue to consider the pros and cons of retention or disposal of this equipment to replace it with newer equipment. Chipset's current production capacity enables it to convert 3,750,000 cm² of silicon each year. A disposal decision depends on any streamlining in the current production process to improve yields. Additional equipment purchases are only available in increments to process 250,000 cm² of silicon wafers.

Five Forces Analysis to Define Strategic Alternatives

▶ LO 1

Explain how the relative strength of competitive forces helps managers identify strategic alternatives.

Michael Porter, a Harvard University business professor and leading expert on strategy, has identified five competitive forces that all corporations face. A competent analysis of Porter's five forces is key to a successful strategic decision. The corporate team must examine (1) competitors, (2) potential entrants into the market, (3) equivalent products, (4) the price-setting power of customers, and (5) the price-setting power of suppliers.[2] A rigorous and disciplined analysis will enable the corporate team to identify the level of competitive rivalry in its business environment and how best to exploit its own core competence to outperform its rivals. Porter's five forces are illustrated in Exhibit 13-1, and we look at each in detail below.

A common tool in formulating strategy is called SWOT (strengths, weaknesses, opportunities, and threats) analysis. The approach stresses examining an organization's internal factors (strengths and weaknesses) and external factors (opportunities and threats).

---

[1] See R.S. Kaplan and D.P. Norton, *The Balanced Scorecard* (Cambridge: Harvard Business School Press, 1996); R.S. Kaplan and D.P. Norton, *The Strategy-Focused Organization: How Balanced Scorecard Companies Thrive in the New Business Environment* (Boston: Harvard Business School Press, 2001); and R.S. Kaplan and D.P. Norton, *Strategy Maps: Converting Intangible Assets into Tangible Outcomes* (Boston: Harvard Business School Press, 2004).

[2] M. Porter, *Competitive Strategy* (New York: Free Press, 1980); M. Porter, *Competitive Advantage* (New York: Free Press, 1985); and M. Porter, "What Is Strategy?" *Harvard Business Review* (November–December 1996): 61–78.

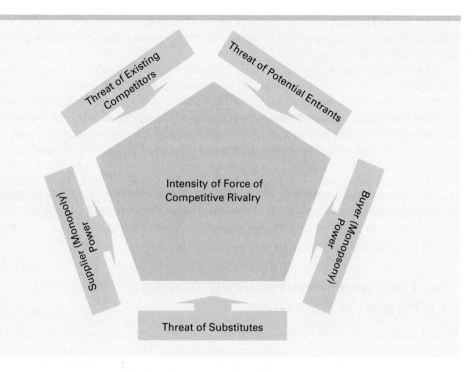

Chipset, a maker of LICDs, produces a single product: the high performance LCX1 chip. A "Five Forces" analysis for Chipset includes the following:

1. *Competitors.* The LCX1 model faces severe competition with respect to price, timely delivery, and quality. Companies in the industry have high fixed costs and persistent pressures to reduce selling prices and utilize capacity fully. Price reductions spur growth because they make LICDs a cost-effective option in new applications.

2. *Potential entrants into the market.* The small profit margins and high capital costs discourage new entrants. Moreover, incumbent companies such as Chipset are further down the learning curve with respect to lowering costs and building close relationships with customers and suppliers.

3. *Equivalent products.* Chipset tailors LCX1 to customer needs and lowers prices by continuously improving LCX1's design and processes to reduce production costs. This reduces the risk of equivalent products or new technologies replacing LCX1.

4. *Bargaining power of customers.* Customers, such as EarthLink and Verizon, negotiate aggressively with Chipset and its competitors to keep prices down because they buy large quantities of product.

5. *Bargaining power of input suppliers.* To produce LCX1, Chipset requires high-quality materials (such as silicon wafers, pins for connectivity, and plastic or ceramic packaging) and skilled engineers, technicians, and manufacturing labour. The skill sets suppliers and employees bring give them bargaining power to demand higher prices and wages.

In summary, large numbers of competitors, low barriers to new entrants, readily available substitutes, and high price-setting power of customers and suppliers can result in higher cost and lower revenue. Corporations that must accept the price customers are willing to pay and the costs monopsony suppliers can charge are called price takers. In this situation, the forces combine to generate high-intensity competitive rivalry and low profit margins. The strategic choice discussed in this chapter is between product differentiation (or value leadership) and cost leadership.

Value leadership strategies succeed when the customer perceives the corporation's output as having either superior or uniquely desirable attributes for which they will pay a higher price. The ability for a corporation to offer desirable products is called **product differentiation**. Value leadership can help assure long-term profitability when a company can differentiate its product successfully.

Corporations can implement a value leadership strategy by closely investigating and analyzing the preferences of their consumers. As competitors develop substitutes and patents expire, corporations can sustain their competitive advantage through innovation.

Cost leadership strategies succeed when a corporation can produce products that are at least equal to others in the market at the lowest cost. A cost leadership strategy often leads to highly automated processes to mass produce large volumes of products. Given a specific fixed cost of capacity, the greater the volume of output produced and sold in the relevant range, the more advantageous are the economies of scale. Corporations may choose to grow by expanding existing capacity. Or they can design different products that can be produced using the same equipment and plant. This is called **economies of scope**. For example, a decision to introduce different product lines of shampoo for oily, dry, and normal hair will exploit economies of scope.

The Decision Framework Applied to Chipset's Strategy

▶ **LO 2**

Understand reengineering.

We can apply the decision framework to many internal operating decisions, from how to select a pricing method to how to design a cost system. This versatile framework is also a reliable guide to selecting an appropriate strategy. The central message of Porter's work is that companies that are unwilling or incapable of deciding will not thrive relative to their competitors who do make a strategic decision. The strategic choice is described using information specific to Chipset.

From its analysis of the competitive environment, Chipset has summarized its strengths in process and product design as well as identified the unique scaleability attribute of its LCX1 product. New opportunities have arisen for Chipset to customize its LXC1 slightly and make it suitable for a different use in digital subscriber lines (DSL). Expanding to a different market without extensive customization will enable Chipset to exploit economies of scope. Before acting, however, the top management team applies the decision framework to decide which value or cost leadership strategy to pursue.

Step 1: Identify the problem. Chipset's managers understand they must choose one of two basic strategies—*value* or *cost leadership*. There are elements of customization at Chipset, but the important attribute designed into its product is that the chips can be linked in arrays to boost performance and power of different devices. Chipset's competitors also provide customized designs and unique product features for their customers, but their products lack scaleability. To fuel future growth, Chipset must decide between either its current core competence or committing to development of innovative highly customized products for which customers will pay more.

Step 2: Gather and analyze relevant information. Chipset gathers intelligence data about its competitor, Visilog, and market data from customers to improve Chipset's understanding of the environment. Top management analyzes the new data and produces the **customer preference map** shown in Exhibit 13-2. The y-axis describes various desirable attributes of the LCX1, which customers perceive as adding value. The x-axis compares the ratings of important attributes from (1) poor to (5) very good for both Chipset and Visilog. The collected data indicates that Visilog has chosen value (product) leadership. The map highlights the tradeoffs for each company.

Chipset's LCX1 chip has an advantage in terms of price, customer service, and scaleability. In terms of scaleability, Chipset's LCX1 technology allows Chipset's customers to achieve different performance levels by simply altering the number of LCX1 units in the product. Visilog's customized chips, though not scaleable, are individually faster and more powerful.

Step 3: Make predictions about the future. LCX1 is somewhat differentiated from competing products, but it is not unique. If Chipset were to pursue unique product development, it would be competing against giants in the microchip industry such as Intel

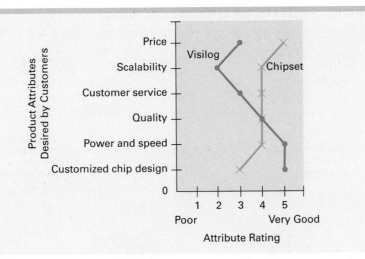

Exhibit 13-2 Customer Preference Map for LICDs

and AMD who already possess a competitive advantage in R&D. Differentiating LCX1 further is costly but profitable if the life cycle for the product would result in satisfactory ROI and Chipset's customers would pay. But product life cycles are as short as 90 days. Chips are obsolete almost as soon as they are marketed, and customers know they can wait only a short time for a superior product. They will not pay a premium price adequate to reach an above average ROI. The alternative strategy is cost leadership.

Step 4: Make the decision between the two strategies. In a highly automated manufacturing process, Chipset can enjoy cost reduction from economies of scale and scope. Chipset's current engineering staff is more skilled at making product and process improvements than at creatively designing new products and technologies. Their talent, however, has enabled Chipset to exploit its equipment capacity more effectively and keep costs lower than competitors. In addition, Chipset scores "very good" on pricing, while Visilog ranks only average. Chipset concludes it will retain the scaleable design of LCX1 but lower its price and improve quality and customer service. Chipset concludes it should follow a *cost leadership* strategy. Chipset will not purchase more capacity but instead will increase its yield.

Step 5: Implement the decision, evaluate performance, and learn. To achieve its cost leadership strategy, Chipset must improve its own internal production process and increase yield. Producing more chips is one way this company will drive down its full absorption cost. But strategy requires some integration of product and process development. Chipset can rely on its core competence, the process engineers, and the skill of its workers, but as change is implemented Chipset must ensure it retains this human capital. There are other important value functions where operations will change in a coordinated way to focus on implementing the strategy smoothly and cost-effectively. As the company reengineers and simplifies both product and processes to reduce opportunities for error, improve quality, and speed up the production cycle, some retraining of Chipset's labour will be needed.

Chipset's engineering changes will be driven by customers' requirements, sustaining scaleability, and cost reduction through reengineering and retraining. There are choices to be made as to how to implement the decision. Chipset decides it would be sensible to avoid the loss of morale from downsizing. Instead, to retain its human capital, Chipset will pay to retrain experienced workers in quality control. Retraining will be consistent with Chipset's history of placing a high value on its people and giving them new opportunities.

Strategy Maps and the Balanced Scorecard

The objectives and measures Chipset's managers choose for each perspective relates to the action plans for furthering Chipset's cost leadership strategy: *improving quality* and *reengineering processes*.

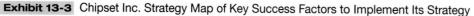

Exhibit 13-3 Chipset Inc. Strategy Map of Key Success Factors to Implement Its Strategy

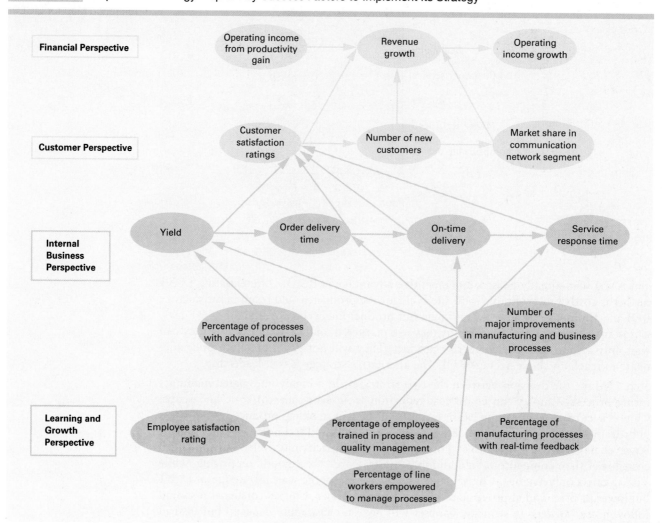

A useful first step in designing a BSC is a *strategy map*. A **strategy map** is a diagram that describes how an organization creates value by connecting strategic objectives in explicit cause-and-effect relationships with each other in the financial, customer, internal business process, and learning and growth perspectives. Exhibit 13-3 presents Chipset's strategy map. Follow the arrows to see how a strategic objective affects other strategic objectives. For example, empowering the workforce helps align employee and organization goals and improves processes. Employee and organizational alignment also helps improve processes that improve manufacturing quality and productivity, reduce customer delivery time, meet specified delivery dates, and improve post-sales service, all of which increase customer satisfaction. Improving manufacturing quality and productivity grows operating income and increases customer satisfaction that, in turn, increases market share, operating income, and shareholder value.

Chipset's most important change to implement will be to reengineer business processes. **Reengineering** (or **redesigning**) is the fundamental rethinking and redesign of business processes to achieve improvements in critical measures such as cost, quality, speed, and customer satisfaction. The different activities that occur at each tier of the strategy map are often referred to as **key success factors** (KSFs), which are activities necessary for the successful execution of a strategy. The strategy map is a way to succinctly illustrate the KSFs that are interdependent at Chipset. The organization will want to obtain feedback to measure the success or failure of their redesign efforts. One approach, the BSC, will produce required feedback to assess the success of the strategy.

Balanced Scorecard: Measures of Performance

The **balanced scorecard** (BSC) is a way to assess how coherently corporate strategy has been implemented in day-to-day operations. It provides a reliable and multidimensional measure of how effectively and efficiently managers have utilized corporate resources—an evaluation of the quality of stewardship. First introduced in 1996 by R.S. Kaplan and D.P. Norton, the BSC links short-term operating outcomes to long-run goals. Exhibit 13-4 illustrates measures that Chipset chose, consistent with both the measures and the four perspectives presented in Exhibit 13-3.

The essence of a good BSC is that it represents the interdependencies among key performance factors (KPFs) using financial and nonfinancial performance measures. The BSC justifies the benefit of nonfinancial measures of corporate success in areas where no financial measures are available, but which actually enhance profits. For example, one study reported how an antenna installation company used customer satisfaction surveys to identify an important KPF: a shortened installation cycle time.[3] By improving its internal process, the company also shortened its cash cycle between accepting the customer's order and receiving payment. By shortening the cycle between order-taking, producing, shipping, invoicing, and collection, there is more time to complete more orders and there is also more time to increase the volume of Chipset's customers and increase market share.

► **LO 3**

Understand the four perspectives of the balanced scorecard.

Four Perspectives of the Balanced Scorecard

The measures chosen by Chipset in the context of its strategy can be seen in Exhibit 13-4 and can be described in terms of the BSC as

1. **Financial perspective.** This perspective evaluates the profitability of the strategy and the creation of shareholder value. Because Chipset's key strategic initiatives are cost reduction relative to competitors' costs and sales growth, the financial perspective focuses on how much operating income results from reducing costs and selling more units of LCX1.

2. **Customer perspective.** This perspective identifies targeted customer and market segments and measures the company's success in these segments. To monitor its customer objectives, Chipset uses measures such as market share in the communication-networks segment, number of new customers, and customer-satisfaction ratings.

3. **Internal-business-process perspective.** This perspective focuses on internal operations that create value for customers that, in turn, help achieve financial performance. Chipset determines internal-business-process improvement targets after benchmarking against its main competitors using information from published financial statements, prevailing prices, customers, suppliers, former employees, industry experts, and financial analysts. The internal-business-process perspective comprises three sub-processes:

   ■ *Innovation process:* Creating products, services, and processes that will meet the needs of customers is a very important process for companies that follow a product-differentiation strategy and must constantly design and develop innovative new products to remain competitive in the marketplace. Chipset's innovation focuses on improving its manufacturing capability and process controls to lower costs and improve quality. Chipset measures innovation by the number of improvements in manufacturing processes and percentage of processes with advanced controls.

   ■ *Operations process:* This process involves producing and delivering existing products and services that will meet the needs of customers. Chipset's strategic initiatives are (a) improving manufacturing quality, (b) reducing delivery time to customers, and (c) meeting specified delivery dates so it measures yield, order-delivery time, and on-time deliveries.

[3] R.E. Paladino, "Balanced Forecasts Drive Value," *Strategic Finance* (January, 2005): 37–42.

Exhibit 13-4 Specific BSC Measures Consistent with Chipset's Strategy

Financial Perspective
Maximize Shareholder Value

Increase Operating Income (OI)

Activities that Change	Measures	Budget (prediction)	Actual Performance
More effective capacity use	Improve yield	$2,000,000 savings	$2,012,500
Reduce unitized fixed cost	Increase OI growth	$3,000,000 increase	$3,420,000
Strengthen customer relationships	Increase revenue	6%	6.48%[a]

[a](Revenue in 2019 − Revenue in 2018) ÷ Revenue in 2018 = ($28.75 mil − $27 mil) ÷ $27 mil = 6.48%

Customer Perspective
Give the Customer Value-Added

Increase LCX1 Versatility To Meet Needs of New Customers

Activities that Change	Measures	Budget (prediction)	Actual Performance
Identify attributes clients need	Market share	6%	7%
Identify new groups of clients	Quantity of new groups	1	1[b]
Increase focus on the client	Customer satisfaction	90% give top 2 ratings	87%

[b]One new group of customers obtained for a new application of the product.

Internal Business Process Perspective
Manage Key Success Factors in All Business Processes

Streamline Key Success Factors in All Business Functions

Activities that Change	Measures	Budget (prediction)	Actual Performance
Decrease service cycle time	Time to complete a job	≤ 4 hours	≤ 3 hours
Increase quality and yield	Yield	78%	79.3%
Decrease delivery cycle time	Order-delivery time	≤ 30 days	≤ 30 days
Increase on-time deliveries	On-time delivery ratio	92%	90%
Streamline business process	Quantity of innovations	5	5
Improve quality control	Advanced controls ratio	75%	75%

Learning, Growth Perspective
Align Employee and Corporate Goals

Develop and Empower Teamwork Among Employees

Activities that Change	Measures	Budget (prediction)	Actual Performance
Increase ratio of improved team performance from workers' suggestions	Employee satisfaction	80% give top 2 ratings	88%
Increase front-line workers' scope of decision making	Ratio of workers' decisions to total decisions	85%	90%
Increase training programs	Ratio of employees trained to total	90%	92%
Increase independent data searches for benchmarks	Ratio of real-time feedback to total processes	80%	80%

Concepts in Action | Balanced Scorecard Helps Infosys Transform into a Leading Consultancy

Namas Bhojani/Bloomberg/Getty Images

Bangalore-based Infosys is a market leader in information technology outsourcing, constantly under pressure to expand to meet increased client demand. Infosys invested in many new areas including business process outsourcing, project management, and management consulting. This put Infosys in direct competition with established consulting firms such as IBM and Accenture.

Led by CEO Kris Gopalakrishnan, the company developed an integrated management structure that would help align these new, diverse initiatives. Infosys turned to the BSC to provide a framework the company could use to formulate and monitor its strategy. The BSC measures corporate performance along four dimensions—financial, customer, internal business process, and learning and growth.

The BSC immediately played a role in the transformation of Infosys. The executive team used the scorecard to guide discussion during its meetings. The continual process of adaptation, execution, and management that the scorecard fostered helped the team respond to, and even anticipate, its clients' evolving needs. Eventually, use of the scorecard for performance measurement spread to the rest of the organization, with monetary incentives linked to the company's performance along the different dimensions.

Over time, the BSC became part of the Infosys culture. In recent years, Infosys has begun using the BSC concept to create "relationship scorecards" for many of its largest clients. Using the scorecard framework, Infosys began measuring its performance for key clients not only on project management and client satisfaction, but also on repeat business and anticipating clients' future strategic needs.

The BSC helped successfully steer the transformation of Infosys from a technology outsourcer to a sustainable market-leading business consultancy. Revenues in the fiscal year ending 2016 were US$9.5 billion (up 9% from the previous year). The company decreased per capita energy use by 6.5% and increased the number of higher education opportunities by more than 10%, with a goal of providing company-wide access, all the while increasing customer acquisition and customer retention.

Source: Infosys Sustainability Report 2015–2016 (https://www.infosys.com/sustainability/Documents/infosys-sustainability-report-2015-16.pdf).

- *Postsales-service process:* This process involves providing service and support to the customer after the sale of a product or service. Chipset monitors how quickly and accurately it is responding to customer-service requests.

4. **Learning-and-growth perspective.** This perspective identifies the capabilities the organization must excel at to achieve superior internal processes that in turn create value for customers and shareholders. Chipset's learning and growth perspective emphasizes three capabilities: (1) information-system capabilities, measured by the percentage of manufacturing processes with real-time feedback; (2) employee capabilities, measured by the percentage of employees trained in process and quality management; and (3) motivation, measured by employee satisfaction and the percentage of manufacturing and sales employees (line employees) empowered to manage processes.

Nonfinancial BSC Measures at Chipset

The BSC takes into account not only financial targets but also targets based on social, legal, and environmental perspectives. Today, companies must respond to increasingly complex arrays of customer demands for social, legal, and environmental as well as financial sustainability. This multidimensional demand for corporate sustainability has led companies like Pearson PLC to produce three annual reports. One is the familiar financial report, the second is their social responsibility report, and the third is their environmental sustainability report. Global companies take the triple bottom line seriously. Recent research provides evidence that investors recognize and reward companies that implement best practices. The shareholders are rewarded because the market value of these firms is higher than firms that ignore social and environmental sustainability practices.[4]

For example, Pearson PLC pursues an environmental strategy to achieve climate neutrality with respect to carbon emissions. The company will measure its unavoidable CO_2 emissions and has pledged to generate outputs that absorb as many tonnes of CO_2 as Pearson emits. Since 2007, the company has reduced its emissions from 1.62 to 1.04 tonnes per full-time employee on a like-for-like basis that excludes acquisitions. In 2007 Pearson set a target of 95% recycling and reuse of unsold product, but by 2009 Pearson had exceeded this and achieved 99%. Pearson has also reduced its use of plastic in packaging by 85% since implementing its strategy.

Customers have successfully gained corporate attention using social media to expose companies such as Nike and IKEA, which have employed child labour in offshore factories. Tyson Foods, a global food processor, found its unhygienic slaughtering and processing practices posted on YouTube by People for the Ethical Treatment of Animals (PETA). PETA continues its internet campaign against YUM!, the owner of Kentucky Fried Chicken, to replace Tyson Foods as its supplier.

The Brundtland Commission[5] defined a sustainable society as one where "the current generation meets its needs without jeopardizing the ability of future generations to meet their needs."

There are a wide variety of opinions on this issue. Some believe that managers should only focus on long-run financial performance and not be distracted by pursuing social and environmental goals beyond the minimum levels required by law. Others believe that managers must act to attain environmental and social objectives beyond what is legally required, while achieving good financial performance—often called the *triple bottom line*—as part of a company's social responsibility. Still others believe that there is no conflict between achieving social and environmental goals and long-run financial performance.

Many managers recognize that good environmental and social performance helps to attract and inspire outstanding employees, improve employee safety and health, increase productivity, and lower operating costs. Environmental and social performance also enhances a company's reputation with socially conscious customers and investors and boosts its image with governments and citizens, all contributing to long-run financial performance. Experienced financial analysts are publishing favourable reports about companies with strong environmental and social performance because of their greater transparency and engagement with multiple stakeholders. A distinguishing organizational characteristic of companies that emphasize environmental and social performance is their long-term orientation. Some recent research suggests that taking the long-term view and engaging with multiple stakeholders results in superior financial performance. Companies, such as Natura, China Light & Power, and Dow Chemical, that focus on the triple bottom line of financial, environmental, and social performance benefit from innovating in technologies, processes, products, and business models to reduce the tradeoffs between financial and sustainability goals. These companies also build transformational and transitional leadership and change capabilities needed to implement the strategies to achieve the triple bottom line.

---

[4] S-F. Lo, H-J. Sheu, "Is Corporate Sustainability a Value-Increasing Strategy for Business?" *Corporate Governance* 15.2 (March 2007): 345–358.

[5] The Brundtland Commission was set up by the United Nations as the World Commission on Environment and Development. It issued its report, *Our Common Future*, in 1987.

The BSC has changed how management teams understand the way to improve profits and requires careful understanding of the interdependence between the firm and its competitive environment. When companies go offshore and source their materials, labour, and merchandise globally, they are held accountable for the practices of all their business partners. **Enterprise risk management (ERM)** expands triple bottom line responsibility beyond the firm itself. The purpose of ERM is to identify risk and align the firm's strategy and measures of success using many different measures. This is the power of the BSC.

13.1 TRY IT! ⊕

Ronaldo Associates is a construction engineering firm that prepares detailed construction drawings for single family homes. The market for this service is very competitive. To compete successfully Ronaldo must deliver quality service at low cost. Ronaldo presents the following data for 2016 and 2017.

	2016	2017
1. Number of jobs billed	400	500
2. Selling price per job	$ 3,200	$ 3,100
3. Engineering labour-hours	24,000	27,000
4. Cost per engineering labour-hour	$ 35	$ 36
5. Engineering support capacity (number of jobs the firm can do)	600	600
6. Total cost of engineering support (space rent, equipment etc.)	$180,000	$192,000
7. Engineering support-capacity cost per job (row 6 ÷ row 5)	$ 300	$ 320

Engineering labour-hour costs are variable costs. Engineering support costs for each year depend on the engineering support capacity that Ronaldo chooses to maintain each year (that is, the number of jobs it can do each year). Engineering support costs do not vary with the actual number of jobs done in a year.

Required

1. Calculate the operating income of Ronaldo Associates in 2016 and 2017.
2. Calculate the growth, price-recovery, and productivity components that explain the change in operating income from 2016 to 2017.
3. Comment on your answer in requirement 2. What do these components indicate?

Implementing a Balanced Scorecard

To successfully implement a BSC requires commitment and leadership from top management. At Chipset, the BSC team (headed by the vice-president of strategic planning) conducted interviews with senior managers; questioned executives about customers, competitors, and technological developments; and sought proposals for BSC objectives across the four perspectives. The team then met to discuss the responses and to build a prioritized list of objectives.

In a meeting with all senior managers, the team sought to achieve consensus on the scorecard objectives. Senior management was then divided into four groups, with each group being responsible for one of the perspectives. In addition, each group broadened the base of inputs by including representatives from the next-lower levels of management and key functional managers. The groups identified measures for each objective and the sources of information for each measure. The groups then met to finalize scorecard objectives, measures, targets, and the initiatives to achieve the targets. Management accountants played an important role in the design and implementation of the BSC, particularly in determining measures to represent the realities of the business. This required management accountants to understand the economic environment of the industry, Chipset's customers and competitors, and internal business issues such as human resources, operations, and distribution.

The final BSC was communicated to all employees, and managers made sure that employees understood the scorecard and the scorecard process. Sharing the scorecard allowed engineers and operating personnel, for example, to understand the reasons for customer satisfaction and dissatisfaction and to make suggestions for improving internal processes directly aimed at satisfying customers and implementing Chipset's strategy. Too often, scorecards are seen only by a select group of managers. By limiting the scorecard's exposure, an organization loses the opportunity for widespread organization engagement and alignment.

Chipset (like Cigna Property, Casualty Insurance, and Wells Fargo) also encourages each department to develop its own scorecard that ties into Chipset's main scorecard. For example, the quality control department's scorecard has measures that its department managers use to improve yield. Department scorecards help align the actions of each department to implement Chipset's strategy. Companies frequently use BSCs to evaluate and reward managerial performance and to influence managerial behaviour. Using the BSC for performance evaluation widens the performance management lens and motivates managers to give greater attention to nonfinancial drivers of performance. Surveys indicate, however, that companies continue to assign more weight to the financial perspective (55%) than to the other perspectives—customer (19%), internal business process (12%), and learning and growth (14%).

Companies cite several reasons for the relatively smaller weight on nonfinancial measures: difficulty evaluating the relative importance of nonfinancial measures; challenges in measuring and quantifying qualitative, nonfinancial data; and difficulty in compensating managers despite poor financial performance. Many companies, however, are giving greater weight to nonfinancial measures in promotion decisions because they believe that nonfinancial measures (such as customer satisfaction, process improvements, and employee motivation) better assess a manager's potential to succeed at senior levels of management. For the BSC to be effective, managers must view it as fairly assessing and rewarding all important aspects of a manager's performance and promotion prospects.

Features of a Good Balanced Scorecard

A good BSC design has several features:

■ It tells the story of a company's strategy by clarifying a limited sequence of orderly relationships among KSFs. People have cognitive limits; therefore, a good BSC focuses on a limited set of linked measures that, if improved in an orderly way, will increase profitability.

■ The BSC communicates the strategy to all members of the organization by translating the strategy into a coherent and linked set of understandable and measurable operational targets. Guided by the BSC, managers and employees take actions and make decisions that aim to achieve the company's strategy. To focus these actions, some companies, such as Mobil and Bank of Montreal, have developed BSCs at the division and department levels.

■ Improvements in nonfinancial performance measures usually lead to improvements in financial performance measures. In not-for-profit enterprises, nonfinancial factors measure the achievement of almost all key objectives.

■ The BSC limits the number of measures used by identifying only the most critical KSF. Avoiding a proliferation of measures focuses management's attention on those that are central to strengthening the corporation's core competence. Although strategy is stable in the long term, KSFs may change over time and so too must the BSC measures.

- The BSC highlights suboptimal tradeoffs that managers may make when they fail to consider operational and financial measures together. For example, a company for which innovation is central to product differentiation could achieve superior short-run financial performance by reducing money spent on R&D. A good BSC would signal that the short-run financial performance may have been achieved by taking actions that hurt future financial performance because a leading indicator of that performance, R&D spending and R&D output, has declined.

Pitfalls When Implementing a Balanced Scorecard

Pitfalls to avoid when implementing a BSC include the following:

- Strategy requires knowledge of how orderly changes in a corporation can better assure success in a changing competitive environment. Orderly change focuses on shoring up the weak KSFs and nourishing the strong KSFs that sustain core competence. A critical challenge is to identify the strength and speed of the orderly changes among the nonfinancial and financial measures. Management must gather evidence of these linkages over time. Evolving the BSC over time avoids the paralysis by analysis associated with trying to design the "perfect" scorecard at the outset.

- Scarce corporate resources means tradeoffs or priority-setting must occur among various strategic goals. For example, emphasizing quality and on-time performance beyond a point may not be worthwhile—improving these objectives may be inconsistent with profit maximization.

- The BSC includes the intangible achievement of good management of intellectual capital. Qualitative or subjective measures such as interviews and surveys to assess intellectual and corporate sustainability achievements provide a rich basis upon which to assess progress.

- Intangible costs are extremely difficult to estimate, but intangible benefits even more so. Nonfinancial measures of the benefits of improved information technology, advocacy of human rights, and reduction of carbon emissions are not standardized. Management accountants play a large liaison role in translating qualitative measures made by technical experts into financial measures of benefit.

- Managers tend to focus on what their performance is measured by rather than corporate success. Excluding nonfinancial measures when evaluating performance will reduce the significance and importance given to managing nonfinancial BSC measures. Many of the nonfinancial measures serve as leading indicators of future financial performance. The Chipset example will show how improvements in nonfinancial factors lead to improvements in financial factors.

Strategic Analysis of Operating Income

Having implemented some changes, Chipset can measure its actual achievement against benchmarks in the BSC budget targets shown in Exhibit 13-4. The comparisons in this section are important to strategic cost management, which identifies the use of cost information to measure the successful implementation of a strategy. Performance indicators isolate and measure contributions to favourable operating income change arising from the choice of a cost leadership strategy apart from those arising from industry change and product customization.

Chipset has focused on comparing actual operating performance over two different time periods and explicitly linking the performance to strategic choices. Improvements in performance measures will be interpreted as successful implementation of strategy. While Chipset has chosen cost leadership, more complex companies with portfolios of product and service bundles may select more complex strategies. When value leadership is selected, these types of companies cannot simply ignore cost—cost leadership is important

▶ **LO 4**

Evaluate strategic success at implementing a cost leadership strategy using balanced scorecard measures.

to profitability for any company. The difference will lie in the BSC measures of success when implementing the selected strategy.

The following simplified example illustrates how operating-income changes between two years can be divided into components that can describe how successful a company has been with regard to cost leadership, product differentiation, and growth.[6] From the first two tables, notice that Chipset has reduced its unit sales price from $27 to $25 but increased its operating income.

	2018	2019
1. Units of LCX1 produced and sold	1,000,000	1,150,000
2. Selling price	$27	$25
3. Direct materials (square centimetres of silicon wafers)	3,000,000	2,900,000
4. Direct material cost per square centimetre	$1.40	$1.50
5. Manufacturing processing capacity (in square centimetres of silicon wafer)	3,750,000	3,500,000
6. Conversion costs (all manufacturing costs other than direct material costs)	$16,050,000	$15,225,000
7. Conversion cost per unit of capacity (Row 6 ÷ Row 5)	$4.28	$4.35
8. R&D employees	40	39
9. R&D costs	$4,000,000	$3,900,000
10. R&D cost per employee (Row 9 ÷ Row 8)	$100,000	$100,000

Chipset implemented key elements of its strategy late in 2018 and early 2019, expecting financial improvement by late 2019. In a more complex analysis, Chipset could evaluate its progress across all three years. This emphasizes that implementation of a strategic plan occurs over several years, and immediate improvement is inconsistent with the long-term strategic perspective. Chipset provides the following additional information:

■ Annual conversion costs depend on the total capacity (measured as square centimetres of silicon wafers, or practical capacity of the LCX1, that *can* be produced). This capacity cost is fixed. The direct manufacturing labour costs are relatively small compared to capacity costs and are based on time worked, not output quantity produced. Capacity costs can *only* be reduced by selling equipment, laying workers off, or reassigning them to non-manufacturing tasks.

■ The amount spent on R&D is discretionary. Chipset's managers decide on this at the beginning of each year. The R&D work does not depend on the quantity of LCX1 produced. Engineers earn approximately $100,000 annually.

■ Marketing and sales non-manufacturing costs are small relative to other costs. The company has 10 customers who purchase roughly the same quantity of LCX1 in a year. Engineers work closely with customers to provide continuous improvements that meet the customers' needs. The customer relationship manager works with the engineers and the production department to ensure Chipset can fill the order according to the requirements of the customer. This cross-functional approach recognizes the interdependence of design, sales, and production and assures customer satisfaction. It costs approximately $80,000 to support each customer.

■ The investment base and asset structure are not materially different in the years 2018 and 2019. Operating income for each year is as follows:

---

[6] For other details, see R. Banker, S. Datar, and R. Kaplan, "Productivity Measurement and Management Accounting," *Journal of Accounting, Auditing and Finance* (1989): 528–554; and A. Hayzen and J. Reeve, "Examining the Relationships in Productivity Accounting," *Management Accounting Quarterly* (2000).

	2018	2019
Revenue		
($27 per unit × 1,000,000 units; $25 per unit × 1,150,000 units)	$27,000,000	$28,750,000
Costs		
Direct material costs		
($1.40/sq. cm. × 3,000,000 sq. cm.; $1.50/sq. cm. × 2,900,000 sq. cm.)	4,200,000	4,350,000
Conversion costs		
($4.28/sq. cm. × 3,750,000 sq. cm.; $4.35/sq. cm. × 3,500,000 sq. cm.)	16,050,000	15,225,000
R&D costs ($100,000 × 40 employees; $100,000 × 39 employees)	4,000,000	3,900,000
Total costs	24,250,000	23,475,000
Operating income	$ 2,750,000	$ 5,275,000
Change in operating income		↑ $2,525,000 F ↑

Chipset now wants to evaluate how much of this $2,525,000 increase in operating income can be attributed to successful implementation of the company's strategy.[7] To do so, it must examine three main analysis components: growth, price recovery, and productivity. Each component will be isolated from the favourable or unfavourable variance generated by the others.

The Growth Component

The growth component measures the increase in revenues minus the increase in costs from selling more units of LCX1 in 2019 (1,150,000 units) than in 2018 (1,000,000 units). That is, the output prices, input prices, efficiencies, and capacities of 2018 are assumed to continue into 2019. This isolates the effect of increased sales volume from all other revenue effects.

Revenue Effect of Growth

$$\text{Revenue effect of growth} = \left(\begin{array}{c}\text{Actual units of} \\ \text{output sold} \\ \text{in 2019}\end{array} - \begin{array}{c}\text{Actual units of} \\ \text{output sold} \\ \text{in 2018}\end{array}\right) \times \begin{array}{c}\text{Selling} \\ \text{price} \\ \text{in 2018}\end{array}$$

$$= (1,150,000 \text{ units} - 1,000,000 \text{ units}) \times \$27 \text{ per unit}$$

$$= \$4,050,000 \text{ F}$$

This component is favourable (F) because it increases operating income, all other things held equal. Decreases in operating income are unfavourable (U). The analysis assumes that in this highly competitive environment the 2018 selling price continued into 2019.

Cost Effect of Growth

Of course, to produce the higher output sold in 2019, more inputs would be needed. The cost increase from growth measures the amount by which costs in 2019 would have increased (1) if the relationship between inputs and outputs that existed in 2018 had continued in 2019, and (2) if prices of inputs in 2018 had continued in 2019. We use 2018 input–output relationships and 2018 input prices because the goal is to isolate the increase in costs caused solely by the growth in units sold of 150,000 units of LCX1 between 2018 and 2019.

$$\text{Cost effect of growth for variable costs} = \left(\begin{array}{c}\text{Units of input} \\ \text{required to} \\ \text{produce 2019} \\ \text{output in 2018}\end{array} - \begin{array}{c}\text{Actual units of} \\ \text{input used} \\ \text{to produce} \\ \text{2018 output}\end{array}\right) \times \begin{array}{c}\text{Input} \\ \text{price} \\ \text{in 2018}\end{array}$$

[7] The manufacturing conversion cost pool is almost 100% fixed cost. Chipset's strategy is cost leadership. It will improve profit by increasing the quantity of saleable LCX1. It will redesign the production process without spending more money to increase capacity.

$$\begin{array}{l}\text{Cost effect of}\\ \text{growth for}\\ \text{direct materials}\end{array} = \left(3{,}000{,}000 \text{ sq. cm.} \times \dfrac{1{,}150{,}000 \text{ units}}{1{,}000{,}000 \text{ units}} - 3{,}000{,}000 \text{ sq. cm.}\right) \times \$1.40 \text{ per sq. cm.}$$

$$= (3{,}450{,}000 \text{ sq. cm.} - 3{,}000{,}000 \text{ sq. cm.}) \times \$1.40 \text{ per sq. cm.} = \$630{,}000 \text{ U}$$

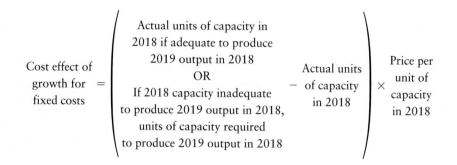

$$\begin{array}{l}\text{Cost effect of}\\ \text{growth for}\\ \text{conversion costs}\end{array} = (\$3{,}750{,}000 \text{ sq. cm.} - 3{,}750{,}000 \text{ sq. cm}) \times \$4.28 \text{ per sq. cm.} = \$0$$

All conversion costs are fixed at practical capacity of 3,750,000 cm² of silicon wafers at a total cost of $16,050,000, or $4.28/cm². In 2018, Chipset would have needed 3,450,000 cm² of direct materials to produce 3,450,000 LCX1. The actual quantity produced is within the relevant range with no additional capacity cost or conversion cost.

The R&D costs, however, are discretionary but would not change in 2018 even if Chipset had produced and sold a larger quantity of LCX1:

$$\begin{array}{l}\text{Cost effect of}\\ \text{growth for}\\ \text{R\&D costs}\end{array} = (40 \text{ employees} - 40 \text{ employees}) \times 100{,}000 \text{ per employee} = \$0$$

In summary, the net increase in operating income as a result of growth equals:

Revenue effect of growth		$4,050,000 F
Cost effect of growth		
Direct material costs	$630,000 U	
Conversion costs	0	
R&D costs	0	630,000 U
Change in operating income due to growth		$3,420,000 F

The Price-Recovery Component

The price-recovery component of operating income measures the change in revenues and the change in costs to produce the 1,150,000 units of LCX1 manufactured in 2019 as a result of the change in the prices of LCX1.

Revenue Effect of Price Recovery

Note that this calculation focuses on the decrease in the price of LCX1 between 2018 and 2019. The objective of the revenue effect of price recovery is to isolate the change in revenue between 2018 and 2019 due solely to the change in selling prices.

$$\begin{array}{l}\text{Revenue effect}\\ \text{of product differentiation}\\ \text{component}\end{array} = \left(\begin{array}{l}\text{Selling price}\\ \text{in 2019}\end{array} - \begin{array}{l}\text{Selling price}\\ \text{in 2018}\end{array}\right) \times \begin{array}{l}\text{Actual units of}\\ \text{output sold}\\ \text{in 2019}\end{array}$$

$$= (\$25 - \$27) \times 1{,}150{,}000 = \$2{,}300{,}000 \text{ U}$$

Cost Effect of Price Recovery

This calculation focuses on the effect of changes in the prices of inputs. Because of the anticipated change in manufacturing conversion costs, these fixed costs must be considered to capture the full cost effect of price recovery. The cost of direct materials required to produce 3,450,000 cm² has already been considered when calculating the cost effect of growth.

$$\begin{matrix} \text{Cost effect of} \\ \text{price recovery for} \\ \text{variable costs} \end{matrix} = \begin{pmatrix} \text{Input price} \\ \text{in 2019} \end{pmatrix} - \begin{pmatrix} \text{Input price} \\ \text{in 2018} \end{pmatrix} \times \begin{matrix} \text{Units} \\ \text{required to} \\ \text{produce 2019} \\ \text{output in 2018} \end{matrix}$$

$$\begin{matrix} \text{Cost effect of} \\ \text{price recovery for} \\ \text{direct materials} \end{matrix} = (\$1.50 \text{ per sq. cm.} - \$1.40 \text{ per sq. cm.}) \times 3,450,000 \text{ sq. cm.} = \$345,000 \text{ U}$$

The cost effect of price recovery for fixed costs is

$$\begin{matrix} \text{Cost effect of} \\ \text{price recovery for} \\ \text{fixed costs} \end{matrix} = \begin{pmatrix} \text{Price per} \\ \text{unit of} \\ \text{capacity} \\ \text{in 2019} \end{pmatrix} - \begin{pmatrix} \text{Price per} \\ \text{unit of} \\ \text{capacity} \\ \text{in 2018} \end{pmatrix} \times \begin{matrix} \text{Actual units of capacity in} \\ \text{2018, if adequate to produce} \\ \text{2019 output in 2018} \\ \text{OR} \\ \text{If 2018 capacity inadequate to} \\ \text{produce 2019 output in 2018,} \\ \text{units of capacity required to} \\ \text{produce 2019 output in 2018} \end{matrix}$$

The cost effects of price recovery conversion and R&D fixed costs are

Conversion costs = ($4.35 per cm² − $4.28 per cm²) × 3,750,000 cm² = $262,500 U

R&D costs = ($100,000 per employee − $100,000 per employee) × 40 employees = $0

In summary, the net decrease in operating income attributable to price recovery when there is adequate capacity and R&D employees are constant is

Revenue effect of price recovery		$2,300,000 U
Cost effect of price recovery		
Direct material costs	$345,000 U	
Conversion costs	262,500 U	
R&D costs	0	607,500 U
Change in operating income due to price recovery		$2,907,500 U

The Productivity Component

Productivity is the ratio of finished output units divided by input quantity. The contribution of productivity to the change in operating income uses current input costs in 2019. There is no revenue effect because the focus is on cost. The first calculation isolates the decrease in variable costs arising from use of fewer inputs, improved input mix, and less capacity compared to those used in 2018.

$$\begin{matrix} \text{Cost effect of} \\ \text{productivity for} \\ \text{variable costs} \end{matrix} = \begin{pmatrix} \text{Actual units of} \\ \text{input used} \\ \text{to produce} \\ \text{2019 output} \end{pmatrix} - \begin{pmatrix} \text{Units of input} \\ \text{required to} \\ \text{produce 2019} \\ \text{output in 2018} \end{pmatrix} \times \begin{matrix} \text{Input} \\ \text{price} \\ \text{in 2019} \end{matrix}$$

Direct material costs = (2,900,000 − 3,450,000) × $1.50 = $825,000 F.

Chipset's quality and yield improvements reduced the quantity of direct materials (inputs) required to generate higher productivity in 2019 relative to 2018:

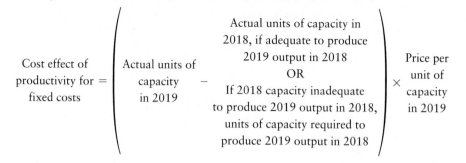

$$\begin{pmatrix} \text{Cost effect of} \\ \text{productivity for} \\ \text{fixed costs} \end{pmatrix} = \left(\begin{array}{c} \text{Actual units of} \\ \text{capacity} \\ \text{in 2019} \end{array} - \begin{array}{c} \text{Actual units of capacity in} \\ \text{2018, if adequate to produce} \\ \text{2019 output in 2018} \\ \text{OR} \\ \text{If 2018 capacity inadequate} \\ \text{to produce 2019 output in 2018,} \\ \text{units of capacity required to} \\ \text{produce 2019 output in 2018} \end{array} \right) \times \begin{array}{c} \text{Price per} \\ \text{unit of} \\ \text{capacity} \\ \text{in 2019} \end{array}$$

Based on the 2018 data and these analyses, the cost effects of fixed conversion costs on productivity are

Conversion costs =   (3,500,000 sq. cm. − 3,750,000 sq. cm.) × $4.35 per sq. cm. = $1,087,500 F

R&D costs =   (39 employees − 40 employees) × $100,000 per employee = $100,000 F

Chipset's managers decreased manufacturing capacity in 2019 to 3,500,000 cm². They accomplished this by selling off old equipment and retraining manufacturing workers to perform non-manufacturing tasks. One R&D manager voluntarily left Chipset and was not replaced, which reduced R&D expense. In summary, the net increase in operating income attributable to productivity is

Cost effect of productivity	
Direct material costs	$ 825,000 F
Conversion costs	1,087,500 F
R&D costs	100,000 F
Change in operating income due to productivity	$2,012,500 F

The productivity component reveals that Chipset increased its operating income in several ways consistent with the strategy of cost leadership. Chipset improved quality and yield, and reduced capacity costs. The company can conduct a more detailed analysis of partial and total factor productivity changes to obtain a deeper understanding of the effectiveness of Chipset's cost leadership strategy.

Further Analysis of Growth, Price-Recovery, and Productivity Components

Exhibit 13-5 summarizes the growth, price-recovery, and productivity components that contributed to a total favourable variance in operating income in 2019. As in all variance and profit analysis, the thoughtful analyst will want to look at the sources of operating income more closely. For instance, in the Chipset example growth may have been helped by an increase in industry market size. Therefore, at least a part of the increase in operating income may be attributable to favourable economic conditions in the industry rather than to any successful implementation of strategy. Some of the growth may also have come as a result of a management decision at Chipset to take advantage of its productivity gains by cutting prices. In this case, the increase in operating income from cost leadership equals the productivity gain, plus any increase in operating income from growth in market share attributable to productivity improvements, minus any decrease in operating income from a strategic decision to lower prices.

To illustrate these ideas, consider again the Chipset example and the following additional information:

■ The market growth rate in the industry is 10%. That is, of the 150,000 (= 1,150,000 − 1,000,000) units of increased sales of LCX1 between 2018 and 2019, 100,000 (= 10% × 1,000,000) units are due to an increase in industry market size (which

Exhibit 13-5 Strategic Analysis of Profitability

	Income Statement Amounts in 2018 (1)	Revenue and Cost Effects of Growth Component in 2019 (2)	Revenue and Cost Effects of Price-Recovery Component in 2019 (3)	Cost Effect of Productivity Component in 2019 (4)	Income Statement Amounts in 2019 (5) = (1) + (2) + (3) − (4)
Revenue	$27,000,000	$4,050,000 F	$2,300,000 U	—	$28,750,000
Costs	24,250,000	630,000 U	607,500 U	$2,012,500 F	23,475,000
Operating income	$ 2,750,000	$3,420,000 F	$2,907,500 U	$2,012,500 F	$ 5,275,000
			$2,525,000 F		

Change in operating income

Chipset would have benefited from regardless of its productivity gains), and the remaining 50,000 units are due to an increase in market share.

- There was a $1.35 or 5% decrease in the target price of LCX1 ($0.05 \times \$27 = \$1.35$). The remaining decrease of $0.65 arose from taking advantage of Chipset's productivity gain. As a result, Chipset's total reduction in unit sales price was $2 (= \$1.35 + \$0.65$).

Clearly, some of the improvement came from a growth in market size rather than any action by Chipset. This effect can be calculated as follows:

$$\$3,420,000 \text{ (Exhibit 13-5, column 2)} \times \frac{100,000 \text{ units}}{150,000 \text{ units}} = \$2,280,000 \text{ F}$$

Lacking a differentiated product, Chipset is unable to pass along increases in input prices to its customers. The effect of product differentiation on operating income is

Change in operating income due to a decline in the selling price of LCX1 (other than the strategic reduction in price included as part of the cost-leadership component) $1.35/unit × 1,150,000 units	$1,552,500 U
Change in prices of inputs (cost effect of price recovery)	607,500 U
Change in operating income due to product differentiation	$2,160,000 U

The change in operating income between 2018 and 2019 due to implementing the cost leadership strategy is

Productivity component	$2,012,500 F
Effect of strategic decision to reduce price ($0.65/unit × 1,150,000 units)	747,500 U
Growth in market share due to productivity improvement and strategic decision to reduce prices $3,420,000 (Exhibit 13-5, column 2) × $\frac{50,000 \text{ units}}{150,000 \text{ units}}$	1,140,000 F
Change in operating income due to cost leadership	$2,405,000 F

In summary, the change in operating income between 2018 and 2019 is

Change due to industry market size	$2,280,000 F
Change due to product differentiation	2,160,000 U
Change due to cost leadership	2,405,000 F
Change in operating income	$2,525,000 F

Under different assumptions of how changes in prices affect the quantity of LCX1 sold, the analyst will attribute different amounts to the different measures. The important point, though, is that the productivity gains of $2,012,500 Chipset made in 2019 were key to the operating income increases in 2019.

Specific Productivity Improvement Measures

► **LO 5**

Analyze the results from specific productivity and capacity control strategies to achieve balanced scorecard expectations.

Productivity measures the relationship between actual outputs produced and actual inputs used (both quantities and costs). The lower the quantity of inputs for a given quantity of outputs (or the higher the outputs for a given quantity of inputs), the higher the level of productivity. Measuring productivity improvements over time highlights the specific output–input relationships that contribute to cost leadership.

Partial productivity, the most frequently used productivity measure, compares the quantity of output produced with the quantity of an individual input used. The higher the ratio, the greater the productivity. In its most common form, partial productivity is expressed as a ratio:

$$\text{Partial productivity} = \frac{\text{Quantity of output produced}}{\text{Quantity of input used}}$$

Consider only direct materials productivity at Chipset in the year 2019.

$$\begin{aligned} \frac{\text{Direct materials}}{\text{partial productivity}} &= \frac{\text{Quantity of LCX1 units produced during 2019}}{\text{Quantity of direct materials used to produce LCX1 in 2019}} \\[2mm] &= \frac{1{,}150{,}000 \text{ units of LCX1}}{2{,}900{,}000 \text{ sq. cm. of direct materials}} \\[2mm] &= 0.397 \text{ units of LCX1 per sq. cm. of direct materials} \end{aligned}$$

Direct materials partial productivity ignores Chipset's other inputs, manufacturing conversion costs and R&D. Partial productivity measures become meaningful when comparisons are made that examine productivity changes over time, either across several facilities or relative to a benchmark. Exhibit 13-6 presents partial productivity measures for Chipset's various inputs for 2018 and 2019 using information from the productivity calculations. These measures compare the actual inputs used in the year 2019 to produce 1,150,000 units of LCX1 with the inputs that would have been used in 2019 had the input-output relationship from 2018 continued in 2019.

Partial productivity measures differ between fixed and variable costs of inputs. For fixed-cost inputs such as manufacturing conversion capacity, partial productivity will measure the reduction in overall capacity from 2018 to 2019 (3,750,000 cm^2 of silicon wafers to 3,500,000 cm^2) regardless of the actual capacity used in each year. A major advantage of partial productivity measures is that they focus on a single input. As a result, they are simple to calculate and easily understood by operations personnel.

Managers and supervisors examine these numbers to understand the reasons underlying productivity changes from one period to the next. Various possibilities are improved

Exhibit 13-6 Comparing Chipset's Partial Productivities in 2018 and 2019

Input (1)	Partial Productivity in 2019 (2)	Comparable Partial Productivity Based on 2018 Input- Output Relationships (3)	Percentage Change from 2018 to 2019 (4)
Direct materials	$\frac{1{,}150{,}000}{2{,}900{,}000} = 0.397$	$\frac{1{,}150{,}000}{3{,}450{,}000} = 0.333$	$\frac{0.397 - 0.333}{0.333} = 19.2\%$
Manufacturing conversion capacity	$\frac{1{,}150{,}000}{3{,}500{,}000} = 0.329$	$\frac{1{,}150{,}000}{3{,}750{,}000} = 0.307$	$\frac{0.329 - 0.307}{0.307} = 7.2\%$
R&D	$\frac{1{,}150{,}000}{39} = 29{,}487$	$\frac{1{,}150{,}000}{40} = 28{,}750$	$\frac{29{,}487 - 28{,}750}{28{,}750} = 2.6\%$

training and lower turnover (learning and growth), increased incentives to suggest productivity improvements, changes in the production process, higher quality inputs, substitution of machine- for labour-hours, and advanced quality control (internal business process). One drawback, of course, is the interdependencies illustrated in Exhibit 13-3, whereby improvement in one measure will lead to improvements in other related measures. This is why a different approach is needed to ensure that an isolated change in fact improved total productivity.

Total factor productivity (TFP), or total productivity, considers the result of changing all inputs simultaneously. TFP is the ratio of the quantity of output produced to the costs of all inputs used, where the inputs are combined on the basis of current period prices.

$$\text{Total factor productivity} = \frac{\text{Quantity of output produced}}{\text{Costs of all inputs used}}$$

TFP considers all inputs simultaneously and also considers the tradeoffs across inputs based on current input prices. Do not be tempted to think of all productivity measures as physical measures lacking financial content—how many units of output are produced per unit of input. Total factor productivity is intricately tied to minimizing total cost—a financial objective. We next measure changes in TFP at Chipset from 2018 to 2019.

Calculating and Comparing Total Factor Productivity

We first calculate Chipset's TFP in 2019 using 2019 prices and 1,150,000 units of output produced (using information from the first column of the productivity component calculations).

$$\begin{aligned}\frac{\text{Total factor productivity}}{\text{for 2019 using 2019 prices}} &= \frac{\text{Quantity of output produced in 2019}}{\text{Costs of inputs used in 2019 based on 2019 prices}} \\[1em]
&= \frac{1,150,000}{(2,900,000 \times \$1.50) + (3,500,000 \times \$4.35) + (39 \times \$100,000)} \\[1em]
&= \frac{1,150,000}{\$23,475,000} \\[1em]
&= 0.048988 \text{ units of output per dollar of input cost}\end{aligned}$$

By itself, the 2019 TFP of 0.048988 units of LCX1 per dollar of input is not particularly helpful. We need something to compare it against. One alternative is to compare TFPs of other similar companies in 2019. However, finding similar companies and obtaining accurate comparable data is often difficult. Companies therefore usually compare their own TFP over time.

In the Chipset example, we use as a benchmark TFP the inputs that Chipset would have used in 2018 to produce 1,150,000 units of LCX1 at 2019 prices (that is, we use the costs calculated from the second column in the productivity component calculations. The 2019 prices are used because using the current year's (2019) prices in both calculations controls for input price differences and focuses the analysis on the adjustments the manager made in the quantities of inputs in response to changes in prices.

$$\begin{aligned}\frac{\text{Benchmark}}{\text{TFP}} &= \frac{\text{Quantity of output produced in 2019}}{\text{Costs of inputs that would have been used in 2018 to produce 2019 output}} \\[1em]
&= \frac{1,150,000}{(3,450,000 \times \$1.50) + (3,750,000 \times \$4.35) + (40 \times \$100,000)} \\[1em]
&= \frac{1,150,000}{\$25,487,500} \\[1em]
&= 0.045120 \text{ units of output per dollar of input cost}\end{aligned}$$

Using 2019 prices, total factor productivity increased 8.6% [= (0.048988 − 0.045120) ÷ 0.045120] from 2018 to 2019. The gain in TFP occurs because Chipset increases the partial productivities of individual inputs and, consistent with its strategy, seeks the least expensive combination of inputs to produce LCX1.

A major advantage of TFP is that it measures the combined productivity of all inputs used to produce output. Therefore, it explicitly considers gains from using fewer physical inputs as well as substitution among inputs. Managers can analyze these numbers to understand the reasons for changes in TFP. For example, Chipset's managers will try to evaluate whether the increase in TFP from 2018 to 2019 was due to better human resource management practices, higher quality of materials, or improved manufacturing methods. Chipset will adopt the most successful practices and use TFP measures to implement and evaluate strategy by setting targets and monitoring trends.

Many companies, such as Monsanto, a manufacturer of fibres, and Motorola, a microchip manufacturer, use both partial productivity and total factor productivity to evaluate performance. *Partial productivity and TFP measures work best together because the strengths of one are the weaknesses of the other.*

Downsizing and the Management of Processing Capacity

Fixed costs are tied to capacity. Unlike variable costs, fixed costs do not change automatically with changes in activity level (for example, fixed conversion costs do not change with changes in the quantity of silicon wafers started into production). Managers reduce capacity-based fixed costs by measuring and managing unused capacity. **Unused capacity** is the amount of productive capacity available over and above the productive capacity employed to meet consumer demand in the current period. To understand unused capacity, it is necessary to distinguish between *engineered costs* and *discretionary costs*.

Engineered and Discretionary Costs

Engineered costs result from a cause-and-effect relationship between the cost driver— output—and the (direct or indirect) resources used to produce that output. Engineered costs have a detailed, physically observable, and repetitive relationship with output. In the Chipset example, direct material costs are *direct engineered costs*. Conversion costs are an example of *indirect engineered costs*. Consider 2019. The output of 1,150,000 units of LCX1 and the efficiency with which inputs are converted into outputs result in 2,900,000 square centimetres of silicon wafers being started into production. Manufacturing-conversion-cost resources used equal $12,615,000 (= $4.35 per sq. cm. × 2,900,000 sq. cm.), but actual conversion costs ($15,225,000) are higher because Chipset has manufacturing capacity to process 3,500,000 square centimetres of silicon wafer ($4.35 per sq. cm. × 3,500,000 sq. cm. = $15,225,000). Although these costs are fixed in the short run, over the long run there is a cause-and-effect relationship between output and manufacturing capacity required (and conversion costs needed). In the long run, Chipset will try to match its capacity to its needs.

Discretionary costs have two important features: (1) They arise from periodic (usually annual) decisions regarding the maximum amount to be incurred; and (2) they have no measurable cause-and-effect relationship between output and resources used. There is often a delay between when a resource is acquired and when it is used. Examples of discretionary costs include advertising, executive training, R&D, and corporate-staff department costs such as legal, human resources, and public relations. Unlike engineered costs, the relationship between discretionary costs and output is unknown because it is nonrepetitive and nonroutine. A noteworthy aspect of discretionary costs is that managers are seldom confident that the "correct" amounts are being spent. William Hesketh Lever, the founder of Lever Brothers, an international consumer-products company, once noted, "Half the money I spend on advertising is wasted; the trouble is, I don't know which half!"

Identifying Unused Capacity for Engineered and Discretionary Overhead Costs

Identifying unused capacity is very different for engineered costs compared to discretionary costs. Consider engineered conversion costs.

At the start of 2019, Chipset had capacity to process 3,750,000 square centimetres of silicon wafers. Quality and productivity improvements made during 2018 enabled Chipset to produce 1,150,000 units of LCX1 by processing 2,900,000 square centimetres of silicon wafers. Unused manufacturing capacity is 850,000 (= 3,750,000 − 2,900,000) square centimetres of silicon-wafer processing capacity at the beginning of 2019. At the 2019 conversion cost of $4.35 per square centimetre,

$$\begin{array}{l} \text{Cost of} \\ \text{unused capacity} \end{array} = \begin{array}{l} \text{Cost of capacity} \\ \text{at the beginning} \\ \text{of the year} \end{array} - \begin{array}{l} \text{Manufacturing resources} \\ \text{used during the year} \end{array}$$

$$= (3,750,000 \text{ sq. cm.} \times \$4.35 \text{ per sq. cm.}) - (2,900,000 \text{ sq. cm.} \times \$4.35 \text{ per sq. cm.})$$

$$= \$16,312,500 - \$12,615,000 = \$3,697,500$$

The absence of a cause-and-effect relationship makes identifying unused capacity for discretionary costs difficult. For example, management cannot determine the R&D resources used for the actual output produced. And without a measure of capacity used, it is not possible to compute unused capacity.

Managing Unused Capacity

What actions can Chipset management take when it identifies unused capacity? In general, it has two alternatives: eliminate unused capacity or grow output to utilize the unused capacity.

In recent years, many companies have *downsized* in an attempt to eliminate unused capacity. **Downsizing** (also called **rightsizing**) is an integrated approach of configuring processes, products, and people to match costs to the activities that need to be performed to operate effectively and efficiently in the present and future. Companies such as AT&T, Delta Airlines, Ford Motor Company, and IBM have downsized to focus on their core businesses and have instituted organization changes to increase efficiency, reduce costs, and improve quality. However, downsizing often means eliminating jobs, which can adversely affect employee morale and the culture of a company.

Consider Chipset's alternatives with respect to its unused manufacturing capacity. Because it needed to process 2,900,000 square centimetres of silicon wafers in 2019, it could have reduced capacity to 3,000,000 square centimetres (Chipset can add or reduce manufacturing capacity in increments of 250,000 sq. cm.), resulting in cost savings of $3,262,500 [= (3,750,000 sq. cm. − 3,000,000 sq. cm.) × $4.35 per sq. cm.]. Chipset's strategy, however, is not just to reduce costs but also to grow its business. So early in 2019, Chipset reduces its manufacturing capacity by only 250,000 square centimetres from 3,750,000 square centimetres to 3,500,000 square centimetres saving $1,087,500 (= $4.35 per sq. cm. × 250,000 sq. cm.). It retains some extra capacity for future growth. By avoiding greater reductions in capacity, it also maintains the morale of its skilled and capable workforce. The success of this strategy will depend on Chipset's achieving the future growth it has projected.

Because identifying unused capacity for discretionary costs, such as R&D costs, is difficult, downsizing or otherwise managing this unused capacity is also difficult. Management must exercise considerable judgment in deciding the level of R&D costs that would generate the needed product and process improvements. Unlike engineered costs, there is no clear-cut way to know whether management is spending too much (or too little) on R&D.

Pulling it all Together—Problem for Self-Study

(Try to solve this problem before examining the solution that follows.)

Problem

Following a strategy of product differentiation, Westwood Corporation makes a high-end kitchen range hood, KE8. Westwood presents the following data for the years 2018 and 2019.

	2018	2019
1. Units of KE8 produced	40,000	42,000
2. Selling price	$100	$110
3. Direct materials (m²)	120,000	123,000
4. Direct materials costs per m²	$10	$11
5. Manufacturing capacity for KE8	50,000 units	50,000 units
6. Total manufacturing conversion costs	$1,000,000	$1,100,000
7. Manufacturing conversion costs per unit of capacity (Row 6 ÷ Row 5)	$20	$22
8. Selling and customer-service capacity	30 customers	29 customers
9. Total selling and customer-service costs	$720,000	$725,000
10. Cost per customer of selling and customer-service capacity (Row 9 ÷ Row 8)	$24,000	$25,000

Westwood produces no defective units, but it wants to reduce direct materials usage per unit of KE8 in 2019. Manufacturing conversion costs in each year depend on production capacity defined in terms of KE8 units that can be produced. Selling and customer-service costs depend on the number of customers that the customer and service functions are designed to support. Westwood has 23 customers in 2018 and 25 customers in 2019. The industry market size for high-end kitchen range hoods increased 5% from 2018 to 2019.

Required ▶

❶ 1. Describe briefly key elements that you would include in Westwood's BSC.

❷ 2. How would improved corporate governance improve Westwood's corporate competitiveness?

❸ 3. How would BSC measures of environmental sustainability contribute to Westwood's enterprise risk management?

❹ 4. Calculate the growth, price-recovery, and productivity components of changes in operating income between 2018 and 2019.

❶ 5. Without doing any more calculations, explain in a few sentences whether Westwood was successful in implementing its strategy.

Solution

1. Key elements that Westwood should include in its BSC are

- *Financial perspective.* Operating income growth from charging higher prices on KE8.

- *Customer perspective.* Market share in high-end kitchen range market and customer satisfaction.

- *Internal-business perspective.* Manufacturing quality, order-delivery time, on-time delivery, and new product features added.

- *Learning-and-growth perspective.* Development time for designing new products and improving manufacturing processes.

2. Improving any one of the five dimensions of corporate governance improves the others. Improved corporate governance also improves competitiveness because all the factors affect customer, financial, and intellectual capital management.

3. Increasingly countries are enacting legislation that requires reclamation, recycling, and remediation activities be paid for by companies causing the need for these activities. The risk to the enterprise is that its current life-cycle pricing practices fail to include reasonable estimates of environmental life-cycle costs. Global companies need to measure their performance in a BSC format to provide relevant information to improve their strategy to respond to mandatory compliance with new legislation— good corporate governance.

4. Operating income for each year is as follows:

	2018	2019
Revenue ($100 × 40,000; $110 × 42,000)	$4,000,000	$4,620,000
Costs		
Direct materials costs ($10 × 120,000; $11 × 123,000)	1,200,000	1,353,000
Manufacturing conversion costs ($20 × 50,000; $22 × 50,000)	1,000,000	1,100,000
Selling and customer-service costs ($24,000 × 30; $25,000 × 29)	720,000	725,000
Total costs	2,920,000	3,178,000
Operating income	$1,080,000	$1,442,000
Change in operating income	↓ $362,000 F ↓	

The Growth Component

$$\frac{\text{Revenue effect of}}{\text{growth component}} = \left(\begin{array}{c} \text{Actual units of output} \\ \text{sold in 2019} \end{array} - \begin{array}{c} \text{Actual units of output} \\ \text{sold in 2018} \end{array} \right) \times \begin{array}{c} \text{2018 output} \\ \text{price} \end{array}$$

$$= (42{,}000 - 40{,}000) \times \$100 = \$200{,}000 \text{ F}$$

$$\begin{array}{c} \text{Cost effect} \\ \text{of growth} \\ \text{component} \end{array} = \left(\begin{array}{c} \text{Actual units of input/capacity that} \\ \text{would have been used to produce} \\ \text{year 2019 output, assuming the} \\ \text{same input-output relationship} \\ \text{that existed in 2018} \end{array} - \begin{array}{c} \text{Actual units of} \\ \text{input/capacity to} \\ \text{produce 2018} \\ \text{output} \end{array} \right) \times \begin{array}{c} \text{Year} \\ \text{2018} \\ \text{prices} \end{array}$$

Direct materials costs that would be required in 2018 to produce 42,000 units instead of the 40,000 units produced in 2018, assuming the 2018 input-output relationship continued into 2019, equal 126,000 m² (= 120,000/40,000 × 42,000). Manufacturing conversion costs and selling and customer-service costs will not change since adequate capacity exists in 2018 to support year 2019 output and customers.

The cost effects of growth component are

Direct materials costs	(126,000 – 120,000) × $10	=	$60,000 U
Manufacturing conversion costs	(50,000 – 50,000) × $20	=	0
Selling and customer-service costs	(30 – 30) × $24,000	=	0
Cost effect of growth component			$60,000 U

In summary, the net increase in operating income as a result of the growth component equals

Revenue effect of growth component	$200,000 F
Cost effect of growth component	60,000 U
Increase in operating income due to growth component	$140,000 F

The Price-Recovery Component

$$\begin{array}{l}\text{Revenue effect of}\\ \text{product differentiation} = \left(\begin{array}{c}\text{Output price} \\ \text{in 2019}\end{array} - \begin{array}{c}\text{Output price}\\ \text{in 2018}\end{array}\right) \times \begin{array}{c}\text{Actual units of}\\ \text{output sold}\\ \text{in 2019}\end{array}\\ \text{component}\end{array}$$

$$= (\$110 - \$100) \times 42{,}000 = \$420{,}000 \text{ F}$$

$$\begin{array}{l}\text{Cost effect}\\ \text{of product} = \left(\begin{array}{c}\text{Input price}\\ \text{in 2019}\end{array} - \begin{array}{c}\text{Input price}\\ \text{in 2018}\end{array}\right) \times \begin{array}{c}\text{Actual units of input/capacity that}\\ \text{would have been used to produce}\\ \text{year 2019 output, assuming the}\\ \text{same input-output relationship}\\ \text{that existed in 2018}\end{array}\\ \text{differentiation}\end{array}$$

Direct materials costs	($11 − $10) × 126,000	=	$126,000 U
Manufacturing conversion costs	($22 − $20) × 50,000	=	100,000 U
Selling and customer-service costs	($25,000 − $24,000) × 30	=	30,000 U
Total cost effect of price-recovery component			$256,000 U

In summary, the net increase in operating income as a result of the price-recovery component equals

Revenue effect of price-recovery component	$420,000 F
Cost effect of price-recovery component	256,000 U
Increase in operating income due to price-recovery component	$164,000 F

The Productivity Component

$$\begin{array}{l}\text{Productivity/}\\ \text{cost leadership} = \left(\begin{array}{c}\text{Actual units of}\\ \text{input/capacity to}\\ \text{produce year}\\ \text{2019 input}\end{array} - \begin{array}{c}\text{Actual units of input/capacity}\\ \text{that would have been used to}\\ \text{produce year 2019 output}\\ \text{assuming the same input-}\\ \text{output relationship that}\\ \text{existed in 2018}\end{array}\right) \times \begin{array}{c}\text{Year}\\ \text{2019}\\ \text{prices}\end{array}\\ \text{component}\end{array}$$

The productivity component of cost changes are

Direct materials costs	(123,000 − 126,000) × $11	=	$33,000 F
Manufacturing conversion costs	(50,000 − 50,000) × $22	=	0
Selling and customer-service costs	(29 − 30) × $25,000	=	25,000 F
Increase in operating income due to productivity component			$58,000 F

The change in operating income between 2018 and 2019 can be analyzed as follows:

	Statement of Comprehensive Income Amounts in 2018 (1)	Revenue and Cost Effects of Growth Component in 2019 (2)	Revenue and Cost Effects of Price-Recovery Component in 2019 (3)	Cost Effect of Productivity Component in 2019 (4)	Statement of Comprehensive Income Amounts in 2019 (5) = (1) + (2) + (3) + (4)
Revenue	$4,000,000	$200,000 F	$420,000 F	—	$4,620,000
Costs	2,920,000	60,000 U	256,000 U	$58,000 F	3,178,000
Operating income	$1,080,000	$140,000 F	$164,000 F	$58,000 F	$1,442,000
	↓		$362,000 F		↓

Change in operating income

5. The analysis of operating income indicates that Westwood was successful in implementing its product differentiation strategy. The company was able to continue to charge a premium price for KE8. Westwood was also able to earn additional operating income from improving its productivity. The growth in units (from 40,000 to 42,000) was attributable entirely to the 5% increase in market size rather than Westwood's product differentiation strategy.

Decision Points

The following question-and-answer format summarizes the chapter's learning objectives. Each point presents a key question, and the guidelines are the answer to that question.

Learning Objectives	Guidelines
1. How does the relative strength of competitive forces help managers identify strategic alternatives?	Porter's five forces analysis indicates two potential strategies. One is value leadership, appropriate when customers will pay a premium price for unique or highly differentiated products. The second is cost leadership, appropriate when there are plenty of substitutes for a commodity product and many competitors. Corporations selecting the strategy appropriate to the customer's willingness to pay will open an opportunity for superior ROI. Target pricing begins with a target ROI, given the customer's target price. This drives the calculation of the target operating income margin percentage from which are derived the target costs. In a commodity market where cost leadership is the appropriate strategy, improving the operating income margin percentage depends on avoiding the "stuck in the middle" situation.
2. What is reengineering?	Reengineering is a process of examining business processes at the most basic level with the possibility of engaging in holistic change. It involves redesigning business processes to improve performance by reducing cost and improving quality.
3. What are the four perspectives of the BSC?	These four measures include the customer-service perspective, which relates to design and selection of products. The second is the internal process perspective or design of products and production processes to meet customer expectations. The third is the learning and growth perspective, which influences the rate of innovation and successful implementation of products and processes to meet customer expectations. Aligning these three will result in improvement in the fourth perspective, financial results.
4. How is strategic success measured?	Strategic success can be measured by growth, price-recovery, and productivity components of improved operating income. A company is considered successful in implementing its strategy when changes in operating income align closely with that strategy.
5. How are BSC expectations achieved?	Analyze an organization within the framework of the performance and operations of financial management, customer relations and service, internal business processes, and learning and growth.

Terms to Learn

This chapter and the Glossary at the end of the book contain definitions of the following important terms:

balanced scorecard (BSC) **(p. 529)**
cost leadership **(p. 526)**
customer perspective **(p. 529)**
customer preference
  map **(p. 526)**
discretionary costs **(p. 544)**
downsizing **(p. 545)**
economies of scope **(p. 526)**
engineered costs **(p. 544)**

enterprise risk management
  (ERM) **(p. 533)**
financial perspective **(p. 529)**
internal-business-process
  perspective **(p. 529)**
key success factors **(p. 528)**
learning-and-growth perspective **(p. 531)**
partial productivity **(p. 542)**
product differentiation **(p. 526)**

redesigning **(p. 528)**
reengineering **(p. 528)**
rightsizing **(p. 545)**
scaleability **(p. 524)**
strategy **(p. 524)**
strategy map **(p. 528)**
total factor productivity (TFP) **(p. 543)**
unused capacity **(p. 544)**
value leadership **(p. 525)**

Assignment Material

MyLab Accounting Make the grade with MyLab Accounting: The Short-Answer Questions, Exercises, and Problems marked with a ⊕ can be found on MyLab Accounting. You can practise them as often as you want, and most feature step-by-step guided instructions to help you find the right answer.

Short-Answer Questions

⊕ **13-1** Define *strategy*.
⊕ **13-2** Describe the five key forces to consider when analyzing an industry.
⊕ **13-3** Describe two generic strategies.
⊕ **13-4** What is a customer preference map, and why is it useful?
⊕ **13-5** What is reengineering?
⊕ **13-6** What are four key perspectives in the BSC?
⊕ **13-7** What is a strategy map?
⊕ **13-8** Describe three features of a good BSC.
⊕ **13-9** What are three important pitfalls to avoid when implementing a BSC?
⊕ **13-10** Describe three key components of a strategic analysis of operating income.
⊕ **13-11** What is the difference between a stakeholder and a shareholder?
⊕ **13-12** How does an engineered cost differ from a discretionary cost?
⊕ **13-13** What is downsizing?
⊕ **13-14** "We are already measuring total factor productivity. Measuring partial productivity would be of no value." Do you agree? Comment briefly.

Exercises

⊕ **13-15 Terminology.** A number of terms are listed below:

engineered costs	economies of scale	customer perspective
key success factors (KSF)	enterprise risk management (ERM)	economies of scope
organic revenue	internal-process perspective	financial perspective
strategy	product differentiation	learning/growth
balanced scorecard (BSC)	value leadership	perspective
cost leadership	competitive advantage	reengineering

Required

Select the terms from the above list to complete the following sentences.

Any management team must understand how it creates value for its customers and decide how to accomplish this goal better than all its competitors. This is a decision about _____. For exciting new products and products with no substitutes, consumers are willing to pay a premium price. Focusing on inventing and commercializing products with unique attributes is a _____ _____ (or _____ _____) strategy. For most mass-produced products sold by many competitors, consumers readily find substitutes. _____ _____ is the alternative strategy that improves profitability and ROI through _____ _____ _____ and _____ _____ _____. Usually this means the management team will work on increasing the quantity of output using the same capacity. The fixed cost per unit produced will decrease, and, if price is fixed, then profit will increase. Often cost leadership (or reduction) is achieved by _____ the production process. Growth can also be achieved by producing similar but not identical products, and this is _____ _____ growth that provides economies of scope.

Competitive advantage is identified by a resource or set of resources available to a company that enable it to execute its business activities more profitably than other competitors. Management teams must align the choice of strategy with the competitive advantage to implement a strategy well. The resources that provide competitive advantage are called _____ _____ _____ (_____).

To obtain feedback on how successful the implementation of strategy is, a _____ _____ (_____) is often used. The BSC is the foundation of more technologically intensive _____ _____ _____ (_____) systems. The BSC and ERM require refined cost reporting systems. The BSC measures success from four perspectives: _____ _____, _____ _____ _____, _____/_____, and of course _____ _____. The BSC approach provides a more detailed basis upon which to evaluate the success of implementation of strategy.

🌐 **13-16 Balanced scorecard.** La Flamme Corporation manufactures corrugated cardboard boxes. It competes and plans to grow by producing high-quality boxes at a low price that are delivered to customers in a timely manner. Many other manufacturers produce similar boxes. La Flamme believes that continuously improving its manufacturing processes and having satisfied employees are critical to implementing its strategy in 2018.

◀ LO 1

Required

1. Is La Flamme's 2018 strategy one of product differentiation or cost leadership? Explain briefly.
2. Portage Corporation, a competitor of La Flamme, manufactures corrugated boxes with more designs and colour combinations than La Flamme at a higher price. Portage's boxes are of high quality but require more time to produce and so have longer delivery times. Draw a simple customer preference map for La Flamme and Portage using the attributes of price, delivery time, quality, and design.
3. Indicate two measures you would expect to see under each perspective in La Flamme's BSC for 2018. Use a strategy map to explain your answer.

🌐 **13-17 Analysis of growth, price-recovery, and productivity components** (continuation of Exercise 13-16). An analysis of La Flamme's operating income changes between 2018 and 2019 shows the following:

◀ LO 1

Operating income for 2019	$1,700,000
Add growth component	80,000
Deduct price-recovery component	(60,000)
Add productivity component	180,000
Operating income for 2018	$1,900,000

The industry market size for corrugated boxes did not grow in 2019, input prices did not change, and La Flamme reduced the price of its boxes in line with the market.

Required

1. Was La Flamme's gain in operating income in 2019 consistent with the strategy you identified in requirement 1 of Exercise 13-16?
2. Explain the productivity component. In general, does it represent savings in only variable costs, only fixed costs, or both variable and fixed costs?

⊕ **13-18 Strategy, balanced scorecard.** Grey Corporation makes a special-purpose D4H machine used in the textile industry. Grey has designed the D4H machine for 2018 to be distinct from its competitors. It has been generally regarded as a superior machine. Grey presents the following data for the years 2018 and 2019.

	2018	2019
1. Units of D4H produced and sold	200	210
2. Selling price	$40,000	$42,000
3. Direct materials (kilograms)	300,000	310,000
4. Direct material cost per kilogram	$8.00	$8.50
5. Manufacturing capacity (units of D4H)	250	250
6. Total conversion costs	$2,000,000	$2,025,000
7. Conversion cost per unit of capacity	$8,000	$8,100
8. Selling and customer-service capacity	100 customers	95 customers
9. Total selling and customer-service costs	$1,000,000	$940,500
10. Selling and customer-service capacity cost per customer	$10,000	$9,900
11. Design staff	12	12
12. Total design costs	$1,200,000	$1,212,000
13. Design cost per employee	$100,000	$101,000

Grey produces no defective machines, but it wants to reduce direct materials usage per D4H machine in 2019. Manufacturing conversion costs in each year depend on production capacity defined in terms of D4H units that can be produced, not the actual units of D4H produced. Selling and customer-service costs depend on the number of customers that Grey can support, not the actual number of customers Grey serves. Grey has 75 customers in 2018 and 80 customers in 2019. At the start of each year, management uses its discretion to determine the number of design staff for the year. The design staff and costs have no direct relationship with the quantity of D4H produced or the number of customers to whom D4H is sold.

Required

1. Is Grey's strategy one of product differentiation or cost leadership? Explain briefly.
2. Describe briefly key elements that you would include in Grey's BSC and the reasons for doing so.

LO 4 ▶

1. Change in operating income, $607,500 F

⊕ **13-19 Strategic analysis of operating income.** Refer to the information in Exercise 13-18.

Required

1. Calculate the change in operating income of Grey Corporation in 2018 and 2019.
2. Calculate the growth, price-recovery, and productivity components of changes in operating income between 2018 and 2019.
3. Comment on your answer in requirement 2. What do these components indicate?

LO 5 ▶

Change in operating income from industry market-size factor, $168,000 F

⊕ **13-20 Analysis of growth, price-recovery, and productivity components** (continuation of Exercise 13-19). Suppose that between 2018 and 2019 the market for Grey's special-purpose machines grew at 3%. All increases in market share (that is, sales increases greater than 3%) are the result of Grey's strategic actions.

Required

Calculate how much of the change in operating income between 2018 and 2019 is due to industry market-size factors, cost leadership, and product differentiation. How successful has Grey been in implementing its strategy? Explain.

LO 5 ▶

1. a. Amount of unused manufacturing capacity, 40 units

⊕ **13-21 Identifying and managing unused capacity.** Refer to the Grey Corporation information in Exercise 13-18.

Required

1. Where possible, calculate the amount and cost of unused capacity for (a) manufacturing, (b) selling and customer service, and (c) design at the beginning of 2019 based on 2019 production. If you could not calculate the amount and cost of unused capacity, indicate why not.
2. Suppose Grey can add or reduce its manufacturing capacity in increments of 30 units. What is the maximum amount of costs that Grey could save by downsizing manufacturing capacity?
3. Grey, in fact, does not eliminate any of its unused manufacturing capacity. Why might Grey not downsize?

⊕ 13-22 Balanced scorecard. Following is a random-order listing of perspectives, strategic objectives, and performance measures for the BSC.

◄ LO 3

Perspectives	Performance Measures
Internal business process	Percentage of defective product units
Customer	Return on assets
Learning and growth	Number of patents
Financial	Employee turnover rate
	Net income
Strategic Objectives	Customer profitability
	Percentage of processes with real-time feedback
Acquire new customers	Return on sales
Increase shareholder value	Average job-related training-hours per employee
Retain customers	Return on equity
Improve manufacturing quality	Percentage of on-time deliveries by suppliers
Develop profitable customers	Product cost per unit
Increase proprietary products	Profit per salesperson
Increase information-system capabilities	Percentage of error-free invoices
Enhance employee skills	Customer cost per unit
On-time delivery by suppliers	Earnings per share
Increase profit generated by each salesperson	Number of new customers
Introduce new product	Percentage of customers retained
Minimize invoice error rate	

Required

For each perspective, select those strategic objectives from the list that best relate to it. For each strategic objective, select the most appropriate performance measure(s) from the list.

⊕ 13-23 Strategy, balanced scorecard, service company. Haller Corporation is a small information systems consulting firm that specializes in helping companies implement sales management software. The market for Haller's products is very competitive. To compete, Haller must deliver quality service at a low cost. Haller bills clients in terms of units of work performed, which depends on the size and complexity of the sales management system. Haller presents the following data for the years 2018 and 2019.

◄ LO 4

	2018	2019
1. Units of work performed	60	70
2. Selling price	$ 50,000	$ 48,200
3. Software implementation labour-hours	30,000	32,000
4. Cost per software implementation labour-hour	$ 60	$ 63
5. Software implementation support capacity (units of work)	90	90
6. Total cost of software implementation support	$360,000	$369,000
7. Software implementation support capacity cost per unit of work	$ 4,000	$ 4,100
8. Number of employees doing software development	3	3
9. Total software development costs	$375,000	$390,000
10. Software development cost per employee	$125,000	$130,000

Software implementation labour-hour costs are variable costs. Software implementation support costs for each year depend on the software implementation support capacity (defined in terms of units of work) that Haller chooses to maintain each year. It does not vary with the actual units of work performed each year. At the start of each year, management uses its discretion to determine the number of software-development employees. The software-development staff and costs have no direct relationship with the number of units of work performed.

Required

1. Is Haller Corporation's strategy one of product differentiation or cost leadership?
2. Describe briefly key elements that you would include in Haller's BSC and your reasons for doing so.

🌐 **13-24 Strategic analysis of operating income.** Refer to the information in Exercise 13-23.

Required

1. Calculate the change in operating income of Haller Corporation in 2018 and 2019.
2. Calculate the growth, price-recovery, and productivity components of changes in operating income between 2018 and 2019.
3. Comment on your answer in requirement 2. What do these components indicate?

🌐 **13-25 Analysis of growth, price-recovery, and productivity components** (continuation of Exercise 13-24). Suppose that during 2019 the market for implementing sales management software increased by 5%, and that Haller experiences a 1% decline in prices. Assume that any further decreases in selling prices and increases in market share are strategic choices by Haller's management to implement Haller's cost leadership strategy.

Required

Calculate how much of the change in operating income between 2018 and 2019 is due to industry market-size factors, cost leadership, and product differentiation. How successful has Haller been in implementing its strategy?

🌐 **13-26 Identifying and managing unused capacity.** Refer to the Haller Corporation information in Exercise 13-23.

Required

1. Where possible, calculate the amount and cost of unused capacity for (a) software implementation support and (b) software development at the beginning of 2019, based on units of work to be performed in 2019. If you could not calculate the amount and cost of unused capacity, indicate why not.
2. Suppose Haller can add or reduce its software implementation support capacity in increments of 5 units. What is the maximum amount of costs that Haller could save by downsizing software implementation support capacity?
3. Haller, in fact, does not eliminate any of its unused software implementation support capacity. Why might Haller not downsize?

🌐 **13-27 Growth, price-recovery, and productivity components.** Lakeside T-Shirt Company sells a variety of T-shirts. Lakeside presents the following data for its first two years of operations, 2018 and 2019. For simplicity, assume that all purchasing and selling costs are included in the average cost per T-shirt and that each customer buys one T-shirt.

	2018	2019
Number of T-shirts purchased	200,000	250,000
Number of T-shirts lost	2,000	3,300
Number of T-shirts sold	198,000	246,700
Average selling price	$25.00	$26.00
Average cost per T-shirt	$10.00	$8.50
Administrative capacity in terms of number of customers who can be served	4,000	3,750
Administrative costs	$1,200,000	$1,162,500
Administrative cost per customer	$300	$310
Design staff	5	5
Total design costs	$250,000	$275,000
Design cost per employee	$50,000	$55,000

Required

1. Is Lakeside's strategy one of value or cost leadership? Explain briefly.
2. Describe briefly the key elements Lakeside should include in its BSC and the reasons it should do so.

🌐 **13-28 Strategic analysis of operating income** (continuation of Exercise 13-27).

Required

1. Calculate Lakeside's operating income in both 2018 and 2019.
2. Calculate the growth, price-recovery, and productivity components that explain the change in operating income from 2018 to 2019.
3. Comment on your answers in requirement 2. What do each of these components indicate?

Problems

🌐 **13-29 Balanced scorecard, non-profit, governance.** Sunset Heights Animal Rescue & Protection Society (ANIPAL) is a non-profit organization dedicated to the rescue and protection of domestic animals. It operates several animal shelters in the Sunset Heights area (including animal adoption services), rescues injured or abused domestic animals, and educates volunteers, pet owners, and potential pet owners on animal guardianship.

◀ LO 3

As with all charitable organizations, it is facing increased competition in raising funds and recruiting volunteers. It is also experiencing greater demands for accountability from its donors. Recently it was unable to respond to its board of directors on the costs of running each of its programs and its allocation of funds received to various programs. Although ANIPAL is expected to operate with a balanced budget, it reported an operating deficit last year.

Required

1. Create a BSC for ANIPAL. In your answer, consider the various programs/services ANIPAL provides.
2. What are the corporate governance issues raised, and how might they be addressed?

🌐 **13-30 Strategic analysis of operating income.** Dransfield Company manufactures an electronic component, ZP98. This component is significantly less expensive than similar products sold by Dransfield's competitors. Order-processing time is very short; however, approximately 10% of products are defective and returned by the customer. Returns and refunds are handled promptly. Yorunt Manufacturing, Dransfield's main competitor, has a higher-priced product with almost no defects but a longer order-processing time. Assume that in 2019, Dransfield has changed its processes and trained workers to recognize quality problems and fix them before products are finished and shipped to customers. Quality is now at an acceptable level. Cost per kilogram of materials is about the same as before, but conversion costs are higher, and Dransfield has raised its selling price in line with the market. Sales have increased and returns have decreased. Dransfield's managers attribute this to higher quality and a price that is still less than Yorunt's. Information about the current period (2019) and last period (2018) follows.

◀ LO 4
1. Change in operating income, $36,820 F

	2018	2019
1a. Units of ZP98 produced and sold	5,000	6,250
1b. Units of ZP98 returned	500	225
1c. Net sales in units	4,500	6,025
2. Selling price	$44	$50
3. Direct materials (kilograms) used	2,500	3,125
4. Direct materials cost per kilogram	$10	$10
5. Manufacturing capacity in units of ZP98	8,000	8,000
6. Total conversion costs	$128,000	$184,000
7. Conversion cost per unit of capacity	$16	$23
8. Selling and customer-service capacity	60 customers	60 customers
9. Total selling and customer-service costs	$4,000	$4,180
10. Selling and customer-service capacity cost per customer	$66.67	$69.67
11. Advertising staff	1	1
12. Total advertising costs	$20,000	$24,000
13. Advertising cost per employee	$20,000	$24,000

Conversion costs in each year depend on production capacity defined in terms of ZP98 units that can be produced, not the actual units produced. Selling and customer-service costs depend on the number of customers that Dransfield can support, not the actual number of customers it serves. Dransfield has 50 customers in 2018 and 60 customers in 2019. At the start of each year, management uses its discretion to determine the number of advertising staff for the year. Advertising staff and its costs have no direct relationship with the quantity of ZP98 units produced and sold or the number of customers who buy ZP98.

Required

1. Calculate the change in operating income of Dransfield Company for 2018 and 2019.
2. Calculate the growth, price-recovery, and productivity components that explain the change in operating income from 2018 to 2019.
3. Comment on your answer in requirement 2. What do these components indicate?

LO 5 ▶

Unit increase due to market
share, 1,165

⊕ **13-31 Analysis of growth, price-recovery, and productivity components** (continuation of Exercise 13-30). Suppose that during 2019, the market for ZP98 grew 8%. All increases in market share (that is, sales increases greater than 8%) are the result of Dransfield's strategic actions.

Required

Calculate how much of the change in operating income from 2018 to 2019 is due to the industry market-size factor, product differentiation, and cost leadership. How does this relate to Dransfield's strategy and its success in implementation? Explain.

LO 5 ▶

1. a. Amount of unused capacity,
1,750 units

⊕ **13-32 Identifying and managing unused capacity** (continuation of Exercise 13-30). Refer to the information for Dransfield Company in Exercise 13-30.

Required

1. Calculate the amount and cost of unused capacity for
   a. Manufacturing
   b. Sales and customer service
   c. Advertising

   If you are unable to calculate the amount and cost of unused capacity, explain why.

2. State two reasons Dransfield might downsize and two reasons it might not downsize.
3. Assume Dransfield has several product lines, of which ZP98 is only one. The manager for the ZP98 product line is evaluated on the basis of manufacturing and customer sales and service costs, but not advertising costs. The manager wants to increase capacity for customers because he thinks the market is growing, and this will cost an additional $1,098. However, the manager is not going to use this extra capacity immediately, so he classifies it as advertising cost rather than customer sales and service cost. How will the deliberate misclassification of this cost affect
   a. The operating income overall?
   b. The growth, price-recovery, and productivity components?
   c. The evaluation of the ZP98 manager?

   You are not required to calculate any numbers when answering requirement 3. Only discuss whether it will have a positive, negative, or no effect; and comment on the ethics of the manager's actions.

LO 4 ▶

⊕ **13-33 Balanced scorecard.** Caltex Inc. refines gasoline and sells it through its own Caltex Gas Stations. On the basis of market research, Caltex determines that 60% of the overall gasoline market consists of "service-oriented customers," medium- to high-income individuals who are willing to pay a higher price for gas if the gas stations can provide excellent customer service, such as a clean facility, a convenience store, friendly employees, a quick turnaround, the ability to pay by credit card, and high-octane premium gasoline. The remaining 40% of the overall market are "price shoppers" who look to buy the cheapest gasoline available. Caltex's strategy is to focus on the 60% of service-oriented customers. Caltex's BSC for 2019 follows. For brevity, the initiatives taken under each objective are omitted.

Objectives	Measures	Target Performance	Actual Performance
Financial Perspective			
Increase shareholder value	Operating-income changes from price recovery	$90,000,000	$95,000,000
	Operating-income changes from growth	$65,000,000	$67,000,000
Customer Perspective			
Increase market share	Market share of overall gasoline market	10%	9.5%
Internal-Business-Process Perspective			
Improve gasoline quality	Quality index	94 points	97 points
Improve refinery performance	Refinery-reliability index (%)	91%	91%
Ensure gasoline availability	Product-availability index (%)	99%	100%
Learning-and-Growth Perspective			
Increase refinery process capability	Percentage of refinery processes with advanced controls	88%	90%

Required

1. Was Caltex successful in implementing its strategy in 2019? Explain your answer.
2. Would you have included some measure of employee satisfaction and employee training in the learning-and-growth perspective? Are these objectives critical to Caltex for implementing its strategy? Why or why not? Explain briefly.

3. Explain how Caltex did not achieve its target market share in the total gasoline market but still exceeded its financial targets. Is "market share of overall gasoline market" the correct measure of market share? Explain briefly.

4. Is there a cause-and-effect linkage between improvements in the measures in the internal business-process perspective and the measure in the customer perspective? That is, would you add other measures to the internal-business-process perspective or the customer perspective? Why or why not? Explain briefly.

5. Do you agree with Caltex's decision not to include measures of changes in operating income from productivity improvements under the financial perspective of the BSC? Explain briefly.

🌐 **13-34 Balanced scorecard and strategy.** Scott Company manufactures a DVD player called Orlicon. The company sells the player to discount stores throughout the country. This player is significantly less expensive than similar products sold by Scott's competitors, but the Orlicon offers just DVD playback, compared with DVD and Blu-ray playback offered by competitor Nomad Manufacturing. Furthermore, the Orlicon has experienced production problems that have resulted in significant rework costs. Nomad's model has an excellent reputation for quality.

◀ **LO 5**

Required

1. Draw a simple customer preference map for Scott and Nomad using the attributes of price, quality, and playback features. Use the format of Exhibit 13-2.
2. Is Scott's current strategy that of product differentiation or cost leadership?
3. Scott would like to improve quality and decrease costs by improving processes and training workers to reduce rework. Scott's managers believe the increased quality will increase sales. Draw a strategy map as in Exhibit 13-3 describing the cause-and-effect relationships among the strategic objectives you would expect to see. Present at least two strategic objectives you would expect to see under each balanced scorecard perspective. Identify what you believe are any (a) strong ties, (b) focal points, (c) trigger points, and (d) distinctive objectives. Comment on your structural analysis of the strategy map.
4. For each strategic objective, suggest a measure you would recommend in Scott's balanced scorecard.

🌐 **13-35 Strategic analysis of operating income** (continuation of 13-34). As a result of the actions taken, quality has significantly improved in 2017 while rework and unit costs of the Orlicon have decreased. Scott has reduced manufacturing capacity because capacity is no longer needed to support rework. Scott has also lowered the Orlicon's selling price to gain market share and unit sales have increased. Information about the current period (2017) and last period (2016) follows.

◀ **LO 2**

	2016	2017
1. Units of Orlicon produced and sold	16,000	22,000
2. Selling price	$95	$80
3. Direct materials used (kits*)	20,000	22,000
4. Direct material cost per kit*	$32	$32
5. Manufacturing capacity in kits processed	28,000	26,000
6. Total conversion costs	$560,000	$520,000
7. Conversion cost per unit of capacity (6 ÷ row 5)	$20	$20
8. Selling and customer-service capacity	180 customers	180 customers
9. Total selling and customer-service costs	$27,000	$32,400
10. Selling and customer-service capacity cost per customer (row 9 ÷ row 8)	$150	$180

*A kit is composed of all the major components needed to produce a DVD player.

Conversion costs in each year depend on production capacity defined in terms of kits that can be processed, not the actual kits started. Selling and customer-service costs depend on the number of customers that Scott can support, not the actual number of customers it serves. Scott has 140 customers in 2016 and 160 customers in 2017.

Required

1. Calculate operating income of Scott Company for 2016 and 2017.
2. Calculate the growth, price-recovery, and productivity components that explain the change in operating income from 2016 to 2017.
3. Comment on your answer in requirement 2. What do these components indicate?

LO 4 ▷

🌐 **13-36 Analysis of growth, price-recovery, and productivity components** (continuation of 13-35). Suppose that during 2017, the market for DVD players grew 10%. All increases in market share (that is, sales increases greater than 10%) and decreases in the selling price of the Orlicon are the result of Scott's strategic actions.

Required

Calculate how much of the change in operating income from 2016 to 2017 is due to the industry-market-size factor, product differentiation, and cost leadership. How does this relate to Scott's strategy and its success in implementation? Explain.

LO 4 ▷

1. Direct materials partial productivity, 1.59 wallets/metre

🌐 **13-37 Partial productivity measurement.** Guble Company manufactures wallets from fabric. In 2018, Guble made 2,500,000 wallets using 1,875,000 metres of fabric. In 2019, Guble plans to make 2,650,000 wallets and wants to make fabric use more efficient. At the same time, Guble wants to reduce capacity; capacity in 2018 was 3,000,000 wallets at a total cost of $9,000,000. Guble wants to reduce capacity to 2,800,000 wallets, at a total cost of $8,680,000 in 2019.

   Suppose that in 2019 Guble makes 2,650,000 wallets, uses 1,669,500 metres of fabric, and reduces capacity to 2,800,000 units and costs to $8,680,000.

Required

1. Calculate the partial-productivity ratios for materials and conversion (capacity costs) for 2019, and compare them to a benchmark for 2018 calculated based on 2019 output.
2. How can Guble Company use the information from the partial-productivity calculations?

LO 5 ▷

1. Total factor productivity for 2019 using 2019 prices, 0.1725 units of output/$1 of input

🌐 **13-38 Total factor productivity** (continuation of Exercise 13-37). Refer to the data for Exercise 13-37. Assume the fabric costs $4 per metre in 2019 and $4.10 per metre in 2018.

Required

1. Compute Guble Company's total factor productivity (TFP) for 2019.
2. Compare TFP for 2019 with a benchmark TFP for 2018 inputs based on 2019 output.
3. What additional information does TFP provide that partial productivity measures do not?

Collaborative Learning Cases

LO 4 ▷

2. Change in operating income, $21,300 F

13-39 Strategic analysis of operating income. Halsey Company sells women's clothing. Halsey's strategy is to offer a wide selection of clothes and excellent customer service and to charge a premium price. Halsey presents the following data for 2018 and 2019. For simplicity, assume that each customer purchases one piece of clothing.

	2018	2019
1. Pieces of clothing purchased and sold	40,000	40,000
2. Average selling price	$60	$59
3. Average cost per piece of clothing	$40	$41
4. Selling and customer-service capacity	51,000 customers	43,000 customers
5. Selling and customer-service costs	$357,000	$296,700
6. Selling and customer-service capacity cost per customer (Line 5 ÷ Line 4)	$7 per customer	$6.90 per customer
7. Purchasing and administrative capacity	980 designs	850 designs
8. Purchasing and administrative costs	$245,000	$204,000
9. Purchasing and administrative capacity cost per distinct design (Line 8 ÷ Line 7)	$250 per design	$240 per design

Total selling and customer-service costs depend on the number of customers that Halsey has created capacity to support, not the actual number of customers that Halsey serves. Total purchasing and administrative costs depend on purchasing and administrative capacity that Halsey has created (defined in terms of the number of distinct clothing designs that Halsey can purchase and administer). Purchasing and administrative costs do not depend on the actual number of distinct clothing designs purchased. Halsey purchased 930 distinct designs in 2018 and 820 distinct designs in 2019.

   At the start of 2019, Halsey planned to increase operating income by 10% over operating income in 2018.

Required

1. Is Halsey's strategy one of product differentiation or cost leadership? Explain.
2. Calculate the change in Halsey's operating income in 2018 and 2019.

3. Calculate the growth, price-recovery, and productivity components of changes in operating income between 2018 and 2019.

4. Does the strategic analysis of operating income indicate Halsey was successful in implementing its strategy in 2019? Explain.

13-40 Balanced scorecard, sustainability. Nost Vineyards is a wine manufacturer. It distributes its products to retailers across Canada. Nost's objective is to be the number one distributor of its product lines in Canada. Nost competes against a limited number of Canadian companies but also must compete against several large American vintners. It seeks to increase market share through the delivery of quality products. It believes it can achieve its objectives through high quality control in its manufacturing processes, improved efficiency (particularly relating to yields), and innovation of its products. ◀ **LO 3**

Nost has had problems with employee turnover, both in production and administration. It pays competitive wages but still has struggled managing employee turnover. Employee surveys have determined that employees do not believe the company provides adequate training or support and that employees are unaware of opportunities for advancement.

Required

1. Create a BSC for Nost Vineyards using the traditional four perspectives.

2. What types of sustainability measures would you recommend for Nost?

3. What specific measures could Nost take to address its employee turnover issues?

SOLUTION

◀ **TRY IT!**

Try It 13–1

1. Operating income for each year is as follows:

	2016	2017
Revenues ($3,200 × 400; $3,100 × 500)	$1,280,000	$1,550,000
Costs		
Engineering labour costs ($35 × 24,000; $36 × 27,000)	840,000	972,000
Engineering support costs ($300 × 600; $320 × 600)	180,000	192,000
Total costs	1,020,000	1,164,000
Operating income	$ 260,000	$ 386,000
Change in operating income	↑ $126,000 F ↑	

2.

The Growth Component

$$\text{Revenue effect of growth} = \left(\begin{array}{c} \text{Actual units} \\ \text{of output sold} \\ \text{in 2017} \end{array} - \begin{array}{c} \text{Actual units of} \\ \text{output sold} \\ \text{in 2016} \end{array} \right) \times \begin{array}{c} \text{Selling} \\ \text{price} \\ \text{in 2016} \end{array}$$

$$= (500 - 400) \times \$3,200 = \$320,000$$

$$\text{Cost effect of growth for variable costs} = \left(\begin{array}{c} \text{Units of} \\ \text{input required} \\ \text{to produce} \\ \text{2017 output} \\ \text{in 2016} \end{array} - \begin{array}{c} \text{Actual units} \\ \text{of inputs} \\ \text{used to} \\ \text{produce} \\ \text{2016 output} \end{array} \right) \times \begin{array}{c} \text{Input} \\ \text{price} \\ \text{in 2016} \end{array}$$

$$\text{Cost effect of growth for fixed costs} = \left(\begin{array}{c} \text{Actual units of capacity in} \\ \text{2016 because adequate} \\ \text{capacity exists to produce} \\ \text{2017 output in 2016} \end{array} - \begin{array}{c} \text{Actual} \\ \text{units of} \\ \text{capacity} \\ \text{in 2016} \end{array} \right) \times \begin{array}{c} \text{Price per unit} \\ \text{of capacity} \\ \text{in 2016} \end{array}$$

(Continued)

Engineering labour-hours that would be required in 2017 to complete 500 jobs instead of the 400 jobs done in 2016, assuming the 2016 input-output relationship continued into 2017, equal 30,000 $\left(500\ jobs \times \dfrac{24{,}000\ \text{labour-hours}}{400\ \text{jobs}}\right)$ labour-hours. Engineering support capacity would not change since adequate capacity exists in 2016 to support year 2017 jobs.

The cost effects of growth component are

Engineering labour costs	$(30{,}000 - 24{,}000) \times$ $35 = $210,000 U
Engineering support costs	$(600 - 600) \times$ $300 = $ 0
Cost effect of growth	$210,000 U

In summary, the net increase in operating income as a result of the growth component equals

Revenue effect of growth	$320,000 F
Cost effect of growth	210,000 U
Change in operating income due to growth	$110,000 F

The Price-Recovery Component

$$\begin{matrix} \text{Revenue effect of} \\ \text{price-recovery} \end{matrix} = \left(\begin{matrix} \text{Selling price} \\ \text{in 2017} \end{matrix} - \begin{matrix} \text{Selling price} \\ \text{in 2016} \end{matrix} \right) \times \begin{matrix} \text{Actual units} \\ \text{of output} \\ \text{sold in 2017} \end{matrix}$$

$$= (\$3{,}100 - \$3{,}200) \times 500 = \$50{,}000\ U$$

$$\begin{matrix} \text{Cost effect of} \\ \text{price-recovery for} \\ \text{variable costs} \end{matrix} = \left(\begin{matrix} \text{Input} \\ \text{price in} \\ 2017 \end{matrix} - \begin{matrix} \text{Input} \\ \text{price in} \\ 2016 \end{matrix} \right) \times \begin{matrix} \text{Units of input} \\ \text{required to} \\ \text{produce 2017} \\ \text{output in 2016} \end{matrix}$$

$$\begin{matrix} \text{Cost effect of} \\ \text{price-recovery for} \\ \text{fixed costs} \end{matrix} = \left(\begin{matrix} \text{Price per} \\ \text{unit of} \\ \text{capacity} \\ \text{in 2017} \end{matrix} - \begin{matrix} \text{Price per} \\ \text{unit of} \\ \text{capacity} \\ \text{in 2016} \end{matrix} \right) \times \begin{matrix} \text{Actual units of capacity in} \\ \text{2016 because adequate} \\ \text{capacity exists to produce} \\ \text{2017 output in 2016} \end{matrix}$$

Engineering labour costs	$($36 - $35) \times 30{,}000 = $30,000 U
Engineering support costs	$($320 - $300) \times 600 = 12,000 U
Cost effect of price recovery	$42,000 U

In summary, the net decrease in operating income as a result of the price-recovery component equals

Revenue effect of price-recovery	$50,000 U
Cost effect of price-recovery	42,000 U
Change in operating income due to price recovery	$92,000 U

The Productivity Component

$$\begin{matrix} \text{Cost effect of} \\ \text{productivity for} \\ \text{variable costs} \end{matrix} = \left(\begin{matrix} \text{Actual units of} \\ \text{input used} \\ \text{to produce} \\ \text{2017 output} \end{matrix} - \begin{matrix} \text{Units of input} \\ \text{required to} \\ \text{produce 2017} \\ \text{output in 2016} \end{matrix} \right) \times \begin{matrix} \text{Input} \\ \text{price} \\ \text{in 2017} \end{matrix}$$

$$\begin{matrix} \text{Cost effect of} \\ \text{productivity for} \\ \text{fixed costs} \end{matrix} = \left(\begin{matrix} \text{Actual} \\ \text{units of} \\ \text{capacity} \\ \text{in 2017} \end{matrix} - \begin{matrix} \text{Actual units of capacity in} \\ \text{2016 because adequate} \\ \text{capacity exists to produce} \\ \text{2017 output in 2016} \end{matrix} \right) \times \begin{matrix} \text{Price per} \\ \text{unit of} \\ \text{capacity} \\ \text{in 2017} \end{matrix}$$

The productivity component of cost changes are

Engineering labour costs	$(27{,}000 - 30{,}000) \times \$36 =$	$108,000 F
Engineering support costs	$(600 - 600) \times \$320 =$	0
Change in operating income due to productivity		$108,000 F

The change in operating income between 2016 and 2017 can be analyzed as follows:

	Income Statement Amounts in 2016 (1)	Revenue and Cost Effects of Growth Component in 2017 (2)	Revenue and Cost Effects of Price-Recovery Component in 2017 (3)	Cost Effect of Productivity Component in 2017 (4)	Income Statement Amounts in 2017 (5) = (1) + (2) + (3) + (4)
Revenues	$1,280,000	$320,000 F	$ 50,000 U	—	$1,550,000
Costs	1,020,000	210,000 U	42,000 U	$108,000 F	1,164,000
Operating income	$ 260,000	$110,000 F	$ 92,000 U	$108,000 F	$ 386,000
			$126,000 F		

Change in operating income

3. The analysis of operating income indicates that a significant amount of the increase in operating income resulted from Ronaldo's productivity improvements in 2017. The company had to reduce selling prices while labour costs were increasing, but it was able to increase operating income by improving its productivity. The productivity gains also allowed Ronaldo to be competitive and grow the business. The unfavourable price recovery component indicates that Ronaldo could not pass on increases in labour-related wages via price increases to its customers, very likely because its product was not differentiated from competitors' offerings.

14

Period Cost Application

▶ Learning Objectives

1. Understand the four purposes for period cost allocation and the four criteria to justify the method chosen to allocate the non-manufacturing (period) costs.

2. Evaluate and select between the single- and dual-rate cost methods to apply period costs of support departments.

3. Analyze how the selection of the single- or dual-cost allocation rate affects the calculation of efficiency variance.

4. Evaluate and select among the direct, step-down, and reciprocal methods of allocating support division costs to production divisions.

5. Analyze cost allocation procedures to apply common costs and justify contractual reimbursement terms.

▶ CPA Competencies

This chapter covers material outlined in **Section 3: Management Accounting** of the CPA Competency Map. The Learning Objectives in this chapter have been aligned with the CPA Competency Map to ensure the best coverage possible.

3.3.1 Evaluates cost classifications and costing methods for management of ongoing operations

3.3.2 Evaluates and applies cost management techniques appropriate for specific costing decisions

Good Period Overhead Cost-Application Methods Improve Management Decisions

Cogeco Inc. is a diversified communications company listed on the Toronto stock exchange under the symbol CGO. Cogeco provides communication products and services to consumers and advertisers through cable distribution and radio broadcasting that is primarily based in Ontario and Quebec. As the Canadian telecommunications universe continues to expand and attract more competition, companies like Cogeco need to find effective ways to allocate large amounts of period costs to their products and services.

Careful target pricing will assure Cogeco's continued profitability. Target prices determine Cogeco's target ROI and operating margin percent as well as the constraints on target costing. In the long run, Cogeco's decisions about cost application will signal how costs actually flow to core divisions in proportion to the benefits each division receives. The application of indirect costs will affect the total costs assigned to finished goods or services from core divisions. Decisions at Cogeco about cost-application methods will reflect trade-offs among cost–benefit, simplicity, and economic plausibility.

The purpose of this chapter is to explain and apply techniques to allocate support department costs. These are also called period overhead costs, which financial accountants call operating expenses. Support department cost allocation is treated separately in part because most period costs are excluded from inventoriable costs by financial accounting standards. But prices of the finished output must recover *all* manufacturing and non-manufacturing costs for corporations to remain profitable. Period costs, such as R&D and IT services arising from business functions other than production, are essential to management of an entire corporation. These costs must somehow be assigned to outputs in a way that reflects the truth about economic activities. For example, if there is more than one distinct output and if the non-manufacturing costs of IT services provide different levels of value added to each distinct output, as judged by the customer, then the customer should be willing to pay for that value added. The task of the management team is to select the best method of cost assignment (to each distinct output) that most accurately includes the value added.

Purposes of Cost Allocation

Cost allocation is the alternative used when tracing is not economically feasible. The benefits of most facilities-sustaining costs are not observable and therefore cannot be readily measured. For example, even if the number of square metres of office floors cleaned by the maintenance division could be counted and a cost could be developed, it makes no sense to answer the question "How many square metres of cleaned office floors does it take to manufacture a smartphone?" This makes the logic of cost allocation for many period costs different from the logic behind allocating indirect manufacturing overhead (MOH). The goal is to allocate period costs of non-manufacturing activities proportional to the different levels of benefit provided to each of the users.

The activities of upstream and downstream business functions are often interdependent. As illustrated in Exhibit 14-1, upstream business activities incur preproduction costs, and downstream business activities incur postproduction costs. The activities in customer service, a downstream business function, can sometimes be reduced by spending more on product and process design in R&D, an upstream business function. The sales price of the product or service needs to be high enough to recover all costs, as **full product costing** requires the recovery of all costs generated by all business functions in the value chain.

There is no universal rule to tell accountants how to allocate either manufacturing or non-manufacturing costs. But throughout the text we have consistently noted that, if outputs are identical, a simple average will be an appropriate way to calculate a cost allocation rate. If, however, the outputs (jobs) are not using resources identically, then using a simple average runs the risk of inadvertent over- or undercosting of the product. The threat posed by overcosting and overpricing in a highly competitive market is that customers will not pay a higher price when lower-priced substitutes are readily available. The threat posed by undercosting (and subsequent underpricing) is that you cannot identify why your profits are dropping even as sales volume increases.

Activity-based costing (ABC) relies on an economically plausible relationship between the contributors to the MOH cost pool and the activities of production. As mentioned above, this logic does not readily apply to non-manufacturing or period cost pools.

▶ **LO 1**

Understand the four purposes for period cost allocation and the four criteria to justify the method chosen to allocate the non-manufacturing (period) costs.

Exhibit 14-1 Period Cost Allocation—One Part of the Big Picture

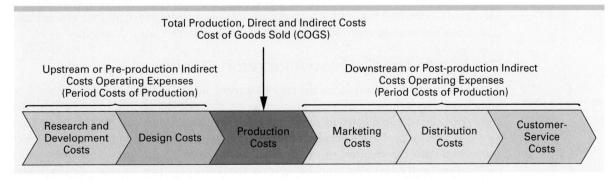

Careful costing of products and services provides four important benefits:

1. It will result in more accurate full-product pricing. In a highly competitive market, this protects market share.

2. It will improve the budgeting process. When companies are price-takers, there is no option to simply raise the price to cover extra costs. A good budget can signal when it is time to exit an unprofitable market as well as showing how to sustain or improve profit.

3. It will allow feedback in the form of periodic variance analysis. This will identify areas that management needs to examine in order to control resource usage.

4. It enables managers to select the most profitable among existing opportunities. When resources are constrained, this capability reduces opportunity cost and maximizes profits.

Four Possible Purposes

Managers face a wide variety of business decisions. Selecting the most appropriate method of allocation will generate higher quality information. The higher the quality of information, the better able the management team will be to select only the costs relevant to different types of decisions. Four possible reasons to allocate period costs appropriately are to

- Provide information for economic decisions.
- Motivate managers and employees.
- Justify either costs or reimbursement internally or externally.
- Measure ASPE/IFRS-compliant income and assets for reports to external parties.

The same combination of costs in the six business functions does not often satisfy each of the four purposes listed. For economic decision purposes, the costs in all six functions (as shown in Exhibit 14-1) should be included. For motivation purposes, costs from more than one function are often excluded. Non-manufacturing support costs are common to many business functions.

For cost reimbursement purposes, contracts will often state any specific business function costs that must be excluded from reimbursement. Cost reimbursement rules governing government contracts may, for example, explicitly exclude marketing costs. For purposes of income and asset measurement, inventoriable costs under ASPE/IFRS include only manufacturing costs. In Canada, R&D and design costs are expensed to the accounting period in which they are incurred unless they can be directly associated solely with a product or service currently generating revenue. Different external parties require the use of different costing rules.

Before undertaking any refinements to the existing costing system, it is important to consider both costs and benefits of the project. The time, aggravation, and money involved in changing the costing system are all too evident. The benefits are less evident. If the decision has been made to proceed, then many choices of contributors to significant period cost pools and cost drivers can be contentious. But rapid advances in technology have reduced the financial costs of collecting and processing timely cost information. Even small companies have either adopted or developed costing systems that use multiple cost allocation bases to improve the quality of information to make decisions.

Criteria to Guide Cost-Allocation Decisions

After identifying the purposes for the cost allocation, managers and management accountants must decide how to allocate costs. Having a reasonable justification for how the costs are to be allocated helps to support the validity and relevance of the costing system. This is a difficult problem since, by definition, many of these period costs have no direct connection with the creation of the product or provision of the service. Without some justification for the cost allocation being used, the costing systems will have little validity.

Exhibit 14-2 Criteria for Cost-Allocation Decisions

1. Cause and Effect. Using this criterion, managers identify the variables that cause resources to be consumed. For example, managers may use hours of testing as the variable when allocating the costs of a quality-testing area to products. Cost allocations based on the cause-and-effect criterion are likely to be the most credible to operating personnel.

2. Benefits Received. Using this criterion, managers identify the beneficiaries of the outputs of the cost object. The costs of the cost object are allocated among the beneficiaries in proportion to the benefits each receives. Consider a corporate-wide advertising program that promotes the general image of the corporation rather than any individual product. The costs of this program may be allocated on the basis of division revenues; the higher the revenues, the higher the division's allocated cost of the advertising program. The rationale behind this allocation is that divisions with higher revenues apparently benefited from the advertising more than divisions with lower revenues and, therefore, ought to be allocated more of the advertising costs.

3. Fairness or Equity. This criterion is often cited in government contracts when cost allocations are the basis for establishing a price satisfactory to the government and its suppliers. Cost allocation here is viewed as a "reasonable" or "fair" means of establishing a selling price in the minds of the contracting parties. For most allocation decisions, fairness is a matter of judgment rather than an operational criterion.

4. Ability to Bear. This criterion advocates allocating costs in proportion to the cost object's ability to bear costs allocated to it. An example is the allocation of corporate executive salaries on the basis of division operating income. The presumption is that the more-profitable divisions have a greater ability to absorb corporate headquarters' costs.

Managers can use one or more of the following criteria to justify their decisions about the design of the costing systems.

Exhibit 14-2 presents four criteria used to guide cost-allocation decisions. These decisions affect both the number of indirect-cost pools and the cost-allocation base for each indirect-cost pool. We emphasize the superiority of the cause-and-effect and the benefits-received criteria, especially when the purpose of cost allocation is to provide information for economic decisions or to motivate managers and employees. Cause and effect is the primary criterion used in activity-based costing applications. ABC systems use the concept of a cost hierarchy to identify the cost drivers that best demonstrate the cause-and-effect relationship between each activity and the costs in the related cost pool. The cost drivers are then chosen as cost-allocation bases.

Fairness and ability-to-bear are less-frequently used and more problematic criteria than cause-and-effect or benefits-received. Fairness is a difficult criterion on which to obtain agreement. What one party views as fair, another party may view as unfair.[1] For example, a university may view allocating a share of general administrative costs to government contracts as fair because general administrative costs are incurred to support all activities of the university. The government may view the allocation of such costs as unfair because the general administrative costs would have been incurred by the university regardless of whether the government contract existed. Perhaps the fairest way to resolve this issue is to understand, as well as possible, the cause-and-effect relationship between the government contract activity and general administrative costs. In other words, fairness is more a matter of judgment than an easily implementable choice criterion.

To get a sense of the issues that arise when using the ability-to-bear criterion, consider a product that consumes a large amount of indirect costs and currently sells for a price equal to its direct costs. This product has no ability to bear any of the indirect costs it uses. However, if the indirect costs it consumes are allocated to other products, these other products are subsidizing the product that is losing money. An integrated airline, for example, might allocate fewer costs to its activities in a highly contested market such as freight transportation,

---

[1] Kaplow and Shavell, in a review of the legal literature, note that "notions of fairness are many and varied. They are analyzed and rationalized by different writers in different ways, and they also typically depend upon the circumstances under consideration. Accordingly, it is not possible to identify a consensus view on these notions . . ." See L. Kaplow and S. Shavell, "Fairness Versus Welfare," *Harvard Law Review* (February 2001); and L. Kaplow and S. Shavell, *Fairness Versus Welfare* (Boston: Harvard University Press, 2002).

thereby subsidizing it via passenger transport. Some airports cross-subsidize costs associated with serving airline passengers through sales of duty-free goods. Such practices provide a distorted view of relative product and service profitability, and have the potential to invite both regulatory scrutiny and competitors' attempts to undercut artificially higher-priced services.

Most importantly, companies must weigh the costs and benefits when designing and implementing their cost allocations. Companies incur costs not only in collecting data but also in taking the time to educate managers about cost allocations. In general, the more complex the cost allocations, the higher these education costs.

The costs of designing and implementing complex cost allocations are highly visible. Unfortunately, the benefits from using well-designed cost allocations—such as enabling managers to make better-informed sourcing decisions, pricing decisions, cost-control decisions, and so on—are difficult to measure. Nevertheless, when making cost allocations, managers should consider the benefits as well as the costs. As costs of collecting and processing information decrease, companies are building more-detailed cost allocations.

Deciding Between Single- and Dual-Rate Cost Methods

▶ **LO 2**

Evaluate and select between the single- and dual-rate cost methods to apply period costs of support divisions.

The management team at Sand Hill Company (SHC) must decide how to cost its two products, notebooks and peripherals. SHC's **core divisions** (**operating division, production division**) produce each product. A core division adds value to output for which the customer will pay. In Exhibit 14-3, IT services, a non-manufacturing cost, is allocated between the two core divisions, Notebook and Peripherals. To simplify the illustration, only the Notebook allocation path is shown in full as the solid blue line.

Note in the illustration the section above the horizontal box (labelled "Products from the Manufacturing Division Direct Cost"). The costs in this area are all overhead costs. The overhead costs are allocated into two distinct groups: Indirect Non-Manufacturing (Period) Costs and Indirect MOH Cost.

Companies distinguish operating departments (and operating divisions) from support departments. An **operating department**, also called a **production department**, directly adds value to a product or service. A **support department**, also called a **service department**, provides the services that assist other internal departments (operating departments and other support departments) in the company. Examples of support departments are information systems and plant maintenance.

Managers face two questions when allocating the costs of a support department to operating departments or divisions: (1) Should fixed costs of support departments be allocated to operating divisions? (2) If fixed costs are allocated, should variable and fixed costs be allocated in the same way? With regard to the first question, most companies believe that fixed costs of support departments should be allocated because the support department needs to incur fixed costs to provide operating divisions with the services they require. Depending on the answer to the second question, there are two approaches to allocating support-department costs: the *single-rate cost-allocation method* and the *dual-rate cost-allocation method*.

Single-Rate and Dual-Rate Methods

▶ **LO 3**

Analyze how the selection of the single- or dual-cost allocation rate affects the calculation of efficiency variance.

The **single-rate method** makes no distinction between fixed and variable costs. It allocates costs in each cost pool (support department in this section) to cost objects (operating divisions in this section) using the same rate per unit of a single allocation base. By contrast, the **dual-rate method** partitions the cost of each support department into two pools, a variable-cost pool and a fixed-cost pool, and allocates each pool using a different cost-allocation base. When using either the single-rate method or the dual-rate method, managers can allocate support-department costs to operating divisions based on either a *budgeted* rate or the eventual *actual* cost rate. The latter approach is neither conceptually preferred nor widely used in practice (we explain why in the next section). Accordingly, we illustrate the single-rate and dual-rate methods next based on the use of *budgeted* rates.

Exhibit 14-3 Full Product Costing at the Edmonton Production Plant of Sand Hill Company

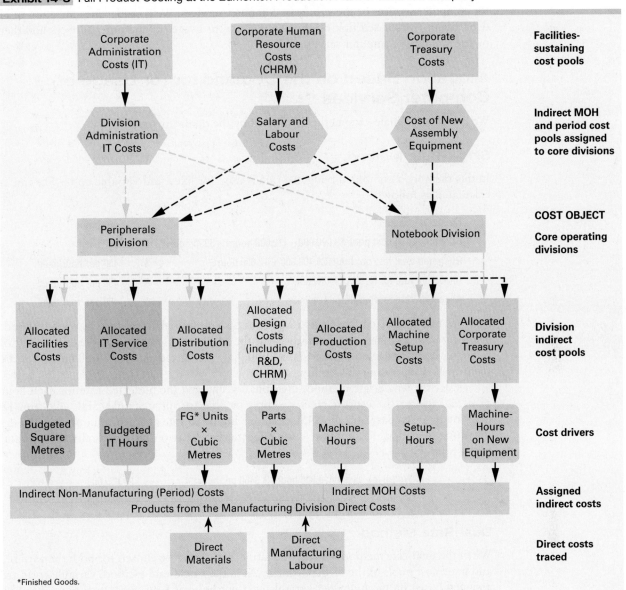

*Finished Goods.

Consider the IT department of SHC. This support department has two users, both operating divisions: the Notebook division and the Peripherals division. The following data relate to the 2018 budget:

Practical capacity	18,750 hours
Fixed costs of operating the computer facility in the 6,000-hour to 18,750-hour relevant range	$3,000,000
Budgeted long-run usage (quantity) in hours:	
Notebook division	8,000 hours
Peripherals division	4,000 hours
Total	12,000 hours
Budgeted variable cost per hour in the 6,000-hour to 18,750-hour relevant range	$200 per hour used
Actual usage in 2018 in hours:	
Notebook division	9,000 hours
Peripherals division	3,000 hours
Total	12,000 hours

The budgeted rates for IT department costs can be computed based on either the demand for computer services or the supply of computer services. We consider the allocation of IT department costs based first on the demand for (or usage of) computer services and then on the supply of computer services.

Allocation Based on the Demand for (or Usage of) Computer Services

We present the single-rate method followed by the dual-rate method.

Single-Rate Method

In this method, a combined budgeted rate is used for fixed and variable costs. The rate is calculated as follows:

Budgeted usage		12,000 hours	
Budgeted total cost pool: $3,000,000 + (12,000 hours × $200/hour)	$5,400,000		
Budgeted total rate per hour: $5,400,000 ÷ 12,000 hours		$	450 per hour used
Allocation rate for Notebook division		$	450 per hour used
Allocation rate for Peripherals division		$	450 per hour used

Note that the budgeted rate of $450 per hour is substantially higher than the $200 budgeted *variable* cost per hour. That's because the $450 rate includes an allocated amount of $250 per hour (budgeted fixed costs, $3,000,000 ÷ budgeted usage, 12,000 hours) for the *fixed* costs of operating the facility.

Under the single-rate method, divisions are charged the budgeted rate for each hour of *actual* use of the central facility. Applying this to our example, SHC allocates IT department costs based on the $450 per hour budgeted rate and actual hours used by the operating divisions. The support costs allocated to the two divisions under this method are as follows:

Notebook division: 9,000 hours × $450 per hour	$4,050,000
Peripherals division: 3,000 hours × $450 per hour	$1,350,000

Dual-Rate Method

When the dual-rate method is used, allocation bases must be chosen for both the variable and fixed cost pools of the IT department. As in the single-rate method, variable costs are assigned based on the *budgeted* variable cost per hour of $200 for *actual* hours used by each division. However, fixed costs are assigned based on *budgeted* fixed costs per hour and the *budgeted* number of hours for each division. Given the budgeted usage of 8,000 hours for the Notebook division and 4,000 hours for the Peripherals division, the budgeted fixed-cost rate is $250 per hour (= $3,000,000 ÷ 12,000 hours), as before. Since this rate is charged on the basis of the *budgeted* usage, however, the fixed costs are effectively allocated in advance as a lump-sum based on the relative proportions of the IT facilities expected to be used by the operating divisions.

The costs allocated to the Notebook division in 2018 under the dual-rate method would be as follows:

Fixed costs: $250 per hour × 8,000 (budgeted) hours	$2,000,000
Variable costs: $200 per hour × 9,000 (actual) hours	1,800,000
Total costs	$3,800,000

The costs allocated to the Peripherals division in 2018 would be as follows:

Fixed costs: $250 per hour × 4,000 (budgeted) hours	$1,000,000
Variable costs: $200 per hour × 3,000 (actual) hours	600,000
Total costs	$1,600,000

Note that each operating division is charged the same amount for variable costs under the single-rate and dual-rate methods ($200 per hour multiplied by the actual hours of use). However, the overall assignment of costs differs under the two methods because the single-rate method allocates fixed costs of the support department based on *actual usage* of computer resources by the operating divisions, whereas the dual-rate method allocates fixed costs based on *budgeted usage*.

We next consider the alternative approach of allocating IT department costs based on the capacity of computer services supplied.

Allocation Based on the Supply of Capacity

We illustrate this approach using the 18,750 hours of practical capacity of the IT department. The budgeted rate is then determined as follows:

Budgeted fixed-cost rate per hour, $3,000,000 ÷ 18,750 hours	$160 per hour
Budgeted variable-cost rate per hour	200 per hour
Budgeted total-cost rate per hour	$360 per hour

Using the same procedures for the single-rate and dual-rate methods as in the previous section, the support cost allocations to the operating divisions are as follows:

Single-Rate Method

Notebook division: $360 per hour × 9,000 (actual) hours	$3,240,000
Peripherals division: $360 per hour × 3,000 (actual) hours	1,080,000
Fixed costs of unused computer capacity:	
$160 per hour × 6,750 hours[a]	1,080,000

[a]6,750 hours = Practical capacity of 18,750 − (9,000 hours used by Notebook division + 3,000 hours used by Peripherals division).

Dual-Rate Method

Notebook division	
Fixed costs: $160 per hour × 8,000 (budgeted) hours	$1,280,000
Variable costs: $200 per hour × 9,000 (actual) hours	1,800,000
Total costs	$3,080,000
Peripherals division	
Fixed costs: $160 per hour × 4,000 (budgeted) hours	$ 640,000
Variable costs: $200 per hour × 3,000 (actual) hours	600,000
Total costs	$1,240,000
Fixed costs of unused computer capacity:	
$160 per hour × 6,750 hours[b]	$1,080,000

[b]6,750 hours = Practical capacity of 18,750 hours − (8,000 hours budgeted to be used by Notebook division + 4,000 hours budgeted to be used by Peripherals division).

When practical capacity is used to allocate costs, the single-rate method allocates only the actual fixed-cost resources used by the Notebook and Peripherals divisions, while the dual-rate method allocates the budgeted fixed-cost resources to be used by the operating divisions. Unused IT department resources are highlighted but usually not allocated to the divisions.[2]

The advantage of using practical capacity to allocate costs is that it focuses management's attention on managing unused capacity. Using practical capacity also avoids burdening the user divisions with the cost of unused capacity of the IT department. In contrast, when costs are allocated on the basis of the demand for computer services, all $3,000,000

---

[2] In our example, the cost of unused capacity under the single-rate and the dual-rate methods coincide (each equals $1,080,000). This occurs because the total actual usage of the facility matches the total expected usage of 12,000 hours. The budgeted cost of unused capacity (in the dual-rate method) can be either greater or lower than the actual cost (in the single-rate method), depending on whether the total actual usage is lower or higher than the budgeted usage.

of budgeted fixed costs, including the cost of unused capacity, are allocated to user divisions. If costs are used as a basis for pricing, then charging user divisions for unused capacity could result in the downward demand spiral (for further discussion, see Chapter 9).

Single-Rate Versus Dual-Rate Method

There are benefits and costs of both the single-rate and dual-rate methods. One benefit of the single-rate method is the low cost to implement it. The single-rate method avoids the often-expensive analysis necessary to classify the individual cost items of a department into fixed and variable categories. Also, by basing the final allocations on the actual usage of central facilities, rather than basing them solely on uncertain forecasts of expected demand, it offers the user divisions some operational control over the charges they bear.

A problem with the single-rate method is that it makes the allocated fixed costs of the support department appear as variable costs to the operating divisions. Consequently, the single-rate method may lead division managers to make outsourcing decisions that are in their own best interest but that may be inefficient from the standpoint of the organization as a whole. Consider the setting where allocations are made on the basis of the demand for computer services. In this case, each user division is charged $450 per hour under the single-rate method (recall that $250 of this charge relates to the allocated fixed costs of the IT department). Suppose an external vendor offers the Notebook division computer services at a rate of $340 per hour, at a time when the IT department has unused capacity. The Notebook division's managers would be tempted to use this vendor because it would lower the division's costs ($340 per hour instead of the $450 per hour internal charge for computer services). In the short run, however, the fixed costs of the IT department remain unchanged in the relevant range (between 6,000 hours of usage and the practical capacity of 18,750 hours). SHC would therefore incur an additional cost of $140 per hour if the managers were to take this offer—the difference between the $340 external purchase price and the true internal variable cost of $200 of using the IT department.

The divergence created under the single-rate method between SHC's interests and those of its division managers is lessened when allocation is done on the basis of practical capacity. The variable cost per hour perceived by the operating division managers is now $360 (rather than the $450 rate when allocation is based on budgeted usage). However, any external offer above $200 (SHC's true variable cost) and below $360 (the single-rate charge per hour) will still result in the user manager preferring to outsource the service at the expense of SHC's overall profits.

A benefit of the dual-rate method is that it signals to division managers how variable costs and fixed costs behave differently. This information guides division managers to make decisions that benefit the organization as a whole, as well as each division. For example, using a third-party computer provider that charges more than $200 per hour would result in SHC's being worse off than if its own IT department were used, because the latter has a variable cost of $200 per hour. Under the dual-rate method, neither division manager has an incentive to pay more than $200 per hour for an external provider because the internal charge for computer services is precisely that amount. By charging the fixed costs of resources budgeted to be used by the divisions as a lump-sum, the dual-rate method succeeds in removing fixed costs from the division managers' consideration when making marginal decisions regarding the outsourcing of services. It thus avoids the potential conflict of interest that can arise under the single-rate method.

Recently, the dual-rate method has been receiving more attention. Resource consumption accounting (RCA), an emerging management accounting system, employs an allocation procedure akin to a dual-rate system. For each cost/resource pool, cost assignment rates for fixed costs are based on practical capacity supplied, while rates for proportional costs (i.e., costs that vary with regard to the output of the resource pool) are based on planned quantities.[3]

---

[3] Other salient features of RCA include the selective use of ABC, the non-assignment of fixed costs when causal relationships cannot be established, and the depreciation of assets based on their replacement cost. RCA has its roots in the nearly 50-year-old German cost accounting system called *Grenzplankostenrechnung* (GPK), which is used by organizations such as Mercedes-Benz, Porsche, and Stihl. For further details, as well as illustrations of the use of RCA and GPK in organizations, see S. Webber and B. Clinton, "Resource Consumption Accounting Applied: The Clopay Case," *Management Accounting Quarterly* (Fall 2004) and B. Mackie, "Merging GPK and ABC on the Road to RCA," *Strategic Finance* (November 2006).

Aberdeen Corporation has one support department, Engineering Services, and two production departments, Machining and Assembly. The following data relate to the 2017 budget for the Engineering Services department:

14.1 TRY IT! ⊕

Practical capacity	8,000 hours
Fixed costs of the Engineering Services department in the 6,000 labour-hour to 8,000 labour-hour relevant range	$280,000
Budgeted usage (quantity) of Engineering Services labour-hours required to support the productions departments:	
Machining department	2,500 hours
Assembly department	4,500 hours
Total	7,000 hours
Budgeted variable cost per Engineering Services labour-hour in the 6,000 labour-hour to 8,000 labour-hour relevant range	$25 per hour used
Actual usage (quantity) of Engineering Services labour-hours required to support the productions departments:	
Machining department	2,000 hours
Assembly department	4,000 hours
Total	6,000 hours

Required

1. Using the single-rate method, calculate the cost to be allocated to the Machining and Assembly departments if the allocation rate is based on budgeted costs and budgeted quantity of Engineering Services and allocated based on actual Engineering Services hours used in each department.

2. Using the dual-rate method, calculate the cost to be allocated to the Machining and Assembly departments if (a) variable costs are allocated based on the budgeted variable cost per hour for actual hours used in each department and (b) fixed costs are allocated based on budgeted fixed costs per hour and the budgeted number of hours for each department.

3. Using the single-rate method, calculate the cost to be allocated to the Machining and Assembly departments if the allocation rate is based on budgeted costs and practical capacity of the Engineering Services department and allocated based on actual Engineering Services hours used in each department.

4. Using the dual-rate method, calculate the cost to be allocated to the Machining and Assembly departments if (a) variable costs are allocated based on the budgeted variable cost per hour for actual hours used in each department and (b) fixed costs are allocated based on budgeted fixed costs and practical capacity of the Engineering Services department. The allocation rate is based on budgeted costs and practical capacity of the Engineering Services department and allocated based on budgeted Engineering Services hours used in each department.

Budgeted Versus Actual Costs, and the Choice of Allocation Base

The allocation methods previously outlined follow specific procedures in terms of the support department costs that are considered as well as the manner in which costs are assigned to the operating departments. In this section, we examine these choices in greater detail and consider the impact of alternative approaches. We show that the decision whether to use actual or budgeted costs, as well as the choice between actual and budgeted usage as allocation base, has a significant impact on the cost allocated to each division and the incentives of the division managers.

Budgeted Versus Actual Rates

In both the single-rate and dual-rate methods, we use *budgeted* rates to assign support department costs (fixed as well as variable costs). An alternative approach would involve using the *actual* rates based on the support costs realized during the period. This method is much less common because of the level of uncertainty it imposes on user divisions. When allocations are made using budgeted rates, managers of divisions to which costs are allocated know with certainty the rates to be used in that budget period. Users can then determine the amount of the service to request and—if company policy allows—whether to use the internal source or an external vendor. In contrast, when actual rates are used for cost allocation, user divisions are kept unaware of their charges until the end of the budget period.

Budgeted rates also help motivate the manager of the support (or supplier) department (for example, the IT department) to improve efficiency. During the budget period, the support department (not the user divisions) bears the risk of any unfavourable cost variances, because user divisions do not pay for any costs or inefficiencies of the supplier department that cause actual rates to exceed budgeted rates.

The manager of the supplier department would likely view the budgeted rates negatively if unfavourable cost variances occur due to price increases outside of his or her control. Some organizations try to identify these uncontrollable factors and relieve the support department manager of responsibility for these variances. In other organizations, the supplier department and the user division agree to share the risk (through an explicit formula) of a large, uncontrollable increase in the prices of inputs used by the supplier department. This procedure avoids imposing the risk completely on either the supplier department (as when budgeted rates are used) or the user division (as in the case of actual rates).

For the rest of this chapter, we will continue to consider only allocation methods that are based on the budgeted cost of support services.

Budgeted Versus Actual Usage

In both the single-rate and dual-rate methods, the variable costs are assigned on the basis of budgeted rates and actual usage. Since the variable costs are directly and causally linked to usage, charging them as a function of the actual usage is appropriate. Moreover, allocating variable costs on the basis of budgeted usage would provide the user departments with no incentive to control their consumption of support services.

What about the fixed costs? Consider the budget of $3,000,000 fixed costs at the IT department of SHC. Recall that budgeted usage is 8,000 hours for the Notebook division and 4,000 hours for the Peripherals division. Assume that actual usage by the Notebook division is always equal to budgeted usage. We consider three cases: when actual usage by the Peripherals division equals (Case 1), is greater than (Case 2), and is less than (Case 3) budgeted usage.

Fixed Cost Allocation Based on Budgeted Rates and Budgeted Usage

This is the dual-rate procedure outlined in the previous section. When budgeted usage is the allocation base, regardless of the actual usage of facilities (i.e., whether Case 1, 2, or 3 occurs), user divisions receive a preset lump-sum fixed cost charge. If rates are based on expected demand ($250 per hour), the Notebook division is assigned $2,000,000 and the Peripherals division, $1,000,000. If rates are set using practical capacity ($160 per hour), the Notebook division is charged $1,280,000, the Peripherals division is allocated $640,000, and the remaining $1,080,000 is the unallocated cost of excess capacity.

The advantage of knowing the allocations in advance is that it helps the user divisions with both short-run and long-run planning. Companies commit to infrastructure costs (such as the fixed costs of a support department) on the basis of a long-run planning horizon; budgeted usage measures the long-run demands of the user divisions for support-department services.

Allocating fixed costs on the basis of budgeted long-run usage may tempt some managers to underestimate their planned usage. Underestimating will result in their divisions bearing a lower percentage of fixed costs (assuming all other managers do not similarly underestimate their usage). To discourage such underestimates, some companies offer bonuses or other rewards—the "carrot" approach—to managers who make accurate forecasts of long-run usage. Other companies impose cost penalties—the "stick" approach—for underestimating long-run usage. For instance, a higher cost rate is charged after a division exceeds its budgeted usage.

Fixed Cost Allocation Based on Budgeted Rates and Actual Usage

Column 2 of Exhibit 14-4 provides the allocations when the budgeted rate is based on expected demand ($250 per hour), while column 3 shows the allocations when practical capacity is used to derive the rate ($160 per hour). Note that each operating division's fixed cost allocation varies based on its actual usage of support facilities. However, variations in actual usage in one division do not affect the costs allocated to the other division. The Notebook division is allocated either $2,000,000 or $1,280,000, depending on the budgeted rate chosen, independent of the Peripherals division's actual usage. Therefore, combining actual usage as the allocation base with budgeted rates provides user divisions with advanced knowledge of rates, as well as control over the costs charged to them.[4]

Note, however, that this allocation procedure for fixed costs is exactly the same as that under the single-rate method. As such, the procedure shares the disadvantages of the single-rate method discussed in the previous section, such as charging excessively high costs, including the cost of unused capacity, when rates are based on expected usage. Moreover, even when rates are based on practical capacity, recall that allocating fixed cost rates based on actual usage induces conflicts of interest between the user divisions and the firm when evaluating outsourcing possibilities.

Allocating Budgeted Fixed Costs Based on Actual Usage

Finally, consider the impact of having actual usage as the allocation base when the firm assigns total budgeted fixed costs to operating divisions (rather than specifying budgeted fixed cost rates, as we have thus far). If the budgeted fixed costs of $3,000,000 are allocated using budgeted usage, we are back in the familiar dual-rate setting. On the other hand, if the actual usage of the facility is the basis for allocation, the charges would equal the amounts in Exhibit 14-4, column 4. In Case 1, the fixed-cost allocation equals the budgeted amount (which is also the same as the charge under the dual-rate method). In Case 2, the fixed-cost allocation is $400,000 less to the Notebook division than the amount based on budgeted usage ($1,600,000 versus $2,000,000). In Case 3, the fixed-cost allocation is $400,000 more to the Notebook division than the amount based on budgeted usage ($2,400,000 versus $2,000,000). Why does the Notebook division receive $400,000 more in costs in Case 3, even though its actual usage equals its budgeted usage? It is because the total fixed costs of $3,000,000 are now spread over 2,000 fewer hours of actual total usage. In other words, the lower usage by the Peripherals division leads to an increase in the fixed costs allocated to the Notebook division. When budgeted fixed costs are allocated based on actual usage, user divisions will not know their fixed cost allocations until the end of the budget period. This method therefore shares the same flaw as those that rely on the use of actual cost realizations rather than budgeted cost rates.

To summarize, there are excellent economic and motivational reasons to justify the precise forms of the single-rate and dual-rate methods considered in the previous section, and in particular, to recommend the dual-rate allocation procedure.

---

[4] The total amount of fixed costs allocated to divisions will in general not equal the actual realized costs. Adjustments for over-allocations and underallocations would then be made.

Exhibit 14-4 Effect of Variations in Actual Usage on Fixed Cost Allocation to Operating Divisions

	(1) Actual Usage		(2) Budgeted Cost Based on Expected Demand[a]		(3) Budgeted Cost Based on Practical Capacity[b]		(4) Allocation of Budgeted Total Fixed Cost	
Case	Notebook	Peripherals	Notebook	Peripherals	Notebook	Peripherals	Notebook	Peripherals
1	8,000 hours	4,000 hours	$2,000,000	$1,000,000	$1,280,000	$640,000	$2,000,000[c]	$1,000,000[d]
2	8,000 hours	7,000 hours	2,000,000	1,750,000	1,280,000	1,120,000	1,600,000[e]	1,400,000[f]
3	8,000 hours	2,000 hours	2,000,000	500,000	1,280,000	320,000	2,400,000[g]	600,000[h]

$$^a \frac{\$3,000,000}{(8,000 + 4,000)\text{ hours}} = \$250 \text{ per hour} \qquad ^b \frac{\$3,000,000}{18,750\text{ hours}} = \$160 \text{ per hour} \qquad ^c \frac{8,000}{(8,000 + 4,000)} \times \$3,000,000 \qquad ^d \frac{4,000}{(8,000 + 4,000)} \times \$3,000,000$$

$$^e \frac{8,000}{(8,000 + 7,000)} \times \$3,000,000 \qquad ^f \frac{7,000}{(8,000 + 7,000)} \times \$3,000,000 \qquad ^g \frac{8,000}{(8,000 + 2,000)} \times \$3,000,000 \qquad ^h \frac{2,000}{(8,000 + 2,000)} \times \$3,000,000$$

Manufacturing Overhead Cost Allocation Methods Are Irrelevant

For ASPE/IFRS-compliant external reporting, there is rarely an issue of cost assignment. Issues may arise, however, in reporting costs for purposes of contract reimbursement. It is the responsibility of the management accountant to point out options to top managers as they negotiate contract terms. This will avoid ambiguity in defining reimbursable costs and expensive litigation. For internal reporting purposes, the cost assignment that best motivates employees may conflict with the highest quality of information for use in economic decisions.

Sustainability in Action   Urban Allocation Decisions

While (seemingly) not as exciting as the marketing department's setting prices and designing promotional campaigns, or the purchasing department's negotiating the best possible prices for inputs, or the manufacturing department's designing an elegant production system, the accounting department's decisions about how to allocate indirect costs are critical to an organization.

The City of Atlanta* undertook an internal audit to examine how indirect costs had been allocated to various civic departments. The audit was initiated after questions were raised by senior managers at two city departments about overcharging of overheads and the transparency of the allocation methods being used.

The City of Atlanta, like many other US cities, follows generally accepted accounting principles for state and local governments. In addition, due to federal regulations regarding federal grant eligibility, it must create an explicit cost allocation plan that does not include specific costs such as for the city council and the mayor's office. As a result, Atlanta's accounting department used a "Full Cost Allocation Plan" and an "A-87 Cost Allocation Plan" prepared by an outside supplier, Maximus, due to the complexities of creating these

allocation plans. The city had paid Maximus $257,000 for a two-year contract (2007–2008) and a renewal (2009) that cost the city $95,000.

After an extensive internal audit, it was concluded that various city departments had, on one hand, been overcharged approximately $11 million but, at the same time, had not been allocated $41.6 million of IT charges arising from the implementation of a city-wide Oracle system. The report stated that "City oversight of contract performance was minimal and the contractor did not perform all required activities."** It also concluded that the method used by Maximus (a reciprocal/step-down hybrid) was overly complex for the city's needs.

The Atlanta example demonstrates the need for systems that are appropriate for the organization and considered fair (by those being charged the allocated costs).

*While the authors look for Canadian examples to illustrate various accounting issues, this example from the United States was so relevant to the topic that it was selected for inclusion in this edition.
**City Auditor's Department, "Performance Audit: Indirect Cost Allocation," December 2009, City of Atlanta, (http://www.atlaudit.org/audits/city-finances-and-administration/indirect-cost-allocation-december-2009).

ASPE/IFRS usually requires the exclusion of all non-manufacturing costs from inventoriable costs. The management team at SHC need not be concerned about actual, budget, or normal methods of assigning period costs to obtain a full product cost. These three methods are only relevant to the assignment of manufacturing overhead costs. For external reporting purposes, all non-manufacturing overhead is expensed in the period in which it occurs and does not accumulate in any inventory. Similarly for contract purposes, it is rare that any customer would pay for period costs. These costs were not incurred primarily to serve a customer and are non-value-added to that customer. In fact, the customer is more likely to demand transparent internal controls be in place to reduce the difficulty of auditing the costs for which the customer was invoiced.

Deciding Among Direct, Step-Down, and Reciprocal Cost Allocation Methods

In many cases, the costs of a division will include costs allocated from other divisions. Rather than use an inappropriate actual unitized fixed cost rate based on actual results, there are three alternatives: *direct, step-down*, and *reciprocal* cost allocation. To simplify, the corporation in the following example contains only two support divisions (maintenance and IT services), and two core or operating divisions in production (machining and assembly).

▶ **LO 4**

Evaluate and select among the direct, step-down, and reciprocal methods of allocating support division costs to production divisions.

Relevance

A strong caution here is to remember that there are no standardized corporate structures. Neither ASPE/IFRS nor the demand for economic plausibility requires identical value chains, identical business functions in each component of the value chain, or identical classification of costs in each component. In centralized corporate structures, most facilities-sustaining activities are undertaken at corporate headquarters. The period cost application methods selected would differ from a decentralized structure.

In decentralized corporate structures, business functions such as R&D will be undertaken at a divisional level. Practically, in the example, R&D incurs significant IT costs as it provides services to each core division. Each corporate situation differs. It takes an alert management accountant to exercise professional judgment when making decisions in costing system design. The decisions must be appropriate to the individual corporation as well as the specific purpose of costing.

Step 1: Identify the problem. Top management at Castleford Engineering Ltd. (CEL) has witnessed profit erosion and suspects its method of allocating product-sustaining MOH and facilities-sustaining IT services is inappropriate. If true, then the costing system itself is failing to reveal the distortions in cost that are undermining CEL's attempts at cost leadership.

Step 2: Gather relevant information. Gathering information reveals that at CEL maintenance services are provided to two different activity centres in the production area: machining and assembly. But maintenance services also repairs and maintains the computers in IT services, which in turn supports maintenance services, machining, and assembly, as shown in Exhibit 14-5.

Costs are accumulated in each division for planning and control purposes. For inventory costing, however, the support division costs of CEL must be allocated to the core divisions. Only the costs contributing to the production of its units can be allocated to inventory and cost of goods sold (COGS), according to ASPE/IFRS. For internal purposes, however, CEL can apply the proportion of cost pools relevant to achieving the purpose for the cost allocation in the first place.

In looking at the percentages in the table in Exhibit 14-5 for plant maintenance (PM), we can see that this support division provides a total of 8,000 hours of support work: 20% (= 1,600 ÷ 8,000) goes to the information technology (IT) support division; 30% (= 2,400 ÷ 8,000) to the core machining division (M); and 50% (= 4,000 ÷ 8,000) to the core assembly division (A). The table also shows a similar situation for the other support

Exhibit 14-5 Data for Allocating Support Department Costs at Castleford Engineering for 2018

	A	B	C	D	E	F
1		SUPPORT		OPERATING		
2		DEPARTMENTS		DEPARTMENTS		
3		Plant	Information			
4		Maintenance	Systems	Machining	Assembly	Total
5	Budgeted manufacturing overhead costs before any interdepartmental cost allocations	$600,000	$116,000	$400,000	$200,000	$1,316,000
6	Support work furnished:					
7	By plant maintenance					
8	Budgeted labour-hours	—	1,600	2,400	4,000	8,000
9	Percentage	—	20%	30%	50%	100%
10	By information systems					
11	Budgeted computer hours	200	—	1,600	200	2,000
12	Percentage	10%	—	80%	10%	100%

division (information systems). It provides 10%, 80%, and 10% of its service (based on the number of computer hours) to the plant maintenance division, machining division, and assembly division, respectively. Under ASPE/IFRS, these costs are classified as inventoriable manufacturing overhead (MOH) costs.

Step 3: Make predictions about the future. As CEL studies its three alternatives for cost allocation, the forecast outcomes will be compared to the economic reality of CEL's production and support activities. The goal for CEL is to adopt the method that best reflects full product costs to assist in more accurate target costing, given their target price, ROI, and operating margin percentage. The company would also try to assess how the managers of the operating division might react to any changes. The managers of the support divisions don't really care about which allocation method is used, since all three methods allocate 100% of the costs of the respective support divisions.

Step 4: Decide on and implement an alternative. The budgeted or predicted data generated by CEL are shown in Exhibit 14-6. This forecast provides the data required to evaluate the three alternative allocation methods—direct, step-down, and reciprocal allocation.

Direct Method

The **direct allocation method** (often called the **direct method**) is simple and intuitive. It is readily explained and inexpensive to implement because little training is required. Any service rendered by one support division to another support division is ignored. The relationship is illustrated in Exhibit 14-6, wherein $11,600 (= $116,000 × 10%) of the IT cost pool is spent to support PM and $120,000 (= $600,000 × 20%) of the PM cost pool that supports IT is ignored. This is a straightforward average costing method but, in total, the machining and assembly core production functions will bear $131,600, but possibly not distributed in a fashion that reflects economic reality. This represents approximately 18% of the PM and IT support cost pools ($131,600 ÷ $716,000).

The budgeted total values of the PM and IT cost pools are constant. The denominators are not the total hours provided by PM and IT, but rather only those hours provided to the core production activities. The denominator is understated, and the cost allocation rate is overstated.

As illustrated, by ignoring the use of the DLH and ITH (IT hours) by the two service divisions, the total cost drivers decrease from 8,000 DLH to 6,400 DLH for PM and from 2,000 ITH to 1,800 ITH for IT services. The total budgeted cost pools remain constant. The cost driver rate for PM becomes $93.75/DLH (= $600,000 ÷ 6,400 DLH) and for IT

Exhibit 14-6 Direct Method of Allocating Support Department Costs at Castleford Engineering for 2018

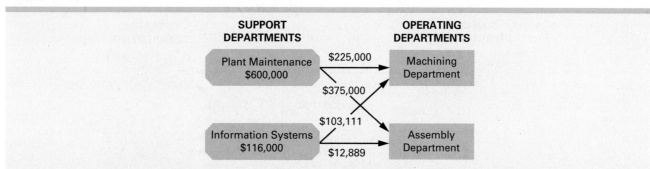

	A	B	C	D	E	F
1		**SUPPORT**		**OPERATING**		
2		**DEPARTMENTS**		**DEPARTMENTS**		
3		**Plant**	**Information**			
4		**Maintenance**	**Systems**	**Machining**	**Assembly**	**Total**
5	Budgeted manufacturing overhead costs before any interdepartmental cost allocations	$ 600,000	$ 116,000	$400,000	$200,000	$1,316,000
6	Allocation of plant maintenance (3/8, 5/8)[a]	(600,000)		225,000	375,000	
7	Allocation of information systems (8/9, I/9)[b]		(116.000)	103,111	12,889	
8	Total budgeted manufacturing overhead of operating departments	$ 0	$ 0	$728,111	$587,889	$1,316,000
9						
10	[a]Base is (2,400 + 4,000) or 6,400 hours; 2,400 ÷ 6,400 = 3/8; 4,000 ÷ 6,400 = 5/8. An equivalent approach is to calculate a budgeted rate for allocating plant maintenance department costs, $600,000 ÷ 6,400 hours = $93.75 per hour. The machining department would then be allocated $225,000 ($93.75 per hour × 2,400 hours) and the assembly department $375,000 ($93.75 per hour × 4,000 hours).					
11	[b]Base is (1,600 + 200), or 1,800 hours; 1,600 ÷ 1,800 = 8/9; 200 ÷ 1,800 = 1/9. An equivalent approach is to calculate a budgeted rate for allocating information systems department costs, $116,000 ÷ 1,800 hours = $64.444 per hour. The machining department would then be allocated $103,111 (= $64.444 per hour × 1,600 hours) and the assembly department $12,889 (= $64.444 per hour × 200 hours). For ease of exposition throughout this section, we will use the fraction of the support department services used by other departments to allocate support department costs to other departments rather than calculate budgeted rates to allocate costs.					

services, approximately $64.44/ITH. The costs applied to machining and assembly on this basis will, of course, include the burden that should be borne by PM and IT services for the costs of each other's support services. This is summarized in Exhibit 14-6.

Step-Down Method

The **step-down method** (sometimes called the **step allocation method,** or **sequential method**) recognizes the cost of services provided by one support division to the other before allocating the remaining services cost pool to the core divisions. The method does not recognize the cost of services provided by each cost pool to the other, though. It assumes that one division is ranked as step 1, another as step 2, and so on. In this example, assume that the PM division is ranked step 1 and the IT division is ranked step 2. Once the PM service costs have been deducted and added to IT services, there is no subsequent inflow of costs of IT services to PM. The smaller PM cost pool and the larger IT services cost pool will then be allocated to machining and assembly.

A decision on how to rank the two service providers must be made on some justifiable basis. Usually the highest *percentage of service* provided to other services is ranked first, followed in order by the others. An alternative would be to rank on the basis of *highest to lowest cost of services* provided to other divisions.

If CEL implemented the step-down method based on hours of service, then the cost of 20% of DLH that the PM division provided to IT would be deducted before allocating the

Exhibit 14-7 **Step-Down Method** of Allocating Support Department Costs at Castleford Engineering for 2018

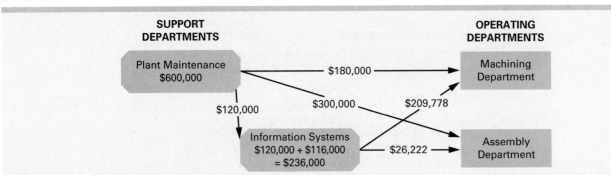

	A	B	C	D	E	F
1		SUPPORT		OPERATING		
2		DEPARTMENTS		DEPARTMENTS		
3		Plant	Information			
4		Maintenance	Systems	Machining	Assembly	Total
5	Budgeted manufacturing overhead costs before any interdepartmental cost allocations	$ 600,000	$116,000	$400,000	$200,000	$1,316,000
6	Allocation of plant maintenance (2/10, 3/10, 5/10)[a]	(600,000)	120,000	180,000	300,000	
7			236,000			
8	Allocation of information systems (8/9, l/9)[b]		(236,000)	209,778	26,222	
9	Total budgeted manufacturing overhead of operating departments	$ 0	$ 0	$789,778	$526,222	$1,316,000
10						
11	[a]Base is (1,600 + 2,400 + 4,000), or 8,000 hours; 1,600 ÷ 8,000 = 2/10; 2,400 ÷ 8,000 = 3/10; 4,000 ÷ 8,000 = 5/10. Instead of using fractions, we could have calculated a budgeted rate for allocating plant maintenance costs to the other departments as described in Exhibit 14-6.					
12	[b]Base is (1,600 + 200), or 1,800 hours; 1,600 ÷ 1,800 = 8/9; 200 ÷ 1,800 = 1/9.					

remainder in the PM cost pool to machining and assembly. IT is ranked second because the IT percentage is only 10% of ITH provided to PM. The total cost to provide 1,600 DLH to IT is $120,000 (= $600,000 × 20%) and the total cost to provide 200 ITH to PM is only $11,600 (= $116,000 × 10%), as shown in Exhibit 14-7. For CEL, both alternatives (percentage of service, or cost) lead to the same sequencing. In the first line of the table, the predicted cost pools are reported. The percentage of ITH to PM is reported as 20% and the dollar value reported in the IT column.

Now the total cost pool of IT more than doubles to $236,000 as shown, but the total cost driver has also decreased slightly to 1,800 ITH. Of course the result is a large increase in the cost allocation rate to approximately $131.11/ITH (= $236,000 ÷ 1,800 ITH). The PM cost pool has decreased by the amount allocated to IT systems and is now $480,000, and the DLH measuring the benefit of PM to core divisions is 6,400 DLH. The cost allocation rate is $75/DLH (= $480,000 ÷ 6,400 DLH).

Following through from PM to machining, the 20% of DLH to serve IT services has been given, leaving 80% of the total PM cost pool, or $480,000, to be applied. The 1,600 DLH have been applied to IT and what remains is 6,400 DLH. The PM cost allocation rate will be $75/DLH (= $480,000 ÷ 6,400 DLH). Machining is budgeted to consume 2,400 DLH, or 30%, of available hours (2,400 DLH ÷ 8,000 DLH) and costs. The cost applied to machining will be $180,000 (either $75/DLH × 2,400 DLH or 30% × $600,000). The remaining cost of 4,000 DLH is applied to assembly. Exhibit 14-7 summarizes this approach; notice that the percentages are determined by the DLH, not the size of the cost pool.

The IT services cost pool has increased by 20% of PM, or $120,000, applied using the step-down method. The IT services cost pool of $236,000 is not adjusted for the

200 ITH of service provided to PM. This means the total cost driver is not 2,000 ITH but rather, consistent with the direct method, it is 1,800 ITH. The cost driver rate is approximately $131.11/ITH (= $236,000 ÷ 1,800 ITH). Of the 1,800 ITH, the assembly activities will consume 200 ITH, or 1/9 of the budgeted hours and costs (200 ITH ÷ 1,800 ITH), or $26,222. The same amount can be calculated using the cost driver rate ($131.11 × 200 = $26,222). The remaining 8/9 of the budgeted ITH and costs (1,600 ITH ÷ 1,800 ITH) will be $209,778 and can be obtained by simple subtraction.

Reciprocal Method—Linear Equation and Solver

The **reciprocal allocation method** takes the step-down method one step further. Where the step-down method recognizes the work that the first ranked support division provides to the other support divisions (but ignores the work that the other support divisions provide to the first ranked support division), the reciprocal method recognizes the work that *all the support* divisions do for each other before allocating costs to the production divisions. The reciprocal method for allocating CEL's support department costs is shown in Exhibit 14-8.

The result is a budgeted complete **reciprocated cost** pool for each support services division. Another term often used is **artificial cost**. This approach is another application of linear programming; as well, either the Solver or Matrix functions in Excel can be used. The drawback for the linear equation method is that it becomes unwieldy in situations

Exhibit 14-8 **Reciprocal Method** of Allocating Support Department Costs Using Linear Equations at Castleford Engineering for 2018

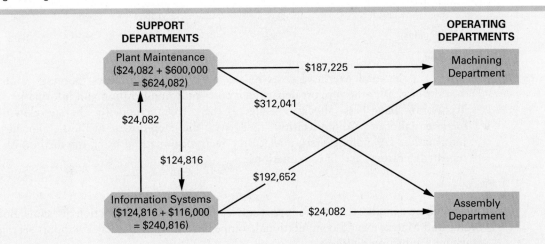

	A	B	C	D	E	F
1		SUPPORT		OPERATING		
2		DEPARTMENTS		DEPARTMENTS		
3		Plant	Information			
4		Maintenance	Systems	Machining	Assembly	Total
5	Budgeted manufacturing overhead costs before any interdepartmental cost allocations	$ 600,000	$ 116,000	$400,000	$200,000	$1,316,000
6	Allocation of plant maintenance (2/10, 3/10, 5/10)[a]	(624,082)	124,816	187,225	312,041	
7	Allocation of information systems (1/10, 8/10, l/10)[b]	24,082	(240,816)	192,652	24,082	
8	Total budgeted manufacturing overhead of operating departments	$ 0	$ 0	$779,877	$536,123	$1,316,000
9						
10	[a]Base is (1,600 + 2,400 + 4,000), or 8,000 hours; 1,600 ÷ 8,000 = 2/10; 2,400 ÷ 8,000 = 3/10; 4,000 ÷ 8,000 = 5/10.					
11	[b]Base is (200 + 1,600 + 200), or 2,000 hours; 200 ÷ 2,000 = 1/10, 1,600 ÷ 2,000 = 8/10; 200 ÷ 2,000 = 1/10.					

● **TRY IT! 14.2**

Montvale Tours provides guided educational tours to college alumni associations. The company is divided into two operating divisions: domestic tours and world tours. Each of the tour divisions uses the services of the company's two support departments: Administration and Information Technology. Additionally, the Administration and Information Technology departments use the services of each other. Data concerning the past year are as follows:

| | Support Departments | | Operating Departments | | |
	Administration	Information Technology	Domestic Tours	World Tours	Total
Budgeted overhead costs before any interdepartmental cost allocations	$400,000	$250,000	$1,300,000	$1,840,000	$3,790,0000
Support work furnished: by Administration					
Budgeted administration salaries	—	$ 88,000	$ 55,000	$ 77,000	$ 220,000
Percentage	—	40%	25%	35%	100%
by Information Technology					
Budgeted IT service hours	600	—	2,200	1,200	4,000
Percentage	15%	—	55%	30%	100%

Required

What are the total overhead costs of the operating departments (domestic and world tours) *after* the support department costs of Administration and Information Technology have been allocated using (a) the direct method, (b) the step-down method (allocate Administration first), (c) the step-down method (allocate Information Technology first), and (d) the reciprocal method using the method of repeated iterations and linear equations?

that are more complex than two support services and two core production divisions. Both Solver and Matrix extend computational competence to any number of support services and core production divisions.

Using matrix algebra in Excel, it is only the reciprocal support division allocations that require this treatment and the goal is to obtain the complete reciprocated or artificial costs in a more efficient manner than using simultaneous equations. No matrix algebra is required to calculate the allocations of support division costs to the two operating divisions.

Linear Equation Method

The simultaneous linear equation method requires three steps:[5]

1. *Express support division costs and reciprocal relationships in linear equation form.* Let PM be the complete reciprocated costs of PM, and IS be the complete reciprocated costs of IS. The relationships are

$$\text{PM} = \$600,000 + 0.1\text{IS} \tag{1}$$

$$\text{IS} = \$116,000 + 0.2\text{PM} \tag{2}$$

---

[5] The reciprocal allocation method requires iteration, a mathematical approach to solving a problem that requires an estimate of the answer in order to begin solving a system of linear equations. By repeatedly substituting improved estimates, the error term in the equations converges to zero, or the best answer. Undertaking reciprocal allocation in Excel, the iteration is automatic.

The 0.1IS term in equation (1) is the percentage of the IS resources consumed by PM. But the IS reciprocated cost pool includes 20% of the PM cost pool. In equation (1) the 10% IS term must be adjusted to include the additional PM costs before solving.

2. *Substitute equation (2) for the term IS in equation (1).* The resulting equation is shown in the first line:

$$PM = \$600,000 + [0.1(\$116,000 + 0.2PM)] \tag{3}$$

$$PM = \$600,000 + \$11,600 + 0.02PM \tag{4}$$

$$0.98PM = \$611,600 \tag{5}$$

$$PM = \$624,082 \tag{6}$$

In equation (4), the known quantities, $600,000 in the PM cost pool and the $11,600 or 10% of the IS cost pool, replace the terms in equation (3). Be careful to notice in equation (3) that the 10% is outside an expression containing two terms, of which one is 0.2PM. Multiplying 0.2PM by 0.1 gives 0.02PM, as shown in equation (4). Equation (4) can be understood as 100%PM = $600,000 + $11,600 + 2%PM. Collecting similar terms and subtracting 2%PM from both sides of the equation gives equation (5), in which only one unknown remains. Dividing both sides of the equation by 0.98 provides the result in equation (6) of PM = $624,082 (= $611,600 ÷ 0.98). This is the *artificial cost* of PM. Next we need to *substitute known values into the IS equation.* The first value is provided by CEL's budget and the second from the artificial cost pool calculated for PM:

$$IS = \$116,000 + 0.2(\$624,082) = \$240,816$$

Where more than two support divisions have reciprocal relationships, either Solver or the Matrix function in Excel can be used to calculate the artificial costs of each support division.

3. *Apply the complete artificial costs of each support division to all other divisions (both support and operating divisions) on the basis of the usage proportions (based on total units of service provided to all divisions).* Consider the IT division, which has a complete reciprocated cost of $240,816. This amount would be applied as follows:

To plant maintenance (1/10 × $240,816)	=	$ 24,082
To machining (8/10 × $240,816), rounded	=	192,652
To assembly (1/10 × $240,816)	=	24,082
Total		$240,816

The artificial cost pool used to download the PM service support costs to machining and assembly is $624,082, and for the IT service support costs is $240,816. Both have expanded to include the costs of PM and IT services reciprocally provided to each other.

One source of confusion to some managers using the reciprocal cost allocation method is why the complete reciprocated (artificial) costs of the support divisions of $864,898 (= $624,082 and $240,816) exceed their budgeted amount of $716,000 ($600,000 and $116,000). The excess of $148,898 ($24,082 for PM and $124,816 for IT) is the total of costs that are reciprocally allocated between support divisions. The total costs allocated to the operating divisions under the reciprocal allocation method remain only $716,000 (= $600,000 + $116,000).

Under the reciprocal method, the cost allocation rates rounded to the nearest dollar are $78/DLH for the PM services and $120/ITH for the IT services.

Which Method to Select?

The table below summarizes the total support division costs allocated to the machining and assembly divisions. Note that, regardless of which one is used, each method allocates the same *total* amount of support division costs ($1,316,000).

	Machining	Assembly	Total
Direct method	$728,111	$587,889	$1,316,000
Step-down method, PM sequenced first	789,778	526,222	1,316,000
Reciprocal method	779,877	536,123	1,316,000

The following table outlines some advantages and disadvantages of each method:

Allocation Method	Advantages	Disadvantages
Direct Method Exhibit 14-6	■ Simple to calculate ■ Easy to understand ■ Inexpensive to implement ■ Does not require support departments to be ranked	■ May not accurately reflect the economic reality of value being added by support division activities ■ Fails to recognize level of activity between support divisions ■ May result in large cost/value distortions
Step-Down Method Exhibit 14-7	■ Simpler than the reciprocal method ■ Recognizes some of the activity between support divisions ■ May be viewed as "fairer" than the direct method ■ If one division provides a majority of the interdivisional support, there is minimal distortion of cost (compared to the direct method)	■ Not as economically plausible as the reciprocal method ■ More complex than the direct method ■ Requires support divisions to be ranked by some method
Reciprocal Method Exhibit 14-8	■ Conceptually, the best method ■ Reflects economic reality of support division activities ■ Does not require support divisions to be ranked	■ Difficult for non-accountants to understand, therefore it may be difficult to justify the numbers ■ Complex to calculate and, as a result, subject to error ■ Most expensive (due to complexity and training requirements)

It may well be that the method a company chooses is the one that can be implemented with the least disruption to operations. For example, if CEL was currently using the direct method, the manager of the machining division would probably resist a change to either of the other two methods (since both result in significantly more support division costs being allocated to machining). Alternatively, if there currently was no allocation taking place and the choice was between the step-down method and the reciprocal method, a manager might argue for the step-down method on the basis that the dollar differences aren't significant and the step-down method is much easier to calculate and explain. However, if the marketplace was extremely competitive and price sensitive and the support division costs were significant, it might make sense to use the reciprocal method in order to get the most accurate picture of value (and costs) added by the support divisions.

Step 5: Implement the decision, evaluate the performance, and learn. Once CEL makes a decision regarding which allocation method to use for its support division costs, it will need to assess the impact of this change. In order to do this, it has to assign the newly calculated cost for the operating divisions (i.e., machining and assembly) to the products that are being produced. Remember that the majority of support division costs have been allocated to the various operating divisions. To assess the impact, CEL has to take the costs that are now residing in the various operating division cost pools and assign them to the products in order to generate a full job/product cost (note that this concept of full product cost is not the same as inventoriable costs because full product cost includes period costs).

Assume that CEL uses machine-hours (DMH) as the machining cost driver, and the total budgeted DMH hours is 4,000. In assembly, the cost driver is direct manufacturing labour-hours (DMLH), and the total budgeted DMLH hours is 3,000. Under the three different overhead cost application methods, the total machining and assembly cost pools assigned to units of finished jobs (goods) differ somewhat. The denominator or cost driver remains constant while the cost pools vary and so, too, do the cost driver rates, as shown:

Support Division Cost Allocation Method	Total Budgeted Costs After Support Overhead Allocation of All Division Costs		Budgeted Overhead Rate per Hour for Product Costing Purposes	
	Machining	**Assembly**	**Machining 4,000 DMH**	**Assembly 3,000 DMLH**
Direct	$728,111	$587,889	$182	$196
Step-down	789,778	526,222	197	175
Reciprocal	779,877	536,123	195	179

These differences in budgeted overhead rates with alternative support division cost allocation methods can be important to managers. For example, consider a cost reimbursement contract that uses 100 machining DMH and 15 assembly DMLH. The support division costs allocated to this contract would be

Direct	$21,140	$182 × 100 + $196 × 15
Step-down	22,325	$197 × 100 + $175 × 15
Reciprocal	22,185	$195 × 100 + $179 × 15

In this example, the use of the step-down method would result in the highest cost reimbursement to CEL. This will benefit CEL only if, when it bids for a job, the client fails to state which of the three methods must be used. If CEL assumes that the step-down method is required, enters a bid, and is accepted—but later is advised that the client required the reciprocal (or worse, the direct method)—a lengthy and costly legal dispute could arise.

With the high cost driver rate for IT services, should the core division managers decide to outsource this service? The method adopted by CEL will affect that decision. Assume all of CEL's IT services are variable. The bid price must be compared to the complete reciprocated or artificial costs for this service of $240,816, not the budgeted IT service cost of $116,000. The reason is that the complete reciprocated costs include the services PM provides to deliver 2,000 hours of computer time to *all* three divisions.

The hourly rate for the complete reciprocated costs is $120.41 (= $240,816 ÷ 2,000 ITH). To be competitive, the third party must bid less than either the hourly rate of $120.41 or the total reciprocated cost of $240,816 to improve the company's operating income. In this case, the relevant costs of shutting down IT are $116,000 plus $124,816 of PM costs because these will no longer be incurred to support IT, making the total relevant cost savings $240,816. This assumes that the PM costs are scalable (will decrease if the division does not have to support IT after it is shut down) and that the $116,000 IT costs are avoidable. Neither the direct nor the step-down method will provide this relevant information for outsourcing decisions.[6]

Allocating Common Costs

We next consider two methods used to allocate **common costs**. A common cost is a cost of operating a facility, operation, activity, or like cost object that is shared by two or more users. A common cost is different from our previous situation (allocating support division costs) in a number of aspects:

▶ **LO 5**

Analyze cost allocation procedures to apply common costs and justify contractual reimbursement terms.

■ There is only one cost to allocate and it is shared by multiple users (versus costs of multiple support divisions that might provide services to each other as well as providing support to production divisions—remember, if there was only one support division you could only use the direct method to allocate the support division's cost pool).

---

[6] Technical issues when using the reciprocal method in outsourcing decisions are discussed in R.S. Kaplan and A.A. Atkinson, *Advanced Management Accounting*, 3rd ed. (Upper Saddle River, N.J.: Prentice Hall, 1998), pp. 73–81.

■ It is typically a fixed or step cost where it would be difficult to select an appropriate cost driver to allocate it. This differs from the support division situation, where their cost pools were allocated by some specific driver (e.g., IT hours, machine-hours, etc.).

Consider Jason Stevens, a student in Winnipeg who has been invited to an interview with an employer in Halifax. The round-trip Winnipeg–Halifax airfare is $1,200. A week before leaving, Stevens is also invited to an interview with an employer in Montreal. The round-trip Winnipeg–Montreal fare is $800. Stevens decides to combine the two recruiting stops into a Winnipeg–Montreal–Halifax trip that will cost $1,500 in airfare. The $1,500 is a common cost that benefits both employers. There are two methods for allocating this common cost between the two potential employers: the stand-alone method and the incremental method.

Stand-Alone Cost Allocation Method

The **stand-alone cost allocation method** uses information pertaining to each cost object as a separate operating entity to determine the cost allocation weights. For the airfare common cost of $1,500, information about the separate (stand-alone) return airfares ($1,200 and $800) is used to determine the allocation weights:

$$\text{Halifax employer: } \frac{\$1,200}{\$1,200 + \$800} \times \$1,500 = 0.60 \times \$1,500 = \$900$$

$$\text{Montreal employer: } \frac{\$800}{\$1,200 + \$800} \times \$1,500 = 0.40 \times \$1,500 = \$600$$

Advocates of this method often emphasize an equity or fairness rationale. That is, fairness occurs because each employer bears a proportionate share of total costs in relation to its individual stand-alone costs.

Incremental Cost Allocation Method

The **incremental cost allocation method** ranks the individual cost objects and then uses this ranking to allocate costs among those cost objects. The first-ranked cost object is termed the *primary party* and is allocated costs up to its cost as a stand-alone entity. The second-ranked cost object is termed the *incremental party* and is allocated the additional cost that arises from there being two users instead of only the primary user. If there are more than two parties, the nonprimary parties will also need to be ranked.

Consider Jason Stevens and his $1,500 airfare cost. Assume that the Halifax employer is viewed as the primary party. Stevens's rationale was that he had already committed to go to Halifax. The cost allocations would then be

Party	Cost Allocated	Costs Remaining to Be Allocated to Other Parties
Halifax (primary)	$1,200	$300 = $1,500 − $1,200
Montreal (incremental)	300	0

The Halifax employer is allocated the full Winnipeg–Halifax airfare. The nonallocated part of the total airfare is allocated to the Montreal employer. Had the Montreal employer been chosen as the primary party, the cost allocations would have been Montreal, $800 (the stand-alone Winnipeg–Montreal return airfare), and Halifax, $700 (= $1,500 − $800). Where there are more than two parties, this method requires them to be ranked and the common costs allocated to those parties in the ranked sequence.

A variation on the incremental approach is to apply a type of *Shapley value* method to allocate the common costs. The Shapley value method involves calculating all of the possible cost allocation combinations resulting from changing the rankings of the various parties and then averaging the amounts. This approach addresses the situation where one party (e.g., Halifax) pays a much larger share of the common cost than the other party. Using the costs from the Stevens example, the possible outcomes are as follows:

Party	Cost Allocated *Halifax* Primary Party	Cost Allocated *Montreal* Primary Party	Average Cost Allocated to Party
Halifax	$1,200	$ 700	$ 950*
Montreal	300	800	550**
Total allocated	$1,500	$1,500	$1,500

*($1,200 + $700) ÷ 2 = $950
**($300 + $800) ÷ 2 = $550

This example assumed that there was an equal weighting of the two parties sharing the common cost. It also assumed only two parties when in fact there might be many more parties sharing a common cost. For an example of how the Shapley value method can be used to allocate a common amount when there are more than two parties involved and there is a weighting of the allocation, please refer to Chapter 16 and the bundled revenue allocation discussion.

Under the incremental method, the primary party typically receives the highest allocation of the common costs. Not surprisingly, most users in common cost situations propose themselves as the incremental (second ranked) party. In some cases, the incremental party is a newly formed "organization" such as a new product line or a new sales territory. Chances for its short-term survival may be enhanced if it bears a relatively low allocation of common costs.

Disputes over how to allocate common costs are often encountered. The final section of this chapter discusses the role of cost data in contracting.

Justifying Reimbursement Costs

Many commercial contracts include clauses that require the use of cost accounting information. Examples include

1. A contract between the Department of National Defence and a company designing and assembling a new fighter plane. The price paid for the plane is based on the contractor's costs plus a preset fixed fee.

2. A research contract between a university and a government agency. The university is reimbursed its direct costs plus an overhead rate that is a percentage of direct costs.

3. A contract between an energy-consulting firm and a hospital. The consulting firm receives a fixed fee plus a share of the energy-cost savings arising from the consulting firm's recommendations.

The areas of dispute between the contracting parties can be reduced by making the "rules of the game" explicit in writing at the time the contract is signed. Such rules of the game include the definition of cost items allowed, the permissible cost-allocation bases, and how differences between budgeted and actual costs are to be handled.

Contracting

There are two main approaches to reimbursing costs as determined by a contract:

1. The *contractor is paid a set price without analysis of actual contract cost data.* This approach is used, for example, where there is competitive bidding, where there is adequate price competition, or where there is an established catalogue with prices quoted for items sold in substantial quantities to the general public.

2. The *contractor is paid after analysis of actual contract cost data.* In some cases, the contract will explicitly state that reimbursement is based on actual allowable costs plus a set fee. This arrangement is a cost-plus contract.

⊕ **TRY IT!** ▸ **14.3**

Essence Company blends and sells designer fragrances. It has a Men's Fragrances division and a Women's Fragrances division, each with different sales strategies, distribution channels, and product offerings. Essence is now considering the sale of a bundled product called Sync consisting of one bottle of Him, a men's cologne, and one bottle of Her, a women's perfume, two of Essence's very successful products. For the most recent year, Essence reported the following:

Product	Retail Price
Him	$ 25.00
Her	$ 50.00
Sync (Him and Her)	$ 60.00

Required

1. Allocate revenue from the sale of each unit of Sync to Him and Her using the following:
   a. The stand-alone revenue-allocation method based on selling price of each product
   b. The incremental revenue-allocation method, with Him ranked as the primary product
   c. The incremental revenue-allocation method, with Her ranked as the primary product
   d. The Shapley value method, assuming equal unit sales of Him and Her
2. Of the four methods in requirement 1, which one would you recommend for allocating Sync's revenues to Him and Her? Explain.

Fairness of Pricing

When uncertainty is high, as in many defence contracts involving new weapons and equipment, contracts are rarely subject to competitive bidding. Why? Because no contractor is willing to assume all the risk. Hence, market-based fixed-price setting fails to attract a contractor, or the resulting price is too outrageously high for the government. So the government assumes a major share of the risks. It negotiates contracts by using costs as a substitute for selling prices that are ordinarily set by suppliers in open markets. In this contracting arena, a cost allocation may be difficult to defend on the basis of any cause-and-effect reasoning. Nonetheless, the contracting parties may still view it as a "reasonable" or "fair" means to help establish a selling price. Some costs become "allowable," but others are "unallowable." An **allowable cost** is a cost that the contract parties agree to include in the costs to be reimbursed. Some contracts specify how allowable costs are to be determined. For example, only economy-class airfares may be allowable in a contract. Other contracts identify cost categories that are nonallowable. For example, the costs of lobbying activities and the costs of alcoholic beverages are not allowable costs on some contracts.

Pulling it all Together—Problem for Self-Study

(Try to solve this problem before examining the solution that follows.)

Problem

This problem illustrates how the costs of two corporate support divisions are allocated to operating divisions.

Computer Horizons budgets the following amounts for its two central corporate support divisions (legal and human resources) in supporting each other and the two manufacturing divisions, the laptop division (LTD) and the workstation division (WSD):

	A	B	C	D	E	F
1		SUPPORT		OPERATING		
2		Legal	Human Resources			
3		Division	Division	LTD	WSD	Total
4	**BUDGETED USAGE**					
5	Legal (hours)	—	250	1,500	750	2,500
6	(Percentages)	—	10%	60%	30%	100%
7	Human resources (hours)	2,500	—	22,500	25,000	50,000
8	(Percentages)	5%	—	45%	50%	100%
9						
10	**ACTUAL USAGE**					
11	Legal (hours)	—	400	400	1,200	2,000
12	(Percentages)	—	20%	20%	60%	100%
13	Human resources (hours)	2,000	—	26,600	11,400	40,000
14	(Percentages)	5%	—	66.5%	28.5%	100%
15	Budgeted fixed overhead costs before any interdivision cost allocations	$360,000	$475,000	—	—	$835,000
16	Actual variable overhead costs before any interdivision cost allocations	$200,000	$600,000	—	—	$800,000

The company needs to improve the accuracy of its cost allocations to improve the competitiveness of its prices.

◄ Required

1. What are other possible reasons a company would undertake improved cost ❶ allocation?
2. What are the possible cost drivers of the legal division? ❷
3. Why might Computer Horizons choose budgeted rather than actual cost allocation ❸ rates for this project?
4. What amount of support division costs for legal and human resources will be allocated ❹ to LTD and WSD using (a) the direct method, (b) the step-down method (allocating the legal division costs first), and (c) the reciprocal method using linear equations?
5. If Computer Horizons were justifying reimbursement from a contract, how would ❺ this project improve its position?

Solution

1. One objective may be to motivate employees through challenging performance targets accompanied by substantial compensation if they are achieved. The effectiveness of using period cost allocation to accomplish this depends on what is perceived as fair by those affected. Generally speaking, if people
   - believe the decision makers and the decision process is undertaken in good faith,
   - are given the opportunity to participate in distributive decision making,
   - have access to relevant information about the consequences, and
   - are treated with respect and sensitivity when they are not beneficiaries, but bear burdens,

   then they will accept that the distribution was fair although it was burdensome for them but not others.

   A second reason is legal, to verify and justify that particular period cost is allowable per specific contract terms. The methods of cost allocation in this chapter can be used to justify beyond reasonable doubt that a cost is allowable. Nevertheless, the same principles of fairness apply and the preferable approach is that the parties of the contract negotiate the allocation method and the specifics of its implementation.

A third reason is to measure income and assets. An additional burden is imposed, however, that the allocation method chosen be justifiable within GAAP if the values of income and assets are publicized. Different methods will impose different costs on different divisions, and this in turn will be reported in segmented statements of income.

2. Cost drivers should be chosen on the basis of their capacity to explain a reasonable proportion of total change in the cost pool. In other words, as the cost pools changes, the cost driver should change in proportion. Choices include sales, assets employed, estimated duration of legal activity. Notice that these choices include an output measure of activity (sales), a capacity input measure (assets employed), and a measure of time (duration of legal activity).

3. The choice of rates can affect managers' behaviour. When budgeted rates are used, the consumers of support resources will know in advance what the pro forma costs will be and this improves their planning.

4. Exhibits 14-6, 14-7, and 14-8 present the computations for allocating the fixed and variable support division costs. A summary of these costs follows:

	Laptop Division (LTD)	Workstation Division (WSD)
(a) Direct Method		
Fixed costs	$465,000	$370,000
Variable costs	470,000	330,000
	$935,000	$700,000
(b) Step-Down Method		
Fixed costs	$458,053	$376,947
Variable costs	488,000	312,000
	$946,053	$688,947
(c) Reciprocal Method		
Fixed costs	$462,513	$372,487
Variable costs	476,364	323,636
	$938,877	$696,123

5. Contractors may price their job prior to it being undertaken and they establish what costs are allowable. An accurate cost allocation project will enable Computer Horizons to understand and separate allowable from other costs. The company will be better able to justify its claim for reimbursement is fair and within the terms of the contract.

Decision Points

The following question-and-answer format summarizes the chapter's learning objectives. Each point presents a key question, and the guidelines are the answer to that question.

Learning Objectives	Guidelines
1. What use is it to allocate period costs?	There are four reasons to calculate the full product, job, or process cost: (a) to provide information for economic decisions, (b) to motivate managers and employees, (c) to justify costs or compute reimbursement, and (d) to measure income and assets for reporting to external parties.

2. Should a manager use the single-rate or the dual-rate cost allocation method?

The single-rate system allocates all support costs based on an average rate. In a highly competitive environment where corporations are price takers, this system overallocates all fixed costs. The dual-rate method separates variable from fixed cost pools. This method reveals the costs of unused capacity, which are not recoverable from customers because this is a non-value-added cost. The dual-rate method enables more accurate target costing.

3. Should actual, normal, or standard costing be applied?

Normal costing is a term used when assigning manufacturing overhead costs. The methods are irrelevant to assigning non-manufacturing costs. GAAP requires period costs be expensed, not accumulated in inventory as value-added to finished goods. The use of either budgeted or actual use of the resource supplied by the support service will affect the assignment of period costs. Allocation of period costs is done for internal purposes.

4. What methods can a manager use to allocate costs of support divisions to one another and to core production divisions?

The three methods are direct, step-down, and reciprocal. The direct method is simple but fails to represent the economic reality of cost flows between support divisions. The step-down method represents support cost flow from one to the other support division in sequence. The economic reality of cost flows is not represented. Both methods will misapply support division costs. Ultimately, costs assigned to products, jobs, or processes will be too high or too low. The reciprocal method fully represents the economic reality of cost flows but is arithmetically more challenging to explain. It is superior to the other two methods because it is consistent, is fair, and more accurately assigns full costs, recoverable when output is sold.

5. What methods can a manager use to allocate common costs to two or more users?

Common costs are the costs of operating a facility, of an activity, or of a cost object that are shared by two or more users. The stand-alone cost allocation method uses information pertaining to each user of the cost object to determine cost allocation weights. The incremental cost allocation method ranks individual users of the cost object and allocates common costs first to the primary user and then to the other incremental users.

Terms to Learn

This chapter and the Glossary at the end of the book contain definitions of the following important terms:

allowable cost (**p. 586**)
artificial costs (**p. 579**)
common costs (**p. 583**)
core divisions (**p. 566**)
direct allocation method (**p. 576**)
direct method (**p. 576**)
dual-rate method (**p. 566**)
full product costing (**p. 563**)

incremental cost allocation method (**p. 584**)
operating department (**p. 566**)
operating division (**p. 566**)
production department (**p. 566**)
production division (**p. 566**)
reciprocal allocation method (**p. 579**)
reciprocated cost (**p. 579**)

sequential method (**p. 577**)
service department (**p. 566**)
single-rate method (**p. 566**)
stand-alone cost allocation method (**p. 584**)
step allocation method (**p. 577**)
step-down method (**p. 577**)
support department (**p. 566**)

Assignment Material

MyLab Accounting Make the grade with MyLab Accounting: The Short-Answer Questions, Exercises, and Problems marked with a ⊕ can be found on MyLab Accounting. You can practise them as often as you want, and most feature step-by-step guided instructions to help you find the right answer.

Short-Answer Questions

🌐 **14-1** "I am going to focus on the customers of my business and leave cost allocation issues to my accountant." Do you agree with this comment by a division president?

🌐 **14-2** Describe how the dual-rate method is useful to division managers in decision making.

🌐 **14-3** What are four purposes of cost allocation?

🌐 **14-4** What criteria might be used to justify cost allocation decisions? Which are the dominant criteria?

🌐 **14-5** What are two basic reasons for a management team to select one period cost allocation method over another?

🌐 **14-6** How do cost–benefit considerations affect choices by a company about the allocation of indirect criteria?

🌐 **14-7** Name three decisions managers face when designing the cost allocation component of an accounting system.

🌐 **14-8** Give examples of bases used to allocate corporate cost pools to the operating divisions of an organization.

🌐 **14-9** Why might a manager prefer that budgeted rather than actual indirect cost allocation rates be used for costs being allocated to her division from another division?

🌐 **14-10** "To ensure unbiased cost allocations, fixed indirect costs should be allocated on the basis of estimated long-run use by user division managers." Do you agree? Why?

🌐 **14-11** Specify the strengths and weaknesses among the three methods of allocating the costs of service divisions to production divisions.

🌐 **14-12** What is theoretically the most defensible method for allocating service division costs?

🌐 **14-13** Distinguish between two methods of allocating common costs.

🌐 **14-14** What is one key method to avoid disputes over allocation of support costs with respect to government contracts?

Exercises

🌐 **14-15 Terminology.** A number of terms are listed below:

artificial cost pools	direct method
core operating division	incremental cost allocation method
dual-rate	stand-alone cost allocation method
sequential method	reciprocal method
price taker	common cost pool
common cost	

Required

Select the terms from the above list to complete the following sentences.

Target pricing is a policy well suited to a highly competitive environment where the corporation is a _____ because customers set the price. Depending on the proportion of fixed costs in the pool, the management team must choose between a _____ or a single-rate cost pool. Cost leadership is an appropriate policy, and the _____ most accurately reflects cost flows from support divisions back and forth among one another and to _____. To implement the reciprocal method, the support cost pools must be arithmetically adjusted to create _____, which are then the basis for all cost allocation.

The _____ is an improvement over the _____ of applying support costs, but only reports the flow of support departments to one another in one direction. The support divisions are first ranked on some basis from highest to lowest flow of either costs or resources then step down from the largest to smallest support division. Then the adjusted support cost pools are allocated to core operating divisions.

A _____ arises when two or more users share benefits from consuming a corporate resource. There are two ways to recognize proportional cost and benefit. The _____ defines each cost object as if it were the only output. The _____ ranks those who share in benefits from incurring the total common cost pool from high to low. The highest ranked is the primary party who bears most of the total shared cost. The remaining incremental parties share the difference of the total common cost pool minus the costs allocated to the primary party. Disputes over the primary party often arise.

LO 1 ▶
1. Overhead rate, 231.9%

🌐 **14-16 Criteria of cost allocation decisions.** Dave Meltzer went to Lake Tahoe for his annual winter vacation. Unfortunately, he broke his ankle severely while skiing and had to spend two days at the Tahoe General Hospital. Meltzer's insurance company received a $4,800 bill for his two-day stay. One item that caught Meltzer's eye was a $10.62 charge for a roll of cotton. Meltzer is a salesman for Johnson & Johnson and knows that the cost to the hospital of the roll of cotton would be in the $2.20 to $3 range. He asked for a breakdown of how the $10.62 charge was derived. The accounting office of the hospital sent him the following information:

a. Invoiced cost of cotton roll	$ 3.20
b. Processing of paperwork for purchase	0.40
c. Supplies room management fee	0.50
d. Operating-room and patient-room handling charge	1.30
e. Administrative hospital costs	1.00
f. Research-related recoupment	0.40
g. Malpractice insurance costs	1.00
h. Cost of treating uninsured patients	2.32
i. Profit component	0.50
Total	$10.62

Meltzer believes the overhead charge is obscene. He comments, "There was nothing I could do about it. When they come in and dab your stitches, it's not as if you can say, 'Keep your cotton roll. I brought my own.'"

Required

1. Compute the overhead rate Tahoe General Hospital charged on the cotton roll.
2. What criteria might Tahoe General use to justify allocation of each of the overhead items (b) through (i) in the preceding list? Examine each item separately, and use the allocation justifications in your answer.
3. What should Meltzer do about the $10.62 charge for the cotton roll?

🌐 **14-17 Single-rate versus dual-rate methods, support department.** The Cincinnati power plant that services all manufacturing departments of Eastern Mountain Engineering has a budget for the coming year. This budget has been expressed in the following monthly terms:

◀ **LO 3**
2. Variable cost pool is $0.20 per hour of expected usage

Manufacturing Department	Needed at Practical Capacity Production Level (Kilowatt-Hours)	Average Expected Monthly Usage (Kilowatt-Hours)
Loretta	13,000	10,000
Bently	21,000	9,000
Melboum	14,000	10,000
Eastmoreland	32,000	11,000
Total	80,000	40,000

The expected monthly costs for operating the power plant during the budget year are $20,000: $8,000 variable and $12,000 fixed.

Required

1. Assume that a single cost pool is used for the power plant costs. What budgeted amounts will be allocated to each manufacturing department if (a) the rate is calculated based on practical capacity and costs are allocated based on practical capacity and (b) the rate is calculated based on expected monthly usage and costs are allocated based on expected monthly usage?
2. Assume the dual-rate method is used with separate cost pools for the variable and fixed costs. Variable costs are allocated on the basis of expected monthly usage. Fixed costs are allocated on the basis of practical capacity. What budgeted amounts will be allocated to each manufacturing department? Why might you prefer the dual-rate method?

🌐 **14-18 Single-rate method, budgeted versus actual costs and quantities.** Chocolat Inc. is a producer of premium chocolate based in Owen Sound. The company has a separate division for each of its two products: dark chocolate and milk chocolate. Chocolat purchases ingredients from Toronto for its dark chocolate division and from Barrie for its milk chocolate division. Both locations are the same distance from Chocolat's Owen Sound plant.

Chocolat Inc. operates a fleet of trucks as a cost centre that charges the divisions for variable costs (drivers and fuel) and fixed costs (vehicle amortization, insurance, and registration fees) of operating the fleet. Each division is evaluated on the basis of its operating income. For 2018, the trucking fleet had a

◀ **LO 3**
1. a. Budgeted rate, $2,300 per round trip

practical capacity of 50 round trips between the Owen Sound plant and the two suppliers. It recorded the following information:

	Budgeted	Actual
Costs of truck fleet	$115,000	$96,750
Number of round trips for dark chocolate division (Owen Sound plant–Toronto)	30	30
Number of round trips for milk chocolate division (Owen Sound plant–Barrie)	20	15

Required

1. Using the single-rate method, allocate costs to the dark chocolate division and the milk chocolate division in these three ways:
   a. Calculate the budgeted rate per round trip and allocate costs based on round trips budgeted for each division.
   b. Calculate the budgeted rate per round trip and allocate costs based on actual round trips used by each division.
   c. Calculate the actual rate per round trip and allocate costs based on actual round trips used by each division.
2. Describe the advantages and disadvantages of using each of the three methods in requirement 1. Would you encourage Chocolat Inc. to use one of these methods? Explain and indicate any assumptions you made.

LO 3 ▶
1. a. Variable indirect cost rate, $1,500 per round trip

14-19 Dual-rate method, budgeted versus actual costs, and practical capacity versus actual quantities (continuation of Exercise 14-18). Chocolat Inc. decides to examine the effect of using the dual-rate method for allocating truck costs to each round trip. At the start of 2018, the budgeted costs were

Variable cost per round trip	$ 1,500
Fixed costs	40,000

The actual results for the 45 round trips made in 2018 were

Variable costs	$60,750
Fixed costs	36,000
	$96,750

Assume all other information to be the same as in Exercise 14-18.

Required

1. Using the dual-rate method, what are the costs allocated to the dark chocolate division and the milk chocolate division when (a) variable costs are allocated using the budgeted rate per round trip and actual round trips used by each division, and when (b) fixed costs are allocated based on the budgeted rate per round trip and round trips budgeted for each division?
2. From the viewpoint of the dark chocolate division, what are the effects of using the dual-rate method rather than the single-rate method?

LO 4 ▶
3. Allocation of Administrative Services on dollar amount ranking is $150,000

14-20 Support-department cost allocation; direct and step-down methods. Phoenix Partners provides management consulting services to government and corporate clients. Phoenix has two support departments—administrative services (AS) and information systems (IS)—and two operating departments—government consulting (GOVT) and corporate consulting (CORP). For the first quarter of 2017, Phoenix's cost records indicate the following:

	A	B	C	D	E	F	G
		Home Insert Page Layout	Formulas	Data	Review View		
1		SUPPORT			OPERATING		
2		AS	IS		GOVT	CORP	Total
3	Budgeted overhead costs before any						
4	interdepartment cost allocations	$600,000	$2,400,000		$8,756,000	$12,452,000	$24,208,000
5	Support work supplied by AS (budgeted head count)	—	25%		40%	35%	100%
6	Support work supplied by IS (budgeted computer time)	10%	—		30%	60%	100%

Required

1. Allocate the two support departments' costs to the two operating departments using the following methods:
   a. Direct method
   b. Step-down method (allocate AS first)
   c. Step-down method (allocate IS first)
2. Compare and explain differences in the support-department costs allocated to each operating department.
3. What approaches might be used to decide the sequence in which to allocate support departments when using the step-down method?

⊕ **14-21 Support-department cost allocation, reciprocal method** (continuation of 14-20). Refer to the data given in Exercise 14-20.

◄ **LO 4**

Administrative Services is $861,538

Required

1. Allocate the two support departments' costs to the two operating departments using the reciprocal method. Use (a) linear equations and (b) repeated iterations.
2. Compare and explain differences in requirement 1 with those in requirement 1 of Exercise 14-21. Which method do you prefer? Why?

⊕ **14-22 Allocating costs of support divisions, step-down and direct methods.** The Bow River Company has prepared division overhead budgets for budgeted-volume levels before allocations as follows:

◄ **LO 3**

The Direct Method, Job 89 allocated costs is $115.89

Support departments:		
Building and grounds	$10,000	
Personnel	1,000	
General plant administration	26,090	
Cafeteria: operating loss	1,640	
Storeroom	2,670	$ 41,400
Operating departments:		
Machining	34,700	
Assembly	48,900	83,600
Total for support and operating departments		$125,000

Management has decided that the most appropriate inventory costs are achieved by using individual division overhead rates. These rates are developed after support division costs are allocated to operating divisions.

Bases for allocation are to be selected from the following:

Department	Direct Manufacturing Labour-Hours	Number of Employees	Square Metres of Floor Space Occupied	Manufacturing Labour-Hours	Number of Requisitions
Building and grounds	0	0	0	0	0
Personnel[a]	0	0	2,000	0	0
General plant administration	0	35	7,000	0	0
Cafeteria: operating loss	0	10	4,000	1,000	0
Storeroom	0	5	7,000	1,000	0
Machining	5,000	50	30,000	8,000	2,000
Assembly	15,000	100	50,000	17,000	1,000
Total	20,000	200	100,000	27,000	3,000

[a]Basis used is number of employees.

Required

1. Using the step-down method, allocate support division costs. Develop overhead rates per direct manufacturing labour-hour for machining and assembly. Allocate the costs of the support divisions in the order given in this problem. Use the allocation base for each support division you think is most appropriate.
2. Using the direct method, rework requirement 1.

3. Based on the following information about two jobs, determine the total overhead costs for each job by using rates developed in (a) requirement 1 and (b) requirement 2.

	Direct Manufacturing Labour-Hours	
	Machining	**Assembly**
Job 88	18	2
Job 89	3	17

4. The company evaluates the performance of the operating division managers on the basis of how well they managed their total costs, including allocated costs. As the manager of the machining department, which allocation method would you prefer from the results obtained in requirements 1 and 2? Explain.

LO 1 ▶

1. Restaurant C actual usage cost allocation, $3,100

🌐 **14-23 Fixed cost allocation.** Three restaurants in a downtown area of a large city have decided to share a valet service and parking lot for their customers. The cost of the service and lot is $10,000 per month. The owners of the restaurants need to decide how to divide the $10,000 cost. The actual usage, planned usage, and practical capacity in the month of May was

Restaurant	Actual Parking Spots Used	Planned Parking Spots	Practical Capacity Parking Spots
A	1,500	1,600	2,000
B	1,400	1,300	1,500
C	1,300	1,100	1,500

Required

1. Allocate the fixed cost to each restaurant using actual, planned, and capacity usage measures.
2. In this situation, which method of allocation makes the most sense?

LO 4 ▶

1. Allocation of HR costs to consumer sales division, $29,080

🌐 **14-24 Direct and step-down allocation.** E-books, an online book retailer, has two operating divisions—corporate sales and consumer sales—and two support divisions—human resources and information systems. Each sales division conducts merchandising and marketing operations independently. E-books uses number of employees to allocate human resources costs and processing time to allocate information systems costs. The following data are available for September 2018:

	Support Divisions		Operating Divisions	
	Human Resources	**Information Systems**	**Corporate Sales**	**Consumer Sales**
Budgeted costs incurred before any interdivision cost allocations	$82,700	$234,400	$998,270	$489,860
Support work supplied by human resources division				
Budgeted number of employees	—	21	42	28
Support work supplied by information systems division				
Budgeted processing time (in minutes)	320	—	1,920	1,600

Required

1. Allocate the support divisions' costs to the operating divisions using the direct method.
2. Rank the support divisions based on the percentage of their services provided to other support divisions. Use this ranking to allocate the support divisions' costs to the operating divisions based on the step-down method.
3. How could you have ranked the support divisions differently?

LO 4 ▶

2. Allocation of HR costs to IS division, $21,702

🌐 **14-25 Reciprocal cost allocation** (continuation of Exercise 14-24). Consider E-books again. The controller of E-books reads a widely used textbook that states "The reciprocal method is conceptually the most defensible." He seeks your assistance.

Required

1. Describe the key features of the reciprocal method.
2. Allocate the support divisions' costs (human resources and information systems) to the two operating divisions using the reciprocal method.
3. In the case presented in this exercise, which method (direct, step-down, or reciprocal) would you recommend? Why?

Problems

🌐 **14-26 Single-rate, dual-rate, and practical capacity allocation.** Total Body Inc. has a new promotional program that offers a free gift-wrapping service for its customers. Total's customer-service division has practical capacity to wrap 7,500 gifts at a budgeted fixed cost of $6,750 each month. The budgeted variable cost to gift wrap an item is $0.50. Although the service is free to customers, a gift-wrapping service cost allocation is made to the division where the item was purchased. The customer-service division reported the following for the most recent month:

◀ **LO 3**
Total cost per gift wrapped, $1.50

Department	Actual Number of Gifts Wrapped	Budgeted Number of Gifts to be Wrapped	Practical Capacity Available for Gift-Wrapping
Women's face wash	2,100	2,475	2,625
Men's face wash	750	825	938
Fragrances	1,575	1,800	1,969
Body wash	525	450	656
Hair products	1,050	1,200	1,312
Total	6,000	6,750	7,500

Required

1. Using the single-rate method, allocate gift-wrapping costs to different divisions in these three ways:
   a. Calculate the budgeted rate based on the budgeted number of gifts to be wrapped, and allocate costs based on the budgeted use (of gift-wrapping services).
   b. Calculate the budgeted rate based on the budgeted number of gifts to be wrapped, and allocate costs based on actual usage.
   c. Calculate the budgeted rate based on the practical gift-wrapping capacity available, and allocate costs based on actual usage.
2. Using the dual-rate method, compute the amount allocated to each division when (a) the fixed-cost rate is calculated using budgeted costs and the practical gift-wrapping capacity, (b) fixed costs are allocated based on budgeted usage of gift-wrapping services, and (c) variable costs are allocated using the budgeted variable cost rate and actual usage.
3. Comment on your results in requirements 1 and 2. Discuss the advantages of the dual-rate method.

🌐 **14-27 Allocating costs to divisions.** Gether Corporation manufactures appliances. It has four divisions: refrigerator, stove, dishwasher, and microwave oven. Each division is located in a different city and the headquarters is located in Mississauga, Ontario. Headquarters incurs a total of $14,255,000 in costs, none of which are direct costs of any of the divisions. Revenues, costs, and facility space for each division are as follows:

◀ **LO 2**
1. Allocation to stove based on square metres, $3,207,375

	Refrigerator	Stove	Dishwasher	Microwave Oven
Revenue	$10,900,000	$18,800,000	$11,500,000	$6,780,000
Direct costs	5,700,000	10,400,000	6,200,000	3,220,000
Segment margin	5,200,000	8,400,000	5,300,000	3,560,000
Square metres of floor space occupied	130,000	90,000	80,000	100,000

Gether wants to allocate the indirect costs of headquarters on the basis of either square metres or segment margin for each division.

Required

1. Allocate the indirect headquarters costs to each division, first using square metres of space and then using segment margin as the allocation base. Calculate the division operating margins after each allocation in dollars and as a percentage of revenue.

2. Which allocation base do you prefer? Why?

3. Should any of the divisions be dropped based on your calculations? Why or why not?

LO 4 ▶ 🌐 **14-28 Support-department cost allocations; single-department cost pools; direct, step-down, and reciprocal methods.** The Martinez Company has two products. Product 1 is manufactured entirely in department X. Product 2 is manufactured entirely in department Y. To produce these two products, the Martinez Company has two support departments: A (a materials-handling department) and B (a power-generating department).

An analysis of the work done by departments A and B in a typical period follows:

	Used by			
Supplied by	**A**	**B**	**X**	**Y**
A	—	400	1,000	600
B	1,500	—	250	750

The work done in department A is measured by the direct labour-hours of materials-handling time. The work done in department B is measured by the kilowatt-hours of power. The budgeted costs of the support departments for the coming year are as follows:

	Department A (Materials Handling)	**Department B (Power Generation)**
Variable indirect labour and indirect materials costs	$300,000	$ 30,000
Supervision	90,000	50,000
Depreciation	30,000	100,000
	$420,000	$180,000
	+ Power costs	+ Materials-handling costs

The budgeted costs of the operating departments for the coming year are $2,500,000 for department X and $1,900,000 for department Y.

Supervision costs are salary costs. Depreciation in department B is the straight-line depreciation of power-generation equipment in its 19th year of an estimated 25-year useful life; it is old, but well-maintained, equipment.

Required

1. What are the allocations of costs of support departments A and B to operating departments X and Y using (a) the direct method, (b) the step-down method (allocate department A first), (c) the step-down method (allocate department B first), and (d) the reciprocal method?
2. An outside company has offered to supply all the power needed by the Martinez Company and to provide all the services of the present power department. The cost of this service will be $80 per kilowatt-hour of power. Should Martinez accept? Explain.

LO 5 ▶ 🌐 **14-29 Common costs.** Tate Inc. and Booth Inc. are two small manufacturing companies that are considering leasing a cutting machine together. If Tate rents the machine on its own, it will cost $26,000. If Booth rents the machine alone, it will cost $14,000. If they rent the machine together, the cost will decrease to $36,000.

Required

1. Calculate Tate's and Booth's respective share of fees under the stand-alone cost-allocation method.
2. Calculate Tate's and Booth's respective share of fees using the incremental cost-allocation method assuming (a) Tate is the primary party and (b) Booth is the primary party.
3. Calculate Tate's and Booth's respective share of fees using the Shapley value method.
4. Which method would you recommend Tate and Booth use to share the fees?

LO 4 ▶ **14-30 Support-department cost allocations; single-department cost pools; direct, step-down, and reciprocal methods.** Sportz, Inc., manufactures athletic shoes and athletic clothing for both amateur and professional athletes. The company has two product lines (clothing and shoes), which are produced in separate manufacturing facilities; however, both manufacturing facilities share the same support services for information technology and human resources. The following shows costs (in thousands) for each manufacturing facility and for each support department.

	Variable Costs	Fixed Costs	Total Costs by Department
Information technology (IT)	$ 1,200	$ 4,000	$ 5,200
Human resources (HR)	800	2,000	2,800
Clothing	5,000	16,000	21,000
Shoes	6,000	9,000	15,000
Total costs	$13,000	$31,000	$44,000

The total costs of the support departments (IT and HR) are allocated to the production departments (clothing and shoes) using a single rate based on the following:

Information technology: Number of IT labour-hours worked by department

Human resources: Number of employees supported by department

Data on the bases, by department, are given as follows:

Department	IT Hours Used	Number of Employees
Clothing	10,080	440
Shoes	7,920	176
Information technology	—	184
Human resources	6,000	—

Required

1. What are the total costs of the production departments (clothing and shoes) *after* the support-department costs of information technology and human resources have been allocated using (a) the direct method, (b) the step-down method (allocate information technology first), (c) the step-down method (allocate human resources first), and (d) the reciprocal method?

2. Assume that all of the work of the IT department could be outsourced to an independent company for $97.50 per hour. If Sportz no longer operated its own IT department, 30% of the fixed costs of the IT department could be eliminated. Should Sportz outsource its IT services?

🌐 **14-31 Stand-alone revenue allocation.** Magic Systems, Inc., sells computer hardware to end consumers. The CX30 is sold as a "bundle," which includes three hardware products: a personal computer (PC) tower, a 26-inch monitor, and a color laser printer. Each of these products is made in a separate manufacturing division of Magic Systems and can be purchased individually as well as in a bundle. Magic Systems sells roughly equal quantities of the three products. The individual selling prices and per unit costs are as follows:

◀ **LO 2**

Computer Component	Individual Selling Price per Unit	Cost per Unit
PC tower	$1,150	$375
Monitor	$ 250	$200
Color laser printer	$ 600	$225
Computer bundle purchase price	$1,500	

Required

1. Allocate the revenue from the computer bundle purchase to each of the hardware products using the stand-alone method based on the individual selling price per unit.
2. Allocate the revenue from the computer bundle purchase to each of the hardware products using the stand-alone method based on cost per unit.
3. Allocate the revenue from the computer bundle purchase to each of the hardware products using the stand-alone method based on physical units (that is, the number of individual units of product sold per bundle).
4. Which basis of allocation makes the most sense in this situation? Explain your answer.

🌐 **14-32 Cost allocation to divisions.** Forber Bakery makes baked goods for grocery stores, and has three divisions: bread, cake, and doughnuts. Each division is run and evaluated separately, but the main headquarters incurs costs that are indirect costs for the divisions. Costs incurred in the main headquarters are

◀ **LO 2**
1. Bread operating income, $4,700,000

Human resources (HR) costs	$1,900,000
Accounting department costs	1,400,000
Rent and amortization	1,200,000
Other	600,000
Total costs	$5,100,000

The Forber upper management currently allocates this cost to the divisions equally. One of the division managers has done some research on ABC and proposes the use of different allocation bases for the different indirect costs—number of employees for HR costs, total revenues for accounting division costs, square metres of space for rent and amortization costs, and equal allocation among the divisions of "other" costs. Information about the three divisions follows:

	Bread	Cake	Doughnuts
Total revenues	$20,900,000	$4,500,000	$13,400,000
Direct costs	14,500,000	3,200,000	7,250,000
Segment margin	$ 6,400,000	$1,300,000	$ 6,150,000
Number of employees	400	100	300
Square metres of space	10,000	4,000	6,000

Required

1. Allocate the indirect costs of Forber to each division equally. Calculate division operating income after allocation of headquarters costs.
2. Allocate headquarters costs to the individual divisions using the proposed allocation bases. Calculate the division operating income after allocation. Comment on the allocation bases used to allocate headquarters costs.
3. Which division manager do you think suggested this new allocation? Explain briefly. Which allocation do you think is "better"?

LO 2 ▶ **14-33 Revenue allocation, bundled products.** Boca Resorts (BR) operates a five-star hotel with a world-class spa. BR has a decentralized management structure, with three divisions:

- Lodging (rooms, conference facilities)
- Food (restaurants and in-room service)
- Spa

Starting next month, BR will offer a two-day, two-person "getaway package" for $1,000. This deal includes the following:

	As Priced Separately
Two nights' stay for two in an ocean-view room	$ 750 ($375 per night)
Two spa treatments (can be used by either guest)	300 ($150 per treatment)
Candlelight dinner for two at BR's finest restaurant	200 ($100 per person)
Total package value	$1,250

Jennifer Gibson, president of the spa division, recently asked the CEO of BR how her division would share in the $1,000 revenue from the getaway package. The spa was operating at 100% capacity. Currently, anyone booking the package was guaranteed access to a spa appointment. Gibson noted that every "getaway" booking would displace $300 of other spa bookings not related to the package. She emphasized that the high demand reflected the devotion of her team to keeping the spa rated one of the "Best 10 Luxury Spas in the World" by *Travel Monthly*. As an aside, she also noted that the lodging and food divisions had to turn away customers during only "peak-season events such as the New Year's period."

Required

1. Using selling prices, allocate the $1,000 getaway-package revenue to the three divisions using:
   a. The stand-alone revenue-allocation method
   b. The incremental revenue-allocation method (with spa first, then lodging, and then food)
2. What are the pros and cons of the two methods in requirement 1?

3. Because the spa division is able to book the spa at 100% capacity, the company CEO has decided to revise the getaway package to only include the lodging and food offerings shown previously. The new package will sell for $800. Allocate the revenue to the lodging and food divisions using the following:
   a. The Shapley value method
   b. The weighted Shapley value method, assuming that lodging is three times as likely to sell as the food

14-34 Support-department cost allocations; direct, step-down, and reciprocal methods. ◄ LO 5
Ballantine Corporation has two operating departments: Eastern Department and Western Department. Each of the operating departments uses the services of the company's two support departments: Engineering and Information Technology. Additionally, the Engineering and Information Technology departments use the services of each other. Data concerning the past year are as follows:

	Support Departments		Operating Departments		
	Engineering	Information Technology	Eastern Department	Western Department	Total
Budgeted overhead costs before any interdepartment cost allocations	$300,000	$250,000	$650,000	$920,000	$2,120,000
Support work furnished:					
By Engineering					
Budgeted Engineering salaries	—	$60,000	$50,000	$90,000	$200,000
Percentage	—	30%	25%	45%	100%
By Information Technology					
Budgeted IT service hours	450	—	1,500	1,050	3,000
Percentage	15%	—	50%	35%	100%

Required
1. What are the total overhead costs of the operating departments (Eastern and Western) *after* the support-department costs of Engineering and Information Technology have been allocated using (a) the direct method, (b) the step-down method (allocate Engineering first), (c) the step-down method (allocate Information Technology first), and (d) the reciprocal method?
2. Which method would you recommend that Ballantine Corporation use to allocate service-department costs? Why?

SOLUTIONS

 TRY IT!

Try It 14–1

1. A combined budgeted rate is used for fixed and variable costs. The rate is calculated as follows:

Budgeted usage of engineering-services labour-hours	7,000 hours	
Budgeted total cost pool: $280,000 + ($25 × 7,000 hours)	$455,000	
Budgeted total rate per hour: $455,000 ÷ 7,000 hours	$65	per hour used

The rate of $65 per hour is used to allocate Engineering-Services department costs to the Machining and Assembly departments.

Under the single-rate method, the Machining and Assembly departments are charged the budgeted rate for each hour of *actual* use of engineering services.

Machining department: $65 per hour × 2,000 hours	$130,000
Assembly department: $65 per hour × 4,000 hours	$260,000

2. Budgeted fixed cost rate per hour = $280,000 ÷ 7,000 hours = $40 per hour

The costs allocated to the Machining Department in 2017 equal

Fixed costs: $40 per hour × 2,500 (budgeted) hours	$100,000
Variable costs: $25 per hour × 2,000 (actual) hours	50,000
Total costs	$150,000

The costs allocated to the Assembly Department in 2017 equal

Fixed costs: $40 per hour × 4,500 (budgeted) hours	$180,000
Variable costs: $25 per hour × 4,000 (actual) hours	100,000
Total costs	$280,000

3. Using the 8,000 hours of practical capacity of the Engineering Services department, the budgeted rate is

Budgeted fixed-cost rate per hour, $280,000 ÷ 8,000 hours	$35 per hour
Budgeted variable-cost rate per hour	25 per hour
Budgeted total-cost rate per hour	$60 per hour

Under the single rate method, the Engineering Services department costs are allocated to the Machining and Assembly departments as follows:

Machining department: $60 per hour × 2,000 (actual) hours	$ 120,000
Assembly department: $60 per hour × 4,000 (actual) hours	240,000
Fixed costs of unused Engineering-Services capacity:	
$35 per hour × 2,000 hours[a]	70,000

4. Under the dual rate method, the Engineering Services department costs are allocated to the Machining and Assembly departments as follows:

Machining Department

Fixed costs: $35 per hour × 2,500 (budgeted) hours	$ 87,500
Variable costs: $25 per hour × 2,000 (actual) hours	50,000
Total costs	$137,500

Assembly Department

Fixed costs: $35 per hour × 4,500 (budgeted) hours	$157,500
Variable costs: $25 per hour × 4,000 (actual) hours	100,000
Total costs	$257,500

Fixed costs of unused Engineering-Services capacity:

$35 per hour × 1,000 hours[b]	$ 35,000

[b]1,000 hours = Practical capacity of 8,000 hours − (2,500 hours budgeted to be used by Machining department + 4,500 hours budgeted to be used by Assembly department).

Try It 14–2

1a. Allocate the total support department costs to the operating departments under the direct allocation method:

	Domestic Tours	World Tours
Departmental Overhead Costs	$1,300,000	$1,840,000
From:		
Administration		
($55,000/$132,000) × $400,000	166,667	
($77,000/$132,000) × $400,000		233,333
Information Technology		
(2,200/3,400) × $250,000	161,765	
(1,200/3,400) × $250,000		88,235
Total Departmental Overhead Costs	$1,628,432	$2,161,568

Total Costs to account for: $3,790,000

b. Allocate the support department costs to the operating departments under the step-down (sequential) allocation method with Administration first sequentially:

	Administration	IT	Domestic Tours	World Tours
Departmental Overhead Costs	$ 400,000	$ 250,000	$1,300,000	$1,840,000
From:				
Administration	$(400,000)			
40% × $400,000		160,000		
25% × $400,000			100,000	
35% × $400,000				140,000
Information Technology		(410,000)		
(2,200/3,400) × $410,000			265,294	
(1,200/3,400) × $410,000				144,706
Total Departmental Costs	$ 0	$ 0	$1,665,294	$2,124,706

Total costs to account for: $3,790,000

c. Allocate the support department costs to the operating departments under the step-down (sequential) allocation method with IT first sequentially:

To:

	IT	Administration	Domestic Tours	World Tours
Departmental Costs	$ 250,000	$400,000	$1,300,000	$1,840,000
From:				
Information Technology	(250,000)			
15% × $250,000		37,500		
55% × $250,000			137,500	
30% × $250,000				75,000
Administration		(437,500)		
(55,000/132,000) × $437,500			182,292	255,208
(77,000/132,000) × $437,500				
Total Departmental Costs	$ 0	$ 0	$1,619,792	$2,170,208

Total costs to account for: $3,790,000

d. Allocate the support department costs to the operating departments under the reciprocal allocation method:

Assign reciprocal equations to the support departments

$$AD = \$400,000 + 0.15\ IT$$
$$IT = \$250,000 + 0.40\ AD$$

Solve the equation to complete the reciprocal costs of the support departments:

$$AD = \$400,000 + 0.15\ IT$$
$$AD = \$400,000 + 0.15\ (\$250,000 + 0.40\ AD)$$
$$AD = \$400,000 + \$37,500 + 0.06\ AD$$
$$0.94\ AD = \$437,500$$
$$AD = \$465,426$$
$$IT = \$250,000 + 0.40\ AD$$
$$IT = \$250,000 + 0.40\ (\$465,426)$$
$$IT = \$250,000 + \$186,170$$
$$IT = \$436,170$$

Allocate reciprocal costs to departments (all numbers rounded to nearest dollar):

	Admin.	IT	Domestic Tours	World Tours
Departmental Costs	$400,000	$250,000	$1,300,000	$1,840,000
Administration	(465,426)			
40% × $465,426		186,170		
25% × $465,426			116,357	
35% × $465,426				$ 162,899
Information Technology		(436,170)		
15% × $436,170	65,426			
55% × $436,170			239,893	
30% × $436,170				130,851
Total Departmental Costs	$ 0	$ 0	$1,656,250	$2,133,750

Costs allocated to the domestic tours department equal $356,250 ($116,357 + $239,893). Costs allocated to the world tours department equal $293,750 ($162,899 + $130,851). Total support department costs to account for $650,000 (Administration, $400,000 + Information Technology, $250,000).

Try It Exhibit 14-2 shows the allocation of the IT and HR department costs to the domestic tours department and to the world tours department using repeated iterations.

Try It 14–3

1a. Under the stand-alone revenue-allocation method, based on selling price, Him will be allocated 33.33% of all revenues, or $20 of the bundled selling price, and Her will be allocated 66.67% of all revenues, or $40 of the bundled selling price, as shown below.

Stand-alone Method, Based on Selling Prices	Him	Her	Total
Selling price	$25	$50	$75
Selling price as a % of total ($25 ÷ $75; $50 ÷ $75)	33.33%	66.67%	100%
Allocation of $60 bundled selling price (33.33% × $60; 66.67% × $60)	$20	$40	$60

	Support Departments		Operating Departments	
	Admin.	IT	Domestic	World
Budgeted manufacturing overhead costs before any interdepartmental cost allocations	$400,000	$250,000	$1,300,000	$1,840,000
1st Allocation of Admin. Dept. (40%, 25%, 35%)[a]	(400,000)	160,000	100,000	140,000
		410,000		
1st Allocation of IT Dept. (15%, 55%, 30%)[b]	61,500	(410,000)	225,500	123,000
2nd Allocation of Admin. Dept. (40%, 25%, 35%)[a]	(61,500)	24,600	15,375	21,525
2nd Allocation of IT Dept. (15%, 55%, 30%)[b]	3,690	(24,600)	13,530	7,380
3rd Allocation of Admin. Dept. (40%, 25%, 35%)[a]	(3,690)	1,476	923	1,291
3rd Allocation of IT Dept. (15%, 55%, 30%)[b]	221	(1,476)	812	443
4th Allocation of Admin. Dept. (40%, 25%, 35%)[a]	(221)	88	55	78
4th Allocation of IT Dept. (15%, 55%, 30%)[b]	13	(88)	49	26
5th Allocation of Admin. Dept. (40%, 25%, 35%)[a]	(13)	5	3	5
5th Allocation of IT Dept. (15%, 55%, 30%)[b]	1	(5)	3	1
6th Allocation of Admin. Dept. (40%, 25%, 35%)[a]	(1)	0	0	1
Total budgeted manufacturing overhead of operating departments	$ 0	$ 0	$1,656,250	$2,133,750

Total accounts allocated and reallocated (the numbers in parentheses in first two columns):
Admin. Dept.: $400,000 + $61,500 + $3,690 + $221 + $13 + $1 = $465,425
IT Dept.: $410,000 + $24,600 + $1,476 + $88 + $5 = $436,169

[a]Base is ($88,000 + $55,000 + $77,000) or $220,000; $88,000 ÷ $220,000 = 40%, $55,000 ÷ $220,000 = 25%, $77,000 ÷ $220,000 = 35%.
[b]Base is (600 + 2,200 + 1,200) or 4,000 IT service-hours; 600 ÷ 4,000 = 15%, 2,200 ÷ 4,000 = 55%, 1,200 ÷ 4,000 = 30%.

TRY IT EXHIBIT 14-2
Reciprocal Method of Allocating Support Department Costs for Montvale Tours Using Repeated Iterations.

1b. Under the incremental revenue-allocation method, with Him ranked as the primary product, Him will be allocated $25 (its own stand-alone selling price), and Her will be allocated $35 of the $60 selling price, as shown below.

Incremental Method (Him rank 1)	Him	Her
Selling price	$25	$50
Allocation of $60 bundled selling price ($25; $35 = $60 − $25)	$25	$35

1c. Under the incremental revenue-allocation method, with Her ranked as the primary product, Her will be allocated $50 (its own stand-alone selling price), and Him will be allocated $10 of the $60 selling price, as shown below.

Incremental Method (Her rank 1)	Him	Her
Selling price	$25	$50
Allocation of $60 bundled selling price ($10 = $60 − $50; $50)	$10	$50

1d. Under the Shapley value method, each product will be allocated the average of its allocations in 1b and 1c. In other words, the average of its allocations when it is the primary product and when it is the secondary product are shown below.

Shapley Value Method	Him	Her
Allocation when Him = Rank 1; Her = Rank 2 (from 1b.)	$25.00	$35.00
Allocation when Her = Rank 1; Him = Rank 2 (from 1c.)	$10.00	$50.00
Average of allocated selling price ($25 + $10) ÷ 2; ($35 + $50) ÷ 2	$17.50	$42.50

2. A summary of the allocations based on the four methods in requirement 1 is shown below.

	Stand-alone (Selling Prices)	Incremental (Him first)	Incremental (Her first)	Shapley
Him	$20	$25	$10	$17.50
Her	40	35	50	42.50
Total for Sync	$60	$60	$60	$60.00

If there is no clear indication of which product is the more "important" product, or if it can be reasonably assumed that the two products are equally important to the company's strategy, the Shapley value method is the fairest of all the methods because it averages the effect of product rank. In this particular case, note that the allocations from the stand-alone method based on selling price are reasonably similar to the allocations from the Shapley value method, so the managers at Essence may well want to use the much simpler stand-alone method. The stand-alone method also does not require ranking the products in the suite, and so it is less likely to cause debates among product managers in the Men's and Women's Fragrance divisions. If, however, one of the products (Him or Her) is clearly the product that is driving sales of the bundled product, then that product should be considered the primary product or weighted more heavily (rather than equally) when applying the Shapley value method.

Cost Allocation: Joint Products and Byproducts

15

Photo courtesy of Hibernia Management and Development Company Ltd

▶ Learning Objectives

1. Distinguish among different types of saleable products, scrap, and toxic waste.

2. Analyze the physical measure and sales value at splitoff methods to allocate joint costs.

3. Analyze the two methods to use when there is no sales value at the splitoff point.

4. Understand the irrelevance of joint costs in the "sell or process further" decision.

5. Identify the strategic implications of a decision to implement one joint cost allocation method.

6. Account for byproducts using two different methods.

Challenges of Joint Cost Allocation

The Hibernia offshore oil field project off the coast of Newfoundland[1] is a joint venture among many companies, including ExxonMobil Canada. The costs of lifting oil from the ocean's floor are shared among the companies investing in this project. The crude oil pumped will be refined into a variety of petroleum products. The lifting costs common to all produced products will be recovered by allocating or sharing these joint costs in some reasonable way. The partners will evaluate two market-based cost allocation methods to identify the more appropriate method that best reflects the facts of the actual proportion of joint resources (and costs) shared among them.

Costing for the more complex case in which two or more products are simultaneously produced involves joint costs. A variety of products share core activities of production up to a point in the production process. After this point, processing the products further involves separate production activities and separate costs. The goal is to choose the cost allocation method that best reflects how the costs actually flow throughout a real economic process. The choice is not often straightforward because corporations allocate costs in ways most appropriate to the business decisions they must make.

▶ CPA Competencies

This chapter covers material outlined in **Section 3: Management Accounting** of the CPA Competency Map. The Learning Objectives in this chapter have been aligned with the CPA Competency Map to ensure the best coverage possible.

3.3.1 Evaluates cost classifications and costing methods for management of ongoing operations

3.3.2 Evaluates and applies cost management techniques appropriate for specific costing decisions

---

[1] Canada Environmental Assessment Agency (http://www.ceaa.gc.ca/default.asp?lang=en&n=d75fb358-1).

Joint-Cost Basics

▶ **LO 1**

Distinguish among different
types of saleable products,
scrap, and toxic waste.

Joint costs are the costs of a production process that yields multiple **main products** simultaneously. A **product** is any output that can be sold at full product cost plus profit, or enables the company to avoid purchasing direct materials. When a process yields many products, the main product is the one with the highest sales value. If two or more products have high sales value, they are called **joint products**. Products of relatively low sales value are called **byproducts**. During production, **scrap**, which has minimal to zero sales value, may also be produced. These relationships are illustrated in Exhibit 15-1.

The processing of poultry, for example, yields feathers, giblets, wings, thighs, and entire birds. Often heads, feet, skin, and internal organs are processed differently and ground as byproducts for use in animal meal. White breast meat, the highest revenue-generating product, is obtained from the front end of the bird; dark meat from the back end. Other edible products include chicken wings and giblets. There are many inedible products that have a diverse set of uses. For example, poultry feathers are used in bedding and sporting goods. Poultry companies use individual product cost information for different customers (e.g., supermarkets, fast food outlets) and the sales mix differs for these customers. A subset of products is placed into frozen storage, which creates demand for individual product cost information for the purpose of inventory valuation.

Byproducts often used to be waste product for which a use has now been found. Scrap may be referred to as waste. Processes in some extractive industries generate toxic

Exhibit 15-1

Classification of Products

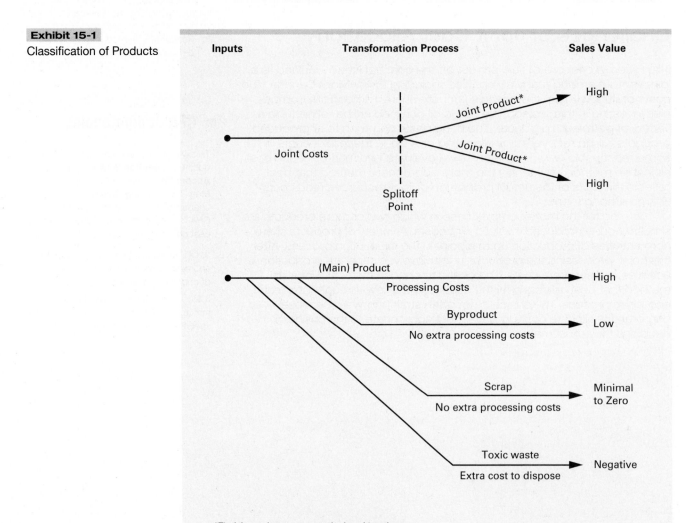

*The joint product process can also have byproducts,
scrap, and toxic waste. These items were omitted simply for clarity.

Exhibit 15-2 Industries
Incurring Joint Costs

Industry	Separable Products at the Splitoff Point
Agriculture and Food Processing	
Cocoa beans	Cocoa butter, cocoa powder, cocoa drink mix, tanning cream
Lambs	Lamb cuts, tripe, hides, bones, fat
Hogs	Bacon, ham, spare ribs, pork roast
Lumber	Lumber of varying grades and shapes
Extractive Industries	
Coal	Coke, gas, benzol, tar, ammonia
Copper ore	Copper, silver, lead, zinc
Petroleum	Crude oil, natural gas, raw LPG
Salt	Hydrogen, chlorine, caustic soda
Chemical Industries	
Raw LPG (liquefied petroleum gas)	Butane, ethane, propane
Crude oil	Gasoline, kerosene, benzene, naphtha
Semiconductor Industry	
Fabrication of silicon-wafer chips	Memory chips of different quality (as to capacity), speed, life expectancy, and temperature tolerance

waste, such as cyanide, lead, toluene, sulphuric acid, or dioxin. **Toxic waste** has negative revenue when the costs of reclamation and remediation are considered. Costs of recovering or disposing of toxic emissions are life-cycle costs that should be added to joint production costs prior to allocating this cost pool to main, joint, or byproducts. Exhibit 15-2 lists a variety of industries in which joint costs are incurred in their production processes.

In joint cost processes, the **splitoff point** is the place in a production process where two or more main products become separately identifiable. **Separable costs** are the full product costs of processing incurred by each identifiable product beyond the splitoff point. Decisions about whether to sell work-in-process at that point or process further can be made at or beyond the splitoff point. In practice, the classification of products versus byproducts is not straightforward and changes over time, especially when prices are volatile.

Different reasons to allocate joint costs include:

■ Calculation of inventoriable costs and cost of goods sold for external financial statements and reports for income tax authorities.

■ Calculation of inventoriable costs and cost of goods sold for internal financial reporting. Such reports are used in division profitability analysis when determining compensation for division managers.

■ Cost reimbursement under contracts when only a portion of a business's products or services is sold or delivered to a single customer (such as a government agency).

■ Customer profitability analysis where individual customers purchase varying combinations of joint products or byproducts as well as other products of the company.

■ Insurance settlement calculations when damage claims made by businesses with joint products, main products, or byproducts are based on cost information.

■ Rate regulation when one or more of the jointly produced products or services is subject to price regulation.

■ Contract litigation in which costs of joint products are key inputs.

Approaches to Allocating Joint Costs

▶ **LO 2**

Analyze the physical measure and sales value at splitoff methods to allocate joint costs.

There are four joint cost allocation methods from which managers may choose. The **physical measure method** allocates joint costs on the basis of their relative proportions *at the splitoff point*, using a common physical measure such as weight or volume of the total production of each product. The **sales value at splitoff method** allocates joint costs on the basis of the relative sales value *at the splitoff point* of the total production in the accounting period for each product.

These two methods may be appropriate when the products can be sold at splitoff, but often the joint product is processed further and there is no selling price at the splitoff point. In these cases, two slightly more complex market methods are more appropriate: the **net realizable value (NRV) method** and the **constant gross margin percentage of NRV method**. The NRV method allocates joint costs on the basis of the *relative net realizable value* (expected final sales value in the ordinary course of business minus the expected separable costs of production and marketing of the total production of the period). The constant gross margin percentage NRV method works in reverse. For each product, the gross margin (based on the overall gross margin percentage) and separable costs are deducted from the final sales value of units produced. The residual amount for each product is its allocation of joint costs.

As with virtually all cost accounting problems, the decision framework can be used to decide on an appropriate cost allocation method.

Step 1: Identify the Problem Farmers Dairy is a producer of dairy products in Canada. There is no competition for Farmers Dairy because the industry is fully regulated in Canada. The Dairy Farmers of Canada sets and announces monthly support prices and quotas for raw milk and milk outputs. The government sets and enforces standards of quality and safety as well as butterfat content that defines the type of output and therefore the price of various milk products.

There are two markets: fluid milks, which account for about 33% of total dairy production, and industrial products such as butter, cheese, and ice cream. One-third of milk output is a commodity, such as 2% partly skimmed milk. People purchase such products on price. There is no shortage of outlets from which milk can be purchased, from retailers such as Shoppers Drug Mart to gas stations. For producers, cost leadership is the appropriate strategy to assure profitability of these finished goods.

The production of milk products starts with the pasteurization of raw milk. At a certain point in the process (the splitoff point—see Exhibit 15-3), a number of different products are created. For the purposes of this example, we will initially limit our analysis to examining two joint products: cream and liquid skim. As a result of this production situation, Farmers Dairy faces two accounting-related challenges.

1. For financial accounting purposes, joint costs (the costs of the production process up to the splitoff point) must be allocated to the various products in inventory and cost of goods sold. ASPE standard 3031.15 and IFRS standard IAS 2.14 require that these costs be "allocated between the products on a rational and consistent basis." The standards further state that "The allocation may be based, for example, on the relative sales value of each product either at the stage in the production process when the products become separately identifiable, or at the completion of production."

2. Regardless of the allocation method required by financial accounting standards, the firm must decide how to treat joint cost for decision-making purposes.

The physical fact is that the initial process of pasteurization cannot be observed without compromising the pasteurized milk's safety. It is not possible until after pasteurization to measure quantities that will flow into further separable joint processes, so pasteurization gives rise to joint costs when raw milk is processed.

Step 2: Gather Information Gathering information from Farmers Dairy's information system for a specific time period, the $345,000 joint costs produced 1,000 hL of cream and 3,000 hL of liquid skim (see Exhibit 15-3).

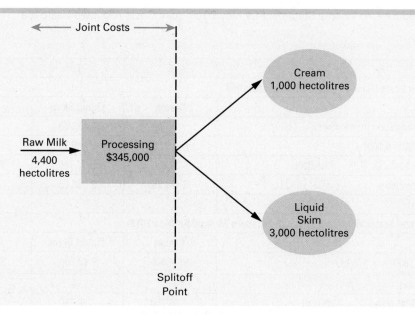

Exhibit 15-3 Farmers Dairy Overview

Farmers Dairy purchases raw milk from individual farms and processes it up to the splitoff point, where two products (cream and liquid skim) are obtained.

Below is some summary data for Farmers Dairy for the month of May 2018:

- Raw milk processed: 4,400 hL of raw milk with a 10% shrinkage of 400 hL due to evaporation and spillage, to net 4,000 hL of cream and liquid skim for sale. One hectolitre equals 100 litres. After the raw milk is received at the Farmers Dairy processing plant, it is separated in machines.

- Inventories: The inventory amounts are shown in the table below.

	A	B	C
1		**Joint Costs**	
2	**Joint costs (costs of 4,400 hL of raw milk and processing to splitoff point)**		$345,000
3		**Cream**	**Liquid Skim**
4	Beginning inventory (hectolitres)	0	0
5	Production (hectolitres)	1,000	3,000
6	Sales (hectolitres)	800	900
7	Ending inventory (hectolitres)	200	2,100
8	Selling price per hectolitre	$155.00	$ 75.00

- Cost of processing 4,400 hL of raw milk and processing it up to the splitoff point to yield 1,000 hL of cream and 3,000 hL of liquid skim: $345,000.

Step 3: Forecast Future Outcomes Farmers Dairy now needs to identify, analyze, and evaluate the four joint cost allocation alternatives, beginning with the two simplest: physical measure and sales value at splitoff. Both joint cost allocation methods can be used for costing the inventory of cream and liquid skim as well as determining cost of goods sold.

Physical Measure Method

Exhibit 15-4 presents summary data for May 2018. Panel A illustrates the allocation of joint costs to individual products to calculate cost per hectolitre of cream and liquid skim for ending inventory valuation. This method allocates joint costs on the basis of total

Exhibit 15-4 Farmers Dairy Product-Line Income Statement for May 2018: Joint Costs Allocated Using the Physical Measure Method

	A	B	C	D
1	**PANEL A: Allocation of Joint Costs Using Physical Measure Method**			
2		**Cream**	**Liquid Skim**	**Total**
3	Physical measure of total production (hectolitres)	1,000	3,000	4,000
4	Weighting (1,000 ÷ 4,000; 3,000 ÷ 4,000)	0.25	0.75	
5	Joint costs allocated (0.25 × $345,000; 0.75 × $345,000)	$ 86,250	$258,750	$345,000
6	Joint production cost per hectolitre	$ 86.25	$ 86.25	
7				
8	**PANEL B: Product-Line Income Statement Using Physical Measure Method for May 2018**			
9		**Cream**	**Liquid Skim**	**Total**
10	Revenues (800 hL × $155/hL; 900 hL × $75/hL)	$124,000	$ 67,500	$191,500
11	Cost of goods sold (joint costs)			
12	Production costs (0.25 × $345,000; 0.75 × $345,000)	86,250	258,750	345,000
13	Deduct ending inventory (200 hL × $86.25/hL; 2,100 hL × $86.25/hL)	(17,250)	(181,125)	(198,375)
14	Cost of goods sold (joint costs)	69,000	77,625	146,625
15	Gross margin	$ 55,000	$ (10,125)	$ 44,875
16	Gross margin percentage (Gross margin ÷ Revenue)	44.4%	−15.0%	23.4%

hectolitres; therefore, the cost per hectolitre is the same for both products ($86.25). Panel B presents the product-line income statement using the physical measure method. The gross margin percentages are 44.4% for cream and a *loss* of 15% for liquid skim.

The advantages of this method are that it is observable, readily verifiable, and (may be) economically plausible. Economic plausibility arises from the actual physical process of production. The different quantities were actually split off during a specific time period. The cost flow reflects the economic fact of production. The average cost allocation rate is applied equally to each unit of input of WIP used in each separable product after splitoff.

The physical measure method may also be appropriate to use in a rate-regulated situation where the accounting information is being used to set the prices (which are based on the costs). This is because this method does not rely on a selling price (unlike the other three methods) to allocate the joint costs.

The disadvantages of the physical measure method are significant:

■ The amount of joint cost allocated to a joint product may have no relationship to the product's economic value. By the very nature of being a high volume output (and thus attracting a large portion of the joint cost), the joint product might have a low sales value (the liquid skim being an example of this situation).

■ Production managers may end up in a situation where, as a result of the joint cost allocation method chosen (in this case the physical measure method), they are responsible for a product line that has a negative gross margin (through no fault of their own). This could cause significant motivational issues for the organization.

■ There can be problems deciding what units of output to include/exclude in the denominator measure (the total amount of physical units to include). For example, should the units of byproduct be included? Typically, the units of byproduct are excluded from the denominator measure.

■ Finding a common unit of physical measure may also be a challenge. For example, in oil production, the same wellhead might produce crude oil and natural gas. If the physical measure method was to be used to allocate the joint cost of extraction, then some common physical unit of measurement would need to be found to combine the number of barrels of oil (typical measure of crude oil output) with the amount of natural gas (measured in cubic feet).

Sales Value at Splitoff Method

In Exhibit 15-5, Panel A, the sales value at splitoff of the May 2018 production is $155,000 for cream and $225,000 for liquid skim.

Simple division of the joint cost pool (the numerator) by total revenue (the denominator) provides an average cost allocation rate. The cost pool is assigned on the basis of each product's percentage of total revenue. This approach uses the sales value of the *entire production of the accounting period* (1,000 hL of cream and 3,000 hL of liquid skim). The reason is that joint costs were incurred on all the units produced, not simply the units sold during the current sales period. Panel B presents the product-line income statement using the sales value at splitoff method.

Both cream and liquid skim have gross margin percentages of 9.2% (the gross margin percentages are always equal under this method). The total revenue includes consideration of both sales price per unit and quantity of inputs physically used to produce each separable product. Revenue recognized during a specific accounting period, however, must be reported product by product. This method is verifiable and economically plausible, but it assumes all products can be sold at splitoff versus being further processed.

Exhibit 15-5 Farmers Dairy Product-Line Income Statement for May 2018: Joint Costs Allocated Using the Sales Value at Splitoff Method

	A	B	C	D
1	**Panel A: Allocation of Joint Costs Using Sales Value at Splitoff Method**			
2		**Cream**	**Liquid Skim**	**Total**
3	Sales value of total production at splitoff point (1,000 hL × $155/hL; 3,000 hL × $75/hL)	$155,000	$225,000	$380,000
4	Weighting ($155,000 ÷ $380,000; $225,000 ÷ $380,000)	40.789%	59.211%	
5	Joint costs allocated (0.40789 × $345,000; 0.59211 × $345,000, rounded)	$140,722	$204,278	$345,000
6	Joint production cost per hectolitre	$140.722	$ 68.093	
7				
8	**PANEL B: Product-Line Income Statement Using Sales Value at Splitoff Method for May 2018**			
9		**Cream**	**Liquid Skim**	**Total**
10	Revenue (800 hL × $155/hL; 900 hL × $75.00/hL)	$124,000	$ 67,500	$191,500
11	Cost of goods available for sale (joint costs) Production costs (0.40789 × $345,000; 0.59211 × $345,000, rounded)	140,722	204,278	345,000
12	Deduct ending inventory (200 hL × $140.722/hL; 2,100 hL × $68.093/hL, rounded)	(28,144)	(142,995)	(171,139)
13	Cost of goods sold (joint costs)	112,578	61,283	173,861
14	Gross margin	$ 11,422	$ 6,217	$ 17,639
15	Gross margin percentage (Gross margin ÷ Revenue, rounded)	9.2%	9.2%	9.2%
16				
17	*Note:* Suppose Farmers Dairy has beginning inventory of cream and liquid skim milk in May 2018. Suppose further that when this inventory is sold, Farmers earns a gross margin different from 9.2%. Then the gross margin percentage for cream and liquid skim milk will be different from the figures shown in the income statement above. The actual value of the gross margin percentage depends on the proportion of sales of each product from beginning inventory and the proportion from current period production.			

Note how the sales value at splitoff method follows the benefits-received criterion of cost allocation: Costs are allocated to products in proportion to their revenue-generating power (expected revenue). This method is both straightforward and intuitive. The difficulty with assuming all products can be sold at splitoff is that there must actually be a market for the joint product separate from finished goods or there is no economic plausibility. Regulated markets can provide shadow prices for these intermediate outputs, but competitive markets do not.

The sales value at splitoff method has the added benefit that all of the joint products (assuming they are sold at the splitoff point) will have a *positive gross margin* (assuming that the total revenues of the joint products less the joint cost results in an overall positive gross margin). Perhaps less beneficial (from the viewpoint of motivating managers) is the fact that all of the joint products using the sales value at splitoff point method will have *the same gross margin*, assuming they are sold at the splitoff point.

⊕ **TRY IT!** ◢ **15.1**

Xavier Chemicals processes resin from fir trees into three products: printing inks, varnishes, and adhesives. During June, the joint costs of processing were $480,000. Additional information is given below:

Product	Units Produced	Sales Value at Splitoff Point
Printing inks	15,000 litres	$120,000
Varnishes	15,000 litres	72,000
Adhesives	7,500 litres	48,000

Determine the amount of joint cost allocated to each product if Xavier uses (a) the physical measure method and (b) the sales value at splitoff method.

Two More Methods to Allocate Joint Cost

▶ **LO 3**

Analyze the two methods to use when there is no sales value at the splitoff point.

In this section, we'll look at the remaining two cost allocation methods for joint costs. These two methods (the NRV method and the constant gross margin percentage of NRV method) should be used to allocate joint costs when there is no selling price available at the splitoff point for one (or more) of the joint products. It is possible to use the physical measure method to allocate the joint costs in this situation (when there is no selling price available for one of the joint products), but the physical measure method is the least defensible of the four methods. The ASPE and IAS standards both state that the joint costs need to be allocated on a "rational and consistent basis." Given the lack of economic rationale for the physical measure method, it is probably the least "rational" of the four methods available.

Let's assume the same situation for Farmers Dairy as above except that both the cream and liquid skim can be processed further. From Farmers Dairy, the following information is known:

■ *Cream → buttercream:* 1,000 hL of cream are further processed to yield 800 hL of buttercream at additional processing (separable) costs of $135,000. Buttercream is sold for $420 per hectolitre.

■ *Liquid skim → condensed milk:* 3,000 hL of liquid skim are further processed to yield 2,000 hL of condensed milk at additional processing costs of $270,000. Condensed milk is sold for $305 per hectolitre.

Sales during the accounting period, May 2018, were 750 hL of buttercream and 1,930 hL of condensed milk. Exhibit 15-6 presents an overview of the basic relationships. Panel A illustrates both the basic relationships in the conversion process from raw milk

Exhibit 15-6 Farmers Dairy: Actual Data for May 2018

PANEL A: Graphical Presentation of Processing

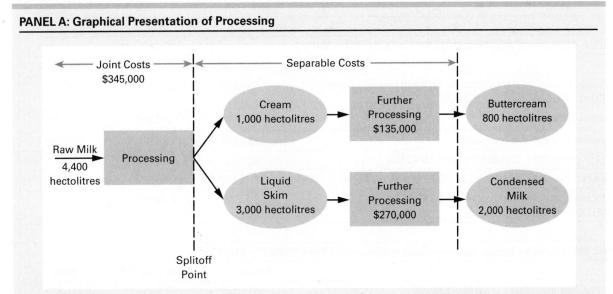

PANEL B: Data

	A	B	C	D	E
1		Joint Costs		**Buttercream**	**Condensed Milk**
2	Joint costs (costs of 4,400 hL fluid milk and processing to splitoff point)	$345,000			
3	Separable cost of processing 1,000 hL cream into 800 hL of buttercream			$135,000	
4	Separable cost of processing 3,000 hL liquid skim into 2,000 hL condensed milk				$270,000
5					
6		**Cream**	**Liquid Skim**	**Buttercream**	**Condensed Milk**
7	Beginning inventory (hectolitres)	0	0	0	0
8	Production (hectolitres)	1,000	3,000	800	2,000
9	Transfer for further processing (hectolitres)	1,000	3,000		
10	Sales (hectolitres)			750	1,930
11	Ending inventory (hectolitres)	0	0	50	70
12	Selling price per hectolitre	$ 155.00	$ 75.00	$ 420.00	$ 305.00

into cream and liquid skim in a joint production process and the separate processing of cream into buttercream as well as liquid skim into condensed milk. Panel B provides the data for this decision.

The actual data for May 2018 are the basis for forecasting how the two alternative cost allocation methods would affect the estimates of gross margin. As reported in Exhibit 15-6, Farmers Dairy sold 750 hL, not 800 hL, of cream, leaving 50 hL in inventory. Only 1,930 hL of condensed milk was sold with 70 hL remaining in finished goods inventory at the end of May.

Net Realizable Value (NRV) Method

The **NRV method** allocates joint costs on the basis of the *NRV* (expected final sales value in the ordinary course of business minus the total expected *separable* costs of production

Exhibit 15-7 Joint-Cost NRV Allocation and Product-Line Income Statement: Farmers Dairy, May 2018

	A	B	C	D
1	**PANEL A: Allocation of Joint Costs Using Net Realizable Value Method**			
2		**Buttercream**	**Condensed Milk**	**Total**
3	Final sales value of total production during the accounting period (800 hL × $420/hL; 2,000 hL × $305/hL)	$336,000	$610,000	$946,000
4	Deduct separable costs	135,000	270,000	405,000
5	Net realizable value at splitoff point	$201,000	$340,000	$541,000
6	Weighting ($201,000 ÷ $541,000; $340,000 ÷ $541,000)	0.371534	0.628466	
7	Joint costs allocated (0.371534 × $345,000; 0.628466 × $345,000, rounded)	$128,179	$216,821	$345,000
8	Production cost per hectolitre ([$128,179 + $135,000] ÷ 800 hL; [$216,821 + $270,000] ÷ 2,000 hL)	$ 328.97	$ 243.41	
9				
10	**PANEL B: Product-Line Income Statement Using Net Realizable Value Method for May 2018**			
11		**Buttercream**	**Condensed Milk**	**Total**
12	Revenue (750 hL × $420/hL; 1,930 hL × $305/hL)	$315,000	$588,650	$903,650
13	Cost of goods sold Joint costs (Panel A, line 7)	128,179	216,821	345,000
14	Separable costs	135,000	270,000	405,000
15	Production costs	263,179	486,821	750,000
16	Deduct ending inventory (50 hL × $328.97; 70 hL × $243.41)	(16,449)	(17,039)	(33,488)
17	Cost of goods sold	246,730	469,782	716,512
18	Gross margin	$ 68,270	$118,868	$187,138
19	Gross margin percentage (Gross margin ÷ Revenue)	21.7%	20.2%	20.7%

and marketing of the total production of the period). This method is an alternative when selling prices for one or more products at splitoff do not exist. Its strength and weakness is that all upstream, production, and downstream separable costs are included in cost of goods sold. While this produces a full product cost, it is also contrary to GAAP and cannot be used for external reporting.

Exhibit 15-7 illustrates the forecast gross margins for both products. Panel A illustrates how joint costs are allocated to individual products to calculate the cost per

● **TRY IT! 15.2**

Red Stripe Company processes tomatoes into ketchup, tomato juice, and canned tomatoes. During the summer of 2017, the joint costs of processing the tomatoes were $2,086,000. The company maintains no inventories. Production and sales information for the summer is as follows:

Product	Cases	Sales Value at Splitoff Point	Separable Costs	Selling Price
Ketchup	100,000	$6 per case	$3 per case	$24 per case
Juice	175,000	8 per case	5 per case	25 per case
Canned	200,000	5 per case	3 per case	10 per case

Determine the amount of joint cost allocated to each product if Red Stripe uses the estimated net realizable value method. What is the cost per case for each product?

hectolitre of buttercream and condensed milk for ending inventory valuation. Panel B presents the product-line income statement using the NRV method. Gross margin percentages are 21.7% for buttercream and 20.2% for condensed milk. The reason is that the total costs are allocated proportionally to the total NRV, as shown in line 6 of the exhibit. A change in one separable cost element will affect both estimated proportions and be spread over the cost of both products.

Constant Gross Margin Percentage of NRV Method

The **constant gross margin percentage of NRV method** works in reverse to the NRV method. For each product, the gross margin (based on the overall gross margin percentage) and total separable costs are deducted from the final sales value of units produced. The residual amount for each product is its allocation of joint costs.

This method allocates joint costs in such a way that the overall gross margin percentage is identical for all the individual products. This method entails three steps:

1. Compute the overall gross margin percentage.

2. Use the overall gross margin percentage and deduct the gross margin from each product's final sales value to obtain the total cost that each product should bear.

3. Deduct the expected separable costs from the total costs to obtain the joint cost allocation.

Exhibit 15-8, Panel A, illustrates these three steps for allocating the $345,000 joint costs between buttercream and condensed milk in the Farmers Dairy example to calculate the cost per hectolitre of buttercream and condensed milk for valuation of ending inventory. Panel B presents the product-line income statement for the constant gross margin percentage NRV method. The tenuous assumption underlying this method is that all the products have the same ratio of cost to sales value. A constant ratio of cost to sales value across products is rarely seen in companies that produce multiple products but have no joint costs.

This variation on the NRV method means the gross margin percentage will be identical for each product, regardless of its separable costs. In effect, products with relatively high separable costs are subsidized because they are assigned a lower proportion of joint costs. This seems counterintuitive if the purpose of cost allocation is to avoid cross-subsidization.

Comparison of the Four Methods

Because the costs are joint in nature, managers cannot use the cause-and-effect criterion in making this choice. Managers cannot be sure what causes what cost when examining joint costs. The purpose of the joint cost allocation is important. Consider rate regulation. Market-based measures are difficult to use in this context. It is circular to use selling prices as a basis for setting prices (rates) and at the same time use selling prices to allocate the costs on which prices (rates) are based. Physical measures represent one joint cost allocation approach appropriate for rate regulation.

In competitive markets, the benefits-received criterion leads to a preference for the *sales value at the splitoff point method* (or other related revenue or market-based methods). Additional benefits of this method include the following:

■ *No anticipation of subsequent management decisions.* The sales value at splitoff method does not presuppose an exact number of subsequent steps undertaken for further processing.

■ *Availability of a meaningful common denominator to compute the weighting factors.* The denominator of the sales value at splitoff method (revenue) is an economically meaningful one. In contrast, there may be no common denominator to implement the physical measure method for all the separable products (for example, when some products are liquids and other products are solids).

Exhibit 15-8 Farmers Dairy Joint Costs Constant Gross Margin Percentage of NRV Allocation, May 2018

	A	B	C	D
1	**PANEL A: Allocation of Joint Costs Using Constant Gross Margin Percentage NRV Method**			
2	**Step 1**			
3	Final sales value of total production during the accounting period (800 hL × $420/hL; 2,000 hL × $305/hL)	$946,000		
4	Deduct joint and separable costs ($345,000 + $135,000 + $270,000)	750,000		
5	Gross margin	$196,000		
6	Gross margin percentage (Gross margin ÷ Revenue) (rounded)	20.719%		
7				
8	**Step 2**	**Buttercream**	**Condensed Milk**	**Total**
9	Final sales value of total production during accounting period (800 hL × $420/hL; 2,000 hL × $305/hL)	$336,000	$610,000	$946,000
10	Deduct gross margin, using constant gross margin percentage (20.719% × $336,000; 20.719% × $610,000)	69,615	126,385	196,000
11	Total production costs	266,385	483,615	750,000
12	**Step 3**			
13	Deduct separable costs	(135,000)	(270,000)	(405,000)
14	Joint costs allocated	$131,385	$213,615	$345,000
15				
16	**PANEL B: Product-Line Income Statement Using Constant Gross Margin Percentage NRV Method for May 2018**			
17		**Buttercream**	**Condensed Milk**	**Total**
18	Revenue (750 hL × $420/hL; 1,930 hL × $305/hL)	$315,000	$588,650	$903,650
19	Cost of goods sold Joint costs (from Panel A, Step 3)	131,385	213,615	345,000
20	Separable costs	135,000	270,000	405,000
21	Production costs	266,385	483,615	750,000
22	*Deduct ending inventory (50 hL × $332.981/hL; 70 hL × $241.808/hL)	(16,649)	(16,927)	(33,576)
23	Cost of goods sold	249,736	466,688	716,424
24	Gross margin	$ 65,264	$121,962	$187,226[1]
25	Gross margin percentage (Gross margin ÷ Revenue)	20.7%	20.7%	20.7%
26				
27	*Total production cost of buttercream ÷ Total production of buttercream	$332.981 per hL		
28	Total production cost of condensed milk ÷ Total production of condensed milk		$241.808 per hL	
29	[1]The total gross margin for this method and NRV method in Exhibit 15-7 should be the same. The difference is due to rounding.			

■ *Simplicity.* The sales value at splitoff method is simple. In contrast, the NRV method can be very complex in operations with multiple products and multiple splitoff points. The total sales value at splitoff is unaffected by any change in the production process after the splitoff point.

However, it is not always feasible to use the sales value at splitoff method because in unregulated markets market prices may not appear until after processing beyond the splitoff point has occurred. In fact, there may be no market for the product at splitoff and thus no sales are possible.

The NRV value method is the predominant choice. Both NRV methods can be used for joint products that have no market value at splitoff. These methods always require assumptions about the quantities or volume of product produced, the unit selling price for each product, the quantity sold, and the dollar value of total separable costs. This is not straightforward because, for example, in petrochemical plants there are alternatives among possible subsequent steps in processing after splitoff. Companies will frequently change further processing to exploit fluctuations in the separable costs of each processing stage or in the selling prices of individual products.

Under the NRV method, each such change in separable costs would affect the joint cost allocation percentages symmetrically. The decrease in one product's separable cost will decrease the NRV cost allocation rate for both products. Any decrease in NRV percentage for the more efficiently processed product will reflect only a portion of the cost savings. Of course, as one NRV percentage decreases, the other increases in the same amount.

Step 4: Decide On and Implement One of the Available Alternatives Farmers Dairy, following common practice, would evaluate the benefits of the cost allocation system. The implementation of NRV influences the quality of information Farmers Dairy would use to evaluate the alternatives of selling or processing further. The best method for internal management decision making is the one that provides the best estimate of gross margin percentage and best helps Farmers Dairy realize a targeted level of profitability. If using the most predominant market-based allocation method provides data inappropriate to the decision situation, then Farmers Dairy is only impairing the quality of data used internally. But, if sales values do exist and Farmers Dairy produces many types of milk product, then it may be best off using the simplest market-based method.

Step 5: Implement the Decision, Evaluate Performance, and Learn All the preceding joint cost allocation methods can be criticized as arbitrary and incomplete simply because they are estimates. As a result, some companies refrain from joint cost allocation entirely. Instead, they carry all inventories at NRV per ASPE/IFRS standards. Revenue on each product is recognized when production is completed. Accountants ordinarily criticize carrying inventories at NRV because this practice contradicts the revenue recognition standard. For large numbers of rapidly changing items, the inventory value is based on a reduction to sales value minus an expected gross margin to estimate NRV (see Exhibit 15-8). This avoids treating cost of goods available for sale as if finished goods were already sold.

15.3 TRY IT!

Consider Red Stripe Company again. With the same information for 2017 as provided in Try It 15-2, calculate the amount of joint cost allocated to each product if Red Stripe uses the constant gross-margin percentage NRV method.

Irrelevance of Joint Costs for Decision Making

No technique for allocating joint product costs should guide management decisions regarding whether a product should be sold at the splitoff point or processed beyond splitoff. When a product is an inevitable result of a joint process, the decision to further process should not be influenced either by the size of the total joint costs or by the portion of the joint costs allocated to particular products. The amount of joint costs incurred up to splitoff ($345,000)—and how it is allocated—is irrelevant in deciding whether to process further. The economic reality is that the joint costs of $345,000 are the same whether or not further processing is done. They do not differ between the two alternatives; therefore, they cannot influence the decision and are irrelevant.

▶ **LO 4**
Understand the irrelevance of joint costs in the "sell or process further" decision.

Exhibit 15-9 Farmers Dairy Product-Line Income Statement for May 2018: No Allocation of Joint Costs

	A	B	C	D
1		**Buttercream**	**Condensed Milk**	**Total**
2	Produced and sold (buttercream, 750 hL × $420/hL; 1,930 hL × $305/hL)	$315,000	$588,650	$903,650
3	Produced but not sold (buttercream 50 hL × $420/hL; 70 hL × $305/hL)	21,000	21,350	42,350
4	Total sales value of production	336,000	610,000	946,000
5	Separable costs (given)	135,000	270,000	405,000
6	Contribution to joint costs and operating income	$201,000	$340,000	541,000
7	Joint costs (given)			345,000
8	Gross margin			$196,000
9	Gross margin percentage (Gross margin ÷ Revenue)			20.719%

Sell or Process Further?

Exhibit 15-9 presents the product-line income statement *with no allocation of joint costs* for the "sell or process further" decision. The separable costs are assigned first, which highlights for managers the cause-and-effect relationship between individual products and the costs incurred to process them. The joint costs are not allocated to buttercream and condensed milk as individual products. The decision to incur additional costs beyond splitoff should be based on the incremental gross margin ($) attainable beyond the splitoff point.

The incremental analysis for these decisions to further process is as follows:

	Buttercream	Condensed Milk	Total
Incremental revenue (buttercream vs. cream: condensed milk vs. liquid skim)	$181,000	$385,000	$566,000
($336 − $155 = $181: $610 − $225 = $385)			
Incremental costs (cream → buttercream: liquid skim → condensed milk)	135,000	270,000	405,000
(separable costs for each product line)			
Incremental gross margin due to processing beyond splitoff point	$ 46,000	$115,000	$161,000
GM as a percentage of the incremental revenue	25.4%	29.9%	28.4%

To make the "sell or process further" decision, two assumptions are necessary.

1. You must assume that all the units of the given product (e.g., cream) are either sold at the splitoff point or processed into the next product line (e.g., buttercream). This is because the separable costs may be added in fixed amounts (e.g., a batch cost to make the buttercream) to further process a given amount of product. In the example above, the comparison is selling 1,000 hL of cream for a total sales value of $155,000 (see Exhibit 15-5, Panel A) or processing the cream further and selling the resulting 800 hL of buttercream for $336,000 (see Exhibit 15-9). Therefore, the incremental revenue is $181,000 (= $336,000 − $155,000). The incremental cost is the separable cost of further processing the cream into buttercream, $135,000 (see Exhibit 15-9).

2. You must assume that firms are more interested in absolute dollar measurements (i.e., the total dollar amount of gross margin) than relative measurements (i.e., the largest gross margin percentage). Otherwise, a firm would be happier with a 75% gross margin on $1 of sales (or $0.75 of gross margin) than with a 25% gross margin

on $1 million of sales (or $250,000 of gross margin). Obviously, given the information in the above table and this assumption (dollars are preferable to percentages), a manager would typically choose to process both product lines further (beyond the splitoff point) because the incremental revenue is positive for both lines. Otherwise, if gross margin percentage was the performance measure that drove decisions, a manager might decide to sell all the products at the splitoff point and show a 23.4% gross margin for the period. This is the situation when the physical measure method is used to allocate joint costs (see Exhibit 15-4). This is distorted to a large degree because of the unsold product that remains in inventory that contains a large amount of the joint costs.

The relevant information for Farmers Dairy is reported in the first column of the table below. If Farmers had incorrectly included allocated joint costs under the NRV method, and if only one product were to be processed further, then the choice would be buttercream because its gross margin is higher than condensed milk's. If the correct incremental data were used, then the choice would be condensed milk, not buttercream, and the potential incremental gross margin would be far higher. By considering irrelevant costs, Farmers Dairy would forgo a very lucrative opportunity to exploit the less lucrative one.

	Gross Margin Percentage		
Product Line	No Allocation	NRV	Constant GM
Buttercream	25.4%	21.7%	20.7%
Condensed milk	29.9	20.2	20.7

Challenges for Management Accountants

There is potential conflict between the cost concepts used for decision making and those used for evaluating the performance of managers. If managers make process-further or sell decisions using an incremental revenue/incremental cost approach, the resulting budgeted product-line income statement using any of the three market methods will show each individual product budgeted to have a positive (or zero) operating income (as long as the incremental costs do not exceed the incremental revenues). In contrast, allocating joint costs using a physical measure can show a manager being responsible for one or more products budgeted to have losses, even though the company has higher operating income by producing those products in a joint-product setting.

Consider again Farmers Dairy and the cost allocation decision between physical measure and sales value at splitoff, with the following change: The selling price per hectolitre of liquid skim increases by 20% (from $75/hL to $90/hL). This change would not affect the joint costs allocated or the cost of goods computed using the physical measure method (see Exhibit 15-4), but it would affect the revenues of the liquid skim product. The revised product-line income statement for May 2018 using the physical measure method is shown below:

> **► LO 5**
>
> Identify the strategic implications of a decision to implement one joint cost allocation method.

	A	B	C	D
1	**Panel B: Product-Line Income Statement Using Physical Measure Method for May 2018**			
2		Cream	Liquid Skim	Total
3	Revenues (800 hL × $155/hL; 900 hL × $90/hL)	$124,000	$ 81,000	$205,000
4	Cost of goods sold (joint costs)			
5	Production costs (0.25 × $345,000; 0.75 × $345,000)	86,250	258,750	345,000
6	Deduct ending inventory (200 hL × $86.25/hL; 2,100 hL × $86.25/hL)	(17,250)	(181,125)	(198,375)
7	Cost of goods sold (joint costs)	69,000	77,625	146,625
8	Gross margin	$ 55,000	$ 3,375	$ 58,375
9	Gross margin percentage (Gross margin ÷ Revenue)	44.4%	4.2%	28.5%

Sustainability in Action | Overcoming the Challenges of Joint Cost Allocation

When you think of companies such as the Ganong Bros. Ltd., Maple Leaf Foods, or Petro-Canada, perhaps the first thing that comes to mind is chocolate truffles, a hot dog at a hockey game, or the high cost of gasoline. You don't think about the management accounting challenges faced daily at these companies. Unfortunately, any allocation process is arbitrary. This gives production managers, who are evaluated on process cost control, the opportunity to lobby for joint cost allocations that assign the lowest joint costs to their division. However, allocating joint costs to please one production division is rarely in the best interests of the company as a whole.

Challenges with joint cost allocations can also arise when two separate companies, such as Exxon-Mobil Canada and Suncor, enter into a joint venture to extract crude oil and natural gas, with one company processing primarily the crude oil and the other processing primarily the natural gas. The contract terms will spell out how joint costs of refining are to be allocated; and such approaches to costing can help

ensure that production processes and volumes are planned to maximize the sustainability of the venture. Management accountants ensure that both parties agree to an understandable and economically plausible method that accurately reflects operations. They are also licensed to audit reports to ensure adherence to the contract terms.

Under these assumptions, the budgeted profit margin for liquid skim product changes dramatically from negative 15.0% to positive 4.2%. On the basis of the initial loss reported using the physical measure method, a manager who is evaluated on product-by-product gross margin information will be reluctant to process the raw milk into cream and liquid skim to avoid having to explain why liquid skim is being produced at a negative gross margin. This also obscures the opportunity to exploit added profitability from processing further into buttercream and condensed milk. Under this method, a price change, which is beyond the processing manager's control, is crucial to improving profitability. Use of a market-based joint cost allocation method avoids this situation.

Accounting for Byproducts

▶ **LO 6**

Account for byproducts using two different methods.

Processes that yield joint products often also yield byproducts—products that have relatively low sales value compared with the sales value of the main or joint product(s). To simplify the discussion of accounting for byproducts, consider a two-product example consisting of a main product and a byproduct.

The Westlake Corporation processes timber into fine-grade lumber and wood chips that are used as mulch in gardens and lawns. Information about these products follows:

■ Fine-grade lumber (the main product)—sells for $505 per thousand board feet (MBF), or $0.505 per board foot

■ Wood chips (the byproduct)—sell for $86 per oven-dried tonne

Data for 2018 are as follows:

	A	B	C	D	E
1		Beginning Inventory	Production	Sales	Ending Inventory
2	Fine-grade lumber, thousand board feet (MBF)	0	4,000	3,700	300
3	Wood chips, oven-dried tonnes	0	700	450	250
4		Softwood	Chips		
5	Prices (per MBF, lumber; per tonne, chips)	$ 505	$ 86		
6		Direct Materials	Conversion	Total	
7	Joint manufacturing costs	$356,000	$1,068,000	$1,424,000	
8	Note: MBF = thousand board feet				

Joint manufacturing costs for these products were $1,424,000, comprising $356,000 for direct materials and $1,068,000 for conversion costs. Both products are sold at the splitoff point without further processing. An overview of Westlake Corporation is shown in Exhibit 15-10.

Two byproduct accounting methods will be presented. Method A (the production byproduct method) recognizes byproducts in the financial statements at the time their production is completed. Method B (the sale byproduct method) delays recognition of byproducts until the time of their sale.[2] Recognition of byproducts at the time of production is conceptually correct. Where recognition at the time of sales occurs in practice, it is usually rationalized on the grounds that the dollar amounts of byproducts are immaterial. Exhibit 15-11 presents the operating income statement of Westlake Corporation under both methods.

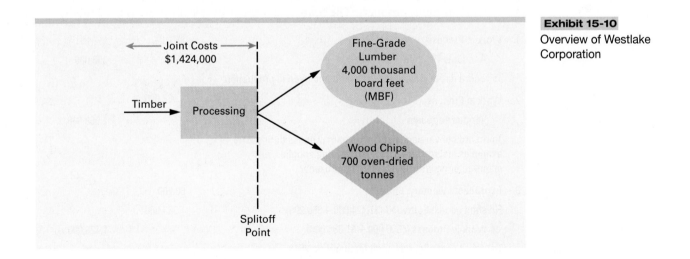

Exhibit 15-10
Overview of Westlake Corporation

---

[2] Further discussion on byproduct accounting methods is in C. Cheatham and M. Green, "Teaching Accounting for Byproducts," *Management Accounting News & Views* (Spring 1988): 14–15; and D. Stout and D. Wygal, "Making Byproducts a Main Product of Discussion: A Challenge to Accounting Educators," *Journal of Accounting Education* (1989): 219–233. See also P.D. Marshall and R.F. Dombrowski, "A Small Business Review of Accounting for Primary Products, Byproducts and Scrap," *The National Public Accountant* (February/March 2003): 10–13.

Exhibit 15-11 Operating Income Statements of Westlake Corporation for 2018 Using the Production and Sales Methods for Byproduct Accounting

	Production Method	Sales Method
Revenue		
Main product fine-grade lumber (3,700 MBF × $505/MBF)	$1,868,500	$1,868,500
Byproduct pulp-quality wood chips (450 tonnes × $86/tonne)	—	38,700
Total revenue	1,868,500	1,907,200
Cost of goods sold		
Total manufacturing costs	1,424,000	1,424,000
Deduct byproduct *sales* value (700 tonnes × $86/tonne)	(60,200)	—
Net manufacturing costs	1,363,800	$1,424,000
Deduct main product ending inventory	(102,285)[a]	(106,800)[b]
Cost of goods sold	1,261,515	1,317,200
Gross margin	$ 606,985	$ 590,000
Gross margin percentage	32.5%	30.9%
Inventoriable costs (end of period)		
300 MBF main product fine-grade lumber	$ 102,285[a]	$ 106,800[b]
250 tonnes byproduct pulp-quality wood chips	$ 21,500[c]	$ 0[d]

[a]($1,363,800 ÷ 4,000) × 300 tonnes = $102,285.
[b]($1,424,000 ÷ 4,000) × 300 tonnes = $106,800.
[c]250 tonnes × $86 per tonne = $21,500 for the remaining tonnes in inventory.
[d]Zero inventory value carried for unsold byproducts under the sales method.

Method A: Byproducts Are Recognized When Production Is Completed

This method recognizes in the financial statements the byproduct—700 tonnes of wood chips—as it is produced in 2018. The NRV from the byproduct is offset against the costs of the main (or joint) products. The following journal entries illustrate this method:

1. Work in Process   356,000
      Accounts Payable   356,000
   To record direct materials purchased and used in production.

2. Work in Process   1,068,000
      Various accounts   1,068,000
   To record conversion costs in the joint process during 2018; examples include energy, manufacturing supplies, all manufacturing labour, and plant amortization.

3. Byproduct Inventory: Chips   60,200
   Finished goods: Softwood ($1,424,000 − $60,200)   1,363,800
      Work in Process ($356,000 + $1,068,000)   1,424,000
   To record cost of goods completed during 2018.

4a. Cost of Goods Sold   1,261,515
      Finished Goods: Softwood   1,261,515
   To record the cost of the main product sold during 2018.

4b. Cash or Accounts Receivable (3,700/MBF × $505/MBF)   1,868,500
      Revenue: Softwood   1,868,500
   To record the sale of the main product during 2018.

5. Cash or Accounts Receivable (450 × $86)	38,700	
Byproduct Inventory: Chips		38,700
To record the sale of the byproduct during 2018.		

Note: Journal entry #5 does not record revenue; it simply reduces the amount of byproduct inventory that was recognized in journal entry #3. The remaining byproduct inventory has a value of $ 21,500 (= $60,200 − $38,700) that would be reported on the statement of financial position at the end of 2018.

This method reports the byproduct inventories of oven-dried wood chips on the statement of financial position at their per-tonne selling price. The production method, everything being equal, is the preferred method. The relevant accounting standards (ASPE 3031.15 and IAS 2.14) state that byproducts "are often measured at net realisable value and this value is deducted from the cost of the main product." That said, if the selling price of the byproduct is volatile and/or hard to predict, it may make sense to use the time of sale method. With the time of sale method, the value of the byproduct does not impact the accounting records until the byproduct is sold.

One variant of this method would be to report byproduct inventory at its NRV reduced by a normal profit margin. When the byproduct inventory is sold in a subsequent period, the statement of comprehensive income would match the selling price with the "net" selling price reported for the byproduct inventory.

Method B: Byproducts Are Recognized at Time of Sale

This method makes no journal entries until sale of the byproduct occurs. Revenues of the byproduct are reported as a revenue item in the statement of comprehensive income at the time of sale. In the Westlake Corporation example, byproduct revenue in 2018 would be $38,700 because only 450 tonnes of chips are sold in 2018.

1. Work in Process	356,000	
Accounts Payable		356,000
To record direct materials purchased and used in production.		
2. Work in Process	1,068,000	
Various accounts		1,068,000
To record conversion costs in the joint process during 2018; examples include energy, manufacturing supplies, all manufacturing labour, and plant amortization.		
3. Finished Goods: Softwood	1,424,000	
Work in Process ($356,000 + $1,068,000)		1,424,000
To record cost of goods completed during 2018.		
4a. Cost of Goods Sold	1,317,200	
Finished Goods: Softwood		1,317,200
To record the cost of the main product sold during 2018.		
4b. Cash or Accounts Receivable (3,700/MBF × $505/MBF)	1,868,500	
Revenue: Softwood		1,868,500
To record the sale of the main product during 2018.		
5. Cash or Accounts Receivable (450 × $86)	38,700	
Revenue: Chips		38,700
To record the sale of the byproduct during 2018.		

Method B is rationalized in practice primarily on the grounds that the dollar amounts of byproducts are immaterial. However, this method permits managers to "manage" reported earnings by timing when they sell byproducts. Managers may stockpile byproducts so that they have the flexibility to give revenues a "boost" at opportune times.

Pulling it all Together—Problem for Self-Study

(Try to solve this problem before examining the solution that follows.)

Problem

Inorganic Chemicals (IC) processes salt into various industrial products. In July 2018, IC incurred joint costs of $100,000 to purchase salt and convert it into two saleable products: caustic soda and chlorine. Although there is an active outside market for chlorine, IC processes all 800 tonnes of chlorine it produces into 500 tonnes of PVC (polyvinyl chloride), which is then sold. There were no beginning or ending inventories of salt, caustic soda, chlorine, or PVC in July. Information for July 2018 production and sales follows:

	A	B	C	D
1		**Joint Costs**		**PVC**
2	Joint costs (costs of salt and processing to splitoff point)		$100,000	
3	Separable cost of processing 800 tonnes chlorine into 500 tonnes PVC			$20,000
4				
5		**Caustic Soda**	**Chlorine**	**PVC**
6	Beginning inventory (tonnes)	0	0	0
7	Production (tonnes)	1,200	800	500
8	Transfer for further processing (tonnes)		800	
9	Sales (tonnes)	1,200		500
10	Ending inventory (tonnes)	0	0	0
11	Selling price per tonne in active outside market (for products not actually sold)		$ 75	
12	Selling price per tonne for products sold	$ 50		$ 200

▶ **Required**

❶ 1. Allocate the joint costs of $100,000 between caustic soda and chlorine under (a) the sales value at splitoff method and (b) the physical measure method.

❷ 2. Allocate the joint costs of $100,000 between caustic soda and PVC under the NRV method.

❸ 3. What is the gross margin percentage of (a) caustic soda and (b) PVC under the three allocation methods?

❹ 4. Lifetime Swimming Pool Products offers to purchase 800 tonnes of chlorine in August 2018 at $75 per tonne. Assume all other production and sales data are the same for August as they were for July. This sale of chlorine to Lifetime would mean that no PVC would be produced by IC in August. How would accepting this offer affect IC's August 2018 operating income?

Solution

1a. Sales value at splitoff method

	A	B	C	D
1	**Allocation of Joint Costs Using Sales Value at Splitoff Method**	**Caustic Soda**	**Chlorine**	**Total**
2	Sales value of total production at splitoff point (1,200 tonnes × $50 per tonne; 800 tonnes × $75 per tonne)	$60,000	$60,000	$120,000
3	Weighting ($60,000 ÷ $120,000; $60,000÷ $120,000)	0.50	0.50	
4	Joint costs allocated (0.50 × $100,000; 0.50 × $100,000)	$50,000	$50,000	$100,000

1b. Physical measures method

	A	B	C	D
1	**Allocation of Joint Costs Using Physical Measure Method**	**Caustic Soda**	**Chlorine**	**Total**
2	Physical measure of total production (tonnes)	1,200	800	2,000
3	Weighting (1,200 tonnes ÷ 2,000 tonnes; 800 tonnes ÷ 2,000 tonnes)	0.60	0.40	
4	Joint costs allocated (0.60 × $100,000; 0.40 × $100,000)	$60,000	$40,000	$100,000

2. Net realizable value method

	A	B	C	D
1	**Allocation of Joint Costs Using Net Realizable Value Method**	**Caustic Soda**	**PVC**	**Total**
2	Final sales value of total production during accounting period	$60,000	$ 100,000	$160,000
3	Deduct separable costs to complete and sell	0	20,000	20,000
4	Net realizable value at splitoff point	$60,000	$ 80,000	$140,000
5	Weighting ($60,000 ÷ $140,000; $80,000 ÷ $140,000)	0.43	0.57	
6	Joint costs allocated (caustic, 0.43 × $100,000; chlorine, 0.57 × $100,000)	$42,857	$ 57,143	$100,000

3a. Caustic soda

	A	B	C	D
1				
2		**Sales Value**	**Physical**	**Net Realizable**
3		**at Splitoff**	**Measure**	**Value**
4	Sales	$60,000	$60,000	$60,000
5	Joint costs	50,000	60,000	42,857
6	Gross margin	$10,000	$ 0	$17,143
7	Gross margin percentage	16.67%	0%	28.57%

3b. PVC

	A	B	C	D
1				
2		**Sales Value**	**Physical**	**Net Realizable**
3		**at Splitoff**	**Measure**	**Value**
4	Sales	$100,000	$100,000	$100,000
5	Joint costs	50,000	40,000	57,143
6	Separable costs	20,000	20,000	20,000
7	Gross margin	$ 30,000	$ 40,000	$ 22,857
8	Gross margin percentage	30.00%	40.00%	22.86%

4. Incremental income from further processing of chlorine into PVC:

Incremental revenue of further processing	
(500 tonnes × $200 per tonne) − (800 tonnes × $75 per tonne)	$40,000
Incremental costs of further processing chlorine into PVC	20,000
Incremental operating income from further processing	$20,000

The operating income of Inorganic Chemicals would be reduced by $20,000 if it sold 800 tonnes of chlorine to Lifetime Swimming Pool Products instead of further processing the chlorine into PVC for sale.

Decision Points

The following question-and-answer format summarizes the chapter's learning objectives. Each point presents a key question, and the guidelines are the answer to that question.

Learning Objectives	Guidelines
1. How can products be distinguished?	Products have positive sales value. Main and joint products have high total sales value at the splitoff point. A byproduct has a comparatively low total sales value at the splitoff point. Products can change from byproducts to joint products when their total sales values significantly increase; they can change from joint products to byproducts when their total sales values significantly decrease. Scrap has no sales value and toxic waste has negative value. Outputs such as dirt and water from extraction industries have no sales value but are used to reclaim land.
2. What methods can be used to allocate joint costs to individual products?	The methods available to allocate joint costs to products are physical measure and sales value at splitoff. There may be no common physical measure upon which to allocate joint costs of products. There may be no market at splitoff and therefore the joint products are not saleable, although revenue would otherwise be a common measure upon which to allocate joint costs.
3. What other market-based methods are used when there is no sales value at splitoff?	Both net realizable value and constant margin percentage of net realizable value can provide a cost allocation base upon which to allocate total product costs when no market exists for joint products at splitoff. Neither method is GAAP-compliant because separable non-manufacturing costs are included in cost of goods available for sale.
4. Why are joint costs irrelevant in the "sell or process further" decision?	Joint costs are deemed irrelevant as these costs have already been incurred at the time of the decision to sell or process further. In other words, they are sunk costs. The decision to sell or process further should rely on the net additional revenue resulting from further processing.
5. What strategic implications arise when basing sell or process-further decisions on allocated joint costs?	Allocated joint costs are irrelevant to any sell or process-further decision. The joint costs, by definition, will not change under either alternative. Including these costs impairs the quality of information upon which this decision will be based. No internal feedback will indicate the managers have incorrectly included an irrelevant cost. In the long term, companies will miss the opportunity to process beyond splitoff and improve operating margin.
6. What methods can be used to account for byproducts?	Byproduct accounting methods differ on whether byproducts are recognized in financial statements at the time of production or at the time of sale. Recognition at the time of production is conceptually correct. Recognition at the time of sale is often used in practice because dollar amounts of byproducts are immaterial.

Terms to Learn

This chapter and the Glossary at the end of the book contain definitions of the following important terms:

byproducts (**p. 606**)

constant gross margin percentage of
  NRV method (**p. 608**)

net realizable value (NRV) method
  (**p. 608**)

joint costs (**p. 606**)

joint products (**p. 606**)

main products (**p. 606**)

physical measure method (**p. 608**)

product (**p. 606**)

sales value at splitoff method (**p. 608**)

scrap (**p. 606**)

separable costs (**p. 607**)

splitoff point (**p. 607**)

toxic waste (**p. 607**)

Assignment Material

MyLab Accounting Make the grade with MyLab Accounting: The Short-Answer Questions, Exercises, and Problems marked with a ⊕ can be found on MyLab Accounting. You can practise them as often as you want, and most feature step-by-step guided instructions to help you find the right answer.

Short-Answer Questions

⊕ **15-1** Give two examples of industries in which joint costs are found. For each example, what are the individual products at or beyond the splitoff point?

⊕ **15-2** What is a joint cost? What is a separable cost?

⊕ **15-3** Distinguish between a joint product and a byproduct.

⊕ **15-4** Why might the number of products in a joint cost setting differ from the number of outputs? Give an example.

⊕ **15-5** Provide three reasons for allocating joint costs to individual products or services.

⊕ **15-6** Why does the sales value at splitoff method use the sales value of the total production in the accounting period and not just the sales value of the products sold?

⊕ **15-7** Describe a situation in which the sales value at splitoff method cannot be used but the NRV method can be used for joint cost allocation.

⊕ **15-8** Distinguish between the sales value at splitoff method and the NRV method.

⊕ **15-9** Give two limitations of the physical measure method of joint cost allocation.

⊕ **15-10** How might a company simplify its use of the NRV method when the final selling prices can vary sizably in an accounting period and management makes frequent changes to the point at which it sells individual products?

⊕ **15-11** Why is the constant gross margin percentage NRV method sometimes called a "joint cost and a profit allocation" method?

⊕ **15-12** "Managers must decide whether a product should be sold at splitoff or processed further. The sales value at splitoff method of joint cost allocation is the best method for generating the information managers need." Do you agree? Why?

⊕ **15-13** "Managers should consider only additional revenues and separable costs when making decisions about selling now or processing further." Do you agree? Why?

⊕ **15-14** Describe two major methods to account for byproducts.

Exercises

⊕ **15-15 Terminology.** A number of terms are listed below:

byproduct	products
constant gross margin percentage	sales value at splitoff
net realizable value	scrap
joint costs	separable costs
main product	splitoff point
physical measure	

Required

Select the terms from the above list to complete the following sentences.

Companies provide value-added to their customers through the sale of their _____. A product is any output or service that can be sold for a price that recovers the total costs to bring the product to the customer plus some reasonable profit. Some production processes yield a _____ with the highest sales price, a _____ that requires little if any further processing but is sold for a far lower price, and _____, which is usually unused direct materials recovered and sold for almost nothing. Two or more products sold at a high price are called joint products. The costs of producing more than one product can be common or _____ plus _____ to complete each product. The _____ determines what pool comprises the joint costs that must be allocated on a reasonable basis. The allocation methods are _____, _____, _____, and _____. The task of the management team is to select the method of joint cost allocation that best represents what actually happened in the physical production process.

LO 1 ▶

1. a. Joint costs allocated to breasts, $33.75

⊕ **15-16 Joint cost allocation, insurance settlement.** Quality Chicken grows and processes chickens. Each chicken is disassembled into five main parts. Information pertaining to production in July 2018 is

Parts	Kilograms of Product	Wholesale Selling Price per Kilogram When Production Is Complete
Breasts	100	$0.55
Wings	20	0.20
Thighs	40	0.35
Bones	80	0.10
Feathers	10	0.05

Joint cost of production in July 2018 was $50.

A special shipment of 80 kilograms of breasts and 30 kilograms of wings has been destroyed in a fire. Quality Chicken's insurance policy provides reimbursement for the cost of the items destroyed. The insurance company permits Quality Chicken to use a joint cost allocation method. The splitoff point is assumed to be at the end of the production process.

Required

1. Compute the cost of the special shipment destroyed using
   a. Sales value at splitoff method.
   b. Physical measure method (kilograms of finished product).
2. What joint cost allocation method would you recommend Quality Chicken use? Explain.

LO 5 ▶

1. Wings ending inventory, $0.49

⊕ **15-17 Joint products and byproducts** (continuation of Exercise 15-16). Quality Chicken is computing the ending inventory values for its July 31, 2018, statement of financial position. Ending inventory amounts on July 31 are 15 kilograms of breasts, 4 kilograms of wings, 6 kilograms of thighs, 5 kilograms of bones, and 2 kilograms of feathers.

Quality Chicken's management wants to use the sales value at splitoff method. However, they want you to explore the effect on ending inventory values of classifying one or more products as a byproduct rather than a joint product.

Required

1. Assume Quality Chicken classifies all five products as joint products. What are the ending inventory values of each product on July 31, 2018?
2. Assume Quality Chicken uses the production method of accounting for byproducts. What are the ending inventory values for each joint product on July 31, 2018, assuming breasts and thighs are the joint products, and wings, bones, and feathers are byproducts?
3. Comment on differences in the results in requirements 1 and 2.

LO 3 ▶

1. Weighting for turpentine, 0.75

⊕ **15-18 Irrelevance of joint costs.** The Vapor Company produces two products, turpentine and methanol (wood alcohol), by a joint process. Joint costs amount to $144,000 per batch of output. Each batch totals 40,000 litres: 25% methanol and 75% turpentine. Both products are processed further without gain or loss in volume. Separable processing costs are methanol, $0.90 per litre; turpentine, $0.60 per litre. Methanol sells for $6.30 per litre. Turpentine sells for $4.20 per litre.

Required

1. How much joint cost per batch should be allocated to turpentine and to methanol, assuming that joint costs are allocated on a physical measure (number of litres at splitoff point) basis?
2. If joint costs are to be assigned on an NRV basis, how much joint cost should be assigned to turpentine and to methanol?
3. Prepare product-line income statements per batch for requirements 1 and 2. Assume no beginning or ending inventories.
4. The company has discovered an additional process by which the methanol (wood alcohol) can be made into laboratory ethanol. The selling price of this product would be $18 a litre. Additional processing would increase separate costs $2.70 per litre (in addition to the $0.90 per litre separable cost required to yield methanol). The company would have to pay excise taxes of 20% on the selling price of the product. Assuming no other changes in cost, what is the joint cost applicable to the ethanol (using the NRV method)? Should the company produce the ethanol? Show your computations.

LO 3 ▶

1. Weighting, cookies, soymeal, 0.556

⊕ **15-19 Joint cost allocation: sell immediately or process further.** Saskatchewan Soy Products (SSP) buys soy beans and processes them into other soy products. Each tonne of soy beans that SSP purchases for $300 can be converted for an additional $200 into 500 lbs of soy meal and 100 gallons of soy oil. A pound of soy meal can be sold at splitoff for $1 and soy oil can be sold in bulk for $4 per gallon.

SSP can process the 500 lbs of soy meal into 600 lbs of soy cookies at an additional cost of $300. Each pound of soy cookies can be sold for $2 per pound. The 100 gallons of soy oil can be packaged at a cost of $200 and made into 400 quarts of Soyola. Each quart of Soyola can be sold for $1.25.

Required

1. Allocate the joint cost to the cookies and the Soyola using
   a. Sales value at splitoff method.
   b. NRV method.
2. Should the company have processed each of the products further? What effect does the allocation method have on this decision?

🌐 **15-20 Net realizable value method.** Convad Company is one of the world's leading corn refiners. It produces two joint products, corn syrup and corn starch, using a common production process. In July 2018, Convad reported the following production and selling price information:

◀ **LO 1**
Joint costs allocated to corn starch, $65,000

	Corn Syrup	Corn Starch	Joint Costs
Joint costs (costs of processing corn to splitoff point)			$325,000
Separable cost of processing beyond splitoff point	$375,000	$93,750	
Beginning inventory (cases)	0	0	
Production and sales (cases)	12,500	6,250	
Ending inventory (cases)	0	0	
Selling price per case	$ 50	$ 25	

Required

Allocate the $325,000 joint costs using the NRV method.

🌐 **15-21 Joint cost allocation, sales value, physical measure, NRV methods.** Instant Foods produces two types of microwavable products—beef-flavoured ramen and shrimp-flavoured ramen. The two products share common inputs such as noodles and spices. The production of ramen results in a waste product referred to as stock, which Instant dumps at negligible costs in a local drainage area. In June 2018, the following data were reported for the production and sales of beef-flavoured and shrimp-flavoured ramen:

◀ **LO 2**
1. Special B joint costs allocated, $60,000

	Joint Costs
Joint costs (costs of noodles, spices, and other inputs and processing to splitoff point)	$240,000

	Beef Ramen	Shrimp Ramen
Beginning inventory (tonnes)	0	0
Production (tonnes)	10,000	20,000
Sales (tonnes)	10,000	20,000
Selling price per tonne	$10	$15

Due to the popularity of its microwavable products, Instant decides to add a new line of products that targets dieters. These new products are produced by adding a special ingredient to dilute the original ramen and are to be sold under the names Special B and Special S, respectively. The monthly data for all the products follow:

	Joint Costs	Special B	Special S
Joint costs (costs of noodles, spices, and other inputs and processing to splitoff point)	$240,000		
Separable costs of processing 10,000 tonnes of beef ramen into 12,000 tonnes of Special B		$48,000	
Separable cost of processing 20,000 tonnes of shrimp ramen into 24,000 tonnes of Special S			$168,000

	Beef Ramen	Shrimp Ramen	Special B	Special S
Beginning inventory (tonnes)	0	0	0	0
Production (tonnes)	10,000	20,000	12,000	24,000
Transfer for further processing (tonnes)	10,000	20,000		
Sales (tonnes)			12,000	24,000
Selling price per tonne	$10	$15	$18	$25

Required

1. Calculate Instant's gross margin percentage for Special B and Special S when joint costs are allocated using
   a. Sales value at splitoff method.
   b. Physical measure method.
   c. Net realizable value method.

2. Recently, Instant discovered that the stock it is dumping can be sold to cattle ranchers at $5 per tonne. In a typical month with the production levels shown above, 4,000 tonnes of stock are produced and can be sold by incurring marketing costs of $10,800. Sherrie Dong, a management accountant, points out that in treating the stock as a joint product and using the sales value at splitoff method the stock product would lose about $2,228 each month, so it should not be sold. How did Dong arrive at that final number, and what do you think of her analysis? Should Instant sell the stock?

🌐 **15-22 Joint cost allocation, process further.** Sinclair Oil & Gas, a large energy conglomerate, jointly processes purchased hydrocarbons to generate three nonsaleable intermediate products: ICR8, ING4, and XGE3. These intermediate products are further processed separately to produce Crude Oil, Natural Gas Liquids (NGL), and Natural Gas (measured in liquid equivalents). An overview of the process and results for August 2018 is shown here. (*Note:* The numbers are small to keep the focus on key concepts.)

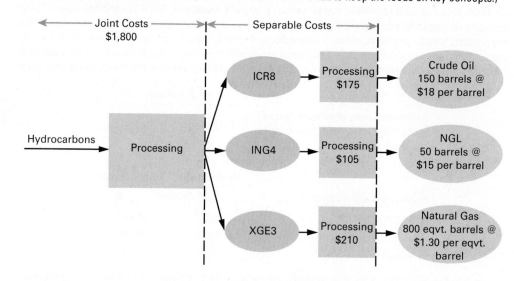

A federal law has recently been passed that taxes crude oil at 30% of operating income. No new tax is to be paid on natural gas liquid or natural gas. Starting August 2018, Sinclair Oil & Gas must report a separate product-line income statement for crude oil. One challenge facing Sinclair Oil & Gas is how to allocate the joint cost of producing the three separate saleable outputs. Assume no beginning or ending inventory.

Required

1. Allocate the August 2018 joint cost among the three products using
   a. Physical measure method.
   b. NRV method.
2. Show the operating income for each product using the methods in requirement 1.
3. Which, if any, method would you use for product emphasis? Explain.
4. Draft a letter to the taxation authorities on behalf of Sinclair Oil & Gas that justifies the joint cost allocation method you recommend Sinclair use.

15-23 Alternative methods of joint cost allocation, ending inventories. The Klein Company operates a simple chemical process to convert a single material into three separate items, referred to here as X, Y, and Z. All three end products are separated simultaneously at a single splitoff point.

◀ LO 1

1. Weight for Z, 0.15

Products X and Y are ready for sale immediately upon splitoff without further processing or any other additional costs. Product Z, however, is processed further before being sold. There is no available market price for Z at the splitoff point.

The selling prices quoted here are expected to remain the same in the coming year. During 2018, the selling prices of the items and the total amounts sold were

- X—120 tonnes sold for $1,500 per tonne.
- Y—340 tonnes sold for $1,000 per tonne.
- Z—475 tonnes sold for $700 per tonne.

The total joint manufacturing costs for the year were $400,000. Klein spent an additional $200,000 to finish product Z.

There were no beginning inventories of X, Y, or Z. At the end of the year, the following inventories of completed units were on hand: X, 180 tonnes; Y, 60 tonnes; Z, 25 tonnes. There was no beginning or ending work in process.

Required

1. Compute the cost of inventories of X, Y, and Z for the purposes of the statement of financial position and the cost of goods sold for operating income statement purposes as of December 31, 2018, using the following joint cost allocation methods:
   a. NRV method.
   b. Constant gross margin percentage NRV method.
2. Compare the gross margin percentages for X, Y, and Z using the two methods given in requirement 1.

15-24 Process further or sell, byproduct. Newcastle Mining Company (NMC) mines coal, puts it through a one-step crushing process, and loads the bulk raw coal onto river barges for shipment to customers.

◀ LO 5

1. Incremental costs, $73,900,000

NMC's management is currently evaluating the possibility of further processing the raw coal by sizing and cleaning it and selling it to an expanded set of customers at higher prices. The option of building a new sizing and cleaning plant is ruled out as being financially infeasible. Instead, Amy Kimbell, a mining engineer, is asked to explore outside contracting arrangements for the cleaning and sizing process. Kimbell puts together the following summary:

Selling price of raw coal	$29 per tonne
Cost of producing raw coal	$22 per tonne
Selling price of sized and cleaned coal	$36 per tonne
Annual raw coal output	10,000,000 tonnes
Percentage of material weight loss in sizing/cleaning coal	6%

	Incremental Costs of Sizing and Cleaning Processes
Direct labour	$800,000 per year
Supervisory personnel	200,000 per year
Heavy equipment: rental, operating, maintenance costs	25,000 per month
Contract sizing and cleaning	3.50 per tonne of raw coal
Outbound rail freight	240 per 60-tonne rail car

Kimbell also learns that 75% of the material loss that occurs in the cleaning and sizing process can be salvaged as coal fines, which can be sold to steel manufacturers for their furnaces. The sale of coal fines is erratic and NMC may need to stockpile it in a protected area for up to one year. The selling price of coal fines ranges from $15 to $24 per tonne and costs of preparing coal fines for sale range from $2 to $4 per tonne.

Required

1. Prepare an analysis to show whether it is more profitable for NMC to continue selling raw bulk coal or to process it further through sizing and cleaning. (Ignore coal fines in your analysis.)
2. How would your analysis be affected if the cost of producing raw coal could be held down to $20 per tonne?
3. Now consider the potential value of the coal fines and prepare an addendum that shows how their value affects the results of your analysis prepared in requirement 1.

LO 5 ▶
1. Total revenues under sales method, $668,000

🌐 **15-25 Accounting for a main product and a byproduct.** Crisps Inc. is a producer of potato chips. A single production process at Crisps Inc. yields potato chips as the main product and a byproduct that can also be sold as a snack. Both products are fully processed by the splitoff point, and there are no separable costs.

For September 2018, the cost of operations is $480,000. Production and sales data are as follows:

	Production (in kilograms)	Sales (in kilograms)	Selling Price per Kilogram
Main product: Potato chips	40,000	32,000	$20
Byproduct	8,000	5,600	5

There were no beginning inventories on September 1, 2018.

Required

1. What is the gross margin for Crisps Inc. under the production method and the sales method of byproduct accounting?
2. What are the inventory costs reported in the statement of financial position on September 30, 2018, for the main product and byproduct under the two methods of byproduct accounting in requirement 1?

LO 5 ▶
1. Net joint costs to be allocated = $$124,800

🌐 **15-26 Joint costs and byproducts.** Royston, Inc., is a large food-processing company. It processes 150,000 pounds of peanuts in the peanuts department at a cost of $180,000 to yield 12,000 pounds of product A, 65,000 pounds of product B, and 16,000 pounds of product C.

- Product A is processed further in the salting department at a cost of $27,000. It yields 12,000 pounds of salted peanuts, which are sold for $12 per pound.
- Product B (raw peanuts) is sold without further processing at $3 per pound.
- Product C is considered a byproduct and is processed further in the paste department at a cost of $12,000. It yields 16,000 pounds of peanut butter, which are sold for $6 per pound.

The company wants to make a gross margin of 10% of revenues on product C and needs to allow 20% of revenues for marketing costs on product C. An overview of operations follows:

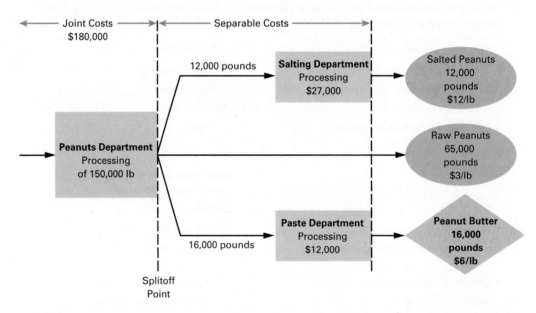

Required

1. Compute unit costs per pound for products A, B, and C, treating C as a byproduct. Use the NRV method for allocating joint costs. Deduct the NRV of the byproduct produced from the joint cost of products A and B.
2. Compute unit costs per pound for products A, B, and C, treating all three as joint products and allocating joint costs by the NRV method.

LO 2 ▶
1. a. Joint costs allocated to posts, $307,692

🌐 **15-27 Joint cost allocation, process further or sell.** Lanigan Lumber Inc. (Lanigan) purchases logs from independent timber contractors and processes the logs into three types of lumber products:

- Studs for residential buildings (walls, ceilings).
- Decorative pieces (fireplace mantels, beams for cathedral ceilings).
- Posts used as support braces (mine support braces, braces for exterior fences on ranch properties).

These products are the result of a joint sawmill process that involves removal of bark from the logs, cutting the logs into a workable size, and then cutting the individual products from the logs.

The joint process results in the following costs of products for a typical month:

Direct materials (rough timber logs)	$ 500,000
Debarking (labour and overhead)	50,000
Sizing (labour and overhead)	200,000
Product cutting (labour and overhead)	250,000
Total joint costs	$1,000,000

Product yields and average sales values on a per-unit basis from the joint process are as follows:

Product	Monthly Output of Materials at Splitoff Point	Fully Processed Selling Price
Studs	75,000 units	$ 8
Decorative pieces	5,000 units	100
Posts	20,000 units	20

The studs are sold as rough-cut lumber after emerging from the sawmill operation without further processing by Lanigan. Also, the posts require no further processing beyond the splitoff point. The decorative pieces must be planed and further sized after emerging from the sawmill. This additional processing costs $100,000 per month and normally results in a loss of 10% of the units entering the process. Without this planing and sizing process, there is still an active intermediate market for the unfinished decorative pieces in which the selling price averages $60 per unit.

Required

1. Based on the information given for Lanigan Lumber, allocate the joint processing costs of $1,000,000 to the three products using
   a. Sales value at splitoff method
   b. Physical measure method (volume in units)
   c. NRV method
2. Prepare an analysis that compares processing the decorative pieces further, as is current practice, with selling them as a rough-cut product immediately at splitoff.
3. Assume the company announced that in six months it will sell the unfinished decorative pieces at splitoff due to increasing competitive pressure. Identify at least three types of likely behaviour that will be demonstrated by the skilled labour in the planing-and-sizing process as a result of this announcement. Include in your discussion how this behaviour could be influenced by management.

Problems

🌐 **15-28 Alternative methods of joint-cost allocation, product-mix decisions.** The Chicago Oil ◀ LO 5
Company buys crude vegetable oil. Refining this oil results in four products at the splitoff point: A, B, C, and D. Product C is fully processed by the splitoff point. Products A, B, and D can individually be further refined into Super A, Super B, and Super D. In the most recent month (November), the output at the splitoff point was as follows:

- Product A, 550,000 gallons
- Product B, 200,000 gallons
- Product C, 150,000 gallons
- Product D, 100,000 gallons

The joint costs of purchasing and processing the crude vegetable oil were $210,000. Chicago had no beginning or ending inventories. Sales of product C in November were $90,000. Products A, B, and D were further refined and then sold. Data related to November are as follows:

	Separable Processing Costs to Make Super Products	Revenues
Super A	$480,000	$750,000
Super B	120,000	300,000
Super D	90,000	150,000

Chicago had the option of selling products A, B, and D at the splitoff point. This alternative would have yielded the following revenues for the November production:

- Product A, $150,000
- Product B, $125,000
- Product D, $135,000

Required

1. Compute the gross-margin percentage for each product sold in November, using the following methods for allocating the $210,000 joint costs:
   a. Sales value at splitoff
   b. Physical measure
   c. NRV
2. Could Chicago Oil have increased its November operating income by making different decisions about the further processing of products A, B, or D? Show the effect on operating income of any changes you recommend.

LO 2 ▶

1. Joint cost allocation for product C, 0.25

🌐 **15-29 Alternative methods of joint cost allocation, product-mix decisions.** The Sunshine Oil Company buys crude vegetable oil. Refining this oil results in four products at the splitoff point: A, B, C, and D. Product C is fully processed by the splitoff point. Products A, B, and D can individually be further refined into Super A, Super B, and Super D. In the most recent month (December), the output at the splitoff point was:

- Product A, 300,000 litres.
- Product B, 100,000 litres.
- Product C, 50,000 litres.
- Product D, 50,000 litres.

The joint costs of purchasing and processing the crude vegetable oil were $100,000. Sunshine had no beginning or ending inventories. Sales of product C in December were $50,000. Products A, B, and D were further refined and then sold. Data related to December are:

	Separable Processing Costs to Make Super Products	Sales
Super A	$200,000	$300,000
Super B	80,000	100,000
Super D	90,000	120,000

Sunshine had the option of selling products A, B, and D at the splitoff point. This alternative would have yielded the following revenues for the December production:

- Product A, $50,000.
- Product B, $30,000.
- Product D, $70,000.

Required

1. Compute the gross margin percentage for each product sold in December, using the following methods for allocating the $100,000 joint costs:
   a. Sales value at splitoff.
   b. Physical measure.
   c. NRV.
2. Could Sunshine have increased its December operating income by making different decisions about the further processing of products A, B, or D? Show the effect on operating income of any changes you recommend.

LO 2 ▶ 🌐 **15-30 Methods of joint-cost allocation, ending inventory.** Garden Labs produces a drug used for the treatment of arthritis. The drug is produced in batches. Chemicals costing $50,000 are mixed and heated, then a unique separation process extracts the drug from the mixture. A batch yields a total of 3,000 gallons of the chemicals. The first 2,500 gallons are sold for human use while the last 500 gallons, which contain impurities, are sold to veterinarians.

The costs of mixing, heating, and extracting the drug amount to $155,000 per batch. The output sold for human use is pasteurized at a total cost of $130,000 and is sold for $600 per gallon. The product sold to veterinarians is irradiated at a cost of $20 per gallon and is sold for $450 per gallon.

In March, Garden, which had no opening inventory, processed one batch of chemicals. It sold 2,000 gallons of product for human use and 300 gallons of the veterinarian product. Garden uses the net realizable value method for allocating joint production costs.

Required

1. How much in joint costs does Garden allocate to each product?
2. Compute the cost of ending inventory for each of Garden's products.
3. If Garden were to use the constant gross-margin percentage NRV method instead, how would it allocate its joint costs?
4. Calculate the gross margin on the sale of the product for human use in March under the constant gross-margin percentage NRV method.
5. Suppose that the separation process also yields 300 pints of a toxic byproduct. Garden currently pays a hauling company $6,000 to dispose of this byproduct. Garden is contacted by a firm interested in purchasing a modified form of this byproduct for a total price of $7,000. Garden estimates that it will cost about $35 per pint to do the required modification. Should Garden accept the offer?

🌐 **15-31 Accounting for a byproduct.** West-Coast Oceanic Water (WOW) desalinates and bottles sea water. The desalinated water is in high demand from a large group of environmentally conscious people on the west coast of Canada. During March, WOW processes 1,000 litres of sea water and obtains 1,000 litres of drinking water and 50 kilograms of sea salt (the rest of the sea water evaporates in the desalinization process). Processing the 1,000 litres of water costs WOW $1,500. WOW sells 600 litres of the desalinated water in 2-litre containers for $8 per container. In addition, WOW sells 40 kilograms of sea salt for $1.20 per kilogram. Due to the relatively small proportion of sea salt, WOW has decided to treat it as a byproduct.

◀ **LO 5**

1. Inventoriable cost of main product, $2.88 per container

Required

1. Assuming WOW accounts for the byproduct using the production method, what is the inventoriable cost for each product and WOW's gross margin?
2. Assuming WOW accounts for the byproduct using the sales method, what is the inventoriable cost for each product and WOW's gross margin?
3. Discuss the difference between the two methods of accounting for byproducts.

🌐 **15-32 Comparison of alternative joint-cost-allocation methods, further-processing decision, chocolate products.** The Rich and Creamy Edibles Factory manufactures and distributes chocolate products. It purchases cocoa beans and processes them into two intermediate products: chocolate-powder liquor base and milk-chocolate liquor base. These two intermediate products become separately identifiable at a single splitoff point. Every 600 pounds of cocoa beans yields 20 gallons of chocolate-powder liquor base and 60 gallons of milk-chocolate liquor base.

◀ **LO 1**

The chocolate-powder liquor base is further processed into chocolate powder. Every 20 gallons of chocolate-powder liquor base yield 680 pounds of chocolate powder. The milk-chocolate liquor base is further processed into milk chocolate. Every 60 gallons of milk-chocolate liquor base yield 1,100 pounds of milk chocolate.

Production and sales data for August 2017 are as follows (assume no beginning inventory):

■ Cocoa beans processed, 27,600 pounds
■ Costs of processing cocoa beans to splitoff point (including purchase of beans), $70,000

	Production	**Sales**	**Selling Price**	**Separable Processing Costs**
Chocolate powder	31,280 pounds	6,800 pounds	$8 per pound	$46,035
Milk chocolate	50,600 pounds	14,400 pounds	$9 per pound	$55,085

Rich and Creamy Edibles Factory fully processes both of its intermediate products into chocolate powder or milk chocolate. There is an active market for these intermediate products. In August 2017, Rich and Creamy Edibles Factory could have sold the chocolate-powder liquor base for $21 a gallon and the milk-chocolate liquor base for $28 a gallon.

Required

1. Calculate how the joint costs of $70,000 would be allocated between chocolate powder and milk chocolate under the following methods:
   a. Sales value at splitoff
   b. Physical measure (gallons)
   c. NRV
   d. Constant gross-margin percentage NRV
2. What are the gross-margin percentages of chocolate powder and milk chocolate under each of the methods in requirement 1?
3. Could Rich and Creamy Edibles Factory have increased its operating income by a change in its decision to fully process both of its intermediate products? Show your computations.

LO 5 ▶   🌐 **15-33 Joint-cost allocation.** SW Flour Company buys 1 input of standard flour and refines it using a special sifting process to 3 cups of baking flour and 9 cups of bread flour. In May 2017, SW bought 12,000 inputs of flour for $89,000. SW spent another $47,800 on the special sifting process.

SW puts the baking flour can be sold for $3.60 per cup and the bread flour for $4.80 per cup.

SW puts the baking flour through a second process so it is super fine. This costs an additional $1.00 per cup of baking flour and the process yields ½ cup of super-fine baking flour for every one cup of baking flour used. The super-fine baking flour sells for $9.60 per cup.

Required

1. Allocate the $136,800 joint cost to the super-fine baking flour and the bread flour using the following:
   a. Physical-measure method (using cups) of joint-cost allocation
   b. Sales value at splitoff method of joint-cost allocation
   c. NRV method of joint-cost allocation
   d. Constant gross-margin percentage NRV method of joint-cost allocation
2. Each of these measures has advantages and disadvantages; what are they?
3. Some claim that the sales value at splitoff method is the best method to use. Discuss the logic behind this claim.

LO 5 ▶   🌐 **15-34 Joint-cost allocation with a byproduct.** The Seattle Recycling Company (SRC) purchases old water and soda bottles and recycles them to produce plastic covers for outdoor furniture. The company processes the bottles in a special piece of equipment that first melts, then reforms the plastic into large sheets that are cut to size. The edges from the cut pieces are sold for use as package filler. The filler is considered a byproduct.

SRC can produce 25 table covers, 75 chair covers, and 5 pounds of package filler from 100 pounds of bottles.

In June, SRC had no beginning inventory. It purchased and processed 120,000 pounds of bottles at a cost of $600,000. SRC sold 25,000 table covers for $12 each, 80,000 chair covers for $8 each, and 5,000 pounds of package filler at $1 per pound.

Required

1. Assume that SRC allocates the joint costs to table and chair covers using the sales value at splitoff method and accounts for the byproduct using the production method. What is the ending inventory cost for each product and gross margin for SRC?
2. Assume that SRC allocates the joint costs to table and chair covers using the sales value at splitoff method and accounts for the byproduct using the sales method. What is the ending inventory cost for each product and gross margin for SRC?
3. Discuss the difference between the two methods of accounting for byproducts, focusing on what conditions are necessary to use each method.

LO 5 ▶   **15-35 Byproduct-costing journal entries** (continuation of 15-34). The accountant for SRC needs to record the information about the joint and byproducts in the general journal, but is not sure what the entries should be. The company has hired you as a consultant to help its accountant.

Required

1. Show journal entries at the time of production and at the time of sale assuming SRC accounts for the byproduct using the production method.
2. Show journal entries at the time of production and at the time of sale assuming SRC accounts for the byproduct using the sales method.

LO 1 ▶   **15-36 Joint-cost allocation, process further or sell.** Arnold Technologies manufactures a variety of flash memory chips at its main plant in Taiwan. Some chips are sold to makers of electronic equipment while others are embedded into consumer products for sale under Arnold's house label, AT. Three of the chips that Arnold produces arise from a common production process. The first chip, Amber, is sold to a maker of smartphones and personal computers. The second chip, Bronze, is intended for a wireless and broadband communication firm. The third chip, Cobalt, is used to manufacture and market a solid-state device under the AT name.

Data regarding these three products for the fiscal year ended April 30, 2017, are given below.

	Amber	Bronze	AT with Cobalt
Units produced	255,000	495,000	750,000
Selling price per unit at splitoff	$ 3.50	$ 2.00	—
Separable costs	—	—	$2,200,000
Final selling price per unit	—	—	$ 8.00

Arnold incurred joint product costs up to the splitoff point of $5,400,000 during the fiscal year.

The head of Arnold, Amanda Peterson, is considering a variety of alternatives that would potentially change the way the three products are processed and sold. Proposed changes for each product are as follows:

- Amber chips can be incorporated into Arnold's own memory stick. However, this additional processing causes a loss of 27,500 units of Amber. The separable costs to further process Amber chips are estimated to be $750,000 annually. The memory stick would sell for $5.50 per unit.
- Arnold's R&D unit has recommended that the company process Bronze further into a 3D vertical chip and sell it to a high-end vendor of datacenter products. The additional processing would cost $1,000,000 annually and would result in 15% more units of product. The 3D vertical chip sells for $4.00 per unit.
- The third chip is currently incorporated into a solid-state device under the AT name. Galaxy Electronics has approached Arnold with an offer to purchase this chip at the splitoff point for $2.40 per unit.

Required

1. Allocate the $5,400,000 joint production cost to Amber, Bronze, and AT with Cobalt using the NRV method.
2. Identify which of the three joint products Arnold should sell at the splitoff point in the future and which of the three the company should process further to maximize operating income. Support your decisions with appropriate computations.

15-37 Methods of joint-cost allocation, comprehensive. Kardash Cosmetics purchases flowers in bulk and processes them into perfume. From a certain mix of petals, the firm uses Process A to generate Seduction, its high-grade perfume, as well as a certain residue. The residue is then further treated, using Process B, to yield Romance, a medium-grade perfume. An ounce of residue typically yields an ounce of Romance. ◀ **LO 5**

In July, the company used 25,000 pounds of petals. Costs involved in Process A, i.e., reducing the petals to Seduction and the residue, were:

Direct Materials — $440,000; Direct Labour — $220,000; Overhead Costs — $110,000.

The additional costs of producing Romance in Process B were:

Direct Materials — $22,000; Direct Labour — $50,000; Overhead Costs — $40,000.

During July, Process A yielded 7,000 ounces of Seduction and 49,000 ounces of residue. From this, 5,000 ounces of Seduction were packaged and sold for $109.50 an ounce. Also, 28,000 ounces of Romance were processed in Process B and then packaged and sold for $31.50 an ounce. The other 21,000 ounces remained as residue. Packaging costs incurred were $137,500 for Seduction and $196,000 for Romance. The firm has no beginning inventory on July 1.

If it so desired, the firm could have sold unpackaged Seduction for $56 an ounce and the residue from Process A for $24 an ounce.

Required

1. What is the joint cost of the firm to be allocated to Seduction and Romance?
2. Under the physical measure method, how would the joint costs be allocated to Seduction and Romance?
3. Under the sales value at splitoff method, what portion of the joint costs would be allocated to Seduction and Romance, respectively?
4. What is the estimated net realizable value per ounce of Seduction and Romance?
5. Under the net realizable value method, what portion of the joint costs would be allocated to Seduction and Romance, respectively?
6. What is the gross margin percentage for the firm as a whole?
7. Allocate the joint costs to Seduction and Romance under the constant gross-margin percentage NRV method.
8. If you were the manager of Kardash Cosmetics, would you continue to process the petal residue into Romance perfume? Explain your answer.

Collaborative Learning Cases

15-38 Usefulness of joint cost allocation. In the United States, organ procurement organizations (OPOs), transplant centres, and the medical professions coordinate the organ donation process. The US government pays for this treatment through its Medicare program. What price should the US government pay for these organs from the taxes it collects from all citizens? Often multiple organs are removed from a single donor, meaning that there are joint costs such as operating room time, surgeons' fees, and medications to preserve the organs. The OPOs insist all costs be allocated to each organ, irrespective of whether the organ is actually collected for transplant. For example, lung and kidney donations may be planned, but ◀ **LO 1**

the surgeon discovers postmortem that the lungs are not viable. A portion of joint costs will still be assigned to the lungs; otherwise, total costs of the donation would be assigned to the kidneys.

The payer, the US government, does not want to pay the joint costs assigned to the lungs. The Medicare program pays only for transplanted organs. Over 62% of all kidney transplants are paid for by Medicare. Six years ago, a government audit revealed that, of the total of $80 million in organ acquisition costs, $47 million were unallowable and unsupported.[3]

Some organs, such as one kidney, part of a liver, part of a lung, bone marrow, and stem cells, can be recovered from live donors. The recovery of these organs requires major surgery and patients are anaesthetized. The surgeon ensures the donor's organs are suffused with a protective chemical and removes the organ. The donated organ is preserved in a chemical and placed in a refrigerated container for immediate transport. The donor often recovers after two to five days in hospital.

In contrast, stem cells are recovered from live donors who receive medication to increase the number of stem cells in the blood for four to five days prior to the transplant. The process is similar to a blood donation. The stem cells are extracted from whole blood removed intravenously from the donor's arm. The rest of the blood is returned to the donor while the stem cells are sealed in plastic packs, placed in a special container, and transported to the recipient. The donor usually returns home to rest for the remainder of the day before resuming normal life. The stem cells are injected intravenously into the recipient's arm.

Required

Form groups of two or more students to complete the following requirements.

1. Of the reasons to use acceptable methods to allocate joint costs, which ones are relevant in this case?
2. What costs are incurred beyond the splitoff point that differ between these two types of donations?
3. What would the separable costs be?
4. In Canada, where all medically necessary care is paid for from tax revenue, of what relevance is joint cost allocation?

LO 2 ▶

1. a. Total production costs of deluxe model, $19,694

15-39 Joint cost allocation. Flash Chip Company (FCC) produces memory modules in a two-step process: chip fabrication and module assembly.

In chip fabrication, each batch of raw silicon wafers yields 500 standard chips and 500 deluxe chips. Chips are classified as standard or deluxe on the basis of their density (the number of memory bits on each chip). Standard chips have 500 memory bits per chip, and deluxe chips have 1,000 memory bits per chip. Joint costs to process each batch are $24,000.

In module assembly, each batch of standard chips is converted into standard memory modules at a separately identified cost of $1,000 and then sold for $8,500. Each batch of deluxe chips is converted into deluxe memory modules at a separately identified cost of $1,500 and then sold for $25,000.

Required

1. Allocate joint costs of each batch to deluxe modules and standard modules using (a) the NRV method, (b) the constant gross margin percentage NRV method, and (c) the physical measure method, based on the number of memory bits. Which method should FCC use?
2. FCC can process each batch of 500 standard memory modules to yield 400 DRAM modules at an additional cost of $1,600. The selling price per DRAM module would be $26. Assume FCC uses the physical measure method. Should FCC sell the standard memory modules or the DRAM modules?

TRY IT! ▶

SOLUTIONS

Try It 15–1

(a)

Product	Units Produced	Percentage	Joint Costs	Allocated
Printing inks	15,000 litres	40 %	$480,000 =	$192,000
Varnishes	15,000 litres	40 %	480,000 =	192,000
Adhesives	7,500 litres	20 %	480,000 =	96,000
Totals	37,500 litres	100%		$480,000

---

[3] Department of Health and Human Services Centers for Medicare & Medicaid Services, "Ruling No.: CMS-1543-R," December 21, 2006; Department of Health and Human Services, Office of Inspector General, "Review of Organ Acquisition Costs Claimed by Certified Transplant Centers (A-09-05-00034)," September 28, 2006; and J. Warren, "CMS Enforcement of Rule Covering Organ Acquisition Fees Could Shut Down Some OPOs, Transplant Centers," *Transplant News*, April 28, 2003.

(b)

Product	Sales Value at Splitoff Point	Percentage	Joint Costs	Allocated
Printing inks	$120,000	50 %	$480,000 =	$240,000
Varnishes	72,000	30 %	480,000 =	144,000
Adhesives	48,000	20 %	480,000 =	96,000
Totals	$240,000	100%		$480,000

Try It 15–2

Product	Final Sales Value	Separable Costs	Net Realizable Value	Percentage
Ketchup	$2,400,000	$ 300,000	$2,100,000	30
Juice	4,375,000	875,000	3,500,000	50
Canned	2,000,000	600,000	1,400,000	20
Totals	$8,775,000	$1,775,000	$7,000,000	100

Product	Percentage	Joint Costs	Allocated	Separable Costs	Product Costs
Ketchup	30% ×	$2,086,000 =	$ 625,800 +	$300,000 =	$ 925,800
Juice	50% ×	2,086,000 =	1,043,000 +	875,000 =	1,918,000
Canned	20% ×	2,086,000 =	417,200 +	600,000 =	1,017,200

Cost per case: Ketchup = $925,800/100,000 = $9.26

Juice = $1,918,000/175,000 = $10.96

Canned = $1,017,200/200,000 = $5.09

Try It 15–3

The overall gross margin is the difference between the total estimated net realizable value ($7,000,000) and the joint costs ($2,086,000), or $4,914,000.

The gross margin percentage is $4,914,000/$8,775,000 = 56%.

Product	Final Sales Value	Less Gross Margin	Total Production Costs	Less Separable Costs	Joint Costs Allocated
Ketchup	$2,400,000	$1,344,000	$1,056,000	$ 300,000	$ 756,000
Juice	4,375,000	2,450,000	1,925,000	875,000	1,050,000
Canned	2,000,000	1,120,000	880,000	600,000	280,000
Totals	$8,775,000	$4,914,000	$3,861,000	$1,775,000	$2,086,000

16

Revenue and Customer Profitability Analysis

► Learning Outcomes

1. Select a method and allocate revenue from a product bundle to its distinct components.

2. Apply an activity-based costing (ABC) system to allocate costs when the customer is the cost object.

3. Calculate and interpret four levels of contribution margin variance analyses.

4. Generate a customer profitability profile.

5. Analyze relevant profitability data, and decide whether to drop or add customers or branches.

► CPA Competencies

This chapter covers material outlined in **Section 3: Management Accounting** of the CPA Competency Map. The Learning Objectives in this chapter have been aligned with the CPA Competency Map to ensure the best coverage possible.

3.2.1 Develops or evaluates information inputs for operational plans, budgets, and forecasts

3.2.2 Prepares, analyzes, or evaluates operational plans, budgets, and forecasts

3.2.3 Computes, analyzes, or assesses implications of variances

3.4.1 Evaluates sources and drivers of revenue growth

Revenue

Royalty contracts are by and large revenue-sharing contracts. Oil companies pay a percentage of revenue to governments from whom they lease mineral development rights. Publishers pay royalties to their authors. Recording companies pay royalties to recording artists.

Video games present a particularly challenging problem when it comes to revenue distribution. Games such as Minecraft® are sold across multiple platforms (Mac, Xbox 360 and One, PlayStation 4, as well as mobile devices) and in multiple countries.[1] With more than 75 million players around the world and over $1 billion in revenues, the question of how to share Minecraft® revenues between the original developers, the software distributors, and game console manufacturers is critical to all the parties involved in this hugely successful venture.

Government, too, allocates tax revenue to different ministries. In specific cases, such as gambling revenue, the government allocates contracted amounts to non-profit service organizations. The achievements of these non-profits are then measured by government relative to commitments the organizations have made. The government will continue to fund those which are effective and meet their commitments.

---

[1] J. Gaudiosi, "Mojang expands its Minecraft virtual empire brick by brick," CNNMoney (http://tech.fortune.cnn.com/2013/11/12/minecraft-mojang).

Revenue Allocation and Bundled Products

► **LO 1**

Select a method and allocate revenue from a product bundle to its distinct components.

Revenues are inflows of assets (almost always cash or accounts receivable) received for products or services provided to customers. Just as costs can be allocated to specific products, services, customers, or some other more relevant cost object, so too can revenues. **Revenue allocation** occurs when revenues must be assigned to distinct types of sales, but it is not economically feasible to trace the revenue (which would result in a more accurate assignment of revenues to products). The more accurate the assignment of revenue, the more reliable and relevant is the information on which many new product introductions and product-mix decisions are made.

Companies combine or create bundles (or suites) of outputs to generate more value added for customers without incurring added costs. In this way, the bundle responds to the desire for a customized product and at the same time provides the supplier with economies of scope.

Governments also use revenue-allocation formulas to distribute tax revenue to various programs such as university education and health care. Government determination of how revenue is allocated will make a significant difference to people who require those services. For example, the allocation of casino revenue retained by one First Nations band in Alberta (see Sustainability in Action box) illustrates how allocation can affect

Sustainability in Action | Revenue Allocation by the Government and First Nations

First Nations casinos on reserves in Alberta are regulated under the Alberta Gaming and Liquor Commission (AGLC). Gaming license fees pay for the commission's operating costs. Net of winnings paid, commissions, and a percentage paid to the federal government, the Alberta Lottery Fund (ALF), and the First Nations Development Fund Grant Program (FNDF) share the proceeds from slot machines. In 2009–2010, total proceeds from casinos were $234 million, of which some were First Nations casinos (see the first pie chart).

The government transfers responsibility and control of 30% of revenue distribution back to the FNDF. The AGLC retains the other 70%. The revenue flowing from gaming to First Nations groups is considered charitable gaming proceeds. The government regulates how these proceeds should be allocated by the First Nations groups. The second pie-chart illustrates the distribution by First Nations groups to safety, addiction treatment, subsidized housing and services, seniors and elder support, cultural events, and life skills training.

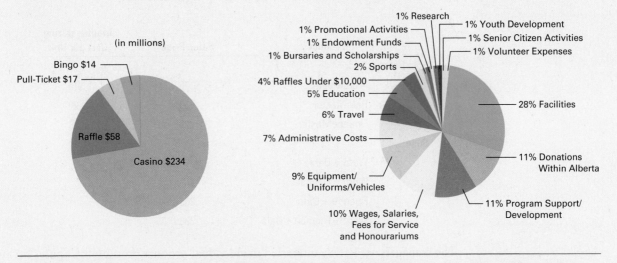

Source: Alberta Gaming Research Institute, "Revenue Allocation," May 1, 2007 (http://www.abgaminginstitute.ualberta.ca/Alberta_casinos_ revenue_allocation.cfm); Alberta Gaming Research Institute, "Quick Facts—Gaming," (http://www.gaming.gov.ab.ca/pdf/quickfacts/quickfacts_ gaming.pdf); Alberta Gaming and Liquor Commission, "Charitable Gaming in Review: Supporting Our Communities 2008–2009" (http://www.aglc.ca/ pdf/charitable_gaming/2008_2009_charitable_gaming_report.pdf); Alberta Gaming and Liquor Commission, "2009–2010 Charitable Gaming in Review" (http://www.aglc.ca/pdf/charitable_gaming/2009_2010_charitable_gaming_report.pdf, pp. 1, 14).

individuals in a group. The band retains about 30% of total casino revenue net of prizes paid out. This band then makes quarterly payments to its eligible beneficiaries, those agencies approved for funding by the government.

Internal revenue allocation arises when companies sell product bundles. A **product bundle** is a combination of two or more products or services sold together for a single price. For example, Shaw Communications bundles its high-speed internet access with its cable TV and telephone service at a price lower than if each service is sold separately. The bundled price is set to meet the customer's expectation of value-added, especially when competition is intense and companies are price takers.

The single price for the bundled product is typically less than the sum of the prices of the products in the bundle, should they be purchased separately. The company can be very profitable when a lower price drives higher consumer demand that requires a higher volume of production. The increased production gives rise to a lower unitized cost per output, which improves the company's gross margin percentage.

Deciding on a Revenue-Allocation Method

Where individual department or division managers have revenue or profit responsibilities for individual products, the issue is how to *fairly* allocate the bundled revenue amount among the individual products in the bundle. Let's look at an example. SG Company develops, sells, and supports three software packages both individually and as bundled products:

1. *WordMaster.* Current version is WordMaster 5.0, which was released 36 months ago. WordMaster was the company's initial product.

2. *DataMaster.* Current version is DataMaster. 3.0, which was released 18 months ago.

3. *FinanceMaster.* Current version is FinanceMaster 2.0. This product, the company's most recent addition, has been its most successful. The 2.0 version was released 2 months ago.

SG's management team must decide how to allocate revenue from its bundled product ("suite") sales. The team will decide between the two most common methods, which are the stand-alone and incremental revenue allocation methods. The team should choose the method that best reflects the economic reality of how much revenue each component generates. For internal purposes, the more representationally faithful the method, the higher the quality of information SG will have to make other operating decisions. SG's reliable MIS provides ready access to data for both unit prices and costs:

Product	Sales Price	Manufacturing Cost per Unit
Stand-alone		
WordMaster	$125	$18
DataMaster	150	20
FinanceMaster	225	25
Suite		
Word + Data	220	
Word + Finance	280	
Finance + Data	305	
Word + Finance + Data	380	

The managers are keenly interested in individual-product profitability figures because they operate separate profit centres for each product. Their performance evaluation and remuneration depend on profits at, or larger than, predicted (budgeted). SG's Software Department engineers are also organized on an individual product basis and receive a bonus based on percentage of product profitability. It is straightforward for managers to predict that if the revenue per unit decreases when their products are sold in a bundle, with no other change, their profit will decrease along with their remuneration. Strategically, bundling products can increase overall corporate profitability, but only if the bundling causes volumes to increase.

The stand-alone and incremental methods are two of the alternatives from which SG's management team can choose. Each method is analogous to cost allocation methods. After choosing, SG will be able to determine how well actual performance met expectations. In this way, they can learn how to improve performance and align incentives more appropriately.

Stand-Alone Revenue-Allocation Methods

The **stand-alone revenue-allocation method** is a weighted-average method. SG will use *product*-specific information about products in the bundle to determine the weights used to allocate the bundled revenues to each distinct product. The term *stand-alone* refers to the product as a separate (non-suite) item. There are alternative ways to calculate the weights.

The following are four of the more common allocation bases used:

■ Selling price of each (separate) unit in the bundle (suite)

■ Manufacturing cost of each unit in the bundle

■ Number of physical units of each type of product in the bundle

■ Product revenue for each product line in the bundle

The allocation base chosen (from the four listed above) creates the weighting (percentage) used to allocate the bundled price to each of the separate products. For simplicity's sake, the following example assumes a two-product bundle (WordMaster and FinanceMaster) that sells for $280.

1. *Selling prices.* The individual selling prices are used to calculate the percentage of the bundled price to allocate to that product. See the table below for details of the calculations.

   This method recognizes the different contribution to revenue made by each unit, but fails to recognize any difference in the stand-alone pricing policies or strategic classification of each product. One may be a commodity while the other may be a differentiated product. One may be the result of target pricing while the other may be the result of cost-plus pricing.

2. *Unit manufacturing costs.* The individual manufacturing costs are used to calculate the percentage of the bundled price to allocate to that product. See the table below for details of the calculations.

   This method will only be as reliable as the costing system used at SG; otherwise, SG runs the risk of unintentional cross-subsidization. Traditional single overhead cost pool systems often fail to reliably assign shared costs when there is unequal benefit to distinct products. This may result in one product being overcosted and the other undercosted.

3. *Physical units.* The number of physical units of each product that are included in the bundled suite are used to calculate the percentage of the bundled price to allocate to the individual products. In this case, since there is one unit of WordMaster and one unit of FinanceMaster in the bundled suite, there is an equal allocation (50/50) of the bundled price. See the table below for details of the calculations.

   This method has the benefit of simplicity, but it is not sensible if the products in a bundle have materially different unit sales prices. For example, selling a bundle made up of a dishwasher plus a box of detergent and then allocating the revenue per bundle 50/50 overweights the allocated detergent revenue and underallocates the dishwasher revenue. The disproportionate amount of cost compared to the revenue generated by the sale of a box of detergent is what makes this method inappropriate for this product bundle. This method would also be inappropriate when the retailer bundles products and services, such as special insurance with the product, because the components of the bundle are not both physical units.

4. *Total product-line revenues.* Total product-line revenues capture the quantity of each product sold as well as the selling price of the individual products. Assume that the

product-line revenue is $28 million for WordMaster and $7 million for FinanceMaster. These revenues will be used to calculate the percentage of the bundled price to allocate to the individual products. See the table below for details of the calculations.

Product-line revenues are a good indicator of the overall popularity of each individual product. This may be a reasonable way to allocate the bundled revenues if one believes that the more popular product (in terms of total revenues) will positively impact the sales of the bundled products and, therefore, should be allocated a larger portion of the bundled revenues. However, if the products are at different points in their product life cycle, this may not be an appropriate method to allocate the bundled revenues. For example, if the lower product-line revenue attributed to FinanceMaster is, in part, due to its being released only two months ago, then the total product-line revenue method would be judged to be unfair. It may be the case that the unit selling price weights are the best available external indicators of the benefits received from the various products in the bundles. Market-based weights (e.g., total revenues or individual selling prices) place products in their external competitive context, which would support the firm's strategic intent.

These four approaches to determining weights with the stand-alone method yield the following revenue allocations to individual products:

| | | | $280 Bundled Price Allocation | |
Allocation Basis	Product Specific Information	Calculations	WordMaster	FinanceMaster
Selling price	WordMaster, $125*	Word: $\dfrac{\$125}{\$125 + \$225} \times \$280 = 0.357 \times \$280 = \$100$	$100	
	FinanceMaster, $225*	Finance: $\dfrac{\$225}{\$125 + \$225} \times \$280 = 0.643 \times \$280 = \$180$		$180
Unit manufacturing cost	WordMaster, $18*	Word: $\dfrac{\$18}{\$18 + \$25} \times \$280 = 0.419 \times \$280 = \$117$	117	
	FinanceMaster, $25*	Finance: $\dfrac{\$25}{\$18 + \$25} \times \$280 = 0.581 \times \$280 = \$163$		163
Physical units	WordMaster, 1.0 unit	Word: $\dfrac{1}{1 + 1} \times \$280 = 0.50 \times \$280 = \$140$	140	
	FinanceMaster, 1.0 unit	Finance: $\dfrac{1}{1 + 1} \times \$280 = 0.50 \times \$280 = \$140$		140
Product line revenues	Wordmaster, $28 million	Word: $\dfrac{\$28 \text{ million}}{\$28 \text{ million} + \$7 \text{ million}} \times \$280 = 0.80 \times \$280 = \$224$	224	
	FinanceMaster, $7 million	Finance: $\dfrac{\$7 \text{ million}}{\$28 \text{ million} + \$7 \text{ million}} \times \$280 = 0.20 \times \$280 = \$56$		56

*Provided in previous table.

If SG has a cost-plus pricing policy, then unit manufacturing costs may be the best choice. If SG has a target pricing policy, then product-line revenues may be the best choice. Each choice will be consistent with internal pricing policies. The method that reflects the economic reality of what each product contributes to SG's profitability, consistent with the competitive intensity and SG's strategy, will be the best guide in this management decision.

Incremental Revenue-Allocation Method

The **incremental revenue-allocation method** ranks the individual products in a bundle and then uses this ranking to allocate the bundled revenues to these individual products. The first-ranked product is termed the *primary product* in the bundle, the second-ranked product is termed the *first incremental product*, the third-ranked product is the *second incremental product*, and so on.

How is the ranking of products in the incremental revenue-allocation method determined? One approach is to survey customers on the relative importance of individual products in their decision to purchase the bundled products. A second approach is to use internal data on recent stand-alone performance of the individual products in the bundle. A third approach is for top management to decide the rankings based on their knowledge or intuition.

Consider again the pricing of the Word and Finance suite. Assume WordMaster is designated as the primary product. If the suite revenue exceeds the stand-alone revenue of the primary product, the primary product is allocated 100% of its stand-alone revenue. This is the case for the Word and Finance suite. The suite revenue of $280 exceeds the stand-alone revenue of $125 for WordMaster; WordMaster is allocated revenues of $125, with the remaining or residual revenue of $155 (= $280 − $125) allocated to FinanceMaster:

Product	Revenue Allocated	Cumulative Revenue Allocated
WordMaster	$125	$125
FinanceMaster ($280 − $125)	155	280
Total	$280	

Clearly, the ranking of the individual products in the suite is a key factor in determining the revenues allocated to individual products. Under the incremental revenue-allocation method, all managers of the revenue object want to be the first-ranked user, because the first-ranked user will be allocated a larger portion of the revenues. If FinanceMaster were the primary product, the revenue allocated would be $225 (stand-alone sales price), not $155, and WordMaster would be allocated $55, not $125. The differences between these two allocations are material for managers who may be paid on the basis of new revenue generated or total revenue generated. This is called a **zero-sum game**, which is where what one gains, the other loses. This is another example where the purpose of allocation must be clear and one allocation method is not satisfactory to achieve all purposes.

One approach to solving the problem of who gets ranked as the primary product (and thus, gets the largest share of the allocated revenue) is the *Shapley value method*. It allocates an average of the possible allocated revenues based under different scenarios (i.e., what revenue would the product get if it were ranked primary, first incremental, second incremental, and so on). If SG sells *equal* quantities of WordMaster and FinanceMaster, then the *Shapley value* method allocates the average of the revenues allocated as the primary and first incremental products:

$$\text{WordMaster:} \quad \frac{\$125 + \$55}{2} = \$180 \div 2 = \$90$$

$$\text{FinanceMaster:} \quad \frac{\$225 + \$155}{2} = \$380 \div 2 = \$190$$

$$\text{Total} \qquad\qquad\qquad = \$280$$

But what if the sales quantities are not equal? For example, in the most recent quarter, SG sells 80,000 units of WordMaster and 20,000 units of FinanceMaster. Because SG sells four times as many units of WordMaster, its managers believe that the sales of the Word and Finance suite are four times more likely to be driven by WordMaster as the primary product. The *weighted Shapley value* method takes this into account by weighting the revenue allocations when WordMaster is the primary product four times as much as when FinanceMaster is the primary product:

$$\text{WordMaster:} \quad \frac{(\$125 \times 4) + (\$55 \times 1)}{(4 + 1)} = \frac{\$555}{5} = \$111$$

$$\text{FinanceMaster:} \quad \frac{(\$225 \times 1) + (\$155 \times 4)}{(4 + 1)} = \frac{\$845}{5} = \$169$$

$$\text{Total} \qquad\qquad\qquad\qquad = \$280$$

When there are more than two products in the suite, the incremental revenue-allocation method allocates suite revenues sequentially. Assume WordMaster is the primary product in SG's three-product suite (Word + Finance + Data). FinanceMaster is the first incremental product, and DataMaster is the second incremental product. This suite sells for $380. The allocation of the $380 suite revenues proceeds as follows:

Product	Revenue Allocated	Cumulative Revenue Allocated
WordMaster	$125	$125
FinanceMaster ($280 – $125)	155	$280 (price of Word + Finance suite)
DataMaster ($380 – $280)	100	$380 (price of Word + Finance + Data suite)
Total	$380	

Now, instead, suppose WordMaster is the primary product, DataMaster is the first incremental product, and FinanceMaster is the second incremental product:

Product	Revenue Allocated	Cumulative Revenue Allocated
WordMaster	$125	$125
DataMaster ($220 – $125)	95	$220 (price of Word + Data suite)
FinanceMaster ($380 – $220)	160	$380 (price of Word + Data + Finance suite)
Total	$380	

The ranking of the individual products in the suite determines the revenues allocated to them. Product managers at SG would likely differ on how they believe their individual products contribute to sales of the suite products. It is possible that each product manager would claim to be responsible for the primary product in the Word and Finance and Data suite!

Calculating the *Shapley value* mitigates this problem because each product is considered as a primary, first-incremental, and second-incremental product. *Assuming equal weights* on all products, the revenue allocated to each product is an average of the revenues calculated for each product under these different assumptions: FinanceMaster, $180; WordMaster, $87.50; and DataMaster, $112.50:

Product Ranking			Revenues Allocated to Each Product		
FinanceMaster	WordMaster	DataMaster	FinanceMaster	WordMaster	DataMaster
Primary	1st Incremental	2nd Incremental	$225	$ 55	$100
				($280 – $225)	($380 – $225 – $55)
Primary	2nd Incremental	1st Incremental	$225	$ 75	$ 80
				($380 – $225 – $80)	($305 – $225)
1st Incremental	Primary	2nd Incremental	$155	$125	$100
			($280 – $125)		($380 – $125 – $155)
2nd Incremental	Primary	1st Incremental	$160	$125	$ 95
			($380 – $125 – $95)		($220 – $125)
1st Incremental	2nd Incremental	Primary	$155	$ 75	$150
			($305 – $150)	($380 – $150 – $155)	
2nd Incremental	1st Incremental	Primary	$160	$ 70	$150
			($380 – $150 – $70)	($220 – $150)	
Total:			$1,080	$525	$675
Average Revenue Allocated:			$1,080 ÷ 6 = $180	$525 ÷ 6 = $87.50	$675 ÷ 6 = $112.50

In contrast, because the stand-alone revenue-allocation method does not require rankings of individual products in the suite, that method is less likely to cause debates among product managers. An inappropriate method will bias and degrade the usefulness of internal information for decision making. In the design of a defensible internal control system, it is essential to assess allocation method choices to ensure good corporate governance.

Not one of the methods, however, changes the economic reality that any bundled suite of products will generate a lower unit sales price *per product* than the revenue generated when products are sold individually. The techniques of revenue allocation fail to resolve the incentives problem. SG must encourage managers to accept and willingly promote sales of the suite, which aligns with corporate profitability even at the (possible) expense of maximizing their personal remuneration. Otherwise, the gain in corporate profit will be very short-term as the best managers and software engineers leave SG to work for its competitors.

Other Revenue-Allocation Methods

Management's judgment is an alternative method of revenue allocation. The difficulty is in ensuring that the method is defensible by the CEO and CFO, who must provide written assurance of the quality of internal control. For example, the president of one software company decided to issue a set of revenue-allocation weights because the managers of the three products in the bundle could not agree.

The factors the president considered included stand-alone selling prices (all three were very similar), stand-alone unit sales (A and B were over 10 times more than C), product ratings by independent experts, and consumer awareness. The Product C manager complained that his 10% weighting dramatically short-changed the contribution of Product C to suite revenues. The president responded that its inclusion in the suite greatly increased consumer exposure to Product C, with the result that Product C's total revenues would be far larger (even with only 10% of suite revenues) than had it not been included in the suite at all.

ABC: The Cost Object is the Customer

▶ **LO 2**

Apply an activity-based costing (ABC) system to allocate costs when the customer is the cost object.

Managers solve problems—where there are no problems there is no need to manage anything. We have assumed for our next example that the company Spring Distribution, which sells bottled water, has decided upon a cost leadership strategy. The management team at Spring Distribution makes decisions as they receive feedback on how successfully they have implemented their cost leadership strategy.

Spring Distribution has two distinct distribution channels: (1) a wholesale distribution channel, in which the wholesaler sells to supermarkets, drugstores, and other stores, and (2) a retail distribution channel for a small number of business customers. Consistent with its cost leadership strategy, the company has an ABC system. The system has improved the management team's understanding of how the overhead costs of shared resources can be assigned proportionally to benefits provided to each distinct customer service.

The MIS can also provide data that enables Spring Distribution to assign the overhead cost pools proportionally to the benefits received by its customers. By selecting the customer as a cost object, the management team can rank their customers in order of total costs to provide services to each. We begin by analyzing ABC customer cost assignment, then proceed to revenue analysis to determine customer profitability. The cost object is neither an output nor an activity but rather a customer.

Customer ABC Analysis

In the *cost hierarchy* concept, costs are categorized into different cost pools arising from shared use of common resources (overhead). The beneficiaries sharing the resources can be distinguished because they do not share equally. The cost allocation base or cost driver for each cost pool measures the amount of benefit received. In an ABC system where the customer is the cost object, shared costs are classified into five categories:

1. *Customer output unit-level costs*—costs of activities to sell each output unit to a customer. An example for Spring is product-handling costs of each case sold.

2. *Customer batch-level costs*—costs of activities that are related to a group of units (cases) sold to a customer. Examples are costs incurred to process orders or to make Spring's two types of deliveries.

3. *Customer-sustaining costs*—costs of activities to support individual customers, regardless of the number of units or batches of product delivered to the customer. Examples are the downstream costs of visits to customers or costs of displays at customer sites after Spring's distribution activity.

4. *Distribution-channel costs*—costs of activities related to a particular distribution channel rather than to each unit of product, each batch of product, or specific customers. An example is the salary of the manager of Spring's retail distribution channel.

5. *Facility/corporate-sustaining costs*—costs of activities that cannot be traced to individual customers or distribution channels. Examples are top-management and general-administration costs.

Spring uses its customer-cost hierarchy to assist managers in decisions made at different levels in this hierarchy. We will now consider decisions made at the *individual customer level*. Note from these descriptions that four of the five levels of Spring's cost hierarchy closely parallel the cost hierarchy described in Chapter 5, except that Spring focuses on customers, whereas the cost hierarchy in Chapter 5 focused on products. Spring has one additional cost hierarchy category: distribution-channel costs, for the costs it incurs to support its wholesale and retail distribution channels.

First consider customer revenues. Data from Spring Distribution's MIS for four customers are reported for June 2018 in Exhibit 16-1. One observation from these data suggests that Spring Distribution should track future sales to Customer G to confirm that the $1.20-per-case discount translates into higher future sales. Managers find customer profitability analysis useful for several reasons. First, it frequently highlights how vital a small set of customers is to total profitability. Managers need to ensure that the interests of these customers receive high priority. Microsoft uses the phrase "not all revenue dollars are endowed equally in profitability" to stress this key point. Second, when a customer is ranked in the "loss category," managers can focus on ways to make future business with this customer more profitable.

Spring is particularly interested in analyzing customer-level indirect costs that are incurred in the first three categories of the customer-cost hierarchy: customer output unit-level costs, customer batch-level costs, and customer-sustaining costs. Spring believes that it can work with customers to reduce these costs. It believes that customer actions will have less impact on distribution-channel and corporate-sustaining costs.

Exhibit 16-1 Customer Profitability Analysis for Four Customers of Spring Distribution for June 2018

	A	B	C	D	E
1		CUSTOMER			
2		A	B	G	J
3	Units sold	42,000	33,000	2,900	2,500
4	List selling price	$ 14.40	$ 14.40	$ 14.40	$ 14.40
5	Price discount	0.96	0.24	1.20	—
6	Invoice price	$ 13.44	$ 14.16	$ 13.20	$ 14.40
7	Revenues (Row 3 × Row 6)	$564,480	$467,280	$38,280	$36,000

The five activity areas used to collect costs for selling-related costs, cost drivers, and rates are as follows:

Activity Area	Cost Rate and Driver	Cost Hierarchy Category
Product handling	$0.50 per case sold	Customer output-unit-level costs
Order taking	100 per purchase order	Customer batch-level costs
Delivery vehicles	2 per delivery kilometre traveled	Customer batch-level costs
Rush deliveries	300 per expedited delivery	Customer batch-level costs
Visits to customers	80 per sales visit	Customer-sustaining costs

The table below provides information on the quantity of cost driver consumed or used by each customer:

	Customer			
	A	B	G	J
Number of purchase orders	30	25	15	10
Number of deliveries	60	30	20	15
Kilometres traveled per delivery	5	12	20	6
Number of rush deliveries	1	—	2	—
Number of visits to customers	6	5	4	3

Spring Distribution can use the information on ABC in Exhibit 16-2 to assist its customers in reducing their consumption of the cost drivers. Consider a comparison of Customer G with Customer A: Customer G's total purchases (2,900 cases) are only 7% the size of Customer A's total purchases (42,000 cases). Customer G, however, requires one-half the number of purchase orders, two-thirds the number of visits, one-third the number of deliveries, and double the number of rush deliveries. To improve the profitability of Customer G, Spring must encourage this customer to request fewer customer visits and rush deliveries as well as larger but fewer purchases.

Exhibit 16-2 Customer Profitability Analysis for Four Customers of Spring Distribution for June 2018

	A	B	C	D	E
1			CUSTOMER		
2		A	B	G	J
3	Revenues at list price: $14.40 × 42,000; 33,000; 2,900; 2,500	$604,800	$475,200	$41,760	$36,000
4	Price discount: $0.96 × 42,000; $0.24 × 33,000; $1.20 × 2,900; $0 × 2,500	40,320	7,920	3,480	—
5	Revenues at actual price	564,480	467,280	38,280	36,000
6	Cost of goods sold: $12 × 42,000; 33,000; 2,900; 2,500	504,000	396,000	34,800	30,000
7	Gross margin	60,480	71,280	3,480	6,000
8	Customer-level operating costs				
9	Product handling: $0.50 × 42,000; 33,000; 2,900; 2,500	21,000	16,500	1,450	1,250
10	Order taking: $100 × 30; 25; 15; 10	3,000	2,500	1,500	1,000
11	Delivery vehicles: $2 × (5 × 60); (12 × 30); (20 × 20); (6 × 15)	600	720	800	180
12	Rush deliveries: $300 × 1; 0; 2; 0	300	—	600	—
13	Visits to customers: $80 × 6; 5; 4; 3	480	400	320	240
14	Total customer-level operating costs	25,380	20,120	4,670	2,670
15	Customer-level operating income	$ 35,100	$ 51,160	$(1,190)	$ 3,330

Exhibit 16-3 Operating Income Statement for Spring Distribution in 2018

	A	B	C	D	E	F	G	H	I	J	K	L	M	N
1		CUSTOMER DISTRIBUTION CHANNELS												
2		Wholesale Customers						Retail Customers						
3		Total	Total	A1	A2	A3	•	Total	Aa		Ba		Ga	Ja
4		(1) = (2) + (7)	(2)	(3)	(4)	(5)	(6)	(7)	(8)		(9)		(10)	(11)
5	Revenues (at actual prices)	$12,138,120	$10,107,720	$1,946,000	$1,476,000	•	•	$2,030,400	$564,480		$467,280		•	•
6	Customer-level costs	11,633,760	9,737,280	1,868,000	1,416,000	•	•	1,896,480	529,380	b	416,120	b	•	•
7	Customer-level operating income	504,360	370,440	$ 78,000	$ 60,000	•	•	133,920	$ 35,100		$ 51,160		•	•
8	Distribution-channel costs	160,500	102,500					58,000						
9	Distribution-channel operating income	343,860	$ 267,940					$ 75,920						
10	Corporate-sustaining costs	263,000												
11	Operating income	$ 80,860												
12														
13	aFull details are presented in Exhibit 16-2.													
14	bCost of goods sold + Total customer-level operating costs from Exhibit 16-2.													
15	• Indicates that the data has been omitted in order to condense the exhibit.													

The ABC system underlying Exhibit 16-2 provides a road map to facilitate less use of cost drivers by a customer to promote cost reduction. Another advantage of ABC is that it highlights a second way cost reduction can be promoted by Spring Distribution—Spring can take actions to reduce the costs in each of its own activity areas. For example, order taking currently is estimated to cost $100 per purchase order. By making its own ordering process more efficient (such as having its customers order electronically), Spring can reduce its costs even if its customers make the same number of orders.

Exhibit 16-3 reports Spring Distribution's monthly operating income. The hierarchical format in Exhibit 16-3 distinguishes among various degrees of objectivity when allocating costs, and it dovetails with the different levels at which decisions are made and performance is evaluated. The issue of when and what costs to allocate is another example of the "different costs to match the economic facts" idea emphasized throughout the text.

The customer-level operating incomes of Customers A and B in Exhibit 16-2 are shown in columns I and K of Exhibit 16-3. In contrast to this presentation, some managers and management accountants advocate fully allocating all costs to customers and distribution channels so that

- The sum of operating incomes of all customers in a distribution channel (segment) equals the operating income of the distribution channel.

- The sum of the distribution-channel operating incomes equals companywide operating income.

The justification is that customers and products must eventually be profitable on a full-product (or service) cost basis. For some decisions, such as pricing, allocating all costs ensures that long-run prices are set at a level to cover the cost of all resources used to produce and sell products. In an intensely competitive environment, Spring Distribution's management team would likely choose a target pricing policy. As a price taker, this would ensure Spring would not lose profitable customers because it mispriced its distribution service.

Consider corporate-sustaining costs such as top-management and general-administration costs. Spring's managers have concluded that there is neither a cause-and-effect nor a benefits-received relationship between any cost-allocation base and corporate-sustaining costs. Consequently, allocation of corporate-sustaining costs serves no useful purpose in decision making, performance evaluation, or motivation. For example, suppose Spring allocated the $263,000 of corporate-sustaining costs to its distribution channels: $173,000 to the wholesale channel and $90,000 to the retail channel. Using information from Exhibit 16-3, the retail channel would then show a loss of $14,080 (= $75,920 − $90,000).

If this situation persisted in subsequent months, should Spring shut down the retail distribution channel? No, because if retail distribution were discontinued, corporate-sustaining costs would be unaffected. Allocating corporate-sustaining costs to distribution channels could give the misleading impression that the $14,080 loss could be avoided if the retail channel was discontinued. A similar argument could also be made about the danger of allocating the distribution channel costs out to the individual customers. Given that many of the distribution-channel costs are fixed and not responsive to changes in individual customer volume, it could be misleading to allocate the costs to individual customers, discover that it now looks like one of the customers is unprofitable, and then drop the customer only to realize that the distribution-channel costs haven't changed and now must be covered by fewer customers.

16.1 TRY IT! ⊕

Dexter Inc. has only two retail and two wholesale customers. Information relating to each customer for 2016 follows:

	Wholesale Customers		Retail Customers	
	West Region Wholesaler	East Region Wholesaler	Hudson Inc.	Pentel Corp
Revenues at list prices	$750,000	$1,180,000	$350,000	$260,000
Discounts from list prices	51,600	79,200	19,800	6,180
Cost of goods sold	570,000	1,020,000	298,000	190,000
Delivery costs	29,100	23,420	16,460	14,290
Order processing costs	12,640	16,960	9,360	7,260
Cost of sales visit	12,600	10,240	9,240	8,150

Required
Calculate customer-level operating income.

Contribution Margin Variance Analyses

In this section we will calculate variances that use revenue and contribution margin information as a key input. Profitability analysis requires thorough understanding of the causes of both revenue and costs. The finer or more detailed the analyses of what caused unexpected outcomes, the more relevant the information available to managers who must remedy the situation.

Selling-price variances are only reflected on the flexible budget side of a variance analysis since there is no selling-price variance on the sales-volume side of the variance analysis. When looking at the sales-volume side of a variance analysis, it is possible to look at changes in revenues and the subsequent impact on operating income, but you would also have to take into account the corresponding changes in costs in order to have any clear picture of the impact on the firm's operating income. Since both revenues and costs are at their budgeted amounts on the sales-volume side of the analysis, it is just as easy (and more directly informative) to use a contribution margin analysis (selling price less variable costs)

▶ **LO 3**

Calculate and interpret four levels of contribution margin variance analyses.

instead of a revenue analysis. This is true because, on the sales-volume side of the analysis, the fixed costs don't change with different levels of sales, so any change in contribution margin will have a direct (and equal) effect on the operating income.

Spring's MIS separates all variable customer-level costs from distribution-channel and corporate-sustaining costs, which are classified as fixed costs. To simplify the sales-variance analysis and calculations, we assume that all Spring's variable costs are variable with respect to units (cases) sold. One consequence is that average batch sizes remain the same as the total cases sold vary. Without this assumption, the analysis would become more complex and would have to be done using the ABC-variance analysis approach.

Two variables explain revenue differences across the four customers presented in Exhibits 16-1 and 16-2: (1) the volume of bottles purchased and (2) the magnitude of price discounting.

Price discounting is the reduction of selling prices below listed levels to encourage an increase in purchases by customers. It is important to remember that the management team has selected a cost leadership strategy that requires minimizing cost. When customers set price, the company that delivers on the value proposition at the least cost will have a higher profit. Spring Distribution's management team could engage in a price war to capture volume, but this is extremely risky in a competitive market. Assuming that this company is a cost leader, price discounting can only hurt profit as its competitors retaliate by lowering their price to match or beat that of Spring Distribution.

Price discounts are a function of multiple factors, including

- sales volume purchased by that customer (more volume usually means more discount)
- desirability of attracting a specific customer (discounts can be used as incentives)
- current market conditions (discounts can allow for temporary price adjustments that don't change the regular, listed price)

At no time should price discounts run afoul of the law by way of price discrimination, predatory pricing, or collusive pricing. Price discounts can also be unethical—for example, when discounts are given by pharmaceutical representatives to doctors to encourage them to prescribe a particular drug. That said, price discounts can be an effective tool to attract price-sensitive customers without having to revert to "across-the-board," publicly announced cuts to the product's list price.

Companies that record only the invoice price in their information system would not be able to readily track the magnitude of their price discounting (except in the extreme case of a single-product company with a constant list price in the accounting period).[2] In the Spring example below, the price discounting shows up as a cost. This is because sales discounts are a contra-account to sales, and therefore the discount has a debit balance (opposite to the revenue/sales account's credit balance). In a variance analysis situation, the sales discount account's debit balance is reflected as a cost of the unit being sold. In the table below, we can see that the actual variable cost of the retail channel is $13.17 per unit versus the budgeted cost of $13.12. In this situation, this extra cost is due to the price discounting in the retail channel. While the difference is subtle, a change in the selling price (say, due to changes in the overall market conditions) should be reflected as a selling price variance, while price discounts being offered should be reflected as an expense (or contra-revenue) and analyzed accordingly. Tracking discounts by customer, and by salesperson, can provide valuable information about ways to improve customer profitability. For example, companies may institute a corporate policy to ensure that any volume-based price discounting policy is enforced for customers with decreasing volume as well as those with increasing volume. It may also require its salespeople to obtain approval before giving large discounts to customers not normally qualifying for them. In addition, it could track the future sales of customers that its salespeople argue warrant a sizable price discount due to their predicted "high growth potential."

---

[2] Further analysis of customer revenues could distinguish between gross revenues and net revenues. This approach would highlight differences across customers in sales returns. Additional discussion of ways to analyze revenue differences across customers is in R.S. Kaplan and R. Cooper, *Cost and Effect* (Boston, Mass.: Harvard Business School Press, 1998), Chapter 10.

The following information, from Spring Distribution's MIS, will be used to calculate several variances for the company. Budget and actual data for June 2018 are shown in the table below:

	Budget Data for June 2018					
	Selling Price per Unit (1)	Variable Cost per Unit (2)	Contribution Margin per Unit (3) = (1) − (2)	Sales Volume in Units (4)	Sales Mix (Based on Units) (5)	Contribution Margin (6) = (3) × (4)
Wholesale channel	$13.37	$12.88	$0.49	712,000	80%[a]	$348,880
Retail channel	14.10	13.12	0.98	178,000	20%	174,440
Total				890,000	$100%	$523,320

"Unit" in the column headings refers to a case of 24 bottles
[a]Percentage of unit sales to wholesale channel = 712,000 units ÷ 890,000 total units = 80%.

	Actual Data for June 2018					
	Selling Price per Unit (1)	Variable Cost per Unit (2)	Contribution Margin per Unit (3) = (1) − (2)	Sales Volume in Units (4)	Sales Mix (Based on Units) (5)	Contribution Margin (6) = (3) × (4)
Wholesale channel	$13.37	$12.88	$0.49	756,000	84%	$370,440
Retail channel	14.10	13.17	0.93	144,000	16%	133,920
Total				900,000	100%	$504,360

Static-Budget Contribution Margin Variance

Recall from Chapter 7 that the *static-budget contribution margin variance* is calculated as

Static-budget contribution margin variance = Actual results – Static budget amount

Our analysis focuses on the difference between actual and budgeted contribution margins (column 6 in the preceding tables). The total static-budget variance is $18,960 U (actual contribution margin of $504,360 − budgeted contribution margin of $523,320). Managers can gain more insight about the static-budget variance by subdividing it into the flexible-budget variance and the sales-volume variance.

Flexible-Budget and Sales-Volume Contribution Margin Variances

Flexible-Budget Variance

The *flexible-budget contribution margin variance* is a Level 2 variance calculated as:

Flexible-budget contribution margin variance = Actual results − Flexible-budget amount

The flexible-budget variance is the difference between an actual result and the corresponding flexible-budget amount based on actual output level in the budget period. The flexible-budget contribution margin (CM) is equal to budgeted CM per unit (case) times actual units (cases) sold of each product. Exhibit 16-4, column D, shows the flexible-budget calculations. The flexible budget measures the CM that Spring would have budgeted for the actual quantities of cases sold. The flexible-budget variance is the difference between columns B and D in Exhibit 16-4.

Recall that the levels of detail introduced in Chapter 7 included the static-budget variance (Level 1), the flexible-budget variance (Level 2), and the sales-volume variance (Level 2). The sales-volume variance can be further separated into sales-mix and sales-quantity variance, which are Level 3 variances.[3] Exhibit 16-4 illustrates how to reconcile

---

[3] The presentation of the variances in this chapter draws on teaching notes prepared by J.K. Harris.

Exhibit 16-4 Flexible-Budget and Sales-Volume Contribution Margin Variance Analysis of Spring Distribution for June 2018

	A	B	C	D	E	F	G
1		Actual Results:		Flexible Budget:		Static Budget:	
2		Actual Units of		Actual Units of		Budgeted Units of	
3		All Products Sold ×		All Products Sold ×		All Products Sold ×	
4		Actual Sales Mix ×		Actual Sales Mix ×		Budgeted Sales Mix ×	
5		Actual Contribution		Budgeted Contribution		Budgeted Contribution	
6		Margin per Unit		Margin per Unit		Margin per Unit	
7		(1)		(2)		(3)	
8	Wholesale	900,000 × 0.84 × $0.49 =	$370,440	900,000 × 0.84 × $0.49 =	$370,440	890,000 × 0.80 × $0.49 =	$348,880
9	Retail	900,000 × 0.16 × $0.93 =	133,920	900,000 × 0.16 × $0.98 =	141,120	890,000 × 0.20 × $0.98 =	174,440
10			$504,360		$511,560		$523,320
11			↑	$7,200 U	↑	$11,760 U	↑
12	Level 2			Flexible-budget CM variance		Sales-volume CM variance	
13			↑		$ 18,960	U	↑
14	Level 1			Static-budget CM variance			
15							
16							

Levels 1 and 2 CM variance analyses for the current sales mix of products sold through the two distribution channels.

The key difference between columns B and D is that actual units sold of each product is multiplied by actual CM per unit in column B and budgeted CM per unit in column D. The $7,200 U flexible-budget variance arises because actual CM on retail sales of $0.93 per case is lower than the budgeted amount of $0.98 per case. Spring's management is aware that this difference of $0.05 per case resulted from excessive price discounts, and they have put controls in place to reduce discounts in the future.

Special attention is paid to companies with multiple products or services and to companies selling the same product or service in multiple distribution channels. Companies such as Cisco, GE, and Hewlett-Packard perform similar analyses because they sell their products through multiple distribution channels—for example, via the internet, over the telephone, and in retail stores.

● **TRY IT! 16.2** ▶ Dexter Inc. has only two retail and two wholesale customers. Information relating to each customer for 2016 follows:

	Wholesale Customers		Retail Customers	
	West Region Wholesaler	East Region Wholesaler	Hudson Inc.	Pentel Corp
Revenues at list prices	$750,000	$1,180,000	$350,000	$260,000
Discounts from list prices	51,600	94,200	19,800	6,180
Cost of goods sold	570,000	1,020,000	298,000	190,000
Delivery costs	29,100	23,420	16,460	14,290
Order processing costs	12,640	16,960	9,360	7,260
Cost of sales visit	12,600	10,240	9,240	8,150

Enviro-Tech's annual distribution-channel costs are $36,000 for wholesale customers and $14,000 for retail customers. The company's annual corporate-sustaining costs are $48,000. The company allocates distribution channel cost to customers in each channel on the basis of revenues (at actual prices). It allocates corporate overhead costs (1) to distribution channels based on channel operating incomes, if positive and (2) from channels to customers based on channel operating income if positive.

Required

Prepare a customer profitability report based on fully-allocated costs.

Sales-Volume Contribution Margin Variance

The *sales-volume contribution margin variance* is calculated as

$$\begin{array}{c}\text{Sales-Volume} \\ \text{contribution margin} \\ \text{variance}\end{array} = \left(\begin{array}{c}\text{Actual sales} \\ \text{quantity in units}\end{array} - \begin{array}{c}\text{Static-budget sales} \\ \text{quantity in units}\end{array}\right) \times \begin{array}{c}\text{Budgeted contribution} \\ \text{margin per unit}\end{array}$$

The sales-volume variance shows the effect of the difference between the actual and budgeted quantity of the variable used to "flex" the flexible budget. The sales-volume variance of $11,760 U is the difference between columns E and G in Exhibit 16-4. Exhibit 16-5 presents these calculations in graphic format.

Campbell Corp. buys and sells two types of sunglasses in New York: Duma and Kool. Budgeted and actual results for 2017 are as follows:

| Product | Budget for 2017 | | | Actual for 2017 | | |
	Selling Price	Variable Cost per Unit	Units Sold	Selling Price	Variable Cost per Carton	Cartons Sold
Duma	$20	$16	88,000	$18	$15	90,000
Kool	$23	$18	132,000	$25	$19	110,000

Required

Compute the total sales-volume variance, the total sales-mix variance, and the total sales-quantity variance. (Calculate all variances in terms of contribution margin.) Show results for each product in your computations.

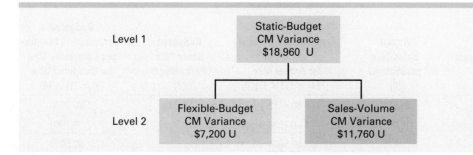

Exhibit 16-5 Overview of Levels 1 and 2 Contribution Margin Variances for June 2018

Interpretation of Levels 1 and 2 Contribution Margin Variance

The flexible-budget variance of $7,200 U arose because the actual Q produced and sold either cost more than it should have or the selling price was lower than the budgeted amount. Further variance analysis would help to isolate the cause of the unfavourable variance (see Chapters 7 and 8 for selling-price variance, direct materials variance, direct manufacturing labour variance, and variable overhead variance). In this case, we already know that it was due to price discounting. However, the $11,760 U sales-volume CM variance is also a concern. Although the *quantity sold was more* than budget (900,000 cases versus 890,000 cases), the *operating income went down* (by the amount of the CM variance). To examine the sale-volume CM variance in more detail, it is necessary to inspect the relevant Level 3 components: sales-mix variance and sales-quantity variance.

Sales-Mix and Sales-Quantity Contribution Margin Variances

The **sales-mix contribution margin variance** is one of the Level 3 variances calculated as the difference between two amounts: (1) the budgeted amount for the actual sales mix and (2) the budgeted amount for the budgeted sales mix. In the case of CM variances, the managers of each product would have some discretion in how their individual and product bundles were sold. The formula for computing the sales-mix variance in terms of the CM for Spring is

$$\begin{array}{c}\text{Sales-mix} \\ \text{contribution margin} \\ \text{variance}\end{array} = \begin{array}{c}\text{Actual units of} \\ \text{all products sold}\end{array} \times \left(\begin{array}{c}\text{Actual sales-} \\ \text{mix percentage}\end{array} - \begin{array}{c}\text{Budgeted sales-} \\ \text{mix percentage}\end{array}\right) \times \begin{array}{c}\text{Budgeted} \\ \text{contribution} \\ \text{margin per unit}\end{array}$$

	Actual Units of All Products Sold	×	(Actual Sales Mix Percentage	−	Budgeted Sales-Mix Percentage)	×	Budgeted Contribution Margin per Unit	=	Sales-Mix Contribution Margin Variance
Wholesale	900,000 units	×	(84.00%	−	80.00%)	×	$0.49 per unit	=	$ 17,640 F
Retail	900,000 units	×	(16.00%	−	20.00%)	×	$0.98 per unit	=	$ 35,280 U
Total sales-mix variance									$ 17,640 U

A favourable sales-mix variance arises for the wholesale channel because the 84% actual sales-mix percentage exceeds the 80% budgeted sales-mix percentage. In contrast, the retail channel has an unfavourable variance because the 16% actual sales-mix percentage is less than the 20% budgeted sales-mix percentage. The sales-mix variance is unfavourable because actual sales mix shifted toward the less-profitable wholesale channel relative to budgeted sales mix. Remember that if one product line increases its share of the sales mix (i.e., has a favourable sales-mix variance), then at least one other product must decrease its share of the sales-mix (i.e., have an unfavourable sales-mix variance).

The concept underlying the sales-mix variance is best explained in terms of budgeted CM per composite unit of the sales mix. A **composite unit** is a hypothetical unit with weights based on the mix of individual units. For actual sales mix, the composite unit consists of 0.84 units of sales to the wholesale channel and 0.16 units of sales to the retail channel. For budgeted sales mix, the composite unit consists of 0.80 units of sales to the wholesale channel and 0.20 units of sales to the retail channel. The table below reports budgeted CM per composite unit, computed in columns 3 and 5, for actual and budgeted mix:

	Budgeted Contribution Margin per Unit (1)	Actual Sales-Mix percentage (2)	Budgeted Contribution Margin per Unit for Actual Mix (3) = (1) × (2)	Budgeted Sales-Mix Percentage (4)	Budgeted Contribution Margin per Composite Unit for Budgeted Mix (5) = (1) × (4)
Wholesale	$0.49	84.00%	$0.4116	80.00%	$0.3920
Retail	0.98	16.00	0.1568	20.00	0.1960
			$0.5684		$0.5880

Actual sales mix has a budgeted CM per composite unit of $0.5684. Budgeted sales mix has a budgeted CM per composite unit of $0.5880. Budgeted CM per composite unit can be computed in another way by dividing total budgeted CM of $523,320 by total budgeted units of 890,000: $523,320 ÷ 890,000 units = $0.5880 per unit. The effect of the sales-mix shift for Spring is to decrease budgeted CM per composite unit by $0.0196 ($0.5880 − $0.5684). For the 900,000 units actually sold, this decrease translates to a $17,640 U sales-mix variance ($0.0196 per unit × 900,000 units).

The **sales-quantity contribution margin variance** is the difference between two amounts: (1) the budgeted CM based on actual units sold of all products and the budgeted mix and (2) the CM in the static budget (which is based on the budgeted units to be sold of all products and the budgeted mix). The formula for calculating the sales-quantity CM variance in terms of CM is

$$\begin{matrix} \text{Sales-quantity} \\ \text{contribution margin} \\ \text{variance} \end{matrix} = \left(\begin{matrix} \text{Actual units of} \\ \text{all products sold} \end{matrix} - \begin{matrix} \text{Budgeted units of} \\ \text{all products sold} \end{matrix} \right) \times \begin{matrix} \text{Budgeted sales-} \\ \text{mix percentage} \end{matrix} \times \begin{matrix} \text{Budgeted} \\ \text{contribution} \\ \text{margin per unit} \end{matrix}$$

	(Actual Units of All Products Sold	−	Budgeted Units of All Products Sold)	×	Budgeted Sales- Mix Percentage	×	Budgeted Contribution Margin per Unit	=	Quantity Variance
Wholesale	(900,000	−	890,000)	×	80.00%	×	$0.49 per unit	=	$3,920 F
Retail	(900,000	−	890,000)	×	20.00%	×	$0.98 per unit	=	1,960 F
Total sales-quantity contribution margin variance									$5,880 F

Exhibit 16-6 reports the results of the Levels 2 and 3 variance analyses in columnar format.

The sales-quantity CM variance is one where the individual components of the variance (the separate product lines) always move in the same direction. For example, if the overall sales-quantity variance is favourable (i.e., more units were sold than were originally budgeted for), then *all* the individual products will also have a favourable sales-quantity CM variance, and vice versa. Spring sold 10,000 more cases than were budgeted, resulting in a $5,880 F sales-quantity variance (also equal to budgeted CM per composite unit for the budgeted sales mix times the additional cases sold, $0.5880 × 10,000). Exhibit 16-7 illustrates graphically how to reconcile Level 3 and Level 2 variances.

Exhibit 16-6 Sales-Mix and Sales-Quantity Contribution Margin Variance Analysis of Spring Distribution for June 2018

	A	B	C	D	E	F	G
1		Flexible Budget:				Static Budget:	
2		Actual Units of		Actual Units of		Budgeted Units of	
3		All Products Sold ×		All Products Sold ×		All Products Sold ×	
4		Actual Sales Mix ×		Budgeted Sales Mix ×		Budgeted Sales Mix ×	
5		Budgeted Contribution		Budgeted Contribution		Budgeted Contribution	
6		Margin per Unit		Margin per Unit		Margin per Unit	
7		(1)		(2)		(3)	
8	Wholesale	900,000 × 0.84 × $0.49 =	$370,440	900,000 × 0.80 × $0.49 =	$352,800	890,000 × 0.80 × $0.49 =	$348,880
9	Retail	900,000 × 0.16 × $0.98 =	141,120	900,000 × 0.20 × $0.98 =	176,400	890,000 × 0.20 × $0.98 =	174,440
10			$511,560		$529,200		$523,320
11			↑	$17,640 U	↑	$5,880 F	↑
12	Level 3			Sales-mix variance		Sales-quantity variance	
13			↑		$ 11,760 U		↑
14	Level 2			Sales-volume variance			

Exhibit 16-7 Overview of Levels 1, 2 and 3 Contribution Margin Variances for Spring Distribution for June 2018

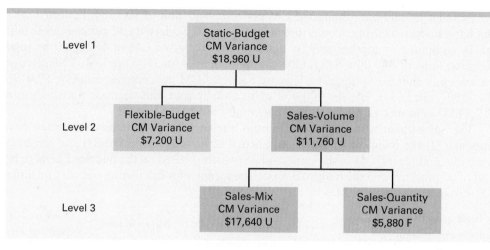

Interpretation of Level 3 Revenue Variances

Managers should probe why the $17,640 U sales-mix variance occurred in June 2018. Is it because

- The economy changed and retail customers were more difficult to find than originally anticipated?
- A competitor in the retail channel provided the same (or better) service at a lower price?
- The original projections for the sales mix were estimated without adequate research?
- Things were much better in the wholesale channel as the sales mix changed and the number of cases sold in the wholesale channel was more than the original budget?

Sales depend on overall demand for the industry's products as well as the company's share of the market for bottled water. Assume that Spring derived its total unit sales budget for 2018 from a management estimate of a 25% market share and a total industry sales forecast of 3,560,000 units (0.25 × 3,560,000 units = 890,000 units). For June 2018, actual industry sales were 4,000,000, and Spring's actual market share was 22.5% (900,000 ÷ 4,000,000 = 0.225 or 22.5%).

Managers would want to determine the reasons for the increase in sales. Did higher sales come as a result of a competitor's distribution problems? Better customer service? Or growth in the overall market? Further insight into the causes of the sales-quantity variance can be gained by analyzing changes in Spring's share of the total market available relative to any change in the size of the entire market.

Market-Share Variance

The **market-share variance** is one of the Level 4 variances calculated as the difference between two amounts: (1) the actual market size in units, times the *actual market share*, calculated using the budgeted per composite unit for the budgeted mix, and (2) the actual market size in units, times the *budgeted market share*, calculated using the budgeted per composite unit for the budgeted mix. The formula for computing the market-share variance in terms of CM for Spring is

$$\begin{array}{c}\text{Market share} \\ \text{contribution margin} \\ \text{variance}\end{array} = \begin{array}{c}\text{Actual market} \\ \text{size in units}\end{array} \times \left(\begin{array}{c}\text{Actual} \\ \text{market share}\end{array} - \begin{array}{c}\text{Budgeted} \\ \text{market share}\end{array}\right) \times \begin{array}{c}\text{Budgeted contribution} \\ \text{margin per composite} \\ \text{unit for budgeted mix}\end{array}$$

$$= 4,000,000 \text{ units (cases)} \times (0.225 - 0.25) \times \$0.5880 \text{ per unit (case)}$$

$$= \$58,800 \text{ U}$$

The budgeted CM per composite unit for the budgeted mix (also known as budgeted average CM per unit) is calculated using the approach outlined earlier in this chapter.

Market-Size Contribution Margin Variance

The **market-size contribution margin variance** is the difference between two amounts: (1) the amount based on the *actual market size in units,* times the budgeted market share, and budgeted CM per composite unit for budgeted mix, and (2) the static-budget amount based on the *budgeted market size in units,* times the budgeted market share, and budgeted CM per composite unit for budgeted mix. The formula for computing the market-size variance in terms of CM for Spring is

$$\begin{matrix} \text{Market-size} \\ \text{contribution margin} \\ \text{variance} \end{matrix} = \left(\begin{matrix} \text{Actual market} \\ \text{size in units} \end{matrix} - \begin{matrix} \text{Budgeted market} \\ \text{size in units} \end{matrix} \right) \times \begin{matrix} \text{Budgeted} \\ \text{market share} \end{matrix} \times \begin{matrix} \text{Budgeted contribution} \\ \text{margin per composite} \\ \text{unit for budgeted mix} \end{matrix}$$

$$= (4,000,000 \text{ units (cases)} - 3,560,000) \times 0.25 \times \$0.5880$$

$$= \$64,680 \text{ F}$$

The market-size CM variance is favourable because actual market size, or total consumer demand, increased 440,000 cases, or 12.4%,[4] compared to budgeted market size. Managers should probe the reasons for the market-share and market-size variances for June 2018. Was the $58,800 U market-share variance because of competitors providing better service and offering a lower price? Did Spring's products experience quality-control problems that were the subject of negative media coverage? Is the $64,680 F market-size variance because of an increase in market size that can be expected to continue in the future? If yes, Spring has much to gain by attaining or exceeding its budgeted 25% market share. The reconciliation of Level 4 to Level 3 variance is reported in Exhibit 16-8.

Exhibit 16-8 Level 4 Contribution Margin Variance Analysis of Spring Distribution for June 2018

	A	B	C	D	E	F
1						**Static Budget:**
2		**Actual Market Size ×**		**Actual Market Size ×**		**Budgeted Market Size ×**
3		**Actual Market Share ×**		**Budgeted Market Share ×**		**Budgeted Market Share ×**
4		**Budgeted Average**		**Budgeted Average**		**Budgeted Average**
5		**Contribution Margin**		**Contribution Margin**		**Contribution Margin**
6		**per Unit**		**per Unit**		**per Unit**
7		4,000,000 × 0.225[a] × $0.5880[b]		4,000,000 × 0.25[c] × $0.5880[b]		3,560,000 × 0.25[c] × $0.5880[b]
8		$529,200		$588,000		$523,320
9						
10		↑	$58,800 U	↑	$64,680 F	↑
11	Level 4		Market-share CM variance		Market-size CM variance	
12		↑				↑
13				$5,880 F		
14	Level 3			Sales-quantity CM variance		
15						
16	F = favourable effect on operating income; U = unfavourable effect on operating income.					
17	[a]Actual market share: 900,000 units ÷ 4,000,000 units = 0.225 or 22.5%.					
18	[b]Budgeted average contribution margin per unit: $523,320 ÷ 890,000 units = $0.5880 per unit.					
19	[c]Budgeted market share: 890,000 ÷ 3,560,000 units = 0.25 or 25%.					

---

[4] $(4,000,000 - 3,560,000) \div 3,560,000 = 0.124 \text{ or } 12.4\%$

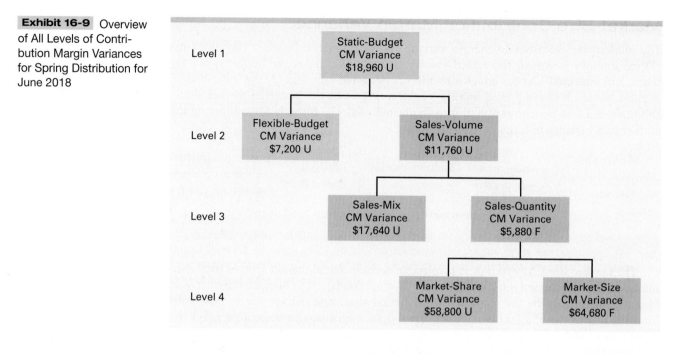

Spring Distribution's management team is now in a position to use its four-level CM variance analysis, along with its ABC customer cost analyses, to produce a customer profitability profile. Exhibit 16-9 presents an overview of the Level 1 to Level 4 variances and how each level of variance reconciles to the others.

 **TRY IT! 16.4**

Campbell Corp. buys and sells two types of sunglasses in New York: Duma and Kool. Budgeted and actual results for 2017 are as follows:

Product	Budget for 2017			Actual for 2017		
	Selling Price	Variable Cost per Unit	Units Sold	Selling Price	Variable Cost per Carton	Cartons Sold
Duma	$20	$16	88,000	$18	$15	90,000
Kool	$23	$18	132,000	$25	$19	110,000

Campbell Corp. prepared the budget for 2017 assuming an 11% market share based on total sales of 2,000,000 units in New York. However, actual total sales volume in New York was 2,500,000 units.

Required

Calculate the market-share and market-size variances for Campbell Corp. in 2017. (Calculate all variances in terms of contribution margin.) Comment on the results.

Interpretation of Level 4 Contribution Margin Variances

Some companies place more emphasis on the market-share variance than the market-size variance when evaluating their managers. That's because they believe the market-size variance is influenced by economy-wide factors and shifts in consumer preferences that are outside the managers' control, whereas the market-share variance measures how well managers performed relative to their peers. Be cautious when computing the market-size variance and the market-share variance. Reliable information on market size and market share is available for some but not all industries. The automobile, computer, and television industries are cases in which market-size and market-share statistics are widely available. In other industries, such as management consulting and personal financial planning, information about market size and market share is far less reliable.

The managerial task, based on this feedback, is to decide upon the best response. The unfavourable variances have only revealed what occurred, not how it occurred. If there is a controllable cause, then the team will find an operating remedy. If there is an uncontrollable cause, then the best decision may be to change the budget and deal with a new set of expectations, as unfavourable as they may be.

Market-share and market-size variances reveal generally what variances are controllable and uncontrollable. In a competitive market it is rare that a single company can control market size. The demand for a product or a service depends on consumer preference.

Thus, an unfavourable *market size variance has strategic implications*. For example, the recently reduced demand for SUVs may imply a long-term decision to change capacity. The cause of the reduced market size, high fuel prices, is beyond the control of vehicle manufacturers. Another potential remedy is innovative use of alternative, less expensive fuels, which requires redesign of the internal combustion engine. A third alternative would be to expand into adjacent product markets and simply harvest the benefits of the capacity already in place.

In contrast, an unfavourable *market-share variance has operating implications*. The reduced demand for products made by a specific company with no accompanying reduction in market size provides different relevant information. Remedies include improved understanding of the value proposition, improved product attributes, or improved timeliness.

Concepts in Action

Variance Analysis and Standard Costing Help Sandoz Manage Its Overhead Costs

Sandoz, the $10.1 billion generics division of Swiss-based Novartis AG, is the world's second largest generic drug manufacturer. Generic pharmaceuticals help reduce the cost of health care around the world. In the United States in 2016, for example, 88% of all prescription drugs dispensed were generics, but they accounted for only 28% of total drug costs. Market pricing pressure means that Sandoz operates on razor-thin margins. As a result, the company must ensure that managers have a full and accurate understanding of its costs, including an accounting for overhead costs. Sandoz uses standard costing and variance analysis to manage its overhead costs.

Each year, Sandoz prepares an overhead budget based on a detailed production plan, planned overhead spending, and other factors. Sandoz then uses ABC to assign budgeted overhead costs to different work centres (for example, mixing, blending, tableting, testing, and packaging). Finally, overhead costs are assigned to products based on the activity levels required by each product at each work centre. The resulting standard product cost is used in product profitability analysis and as a basis for making pricing decisions. The two main focal points in Sandoz's performance analyses are overhead absorption analysis and manufacturing overhead variance analysis.

Each month, Sandoz uses absorption analysis to compare actual production and actual costs to the standard costs of processed inventory. The monthly analysis evaluates two key trends:

1. Are costs in line with the budget? If not, the reasons are examined and the accountable managers are notified.
2. Are production volume and product mix conforming to plan? If not, Sandoz reviews and adjusts machine capacities and the absorption trend is deemed to be permanent.

Manufacturing overhead variances are examined at the work centre level. These variances help determine when equipment is not running as expected so it can be repaired or replaced. Variances also help in identifying inefficiencies in processing and setup and cleaning times, which leads to more efficient ways to use equipment. Sometimes, the manufacturing overhead variance analysis leads to the review and improvement of the standards themselves—a critical element in planning the level of plant capacity. Management also reviews current and future capacity on a monthly basis to identify constraints and future capital needs.

Sources: Novartis AG, 2016 Form 20-F (Basel, Switzerland: Novartis AG, 2016); IMS Institute for Healthcare Informatics/Generic *Pharmaceutical Association, Generic Drug Savings in the United States*, November 2016; Conversations with, and documents prepared by, Eric Evans and Erich Erchr of Sandoz, 2004; Conversations with, and documents prepared by, Tobias Hestler and Chris Lewis of Sandoz, 2016.

Customer Profitability Analysis

► **LO 4**

Generate a customer profitability profile.

Once a company such as Spring Distribution decides to measure customer profitability, management accountants are responsible for articulating the benefits of such measurements. This can be problematic because the sales groups in most companies are compensated on the basis of revenues, not customer profits. Therefore, the sales force may be reluctant to follow a strategy of serving only profitable customers and taking actions to change the behaviour and buying patterns of those that are unprofitable.

When it comes to customer profitability analysis, the sales force is not the only part of an organization that may pose challenges for management accountants. Line managers are sometimes surprised by which customers are profitable and which are not, because they may assume a company's largest customer is profitable. However, this customer may consume high levels of customer support and actually be unprofitable. Management accountants need to communicate to the sales force and line managers why measuring customer profits is critical to the organization.

We will focus mainly on **customer profitability analysis** in Spring's retail distribution channel. The list selling price in this channel is $14.40 per case (unit), while the purchase cost to Spring is $12 per case. If every case were sold at its list price in this distribution channel, Spring would earn a gross margin of $2.40 per case or a 20% gross margin. This high-percentage contribution by a small number of customers is a common finding in many studies. It highlights the importance of Spring Distribution maintaining good relations with this pivotal set of customers. But, even with this group of highly profitable customers, it may be worthwhile to do an even more detailed profitability analysis.

The data on all customers, retrieved from Spring's MIS, are reported in Exhibit 16-10. Wholesale customers comprise new data, as do the distribution-channel costs and corporate-sustaining costs. The format of Exhibit 16-10 is based on Spring's cost hierarchy. All costs incurred to serve customers are not included in customer-level costs and therefore are not allocated to customers in Exhibit 16-10. Distribution-channel costs such as the $58,000 salary for the manager of the retail distribution channel are not included in customer-level costs and are not allocated to customers (see Exhibit 16-2). Instead, these costs are

Exhibit 16-10 Customer Profitability Analysis for Retail Channel Customers: Spring Distribution, June 2018

	A	B	C	D	E	F
1						Cumulative
2						Customer-Level
3		Customer-				Operating Income
4		Level		Customer-Level	Cumulative	as a % of Total
5		Operating	Customer	Operating Income	Customer-Level	Customer-Level
6	Customer	Income	Revenue	Divided by Revenue	Operating Income	Operating Income
7	Code	(1)	(2)	(3) = (1) ÷ (2)	(4)	(5) = (4) ÷ $133,920
8	B	$ 51,160	$ 467,280	10.95%	$ 51,160	38.20%
9	A	35,100	564,480	6.22	86,260	64.41
10	C	21,070	255,640	8.24	107,330	80.14
11	D	17,580	277,000	6.35	124,910	93.27
12	F	7,504	123,500	6.08	132,414	98.88
13	J	3,330	36,000	9.25	135,744	101.36
14	E	3,176	193,000	1.65	138,920	103.73
15	G	(1,190)	38,280	−3.11	137,730	102.84
16	H	(1,690)	38,220	−4.42	136,040	101.58
17	I	(2,120)	37,000	−5.73	133,920	100.00
18		$133,920	$2,030,400			

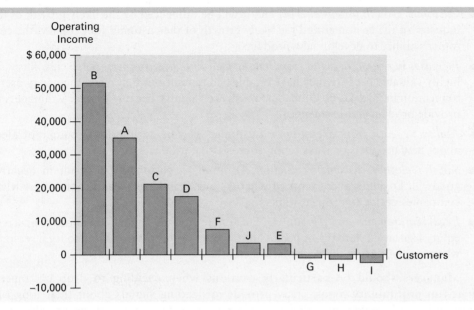

identified as costs of the distribution channel as a whole (see Exhibit 16-3). That is because Spring's management believes that changes in the retail channel manager's salary will not affect the behaviour of a specific customer.

Distribution-channel costs will be affected only by decisions pertaining to the whole channel, such as a decision to discontinue retail distribution. Another reason Spring does not allocate distribution-channel costs to customers is motivation. Spring's managers contend that salespersons responsible for managing individual customer accounts would lose motivation if their bonuses were affected by the allocation to customers of distribution-channel costs over which they have almost no influence.

Exhibit 16-11 ranks customers on customer-level operating income. Three of the four smallest customers (based on revenue) are unprofitable. Moreover, customer E, with revenues of $193,000, is only marginally profitable. Further analysis revealed that a former sales representative gave customer E excessive discounts in an attempt to meet a monthly sales-volume target.

Managers often find the bar chart presentation, like that shown in Exhibit 16-11, to be the most intuitive way to visualize customer profitability. The highly profitable customers clearly stand out. Moreover, the number of loss-customers and the magnitude of their losses are apparent and focus management attention on how to improve the profitability of these loss-customers.

Assessing Customer Value

The "80-20 rule," also known as the Pareto principle,[5] appears to prevail among customers: Of total profit, 80% will come from 20% of the customers. Customer profitability analysis is attention-getting and directs management attention toward maintaining the best possible retention ratio of these customers and transforming the remainder into more profitable customers. The information in Exhibits 16-3 and 16-10 relates to customer profitability in a single accounting period. This is one of several factors that managers should consider in deciding how to allocate resources across customers. Other factors include the following:

- *Short-run and long-run customer profitability.*
- *Customer retention likelihood.* The more likely a customer is to continue doing business with a company, the more valuable the customer is.

---

[5] The Pareto principle or "80–20 rule" comes from the observation that results are frequently not distributed in symmetrical or proportionate fashions. Vilfredo Pareto, an Italian economist, noted this phenomenon when researching Italian land ownership in 1906. He found that approximately 80% of the land was owned by 20% of the population. Since that observation, this ratio has been seen to be repeated in many areas of both nature and business.

- *Customer growth potential.* This factor will be influenced by the likely growth of the industry of the customer and the likely growth of the customer (due to, say, the customer's ability to develop new products).

- *Increases in overall demand from having well-known customers.* Some customers are highly valuable because they have established reputations that make them very useful to mention in sales visits. Other customers are valuable because of their willingness to provide product endorsements.

- *Ability to learn from a customer.* Customers can be an important source of ideas about new products or ways to improve existing products.

- *Salesforce/other customers' reaction.* Dropping a customer can result in negative goodwill. Loyalties and a sense of what is "fair" can have a significant impact when companies decide to drop customers.

- *Legal requirements and regulations.* For some regulated companies, and given current equity legislation, it may not be possible to drop some customers due to legal reasons, whatever their profitability (or lack thereof).

Managers should be particularly cautious when deciding to drop customers. Short-run profitability reports may provide misleading signals about their long-run profitability. Moreover, not all costs assigned to a customer may be variable with respect to short-run reductions in purchases by customers. It is typically *not* the case that a policy of dropping any currently unprofitable customer (sometimes called "revenue shedding") will eliminate, in the short run, all the costs assigned to that customer.

Customer Mix Analysis

▶ **LO 5**

Analyze relevant profitability data, and decide whether to drop or add customers or branches.

The goal of customer profitability analysis is to use high quality data to make decisions that will improve the profitability of a company. This section illustrates relevant-revenue and relevant-cost analyses when different cost drivers are identified for different activities in ABC. This discussion is similar to the relevant cost analysis in Chapter 11 but with a specific emphasis on ABC when the cost object is the customer. The analysis focuses on customer profitability at Allied West, the west coast sales office of Allied Furniture, a wholesaler of specialized furniture.

The MIS at Allied West provides detailed cost information on three customers for the year 2018, as reported in Exhibit 16-12. Allied West wholesales furniture to three local

Exhibit 16-12 Customer Profitability Analysis for Allied West

	Vogel	Brenner	Wisk	Total
Sales	$500,000	$300,000	$ 400,000	$1,200,000
Cost of goods sold	370,000	220,000	330,000	920,000
Materials-handling labour	41,000	18,000	33,000	92,000
Materials-handling equipment cost written off as depreciation	10,000	6,000	8,000	24,000
Rent	14,000	8,000	14,000	36,000
Marketing support	11,000	9,000	10,000	30,000
Purchase orders and delivery processing	13,000	7,000	12,000	32,000
General administration	20,000	12,000	16,000	48,000
Total operating costs	479,000	280,000	423,000	1,182,000
Operating income	$ 21,000	$ 20,000	$ (23,000)	18,000
Allocated corporate costs				24,000
				$ (6,000)

retailers: Vogel, Brenner, and Wisk. Additional information on Allied West's costs for different activities at various levels of the cost hierarchy is as follows:

- Materials-handling labour costs vary with the number of units of furniture shipped to customers.

- Different areas of the warehouse stock furniture for different customers. Materials-handling equipment and depreciation costs on the equipment are identified with individual customer accounts. Any equipment not used remains idle. The equipment has a one-year useful life and zero disposal price.

- Allied West allocates rent costs to each customer account based on the amount of warehouse space occupied by the products to be shipped to that customer.

- Marketing costs vary with the number of sales visits made to customers.

- Purchase order costs vary with the number of purchase orders received; delivery processing costs vary with the number of shipments made.

- Allied West allocates fixed general administration for the Allied West office costs to customers based on dollar sales made to each customer.

The management team's task is to analyze these data, assuming they are faithful to the economic facts of what each customer costs. From the analysis, Allied West can predict the effects of dropping any customer on their profitability.

Drop a Customer

Exhibit 16-12 indicates a loss of $23,000 on sales to Wisk. Allied West's manager believes this loss was occurred because Wisk places many low-volume orders with Allied, resulting in high purchase order, delivery processing, materials-handling, and marketing activity. Allied West is considering several possible actions with respect to the Wisk account: reducing its own costs of supporting Wisk by becoming more efficient, cutting back on some of the services it offers Wisk, charging Wisk higher prices, or dropping the Wisk account. The following analysis focuses on the operating income effect of dropping the Wisk account. The following financial facts are from the ABC system:

1. Dropping the Wisk account will save cost of goods sold, materials-handling labour, marketing support, purchase order, and delivery processing costs incurred on the Wisk account.

2. Dropping the Wisk account will mean that the warehouse space currently occupied by products for Wisk and the materials-handling equipment used to move them will become idle.

3. Dropping the Wisk account will have no effect on fixed general administration costs.

Exhibit 16-13 shows the results of dropping the Wisk account in both "total" and "differential" formats (see Chapter 11). The analysis predicts that Allied West's operating income will be $15,000 lower if it drops the Wisk account. The last column in Exhibit 16-13 indicates in detail why the cost savings from dropping the Wisk account, $385,000, are not enough to offset the loss of $400,000 in revenue. The full cost format provides the explanation. Depreciation, rent, and general administration costs will not change if the Wisk account is dropped.

Assume that there is an alternative use for the warehouse capacity freed up if Wisk is dropped as a customer. Allied has the alternative to lease the extra warehouse space to the Sanchez Corporation, which has offered $20,000 per year for it. Then the $20,000 that Allied would receive would be the opportunity cost of continuing to use the warehouse to service Wisk. Allied would gain $5,000 by dropping the Wisk account ($20,000 from lease revenue minus lost operating income of $15,000).

Before reaching a final decision, however, the management team must examine whether Wisk can be made more profitable. Activities use might be changed such that services supplied to Wisk earn more than the $20,000 from leasing to Sanchez. Allied must also consider qualitative factors, such as the effect of the decision on Allied's reputation with other customers for developing stable, long-run business relationships.

Exhibit 16-13 Relevant-Cost Analysis for Allied West Dropping the Wisk Account

	Amount of Total Revenues and Total Costs		Difference: Incremental (Loss in Revenue and Savings in Costs from Dropping Wisk Account)
	Keep Wisk Account	Drop Wisk Account	
Sales	$1,200,000	$800,000	$(400,000)
Cost of goods sold	920,000	590,000	330,000
Materials-handling labour	92,000	59,000	33,000
Materials-handling equipment cost written off as depreciation	24,000	24,000	—
Rent	36,000	36,000	—
Marketing support	30,000	20,000	10,000
Purchase orders and delivery processing	32,000	20,000	12,000
General administration	48,000	48,000	—
Total operating costs	1,182,000	797,000	385,000
Operating income	$ 18,000	$ 3,000	$ (15,000)

Add a Customer

Suppose that in addition to dropping the Wisk account, Allied is evaluating the profitability of substituting a customer, Loral. Allied is already paying rent of $36,000 for the warehouse and is incurring general administration costs of $48,000. These costs will not change if Loral is added as a customer. Loral is a customer with a profile much like Wisk's. Suppose Allied predicts other revenues and costs of doing business with Loral to be the same as those described under the Wisk column of Exhibit 16-13. Should Allied substitute Loral as a customer?

Exhibit 16-14 predicts that incremental revenues will exceed incremental costs by $7,000. Allied would not prefer to substitute Loral as a customer for Wisk (a $15,000 loss versus a $7,000 gain).

Exhibit 16-14 Relevant-Cost Analysis for Dropping the Wisk Account and Adding the Loral Account

	(Loss in Revenue) and Savings in Costs from Dropping Wisk Account (1)	Incremental Revenue and (Incremental Costs) from Adding Loral Account (2)
Revenue	$(400,000)	$ 400,000
Cost of goods sold	330,000	(330,000)
Materials-handling labour	33,000	(33,000)
Materials-handling equipment cost written off as depreciation	0	(8,000)
Rent	0	0
Marketing support	10,000	(10,000)
Purchase-order and delivery processing	12,000	(12,000)
General administration	0	0
Corporate-office costs	0	0
Total costs	385,000	(393,000)
Effect on operating income (loss)	$ (15,000)	$ 7,000

One key point is that the cost of acquiring new equipment to support the Loral order (written off as depreciation of $8,000 in Exhibit 16-14) is included as a relevant cost. It is relevant because this cost can be avoided if Allied decides not to do business with Loral. Note the critical distinction here. Depreciation cost is irrelevant in deciding whether to drop Wisk as a customer (because it is a past sunk cost), but the purchase cost of the *new* equipment that will then be written off as depreciation in the future is relevant in deciding whether to add Loral as a new customer (this analysis assumes that the materials-handling equipment being used for the Wisk account is not suitable for use on the Loral account).

Drop or Add Branches

Companies periodically confront decisions about discontinuing or adding entire branches or business segments. For example, given Allied West's expected loss of $6,000 (see Exhibit 16-12), should it be closed? Assume that closing Allied West will have no effect on total corporate-office costs. Exhibit 16-15 reports the relevant revenue and cost analyses (in column 1) using the data from the final column in Exhibit 16-12. The revenue losses of $1,200,000 will exceed the cost savings of $1,158,000, leading to a decrease in operating income of $42,000. Allied West should not be closed down.

The key reasons are that closing Allied West will save neither depreciation costs of $24,000, which is a past or sunk cost (see above), nor actual total corporate costs. Corporate costs allocated to various sales offices will change but not decline in total. The $24,000 corporate costs that are no longer allocated to Allied West will have to be allocated to other sales offices. Therefore, the $24,000 of allocated corporate costs should not be included as expected cost savings from closing Allied West.

Now suppose Allied Furniture has the opportunity to open another sales office, Allied South, whose revenues and costs would be identical to Allied West's, including a cost of $25,000 to acquire materials-handling equipment with a one-year useful life and zero disposal value.

Opening this office will have no effect on total corporate costs. Should Allied Furniture open Allied South? Exhibit 16-15, column 2, indicates that it should do so because opening Allied South will increase operating income by $17,000. As before, the cost of new equipment (written off as depreciation) *is* relevant. But the point here is to ignore allocated corporate costs and focus on actual total corporate-office costs. Total corporate costs will not change if Allied South is opened and, hence, these costs are irrelevant.

Exhibit 16-15 Relevant-Revenue and Relevant-Cost Analyses for Closing Allied West and Opening Allied South

	(Loss in Revenue) and Savings in Costs from Closing Allied West (1)	Incremental Revenue and (Incremental Costs) from Opening Allied South (2)
Revenue	$(1,200,000)	$1,200,000
Cost of goods sold	920,000	(920,000)
Materials-handling labour	92,000	(92,000)
Materials-handling equipment cost written off as depreciation	0	(25,000)
Rent	36,000	(36,000)
Marketing support	30,000	(30,000)
Purchase-order and delivery processing	32,000	(32,000)
General administration	48,000	(48,000)
Corporate-office costs	0	0
Total costs	1,158,000	(1,183,000)
Effect on operating income (loss)	$ (42,000)	$ 17,000

Pulling it all Together—Problem for Self-Study

(Try to solve this problem before examining the solution that follows.)

Problem

The Payne Company manufactures two types of vinyl flooring. Budgeted and actual operating data for 2018 are

	Static Budget			Actual Results		
	Commercial	Residential	Total	Commercial	Residential	Total
Unit sales in rolls	20,000	60,000	80,000	25,200	58,800	84,000
Contribution margin	$10,000,000	$24,000,000	$34,000,000	$11,970,000	$24,696,000	$36,666,000

In late 2014, a marketing research firm estimated industry volume for commercial and residential vinyl flooring for 2018 at 800,000 rolls. Actual industry volume for 2018 was 700,000 rolls.

Required ▶ ❸

1. Compute the sales-mix variance and the sales-quantity variance by type of vinyl flooring and in total. (Compute all variances in terms of contribution margins.)

❸ 2. Compute the market-share variance and the market-size variance.

❸ 3. What insights do the variances calculated in requirements 1 and 2 provide about Payne Company's performance in 2018?

Solution

1. Actual sales-mix percentage:

$$\text{Commercial} = 25,200 \div 84,000 = 0.30, \text{ or } 30\%$$

$$\text{Residential} = 58,800 \div 84,000 = 0.70, \text{ or } 70\%$$

Budgeted sales-mix percentage:

$$\text{Commercial} = 20,000 \div 80,000 = 0.25, \text{ or } 25\%$$

$$\text{Residential} = 60,000 \div 80,000 = 0.75, \text{ or } 75\%$$

Budgeted contribution margin per unit:

$$\text{Commercial} = 10,000,000 \div 20,000 \text{ units} = \$500 \text{ per unit}$$

$$\text{Residential} = 24,000,000 \div 60,000 \text{ units} = \$400 \text{ per unit}$$

	Actual Units of All Products Sold	×	(Actual Sales-Mix Percentage − Budgeted Sales-Mix Percentage)	×	Budgeted Contribution Margin per Unit	=	Sales-Mix Variance
Commercial	84,000 units	×	(0.30 − 0.25)	×	$500 per unit	=	$2,100,000 F
Residential	84,000 units	×	(0.70 − 0.75)	×	$400 per unit	=	1,680,000 U
Total sales-mix variance							$ 420,000 F

	(Actual Units of All Products Sold − Budgeted Units of All Products Sold)	×	Budgeted Sales-Mix Percentage	×	Budgeted Contribution Margin per Unit	=	Sales-Quantity Variance
Commercial	(84,000 units − 80,000 units)	×	0.25	×	$500 per unit	=	$ 500,000 F
Residential	(84,000 units − 80,000 units)	×	0.75	×	$400 per unit	=	1,200,000 F
Total sales-quantity variance							$1,700,000 F

2. Actual market share = 84,000 ÷ 700,000 = 0.12, or 12%

   Budgeted market share = 80,000 ÷ 800,000 = 0.10, or 10%

   Budgeted contribution margin per composite unit = $34,000,000 ÷ 80,000 units

$$= \$425 \text{ per unit of budgeted mix}$$

Budgeted contribution margin per composite unit of budgeted mix can also be calculated as

Commercial: $500 per unit × 0.25 =	$125	
Residential: $400 per unit × 0.75 =	300	
Budgeted contribution margin per composite unit	$425	

$$\begin{matrix} \text{Market-share} \\ \text{variance} \end{matrix} = \begin{matrix} \text{Actual} \\ \text{market size} \\ \text{in units} \end{matrix} \times \left(\begin{matrix} \text{Actual} \\ \text{market} \\ \text{share} \end{matrix} - \begin{matrix} \text{Budgeted} \\ \text{market} \\ \text{share} \end{matrix} \right) \times \begin{matrix} \text{Budgeted} \\ \text{contribution margin} \\ \text{per composite unit} \\ \text{for budgeted mix} \end{matrix}$$

$$= 700,000 \text{ units} \times (0.12 - 0.10) \times \$425 \text{ per unit}$$

$$= \$5,950,000 \text{ F}$$

$$\begin{matrix} \text{Market-size} \\ \text{variance} \end{matrix} = \left(\begin{matrix} \text{Actual} \\ \text{market size} \\ \text{in units} \end{matrix} - \begin{matrix} \text{Budgeted} \\ \text{market size} \\ \text{in units} \end{matrix} \right) \times \begin{matrix} \text{Budgeted} \\ \text{market} \\ \text{share} \end{matrix} \times \begin{matrix} \text{Budgeted} \\ \text{contribution margin} \\ \text{per composite unit} \\ \text{for budgeted mix} \end{matrix}$$

$$= (700,000 \text{ units} - 800,000 \text{ units}) \times 0.10 \times \$425 \text{ per unit}$$

$$= \$4,250,000 \text{ U}$$

Note that the algebraic sum of the market-share variance and the market-size variance is equal to the sales-quantity variance: $5,950,000 F + $4,250,000 U = $1,700,000 F.

3. Both the sales-mix variance and the sales-quantity variance are favourable. The favourable sales-mix variance occurred because the actual mix comprised more of the higher-margin commercial vinyl flooring. The favourable sales-quantity variance occurred because the actual total quantity of rolls sold exceeded the budgeted amount.

The company's large favourable market-share variance is due to a 12% actual market share compared with a 10% budgeted market share. The market-size variance is unfavourable because the actual market size was 100,000 rolls less than the budgeted market size. Payne's performance in 2018 appears to be very good.

Although overall market size declined, the company sold more units than budgeted by gaining market share.

Decision Points

The following question-and-answer format summarizes the chapter's learning objectives. Each point presents a key question, and the guidelines are the answer to that question.

Learning Objectives	Guidelines
1. What is product bundling, and why does it give rise to revenue-allocation issues?	Bundling occurs when two or more products (or services) sell together for a single price. There are three methods of revenue allocation, and management teams should choose the method that most closely represents economic reality. Good judgment is needed because the method selected affects remuneration of managers of individual products in the bundle who are often evaluated on product revenues or product operating incomes.

2. Of what relevance is an ABC system to evaluating the relative profitability of customers?

The data provided by an ABC system more readily distinguishes among more and less expensive customer value propositions. Particularly for price takers in an intensely competitive environment, when product/service mix pricing differs among customers, management teams must select those customers who are most profitable to the company.

3. How can Level 3 and 4 contribution margin variances be helpful to a management team?

Calculating Level 3 and 4 contribution margin variances directs attention to what has actually happened relative to what was expected. Contribution margin variances are best explained by marketing, which is responsible for sales volume forecasts and pricing of individual and bundled units. Contribution margin variance analyses are essential to evaluating and ranking product/service profitability.

4. How can a customer profitability profile be used?

The profile enables management teams to more readily select costs relevant to ranking the profitability of individual customers and entire groups of customers. The alternatives of negotiating new prices or reducing customer sustaining costs are clearer.

5. What are the key concepts when making product and customer mix decisions?

Managers should ignore allocated overhead costs when making decisions about discontinuing and adding customers, branches, and segments. They should focus instead on how total costs differ among alternatives.

Terms to Learn

This chapter and the Glossary at the end of the book contain definitions of the following important terms:

composite unit **(p. 656)**
customer profitability analysis
  (p. 662)
incremental revenue-allocation
  method **(p. 644)**
market-share variance
  (p. 658)

market-size contribution margin
  variance **(p. 659)**
price discounting **(p. 652)**
product bundle **(p. 642)**
revenue allocation **(p. 641)**
sales-mix contribution margin
  variance **(p. 656)**

sales-quantity contribution margin
  variance **(p. 657)**
stand-alone revenue-allocation
  method **(p. 643)**
zero-sum game **(p. 645)**

Assignment Material

MyLab Accounting Make the grade with MyLab Accounting: The Short-Answer Questions, Exercises, and Problems marked with a ⊕ can be found on MyLab Accounting. You can practise them as often as you want, and most feature step-by-step guided instructions to help you find the right answer.

Short-Answer Questions

⊕ **16-1** Describe how companies are increasingly facing revenue-allocation decisions.

⊕ **16-2** Distinguish between the stand-alone revenue-allocation method and the incremental revenue-allocation method.

⊕ **16-3** Identify and discuss arguments that individual product managers may put forward to support their preferred revenue-allocation method.

⊕ **16-4** How might a dispute over the allocation of revenues of a bundled product be resolved?

⊕ **16-5** Show how managers can gain insight into the causes of a sales-volume variance by drilling down into the components of this variance.

⊕ **16-6** How can the concept of a composite unit be used to explain why an unfavourable total sales-mix variance of contribution margin occurs?

16-7 Explain why a favourable sales-quantity variance occurs.

16-8 Distinguish between a market-size variance and a market-share variance.

16-9 Why might some companies choose not to compute market-size and market-share variances?

16-10 Why is customer profitability analysis a vitally important topic to managers?

16-11 Are for-profit businesses the only users of revenue allocation? Explain.

16-12 "A customer profitability profile highlights those customers that should be dropped to improve profitability." Do you agree? Explain.

16-13 Give an example of three types of different levels of costs in a customer cost hierarchy.

16-14 How can the extent of price discounting be tracked on a customer-by-customer basis?

Exercises

16-15 Terminology. A number of terms are listed below:

composite unit	customer profitability analysis	incremental
market-share	market-size	sales-mix
sales-quantity	standalone	product bundles

Required

Select the terms from the above list to complete the following sentences.

To satisfy their customers' value proposition and benefit from economies of scale, companies often create customized _____ from individual products. This is also called a _____. The decision the management team needs to make is how to allocate the bundled revenue to each component of the bundle. There are two methods: _____ and _____ revenue allocation. In combination with ABC systems, the management team can examine detailed variance reports of _____, _____, _____, and _____ variance. This informs the team how well they are implementing their strategy. The team can also use the customer as cost object in an ABC system and conduct a(n) _____ to determine whether to drop or add customers, stores, or branches to improve profit.

16-16 Cost allocation and decision making. Reidland Manufacturing has four divisions: Acme, Dune, Stark, and Brothers. Corporate headquarters is in Minnesota. Reidland corporate headquarters incurs costs of $16,800,000 per period, which is an indirect cost of the divisions. Corporate headquarters currently allocates this cost to the divisions based on the revenues of each division. The CEO has asked each division manager to suggest an allocation base for the indirect headquarters costs from among revenues, segment margin, direct costs, and number of employees. The following is relevant information about each division:

◄ LO 1

	Acme	Dune	Stark	Brothers
Revenues	$23,400,000	$25,500,000	$18,600,000	$16,500,000
Direct costs	15,900,000	12,300,000	12,900,000	13,800,000
Segment margin	$ 7,500,000	$13,200,000	$ 5,700,000	$ 2,700,000
Number of employees	6,000	12,000	4,500	1,500

Required

1. Allocate the indirect headquarters costs of Reidland Manufacturing to each of the four divisions using revenues, direct costs, segment margin, and number of employees as the allocation bases. Calculate operating margins for each division after allocating headquarters costs.
2. Which allocation base do you think the manager of the Brothers division would prefer? Explain.
3. What factors would you consider in deciding which allocation base Reidland should use?
4. Suppose the Reidland CEO decides to use direct costs as the allocation base. Should the Brothers division be closed? Why or why not?

16-17 Revenue allocation. Lee Shu-yu Inc. produces and sells DVDs to business people and students who are planning extended stays in China. It has been very successful with two DVDs: *Beginning Mandarin* and *Conversational Mandarin*. It is introducing a third DVD, *Reading Chinese Characters*. It has decided to

◄ LO 1

1. a. Allocated to *RCC*, $36

market its new DVD in two different packages, grouping the *Reading Chinese Characters* DVD with each of the other two language DVDs. Information about the separate DVDs and the packages follows.

DVD	Selling Price
Beginning Mandarin (*BegM*)	$60
Conversational Mandarin (*ConM*)	50
Reading Chinese Characters (*RCC*)	40
BegM + *RCC*	90
ConM + *RCC*	72

Required

1. Using the selling prices, allocate revenues from the *BegM* + *RCC* package to each DVD in that package using (a) the stand-alone method, (b) the incremental method, and (c) the Shapley value method.
2. Using the selling prices, allocate revenues from the *ConM* + *RCC* package to each DVD in that package using (a) the stand-alone method, (b) the incremental method, in either order, and (c) the Shapley value method.
3. Which method is most appropriate for allocating revenues among the DVDs? Why?

LO 2,3 ▶
1. Lower-tier tickets, $14,000 U

🌐 **16-18 Variance analysis, multiple products.** The Penguins play in the North American Ice Hockey League. The Penguins play in the Downtown Arena (owned and managed by the City of Downtown), which has a capacity of 15,000 seats (5,000 lower-tier seats and 10,000 upper-tier seats). The Downtown Arena charges the Penguins a per-ticket charge for use of the facility. All tickets are sold by the Reservation Network, which charges the Penguins a reservation fee per ticket. The Penguins' budgeted contribution margin for each type of ticket in 2018 is computed as follows:

	Lower-Tier Tickets	Upper-Tier Tickets
Selling price	$35	$14
Downtown Arena fee	10	6
Reservation Network fee	5	3
Contribution margin per ticket	$20	$ 5

The budgeted and actual average attendance figures per game in the 2018 season are

	Budgeted Seats Sold	Actual Seats Sold
Lower tier	4,000	3,300
Upper tier	6,000	7,700
Total	10,000	11,000

There was no difference between the budgeted and actual contribution margin for lower-tier or upper-tier seats.

The manager of the Penguins was delighted that actual attendance was 10% above budgeted attendance per game, especially given the depressed state of the local economy in the past six months.

Required

1. Compute the sales-volume variance for each type of ticket and in total for the Penguins in 2018. (Calculate all variances in terms of contribution margins.)
2. Compute the sales-quantity and sales-mix variances for each type of ticket and in total in 2018.
3. Present a summary of the variances in requirements 1 and 2. Comment on the results.

LO 2,3 ▶
1. Sales mix, 80% Plain, 20% Chic

🌐 **16-19 Variance analysis, working backward.** The Guangzhou Corporation (GC) sells two brands of wineglasses, Plain and Chic. GC provides the following information for sales in the month of June 2018:

Static-budget total contribution margin	$5,600
Budgeted units to be sold of all glasses	2,000 units
Budgeted contribution margin per unit of Plain	$ 2 per unit
Budgeted contribution margin per unit of Chic	$ 6 per unit
Total sales-quantity variance	$1,400 U
Actual sales-mix percentage of Plain	60%

All variances are to be computed in contribution-margin terms.

Required

1. Calculate the sales-quantity variances for each product for June 2018.
2. Calculate the individual-product and total sales-mix variances for June 2018. Calculate the individual-product and total sales-volume variances for June 2018.
3. Briefly describe the conclusions you can draw from the variances.

🌐 **16-20 Variance analysis, multiple products.** The PopStop manufactures and sells three soft drinks: Kola, Lima, and Oranga. Budgeted and actual results for 2018 are as follows:

◀ **LO 2**
1. Budgeted sales mix, 16% Kola, 24% Limor, 60% Orlem

	Budget for 2018			Actual for 2018		
Product	Selling Price	Variable Cost per Case	Cases Sold	Selling Price	Variable Cost per Case	Cases Sold
Kola	$6.00	$4.00	400,000	$6.20	$4.50	480,000
Lima	4.00	2.80	600,000	4.25	2.75	900,000
Oranga	7.00	4.50	1,500,000	6.80	4.60	1,620,000

Required

1. Compute the total sales-volume variance, the total sales-mix variance, and the total sales-quantity variance. (Calculate all variances in terms of contribution margin.) Show results for each product in your computations.
2. What inferences can you draw from the variances computed in requirement 1?

🌐 **16-21 Variance analysis, multiple products.** The Chicago Tigers play in the American Ice Hockey League. The Tigers play in the Downtown Arena, which is owned and managed by the City of Chicago. The arena has a capacity of 15,000 seats (5,500 lower-tier seats and 9,500 upper-tier seats). The arena charges the Tigers a per-ticket charge for use of its facility. All tickets are sold by the Reservation Network, which charges the Tigers a reservation fee per ticket. The Tigers' budgeted contribution margin for each type of ticket in 2017 is computed as follows:

◀ **LO 2, 3**
Sales Volume Variance is $8,600 U

	Lower-Tier Tickets	Upper-Tier Tickets
Selling price	$33	$18
Downtown Arena fee	9	6
Reservation Network fee	4	5
Contribution margin per ticket	$20	$7

The budgeted and actual average attendance figures per game in the 2017 season are as follows:

	Budgeted Seats Sold	Actual Seats Sold
Lower tier	4,500	3,300
Upper tier	5,500	7,700
Total	10,000	11,000

There was no difference between the budgeted and actual contribution margin for lower-tier or upper-tier seats.

The manager of the Tigers was delighted that actual attendance was 10% above budgeted attendance per game, especially given the depressed state of the local economy in the past six months.

Required

1. Compute the sales-volume variance for each type of ticket and in total for the Chicago Tigers in 2017. (Calculate all variances in terms of contribution margins.)
2. Compute the sales-quantity and sales-mix variances for each type of ticket and in total in 2017.
3. Present a summary of the variances in requirements 1 and 2. Comment on the results.

🌐 **16-22 Market-share and market-size variances.** Emcee Inc. prepared the budget for 2017 assuming a 20% market share based on total sales in the Midwest region of the United States. The total fruit drinks market was estimated to reach sales of 1.25 million cartons in the region. However, actual total sales volume in the Midwest region was 1.5 million cartons.

◀ **LO 4**

Required

Calculate the market-share and market-size variances for Emcee Inc. in 2017. (Calculate all variances in terms of contribution margin.) Comment on the results.

LO 2,4 ▶
1. Order processing costs for
Generic Inc., $400

⊕ **16-23 Customer profitability, distribution.** Generic Inc. is a distributor of pharmaceutical products. Its ABC system has five activities:

Activity Area	Cost Driver Rate in 2018
1. Order processing	$40 per order
2. Line-item ordering	3 per line item
3. Store deliveries	50 per store delivery
4. Carton deliveries	1 per carton
5. Shelf-stocking	16 per stocking-hour

Rick Flair, the controller of Generic, wants to use this ABC system to examine individual customer profitability within each distribution market. He focuses first on the mom-and-pop single-store distribution market. Two customers are used to exemplify the insights available with the ABC approach. Data pertaining to these two customers in August 2018 are as follows:

	Charlesville Pharmacy	Chapelville Pharmacy
Total orders	13	10
Average line items per order	9	18
Total store deliveries	7	10
Average cartons shipped per store delivery	22	20
Average hours of shelf-stocking per store delivery	0	0.5
Average revenue per delivery	$2,400	$1,800
Average cost of goods sold per delivery	$2,100	$1,650

Required

1. Use the ABC information to compute the operating income of each customer in August 2018. Comment on the results and what, if anything, Flair should do.
2. Flair ranks the individual customers in the mom-and-pop single-store distribution market on the basis of monthly operating income. The cumulative operating income of the top 20% of customers is $55,680. Generic reports operating losses of $21,247 for the bottom 40% of its customers. Make four recommendations that you think Generic should consider in light of this new customer profitability information.

Problems

LO 1,4 ▶
1. Total Customer Revenue
is $13,980

⊕ **16-24 Customer profitability.** Bracelet Delights is a new company that manufactures custom jewelry. Bracelet Delights currently has six customers referenced by customer number: 01, 02, 03, 04, 05, and 06. Besides the costs of making the jewelry, the company has the following activities:

1. **Customer orders.** The salespeople, designers, and jewelry makers spend time with the customer. The cost-driver rate is $42 per hour spent with a customer.
2. **Customer fittings.** Before the jewelry piece is completed, the customer may come in to make sure it looks right and fits properly. Cost-driver rate is $30 per hour.
3. **Rush orders.** Some customers want their jewelry quickly. The cost-driver rate is $90 per rush order.
4. **Number of customer return visits.** Customers may return jewelry up to 30 days after the pickup of the jewelry to have something refitted or repaired at no charge. The cost-driver rate is $40 per return visit.

Information about the six customers follows. Some customers purchased multiple items. The cost of the jewelry is 60% of the selling price.

Customer number	01	02	03	04	05	06
Sales revenue	$850	$4,500	$280	$2,200	$5,500	$650
Cost of item(s)	$510	$2,700	$168	$1,320	$3,300	$390
Hours spent on customer order	3	10	1	8	17	5
Hours on fittings	1	6	0	0	4	0
Number of rush orders	0	2	1	2	3	0
Number of return visits	0	0	0	0	0	1

Required

1. Calculate the customer-level operating income for each customer. Rank the customers in order of most to least profitable and prepare a customer-profitability analysis, as in Exhibits 16-2 and 16-10.
2. Are any customers unprofitable? What is causing this? What should Bracelet Delights do about these customers?

16-25 Customer profitability and ethics. KC Corporation manufactures an air-freshening device called GoodAir, which it sells to six merchandising firms. The list price of a GoodAir is $30, and the full manufacturing costs are $18. Salespeople receive a commission on sales, but the commission is based on number of orders taken, not on sales revenue generated or number of units sold. Salespeople receive a commission of $10 per order (in addition to regular salary).

◀ **LO 1**

KC Corporation makes products based on anticipated demand. KC carries an inventory of GoodAir, so rush orders do not result in any extra manufacturing costs over and above the $18 per unit. KC ships finished product to the customer at no additional charge for either regular or expedited delivery. KC incurs significantly higher costs for expedited deliveries than for regular deliveries. Customers occasionally return shipments to KC, and the company subtracts these returns from gross revenue. The customers are not charged a restocking fee for returns.

Budgeted (expected) customer-level cost driver rates are:

Order taking (excluding sales commission)	$15 per order
Product handling	$1 per unit
Delivery	$1.20 per kilometre driven
Expedited (rush) delivery	$175 per shipment
Restocking	$50 per returned shipment
Visits to customers	$125 per customer

Because salespeople are paid $10 per order, they often break up large orders into multiple smaller orders. This practice reduces the actual order-taking cost by $7 per smaller order (from $15 per order to $8 per order) because the smaller orders are all written at the same time. This lower cost rate is not included in budgeted rates because salespeople create smaller orders without telling management or the accounting department. All other actual costs are the same as budgeted costs.

Information about KC's clients follows:

	AC	DC	MC	JC	RC	BC
Total number of units purchased	225	520	295	110	390	1,050
Number of actual orders	5	20	4	6	9	18
Number of written orders	10	20*	9	12	24	36
Total number of kilometres driven to deliver all products	360	580	350	220	790	850
Total number of units returned	15	40	0	0	35	40
Number of returned shipments	3	2	0	0	1	5
Number of expedited deliveries	0	8	0	0	3	4

*Because DC places 20 separate orders, its order costs are $15 per order. All other orders are multiple smaller orders and so have actual order costs of $8 each.

Required

1. Classify each of the customer-level operating costs as a customer output unit–level, customer batch-level, or customer-sustaining cost.
2. Using the preceding information, calculate the expected customer-level operating income for the six customers of KC Corporation. Use the number of written orders at $15 each to calculate expected order costs.
3. Recalculate the customer-level operating income using the number of written orders but at their actual $8 cost per order instead of $15 (except for DC, whose actual cost is $15 per order). How will KC Corporation evaluate customer-level operating cost performance this period?
4. Recalculate the customer-level operating income if salespeople had not broken up actual orders into multiple smaller orders. Don't forget to also adjust sales commissions.
5. How is the behaviour of the salespeople affecting the profit of KC Corporation? Is their behaviour ethical? What could KC Corporation do to change the behaviour of the salespeople?

LO 4 ▶

1. Customer-level operating
income for customer R, $38,720

16-26 Customer profitability, distribution. Spring Distribution has decided to analyze the profitability of five new customers. It buys bottled water at $12 per case and sells to retail customers at a list price of $14.40 per case. Data pertaining to the five customers are

	Customer				
	P	**Q**	**R**	**S**	**T**
Cases sold	2,080	8,750	60,800	31,800	3,900
List selling price	$14.40	$14.40	$14.40	$14.40	$14.40
Actual selling price	$14.40	$14.16	$13.20	$13.92	$12.96
Number of purchase orders	15	25	30	25	30
Number of customer visits	2	3	6	2	3
Number of deliveries	10	30	60	40	20
Kilometres traveled per delivery	14	4	3	8	40
Number of expedited deliveries	0	0	0	0	1

Activity	Cost Driver Rate
Order taking	$100 per purchase order
Customer visits	80 per customer visit
Deliveries	2 per delivery kilometre traveled
Product handling	0.50 per case sold
Expedited deliveries	300 per expedited delivery

Required

1. Compute the customer-level operating income of each of the five retail customers now being examined (P, Q, R, S, and T). Comment on the results.
2. What insights are gained by reporting both the list selling price and the actual selling price for each customer?
3. What factors should Spring Distribution consider in deciding whether to drop one or more of the five customers?

LO 2 ▶

1. SlatePro actual contribution
percent, 16%

16-27 Variance analysis, sales-mix, and sales-quantity variances. Blank Slate Inc. (BSI) produces tablet computers. BSI markets three different handheld models. SlatePro is a souped-up version for the executive on the go; Slate is a consumer-oriented version; and SlateLite is a stripped down version for the young adult market. You are BSI's senior vice-president of marketing. The CEO has discovered that the total contribution margin came in lower than budgeted, and it is your responsibility to explain to him why results are different from the budget. Budgeted and actual operating data for the company's third quarter of 2018 are as follows:

Budgeted Operating Data, Third Quarter 2018

	Selling Price	Variable Cost per Unit	Contribution Margin per Unit	Sales Volume in Units
SlatePro	$379	$182	$197	12,500
Slate	269	98	171	37,500
SlateLite	149	65	84	50,000
				100,000

Actual Operating Data, Third Quarter 2018

	Selling Price	Variable Cost per Unit	Contribution Margin per Unit	Sales Volume in Units
SlatePro	$349	$178	$171	11,000
Slate	285	92	193	44,000
SlateLite	102	73	29	55,000
				110,000

Required

1. Compute the actual and budgeted contribution margins in dollars for each product and in total for the third quarter of 2018.
2. Calculate the actual and budgeted sales mixes for the three products for the third quarter of 2018.
3. Calculate total sales-volume, sales-mix, and sales-quantity variances for the third quarter of 2018. (Calculate all variances in terms of contribution margins.)
4. Given that your CEO is known to have temper tantrums, you want to be well prepared for this meeting. In order to prepare, write a paragraph or two comparing actual results to budgeted amounts.

⊕ **16-28 Market-share and market-size variances** (continuation of Problem 16-27). Blank Slate's senior vice-president of marketing prepared his budget at the beginning of the third quarter, assuming a 25% market share based on total sales. The total tablet market was estimated by Foolinstead Research to reach sales of 400,000 units worldwide in the third quarter. However, actual sales in the third quarter were 500,000 units.

◀ **LO 2**

1. Budgeted average contribution margin per unit, $130.75

Required

1. Calculate the market-share and market-size variances for BSI in the third quarter of 2018. (Calculate all variances in terms of contribution margins.)
2. Explain what happened based on the market-share and market-size variances.
3. Calculate the actual market size, in units, that would have led to no market-size variance (again using budgeted contribution margin per unit). Use this market-size figure to calculate the actual market share that would have led to a zero market-share variance.

⊕ **16-29 Variance analysis, multiple products.** Momma's Pan Inc. operates a chain of cookie stores. Budgeted and actual operating data for its three Ottawa stores for August 2018 are as follows:

◀ **LO 2, 3**

1. Chocolate chip sales-volume variance, $25,200 F

Budget for August 2018

	Selling Price per Kilogram	Variable Cost per Kilogram	Contribution Margin per Kilogram	Sales Volume in Kilograms
Chocolate chip	$4.50	$2.50	$2.00	45,000
Oatmeal raisin	5.00	2.70	2.30	25,000
Coconut	5.50	2.90	2.60	10,000
White chocolate	6.00	3.00	3.00	5,000
Macadamia nut	6.50	3.40	3.10	15,000
				100,000

Actual for August 2018

	Selling Price per Kilogram	Variable Cost per Kilogram	Contribution Margin per Kilogram	Sales Volume in Kilograms
Chocolate chip	$4.50	$2.60	$1.90	57,600
Oatmeal raisin	5.20	2.90	2.30	18,000
Coconut	5.50	2.80	2.70	9,600
White chocolate	6.00	3.40	2.60	13,200
Macadamia nut	7.00	4.00	3.00	21,600
				120,000

Momma's Pan focuses on contribution margin in its variance analysis.

Required

1. Compute the total sales-volume variance for August 2018.
2. Compute the total sales-mix variance for August 2018.
3. Compute the total sales-quantity variance for August 2018.
4. Comment on your results in requirements 1, 2, and 3.

LO 2, 3 ▶

🌐 **16-30 Cost-hierarchy income statement and allocation of corporate costs to customers.** The Insurance Company insures homeowners in three regions of the United States: Eastern, Midwest, and South. In the past year, several hurricanes hit the Southern region of the United States, requiring payments to insured homeowners.

Management of the company wishes to analyze the profitability of the three key regions and has gathered the following information:

	Eastern	Midwest	South	Total
Revenue	$4,000,000	$2,600,000	$1,800,000	$8,400,000
Customer-level costs	2,920,000	1,768,000	1,674,000	6,362,000
Customer-level operating income	$1,080,000	$ 832,000	$ 126,000	$2,038,000
Customer-level operating income percentage	27.00%	32.00%	7.00%	24.26%

In addition to the customer-level costs above, the company also allocates $750,000 of corporate costs to each region based on the revenues of each region.

Required

1. Prepare a cost-hierarchy income statement for The Insurance Company using the format in Exhibit 16-3 assuming corporate costs are not allocated to each region.
2. Allocate the corporate costs to each region and calculate the income of each region after assigning corporate costs.
3. Should top management of The Insurance Company close down the South region? Explain.
4. What are the advantages and disadvantages of The Insurance Company allocating corporate costs to the regions?

LO 4 ▶

1. Gold Program contribution margin, $12,295,800

16-31 Customer profitability and ABC hierarchy. The Sherriton Hotels chain embarked on a new customer loyalty program in 2018. The 2018 year-end data have been collected, and it is now time for you to determine whether the loyalty program should be continued, discontinued, or perhaps altered to improve loyalty and profitability levels at Sherriton.

Sherriton's loyalty program consists of three different customer loyalty levels. All new customers can sign up for the Sherriton Bronze Card—this card provides guests with a complimentary bottle of wine (cost to the chain is $5 per bottle) and $20 in restaurant coupons each night (cost to the chain is $10). Bronze customers also receive a 10% discount off the nightly rate. The program enables the chain to track a member's stays and activities. Once a customer has stayed and paid for 20 nights at any of the chain's locations worldwide, he or she is upgraded to Silver Customer status. Silver benefits include the bottle of wine (cost to the chain is $5 per bottle), $30 in restaurant coupons (cost to the chain is $15), and 20% off every night from the twenty-first night on. A customer who reaches the 50-night level is upgraded to Gold Customer status. Gold status increases the nightly discount to 30% and replaces the $5 bottle of wine with a bottle of champagne (cost to the chain is $20 per bottle). As well, $40 in restaurant coupons are granted (cost to the chain is $20).

The average full price for one night's stay is $200. The chain incurs variable costs of $65 per night, exclusive of loyalty program costs. Total fixed costs for the chain are $140,580,000. Sherriton operates 10 hotels with, on average, 500 rooms each. All hotels are open for business 365 days a year, and approximate average occupancy rates are around 80%. Following are some loyalty program characteristics:

Loyalty Program	Number of Customers	Average Number of Nights per Customer
Gold	2,673	60
Silver	9,174	35
Bronze	88,330	10
No program	240,900	1

Note that an average Gold Customer would have received the 10% discount for his or her first 20 stays, received the 20% discount for the next 30 stays, and the 30% discount only for the last 10 nights. Assume that all program members signed on to the program the first time they stayed with one of the chain's hotels. Also, assume the restaurants are managed by a 100%-owned subsidiary of Sherriton.

Required

1. Calculate the program contribution margin for each of the three programs, as well as for the group of customers not subscribing to the loyalty program. Which program is the most profitable? Which is the least profitable? Do not allocate fixed costs to individual rooms or specific loyalty programs.
2. Develop an operating income statement for Sherriton for the year ended December 31, 2018.
3. What is the average room rate per night? What are average variable costs per night inclusive of the loyalty program?
4. Explain what drives the profitability (or lack thereof) of the most and least profitable loyalty programs (again, one of these may be the "no program" option).

⊕ **16-32 Customer profitability, customer-cost hierarchy.** Ramish Electronics has only two retail and two wholesale customers. Information relating to each customer for 2018 follows (in thousands):

◀ **LO 5**
1. North America wholesaler customer-level operating income, $58,150

	Wholesale Customers		Retail Customers	
	North America Wholesaler	South America Wholesaler	Big Sam Stereo	World Market
Revenues at list price	$450,000	$580,000	$130,000	$100,000
Discounts from list prices	30,000	40,000	7,000	500
Cost of goods sold	325,000	455,000	118,000	90,000
Delivery costs	450	650	200	125
Order processing costs	800	1,000	200	130
Costs of sales visits	5,600	5,500	2,300	1,350

Ramish's annual distribution-channel costs are $38 million for wholesale customers and $7 million for retail customers. Its annual corporate-sustaining costs, such as salary for top management and general administration costs, are $65 million. There is no cause-and-effect or benefits-received relationship between any cost allocation base and corporate-sustaining costs. That is, corporate-sustaining costs could be saved only if Ramish Electronics were to completely shut down.

Required

1. Calculate customer-level operating income using the format in Exhibit 16-2.
2. Prepare a customer-cost hierarchy report, using the format in Exhibit 16-13.
3. Ramish's management decides to allocate all corporate-sustaining costs to distribution channels: $51 million to the wholesale channel and $14 million to the retail channel. As a result, distribution-channel costs are now $89 million (= $38 million + $51 million) for the wholesale channel and $21 million (= $7 million + $14 million) for the retail channel. Calculate the distribution-channel-level operating income. On the basis of these calculations, what actions, if any, should Ramish's managers take? Explain.

⊕ **16-33 Customer profitability in a manufacturing firm.** Lee Manufacturing makes a component they call P14-31. This component is manufactured only when ordered by a customer, so Lee keeps no inventory of P14-31. The list price is $100 per unit, but customers who place "large" orders receive a 10% discount on price. Currently, the salespeople decide whether an order is large enough to qualify for the discount. When the product is finished, it is packed in cases of 10. When a customer order is not a multiple of 10, Lee uses a full case to pack the partial amount left over (e.g., if Customer C orders 25 units, three cases will be required). Customers pick up the order so Lee incurs costs of holding the product in the warehouse until customer pickup. The customers are manufacturing firms; if the component needs to be exchanged or repaired, customers can come back within 10 days for free exchange or repair.

◀ **LO 4**
Customer A customer-level operating income, $40,485

The full cost of manufacturing a unit of P14-31 is $80. In addition, Lee incurs customer-level costs. Customer-level cost-driver rates are

Order taking	$380 per order
Product handling	10 per case
Warehousing (holding finished product)	55 per day
Rush order processing	520 per rush order
Exchange and repair costs	40 per unit

Information about Lee's five biggest customers follows:

	A	B	C	D	E
Number of units purchased	5,000	2,400	1,200	4,000	8,000
Discounts given	10%	0	10%	0	10% on half the units
Number of orders	10	12	48	16	12
Number of cases	500	240	144	400	812
Days in warehouse (total for all orders)	13	16	0	12	120
Number of rush orders	0	2	0	0	5
Number of units exchanged/repaired	0	30	5	20	95

The salesperson gave Customer C a price discount because, although Customer C ordered only 1,200 units in total, 12 orders (one per month) were placed. The salesperson wanted to reward Customer C for repeat business. All customers except E ordered units in the same order size. Customer E's order quantity varied, so E got a discount some of the time but not all the time.

Required

1. Calculate the customer-level operating income for these five customers. Use the format in Exhibit 16-2. Prepare a customer profitability analysis by ranking the customers from most to least profitable, as in Exhibit 16-10.
2. Discuss the results of your customer profitability analysis. Does Lee have unprofitable customers? Is there anything Lee should do differently with its five customers?

LO 2, 4, 5 ▶
1. Customer 02's customer-level operating income, $900

🌐 **16-34 Customer profitability.** Ring Delights is a new company that manufactures custom jewellery. Ring Delights currently has six customers referenced by customer number: 01, 02, 03, 04, 05, and 06. Besides the costs of making the jewellery, the company has the following activities:

1. Customer orders. The salespeople, designers, and jewellery makers spend time with the customer. The cost driver rate is $40 per hour spent with a customer.
2. Customer fittings. Before the jewellery piece is completed the customer may come in to make sure it looks right and fits properly. Cost driver rate is $25 per hour.
3. Rush orders. Some customers want their jewellery quickly. The cost driver rate is $100 per rush order.
4. Number of customer return visits. Customers may return jewellery up to 30 days after the pickup of the jewellery to have something refitted or repaired at no charge. The cost driver rate is $30 per return visit.

Information about the six customers follows. Some customers purchased multiple items. The cost of the jewellery is 70% of the selling price.

Customer number	01	02	03	04	05	06
Sales revenue	$600	$4,200	$300	$2,500	$4,900	$700
Cost of item(s)	$420	$2,940	$210	$1,750	$3,430	$490
Hours spent on customer order	2	7	1	5	20	3
Hours on fittings	1	2	0	0	4	1
Number of rush orders	0	0	1	1	3	0
Number of return visits	0	1	0	1	5	1

Required

1. Calculate the customer-level operating income for each customer. Rank the customers in order of most to least profitable and prepare a customer profitability analysis, as in Exhibit 16-12.
2. Are any customers unprofitable? What is causing this? What should Ring Delights do with respect to these customers?

🌐 **16-35 Cost-hierarchy income statement and allocation of corporate, division, and channel costs to customers.** Vocal Speakers makes wireless speakers that are sold to different customers in two main distribution channels. Recently, the company's profitability has decreased. Management would like to analyze the profitability of each channel based on the following information:

◀ **LO 5**

	Distribution Channel A	Distribution Channel B	Total
Revenue	$850,000	$910,000	$1,760,000
Customer-level costs	628,000	532,400	1,160,400
Customer-level operating income	$222,000	$377,600	$ 599,600
Customer-level operating income as a percentage of revenue	26.12%	41.49%	34.07%

The company allocates distribution channel costs of marketing and administration as follows:

	Total	Allocation basis
Distribution-channel costs		
Marketing costs	$260,000	Channel revenue
Administration costs	$200,000	Customer-level costs

Based on a special study, the company allocates corporate costs to the two channels based on the corporate resources demanded by the channels as follows: Distribution Channel A, $45,000, and Distribution Channel B, $55,000. If the company were to close a distribution channel, none of the corporate costs would be saved.

Required

1. Calculate the operating income for each distribution channel as a percentage of revenue after assigning customer-level costs, distribution-channel costs, and corporate costs.
2. Should Vocal Speakers close down any distribution channel? Explain briefly including any assumptions that you made.
3. Would you allocate corporate costs to divisions? Why is allocating these costs helpful? What actions would it help you take?

🌐 **16-36 Customer profitability and governance.** Pilt Corporation manufactures a product called the Pilt, which it sells to merchandising firms such as International House of Pilts (IHoP), Pilts-R-Us (PRU), Pilt Marcus (PM), Pilt City (PC), Good Pilts (PP), and Pilt-mart (Pmart). The list price of a Pilt is $40, and the full manufacturing costs are $30. Salespeople receive a commission on sales, but the commission is based on number of orders taken, not on sales revenue generated or number of units sold. Salespeople receive a commission of $20 per order (in addition to regular salary).

◀ **LO 4**
GM customer-level operating incomes, $2,340

Pilt Corporation makes products based on anticipated demand. Pilt Corporation carries an inventory of Pilts, so rush orders do not result in any extra manufacturing costs over and above the $30 per Pilt. Pilt Corporation ships finished product to the customer at no additional charge to the customer for either regular or expedited delivery. Pilt incurs significantly higher costs for expedited deliveries than for regular deliveries.

Expected and actual customer-level cost driver rates are

Order taking (excluding sales commission)	$ 28 per order
Product handling	1 per unit
Delivery	1 per kilometre driven
Expedited (rush) delivery	300 per shipment

Because salespeople are paid $20 per order, they break up large orders into multiple smaller orders. This practice reduces the actual order-taking cost by $16 per smaller order (from $28 per order to $12 per order) because the smaller orders are all written at the same time. This lower cost rate is not included in budgeted rates because salespeople create smaller orders without telling management or the accounting department. Also, salespeople offer customers discounts to entice them to place more orders; PRU and Pmart each receive a 5% discount off the list price of $40.

Information about Pilt's clients follows:

	IHP	PRU	PM	PC	PP	Pmart
Total number of units purchased	200	540	300	100	400	1,000
Number of actual orders	2	12	2	2	4	10
Number of written orders per actual order	2	1*	3	2	4	2
Total number of kilometres driven to deliver all products	80	120	72	28	304	100
Number of expedited deliveries	0	4	0	0	1	3

*Because PRU places 12 separate orders, its order costs are $28 per order. All other orders are multiple smaller orders and so have actual order costs of $12 each.

Required

1. Using the information above, calculate the expected customer-level operating income for the six customers. Use the number of written orders at $28 each to calculate expected order costs.
2. Recalculate the customer-level operating income using the number of written orders but at their actual $12 cost per order instead of $28 (except for PRU, whose actual cost is $28 per order). Detail an approach to evaluate customer-level operating cost performance this period.
3. Recalculate the customer-level operating income if salespeople had not broken up actual orders into multiple smaller orders. Don't forget to also adjust sales commissions.
4. How is the behaviour of the salespeople affecting the profit of Pilt Corporation? Is their behaviour ethical? What could Pilt Corporation do to change the behaviour of the salespeople?

LO 2, 4, 5 ▶   🌐 **16-37 Cost allocation to divisions.** Forber Bakery makes baked goods for grocery stores and has three divisions: bread, cake, and doughnuts. Each division is run and evaluated separately, but the main headquarters incurs costs that are indirect costs for the divisions. Costs incurred in the main headquarters are as follows:

Human resources (HR) costs	$1,900,000
Accounting department costs	1,400,000
Rent and depreciation	1,200,000
Other	600,000
Total costs	$5,100,000

The Forber upper management currently allocates this cost to the divisions equally. One of the division managers has done some research on activity-based costing and proposes the use of different allocation bases for the different indirect costs—number of employees for HR costs, total revenues for accounting department costs, square feet of space for rent and depreciation costs, and equal allocation among the divisions of "other" costs. Information about the three divisions follows:

	Bread	Cake	Doughnuts
Total revenues	$20,900,000	$4,500,000	$13,400,000
Direct costs	14,500,000	3,200,000	7,250,000
Segment margin	$ 6,400,000	$1,300,000	$ 6,150,000
Number of employees	400	100	300
Square feet of space	10,000	4,000	6,000

Required

1. Allocate the indirect costs of Forber to each division equally. Calculate division operating income after allocation of headquarter costs.
2. Allocate headquarter costs to the individual divisions using the proposed allocation bases. Calculate the division operating income after allocation. Comment on the allocation bases used to allocate headquarter costs.
3. Which division manager do you think suggested this new allocation. Explain briefly. Which allocation do you think is "better?"

🌐 **16-38 Allocation of corporate costs to divisions.** Cathy Carpenter, controller of the Sweet and Salty Snacks is preparing a presentation to senior executives about the performance of its four divisions. Summary data related to the four divisions for the most recent year are as follows: ◄ **LO 1**

	Home	Insert	Page Layout	Formulas	Data	Review	View
	A	B	C	D	E	F
1		DIVISIONS					
2		Candy	Nuts	Crackers	Cookies	Total
3	Revenues	$ 870,000	$ 975,000	$ 654,000	$ 501,000	$3,000,000
4	Operating Costs	330,800	378,000	658,000	314,000	1,680,800
5	Operating Income	$ 539,200	$ 597,000	$ (4,000)	$ 187,000	$1,319,200
6						
7	Identifiable assets	$1,800,000	$2,880,000	$1,440,000	$1,080,000	$7,200,000
8	Number of employees	3,600	6,600	2,700	2,100	15,000

Under the existing accounting system, costs incurred at corporate headquarters are collected in a single cost pool ($1.2 million in the most recent year) and allocated to each division on the basis of its actual revenues. The top managers in each division share in a division-income bonus pool. Division income is defined as operating income less allocated corporate costs.

Carpenter has analyzed the components of corporate costs and proposes that corporate costs be collected in four cost pools. The components of corporate costs for the most recent year and Carpenter's suggested cost pools and allocation bases are as follows:

	Home	Insert	Page Layout	Formulas	Data	Review	View
	A	B	C	D	E	F
11	**Corporate Cost Category**	**Amount**	**Suggested Cost Pool**	**Suggested Allocation Base**		
12	Interest on debt	$ 380,000	Cost Pool 1	Identifiable assets		
13	Corporate salaries	200,000	Cost Pool 2			
14	Accounting and control	160,000	Cost Pool 2	Division revenues		
15	General marketing	170,000	Cost Pool 2			
16	Public affairs	150,000	Cost Pool 3	Positive operating income*		
17	Personnel and payroll	140,000	Cost Pool 4	Number of employees		
18	Total	$1,200,000				
19						
20	*Carpenter proposes that this cost be allocated using the operating income (if positive) of divisions,					
21	with only divisions with positive operating income included in the allocation base.					

Required

1. Discuss two reasons why Sweet and Salty Snacks should allocate corporate costs to each division.
2. Calculate the operating income of each division when all corporate costs are allocated based on revenues of each division.
3. Calculate the operating income of each division when all corporate costs are allocated using the four cost pools.
4. How do you think the division managers will receive the new proposal? What are the strengths and weaknesses of Carpenter's proposal relative to the existing single cost-pool method?

LO 1 ▶

1. The weight for Innocence, $220

16-39 Revenue allocation for bundled products. Pétale Parfum (PP) manufactures and sells upscale perfumes. In recent months, PP has started selling its products in bundled form, as well as in individual form. Sales in 2018 of three products that have been sold individually are as follows:

	Retail Price	Units Sold
Stand-alone		
Fraîche	$110	20,000
Désarmer	88	37,500
Innocence	275	20,000
Suite		
Fraîche + Désarmer	165	
Fraîche + Innocence	308	

Required

1. Compute the weights for allocating revenues to each division for each of the bundled products using:
   a. The stand-alone revenue-allocation method based on total revenues of individual products.
   b. The incremental revenue-allocation method, with Innocence ranked 1; Désarmer, 2; and Fraîche, 3, based on retail prices of individual products. According to this ranking, the primary product in a suite has the highest rank, and so on.
2. Recalculate the allocation using the Shapley and the weighted Shapley value methods. What method would you recommend and why?

LO 5 ▶

1. If the Surrey store is closed, Sundry's operating income would increase by $7,000.

⊕ **16-40 Closing and opening stores.** Your Market (YM) runs two convenience stores, one in Vancouver and one in Surrey. Operating income for each store in 2018 follows:

	Vancouver	Surrey
Revenues	$1,070,000	$ 860,000
Operating costs:		
Cost of goods sold	750,000	660,000
Lease rent (renewable each year)	90,000	75,000
Labour (paid on an hourly basis)	42,000	42,000
Depreciation of equipment	25,000	22,000
Utilities (electricity, heating)	43,000	46,000
Allocated corporate overhead	50,000	30,000
Total operating costs	1,000,000	875,000
Operating income (loss)	$ 70,000	$ (15,000)

The equipment has a remaining useful life of one year and zero disposal price. In a senior management meeting, Maria Lopez, the management accountant at Your Market, makes the following comment: "YM can increase its profitability by closing down the Surrey store or by adding more stores like it."

Required

Answer the following questions referring to the preceding data.

1. Calculate YM's operating income if it closes down the Surrey store. By closing down the store, YM can reduce overall corporate overhead costs by $44,000. Is Maria Lopez correct? Explain.

2. Calculate YM's operating income if it opens another store with revenues and costs identical to the Surrey store (including a cost of $22,000 to acquire equipment with a one-year useful life and zero disposal price). Opening this store will increase corporate overhead costs by $4,000. Is Maria Lopez correct? Explain.

🌐 **16-41 Customer profitability in a manufacturing firm.** Mississippi Manufacturing makes a component called B2040. This component is manufactured only when ordered by a customer, so Mississippi keeps no inventory of B2040. The list price is $112 per unit, but customers who place "large" orders receive a 10% discount on price. The customers are manufacturing firms. Currently, the salespeople decide whether an order is large enough to qualify for the discount. When the product is finished, it is packed in cases of 10. If the component needs to be exchanged or repaired, customers can come back within 14 days for free exchange or repair.   ◀ LO 2, 3

The full cost of manufacturing a unit of B2040 is $95. In addition, Mississippi incurs customer-level costs. Customer-level cost-driver rates are:

Order taking	$360 per order
Product handling	$15 per case
Rush-order processing	$560 per rush order
Exchange and repair costs	$50 per unit

Information about Mississippi's five biggest customers follows:

	A	B	C	D	E
Number of units purchased	5,400	1,800	1,200	4,400	8,100
Discounts given	10%	10%	0	10%	10% on half the units
Number of orders	8	16	50	20	18
Number of cases	540	180	120	440	810
Number of rush orders	2	7	1	0	8
Number of units exchanged/repaired	18	70	13	50	200

All customers except E ordered units in the same order size. Customer E's order quantity varied, so E got a discount part of the time but not all the time.

Required

1. Calculate the customer-level operating income for these five customers. Use the format in Exhibit 14-3. Prepare a customer-profitability analysis by ranking the customers from most to least profitable, as in Exhibit 14-4.
2. Discuss the results of your customer-profitability analysis. Does Mississippi have unprofitable customers? Is there anything Mississippi should do differently with its five customers?

🌐 **16-42 Customer profitability, distribution.** Green Paper Delivery has decided to analyze the profitability of five new customers. It buys recycled paper at $20 per case and sells to retail customers at a list price of $26 per case. Data pertaining to the five customers are: ◀ LO 1

	Customer				
	1	2	3	4	5
Cases sold	1,830	6,780	44,500	31,200	1,950
List selling price	$26	$ 26	$ 26	$ 26	$ 26
Actual selling price	$26	$25.20	$24.30	$25.80	$23.90
Number of purchase orders	10	18	35	16	35
Number of customer visits	3	5	12	4	12
Number of deliveries	12	28	65	25	35
Kilometres traveled per delivery	14	4	8	6	45
Number of expedited deliveries	0	0	0	0	3

Green Paper Delivery's five activities and their cost drivers are:

Activity	Cost-Driver Rate
Order taking	$90 per purchase order
Customer visits	$75 per customer visit

Deliveries	$3 per delivery kilometre traveled
Product handling	$1.20 per case sold
Expedited deliveries	$250 per expedited delivery

Required

1. Compute the customer-level operating income of each of the five retail customers now being examined (1, 2, 3, 4, and 5). Comment on the results.
2. What insights do managers gain by reporting both the list selling price and the actual selling price for each customer?
3. What factors should managers consider in deciding whether to drop one or more of the five customers?

Collaborative Learning Case

LO 5 ▶ **16-43 Relevance of variance analyses.** As a producer of wine in the Niagara region, you have the opportunity either to lease vineyards from local grape-growers or to purchase grapes from other farmers. In the past you have purchased grapes from the Okanagan Valley in British Columbia, and from the Sonoma Valley in California.

The quality of wine depends in part on the quality of grapes input to the fermenting process, but your fermenting machinery has a fixed capacity. Any unused capacity in one year cannot be applied to a different use. To obtain the best return, your preference is to operate at practical capacity even if projected demand or normal capacity is higher. An interesting opportunity in the industry is the ability to enter into a contract in the spring to pay a specific dollar value for grapes harvested in the fall.

Financial experts call this a hedging contract because you are protecting yourself against the risk that actual prices in the fall (the spot price) will be higher than your spring contracted price (the strike price). The quantity and quality of grapes harvested each year depend largely on a single uncontrollable factor—the weather. In spring you must decide on the input mix of harvested and purchased grapes that you believe is most likely to make the best use of available practical capacity—but you have no idea what the weather will be in the months before harvest.

A supplier approaches you in the spring with a proposition to sell you grapes and specifies the strike price. This supplier from the Okanagan provides you with a historical trend chart that summarizes the association between weather and yield from the vineyard for the last eight years.

Required

1. Explain your reasons for your contracting decision.
2. Of what use would similar information on your own market share be?

TRY IT! 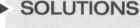 **SOLUTIONS**

Try It 16–1

| | All amounts in thousands of US dollars | | | |
| | Wholesale | | Retail | |
	West Region Wholesaler	East Region Wholesaler	Hudson Inc.	Pentel Corp.
Revenues at list prices	$750,000	$1,180,000	$350,000	$260,000
Price discounts	51,600	79,200	19,800	6,180
Revenues (at actual prices)	698,400	1,100,800	330,200	253,820
Cost of goods sold	570,000	1,020,000	298,000	190,000
Gross margin	128,400	80,800	32,200	63,820
Customer-level operating costs				
Delivery	29,100	23,420	16,460	14,290
Order processing	12,640	16,960	9,360	7,260
Sales visit	12,600	10,240	9,240	8,150
Total customer-level oper. costs	54,340	50,620	35,060	29,700
Customer-level operating. income	$ 74,060	$ 30,180	$ (2,860)	$ 34,120

Try It 16-2

Customer Distribution Channels

(all amounts in $000s)

	Total (all customers) (1) = (2) + (5)	Wholesale Customers — Total Wholesale (2) = (3) + (4)	West Region Wholesaler (3)	East Region Wholesaler (4)	Total Retail (5) = (6) + (7)	Retail Customers — Hudson Inc. (6)	Pentel Corp. (7)
Revenues (at actual prices)	$2,368,220	$1,799,200	$698,400	$1,100,800	$584,020	$330,200	$253,820
Customer-level costs	2,247,720	1,694,960	624,340[1]	1,070,620[1]	552,760	333,060[1]	219,700[a]
Customer-level operating income	135,500	104,240	$ 74,060	$ 30,180	31,260	$ (2,860)	$ 34,120
Distribution-channel costs allocated based on revenues	50,000	36,000	14,092[2]	21,908[2]	14,000	7,915[2]	6,085[2]
Distribution-channel-level operating income	85,500	68,240	59,968	8,272	17,260	(10,775)	28,035
Corporate-sustaining costs allocated to distribution channels based on channel oper. inc.	48,000	38,310[3]			9,690[3]		
Allocation of costs allocated to distribution channel reallocated to customers based on op. inc.			33,666[4]	4,644[4]			9,690
Operating income	$ 37,500	$ 29,930	$ 26,302	$ 3,628	$ 7,570	$(10,775)	$ 18,345

[1] Cost of goods sold + Total customer-level operating costs from Try It 16-1.

[2] $698,400 ÷ $1,784,200 × $36,000 = $14,092; $1,100,800 ÷ $1,784,200 × $36,000 = $21,908; $330,200 ÷ $584,020 × $14,000 = $7,915; $253820 ÷ $584,020 × $14,000 = $6,085.

[3] $68,240 ÷ $85,500 × 48,000 = $38,310; $17,260 ÷ $85,500 × 48,000 = $9,690.

[4] $59,968 ÷ $68,240 × $38,310 = $33,666; $8,272 ÷ $68,240 × $38,310 = $4,644.

Try It 16–3

Budget for 2017

	Variable		Contrib.			
	Selling Price	Cost per Unit	Margin per Unit	Units Sold	Sales Mix	Contribution Margin
	(1)	(2)	(3) = (1) − (2)	(4)	(5)	(6) = (3) × (4)
Duma	$20	$16	$4	88,000	40%	$ 352,000
Kool	23	18	5	132,000	60	660,000
Total				220,000	100%	$1,012,000

Actual for 2017

	Variable		Contrib.			
	Selling Price	Cost per Unit	Margin per Unit	Units Sold	Sales Mix	Contribution Margin
	(1)	(2)	(3) = (1) − (2)	(4)	(5)	(6) = (3) × (4)
Duma	$18	$15	$3	90,000	45%	$270,000
Kool	25	19	6	110,000	55	660,000
Total				200,000	100%	$930,000

The solution to Try It 16-3 presents the sales-volume, sales-quantity, and sales-mix variances for each product and in total for 2017.

$$\text{Sales-volume variance} = \left(\begin{array}{c} \text{Actual} \\ \text{quantity of} \\ \text{units sold} \end{array} - \begin{array}{c} \text{Budgeted} \\ \text{quantity of} \\ \text{units sold} \end{array} \right) \times \begin{array}{c} \text{Budgeted} \\ \text{contribution margin} \\ \text{per unit} \end{array}$$

Duma	=	(90,000 − 88,000) × $4	= $ 8,000 F
Kool	=	(110,000 − 132,000) × $5	= 110,000 U
Total			$102,000 U

$$\text{Sales-quantity variance} = \left(\begin{array}{c} \text{Actual units} \\ \text{of all} \\ \text{products sold} \end{array} - \begin{array}{c} \text{Budgeted units} \\ \text{of all} \\ \text{products sold} \end{array} \right) \times \begin{array}{c} \text{Budgeted} \\ \text{sales-mix} \\ \text{percentage} \end{array} \times \begin{array}{c} \text{Budgeted} \\ \text{contribution margin} \\ \text{per unit} \end{array}$$

Duma	=	(200,000 − 220,000) × 0.40 × $4	= $32,000 U
Kool	=	(200,000 − 220,000) × 0.60 × $5	= 60,000 U
Total			$92,000 U

$$\text{Sales-mix variance} = \begin{array}{c} \text{Actual units of} \\ \text{all products} \\ \text{sold} \end{array} \times \left(\begin{array}{c} \text{Actual} \\ \text{sales-mix} \\ \text{percentage} \end{array} - \begin{array}{c} \text{Budgeted} \\ \text{sales-mix} \\ \text{percentage)} \end{array} \right) \times \begin{array}{c} \text{Budgeted} \\ \text{contribution margin} \\ \text{per unit} \end{array}$$

Duma	=	200,000 × (0.45 − 0.40) × $4	= $40,000 F
Kool	=	200,000 × (0.55 − 0.60) × $5	= 50,000 U
Total			$10,000 U

The breakdown of the unfavourable sales-volume variance of $102,000 shows that the biggest contributor is the 20,000 unit decrease in sales, resulting in an unfavourable sales-quantity variance of $92,000. There is a further unfavourable sales-mix variance of $10,000 in contribution margin as a result of the sales mix shifting in favour of the less profitable Duma (budgeted contribution margin of $4 versus budgeted contribution margin of $5 for Kool).

Try It 16–3

Sales-Mix and Sales-Quantity Variance Analysis of Campbell Corp. for 2017

	Flexible Budget: Actual Units of All Products Sold × Actual Sales Mix × Budgeted Contribution Margin Per Unit	Static Budget: Actual Units of All Products Sold × Budgeted Sales Mix × Budgeted Contribution Margin Per Unit	Budgeted Units of All Products Sold × Budgeted Sales Mix × Budgeted Contribution Margin Per Unit
Duma	$200,000 \times 0.45 \times \$4 = \$360,000$	$200,000 \times 0.4 \times \$4 = \$320,000$	$220,000 \times 0.4 \times \$4 = \$352,000$
Kool	$200,000 \times 0.55 \times \$5 = \underline{550,000}$	$200,000 \times 0.6 \times \$5 = \underline{600,000}$	$220,000 \times 0.6 \times \$5 = \underline{660,000}$
	$\$910,000$	$\$920,000$	$\$1,012,000$

$ 10,000 U $ $ 92,000 U $

Sales-mix variance   Sales-quantity variance

$102,000 U

Sales-volume variance

F = favourable effect on operating income; U = unfavourable effect on operating income

Try It 16–4

	Actual	**Budgeted**
New York sales	2,500,000 units	2,000,000 units
Campbell Corp.	200,000 units	220,000 units
Market share	8%	11%

Average budgeted contribution margin per unit $= (\$4 \times 88,000 + \$5 \times 132,000) \div 220,000$

$= (\$352,000 + 660,000) \div 220,000 = \$4.60$

The solution to Try It 16-4 presents the sales-quantity variance, market-size variance, and market-share variance for 2017.

$$\begin{array}{l} \text{Market share} \\ \text{variance} \end{array} = \begin{array}{l} \text{Actual market} \\ \text{size in units} \end{array} \times \left(\begin{array}{l} \text{Actual} \\ \text{market} \\ \text{share} \end{array} - \begin{array}{l} \text{Budgeted} \\ \text{market} \\ \text{share} \end{array} \right) \times \begin{array}{l} \text{Budgeted contribution} \\ \text{margin per composite} \\ \text{unit for budgeted mix} \end{array}$$

$= 2,500,000 \times (0.08 - 0.11) \times \$4.60$

$= 2,500,000 \times 0.03 \times \$4.60$

$= \$345,000 U$

$$\begin{array}{l} \text{Market-size} \\ \text{variance} \end{array} = \left(\begin{array}{l} \text{Actual} \\ \text{market size} \\ \text{in units} \end{array} - \begin{array}{l} \text{Budgeted} \\ \text{market size} \\ \text{in units} \end{array} \right) \times \begin{array}{l} \text{Budgeted} \\ \text{market} \\ \text{share} \end{array} \times \begin{array}{l} \text{Budgeted contribution} \\ \text{margin per composite} \\ \text{unit for budgeted mix} \end{array}$$

$= (2,500,000 - 2,000,000) \times 0.11 \times \$4.60$

$= 500,000 \times 0.11 \times \$4.60$

$= 253,000 F$

The market share variance is unfavourable because the actual 8% market share was lower than the budgeted 11% market share. The market size variance is favourable because the market size increased 25% [(2,500,000 − 2,000,000) ÷ 2,000,000].

The unfavourable market-share variance was greater than the increase in market size variance, resulting in an unfavourable sales-quantity variance.

Sales-Quantity Variance
$92,000 U

Market-share variance
$345,000 U

Market-size variance
$253,000 F

Process Costing

17

Stringer/Singapore/Reuters

Allocation Affects Net Income—Reliable Estimates Are Important

Royal Dutch Shell is a global explorer and developer of energy sources. It is important to the Shell managers to plan, control, and report their year-to-year profitability. To accomplish this, they must allocate the costs of Royal Dutch Shell's activities to reflect the timing, amount, and costs of those activities. Doing so means that managers can be more confident that the budgeted profits will be realized. The goal of allocation is to match the quantity of actual activities and their timing to the flow of costs incurred from them. However, it is not feasible to trace every single cost to a single activity. Nor is every single activity uniquely linked to a single unit of output. What should the Shell managers do?

Fortunately for the Shell managers, process-costing techniques have been developed that will provide a suitably close and reliable approximation of the timing and flow of costs for a number of Shell's processes.

This chapter introduces the process-costing method of cost allocation, which differs from the job-costing method introduced in Chapter 4.

To review briefly, job costing is appropriate in situations where the product or service is made to the customer's specifications. As a result, different amounts of direct materials and conversion costs are used in the production process for each job. Therefore, the focus of the job-costing system is to accurately accumulate costs to each job since each job can use dramatically different amounts of inputs. The number of units of output is not an issue in the job-costing system because they have been determined by the customer's specifications for that job. The unit cost is then determined by dividing the total accumulated cost for the job by the number of units of output produced for that specific job.

In contrast, in a process-costing system, all units produced are identical (or very similar). The unit cost of a product or service is obtained by assigning the total costs to all the identical or similar units. In a manufacturing process-costing setting, every unit receives the same or similar amounts of direct materials costs, direct manufacturing labour, and indirect manufacturing costs (manufacturing overhead).

One significant characteristic of continuous processes is that the output is homogeneous (i.e., identical). One unit of output is essentially identical to another, such as a litre of milk, a barrel of oil, a printed circuit or smartphone, a T-shirt, or a satellite TV dish. Allocation is a way to assign costs to units of output when it is not feasible to trace costs directly to output. Direct costs are traced, but indirect costs are allocated.

This chapter describes how companies, such as ExxonMobil or Kellogg, use process-costing methods to determine the costs of products or services and to value inventory and the cost of goods sold.

Process Costing and Decision Making

▶ **LO 1**

Distinguish process- from job-costing allocation methods within the decision framework, and apply the weighted-average method of inventory valuation when the beginning work-in-process inventory is zero.

Deciding upon a process-costing system is, in many ways, easier than making other cost allocation decisions. In the simplest system there are only two cost pools. One is the prime cost pool comprising all direct materials (DM) costs. The second is the conversion cost pool comprising all direct manufacturing labour and other indirect manufacturing overhead (MOH) costs. The cost driver for the prime cost pool is straightforward—the quantity of DM used during the accounting period. The cost driver for the conversion cost pool is predetermined as well. The resulting conversion cost rate is a straightforward weighted-average cost of all identical units produced in the time period.

Step 1: Identify the Problem and Uncertainties The accounting problem is to design a cost assignment system that best matches the flow of costs to the flow of physical production of *identical* outputs. The physical processes cannot be directly observed often because it would be unsafe and unprofitable to do so. Moreover, direct observation would fail to reveal how complete each conversion process is for each unit of input remaining in the process. The purpose is to estimate full absorption cost per unit for both work-in-process (WIP) and finished goods (FG) inventory produced during a specific time period.

Step 2: Gather Relevant Information Typically, process-cost accounting makes the following (simplifying) assumptions:

- Both the quantity of DM and the time that DM are added can be observed and reported.
- Conversion (direct labour and overhead) is a joint costing activity throughout this physical transformation.
- The exit of identical units of completed goods can be observed and measured.
- The *quantities* and *costs* of inputs of DM and conversion activities can be reliably measured and reported in the month they are used or consumed.

The task of accountants is to design a costing process to reflect as efficiently and effectively as possible the timing and accumulated costs of physical conversion. It is difficult because all units entering the process at the beginning of a time period accumulate costs until the finished goods can be sold. The costs will only be recovered fully (plus a reasonable profit) through the sale of finished goods.

Step 3: Forecast Future Outcomes One of the accounting challenges with process costing is determining the amount of work done in a given time period (e.g., one month). Because the production process is continuous, there are often units of product (or service) that are incomplete at the end of an accounting period. These units represent ending inventory WIP for that accounting period and, subsequently, beginning inventory WIP for the next accounting period. The units present at any given point in time are typically referred to as **physical units**. While it is relatively straightforward to count these physical units, it is another matter to determine the amount of production work (i.e., DM or conversion costs) that has gone into them. It is important to accurately determine these figures because they will be used as the cost drivers for the DM and the conversion cost pools.

For DM, the process to calculate the amount of work done is relatively easy due to the simplifying assumption typically made by management that DM are 100% consumed at the moment they are added to the production process (this could be at the start of the process, at the end of the process, or at some point in between). In other words, either

- The DM *have been added* (all of them), or
- The DM *have not been added* to the relevant physical unit.

Therefore, if the DM have been added to the process, then the number of physical units also equals the amount of work done to those units. This measure of work is known as an **equivalent unit (EU)**, which expresses a 100% completed unit (for that input).

In contrast (to DM), the amount of conversion effort (direct labour and overhead) that has been applied to a physical unit is assumed to be *added evenly* throughout the production process. As a result, the physical units and the EU for conversion costs will often be different from each other. Therefore, partially completed (with respect to conversion costs) physical units can be expressed as some amount of EU. For example, two physical units that are 50% complete with respect to conversion would be the same as having one physical unit that is 100% complete ($2 \times 50\% = 1.0$). In order to distinguish physical units (that may or may not be complete or may only be partially complete) from the *amount of work* that has been done to those physical units, the term *equivalent unit* is used to quantify the amount of work that has been done. So, we can also state that two physical units that are 50% complete with regard to conversion are the same as one EU of conversion ($2 \times 50\% = 1.0$ EU).

Input quantities of DM can be reliably measured in physical units as well as the DM cost pool. The cost driver rate is readily calculated as the total DM cost pool divided by the total physical units of input to which DM was added. The DM cost pool is called a *prime cost pool*.

Now the rate per unit of *input* is calculated and the costs must be assigned to *output* units. Accountants use engineering reports of actual yield. The yield ratio multiplied by the cost driver rate assigns DM costs to each fully complete output unit. Provided the process is under control and purchase prices are stable, the DM cost assigned should be relatively constant from one time period to the next. A third and fourth level variance analysis will confirm whether or not this is the case.

The remaining costs to transform raw materials into completed units, including any direct manufacturing labour costs, comprise a second indirect cost pool called the conversion cost pool. There may be one conversion cost pool for all stages in a process or a conversion cost pool for each stage. Because the process is highly mechanized, a large part of the cost pool will be fixed manufacturing overhead (FMOH) costs of equipment, insurance, taxes, and so on, in addition to the variable operating costs of production that are not DM costs.

The conversion cost pool is reported monthly in the information system. The percentage complete is also reported and the expected yield on the DM is also known. This enables the management team to calculate the DM cost rate and to use the EU to calculate the conversion cost rate. To calculate the conversion cost rate, divide the total conversion cost pool by the total output measured as EU.

The corporation then subtracts the estimated full absorption cost of finished goods sold to calculate gross margin. Estimated gross margin and cost of goods sold can be compared to budgeted performance to assess if the process and profit are both under control.

Step 4: Make Decisions by Choosing Among Alternatives Engineers and accountants alike know that only finished goods can be sold to recover the production costs plus profit. This means that both the dollar value of assigned costs and the timing of their assignment will affect forecasts of gross margin.

The alternative methods of assigning the conversion cost pool to either WIP or finished goods are

- Weighted-average
- First-in, first-out (FIFO)
- Standard costing

The criterion to focus on when making a decision is which method best tells managers the costs incurred from the physical activities of continuous production in a particular time period. The choice of method affects both the calculation of the conversion cost pool allocation rates and the multiplier used to assign costs to WIP and FG inventories.

Managers must be able to depend on the separation of costs of finished goods available for sale, because these costs can be fully recovered if demand and pricing are appropriate. The inputs remaining in WIP cannot be sold and the costs will remain unrecovered until such time as these inputs are 100% converted and sold. In fact, WIP is an opportunity cost that delays the realization of revenue until the inputs are finally available for sale. Clearly, inventory management is one important path to realizing the maximum profit in any specific time period. This is best achieved when the estimates of conversion costs allocated to WIP and FG inventories are reliable.

Step 5: Implement the Decision, Evaluate Performance, and Learn If accountants have selected the best of the three ASPE/IFRS alternatives available to measure the costs of continuous production processes, then the managers can assess actual-to-forecast performance with some confidence. Forecasts predict reasonable measures of future costs. Budgeted costs are a commitment to the future consumption of resources. When actual reports are compared to predicted, the level of difference will indicate when a process is within or out of control.

In many industries, processes are continuous and production managers are paid bonuses when they perform at or better than their cost targets. The more accurately the process-costing system reflects the physical reality of production, or its economic substance, the fairer will be the remuneration from one time period to the next. The best process cost allocation system will be a reliable basis upon which to price outputs in order to recover all costs.

Process Costing: Alternative Methods

There are three commonly used approaches to calculating the unit costs of production in a process-costing environment. As previously mentioned, they are weighted-average method, FIFO method, and standard costing. However, depending on the product and the type of production environment, the discussion over which method should be used may be moot (unnecessary). If any of the following conditions are present, then there is no material difference between the weighted-average and the FIFO method:

- small (or nonexistent) amounts of WIP inventories, or
- the amounts of WIP are constant from period to period

If either condition is present, there is no need to calculate EU and, as a result, there is no difference between the weighted-average method and the FIFO method of calculating unit costs. This situation is sometimes referred to as *operations costing*. Also, if the company is using standard costs (see Chapter 7 Appendix), then there is no need to consider the issue of whether to use weighted-average or FIFO (even if the two conditions above *are not* present) since all EU will have the same *standard* cost assigned to them.[1] Also, there is some research that indicates that some industries simply calculate unit costs when the information is needed and do not worry about overly-complex calculations of EU of production.

That being said, it is important to understand the concepts and the methodology behind the three methods. The **weighted-average (WA) process-costing method** calculates the average EU cost of the work done to date (regardless of the period in which it was done) and assigns it to the units completed and transferred out (either to the next cost centre/department or to the FG inventory), and to the EU in the ending WIP inventory. In a true continuous process there will always be WIP at each stage of the conversion. The quantity of WIP will be measured in EU based on an estimate of percentage of completion.

The **first-in, first-out (FIFO) process-costing method** assigns the costs of the prior accounting period's EUs that is in the beginning WIP inventory to the *first* EUs completed and transferred out in the *current* accounting period. The method then assigns the *remaining* costs of the current period to the EU added to and converted during that period. The costs of the EU completed and transferred out are kept separate from those remaining in the ending inventory WIP. Of course, these EU and costs become the beginning quantities and costs of the beginning inventory WIP in the next time period.

The **standard-costing method** relies on the standard *input* quantity required to produce one standard output unit. This information might come from the engineers in the production department. The standard costs per input unit typically comes from the purchasing department. The standard input cost times the standard input quantity results in a *standard cost per unit produced*. The standard cost is then multiplied by the percentage of completion of the units to determine the cost allocation to that component of production (i.e., ending WIP, or units completed and transferred).

While all these methods are ASPE/IFRS compliant, when all things are equal, standard costing may be the most effective and efficient method for internal reporting and cost control purposes.

Concepts in Action   NI 52-109—Internal Control System Design

At all levels of management, managers owe a duty of care or stewardship to those whose assets they control. In 2008, the Canadian Securities Administrators (CSA) passed national regulation NI 52-109, which applies to companies listed on any Canadian stock exchange. For every quarter in which a company reports its financial results, the chief executive officer (CEO) must sign a certificate attesting to the quality of the disclosure. The CEOs certify that they have either supervised or designed an internal control system providing reasonable assurance of no material misstatement in the financial disclosure. Process cost allocation affects the cost of goods sold (COGS), and ultimately the net income reported, as well as inventory on the statement of financial position. By applying process costing thoughtfully, management accountants establish a sound foundation for internal control. Failure to conform to internal control standards under NI 52-109 carries heavy financial and social penalties, not only for CEOs but also for accountants who implement the systems.

More recently, the CSA conducted a review of the annual filings submitted by companies and found that over 50% did not meet the standards set out in the regulation. Additionally, 30% of the firms reviewed had to re-file their MD&A (Management Discussion and Analysis) and/or their certificates. The rigour of this review reflects how seriously CSA considers internal controls; and the level of noncompliance indicates that many firms still have significant gaps to overcome.

---

[1] The authors wish to thank Prof. John Parkinson, York University, for pointing out this issue and some relevant research done in this area (process-costing methods in practice). Interested students are directed to John Parkinson, "Accounting for Process Costing Systems," *The Journal of Law & Financial Management*, 2012 Vol. II Issue 2; Jennifer Dosch and Joel Wilson, "Process Costing and Management Accounting in Today's Business Environment," *Strategic Finance*, August, 2010.

The requirements of ASPE/IFRS include not only an initial inventory valuation but also impairment testing. The inventory values must be at the lower of cost or net realizable value. Obsolete or unusable inventories must be deducted from inventory balances. An appropriate process-costing system to assign costs ensures adequate internal control of not only the physical process but also the cost reporting process.

Weighted-Average Method with no Beginning WIP Inventory

► **LO 2**

Contrast the journal entries for a process-costing system when there is and when there is not ending work-in-process inventory using the weighted-average method of inventory valuation.

The easiest way to learn process costing is by example. Consider a continuous process that produces identical circuit boards. Global Defence Inc. manufactures thousands of components for missiles and military equipment. We will focus on the production of one of these components, DG-19. The DG-19 is a critical part in a military defence system to control drones. Global Defence assembles and tests the DG-19.

The assembly process is manual. Completed subassemblies arrive for robot testing and final addition of an expensive printed circuit. Prior to adding the last circuit to the DG-19, thorough quality control and inspection must be done as part of the conversion. These are processes that incur an indirect cost of MOH and are done by robots in a clean room. Either the final component is inserted into the tested subassembly or the subassembly is discarded for rework.

Only those subassemblies that pass the testing process will have the final circuit board added by a robot. The completed DG-19 is immediately transferred to finished goods. All DM form one cost pool, and all conversion costs, including direct manufacturing labour, form the second cost pool, which includes both the assembly and testing process costs. Only the completely converted circuit boards use 100% of the DM.

The process-costing system for DG-19 has a single direct cost category (DM) and a single indirect process cost category (conversion costs). Every effort is made to ensure that all completed DG-19 units are identical and meet a set of demanding performance specifications. DM are added to the process in both departments. In the Assembly department, the DM are added at the start of the assembly process, while in the Testing department, the DM are added at the end of the testing process and are 100% consumed.

Conversion costs are added evenly during both hand assembly and robotic testing processes. Conversion costs include manufacturing labour, indirect materials, security, plant depreciation, insurance, and so on. Basically, conversion costs include all manufacturing costs except DM costs. Exhibit 17-1 summarizes these facts.

The manufacture of the DG-19 component will illustrate three cases:

■ **Case 1:** Process costing with *no beginning inventory (BI) or ending inventory (EI) WIP* of DG-19—that is, all units are started and fully completed by the end of the

Exhibit 17-1 The Illustrated Process at Global Defence Inc.

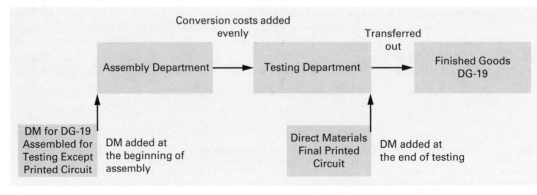

accounting period. This case illustrates the basic averaging-of-costs idea that is a key feature of process-costing systems.

- **Case 2:** Process costing with *no beginning inventory WIP but an ending inventory WIP* of DG-19—that is, some units of DG-19 started during the accounting period are incomplete at the end of the period. This means that no DM have been added to the incomplete circuit boards at the end of hand assembly.

- **Case 3:** Process costing with *both beginning inventory WIP and ending inventory WIP* of DG-19.

Also note that the cases take place in different time periods: Case 1 takes place in January, Case 2 takes place in February, and Case 3 takes place in March. The production process is assumed to be continuous, therefore, if the Assembly department has no ending inventory of WIP in January, it is consistent that February starts with no beginning inventory for WIP. Similarly, if *there is* ending inventory WIP in the Assembly department at the end of February, then there will, logically, be beginning inventory WIP on March 1 in the Assembly department. See the figure below for a visual presentation of these assumptions.

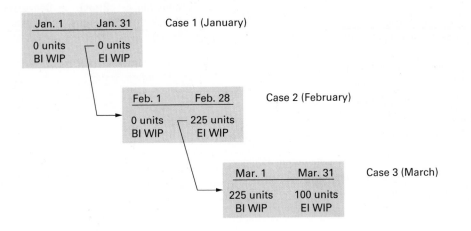

For *Case 1*, on January 1, 2018, the value is $0 for beginning inventory WIP of DG-19 circuit boards and all DM. In January 2018, Global Defence started, completed hand assembly of, and transferred out to the robotic testing phase, 400 DG-19 units. All the DM costs of $32,000 were added and all completed units and costs were transferred out to finished goods. The total costs for January 2018 were

Direct materials costs added during January	$32,000
Conversion costs added during January	24,000
Total Assembly department costs added during January	$56,000

With zero beginning inventory and ending inventory WIP, no inventory valuation is necessary. By averaging, the hand assembly cost per unit of DG-19 would simply be $56,000 ÷ 400 units = $140, itemized as follows:

Direct materials ($32,000 ÷ 400) cost per unit	$ 80
Conversion costs ($24,000 ÷ 400) per unit	60
Assembly department cost per unit	$140

This case shows that in a process-costing system, unit costs can be averaged by dividing total cost in a given accounting period by total units produced in the period. Because all units are identical, there is no reason to believe any single unit would cost more to produce than the other units. All units receive identical amounts of direct materials and conversion costs. If organizations mass-produce standard units, then they

Exhibit 17-2 Summarizing the Flow of Production in Physical Units and Equivalent Units for the Assembly Department of Global Defence Inc. for January 2018—**Case 1, No Beginning WIP Inventory and No Ending WIP Inventory**

	A	B	C	D
1			Equivalent Units	
2	**Flow of Production**	**Physical Units**	**Direct Materials**	**Conversion Costs**
3	Work in progress, beginning	0		
4	Started during January	400		
5	To account for	400		
6				
7	Completed and transferred out during January	400	400	400
8	Work in progress, ending inventory, hand assembly	0		
9	Accounted for	400		
10	Work done in January only		400	400
11				
12		**Total Production Costs**	**Direct Materials**	**Conversion Costs**
13	Costs added in January	$56,000	$32,000	$24,000
14				
15	Divide by equivalent units of work			
16	done in current period		÷ 400	÷ 400
17	Cost per equivalent unit		$ 80	$ 60
18	Total costs to account for	$56,000		
19				
20	Assignment of costs:			
21	Completed and transferred out during January (400 units from EU calculations)	$56,000	400 × ($80 + $60)	
22	Total costs accounted for	$56,000		

can use this basic average-costing approach when there are no incomplete units at the end of each accounting period. Exhibit 17-2 presents another way to summarize this information.

Global Defence—Ending WIP Inventory Valuation Using the Weighted-Average Method

Case 2. In February 2018, Global Defence places another 400 units of DG-19 into production. Recall that there is no beginning inventory of partially completed units in the Assembly department on February 1, 2018, because all units placed into production in January were fully completed by February 1. During February, however, customer delays in placing orders for DG-19 prevented the complete assembly of all units started in February. Only 175 units were completed and transferred out to the Testing department. This means that 225 units remained in the Assembly department's ending inventory WIP at the end of February. The production engineers estimated that the conversion of the 225 units in ending inventory WIP was 60% complete. The total costs for the Assembly department for February 2018 were

Direct materials costs added during February	$32,000
Conversion costs added during February	18,600
Total Assembly department costs added during February	$50,600

	A	B	C	D
			Equivalent Units	
1				
2		**Physical**	**Direct**	**Conversion**
3	**Flow of Production**	**Units**	**Materials**	**Costs**
4	Work in process, beginning	0		
5	Started during February	400		
6	To account for	400		
7				
8	Completed and transferred out during February	175	175	175
9	Work in process, ending inventory, assembly[a]	225		
10	(225 × 100%; 225 × 60%)	—	225	135
11	Accounted for	400	—	—
12	Work done in February only		400	310
13				
14	[a] Degree of completion in this department: direct materials, 100%; conversion costs, 60%.			

Exhibit 17-3
Summarizing the Flow of Production in Physical Units and Equivalent Units for the Assembly Department of Global Defence Inc. for February 2018—**Case 2 Ending WIP Inventory but No Beginning WIP Inventory**

Exhibit 17-3 records flow of production in units. The Physical Units column records the units in beginning WIP inventory (which was 0) and the quantity started in February (which was 400), giving the 400 total units to account for. The quantity completed and transferred out of the Assembly department (175 physical units) and the ending inventory WIP (225 physical units) are then recorded, giving the 400 total quantity accounted for. The Equivalent Units columns report the EU for both the DM and indirect conversion cost pools for the EU completed and transferred out and the units remaining in ending inventory WIP. Exhibit 17-3 shows in detail the calculation of the EU for both the DM and conversion cost pools.

Exhibit 17-4 shows the cost pools and calculation of cost allocation rates per EU. It then shows the assignment of costs to units completed and transferred out, and to partially completed units remaining in ending WIP inventory.

At the top of Exhibit 17-4, the Direct Materials column shows that $32,000 of DM were purchased and should have been added to the 400 units started during February. There was no beginning inventory WIP. Thus the cost rate of DM was $80/EU (= $32,000 ÷ 400 EU from Exhibit 17-3). The Conversion Costs column shows that the conversion cost pool for the Assembly department for February was $18,600. Thus the cost per EU for conversion costs was $60 (= $18,600 ÷ 310 EU from Exhibit 17-3). The total production costs to be accounted for during the month are the sum of the DM and conversion costs, $50,600.

The bottom section of Exhibit 17-4 multiplies the cost rates by the EU in ending inventory WIP and assigned and transferred out to the Testing department. The costs are assigned using the weighted-average method. Recall that the weighted-average is very straightforward because the weights have already been provided in transforming the physical units into EU. The cost allocation rates are already weighted. In the case of the DM cost pool, the weight for both complete and incomplete physical units is 100% or 1. The weight for the conversion cost pool for units transferred out is 1 or 100% and 0.60 or 60% for incomplete units in ending inventory WIP.

Exhibit 17-4 shows that the cost assigned for the 175 completed units is $24,500 (= 175 × $80/EU for DM + 175 × $60/EU for conversion costs). The value of ending inventory WIP is not quite as straightforward to calculate. The DM remain 100% used for the 225 units in ending inventory WIP; therefore, this cost is $18,000 (= 225 EU × $80/EU). Recall that DM are added at the start of the Assembly department's work, therefore any units that have been started are 100% complete for DM. The conversion cost for the 135 EU in ending inventory WIP is $8,100 (= 135 EU × $60/EU).

Exhibit 17-4 Calculating Equivalent Unit Costs and Assigning Costs to Completed Units and Ending WIP, Assembly

	A	B	C	D
1		**Total**		
2		**Production**	**Direct**	**Conversion**
3		**Costs**	**Materials**	**Costs**
4	Cost added in February	$50,600	$32,000	$18,600
5	Divide by equivalent units of work done in current period (Exhibit 17-3)		÷ 400	÷ 310
6	Cost per equivalent unit		$ 80	$ 60
7	Total costs to account for	$50,600		
8	Assignment of costs:			
9	Completed and transferred out (175 units from Exhibit 17-3)	$24,500	175 × ($80 + $60)	
10	Work in process ending inventory, Assembly (225 units)			
11	Direct materials	18,000	(225 × $80)	
12	Conversion costs	8,100	(135 EU from Exhibit 17-4 × $60)	
13	Total work in process	26,100		
14	Total costs accounted for	$50,600		
15				

The total value of ending inventory WIP at the end of February is $26,100 (= $18,000 + $8,100). The completed and transferred-out amount of $24,500 and the ending inventory WIP amount of $26,100 sum to $50,600, the total costs of the Assembly department to account for in February.

Process-costing systems separate costs into cost categories according to the timing of when costs are introduced into the process. Only two cost pools are required in the Global Defence example because all conversion costs are assumed to be added to the process at an even rate over time. If, however, direct manufacturing labour were added to the process at different times than all other conversion costs, then a third cost pool would be necessary. In this situation, we could no longer assume that all conversion activities occur at a uniform rate; therefore, separate estimates of EU would be required for the manufacturing labour and the quality-control assembly processes.

Transferring costs out as reported in the bottom section of Exhibit 17-4 is an accounting process wherein the costs follow the EU through conversion. The methods to value ending inventory WIP are constrained for external reporting purposes by ASPE/IFRS to either the weighted-average or the FIFO (first-in, first-out) method. At this point in the Global Defence example, no decision need be made because the beginning inventory WIP was $0 in both January and February. The choice of methods will make a difference in *Case 3*, however, because there is beginning inventory WIP to be converted and transferred out in March.

Journal Entries

Process-costing journal entries are basically like those made in the job-costing system. That is, DM and conversion costs are accounted for in a similar way as in job-costing systems. The main difference is that, in process costing, there is often more than one ending inventory WIP: In our Global Defence example, there is Work in Process—Assembly and Work in Process—Testing. Global Defence purchases DM as needed, and these materials are delivered directly to the Assembly department. Using dollar amounts from Exhibit 17-4, summary journal entries for the month of February at Global Defence Inc. are as follows:

1. Work in Process—Assembly	32,000	
Accounts Payable		32,000

To record direct materials purchased and used in production during February.

2. Work in Process—Assembly	18,600	
[Various accounts]		18,600

To record assembly department conversion costs for February; examples include energy, manufacturing supplies, all manufacturing labour, and plant depreciation.

3. Work in Process—Testing	24,500	
Work in Process—Assembly		24,500

To record cost of goods completed and transferred from assembly to testing during February.

Exhibit 17-5 shows a general sketch of the flow of costs through the T-accounts. The key T-account, Work in Process—Assembly, shows an ending balance of $26,100.

For presentation in correct financial-reporting format, the dollar values presented in Exhibit 17-4 (and the journal entries) for the Assembly department are reported below:

Global Defence Inc. Schedule of Cost of Goods Manufactured, Assembly Department for the Month Ended:	January 31, 2018 (Case 1) Weighted-Average		February 28, 2018 (Case 2) Weighted-Average	
Direct Materials				
Beginning inventory of direct materials	$ 0		$ 0	
Purchases of direct materials during the month	32,000		32,000	
Cost of direct materials available for use	32,000		32,000	
Ending inventory of direct materials for the month	0		0	
Direct materials used during the month		$32,000		$32,000
All conversion costs	24,000		18,600	
Total conversion costs		24,000		18,600
Manufacturing costs incurred during the month		56,000		50,600
Beginning work-in-process inventory		0		0
Total manufacturing costs to account for		56,000		50,600
Ending work-in-process inventory		0		(26,100)
Cost of goods manufactured—transferred out to Testing department		$56,000		$24,500

In double-entry bookkeeping, this report from the Assembly department represents only half the transaction. The other half is the receipt into inventory of both the physical units and the COGM by the Testing department. The physical units received by the Testing department from the Assembly department are subcomponents, which are DM. The dollar value of the monthly COGM represents the DM transferred in or added to the Testing department's purchases for the month. Strictly speaking, these DM were not purchased from an external party but nevertheless are treated as internal purchases. Ascertaining the correct transfer price is sometimes less straightforward than presented in this chapter.

Exhibit 17-5 Flow of Costs in a Process-Costing System, Assembly Department of Global Defence Inc. for February 2018

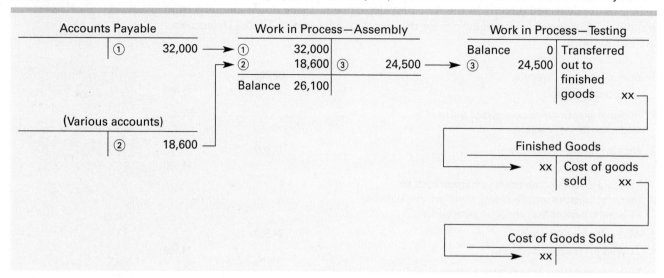

⊕ **TRY IT! 17.1**

Big Band Corporation produces a semiconductor chip used on communications. The direct materials are added at the start of the production process while conversion costs are added uniformly throughout the production process. Big Band had no inventory at the start of June. During the month, it incurred direct materials costs of $935,750 and conversion costs of $4,554,000. Big Band started 475,000 chips and completed 425,000 of them in June. Ending inventory was 50% complete as to conversion costs.

Compute (a) the equivalent units of work done in June, and (b) the total manufacturing cost per chip. Allocate the total costs between the completed chips and those in ending inventory.

Weighted-Average Method with Beginning and Ending WIP Inventory

▶ **LO 3**

Apply the weighted-average method of process costing to calculate the cost of goods manufactured and transferred out when there is both beginning and ending work-in-process inventory.

Case 3. For Case 3, remember there is both a beginning inventory WIP and an ending inventory WIP. At the beginning of March 2018, Global Defence had 225 partially assembled DG-19 physical units in the Assembly department. During March 2018, Global Defence placed another 275 physical units into production. The total physical units in various stages of production during March was 500 (= 225 beginning physical units + 275 physical units), of which 400 were completed and transferred out to the Testing department.

At the end of March 2018, there were 100 physical units remaining in Assembly that were 50% complete. During March, DM costs of $19,800 and conversion costs of $16,380 were added in the Assembly department, for total costs of $36,180 added during March. With a non-zero beginning inventory WIP, a choice must be made with respect to the timing of when either beginning inventory WIP or the new units DM are converted fully and transferred out to the Testing department—weighted-average or FIFO.

The EU calculation in the weighted-average method is only concerned with total EU of work done. The work to complete the EU remaining from last month in March's beginning inventory WIP is not distinguished from those units added and converted this month. All EU fully converted are assumed to be converted at an equal rate in March. The weighted-average method is not fine enough to reflect the physical timing of conversion of beginning inventory WIP in which conversion and DM costs have already been accumulated from new EU. Thus, the stage of completion of the current-period beginning inventory WIP is irrelevant and not used in the computation. The flow of physical units and the calculation of EU for the Assembly department for March 2018 are shown in Exhibit 17-6.

Exhibit 17-6
Summarizing the Flow
of Production in Physical
Units and Equivalent
Units for the Assembly
Department of Global
Defence Inc. for March
2018—**Case 3, Weighted-
Average Method with
Beginning and Ending
WIP Inventory**

	A	B	C	D
1			**Equivalent Units**	
2		**Physical**	**Direct**	**Conversion**
3	**Flow of Production**	**Units**	**Materials**	**Costs**
4	Work in process, beginning inventory, Assembly (February EI WIP, Exhibit 17-3)	225		
5	Started during current period (given)	275		
6	To account for	500		
7	Completed and transferred out during March	400	400	400
8	Work in process, ending inventory, Assembly[a] (given)	100		
9	(100 × 100%; 100 × 50%)		100	50
10	Accounted for	500		
11	Work done to date		500	450
12				
13	[a]Degree of completion in this department: direct materials, 100%; conversion costs, 50%.			

The weighted-average cost is the total of all costs entering the WIP account (regardless of whether it is from beginning WIP or from work started during the period) divided by total EU of work done to date in the Assembly department:

$$\begin{array}{c}\text{EU in beginning} \\ \text{inventory WIP}\end{array} + \begin{array}{c}\text{EU of work done} \\ \text{in current period}\end{array} = \begin{array}{c}\text{EU completed and transferred} \\ \text{out in current period}\end{array} + \begin{array}{c}\text{EU in ending} \\ \text{inventory WIP}\end{array}$$

$$225 + 275 = 400 + 100$$

Exhibit 17-7 shows the calculation of the DM and conversion cost per EU, and the assignment of costs to units either completed and transferred out or remaining in ending

Exhibit 17-7 Calculating Equivalent Unit Costs and Assigning Costs to Completed Units and Ending WIP Inventory for the Assembly Department of Global Defence Inc. for March 2018—**Case 3, Weighted-Average Method with Beginning and Ending WIP Inventory**

	A	B	C	D
1		**Total**		
2		**Production**	**Direct**	**Conversion**
3		**Costs**	**Materials**	**Costs**
4	Work in process, beginning (February EI WIP, Exhibit 17-4)	$26,100	$18,000	$ 8,100
5	Costs added in current period (given)	36,180	19,800	16,380
6	Costs incurred to date		$37,800	$24,480
7	Divide by equivalent units of work done to date (Exhibit 17-6)		÷ 500	÷ 450
8	Cost per equivalent unit of work done to date		$ 75.60	$ 54.40
9	Total costs to account for	$62,280		
10	Assignment of costs:			
11	Completed and transferred out (400 units)	$52,000	(400[a] × $75.60) + (400[a] × $54.40)	
12	Work in process, ending (100 units)	10,280	(100[b] × $75.60) + (50[b] × $54.40)	
13	Total costs accounted for	$62,280		
14				
15	[a]Equivalent units completed and transferred out from Exhibit 17-6.			
16	[b]Equivalent units in ending work in process from Exhibit 17-6.			

inventory WIP. The dollars follow the EU, which are either 100% converted and transferred out to the Testing department, or remain 50% complete in the ending inventory WIP of the Assembly department, allocated on a weighted-average cost per EU. In column C are the EU used to calculate the cost allocation rate for the DM cost pool. In column D are the ending inventory used to calculate the cost allocation rate for the March conversion cost pool. The total costs of March ending inventory WIP are calculated in Exhibit 17-7 as follows:

Direct materials:

100 equivalent units × weighted-average cost per equivalent unit of $75.60		$ 7,560
Conversion costs:		
50 equivalent units × weighted-average cost per equivalent unit of $54.40		2,720
Total costs of ending work in process		$10,280

As shown in Exhibit 17-7, for cost assignment, the completed and transferred-out amount of $52,000 and the ending inventory WIP amount of $10,280 in March, $62,280, are the total costs of the Assembly department to account for in March. It is important to note that the factor for direct materials EU is 100%, or 1, but that is not always the case. It is entirely possible to encounter a conversion process wherein the DM of partially converted units are also only partially used. The factor for DM used is unique and unrelated to the conversion factor. Thus it is possible for partially converted units to have consumed 20% of DM and 75% of conversion inputs, for example.

The following table summarizes the total costs to account for and the $62,280 accounted for in Exhibit 17-7. The arrows indicate that costs of units completed and transferred out and costs of units in ending WIP are calculated using average total costs obtained after merging costs of beginning inventory WIP added in the current period.

Costs to Account for		Costs Accounted for Calculated at Weighted-Average Cost	
Beginning work in process	$26,100	→ Completed and transferred out	$52,000
Costs added in current period	36,180	→ Ending work in process	10,280
Total costs to account for	$62,280	Total costs accounted for	$62,280

The information Global Defence has calculated for the month of March based on the weighted-average method of inventory valuation is summarized below:

Global Defence Inc. **Schedule of Cost of Goods Manufactured, Assembly Department for the Month Ended:**		**March 31, 2018** **Weighted-Average**
Direct materials		
Beginning inventory of direct materials	$ 0	
Purchases of direct materials during the month	19,800	
Cost of direct materials available for use	19,800	
Ending inventory of direct materials for the month	0	
Direct materials used during the month		$19,800
All conversion costs	16,380	
Total conversion costs		16,380
Manufacturing costs incurred during the month		36,180
Beginning work-in-process inventory		26,100
Total manufacturing costs to account for		62,280
Ending work-in-process inventory		(10,280)
Costs of goods manufactured—transferred out to Testing department		$52,000

Using dollar amounts from Exhibit 17-7, summary journal entries for the month of March at Global Defence Inc. are

1. Work in Process—Assembly   19,800

    Accounts Payable   19,800

To record direct materials purchased and used in production during March.

2. Work in Process—Assembly   16,380

    [Various accounts]   16,380

To record Assembly department conversion costs for March; examples include energy, manufacturing supplies, all manufacturing labour, and plant depreciation.

3. Work in Process—Testing   52,000

    Work in Process—Assembly   52,000

To record cost of units completed and transferred from Assembly to Testing during March.

The key T-account, Work in Process—Assembly, would show the following:

Work in Process—Assembly

Beginning inventory, March 1	26,100	③ Transferred out to Work in	
① Direct materials	19,800	Process—Testing	52,000
② Conversion costs	16,380		
Ending inventory, March 31	10,280		

The Stanton Processing Company had work in process at the beginning and end of March 2017 in its Painting Department as follows:

		PERCENTAGE OF COMPLETION	
		Direct Materials	**Conversion Costs**
March 1	(3,000 units)	40%	10%
March 31	(2,000 units)	80%	40%

The company completed 30,000 units during March. Manufacturing costs incurred during March were direct materials costs of $176,320 and conversion costs of $312,625. Inventory at March 1 was carried at a cost of $16,155 (direct materials − $5,380 and conversion costs − $10,775).

Assuming Stanton uses weighted-average costing, determine the equivalent units of work done in March, and calculate the cost of units completed and the cost of units in ending inventory.

First-In, First-Out and Standard-Cost Methods

◀ **LO 4**

Analyze weighted-average, FIFO, and standard-costing methods of inventory valuation of cost of goods manufactured and transferred out.

In contrast to the weighted-average method, the first-in, first-out (FIFO) process-costing method assigns the cost of the prior accounting period's EU in beginning inventory WIP inventory to the first units completed and transferred out. It assigns the cost of equivalent units worked on during the current period first to complete beginning inventory, then to start and complete new units, and finally to units in ending work-in-process inventory. This method assumes that the earliest EU in the WIP—Assembly account are completed first.

A distinctive feature of the FIFO process-costing method is that the costs of work done on beginning inventory WIP before the current period are kept separate from work

Exhibit 17-8

Summarizing the Flow of Production in Physical Units and Equivalent Units for the Assembly Department of Global Defence Inc. for March 2018—**Case 3, FIFO Method with Beginning and Ending WIP Inventory**

	A	B	C	D
			Equivalent Units	
1				
2		**Physical**	**Direct**	**Conversion**
3	**Flow of Production**	**Units**	**Materials**	**Costs**
4	Work in process, beginning (February EI WIP, Exhibit 17-3)	225	(work done before current period)	
5	Started during current period (given)	275		
6	To account for	500		
7	Completed and transferred out during current period:			
8	From beginning work in process[a]	225		
9	[225 × (100% − 100%); 225 × (100% − 60%)]		0	90
10	Started and completed	175[b]		
11	(175 × 100%; 175 × 100%)		175	175
12	Work in process, ending[c] (given)	100		
13	(100 × 100%; 100 × 50%)		100	50
14	Accounted for	500		
15	Work done in March only		275	315
16				
17	[a]Degree of completion in this department: direct materials, 100%; conversion costs, 60%.			
18	[b]400 physical units completed and transferred out minus 225 physical units completed and transferred out from beginning work-in-process inventory.			
19	[c]Degree of completion in this department: direct materials, 100%; conversion costs, 50%.			

done in the current period. Costs incurred in the *current period* and units produced in the *current period* are used to calculate costs per EU of work done in the current period. In contrast, EU and cost-per-EU calculations in the weighted-average method merge the units and costs in beginning inventory WIP with units and costs of work done in the current period, and make no distinction between the units.

The following observations help explain the physical units calculations in Exhibit 17-8:

■ From the March data, 400 physical units were completed during March. The FIFO method assumes that the first 225 of these units were from beginning inventory WIP; thus 175 physical units (= 400 physical units − 225 physical units) must have been started and completed during March.

■ Ending inventory WIP consists of 100 physical units (= 275 physical units started in March − 175 physical units started and completed in March) partially converted in March.

■ Note that the physical units "to account for" equal the physical units "accounted for" (500 units).

Under the FIFO method, the EU calculations focus on only what has been converted in March. Under the FIFO method, the work done in the current period is assumed to first complete the 225 units in beginning WIP. The EU of work done in March on the beginning inventory WIP are computed by multiplying the 225 physical units by the percentage of work remaining to be done to complete these units: 0% for DM because the beginning WIP is 100% complete with respect to DM and 40% for conversion costs, because the beginning WIP is 60% complete with respect to conversion costs. The results are 0 EU (= 225 physical units × 0.0) of work for DM and 90 EU (= 225 physical units × 0.40) for conversion costs.

Next, the work done in the current period is assumed to start and complete the next 175 units. The EU of work done on the 175 physical units started and completed are computed by multiplying 175 units by 100% for both DM and conversion costs, because all work on these units is done in the current period. Therefore, there are 175 EU (= 175 physical units × 1.0) started and completed in March.

Finally, the work done in the current period is assumed to start but leave incomplete the final 100 physical units as ending inventory WIP. The EU of work done on the 100 physical units of ending inventory WIP are calculated by multiplying 100 physical units by 100% for DM (because all DM have been added for these units in the current period) and 50% for conversion costs (because 50% of conversion and corresponding costs have been undertaken and consumed in the current period). The flow of production in physical units and EU is summarized in Exhibit 17-8.

In FIFO, the logic of the flow of costs is that all of February's costs must be transferred out first. The ending inventory WIP from February is 60% converted, which means the remaining 40% conversion must be paid from the conversion cost pool for March. The total conversion cost for March is given as $16,380. The actual conversion EU for March comprise the 90 EU (= 225 physical units $\times$ 0.40) remaining from February, the 175 EU (= 175 physical units $\times$ 1.0) begun and completed in March, and the 50 EU (= 100 physical units $\times$ 0.50) remaining in Assembly. The actual cost allocation rate for March, based on only those conversion costs incurred in March, is $52 [= $16,380 \div (90 + 175 + 50)]$.

Under FIFO, the ending inventory WIP comes from physical units that were started but not fully completed during the current period. The total cost of the 100 partially assembled physical units in ending WIP consists of

Direct materials:	
100 equivalent units $\times$ cost per equivalent unit in March of $72	$7,200
Conversion costs:	
50 equivalent units $\times$ cost per equivalent unit in March of $52	2,600
Total costs of work in process on March 31	$9,800

The diagram below summarizes the flows of each element of total costs to account for and the costs already accounted for of $62,280 in Exhibit 17-9. Notice how under the

Exhibit 17-9 Calculating Equivalent Unit Costs and Assigning Costs to Completed Units and Ending WIP Inventory for the Assembly Department of Global Defence Inc. for March 2018—**Case 3, FIFO Method with Beginning and Ending WIP Inventory**

	A	B	C	D
1		Total		
2		Production	Direct	Conversion
3		Costs	Materials	Costs
4	Work in process, beginning (February EI WIP, Exhibit 17-4)	$26,100	(work done before current period)	
5	Costs added in current period (given)	36,180	$19,800	$16,380
6	Divide by equivalent units of work done in current period (Exhibit 17-8)		÷ 275	÷ 315
7	Cost per equivalent unit of work done in current period		$ 72	$ 52
8	Total costs to account for	$62,280		
9	Assignment of costs:			
10	Completed and transferred out (400 units):			
11	Work in process, beginning (225 units)	$26,100		
12	Costs added to beginning work in process in current period	4,680	$(0^a \times \$72) + (90^a \times \$52)$	
13	Total from beginning inventory	30,780		
14	Started and completed (175 units)	21,700	$(175^b \times \$72) + (175^b \times \$52)$	
15	Total costs of units completed and transferred out	52,480		
16	Work in process, ending (100 units)	9,800	$(100^c \times \$72) + (50^c \times \$52)$	
17	Total costs accounted for	$62,280		
18				
19	[a]Equivalent units used to complete beginning work in process from Exhibit 17-8.			
20	[b]Equivalent units started and completed from Exhibit 17-8.			
21	[c]Equivalent units in ending work in process from Exhibit 17-8.			

FIFO method the layers of beginning WIP and costs added in the current period are kept separate. The arrows indicate where the costs in each layer go (that is, to units completed and transferred out, or to ending WIP). Be sure to include the costs of beginning WIP ($26,100) when calculating the costs of units completed from beginning inventory.

Costs to Account for		Costs Accounted for Calculated on a FIFO Basis	
		Completed and transferred out:	
Beginning work in process	$26,100	Beginning work in process	$26,100
Costs added in current period	36,180	Used to complete beginning work in process	4,680
		Started and completed	21,700
		Completed and transferred out	52,480
		Ending work in process	9,800
Total costs to account for	$62,280	Total costs accounted for	$62,280

Exhibit 17-9 shows the calculation of the DM and conversion cost per EU, and the assignment of costs to units completed and transferred out and to ending inventory WIP using the FIFO method of process costing. The completed and transferred out amount of $52,480 and the ending inventory WIP amount of $9,800 sum to $62,280, the total costs the Assembly department needs to account for in March.

The information Global Defence calculated for the month of March based on the FIFO method of valuation of inventory is summarized below and compared to the amounts obtained using the weighted-average method:

Global Defence Inc. Schedule of Cost of Goods Manufactured, Assembly Department for the Month Ended:	March 31, 2018 Weighted-Average		March 31, 2018 FIFO	
Direct materials				
Beginning inventory of direct materials	$ 0		$ 0	
Purchases of direct materials during the month	19,800		19,800	
Cost of direct materials available for use	19,800		19,800	
Ending inventory of direct materials for the month	0		0	
Direct materials used during the month		$19,800		$19,800
All conversion costs	16,380		16,380	
Total conversion costs		16,380		16,380
Manufacturing costs incurred during the month		36,180		36,180
Beginning work-in-process inventory		26,100		26,100
Total manufacturing costs to account for		62,280		62,280
Ending work-in-process inventory		(10,280)		(9,800)
Cost of goods manufactured—transferred out to Testing department		$52,000		$52,480

The journal entries under the FIFO method parallel the journal entries under the weighted-average method. The only difference is that the entry to record the cost of goods completed and transferred out would be for $52,480 under the FIFO method instead of $52,000 under the weighted-average method.

Only rarely is an application of pure FIFO ever encountered in process costing. As a result, this method should really be called a modified or departmental FIFO method because FIFO is applied within a department to compile the cost of units transferred out, but the units transferred in during a given period are usually carried at a single average unit cost as a matter of convenience. For example, the average cost of units transferred out of the Assembly department is $52,480 ÷ 400$ units $= \$131.20$ per DG-19 unit. The Assembly department uses FIFO to distinguish between monthly batches of production. The succeeding department, Testing, however, costs these units (that consist of costs incurred in February and March) at one average unit cost ($131.20 in this illustration). If this averaging were not done, the attempt to track costs on a pure FIFO basis throughout a series of processes would be unduly cumbersome, if not impossible.

Consider Stanton Processing Company again. With the same information for 2017 as provided in Try It 17-2, redo the problem assuming Stanton uses FIFO costing instead.

 **17.3 TRY IT!** ⊕

Comparing Weighted-Average and FIFO Methods

The following table summarizes the costs assigned to units completed and those still in process under the weighted-average and FIFO process-costing methods for our example:

	Weighted-Average (from Exhibit 17-7)	FIFO (from Exhibit 17-9)	Difference
Cost of units completed and transferred out	$52,000	$52,480	+$480
Work in process, ending	10,280	9,800	− 480
Total costs accounted for	$62,280	$62,280	$ 0

The *weighted-average ending inventory* is higher than the FIFO ending inventory by $480, or 4.9% (= $480 ÷ $9,800). This is a significant difference when aggregated over the many thousands of components that Global Defence makes. The weighted-average method in our example also results in lower COGS and hence higher operating income and higher tax payments than the FIFO method. Differences in EU costs of beginning inventory WIP and work done during the current period account for the differences in weighted-average and FIFO costs. Recall that the cost per EU of beginning inventory WIP was greater than the cost per EU of work done during the period.

For the Assembly department, FIFO assumes that all the higher-cost prior-period units in beginning inventory WIP are the first to be completed and transferred out while ending inventory WIP consists of only the lower-cost current-period units. The weighted-average method, however, smooths out cost per EU by assuming that more of the lower-cost units are completed and transferred out, while some of the higher-cost units are placed in ending inventory WIP. Hence, in this example, the weighted-average method results in a lower cost of units completed and transferred out and a higher ending inventory WIP relative to FIFO.

Unit costs can differ materially between the weighted-average and FIFO methods when (1) the DM or conversion costs per unit vary from period to period and (2) the physical inventory levels of WIP are large in relation to the total number of units transferred out. This means that both gross margin and operating income will differ materially between the two approaches. As companies move toward long-term procurement contracts that smooth out the unit cost differences from one time period to another, and toward eliminating inventory, the difference between these two cost estimates will decrease.

Managers need feedback about their most recent performance (March in this illustration) to plan and improve their future performance. A major advantage of FIFO is that it gives managers actual information from which they can judge their performance in the current period independently from that in the preceding period. Work done during the current period is vital information for these planning and control purposes.

Managers in operations often receive cash bonuses based on minimizing costs. The weighted-average method reports the lowest COGM transferred out for the Assembly department. Notice that regardless of the method chosen, for purposes of deducting COGS to arrive at taxable income, the total cost for the two methods is identical. What is added to ending inventory WIP is deducted from COGM completed and transferred out. There is no tax benefit to either choice. The manager, however, would prefer to report lower rather than higher COGM, and without accounting training could choose FIFO over the weighted-average method. However, as those trained in financial accounting know, this benefit will most likely reverse out in the next accounting time period—the iron law of accruals. Managers who know this should be indifferent between these two methods of process costing.

Computations Under Standard Costing

For an introductory discussion see Chapter 7 and Chapter 8.

As we have mentioned, companies that use process-costing systems produce numerous like or similar units of output. Setting standard quantities for inputs is often relatively straightforward in such companies. Standard costs per input unit may then be assigned to the physical standards to develop standard costs.

One weakness of standard costing, however, is that the standard must be updated when significant changes occur in process, quantity, and/or unit input cost. The overallocation or underallocation of process costs must be prorated prior to the calculation of taxable income.

Weighted-average and FIFO methods become very complicated when used in industries that produce a variety of products. For example, a steel rolling mill uses various steel alloys and produces sheets of various sizes and of various finishes. The items of DM are not numerous, nor are the operations performed. But used in various combinations, they yield so great a variety of products that inaccurate costs for each product result if the broad averaging procedure of historical process costing is used. Similarly, complex conditions are frequently found in plants that manufacture rubber products, textiles, ceramics, paints, and packaged food products. As we shall see, standard costing is especially useful in these situations.

The intricacies of weighted-average and FIFO historical costing methods and the conflicts between them are also eliminated by using standard costs. We again use the Assembly department of Global Defence Inc. as an example, except this time we assign standard costs to the process. The same standard costs apply in February and March of 2018.

We have incomplete units in both beginning inventory WIP and ending inventory WIP. Exhibit 17-8 presented the results of the FIFO method. Exhibit 17-10 summarizes

Exhibit 17-10

Summarizing the Flow of Production in Physical Units and Equivalent Units for the Assembly Department of Global Defence Inc. for March 2018—Standard Costing with Beginning and Ending WIP Inventory

	A	B	C	D
1			Equivalent Units	
2		Physical	Direct	Conversion
3	**Flow of Production**	Units	Materials	Costs
4	Work in process, beginning (February EI WIP, Exhibit 17-3)	225		
5	Started during current period (given)	275		
6	To account for	500		
7	Completed and transferred out during current period:			
8	From beginning work in process[a]	225		
9	[225 × (100% − 100%); 225 × (100% − 60%)]		0	90
10	Started and completed	175[b]		
11	(175 × 100%; 175 × 100%)		175	175
12	Work in process, ending[c] (given)	100		
13	(100 × 100%; 100 × 50%)		100	50
14	Accounted for	500		
15	Work done in March only		275	315
16				
17	[a]Degree of completion in this department: direct materials, 100%; conversion costs, 60%.			
18	[b]400 physical units completed and transferred out minus 225 physical units completed and transferred out from beginning work-in-process inventory.			
19	[c]Degree of completion in this department: direct materials, 100%; conversion costs, 50%.			

the flow of production in both physical units and EU for the standard-costing method of process costing. Notice in Exhibit 17-10 that the standard-costing method also assumes that the earliest EU in beginning inventory WIP are completed first. Work done in the current period for DM is 275 EU. Work done in the current period for conversion costs is 315 EU.

Exhibit 17-11 shows the standard cost per EU, and the assignment of costs to units completed and transferred out and to ending inventory WIP using the standard-costing method of process costing, ending with a summary of variances. The standard-costing method requires *no calculation of the cost allocation rates for either direct materials purchases or conversion costs.* Cost rate per EU are already given as standard costs: direct materials, $74, and conversion costs, $54. The bookkeeping to adjust the COGM and ending inventory WIP for overallocation or underallocation is straightforward, and this method has the added advantage of drawing a manager's attention to unfavourable cost variances. This method provides an opportunity to apply management-accounting analyses of variances to ascertain where the costs of a process require explanation and perhaps remedy.

The total debits to WIP—Assembly differ from total debits to WIP—Assembly under the actual-cost-based weighted-average and FIFO methods. That's because, as in

Exhibit 17-11 Standard Costs per Equivalent Unit and Assigning Costs to Completed Units and Ending WIP Inventory for the Assembly Department of Global Defence Inc. for March 2018—**Case 3, Standard-Costing Method with Beginning and Ending WIP Inventory**

	A	B	C	D
		Total		
		Production	**Direct**	**Conversion**
		Costs	**Materials**	**Costs**
4	Standard cost per equivalent unit (given)		$ 74	$ 54
5	Work in process, beginning (given, Exhibit 17-10)			
6	Direct materials, 225 × $74; Conversion costs, 135 × $54	$23,940	$16,650	$ 7,290
7	Costs added in current period at standard costs			
8	Direct materials, 275 × $74; Conversion costs, 315 × $54	37,360	$20,350	$17,010
9	Total costs to account for	$61,300		
10	Assignment of costs at standard costs:			
11	Completed and transferred out (400 units):			
12	Work in process, beginning (225 units)	$23,940		
13	Costs added to beginning work in process in current period	4,860	$(0^a \times \$74) + (90^a \times \$54)$	
14	Total from beginning inventory	28,800		
15	Started and completed (175 units)	22,400	$(175^b \times \$74) + (175^b \times \$54)$	
16	Total costs of units completed and transferred out	51,200		
17	Work in process, ending (100 units)	10,100	$(100^c \times \$74) + (50^c \times \$54)$	
18	Total costs accounted for	$61,300		
19	Summary of variances for current performance:			
20	Costs added in current period at standard costs (see above)		$20,350	$17,010
21	Actual costs incurred (given)		19,800	16,380
22	Variance		$ 550 F	$ 630 F
23				
24	ᵃEquivalent units used to complete beginning work in process from Exhibit 17-10.			
25	ᵇEquivalent units started and completed from Exhibit 17-10.			
26	ᶜEquivalent units in ending work in process from Exhibit 17-10.			

all standard-costing systems, the debits to the WIP account are at standard costs rather than actual costs. Notice that in comparing Exhibit 17-9 to Exhibit 17-11, all the quantities are identical; it is the rates that change. In Exhibit 17-9 the DM cost allocation rate is $72/EU and the conversion cost allocation rate is $52/EU, while in Exhibit 17-11 the DM standard cost rate is $74/EU and the standard conversion cost rate is $54/EU. The standard costs total is $61,300 in Exhibit 17-11. Using T-accounts, the flow of costs of Global Defence Inc.'s transformation process is illustrated in Exhibit 17-12. Any variance between the standard and actual costs incurred also transfers into and out of the various process accounts.

Accounting for Variances

Process-costing systems using standard costs usually accumulate actual costs separately from the inventory accounts. For example, the actual data are recorded in the first two entries shown below. Recall that Global Defence purchases DM as needed and that these materials are delivered directly to the Assembly department. The total variances are recorded in the next two entries. The final entry transfers out the completed goods at standard costs.

1. Assembly Department Direct Materials Control (at actual)   19,800

       Accounts Payable   19,800

To record direct materials purchased and used in production during March.

This cost control account is debited with actual costs and credited later with standard costs assigned to the units worked on.

2. Assembly Department Conversion Costs Control (at actual)   16,380

       [Various accounts]   16,380

To record Assembly department conversion costs for March.

(Entries 3, 4, and 5 use standard-cost dollar amounts from Exhibit 17-11)

3. Work in Process—Assembly (at standard costs)   20,350

       Direct Materials Variances   550

       Assembly Department Direct Materials Control   19,800

To record actual direct materials used and total direct materials variances.

4. Work in Process—Assembly (at standard costs)   17,010

       Conversion Costs Variances   630

       Assembly Department Conversion Costs Control   16,380

To record actual conversion costs and total conversion costs variances.

5. Work in Process—Testing (at standard costs)   51,200

       Work in Process—Assembly (at standard costs)   51,200

To record cost of units completed and transferred at standard cost from Assembly to Testing.

Variances arise under the standard-costing method, as in entries 3 and 4, because the standard costs assigned to products on the basis of work done in the current period do not usually equal the actual costs incurred in the current period. Variances can be measured and analyzed in little or great detail for feedback, control, and decision-making purposes. Exhibit 17-12 illustrates how the costs flow using T-accounts.

Hybrid-Costing Systems

Product-costing systems must often be designed to fit the particular characteristics of different production systems. Many production systems are a hybrid—they have some

Exhibit 17-12 Flow of Standard Costs in a Process-Costing System, Assembly Department of Global Defence Inc. for March 2018

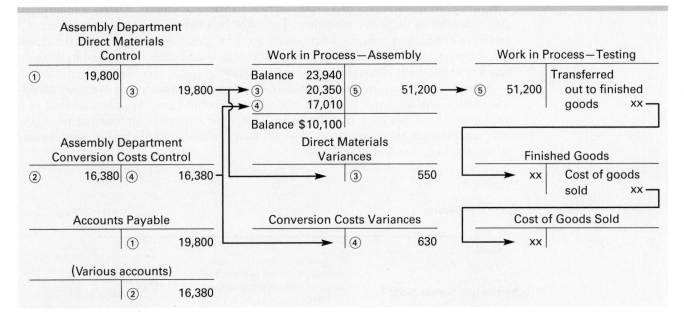

Sustainability in Action

Hybrid Costing for Under Armour 3D Printed Shoes

Under Armour is the fastest growing sportswear company in the world. Known for its high-tech fitness apparel and celebrity endorsers such as Stephen Curry, in 2016 Under Armour introduced customized, 3D-printed shoes to its product lineup.

The Under Armour Architech training shoes feature a 3D-printed midsole that increases stability during exercise. To create the 3D-printed elements, computers create an accurate 3D model of a customer's feet using photographs taken from multiple angles. Under Armour then prints the midsoles in their Baltimore, Maryland, lab and stitches them into the Architech shoes, which are traditionally manufactured ahead of time. The result is a customized pair of shoes tailored for each person's unique feet.

3D printed shoes, like the Architech, use a hybrid costing system. Accounting for the 3D printing of the midsoles and customization requires job costing, but the similar process used to make the shoes they are stitched into lends itself to process costing. The cost of making each pair of shoes is calculated by accumulating all production costs and dividing by the number of shoes made. In other words, while each pair of Architechs is different, the production cost is roughly the same.

The combination of mass production with customized parts is called mass customization, and fosters organizational systems capable of producing much less waste while managing to serve customers more effectively. 3D printing enables mass customization by allowing

customers to tailor specific elements of certain products to their specifications or wants. Along with athletic shoes, 3D printing is letting people create personalized jewellery, earphones, and mobile phone cases. While 3D printing it still in its infancy, by 2020 the market for 3D printers and software is expected to eclipse $20 billion.

Sources: A. Zaleski. 2018. Here's why 2016 could be 3D printing's breakout year. *Fortune*, December 30; J. Kell. 2016. Under Armour debuts first-ever 3D-printed shoes. *Fortune*, March 8; J. Brownlee. What Under Armour's new 3-D-printed shoe reveals about the future of footwear. 2018. *Fast Company*, Co. Design blog, March 25; D. Burrus. 2014. 3D printed shoes: A step in the right direction. *Wired*, September.

features of custom-order manufacturing and other features of mass-production manufacturing. Manufacturers of a relatively wide variety of closely related standardized products tend to use a hybrid system. Typically, in a hybrid costing system, there is a common production system (the products go through the same stages of production) but the materials added to the system are different. Usually this is achieved by running batches of products through the process. Increasingly, due to computerized production lines, the batches are getting smaller or, in some instances, may even be individual units. Consider Ford Motor Company. Automobiles may be manufactured in a continuous flow, but each may be customized with a special combination of engine size, transmission, music system, and so on. Companies develop **hybrid-costing systems** to meet these individual needs.

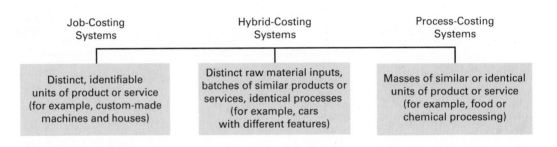

Transferred-in Costs in Process Costing

▶ **LO 5**

Apply process-costing methods to report transferred-in costs and operations costing.

Many process-costing systems have two or more processes in the conversion cycle, as does Global Defence Inc. Ordinarily, as units move from one process to the next, related costs are also transferred by monthly journal entries. If standard costs are used, the accounting for such transfers is relatively simple. However, if weighted-average or FIFO is used, the accounting can become more complex.

To illustrate, we now extend our Global Defence Inc. example to include the next step in the production process, which is undertaken in the Testing department. The process is one of testing and inspection. Once the DG-19 subassemblies pass inspection, additional DM, such as the housing for the closed circuit, complete the unit in readiness for sale to the customer.

Assume conversion costs are added evenly during the testing process. Once units complete the testing process, they are immediately transferred to finished goods. The COGM are added to the cost of goods available for sale (COGAS) and upon sale will become cost of goods sold (COGS). Subcomponents are transferred into Testing after they complete the assembly process. But whereas the Assembly department received subcomponents from an external supplier for conversion, the testing process receives subcomponents from an internal supplier—the assembly process. Conceptually, however, the units transferred into testing are treated like a type of direct material. The costs of all the transferred-in physical units from the Assembly department are, however, called transferred-in costs, not DM costs, for the Testing department. These costs will differ depending upon the choice of weighted-average ($52,000) or FIFO ($52,480) used to estimate the assembly process's COGM and ending inventory WIP.

With respect to the physical units of transferred-in costs, they are 100% complete as beginning inventory WIP for the Testing department. They are not complete with respect to any conversion or any DM added by the Testing department. Unless the transferred-in physical units are 100% converted in the Testing department process, no DM will be added by the Testing department. That is, no unfinished circuits will be placed in their housing unless they successfully pass all tests and quality inspections. DM costs for testing will consist of only those costs incurred to acquire DM from external third parties. These additional DM are added at the end of the testing process.

These data for the process of testing in March 2018 have been reported in the information system:

	A	B	C	D	E
1		**Physical Units**	**Transferred-in**	**Direct**	**Conversion**
2		**(DG-19s)**	**Costs**	**Materials**	**Costs**
3	Work in process, beginning inventory (March 1)	240	$33,600	$ 0	$18,000
4	Degree of completion, beginning work in process		100%	0%	62.5%
5	Transferred-in during March	400			
6	Completed and transferred out during March	440			
7	Work in process, ending inventory (March 31)	200			
8	Degree of completion, ending work in process		100%	0%	80%
9	Total costs added during March				
10	Direct materials and conversion costs			$13,200	$48,600
11	Transferred-in (Weighted-average from Exhibit 17-7)[a]		$52,000		
12	Transferred-in (FIFO from Exhibit 17-9)[a]		$52,480		
13					
14	[a]The transferred-in costs during March are different under the weighted-average method (Exhibit 17-7) and the FIFO method (Exhibit 17-9). In our example, beginning work-in-process inventory of $51,600 (= $33,600 + $0 + $18,000) is the same under both the weighted-average and FIFO inventory methods because we assume costs per equivalent unit to be the same in both January and February. If costs per equivalent unit had been different in the two months, work-in-process inventory at the end of February (beginning of March) would be costed differently under the weighted-average and FIFO methods. The basic approach to process costing with transferred-in costs, however, would still be the same as what we describe in this section.				

Transferred-in costs (or **previous department costs**) are costs incurred in a previous department that are carried forward as part of the product's cost as it moves to a subsequent department for more processing. That is, as the physical units move from one department to the next, their costs per EU move with them. Thus, costs accumulate and those of the testing process include transferred-in costs as well as any additional DM costs and conversion costs added while in the Testing department.

Transferred-in Costs and the Weighted-Average Method

To examine the weighted-average process-costing method with transferred-in costs, we need to add a third column to the EU calculations shown in the process illustrated in Exhibits 17-6 and 17-7. This third column reflects the transferred in EU and related cost calculations.

Exhibit 17-13 shows the flow of production in both physical units and EU. The computations are basically the same as the calculations of EU under the weighted-average method for the Assembly department in Exhibit 17-6, except for the addition of transferred-in costs.

Exhibit 17-14 has been expanded to illustrate the allocation of the DM cost pool using the conversion rates appropriate to the beginning inventory WIP of the Testing department and the good units completed and transferred out this month. The addition of this calculation of the quantity in the cost allocation base for this cost pool is quite straightforward in an all-or-nothing process and was excluded in the Assembly department analysis for this reason. It is more frequently the case that DM are assumed to be added evenly throughout a process. The cost allocation base is always the EU, not the physical units.

Exhibit 17-13 Summarizing the Flow of Production in Physical Units and Equivalent Units Using the Weighted-Average Method of Process Costing for the Testing Department of Global Defence Inc. for March 2018

	A	B	C	D	E
1				Equivalent Units	
2		Physical	Transferred-in	Direct	Conversion
3	**Flow of Production**	Units	Costs	Materials	Costs
4	Work in process, beginning (given)	240	(work done before current period)		
5	Transferred-in during current period (given)	400			
6	To account for	640			
7	Completed and transferred out during current period	440	440	440	440
8	Work in process, ending[a] (given)	200			
9	(200 × 100%; 200 × 0%; 200 × 80%)		200	0	160
10	Accounted for	640			
11	Work done to date		640	440	600
12					
13	[a]Degree of completion in this department: transferred-in costs, 100%; direct materials, 0%; conversion costs, 80%				

Exhibit 17-14 also reports the new cost pool to be considered, the costs transferred in to the Testing department from physical units transferred out by the Assembly department. The transferred-in cost pool consists of two cost elements. The first is the ending inventory WIP of the Testing department, which was 62.5% converted, and 0% of DM

Exhibit 17-14 Calculating Equivalent Unit Costs and Assigning Costs to Completed Units and Ending WIP Inventory for the Testing Department of Global Defence Inc. for March 2018—Weighted-Average Method with Beginning and Ending WIP Inventory

	A	B	C	D	E
1		Total			
2		Production	Transferred-in	Direct	Conversion
3		Costs	Costs	Materials	Costs
4	Work in process, beginning (given)	$ 51,600	$33,600	$ 0	$18,000
5	Costs added in current period (given)	113,800	52,000	13,200	48,600
6	Costs incurred to date		85,600	13,200	66,600
7	Divide by equivalent units of work done to date (Exhibit 17-13)		÷ 640	÷ 440	÷ 600
8	Cost per equivalent unit of work done to date		$133.75	$ 30	$ 111
9	Total costs to account for	$165,400			
10	Assignment of costs:				
11	Completed and transferred out (440 units)	$120,890	(440* × $133.75) + (440* × $30) + (440* × $111)		
12	Work in process, ending (200 units)	44,510	(200[†] × $133.75) + (0[†] × $30) + (160[†] × $111)		
13	Total costs accounted for	$165,400			
14					
15	*Equivalent units completed and transferred out from Exhibit 17-13.				
16	[†]Equivalent units in ending work in process from Exhibit 17-13.				

had been added to these 240 physical units. These units were all transferred into the Testing department from the Assembly department during the month of February. The transferred-in costs remaining in beginning inventory WIP of the Testing department at the beginning of March equal $33,600. No DM were added; therefore, there is $0 reported in the first line of Exhibit 17-14 for DM. The dollar value of conversion costs for the ending inventory WIP in February, and therefore beginning inventory WIP of March for the Testing department, is also given as $18,000 and this is reported in the final column of cost pools in Exhibit 17-14.

The information in Exhibit 17-7 illustrating the March weighted-average costs for the Assembly department reported the total COGM transferred out for the 400 completed physical units was $52,000, which appears as the dollar value of physical units transferred in to the Testing department on the second line of Exhibit 17-14 in the Transferred-in Costs column. Note that the transferred-out units for March from the Assembly department are the same units that are the transferred-in units for March for the Testing department. The total transferred-in, DM, and conversion costs in the Testing department for those 640 units that were either completed or still in-process are $165,400 for the month of March. The dollar amounts in the testing DM and testing conversion cost pools are given as shown.

In Exhibit 17-14, the cost assignment is based on the cost allocation rates shown in the top section of the exhibit. In the bottom section, the first line refers to the EU completed and transferred out to Finished Goods and the second refers to the EU remaining in ending inventory WIP. Notice that 0 DM EU remaining in ending inventory WIP did not consume any DM, the housing for the circuit boards, during March because the DM are added at the end of the Testing department's conversion process. Using the dollar amount from Exhibit 17-14, the journal entry for the transfer out of the Testing department to FG inventory is

Finished Goods	120,890	
Work in Process—Testing		120,890
To transfer units to finished goods inventory.		

Entries to the key T-account, Work in Process—Testing, follow, using information from Exhibit 17-14:

Work in Process—Testing

Beginning inventory, March 1	51,600	Transferred out	120,890
Transferred-in costs	52,000		
Direct materials	13,200		
Conversion costs	48,600		
Ending inventory, March 31	44,510		

Transferred-in Costs and the FIFO Method

To examine the FIFO process-costing method with transferred-in costs, we must refer back to Exhibit 17-9 for both the transferred-out COGM from the Assembly department and the physical units completed and transferred out. It is important to understand that in a series of interdepartmental transfers, each department is regarded as being separate and distinct for accounting purposes. All costs transferred in during a given accounting period are carried at the unit cost figure the previous department transferred out.

Exhibit 17-15 shows the flow of production in both physical units and EU under the FIFO method of process costing. Obviously, the physical unit information remains the same under either the weighted-average or the FIFO method. Other than considering

Exhibit 17-15 Summarizing the Flow of Production in Physical Units and Equivalent Units Using the FIFO Method of Process Costing for the Testing Department of Global Defence Inc. for March 2018

	A	B	C	D	E
1				Equivalent Units	
2		**Physical**	**Transferred-in**	**Direct**	**Conversion**
3	**Flow of Production**	**Units**	**Costs**	**Materials**	**Costs**
4	Work in process, beginning (given)	240	(work done before current period)		
5	Transferred-in during current period (given)	400			
6	To account for	640			
7	Completed and transferred out during current period:				
8	From beginning work in process[a]	240			
9	[240 × (100% − 100%); 240 × (100% − 0%); 240 × (100% − 62.5%)]		0	240	90
10	Started and completed	200[b]			
11	(200 × 100%; 200 × 100%; 200 × 100%)		200	200	200
12	Work in process, ending[c] (given)	200			
13	(200 × 100%; 200 × 0%; 200 × 80%)		200	0	160
14	Accounted for	640			
15	Work done in current period only		400	440	450
16					
17	[a]Degree of completion in this department: transferred-in costs, 100%; direct materials, 0%; conversion costs, 62.5%.				
18	[b]440 physical units completed and transferred out minus 240 physical units completed and transferred out from beginning work-in-process inventory.				
19	[c]Degree of completion in this department: transferred-in costs, 100%; direct materials, 0%; conversion costs, 80%.				

transferred-in costs, the computations of EU are basically the same as those under the FIFO method for the Assembly department shown in Exhibit 17-8.

Exhibit 17-16 shows the calculation of the transferred-in DM, and conversion cost per EU, and the assignment of costs to units completed and transferred out and to ending inventory WIP using the FIFO method of process costing. The per-unit transferred-in costs added during the month of March are simply the transferred-in costs for March divided by the number of units transferred in during March ($52,480 ÷ 400 EU = $131.20/EU). The DM costs added in the Testing department are calculated based on the 440 EU completed and transferred out this month. Conversion costs of testing are divided by the total EU finished in the current time period, which have been calculated in Exhibit 17-15 as 450 EU.

The reasoning for using only $52,480 in the Transferred-in, $13,200 in the Direct Materials, and $48,600 in the Conversion cost pools is that these are the only relevant costs for the month of March in the Testing department using FIFO. Based on the appropriate cost allocation rates, the costs are assigned using the appropriate EU beginning with the 90 EU to be converted from beginning inventory WIP first (240 physical units multiplied by (1 − 62.5%) = 90 EU). Notice that DM are added to 240 EU because these 240 physical units must be 100% converted before the Testing department adds any DM at all.

In Exhibit 17-16, the total costs to account for and accounted for of $165,880 under the FIFO method differ from the corresponding amounts under the weighted-average method of $165,400 because of the different costs of completed units transferred in from the Assembly department under the two methods ($52,480 under FIFO and $52,000 under weighted-average).

Exhibit 17-16 Calculating Equivalent Unit Costs and Assigning Costs to Completed Units and Ending WIP Inventory for the Testing Department of Global Defence Inc. for March 2018—FIFO Method with Beginning and Ending WIP Inventory

	A	B	C	D	E
		Total			
		Production	Transferred-in	Direct	Conversion
		Costs	Costs	Materials	Costs
4	Work in process, beginning (given)	$ 51,600	(work done before current period)		
5	Costs added in current period (given)	114,280	$52,480	$13,200	$48,600
6	Divide by equivalent units of work done in current period (Exhibit 17-15)		÷ 400	÷ 440	÷ 450
7	Cost per equivalent unit of work done in current period		$131.20	$ 30	$ 108
8	Total costs to account for	$165,880			
9	Assignment of costs:				
10	Completed and transferred out (440 units)				
11	Work in process, beginning (240 units)	$ 51,600			
12	Costs added to beginning work in process in current period	16,920	$(0^a \times \$131.20) + (240^a \times \$30) + (90^a \times \$108)$		
13	Total from beginning inventory	68,520			
14	Started and completed (200 units)	53,840	$(200^b \times \$131.20) + (200^b \times \$30) + (200^b \times \$108)$		
15	Total costs of units completed and transferred out	122,360			
16	Work in process, ending (200 units)	43,520	$(200^c \times \$131.20) + (0^c \times \$30) + (160^c \times \$108)$		
17	Total costs accounted for	$165,880			
18					
19	^{a}Equivalent units used to complete beginning work in process from Exhibit 17-15.				
20	^{b}Equivalent units started and completed from Exhibit 17-15.				
21	^{c}Equivalent units in ending work in process from Exhibit 17-15.				

Using the dollar amount from Exhibit 17-16, the journal entry for the transfer out to FG inventory is

Finished Goods	122,360	
Work in Process—Testing		122,360
To transfer units to finished goods inventory.		

Entries to the key T-account, Work in Process—Testing, follow, using information from Exhibit 17-16:

Work in Process—Testing

Beginning inventory, March 1	51,600	Transferred out	122,360
Transferred-in costs	52,480		
Direct materials	13,200		
Conversion costs	48,600		
Ending inventory, March 31	43,520		

The dollar values using the weighted-average and FIFO methods reported in Exhibits 17-15 and 17-16 for the Testing department are summarized and compared for the month of March.

Global Defence Inc. **Schedule of Cost of Goods Manufactured,** **Testing Department for the Month Ended:**	**March 31, 2018** **Weighted-Average**		**March 31, 2018** **FIFO**	
Direct materials				
Beginning inventory of direct materials	$ 0		$ 0	
Purchases of direct materials during the month	13,200		13,200	
Cost of direct materials available for use	13,200		13,200	
Ending inventory of direct materials for the month	0		0	
Direct materials used during the month		$ 13,200		$ 13,200
All conversion costs	48,600		48,600	
Total conversion costs		48,600		48,600
Manufacturing costs incurred during the month		61,800		61,800
Beginning work-in-process inventory		51,600		51,600
Transferred-in cost of goods manufactured from assembly		52,000		52,480
Total manufacturing costs to account for		165,400		165,880
Ending work-in-process inventory		(44,510)		(43,520)
Cost of goods manufactured—transferred out to finished goods		$120,890		$120,360

Common Mistakes with Transferred-in Costs

Here are some common pitfalls to avoid when accounting for transferred-in costs:

1. Remember that transferred-in costs from previous departments are cost pools that must be added into your calculations.

2. In calculating costs to be transferred on a FIFO basis, do not overlook the costs assigned at the beginning of the period to units that were in process but are now included in the units transferred out. For example, do not overlook the $51,600 in Exhibit 17-16.

3. The cost allocation rates most likely will fluctuate from month to month because they are based on actual costs incurred. Therefore, transferred units may contain batches accumulated at different unit costs. For example, the 400 units transferred in at $52,480 in Exhibit 17-16 using the FIFO method consist of units that have different unit costs for direct materials and conversion costs when these units were worked on in the Assembly department (see Exhibit 17-9). Remember, however, that when these units are transferred in to the Testing department, they are at one average unit cost of $131.20 (= $52,480 ÷ 400), as in Exhibit 17-16.

4. Units may be measured in different terms in different departments. Consider each department separately. For example, unit costs could be based on kilograms in the first department and litres in the second; therefore, as units are received by the second department, their measurements would need to be converted to litres to ensure comparable cost allocation bases and rates.

Pulling it all Together—Problem for Self-Study

(Try to solve this problem before examining the solution that follows.)

Problem

Allied Chemicals operates a thermo-assembly process as the second of three processes at its plastics plant. Direct materials in thermo-assembly are added at the end of the process. Conversion costs are added evenly during the process. The following data pertain to the Thermo-Assembly department for 2018.

A	B	C	D	E
1	Physical	Transferred-in	Direct	Conversion
2	Units	Costs	Materials	Costs
3 Work in process, beginning inventory	50,000			
4 Degree of completion, beginning work in process		100%	0%	80%
5 Transferred in during current period	200,000			
6 Completed and transferred out during current period	210,000			
7 Work in process, ending inventory	?			
8 Degree of completion, ending work in process		100%	0%	40%

Compute equivalent units under (1) the weighted-average method and (2) the FIFO method. ❶ ❷ ❸ ❹ ◀ **Required**

Solution

1. The weighted-average method uses equivalent units of work done to date to compute cost per equivalent unit. The calculation of equivalent units follows:

	A	B	C	D	E
1			Equivalent Units		
2		Physical	Transferred-in	Direct	Conversion
3	**Flow of Production**	Units	Costs	Materials	Costs
4	Work in process, beginning (given)	50,000			
5	Transferred in during current period (given)	200,000			
6	To account for	250,000			
7	Completed and transferred out during current period	210,000	210,000	210,000	210,000
8	Work in process, ending[a]	40,000[b]			
9	(40,000 × 100%; 40,000 × 0%; 40,000 × 40%)		40,000	0	16,000
10	Accounted for	250,000			
11	Work done to date		250,000	210,000	226,000
12					
13	[a]Degree of completion in this department: transferred-in costs, 100%; direct materials, 0%; conversion costs, 40%.				
14	[b]250,000 physical units to account for minus 210,000 physical units completed and transferred out.				

2. The FIFO method uses equivalent units of work done in the current period only to compute cost per equivalent unit. The calculations of equivalent units follow:

	A	B	C	D	E
1				Equivalent Units	
2		Physical	Transferred-in	Direct	Conversion
3	**Flow of Production**	Units	Costs	Materials	Costs
4	Work in process, beginning (given)	50,000			
5	Transferred in during current period (given)	200,000			
6	To account for	250,000			
7	Completed and transferred out during current period:				
8	From beginning work in process[a]	50,000			
9	[50,000 × (100% − 100%); 50,000 × (100% − 0%); 50,000 × (100% − 80%)]	0	50,000	10,000	
10	Started and completed	160,000[b]			
11	(160,000 × 100%; 160,000 × 100%; 160,000 × 100%)		160,000	160,000	160,000
12	Work in process, ending[c]	40,000[d]			
13	(40,000 × 100%; 40,000 × 0%; 40,000 × 40%)		40,000	0	16,000
14	Accounted for	250,000			
15	Work done in current period only		200,000	210,000	186,000
16					
17	[a]Degree of completion in this department: transferred-in costs, 100%; direct materials, 0%; conversion costs, 80%.				
18	[b]210,000 physical units completed and transferred out minus 50,000 physical units completed and transferred out from beginning work-in-process inventory.				
19	[c]Degree of completion in this department: transferred-in costs, 100%; direct materials, 0%; conversion costs, 40%.				
20	[d]250,000 physical units to account for minus 210,000 physical units completed and transferred out.				

Decision Points

The following question-and-answer format summarizes the chapter's learning objectives. Each point presents a key question, and the guidelines are the answer to that question.

Learning Objectives	Guidelines
1. What are the key differences that distinguish job from process costing?	The motivation to use job costing is that different jobs consume different resources at different rates; therefore, their costs differ. Indirect cost assignment systems are designed to report these differences in an economic, effective, and efficient way. The cost object is the job. The motivation to use process costing is that all outputs consume virtually identical resources at constant rates; therefore, the costs of outputs are identical. Indirect cost assignment systems are designed to accumulate and match the costs of each process to the physical conversion occurring during the process. The cost object is the process.
2. How are costs assigned to units completed and units in ending WIP using the weighted-average method?	The weighted-average method is one of three methods used to assign costs to either completed units that have moved on to the next process (finished) or to work-in-process (WIP) inventory. The cost driver is equivalent units, and all cost allocation rates are calculated on a cost per equivalent unit. Each cost pool (e.g., direct materials, conversion costs) is assigned on the basis of the equivalent units either completed or remaining in ending WIP inventory. The main difference in journal entries is that, in a process-costing system, there is a separate WIP account for each process.

3. What is a transferred-out cost?

The physical flow of raw materials through different processes of conversion is matched by the transfer of accumulated costs out of one process (for 100% completed conversion of the inputs), and into the account for the next process. No cost disappears but rather accumulates and is transferred to the next stage of the process.

4. What are the first-in, first-out method and standard-costing method of process costing?

The first-in, first-out (FIFO) method computes unit costs based on costs incurred during the period and equivalent units of work done in the current period. FIFO assigns the costs of the beginning WIP inventory to the first units completed and assigns the costs of the equivalent units worked on during the current period first to complete beginning inventory, next to started and completed new units, and finally to units in ending WIP inventory. Under the standard-costing method, cost allocation rates are already in place as standard costs per unit when assigning cost to units completed and to units in ending WIP inventory. Standard costing is not an ASPE/IFRS-compliant method to value inventories or costs for external reporting purposes.

5. What is a transferred-in cost?

The costs of goods manufactured, those physical units completed in a prior conversion process, are transferred out of the prior department during the current time period. These become the transferred-in costs for the next department in the conversion process.

Terms to Learn

This chapter and the Glossary at the end of the book contain definitions of the following important terms:

equivalent unit (EU) **(p. 693)**

first-in, first-out (FIFO) process-costing
  method **(p. 695)**

hybrid-costing systems **(p. 714)**

physical units **(p. 693)**

previous department
  costs **(p. 715)**

standard-costing method **(p. 695)**

transferred-in costs **(p. 715)**

weighted-average (WA)
  process-costing method **(p. 695)**

Assignment Material

MyLab Accounting Make the grade with MyLab Accounting: The Short-Answer Questions, Exercises, and Problems marked with a ⊕ can be found on MyLab Accounting. You can practise them as often as you want, and most feature step-by-step guided instructions to help you find the right answer.

Short-Answer Questions

⊕ **17-1** Give three examples of industries that often use process-costing systems.

⊕ **17-2** In process costing, why are costs often divided into two main classifications?

⊕ **17-3** Explain equivalent units. Why are equivalent-unit calculations necessary in process costing?

⊕ **17-4** State two conditions under which computing equivalent units will make a material difference to reported inventory amounts.

⊕ **17-5** Describe the distinctive characteristic of weighted-average computations in assigning costs to units completed and ending work in process.

⊕ **17-6** Describe the distinctive characteristic of FIFO computations in assigning costs to units completed and ending work in process.

⊕ **17-7** Identify the main difference between journal entries in process costing and the ones in job costing.

⊕ **17-8** "Standard-cost procedures are particularly applicable to process-costing situations." Do you agree? Why?

⊕ **17-9** Why should the accountant distinguish between transferred-in costs and additional direct materials costs for each subsequent department in a process-costing system?

⊕ **17-10** "Transferred-in costs are those incurred in the preceding accounting period." Do you agree? Explain.

⊕ **17-11** "There's no reason for me to get excited about the choice between the weighted-average and FIFO methods in my process-costing system. I have long-term contracts with my materials suppliers at fixed prices." State the conditions under which you would (a) agree and (b) disagree with this statement, made by a plant controller. Explain.

Exercises

⊕ **17-12 Terminology.** A number of terms are listed below:

equivalent unit (EU)	first-in, first-out (FIFO)
weighted-average process-costing method	standard-costing method

Required

Select the terms from the above list to complete the following sentences.

In process costing, the cost object is the entire production process. The method is used for mass-produced items that are identical. That is why a weighted average can be used to calculate the ratio of work in process to finished goods. A common denominator must be found because a physical unit 100% converted has cost more to produce than one that is only 50% converted and remains in work-in-process inventory. The benefits of the conversion process are unequally shared between the items in each type of inventory. The average conversion rate is calculated using a denominator called an _____ ( ). Three methods assign conversion costs to finished goods and work in process. The choice of method should be made by the management team such that the method is economically plausible. The method reflects the facts of the economic outcome of the production process in a specified time period. The three methods are _____ ( ) method, the _____, and the _____ .

LO 1 ▶
1. Unit cost, $154.80

⊕ **17-13 Equivalent units, zero beginning inventory.** A&A Inc. is a manufacturer of digital cameras. It has two departments: assembly and testing. In January 2018, the company incurred $900,000 on direct materials and $957,600 on conversion costs, for a total manufacturing cost of $1,857,600.

Required

1. Assume there was no beginning inventory of any kind on January 1, 2018. During January, 12,000 cameras were placed into production and all 12,000 were fully completed at the end of the month. What is the unit cost of an assembled camera in January 2018?
2. Assume that during February, 12,000 cameras were placed into production. Further assume the same total assembly costs for January are also incurred in February 2018, but only 9,000 cameras are fully completed at the end of February. All direct materials have been added to the remaining 3,000 cameras. However, on average, these remaining 3,000 cameras are only 50% complete as to conversion costs. (a) What are the equivalent units for direct materials and conversion costs and their respective costs per equivalent unit for February? (b) What is the unit cost of an assembled camera in February 2018?
3. Explain the difference in your answers to requirements 1 and 2.

LO 2 ▶
1. Work-in-process Assembly DR, $750,000

⊕ **17-14 Journal entries** (continuation of Exercise 17-13).

Required

Prepare summary journal entries for the use of direct materials and incurrence of conversion costs. Also prepare a journal entry to transfer out the cost of goods completed. Show the postings to the Work-in-Process account.

🌐 **17-15 Zero beginning inventory, materials introduced in middle of process.** Roary Chemicals has a mixing department and a refining department. Its process-costing system in the mixing department has two direct materials cost categories (Chemical P and Chemical Q) and one conversion costs pool. The following data pertain to the mixing department for July 2018:

◀ **LO 1**
1. Equivalent units, conversion costs, 45,000

Physical Units:	
Work in process, July 1	0
Units started	50,000
Completed and transferred to	
refining department	35,000
Costs:	
Chemical P	$250,000
Chemical Q	70,000
Conversion costs	135,000

Chemical P is introduced at the start of operations in the mixing department, and Chemical Q is added when the product is three-quarters completed in the mixing department. Conversion costs are added evenly during the process. The ending work in process in the mixing department is two-thirds completed.

Required

1. Compute the equivalent units in the mixing department for July 2018 for each cost category.
2. Compute (a) the cost of goods completed and transferred to the refining department during July and (b) the cost of work in process as of July 31, 2018.
3. Would there be any difference in your calculations of equivalent units if you used a weighted-average approach versus the FIFO approach? What is the reason for this?

🌐 **17-16 Weighted-average method, assigning costs.** Bio Doc Corporation is a biotech company that makes a cancer-treatment drug in a single processing department. Direct materials are added at the start of the process. Conversion costs are added evenly during the process. Bio Doc uses the weighted-average method of process costing. The following information for July 2018 is available:

◀ **LO 3**
1. Equivalent units of conversion costs, 52,500.

	Physical Units	Equivalent Units	
		Direct Materials	Conversion Costs
Work in process, July 1*	12,500	12,500	8,750
Started during July	50,000		
Completed and transferred out during July	42,500	42,500	42,500
Work in process, July 31†	20,000	20,000	10,000

*Degree of completion: direct materials, 100%; conversion costs, 70%.
†Degree of completion: direct materials, 100%; conversion costs, 50%.

Total Costs for July 2018		
Work in process, beginning		
Direct materials	$75,000	
Conversion costs	87,500	$162,500
Direct materials added during July		325,000
Conversion costs added during July		463,750
Total costs to account for		$951,250

Required

1. Calculate the cost per equivalent unit for direct materials and conversion costs.
2. Summarize total costs to account for, and assign total costs to units completed (and transferred out) and to units in ending work in process.

LO 4 ▷
1. Direct materials cost per equivalent unit, $7

🌐 **17-17 FIFO method, assigning costs.** Refer to the information in Exercise 17-16.

Required

Do Exercise 17-16 using the FIFO method. Note that you first need to calculate the equivalent units of work done in the current period (for direct materials and conversion costs) to complete beginning work in process, to start and complete new units, and to produce ending work in process.

LO 4 ▷
2. Total direct materials cost variance, $20,000 U

🌐 **17-18 Standard-costing method, assigning costs.** Refer to the information in Exercise 17-16. Suppose Bio Doc determines standard costs of $6.60 per equivalent unit for direct materials and $10.40 per equivalent unit for conversion costs for both beginning work in process and work done in the current period.

Required

1. Do Exercise 17-16 using the standard-costing method. Note that you first need to calculate the equivalent units of work done in the current period (for direct materials and conversion costs) to complete beginning work in process, to start and complete new units, and to produce ending work in process.
2. Compute the total direct materials and conversion costs variances for July 2018.

LO 3 ▷
2. Direct materials cost per equivalent unit, $701,837.80

🌐 **17-19 Weighted-average method, equivalent units and unit costs.** Consider the following data for the assembly division of a satellite manufacturer:

	Physical Units (satellites)	Direct Materials	Conversion Costs
Beginning work in process (May 1)*	8	$ 5,426,960	$ 1,001,440
Started in May 2018	55		
Completed during May 2018	51		
Ending work in process (May 31)†	12		
Costs added during May 2018		$35,420,000	$15,312,000

*Degree of completion: direct materials, 90%; conversion costs, 40%.

†Degree of completion: direct materials, 60%; conversion costs, 30%.

The assembly division uses the weighted-average method of process costing.

Required

1. Compute equivalent units for direct materials and conversion costs. Show physical units in the first column of your schedule.
2. Calculate cost per equivalent unit for direct materials and conversion costs.

LO 3 ▷
Conversion cost per equivalent unit of work done to date, $298,780.95

🌐 **17-20 Weighted-average method, assigning costs** (continuation of Exercise 17-19).

Required

For the data in Exercise 17-19, summarize total costs to account for, and assign these costs to units completed (and transferred out) and to units in ending work in process.

LO 4 ▷
2. Direct materials cost per equivalent unit, $694,510

🌐 **17-21 FIFO method, equivalent units and unit costs.** Refer to the information in Exercise 17-19. Suppose the assembly division uses the FIFO method of process costing instead of the weighted-average method.

Required

1. Compute equivalent units for direct materials and conversion costs. Show physical units in the first column of your schedule.
2. Calculate cost per equivalent unit for direct materials and conversion costs.

LO 4 ▷
Total cost of work in process, $6,072,908

🌐 **17-22 FIFO method, assigning costs** (continuation of Exercise 17-21).

Required

For the data in Exercise 17-19, use the FIFO method to summarize total costs to account for, and assign these costs to units completed and transferred out, and to units in ending work in process.

LO 4 ▷
Equivalent units of work done in current period for Direct materials is 100,000

🌐 **17-23 Standard-costing with beginning and ending work in process.** Lawrence Company is a manufacturer of contemporary door handles. The vice president of Design attends home shows twice a year so the company can keep current with home trends. Because of its volume, Lawrence uses process costing to account for production. Costs and output figures for August are as follows:

Lawrence Company's Process Costing
for the Month Ended August 31, 2017

	Units	Direct Materials	Conversion Costs
Standard cost per unit		$ 5.75	$ 12.25
Work in process, beginning inventory (Aug. 1)	15,000	$ 86,250	$ 55,125
Degree of completion of beginning work in process		100%	30%
Started in August	100,000		
Completed and transferred out	95,000		
Work in process, ending inventory (Aug. 31)	20,000		
Degree of completion of ending work in process		100%	80%
Total costs added during August		$569,000	$1,307,240

Required

1. Compute equivalent units for direct materials and conversion costs. Show physical units in the first column of your schedule.
2. Compute the total standard costs of handles transferred out in August and the total standard costs of the August 31 inventory of work in process.
3. Compute the total August variances for direct materials and conversion costs.
4. Prepare summarized journal entries to record both the actual costs and standard costs for direct materials and conversion costs, including the variances for both production costs.

🌐 **17-24 Transferred-in costs, weighted-average method.** Asaya Clothing Inc. is a manufacturer of winter clothes. It has a knitting department and a finishing department. This exercise focuses on the finishing department. Direct materials are added at the end of the process. Conversion costs are added evenly during the process. Asaya uses the weighted-average method of process costing. The information for June 2018 is shown below.

◀ **LO 4**
3. Total cost to account for work in process, $363,000

	Physical Units (tonnes)	Transferred-in Costs	Direct Materials	Conversion Costs
Work in process, beginning inventory (June 1)	75	$ 75,000	$ 0	$30,000
Degree of completion, beginning work in process		100%	0%	60%
Transferred in during June	135			
Completed and transferred out during June	150			
Work in process, ending inventory (June 30)	60			
Degree of completion, ending work in process		100%	0%	75%
Total costs added during June		$142,500	$37,500	$78,000

Required

1. Calculate equivalent units (tonnes) of transferred-in costs, direct materials, and conversion costs.
2. Summarize total costs to account for, and calculate the cost per equivalent unit for transferred-in costs, direct materials, and conversion costs.
3. Assign total costs to units completed (and transferred out) and to units in ending work in process.

🌐 **17-25 Transferred-in costs, FIFO method.** Refer to the information in Exercise 17-24. Suppose that Asaya uses the FIFO method instead of the weighted-average method in all of its departments. The only changes to Exercise 17-24 under the FIFO method are that the total transferred-in costs of beginning work in process on June 1 are $60,000 (instead of $75,000) and total transferred-in costs added during June are $130,800 (instead of $142,500).

◀ **LO 5**
3. Total cost of work in process, ending, $81,534

Required

Do Exercise 17-24 using the FIFO method. Note that you first need to calculate the equivalent units of work done in the current period (for transferred-in costs, direct materials, and conversion costs) to complete beginning work in process, to start and complete new units, and to produce ending work in process.

LO 3 ▷
Direct materials equivalent
units, 532

⊕ **17-26 Weighted-average method, equivalent units and unit costs.** Consider the following data for the assembly division of Fenton Watches Inc.:

	Physical Units	Direct Materials	Conversion Costs
Beginning work in process (May 1)*	80	$ 493,360	$ 91,040
Started in May 2018	500		
Completed during May 2018	460		
Ending work in process (May 31)†	120		
Costs added during May 2018		$3,220,000	$1,392,000

*Degree of completion: direct materials, 90%; conversion costs, 50%.
† Degree of completion: direct materials, 60%; conversion costs, 30%.

The assembly division uses the weighted-average method of process costing.

Required

Compute equivalent units for direct materials and conversion costs. Show physical units in the first column of your schedule.

LO 3 ▷
Total cost of work in process,
ending $610,200

⊕ **17-27 Weighted-average method, assigning costs** (continuation of Exercise 17-26).

Required

For the data in Exercise 17-26, summarize total costs to account for, calculate cost per equivalent unit for direct materials and conversion costs, and assign total costs to units completed (and transferred out) and to units in ending work in process.

LO 4 ▷
Direct materials equivalent
units, 460

⊕ **17-28 FIFO method, equivalent units.** Refer to the information in Exercise 17-26. Suppose the assembly division at Fenton Watches Inc. uses the FIFO method of process costing instead of the weighted-average method.

Required

Compute equivalent units for direct materials and conversion costs. Show physical units in the first column of your schedule.

LO 4 ▷
Total cost of work in process,
ending, $612,000

⊕ **17-29 FIFO method, assigning costs** (continuation of Exercise 17-28).

Required

For the data in Exercise 17-26, use the FIFO method to summarize total costs to account for, calculate cost per equivalent unit for direct materials and conversion costs, and assign total costs to units completed (and transferred out) and to units in ending work in process.

Problems

LO 2 ▷

⊕ **17-30 Weighted-average method.** McKnight Handcraft is a manufacturer of picture frames for large retailers. Every picture frame passes through two departments: the assembly department and the finishing department. This problem focuses on the assembly department. The process-costing system at McKnight has a single direct-cost category (direct materials) and a single indirect-cost category (conversion costs). Direct materials are added when the assembly department process is 10% complete. Conversion costs are added evenly during the assembly department's process.

McKnight uses the weighted-average method of process costing. Consider the following data for the assembly department in April 2017:

	Physical Unit (Frames)	Direct Materials	Conversion Costs
Work in process, April 1a	60	$ 1,530	$ 156
Started during April 2017	510		
Completed during April 2017	450		
Work in process, April 30b	120		
Total costs added during April 2017		$17,850	$11,544

aDegree of completion: direct materials, 100%; conversion costs, 40%.
bDegree of completion: direct materials, 100%; conversion costs, 15%.

Required

1. Summarize the total assembly department costs for April 2017, and assign them to units completed (and transferred out) and to units in ending work in process.
2. What issues should a manager focus on when reviewing the equivalent units calculation?

⊕ **17-31 FIFO method** (continuation of 17-30). ◀ **LO 2**

Required

1. Complete Problem 17-30 using the FIFO method of process costing.
2. If you did Problem 17-30, explain any difference between the cost of work completed and transferred out and the cost of ending work in process in the assembly department under the weighted-average method and the FIFO method. Should McKnight's managers choose the weighted-average method or the FIFO method? Explain briefly.

17-32 Standard costing, journal entries. The Warner Company manufactures reproductions of expensive sunglasses. Warner uses the standard-costing method of process costing to account for the production of the sunglasses. All materials are added at the beginning of production. The costs and output of sunglasses for May 2017 are as follows: ◀ **LO 2**

	Physical Units	% of Completion for Conversion Costs	Direct Materials	Conversion Costs
Work in process, beginning	22,000	60%	$ 48,400	$ 33,000
Started during May	95,000			
Completed and transferred out	87,000			
Work in process, ending	30,000	75%		
Standard cost per unit			$ 2.20	$ 2.50
Costs added during May			$207,500	$238,000

Required

1. Compute equivalent units for direct materials and conversion costs. Show physical units in the first column of your schedule.
2. Compute the total standard costs of sunglasses transferred out in May and the total standard costs of the May 31 inventory of work in process.
3. Compute the total May variances for direct materials and conversion costs.
4. Prepare summarized journal entries to record both the actual costs and standard costs for direct materials and conversion costs, including the variances for both production costs.

⊕ **17-33 Transferred-in costs, weighted-average method.** Spelling Sports, which produces basketballs, has two departments: cutting and stitching. Each department has one direct-cost category (direct materials) and one indirect-cost category (conversion costs). This problem focuses on the stitching department. ◀ **LO 5**

Basketballs that have undergone the cutting process are immediately transferred to the stitching department. Direct material is added when the stitching process is 70% complete. Conversion costs are added evenly during stitching operations. When those operations are done, the basketballs are immediately transferred to Finished Goods.

Spelling Sports uses the weighted-average method of process costing. The following is a summary of the March 2017 operations of the stitching department:

	Home	Insert	Page Layout	Formulas	Data	Review	View		
	A				B	C	D		E
1					Physical Units (basketballs)	Transferred-In Costs	Direct Materials		Conversion Costs
2	Beginning work in process				17,500	$ 45,360	$ 0		$17,660
3	Degree of completion, beginning work in process					100%	0%		60%
4	Transferred in during March 2017				56,000				
5	Completed and transferred out during March 2017				52,000				
6	Ending work in process, March 31				21,500				
7	Degree of completion, ending work in process					100%	0%		20%
8	Total costs added during March					$154,560	$28,080		$89,310

Required

1. Summarize total stitching department costs for March 2017, and assign these costs to units completed (and transferred out) and to units in ending work in process.
2. Prepare journal entries for March transfers from the cutting department to the stitching department and from the stitching department to Finished Goods.

🌐 **17-34 Transferred-in costs, FIFO method.** Refer to the information in Problem 17-33. Suppose that Spelling Sports uses the FIFO method instead of the weighted-average method. Assume that all other information, including the cost of beginning WIP, is unchanged.

Required

1. Using the FIFO process-costing method, complete Problem 17-33.
2. If you did Problem 17-33, explain any difference between the cost of work completed and transferred out and the cost of ending work in process in the stitching department under the weighted-average method and the FIFO method.

🌐 **17-35 Weighted-average method.** Porter Handcraft is a manufacturer of picture frames for large retailers. Every picture frame passes through two departments: assembly and finishing. This problem focuses on the assembly department. The process-costing system at Porter has a single direct cost category (direct materials) and a single indirect cost category (conversion costs). Direct materials are added when the assembly department process is 10% complete. Conversion costs are added evenly during the assembly department's process.

Porter uses the weighted-average method of process costing. Consider the following data for the assembly department in April 2018:

	Physical Units (frames)	Direct Materials	Conversion Costs
Work in process, April 1*	75	$ 1,775	$ 135
Started during April 2018	550		
Completed during April 2018	500		
Work in process, April 30†	125		
Costs added during April 2018		$17,600	$10,890

*Degree of completion: direct materials, 100%; conversion costs, 40%.
† Degree of completion: direct materials, 100%; conversion costs, 20%.

Required

Summarize the total assembly department costs for April 2018, and assign total costs to units completed (and transferred out) and to units in ending work in process.

🌐 **17-36 Journal entries** (continuation of Problem 17-35).

Required

Prepare a set of summarized journal entries for all April transactions affecting Work in Process—Assembly. Set up a T-account for Work in Process—Assembly, and post the entries to it.

17-37 FIFO method (continuation of Problem 17-35).

Required

Do Problem 17-36 using the FIFO method of process costing. If you did Problem 17-35, explain any difference between the cost of work completed and transferred out and the cost of ending work in process in the assembly department under the weighted-average method and the FIFO method.

🌐 **17-38 Transferred-in costs, weighted-average method.** Choice Books Inc. has two departments: printing and binding. Each department has one direct cost category (direct materials) and one indirect cost category (conversion costs). This problem focuses on the binding department. Books that have undergone the printing process are immediately transferred to the binding department. Direct materials are added when the binding process is 80% complete. Conversion costs are added evenly during binding operations. When those operations are done, the books are immediately transferred to finished goods. Choice Books Inc. uses the weighted-average method of process costing. The following is a summary of the April 2018 operations of the binding department.

	Physical Units (books)	Transferred-in Costs	Direct Materials	Conversion Costs
Beginning work in process	900	$ 32,775	$ 0	$15,000
Degree of completion, beginning work in process		100%	0%	40%
Transferred in during April 2018	2,700			
Completed and transferred out during April	3,000			
Ending work in process (April 30)	600			
Degree of completion, ending work in process		100%	0%	60%
Total costs added during April		$144,000	$26,700	$69,000

Required

1. Summarize the total binding department costs for April 2018, and assign these costs to units completed (and transferred out) and to units in ending work in process.
2. Prepare journal entries for April transfers from the printing department to the binding department and from the binding department to finished goods.

🌐 **17-39 Transferred-in costs, weighted-average method.** Hoffman Company, as you know, is a manufac- ◀ **LO 5**
turer of car seats. Each car seat passes through the assembly department and testing department. This problem focuses on the testing department. Direct materials are added when the testing department process is 90% complete. Conversion costs are added evenly during the testing department's process. As work in assembly is completed, each unit is immediately transferred to testing. As each unit is completed in testing, it is immediately transferred to Finished Goods.

Hoffman Company uses the weighted-average method of process costing. Data for the testing department for October 2017 are as follows:

	Physical Units (Car Seats)	Transferred-In Costs	Direct Materials	Conversion Costs
Work in process, October 1[a]	5,500	$2,931,000	$ 0	$ 499,790
Transferred in during October 2017	?			
Completed during October 2017	29,800			
Work in process, October 31[b]	1,700			
Total costs added during October 2017		$8,094,000	$10,877,000	$4,696,260

[a]Degree of completion: transferred-in costs,?%; direct materials,?%; conversion costs, 65%.
[b]Degree of completion: transferred-in costs,?%; direct materials,?%; conversion costs, 45%.

Required

1. What is the percentage of completion for (a) transferred-in costs and direct materials in beginning work-in-process inventory and (b) transferred-in costs and direct materials in ending work-in-process inventory?
2. For each cost category, compute equivalent units in the testing department. Show physical units in the first column of your schedule.
3. For each cost category, summarize total testing department costs for October 2017, calculate the cost per equivalent unit, and assign costs to units completed (and transferred out) and to units in ending work in process.
4. Prepare journal entries for October transfers from the assembly department to the testing department and from the testing department to Finished Goods.

🌐 **17-40 Transferred-in costs, FIFO method** (continuation of 17-39). Refer to the information in Problem 17-39. ◀ **LO 5**
Suppose that Hoffman Company uses the FIFO method instead of the weighted-average method in all of its departments. The only changes to Problem 17-39 under the FIFO method are that total transferred-in costs of beginning work in process on October 1 are $2,879,000 (instead of $2,931,000) and that total transferred-in costs added during October are $9,048,000 (instead of $8,094,000).

Required

Using the FIFO process-costing method, complete Problem 17-39.

LO 4 ▶ 🌐 **17-41 Weighted-average method.** Hoffman Company manufactures car seats in its Boise plant. Each car seat passes through the assembly department and the testing department. This problem focuses on the assembly department. The process-costing system at Hoffman Company has a single direct-cost category (direct materials) and a single indirect-cost category (conversion costs). Direct materials are added at the beginning of the process. Conversion costs are added evenly during the process. When the assembly department finishes work on each car seat, it is immediately transferred to testing.

Hoffman Company uses the weighted-average method of process costing. Data for the assembly department for October 2017 are as follows:

	Physical Units (Car Seats)	Direct Materials	Conversion Costs
Work in process, October 1[a]	4,000	$1,248,000	$ 241,650
Started during October 2017	22,500		
Completed during October 2017	26,000		
Work in process, October 31[b]	500		
Total costs added during October 2017		$4,635,000	$2,575,125

[a]Degree of completion: direct materials,?%; conversion costs, 45%.
[b]Degree of completion: direct materials,?%; conversion costs, 65%.

Required

1. For each cost category, compute equivalent units in the assembly department. Show physical units in the first column of your schedule.
2. What issues should the manager focus on when reviewing the equivalent-unit calculations?

LO 5 ▶ 🌐 **17-42 Journal entries** (continuation of 17-41).

Required

Prepare a set of summarized journal entries for all October 2017 transactions affecting Work in Process—Assembly. Set up a T-account for Work in Process—Assembly and post your entries to it.

LO 5 ▶ 🌐 **17-43 FIFO method** (continuation of 17-41).

Required

1. Do Problem 17-42 using the FIFO method of process costing. Explain any difference between the cost per equivalent unit in the assembly department under the weighted-average method and the FIFO method.
2. Should Hoffman's managers choose the weighted-average method or the FIFO method? Explain briefly.

Collaborative Learning Cases

LO 3 ▶ **17-44 Equivalent-unit computations, benchmarking, governance.** Margaret Major is the corporate controller of Leisure Suits. Leisure Suits has 20 plants worldwide that manufacture basic suits for retail stores. Each plant uses a process-costing system. At the end of each month, each plant manager submits a production report and a production cost report. The production report includes the plant manager's estimate of the percentage of completion of the ending work in process as to direct materials and conversion costs. Major uses these estimates to compute the equivalent units of work done in each plant and the cost per equivalent unit of work done for both direct materials and conversion costs in each month. Plants are ranked from 1 to 20 in terms of (a) cost per equivalent unit of direct materials and (b) cost per equivalent unit of conversion costs. Each month, Major uses a report that she calls "Benchmarking for Efficiency Gains at Leisure Suits." The three top-ranked plants on each category receive a bonus and are written up as the best in their class in the company newsletter.

Major has been pleased with the success of her benchmarking program. However, she has heard some disturbing news. She has received some unsigned letters stating that two plant managers have been manipulating their monthly estimates of percentage of completion in an attempt to obtain "best in class" status.

Required

1. How and why might plant managers "manipulate" their monthly estimates of percentage of completion?
2. Major's first instinct is to contact each plant controller and discuss the problem raised by the unsigned letters. Is that a good idea?
3. Assume that the plant controller's primary reporting responsibility is to the plant manager and that each plant controller receives the phone call from Major mentioned in requirement 2. What is the ethical responsibility of each plant controller (a) to Margaret Major and (b) to Leisure Suits in relation to the equivalent unit information each plant provides for the "Benchmarking for Efficiency" report?
4. How might Major gain some insight into whether the equivalent-unit figures provided by particular plants are being manipulated?

17-45 Operation costing. Farkas Shoes, a high-end shoe manufacturer, produces two lines of shoes for women. The shoes are identical in design, but differ in the materials used and the trim added to the shoes. The basic shoes are made from a synthetic leather, have a synthetic insole, and have plain buttons decorating the upper. The elaborate shoes are made from genuine leather, have a special insole, and have creative buttons applied to the upper. Each shoe is assumed to use an identical amount of conversion costs for a given operation. Work orders 10399 and 10400 are representative work orders for the two types of shoes.

◀ LO 5
1. Budgeted conversion cost per pair of shoes, operation 4, $2.10 per pair

Farkas Shoes
Selected Work Orders
for the Month Ended February 28, 2018

	Work Order 10399	Work Order 10400
Quantity (pairs of shoes)	1,000	150
Direct materials	Synthetic leather	Genuine leather
	Synthetic insole	FitDry insole
	Plain buttons	Creative buttons
Operations		
1. Cut leather	Use	Use
2. Shape leather	Use	Use
3. Treat leather	Do not use	Use
4. Sew shoes	Use	Use
5. Machine application of buttons	Use	Do not use
6. Hand application of buttons	Do not use	Use

Selected budget information for February follows:

	Basic	Elaborate	Total
Units	30,000	2,250	32,250
Direct material costs	$390,000	63,000	$453,000

Budgeted conversion costs for each operation for February follow:

Operation 1	$145,125	Operation 4	$67,725
Operation 2	58,050	Operation 5	13,500
Operation 3	4,275	Operation 6	2,025

Required

1. Using budgeted pairs of shoes as the denominator, calculate the budgeted conversion cost rates for each of the six operations.
2. Using the information in requirement 1, calculate the budgeted cost of goods manufactured for the two February work orders.
3. Based on the two representative work orders for February, calculate the budgeted cost of each pair of shoes.

TRY IT! ►

SOLUTIONS

Try It 17–1

(a) Equivalent units for direct materials = 475,000

Equivalent units for conversion costs = 425,000 completed + (50,000 × 50%) = 450,000

(b) Cost per equivalent unit:

Direct materials = $ 935,750/475000 = $ 1.97

Conversion costs = $4,554,000/450,000 = $10.12

Total cost = $12.09

Cost of completed units = 425,000 × $12.09 = $5,138,250

Cost of ending WIP:

Direct materials:	50,000 × $1.97 =	$ 98,500
Conversion costs:	25,000 × $10.12 =	$253,000
		$351,500

Try It 17–2

Note that units started during March = 30,000 + 2,000 – 3,000 = 29,000

Summarize the Flow of Physical Units and Compute Output in Equivalent Units;

		(Step 2)	
		Equivalent Units	
	(Step 1)		
	Physical	**Direct**	**Conversion**
Flow of Production	**Units**	**Materials**	**Costs**
Work in process beginning (given)	3,000		
Started during current period	29,000		
To account for	32,000		
Completed and transferred out during current period	30,000	30,000	30,000
Work in process, ending* (2,000 × 80%; 2,000 × 40%)	2,000	1,600	800
Accounted for	32,000		
Equivalent units of work done to date		31,600	30,800

Summarize the total costs to account for, compute the cost per equivalent unit, and assign costs to the units completed and units in ending work-in-process inventory.

		Total Production Costs	Direct Materials	Conversion Costs
(Step 3)	Work in process, beginning (given)	$ 16,155	$ 5,380	$ 10,775
	Costs added in current period (given)	488,945	176,320	312,625
	Total costs to account for	$505,100	$181,700	$323,400
(Step 4)	Costs incurred to date		$181,700	$323,400
	Divide by equivalent units of work done to date		÷ 31,600	÷ 30,800
	Cost per equivalent unit of work done to date		$ 5.75	$ 10.50
(Step 5)	Assignment of costs: Completed and transferred out (30,000 units)	$487,500	(30,000 × $5.75) +	(30,000 × $10.50)
	Work in process, ending (2,000 units)	17,600	(1,600 × $5.75) +	(800 × $10.50)
	Total costs accounted for	$505,100	$181,700 +	$323,400

Try It 17–3

Summarize the flow of physical units, and compute output in equivalent units.

	(Step 1) Physical Units	(Step 2) Equivalent Units	
Flow of Production		**Direct Materials**	**Conversion Costs**
Work in process, beginning (given)	3,000	(work done before current period)	
Started during current period (given)	29,000		
To account for	32,000		
Completed and transferred out during current period:			
From beginning work in process	3,000		
3,000 × (100% – 40%); 3,000 × (100% – 10%)		1,800	2,700
Started and completed	27,000		
27,000 × 100%, 27,000 × 100%		27,000	27,000
Work in process, ending* (given)	2,000		
2,000 × 80%; 2,000 × 40%		1,600	800
Accounted for	32,000		
Equivalent units of work done in current period		30,400	30,500

Summarize the total costs to account for, compute the cost per equivalent unit, and assign costs to the units completed and units in ending work-in-process inventory.

		Total Production Costs	Direct Materials	Conversion Costs
(Step 3)	Work in process, beginning (given)	$ 16,155	$ 5,380	$ 10,775
	Costs added in current period (given)	488,945	176,320	312,625
	Total costs to account for	$505,100	$181,700	$323,400
(Step 4)	Costs added in current period		$176,320	$312,625
	Divide by equivalent units of work done in current period		÷ 30,400	÷ 30,500
	Cost per equivalent unit of work done to date		$ 5.80	$ 10.25

		Total Production Costs	Direct Materials	Conversion Costs
(Step 5)	Assignment of costs:			
	Completed and transferred out (30,000 units):			
	Work in process, beginning (3,000 units)	$ 16,155	$5,380 + $10,775	
	Costs added to beginning work in process in current period	38,115	(1,800 × $5.80) + (2,700 × $10.25)	
	Total from beginning inventory	54,270		
	Started and completed (27,000 units)	433,350	(27,000 × $5.80) + (27,000 × $10.25)	
	Total cost of units completed and transferred out	487,620		
	Work in process, ending (2,000 units)	17,480	(1,600 × $5.80) + (800 × $10.25)	
	Total costs accounted for	$505,100	$181,700 + $323,400	

Spoilage, Rework, and Scrap

18

Sergio Azenha/Alamy Stock Photo

Airbag Rework Sinks Honda's Record Year

In 2015, Japanese automobile manufacturer Honda Motor Corp. set many company sales records. In the United States, Honda sold a record 1.6 million cars. In China, it sold 1 million cars in a year for the first time. Despite these record sales, Honda's profits were down sharply. Why? Huge rework costs associated with recalling millions of cars with defective airbags.

By the end of 2015, Honda was forced to recall more than 25 million of its vehicles worldwide. Each of the vehicles had potentially defective airbags supplied by Takata Corporation. Airbag inflators use an explosive propellant similar to gunpowder to deploy airbags in the event of a crash. Because of defects in the manufacturing process, the propellant in millions of Takata inflators can degrade over time and explode at random. When that happens, the airbag's metal housing can rupture, sending lethal shrapnel into the car. Ten deaths were linked to failed Takata airbags.

With so many vehicles requiring rework, Honda's recall costs soared. Honda spent $2.6 billion on recall-related expenses, including rework costs associated with replacing defective Takata airbags, compensation for Honda dealers, and legal expenses. Billions of dollars in future rework costs are anticipated, as well. As a result, Honda announced that it would no longer use Takata airbags for its new vehicles under development.

For Honda, Takata and other companies, the costs of producing defective output can be enormous. Accordingly, companies are increasingly focused on improving the quality of, and reducing defects in, their products, services, and activities. A rate of defects regarded

▶ Learning Objectives

1. Distinguish among spoilage, rework, and scrap, and apply the appropriate methods to account for normal and abnormal spoilage.

2. Apply process-costing methods to account for spoilage using weighted-average and first-in, first-out (FIFO) methods.

3. Apply the standard-costing method to account for spoilage.

4. Allocate costs of normal spoilage.

5. Apply job cost allocation procedures to account for spoilage in job costing.

6. Apply cost allocation procedures to account for reworked units and scrap.

▶ CPA Competencies

This chapter covers material outlined in **Section 3: Management Accounting** of the CPA Competency Map. The Learning Objectives in this chapter have been aligned with the CPA Competency Map to ensure the best coverage possible.

3.3.1 Evaluates cost classifications and costing methods for management of ongoing operations

3.3.2 Evaluates and applies cost management techniques appropriate for specific costing decisions

Sources: Y. Kubota. 2016. Honda Motor Profit Slides on Recall Costs, *The Wall Street Journal* (January 29); Y. Kubota. 2015. Honda Air-Bag Recall Costs Take a Toll, *The Wall Street Journal* (November 4); H. Tabuchi. 2016. Honda Expands Recall of Takata Airbags as Its Longtime Partner's Crisis Widens, *The New York Times* (February 3).

as normal in the past is no longer tolerable, and companies strive for ongoing improvements in quality. Firms in industries as varied as construction (Skanska), aeronautics (Lockheed Martin), product development software (Dassault Systemes), and specialty food (Tate & Lyle) have set zero-defects goals. Reducing defects, and the waste associated with them, is also a key element of the sustainability programs now in place at many enlightened organizations and government bodies.

In this chapter, we focus on three types of costs that arise as a result of defects—spoilage, rework, and scrap—and ways to account for them. We also describe how to determine (1) the cost of products, (2) cost of goods sold, and (3) inventory values when spoilage, rework, and scrap occur.

Defining and Accounting for Spoilage, Rework, and Scrap

▶ **LO 1**

Distinguish among spoilage, rework, and scrap, and apply the appropriate methods to account for normal and abnormal spoilage.

The terms *spoilage*, *rework*, and *scrap* are not interchangeable. For a financial accountant, the costs must be classified differently because under ASPE/IFRS different transactions give rise to each type of cost. Some amount of spoilage, rework, or scrap is an inherent part of many production processes. One example is semiconductor manufacturing, in which the products are so complex and delicate that some spoiled units are invariably produced and cannot be reworked.

Spoilage refers to output that fails to attain either a specified performance level or standard of composition. For example, in fermenting beer, hops are added to wort[1] for flavour. Hops also inhibit the growth of spoilage bacteria that would ruin the taste of the final product. Other examples are broken silicon wafers, T-shirts sold as "seconds" at outlet malls, and defective aluminum cans.

Rework is the conversion of production rejects into reusable products of the same or lower quality.[2] For example, cooked sausage ends can be reprocessed into pizza topping. Leftover ground raw poultry can be cooked and processed into chili. Damaged motherboards can also be reworked.

Scrap is a residual material that results from manufacturing a product. Scrap such as hard candy chips can be reheated and reused in new batches.[3] Scrap such as silicon templates that remain after parts are stamped can also be reused. Scrap has minimal total sales value compared with the total sales value of the product. In some situations the firm may have to pay to have the scrap removed. In this case, it is usually referred to as waste or refuse.

Exhibit 18-1 illustrates these differences graphically. Often these costs are locked in during the design of a product. Processes with a few simple steps are less prone to spoilage and defects than those with many complex steps. To minimize cost, managers want to determine the costs of spoilage and distinguish between the costs of normal and abnormal spoilage (illustrated under Spoilage in Exhibit 18-1). Eliminating the unrecoverable spoilage costs can result from improving the efficiency and effectiveness of production processes.

Normal spoilage arises under efficient operating conditions as a result of predictable rates of failure in a production process. Normal spoilage may be a locked-in cost, which managers accept when they invest in equipment with a specific failure rate. These costs are not considered controllable or avoidable. ASPE/IFRS permits the costs of normal spoilage to be included in the costs of goods manufactured (COGM). The cost is transferred to cost of goods sold when the good units are sold. The normal spoilage rate should be computed using the total good units completed as the base, not the total actual units

---

[1] *Wort* refers to the mixture of malt and other grains with water that is ready for fermentation (http://www.microbiologyproce-dure.com/industrial-microbiology/beer-manufacturing.htm).

[2] http://www.gov.mb.ca/agriculture/foodsafety/processor/cfs02s112.html; S.D.P. Flapper and R.H. Teunter, "Logistic planning of rework with deteriorating work-in-process," *International Journal of Production Economics*, 88.11 (2004): 51–19.

[3] http://www.allbusiness.com/wholesale-trade/merchant-wholesalers-nondurable/550143-1.html.

Exhibit 18-1 Classification of Spoilage, Rework, and Scrap

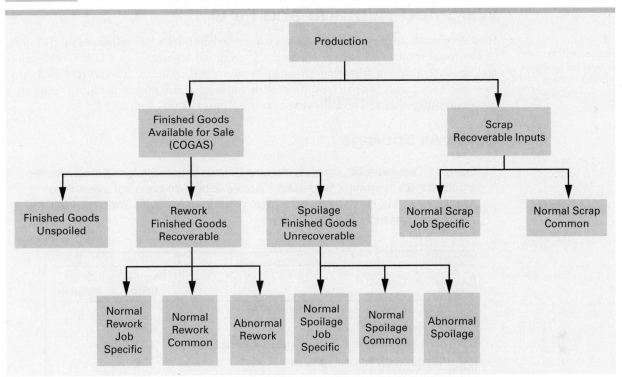

started (into production/process), because total units started also includes any *abnormal* spoilage in addition to normal spoilage.

Abnormal spoilage is spoilage that is unexpected under efficient operating conditions but is regarded as controllable and avoidable. Food contamination from salmonella, listeria, or *E. coli* bacteria are an example of abnormal spoilage. Automobile recalls are a second example. Diligent hygiene and machine maintenance can prevent unexpected outbreaks and breakdowns. The cost of abnormal spoilage can extend well beyond the immediate cost of the offending product. Take the case of Maple Leaf Foods, which in 2008 reported a one-time cost of $19 million for the retrieval and destruction of meat tainted with listeria *plus* an estimated $40 million–$50 million loss due to reduced sales, reduced margins, and increased costs,[4] or the more recent situation in 2013 when Costco had to recall ground beef sold at stores in Alberta, British Columbia, Manitoba, and Saskatchewan.[5] Abnormal spoilage costs are written off as losses of the accounting period in which detection of the spoiled units occurs. For the most informative internal feedback, the Loss from Abnormal Spoilage account should appear in a detailed statement of comprehensive income as a separate line item and not be buried as an indistinguishable part of the COGM.

Many companies, such as Toyota Motor Corporation, adhere to a perfection standard as a part of their emphasis on total quality control. Their ideal goal is zero defects. Hence, all spoilage would be treated as abnormal. Issues about accounting for spoilage arise in both process-costing and job-costing systems. We will first present the accounting for spoilage in process-costing systems because it is an extension of the discussion of process costing found in Chapter 17.

[4] K. Owram. 2009. Meat scandal fallout eases for Maple Leaf Foods, *Toronto Star*, (http://www.thestar.com/business/2009/02/24/meat_scandal_fallout_eases_for_maple_leaf_foods.html) February 24.

[5] J. Cotter. 2013. Canada's food safety watchdog orders fourth *E. coli* beef recall this month, Global News (http://globalnews.ca/news/909041/canadas-food-safety-watchdog-orders-fourth-e-coli-beef-recall) October 17.

Spoilage in Process Costing Using Weighted-Average and FIFO

► **LO 2**
Apply process-costing methods to account for spoilage using weighted-average and first-in, first-out (FIFO) methods.

How do process-costing systems account for spoiled units? We have already said that units of abnormal spoilage should be counted and recorded separately in a Loss from Abnormal Spoilage account. But what about units of normal spoilage? The correct method is to count these units when computing both physical and equivalent output units in a process-costing system. The following example illustrates this approach.

Count All Spoilage

Example 1: Chipmakers, Inc., manufactures computer chips for television sets. All direct materials are added at the beginning of the production process. To highlight issues that arise with normal spoilage, we assume there's no beginning inventory and focus only on the direct materials costs. The following data are for May 2017.

	A	B	C
1		**Physical Units**	**Direct Materials**
2	Work in process, beginning inventory (May 1)	0	
3	Started during May	10,000	
4	Good units completed and transferred out during May	5,000	
5	Units spoiled (all normal spoilage)	1,000	
6	Work in process, ending inventory (May 31)	4,000	
7	Direct materials costs added in May		$270,000

Spoilage is detected upon completion of the process and has zero net disposal value.

An **inspection point** is the stage of the production process at which products are examined to determine whether they are acceptable or unacceptable units. Spoilage is typically assumed to occur at the stage of completion where inspection takes place. As a result, the spoiled units in our example are assumed to be 100% complete for direct materials.

Exhibit 18-2 calculates and assigns the cost of the direct materials used to produce both good units and units of normal spoilage. Overall, Chipmakers generated 10,000 equivalent units of output: 5,000 equivalent units in good units completed (5,000 physical

Exhibit 18-2 Using Equivalent Units to Account for the Direct Materials Costs of Good and Spoiled Units for Chipmakers, Inc., for May 2017

	A	B
1		**Approach Counting Spoiled Units When Computing Output in Equivalent Units**
2	Costs to account for	$270,000
3	Divide by equivalent units of output	÷10,000
4	Cost per equivalent unit of output	$ 27
5	Assignment of costs:	
6	Good units completed (5,000 units × $27 per unit)	$135,000
7	Add normal spoilage (1,000 units × $27 per unit)	27,000
8	Total costs of good units completed and transferred out	162,000
9	Work-in-process, ending (4,000 units × $27 per unit)	108,000
10	Costs accounted for	$270,000

units $\times$ 100%), 4,000 units in ending work in process (4,000 physical units $\times$ 100%), and 1,000 equivalent units in normal spoilage (1,000 physical units $\times$ 100%). Given total direct material costs of $270,000 in May, this yields an equivalent-unit cost of $27. The total cost of good units completed and transferred out, which includes the cost of normal spoilage, is then $162,000 (6,000 equivalent units $\times$ $27). The ending work in process is assigned a cost of $108,000 (4,000 equivalent units $\times$ $27).

Notice that the 4,000 units in ending work in process are not assigned any of the costs of normal spoilage because they have not yet been inspected. Undoubtedly some of the units in ending work in process will be found to be spoiled after they are completed and inspected in the next accounting period. At that time, their costs will be assigned to the good units completed in that period. Notice too that Exhibit 18-2 delineates the cost of normal spoilage as $27,000. By highlighting the magnitude of this cost, the approach helps to focus management's attention on the potential economic benefits of reducing spoilage.

Five-Step Procedure for Process Costing with Spoilage

Example 2: Anzio Company manufactures a recycling container in its forming department. Direct materials are added at the beginning of the production process. Conversion costs are added evenly during the production process. Some units of this product are spoiled as a result of defects, which are detectable only upon inspection of finished units. Normally, spoiled units are 10% of the finished output of good units. That is, for every 10 good units produced, there is 1 unit of normal spoilage. Summary data for July 2017 are as follows:

	A	B	C	D	E
1		Physical Units (1)	Direct Materials (2)	Conversion Costs (3)	Total Costs (4) = (2) + (3)
2	Work in process, beginning inventory (July 1)	1,500	$12,000	$ 9,000	$ 21,000
3	Degree of completion of beginning work in process		100%	60%	
4	Started during July	8,500			
5	Good units completed and transferred out during July	7,000			
6	Work in process, ending inventory (July 31)	2,000			
7	Degree of completion of ending work in process		100%	50%	
8	Total costs added during July		$76,500	$89,100	$165,600
9	Normal spoilage as a percentage of good units	10%			
10	Degree of completion of normal spoilage		100%	100%	
11	Degree of completion of abnormal spoilage		100%	100%	

We can slightly modify the five-step procedure for process costing used in Chapter 17 to include the costs of Anzio Company's spoilage.

Step 1: Summarize the Flow of Physical Units of Output. Identify the number of units of both normal and abnormal spoilage.

$$\text{Total Spoilage} = \begin{pmatrix} \text{Units in beginning} \\ \text{work-in-process} + \text{Units started} \\ \text{inventory} \end{pmatrix} - \begin{pmatrix} \text{Good units} & \text{Units in ending} \\ \text{completed and} + \text{work-in-process} \\ \text{transferred out} & \text{inventory} \end{pmatrix}$$

$$= (1{,}500 + 8{,}500) - (7{,}000 + 2{,}000)$$

$$= 10{,}000 - 9{,}000$$

$$= 1{,}000 \text{ units}$$

Recall that Anzio Company's normal spoilage is 10% of good output. So, the number of units of normal spoilage equals 10% of the 7,000 units of *good* output, or 700 units. With this information, we can then calculate the number of units of abnormal spoilage:

$$\text{Abnormal spoilage} = \text{Total spoilage} - \text{Normal spoilage}$$
$$= 1{,}000 \text{ units} - 700 \text{ units}$$
$$= 300 \text{ units}$$

Step 2: Compute the Output in Terms of Equivalent Units. Managers compute the equivalent units for spoilage the same way they compute equivalent units for good units. All spoiled units are included in the computation of output units. Because Anzio's inspection point is at the completion of production, the same amount of work will have been done on each spoiled and each completed good unit.

Step 3: Summarize the Total Costs to Account For. The total costs to account for are all the costs debited to Work in Process. The details for this step are similar to Step 3 in Chapter 17.

Step 4: Compute the Cost per Equivalent Unit. This step is similar to Step 4 in Chapter 17.

Step 5: Assign Costs to the Units Completed, Spoiled Units, and Units in Ending Work-in-Process Inventory. This step now includes computing of the cost of spoiled units as well as the cost of good units.

Weighted-Average Method and Spoilage

Exhibit 18-3, Panel A, presents Steps 1 and 2 to calculate the equivalent units of work done to date and includes calculations of equivalent units of normal and abnormal spoilage. Exhibit 18-3, Panel B, presents Steps 3, 4, and 5 (together called the production-cost worksheet).

In Step 3, managers summarize the total costs to account for. In Step 4, they calculate the cost per equivalent unit using the weighted-average method. Note how, for each cost category, the costs of beginning work in process and the costs of work done in the current period are totaled and divided by equivalent units of all work done to date to calculate the weighted-average cost per equivalent unit. In the final step, managers assign the total costs to completed units, normal and abnormal spoiled units, and ending inventory by multiplying the equivalent units calculated in Step 2 by the cost per equivalent unit calculated in Step 4. Also note that the $13,825 costs of normal spoilage are added to the costs of the good units completed and transferred out.

$$\begin{array}{l}\text{Cost per good unit} \\ \text{completed and transferred} \\ \text{out of the process}\end{array} = \frac{\text{Total costs transferred out (including normal spoilage)}}{\text{Number of good units produced}}$$

$$= \$152{,}075 \div 7{,}000 \text{ good units} = \$21.725 \text{ per good unit}$$

This amount is not equal to $19.75 per good unit, the sum of the $8.85 cost per equivalent unit of direct materials plus the $10.90 cost per equivalent unit of conversion costs. That's because the cost per good unit equals the sum of the direct materials and conversion costs per equivalent unit, which is $19.75, plus a share of normal spoilage, $1.975 ($13,825 ÷ 7,000 good units), for a total of $21.725 per good unit. The $5,925 costs of abnormal spoilage are charged to the Loss from Abnormal Spoilage account and do not appear in the costs of good units.[6]

FIFO Method and Spoilage

Exhibit 18-4, Panel A, presents Steps 1 and 2 using the FIFO method, which focuses on equivalent units of work done in the current period. Exhibit 18-4, Panel B, presents Steps 3, 4, and 5. Note how when assigning costs, the FIFO method keeps the costs of the

---

[6] The actual costs of spoilage (and rework) are often greater than the costs recorded in the accounting system because the opportunity costs of disruption of the production line, storage, and lost contribution margins are not recorded in accounting systems. Chapter 19 discusses these opportunity costs from the perspective of cost management.

Exhibit 18-3 Weighted-Average Method of Process Costing with Spoilage for the Forming Department for July 2017

PANEL A: Summarize the Flow of Physical Units and Compute Output in Equivalent Units

	A	B	C	D
1		(Step 1)	(Step 2)	
2			Equivalent Units	
3	**Flow of Production**	**Physical Units**	**Direct Materials**	**Conversion Costs**
4	Work in process, beginning (given, p. 743)	1,500		
5	Started during current period (given, p. 743)	8,500		
6	To account for	10,000		
7	Good units completed and transferred out during the current period	7,000	7,000	7,000
8	Normal Spoilage[a]	700		
9	(700 × 100%; 700 × 100%)		700	700
10	Abnormal Spoilage[b]	300		
11	(300 × 100%; 300 × 100%)		300	300
12	Work in process, ending[c] (given, p. 743)	2,000		
13	(2,000 × 100%; 2,000 × 50%)		2,000	1,000
14	Accounted for	10,000		
15	Equivalent units of work done to date		10,000	9,000
16				
17	[a]Normal spoilage is 10% of good units transferred out: 10% × 7,000 = 700 units. Degree of completion of normal spoilage in this			
18	department: direct materials, 100%; conversion costs, 100%.			
19	[b]Abnormal spoilage = Total spoilage − Normal spoilage = 1,000 − 700 = 300 units. Degree of completion of abnormal			
20	spoilage in this department: direct materials, 100%; conversion costs, 100%.			
21	[c]Degree of completion in this department: direct materials, 100%; conversion costs, 50%.			

PANEL B: Summarize the Total Costs to Account For, Compute the Cost per Equivalent Unit, and Assign Costs to the Units Completed, Spoiled Units, and Units in Ending Work-in-Process Inventory

	A	B	C	D	E	F
1			**Total Production Costs**	**Direct Materials**		**Conversion Costs**
2	(Step 3)	Work in process, beginning (given, p. 743)	$ 21,000	$12,000	+	$ 9,000
3		Costs added in current period (given, p. 743)	165,600	76,500	+	89,100
4		Total costs to account for	$186,600	$88,500	+	$98,100
5						
6	(Step 4)	Costs incurred to date		$88,500		$98,100
7		Divide by equivalent units of work done to date (Panel A)		÷10,000		÷9,000
8		Cost per equivalent unit		$ 8.85		$ 10.90
9						
10	(Step 5)	Assignment of costs:				
11		Good units completed and transferred out (7,000 units)				
12		Costs before adding normal spoilage	$138,250	(7,000[d] × $8.85)	+	(7,000[d] × $10.90)
13		Normal spoilage (700 units)	13,825	(700[d] × $8.85)	+	(700[d] × $10.90)
14	(A)	Total costs of good units completed and transferred out	152,075			
15	(B)	Abnormal spoilage (300 units)	5,925	(300[d] × $8.85)	+	(300[d] × $10.90)
16	(C)	Work in process, ending (2,000 units)	28,600	(2,000[d] × $8.85)	+	(1,000[d] × $10.90)
17	(A) + (B) + (C)	Total costs accounted for	$186,600	$88,500	+	$98,100
18						
19	[d]Equivalent units of direct materials and conversion costs calculated in step 2 in Panel A.					

Exhibit 18-4 First-In, First-Out (FIFO) Method of Process Costing with Spoilage for the Forming Department for July 2017

PANEL A: Summarize the Flow of Physical Units and Compute Output in Equivalent Units

	A	B	C	D
1		(Step 1)	(Step 2)	
2			Equivalent Units	
3	Flow of Production	Physical Units	Direct Materials	Conversion Costs
4	Work in process, beginning (given, p. 743)	1,500		
5	Started during current period (given, p. 743)	8,500		
6	To account for	10,000		
7	Good units completed and transferred out during current period			
8	From beginning work in process[a]	1,500		
9	[1,500 × (100% − 100%); 1,500 × (100% − 60%)]		0	600
10	Started and completed	5,500[b]		
11	(5,500 × 100%; 5,500 × 100%)		5,500	5,500
12	Normal Spoilage[c]	700		
13	(700 × 100%; 700 × 100%)		700	700
14	Abnormal Spoilage[d]	300		
15	(300 × 100%; 300 × 100%)		300	300
16	Work in process, ending[e] (given, p. 743)	2,000		
17	(2,000 × 100%; 2,000 × 50%)		2,000	1,000
18	Accounted for	10,000		
19	Equivalent units of work in current period		8,500	8,100
20				
21	[a]Degree of completion in this department: direct materials, 100%; conversion costs, 60%.			
22	[b]7,000 physical units completed and transferred out minus 1,500 physical units completed and transferred out from beginning			
23	work-in-process inventory.			
24	[c]Normal spoilage is 10% of good units transferred out; 10% × 7,000 = 700 units. Degree of completion of normal spoilage in this			
25	department: direct materials, 100%; conversion costs, 100%.			
26	[d]Abnormal spoilage = Total spoilage − Normal spoilage = 1,000 − 700 = 300 units. Degree of completion of abnormal spoilage			
27	in this department: direct materials, 100%; conversion costs, 100%.			
28	[e]Degree of completion in this department: direct materials, 100%; conversion costs, 50%.			

PANEL B: Summarize the Total Costs to Account For, Compute the Cost per Equivalent Unit, and Assign Costs to the Units Completed, Spoiled Units, and Units in Ending Work-in-Process Inventory

	A	B	C	D	E	F
1			Total Production Costs	Direct Materials		Conversion Costs
2	(Step 3)	Work in process, beginning (given, p. 743)	$ 21,000	$12,000		$ 9,000
3		Costs added in current period (given, p. 743)	165,600	76,500		89,100
4		Total costs to account for	$186,600	$88,500		$98,100
5	(Step 4)	Costs added in current period		$76,500		$89,100
6		Divide by equivalent units of work done in current period (Panel A)		÷8,500		÷8,100
7		Cost per equivalent unit		$ 9		$ 11
8	(Step 5)	Assignment of costs:				
9		Good units completed and transferred out (7,000 units)				
10		Work in process, beginning (1,500 units)	$ 21,000	$12,000	+	$ 9,000
11		Costs before adding normal spoilage	6,600	(0[f] × $9)	+	(600[f] × $11)
12		Total from beginning inventory before normal spoilage	27,600			
13		Started and completed before normal spoilage (5,500 units)	110,000	(5,500[f] × $9)	+	(5,500[f] × $11)
14		Normal spoilage (700 units)	14,000	(700[f] × $9)	+	(700[f] × $11)
15	(A)	Total costs of good units completed and transferred out	151,600			
16	(B)	Abnormal spoilage (300 units)	6,000	(300[f] × $9)	+	(300[f] × $11)
17	(C)	Work in process, ending (2,000 units)	29,000	(2,000[f] × $9)	+	(1,000[f] × $11)
18	(A) + (B) + (C)	Total costs accounted for	$186,600	$88,500	+	$98,100
19						
20	[f]Equivalent units of direct materials and conversion costs calculated in step 2 in Panel A.					

beginning work in process separate and distinct from the costs of the work done in the current period. All spoilage costs are assumed to be related to units completed during the period, using the unit costs of the current period.[7]

Note *The standard-costing method is illustrated in the Appendix to this chapter.*

Regardless of the method managers choose to assign conversion costs, the COGM, COGAS, and COGS must conform to ASPE/IFRS for valuation of inventory. The three methods presented are in conformance, and all three methods arrive at the identical total actual costs added during the month of July.

18.1 TRY IT! ⊕

Azure Textiles Company makes silk banners and uses the weighted-average method of process costing. Direct materials are added at the beginning of the process, and conversion costs are added evenly during the process. Spoilage is detected upon inspection at the completion of the process. Spoiled units are disposed of at zero net disposal value.

	Physical Units (Banners)	Direct Materials	Conversion Costs
Work in process, July 1[a]	1,000	$ 1,423	$ 1,110
Started in July 2017	?		
Good units completed and transferred out in July	9,000		
Normal spoilage	100		
Abnormal spoilage	50		
Work in process, July 31[b]	2,000		
Total costs added during July 2017		$12,180	$27,750

[a] Degree of completion: direct materials, 100%; conversion costs, 50%.
[b] Degree of completion: direct materials, 100%; conversion costs, 30%.

Determine the equivalent units of work done in July, and calculate the cost of units completed and transferred out (including normal spoilage), the cost of abnormal spoilage, and the cost of units in ending inventory.

Sustainability in Action | Managing Waste and Environmental Costs at Toyota

In its 2013 North America Environmental Report, Toyota stated that its

> values are outlined in the Guiding Principles and Earth Charter. The Guiding Principles challenge the company to "be a good corporate citizen," "dedicate ourselves to providing clean and safe products," and "pursue growth in harmony with the global community." Environmental responsibility is key to each of these.[8]
>
> Later in the report, Toyota specifically identifies *rework and scrap* as one of the seven sources of waste.

As a result of Toyota's ongoing and strategic approach to scrap and waste reduction

- Toyota is saving 319,000 pounds of paper, through paperless offices and transactions.
- Ten of Toyota's North American plants have achieved "zero waste to landfill" status, and recycle 95% of non-salable waste.
- Toyota relies heavy on copper in its automobiles, and has established facilities to recycle enough copper to be used in 1.2 million cars.

---

[7] To simplify calculations under FIFO, spoiled units are accounted for as if they were started in the current period. Although some of the beginning work in process probably did spoil, all spoilage is treated as if it came from current production.

[8] Excerpt from 2013 Environmental Report, Toyota North America. Copyright © 2013 by Toyota Motor. Used by permission of Toyota Motor.

⊕ **TRY IT!** ▶ **18.2** Consider Azure Textiles Company. With the same information for July 2017 as provided in Try It 18-1, redo the problem assuming Azure uses FIFO costing instead.

Journal Entries

The information from the exhibits above supports the following journal entries to transfer good units completed to finished goods and to recognize the loss from abnormal spoilage.

	Weighted Average		FIFO		Standard	
1. Finished Goods	152,075		151,600		146,300	
Work-in-Process—Forming		152,075		151,600		146,300
To transfer good units completed in July.						
2. Loss from Abnormal Spoilage	5,925		6,000		5,700	
Work-in-Process—Forming		5,925		6,000		5,700
To recognize abnormal spoilage detected in July.						
3. Work-in-Process—Forming (at standard costs)					72,250	
Direct Materials Variances					4,250	
Forming Department Direct Materials Control						76,500
To record actual direct materials used and total direct materials variances.						
4. Work-in-Process—Forming (at standard costs)					85,050	
Conversion Costs Variance					4,050	
Forming Department Conversion Costs Control						89,100
To record actual conversion costs and total conversion cost variances.						

Inspection Points and Allocating Costs of Normal Spoilage

▶ **LO 4**

Allocate costs of normal spoilage.

Spoilage might occur at various stages of a production process, but it is typically detected only at one or more inspection points. The cost of spoiled units equals all costs incurred in producing them up to the point of inspection. When spoiled goods have a disposal value (for example, carpeting sold as "seconds"), we compute a net cost of the spoilage by deducting the disposal value from the costs of the spoiled goods.

The unit costs of normal and abnormal spoilage are the same when the two are detected at the same inspection point. This is the case in our Anzio Company example, where inspection occurs only upon completion of the units. However, situations may arise when abnormal spoilage is detected at a different point than normal spoilage. Consider shirt manufacturing. Normal spoilage in the form of defective shirts is identified upon inspection at the end of the production process. Now suppose a faulty machine causes many defective shirts to be produced at the halfway point of the production process. These defective shirts are abnormal spoilage and occur at a different point in the production process than normal spoilage. Then the per-unit cost of the abnormal spoilage, which is based on costs incurred up to the halfway point of the production process, differs from the per-unit cost of normal spoilage, which is based on costs incurred through the end of the production process.

The costs of abnormal spoilage are separately accounted for as losses of the accounting period in which they are detected. However, recall that normal spoilage costs are added to the costs of good units, which raises an additional issue: Should normal spoilage costs be allocated between completed units and ending work-in-process inventory? *The common approach is to presume that normal spoilage occurs at the inspection point in the production cycle and to allocate its cost over all units that have passed that point during the accounting period.*

Anzio Company inspects units only at the end of the production process. So, the units in ending work-in-process inventory are not assigned any costs of normal spoilage. Suppose Anzio were to inspect units at an earlier stage. Then, if the units in ending work in process have passed the inspection point, the costs of normal spoilage would be allocated to units in ending work in process as well as to completed units. For example, if the inspection point is at the halfway point of production, then any ending work in process that is at least 50% complete would be allocated a full measure of the normal spoilage costs, and those spoilage costs would be calculated on the basis of all costs incurred up to the inspection point. However, if the ending work-in-process inventory is less than 50% complete, no normal spoilage costs would be allocated to it.

To better understand these issues, assume Anzio Company inspects units at various stages in the production process. How does this affect the amount of normal and abnormal spoilage? As before, consider the forming department, and recall that direct materials are added at the start of production, whereas conversion costs are added evenly during the process.

Consider three different cases: Inspection occurs at (1) the 20%, (2) the 55%, or (3) the 100% completion stage. The last option is the one we have analyzed so far (see Exhibit 18-3). Assume that normal spoilage is 10% of the good units passing inspection. A total of 1,000 units are spoiled in all three cases. Normal spoilage is computed on the basis of the number of *good units* that pass the inspection point *during the current period*. The following data are for July 2017. Note how the number of units of normal and abnormal spoilage changes depending on when inspection occurs.

A	B	C	D
	Physical Units: Stage of Completion at Which Inspection Occurs		
Flow of Production	**20%**	**55%**	**100%**
Work in process, beginning[a]	1,500	1,500	1,500
Started during July	8,500	8,500	8,500
To account for	10,000	10,000	10,000
Good units completed and transferred out			
(10,000 – 1,000 spoiled – 2,000 ending)	7,000	7,000	7,000
Normal spoilage	750[c]	550[d]	700[e]
Abnormal spoilage (1,000 – normal spoilage)	250	450	300
Work in process, ending[b]	2,000	2,000	2,000
Accounted for	10,000	10,000	10,000
[a]Degree of completion in this department: direct materials, 100%; conversion costs, 60%.			
[b]Degree of completion in this department: direct materials, 100%; conversion costs, 50%.			
[c]10% × (8,500 units started – 1,000 units spoiled), because only the units started passed the 20% completion inspection point in the current period. Beginning work in process is excluded from this calculation because, being 60% complete at the start of the period, it passed the inspection point in the previous period.			
[d]10% × (8,500 units started – 1,000 units spoiled – 2,000 units in ending work in process). Both beginning and ending work in process are excluded since neither was inspected this period.			
[e]10% × 7,000, because 7,000 units are fully completed and inspected in the current period.			

The following diagram shows the flow of physical units for July and illustrates the normal spoilage numbers in the table. Note that 7,000 good units are completed and transferred out—1,500 from beginning work in process and 5,500 started and completed during the period—while 2,000 units are in ending work in process.

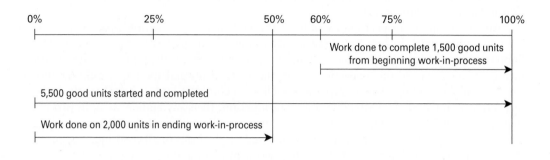

To see the number of units passing each inspection point, consider in the diagram the vertical lines at the 20%, 55%, and 100% inspection points. Note that the vertical line at 20% crosses two horizontal lines—5,500 good units started and completed and 2,000 units in ending work in process—for a total of 7,500 good units. (The 20% vertical line does not cross the line representing work done on the 1,500 good units completed from beginning work in process because these units are already 60% complete at the start of the period and, hence, are not inspected this period.) Normal spoilage equals 10% of 7,500 = 750 units. On the other hand, the vertical line at the 55% point crosses just the second horizontal line, indicating that only 5,500 good units pass this point. Normal spoilage in this case is 10% of 5,500 = 550 units. At the 100% point, the normal spoilage is 10% of 7,000 (1,500 + 5,500) good units = 700 units.

Exhibit 18-5 shows how equivalent units are computed under the weighted-average method if units are inspected at the 20% completion stage. The calculations depend on the direct materials and conversion costs incurred to get the units to this inspection point. The spoiled units have 100% of their direct materials costs and 20% of their conversion costs. Because the ending work-in-process inventory has passed the inspection point, these units are assigned the normal spoilage costs, just like the units that have been completed and transferred out. For example, the conversion costs of units completed and transferred out include the conversion costs for 7,000 good units produced plus 20% × (10% × 5,500) = 110 equivalent units of normal spoilage. *We multiply by 20% to obtain the equivalent units of normal spoilage because the conversion costs are only 20% complete at the inspection point.* The conversion costs of the ending work-in-process inventory include the conversion costs of 50% of 2,000 = 1,000 equivalent good units plus 20% × (10% × 2,000) = 40 equivalent units of normal spoilage. Thus, the equivalent units of normal spoilage accounted for are 110 equivalent units related to the units completed and transferred out plus 40 equivalent units related to the units in ending work in process, for a total of 150 equivalent units, as Exhibit 18-5 shows.

Early inspections can help prevent any further costs being wasted on units that are already spoiled. For example, suppose the units can be inspected when they are 70% complete rather than 100% complete. If the spoilage occurs prior to the 70% point, a company can avoid incurring the final 30% of conversion costs on the spoiled units. While not applicable in the Anzio example, more generally a company can also save on the packaging or other direct materials that are added after the 70% stage. The downside to conducting inspections at too early a stage is that units spoiled at later stages of the process may go undetected. It is for these reasons that firms often conduct multiple inspections and also empower workers to identify and resolve defects on a timely basis.

Exhibit 18-5 Computing Equivalent Units with Spoilage Using the Weighted-Average Method of Process Costing with Inspection at 20% of Completion for the Forming Department for July 2017

	A	B	C	D
1		(Step 1)	(Step 2)	
2			Equivalent Units	
3	**Flow of Production**	**Physical Units**	**Direct Materials**	**Conversion Costs**
4	Work in process, beginning[a]	1,500		
5	Started during current period	8,500		
6	To account for	10,000		
7	Good units completed and transferred out:	7,000	7,000	7,000
8	Normal Spoilage	750		
9	(750 × 100%; 750 × 20%)		750	150
10	Abnormal Spoilage	250		
11	(250 × 100%; 250 × 20%)		250	50
12	Work in process, ending[b]	2,000		
13	(2,000 × 100%; 2,000 × 50%)		2,000	1,000
14	Accounted for	10,000		
15	Equivalent units of work done to date		10,000	8,200
16				
17	[a]Degree of completion: direct materials, 100%; conversion costs, 60%.			
18	[b]Degree of completion: direct materials, 100%; conversion costs, 50%.			

18.3 TRY IT! ⊕

Normal spoilage is 6% of the good units passing inspection in a forging process. In March, a total of 10,000 units were spoiled. Other data include units started during March, 120,000; work in process, beginning, 14,000 units (20% completed for conversion costs); and work in process, ending, 11,000 units (70% completed for conversion costs).

Compute the normal and abnormal spoilage in units, assuming the inspection point is at (a) the 15% stage of completion, (b) the 40% stage of completion, and (c) the 100% stage of completion.

Job Costing and Spoilage

The concepts of normal and abnormal spoilage also apply to job-costing systems. Abnormal spoilage is usually regarded as controllable by the manager. It is separately identified with the goal of eliminating it altogether. Costs of abnormal spoilage are not considered to be product manufacturing costs and are written off as costs of the period in which detection occurs. Normal or expected spoilage in job-costing systems, however, is considered part of normal manufacturing costs, although increasingly managers are tolerating only small amounts of spoilage as normal. When assigning costs, job-costing systems generally distinguish normal spoilage *attributable to a specific job* from normal spoilage *common to all jobs*.

We illustrate the accounting for spoilage in job costing using the following example:

▶ **LO 5**

Apply job cost allocation procedures to account for spoilage in job costing.

Example 3: In Hull Machine Shop, five aircraft parts out of a job lot of 50 aircraft parts are spoiled. Costs assigned up to the point of inspection are $100 per unit. Hull calculates these costs on the basis of its inventory costing assumptions—weighted-average, FIFO, or standard costs. We do not, however, emphasize cost-flow assumptions in our presentation here or in subsequent sections. The current disposal price of the spoiled parts is estimated to be $30 per part. When the spoilage is detected, the spoiled goods are inventoried at $30 per unit.

Normal Spoilage Common to All Jobs

In some cases, spoilage may be considered a normal characteristic of a given production cycle. The spoilage inherent in the process only coincidentally occurs when a specific job is being worked on. The spoilage then is not attributable, and hence is not charged, to the specific job. Instead, it is costed as manufacturing overhead. The budgeted manufacturing overhead allocation rate includes a provision for normal spoilage cost. Therefore, normal spoilage cost is spread, through overhead allocation, over all jobs rather than loaded on specific jobs only.[9]

Materials Control (spoiled goods at current disposal value): 5 × $30	150	
Manufacturing Department Overhead Control (normal spoilage): 5 × $70	350	
Work-in-Process Control (specific job): 5 × $100		500

Normal Spoilage Attributable to a Specific Job

When normal spoilage occurs because of the specifications of a specific job, that job bears the cost of the spoilage reduced by the current disposal value of that spoilage. The journal entry to recognize the disposal value of the salvage (items in parentheses indicate subsidiary postings) is as follows:

Materials Control (spoiled goods at current disposal value): 5 × $30	150	
Work-in-Process Control (specific job): 5 × $30		150

The effect of this accounting is that the net cost of the normal spoilage, $350 (= $500 − $150), becomes a direct cost of the 45 (= 50 − 5) good units produced. This is because the net costs of the spoiled units ($350) still remains as part of the WIP cost of the 45 good units.

Abnormal Spoilage

If the spoilage is abnormal, the net loss is highlighted to management by charging the loss to an abnormal loss account:

Materials Control (spoiled goods at current disposal value): 5 × $30	150	
Loss from Abnormal Spoilage: 5 × $70	350	
Work-in-Process Control (specific job): 5 × $100		500

The different approaches to spoilage in a job-costing system can be summarized in the following table:

	Normal or Abnormal?	
Specific or Common?	**Normal spoilage**	**Abnormal spoilage**
Specific to a particular job	Cost *remains* in the specific job (value of any current disposal is removed from account and debited to *Materials Control*)	Cost is *removed* from the specific job and charged to an *Abnormal Loss* account and reported as a period cost
Common to all jobs	Cost is *removed* from the specific job and charged to *MOH Control* (actual OH incurred account)	Cost is *removed* from the specific job and charged to an *Abnormal Loss* account and reported as a period cost

---

[9] Note that costs *already assigned to products* are being charged back to Manufacturing Overhead Control, which generally accumulates only costs incurred, not both costs incurred and costs already assigned.

Reworked Units and Scrap

Reworked units are unacceptable units of production that are subsequently reworked into good units and sold. The cost of rework is frequently material and therefore included in COGM.

▶ **LO 6**

Apply cost allocation procedures to account for reworked units and scrap.

Consider the Hull Machine Shop data (Example 3). Assume that the five spoiled parts used in our Hull Machine Shop illustration are reworked. The journal entry for the $500 of total costs (details of costs assumed) assigned to the five spoiled units *before* considering rework costs is as follows:

Work-in-Process Control	500	
Materials Control		200
Wages Payable		200
Manufacturing Overhead Allocated		100

Assume that rework costs equal $190 (DM, $40; direct labour, $100; manufacturing overhead, $50).

Normal Rework Common to All Jobs

When rework is normal and not attributable to any specific job, the costs of rework are charged to manufacturing overhead and spread, through overhead allocation, over all jobs.

Manufacturing Department Overhead Control (rework)	190	
Materials Control		40
Wages Payable		100
Manufacturing Overhead Allocated		50

Notice that the Manufacturing Overhead Control (MOH Control) and Manufacturing Overhead Allocated (MOH Allocated) are in the same journal entry. MOH Control is debited because the normal rework is common to all jobs and is not attributable to a specific job. In this case, the additional MOH costs incurred to rework the units (for example, utilities, materials handling, inspection) are spread over all jobs by including an allowance for estimated rework when the MOH allocation rate was estimated. This allowance is credited to MOH Allocated.

Normal Rework Attributable to a Specific Job

If the rework is normal but occurs because of the requirements of a specific job, the rework costs are charged to that job. The journal entry is as follows:

Work-in-Process Control (specific job)	190	
Materials Control		40
Wages Payable		100
Manufacturing Overhead Allocated		50

Abnormal Rework

If the rework is abnormal, it is highlighted to management by charging abnormal rework to a separate loss account.

Loss from Abnormal Rework	190	
Materials Control		40
Wages Payable		100
Manufacturing Overhead Allocated		50

Accounting for rework in process costing only requires abnormal rework to be distinguished from normal rework. Abnormal rework is accounted for as in job costing. Since masses of similar units are manufactured, accounting for normal rework follows the accounting described for normal rework common to all jobs.

Costing rework highlights the resources wasted on activities that would not have to be undertaken if the product were made correctly. It prompts management to seek ways to reduce rework—for example, by designing new products or processes, training workers, or investing in new machines. Calculating rework costs helps management perform cost–benefit analyses for various alternatives. To emphasize the importance of eliminating rework and to simplify the accounting, some companies expense all rework, including the costs of normal rework, as an expense of the current period.

Accounting for Scrap

Scrap is a product that has minimal (frequently zero) sales value compared with the sales value of the main or joint product(s). It is possible for scrap to have a detrimental impact, or have negative value, for instance in the case of toxic waste. Please see Chapter 15 for a discussion of this aspect of accounting for scrap.

There are two major aspects of accounting for scrap:

■ Planning and control, including physical tracking.

■ Inventory costing, including when and how to affect operating income.

Initial entries to scrap records are most often in physical or nonfinancial terms such as in kilograms or units. In various industries, items such as stamped-out metal sheets are quantified by weighing, counting, or some other expedient means. Scrap records not only help measure efficiency, but also often focus on a tempting source for theft. Scrap reports are prepared as source documents for periodic summaries of the amount of actual scrap compared with budgeted norms or standards. Scrap is either sold or disposed of quickly, or stored in some routine way for later sale, disposal, or reuse.

The tracking of scrap often extends into the financial records. Most companies maintain a distinct cost for scrap somewhere in their cost accounting system. The issues here regarding the accounting for byproducts are

■ When should any value of scrap be recognized in the accounting records: at the time of production of scrap or at the time of sale of scrap?

■ How should revenue from scrap be accounted for?

To illustrate, we extend our Hull Machine Shop example by assuming that the manufacture of aircraft parts generates scrap. We further assume that the normal scrap from a job lot has a total sales value of $45.

Recognizing Scrap at the Time of Sale

When scrap is sold, the simplest accounting is to regard scrap sales as a separate line item of Other Revenues. This approach would be appropriate if the amount *was not material* and if the scrap was sold soon after it was produced. The journal entry is

Sale of scrap:	Cash or Accounts Receivable	45	
	Sales of Scrap		45

When the dollar amount of scrap *is material* and the scrap is sold quickly after its production, the accounting depends on whether the scrap is attributable to a specific job or common to all jobs.

Scrap Attributable to a Specific Job

Job-costing systems sometimes trace the sales of scrap to the jobs that yielded the scrap. This method is used only when the tracing can be done in an economically feasible way.

For example, Hull Machine Shop and particular customers may reach an agreement that provides for charging specific jobs with all rework or spoilage costs, and for crediting these jobs with all scrap sales that arise from them. The journal entry is

Scrap returned to storeroom:	[No journal entry. Memo of quantity received and related job is entered in the inventory record.]		
Sale of scrap:	Cash or Accounts Receivable	45	
	Work-in-Process Control (specific job)		45

Unlike spoilage and rework, there is no cost attached to the scrap, and hence no normal or abnormal scrap. All scrap sales, whatever the amount, are credited to the specific job. Scrap sales reduce the costs of the job. In job costing, the cost of scrap is already in the WIP account for each job generating the scrap. These costs are already accounted for, and therefore no journal entry is necessary to explicitly record the cost of scrap. When the scrap is sold, however, the WIP account must be decreased (credited) to reduce the cost of the job by the amount of the scrap's disposal value.

Scrap Common to All Jobs

In this case, scrap is not linked with any particular job or product. Instead, all products bear production costs without any credit for scrap revenues except in an indirect manner: Expected scrap revenues are considered when setting the budgeted manufacturing overhead rate. Thus the budgeted manufacturing overhead rate is lower than it would be if the overhead budget had not been reduced by the expected scrap revenues. The journal entry is

Scrap returned to storeroom:	No journal entry		
	Notation of quantity received and related job entered in the inventory record		
Sale of scrap:	Cash or Accounts Receivable	45	
	Manufacturing Overhead Control		45
	Posting made to subsidiary ledger—"Sales of Scrap" column on department cost record		

This method of accounting for scrap is also used in process accounting when the dollar amount of scrap is immaterial, because the scrap in process accounting is common to the manufacture of all the identical or similar units produced (and cannot be identified with specific units).

Recognizing Scrap at the Time of Production

Our preceding illustrations assume that scrap returned to the storeroom is sold or disposed of quickly and hence not assigned an inventory cost figure. Scrap, however, sometimes has a significant market value, and the time between storing it and selling or reusing it can be quite long. Under these conditions, the company is justified in inventorying scrap at a conservative estimate of net realizable value so that production costs and related scrap recovery may be recognized in the same accounting period. Some companies tend to delay sales of scrap until the market price is most attractive. Volatile price fluctuations are typical for scrap metal. If scrap inventory becomes significant, it should be inventoried at some "reasonable value"—a difficult task in the face of volatile market prices.

Scrap Attributable to a Specific Job

The journal entry in the Hull Machine Shop example is

Scrap returned to storeroom:	Materials Control	45	
	Work-in-Process Control (specific job)		45

Scrap Common to All Jobs

The journal entry in this case is

Scrap returned to storeroom:	Materials Control	45	
	Manufacturing Department Overhead Control		45

Observe that the Materials Control account is debited in place of Cash or Accounts Receivable.

When this scrap is sold, the journal entry is

Sale of scrap:	Cash or Accounts Receivable	45	
	Materials Control		45

Scrap is sometimes reused as DM rather than sold as scrap. Then it should be debited to Materials Control as a class of DM and carried at its estimated net realizable value. For example, the entries when the scrap generated is common to all jobs are

Scrap returned to storeroom:	Materials Control	45	
	Manufacturing Department Overhead Control		45
Reuse of scrap:	Work-in-Process Control (specific job)	45	
	Materials Control		45

The accounting for scrap under process costing follows the accounting for jobs when scrap is common to all jobs since process costing is used to cost the mass manufacture of similar units. The high cost of scrap focuses management's attention on ways to reduce scrap and to use it more profitably. For example, General Motors has redesigned its plastic injection moulding processes to reduce the scrap plastic that must be broken away from its moulded parts. General Motors also regrinds and reuses the plastic scrap as DM, saving substantial input costs.

Pulling it all Together—Problem for Self-Study

(Try to solve this problem before examining the solution that follows.)

Problem

Burlington Textiles has some spoiled goods that had an assigned cost of $40,000 and zero net disposal value.

Required ▶ Prepare a journal entry for each of the following conditions under (a) process costing (Department A) and (b) job costing:

❷ ❺ 1. Abnormal spoilage of $40,000

❷ ❺ 2. Normal spoilage of $40,000 regarded as common to all operations

❷ ❻ 3. Normal spoilage of $40,000 regarded as attributable to specifications of a particular job

Solution

(a) Process Costing			(b) Job Costing		
1. Loss from Abnormal Spoilage	40,000		Loss from Abnormal Spoilage	40,000	
Work-in-Process—Dept. A		40,000	Work-in-Process Control (specific job)		40,000
2. No entry until units are complete and transferred out; then the normal spoilage costs are transferred as part of the cost of good units.			Manufacturing Overhead Control	40,000	
			Work-in-Process Control (specific job)		40,000
Work-in-Process—Dept. A	40,000				
Work-in-Process—Dept. A		40,000			
3. Not applicable			No entry. Normal spoilage cost remains in Work-in-Process Control (specific job)		

Decision Points

The following question-and-answer format summarizes the chapter's learning objectives. Each point presents a key question, and the guidelines are the answer to that question.

Learning Objectives

Guidelines

1. What are spoilage, rework, and scrap?

Spoilage refers to units of production that do not meet the standards required by customers for good units and that are discarded or sold for reduced prices. Rework is unacceptable units that are subsequently repaired and sold as acceptable finished goods. Scrap is material left over when making a product; it has low sales value compared with the sales value of the main product. Normal spoilage is uncontrollable and unavoidable. Abnormal spoilage is both controllable and avoidable. IFRS/ASPE permits costs of normal spoilage in the cost of goods manufactured but abnormal spoilage must be recorded as a loss for the accounting period in which it is detected.

2. How do the weighted-average method and FIFO method of process costing differ in calculating the costs of good units and spoilage?

The weighted-average method combines costs in beginning inventory with costs of the current period when determining the costs of good units (which include a normal spoilage amount) and the costs of abnormal spoilage. The FIFO method keeps separate the costs in beginning inventory from the costs of the current period when determining the costs of good units (which include a normal spoilage amount) and the costs of abnormal spoilage.

3. How does the standard-costing method of process costing calculate the costs of good units and spoilage?

The standard-costing method uses standard costs to determine the costs of good units (which include a normal spoilage amount) and the costs of abnormal spoilage.

4. How are costs of normal spoilage allocated?

Normal spoilage is inherent in a given production process. Normal spoilage specific to a job should be assigned to that job. When common to all jobs, spoilage should be allocated as part of manufacturing overhead.

5. How do job-costing systems account for spoilage and rework?

Normal spoilage specific to a job is assigned to that job or, if common to all jobs, it is allocated as part of manufacturing overhead. Loss from abnormal spoilage is recorded as a cost of the accounting period in which it is detected. Completed reworked units should be indistinguishable from non-reworked good units. Normal rework can be assigned to a specific job, or, if common to all jobs, as part of manufacturing overhead. Abnormal rework is written off as a cost of the accounting period in which it is detected.

Learning Objectives	Guidelines
6. How is scrap accounted for?	Scrap is recognized in the accounting records either at the time of its sale or at the time of its production. Sale of scrap, if immaterial, is often recognized as other revenue. If material, the sale of scrap or its net realizable value reduces the cost of a specific job, or, if common to all jobs, reduces manufacturing overhead.

Appendix 18A

Standard-Costing Method and Spoilage

▶ **LO 3**
Apply the standard-costing method to account for spoilage.

The standard-costing method (see Exhibit 18A-1) simplifies the computations for normal and abnormal spoilage. To illustrate, we return to the Anzio Company example in the chapter. Suppose Anzio develops the following standard costs per unit for work done in the forming department in July 2017:

Direct materials	$ 8.50
Conversion costs	10.50
Total manufacturing cost	$19.00

Assume the same standard costs per unit also apply to the beginning inventory: 1,500 $(1,500 \times 100\%)$ equivalent units of direct materials and 900 $(1,500 \times 60\%)$ equivalent units of conversion costs. Hence, the beginning inventory at standard costs is as follows:

Direct materials, 1,500 units $\times$ $8.50 per unit	$12,750
Conversion costs, 900 units $\times$ $10.50 per unit	9,450
Total manufacturing costs	$22,200

Exhibit 18A-1, Panel A, presents Steps 1 and 2 for calculating physical and equivalent units. These steps are the same as for the FIFO method described in Exhibit 18-4. Exhibit 18A-1, Panel B, presents Steps 3, 4, and 5.

The costs to account for in Step 3 are at standard costs and, hence, they differ from the costs to account for under the weighted-average and FIFO methods, which are at actual costs. In Step 4, cost per equivalent unit is simply the standard cost: $8.50 per unit for direct materials and $10.50 per unit for conversion costs. The standard-costing method makes calculating equivalent-unit costs unnecessary, so it simplifies process costing. In Step 5, managers assign standard costs to units completed (including normal spoilage), to abnormal spoilage, and to ending work-in-process inventory by multiplying the equivalent units calculated in Step 2 by the standard costs per equivalent unit presented in Step 4. This enables managers to measure and analyze variances in the manner described in the appendix to Chapter 17 (pages 691–736).[10]

Finally, note that the journal entries corresponding to the amounts calculated in Step 5 are as follows:

Finished Goods	146,300	
Work in Process—Forming		146,300
To record transfer of good units completed in July.		
Loss from Abnormal Spoilage	5,700	
Work in Process—Forming		5,700
To record abnormal spoilage detected in July.		

---

[10] For example, from Exhibit 18A-1, Panel B, the standard costs for July are direct materials used, $8,500 \times $8.50 = $72,250$, and conversion costs, $8,100 \times $10.50 = $85,050$. From page 741, the actual costs added during July are direct materials, $76,500, and conversion costs, $89,100, resulting in a direct materials variance of $72,250 - $76,500 = $4,250$ U and a conversion costs variance of $85,050 - $89,100 = $4,050$ U. These variances could then be subdivided further as in Chapters 7 and 8; the abnormal spoilage would be part of the efficiency variance.

Exhibit 18A-1 Use of Standard Cost in Process Costing with Spoilage—Forming Department of Anzio Company for July 2017

	A	B	C	D
1	**PANEL A: Summarize Output in Physical Units and Compute Equivalent Units**			
2			**Equivalent Units**	
3		**Physical**	**Direct**	**Conversion**
4	**Flow of Production**	**Units**	**Materials**	**Costs**
5	Work-in-process, beginning balance (given)	1,500		
6	Started during current period (given)	8,500		
7	To account for	10,000		
8	Good units completed and transferred out during the current period			
9	From beginning work-in-process inventory[a]	1,500		
10	1,500 × (100% − 100%); 1,500 × (100% − 60%)		—	600
11	Started and completed[b]	5,500		
12	5,500 × 100%; 5,500 × 100%		5,500	5,500
13	Normal spoilage[c]	700		
14	700 × 100%; 700 × 100%		700	700
15	Abnormal spoilage[d]	300		
16	300 × 100%; 300 × 100%		300	300
17	Work-in-process, ending balance[e] (given)	2,000		
18	2,000 × 100%; 2,200 × 50%		2,000	1,000
19	Accounted for	10,000		
20	Work done in current period only		8,500	8,100
21				
22	[a]Degree of completion for beginning inventory WIP: direct materials, 100%; conversion costs, 60%.			
23	[b]7,000 physical units completed and transferred out minus 1,500 physical units completed and transferred from beginning inventory WIP.			
24	[c]Normal spoilage is 10% of good units transferred out: 10% × 7,000 = 700 units. Degree of completion of			
25	normal spoilage in this department: direct materials 100%; conversion costs 100%.			
26	[d]Abnormal spoilage = Actual spoilage − Normal spoilage = 1,000 − 700 = 300 units. Degree of completion			
27	of abnormal spoilage in this department: direct materials 100%; conversion costs, 100%.			
28	[e]Degree of completion for ending inventory WIP: direct materials 100%; conversion costs, 50%.			
29	**PANEL B: Standard Cost per Equivalent Unit, Summarize Total Costs to Account for,**			
30	**and Assign Total Costs to Units Completed, to Spoiled Units, and to Units in Ending Work-in-Process**			
31		**Total**		
32		**Production**	**Direct**	**Conversion**
33		**Costs**	**Materials**	**Costs**
34	Standard cost per equivalent unit (given)	$ 19.00	$ 8.50	$ 10.50
35	Work-in-process, beginning balance (given)	$ 22,200		
36	Costs added in the current period (at standard)	157,300	= $72,250[g] +	$85,050[h]
37	Total costs to account for	$179,500		
38	Cost per equivalent unit (at standard)		$ 8.50	$ 10.50
39	Assignment of costs:			
40	Good units completed and transferred out (7,000 units):			
41	Work-in-process beginning balance (1,500 units)	$ 22,200		
42	Costs added in current period[f] (0 × $8.50; 600 × $10.50)	6,300	= $ — +	$ 6,300
43	Total from beginning inventory before normal spoilage	28,500		
44	Started and completed before normal spoilage (5,500 units)	104,500	= 46,750 +	57,750
45	Normal spoilage (700 units)	13,300	= 5,950 +	7,350
46	A Total costs of good units completed and transferred out	146,300		
47	B Abnormal spoilage (300 units)	5,700	= 2,550 +	3,150
48	C Work-in-process, ending balance (2,000 × $8.50; 1,000 × $10.50)	27,500	= 17,000 +	10,500
49	A + B + C Total costs accounted for	$179,500	$72,250	$85,050
50	Summary of variances for current performance:			
51	Costs added in current period at standard costs (see above)		$72,250	$85,050
52	Actual costs incurred (given)		76,500	89,100
53	Variance		$ (4,250) U	$ (4,050) U
54				
55	[f]Equivalent units of direct materials and conversion costs calculated in Panel A.			
56	[g]8,500 equivalent units × $8.50.			
57	[h]8,100 equivalent units × $10.50.			

Exhibit 18A-2 Standard-Costing Method of Process Costing with Spoilage for the Forming Department for July 2017

PANEL A: Summarize the Flow of Physical Units and Compute Output in Equivalent Units

	A	B	C	D
1		**(Step 1)**	**(Step 2)**	
2			**Equivalent Units**	
3	**Flow of Production**	**Physical Units**	**Direct Materials**	**Conversion Costs**
4	Work in process, beginning (given, p. 743)	1,500		
5	Started during current period (given, p. 743)	8,500		
6	To account for	10,000		
7	Good units completed and transferred out during current period			
8	From beginning work in process[a]	1,500		
9	[1,500 × (100% − 100%); 1,500 × (100% − 60%)]		0	600
10	Started and completed	5,500[b]		
11	(5,500 × 100%; 5,500 × 100%)		5,500	5,500
12	Normal spoilage[c]	700		
13	(700 × 100%; 700 × 100%)		700	700
14	Abnormal spoilage[d]	300		
15	(300 × 100%; 300 × 100%)		300	300
16	Work in process, ending[e] (given, p. 743)	2,000		
17	(2,000 × 100%; 2,000 × 50%)		2,000	1,000
18	Accounted for	10,000		
19	Equivalent units of work done in current period		8,500	8,100
20				
21	[a]Degree of completion in this department: direct materials, 100%; conversion costs, 60%.			
22	[b]7,000 physical units completed and transferred out minus 1,500 physical units completed and transferred out from beginning			
23	work-in-process inventory.			
24	[c]Normal spoilage is 10% of good units transferred out; 10% × 7,000 = 700 units. Degree of completion of normal spoilage in this			
25	department: direct materials, 100%; conversion costs, 100%.			
26	[d]Abnormal spoilage = Total spoilage − Normal spoilage = 1,000 − 700 = 300 units. Degree of completion of abnormal spoilage			
27	in this department: direct materials, 100%; conversion costs, 100%.			
28	[e]Degree of completion in this department: direct materials, 100%; conversion costs, 50%.			

PANEL B: Summarize the Total Costs to Account For, Compute the Cost per Equivalent Unit, and Assign Costs to the Units Completed, Spoiled Units, and Units in Ending Work-in-Process Inventory

	A	B	C	D	E	F
1			**Total Production Costs**	**Direct Materials**		**Conversion Costs**
2	(Step 3)	Work in process, beginning (given, p. 758)	$ 22,200	(1,500 × $8.50)		(900 × $10.50)
3		Costs added in current period (given, p. 759)	157,300	(8,500 × $8.50)		(8,100 × $10.50)
4		Total costs to account for	$179,500	$85,000		$94,500
5	(Step 4)	Standard costs per equivalent unit (given, p. 758)	$ 19.00	$ 8.50		$ 10.50
6	(Step 5)	Assignment of costs:				
7		Good units completed and transferred out (7,000 units)				
8		Work in process, beginning (1,500 units)	$ 22,200	(1,500 × $8.50)	+	(900 × $10.50)
9		Costs added to beginning work in process in current period	6,300	(0[f] × $8.50)	+	(600[f] × $10.50)
10		Total from beginning inventory before normal spoilage	28,500			
11		Started and completed before normal spoilage (5,500 units)	104,500	(5,500[f] × $8.50)	+	(5,500[f] × $10.50)
12		Normal spoilage (700 units)	13,300	(700[f] × $8.50)	+	(700[f] × $10.50)
13	(A)	Total costs of good units completed and transferred out	146,300			
14	(B)	Abnormal spoilage (300 units)	5,700	(300[f] × $8.50)	+	(300[f] × $10.50)
15	(C)	Work in process, ending (2,000 units)	27,500	(2,000[f] × $8.50)	+	(1,000[f] × $10.50)
16	(A) + (B) + (C)	Total costs accounted for	$179,500	$85,000	+	$94,500
17						
18	[f]Equivalent units of direct materials and conversion costs calculated in step 2 in Panel A.					

Terms to Learn

This chapter and the Glossary at the end of the book contain definitions of the following important terms:

abnormal spoilage **(p. 739)**

inspection point **(p. 740)**

normal spoilage **(p. 738)**

rework **(p. 738)**

scrap **(p. 738)**

spoilage **(p. 738)**

Assignment Material

MyLab Accounting Make the grade with MyLab Accounting: The Short-Answer Questions, Exercises, and Problems marked with a ⊕ can be found on MyLab Accounting. You can practise them as often as you want, and most feature step-by-step guided instructions to help you find the right answer.

Short-Answer Questions

18-1 Why is there an unmistakable trend in manufacturing to improve quality?

18-2 Distinguish among spoilage, reworked units, and scrap.

18-3 "Normal spoilage is planned spoilage." Discuss.

18-4 "Costs of abnormal spoilage are losses." Explain.

18-5 "What has been regarded as normal spoilage in the past is not necessarily acceptable as normal spoilage in the present or future." Explain.

18-6 "Units of abnormal spoilage are inferred rather than identified." Explain.

18-7 "In accounting for spoiled goods, we are dealing with cost assignment rather than cost incurrence." Explain.

18-8 "Total input includes abnormal as well as normal spoilage and is, therefore, inappropriate as a basis for computing normal spoilage." Do you agree? Explain.

18-9 "The point of inspection is the key to the allocation of spoilage costs." Do you agree? Explain.

18-10 "The unit cost of normal spoilage is the same as the unit cost of abnormal spoilage." Do you agree? Explain.

18-11 "In job costing, the costs of normal spoilage that occur while a specific job is being done are charged to the specific job." Do you agree? Explain.

18-12 "The costs of reworking defective units are always charged to the specific jobs where the defects were originally discovered." Do you agree? Explain.

18-13 "Abnormal rework costs should be charged to a loss account, not to manufacturing overhead." Do you agree? Explain.

18-14 When is a company justified in inventorying scrap?

Exercises

18-15 Terminology. A number of terms are listed below:

abnormal spoilage

normal spoilage

scrap

inspection point

rework

Required

Select the terms from the above list to complete the following sentences.

There is no perfect machine, nor is there a perfect manufacturing process. That is why each process has at least one _____to assess the output quality and send the units back for _____and ultimately prepare for sale, or _____ them. Costs of reworked units are non-value-added for the customer, who will, therefore, not pay for them. The company bears this cost. The difference between _____ and _____ is in accounting for the costs. _____ is predictable but unavoidable; therefore, ASPE/IFRS allows this cost in cost of goods manufactured. _____ is avoidable but unpredictable and ASPE/IFRS requires this cost to be expensed. These costs did not produce an asset from which future revenue will be recovered and therefore are not part of cost of goods manufactured.

LO 1 ▷

1. Normal spoilage, 6,600 units

⊕ **18-16 Normal and abnormal spoilage in units.** The following data, in physical units, describe a grinding process for January:

Work-in-process, beginning	19,000
Started during current period	150,000
To account for	169,000
Spoiled units	12,000
Good units completed and transferred out	132,000
Work-in-process, ending	25,000
Accounted for	169,000

Inspection occurs at the 100% completion stage. Normal spoilage is 5% of the good units passing inspection.

Required

1. Compute the normal and abnormal spoilage in units.
2. Assume that the equivalent-unit cost of a spoiled unit is $20. Compute the amount of potential savings if all spoilage were eliminated, assuming that all other costs would be unaffected. Comment on your answer.

LO 2 ▷

Total equivalent units for conversion costs, 9,750 EU

⊕ **18-17 Weighted-average method, spoilage, equivalent units.** (CMA, adapted) Consider the following data for November 2018 from Grey Manufacturing Company, which makes silk pennants and uses a process-costing system. All direct materials are added at the beginning of the process, and conversion costs are added evenly during the process. Spoilage is detected upon inspection at the completion of the process. Spoiled units are disposed of at zero net disposal price. Grey Manufacturing Company uses the weighted-average method of process costing.

	Physical Units (pennants)	Direct Materials	Conversion Costs
Work-in-process, November 1*	1,000	$ 1,423	$ 1,110
Started during November 2018	?		
Good units completed and transferred out during November 2018	9,000		
Normal spoilage	100		
Abnormal spoilage	50		
Work-in-process, November 30†	2,000		
Total costs added during November 2018		$12,180	$27,750

*Degree of completion: direct materials, 100%; conversion costs, 50%.
†Degree of completion: direct materials, 100%; conversion costs, 30%.

Required

Compute the equivalent units of work done in the current period for direct materials and conversion costs. Show physical units in the first column of your schedule.

LO 2 ▷

Conversion cost per equivalent unit, $2.96

⊕ **18-18 Weighted-average method, assigning costs** (continuation of Exercise 18-17).

Required

For the data in Exercise 18-17, summarize total costs to account for, calculate the cost per equivalent unit for direct materials and conversion costs, and assign total costs to units completed and transferred out (including normal spoilage), to abnormal spoilage, and to units in ending work-in-process.

LO 2 ▷

Total equivalent units for conversion costs in current period only, 9,250 EU

⊕ **18-19 FIFO method, spoilage, equivalent units.** Refer to the information in Exercise 18-17. Suppose Grey Manufacturing Company uses the FIFO method of process costing instead of the weighted-average method.

Required

Compute equivalent units for direct materials and conversion costs. Show physical units in the first column of your schedule.

⊕ 18-20 FIFO method, assigning costs (continuation of Exercise 18-19).

◀ **LO 2**
Conversion cost per equivalent unit, $3

Required

For the data in Exercise 18-19, use the FIFO method to summarize total costs to account for, calculate the cost per equivalent unit for direct materials and conversion costs, and assign total costs to units completed and transferred out (including normal spoilage), to abnormal spoilage, and to units in ending work-in-process.

⊕ 18-21 Weighted-average method, spoilage. Winding River Company makes wooden toys in its forming department, and it uses the weighted-average method of process costing. All direct materials are added at the beginning of the process, and conversion costs are added evenly during the process. Spoiled units are detected upon inspection at the end of the process and are disposed of at zero net disposal value. Summary data for August 2018 are as follows:

◀ **LO 2**
1. Total equivalent units for conversion costs, 11,550 EU

	A	B	C	D
1		Physical Units	Direct Materials	Conversion Costs
2	Work-in-process, beginning inventory (August 1)	2,000	$17,700	$10,900
3	Degree of completion of beginning work-in-process		100%	50%
4	Started during August	10,000		
5	Good units completed and transferred out during August	9,000		
6	Work-in-process, ending inventory (August 31)	1,800		
7	Degree of completion of ending work-in-process		100%	75%
8	Total costs added during August		$81,300	$93,000
9	Normal spoilage as a percentage of good units	10%		
10	Degree of completion of normal spoilage		100%	100%
11	Degree of completion of abnormal spoilage		100%	100%

Required

1. For each cost category, calculate equivalent units. Show physical units in the first column of your schedule.
2. Summarize total costs to account for, calculate cost per equivalent unit for each cost category, and assign total costs to units completed and transferred out (including normal spoilage), to abnormal spoilage, and to units in ending work-in-process.

⊕ 18-22 Standard-costing method, spoilage, and journal entries. Aaron Inc. is a manufacturer of vents for water heaters. The company uses a process-costing system to account for its work-in-process inventories. When Job 512 was being processed in the machining department, a piece of sheet metal was off-centre in the bending machine and two vents were spoiled. Because this problem occurs periodically, it is considered normal spoilage and is consequently recorded as an overhead cost. Because this step comes first in the procedure for making the vents, the only costs incurred were $500 for direct materials. Assume the sheet metal cannot be sold, and its cost has already been recorded as part of the work-in-process inventory.

◀ **LO 3**
Manufacturing Overhead Control (normal spoilage), DR 500

Required

Prepare the journal entries to record the spoilage incurred.

⊕ 18-23 Recognition of loss from spoilage. Spheres Toys manufactures globes at its San Fernando facility. The company provides you with the following information regarding operations for April 2017:

◀ **LO 1**
1. The unit cost of making the 20,000 globes = $40 per unit

Total globes manufactured	20,000
Globes rejected as spoiled units	750
Total manufacturing cost	$800,000

Assume the spoiled units have no disposal value.

Required

1. What is the unit cost of making the 20,000 globes?
2. What is the total cost of the 750 spoiled units?
3. If the spoilage is considered normal, what is the increase in the unit cost of good globes manufactured as a result of the spoilage?
4. If the spoilage is considered abnormal, prepare the journal entries for the spoilage incurred.

LO 2 ▶
1. Total equivalent units for conversion costs, 2,880 units

⊕ **18-24 Weighted-average method, spoilage.** Chipcity Inc. is a fast-growing manufacturer of computer chips. Direct materials are added at the start of the production process. Conversion costs are added evenly during the process. Some units of this product are spoiled as a result of defects not detectable before inspection of finished goods. Spoiled units are disposed of at zero net disposal value. Chipcity uses the weighted-average method of process costing.

Summary data for September 2018 are

	Physical Units (computer chips)	Direct Materials	Conversion Costs
Work-in-process, beginning inventory (Sept. 1)	600	$ 96,000	$ 15,300
Degree of completion of beginning WIP		100%	30%
Started during September	2,550		
Good units completed and transferred out during September	2,100		
Work-in-process, ending inventory (Sept. 30)	450		
Degree of completion of ending WIP		100%	40%
Total costs added during September		$567,000	$230,400
Normal spoilage as a percentage of good units	15%		
Degree of completion of normal spoilage		100%	100%
Degree of completion of abnormal spoilage		100%	100%

Required

1. For each cost category, compute equivalent units. Show physical units in the first column of your schedule.
2. Summarize total costs to account for, calculate cost per equivalent unit for each cost category, and assign total costs to units completed and transferred out (including normal spoilage), to abnormal spoilage, and to units in ending work-in-process.

LO 2 ▶
1. Equivalent units for conversion costs for the current period, 2,700 units

⊕ **18-25 FIFO method, spoilage.** Refer to the information in Exercise 18-24.

Required

Do Exercise 18-24 using the FIFO method of process costing.

LO 3 ▶
2. Total costs to account for, $846,000

⊕ **18-26 Standard-costing method, spoilage.** Refer to the information in Exercise 18-24. Suppose Chipcity determines standard costs of $200 per equivalent unit for direct materials and $75 per equivalent unit for conversion costs for both beginning work-in-process and work done in the current period.

Required

Do Exercise 18-24 using the standard-costing method.

LO 4 ▶
1. Unit cost of remaining cases, $6

⊕ **18-27 Spoilage and job costing.** Bamber Kitchens produces a variety of items in accordance with special job orders from hospitals, plant cafeterias, and university dormitories. An order for 2,500 cases of mixed vegetables costs $6 per case: direct materials, $3; direct manufacturing labour, $2; and manufacturing overhead allocated, $1. The manufacturing overhead rate includes a provision for normal spoilage. Consider each requirement independently.

Required

1. Assume that a labourer dropped 200 cases. Suppose that part of the 200 cases could be sold to a nearby prison for $200 cash. Prepare a journal entry to record this event. Calculate and explain briefly the unit cost of the remaining 2,300 cases.
2. Refer to the original data. Tasters at the company reject 200 of the 2,500 cases. The 200 cases are disposed of for $400. Assume that this rejection rate is considered normal. Prepare a journal entry to record this event, and

   a. Calculate the unit cost if the rejection is attributable to exacting specifications of this particular job.
   b. Calculate the unit cost if the rejection is characteristic of the production process and is not attributable to this specific job.
   c. Are unit costs the same in requirements 2a and 2b? Explain your reasoning briefly.

3. Refer to the original data. Tasters rejected 200 cases that had insufficient salt. The product can be placed in a vat, salted, and reprocessed into jars. This operation, which is considered normal, will cost $200. Prepare a journal entry to record this event, and

   a. Calculate the unit cost of all the cases if this additional cost was incurred because of the exacting specifications of this particular job.

b. Calculate the unit cost of all the cases if this additional cost occurs regularly because of difficulty in seasoning.

c. Are unit costs the same in requirements 3a and 3b? Explain your reasoning briefly.

🌐 **18-28 Reworked units, costs of rework.** Heyer Appliances assembles dishwashers at its plant in Tuscaloosa, Alabama. In February 2017, 60 circulation motors that cost $110 each (from a new supplier who subsequently went bankrupt) were defective and had to be disposed of at zero net disposal value. Heyer Appliances was able to rework all 60 dishwashers by substituting new circulation motors purchased from one of its existing suppliers. Each replacement motor cost $125.

◀ **LO 6**

Required

1. What alternative approaches are there to account for the materials cost of reworked units?
2. Should Heyer Appliances use the $110 circulation motor or the $125 motor to calculate the cost of materials reworked? Explain.
3. What other costs might Heyer Appliances include in its analysis of the total costs of rework due to the circulation motors purchased from the (now) bankrupt supplier?

🌐 **18-29 Scrap, job-order costing.** Mendola Corp. has an extensive job-costing facility that uses a variety of metals. Consider each requirement independently.

◀ **LO 4, 5**
1. Job 372 Work-in-Process Control, CR $490

Required

1. Job 372 uses a particular metal alloy that is not used for any other job. Assume that scrap is material in amount and sold for $490 quickly after it is produced. Prepare the journal entry.
2. The scrap from Job 372 consists of a metal used by many other jobs. No record is maintained of the scrap generated by individual jobs. Assume that scrap is accounted for at the time of its sale. Scrap totalling $4,000 is sold. Prepare two alternative journal entries that could be used to account for the sale of scrap.
3. Suppose the scrap generated in requirement 2 is returned to the storeroom for future use, and a journal entry is made to record the scrap. A month later, the scrap is reused as direct material on a subsequent job. Prepare the journal entries to record these transactions.

Problems

🌐 **18-30 Weighted-average method, spoilage.** The White Crab Company is a food-processing company based in PEI. It operates under the weighted-average method of process costing and has two departments: cleaning and packaging. For the cleaning department, conversion costs are added evenly during the process, and direct materials are added at the beginning of the process. Spoiled units are detected upon inspection at the end of the process and are disposed of at zero net disposal value. All completed work is transferred to the packaging department. Summary data for May follow:

◀ **LO 2**
1. Normal spoilage equivalent units, conversion costs, 1,850 units

	A	B	C	D
1	**The White Crab Company: Cleaning Department**	**Physical Units**	**Direct Materials**	**Conversion Costs**
2	Work-in-process, beginning inventory (May 1)	2,500	$ 2,500	$ 2,000
3	Degree of completion of beginning work-in-process		100%	80%
4	Started during May	22,500		
5	Good units completed and transferred out during May	18,500		
6	Work-in-process, ending inventory (May 31)	4,000		
7	Degree of completion of ending work-in-process		100%	25%
8	Total costs added during May		$22,500	$20,000
9	Normal spoilage as a percentage of good units	10%		
10	Degree of completion of normal spoilage		100%	100%
11	Degree of completion of abnormal spoilage		100%	100%

Required

For the cleaning department, summarize total costs to account for, and assign total costs to units completed and transferred out (including normal spoilage), to abnormal spoilage, and to units in ending work-in-process. Carry unit-cost calculations to four decimal places when necessary. Calculate final totals to the nearest dollar. (Problem 18-32 explores additional facets of this problem.)

LO 2 ▷
EU of direct materials, 22,500

⊕ **18-31 FIFO method, spoilage.** Refer to the information in Problem 18-30.

Required

Do Problem 18-30 using the FIFO method of process costing. (Problem 18-33 explores additional facets of this problem.)

LO 2 ▷
EU of direct materials, work done
to date, 16,000

⊕ **18-32 Weighted-average method, packaging department** (continuation of Problem 18-30). In White Crab Company's packaging department, conversion costs are added evenly during the process, and direct materials are added at the end of the process. Spoiled units are detected upon inspection at the end of the process and are disposed of at zero net disposal value. All completed work is transferred to the next department. The transferred-in costs for May equal the total cost of good units completed and transferred out in May from the cleaning department, which were calculated in Problem 18-30 using the weighted-average method of process costing. Summary data for May follow:

	A	B	C	D	E
1	**The White Crab Company: Packaging Department**	**Physical Units**	**Transferred-in Costs**	**Direct Materials**	**Conversion Costs**
2	Work-in-process, beginning inventory (May 1)	7,500	$16,125	$ 0	$ 6,125
3	Degree of completion of beginning work-in-process		100%	0%	80%
4	Started during May	18,500			
5	Good units completed and transferred out during May	15,000			
6	Work-in-process, ending inventory (May 31)	10,000			
7	Degree of completion of ending work-in-process		100%	0%	25%
8	Total costs added during May		?	$1,600	$12,375
9	Normal spoilage as a percentage of good units	5%			
10	Degree of completion of normal spoilage			100%	100%
11	Degree of completion of abnormal spoilage			100%	100%

Required

For the packaging department, use the weighted-average method to summarize total costs to account for and assign total costs to units completed and transferred out (including normal spoilage), to abnormal spoilage, and to units in ending work-in-process.

LO 2 ▷
Transferred-in costs EU in current
period only, 18,500

⊕ **18-33 FIFO method, packaging department** (continuation of Problem 18-31). Refer to the information in Problem 18-32 except for the transferred-in costs for May, which equal the total cost of good units completed and transferred out in May from the cleaning department, which were calculated in Problem 18-31 using the FIFO method of process costing.

Required

For the packaging department, use the FIFO method to summarize total costs to account for, and assign total costs to units completed and transferred out (including normal spoilage), to abnormal spoilage, and to units in ending work-in-process.

LO 4, 5 ▷

⊕ **18-34 Spoilage in job costing.** Jellyfish Machine Shop is a manufacturer of motorized carts for vacation resorts.

Patrick Cullin, the plant manager of Jellyfish, obtains the following information for Job #10 in August 2017. A total of 46 units were started, and 6 spoiled units were detected and rejected at final inspection, yielding 40 good units. The spoiled units were considered to be normal spoilage. Costs assigned prior to the inspection point are $1,100 per unit. The current disposal price of the spoiled units is $235 per unit. When the spoilage is detected, the spoiled goods are inventoried at $235 per unit.

Required

1. What is the normal spoilage rate?
2. Prepare the journal entries to record the normal spoilage, assuming the following:
   a. The spoilage is related to a specific job.
   b. The spoilage is common to all jobs.
   c. The spoilage is considered to be abnormal spoilage.

LO 2 ▷
1. Normally spoiled units, 210

⊕ **18-35 Weighted-average method, spoilage.** Rounder specializes in the manufacture of ball bearings for aircraft. Direct materials are added at the start of the production process. Conversion costs are added evenly during the process. Some units of this product are spoiled as a result of defects not detectable before inspection of finished goods. Normally, the spoiled units are 15% of the good units transferred out. Spoiled units are disposed of at zero net disposal price.

Rounder uses the weighted-average method of process costing. Summary data for September 2018 are

	Physical Units	Direct Materials	Conversion Costs
Work-in-process, September 1*	400	$ 76,800	$ 12,240
Started during September 2018	1,700		
Good units completed and transferred out during September 2018	1,400		
Work-in-process, September 30†	300		
Costs added during September 2018		$453,600	$184,320

*Degree of completion: direct materials, 100%; conversion costs, 30%.
†Degree of completion: direct materials, 100%; conversion costs, 40%.

Required

1. For each cost element, compute the equivalent units. Show physical units in the first column.
2. For each cost element, calculate the cost per equivalent unit.
3. Summarize the total costs to account for, and assign these costs to units completed and transferred out (to normal spoilage), to abnormal spoilage, and to units in ending work-in-process.

🌐 **18-36 FIFO method, spoilage.** Refer to the information in Problem 18-35.

Required

Repeat question 1 from Problem 18-35 using the FIFO method of process costing.

🌐 **18-37 Standard-costing method, spoilage.** Refer to the information in Problem 18-35. Suppose Rounder determines standard costs of $246 per (equivalent) unit for direct materials and $96 per (equivalent) unit for conversion costs for both beginning work-in-process and work done in the current period.

Required

Repeat question 2 from Problem 18-35 using standard costs.

🌐 **18-38 Physical units, inspection at various stages of completion.** Normal spoilage is 6% of the good units passing inspection in a forging process. In March, a total of 10,000 units were spoiled. Other data include units started during March, 120,000; work-in-process, beginning, 14,000 units (20% completed for conversion costs); work-in-process, ending, 11,000 units (70% completed for conversion costs).

Required

In columnar form, compute the normal and abnormal spoilage in units, assuming the inspection point is at (a) the 15% stage of completion, (b) the 40% stage of completion, and (c) the 100% stage of completion.

🌐 **18-39 Weighted-average method, inspection at 80% completion.** Ottawa Manufacturing is a furniture manufacturer with two departments: moulding and finishing. The company uses the weighted-average method of process costing. In August, the following data were recorded for the finishing department:

Units of beginning work-in-process inventory	12,500
Percentage completion of beginning work-in-process units	25%
Cost of direct materials in beginning work-in-process	$ 0
Units started	87,500
Units completed	62,500
Units in ending inventory	25,000
Percentage completion of ending work-in-process units	95%
Spoiled units	12,500
Total costs added during current period:	
Direct materials	$819,000
Direct manufacturing labour	$794,500
Manufacturing overhead	$770,000
Work in process, beginning:	
Transferred-in costs	$103,625
Conversion costs	$ 52,500
Cost of units transferred in during current period	$809,375

◀ **LO 2**
DM cost added in period is $453,600, therefore, the DM costs to account for (under FIFO) is $453,600

◀ **LO 3**
Direct materials total costs to be accounted for, $418,200

◀ **LO 3**
Normal spoilage at 40%, 7,440 units

◀ **LO 3**
Abnormal spoilage, 3,750 units

Conversion costs are added evenly during the process. Direct materials costs are added when production is 90% complete. The inspection point is at the 80% stage of production. Normal spoilage is 10% of all good units that pass inspection. Spoiled units are disposed of at zero net disposal value.

Required

For August, summarize total costs to account for, and assign these costs to units completed and transferred out (including normal spoilage), to abnormal spoilage, and to units in ending work-in-process.

🌐 **18-40 Spoilage in job costing.** Tee Time Machine Shop is a manufacturer of motorized carts for vacation resorts. Pat Cruz, the plant manager of Tee Time, obtains the following information for Job #10 in August 2018. A total of 45 units were started, and 5 spoiled units were detected and rejected at final inspection, yielding 40 good units. The spoiled units were considered to be normal spoilage. Costs assigned prior to the inspection point are $1,000 per unit. The current disposal price of the spoiled units is $200 per unit. When the spoilage is detected, the spoiled goods are inventoried at $200 per unit.

Required

1. What is the normal spoilage rate?
2. Prepare the journal entries to record the normal spoilage, assuming
   a. The spoilage is related to a specific job.
   b. The spoilage is common to all jobs.
   c. The spoilage is considered to be abnormal spoilage.

🌐 **18-41 Rework in job costing, journal entry** (continuation of Problem 18-40). Assume that the five spoiled units of Tee Time Machine Shop's Job #10 can be reworked for a total cost of $1,800. A total cost of $5,000 associated with these units has already been assigned to Job #10 before the rework.

Required

Prepare the journal entries for the rework, assuming

1. a. The rework is related to a specific job.
   b. The rework is common to all jobs.
   c. The rework is considered to be abnormal.

🌐 **18-42 Scrap at time of sale or at time of production, journal entries** (continuation of Problem 18-41). Assume that Job #10 of Tee Time Machine Shop generates normal scrap with a total sales value of $300 (it is assumed that the scrap returned to the storeroom is sold quickly).

Required

Prepare the journal entries for the recognition of scrap, assuming

1. a. The value of scrap is immaterial and scrap is recognized at the time of sale.
   b. The value of scrap is material, is related to a specific job, and is recognized at the time of sale.
   c. The value of scrap is material, is common to all jobs, and is recognized at the time of sale.
   d. The value of scrap is material, scrap is recognized as inventory at the time of production, and is recorded at its net realizable value.

🌐 **18-43 Job costing, rework.** Industrial Fire (IF) Corporation is a manufacturer of computer chips based in Nepean. It manufactures two types of computer chips, CS1 and CS2. The costs of manufacturing each CS1 chip, excluding rework costs, are direct materials, $60; direct manufacturing labour, $12; and manufacturing overhead, $38. Defective units are sent to a separate rework area. Rework costs per CS1 chip are direct materials, $12; direct manufacturing labour, $9; and manufacturing overhead, $15.

In August 2018, IF manufactured 1,000 CS1 chips and 500 CS2 chips; 80 of the CS1 chips and none of the CS2 chips required rework. IF classifies 50 of the CS1 chips reworked as normal rework caused by inherent problems in its production process that coincidentally occurred only during the production of CS1. Hence the rework costs for these 50 CS1 chips are normal rework costs not specifically attributable to the CS1 product. IF classifies the remaining 30 units of CS1 chips reworked as abnormal rework. IF allocates manufacturing overhead on the basis of machine-hours required to manufacture CS1 and CS2. Each CS1 and CS2 chip requires the same number of machine-hours.

Required

1. Prepare journal entries to record the accounting for the cost of the spoiled chips and for rework.
2. What were the total rework costs of CS1 chips in August 2018?

18-44 Job costing, classifying spoilage, ethics. Flextron Company is a contract manufacturer for a variety of pharmaceutical and over-the-counter products. It has a reputation for operational excellence and boasts a normal spoilage rate of 2% of normal input. Normal spoilage is recognized during the budgeting process and is classified as a component of manufacturing overhead when determining the overhead rate.

Lynn Sanger, one of Flextron's quality control managers, obtains the following information for Job No. M102, an order from a consumer products company. The order was completed recently, just before the close of Flextron's fiscal year. The units will be delivered early in the next accounting period. A total of 128,500 units were started, and 6,000 spoiled units were rejected at final inspection, yielding 122,500 good units. Spoiled units were sold at $4 per unit. Sanger indicates that all spoilage was related to this specific job.

The total costs for all 128,500 units of Job No. M102 follow. The job has been completed, but the costs are yet to be transferred to Finished Goods.

Direct materials	$ 979,000
Direct manufacturing labour	840,000
Manufacturing overhead	1,650,500
Total manufacturing costs	$3,469,500

Required

1. Calculate the unit quantities of normal and abnormal spoilage.
2. Prepare the journal entries to account for Job No. M102, including spoilage, disposal of spoiled units, and transfer of costs to the Finished Goods account.
3. Flextron's controller, Vince Chadwick, tells Marta Suarez, the management accountant responsible for Job No. M102, the following: "This was an unusual job. I think all 6,000 spoiled units should be considered normal." Suarez knows that the work involved in Job No. M102 was not uncommon and that Flextron's normal spoilage rate of 2% is the appropriate benchmark. She feels Chadwick made these comments because he wants to show a higher operating income for the year.

   a. Prepare journal entries, similar to requirement 2, to account for Job No. M102 if all spoilage were considered normal. How will operating income be affected if all spoilage is considered normal?
   b. What should Suarez do in response to Chadwick's comment?

⊕ **18-45 Physical units, inspection at various stages of completion.** Normal spoilage is 7% of the good units passing inspection in a forging process. In March, a total of 12,000 units were spoiled. Other data include units started during March, 129,000; work-in-process, beginning, 16,000 units (20% completed for conversion costs); work-in-process, ending, 13,000 units (70% completed for conversion costs).

◄ **LO 3**
Normal spoilage at 15%, 8,190 units

Required

In columnar form, compute the normal and abnormal spoilage in units, assuming inspection at 15%, 40%, and 100% stages of completion.

⊕ **18-46 Job costing, scrap.** Buckwold Corporation makes two different types of hubcaps for cars–HM3 and JB4. Circular pieces of metal are stamped out of steel sheets (leaving the edges as scrap), formed, and finished. The stamping operation is identical for both types of hubcaps. During May, Buckwold manufactured 20,000 units of HM3 and 10,000 units of JB4. In May, manufacturing costs per unit of HM3 and JB4 before accounting for the scrap are as follows:

◄ **LO 5**
1. Journal entry DR Materials Control, 8,400

	HM3	JB4
Direct materials	$12.00	$18.00
Direct manufacturing labour	3.60	4.80
Materials-related manufacturing overhead (materials handling, storage, etc.)	2.40	3.60
Other manufacturing overhead	7.20	9.60
Unit manufacturing costs	$25.20	$36.00

Materials-related manufacturing costs are allocated to products at 20% of direct materials costs. Other manufacturing overhead is allocated to products at 200% of direct manufacturing labour costs. Since the same metal sheets are used to make both types of hubcaps, Buckwold maintains no records of the scrap generated by the individual products. Scrap generated during manufacturing is accounted for at the time it is returned to the storeroom as an offset to materials-related manufacturing overhead. The value of scrap generated during May and returned to the storeroom was $8,400.

Required

1. Prepare a journal entry to summarize the accounting for scrap during May.
2. Suppose the scrap generated in May was sold in June for $8,400. Prepare a journal entry to account for this transaction.
3. What adjustments, if any, would you make for scrap when calculating the manufacturing cost per unit for HM3 and JB4 in May? Explain.

Collaborative Learning Case

LO 2 ▶
1. Total equivalent units for conversion costs, 78,500 EU

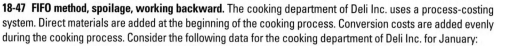

18-47 FIFO method, spoilage, working backward. The cooking department of Deli Inc. uses a process-costing system. Direct materials are added at the beginning of the cooking process. Conversion costs are added evenly during the cooking process. Consider the following data for the cooking department of Deli Inc. for January:

	Physical Units	Direct Materials	Conversion Costs
Work-in-process, January 1*	10,000	$ 264,000	$ 36,000
Started during January	74,000		
Good units completed and transferred out during January	61,000		
Spoiled units	8,000		
Work-in-process, January 31	15,000		
Costs added during January		$1,776,000	$1,130,400
Cost per equivalent unit of work done in January		$ 24	$ 14.40

*Degree of completion: direct materials, 100%; conversion costs, 25%.

Deli uses the FIFO method of process costing. Inspection occurs when production is 100% completed. Normal spoilage is 11% of good units completed and transferred out during the current period.

Instruction

Form pairs of students to complete the following requirements.

Required

1. For each cost category, compute equivalent units of work done in the current period (January).
2. For each cost category, compute equivalent units of work done to complete beginning work-in-process inventory, to start and complete new units, for normal and abnormal spoilage units, and to produce ending work-in-process inventory.
3. For each cost category, calculate the percentage of completion of ending work-in-process inventory.
4. Summarize total costs to account for, and assign these costs to units completed (and transferred out), normal spoilage, abnormal spoilage, and ending work-in-process.

TRY IT! ▶

SOLUTIONS

Try It 18–1

Units started during July = 9,000 + 100 + 50 + 2,000 − 1,000 = 10,150
Summarize the flow of physical units, and compute output in equivalent units.

Flow of Production	(Step 1) Physical Units	(Step 2) Equivalent Units	
		Direct Materials	Conversion Costs
Work in process, beginning (given)	1,000		
Started during current period	10,150		
To account for	11,150		
Good units completed and transferred out during current period:	9,000	9,000	9,000
Normal spoilage*	100		
100 × 100%; 100 × 100%		100	100
Abnormal spoilage†	50		
50 × 100%; 50 ×100%		50	50
Work in process, ending‡ (given)	2,000		
2,000 × 100%; 2,000 × 30%		2,000	600
Accounted for	11,150		
Equivalent units of work done to date		11,150	9,750

*Degree of completion of normal spoilage in this department: direct materials, 100%; conversion costs, 100%.
†Degree of completion of abnormal spoilage in this department: direct materials, 100%; conversion costs, 100%.
‡Degree of completion in this department: direct materials, 100%; conversion costs, 30%.

Summarize the total costs to account for, compute the cost per equivalent unit, and assign costs to the units completed, spoiled units, and units in ending work-in-process inventory.

		Total Production Costs	Direct Materials	Conversion Costs
(Step 3)	Work in process, beginning (given)	$ 2,533	$ 1,423	$ 1,110
	Costs added in current period (given)	39,930	12,180	27,750
	Total costs to account for	$42,463	$ 13,603	$28,860
(Step 4)	Costs incurred to date		$ 13,603	$28,860
	Divided by equivalent units of work done to date		÷11,150	÷ 9,750
	Cost per equivalent unit		$ 1.22	$ 2.96
(Step 5)	Assignment of costs			
	Good units completed and transferred out (9,000 units)			
	Costs before adding normal spoilage	$37,620	$(9,000 × $1.22) + (9,000 × $2.96)$	
	Normal spoilage (100 units)	418	$(100 × $1.22) + (100 × $2.96)$	
(A)	Total cost of good units completed & transf. out	38,038		
(B)	Abnormal spoilage (50 units)	209	$(50 × $1.22) + (50 × $2.96)$	
(C)	Work in process, ending (2,000 units)	4,216	$(2,000 × $1.22) + (600 × $2.96)$	
(A) + (B) + (C)	Total costs accounted for	$42,463	$13,603 + $28,860	

Try It 18–2

Summarize the flow of physical units, and compute output in equivalent units.

	(Step 1)	(Step 2) Equivalent Units	
Flow of Production	Physical Units	Direct Materials	Conversion Costs
Work in process, beginning (given)	1,000		
Started during current period	10,150		
To account for	11,150		
Good units completed and transferred out during current period: From beginning work in process‖	1,000		
1,000 × (100% −100%); 1,000 × (100% − 50%)		0	500
Started and completed	8,000#		
8,000 × 100%; 8,000 × 100%		8,000	8,000
Normal spoilage*	100		
100 × 100%; 100 × 100%		100	100
Abnormal spoilage†	50		
50 × 100%; 50 × 100%		50	50
Work in process, ending‡	2,000		
2,000 × 100%; 2,000 × 30%		2,000	600
Accounted for	11,150		
Equivalent units of work done in current period		10,150	9,250

‖ Degree of completion in this department: direct materials, 100%; conversion costs, 50%.

9,000 physical units completed and transferred out minus 1,000 physical units completed and transferred out from beginning work-in-process inventory.

* Degree of completion of normal spoilage in this department: direct materials, 100%; conversion costs, 100%.

† Degree of completion of abnormal spoilage in this department: direct materials, 100%; conversion costs, 100%.

‡ Degree of completion in this department: direct materials, 100%; conversion costs, 30%.

Summarize the total costs to account for, compute the cost per equivalent unit, and assign costs to the units completed, spoiled units, and units in ending work-in-process inventory.

		Total Production Costs	Direct Materials	Conversion Costs
(Step 3)	Work in process, beginning (given)	$ 2,533	$ 1,423	$ 1,110
	Costs added in current period (given)	39,930	12,180	27,750
	Total costs to account for	$42,463	$13,603	$28,860
(Step 4)	Costs added in current period		$12,180	$27,750
	Divided by equivalent units of work done in current period		÷10,150	÷9,250
	Cost per equivalent unit		$ 1.20	$ 3
(Step 5)	Assignment of costs:			
	Good units completed and transferred out (9,000 units)			
	Work in process, beginning (1,000 units)	$ 2,533	$1,423 + $1,110	
	Costs added to beg. work in process in current period	1,500	(0 × $1.20) + (500 × $3)	
	Total from beginning inventory before normal spoilage	4,033		
	Started and completed before normal spoilage (8,000 units)	33,600	(8,000 × $1.20) + (8,000 × $3)	
	Normal spoilage (100 units)	420	(100 × $1.20) + (100 × $3)	
(A)	Total costs of good units completed and transferred out	38,053		
(B)	Abnormal spoilage (50 units)	210	(50 × $1.20) + (50 × $3)	
(C)	Work in process, ending (2,000 units)	4,200	(2,000 × $1.20) + (600 × $3)	
(A) + (B) + (C)	Total costs accounted for	$42,463	$13,603 + $28,860	

Try It 18–3

	Inspection at 15%	Inspection at 40%	Inspection at 100%
Work in process, beginning (20%)*	14,000	14,000	14,000
Started during March	120,000	120,000	120,000
To account for	134,000	134,000	134,000
Good units completed and transferred out	113,000[a]	113,000[a]	113,000[a]
Normal spoilage	6,600[b]	7,440[c]	6,780[d]
Abnormal spoilage (10,000 − normal spoilage)	3,400	2,560	3,220
Work in process, ending (70%)*	11,000	11,000	11,000
Accounted for	134,000	134,000	134,000

*Degree of completion for conversion costs of the forging process at the dates of the work-in-process inventories
[a] 14,000 beginning inventory + 120,000 − 10,000 spoiled − 11,000 ending inventory = 113,000
[b] 6% × (113,000 − 14,000 + 11,000) = 6% × 110,000 = 6,600
[c] 6% × (113,000 + 11,000) = 6% × 124,000 = 7,440
[d] 6% × 113,000 = 6,780

Inventory Cost Management Strategies

19

Frank Augstein/AP Images

VW Adjusts Production

Volkswagen (VW), the German auto maker, built its reputation on man-ufacturing reliable cars. As part of an aggressive strategy focused on sustainability, VW marketed many of its diesel-engine cars as "clean." The company experienced year over year sales growth with the popularity and perceived reliability of its products.

In mid-2015, reports began to emerge accusing VW of falsifying the emissions data on its automobiles, questioning how truly "clean" they were. VW itself conceded there were irregularities in the information. By September 2015, VW had agreed to multiple rounds of settlements with dealers that had sold the cars and customers who had purchased what they assumed were environmentally friendly vehicles. VW sales revenues began a steady decline after the story broke.

Beyond lost revenue, VW's once vaunted image took a serious hit. As the crisis unfolded, the company was slow to take responsibility for the problems. It then faced the long and difficult task of restoring its credibility and assuring owners and new-car shoppers that it had fixed the problems. The company established a quality committee, added a brake override system, expanded quality training, and increased testing. It reduced engine types and product features to simplify work and focus on quality. Questions remain in the industry as to whether VW can rebuild its tarnished brand.

The VW example vividly illustrates the importance of quality. This chapter presents two ways in which companies gain a competitive advantage. It first addresses quality as a competitive tool, looking at quality from the financial perspective, the customer perspective, the internal-business-process per-spective, and the learning-and-growth perspective before discussing the evaluation of quality performance. Next it addresses time as a competitive tool and focuses on customer-response time, on-time performance, time drivers, and financial and nonfinancial measures of time.

Sources: D. Shepardson. 2015. Volkswagen will pay $1.21 billion to settle U.S. dealer claims, *Reuters* (http://www.reuters.com/article/us-volkswagen-emissions-idUSKCN1202QS) September 30; R. Hotten. 2015. Volkswagen: The scandal explained, *BBC News* (http://www.bbc.com/news/business-34324772) December 10.

▶ **Learning Objectives**

1. Evaluate relevant data and decide on the economic order quantity (EOQ).

2. Resolve conflicts that can arise from results of EOQ and performance models.

3. Analyze the relevant benefits and costs of JIT alternatives.

4. Differentiate a materials requirements planning (MRP) strategy from an enterprise resource planning (ERP) strategy of supply-chain management.

5. Evaluate and decide upon an appropriate backflush costing method.

▶ **CPA Competencies**

This chapter covers material outlined in **Section 3: Management Accounting** of the CPA Competency Map. Specifically, this chapter addresses *Section 3.3 Cost Management* and knowledge from *Section 5.2.1* around working capital and inventory level management. The Learning Objectives in this chapter have been aligned with the CPA Competency Map to ensure the best coverage possible.

3.1.2 Evaluates the types of informa-tion systems used and the role they play in an organization

3.1.3 Recommends improvements to reporting systems to meet information needs

3.3.1 Evaluates cost classifications and costing methods for management of ongoing operations

3.3.2 Evaluates and applies cost management techniques appropriate for specific costing decisions

3.3.3 Recommends changes identified by applying process improvement methodologies

5.2.1 Evaluates the entity's cash flow and working capital (c)

In this chapter, three supply-chain strategies are presented, compared, and contrasted. Supply-chain management is a strategy. The buyer and suppliers act in partnership, sharing otherwise sensitive and confidential information to reduce partnership costs below what could be achieved separately. There are several alternatives, and the goal is to manage and control the cost of inventory yet ensure a smooth flow of production. Retail and manufacturing companies alike need to manage their cost of goods sold (COGS) as well as revenue as they meet the demand of customers and maximize revenue. Under just-in-time materials requirement planning and backflush costing methods of accounting for inventory, the trade-offs among various costs differ, but the goals remain constant.

Inventory Management

► **LO 1**

Evaluate relevant data and decide on the economic order quantity (EOQ).

Inventory management is the planning, coordinating, and control activities related to the flow of inventory into, through, and from the organization. Costs associated with goods for resale include opportunity costs of which the management accountant is aware but which are not recorded in the financial accounting management information system (MIS). Consider retailers where the cost of goods sold constitutes the largest single cost item. The following breakdown of operations for two major retailers is illustrative:

	Loblaw Companies	Sobeys Inc.
Sales	100.0%	100.0%
Cost of Goods Sold	91.9	95.9
Depreciation and amortization	1.8	1.4
Interest and taxes	2.6	1.1
Net income	3.7%	1.6%

With a high level of perishable inventory and low net income percentage, managers in the grocery retail industry must make accurate decisions regarding the purchasing and managing of goods for sale or incur avoidable costs of spoilage. Dry good inventories also require a cash outflow to suppliers, and the shorter the cash-to-cash cycle, the higher will be the revenue for these retailers.

Costs Associated with Goods for Sale

The descriptions of the cost categories indicate that some of the relevant costs for making inventory decisions and managing goods for sale are not available in existing accounting systems. The following cost categories are important when managing inventories and goods for sale:

- **Purchasing costs** consist of the acquisition costs of goods acquired from suppliers including freight in, the transportation costs. These direct costs usually make up the largest single cost category of goods for sale. Supplier credit terms, discounts for different purchase order sizes, and frequency of ordering affect purchasing costs.

- **Ordering costs** consist of the costs to prepare and issue a purchase order. These support department overhead costs vary with the number of purchase orders processed, special processing, receiving, inspection, and payment costs.

- **Carrying costs** arise when a business holds inventories of goods for sale. These manufacturing overhead costs include the costs associated with storage, such as storage space rental and insurance, obsolescence, and spoilage, which are reported by the financial accounting management information system (MIS). Also relevant for managers are the opportunity costs of the investment tied up in inventory.

- **Stockout costs** occur when a company runs out of an item for which there is customer demand. A company may respond to the shortfall or stockout by expediting an order from a supplier. Expediting costs of a stockout include the additional ordering costs plus any associated transportation costs. Alternatively, the company may lose a sale due to the stockout. In this case, stockout costs include the opportunity cost of the lost contribution margin on the sale plus any contribution margin lost on future sales hurt by customer ill-will caused by the stockout.

■ **Costs of quality (COQ)** often are divided into four categories: (a) prevention costs, (b) appraisal costs, (c) internal failure costs, and (d) external failure costs.

■ **Shrinkage costs** arise from theft, embezzlement, misclassifications, and clerical errors. This cost is measured by the difference between the cost of inventory recorded without theft or other incidents and the cost of inventory physically counted. Shrinkage is often an important performance measure by which management effectiveness is evaluated. In grocery retail the operating margin is very small—approximately 2%. Control of inventory shrinkage is one of a store manager's prime responsibilities. To make up for a loss of $1,000 due to shrinkage, a store would have to earn an additional $50,000 in revenue ($1,000 ÷ 0.02 = $50,000).

Information technology—such as the scheduling, inventory control, and costing system software provided by Seradex and bar code and radio-frequency identification (RFID) on items—increases reliability and timeliness of inventory data. For example, bar-coding technology is a low-cost way to capture purchases and sales of individual units. This creates an instantaneous record of inventory movements and helps in the management of purchasing, carrying, and stockout costs. In the sections that follow, we consider how to calculate relevant costs for different inventory-related decisions.

Economic Order Quantity Procurement Model

For manufacturers, procurement is the placement of a purchase order in enough time to ensure continuous processing. The first major decision in managing goods for sale is deciding how much of a given product to order. The management team can use an **economic order quantity (EOQ)** procurement model to calculate the optimal quantity of inventory to order. The simplest version of this model incorporates only ordering costs and carrying costs into the calculation. Assume the following:

■ The same fixed quantity is ordered at each reorder point.

■ Demand, ordering costs, and carrying costs are certain. The **purchase order lead time**—the time between the placement of an order and its delivery—is also certain.

■ Purchasing costs per unit are unaffected by the quantity ordered. This assumption makes purchasing costs irrelevant to determining EOQ, because purchasing costs of all units acquired will be the same, whatever the order size in which the units are ordered.

■ No stockouts occur. One justification for this assumption is that the costs of a stockout are prohibitively high. We assume that to avoid these potential costs, management always maintains adequate inventory so that no stockout can occur.

■ In deciding the size of the purchase order, management considers the cost of quality and shrinkage only to the extent that these costs affect ordering costs or carrying costs.

Given these assumptions, EOQ analysis ignores purchasing costs, stockout costs, and quality costs. To determine EOQ, we minimize the relevant ordering and carrying costs (those ordering and carrying costs that are affected by the quantity of inventory ordered):

Total relevant costs = Total relevant order costs + Total relevant carrying costs

Example: DVDWorld, a retailer, sells packages of blank DVDs to its customers. It purchases packages of DVDs from Sontek at $14 a package. Sontek pays all incoming freight. No incoming inspection is necessary, as Sontek has a superb reputation for delivering quality merchandise. Annual demand is 13,000 packages, at a rate of 250 packages per week. DVDWorld requires a 15% annual return on investment. The purchase order lead time is 2 weeks. The following cost data are available:

Relevant ordering costs per purchase order		$200.00
Relevant carrying costs per package per year:		
Required annual return on investment, 15% × $14	$2.10	
Relevant insurance, materials handling, breakage, etc., per year	3.10	$ 5.20

Note Carrying costs are higher than you may think. In many companies, average annual carrying costs exceed 30% of purchasing costs. In the DVDWorld example, annual carrying costs are 37% (= $5.20 ÷ $14) of purchasing costs.

What is the EOQ of packages of DVDs? The formula underlying the EOQ model is

Number of purchase orders per period (one year)

$$= \frac{\text{Demand in units for a period (one year)}}{\text{Size of each order (order quantity)}} = \frac{D}{Q}$$

Average inventory in units $= \dfrac{Q}{2}$, because each time the inventory goes down to 0, an order for Q units is received. The inventory varies from Q to 0, so the average inventory is $\dfrac{0 + Q}{2}$.

P = Relevant ordering cost per purchase order

C = Relevant carrying cost of one unit in stock for the time period used for D (one year)

For any order quantity, Q,

$$\text{Annual relevant ordering costs} = \left(\begin{array}{c} \text{Number of} \\ \text{purchase orders} \times \\ \text{per year} \end{array} \begin{array}{c} \text{Relevant ordering} \\ \text{cost per} \\ \text{purchase order} \end{array} \right) = \left(\frac{D}{Q} \times P \right)$$

$$\text{Annual relevant carrying costs} = \left(\begin{array}{c} \text{Average inventory} \\ \text{in units} \end{array} \times \begin{array}{c} \text{Annual} \\ \text{relevant carrying} \\ \text{cost per unit} \end{array} \right) = \left(\frac{Q}{2} \times C \right)$$

$$\text{Annual relevant total costs} = \begin{array}{c} \text{Annual} \\ \text{relevant ordering} \\ \text{costs} \end{array} + \begin{array}{c} \text{Annual} \\ \text{relevant carrying} \\ \text{costs} \end{array} = \left(\frac{D}{Q} \times P \right) + \left(\frac{Q}{2} \times C \right)$$

The order quantity that minimizes annual relevant total costs is

$$\text{EOQ} = \sqrt{\frac{2DP}{C}}$$

The formula indicates that the EOQ increases with demand and ordering costs and decreases with carrying costs. Notice the square root in this equation. Either an exponent or a square root signals that the relationship is nonlinear—it is a curve, as illustrated in Exhibit 19-1. We can use this formula to determine the EOQ for DVDWorld as follows:

$$\text{EOQ} = \sqrt{\frac{2 \times 13{,}000 \times \$200}{\$5.20}} = \sqrt{1{,}000{,}000} = 1{,}000 \text{ packages}$$

Therefore, DVDWorld should order 1,000 DVD packages each time to minimize total ordering and carrying costs. The total annual relevant costs (TRC) for any order quantity Q can be calculated using this formula:

$$\text{TRC} = \begin{array}{c} \text{Total annual relevant} \\ \text{ordering costs} \end{array} + \begin{array}{c} \text{Total annual relevant} \\ \text{carrying costs} \end{array}$$

$$= \begin{array}{c} \text{Number of} \\ \text{purchase orders} \times \\ \text{per year} \end{array} \begin{array}{c} \text{Relevant} \\ \text{ordering costs per} \\ \text{purchase order} \end{array} + \begin{array}{c} \text{Average inventory} \\ \text{in units} \end{array} \times \begin{array}{c} \text{Annual relevant} \\ \text{carrying costs of} \\ \text{1 unit for a year} \end{array}$$

$$= \left(\frac{D}{Q} \right) \times P + \left(\frac{Q}{2} \right) \times C = \frac{DP}{Q} + \frac{QC}{2}$$

(Note that in this formula, Q can be any order quantity, not just the EOQ.) When $Q = 1{,}000$ units,

$$\text{TRC} = \frac{13{,}000 \times \$200}{1{,}000} + \frac{1{,}000 \times \$5.20}{2}$$

$$= \$2{,}600 + \$2{,}600 = \$5{,}200$$

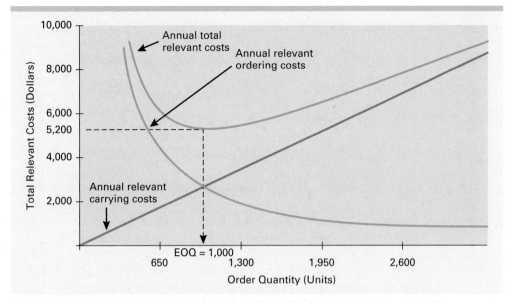

Exhibit 19-1 Ordering Costs and Carrying Costs for DVDWorld

The number of deliveries each time period (in our example, one year) is

$$\frac{D}{\text{EOQ}} = \frac{13,000}{1,000} = 13 \text{ deliveries}$$

Exhibit 19-1 shows a graph analysis of the total annual relevant costs of ordering (DP/Q) and carrying inventory $(QC/2)$. The larger the order quantity, the higher the annual relevant carrying costs, but the lower the annual relevant ordering costs. *The total annual relevant costs are at a minimum where total relevant ordering costs and total relevant carrying costs are equal* (in the DVDWorld example, each equals $2,600).

When to Order, Assuming Certainty

The second major decision in dealing with cost of goods available for sale is when to order. The **reorder point** is the quantity level of the inventory on hand that triggers a new order. The reorder point is simplest to compute when both demand and lead time are certain:

$$\text{Reorder point} = \frac{\text{Number of units sold}}{\text{per unit of time}} \times \text{Purchase order lead time}$$

Consider our DVDWorld example. We choose a week as the unit of time:

Economic order quantity	1,000 packages
Number of units sold per week	250 packages
Purchase order lead time	2 weeks

Thus,

$$\text{Reorder point} = \frac{\text{Number of units sold}}{\text{per unit of time}} \times \text{Purchase order lead time}$$
$$= 250 \times 2 = 500 \text{ packages}$$

DVDWorld will order 1,000 packages of DVDs each time its inventory stock falls to 500 packages. The graph in Exhibit 19-2 presents the behaviour of the inventory level of DVD packages, assuming demand occurs uniformly throughout each week.[1] If the purchase order lead time is 2 weeks, a new order will be placed when the inventory level reaches 500 DVD packages so that the 1,000 packages ordered are received at the time inventory reaches zero.

---

[1] This handy but special formula does not apply when the receipt of the order fails to increase inventory to the reorder-point quantity (for example, when the lead time is 3 weeks and the order is a 1-week supply). In these cases, orders will overlap.

Exhibit 19-2 Inventory Level of DVD Packages for DVDWorld*

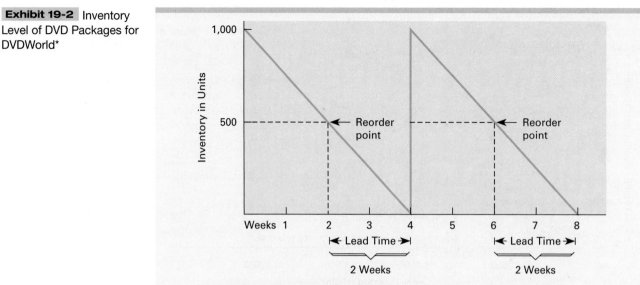

*This exhibit assumes that demand and purchase order lead time are certain:
Demand = 250 DVD packages per week
Purchase order lead time = 2 weeks

TRY IT! 19.1

Spears Canada needs 1,000 ice-cream makers per year. The cost of each ice-cream maker is $80. Ordering cost is $120 per order, and the carrying cost is 40%. What is the economic order quantity?

Safety Stock

When retailers are uncertain about the demand, the lead time, or the quantity that suppliers can provide, they often hold safety stock. **Safety stock** is inventory held at all times regardless of inventory ordered using EOQ. Like a capacity cushion, safety stock is a buffer against unexpected increases in demand or lead time and unavailability of stock from suppliers.

If stockout costs are very high, DVDWorld will hold a safety stock of 300 packages and incur higher carrying costs. The 300 packages equal the maximum excess demand of 150 (= 400 − 250) packages per week multiplied by the 2 weeks of purchase order lead time. If stockout costs are minimal, DVDWorld will hold no safety stocks and avoid incurring the additional carrying costs.

A frequency distribution based on prior daily or weekly levels of demand forms the basis for computing safety-stock levels. Assume that one of the following levels of demand will occur over the 2-week purchase order lead time at DVDWorld.

Total Demand for Two Weeks	Units						
	200	300	400	500	600	700	800
Probability (sums to 1.00)	0.06	0.09	0.20	0.30	0.20	0.09	0.06

The most likely level of demand for the 2-week period is 500 units, because it is assigned the highest probability of occurrence. There is also a 0.35 probability that demand will be between 600, 700, and 800 packages (0.20 + 0.09 + 0.06 = 0.35).

If a customer calls DVDWorld to buy DVDs, and the store has none in stock, it can rush order them to the customer at a cost to DVDWorld of $4 per package. The relevant stockout costs in this case are $4 per package. The optimal safety stock level is the quantity of safety stock that minimizes the sum of the relevant annual stockout and carrying costs. Recall that the relevant carrying costs for DVDWorld are $5.20 per unit per year.

Exhibit 19-3 Computation of Safety Stock for DVDWorld When Reorder Point Is 500 Units

	A	B	C	D	E	F	G	H	I
1	Safety	Demand							
2	Stock	Levels			Relevant	Number of	Expected	Relevant	Relevant
3	Level	Resulting	Stockout	Probability	Stockout	Orders	Stockout	Carrying	Total
4	in Units	in Stockouts	in Units^a	of Stockout	Costs^b	per Year^c	Costs^d	Costs^e	Costs
5	(1)	(2)	(3) = (2) − 500 − (1)	(4)	(5) = (3) × \$4	(6)	(7) = (4) × (5) × (6)	(8) = (1) × \$5.20	(9) = (7) + (8)
6	0	600	100	0.20	\$ 400	13	\$1,040		
7		700	200	0.09	800	13	936		
8		800	300	0.06	1,200	13	936		
9							\$2,912	\$ 0	\$2,912
10	100	700	100	0.09	400	13	\$ 468		
11		800	200	0.06	800	13	624		
12							\$1,092	\$ 520	\$1,612
13	200	800	100	0.06	400	13	\$ 312	\$1,040	\$1,352
14	300	—	—	—	—	—	\$ 0^f	\$1,560	\$1,560
15									
16	^{a}Demand level resulting in stockouts − Inventory available during lead time (excluding safety stock), 500 units − Safety stock.								
17	^{b}Stockout in units × Relevant stockout costs of \$4 per unit.								
18	^{c}Annual demand, 13,000 ÷ 1,000 EOQ = 13 orders per year.								
19	^{d}Probability of stockout × Relevant stockout costs × Number of orders per year.								
20	^{e}Safety stock × Annual relevant carrying costs of \$5.20 per unit (assumes that safety stock is on hand at all times and that there is no overstocking caused by decreases in expected usage).								
21	^{f}At a safety stock level of 300 units, no stockouts will occur and, hence, expected stockout costs = \$0.								

Exhibit 19-3 presents the total annual relevant stockout and carrying costs when the reorder point is 500 units. We need only consider safety stock levels of 0, 100, 200, and 300 units, since demand will exceed the 500 units of stock available at reordering by 0 if demand is 500, by 100 if demand is 600, by 200 if demand is 700, and by 300 if demand is 800. The total annual relevant stockout and carrying costs would be minimized at $1,352 when a safety stock of 200 packages is maintained. DVDWorld's total inventory of DVDs at the time of reordering its EOQ of 1,000 units would be 700 units (the reorder point of 500 units plus the safety stock of 200 units).

Just-in-Time Procurement and EOQ Model Parameters

Just-in-time (JIT) purchasing is a strategy to purchase goods or materials such that a delivery immediately precedes demand or use. JIT is a different inventory management model to minimize the cost of inventories. Ideally, the manufacturer waits for the customer to order and pay for the finished goods, then initiates manufacturing. It is a customer demand-pull strategy rather than a supply-push strategy of production. JIT requires organizations to restructure their relationships with suppliers and place smaller, more frequent purchase orders. JIT can be implemented in both the retail and manufacturing sectors of the economy.

Companies moving toward JIT procurement argue that the cost of carrying inventories (parameter C in the EOQ model) has been dramatically underestimated in the past. This cost includes storage costs, spoilage, obsolescence, and opportunity costs such as investment tied up in inventory. The cost of placing a purchase order (parameter P in the EOQ model) has also been reevaluated. Three factors are causing sizable reductions in P:

■ Companies are increasingly establishing long-run purchasing arrangements in which price and quality dimensions that apply over an extended period are agreed to by both parties. Individual purchase orders occur without any additional negotiation over price or quality in this period.

■ Companies have increased their use of electronic links, such as the internet, to place purchase orders. Electronic commerce (e-commerce) is one of the fastest growing

Exhibit 19-4 Sensitivity of EOQ to Variations in Relevant Ordering and Carrying Costs for DVDWorld

Exhibit 19-4 Sensitivity of EOQ to Variations in Relevant Ordering and Carrying Costs for DVDWorld

	A	B	C	D	E
1	**Relevant Carrying**	**Annual Demand (D) = 13,000 units**			
2	**Costs per Package**	**Relevant Ordering Costs per Purchase Order (P)**			
3	**per Year (C)**	**$200**	**$150**	**$100**	**$30**
4	$ 5.20	EOQ = 1,000	EOQ = 866	EOQ = 707	EOQ = 387
5	7.00	862	746	609	334
6	10.00	721	624	510	279
7	15.00	589	510	416	228

areas of the internet. The cost of placing some orders on the internet is estimated at as much as one one-hundredth the cost of placing orders by telephone or by mail.

■ Companies are increasing the use of purchase cards (similar to consumer credit cards like VISA and MasterCard). Purchasing personnel are given total dollar limits or individual transaction dollar limits. As long as personnel stay within these limits, the traditional labour-intensive procurement approval mechanisms are not required.

Both increases in the carrying cost (C) and decreases in the ordering cost per purchase order (P) result in smaller EOQ amounts. Exhibit 19-4 analyzes the sensitivity of DVDWorld's EOQ to illustrate the economics of smaller and more frequent purchase orders. The analysis presented in Exhibit 19-4 supports JIT procurement—that is, having a smaller EOQ and placing more frequent orders—as relevant carrying costs increase and relevant ordering costs per purchase order decrease.

Lean manufacturing is most financially feasible when availability and prices of inputs are relatively constant and production cycles are well controlled.

Concepts in Action   Overcoming Wireless Data Bottlenecks

The wired world is quickly going wireless. In addition to the smartphone boom, emerging devices including e-book readers, iPads and other tablets, and machine-to-machine appliances (the so-called "internet of things") will add to rapidly growing data traffic. Cisco recently forecast that data traffic will grow at a compound rate of 66% from 885 petabytes per month in 2012 to 11.2 exabytes per month by 2017, a nearly thirteen-fold increase. (An exabyte is equal to 1,024 petabytes, or 1 billion gigabytes.)

This astronomical growth already causes mobile bottlenecks caused by too many users trying to transfer mobile data at the same time in a given area. These bottlenecks are most harmful to companies, such as Amazon.com and eBay, buying and selling products and services over the mobile internet. To relieve mobile bottlenecks, wireless providers and other high-tech companies are deploying more efficient mobile broadband networks, such as 4G LTE, and are working on complementary technologies that automatically choose the best available wireless network to increase capacity. Some technology providers also offer Wi-Fi direct, which allows mobile users to freely transfer video, music, and photos between mobile devices without choking up valuable bandwidth. Companies and government agencies around the world are also trying to increase the wireless broadband spectrum. In the United States, for example, current holders of spectrum—such as radio stations and government agencies—are being encouraged to sell or share their excess capacity to wireless providers in exchange for a share of the profits.

Sources: Cisco Systems, Inc. 2013. "Cisco Visual Networking Index: Global Mobile Data Traffic Forecast Update, 2012–2017" (February 6); C. Edwards. 2010. Wifi Direct Seen as Way to Alleviate Network Congestion, *Bloomberg Businessweek* (January 7); J. Morris. 2010."CTIA: More Spectrum, and Other Ways to Break the Wireless Data Bottleneck, *ZDNet*, "Laptops & Desktops" blog (March 24); G. Pyle. 2010. Wireless Growth Leading to Bottlenecks, *Buffalo News* (May 9); D. Yardon, Federal Agencies Urged to Free Up Airwaves, *The Wall Street Journal* (June 14).

Companies implementing lean production systems manage inventories by eliminating (or at least minimizing) them. The main features in a lean production system are as follows:

- Production is organized in **manufacturing cells**, a grouping of all the different types of equipment used to make a given product. Materials move from one machine to another where various operations are performed in sequence. Materials-handling costs are minimized.

- Workers are hired and trained to be multiskilled and capable of performing a variety of operations and tasks including minor repairs and routine maintenance of equipment. This training adds greatly to the flexibility of the plant.

- Defects are aggressively eliminated through total quality management (TQM). Because of the tight links between stages in the production line, and the minimal inventories at each stage, defects arising at one stage quickly affect other stages in the line. JIT creates an urgency for solving problems immediately and eliminating the root causes of defects as quickly as possible. TQM is an essential component of any JIT production system.

- *Setup time*, which is the time required to get equipment, tools, and materials ready to start the production of a component or product, is reduced. Simultaneously, *manufacturing lead time*—which is the amount of time from when an order is ready to start on the production line (ready to be set up) to when it becomes a finished good— is reduced. Reducing setup time makes production in smaller batches economical, which in turn reduces inventory levels. Reducing manufacturing lead time enables a company to respond more quickly to changes in customer demand.

Challenges in Supply-Chain Cost Management

The level of inventories held by retailers is influenced by demand patterns of their customers and supply relationships with their distributors, manufacturers, suppliers, and so on. The term *supply chain* describes the flow of goods, services, and information from cradle to grave (womb to tomb), regardless of whether those activities occur in the same organization or among other organizations. One point well documented in supply-chain analysis is that there are significant total gains to companies in this supply chain from coordinating their activities and sharing information.

▶ **LO 2**

Resolve conflicts that can arise from results of EOQ and performance models.

Procter & Gamble's (P&G) experience with its Pampers product illustrates the gains from supply-chain coordination. Retailers selling Pampers encounter some variability in weekly demand, despite babies consuming diapers at a relatively steady rate. However, there was pronounced variability in retailers' orders to the manufacturer (P&G), and even more variability in orders by P&G to its own suppliers. Trade promotions worsened the situation because retailers took advantage of lower prices to increase their inventory for future sales. One result was that high levels of inventory were often held at various stages in the supply chain.

P&G responded by sharing information as well as planning and coordinating activities throughout its supply chain. The retailers shared their daily sales information about Pampers with P&G, their distributors, and their suppliers. This updated sales information reduced the level of uncertainty that manufacturers and the manufacturers' suppliers had about retail demand for Pampers.

The reduction in demand uncertainty led to fewer stockouts at the retail level, reduced inventory of unsold Pampers at P&G, reduced expedited manufacturing orders, and lowered inventories being held by each company in the supply chain. The benefits of supply-chain coordination at P&G have been so great that retailers such as Walmart have contracted with P&G to manage Walmart's retail inventories on a JIT basis. This practice is called *supplier- or vendor-managed inventory*. Supply-chain management is, however, not without its challenges.

Estimating Relevant Costs of a Supply Chain

Obtaining accurate estimates of the cost parameters used in the EOQ decision model is a challenging task. For example, the relevant annual carrying costs of inventory consist of *incremental or outlay costs plus the opportunity cost of capital*.

The relevant incremental costs of carrying inventory are those costs that vary with the quantity of inventory held—for example, insurance, property taxes, costs of obsolescence, costs of breakage, shrinkage, warehouse rent, and salaries paid to warehouse workers. Salaries paid to clerks, storekeepers, and materials handlers, however, are irrelevant if they are unaffected by changes in inventory levels.

The relevant opportunity cost of capital is the return forgone by investing capital in inventory rather than elsewhere. It is calculated as the required rate of return multiplied by those costs per unit that vary with the number of units purchased and that are incurred at the time the units are received. Examples of these costs per unit are purchase price, incoming freight, and incoming inspection.

Opportunity costs are not calculated on investments (for example, a building) if these investments are unaffected by changes in inventory levels. In the case of stockouts, calculating the relevant opportunity costs requires an estimate of the lost contribution margin on that sale as well as on future sales hurt by customer ill-will resulting from the stockout. Relevant ordering costs are only those ordering costs that change with the number of orders placed (for example, costs of preparing and issuing purchase orders and receiving and inspecting materials).

Cost of a Prediction Error

Predicting relevant costs is difficult and requires care. Managers understand that their projections will seldom be flawless. This leads to the question: What is the cost of an incorrect prediction when actual relevant costs are different from the relevant predicted costs used for decision making?

Suppose DVDWorld's relevant ordering costs per purchase order are $100 instead of the predicted $200. We can calculate the cost of this prediction error in a logical manner, as follows:

Note This is a benchmark.

■ *Compute the monetary outcome from the best action that could have been taken, given the actual amount of the cost input.* The appropriate inputs are $D = 13,000$ units, $P = \$100$, and $C = \$5.20$. The EOQ size is

$$EOQ = \sqrt{\frac{2DP}{C}}$$
$$= \sqrt{\frac{2 \times 13,000 \times \$100}{\$5.20}} = \sqrt{500,000}$$
$$= 707 \text{ packages (rounded)}$$

The total annual relevant cost when EOQ = 707 is

$$TRC = \frac{DP}{Q} + \frac{QC}{2}$$
$$= \frac{13,000 \times \$100}{707} + \frac{707 \times \$5.20}{2}$$
$$= \$1,839 + \$1,838 = \$3,677$$

■ *Compute the monetary outcome from the best action on the basis of the incorrect amount of the predicted cost input.* The planned action when the relevant ordering costs per purchase order are predicted to be $200 is to purchase 1,000 packages in each order. The total annual relevant costs using this order quantity when $D = 13,000$ units, $P = \$100$, and $C = \$5.20$ are

$$TRC = \frac{13,000 \times \$100}{1000} + \frac{1,000 \times \$5.20}{2}$$
$$= \$1,300 + \$2,600 = \$3,900$$

■ *Compute the difference between the monetary outcomes.*

	Monetary Outcome
Step 1	$3,677
Step 2	3,900
Difference	$ (223)

The cost of the prediction error is only \$223, or just over 6% of the relevant total costs of \$3,677 because the total annual relevant costs curve in Exhibit 19-1 is relatively flat over the range of order quantities from 650 to 1,300. *An important feature of the EOQ model is that the total relevant costs are rarely sensitive to minor variations in cost predictions. The square root in the EOQ model reduces the sensitivity of the decision to errors in predicting its inputs.*

Spears Canada needs 1000 ice-cream makers per year. The cost of each ice-cream maker is \$80. Ordering cost is \$120 per order, the carrying cost is 40%, and the lead time is 8 days. What is the reorder point?

19.2 TRY IT!

Goal-Congruence Issues

Goal-congruence issues can arise when there is an inconsistency between the decision model and the model used to evaluate the performance of the person implementing the decision. For example, the absence of recorded opportunity costs in conventional accounting systems raises the possibility of a conflict between the EOQ model's optimal order quantity and the order quantity that the purchasing manager, evaluated on conventional accounting numbers, regards as optimal.

If annual carrying costs are excluded when evaluating the performance of managers, the managers may favour purchasing a larger order quantity than the EOQ decision model indicates is optimal. Companies such as Coca-Cola and Walmart resolve this conflict by designing the performance evaluation system so that the carrying costs, including a required return on investment, are charged to the appropriate manager.

Relevance and the JIT Strategy of Supply-Chain Management

► **LO 3**

Analyze the relevant benefits and costs of JIT alternatives.

The JIT purchasing model is not guided solely by the EOQ model. As discussed earlier, the EOQ model is designed to emphasize only the trade-off between carrying and ordering costs. Inventory management extends beyond ordering and carrying costs to include purchasing costs, stockout costs, and quality costs. The quality of materials and goods and timely deliveries are important motivations for using JIT purchasing, and stockout costs are an important concern. We add these features as we move from the EOQ decision model to present the JIT purchasing model.

DVDWorld has recently established an internet business-to-business (B2B) purchase-order link with Sontek. DVDWorld initiates a purchase order for DVDs by a single computer entry. Payments are made electronically for batches of deliveries, rather than for each individual delivery. These changes reduce the ordering cost from \$200 to only \$2 per purchase order! DVDWorld will use the internet purchase-order link whether or not it shifts to a JIT strategy. DVDWorld is negotiating to have Sontek deliver 100 packages of DVDs 130 times per year (5 times every 2 weeks), instead of delivering 1,000 packages 13 times per year, as shown in Exhibit 19-3. Sontek is willing to make these frequent deliveries, but it would add \$0.02 to the price per DVD package. DVDWorld's required rate of return on investment remains at 15%. Assume the annual relevant carrying cost of insurance, materials handling, shrinkage, breakage, and the like remains at \$3.10 per package per year.

Suppose that DVDWorld incurs no stockout costs under its current purchasing policy because demand and purchase order lead times over each 4-week period are certain. DVDWorld's major concern is that lower inventory levels from implementing JIT purchasing will lead to more stockouts because demand variations and delays in supplying DVDs are more likely to occur in the short time intervals between supplies under JIT purchasing. Sontek assures DVDWorld that its new manufacturing processes enable it

Exhibit 19-5 Annual Relevant Costs of Current Purchasing Policy and JIT Purchasing Policy for DVDWorld

	A	B	C
1		Relevant Costs Under	
2		Current	JIT
3		Purchasing	Purchasing
4	**Relevant Item**	Policy	Policy
5	Purchasing costs		
6	$14 per unit $\times$ 13,000 units per year	$182,000	
7	$14.02 per unit $\times$ 13,000 units per year		$182,260
8	Ordering costs		
9	$200 per order $\times$ 13 orders per year	2,600	
10	$2 per order $\times$ 130 orders per year		260
11	Opportunity carrying costs, required return on investment		
12	0.15 per year $\times$ $14 cost per unit $\times$ 250[a] units of average inventory per year	525	
13	0.15 per year $\times$ $14.02 cost per unit $\times$ 250[b] units of average inventory per year		526
14	Other carrying costs (insurance, materials handling, breakage, and so on)		
15	$3.10 per unit per year $\times$ 250[a] units of average inventory per year	775	
16	$3.10 per unit per year $\times$ 150[c] units of average inventory per year		465
17	Stockout costs		
18	$4 per unit $\times$ 0 units per year	—	
19	$4 per unit $\times$ 150 units per year	—	600
20	Total annual relevant costs	$185,900	$184,111
21	Annual difference in favour of JIT purchasing	$1,789	
22	[a]Average inventory = 1,000 ÷ 52/13 = 250		
23	[b]Average inventory = 100/week $\times$ 2.5 orders/week = 250		
24	[c]Maximum demand 400/week − average inventory 250/week = 150		

to respond rapidly to changing demand patterns. Consequently, stockouts may not be a serious problem. DVDWorld expects to incur stockout costs on 150 DVD packages each year under a JIT purchasing policy. In the event of a stockout, DVDWorld will have to rush-order DVD packages at a cost of $4 per package. Should DVDWorld implement JIT purchasing?

Exhibit 19-5 compares (1) the incremental costs DVDWorld incurs when it purchases DVDs from Sontek under its current purchasing policy with (2) the incremental costs DVDWorld would incur if Sontek supplied DVDs under a JIT policy. The difference in the two incremental costs is the relevant savings of JIT purchasing. In other methods of comparing the two purchasing policies, the analysis would include only the relevant costs—those costs that differ between the two alternatives. Exhibit 19-5 shows a net cost savings of $1,789 per year from shifting to a JIT purchasing policy.

Companies that implement JIT purchasing choose their suppliers carefully and develop long-term supplier relationships. Some suppliers are better positioned than others to support JIT purchasing. For example, Frito-Lay, a supplier of potato chips and other snack foods, has a corporate strategy that emphasizes service, consistency, freshness, and quality of the delivered products. As a result, the company makes deliveries to retail outlets more frequently than many of its competitors.

What are the relevant total costs when choosing suppliers? Consider again DVDWorld. Denton Corporation, another supplier of DVDs, offers to supply all of DVDWorld's needs at a price of $13.80 per package, less than Sontek's price of $14.02, under the same JIT delivery terms that Sontek offers. Denton proposes an internet purchase-order link identical to Sontek's link, making DVDWorld's ordering cost $2 per purchase order. DVDWorld's relevant cost of insurance, materials handling, breakage, and the like would be $3.00 per package per year if it purchases from Denton, versus $3.10 if it purchases from Sontek. Should DVDWorld buy from Denton? To answer this, we need to consider the relevant costs of quality and delivery performance.

DVDWorld has used Sontek in the past and knows that Sontek will deliver quality disks on time. In fact, DVDWorld does not even inspect the DVD packages that Sontek supplies and therefore incurs zero inspection costs. Denton, however, does not enjoy such a sterling reputation for quality. DVDWorld anticipates the following negative aspects of using Denton:

- Inspection cost of $0.05 per package.
- Average stockouts of 150 and 360 packages per year for Sontek and Denton respectively, requiring rush orders at an additional cost of $4 per package.
- Product returns of 2.5% of all Denton packages sold due to poor disk quality.

DVDWorld estimates an additional cost of $10 to handle each returned package. Exhibit 19-6 shows the relevant total costs of purchasing 13,000 units from Sontek and Denton. Even though Denton is offering a lower price per package, there is a net cost savings of $1,847 per year by purchasing disks from Sontek. Selling Sontek's high-quality

Exhibit 19-6 Annual Relevant Costs of Purchasing from Sontek and Denton

	A	B	C
		Relevant Costs of Purchasing from	
1			
2	**Relevant Item**	**Sontek**	**Denton**
3	Purchasing costs		
4	$14.02 per unit × 13,000 units per year	$182,260	
5	$13.80 per unit × 13,000 units per year		$179,400
6	Ordering costs		
7	$2 per order × 130 orders per year	260	
8	$2 per order × 130 orders per year		260
9	Inspection costs		
10	No inspection necessary	—	
11	$0.05 per unit × 13,000 units per year		650
12	Opportunity carrying costs, required return on investment		
13	0.15 per year × $14.02 × 250[a] units of average inventory per year	526	
14	0.15 per year × $13.80 × 250[a] units of average inventory per year		518
15	Other carrying costs (insurance, materials handling, breakage, etc.)		
16	$3.10 per unit per year × 250[a] units of average inventory per year	775	
17	$3 per unit per year × 250[a] units of average inventory per year		750
18	Stockout costs		
19	$4 per unit × 150 units per year	600	
20	$4 per unit × 360 units per year		1,440
21	Customer returns costs		
22	No customer returns	—	
23	$10 per unit returned × 2.5% units returned × 13,000 units		3,250
24	Total annual relevant costs	$184,421	$186,268
25	Annual difference in favour (disfavour) of Sontek	↑ $1,847 ↑	
26	[a]Average inventory = 100/week × 2.5 orders per week = 250		

disks also enhances DVDWorld's reputation and increases customer goodwill, which could lead to higher sales and profitability in the future.

Performance Measures and Control

To manage and reduce inventories, the management accountant must also design performance measures to evaluate and control JIT production. Examples of information the management accountant may use are as follows:

- Personal observation by production line workers and team leaders.
- Financial performance measures such as the inventory turnover ratio (COGS ÷ average inventory), which is expected to increase.
- Nonfinancial performance measures of time, inventory, and quality, such as manufacturing lead time, units produced per hour, and days inventory is on hand.
- Manufacturing lead time, expected to decrease.
- Units produced per hour, expected to increase.
- Total setup time for machines, expected to decrease total manufacturing time.
- Number of units requiring rework or scrap, expected to decrease total number of units started and completed.

Personal observation and nonfinancial performance measures are the dominant methods of control. These methods are the most timely, intuitive, and easy-to-comprehend measures of plant performance. Rapid, meaningful feedback is critical because the lack of buffer inventories in a demand-pull system creates added urgency to detect and solve problems quickly.

Inventory Management: MRP and ERP

► **LO 4**

Differentiate a materials requirements planning (MRP) strategy from an enterprise resource planning (ERP) strategy of supply-chain management.

We now consider another widely used type of inventory system—**materials requirements planning (MRP)**. A key feature of MRP is its push-through approach, whereas JIT is a demand-pull approach. MRP manufactures finished goods for inventory on the basis of demand forecasts. MRP uses (1) demand forecasts for the final products; (2) a bill of materials outlining the materials, components, and subassemblies for each final product; and (3) the quantities of materials, components, finished products, and product inventories to predetermine the necessary outputs at each stage of production.

Panasonic Corporation of North America is a supply-chain partner with Best Buy. Panasonic used to wait for orders from Best Buy and then initiate the process of filling the order. Now Best Buy collects information on sales of all Panasonic items at its stores' point-of-sale (POS) checkout stations. Best Buy's computers transmit this information to a unit of i2 Technologies Inc. in India. i2 Technologies provides forecasting and other supply-chain analytics to Panasonic. The forecast of demand, modelled on Best Buy's actual sales of Panasonic products, is now transmitted electronically from i2 to Panasonic. i2 Technologies's forecasts are the basis for Panasonic's production schedule. This illustrates how forecast demand pushes production.

Taking into account the lead time required to purchase materials and to manufacture components and finished products, a master production schedule specifies the quantity and timing of each item to be produced. Once scheduled production starts, the output of each department is pushed through the production line whether it is needed or not. The result is often an accumulation of inventory at workstations that receive work they are not yet ready to process.

A major cause of unsuccessful attempts to implement MRP systems has been the problem of collecting and updating inventory records. Calculating the full cost of carrying finished goods inventory motivates other actions. For example, instead of storing product at multiple (and geographically dispersed) warehouses, National Semiconductor contracted with FedEx to airfreight its microchips from a central location in Singapore to customer sites worldwide. The change enabled National to move products from plant to customer in 4 days rather than 45, and to reduce distribution costs from 2.6% to 1.9% of revenues.

These benefits subsequently led National to outsource all its logistics to FedEx, including shipments among its own plants in the United States, Scotland, and Malaysia.[2]

Enterprise Resource Planning (ERP) Systems[3]

For both MRP and JIT supply-chain strategies, the most important resource is effective and efficient communication of relevant information. The speed of information flow from buyers to suppliers is a problem for large companies with fragmented information systems. Systems to program and control manufacturing do not communicate with those tracking inventory, for example. These incompatible systems are spread across the business functions of the value chain.

Enterprise resource planning (ERP) systems improve internal business process flows of information enabling effective inventory cost control. An ERP system is an integrated set of software modules including accounting, distribution, manufacturing, purchasing, human resources, and other functions. An ERP system integrates all the information from a company into a single database that collects data and feeds it into applications supporting all of a company's business activities. All internal software operations receive data in real time, heightening the visibility of the interdependencies and bottlenecks in the entire business process. With an ERP system, companies can choose a supply-chain strategy that demands accurate and timely sharing of information to parties external to the company.

For example, using an ERP system, a salesperson can generate a contract for a customer in Germany, verify the customer's credit limits, and place a production order. The system schedules manufacturing in, say, Brazil, requisitions materials from inventory, orders components from suppliers, and schedules shipment. It also credits sales commissions to the salesperson and records all the costing and financial accounting information.

ERP systems give low-level managers, workers, customers, and suppliers access to operating information. This benefit, coupled with tight coordination across business functions, enables ERP systems to rapidly shift manufacturing and distribution plans in response to changes in supply and demand. Companies believe that an ERP system is essential to support JIT and MRP initiatives because of the effect it has on lead times. Using an ERP system, Autodesk, a maker of computer-aided design software, reduced order lead times from 2 weeks to 1 day; Fujitsu reduced lead times from 18 to 1.5 days.

Although the tight coupling of systems throughout a business streamlines administrative and financial processes and saves costs, it can also make the system large and unwieldy. Because of their complexity, suppliers of ERP systems[4] such as SAP, Baan, Peoplesoft, and Oracle provide software packages that are standard but that can be customized, although at considerable cost. Without some customization, unique and distinctive features that confer strategic advantage will not be available. The challenge when implementing ERP systems is to strike the right balance between systems that are common across all of a company's business and geographical locations and systems that for strategic reasons are designed to be unique.

Backflush Costing

Organizing manufacturing in cells, reducing defects and manufacturing cycle time, and ensuring timely delivery of materials enables purchasing, production, and sales to occur in quick succession with minimal inventories. The absence of inventories makes choices about cost-flow assumptions (such as weighted average or FIFO) or inventory costing methods (such as absorption or variable costing) unimportant: All manufacturing costs of the accounting period flow directly into COGS. The rapid conversion of direct materials into finished goods that are immediately sold greatly simplifies the costing system.

▶ **LO 5**

Evaluate and decide upon an appropriate backflush costing method.

---

[2] C.F. Kemerer (Ed.). (1998). *Information Technology and Industrial Competitiveness: How IT Shapes Competition.* Boston, MA: Kluwer Academic Publishers.

[3] For an excellent discussion, see T.H. Davenport, "Putting the Enterprise into the Enterprise System," *Harvard Business Review*, July–August 1998; also see A. Cagilo, "Enterprise Resource Planning Systems and Accountants: Towards Hybridization?" *European Accounting Review*, May 2003.

[4] Even the smallest business can afford an ERP system. At internet sites like SourceForge (http://sourceforge.net), free ERP and other open-source software can be downloaded.

Simplified Normal or Standard Costing

Traditional and standard costing systems use **sequential tracking** (also called **synchronous tracking**), which is any product costing method in which the accounting system entries occur in the same order as actual purchases and production. The traditional methods of accounting for manufacturing costs using either weighted average or FIFO are IFRS/ASPE-compliant. One accounting report for a specified time period can serve two purposes—external reporting and internal planning and control. But the traditional system is accrual rather than cash-based.

These traditional systems track costs sequentially as products pass from direct materials, to WIP, to finished goods, and finally to sales, as shown here. Some have called this the "just in case" system.

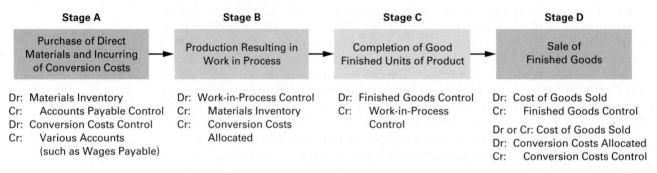

A sequential-tracking costing system has four *trigger points*, corresponding to Stages A, B, C, and D. A **trigger point** is a stage in the cycle, from purchase of direct materials and incurring of conversion costs (Stage A) to sale of finished goods (Stage D), at which journal entries are made in the accounting system. The journal entries (with Dr. representing debits and Cr. representing credits) for each stage are displayed below the box for that stage.

An alternative approach to sequential tracking is backflush costing. **Backflush costing** is a costing system that omits recording some of the journal entries relating to the stages from purchase of direct materials to the sale of finished goods. When journal entries for one or more stages are omitted, the journal entries for a subsequent stage use normal or standard costs to work backward to "flush out" the costs in the cycle for which journal entries were *not* made. When inventories are minimal, as in JIT production systems, backflush costing simplifies costing systems without losing much information.

Consider the following data for the month of April for Silicon Valley Computer (SVC), which produces keyboards for personal computers.

■ There are no beginning inventories of direct materials and no beginning or ending WIP inventories.

■ SVC has only one direct manufacturing cost category (direct materials) and one indirect manufacturing cost category (conversion costs). All manufacturing labour costs are included in conversion costs.

■ From its bill of materials and an operations list (description of operations to be undergone), SVC determines that the standard direct materials cost per keyboard unit is $19 and the standard conversion cost is $12.

■ SVC purchases $1,950,000 of direct materials. To focus on the basic concepts, we assume SVC has no direct materials variances. Actual conversion costs equal $1,260,000. SVC produces 100,000 good keyboard units and sells 99,000 units.

■ Any underallocated or overallocated conversion costs are written off to COGS at the end of April.

We use three examples to illustrate backflush costing. *They differ in the number and placement of trigger points.*

> **Example 1:** The three trigger points for journal entries are purchase of direct materials and incurring of conversion costs (Stage A), completion of good finished units of product (Stage C), and sale of finished goods (Stage D).

Note that there is no journal entry for production resulting in work in process (Stage B) because JIT production has minimal work in process.

SVC records two inventory accounts:

Type	Account Title
Combined materials inventory and materials in work in process	Materials and In-Process Inventory Control
Finished goods	Finished Goods Control

Exhibit 19-7, Panel A, summarizes the journal entries for Example 1 with three trigger points: purchase of direct materials and incurring of conversion costs, completion of good finished units of product, and sale of finished goods (and recognizing under- or overallocated costs). For each stage, the backflush costing entries for SVC are shown on the left. The comparable entries under sequential tracking (costing) are shown on the right.

Consider first the entries for purchase of direct materials and incurring of conversion costs (Stage A). As described earlier, the inventory account under backflush costing combines direct materials and WIP. When materials are purchased, these costs increase (are debited to) Materials and In-Process Inventory Control. Under the sequential tracking approach, the direct materials and Work in Process accounts are separate, so the purchase of direct materials is debited to Materials Inventory Control. Actual conversion costs are recorded as incurred under backflush costing, just as in sequential tracking, and they increase (are debited to) Conversion Costs Control.

Next consider the entries for production resulting in WIP (Stage B). Recall that 100,000 units were started into production in April and that the standard cost for the units produced is $31 (= $19 direct materials + $12 conversion costs) per unit. Under backflush costing, no entry is recorded in Stage B because WIP inventory is minimal and all units are quickly converted to finished goods. Under sequential tracking, WIP inventory is increased as manufacturing occurs and later decreased as manufacturing is completed and the product becomes a finished good.

The entries to record completion of good finished units of product (Stage C) give backflush costing its name. Costs have not been recorded sequentially with the flow of product along its production route through WIP and finished goods. Instead, the output trigger point reaches *back* and pulls (*"flushes"*) the standard direct materials costs from Materials and In-Process Inventory Control and the standard conversion costs for manufacturing the finished goods. Under the sequential tracking approach, Finished Goods Control is debited (increased) and Work-in-Process Control is credited (decreased) as manufacturing is completed and finished goods are produced. The net effect of Stages B and C under sequential tracking is the same as the effect under backflush costing (except for the name of the inventory account).

Finally consider entries to record the sale of finished goods (and under- or overallocated conversion costs) (Stage D). The standard cost of 99,000 units sold in April equals $3,069,000 (= 99,000 units × $31 per unit). The entries to record the cost of finished goods sold are exactly the same under backflush costing and sequential tracking.

Companies that use backflush costing typically have low inventories, so proration of under- or overallocated conversion costs between WIP, finished goods, and COGS is seldom necessary. Many companies write off under- or overallocated conversion costs to COGS only at the end of the fiscal year. Other companies, like SVC, record the write-off monthly. The journal entry to dispose of the difference between actual conversion costs incurred and standard conversion costs allocated is exactly the same under backflush costing and sequential tracking.

The April 30 ending inventory balances under backflush costing are as follows:

Materials and In-Process Inventory Control ($1,950,000 − $1,900,000)	$50,000
Finished Goods Control, 1,000 units × $31/unit ($3,100,000 − $3,069,000)	31,000
Total	$81,000

The April 30 ending inventory balances under sequential tracking would be exactly the same except that the inventory account would be Materials Inventory Control. Exhibit 19-7, Panel B, provides a general-ledger overview of this version of backflush costing.

Exhibit 19-7 Journal Entries and General Ledger Overview for Backflush Costing and Journal Entries for Sequential Tracking with Three Trigger Points: Purchase of Direct Materials and Incurring of Conversion Costs, Completion of Good Finished Units of Product, and Sale of Finished Goods

---

PANEL A: Journal Entries

	Backflush Costing			Sequential Tracking		

Stage A: Record Purchase of Direct Materials and Incurring of Conversion Costs

1. Record Direct Materials Purchased.

| Entry (A1) | Materials and In-Process Inventory Control | 1,950,000 | | Materials Inventory Control | 1,950,000 | |
| | Accounts Payable Control | | 1,950,000 | Accounts Payable Control | | 1,950,000 |

2. Record Conversion Costs Incurred.

Entry (A2)	Conversion Costs Control	1,260,000		Conversion Costs Control	1,260,000	
	Various accounts (such as Wages			Various accounts (such as Wages		
	Payable Control)		1,260,000	Payable Control)		1,260,000

Stage B: Record Production Resulting in Work in Process.

Entry (B1)	No Entry Recorded			Work-in-Process Control	3,100,000	
				Materials Inventory Control		1,900,000
				Conversion Costs Allocated		1,200,000

Stage C: Record Cost of Good Finished Units Completed.

Entry (C1)	Finished Goods Control	3,100,000		Finished Goods Control	3,100,000	
	Materials and In-Process Inventory Control		1,900,000	Work-in-Process Control		3,100,000
	Conversion Costs Allocated		1,200,000			

Stage D: Record Cost of Finished Goods Sold (and Under- or Overallocated Conversion Costs).

1. Record Cost of Finished Goods Sold.

| Entry (D1) | Cost of Goods Sold | 3,069,000 | | Cost of Goods Sold | 3,069,000 | |
| | Finished Goods Control | | 3,069,000 | Finished Goods Control | | 3,069,000 |

2. Record Underallocated or Overallocated Conversion Costs.

Entry (D2)	Conversion Costs Allocated	1,200,000		Conversion Costs Allocated	1,200,000	
	Cost of Goods Sold	60,000		Cost of Goods Sold	60,000	
	Conversion Costs Control		1,260,000	Conversion Costs Control		1,260,000

PANEL B: General Ledger Overview for Backflush Costing

The coding that appears in parentheses for each entry indicates the stage in the production process that the entry relates to as presented in the text.

The elimination of the typical Work-in-Process Control account reduces the amount of detail in the accounting system. Units on the production line may still be tracked in physical terms, but there is "no assignment of costs" to specific work orders while they are in the production cycle. In fact, there are no work orders or labour-time records in the accounting system.

The three trigger points to make journal entries in Example 1 will lead SVC's backflush costing system to report costs that are similar to the costs reported under sequential tracking when SVC has minimal WIP inventory. In Example 1, any inventories of direct materials or finished goods are recognized in SVC's backflush costing system when they first appear (as would be done in a costing system using sequential tracking). International Paper Company uses a method similar to Example 1 in its specialty papers plant.

Accounting for Variances

Accounting for variances between actual and standard costs is basically the same under all standard-costing systems. Suppose that in Example 1, SVC had an unfavourable direct materials price variance of $42,000. Then the journal entry would be as follows:

Materials and In-Process Inventory Control	1,950,000	
Direct Materials Price Variance	42,000	
Accounts Payable Control		1,992,000

Direct materials costs are often a large proportion of total manufacturing costs, sometimes well over 60%. Consequently, many companies will at least measure the direct materials efficiency variance in total by physically comparing what remains in direct materials inventory against what should remain based on the output of finished goods for the accounting period. In our example, suppose that such a comparison showed an unfavourable materials efficiency variance of $30,000. The journal entry would be as follows:

Direct Materials Efficiency Variance	30,000	
Materials and In-Process Inventory Control		30,000

The under- or overallocated conversion costs are split into various overhead variances (spending variance, efficiency variance, and production-volume variance). Each variance is closed to Cost of Goods Sold, if it is immaterial in amount.

Example 2: The two trigger points are purchase of direct materials and incurring of conversion costs (Stage A) and sale of finished goods (Stage D).

This example uses the SVC data to illustrate a backflush costing that differs more from sequential tracking than the backflush costing in Example 1. This example and Example 1 have the same first trigger point, purchase of direct materials and incurring of conversion costs. But the second trigger point in Example 2 is the sale, not the completion, of finished goods. *Note that in this example, there are no journal entries for production resulting in work in progress (Stage B) and completion of good finished units of product (Stage C) because there are minimal WIP and finished goods inventories.*

In this example, there is only one inventory account: direct materials, whether they are in storerooms, in process, or in finished goods.

Type	Account Title
Combines direct materials inventory and any direct materials in work-in-process and finished goods inventories	Inventory Control

Exhibit 19-8, Panel A, summarizes the journal entries for Example 2 with two trigger points: purchase of direct materials and incurring of conversion costs, and sale of finished goods (and recognizing under- or overallocated costs). As in Example 1, for each stage, the backflush costing entries for SVC are shown on the left. The comparable entries under sequential tracking are shown on the right.

The entries for direct materials purchased and conversion costs incurred (Stage A) are the same as in Example 1, except that the inventory account is called Inventory Control. As in Example 1, no entry is made to record production of WIP inventory (Stage B)

Exhibit 19-8 Journal Entries and General Ledger Overview for Backflush Costing and Journal Entries for Sequential Tracking with Two Trigger Points: Purchase of Direct Materials and Incurring of Conversion Costs and Sale of Finished Goods

---

PANEL A: Journal Entries

	Backflush Costing			Sequential Tracking	

Stage A: Record Purchase of Direct Materials and Incurring of Conversion Costs

1. Record Direct Materials Purchased.

Entry (A1)	Inventory: Control	1,950,000		Materials Inventory Control	1,950,000	
	Accounts Payable Control		1,950,000	Accounts Payable Control		1,950,000

2. Record Conversion Costs Incurred.

Entry (A2)	Conversion Costs Control	1,260,000		Conversion Costs Control	1,260,000	
	Various accounts (such as Wages			Various accounts (such as Wages		
	Payable Control)		1,260,000	Payable Control)		1,260,000

Stage B: Record Production Resulting in Work in Process.

Entry (B1)	No Entry Recorded			Work-in-Process Control	3,100,000	
				Materials Inventory Control		1,900,000
				Conversion Costs Allocated		1,200,000

Stage C: Record Cost of Good Finished Units Completed.

Entry (C1)	No Entry Recorded			Finished Goods Control	3,100,000	
				Work-in-Process Control		3,100,000

Stage D: Record Cost of Finished Goods Sold (and Under- or Overallocated Conversion Costs).

1. Record Cost of Finished Goods Sold.

Entry (D1)	Cost of Goods Sold	3,069,000		Cost of Goods Sold	3,069,000	
	Inventory Control		1,881,000	Finished Goods Control		3,069,000
	Conversion Costs Allocated		1,188,000			

2. Record Underallocated or Overallocated Conversion Costs.

Entry (D2)	Conversion Costs Allocated	1,188,000		Conversion Costs Allocated	1,200,000	
	Cost of Goods Sold	72,000		Cost of Goods Sold	60,000	
	Conversion Costs Control		1,260,000	Conversion Costs Control		1,260,000

PANEL B: General Ledger Overview for Backflush Costing

The coding that appears in parentheses for each entry indicates the stage in the production process that the entry relates to as presented in the text.

because WIP inventory is minimal. When finished goods are completed (Stage C), no entry is recorded because the completed units are expected to be sold quickly and finished goods inventory is expected to be minimal. As finished goods are sold (Stage D), the COGS is calculated as 99,000 units sold × $31 per unit = $3,069,000, which is composed of direct material costs (99,000 units × $19 per unit = $1,881,000) and conversion costs allocated (99,000 units × $12 per unit = $1,188,000). This is the same COGS calculated under sequential tracking as described in Example 1.

Under this method of backflush costing, conversion costs are not inventoried because no entries are recorded when finished goods are produced in Stage C. That is, compared with sequential tracking, Example 2 does not assign $12,000 (= $12 per unit × 1,000 units) of conversion costs to finished goods inventory produced but not sold. Of the $1,260,000 in conversion costs, $1,188,000 is allocated at standard cost to the units sold. The remaining $72,000 (= $1,260,000 − $1,188,000) of conversion costs is underallocated. Entry (D2) presents the journal entry if SVC, like many companies, writes off these under-allocated costs monthly as additions to COGS.

The April 30 ending balance of Inventory Control is $69,000 (= 1,950,000 − $1,881,000). This balance represents the $50,000 direct materials still on hand plus $19,000 direct materials embodied in the 1,000 good finished units manufactured but not sold during the period. Exhibit 19-8, Panel B, provides a general-ledger overview of Example 2. The approach described in Example 2 closely approximates the costs computed using sequential tracking when a company holds minimal WIP and finished goods inventories.

Toyota's cost accounting system at its Woodstock plant is similar to this example. Two advantages of this system are (1) it removes the incentive for managers to produce for inventory because conversion costs are recorded as period costs instead of inventoriable costs and (2) it focuses managers on sales.

Example 3: The two trigger points are completion of good finished units of product (Stage C) and sale of finished goods (Stage D).

This example has two trigger points. In contrast to Example 2, the first trigger point in Example 3 is delayed until Stage C, SVC's completion of good finished units of product. *Note that in this example, there are no journal entries for purchase of direct materials and incurring of conversion costs (Stage A) and production resulting in WIP (Stage B) because there are minimal direct materials and WIP inventories.*

Exhibit 19-9, Panel A, summarizes the journal entries for Example 3 with two trigger points: completion of good finished units of product and sale of finished goods (and recognizing under- or overallocated costs). As in Examples 1 and 2, for each stage, the backflush costing entries for SVC are shown on the left. The comparable entries under sequential tracking are shown on the right.

No entry is made for direct materials purchases of $1,950,000 (Stage A) because the acquisition of direct materials is not a trigger point in this form of backflush costing. As in Examples 1 and 2, actual conversion costs are recorded as incurred and no entry is made to record production resulting in WIP inventory (Stage B). The cost of 100,000 good finished units completed (Stage C) is recorded at standard cost of $31 (= $19 direct materials + $12 conversion costs) per unit as in Example 1 except that Accounts Payable Control is credited (instead of Materials and In-Process Inventory Control) because no entry had been made when direct materials were purchased in Stage A. Note that at the end of April, $50,000 of direct materials purchased have not yet been placed into production ($1,950,000 − $1,900,000 = $50,000), nor has the cost of those direct materials been entered into the inventory-costing system. The Example 3 version of backflush costing is suitable for a JIT production system in which both direct materials inventory and WIP inventory are minimal. As finished goods are sold (Stage D), the COGS is calculated as 99,000 units sold × $31 per unit = $3,069,000. This is the same COGS calculated under sequential tracking. Finished Goods Control has a balance of $31,000 under both this form of backflush costing and sequential tracking. The journal entry to dispose of the difference between actual conversion costs incurred and standard conversion costs allocated is the same under backflush costing and sequential tracking. The only difference between this form of backflush costing and sequential tracking is that direct materials inventory

Exhibit 19-9 Journal Entries and General Ledger Overview for Backflush Costing and Journal Entries for Sequential Tracking with Two Trigger Points: Completion of Good Finished Units of Product and Sale of Finished Goods

---

PANEL A: Journal Entries

	Backflush Costing			Sequential Tracking	

Stage A: Record Purchase of Direct Materials and Incurring of Conversion Costs.

1. Record Direct Materials Purchased.

Entry (A1)	No Entry Recorded		Materials Inventory Control	1,950,000	
			Accounts Payable Control		1,950,000

2. Record Conversion Costs Incurred.

Entry (A2)	Conversion Costs Control	1,260,000	Conversion Costs Control	1,260,000	
	Various accounts (such as Wages		Various accounts (such as Wages		
	Payable Control)	1,260,000	Payable Control)		1,260,000

Stage B: Record Production Resulting in Work in Process.

Entry (B1)	No Entry Recorded		Work-in-Process Control	3,100,000	
			Materials Inventory Control		1,900,000
			Conversion Costs Allocated		1,200,000

Stage C: Record Cost of Good Finished Units Completed.

Entry (C1)	Finished Goods Control	3,100,000	Finished Goods Control	3,100,000	
	Accounts Payable Control	1,900,000	Work-in-Process Control		3,100,000
	Conversion Costs Allocated	1,200,000			

Stage D: Record Cost of Finished Goods Sold (and Under- or Overallocated Conversion Costs).

1. Record Cost of Finished Goods Sold.

Entry (D1)	Cost of Goods Sold	3,069,000	Cost of Goods Sold	3,069,000	
	Finished Goods Control	3,069,000	Finished Goods Control		3,069,000

2. Record Underallocated or Overallocated Conversion Costs.

Entry (D2)	Conversion Costs Allocated	1,200,000	Conversion Costs Allocated	1,200,000	
	Cost of Goods Sold	60,000	Cost of Goods Sold	60,000	
	Conversion Costs Control	1,260,000	Conversion Costs Control		1,260,000

PANEL B: General Ledger Overview for Backflush Costing

The coding that appears in parentheses for each entry indicates the stage in the production process that the entry relates to as presented in the text.

of $50,000 (and the corresponding Accounts Payable Control) is not recorded, which is no problem if direct materials inventories are minimal. Exhibit 19-9, Panel B, provides a general-ledger overview of Example 3.

Special Considerations in Backflush Costing

The accounting illustrated in Examples 1, 2, and 3 above does not strictly adhere to the IFRS/ASPE of external reporting. For example, WIP (an asset) exists but is not recognized in the accounting system. Advocates of backflush costing, however, cite the materiality concept in support of these versions of backflushing. They claim that if inventories are low or their total costs are not subject to significant change from one accounting period to the next, operating income and inventory costs developed in a backflush costing system will not differ materially from the results generated by a system that adheres to generally accepted accounting principles.

Suppose material differences in operating income and inventories do exist between the results of a backflush costing system and those of a conventional standard costing system. An adjustment can be recorded to make the backflush numbers satisfy external reporting requirements. For example, the backflush entries in Example 2 would result in expensing all conversion costs as a part of COGS ($1,188,000 at standard costs + $72,000 write-off of underallocated conversion costs = $1,260,000). But suppose conversion costs were regarded as sufficiently material in amount to be included in Inventory Control. Then entry (e), closing the Conversion Costs accounts, would change as shown:

Original entry (e)	Conversion Costs Allocated	1,188,000	
	Cost of Goods Sold	72,000	
	Conversion Costs Control		1,260,000
Revised entry (e)	Conversion Costs Allocated	1,188,000	
	Inventory Control (1,000 units $\times$ $12)	12,000	
	Cost of Goods Sold	60,000	
	Conversion Costs Control		1,260,000

Criticisms of backflush costing focus mainly on the absence of audit trails—the ability of the accounting system to pinpoint the uses of resources at each step of the production process. The absence of large amounts of materials and WIP inventory means that managers can keep track of operations by personal observations, computer monitoring, and nonfinancial measures.

Sustainability in Action   Inventory Management as Strategy

Inventory management is an important part of business, as its many different factors can have a significant impact on a company's bottom line. What inventory valuation method is chosen or who a company's suppliers are can have a big impact on the value of inventory and the company's net income.

IBM is one of the biggest and best known technology firms in the world. Today, it sells mainframe computers and consulting services to clients, and its supply chain encompasses thousands of suppliers all over the world. Traditionally, IBM's supply chain was very linear, starting with parts on one end of the supply

chain and ending with finished goods on the other end. This was inefficient and so IBM decided to integrate its supply chain within every part of the company. This allows better communication between different parts of the company and leads to less inventory and returns. By reducing the need to store large amounts of inventory through an integrated supply chain, IBM is able to cut costs, reduce waste, and save money.

Source: M. Shacklett, "IBM evolves a globally integrated supply chain," *World Trade*, WT 100, 25(5), 32–35 (http://search.proquest.com/docview/1018147932?accountid=13908).

What are the implications of JIT and backflush costing systems for ABC systems? Simplifying the production process, as in a JIT system, makes more of the costs direct and so reduces the extent of overhead cost allocations. Simplified ABC systems are often adequate for companies implementing JIT. But even these simpler ABC systems can enhance backflush costing. Costs from ABC systems give relatively more accurate budgeted conversion costs per unit for different products, which are then used in the backflush costing system. The activity-based cost data are also useful for product costing, decision making, and cost management.

Lean Accounting

Another approach for simplified product costing in JIT (or lean production) systems is *lean accounting*. Successful JIT production requires companies to focus on the entire value chain of business functions (from suppliers to manufacturing to customers) in order to reduce inventories, lead times, and waste. The emphasis on improvements throughout the value chain has led some JIT companies to develop organization structures and costing systems that focus on **value streams**, which are all the value-added activities needed to design, manufacture, and deliver a given product or product line to customers. For example, a value stream can include the activities needed to develop and engineer products, advertise and market those products, process orders, purchase and receive materials, manufacture and ship orders, bill customers, and collect payments. The focus on value streams is aided by the use of manufacturing cells in JIT systems that group together the operations needed to make a given product or product line.

Lean accounting is a costing method that supports creating value for customers by costing the value streams, as distinguished from individual products or departments, thereby eliminating waste in the accounting process.[5] If multiple, related products are made in a single value stream, product costs for the individual products are not computed. Actual costs are directly traced to the value stream and standard costs and variances are not computed. Tracing direct costs to value streams is simple because companies using lean accounting dedicate resources to individual value streams.

Consider the following product costs for Allston Company, which makes two models of refrigerators in one manufacturing cell and two models of ovens in another manufacturing cell.

	Refrigerator		Ovens	
	Model A	**Model B**	**Model C**	**Model D**
Revenues	$600,000	$700,000	$800,000	$550,000
Direct materials	340,000	400,000	410,000	270,000
Direct manufacturing labour	70,000	78,000	105,000	82,000
Manufacturing overhead costs (e.g., equipment lease, supervision, and unused facility costs)	112,000	130,000	128,000	103,000
Rework costs	15,000	17,000	14,000	10,000
Design costs	20,000	21,000	24,000	18,000
Marketing and sales costs	30,000	33,000	40,000	28,000
Total costs	587,000	679,000	721,000	511,000
Operating income	$ 13,000	$ 21,000	$ 79,000	$ 39,000
Direct materials purchased	$350,000	$420,000	$430,000	$285,000
Unused facility costs	$ 22,000	$ 38,000	$ 18,000	$ 15,000

---

[5] See B. Baggaley, "Costing by Value Stream," *Journal of Cost Management* (May–June 2003).

Using lean accounting principles, Allston calculates value-stream operating costs and operating income for refrigerators and ovens, not individual models, as follows:

	Refrigerators	Ovens
Revenues		
($600,000 + $700,000; $800,000 + $550,000)	$1,300,000	$1,350,000
Direct material purchases		
($350,000 + $420,000; $430,000 + $285,000)	770,000	715,000
Direct manufacturing labour		
(70,000 + $78,000; $105,000 + $82,000)	148,000	187,000
Manufacturing overhead (after deducting unused facility costs)		
($112,000 − $22,000) + ($130,000 − $38,000);		
($128,000 − $18,000) + $103,000 − $15,000)	182,000	198,000
Design costs		
($20,000 + $21,000; $24,000 + $18,000)	41,000	42,000
Marketing and sales costs		
($30,000 + $33,000; $40,000 + $28,000)	63,000	68,000
Total value stream operating costs	1,204,000	1,210,000
Value stream operating income	$ 96,000	$ 140,000

Allston Company, like many lean accounting systems, expenses the costs of all purchased materials in the period in which they are bought to signal that direct materials and WIP inventory need to be reduced. In our example, the cost of direct material purchases under lean accounting exceeds the cost of direct materials used in the operating income statement.

Facility costs (such as depreciation, property taxes, and leases) are allocated to value streams based on the square footage used by each value stream to encourage managers to use less space for holding and moving inventory. Note that unused facility costs are subtracted when calculating manufacturing overhead costs of value streams. These costs are instead treated as plant or business unit expenses. Excluding unused facility costs from value stream costs means that only those costs that add value are included in value-stream costs.

Moreover, increasing the visibility of unused capacity costs creates incentives to reduce these costs or to find alternative uses for capacity. Allston Company excludes rework costs when calculating value-stream costs and operating income because these costs are non-value-added costs. Companies also exclude from value stream costs common costs such as corporate or support department costs that cannot reasonably be assigned to value streams.

The analysis indicates that while total cost for refrigerators is $1,266,000 (= $587,000 + $679,000), the value stream cost using lean accounting is $1,204,000 (= 95.1% of $1,266,000), indicating significant opportunities for improving profitability by reducing unused facility and rework costs, and by purchasing direct materials only as needed for production. Ovens portray a different picture. Total cost for ovens is $1,232,000 (= $721,000 + $511,000), while the value-stream cost using lean accounting is $1,210,000 (= 98.2% of $1,232,000). The ovens value stream has low unused facility and rework costs and is more efficient.

Lean accounting is much simpler than traditional product costing. Why? Because calculating actual product costs by value streams requires less overhead allocation. Compared to traditional product costing methods, the focus on value streams and costs is consistent with the emphasis of JIT and lean production on improvements in the value chain from suppliers to customers. Moreover, the practices that lean accounting encourages (such as reducing direct material and WIP inventories, improving quality, using less space, and eliminating unused capacity) reflect the goals of JIT production.

A potential limitation of lean accounting is that it does not compute costs for individual products. Critics charge that this limits its usefulness for decision making. Proponents of lean accounting argue that the lack of individual product costs is not a problem because most decisions are made at the product line level rather than the individual product level, and that pricing decisions are based on the value created for the customer (market prices) and not product costs.

Another criticism is that lean accounting excludes certain support costs and unused capacity costs. As a result, the decisions based on only value stream costs will look profitable because they do not consider all costs. Supporters argue that lean accounting overcomes this problem by adding a larger markup on value stream costs to compensate for some of these excluded costs. Moreover, in a competitive market, prices will eventually settle at a level that represents a reasonable markup above value stream costs because customers will be unwilling to pay for non-value-added costs. The goal must therefore be to eliminate non-value-added costs. A final criticism is that lean accounting, like backflush costing, does not correctly account for inventories under generally accepted accounting principles (IFRS/ASPE). However, proponents are quick to point out that in lean accounting environments, WIP and finished goods inventories are immaterial from an accounting perspective.

Pulling it all Together—Problem for Self-Study

(Try to solve this problem before examining the solution that follows.)

Problem 1

Lee Company has a Singapore plant that manufactures MP3 players. One component is an XT chip. Expected demand is for 5,200 of these chips in March 2018. Lee estimates the ordering cost per purchase order to be $250. The monthly carrying cost for one unit of XT in stock is $5.

Required ▶

❶ 1. Compute the EOQ for the XT chip.
❶ 2. Compute the number of deliveries of XT in March 2018.
❷ 3. What are some conflicts that can arise from the use of an EOQ model?
❸ 4. Identify relevant costs and benefits of a JIT strategy.
❹ 5. What is the key difference between MRP and JIT supply-chain management strategies?
❺ 6. What resource is essential to successful implementation of either MRP or JIT strategies?

Solution

1.
$$EOQ = \sqrt{\frac{2 \times 5,200 \times \$250}{\$5}}$$
$$= 721 \text{ chips (rounded)}$$

2. Number of deliveries = $5,200 \div 721 = 8$ (rounded up)
3. The EOQ model focuses on the trade-off between carrying and ordering costs but ignores purchasing, stockout, and quality costs. A performance measure for the purchasing manager could be a purely financial accounting measure that excludes the opportunity cost of misstating the EOQ. The EOQ optimal solution and the optimal performance threshold will not match because opportunity cost is included in considering the best EOQ. A similar problem arises if annual carrying costs of excess inventory are excluded from the performance measure for purchasing managers.
4. Relevant costs include purchasing, ordering, carrying, stockout, and opportunity costs. Financial accounting standards determine the methods of accounting for all but opportunity costs for purposes of external reporting. COGS and inventory valuation methods are standardized. For internal purposes, however, trade-offs are required between incurring one type versus another of opportunity costs. Management accountants have the expertise required to provide this relevant information.
5. A JIT supply-chain management strategy is based on demand-pull. The demand, an order for goods, initiates the system to supply goods. An MRP supply-chain management strategy is based on demand-push, wherein a forecast of demand is sent directly to the supplier rather than an order. The demand forecast initiates the system to supply goods.

6. Both the JIT and MRP supply-chain strategies require effective information sharing. Often the information stored by one business function software in a company cannot be readily transmitted to another, which incurs delay. An ERP information system collects information from different computer systems into a single database and removes delay.

Problem 2

Littlefield Company uses a backflush costing system with three trigger points:
- Purchase of direct materials
- Completion of good finished units of product
- Sale of finished goods

There are no beginning inventories. Information for April 2018 is

Direct materials purchased	$ 880,000
Direct materials used	850,000
Conversion costs incurred	422,000
Conversion costs allocated	400,000
Costs transferred to finished goods	1,250,000
Cost of goods sold	1,190,000

◀ **Required**

1. Prepare journal entries for April (without disposing of under- or overallocated conversion costs). Assume there are no direct materials variances.
2. Under an ideal JIT production system, how would the amounts in your journal entries differ from the journal entries in requirement 1?

Solution

1. Journal entries for April are:

Entry (a)	Inventory: Materials and In-Process Control	880,000	
	Accounts Payable Control		880,000
	(direct materials purchased)		
Entry (b)	Conversion Costs Control	422,000	
	Various accounts (such as Wages Payable Control)		$ 422,000
	(conversion costs incurred)		
Entry (c)	Finished Goods Control	1,250,000	
	Inventory: Materials and In-Process Control		850,000
	Conversion Costs Allocated		400,000
	(standard cost of finished goods completed)		
Entry (d)	Cost of Goods Sold	1,190,000	
	Finished Goods Control		1,190,000
	(standard costs of finished goods sold)		

2. Under an ideal JIT production system, if the manufacturing lead time per unit is very short, there could be zero inventories at the end of each day. Entry (c) would be $1,190,000 finished goods production (to match finished goods sold in entry (d)), not $1,250,000. If the marketing department could only sell goods costing $1,190,000, the JIT production system would call for direct materials purchases and conversion costs of lower than $880,000 and $422,000, respectively, in entries (a) and (b).

Decision Points

The following question-and-answer format summarizes the chapter's learning objectives. Each point presents a key question, and the guidelines are the answer to that question.

Learning Objectives	Guidelines
1. How do managers use the EOQ model?	The EOQ decision model calculates the optimal quantity of inventory to order by balancing ordering and carrying costs. The larger the order quantity, the higher the annual carrying costs and the lower the annual ordering costs. The EOQ model includes both costs recorded in the financial accounting system and opportunity costs not recorded in the financial accounting system.
2. How can companies reduce the conflict between the EOQ decision model and the models used for performance evaluation?	The opportunity cost of investment tied up in inventory is a key input in the EOQ decision model. Some companies include opportunity costs when evaluating managers so that the EOQ decision model is consistent with the performance evaluation model.
3. What are the features of a JIT strategy of supply-chain management?	A JIT strategy is based on demand-pull. Five features of a JIT production system are (a) organizing production in manufacturing cells, (b) hiring and training multiskilled workers, (c) emphasizing total quality management, (d) reducing manufacturing lead time and setup time, and (e) building strong supplier relationships.
4. How do MRP systems differ from ERP systems?	MRP systems use a "push-through" approach that manufactures finished goods for inventory on the basis of demand forecasts. ERP systems are information management systems that consolidate data from different computer systems into a single database.
5. How does backflush costing simplify job costing?	Backflush costing delays recording some of the journal entries relating to the cycle from purchase of direct materials to the sale of finished goods. Traditional job-costing systems use sequential tracking, in which recording of the journal entries occurs in the same order as actual purchases and progress in production. Most backflush costing systems do not record journal entries for the work-in-process stage of production. Some backflush costing systems also do not record entries for either the purchase of direct materials or the completion of finished goods.

Terms to Learn

This chapter and the Glossary at the end of the book contain definitions of the following important terms:

backflush costing **(p. 786)**
carrying costs **(p. 772)**
costs of quality (COQ) **(p. 773)**
economic order quantity (EOQ) **(p. 773)**
enterprise resource planning (ERP)
  (p. 785)
inventory management **(p. 772)**
just-in-time (JIT) purchasing **(p. 777)**

lean accounting **(p. 794)**
manufacturing cells **(p. 779)**
materials requirements planning
  (MRP) **(p. 784)**
ordering costs **(p. 772)**
purchase order lead time **(p. 773)**
purchasing costs **(p. 772)**
reorder point **(p. 775)**

safety stock **(p. 776)**
sequential tracking **(p. 786)**
shrinkage costs **(p. 773)**
stockout costs **(p. 772)**
synchronous tracking **(p. 786)**
trigger point **(p. 786)**
value streams **(p. 794)**

Assignment Material

MyLab Accounting Make the grade with MyLab Accounting: The Short-Answer Questions, Exercises, and Problems marked with a 🌐 can be found on MyLab Accounting. You can practise them as often as you want, and most feature step-by-step guided instructions to help you find the right answer.

Short-Answer Questions

🌐 **19-1** Why do better decisions regarding the purchasing and managing of goods for sale frequently cause dramatic percentage increases in net income?

🌐 **19-2** Name five cost categories that are important in managing goods for sale in a retail organization.

🌐 **19-3** What five assumptions are made when using the simplest version of the EOQ decision model?

🌐 **19-4** Give examples of costs included in annual carrying costs of inventory when using the EOQ decision model.

🌐 **19-5** Give three examples of opportunity costs that typically are not recorded in accounting systems, although they are relevant to the EOQ model.

🌐 **19-6** What are the steps in computing the cost of a prediction error when using the EOQ decision model?

🌐 **19-7** Why might goal-congruence issues arise when an EOQ model is used to guide decisions on how much to order?

🌐 **19-8** Describe JIT purchasing and its benefits.

🌐 **19-9** What are three factors causing reductions in the cost to place purchase orders of materials?

🌐 **19-10** What is supply-chain analysis, and how can it benefit manufacturers and retailers?

🌐 **19-11** What are some obstacles to companies adopting a supply-chain approach?

🌐 **19-12** What are the main features in a JIT production system?

🌐 **19-13** Distinguish job-costing systems using sequential tracking from backflush costing.

🌐 **19-14** Describe three different versions of backflush costing.

Exercises

🌐 **19-15 Terminology.** A number of terms are listed below:

backflush costing	carrying costs
economic order quantity	enterprise resource planning (ERP)
inventory management	just-in-time (JIT) production
just-in-time (JIT) purchasing	lean production
ordering costs	purchasing costs
reorder point	shrinkage costs
stockout costs	synchronous tracking
trigger points	safety stock

Required

Select the terms from the above list to complete the following sentences.

Supply-chain strategy decisions determine _____ activities. Managing inventory involves the identification of three relevant costs: _____, _____, and _____. One strategy of _____ will match to a production decision of _____ or _____ production. This JIT purchasing strategy will minimize _____ of inventory and reduce or eliminate both _____ and _____ but may increase _____. The goal of the management team is to minimize the overall combination of costs associated with inventory management. Any inventory management model requires careful analysis to identify the _____, the _____, and the _____. The management team requires high-quality information in a database of the type found in _____ systems. These systems are demand-pull systems. Implementing a good demand-pull system requires a highly coordinated information flow that supports lean production. Lean production (JIT) can eliminate inventory and therefore _____ is appropriate.

With no WIP or materials inventories, the need for sequential or _____ of costs of production through the inventories is no longer necessary. Instead _____ are identified such as materials purchase and completion of quality finished goods. Costs transfer at only these two trigger points from the Direct Materials to the Finished Goods inventory.

LO 1 ▶

1. EOQ ≈ 1000 jerseys

19-16 EOQ for retailer. Fan Base (FB) operates a megastore featuring sports merchandise. It uses an EOQ decision model to make inventory decisions. It is now considering inventory decisions for its soccer jerseys product line. This is a highly popular item. Data for 2018 are

Expected annual demand for soccer jerseys	20,000
Ordering cost per purchase order	$200
Carrying cost per year	$ 8 per jersey

Each jersey costs FB $40 and sells for $80. The $8 carrying cost per jersey per year comprises the required return on investment of $4.80 (= 12% of $40 purchase price) plus $3.20 in relevant insurance, handling, and theft-related costs. The purchasing lead time is 7 days. FB is open 365 days a year.

Required

1. Calculate the EOQ.
2. Calculate the number of orders that will be placed each year.
3. Calculate the reorder point.

LO 1 ▶

1. EOQ ≈ 388 jerseys

19-17 EOQ, effect of parameter changes (continuation of Exercise 19-16). Athletic Textiles (AT) manufactures the soccer jerseys that Fan Base (FB) sells to its customers. AT has recently installed computer software that enables its customers to conduct "one-stop" purchasing using state-of-the-art website technology. FB's ordering cost per purchase order will be $30 using this new technology.

Required

1. Calculate the EOQ for the soccer jerseys using the revised ordering cost of $30 per purchase order. Assume all other data from Exercise 19-16 are the same. Comment on the result.
2. Suppose AT proposes to "assist" FB. AT will allow FB customers to order directly from the AT website. AT would ship directly to these customers. AT would pay $10 to FB for every soccer jersey purchased by one of FB's customers. Comment qualitatively on how this offer would affect inventory management at FB. What factors should FB consider in deciding whether to accept AT's proposal?

LO 1 ▶

1. EOQ ≈ 1,789 metres

19-18 EOQ for a retailer. The Cloth Centre sells fabrics to a wide range of industrial and consumer users. One of the products it carries is denim cloth, used in the manufacture of jeans and carrying bags. The supplier for the denim cloth pays all incoming freight. No incoming inspection of the denim is necessary because the supplier has a track record of delivering high-quality merchandise. The purchasing officer of the Cloth Centre has collected the following information:

Annual demand for denim cloth	20,000 metres
Ordering cost per purchase order	$160
Carrying cost per year	20% of purchase costs
Safety-stock requirements	None
Cost of denim cloth	$10 per metre

The purchasing lead time is 2 weeks. The Cloth Centre is open 250 days a year (50 weeks for 5 days a week).

Required

1. Calculate the EOQ for denim cloth.
2. Calculate the number of orders that will be placed each year.
3. Calculate the reorder point for denim cloth.

LO 1 ▶

1. EOQ ≈ 600 units

19-19 EOQ for manufacturer. Lakeland Company, which produces lawn mowers, purchases 18,000 units of a rotor blade part each year at a cost of $60 per unit. Lakeland requires a 15% annual rate of return on investment. In addition, the relevant carrying cost (for insurance, materials handling, breakage, and so on) is $6 per unit per year. The relevant ordering cost per purchase order is $150.

Required

1. Calculate Lakeland's EOQ for the rotor blade part.
2. Calculate Lakeland's annual relevant ordering costs for the EOQ calculated in requirement 1.
3. Calculate Lakeland's annual relevant carrying costs for the EOQ calculated in requirement 1.
4. Assume that demand is uniform throughout the year and known with certainty so that there is no need for safety stocks. The purchase-order lead time is half a month. Calculate Lakeland's reorder point for the rotor blade part.

⊕ **19-20 Sensitivity of EOQ to changes in relevant ordering and carrying costs.** Hall Company's annual demand for Model X253 is 10,000 units. The company is unsure about the relevant carrying cost per unit per year and the relevant ordering cost per purchase order. This table presents six possible combinations of carrying and ordering costs.

◀ **LO 1**

1. EOQ ($D = \$10$, $C = \$300$), 775

Relevant Carrying Cost per Unit per Year	Relevant Ordering Cost per Purchase Order
$10	$300
10	200
15	300
15	200
20	300
20	200

Required

1. Determine EOQ for each of the relevant ordering and carrying-cost alternatives.
2. How does your answer to requirement 1 give insight into the impact on EOQ of changes in relevant ordering and carrying costs?

⊕ **19-21 Inventory management and the balanced scorecard.** Devin Sports Cars (DSC) has implemented a balanced scorecard to measure and support its JIT production system. In the learning and growth category, DSC measures the percentage of employees who are cross-trained to perform a wide variety of production tasks. Internal business process measures are inventory turns and on-time delivery. The customer perspective is measured using a customer satisfaction measure, and financial performance using operating income. DSC estimates that if it can increase the percentage of cross-trained employees by 5%, the resulting increase in labour productivity will reduce inventory-related costs by $100,000 per year and shorten delivery times by 10%. The 10% reduction in delivery times, in turn, is expected to increase customer satisfaction by 5%, and each 1% increase in customer satisfaction is expected to increase revenues by 2% due to higher prices.

◀ **LO 2**

1. Increased operating profit, $600,000

Required

1. Assume that budgeted revenues in the coming year are $5,000,000. Ignoring the costs of training, what is the expected increase in operating income in the coming year if the number of cross-trained employees is increased by 5%?
2. What is the most DSC would be willing to pay to increase the percentage of cross-trained employees if it is only interested in maximizing operating income in the coming year?
3. What factors other than short-term profits should DSC consider when assessing the benefits from employee cross-training?

⊕ **19-22 JIT production, relevant benefits, relevant costs.** The Colonial Hardware Company manufactures specialty brass door handles at its Lynchburg plant. Colonial is considering implementing a JIT production system. The following are the estimated costs and benefits of JIT production:

◀ **LO 3**

Annual difference in favour of JIT production = $630,000

a. Annual additional tooling costs would be $200,000.
b. Average inventory would decline by 80% from the current level of $2,000,000.
c. Insurance, space, materials-handling, and setup costs, which currently total $600,000 annually, would decline by 25%.
d. The emphasis on quality inherent in JIT production would reduce rework costs by 30%. Colonial currently incurs $400,000 in annual rework costs.
e. Improved product quality under JIT production would enable Colonial to raise the price of its product by $8 per unit. Colonial sells 40,000 units each year.

Colonial's required rate of return on inventory investment is 15% per year.

Required

1. Calculate the net benefit or cost to Colonial if it adopts JIT production at the Lynchburg plant.
2. What nonfinancial and qualitative factors should Colonial consider when making the decision to adopt JIT production?
3. Suppose Colonial implements JIT production at its Lynchburg plant. Give examples of performance measures Colonial could use to evaluate and control JIT production. What would be the benefit of Colonial implementing an enterprise resource planning (ERP) system?

LO 5 ▶

1. Finished Goods Control DR, 3,484,000

⊕ **19-23 Backflush costing and JIT production.** Road Warrior Corporation assembles handheld computers that have scaled-down capabilities of laptop computers. Each handheld computer takes 6 hours to assemble. Road Warrior uses a JIT production system and a backflush costing system with three trigger points:

■ Purchase of direct materials.
■ Completion of good finished units of product.
■ Sale of finished goods.

There are no beginning inventories of materials or finished goods. The following data are for August 2018:

Direct materials purchased	$2,754,000
Direct materials used	2,733,600
Conversion costs incurred	723,600
Conversion costs allocated	750,400

Road Warrior records direct materials purchased and conversion costs incurred at actual costs. When finished goods are sold, the backflush costing system "pulls through" standard direct material cost ($102 per unit) and standard conversion cost ($28 per unit). Road Warrior produced 26,800 finished units in August 2018 and sold 26,400 units. The actual direct material cost per unit in August 2018 was $102, and the actual conversion cost per unit was $27.

Required

1. Prepare summary journal entries for August 2018 (without disposing of under- or overallocated conversion costs, there should be four entries).
2. Post the entries in requirement 1 to T-accounts for applicable Inventory: Materials and In-Process Control, Finished Goods Control, Conversion Costs Control, Conversion Costs Allocated, and Cost of Goods Sold.
3. Under an ideal JIT production system, how would the amounts in your journal entries differ from those in requirement 1?

LO 5 ▶

1. Cost of Goods Sold DR, 3,432,000

⊕ **19-24 Backflush costing, two trigger points, materials purchase and sale** (continuation of Exercise 19-23). Assume the same facts as in Exercise 19-23, except that Road Warrior now uses a backflush costing system with the following two trigger points:

■ Purchase of direct materials.
■ Sale of finished goods.

The Inventory Control account will include direct materials purchased but not yet in production, materials in work in process, and materials in finished goods but not sold. No conversion costs are inventoried. Any under- or overallocated conversion costs are written off monthly to Cost of Goods Sold.

Required

1. Prepare summary journal entries for August, including the disposition of under- or overallocated conversion costs.
2. Post the entries in requirement 1 to T-accounts for Inventory Control, Conversion Costs Control, Conversion Costs Allocated, and Cost of Goods Sold.

LO 5 ▶

1. Conversion Costs Allocated $750,400

⊕ **19-25 Backflush costing, two trigger points, completion of production and sale** (continuation of Exercise 19-24). Assume the same facts as in Exercise 19-24, except now Road Warrior uses only two trigger points, the completion of good finished units of product and the sale of finished goods. Any under- or overallocated conversion costs are written off monthly to Cost of Goods Sold.

Required

1. Prepare summary journal entries for August, including the disposition of under- or overallocated conversion costs.
2. Post the entries in requirement 1 to T-accounts for Finished Goods Control, Conversion Costs Control, Conversion Costs Allocated, and Cost of Goods Sold.

Problems

🌐 **19-26 Effect of different order quantities on ordering costs and carrying costs, EOQ.** Koala Blue, a retailer of bed and bath linen, sells 234,000 packages of Mona Lisa designer sheets each year. Koala Blue incurs an ordering cost of $81 per purchase order placed with Mona Lisa Enterprises and an annual carrying cost of $11.70 per package. Liv Carrol, purchasing manager at Koala Blue, seeks your help: She wants to understand how ordering and carrying costs vary with order quantity.

◀ **LO 1**
1. Total relevant costs, scenario 1, $26,325

	Scenario				
	1	**2**	**3**	**4**	**5**
Annual demand (packages)	234,000	234,000	234,000	234,000	234,000
Cost per purchase order	$ 81	$ 81	$ 81	$ 81	$ 81
Carrying cost per package per year	$ 11.70	$ 11.70	$ 11.70	$ 11.70	$ 11.70
Quantity (packages) per purchase order	900	1,500	1,800	2,100	2,700
Number of purchase orders per year					
Annual relevant ordering costs					
Annual relevant carrying costs					
Annual total relevant costs of ordering and carrying inventory					

Required

1. Complete the preceding table for Liv Carrol. What is the EOQ? Comment on your results.
2. Mona Lisa is about to introduce a web-based ordering system for its customers. Liv Carrol estimates that Koala Blue's ordering costs will be reduced to $49 per purchase order. Calculate the new EOQ and the new annual relevant costs of ordering and carrying inventory.
3. Liv Carrol estimates that Koala Blue will incur a cost of $2,000 to train its two purchasing assistants to use the new Mona Lisa system. Help Liv Carrol present a case to upper management showing that Koala Blue will be able to recoup its training costs within the first year of adoption.

🌐 **19-27 EOQ, uncertainty, safety stock, reorder point.** Clarkson Shoe Co. produces and sells excellent quality walking shoes. After production, the shoes are distributed to 20 warehouses around the country. Each warehouse services approximately 100 stores in its region. Clarkson uses an EOQ model to determine the number of pairs of shoes to order for each warehouse from the factory. Annual demand for warehouse OR2 is approximately 120,000 pairs of shoes. The ordering cost is $275 per order. The annual carrying cost of a pair of shoes is $2.40 per pair.

◀ **LO 2**
2. Weekly demand, 2,500 pairs of shoes

Required

1. Use the EOQ model to determine the optimal number of pairs of shoes per order.
2. Assume monthly demand is 10,000 shoes and each month consists of approximately 4 weeks. If it takes 1 week to receive an order, at what point should warehouse OR2 reorder shoes?
3. Although OR2's average monthly demand is 10,000 pairs of shoes (120,000 ÷ 12 months), demand each month may vary from the average by up to 20%. To handle the variation in demand, Clarkson has decided that OR2 should maintain enough safety stock to cover any demand level. How much safety stock should warehouse OR2 hold? How will this affect the reorder point and reorder quantity?
4. What is the total relevant ordering and carrying costs with safety stock and without safety stock?

🌐 **19-28 MRP and ERP.** MacroHard Corp. produces J-Pods, music players that can download thousands of songs. MacroHard forecasts that demand in 2017 will be 48,000 J-Pods. The variable production cost of each J-Pod is $50. Due to the large $50,000 cost per setup, MacroHard plans to produce J-Pods once a month in batches of 4,000 each. The carrying cost of a unit in inventory is $20 per year.

◀ **LO 4**
1. Annual cost of producing and carrying J-Pods in inventory, $3,040,000

Required

1. Using an MRP system, what is the annual cost of producing and carrying J-Pods in inventory? (Assume that, on average, half of the units produced in a month are in inventory.)
2. A new manager at MacroHard has suggested that the company use the EOQ model to determine the optimal batch size to produce. (To use the EOQ model, MacroHard needs to treat the setup cost in the same way it would treat ordering cost in a traditional EOQ model.) Determine the optimal batch size and number of batches. Round up the number of batches to the nearest whole number. What would be the annual cost of producing and carrying J-Pods in inventory if it uses the optimal batch size?
3. MacroHard is also considering switching from an MRP system to a JIT system. This will result in producing to demand in batch sizes of 500 J-Pods. The frequency of production batches will force

MacroHard to reduce setup time and will result in a reduction in setup cost. The new setup cost will be $5,000 per setup. What is the annual cost of producing and carrying J-Pods in inventory under the JIT system?

4. Compare the models analyzed in the previous parts of the problem. What are the advantages and disadvantages of each?

LO 2 ▶ ⊕ **19-29 Effect of management evaluation criteria on EOQ model.** Computer Depot purchases one model of computer at a wholesale cost of $300 per unit and resells it to end consumers. The annual demand for the company's product is 600,000 units. Ordering costs are $1,200 per order and carrying costs are $75 per computer, including $30 in the opportunity cost of holding inventory.

Required

1. Compute the optimal order quantity using the EOQ model.
2. Compute (a) the number of orders per year and (b) the annual relevant total cost of ordering and carrying inventory.
3. Assume that when evaluating the manager, the company excludes the opportunity cost of carrying inventory. If the manager makes the EOQ decision excluding the opportunity cost of carrying inventory, the relevant carrying cost would be $45, not $75. How would this affect the EOQ amount and the actual annual relevant cost of ordering and carrying inventory?
4. What is the cost impact on the company of excluding the opportunity cost of carrying inventory when making EOQ decisions? Why do you think the company currently excludes the opportunity costs of carrying inventory when evaluating the manager's performance? What could the company do to encourage the manager to make decisions more congruent with the goal of reducing total inventory costs?

LO 2 ▶ **19-30 EOQ, uncertainty, safety stock, reorder point.** Stewart Corporation is a major automobile manufacturer. It purchases steering wheels from Coase Corporation. Annual demand is 10,400 steering wheels per year or 200 steering wheels per week. The ordering cost is $100 per order. The annual carrying cost is $13 per steering wheel. It currently takes 1.5 weeks to supply an order to the assembly plant.

Required

1. What is the optimal number of steering wheels that Stewart's managers should order according to the EOQ model?
2. At what point should managers reorder the steering wheels, assuming that both demand and purchase-order lead time are known with certainty?
3. Now assume that demand can vary during the 1.5-week purchase-order lead time. The following table shows the probability distribution of various demand levels:

Total Demand for Steering Wheels for 1.5 Weeks	Probability of Demand (sums to 1)
100	0.15
200	0.20
300	0.40
400	0.20
500	0.05

If Stewart runs out of stock, it would have to rush order the steering wheels at an additional cost of $9 per steering wheel. How much safety stock should the assembly plant hold? How will this affect the reorder point and reorder quantity.

LO 3 ▶

1. Relevant costs under JIT purchasing policy, $156,500.

⊕ **19-31 JIT purchasing, relevant benefits, relevant costs.** (CMA, adapted) The CH Holling Corporation (CHH) is an automotive supplier that uses automatic turning machines to manufacture precision parts from steel bars. CHH's inventory of raw steel averages $600,000. John Oates, president of CHH, and Helen Gorman, CHH's controller, are concerned about the costs of carrying inventory. The steel supplier is willing to supply steel in smaller lots at no additional charge. Gorman identifies the following effects of adopting a JIT inventory program to virtually eliminate steel inventory:

■ Without scheduling any overtime, lost sales due to stockouts would increase by 35,000 units per year. However, by incurring overtime premiums of $40,000 per year, the increase in lost sales could be reduced to 20,000 units per year. This would be the maximum amount of overtime that would be feasible for the company.

■ Two warehouses currently used for steel bar storage would no longer be needed. The company rents one warehouse from another company under a cancellable leasing arrangement at an annual cost of $60,000. The company owns the other warehouse and contains 12,000 square metres. Three-quarters of the space in the owned warehouse could be rented for $1.50 per square metre per year. Insurance and property tax costs totalling $14,000 per year would be eliminated.

The required rate of return on investment is 20% per year, and budgeted income statement for the year ending December 31, 2018, (in thousands) is as follows:

CH Holling Corporation Budgeted Income Statement
For the Year Ending December 31, 2018
(in thousands)

Revenue (900,000 units)		$10,800
Cost of goods sold		
Variable costs	$4,050	
Fixed costs	1,450	
Total costs of goods sold		5,500
Gross margin		5,300
Marketing and distribution costs		
Variable costs	900	
Fixed costs	1,500	
Total marketing and distribution costs		2,400
Operating income		$ 2,900

Required

1. Calculate the estimated dollar savings (loss) that would result in 2018 from the adoption of JIT purchasing.
2. Identify and explain other factors that should be considered before deciding whether to adopt JIT purchasing.

⊕ **19-32 Supply-chain effects on total relevant inventory cost.** Cow Spot Computer Co. outsources the production of motherboards for its computers. It has narrowed down its choice of suppliers to two companies: Maji and Induk. Maji is an older company with a good reputation, while Induk is a newer company with cheaper prices. Given the difference in reputation, 5% of the motherboards will be inspected if they are purchased from Maji, but 25% of the motherboards will be inspected if they are purchased from Induk. The following data refer to costs associated with Maji and Induk.

◀ **LO 3**
1. Total costs Maji, $935,680

	Maji	Induk
Number of orders per year	50	50
Annual motherboards demanded	10,000	10,000
Price per motherboard	$ 93	$ 90
Ordering cost per order	$ 10	$ 8
Inspection cost per unit	$ 5	$ 5
Average inventory level	100 units	100 units
Expected number of stockouts	100	300
Stockout cost (cost of rush order) per stockout	$ 5	$ 8
Units returned by customers for replacing motherboards	50	500
Cost of replacing each motherboard	$ 20	$ 20
Required annual return on investment	10%	10%
Other carrying cost per unit per year	$ 2.50	$ 2.50

Required

1. What is the relevant cost of purchasing from Maji and Induk?
2. What factors other than cost should Cow Spot consider?

⊕ **19-33 Backflush costing and JIT production.** The Acton Corporation manufactures electrical meters. For August, there were no beginning inventories of direct materials and no beginning or ending work in process. Acton uses a JIT production system and backflush costing with three trigger points for making entries in the accounting system:

◀ **LO 5**
1. Finished Goods Control DR, 945,000

- Purchase of direct materials—debited to Inventory: Materials and In-Process Control
- Completion of good finished units of product—debited to Finished Goods Control
- Sale of finished goods

Acton's August standard cost per meter is direct material, $25; and conversion cost, $20. The following data apply to August manufacturing:

Direct materials purchased	$550,000
Conversion costs incurred	$440,000
Number of finished units manufactured	21,000
Number of finished units sold	20,000

Required

1. Prepare summary journal entries for August (without disposing of under- or overallocated conversion costs). Assume no direct materials variances.
2. Post the entries in requirement 1 to T-accounts for Inventory: Materials and In-Process Control, Finished Goods Control, Conversion Costs Control, Conversion Costs Allocated, and Cost of Goods Sold.

LO 5 ▶

1. Cost of Goods Sold DR, 900,000

⊕ **19-34 Backflush, two trigger points, materials purchase and sale** (continuation of Problem 19-33). Assume that the second trigger point for Acton Corporation is the sale—rather than the completion—of finished goods. Also, the inventory account is confined solely to direct materials, whether these materials are in a storeroom, in work in process, or in finished goods. No conversion costs are inventoried. They are allocated to the units sold at standard costs. Any under- or overallocated conversion costs are written off monthly to Cost of Goods Sold.

Required

1. Prepare summary journal entries for August, including the disposition of under- or overallocated conversion costs. Assume no direct materials variances.
2. Post the entries in requirement 1 to T-accounts for Inventory Control, Conversion Costs Control, Conversion Costs Allocated, and Cost of Goods Sold.

LO 5 ▶

1. Conversion Costs Allocated $420,000

⊕ **19-35 Backflush, two trigger points, completion of production and sale** (continuation of Problem 19-33). Assume the same facts as in Problem 19-33 except now there are only two trigger points: the completion of good finished units of product and the sale of finished goods.

Required

1. Prepare summary journal entries for August, including the disposition of under- or overallocated conversion costs. Assume no direct materials variances.
2. Post the entries in requirement 1 to T-accounts for Finished Goods Control, Conversion Costs Control, Conversion Costs Allocated, and Cost of Goods Sold.

LO 3 ▶

2. Value stream operating income, mechanical devices, $227

⊕ **19-36 Lean accounting.** LockTite (LT) has introduced a JIT production process and is considering the adoption of lean accounting principles to support its new production philosophy. The company has two product lines: mechanical devices and electronic devices. Two individual products are made in each line. The company's traditional cost accounting system allocates all plant-level overhead costs to individual products. Product-line overhead costs are traced directly to product lines, and then allocated to the two individual products in each line. Equipment costs are directly traced to products. The latest accounting report using traditional cost accounting methods included the following information (in thousands of dollars).

	Mechanical Devices		Electronic Devices	
	Product A	**Product B**	**Product C**	**Product D**
Sales	$700	$500	$900	$450
Direct materials (based on quantity used)	200	100	250	75
Direct manufacturing labour	150	75	200	60
Equipment costs	90	125	200	100
Allocated product-line overhead	110	60	125	50
Allocated plant-level overhead	50	35	80	25
Operating income	$100	$105	$ 45	$140

LT has determined that each of the two product lines represents a distinct value stream. It has also determined that $120,000 of the allocated plant-level overhead costs represents occupancy costs. Product A occupies 20% of the plant's square footage, Product B occupies 20%, Product C occupies 30%, and Product D occupies 15%. The remaining square footage is occupied by plant administrative functions or is not being used. Finally, LT has decided that direct material should be expensed in the period in which it is purchased, rather than when the material is used. According to purchasing records, direct material purchase costs during the period were

	Mechanical Devices		**Electronic Devices**	
	Product A	**Product B**	**Product C**	**Product D**
Direct materials (purchases)	$190	$125	$250	$90

Required

1. What are the cost objects in LT's lean accounting system? Which of LT's costs would be excluded when computing operating income for these cost objects?
2. Compute operating income for the cost objects identified in requirement 1 using lean accounting principles. Why does operating income differ from the operating income computed using traditional cost accounting methods?

🌐 **19-37 EOQ conflicts.** Ralph Menard is the owner of a truck repair shop. He uses an EOQ model for each of his truck parts. He initially predicts the annual demand for heavy-duty tires to be 2,000. Each tire has a purchase price of $60. The incremental ordering costs per purchase order are $48. The incremental carrying costs per year are $4.80 per unit plus 10% of the supplier's purchase price.

◀ **LO 2**
1. Annual relevant ordering and carrying costs, $1,440

Required

1. Calculate the EOQ for heavy-duty tires, along with the sum of annual relevant ordering costs and carrying costs.
2. Suppose Menard is correct in all his predictions except the purchase price. (He ignored a new law that abolished tariff duties on imported heavy-duty tires, which led to lower prices from foreign competitors.) If he had been a faultless predictor, he would have foreseen that the purchase price would drop to $36 at the beginning of the year and would be unchanged throughout the year. What is the cost of the prediction error?

🌐 **19-38 Backflush costing.** The Ronowski Company produces telephones. For June, there were no beginning inventories of raw materials and no beginning and ending work in process. Ronowski uses a JIT production system and backflush costing with three trigger points for making entries in its accounting system:

◀ **LO 5**
1. Conversion Costs Control DR, 3,696,000

- Purchase of direct (raw) materials
- Completion of good finished units of product
- Sale of finished goods

Ronowski's June standard cost per unit of telephone product is direct materials, $31.20; conversion costs, $18. There are three inventory accounts:

- Inventory: Raw
- Inventory: In-Process Control
- Finished Goods Control

The following data apply to June manufacturing:

Raw materials purchased	$6,360,000
Conversion costs incurred	$3,696,000
Number of finished units manufactured	200,000
Number of finished units sold	192,000

Required

1. Prepare summary journal entries for June (without disposing of under- or overallocated conversion costs). Assume no direct materials variances.
2. Post the entries in requirement 1 to T-accounts for applicable Inventory Control, Conversion Costs Control, Conversion Costs Allocated, and Cost of Goods Sold.

LO 3 ▶

Total annual relevant costs, Big
Red, $738,940

⊕ **19-39 Supplier evaluation and relevant costs of quality and timely deliveries.** Copeland Sporting Goods is evaluating two suppliers of footballs: Big Red and Quality Sports. Pertinent information about each potential supplier follows:

Relevant Item	Big Red	Quality Sports
Purchase price per unit (case)	$ 60.00	$ 61.20
Ordering costs per order	$ 7.20	$ 7.20
Inspection costs per unit	$ 0.02	$ 0.00
Insurance, material handling, and so on per unit per year	$ 4.00	$ 4.50
Annual demand	12,000 units	12,000 units
Average quantity of inventory held during the year	100 units	100 units
Required return on investment	15%	15%
Stockout costs per unit	$ 24	$ 12
Stockout units per year	350 units	60 units
Customer returns	300 units	25 units
Customer-return costs per unit	$ 30	$ 30

Required

Calculate the relevant costs of purchasing (1) from Big Red and (2) from Quality Sports using the format of Exhibit 19-7. From whom should Copeland buy footballs?

LO 4 ▶

⊕ **19-40 Supply chain effects on total relevant inventory cost.** Peach Computer Co. outsources the production of motherboards for its computers. It is currently deciding which of two suppliers to use: Alpha or Beta. Due to differences in the product failure rates in the two companies, 5% of motherboards purchased from Alpha will be inspected and 25% of motherboards purchased from Beta will be inspected. The following data refer to costs associated with Alpha and Beta:

	Alpha	Beta
Number of orders per year	50	50
Annual motherboards demanded	10,000	10,000
Price per motherboard	$ 108	$ 105
Ordering cost per order	$ 13	$ 10
Inspection cost per unit	$ 6	$ 6
Average inventory level	100 units	100 units
Expected number of stockouts	100	300
Stockout cost (cost of rush order) per stockout	$ 4	$ 6
Units returned by customers for replacing motherboards	50	500
Cost of replacing each motherboard	$ 30	$ 30
Required annual return on investment	10%	10%
Other carrying cost per unit per year	$ 3.50	$ 3.50

Required

1. What is the relevant cost of purchasing from Alpha and Beta?
2. What factors other than cost should Peach consider?

LO 5 ▶

⊕ **19-41 Backflush costing and JIT production.** The Grand Meter Corporation manufactures electrical meters. For August, there were no beginning inventories of direct materials and no beginning or ending work in process. Grand Meter uses a JIT production system and backflush costing with three trigger points for making entries in the accounting system:

■ Purchase of direct materials and incurring of conversion costs
■ Completion of good finished units of product
■ Sale of finished goods

Grand Meter's August standard cost per meter is direct materials, $25, and conversion cost, $20. Grand Meter has no direct materials variances. The following data apply to August manufacturing:

Direct materials purchased	$550,000	Number of finished units manufactured	21,000
Conversion costs incurred	$440,000	Number of finished units sold	20,000

Required

1. Prepare summary journal entries for August (without disposing of under- or overallocated conversion costs). Assume no direct materials variances.
2. Post the entries in requirement 1 to T-accounts for Materials and In-Process Inventory Control, Finished Goods Control, Conversion Costs Control, Conversion Costs Allocated, and Cost of Goods Sold.

🌐 **19-42 Purchase order size for retailer, EOQ, JIT purchasing.** The 24-Hour Mart operates a chain of supermarkets. Its best-selling soft drink is Fruitslice. Demand (D) in April for Fruitslice at its Regina supermarket is estimated to be 7,200 cases (24 cans in each case). In March, the Regina supermarket estimated the ordering costs per purchase order (P) for Fruitslice to be $36. The carrying costs ($C$) of each case of Fruitslice in inventory for a month were estimated to be $1.20. At the end of March, the Regina 24-Hour Mart reestimated its carrying costs to be $1.80 per case per month to take into account an increase in warehouse-related costs.

◀ **LO 1**

1. a. EOQ, 658 cases

During March, 24-Hour Mart restructured its relationship with suppliers. It reduced the number of suppliers from 600 to 180. Long-term contracts were signed only with those suppliers that agreed to make product quality checks before shipping. Each purchase order would be made by linking into the suppliers' computer network. The Regina 24-Hour Mart estimated that these changes would reduce the ordering costs per purchase order to $6. The 24-Hour Mart is open 30 days in April.

Required

1. Calculate the EOQ in April for Fruitslice. Use the EOQ model, and assume in turn that

    a. $D = 7,200$; $P = 36; $C = 1.20
    b. $D = 7,200$; $P = 36; $C = 1.80
    c. $D = 7,200$; $P = 6; $C = 1.80

2. How does your answer to requirement 1 give insight into the retailer's movement toward JIT purchasing policies?

Collaborative Learning Case

19-43 Backflushing. The following conversation occurred between Brian Richardson, plant manager at Glendale Engineering, and Charles Cheng, plant controller. Glendale manufactures automotive component parts, such as gears and crankshafts, for automobile manufacturers. Richardson has been very enthusiastic about implementing JIT and about simplifying and streamlining production and other business processes.

◀ **LO 5**

"Charles," Richardson began, "I would like to substantially simplify our accounting in the new JIT environment. Can't we just record one journal entry at the time we ship products to our customers? I don't want to have our staff spending time tracking inventory from one stage to the next, when we have as little inventory as we do."

"Brian," Cheng said, "I think you are right about simplifying the accounting, but we still have a fair amount of direct materials and finished goods inventory that varies from period to period, depending on the demand for specific products. Doing away with all inventory accounting may be a problem."

"Well," Richardson replied, "you know my desire to simplify, simplify, simplify. I know that there are some costs of oversimplifying, but I believe that, in the long run, simplification pays dividends. Why don't you and your staff study the issues involved, and I will put it on the agenda for our next management meeting."

Required

1. What version of backflush costing would you recommend that Cheng adopt? Remember Richardson's desire to simplify the accounting as much as possible. Develop support for your recommendation.
2. Think about the three versions of backflush costing shown in this chapter. These versions differ with respect to the number and types of trigger points used. Suppose your goal of implementing backflush costing is to simplify the accounting, but only if it closely matches the sequential-tracking approach. Which version of backflush costing would you propose if

    a. Glendale had no direct materials and no work-in-process inventories but did have finished goods inventory?
    b. Glendale had no work-in-process and no finished goods inventories but did have direct materials inventory?
    c. Glendale had no direct materials, no work-in-process, and no finished goods inventories?

3. Adler et al. argue the reporting needs of manufacturing systems are not satisfactorily met through the use of backflush accounting systems.[6] Perpetual costing systems provide more valuable data and realistic costing information, which is more in keeping with modern manufacturing techniques. Comment on the use of perpetual versus backflush costing systems and their applicability.

TRY IT! ▶ SOLUTIONS

Try It 19–1

$$EOQ = \sqrt{\frac{2DP}{C}}$$

(D)emand = 1000

(P) Cost of Order = $120

(Carrying) Cost of ice-cream maker = $80 × 40% = $32

$\sqrt{(2 \times 1000 \times 120)/(80 \times 40\%)}$

= 86.6 ~ 87 ice-cream makers

Try It 19-2

(D)emand = 1000

And assuming Spears uses an operating calendar of 365 days per year, the average daily demand would equal

1000/365 = 2.74

The reorder point = daily demand × lead time

2.74 × 8 = 21.92 ~ 22 units.

[6] R. Adler, A.M. Everett, and M. Waldron. (2000, June). "Advanced management accounting techniques in manufacturing: utilization, benefits, and barriers to implementation." In *Accounting Forum* (Vol. 24, No. 2, pp. 131–150). Blackwell Publishers Ltd.

Capital Budgeting: Methods of Investment Analysis

20

2009fotofriends/Shutterstock

Cedar Fair Entertainment Company and Capital Investments

Cedar Fair Entertainment Company is the leading operator of amusement parks in Canada and the United States, entertaining over 23 million guests each year. The company's most well-known Canadian property is Canada's Wonderland in Ontario. The park has some of the largest roller coasters in the world, as well as an abundance of non-coaster rides and activities. The newest roller coaster, "The Leviathan," which opened in 2013, cost US$28 million to build. The company doesn't mind the cost, as long as there is sufficient return.

According to Cedar Point's vice president and general manager, "It's innovative thrills, like those our visitors will experience on the Leviathan, that keep them coming back year after year, earning us the honor of 'Best Amusement Park in the World.'" The company's CEO views the strategic investments in new rides and attractions as one of the keys to the company's ongoing success.

Source: Cedarpoint.com; Cedar Fair, L.P. 2012 10(K) filing, http://www.goldenticketawards.com/pdfs/at_goldenticket_2018_web.pdf.

▶ Learning Objectives

1. Apply the concept of the time value of money to capital budgeting decisions.

2. Evaluate discounted cash flow (DCF) and non-DCF methods to calculate rate of return (ROR).

3. Analyze the impact of income taxes on discounted cash flows and capital budgeting decisions.

4. Apply the concept of relevance to DCF methods of capital budgeting.

5. Assess the complexities in capital budgeting within an interdependent set of value-chain business functions.

6. Apply the concept of defensive strategic investment to the capital budgeting process.

▶ CPA Competencies

This chapter covers material outlined in **Section 3: Management Accounting** of the CPA Competency Map. The Learning Objectives in this chapter have been aligned with the CPA Competency Map to ensure the best coverage possible.

3.2.1 Develops or evaluates information inputs for operational plans, budgets, and forecasts

3.2.2 Prepares, analyzes, or evaluates operational plans, budgets, and forecasts

3.2.3 Computes, analyzes, or assesses implications of variances

3.4.1 Evaluates sources and drivers of revenue growth

Capital Budgeting and Decision Making (5DM Approach)

Capital budgeting is the process of making long-run planning decisions for investments in projects. In much of accounting, income is calculated on a period-by-period basis. However, in choosing investments, managers often must make a selection from among a group of multiple projects, each of which may span several periods. Exhibit 20-1 illustrates these two different, yet intersecting, dimensions of cost analysis: (1) horizontally across, as the *project dimension*, which depicts the life span of the project, and (2) vertically upward, as the *accounting-period dimension*, which depicts the accounting period (in this case a year). Each project is represented as a horizontal rectangle starting and ending at different times and stretching over time spans longer than one year. The vertical rectangle for the 2017 accounting period, for example, represents the dimensions of income determination and routine annual planning and control that were ongoing that year.

Capital budgeting analyzes each project by considering all of the cash flows in the life of the investment, from the initial expenditures through the termination of the project. In this fashion, it is analogous to life-cycle budgeting and costing. For example, when Samsung considers a new line of smartphones, it begins by estimating all potential revenues from the new line as well as any costs that will be incurred along its life cycle. Only after examining the potential costs and benefits across all of the business functions in the value chain, from research and development (R&D) to customer service, across the entire life span of the new project, does Samsung decide whether the new model is a wise investment.

The 5DM model demonstrates how capital budgeting is both a decision-making and a control tool.

Step 1: Identify Projects *Identify potential capital investments that agree with the organization's strategy.*	For example, when Samsung sought a strategy of product differentiation in the form of the *phablet*, the Samsung Galaxy II, it listed possible upgrades and changes from its present offering. Alternatively, a strategy of cost leadership could be promoted by projects that improve productivity and efficiency in its low cost model offerings.
Step 2: Obtain Information *Gather information from all parts of the value chain to evaluate alternative projects.*	In this step, marketing is queried for potential revenue numbers, plant managers are asked about assembly times, and suppliers are consulted about prices and the availability of key components. Some projects may even be rejected at this stage. For example, suppose Samsung learns that the phablet simply cannot be built using existing production lines. It may opt to cancel the project altogether.

Exhibit 20-1 The Project and Time Dimensions of Capital Budgeting

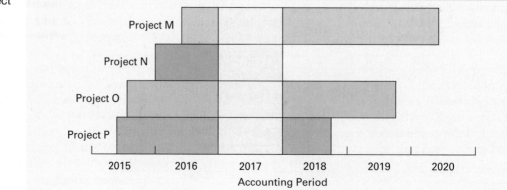

Step 3: Make Predictions *Forecast all potential cash flows attributable to the alternative projects.*

Capital investment projects generally involve substantial initial outlays, which are recouped over time through annual cash inflows and the disposal values at the termination of the project. As a result, they require the firm to make forecasts of cash flows several years into the future to estimate if the investment will be worth the cost.

Step 4: Make Decisions by Choosing Among Alternatives *Determine which investment yields the greatest benefit and the least cost to the organization.*

Using the quantitative information obtained in step 3 (which is typically limited to financial information), managers use their judgment and intuition to factor in qualitative information and strategic considerations as well. For example, even if a proposed new line of low cost phones meets its financial targets on a standalone basis, Samsung might decide not to pursue it further if it feels that the new model will lessen the value of the firm's brand.

Step 5: Implement the Decision, Evaluate Performance, and Learn *Given the complexities of capital investment decisions and the long time horizons they span, this stage can be separated into two phases:*

Phase 1: Obtain funding and make the investments selected in step 4.

Sources of funding include internally generated cash flow as well as equity and debt securities sold in capital markets. Managers must examine the most cost effective strategy to generate capital within the firm's capabilities and consistent with its overall strategy.

Phase 2: Track realized cash flows, compare against estimated numbers, and revise plans if necessary.

As the cash outflows and inflows begin to accumulate, managers can verify whether the predictions made in step 3 agree with the actual flows of cash from the project. When Microsoft initially released the new *Surface* tablet, its realized sales were substantially lower than the original demand estimates. Microsoft responded by adjusting supplies and raw materials and manufacturing fewer devices, reflective of demand.

To illustrate capital budgeting, consider Top-Spin tennis racquets. Top-Spin was one of the first major tennis-racquet producers to introduce graphite in its racquets. This allowed Top-Spin to produce some of the lightest and stiffest racquets in the market. However, new carbon-fibre impregnated racquets are even lighter and stiffer than their graphite counterparts. Top-Spin has always been an innovator in the tennis-racquet industry, and wants to stay that way, so in step 1, it identifies the carbon fibre racquet project. During information gathering (step 2), the company learns that it could feasibly begin using carbon-fibre in its racquets as early as 2019, if it replaces one of its graphite forming machines with a carbon-fibre weaving machine. After collecting additional data, Top-Spin begins to forecast future cash flows if it invests in the new machine (step 3). Top-Spin estimates that it can purchase a carbon-fibre weaving machine with a useful life of five years for a net after-tax initial investment of $379,100, which is calculated as follows:

Cost of new machine	$390,000
Investment in working capital	9,000
Cash flow from disposing of existing machine (after-tax)	(19,900)
Net initial investment for new machine	$379,100

> **Note** *Working capital* refers to the difference between current assets and current liabilities, and it represents the capital used in the firm's day-to-day operations.

New projects often necessitate additional investments in current assets such as inventories and receivables. In the case of Top-Spin, the purchase of the new machine is accompanied by an outlay of $9,000 for supplies and spare parts inventory. At the end of the project, the $9,000 in supplies and spare parts inventory is liquidated, resulting in a cash inflow. However, the machine itself is believed to have no terminal disposal value after five years.

Managers estimated that by introducing carbon-fibre impregnated racquets, operating cash inflows (cash revenues minus cash operating costs) will increase by $100,000 (after tax) in the first four years and $91,000 in year 5. To simplify the analysis, suppose that all cash flows occur at the end of each year. Note that cash flow at the end of the fifth year also increases by $100,000: $91,000 in operating cash inflows and $9,000 in working capital.

Management next calculates the costs and benefits of the proposed project. This chapter discusses four capital budgeting methods to analyze financial information:

1. Net present value (NPV)
2. Internal rate of return (IRR)
3. Payback
4. Accrual accounting rate of return (AARR)

Both the net NPV and IRR methods use *discounted cash flows*, which we discuss in the following section.

A Note on Sources of Capital and Timing of Investments

Financing is most often the treasury function of an organization. Once the investment decision is made, then the financing must be acquired. Again this is an information-gathering process, and if financing is unavailable, this will change the investment decision. In reality, financing opportunities are often investigated simultaneously with the formal analyses of the costs and benefits of various investments. One reason is that interest expense is a cash cost of any investment financed by debt.

When a company such as Top-Spin finally makes a decision and moves forward with an investment, careful thought must be applied in choosing the source of capital to fund the project (step 5). These choices must be consistent with the company's overall strategy and within any constraints (e.g., an agreement with a debt-holder that it will take on no more debt). Long-term investments are appropriately financed by long-term capital to avoid the opportunity costs of spending too much cash immediately and jeopardizing the liquidity of the corporation. Good long-term debt contracts match the timing of cash outflows to pay obligations somewhat closely to the timing of predicted cash inflows. For example, an investment with a useful life of 25 years would be financed by a 25-year long-term debt contract. Sources of financing can also include internally generated cash flow from operations. However, this must be adequate to cover any working capital outlays in the first year of a long-term investment because long-term investments rarely generate cash inflow in their early years.

Discounted Cash Flows and the Time Value of Money

▶ **LO 2**

Evaluate discounted cash flow (DCF) and non-DCF methods to calculate rate of return (ROR).

Discounted cash flow (DCF) methods measure all expected future cash inflows and outflows of a project discounted back to the present point in time. DCF focuses on *cash* inflows and outflows rather than on *operating income* as used in conventional accrual accounting. Cash is invested now with the expectation of receiving a greater amount of cash in the future. It is important to understand that accrual accounting estimates of value are reported on the statement of comprehensive income and statement of financial position according to generally accepted accounting principles (IFRS or ASPE). Cash flow will not equal either operating or net income for the current period. Companies without cash to fulfill their contractual obligations are either insolvent or bankrupt. Therefore, the management team must focus on predicted cash flow when creating a capital budget. The predicted timing and amount of cash inflow and outflow is especially important.

The key feature of DCF methods is the application of the **time value of money**. This method estimates how a dollar (or any other monetary unit) received today is worth more than a dollar received at any future time. The reason is that $1 received today can be invested at, for example, 10% per year so that it grows to $1.10 at the end of one year. The time value of money is the opportunity cost (the return of $0.10 forgone per year) from not having the money today. In this example, $1 received one year from now is worth $1 ÷ 1.10 = $0.9091 today. Similarly, $100 received one year from now will be weighted by 0.9091 to yield a DCF of $90.91, which is the value today of the $100 to be received next year.

The longer the time horizon (e.g., a project spanning 15 years as compared to a project spanning 5 years) results in a higher level of uncertainty. In practical terms, the risk increases the longer it takes to collect the long-term returns of a project, and the greater the potential that those returns may not be realized. In this way, DCF methods explicitly weigh cash flows by the time value of money. Note that DCF focuses exclusively on cash inflows and outflows rather than on operating income as determined by accrual accounting. The compound interest tables and formulas used in DCF analysis are in Appendix A.

The two DCF methods we describe are the NPV method and the IRR method. Both DCF methods use what is called the **required rate of return (RRR)**, which is the minimum acceptable annual ROR on an investment. The RRR is internally set, usually by upper management, and typically reflects the return that an organization could expect to receive elsewhere for an investment of comparable risk. The RRR is also called the **discount rate, hurdle rate, cost of capital,** or **opportunity cost of capital**. Suppose the CFO at Top-Spin has set the RRR for the firm's investments at 8% per year; it would affect NPV and IRR.

Net Present Value Method

The **net present value (NPV) method** calculates the expected financial gain or loss from a project by discounting all expected future cash inflows and outflows back to the present point in time using the RRR. Only projects with a positive NPV are acceptable because the return from these projects exceeds the cost of capital (the return available by investing the capital elsewhere). Managers prefer projects with higher NPVs to projects with lower NPVs, if all other things are equal.

To use the NPV method, apply the first three steps of the 5DM as follows:

Step 1: Identify the scope and form of the project, including an estimate of the *initial* cost of the investment. The focus should be on identifying projects that are consistent with the organization's strategy (e.g., cost leadership, market expansion, or product differentiation).

Step 2: Collect the relevant information on the project(s) including estimates from marketing on revenues and market impact and information from production departments on cash outflows, and investigate possible sources and costs of capital to invest in the project. You can include this information in your NPV model by sketching out the relevant cash inflows and outflows, and include the basic project information such as initial investment and useful life (see Exhibit 20-2).

The right side of Exhibit 20-2 shows how these cash flows are portrayed. Outflows appear in parentheses. Note that Exhibit 20-2 includes the outflow for the new machine at year 0, the time of the acquisition. The NPV method focuses only on cash flows in any form, which can include operations, purchase or sale of equipment, or investment or recovery of working capital. The discount factor is determined by choosing the correct compound interest table from Appendix A. In our example, we are looking for the present value of $1, and so we will refer to Table 2. If we use Table 2, we find the discount factors for periods 1–5 under the 8% column presents the five discount factors. We can discount each year's cash flow separately using Table 2 (Appendix A).

Exhibit 20-2 Forecast of Project Cash Flows

	A	B	C	D	E	F	G	H	I
1			Net initial investment	$379,100					
2	Project Information		Useful life	5 years		Sketch the Cash Flows			
3			Annual cash inflow	$100,000					
4			Required rate of return	8%					
5									
6		Present Value	Present Value of		Sketch of Relevant Cash Flows at End of Each Year				
7		of Cash Flow	$1 Discounted at 8%	0	1	2	3	4	5
8	Approach 1: Discounting Each Year's Cash Flow Separately[a]								
9	Net initial investment	$(379,100) ◄	1.000 ◄	$(379,100)					
10		92,600 ◄	0.926 ◄		$100,000				
11		85,700 ◄	0.857 ◄			$100,000			
12	Annual cash inflow	79,400 ◄	0.794 ◄				$100,000		
13		73,500 ◄	0.735 ◄					$100,000	
14		68,100 ◄	0.681 ◄						$100,000
15	NPV if new machine purchased	$ 20,200							
16									
17	Approach 2: Using Annuity Table[b]				Discount and Sum Cash Flows				
18	Net initial investment	$(379,100) ◄	1.000 ◄	$(379,100)					
19					$100,000	$100,000	$100,000	$100,000	$100,000
20									
21	Annual cash inflow	399,300 ◄	3.993 ◄						
22	NPV if new machine purchased	$ 20,200							
23									
24	*Note:* Parentheses denote relevant cash outflows throughout all exhibits in Chapter 20.								
25	[a]Present values from Table 2, Appendix A at the end of the book. For example, $0.857 = 1 \div (1.08)^2$.								
26	[b]Annuity present value from Table 4, Appendix A. The annuity value of 3.993 is the sum of the individual discount rates $0.926 + 0.857 + 0.794 + 0.735 + 0.681$.								

Step 3: The forecast of the project cash flows is determined through the application of the NPV method as depicted in Exhibit 20-2:

i. Calculate the outflow for the investment at the start of year 1 (also referred to as end of year 0). For Top-Spin, this is the acquisition of a new machine.

ii. Trace the unadjusted cash inflows and outflows over the life of the project.

iii. Discount the cash flows using the compound interest table from Appendix A (Table 2). In the Top-Spin example, we can discount each year's cash flow separately, and we find the discount factors for periods 1–5 under the 8% column. To obtain the present value amount, multiply each discount factor by the corresponding amount represented by the arrow on the right in Exhibit 20-2 ($379,100 × 1.000; $100,000 × 0.926; and so on to $100,000 × 0.681) and then sum these five amounts together. Subtracting the initial investment then reveals the NPV of the project as $20,200 (= $399,300 − $379,100).

Based on this calculation, we could conclude that the project is a good choice *financially*. However, other considerations must be examined in step 4 of the 5DM that are based on qualitative or non-financial information and manager's judgment.

An Alternative Route to the Solution

Because the investment in the new machine produces a series of equal cash flows ($100,000) at equal time intervals (once a year for five years), it constitutes an *annuity*. Because the cash flows are uniform, Appendix A, Table 4 (concerning the present value of an annuity) can be used to compute the value of the investment. Under this approach, we find that the annuity factor for five periods under the 8% column is 3.993, which is the sum of the five discount factors used in the approach described above. We multiply the uniform annual cash inflow ($100,000) by this factor to obtain the present value of the inflows ($399,300). The annuity approach can only be used with uniform cash flows.

Exhibit 20-3 Internal Rate of Return Method: Top-Spin's Carbon-Fibre Machine

	A	B	C	D	E	F	G	H	I
1			Net initial investment	$379,100					
2			Useful life	5 years					
3			Annual cash inflow	$100,000					
4			Annual discount rate	10%					
5									
6		Present Value	Present Value of		Sketch of Relevant Cash Flows at End of Each Year				
7		of Cash Flow	$1 Discounted at 10%	0	1	2	3	4	5
8	Approach 1: Discounting Each Year's Cash Flow Separately[b]								
9	Net initial investment	$(379,100) ◄	1.000 ◄	$(379,100)					
10		90,900 ◄	0.909 ◄		$100,000				
11		82,600 ◄	0.826 ◄			$100,000			
12	Annual cash inflow	75,100 ◄	0.751 ◄				$100,000		
13		68,300 ◄	0.683 ◄					$100,000	
14		62,100 ◄	0.621 ◄						$100,000
15	NPV if new machine purchased[c]	$ 0							
16	(the zero difference proves that								
17	the internal rate of return is 10%)								
18									
19	Approach 2: Using Annuity Table								
20	Net initial investment	$(379,100) ◄	1.000 ◄	$(379,100)					
21					$100,000	$100,000	$100,000	$100,000	$100,000
22									
23	Annual cash inflow	379,100 ◄	3.791[d] ◄						
24	NPV if new machine purchased	$ 0							
25									
26	Note: Parentheses denote relevant cash outflows throughout all exhibits in Chapter 20.								
27	[a]The internal rate of return is computed by methods explained on pp. 758–759.								
28	[b]Present values from Table 2, Appendix A at the end of the book.								
29	[c]Sum is $(100) due to rounding. We round to $0.								
30	[d]Annuity present value from Table 4, Appendix A. The annuity table value of 3.791 is the sum of the individual discount rates								
31	0.909 + 0.826 + 0.751 + 0.683 + 0.621, subject to rounding.								

Assumptions about the timing and amount of cash flows are extremely important. If you use a programmable calculator or a popular spreadsheet program to calculate NPV, you may obtain a slightly different answer than if you use a compound interest table. The reason is that the compound interest table in Appendix A assumes the cash inflow all occurs at the *end* of each year, whereas many programs default to assume the inflow occurs at the beginning of each year. Most programs include an option to choose your assumption about the timing of cash inflows and the number of decimal places.

Internal Rate of Return Method

The **internal rate of return (IRR)** method calculates the discount rate at which the value of all expected cash inflows equals the present value of an investment's expected cash outflows. That is, the IRR is the discount rate that makes NPV = $0.

Exhibit 20-3 presents the cash flows and shows the calculation of NPV using a 10% annual discount rate for Top-Spin's carbon-fibre project. At a 10% discount rate, the NPV of the project is $0, therefore the IRR is 10% per year. IRR is sometimes called the **time-adjusted rate of return**.

Managers most often determine the discount rate that yields an NPV of $0 by using a financial calculator or computer program such as Microsoft Excel or Apple Numbers to provide the IRR. The following trial-and-error approach can also provide the answer.

Step 1: Use a discount rate, and calculate the project's NPV.

Step 2: If the calculated NPV is less than zero, use a lower discount rate. (A *lower* discount rate will *increase* NPV. Remember that we are trying to find a discount rate for which NPV = $0.) If the NPV is greater than zero, use a higher discount rate to lower the NPV. Keep adjusting the discount rate until NPV = $0. In the Top-Spin example, a discount rate of 8% yields an NPV of +$20,200 (see Exhibit 20-2). A discount rate of 12% yields an NPV of −$18,600 (= 3.605, the present value annuity factor from Table 4, multiplied by $100,000, minus $379,100). Therefore, the discount rate that makes NPV = $0 must lie between 8% and 12%. We use 10% and get NPV = $0. Hence, the IRR is 10% per year.

The step-by-step computations of IRR are easier when the cash inflows are constant, as in our Top-Spin example.

An algebraic method can be adopted to solve for IRR. To do this, we must determine what factor *F* in Table 4 (in Appendix A) will satisfy the following equation:

$$\$379,100 = \$100,000\,F$$

$$\frac{\$379,100}{\$100,000} = F$$

$$3.791 = F$$

On the five-period line of Table 4, find the percentage column that is closest to 3.791. It is exactly 10%. If the factor (*F*) falls between the factors in two columns, straight-line interpolation is used to approximate IRR. Alternatively, a spreadsheet such as MS-Excel can be used to determine the IRR with a solver (pre-programmed) function.

Note *Interpolation* is a simple method of estimating an unknown value that is assumed to be in a straight line (linear) relationship between the known points. It essentially means averaging the two known rates over the period to approximate the unknown value. (For an illustration of interpolation, see requirement 1 of the Problem for Self-Study at the end of this chapter.)

A project is accepted only if the IRR equals or exceeds the RRR. In the Top-Spin example, the carbon-fibre machine has an IRR of 10%, which is greater than the required rate of 8%. On the basis of financial factors, Top-Spin should invest in the new machine. In general, the NPV and IRR decision rules result in consistent project acceptance or rejection decisions. If IRR exceeds the required return, then the project has a positive NPV (favouring acceptance). If IRR equals the required return, NPV = $0, so project acceptance and rejection yield the same value. If IRR is less than the required return, NPV is negative (favouring rejection). Obviously, managers prefer projects with higher IRRs to projects with lower IRRs, if all other things are equal. The IRR of 10% means the cash inflows from the project are adequate both to recover the net initial investment in the project and to earn a return of exactly 10% on the investment tied up in the project over its useful life.

Comparison of Net Present Value and Internal Rate of Return Methods

The NPV method is generally regarded as the preferred method for project selection decisions. The NPV measure for a project captures the value (in today's dollars) of the surplus the project generates for the firm's shareholders, over and above the RRR.[1]

One advantage of the NPV method is that it expresses computations in dollars, not in percentages. Therefore, the sum of NPVs of individual projects will provide the NPV of a combination or portfolio of projects. In contrast, IRRs of individual projects cannot be added or averaged to represent the IRR of several projects.

A second advantage is that the NPV of a project can always be computed and expressed as a unique number. Under the IRR method, it is possible that more than one IRR may exist for a given project. This is possible because there may be multiple discount rates that equate the NPV of a set of cash flows to zero. This is especially true in cases of non-uniform cash flows—when in one year the cash flows may be negative (outflows), and in another they may be positive (inflows). In such cases, it is difficult to know which of the IRR estimates should be compared to the firm's RRR.

---

[1] More detailed explanations of the preeminence of the NPV criterion can be found in corporate finance texts.

A third advantage of the NPV method is that it can be used when the required return varies over the life of a project. Suppose Top-Spin's management sets an RRR of 9% per year in years 1 and 2 and 12% per year in years 3, 4, and 5. Total present value of the cash inflows can be calculated as $378,100 (computations not shown). It is not possible to use the IRR method in this case, because different RRRs in different years mean there is no single RRR that the IRR (a single figure) can be compared against to decide if the project should be accepted or rejected.

Finally, there are specific settings in which the IRR method is prone to indicating erroneous decisions (e.g., comparing mutually exclusive projects with unequal lives or unequal levels of initial investment). The IRR method implicitly assumes that project cash flows can be reinvested at the *project's* ROR. The NPV method, in contrast, accurately assumes that project cash flows can only be reinvested at the *company's* RRR. However, despite its limitations, surveys report widespread use of the IRR method.[2]

Sensitivity Analysis

To present the basics of the NPV and IRR methods, we have assumed that the expected values of cash flows will occur *for certain*. In reality, there is substantial uncertainty associated with the prediction of future cash flows. To examine how a result will change if the predicted financial outcomes are not achieved or if an underlying assumption changes, managers use *sensitivity analysis*, or a "what-if" technique. A common way to apply sensitivity analysis in capital budgeting decisions is to vary each of the inputs to the NPV calculation by a certain percentage (for example, increasing revenues by 10% or decreasing costs by 5%) and to assess the effect of the change on the project's NPV. Sensitivity analysis can take on other forms as well, such as considering broader changes in the political, social, or technological environments.

Suppose the manager at Top-Spin believes that forecasted cash flows are difficult to predict. She asks, "What are the minimum annual cash inflows that make the investment in a new carbon-fibre machine acceptable? That is, what inflows lead to an NPV of $0?"

For the data in Exhibit 20-2, let A = Annual cash flow and let NPV = $0. Net initial investment is $379,100, and the present value factor at the 8% required annual rate of return for a five-year annuity of $1 is 3.993. Then,

$$NPV = \$0$$
$$3.993\,A - \$379,100 = \$0$$
$$3.993\,A = \$379,100$$
$$A = \$94,941$$

At the discount rate of 8% per year, the annual (after tax) cash inflows can decrease to $94,941 (a decline of $100,000 − $94,941 = $5,059) before the NPV falls to $0. If the manager believes she can attain annual cash inflows of at least $94,941, she can justify investing in the carbon-fibre machine on financial grounds.

Exhibit 20-4 shows that variations in the annual cash inflows or the RRR significantly affect the NPV of the carbon-fibre machine project. NPVs can also vary with different useful lives of a project. Sensitivity analysis helps managers to focus on variables that are sensitive, or have higher potential to change, and require careful attention.

Exhibit 20-4 Net Present Value Under Different Assumptions of Cash Flows and Required Rates of Return

	A	B	C	D	E	F
1	**Required**	**Annual Cash Flows**				
2	**Rate of Return**	**$ 80,000**	**$ 90,000**	**$100,000**	**$110,000**	**$120,000**
3	6%	$ (42,140)	$ (20)	$ 42,100	$ 84,220	$126,340
4	8%	$ (59,660)	$ (19,730)	$ 20,200	$ 60,130	$100,060
5	10%	$ (75,820)	$ (37,910)	$ 0	$ 37,910	$ 75,820
6						
7	[a]All calculated amounts assume the project's useful life is five years.					

[2] In a recent survey, John Graham and Campbell Harvey found that 75.7% of CFOs always or almost always used IRR for capital budgeting decisions, while a slightly smaller number, 74.9%, always or almost always used the NPV criterion.

Income Tax and DCF in Capital Budgeting

► **LO 3**

Analyze the impact of income taxes on discounted cash flows and capital budgeting decisions.

Income taxes are mandatory cash disbursements and therefore are an important cash flow consideration. Income taxes almost always influence the amount and/or the timing of cash flows. Their basic role in capital budgeting is no different from that of any other cash disbursement. Income tax rates are progressive and depend on the amount of pretax income, with larger pretax income being taxed at higher rates. In capital budgeting, the relevant rate is the marginal income tax rate, that is, the tax rate paid on additional amounts of pretax income.

Suppose corporations pay income taxes of 15% on the first $50,000 of pretax income and 30% on pretax income over $50,000. The *marginal income tax rate* of a company with $75,000 of pretax income is 30%, because 30% of any *additional* income over $50,000 will be paid in taxes. In contrast, the company's *average income tax rate* is only 20% (15% × $50,000 + 30% × $25,000 = $15,000 ÷ $75,000 of pretax income). When we assess tax effects of capital budgeting decisions, we will always use the *marginal* tax rate because that is the rate applied to the incremental cash flows generated by a proposed project.

The impact of income taxes on operating cash flows is straightforward. If a capital project results in a reduction in costs—for example, an annual cost saving of $60,000— then the company's taxable income will increase by $60,000, all other things being equal. If the company has a marginal tax rate of 40%, then the company's income taxes will increase by $24,000 (= $60,000 × 0.40). A net annual after-tax savings of $36,000 results (= $60,000 − $24,000). This means the after-tax savings can be calculated quickly as $60,000 × (1 − the tax rate) or $60,000 × 0.60 = $36,000. Similarly, if operating expenses increase by $250,000, then the taxable income will decrease by $250,000. If the company has a 40% marginal tax rate, then the tax saving will be $100,000 (= $250,000 × 0.40).

Tax Shields and the Effect on Investment Cash Flows

Organizations that pay income taxes use generally accepted accounting principles (e.g., IFRS or ASPE, depending on the organization) to report their net income to the public. This permits managers to choose among depreciation methods in order to be able to present the most accurate data. The Canada Revenue Agency (CRA) does not permit this. Instead, tax laws require corporations to deduct capital cost allowance (CCA), not depreciation, when calculating their taxable income.

The Income Tax Act (ITA) assigns all depreciable capital purchases to a CCA class.[3] For example, a desk would qualify as a Class 8 asset and is in a class that includes furniture, tools costing $500 or more each, appliances, refrigeration equipment, photocopiers, fax machines, and telephone equipment. It also includes data network infrastructure equipment and systems software acquired prior to March 23, 2004, outdoor advertising signs, and other business equipment not specified as a different class. Companies may claim *up to* the amounts specified for an asset in any given class of tangible assets as detailed by CRA publications (but do not have to claim the full amount).[4] Companies may choose to carry unused CCA balances forward to future years when they have greater anticipated incomes (and thus, greater tax burdens).

Application in Capital Budgeting

The initial cost of the investment is the opening balance of what is called *undepreciated capital cost* (UCC). The CCA in any given year is deducted from the balance of the UCC, and thus the value of the investment has a declining balance for tax purposes. The CCA for a subsequent year is based on the CCA rate multiplied by the *new* UCC balance.

---

[3] The income tax statutes for intangible assets such as patents, copyrights, goodwill, and trademarks differ, as does the terminology. The eligible capital expenditure is the acquisition cost of the intangible asset. The eligible capital property is 75% of the acquisition cost of the intangible asset. The full cost is not deductible because the asset is considered to provide indefinite benefit. Intangible assets, by definition, have an indefinite useful life, and the annual deduction is called the cumulative eligible capital amount (CECA), calculated at 7% on a declining balance basis.

[4] For asset classes and capital allowances see Canada Revenue Agency Classes of depreciable property: http://www.cra-arc.gc.ca/tx/bsnss/tpcs/slprtnr/rprtng/cptl/menu-eng.html.

Exhibit 20-5
Calculation of CCA
Amounts for Years 1–4

	A	B	C	D
1		**CCA Rate**	20%	
2				
3				
4	Year	Purchase	CCA	UCC
5	0	$60,000		$60,000
6	1		$ 6,000	$54,000
7	2		$10,800	$43,200
8	3		$ 8,640	$34,560
9	4		$ 6,912	$27,648

Exhibit 20-5 shows the calculation of CCA amounts of a $60,000 Class 8 asset (CCA rate of 20%) over the first four years of the asset's life. When making these calculations, organizations must adhere to the **half-year rule**. The half-year rule assumes that all capital additions are purchased in the middle of the year, and thus only one-half of the stated CCA rate is allowed in the first year.

The starting UCC value of the asset is $60,000. The CCA dollar amount for year 1 is equal to the starting UCC multiplied by one-half the CCA rate, in this case 10% (= 20% × ½). The CCA rate for year 2 is determined by calculating the new UCC of $54,000—the previous year's UCC less the dollar value of the CCA (= $60,000 − $6,000). The new UCC is multiplied by the CCA rate for the asset (20%), which equals $10,800.

The CCA of each year is deducted in the calculation of a company's taxable income. Thus, the CCA is not a cash flow, but a tax savings, commonly called a *tax shield*. To determine the capital cost allowance for each year, the CCA must be multiplied by the company's marginal tax rate. If the marginal tax rate is 40% in the above example, the after-tax implications of the tax shield in year 1 would be $2,400 (= $6,000 × 40%). It is important to note that adjustments to the UCC are made based on *pretax* dollars.

In order to understand the impact of the tax shield in future years, it is necessary to discount the CCA in a similar fashion as any cash flow might be discounted. For instance, if the required return in the example above was 10%, the present value of the tax shield in year 2 would be ($10,800 × 40%) × 0.826 (the present value of $1 in two years at 10%) = $3,568.

Finally, the disposition of an asset at the end of its useful life must be considered in terms of the NPV of an investment, cash inflows (revenue from the disposal of the asset, called *salvage value*), and the loss of the tax shield now that the asset is no longer owned. The complete impact on the present value of an investment of the CCA tax shield can be calculated using the formula:

$$\text{PV tax shield on CCA} = \frac{CdT}{d+r} \times \frac{1+0.5r}{1+r} - \frac{SdT}{d+r} \times \frac{1}{(1+r)^n}$$

where

C = Cost of investment
d = CCA tax rate
T = Corporate tax rate
r = Discount rate
n = Number of periods in the project
S = Salvage value

To understand the implications of income tax and the tax shield generated by the CCA on capital budgeting and investment decisions, consider the following example.

Example Motor Corporation has purchased a CCA Class 8 asset (CCA rate of 20%) for $60,000, which is expected to generate savings in the amount of $25,000 per year. The useful life of the asset is four years and the asset will have a salvage value of $10,000 at the end of its life. The RRR is 10%, and the marginal tax rate for the company is 40%.

To calculate the present value of the investment in the above example, we rely on the present value of an annuity formula and the tax shield formula:

1. The NPV of Motor Corporation's investment is

$$\text{NPV of investment} = \text{PV of the cash flow} + \text{PV of tax shield} - \text{Initial cost of investment} + \text{Salvage value}$$

2. The cash inflow, in this case, an annuity, is the after-tax savings, which can be calculated using Table 4 from Appendix A:

Annual savings $\times$ (1 $-$ Tax rate) $\times$ PV of annuity (10%; 4 years)

$= \$25,000 \times (1 - 0.4) \times 3.170$

$= \$25,000 \times 0.6 \times 3.170$

$= 47,550$

3. The tax shield can be calculated using the above formula as

$$\text{PV tax shield on CCA} = \frac{CdT}{d + r} \times \frac{1 + 0.5r}{1 + r} - \frac{SdT}{d + r} \times \frac{1}{(1 + r)^n}$$

PV tax shield on CCA

$$= \frac{(\$60,000)(20\%)(40\%)}{20\% + 10\%} \times \frac{1 + 0.5(10\%)}{1 + 10\%} - \frac{(\$10,000)(20\%)(40\%)}{20\% + 10\%} \times \frac{1}{(1 + 10\%)^4}$$

$= \$13,451$

4. The salvage value can be calculated as the present value of income (Appendix A, Table 2).

Salvage value $\times$ PV of \$1(10%; 4 years)

$= \$10,000 \times 0.683$

$= \$6,830$

5. Therefore, the NPV of the investment is

NPV of investment $= \$47,550 + \$13,451 - \$60,000 + \$6,830$

$= \$7,831$

This positive NPV would suggest the asset is a worthwhile investment. Because of rounding error, there will often be slight variations between the NPV as calculated through the formula method and through the time line method. The error should not be treated as material to the calculation or the decision.

As an alternative to the formula method displayed above for calculating an asset's NPV inclusive of the CCA tax shield, a time line model can be constructed as shown in Exhibit 20-6.

The columns on the right show the pretax savings generated by the new machine (\$25,000 per year) and the after-tax impact of savings (\$25,000 $\times$ (1 $-$ 0.4) = \$15,000). Note that year 4 has an additional cash flow in the form of revenue generated from the disposal of the asset (which also must be corrected for the time value of money). The present values of the yearly cash flows are then summed (\$54,378) and added to the present value of the tax shield (\$13,451). This results in an NPV for the investment of \$7,829.

Relevant Information and DCF

▶ **LO 4**

Apply the concept of relevance to DCF methods of capital budgeting.

One of the biggest challenges in capital budgeting, particularly in DCF analysis, is determining which cash flows are relevant in making an investment selection. Relevant cash flows are the differences in expected future cash flows as a result of making the investment. A capital investment project typically has three categories of cash flows: (1) net initial investment in the project, which includes the acquisition of assets and any associated additions to working capital, minus the after-tax cash flow from the disposal of

Exhibit 20-6 A Time Line Model

	A	B	C	D	E	F	G	H
1								
2		Initial Cost		$ 60,000				
3		Yearly Savings		$ 25,000				
4		Required Return		10%				
5		Tax Rate		40%				
6		CCA Rate		20%				
7		Salvage Value		$ 10,000				
8								
9								
10			Present Value		Year			
11				0	1	2	3	4
12	Initial Cost		–$60,000	–$60,000				
13								
14	Savings				$25,000	$25,000	$25,000	$25,000
15	After Tax Savings				$15,000	$15,000	$15,000	$15,000
16	Salvage							$10,000
17	Total Cash Flows				$15,000	$15,000	$15,000	$25,000
18								
19	PV of Cash Flows				$13,636	$12,397	$11,270	$17,075
20								
21	Sum of PV of Cash Flows		$ 54,378					
22	PV of Tax Shield		$ 13,451					
23								
24	NPV of Investment		$ 7,829					
25								

existing assets; (2) after-tax cash flow from operations (including income tax cash savings from annual depreciation deductions); and (3) after-tax cash flow from terminal disposal of an asset and recovery of working capital.

1. Net Initial Investment

Three components of net initial investment cash flows are (a) cash outflow to purchase the machine, (b) cash outflow for working capital, and (c) after-tax cash inflow from current disposal of the old machine.

1a. *Initial machine investment*

These outflows, made for purchasing plant and equipment, occur at the beginning of the project's life and include cash outflows for transporting and installing the equipment.

1b. *Initial working-capital investment*

Initial investments in plant and equipment are usually accompanied by additional investments in working capital. These additional investments take the form of current assets, such as accounts receivable and inventories, minus current liabilities, such as accounts payable. Working-capital investments are similar to plant and equipment investments in that they require cash. The magnitude of the investment generally increases as a function of the level of additional sales generated by the project. However, the exact relationship varies based on the nature of the project and the operating cycle of the industry.

1c. *After-tax cash flow from current disposal of old machine*   Any cash received from disposal of the old machine is a relevant cash inflow (in year 0). That's because it is an expected future cash flow that differs between the alternatives of investing and not investing in the new machine.

2. Cash Flow from Operations

This category includes the difference between successive years' cash flow from operations. Organizations make capital investments to generate future cash inflows.

2a. *Annual after-tax cash flow from recurring operations*   Cash inflows may result from savings in operating costs or from producing and selling additional goods. Annual cash flow from operations can be net outflows in some years. Cash outflows can include overhead or expenses related to the new investment.

Focus on cash flows from operations, *not* revenues and expenditures as reported in financial statements.

2b. *Income tax cash savings from annual CCA.*   Deductions for CCA, in effect, partially offset the cost of acquiring new assets. The additional annual CCA deduction results in incremental income tax cash savings.

3. Terminal Disposal of Investment

The disposal of the new investment generally increases cash inflow when the project terminates. Errors in forecasting terminal disposal value are seldom critical for long-duration

---

Sustainability in Action   Capital Budgeting for Sustainable Business

The Tennessee Valley Authority (TVA) is the United States's largest public power provider and is wholly owned by the US government. Although owned by the federal government, TVA is not financed with tax dollars; rather, the utility's funding comes from the sale of power to its customers. Recently, TVA faced a difficult strategic decision: ensuring sufficient power generation while continuing to provide affordable power to a growing number of customers in its service area.

At the same time, TVA was replacing a significant part of its existing power generation capability. TVA previously announced plans to retire multiple coal power plants by 2018 to reach its goal of becoming a clean energy leader. Potential sources of new power generation included the construction of nuclear, natural gas, coal, wind, and solar plants. The power generation options had differing costs, expected cash flows, and useful lives. Moreover, TVA's construction decisions were constrained by a limited capital budget. TVA turned to NPV and IRR calculations to guide its decision making.

After extensive calculations, TVA discovered that the NPVs and IRRs of natural gas, nuclear, and wind plants were positive. The NPVs of solar and coal plants were negative, and their IRRs were below TVA's cost of capital (calculated as the current yield to maturity on 30-year government debt plus an added 1% premium). In 2012, four renewable wind-power sources located in Kansas, Illinois, and Iowa began delivery to the TVA power grid and construction began on a new gas-fired combustion turbine/combined cycle generating power plant.

Ritu Manoj Jethani/Shutterstock

Additionally, the Watts Bar Unit 2 nuclear power generator was scheduled to begin operation in 2015. Construction on the unit, which started in the mid-1980s, was resumed with updated technologies. TVA is also developing a smart grid deployment plan that will help customers better understand the costs and benefits of these new power sources.

Sources: "TVA Releases Cost, Schedule Estimates for Watts Bar Nuclear Unit 2," Tennessee Valley Authority press release (Knoxville, TN, April 5, 2012); B. Wood, S. Isbell, and C. Larson, "The Tennessee Valley Authority: The Cost of Power," *IMA Educational Case Journal*, Vol. 5, No. 4 (Montvale, NJ: Institute of Management Accountants, Inc., December 2012).

projects, because the present values of amounts to be received in the distant future are usually small. Two components of the terminal disposal value of an investment are (a) after-tax cash flow from terminal disposal of machines and (b) after-tax cash flow from recovery of working capital.

3a. *After-tax cash flow from terminal disposal of machines* — At the end of the useful life of the project, the machine's terminal disposal value may be $0 or an amount considerably less than the net initial investment. The relevant cash inflow is the difference in expected after-tax cash inflow from terminal disposal at the end of five years under the two alternatives of purchasing the new machine or keeping the old machine.

3b. *After-tax cash flow from terminal recovery of working-capital investment* — The initial investment in working capital is usually fully recouped when the project is terminated. At that time, inventories and accounts receivable necessary to support the project are no longer needed. If a company receives cash equal to the book value of its working capital, there is no gain or loss on working capital and, hence, no tax consequences.

Exhibit 20-7 presents the relevant cash inflows and outflows for Motor Corporation's decision to purchase the new machine as described earlier in the chapter. Assume that Motor Corporation has to make a $10,000 outlay of working capital at the beginning of the project, which it will fully recoup in the final year.

Exhibit 20-7 Relevant Information in Motor Corporation's Decision to Invest

	A	B	C	D	E	F	G	H	I	J
1										
2			Initial Cost			$60,000				
3			Yearly Savings			$25,000				
4			Required Return			10%				
5			Tax Rate			40%				
6			CCA Rate			20%				
7			Salvage Value			$10,000				
8										
9										
10					**Present Value**			Year		
11						0	1	2	3	4
12	1a	Initial Cost			− $60,000	$60,000				
13	1b	Initial Working Capital Investment			− $10,000					
14		Savings					$25,000	$25,000	$25,000	$25,000
15	2a	After Tax Savings					$15,000	$15,000	$15,000	$15,000
16	3a	Salvage								$10,000
17	3b	Working Capital Recapture								$10,000
18		Total Cash Flows					$15,000	$15,000	$15,000	$35,000
19										
20		PV of Cash Flows					$13,636	$12,397	$11,270	$23,905
21										
22		Sum of PV of Cash Flows			$ 61,208					
23	2b	PV of Tax Shield			$ 13,451					
24										
25		NPV of Investment			$ 4,659					

The columns on the right show the pretax savings generated by the new machine ($25,000 per year), and the after-tax impact of savings ($25,000 × (1 − 0.4) = $15,000). Note that year 4 has additional cash flows in the form of revenue generated from the disposal of the asset and the recapture of working capital (which also must be corrected for the time value of money). The present values of the yearly cash flows are then summed ($54,378) and added to the present value of the tax shield ($13,451). Thus, the present value of the cash inflows is $64,659. To arrive at the NPV of $4,659, we must subtract the cash outflows represented by the initial capital investment in the machine ($60,000) and the initial investment in working capital ($10,000).

TRY IT! 20.1

DigiServe is considering investing in a roof-top solar network to generate its own power. Any unused power will be sold back to the local utility company. Between cost savings and new revenues, the company expects to generate $1,500,000 per year in net cash inflows from the solar network installation. The turbine would cost $8 million and is expected to have a 20-year useful life with no residual value. Calculate (i) the IRR and (ii) the NPV assuming the company uses a 12% hurdle rate.

Non-DCF Methods in Capital Budgeting

► LO 5

Assess the complexities in capital budgeting within an interdependent set of value-chain business functions.

DCF methods for capital budgeting focus on the application of the time value of money as a means of estimating risk and probable returns from investments. The primary advantage of these techniques is the ability to accommodate risk, inflation, and sensitivity in the decision model. However, both NPV and IRR can be cumbersome calculations, and alternatives to DCF methods do exist and are dramatically simpler. The two methods addressed here are the payback period and the AARR.

Payback Period

The **payback method** measures the time it will take to recoup the initial investment in a project in the form of net cash inflows. Like NPV and IRR, the payback method includes all sources of cash inflows (operations, disposal of equipment, or recovery of working capital). The payback method returns an answer in a number of periods (to recoup investment) rather than a dollar value of profitability or an ROR as in the case of NPV and IRR, respectively.

Payback Period and Uniform Cash Flows

Payback is simpler to calculate when a project has uniform cash flows, as opposed to non-uniform cash flows. In the Top-Spin example, the carbon-fibre machine costs $379,100, has a five-year expected useful life, and generates $100,000 *uniform* cash flow each year. Calculation of the payback period is as follows:

$$\text{Payback} = \frac{\text{Net initial investment}}{\text{Increase in cash flows}}$$

$$= \frac{\$379,100}{\$100,000}$$

$$= 3.8 \text{ years (rounded for simplicity)}$$

The payback method highlights liquidity, which is often an important factor in capital budgeting decisions. Managers prefer projects with shorter paybacks (more liquid) to projects with longer paybacks, if all other things are equal. Projects with shorter payback periods give the organization more flexibility because funds for other projects become available sooner. Additionally, managers are less confident about cash flow predictions that stretch far into the future.

The major strength of the payback method is that it is easy to understand. Like the DCF methods described previously, the payback method is not affected by accrual accounting conventions like depreciation. Advocates of the payback method argue that it is a handy measure when (1) estimates of profitability are not crucial and preliminary screening of many proposals is necessary and (2) the predicted cash flows in later years of the project are highly uncertain.

Unlike the NPV and IRR methods, where management selects a ROR, under the payback method, management chooses a cutoff period for a project. Projects with a payback period that is less than the cutoff period are considered acceptable, and those with a payback period that is longer than the cutoff period are rejected. Japanese companies favour the payback method over other methods and use cutoff periods ranging from three to five years depending on the risks involved with the project. In general, modern risk management calls for using shorter cutoff periods for riskier projects.

Two major weaknesses of the payback method are (1) it neglects the time value of money and (2) it neglects to consider project cash flows after the net initial investment is recovered. Consider our discussion earlier about Top-Spin, and an alternative to the $379,100 machine mentioned. Assume that another machine, with a three-year useful life and zero terminal disposal price, requires only a $300,000 net initial investment and will also result in cash inflows of $100,000 per year. First, compare the two payback periods:

$$\text{Payback period for machine 1:} \quad = \frac{\$379,100}{\$100,000} = 3.791 \text{ years}$$

$$\text{Payback period for machine 2:} = \frac{\$300,000}{\$100,000} = 3.000 \text{ years}$$

The payback criterion would favour buying the $300,000 machine, because it has a shorter payback. In fact, if the cutoff period is three years, then Top-Spin would not acquire machine 1 because it fails to meet the payback criterion. Consider next the NPV of the two investment options using Top-Spin's 8% RRR for the investment. At a discount rate of 8%, the NPV of machine 2 is −$42,300 (calculated as 2.577, the present value annuity factor for three years at 8% from Table 4, multiplied by $100,000 equals $257,700, minus the net initial investment of $300,000). Machine 1, as we know, has a positive NPV of $20,200 (from Exhibit 20-3). The NPV criterion suggests that Top-Spin should acquire machine 1. Machine 2, with a negative NPV, would fail to meet the NPV criterion. The payback method gives a different answer from the NPV method because the payback method (1) does not consider cash flows after the payback period and (2) does not discount cash flows.

An additional concern with the payback method is that choosing too short a cutoff period for project acceptance may promote the selection of only short-lived projects; the organization will tend to reject long-term, positive-NPV projects. This would prove particularly problematic in the pharmaceutical industry where drug development projects often run more than 15 years. Companies often use both the payback and DCF methods to select positive NPV projects with an acceptably short payback period.

Non-Uniform Cash Flows

When annual cash inflows are *not uniform*, the payback computation takes a cumulative form. The years' net cash inflows are accumulated until the amount of the net initial investment has been recovered. Assume that Venture Law Group is considering the purchase of videoconferencing equipment for $150,000. The equipment is expected to provide total cash savings of $380,000 over the next five years, due to reduced travel costs and more effective use of associates' time. The cash savings occur uniformly throughout each year, but non-uniformly across years. Payback occurs during the third year:

Year	Cash Savings	Cumulative Cash Savings	Net Initial Investment Yet to Be Recovered at the End of the Year
0	—	—	$150,000
1	$ 50,000	$ 50,000	100,000
2	60,000	110,000	40,000
3	80,000	190,000	—
4	90,000	280,000	—
5	100,000	380,000	—

Straight-line interpolation within the third year, which has cash savings of $80,000, reveals that the final $40,000 needed to recover the $150,000 investment (that is, $150,000 – $110,000 recovered by the end of year 2) will be achieved halfway through year 3 (in which $80,000 of cash savings occur):

$$\text{Payback} = 2 \text{ years} + \left(\frac{\$40,000}{\$80,000} \times 1 \text{ year} \right) = 2.5 \text{ years}$$

The videoconferencing example has a single cash outflow of $150,000 at year 0. Where a project has multiple cash outflows occurring at different points in time, these outflows are subtracted from revenue or savings inflows to derive a net cash outflow figure. The net cash flow is used to calculate the payback period. No adjustment is made for the time value of money when adding these cash outflows in computing the payback period.

Accrual Accounting Rate of Return

The **accrual accounting rate of return (AARR)** is an accounting measure of income divided by an accounting measure of investment. It is also called **accounting rate of return** or **return on investment (ROI)**. Note that NPV, IRR, and payback are all based on cash flows, whereas AARR is based on accrual accounting. AARR is calculated as follows:

$$\text{AARR} = \frac{\text{Increase in after-tax income} - \text{Depreciation associated with the project}}{\text{Net initial investment}}$$

Consider the following example. A company expects to make a total investment of $300,000 in an asset, which has a zero terminal disposal price and terminates in five years. The asset will generate $90,000 in after-tax revenue.

The AARR is computed as follows. The numerator is equal to the after-tax income, less the depreciation of the asset. Using straight-line depreciation, the yearly depreciation is $60,000; thus, the numerator is $90,000 – $60,000 = $30,000. The net initial investment is $300,000. The AARR is equal to

$$\text{AARR} = \frac{\$90,000 - \$60,000}{\$300,000}$$

$$= \frac{\$30,000}{\$300,000} = 10\%$$

In practice; there are variations on this formula. Some companies use "increase in expected average annual operating income" in the numerator and/or "average investment per year" in the denominator. The AARR method focuses on how investment decisions affect operating income numbers routinely reported by organizations. The AARR of 10% indicates the rate at which a dollar of investment generates operating income.

20.2 **TRY IT!**

DigiServe is considering investing in a roof-top solar network to generate its own power. Any unused power will be sold back to the local utility company. Between cost savings and new revenues, the company expects to generate $1,500,000 per year in net cash inflows from the solar network installation. The turbine would cost $8 million and is expected to have a 20-year useful life with no residual value. Calculate the payback period and the AARR.

Strategic Factors in Capital Budgeting Decisions

A company's strategy is the source of its strategic capital budgeting decisions. Strategic investments may be undertaken offensively to grow market share and profitability, or defensively to avoid impairing a company's competitive advantage. The fourth step in the 5DM model as it relates to capital budgeting is the application of the manager's judgment in evaluating the financial information examined in the third step and balancing that against qualitative and other quantitative information. Capital investment decisions that are strategic in nature require managers to study a broad range of factors that may be difficult to estimate.

▶ **LO 6**

Apply the concept of defensive strategic investment to the capital budgeting process.

The factors that companies consider for strategic investment decisions are far broader than costs alone (see Exhibit 20-8). For example, the reasons for introducing computer-integrated manufacturing (CIM) technology—faster response time, higher product quality, and greater flexibility in meeting changes in customer preferences—are often to increase revenues and contribution margins. Ignoring the revenue effects underestimates the financial benefits of CIM investments. However, the revenue benefits of technology investments of this sort are often difficult to quantify in financial terms that can be applied in an NPV model. Nevertheless, competitive and revenue advantages are important managerial considerations when introducing CIM.

Exhibit 20-8 presents examples of the broader set of factors that companies must examine. Predicting the full set of costs also presents problems. Three classes of costs are difficult to measure and are often underestimated:

1. Costs associated with a reduced competitive position in the industry. If other companies in the industry are investing in CIM, a company not investing in CIM will probably suffer a decline in market share because of its inferior quality and slower delivery performance. Several companies in the machine tool industry that continued to use a conventional manufacturing approach experienced rapid drops in market share after their competitors introduced CIM.

2. Costs of retraining the operating and maintenance personnel to handle the automated facilities.

3. Costs of developing and maintaining the software and maintenance programs to operate the automated manufacturing activities.

Examples of Financial Outcomes	Examples of Nonfinancial and Qualitative Outcomes
Lower direct labour costs	Reduction in manufacturing cycle time
Lower hourly support labour costs	Increase in manufacturing flexibility
Less scrap and rework	Increase in business risk due to higher fixed cost structure
Lower inventory costs	Improved product delivery and service
Increase in software and related costs	Reduction in product development time
Higher costs of retraining personnel	Faster response to market changes
	Increased learning by workers about automation
	Improved competitive position in the industry

Exhibit 20-8 Factors Considered in Making Capital Budgeting Decisions for CIM Projects

Customer Value and Capital Budgeting

To remain competitive, companies must keep their profitable customers and gain new ones. Consider Potato Supreme, which makes potato products for sale to retail outlets. It is currently analyzing two of its customers: Shine Stores and Always Open. Potato Supreme predicts the following cash flow from operations, net of income taxes (in thousands), from each customer account for the next five years:

	2018	2019	2020	2021	2022
Shine Stores	$1,450	$1,305	$1,175	$1,058	$ 950
Always Open	690	1,160	1,900	2,950	4,160

Which customer is more valuable to Potato Supreme?

Looking at only the first year, 2018, Shine Stores provides more than double the cash flow compared to Always Open ($1,450 versus $690). A different picture emerges, however, when looking over the entire five-year horizon. Using Potato Supreme's 10% RRR, the NPV of the Always Open customer is $7,610, compared to $4,591 for Shine Stores (computations not shown). These NPV amounts are calculated using the 10% NPV of $1,318 (= $1,450 × 0.909) for Shine Stores and $627 (= $690 × 0.909) for Always Open.

Note how NPV captures in its estimate of customer value the future growth of Always Open. Potato Supreme uses this information to allocate more resources and salespeople to service the Always Open account. Potato Supreme can also use NPV calculations to examine the effects of alternative ways of increasing customer loyalty and retention, such as introducing frequent-purchaser cards.

Concepts in Action | Capital Budgeting at Disney

The Walt Disney Company, one of the world's leading entertainment producers with $42 billion in 2012 revenue, spends about $1 billion annually in capital investments on its theme park business. These funds are invested in new theme parks, rides and attractions, and other park construction and improvements.

Years ago, Disney developed a robust capital budgeting approval process. Project approval relied heavily on projected returns on capital investment as measured by NPV and IRR calculations. This worked well for Disney's investments in its domestic theme park business, but the company experienced challenges when it considered building the DisneySea theme park near Tokyo, Japan.

While capital budgeting in the United States relies on discounted cash flow analysis, Japanese firms frequently use the average accounting return (AAR) method instead. AAR is analogous to an AARR measure based on average investment. However, it focuses on the first few years of a project (five years, in the case of DisneySea) and ignores terminal values.

Disney discovered that the difference in capital budgeting techniques between US and Japanese firms reflected the difference in corporate governance in the two countries. The use of NPV and IRR in the United States underlined a focus on shareholder-value maximization. On the other hand, the preference for AAR in Japan reflected the importance of achieving complete consensus among all parties affected by the investment decision.

When the DisneySea project was evaluated, it was found to have a positive NPV but a negative AAR. To account for the differences in philosophies and capital budgeting techniques, managers at Disney introduced a third calculation method called average cash flow return (ACFR). This hybrid method measured the average cash flow over the first five years, with the asset assumed to be sold for book value at the end of that period at a fraction of the initial investment in the project. The resulting ratio was found to exceed the return on Japanese government bonds and hence to yield a positive return for DisneySea. As a result, the park was constructed next to Tokyo Disneyland and has since become a profitable addition to Disney's Japanese operations.

Sources: M. Misawa, "Tokyo Disneyland and the DisneySea Park: Corporate Governance and Differences in Capital Budgeting Concepts and Methods Between American and Japanese Companies," University of Hong Kong No. HKU568 (Hong Kong: University of Hong Kong Asia Case Research Center, 2006); The Walt Disney Company, *2012 Annual Report* (Burbank, CA: The Walt Disney Company, 2013).

A comparison of year-to-year changes in customer NPV estimates highlights whether managers have been successful in maintaining long-run profitable relationships with their customers. Suppose the NPV of Potato Supreme's customer base declines 15% in one year. Management can then examine the reasons for the decline, such as aggressive pricing by competitors, and devise new product development and marketing strategies for the future.

Cell phone companies Rogers and TELUS use NPV analyses to examine their strategy, which is focused on attempting to enroll customers for multiple years of service. The initial costs of marketing, providing a phone at a subsidized price, and other expenses are balanced against the estimated future service payments customers will make over the life of the contract. The objective is to prevent "customer churn," customers switching frequently from one company to another. The higher the probability of customer churn, the lower the NPV of the customer to the telecommunications company.

Investment in Research and Development

Companies such as Samsung, a global leader in designing, manufacturing, and marketing innovative wireless mobile devices like the Galaxy Tab and the Galaxy II, regard research and development (R&D) projects as important strategic investments. R&D payoffs are not only more uncertain than other investment projects, but also will often occur far into the future. Most companies engaged in these types of investment projects stage their R&D so they have the choice to increase or decrease their investment at different points in time based on its success. This option feature of R&D investments—called *real options*—is an important aspect of R&D investments and increases the NPV of these investments. That's because a company can limit its losses when things are going badly and take advantage of new opportunities when things are going well.

Capital Budgeting and Control: Evaluation and Application

The final step of capital budgeting begins with implementing the decision, or managing the project. This includes management control of the investment activity itself, as well as management control of the project as a whole. Capital budgeting projects, such as purchasing a carbon-fibre machine or videoconferencing equipment, are easier to implement than projects involving building shopping malls or manufacturing plants. The building projects are more complex, so monitoring and controlling the investment schedules and budgets are critical to successfully completing the investment activity.

▶ **LO 6**

Apply the concept of defensive strategic investment to the capital budgeting process.

Management Control: Performance Evaluation

Ideally managers should be evaluated on a project-by-project basis, which examines how well they achieve the amounts and timing of forecasted cash flows. In practice, however, managers are often evaluated based on aggregate information, especially when multiple projects are underway at any point in time. It is important then to ensure that the method of evaluation does not conflict with the use of the NPV method for making capital budgeting decisions.

For example, suppose that Top-Spin uses the AARR generated in each period to assess managerial performance. We know from the NPV method that the manager of the racquet production plant should purchase the carbon-fibre machine because it has a positive NPV. Despite that, the project may be rejected if the AARR on the net initial investment is lower than the minimum accounting rate of return the manager is required to achieve.

There is an inconsistency between using the NPV method as best for capital budgeting decisions and then using a different method to evaluate performance. This inconsistency means managers are tempted to make capital budgeting decisions on the basis of the method by which they are being evaluated, rather than the method best suited to the organization.

Other conflicts between decision making and performance evaluation persist even if a company uses similar measures for both purposes. If the AARR on the carbon-fibre machine exceeds the minimum required AARR but is below the current AARR of the production plant, the manager may still be tempted to reject purchase of the carbon-fibre machine because the lower AARR of the carbon-fibre machine will reduce the AARR of the entire plant and hurt the manager's reported performance. Or, consider an example where the cash inflows from the carbon-fibre machine occur mostly in the later years of the project. Then, even if the AARR on the project exceeds the current AARR of the plant (as well as the minimum required return), the manager may still reject the purchase since it will have a negative effect on the realized AARR for the first few years.

Management Control: The Investment Activity

Assumptions made by managers of a company drive the evaluation of alternative investments. A company may develop a simple DCF analysis using, for example, a 12% discount rate for all projects. As a company grows globally, risks of otherwise identical projects can vary widely, and the issue of currency repatriation (reporting foreign revenue and cost in domestic currency) and political instability affect many countries. Expansion by a Canadian energy producer into Argentina or Somalia, for example, carries higher risk than expansion into the Gulf of Mexico.

Failing to adjust assumptions about the RRR to account for higher risk, such as regulatory and currency risk, produces a biased valuation of investment alternatives. Another factor that creates fundamental difficulties for applying analytic models of domestic investments to overseas expansion is the increasing complexity of international financing. Global expansion strategies require a capital budgeting process that evaluates each proposed investment as a distinct opportunity with unique risks. A single discount rate does not fit all alternatives.

An approach could begin by considering representatives from various countries and deriving a weighted average cost of capital (WACC) for each project. WACC is covered in introductory finance courses. Briefly, WACC calculations require measuring all of the constituent parts of financing for projects: the cost of debt, the target capital structure, the local-country tax rates, and an appropriate cost of equity.[5]

To capture the country-specific risks in foreign markets, one approach is to calculate a cost of debt and a cost of equity for each representative project using domestic data. The risk-free investment is assessed using the difference between the yield on local government bonds and the yield on corresponding domestic government Treasury bonds to both the cost of debt and the cost of equity. The difference, or sovereign spread, can approximate the incremental borrowing costs (and market risk) in the local country. This approach is a more sophisticated way to think about capital budgeting risk and its cost of capital around the world.

Management Control: The Post-Investment Audit

A post-investment audit compares the predictions of investment costs and outcomes made at the time a project was selected to the actual results. It provides management with feedback about the investment's performance. Suppose, for example, that actual outcomes (operating cash savings from the graphite machine in the Top-Spin example) are much lower than predicted outcomes. Management must then investigate whether this occurred because the original estimates were overly optimistic or because there were problems in implementing the project. Both types of problems are a concern.

Optimistic estimates are a concern because they may result in the acceptance of a project that would otherwise have been rejected. To discourage optimistic estimates, companies like DuPont maintain records comparing actual performance to the estimates made by individual managers when seeking approval for capital investments. DuPont believes that post-investment audits discourage managers from making unrealistic forecasts. Problems in implementing a project—such as weak project management, poor quality control, or inadequate marketing—are an obvious concern because the returns from the project will not meet expectations. Post-investment audits can point to areas requiring corrective action.

However, post-investment audits require thoughtfulness and care. They should be done only after project outcomes have stabilized because performing audits too early may

---

[5] Based on "Globalizing the Cost of Capital and Capital Budgeting at AES," Harvard Business School Case No. 9-204-109.

yield misleading feedback. Obtaining actual results to compare against estimates is often not easy. For example, additional revenues from the new carbon-fibre technology may not be comparable to the estimated revenues, because in any particular season the rise or fall of a tennis star can greatly affect the popularity of the sport and the subsequent demand for racquets. Alternatively, increased traffic because of the carbon-fibre products may boost other products' sales. A better evaluation might look at the average revenues across a couple of seasons.

The IFRS require an annual post-investment review. Upon review, if the carrying value (acquisition cost less accumulated depreciation) materially misstates the long-term investment or liability values, then an impairment must be reported. The reported values must also be adjusted along with explanatory notes informing investors of the key changes in assumptions that explain the impairment. In subsequent years, if a reversal occurs with the impaired asset (and its fair market value exceeds the carrying value), then reporting must be adjusted to reflect the higher value. This change to financial accounting standards will lead to a new demand for the skills in applying management accounting methods long used in capital budgeting and forecasts to retrospective reporting of performance on the statement of financial position.

The 5DM Model: A Capital Budgeting Review

Step 1: Identify Projects

Identify potential capital investments that agree with the organization's strategy.

When seeking out and identifying projects, it is important to focus on the organization's mission and vision. Seeking projects that are aligned with the strategy of the organization and will help achieve the mission are more likely to be successful.

Step 2: Obtain Information

Gather information from all parts of the value chain to evaluate alternative projects.

The information gathered here can come from a variety of sources in the value chain, including R&D, production, and customer service. Information gathered here will be used in steps 3 and 4 to make effective capital budgeting decisions.

Step 3: Make Predictions

Forecast all potential cash flows attributable to the alternative projects.

Capital investments require the firm to make forecasts of cash flows several years into the future. Factors that should be included are initial cost of the investment, regular or irregular cash flows (in and out), the impact of income taxes, working capital flows, and other financial data from the organization and the economy. The tools we focus on in capital budgeting are NPV, IRR, payback period, and AARR.

Step 4: Make Decisions by Choosing Among Alternatives

Determine which investment yields the greatest benefit and the least cost to the organization.

Financial information is never enough to make the decision about a capital investment. It is necessary that managers use judgment in evaluating other forms of information that may impact the organization, such as societal and technological trends (i.e., social fashion or obsolescence); stakeholder requirements (i.e., investments that have non-monetary and subjective value); and other factors.

Stage 5: Implement the Decision, Evaluate Performance, and Learn

Given the complexities of capital investment decisions and the long time horizons they span, this stage can be separated into two phases:

Phase 1: Obtain funding and make the investments selected in step 4.

Sources of funding include internally generated cash flow as well as equity and debt securities sold in capital markets. Managers must examine the most cost effective strategy to generate capital within the firm's strategy and capabilities.

Phase 2: Track realized cash flows, compare against estimated numbers, and revise plans if necessary.

As the cash outflows and inflows begin to accumulate, managers can verify whether the predictions made in step 3 agree with the actual flows of cash from the project. Control and evaluation must be exercised judiciously to ensure that the project unfolds as intended.

Pulling it all Together—Problem for Self-Study

(Try to solve this problem before examining the solution that follows.)

Problem

Marist Sails is considering purchasing a new machine to sew sails for high performance racing yachts to complement its existing product line of sails for cruising, or "day sailing" yachts. Assume that the expected annual cash inflows from new sails will be $130,000. A $379,100 net initial investment is required, and the machine has a five-year useful life and an 8% required rate of return. When calculating breakeven time, assume that the investment will occur immediately after management approves the project.

Compute the following:

Required ▶ ❶❷ 1. Discounted cash flow
   a. Net present value
   b. Internal rate of return
   ❸ c. Net present value assuming a Class 8 asset (CCA of 20%), a tax rate of 40%, and a salvage value of $50,000.
   ❷ 2. Payback period
   ❷ 3. Accrual accounting rate of return on net initial investment
   ❷ 4. Calculate the payback period using discounted cash flows. Assume (for calculation purposes) that cash outflows and cash inflows occur at the end of each period.
   ❹ 5. To what five areas would you direct your attention when assessing relevant from irrelevant cash flows for two alternative long-term investments?
   ❺ 6. What prominent change in financial accounting standards has contributed to the importance of the interconnection of management accounting and financial reporting processes?
   ❻ 7. Aside from a growth strategy, for what other reason might managers undertake new investment?

Solution

1. a. NPV = ($130,000 × 3.993) − $379,100
          = $519,090 − $379,100 = $139,990
   b. There are several approaches to computing the IRR. One is to use a calculator with an IRR function; this gives an IRR of 21.16%. An alternative approach is to use Table 4 in Appendix A:

$$\$379,100 = \$130,000 \, F$$

$$F = \frac{\$379,100}{\$130,000} = 2.916$$

On the five-period line of Table 4, the column closest to 2.916 is 22%. To obtain a more accurate number, straight-line interpolation can be used:

	Present Value	**Factors**
20%	2.991	2.991
IRR	—	2.916
22%	2.864	—
Difference	0.127	0.075

$$\text{IRR} = 20\% + \frac{0.075}{0.127}(2\%) = 21.18\% \quad \text{(difference due to rounding of PV factor to 3 decimals)}$$

c.

NPV = Operational Cash Flows	= $\$130,000 \times 3.993$	=	\$519,090
+ Tax Shield	= See below	=	94,580
+ PV of Salvage	= $\$50,000 \times 0.681$	=	34,050
− Initial Investment		=	(389,100)
+ PV of WC recapture	= $\$10,000 \times 0.681$	=	6,810
		=	$\underline{\underline{\$265,430}}$

Tax Shield Calculation

$$\text{PV tax shield on CCA} = \frac{CdT}{d+r} \times \frac{1+0.5r}{1+r} - \frac{SdT}{d+r} \times \frac{1}{(1+r)^n}$$

PV tax shield on CCA

$$= \frac{(\$379,100)(20\%)(40\%)}{20\% + 8\%} \times \frac{1+0.5(8\%)}{1+8\%} - \frac{(\$50,000)(20\%)(40\%)}{20\% + 8\%} \times \frac{1}{(1+8\%)^5}$$

2. $\text{Payback} = \dfrac{\text{Net initial investment}}{\text{Uniform increase in annual cash flows}}$

$= \$379,100 \div \$130,000 = 2.92 \text{ years}$

3. $\text{AARR} = \dfrac{\text{Increase in expected average annual operating income}}{\text{Net initial investment}}$

Increase in expected average
annual operating income $= [(\$130,000 \times 4) + \$120,000] \div 5$
$= \$128,000$

Average annual depreciation $= \$372,890 \div 5 = \$74,578$

Increase in expected average
annual operating income $= \$128,000 - \$74,578 = \$53,422$

$$\text{AARR} = \frac{\$53,422}{\$379,100} = 14.09\%$$

4. Payback using discounted cash flow computations is as follows:

Year	PV Discount Factor at 8% (1)	Investment Cash Outflows (2)	PV of Investment Cash Outflows* (3) = (1) × (2)	Cumulative PV of Investment Cash Outflows* (4)	Cash Inflows (5)	PV of Cash Inflows* (6) = (1) × (5)	Cumulative PV of Cash Inflows* (7)
0	1.000	\$379,100	\$379,100	\$379,100			
1	0.926				\$130,000	\$120,380	\$120,380
2	0.857				130,000	111,410	231,790
3	0.794				130,000	103,220	335,010
4	0.735				130,000	95,550	430,560
5	0.681				130,000	88,530	519,090

*At year 0.

$$\text{BET} = 3 \text{ years} + \frac{(\$379,100 - \$335,010)}{\$95,550}$$

$$= 3 \text{ years} + \frac{44,090}{95,550}$$

$$= 3.46 \text{ years}$$

5. The five areas where cash flows may differ are the cost of initial investment, including working capital requirements; liquidation values of any old investments; recurring cash flows; overhead costs, including depreciation (or CCA); and the terminal disposal price.

6. The convergence from national to international financial accounting and reporting standards now requires an annual post-investment audit. In addition, new standards for long-term liabilities require an annual review of their carrying value as well as an annual impairment test for long-term assets. The methods of capital budgeting are now recommended for use in valuation for financial reporting purposes.

7. Strategically, if competitors are undertaking specific types of long-term investments, failing to do so is highly likely to put a firm at a competitive disadvantage. An example is upgrading management information and control systems. A defensive strategy is to upgrade if all competitors are doing so. Thus, investments may be for growth or defence.

Decision Points

The following question-and-answer format summarizes the chapter's learning objectives. Each point presents a key question, and the guidelines are the answer to that question.

Learning Objectives	Guidelines
1. What does the term *time value of money* recognize?	The term recognizes that money received earlier is worth more because of the returns that can be generated sooner.
2. What are the disadvantages of DCF and non-DCF (payback and AARR) methods of capital budgeting?	The NPV method computes a result in dollars, not percentages, and can be used where the required rates of return vary over the life of the project. The payback method neglects any cash flow after the payback period and the time value of money. The AARR is an after-tax operating income divided by a measure of the investment. The AARR does not consider the time value of money. The payback and AARR methods are nondiscounted cash flow methods, whereas the NPV and IRR are discounted cash flow methods.
3. Analyze the impact of income taxes on discounted cash flows and capital budgeting decisions.	Under the ITA organizations can deduct a CCA, rather than depreciation, from income before taxes. This creates a tax savings, commonly called a *tax shield*. The amount of the tax shield is a material consideration in evaluating the cash inflows and outflows of an investment.
4. What does *relevance* mean in DCF analyses?	*Relevance* in this context means cash flow. No accruals, sunk cost, or cash flows unchanged by alternatives are relevant when these capital budgeting methods are applied. All cash flow is treated identically irrespective of its source from operations, financing, or disinvestment.

5. What conflicts can arise between using discounted cash flow methods for capital budgeting decisions and accrual accounting for performance evaluation? How can these conflicts be reduced?

Frequently, the decision made using a DCF method will not report good "operating income" results in the project's early years under accrual accounting. For this reason, managers are tempted not to use DCF methods even though the decisions based on them would be the best for the company over the long run. This conflict can be reduced by evaluating managers on a project-by-project basis, looking at their ability to achieve the amounts and timing of forecast cash flows.

6. What are the implications of a defensive long-term investment?

A defensive strategic or long-term investment is made for purposes of defending market share. The quantitative and non-quantitative factors are secondary to this purpose. One very great difficulty is properly identifying and assessing the long-term opportunity cost of lost market-share.

Appendix 20A

Capital Budgeting and Inflation

Examples discussed earlier do not include adjustments for inflation in the relevant revenues and costs. **Inflation** is the decline in the general purchasing power of the monetary unit, such as dollars. An inflation rate of 10% per year means that an item bought for $100 at the beginning of the year will cost $110 at the end of the year.

Why is it important to account for inflation in capital budgeting? Because declines in the general purchasing power of the monetary unit will inflate future cash flows above what they would have been in the absence of inflation. These inflated cash flows will cause the project to look better than it really is unless the analyst recognizes that the inflated cash flows are measured in dollars that have less purchasing power than the dollars that were initially invested. When analyzing inflation, distinguish real rate of return from nominal rate of return:

Real rate of return is the rate of return demanded to cover investment risk if there is no inflation. The real rate is made up of two elements: (a) a risk-free element (that's the pure rate of return on risk-free long-term government bonds when there is no expected inflation) and (b) a business-risk element (that's the risk premium demanded for bearing risk).

Nominal rate of return is the rate of return demanded to cover investment risk and the decline in general purchasing power of the monetary unit as a result of expected inflation. The nominal rate is made up of three elements: (a) a risk-free element when there is no expected inflation, (b) a business-risk element, and (c) an inflation element. Items (a) and (b) make up the real rate of return to cover investment risk. The inflation element is the premium above the real rate. The rates of return earned in the financial markets are nominal rates, because investors want to be compensated both for the investment risks they take and for the expected decline in the general purchasing power, as a result of inflation, of the money they get back.

Assume that the real rate of return for investments in high-risk cellular data-transmission equipment at Network Communications is 20% per year and that the expected inflation rate is 10% per year. Nominal rate of return is as follows:

$$\text{Nominal rate} = (1 + \text{Real rate})(1 + \text{Inflation rate}) - 1$$

$$= (1 + 0.20)(1 + 0.10) - 1$$

$$= (1.20 \times 1.10) - 1 = 1.32 - 1 = 0.32, \text{ or } 32\%$$

Nominal rate of return is related to the real rate of return and the inflation rate:

Real rate of return	0.20
Inflation rate	0.10
Combination (0.20 × 0.10)	0.02
Nominal rate of return	0.32

Note that the nominal rate, 0.32, is slightly higher than 0.30, the real rate (0.20) plus the inflation rate (0.10). That's because the nominal rate recognizes that inflation of 10% also decreases the purchasing power of the real rate of return of 20% earned during the year. The combination component represents the additional compensation investors seek for the decrease in the purchasing power of the real return earned during the year because of inflation.[6]

Net Present Value Method and Inflation

When incorporating inflation into the NPV method, the key is *internal consistency*. There are two internally consistent approaches:

1. **Nominal approach**—predicts cash inflows and outflows in nominal (or, stated) monetary units *and* uses a nominal rate as the required rate of return
2. **Real approach**—predicts cash inflows and outflows in real monetary units *and* uses a real rate as the required rate of return

We will limit our discussion to the simpler nominal approach. Consider an investment that is expected to generate sales of 100 units and a net cash inflow of $1,000 ($10 per unit) each year for two years *absent inflation*. Assume cash flows occur at the end of each year. If inflation of 10% is expected each year, net cash inflows from the sale of each unit would be $11 (= $10 × 1.10) in year 1 and $12.10 (= $11 × 1.10, or $10 × (1.10)^2) in year 2, resulting in net cash inflows of $1,100 in year 1 and $1,210 in year 2. The net cash inflows of $1,100 and $1,210 are nominal cash inflows because they include the effects of inflation. *Nominal cash flows are the cash flows that are recorded in the accounting system.* The cash inflows of $1,000 each year are real cash flows. The accounting system does not record these cash flows. The nominal approach is easier to understand and apply because it uses nominal cash flows from accounting systems and nominal rates of return from financial markets.

Assume that Network Communications can purchase equipment to make and sell a cellular data-transmission product at a net initial investment of $750,000. It is expected to have a four-year useful life and no terminal disposal value. An annual inflation rate of 10% is expected over this four-year period. Network Communications requires an after-tax nominal rate of return of 32%. The following table presents the predicted amounts of real (that's assuming no inflation) and nominal (that's after considering cumulative inflation) net cash inflows from the equipment over the next four years (excluding the $750,000 investment in the equipment and before any income tax payments):

Year (1)	Before-Tax Cash Inflows in Real Dollars (2)	Cumulative Inflation Rate Factor[a] (3)	Before-Tax Cash Inflows in Nominal Dollars (4) = (2) × (3)
1	$500,000	$(1.10)^1 = 1.1000$	$550,000
2	600,000	$(1.10)^2 = 1.2100$	726,000
3	600,000	$(1.10)^3 = 1.3310$	798,600
4	300,000	$(1.10)^4 = 1.4641$	439,230

[a]$1.10 = 1.00 + 0.10$ inflation rate.

---

[6] The real rate of return can be expressed in terms of the nominal rate of return as follows:

$$\text{Real rate} = \frac{(1 + \text{Nominal rate})}{(1 + \text{Inflation rate})} - 1 = \frac{1 + 0.32}{1 + 0.10} - 1 = 0.20, \text{ or } 20\%$$

Exhibit 20A-1 Net Present Value Method Using Nominal Approach to Inflation for Network Communications's New Equipment

	A	B	C	D	E	F	G	H	I	J	K	L
						Present	Present Value					
1						Value of	Discount Factor[a] at		Sketch of Relevant Cash Flows at End of Each Year			
2						Cash Flow	32%	0	1	2	3	4
3												
4	1.	Net initial investment										
5		Year	Investment Outflows									
6		0	$(750,000)			$(750,000)	← 1.000 ←	$(750,000)				
7	2a.	Annual after-tax cash flow from										
8		operations (excluding the depreciation effect)										
9			Annual		Annual							
10			Before-Tax	Income	After-Tax							
11			Cash Flow	Tax	Cash Flow							
12		Year	from Operations	Outflows	from Operations							
13		(1)	(2)	(3) = 0.40 x (2)	(4) = (2) − (3)							
14		1	$550,000	$220,000	$330,000	250,140	← 0.758 ←		$330,000			
15		2	726,000	290,400	435,600	250,034	← 0.574 ←			$435,600		
16		3	60798,0	319,440	479,160	208,435	← 0.435 ←				$479,160	
17		4	439,230	175,692	263,538	86,704	← 0.329 ←					$263,538
18						795,313						
19	2b.	Income tax cash savings from annual										
20		depreciation deductions										
21		Year	Depreciation	Tax Cash Savings								
22		(1)	(2)	(3) = 0.40 x (2)								
23		1	$187,500[b]	$75,000		56,850	← 0.758 ←		$75,000			
24		2	187,500	75,000		43,050	← 0.574 ←			$75,000		
25		3	187,500	75,000		32,625	← 0.435 ←				$75,000	
26		4	187,500	75,000		24,675	← 0.329 ←					$75,000
27						157,200						
28		NPV if new equipment purchased				$202,513						
29												
30												
31		[a]The nominal discount rate of 32% is made up of the real rate of return of 20% and the inflation rate of 10% [(1 + 0.20) (1 + 1.10)] − 1 = 0.32.										
32		[b]$750,000 ÷ 4 = $187,500										

We continue to make the simplifying assumption that cash flows occur at the end of each year. The income tax rate is 40%. For tax purposes, the cost of the equipment will be depreciated using the straight-line method.

Exhibit 20A-1 shows the calculation of NPV using cash flows in nominal dollars and using a nominal discount rate. The calculations in Exhibit 20A-1 include the net initial machine investment, annual after-tax cash flows from operations (excluding the depreciation effect), and income tax cash savings from annual depreciation deductions. The NPV is $202,513 and, based on financial considerations alone, Network Communications should purchase the equipment.

Appendix 20B

The Weighted Average Cost of Capital

A commonly used discount rate in capital budgeting analysis is the WACC. The WACC represents the cost of funds and is dependent on the capital structure of the organization. An important assumption is that the risk associated with any particular investment will be close to the average risk of the firm.

The optimal capital structure is most often defined as the proportion of debt and equity that maximizes the value of the organization. To determine the WACC, the capital structure of the organization is examined and the cost of each individual source of financing is calculated and then weighted by its relative proportion in the total capital structure.

Determining Costs of Sources of Capital Structure

1. After-tax cost of debt = $k_d = k(1 - t)$
   where

   k = interest rate
   t = corporate tax rate

2. The cost of preferred shares is derived from the present value of a perpetuity and is as follows:

   Cost of preferred shares = $k_p = \dfrac{D}{P}$

   where

   D = annual dividends paid per share
   P = the market value of one preferred share

3. Common shares can be valued using the dividend growth model (also called the Gordon Model) or the capital asset pricing model (CAPM). For our purposes the more commonly used approach will be adopted, namely the CAPM.

   $$k_e = R_f + \beta(R_m - R_f)$$

   where:

   R_f = the risk-free rate of the market
   β = a measure of the volatility of a particular investment relative to the market
   R_m = the risk of the organization

   $$\text{WACC} = \left(\dfrac{D}{C}\right)k_d + \left(\dfrac{P}{C}\right)k_p + \left(\dfrac{E}{C}\right)k_e$$

   where

   D = market value of debt outstanding
   P = market value of preferred stock outstanding
   E = market value of common equity outstanding
   C = the total amount of capital available to the firm

Example: Suppose an organization with a 40% tax rate has the following capital structure:

- $400,000 debt (yield to maturity is 10%)
- $200,000 preferred shares ($12 dividend and a market price of $96)
- $400,000 common equity (The company's β is 2 with a risk premium of 7.5%, where the risk-free rate is 5%)

The WACC can be determined as follows:

Cost of debt = $kb = k(1 - T) = 0.10 \times (1 - 0.4) = 6.0\%$

Cost of preferred = $kp = \dfrac{Dp}{Pp} = \dfrac{\$12}{\$96} = 12.5\%$

Cost of common shares = $k_e = R_f + \beta(R_m - R_f) = 5 + (2(7.5)) = 20\%$

Weighted average cost of capital

$$= \left(\dfrac{40}{100} \times 6\%\right) + \left(\dfrac{20}{100} \times 12.5\%\right) + \left(\dfrac{40}{100} \times 20\%\right)$$

$$= 2.4\% + 2.5\% + 8\%$$

$$= 12.9\%$$

Terms to Learn

This chapter and the Glossary at the end of the book contain definitions of the following important terms:

accounting rate of return **(p. 828)**
accrual accounting rate of return
  (AARR) **(p. 828)**
capital budgeting **(p. 812)**
cost of capital **(p. 815)**
discount rate **(p. 815)**
discounted cash flow (DCF) **(p. 814)**
half-year rule **(p. 821)**

hurdle rate **(p. 815)**
inflation **(p. 837)**
internal rate of return (IRR) **(p. 817)**
net present value (NPV) **(p. 815)**
nominal approach **(p. 838)**
nominal rate of return **(p. 837)**
opportunity cost of capital **(p. 815)**
payback method **(p. 826)**

real approach **(p. 838)**
real rate of return **(p. 837)**
required rate of return (RRR) **(p. 815)**
return on investment (ROI) **(p. 828)**
time-adjusted rate of return **(p. 817)**
time value of money **(p. 815)**

Assignment Material

MyLab Accounting Make the grade with MyLab Accounting: The Short-Answer Questions, Exercises, and Problems marked with a ⊕ can be found on MyLab Accounting. You can practise them as often as you want, and most feature step-by-step guided instructions to help you find the right answer.

Short-Answer Questions

20-1 "Capital budgeting has the same focus as accrual accounting." Do you agree? Explain.

20-2 List and briefly describe each of the six parts in the capital budgeting decision process.

20-3 What is the essence of the discounted cash flow method?

20-4 "Only quantitative outcomes are relevant in capital budgeting analyses." Do you agree? Explain.

20-5 How can sensitivity analysis be incorporated in DCF analysis?

20-6 What is the payback method? What are its main strengths and weaknesses?

20-7 Describe the AARR method. What are its main strengths and weaknesses?

20-8 "The trouble with discounted cash flow techniques is that they ignore depreciation costs." Do you agree? Explain.

20-9 "Let's be more practical. DCF is not the gospel. Managers should not become so enchanted with DCF that strategic considerations are overlooked." Do you agree? Explain.

20-10 "The net present value method is the preferred method for capital budgeting decisions. Therefore, managers will always use it." Do you agree? Explain.

20-11 "All overhead costs are relevant in NPV analysis." Do you agree? Explain.

20-12 List and briefly describe the five major categories of cash flows included in capital investment projects.

20-13 "Managers' control of job projects generally focuses on four critical success factors." Identify those factors.

20-14 Bill Watts, president of Western Publications, accepts a capital-budgeting project advocated by Division X. This is the division in which the president spent his first 10 years with the company. On the same day, the president rejects a capital-budgeting project proposal from Division Y. The manager of Division Y is incensed. She believes that the Division Y project has an IRR at least 10 percentage points above that of the Division X project. She comments, "What is the point of all our detailed DCF analysis? If Watts is panting over a project, he can arrange to have the proponents of that project massage the numbers so that it looks like a winner." What advice would you give the manager of Division Y?

Exercises

20-15 Terminology. A number of terms are listed below:

accounting rate of return	accrual accounting rate of return (AARR)
adjusted rate of return	capital budgeting
discount rate	discounted cash flow (DCF)
hurdle rate	internal rate of return (IRR)
investment decision	investments
net present value (NPV)	payback method
opportunity cost of capital	required rate of return (RRR)
rate of return (ROR)	time-adjusted rate of return
return on investment (ROI)	

Required

Select the terms from the above list to complete the following sentences.

The goal of _____ _____ is to provide capacity in a planned and orderly manner that will match the predicted demand growth of the company and achieve a targeted _____ ____ __ _____ on these investments. The determination of the ROR links closely to the operating income or profit on sales. That is why _____ affect the statement of financial position, the statement of comprehensive income, and the statement of cash flows. Capital budgeting requires a careful analysis of the amount and timing of cash outflows and cash inflows. There are four methods from which a management team can choose: ____ _____ _____ _____, _____ _____ _____ __ _____, _____, _____ _____ ____ __ _____ (or _____ __ _____). The first two methods require the calculation of discounted cash flow. The NPV method requires that the management team determine what its _____ _____ _____ (___) must be (also called the discount rate, hurdle rate, or opportunity cost of capital). This discount rate is the return the team could expect from investing in a different project of similar risk. In contrast the IRR (sometimes called the _____ _____ __ _____) is fully determined by cash inflow and outflow. It is the rate at which the discounted net cash flow is zero. The _____ is based on nominal, not discounted, cash flow. It is simply the total investment divided by cash inflow to determine the time it takes to recover the cost of the investment. The ____ is calculated by dividing the increase in an accrual, expected average operating income, by the cost of the initial investment.

LO 1, 3 ▶

1. At 5 years you will have $66,911 (rounded)

20-16 Exercises in compound interest, no income taxes. To be sure that you understand how to use the tables in Appendix A at the end of this book, solve the following exercises. Ignore income tax considerations.

Required

1. You have just won $50,000. How much money will you accumulate at the end of 5 years if you invest it at 6% compounded annually? At 12%?

2. Twelve years from now, the unpaid principal of the mortgage on your house will be $249,600. How much do you need to invest today at 6% interest compounded annually to accumulate the $249,600 in 12 years?

3. If the unpaid mortgage on your house in 12 years will be $249,600, how much money do you need to invest at the end of each year at 6% to accumulate exactly this amount at the end of the 12th year?

4. You plan to save $4,800 of your earnings at the end of each year for the next 8 years. How much money will you accumulate at the end of the 8th year if you invest your savings compounded at 4% per year?

5. You have just turned 65 and an endowment insurance policy has paid you a lump sum of $400,000. If you invest the sum at 6%, how much money can you withdraw from your account in equal amounts at the end of each year so that at the end of 7 years (age 72), there will be nothing left?

6. You have estimated that for the first 6 years after you retire you will need a cash inflow of $48,000 at the end of each year. How much money do you need to invest at 4% at your retirement age to obtain this annual cash inflow? At 6%?

7. The following table shows two schedules of prospective operating cash inflows, each of which requires the same net initial investment of $18,000 now:

	Annual Cash Inflows	
Year	**Plan A**	**Plan B**
1	$ 2,000	$ 3,000
2	3,000	5,000
3	4,000	9,000
4	7,000	5,000
5	9,000	3,000
Total	$25,000	$25,000

The required rate of return is 6% compounded annually. All cash inflows occur at the end of each year. In terms of net present value, which plan is more desirable? Show your computations.

⊕ 20-17 Capital budgeting methods, no income taxes. Lethbridge Company runs hardware stores in Alberta. Lethbridge's management estimates that if it invests $180,000 in a new computer system, it can save $60,000 in annual cash operating costs. The system has an expected useful life of five years and no terminal disposal value. The required rate of return is 12%. Ignore income tax issues in your answers. Assume all cash flows occur at year-end except for initial investment amounts.

◀ **LO 1, 2**
1. a. Discount factor for 12% over 5 years, 3.605

Required

1. Calculate the following for the new computer system:

   a. NPV
   b. Payback period
   c. IRR
   d. AARR based on the net initial investment (assume straight-line depreciation)

2. What other factors should Lethbridge Company consider in deciding whether to purchase the new computer system?

⊕ 20-18 Capital budgeting methods, no income taxes. City Hospital, a nonprofit organization, estimates that it can save $28,000 a year in cash operating costs for the next 10 years if it buys a special-purpose eye-testing machine at a cost of $110,000. No terminal disposal value is expected. City Hospital's required rate of return is 14%. Assume all cash flows occur at year-end except for initial investment amounts. City Hospital uses straight-line depreciation.

◀ **LO 1, 2**
1. The Payback Period is 3.93 years

Required

1. Calculate the following for the special-purpose eye-testing machine:

   a. Net present value
   b. Payback period
   c. Internal rate of return
   d. Accrual accounting rate of return based on net initial investment
   e. Accrual accounting rate of return based on average investment

2. What other factors should City Hospital consider in deciding whether to purchase the special-purpose eye-testing machine?

⊕ 20-19 New equipment purchase. Norberto Garcia, general manager of the Argentinean subsidiary of Innovation Inc., is considering the purchase of new industrial equipment to improve efficiency at its Cordoba plant. The equipment has an estimated useful life of five years. The estimated cash flows for the equipment are shown in the table that follows, with no anticipated change in working capital. Innovation has a 12% required rate of return. Assume depreciation is calculated on a straight-line basis. Assume all cash flows occur at year-end except for initial investment amounts.

◀ **LO 4**
1. a. NPV = $32,656

Initial investment	$80,000
Annual cash flow from operations (excluding the depreciation effect)	31,250
Cash flow from terminal disposal of equipment	0

Required

1. Calculate (a) NPV, (b) payback period, and (c) IRR.
2. Compare and contrast the capital budgeting methods in requirement 1.
3. The controller of Innovation Inc. received Garcia's estimates but adjusted them to capture the added risk of doing the project in Argentina. Recalculate item 1 with a required rate of return of 20%, and explain if the project will be approved by Innovation Inc. for its Argentinean subsidiary.

⊕ 20-20 Payback methods, even and uneven cash flows. Sage Laundromat is trying to enhance the services it provides to customers, mostly college students. It is looking into the purchase of new high-efficiency washing machines that will allow for the laundry's status to be checked via smartphone.

Sage estimates the cost of the new equipment at $159,000. The equipment has a useful life of 9 years. Sage expects cash fixed costs of $80,000 per year to operate the new machines, as well as cash variable costs in the amount of 5% of revenues. Sage evaluates investments using a cost of capital of 10%.

◀ **LO 1, 2**
Net annual cash flow is $53,000

Required

1. Calculate the payback period and the discounted payback period for this investment, assuming Sage expects to generate $140,000 in incremental revenues every year from the new machines.

2. Assume instead that Sage expects the following uneven stream of incremental cash revenues from installing the new washing machines:

	A	B	C	D	E	F	G	H	I	J
1	Year	1	2	3	4	5	6	7	8	9
2	Projected Revenue	$90,000	$120,000	$125,000	$85,000	$150,000	$210,000	$130,000	$140,000	$190,000

Based on this estimated revenue stream, what are the payback and discounted payback periods for the investment?

LO 1 ▶

1. Plan 1 NPV, ($3,901,725)

20-21 Comparison of projects, no income taxes. Genetech Corporation is a rapidly growing biotech company that has a required rate of return of 12%. It plans to build a new facility in Halifax, NS. The building will take two years to complete. The building contractor offered Genetech a choice of three payment plans, as follows:

- **Plan I** Payment of $375,000 at the time of signing the contract and $4,425,000 upon completion of the building. The end of the second year is the completion date.

- **Plan II** Payment of $1,500,000 at the time of signing the contract and $1,500,000 at the end of each of the two succeeding years.

- **Plan III** Payment of $150,000 at the time of signing the contract and $1,500,000 at the end of each of the three succeeding years.

Required

1. Using the NPV method, calculate the comparative cost of each of the three payment plans being considered by the company.

2. Which payment plan should the company choose? Explain.

3. Discuss the financial factors, other than the cost of the plan and the nonfinancial factors that should be considered in selecting an appropriate payment plan.

LO 2 ▶

1.b. Project A has a Payback period of 3 years.

20-22 Payback and NPV methods, no income taxes. Andrews Construction is analyzing its capital expenditure proposals for the purchase of equipment in the coming year. The capital budget is limited to $6,000,000 for the year. Lori Bart, staff analyst at Andrews, is preparing an analysis of the three projects under consideration by Corey Andrews, the company's owner.

	A	B	C	D
1		**Project A**	**Project B**	**Project C**
2	**Projected cash outflow**			
3	Net initial investment	$3,000,000	$1,500,000	$4,000,000
4				
5	**Projected cash inflows**			
6	Year 1	$1,000,000	$400,000	$2,000,000
7	Year 2	1,000,000	900,000	2,000,000
8	Year 3	1,000,000	800,000	200,000
9	Year 4	1,000,000		100,000
10				
11	Required rate of return	10%	10%	10%

Required

1. Because the company's cash is limited, Andrews thinks the payback method should be used to choose between the capital budgeting projects.

   a. What are the benefits and limitations of using the payback method to choose between projects?

   b. Calculate the payback period for each of the three projects. Ignore income taxes. Using the payback method, which projects should Andrews choose?

2. Bart thinks that projects should be selected based on their NPVs. Assume all cash flows occur at the end of the year except for initial investment amounts. Calculate the NPV for each project. Ignore income taxes.

3. Which projects, if any, would you recommend funding? Briefly explain why.

🌐 **20-23 Equipment replacement, no income taxes.** Dublin Chips is a manufacturer of prototype chips based in Dublin, Ireland. Next year, in 2018, Dublin Chips expects to deliver 615 prototype chips at an average price of $95,000. Dublin Chips' marketing vice president forecasts growth of 65 prototype chips per year through 2024. That is, demand will be 615 in 2018, 680 in 2019, 745 in 2020, and so on.

◀ **LO 3**
2. Payback Period is 3.12 years

The plant cannot produce more than 585 prototype chips annually. To meet future demand, Dublin Chips must either modernize the plant or replace it. The old equipment is fully depreciated and can be sold for $4,200,000 if the plant is replaced. If the plant is modernized, the costs to modernize it are to be capitalized and depreciated over the useful life of the updated plant. The old equipment is retained as part of the modernize alternative. The following data on the two options are available:

	Modernize	Replace
Initial investment in 2018	$35,300,000	$66,300,000
Terminal disposal value in 2024	$ 7,500,000	$16,000,000
Useful life	7 years	7 years
Total annual cash operating costs per prototype chip	$78,500	$66,000

Dublin Chips uses straight-line depreciation, assuming zero terminal disposal value. For simplicity, we assume no change in prices or costs in future years. The investment will be made at the beginning of 2018, and all transactions thereafter occur on the last day of the year. Dublin Chips' required rate of return is 14%.

There is no difference between the modernize and replace alternatives in terms of required working capital. Dublin Chips has a special waiver on income taxes until 2024.

Required

1. Sketch the cash inflows and outflows of the modernize and replace alternatives over the 2018–2024 period.
2. Calculate the payback period for the modernize and replace alternatives.
3. Calculate net present value of the modernize and replace alternatives.
4. What factors should Dublin Chips consider in choosing between the alternatives?

🌐 **20-24 DCF, accrual accounting rate of return, working capital, evaluation of performance, no income taxes.** Century Lab plans to purchase a new centrifuge machine for its Manitoba facility. The machine costs $137,500 and is expected to have a useful life of eight years, with a terminal disposal value of $37,500. Savings in cash operating costs are expected to be $31,250 per year. However, additional working capital is needed to keep the machine running efficiently. The working capital must continually be replaced, so an investment of $10,000 needs to be maintained at all times, but this investment is fully recoverable (will be "cashed in") at the end of the useful life. Century Lab's required rate of return is 14%. Ignore income taxes in your analysis. Assume all cash flows occur at year-end except for initial investment amounts.

◀ **LO 3**
1. Present value of terminal disposal of machine, 13,163

Required

1. Calculate NPV.
2. Calculate IRR.
3. Calculate AARR based on net initial investment. Assume straight-line depreciation.
4. You have the authority to make the purchase decision. Why might you be reluctant to base your decision on the DCF methods?

🌐 **20-25 DCF, sensitivity analysis, no income taxes.** (CMA, adapted) Sentax Corporation is an international manufacturer of fragrances for women. Management at Sentax is considering expanding the product line to men's fragrances. From the best estimates of the marketing and production managers, annual sales (all for cash) for this new line are 2,000,000 units at $100 per unit; cash variable cost is $50 per unit; and cash fixed costs are $18,000,000 per year. The investment project requires $100,000,000 of cash outflow and has a project life of 4 years.

◀ **LO 2**
1. Cash Flow from Operations is $82,000,000

At the end of the 4-year useful life, there will be no terminal disposal value. Assume all cash flows occur at year-end except for initial investment amounts.

Men's fragrance is a new market for Sentax, and management is concerned about the reliability of the estimates. The controller has proposed applying sensitivity analysis to selected factors. Ignore income taxes in your computations. Sentax's required rate of return on this project is 16%.

Required

1. Calculate the net present value of this investment proposal.
2. Calculate the effect on the net present value of the following two changes in assumptions. (Treat each item independently of the other.)
   a. 20% reduction in the selling price
   b. 20% increase in the variable cost per unit
3. Discuss how management would use the data developed in requirements 1 and 2 in its consideration of the proposed capital investment.

LO 3 ▶
1. Present Value $6,200

⊕ **20-26 DCF, accrual accounting rate of return, working capital, evaluation of performance, no income taxes.** Homer Inc. plans to purchase a new rendering machine for its animation facility. The machine costs $102,500 and is expected to have a useful life of eight years, with a terminal disposal value of $22,500. Savings in cash operating costs are expected to be $22,250 per year. However, additional working capital is needed to maintain the operations of the rendering machine. The working capital must continually be replaced, so an investment of $10,000 needs to be maintained at all times, but this investment is fully recoverable (will be "cashed in") at the end of the useful life. Homer Inc.'s required rate of return is 12%. Ignore income taxes in your analysis. Assume all cash flows occur at year-end except for initial investment amounts. Homer Inc. uses straight-line depreciation for its machines.

Required

1. Calculate NPV.
2. Calculate IRR.
3. Calculate AARR based on net initial investment.
4. Calculate AARR based on average investment.
5. You have the authority to make the purchase decision. Why might you be reluctant to base your decision on the DCF methods?

LO 3 ▶
1. NPV is $33,235

⊕ **20-27 NPV and AARR, goal-congruence issues.** Liam Mitchell, a manager of the Plate Division for the Harvest Manufacturing company, has the opportunity to expand the division by investing in additional machinery costing $495,000. He would depreciate the equipment using the straight-line method and expects it to have no residual value. It has a useful life of 9 years. The firm mandates a required after-tax rate of return of 14% on investments. Liam estimates annual net cash inflows for this investment of $130,000 before taxes and an investment in working capital of $5,000 that will be returned at the project's end. Harvest's tax rate is 30%.

Required

1. Calculate the net present value of this investment.
2. Calculate the accrual accounting rate of return based on net initial investment for this project.
3. Should Liam accept the project? Will Liam accept the project if his bonus depends on achieving an accrual accounting rate of return of 14%? How can this conflict be resolved?

LO 3 ▶
Cash Flows in 2017 is $450,000

⊕ **20-28 Customer value.** Ortel Telecom sells telecommunication products and services to a variety of small businesses. Two of Ortel's key clients are Square and Cloudburst, both fast-growing technology start-ups located in New York City. Ortel has compiled information regarding its transactions with Square and Cloudburst for 2017, as well as its expectations regarding their interactions over the next 3 years:

	A	B	C	D	E
	Home	Insert	Page Layout	Formulas	Data	Review
	A	B	C	D	E
1		Expected Annual Percentage Increase		2017	
2		Square	Cloudburst	Square	Cloudburst
3	Sales Revenues	6%	5.5%	$567,000	$3,510,000
4	Cost of Sales	5%	4.5%	$364,800	$3,060,000
5	Net cash flow			$202,200	$ 450,000

Ortel's transactions with Square and Cloudburst are in cash. Assume that they occur at year-end. Ortel is headquartered in the Cayman Islands and pays no income taxes. The owners of Ortel insist on a required rate of return of 12%.

Required

1. What is the expected net cash flow from Square and Cloudburst for the next 3 years?
2. Based on the net present value from cash flows over the next 3 years, is Cloudburst or Square a more valuable customer for Ortel?
3. Cloudburst threatens to switch to another supplier unless Ortel gives a 10% price reduction on all sales starting in 2018. Calculate the 3-year NPV of Cloudburst after incorporating the 10% discount. Should Ortel continue to transact with Cloudburst? What other factors should it consider before making its final decision?

⊕ **20-29 Estimated cash flows, tax minimization, calculated depreciation.** Crazy Mama manufactures baby furniture, clothing, strollers, and accessories. In the current year the company plans on purchasing a new machine to improve the quality and efficiency of production. Crazy Mama has prepared estimates of future cash flows over the following four years, at which point it will sell the machine for $10,000. The company focuses on tax minimization and calculated depreciation over the four years using the straight-line method, a useful life of four years, and a residual value of $0.

◀ **LO 2**
NPV is ($143,474)

	Relevant Cash Flows at End of Each Year				
	Today	1	2	3	4
Initial investment	(222,000)				
Annual cash flows from operations		23,000	23,000	23,000	23,000
(excluding depreciation)					
Cash flow from sale of machine					10,000
Required return on investment	10%				
Income tax rate	35%				
Depreciation method	straight-line				
CCA rate declining balance for income tax purposes					
All CF occur at end of year except for the initial investment.					

1. Calculate the NPV of the investment.
2. Should the company purchase the new machine?

⊕ **20-30 Internal rate of return in capital budgeting.** Crazy Mama has just heard about payback period and IRR. Assume the CCA rate is 20%, and refer to the following information to answer the questions below.

◀ **LO 2**
1. Payback Period is 1.4 years

	Relevant Cash Flows at End of Each Year				
	Today	1	2	3	4
Initial investment	(22,200)				
Annual cash flows from operations		23,000	23,000	23,000	23,000
(excluding depreciation)					
Cash flow from sale of machine					10,000
Required return on investment	0.10				
Income tax rate	0.35				
Depreciation method	straight-line				
CCA rate declining balance for income tax purposes					

  1. Calculate the payback period.

  2. Compare the payback method with the NPV method. Describe a situation where the payback method would be more appropriate to evaluate a capital budgeting decision.

LO 2, 5 ▶
NPV is $22,527

● **20-31 Capital budgeting and NPV.** Candid Candles manufactures scented candles. There most popular scents are lemon biscotti and raspberry whipped cream. The company is looking into purchasing an automated wick cutter to bolster production. The machine would cost $8,000 and could be sold for scrap metal four years later for $2,000.

  1. Calculate the NPV of the investment using the following information.

	Relevant Cash Flows at End of Each Year				
	Today	1	2	3	4
Initial investment	(8,000)				
Annual cash flows from operations (excluding depreciation)		15,000	15,000	15,000	15,000
Cash flow from sale of machine					2,000

Required return on investment	0.10
Income tax rate	0.40
Depreciation method	straight-line
CCA rate declining balance for income tax purposes	0.15
All CF occur at end of year except for the initial investment.	

  2. Candid Candles will only invest in machines that can break even on the investment within the first year. Based on the payback period, should Candid Candles purchase the machine?

LO 2, 5 ▶
2. NPV is $18,093,25

● **20-32 Capital Budgeting and NPV.** Chicks with Kicks is a boxing club for women. The club manufactures all of its own punching bags out of high-quality leather and sand from Los Roques, one of Venezuela's most beautiful beaches. The company is considering investing in a sand refining machine to improve the quality of its punching bags. Details about the machine investment are as follows:

Cost of new machine	$150,000.00

The expected improvements from the new machine would allow for an increase in membership fees. The CFO expects cash flows from the investment in the first three years to be $89,000, $91,000, and $101,000. The company is subject to a 40% tax rate and has a required rate of return of 15% for all investment projects.

  1. What is the total present value of the predicted cash inflows from the new machine?

  2. Is the investment profitable?

LO 2, 5 ▶
2. NPV is $18,975.47

● **20-33 Capital budgeting, NPV, and economic factors.** Chicks with Kicks has requested another report in addition to the NPV report you completed in Exercise 20-32. Details about the machine investment are as follows:

Cost of new machine	$150,000.00
CCA rate	25%
Disposal value	$11,000.00
Useful life	3 years

The expected improvements from the new machine would allow for an increase in membership fees. The CFO expects cash flows from the investment in the first three years to be $89,000, $91,000, and $101,000. The company is subject to a 40% tax rate and has a required rate of return of 15% for all investment projects.

1. The current required rate of return of 15% per year does not include an adjustment of 2% for inflation. Calculate the real rate of return.
2. The CFO has asked you to recalculate the NPV of the investment using the real rate of return.

20-34 Capital budgeting and NPV. Funky Beats manufactures high-quality headphones for music lovers of all styles. The company requires a payback period of less than five years for any capital budgeting decisions.

◀ **LO 2, 5**
2. NPV is ($36,123)

	Relevant Cash Flows at End of Each Year				
	Today	1	2	3	4
Initial investment	(132,000)				
Annual cash flows from operations (excluding depreciation)		40,000	40,000	40,000	40,000
Cash flow from sale of machine					–
Required return on investment	0.10				
Income tax rate	0.40				
Depreciation method	straight-line				
CCA rate declining balance for income tax purposes	0.30				
All CF occur at end of year except for the initial investment.					

1. Does the project meet the requirements?
2. Is the investment profitable? Hint: Calculate NPV.
3. Could you know the amount of tax shield lost on disposal without doing any calculations? Why should the payback period not be the sole basis for a capital budgeting decision?

20-35 Capital budgeting, NPV, and IRR. Spooked is a Halloween decorations manufacturer planning to purchase a new packing machine for $120,000 with a useful life of 15 years and a terminal value of $10,000. Savings due to the machine are expected to be $23,000 per year, however, parts of the machine must be replaced every year so a working capital investment of $5,000 must be maintained. This amount will be recoverable upon disposal. Required rate of return is 12%. All cash flows occur at year-end except for the initial investment. Ignore income taxes in your analysis.

◀ **LO 2, 5**
1. NPV is $34,394.78

1. Calculate NPV
2. Describe two methods to determine the IRR.
3. Without using the methods in requirement 2, state whether the IRR will be lower or higher than 9%. How do you know?
4. Calculate AARR based on net initial investment.

20-36 DCF, accrual accounting rate of return, working capital, evaluation of performance, no income taxes. Laverty Clinic plans to purchase a new centrifuge machine for its New York facility. The machine costs $94,000 and is expected to have a useful life of 6 years, with a terminal disposal value of $9,000. Savings in cash operating costs are expected to be $24,900 per year. However, additional working capital is needed to keep the machine running efficiently. The working capital must continually be replaced, so an investment of $4,000 needs to be maintained at all times, but this investment is fully recoverable (will be "cashed in") at the end of the useful life. Laverty Clinic's required rate of return is 12%. Ignore income taxes in your analysis. Assume all cash flows occur at year-end except for initial investment amounts. Laverty Clinic uses straight-line depreciation for its machines.

◀ **LO 2**
1. NPV is $10,955

Required

1. Calculate net present value.
2. Calculate internal rate of return.
3. Calculate accrual accounting rate of return based on net initial investment.
4. Calculate accrual accounting rate of return based on average investment.
5. You have the authority to make the purchase decision. Why might you be reluctant to base your decision on the DCF methods?

LO 5 ▶

1. Payback Period for Project A is 3 years

🌐 **20-37 Payback and NPV methods, no income taxes.** (CMA, adapted) Andrews Construction is analyzing its capital expenditure proposals for the purchase of equipment in the coming year. The capital budget is limited to $5,000,000 for the year. Lori Bart, staff analyst at Andrews, is preparing an analysis of the three projects under consideration by Corey Andrews, the company's owner.

	A	B	C	D
		Project A	**Project B**	**Project C**
2	**Projected cash outflow**			
3	Net initial investment	$3,000,000	$1,500,000	$4,000,000
4				
5	**Projected cash inflows:**			
6	Year 1	$1,000,000	$ 400,000	$2,000,000
7	Year 2	1,000,000	900,000	2,000,000
8	Year 3	1,000,000	800,000	200,000
9	Year 4	1,000,000		100,000
10				
11	Required rate of return	10%	10%	10%

Required

1. Because the company's cash is limited, Andrews thinks the payback method should be used to choose between the capital budgeting projects.

   a. What are the benefits and limitations of using the payback method to choose between projects?
   b. Calculate the payback period for each of the three projects. Ignore income taxes. Using the payback method, which projects should Andrews choose?

2. Bart thinks that projects should be selected based on their NPVs. Assume all cash flows occur at the end of the year except for initial investment amounts. Calculate the NPV for each project. Ignore income taxes.

3. Which projects, if any, would you recommend funding? Briefly explain why.

LO 5 ▶

1. Total PV of PLan 1 is $(3,789,300)

🌐 **20-38 Comparison of projects, no income taxes.** (CMA, adapted) New Pharm Corporation is a rapidly growing biotech company that has a required rate of return of 14%. It plans to build a new facility in Santa Clara County. The building will take 2 years to complete. The building contractor offered New Pharm a choice of three payment plans, as follows:

■ **Plan I:** Payment of $175,000 at the time of signing the contract and $4,700,000 upon completion of the building. The end of the second year is the completion date.

■ **Plan II:** Payment of $1,625,000 at the time of signing the contract and $1,625,000 at the end of each of the two succeeding years.

■ **Plan III:** Payment of $325,000 at the time of signing the contract and $1,500,000 at the end of each of the three succeeding years.

Required

1. Using the net present value method, calculate the comparative cost of each of the three payment plans being considered by New Pharm.
2. Which payment plan should New Pharm choose? Explain.
3. Discuss the financial factors, other than the cost of the plan, and the nonfinancial factors that should be considered in selecting an appropriate payment plan.

LO 1 ▶

2. Payback Period is 2.86 years

🌐 **20-39 Capital budgeting with uneven cash flows, no income taxes.** America Cola is considering the purchase of a special-purpose bottling machine for $65,000. It is expected to have a useful life of 4 years with no terminal disposal value. The plant manager estimates the following savings in cash operating costs:

Year	Amount
1	$25,000
2	22,000
3	21,000
4	20,000
Total	$88,000

America Cola uses a required rate of return of 18% in its capital budgeting decisions. Ignore income taxes in your analysis. Assume all cash flows occur at year-end except for initial investment amounts. Calculate the following for the special-purpose bottling machine:

Required

1. Net present value
2. Payback period
3. Discounted payback period
4. Internal rate of return (using the interpolation method)
5. Accrual accounting rate of return based on net initial investment (Assume straight-line depreciation. Use the average annual savings in cash operating costs when computing the numerator of the accrual accounting rate of return.)

🌐 **20-40 New equipment purchase, income taxes.** Anna's Bakery plans to purchase a new oven with an estimated useful life of four years. The estimated pretax cash flows for the oven are as shown in the table that follows, with no anticipated change in working capital. Anna's Bakery has a 12% after-tax required rate of return and a 40% income tax rate. Assume depreciation is calculated on a straight-line basis for accounting purposes using the initial oven investment and estimated terminal disposal value of the oven. Assume all cash flows occur at year-end except for initial investment amounts. Equipment is subject to 20% CCA rate declining balance for income tax purposes.

◀ **LO 5**

1. a. Total present value of recurring after-tax operating savings, $65,599

	Relevant Cash Flows at End of Each Year				
	0	**1**	**2**	**3**	**4**
Initial machine investment	$(95,000)				
Annual cash flow from operations (excluding the depreciation effect)		$36,000	$36,000	$36,000	$36,000
Cash flow from terminal disposal of oven					0

Required

1. Calculate (a) NPV, (b) payback period, and (c) IRR.
2. Compare and contrast the capital budgeting methods in requirement 1.

Problems

🌐 **20-41 Capital budgeting methods, no income taxes.** Yummy Candy Company is considering purchasing a second chocolate dipping machine in order to expand their business. The information Yummy has accumulated regarding the new machine is:

◀ **LO 1**

Cost of the machine	$80,000
Increased annual contribution margin	$15,000
Life of the machine	10 years
Required rate of return	6%

Yummy estimates they will be able to produce more candy using the second machine and thus increase their annual contribution margin. They also estimate there will be a small disposal value of the machine but the cost of removal will offset that value. Ignore income tax issues in your answers. Assume all cash flows occur at year-end except for initial investment amounts.

Required

1. Calculate the following for the new machine:

   a. Net present value

   b. Payback period

   c. Discounted payback period

   d. Internal rate of return (using the interpolation method)

   e. Accrual accounting rate of return based on the net initial investment (assume straight-line depreciation)

2. What other factors should Yummy Candy consider in deciding whether to purchase the new machine?

LO 1, 2 ▶

1. Cash inflow from operations, $10,000,000

🌐 **20-42 DCF, sensitivity analysis, no income taxes.** LVT is an international manufacturer of fragrances for women. Management at LVT is considering expanding the product line to men's fragrances. From the best estimates of the marketing and production managers, annual sales (all for cash) for this new line are 1,000,000 units at $25 per unit; cash variable cost is $10 per unit; cash fixed cost is $5,000,000 per year. The investment project requires $30,000,000 of cash outflow and has a project life of five years.

At the end of the five-year useful life, there will be no terminal disposal value. Assume all cash flows occur at year-end except for initial investment amounts.

Men's fragrance is a new market for LVT, and management is concerned about the reliability of the estimates. The controller has proposed applying sensitivity analysis to selected factors. Ignore income taxes in your computations. LVT's required rate of return on this project is 14%.

Required

1. Calculate the NPV of this investment proposal.

2. Calculate the effect on the NPV of the following two changes in assumptions. (Treat each item independently of the other.)

   a. 5% reduction in the selling price.

   b. 5% increase in the variable cost per unit.

3. Discuss how management would use the data developed in requirements 1 and 2 in its consideration of the proposed capital investment.

LO 1, 2 ▶

1. Present value of net cash inflows, $51,520

🌐 **20-43 NPV, IRR, and sensitivity analysis.** Fluffy Cupcake Company is considering expanding by buying a new (additional) machine that costs $42,000, has zero terminal disposal value, and has a 10-year useful life. It expects the annual increase in cash revenues from the expansion to be $23,000 per year. It expects additional annual cash costs to be $16,000 per year. Its cost of capital is 6%. Ignore taxes.

Required

1. Calculate the NPV and IRR for this investment.

2. Assume the finance manager of Fluffy Cupcake Company is not sure about the cash revenues and costs. The revenues could be anywhere from 10% higher to 10% lower than predicted. Assume cash costs are still $16,000 per year. What are NPV and IRR at the high and low points for revenue?

3. The finance manager thinks that costs will vary with revenues, and if the revenues are 10% higher, the costs will be 7% higher. If the revenues are 10% lower, the costs will be 10% lower. Recalculate the NPV and IRR at the high and low revenue points with this new cost information.

4. The finance manager has decided that the company should earn 2% more than the cost of capital on any project. Recalculate the original NPV in requirement 1 using the new discount rate.

LO 3 ▶

1. Present value if Part No. 789 is purchased, $(7,916)

20-44 Relevance and DCF. The Dannich Company currently makes as many units of Part No. 789 as it needs. David Lin, general manager of the Dannich Company, has received a bid from the Gabriella Company for making Part No. 789. Current plans call for Gabriella to supply 1,000 units of Part No. 789 per year at $60 a unit. Gabriella can begin supplying on January 1, 2018, and continue for five years, after which time Dannich will not need the part. Gabriella can accommodate any change in Dannich's demand for the part and will supply it for $60 a unit, regardless of quantity.

Jacqueline Tyson, the controller of the Dannich Company, reports the following costs for manufacturing 1,000 units of Part No. 789:

Direct materials	$26,400
Direct manufacturing labour	13,200
Variable manufacturing overhead	8,400
Depreciation on machine	12,000
Product and process engineering	4,800
Rent	2,400
Allocation of general plant overhead costs	6,000
Total costs	$73,200

The following additional information is available:

a. Part No. 789 is made on a machine used exclusively for the manufacture of Part No. 789. The machine was acquired on January 1, 2018, at a cost of $72,000. The machine has a useful life of six years and zero terminal disposal price. Depreciation is calculated on the straight-line method.

b. The machine could be sold today for $18,000.

c. Product and process engineering costs are incurred to ensure that the manufacturing process for Part No. 789 works smoothly. Although these costs are fixed in the short run, with respect to units of Part No. 789 produced, they can be saved in the long run if this part is no longer produced. If Part No. 789 is outsourced, product and process engineering costs of $4,800 will be incurred for 2016 but not thereafter.

d. Rent costs of $2,400 are allocated to products on the basis of the floor space used for manufacturing the product. If Part No. 789 is discontinued, the space currently used to manufacture it would become available. The company could then use the space for storage purposes and save $1,200 currently paid for outside storage.

e. General plant overhead costs are allocated to each department on the basis of direct manufacturing labour dollars. These costs will not change in total. But no general plant overhead will be allocated to Part No. 789 if the part is outsourced.

Assume that Dannich requires a 12% rate of return for this project.

Required

1. Should David Lin outsource Part No. 789? Prepare a quantitative analysis.
2. Describe any sensitivity analysis that seems advisable, but you need not perform any sensitivity calculations.
3. What other factors should Lin consider in making a decision?
4. Lin is particularly concerned about his bonus for 2018. The bonus is based on Dannich's accounting income. What decision will Lin make if he wants to maximize his bonus in 2018?

🌐 **20-45 NPV and customer profitability, no taxes.** Christen Granite sells granite countertops to the construction industry. Christen Granite has three customers: Homebuilders, a small construction company that builds private luxury homes; Kitchen Constructors, a company that designs and builds kitchens for hospitals and hotels; and Subdivision Erectors, a construction company that builds large subdivisions in major metro suburbs. Following are Christen Granite's revenue and cost data by customer for the year ended December 31, 2016:

◀ **LO 5**
1. 2017 Homebuilders cash flow from operations, $16,764

	Homebuilders	Kitchen Constructors	Subdivision Erectors
Revenues	$54,000	$390,000	$1,032,000
Cost of goods sold	26,400	216,000	660,000
Operating costs	12,000	90,000	282,000

Operating costs include order processing, sales visits, delivery, and special delivery costs. Christen estimates that revenue and costs will increase as follows on an annual basis:

	Homebuilders	Kitchen Constructors	Subdivision Erectors
Revenues	5%	15%	8%
Cost of goods sold	4%	4%	4%
Operating costs	4%	4%	4%

Required

1. Calculate operating income per customer for 2016 and for each year of the 2017–2021 period.
2. Christen estimates the value of each customer by calculating the customer's projected NPV over the next five years (2017–2021). Use the operating incomes calculated above to compute the value of all three customers. Christen uses a 10% discount rate.
3. Recently, Kitchen Constructors (KC), Christen's most valuable customer, has been threatening to leave. Lawson Tops, Christen's fiercest competitor, has offered KC a greater discount. KC demands a 20% discount from Christen if the latter wants to keep KC's business. At the same time, Christen reevaluates the KC account and anticipates annual revenue increases of only 5% thereafter. Should Christen grant KC the 20% discount? What is the five-year value of KC after incorporating the 20% discount? What other factors should Christen consider before making a final decision?
4. What are the possible adverse effects of caving in to KC's pressure?

LO 1, 2 ▶

1. Net annual cash inflow, $30,000

20-46 Payback, even and uneven cash flows. You have the opportunity to expand your business by purchasing new equipment for $189,000. You expect to incur fixed costs of $96,000 per year to use this new equipment, and you expect to incur variable costs in the amount of approximately 10% of annual revenues.

Required

1. Calculate the payback period for this investment assuming you will generate $140,000 in cash revenues every year.
2. Assume you expect the following revenue stream for this investment:

Year 1: $ 90,000	Year 4: $155,000	Year 7: $140,000
Year 2: 115,000	Year 5: 170,000	Year 8: 125,000
Year 3: 130,000	Year 6: 180,000	Year 9: 80,000

Based on this estimated revenue stream, what is the payback period for this investment?

LO 1, 2, 4 ▶

1. Present value of initial investments, ($325,000)

⊕ **20-47 NPV and AARR, goal-congruence issues.** Nate Stately, a manager of the Plate division for the Great Slate Manufacturing Company, has the opportunity to expand the division by investing in additional machinery costing $320,000. He would depreciate the equipment using the straight-line method and expects it to have no residual value. It has a useful life of six years. The firm mandates a required rate of return of 16% on investments. Nate estimates annual net cash inflows for this investment of $100,000 and an investment in working capital of $5,000 that will be returned at the project's end.

Required

1. Calculate the NPV of this investment.
2. Calculate the AARR for this investment.
3. Should Nate accept the project? Will Nate accept the project if his bonus depends on achieving an AARR of 16%? How can this conflict be resolved?

LO 3, 4 ▶

1. Annual cash flow from operations with new equipment, $760,000

⊕ **20-48 Recognizing cash flows for capital investment projects, NPV.** Met-All Manufacturing manufactures over 20,000 different products made from metal, including building materials, tools, and furniture parts. The manager of the Furniture Parts division has proposed that his division expand into bicycle parts as well. The Furniture Parts division currently generates cash revenues of $4,700,000 and incurs cash costs of $3,600,000, with an investment in assets of $12,090,000. One-quarter of the cash costs are direct labour.

The manager estimates that the expansion of the business will require an investment in working capital of $45,000. Because the company already has a facility, there would be no additional rent or purchase costs for a building, but the project would generate an additional $420,000 in annual cash overhead. Moreover, the manager expects annual materials cash costs for bicycle parts to be $1,700,000, and labour for the bicycle parts to be about the same as the labour cash costs for furniture parts.

The Controller of Met-All, working with various managers, estimates that the expansion would require the purchase of equipment with a $5,000,000 cost and an expected disposal value of $400,000 at the end of its 10-year useful life. Depreciation would occur on a straight-line basis.

The CFO of Met-All determines the firm's cost of capital as 12%. The CFO's salary is $460,000 per year. Adding another division will not change that. The CEO asks for a report on expected revenue for the project, and is told by the marketing department that it might be able to achieve cash revenue of $3,750,000 annually from bicycle parts. Met-All Manufacturing has a tax rate of 30%.

Required

1. Separate the cash flows into four groups: (1) net initial investment cash flows, (2) cash flows from operations, (3) cash flows from terminal disposal of investment, and (4) cash flows not relevant to the capital budgeting problem.
2. Calculate the NPV of the expansion project and comment on your analysis.

LO 3, 4 ▶

2. Annual cash flow from operations, $9,320

20-49 Recognizing cash flows for capital investment projects. Ludmilla Quagg owns a fitness centre and is thinking of replacing the old Fit-O-Matic machine with a brand new Flab-Buster 3000. The old Fit-O-Matic has a historical cost of $50,000 and accumulated depreciation of $46,000, but has a trade-in value of $5,000. It currently costs $1,200 per month in utilities and another $10,000 a year in maintenance to run the Fit-O-Matic. Ludmilla feels that the Fit-O-Matic can be used for another 10 years, after which it would have no salvage value.

The Flab-Buster 3000 would reduce the utilities costs by 30% and cut the maintenance cost in half. The Flab-Buster 3000 costs $98,000, has a 10-year life, and has an expected disposal value of $10,000 at the end of its useful life. Ludmilla charges customers $10 per hour to use the fitness centre. Replacing the fitness machine will not affect the price of service or the number of customers she can serve.

Ludmilla also looked at replacing the Fit-O-Matic with a Walk-N-Pull Series 3, which costs $78,000. However, she prefers the Flab-Buster 3000.

Required

1. Ludmilla wants to evaluate the Flab-Buster 3000 project using capital budgeting techniques, but does not know how to begin. To help her, read through the problem and separate the cash flows into four groups: (1) net initial investment cash flows, (2) cash flow savings from operations, (3) cash flows from terminal disposal of investment, and (4) cash flows not relevant to the capital budgeting problem.
2. Assuming a required rate of return of 8%, and straight-line depreciation over remaining useful life of machines, should Ludmilla buy the Flab-Buster 3000?

20-50 Defensive and offensive strategies in capital budgeting. (CMA, adapted) The management of Kleinburg Industrial Bakery is analyzing two competing investment projects and it must decide which one can be done immediately and which one can be postponed for at least a year. The details of each proposed investment are shown below.

The bakery has a 12% required rate of return to evaluate all investments that directly impact operations and amortizes the investment in plant and equipment using straight-line depreciation over 10 years on the difference between the initial investment and terminal disposal price.

◀ **LO 5**
1. Present value, years 1–9 cash inflows, increase capacity project, $2,131,200

Required

1. Calculate the NPV of each proposal.
2. Which project should the bakery choose on the basis of the NPV calculations?
3. Mention which strategic factors must be considered by the managers when ranking the projects.

	Project: Increase Capacity to Serve New Markets	Project: Upgrade Customer Service
Proposed by	Production manager	Sales and marketing manager
Rationale	Assets are operating at full capacity and we are unable to attend to all the demand, therefore we need to expand our facilities to produce more kilograms.	The fleet of trucks and vans need to be upgraded with tracking devices and remote connections to flex the planning of routes. The new software will allow the company to be paperless and respond faster to customers' requests.
Investment	$600,000	$345,000
Working capital	$ 50,000	$150,000
Terminal disposal value	$60,000	None
Expected useful life	10 years	5 years
Expected increase in operating income	$400,000	$80,000
Expected savings in administrative costs	None	$40,000

Collaborative Learning Cases

20-51 Net present value, internal rate of return, sensitivity analysis. Francesca Freed wants a Burg-N-Fry franchise. The buy-in is $500,000. Burg-N-Fry headquarters tells Francesca that typical annual operating costs are $160,000 (cash) and that she can bring in "as much as" $260,000 in cash revenues per year. Burg-N-Fry headquarters also wants her to pay 10% of her revenues to them per year. Francesca wants to

◀ **LO 1, 2, 3, 4, 5**
1. Annual net cash inflows, periods 1–12, $74,000

earn at least 8% on the investment, because she has to borrow the $500,000 at a cost of 6%. Use a 12-year window, and ignore taxes.

Required

1. Find the NPV and IRR of this investment, given the information that Burg-N-Fry has given Francesca.

2. Francesca is nervous about the "as much as" statement from Burg-N-Fry, and worries that the cash revenues will be lower than $260,000. Repeat requirement 1 using revenues of $240,000 and $220,000.

3. Francesca thinks she should try to negotiate a lower payment to the Burg-N-Fry headquarters, and also thinks that if revenues are lower than $260,000, her costs might also be lower by about $10,000. Repeat requirement 2 using $150,000 as annual cash operating cost and a payment to Burg-N-Fry of only 6% of sales revenues.

4. Discuss how the sensitivity analysis will affect Francesca's decision to buy the franchise. Why don't you have to recalculate the IRR if you change the desired (discount) interest rate?

LO 1, 2, 3, 4, 5 ▶
1. Top Line unit contribution margin, $20

20-52 Relevant costs, capital budgeting, strategic decision. (M. Porporato, adapted) Beauberg is a family-owned company that has been making microwaves for almost 20 years. The company's production line includes 10 models, ranging from a basic model to a deluxe stainless-steel model. Most of its sales are through independently owned retailers in medium-size towns in central Canada, giving the microwaves an image of high quality and price. However, industry sales have been stagnant and those of Beauberg have been falling in the past two years due to the Asian brands. Currently Beauberg sells 75,000 units per year at an average price of $120 each with variable unit costs of $60 (of which materials is $30). As a result, Beauberg is operating its plant at about 75% of a one-shift capacity, although in its "golden years" in the early 1990s it was operating at 75% of a two-shift capacity.

In the spring of 2016, Oh Mart, a chain of large supermarkets, approached Beauberg's CEO and asked about the possibility of producing microwaves for them. The microwaves will be sold under the Oh Mart house brand, called Top Line. They are offering a five-year contract that could be automatically extended on a year-to-year basis, unless one party gives the other at least three months' notice that it does not wish to extend the contract. The deal is for 24,000 units per year with a unit price of $90 each. Oh Mart does not want title on a microwave to pass from Beauberg to Oh Mart until the microwave is shipped to a specific Oh Mart store. Additionally, Oh Mart wants the Top Line microwaves to be somewhat different in appearance from Beauberg's other microwaves. These requirements would increase Beauberg's purchasing, inventorying, and production costs.

In order to be able to give an answer to Oh Mart, knowing that they had no room to negotiate, Beauberg managers gathered the following information:

1. First-year costs of producing Top Line microwaves:

Materials (includes items specific to Oh Mart models)	$40
Labour (same as with regular microwaves)	20
Overhead at 100% of labour (50% is variable; the 100% rate is based on a volume of 100,000 units per year)	20
Total unit cost	$80

2. Related added inventories (the cost of financing them is estimated to be close to 15% per year):

Materials:	two-month supply (a total of 4,000 units)
Work in process:	1,000 units, half completed (but all materials for them issued)
Finished goods:	500 units (awaiting next carload lot shipment to an Oh Mart central warehouse in Concord, Ontario)

3. Impact on Beauberg's regular sales. Beauberg's sales over the next two years are expected to be about 75,000 units a year if it forgoes the Oh Mart deal, based on the CEO's estimates after launching a new "top of the line" microwave. If Beauberg accepts the deal, it would lose about 5,000 units of the regular sales volume a year, since its retail distribution is quite strong in Oh Mart market

regions. These estimates do not include the possibility that a few of Beauberg's current dealers might drop its line if they find out that Beauberg is making microwaves for Oh Mart with a lower selling price.

Instructions

Form groups of three students to complete the following requirements.

Requirements

1. Determine if the proposal by Oh Mart will increase Beauberg's net income in the next year.
2. Calculate the total value of the contract (suppose there is no renewal after the fifth year).
3. On the basis of the NPV criterion, should Beauberg accept the offer?
4. Estimate the strategic consequences of accepting the proposal (consider the current situation of the industry, Beauberg positioning, image, distribution, and production issues).

SOLUTIONS

TRY IT!

Try It 20–1

IRR

The easiest way to calculate the IRR is by using the IRR function in Excel, which results in an IRR of 18.07%.

Alternatively, you can look for the annuity PV factor for $n = 20$ that is closest to the following:

$$\text{Initial investment} / \text{Amount of each equal net cash inflow}$$

$$= \$8,000,000/\$1,500,000$$

$$= 5.33$$

The annuity PV factor at $n = 20$ that is closest to 5.33 occurs when $i = 18\%$. At 18%, the annuity PV factor is 5.353. Thus, the IRR of the wind turbine is close to 18%.

NPV

The NPV is the difference between the present value of the wind turbine's future net cash flows ($750,000 per year for 20 years) and the cost of the initial investment ($4 million). It can be found using the annuity PV factor for $i = 12\%$, $n = 20$, as follows:

$$\text{(Present value of an annuity (at 12\% discount for 20 years))} \times \text{Net Cash Flow} - \text{Initial Investment}$$

$$= \text{(PV Annuity factor} \times \text{Cash Flow)} - \text{Initial Investment}$$

$$= (7.469 \times 1,500,000) - \$8,000,000$$

$$= \$3,203,500$$

Try It 20–2

Payback

Since the net cash inflows are expected to be equal each year, payback is calculated as follows:

$$\text{Payback period} = \text{Initial investment} / \text{Expected annual net cash inflow}$$

$$= \$8,000,000 / \$1,500,000$$

$$= 5.33 \text{ years}$$

ARR

ARR is calculated as follows: ARR = (Average annual net cash inflow − Annual depreciation expense) / Initial investment

The ARR focuses on the operating income generated from the investment, not the net cash inflow from the investment. Thus, to use this formula, we need to find the annual depreciation expense, which will be used to reconcile net cash inflows back to operating income:

$$\text{Annual depreciation} = \$8 \text{ million} / 20 \text{ years}$$
$$= \$400,000$$

Now we calculate ARR as follows:

$$\text{ARR} = (\$1,500,000 - \$400,000) / \$8,000,000$$
$$= 13.75\%$$

Transfer Pricing and Multinational Management Control Systems

Rawpixel.com/Shutterstock

▶ Learning Objectives

1. Integrate the accounting internal control system assurance framework with existing legislation.

2. Apply transfer-pricing processes.

3. Assess the market-based transfer price method.

4. Apply relevant costs and tax considerations to evaluate the selection of cost-based and negotiated transfer prices.

5. Analyze income tax considerations in multinational transfer pricing.

Software Multinationals and Transfer Pricing

Transfer pricing is a strategy adopted in several industries, including the software industry. Transfer prices are the prices that one related entity charges to another related entity for goods or services (such as two divisions or subsidiaries of a multinational corporation). These strategies are often adopted to minimize tax liabilities. However, these strategies can sometimes be seen as unfair manipulation of earnings in the eyes of governments that rely on tax revenues.

Recently, the European Union ruled the business operations of Apple with respect to the tax arrangements offered in Ireland suggest the software giant has an outstanding tax bill of US$14.5 billion. The European Union claims to be concerned that revenues are unfairly being directed to low tax regions within Europe allowing these corporations to lessen their tax liability.

▶ CPA Competencies

This chapter covers material outlined in **Section 3: Management Accounting** of the CPA Competency Map. The Learning Objectives in this chapter have been aligned with the CPA Competency Map to ensure the best coverage possible.

3.3.2 Evaluates and applies cost management techniques appropriate for specific costing decisions

3.4.1 Evaluates sources and drivers of revenue growth

3.7.1 Analyzes the implications of management incentive schemes and employee compensation methods

---

V. Houlder. 2016. Apple's EU tax dispute explained, *Financial Times* (August 29) http://www.ft.com/cms/s/2/3e0172a0-6e1b-11e6-9ac1-1055824ca907.html#axzz4JQR5H5Dn.

Management Control Systems

▶ **LO 1**

Integrate the accounting internal control system assurance framework with existing legislation.

A **management control system** is a means of gathering and using information to aid and coordinate the planning and control decisions throughout an organization and to guide the behaviour of its managers and other employees. Some companies design their management control system around the concept of the balanced scorecard. For example, Scotiabank's management control system contains financial and nonfinancial information in each of the four perspectives of the balanced scorecard. Well-designed management control systems use information both from within the company, such as net income and employee satisfaction, and from outside the company, such as stock price and customer satisfaction.

Formal and Informal Systems

Management control systems consist of formal and informal control systems. The **formal management control system** of a company includes explicit rules, procedures, performance measures, and incentive plans that guide the behaviour of its managers and other employees. The formal control system comprises several systems, such as the management accounting system (which provides information regarding costs, revenues, and income), the human resources systems (which provide information on recruiting, training, absenteeism, and accidents), and the quality systems (which provide information on yield, defective products, and late deliveries to customers).

The **informal management control system** includes shared values, loyalties, and mutual commitments among members of the organization; company culture; and the unwritten norms about acceptable behaviour for managers and other employees. Examples of company slogans that reinforce values and loyalties are "At Ford, Quality Is Job 1" and "At Home Depot, Low Prices Are Just the Beginning."

Effective Management Control

To be effective, management control systems should be closely aligned with the organization's strategies and goals. Two examples of strategies at ExxonMobil are (1) providing innovative products and services to increase market share in key customer segments (by targeting customers who are willing to pay more for faster service, better facilities, and well-stocked convenience stores) and (2) reducing costs and targeting price-sensitive customers. Should ExxonMobil decide to pursue the former strategy, the management control system must then reinforce this goal, and ExxonMobil should tie managers' rewards to achieving the targeted measures.

Management control systems should also be designed to support the organizational responsibilities of individual managers. Different levels of management at ExxonMobil need different kinds of information to perform their tasks. For example, top management needs stock price information to evaluate how much shareholder value the company has created. Stock price, however, is less important for line managers supervising individual refineries. They are more concerned with obtaining information about on-time delivery of gasoline, equipment downtime, product quality, number of days lost to accidents and environmental problems, cost of gasoline, and employee satisfaction. Similarly, marketing managers are more concerned with information about service at gas stations, customer satisfaction, and market share.

Effective management control systems should also motivate managers and other employees. **Motivation** is the desire to attain a selected goal (the goal-congruence aspect) combined with the resulting pursuit of that goal (the effort aspect). **Goal congruence** exists when individuals and groups work toward achieving the organization's goals—that is, managers working in their own best interest take actions that align with the overall goals of top management. Suppose the goal of ExxonMobil's top management is to maximize operating income. If the management control system evaluates the refinery manager only on the basis of costs, the manager may be tempted to make decisions that minimize cost but overlook product quality or timely delivery to retail stations. This oversight is unlikely to maximize operating income of the company as a whole. In this case, the management control system will not achieve goal congruence.

Effort is the extent to which managers strive or endeavour to achieve a goal. Effort goes beyond physical exertion, such as a worker producing at a faster rate, to include mental actions as well. For example, effort includes the diligence or acumen with which a manager gathers and analyzes data before authorizing a new investment. It is impossible to directly observe or reward effort. As a result, management control systems motivate employees to exert effort by rewarding them for the achievement of observable goals, such as profit targets or stock returns. This induces managers to exert effort because higher levels of effort increase the likelihood that the goals are achieved. The rewards can be monetary (such as cash, shares of company stock, use of a company car, or membership in a club) or nonmonetary (such as a better title, greater responsibility, or authority over a larger number of employees).

Organizational Structure and Decentralization

Management control systems must fit an organization's structure. An organization whose structure is decentralized has additional issues to consider for its management control system to be effective. **Decentralization** is the freedom for managers at lower levels of the organization to make decisions. **Autonomy** is the degree of freedom to make decisions. The greater the freedom, the greater the autonomy of any given **subunit**, which can be any part of an organization—a large division, such as the refining division of ExxonMobil; or a small group, such as a two-person advertising department of a local clothing chain. Companies try to choose the degree of decentralization that maximizes benefits over costs. From a practical standpoint, top management can seldom quantify either the benefits or the costs of decentralization. Still, the cost–benefit approach helps management focus on the key issues.

Benefits of Decentralization	Costs of Decentralization
1. *Creates greater responsiveness to needs of a subunit's customers, suppliers, and employees.* Compared with top managers, subunit managers are better informed about their customers, competitors, suppliers, and employees, as well as about local factors that affect performance.	1. *Leads to suboptimal decision making.* This cost arises because top management has given up control over decision making. Subunit managers may unintentionally make decisions not congruent with the overall strategy of the firm.
2. *Leads to gains from faster decision making by subunit managers.* Decentralization speeds decision making, creating a competitive advantage over centralized organizations.	2. *Focuses the manager's attention on the subunit rather than the company as a whole.* Individual subunit managers may regard themselves as competing with managers of other subunits in the same company as if they were external rivals.
3. *Increases motivation of subunit managers.* Subunit managers are more motivated and committed when they can exercise initiative.	3. *Results in duplication of output.* If subunits provide similar products or services, they may unnecessarily duplicate expenditures and artificially increase overall organizational cost.
4. *Assists management development and learning.* Decentralized units provide a training ground for junior members and an opportunity for champions to fight for their ideas.	
5. *Sharpens the focus of subunit managers and broadens the reach of top management.* In a decentralized setting, the manager of a subunit has a concentrated focus.	

Decentralization in Multinational Companies

Multinational companies (MNCs)—companies that operate in multiple countries—are often decentralized because centralized control of a company with subunits around the world is often physically and practically impossible. Also, language, customs, cultures, business practices, rules, laws, and regulations vary significantly across countries. Decentralization enables managers in different countries to make decisions that exploit their knowledge of local business and political conditions, and to deal with uncertainties in their individual environments. For example, Philips, a global electronics company headquartered in the Netherlands, delegates marketing and pricing decisions for its television business in the Indian and Singaporean markets to the managers in those countries.

Multinational corporations often rotate managers among foreign locations and corporate headquarters. Job rotation combined with decentralization helps develop managers' abilities to operate in the global environment.

There are also drawbacks to decentralizing MNCs, however. One of the most important is the lack of control and the resulting risks. Barings PLC, a British investment banking firm, went bankrupt and had to be sold when one of its traders in Singapore caused the firm to lose more than £1 billion on unauthorized trades that were not detected until after the trades were made. Similarly, a trader at Sumitomo Corporation racked up $2.6 billion in copper-trading losses because poor controls failed to detect the magnitude of the trader's activities. Multinational corporations that implement decentralized decision making usually design their management control systems to measure and monitor division performance. Information and communications technology helps the flow of information for reporting and control.

Decisions About Responsibility Centres

To measure the performance of subunits in centralized or decentralized organizations, the management accounting control system uses one or a mix of the four types of responsibility centres:

- *Cost centre:* Manager accountable for costs only.
- *Revenue centre:* Manager accountable for revenues only.
- *Profit centre:* Manager accountable for revenues and costs.
- *Investment centre:* Manager accountable for investments, revenues, and costs.

A common misconception is that the term *profit centre* (and, in some cases, *investment centre*) is a synonym for a decentralized subunit and that *cost centre* is a synonym for a centralized subunit. *Profit centres can be coupled with a highly centralized organization, and cost centres can be coupled with a highly decentralized organization.* For

---

Concepts in Action—Strategy | Transfer-Pricing Dispute Temporarily Stops the Flow of Fiji Water

Fiji Water LLC, a US-based company, was engaged in a fierce transfer-pricing dispute with the government of the Fiji Islands, where its water bottling plant is located. While Fiji Water is produced in the Fiji Islands and accounts for 20% of the country's exports, all other activities in the company's value chain—importing, distributing, and retailing—occur in the 40 countries where Fiji Water is sold. Over time, the Fiji Islands' government became concerned that Fiji Water was engaging in transfer-price manipulations, selling the water shipments produced in the Fiji Islands at a very low price to the company's US headquarters.

As a result, the Fiji Islands Revenue and Customs Authority (FIRCA) halted Fiji Water exports and accused the company of transfer-price manipulations. FIRCA's chief executive, Jitoko Tikolevu, said, "The wholly US-owned Fijian subsidiary sold its water exclusively to its US parent at the declared rate, in Fiji, of $4 a carton. In the US, though, the same company then sold it for up to $50 a carton." Fiji Water immediately filed a lawsuit against FIRCA with the High Court of Fiji arguing that on a global basis it sold each carton of water

for $20 to $28 and did not make a profit due to "heavy investments in assets, employees, and marketing necessary to aggressively grow a successful branded product."

The transfer-pricing dispute between FIRCA and Fiji Water was ultimately resolved through taxation. While Fiji Water maintained its previous transfer price of $4 for water produced at its bottling plant in the Fiji Islands, the Fijian government implemented a new 15-cents-per-litre excise tax—up from one-third of one cent—on water extracted by Fiji Water. While the company initially disputed the new tax, the company eventually agreed to pay the new levy. As this high-profile case demonstrates, transfer-pricing formulas and taxation details remain a contentious issue for governments and countries around the globe.

Sources: A. Bloxham. 2011. Fiji Water Accused of Environmentally Misleading Claims, *The Telegraph* (June 20); P. Chapman. 2010. Fiji Water Reopens Pacific Bottling Plant, *The Telegraph* (December 1); Robert Matau. 2008. Fiji Water Explains Saga, *Fiji Times* (February 9); J. McMaster and J. Novak, "Fiji Water and Corporate Social Responsibility—Green Makeover or 'Green-washing'?" The University of Western Ontario Richard Ivey School of Business Case No. 909A08 (London, Ontario: Ivey Publishing, 2009).

example, managers in a division organized as a profit centre may have little leeway in making decisions. They may need to obtain approval from corporate headquarters for any expenditure over, say, $10,000 and may be forced to accept central staff "advice." In another company, divisions may be organized as cost centres, but their managers may have great latitude on capital expenditures and on where to purchase materials and services. In short, the labels "profit centre" and "cost centre" are independent of the degree of decentralization in an organization.

Nova Scotia Lumber has a raw lumber division and a finished lumber division. The variable costs are as follows: raw lumber division: $100 per 100 board-feet of raw lumber; and finished lumber division: $125 per 100 board-feet of finished lumber. Raw lumber can be sold at $225 per 100 board-feet. Finished lumber can be sold at $375 per 100 board-feet.

   Based on a calculation of operating income, is it more profitable for Nova Scotia Lumber to produce and sell raw lumber or transfer to another division to produce finished lumber?

Transfer Pricing

For both job and process costing, **intermediate products** in a multi-stage production process are transferred from one production stage to another. An intermediate product is an unfinished product transferred from one subunit to another subunit of the same organization. The cost of goods manufactured (COGM), a large proportion of which is allocated manufacturing overhead (MOH), is also transferred.

▶ **LO 2**

Apply transfer-pricing processes.

Transfer pricing refers to the prices one division in a company charges another division in the same company for products and services. This practice is often controversial, with governments frequently intervening to alter the prices companies charge. In Romania, tax authorities frequently question the transfer prices set by multinational companies in that country. Typically this results in adjustments to transfer prices that are paid for by taxpayers. Romania enacted rules to allow advance pricing agreements (APA) where taxpayers can make arrangements with tax authorities to better manage transfer prices. While this has not resulted in the benefits it intended, the number of audits concerning transfer pricing with MNCs has increased. The APA process is time consuming, with tax authorities working to reduce the time involved in the process. Companies operating in Romania frequently transfer goods into the country at low prices and export them at high prices. However, while government controls are in place to regulate transfer pricing in Romania, they are not always taken seriously, which reduces their effectiveness.

In decentralized organizations, much of the decision-making power resides in the individual subunits. In these cases, the management control system often uses transfer prices to coordinate the actions of the subunits and to evaluate their performance. A **transfer price** is the price one subunit (department or division) charges for a product or service supplied to another subunit of the same organization. If, for example, a car manufacturer has a separate division that manufactures engines, the transfer price is the price the engine division charges when it transfers engines to the car assembly division. The transfer price creates revenues for the selling subunit (the engine division in our example) and purchase costs for the buying subunit (the assembly division in our example), affecting each subunit's operating income. These operating incomes can be used to evaluate subunits' performances and to motivate their managers. The product or service transferred between subunits of an organization is called an intermediate product. This product may either be further worked on by the receiving subunit (as in the engine example) or, if transferred from production to marketing, be sold to an external customer.

The rationale for transfer prices is that subunit managers (such as the manager of the engine division) need only focus on how their decisions will affect their subunit's performance without evaluating their impact on companywide performance. In this sense, transfer prices ease the subunit managers' information-processing and decision-making tasks. In a well-designed transfer-pricing system, a manager focuses on optimizing subunit performance (the performance of the engine division), and in so doing optimizes the performance of the company as a whole.

Cooperation among subunits to maximize net profit could include deliberate over- or understatement of the transfer price to minimize tax. The problem is that in this related-party transaction, the cost to the purchasing subunit is deductible from taxable income, and the transfer price received by the supplying subunit is revenue added to taxable income. Transfer prices affect the cash taxes collected by each country. A taxable income of $100 million in Canada would result in approximately $40 million in tax, but the same $100 million in Barbados would incur approximately $2.7 million of tax.

If the Barbadian subunit transferred nearly finished goods to Canada at, for example, $90 million, the MNC's taxable income in Canada would decrease to $10 million and the tax liability would be only $4 million, for a saving in Canada of approximately $36 million.[1] The CRA, along with other national tax authorities, is vitally interested in internal transfer prices for this reason. In the transfer-pricing process, national tax authorities are dominant partners and can enforce their opinion of the appropriate price.

Alternative Transfer-Pricing Methods

The CRA has adopted the **Organisation for Economic Co-operation and Development** (OECD) Hierarchy of Methods for transfer pricing, which ranks in preference the methods of transfer pricing. For a corporation, however, the goal when selecting a transfer-pricing method should be to reflect the economic facts of operations. There are three general methods for determining transfer prices:

1. *Market-based transfer prices.* Top management may choose to set the internal price based on a similar product or service publicly listed, or the external price that a subunit charges to outside customers.

2. *Cost-based transfer prices.* Top management may choose a transfer price based on the cost of producing the product in question. Examples include variable production cost, variable and fixed production costs, and full cost of the product. Sometimes, the cost-based transfer price includes a markup or profit margin that represents a return on subunit investment.

3. *Negotiated transfer prices.* In some cases, the subunits of a company are free to negotiate the transfer price between themselves and then to decide whether to buy and sell internally or deal with outside parties.

Criteria for Evaluating Transfer Prices

As in all management control systems, transfer prices should help achieve a company's strategies and goals and fit its organization structure. We describe four criteria to evaluate transfer pricing:

1. Transfer prices should promote goal congruence.

2. They should induce managers to exert a high level of effort. Subunits selling a product or service should be motivated to hold their costs down; subunits buying the product or service should be motivated to acquire and use inputs efficiently.

3. The transfer price should help top management evaluate the performance of individual subunits.

4. If top management favours a high degree of decentralization, transfer prices should preserve a high degree of subunit autonomy in decision making. That is, a subunit manager seeking to maximize the operating income of the subunit should have the freedom to transact with other subunits of the company (on the basis of transfer prices) or to transact with external parties.

---

[1] D.C. Hill, *CMA Management*, 81.1 (2007): 36–39.

Concepts in Action—Strategy   US$3.4 Billion Is an Incentive

On May 30, 2008, the Tax Court of Canada decided that the Canadian subsidiary GlaxoSmithKline Inc. (GSKI), of the UK parent company Glaxo Group Ltd., had used an inappropriate transfer-pricing method during the years 1990–1993. The values involved decreased GSKI's taxable Canadian income by hundreds of millions of dollars.

The active ingredient of the drug product Zantac was purchased by GSKI from a Swiss affiliate. The Canadian manufacturers produced the drug for approximately $190 to $305 per kilogram, whereas the price paid to the Swiss affiliate was approximately $1,500 to $1,650 per kilogram. A 6% royalty on each purchase was remitted by GSKI to the UK parent under a licensing agreement. The UK parent then paid a 25% withholding tax to the UK government. This exceeds the UK/Canada tax treaty amount of 10%.

The Canada Revenue Agency (CRA) successfully argued that the comparable uncontrolled price (CUP) method should have applied to the transfer price

estimate where GSKI had applied the resale price method (RSP). The decision hinged on two facts: first, what a reasonable price would have been in an arm's-length transaction; second, if the additional 6% royalty paid to the UK parent should be included in the transfer price.

In this case, it was successfully argued by CRA that "reasonable" meant the highest generic price for which the ingredient was sold in Canada. It also argued successfully to separate the supply and licensing contracts to consider the supply contract on its own and exclude the royalty from the total transfer price. The CRA has proposed an adjustment of $51.5 million payable by GSKI, which has appealed the decision to the Federal Court of Appeal.

The US Internal Revenue Service (IRS) has already settled a 14-year claim against the US affiliate of this company. At issue again was the use of inappropriate transfer pricing for ingredients for various drugs, including Zantac. This case was settled on September 11, 2006, with a negotiated settlement of $3.4 billion.

First, the decision upholds the use of the OECD hierarchy of transfer-pricing methods. Second, the court successfully narrowed the case to a decision on the supply price and excluded other contracts as irrelevant in assessing the appropriate transfer price. Third, the court decided that the analysis by GSKI's Canadian tax experts was unreasonable, relying instead on US and Canadian Crown experts.

Sources: The Economist, January 29, 2004; KPMG, "GlaxoSmithKline—Tax Court Prescribes Bitter Pill in Transfer Pricing Case," http://www.kpmg.ca/en/services/tax/tp60/tp60_0803.html; Fasken Martineau, "Tax Court of Canada issues *GlaxoSmithKline* decision," http://www.fasken.com/tax-court-of-canada-issues-iglaxosmithklinei-decision-07-11-2008; Fraser Milner Casgrain LLP, "Focus on Tax—*GlaxoSmithKline Inc. v. The Queen,*" http://www.fmc-law.com/Publications/Tax_SteevesC_Focus_On_Tax_June2008.aspx.

Transfer Pricing in Practice

An illustration of transfer pricing can be seen in the case of Northern Petroleum of Calgary, Alberta, which operates two divisions (the transportation and refining divisions) as profit centres. The transportation division manages the operation of a pipeline that transports crude oil from the Calgary area to Sarnia, Ontario, where the refining division processes crude oil into gasoline. (For simplicity, assume that gasoline is the only saleable product the refinery makes and that it takes two barrels of crude oil to yield one barrel of gasoline.)

Variable costs in each division are variable with respect to a single cost driver: barrels of crude oil transported by the transportation division and barrels of gasoline produced by the refining division. The fixed cost per unit is based on the budgeted annual fixed costs and practical capacity of crude oil that can be transported by the transportation division, and the budgeted fixed costs and practical capacity of gasoline that can be produced by the refining division.

■ The production division can sell crude oil to outside parties in the Calgary area at $72 per barrel.

Exhibit 21-1 Operating Data for Northern Petroleum

	A	B	C	D	E	F	G	H
1								
2				**Transportation Division**				
3				Variable cost per barrel of crude oil	$ 1			
4	Contact price per barrel of crude oil supplied in Calgary =	$72 →		Fixed cost per barrel of crude oil	3			
5				Full cost per barrel of crude oil	$ 4			
6								
7								
8				Barrels of crude oil transferred				
9								
10								
11				**Refining Division**				
12	Market price per barrel of crude oil supplied to Sarnia refinery =	$85 →		Variable cost per barrel of gasoline	$ 8		Market price per barrel of gasoline sold to external =	$190
13				Fixed cost per barrel of gasoline	6	→	parties	
14				Full cost per barrel of gasoline	$14			
15								

- The transportation division "buys" crude oil from the production division, transports it to Sarnia, and then "sells" it to the refining division. The pipeline from Calgary to Sarnia has the capacity to carry 40,000 barrels of crude oil per day.

- The refining division has been using its total practical capacity, operating at 30,000 barrels of crude oil a day, using oil delivered by both the transportation division (an average of 10,000 barrels per day) and other external suppliers who also deliver to the Sarnia refinery (an average of 20,000 barrels per day, at $85 per barrel).

- The refining division sells the gasoline it produces at $190 per barrel.

Exhibit 21-1 summarizes Northern Petroleum's variable and fixed costs per barrel of crude oil in the transportation division and variable and fixed costs per barrel of gasoline in the refining division, the external market prices of buying crude oil, and the external market price of selling gasoline. What's missing in the exhibit is the actual transfer price from the transportation division to the refining division. This transfer price will vary depending on the transfer-pricing method used. Transfer prices from the transportation division to the refining division under each of the three methods are as follows:

1. Market-based transfer price of $85 per barrel of crude oil based on the competitive market price in Calgary.

2. Cost-based transfer prices at, say, 105% of full cost, where full cost is the cost of the crude oil purchased plus the transportation division's own variable and fixed costs (from Exhibit 21-1): $1.05 \times (\$72 + \$1 + \$3) = \$79.80$.

3. Hybrid transfer price of $83 per barrel of crude oil, which is between the market and cost-based transfer prices and is established through agreement of management.

Exhibit 21-2 presents divisional operating incomes per 100 barrels of crude oil purchased under each transfer-pricing method. Transfer prices create income for the selling division and corresponding costs for the buying division that cancel out when division results are consolidated for the company as a whole. Northern Petroleum's total operating income from purchasing, transporting, and refining the 100 barrels of crude oil and selling the 50 barrels of gasoline is the same, $1,200, regardless of the internal transfer prices used.

The operating income of the transportation division is $520 more (= $900 − $380) if transfer prices are based on market prices rather than on 105% of full cost. The operating income of the refining division is $520 more (= $820 − $300) if transfer prices are based on 105% of full cost rather than market prices. If the transportation division's sole

Exhibit 21-2 Division Operating Income of Northern Petroleum for 100 Barrels of Crude Oil Under Alternative Transfer-Pricing Methods

	A	B	C	D	E	F	G
1	**Production and Sales Data**						
2	Barrels of crude transferred =	100					
3	Barrels of gasoline sold =	50					
4		**Internal Transfers**		**Internal Transfers at**			**Internal Transfers at**
5		**at Market Price of**		**105% of Full Cost =**			**Negotiated Price of**
6		**$85.00**		**$79.80**			**$83.00**
7		**per Barrel**		**per Barrel**			**per Barrel**
8	**Transportation Division**						
9	Revenue: 100 × $85; $79.80; $83	$8,500		$7,980			$8,300
10	Costs						
11	Crude oil						
12	$72 × 100 barrels of crude oil	7,200		7,200			7,200
13	Division variable costs						
14	$1 × 100 barrels of crude oil	100		100			100
15	Division fixed costs						
16	$3 × 100 barrels of crude oil	300		300			300
17	Total division costs	7,600		7,600			7,600
18	Division operating income	$ 900		$ 380			$ 700
19	Operating margin	10.59%		4.76%			8.43%
20							
21	**Refining Division**						
22	Revenues: $190 × 50	$9,500		$9,500			$9,500
23	Costs						
24	Transferred-in costs: 100 × $85; $79.80; $83	8,500		7,980			8,300
25	Division variable costs						
26	$8 × 50 barrels of gasoline	400		400			400
27	Division fixed costs						
28	$6 × 50 barrels of gasoline	300		300			300
29	Total division costs	9,200		8,680			9,000
30	Division operating income	$ 300		$ 820			$ 500
31	Operating margin	3.16%		8.63%			5.26%
32	Total operating income for Northern Petroleum	$1,200		$1,200			$1,200

criterion were to maximize its own division operating income, it would favour transfer prices at market prices. In contrast, the refining division would prefer transfer prices at 105% of full cost to maximize its own division operating income. The negotiated transfer price of $82 is between the 105% of full cost and market-based transfer prices. It splits the $1,200 of operating income between the divisions, and could arise as a result of negotiations between the transportation and refining division managers.

It's not surprising that subunit managers, especially those whose compensation or promotion directly depends on subunit operating income, take considerable interest in setting transfer prices. To reduce the excessive focus of subunit managers on their own subunits, many companies compensate subunit managers on the basis of both subunit and companywide operating incomes.

Interprovincial Transfers and Taxes

Top management at Northern Petroleum transferred intermediate goods interprovincially. The corporate tax rates in Alberta are the lowest in Canada, whereas Ontario has the highest provincial corporate tax rates in the country. From the company's perspective, the split of taxable income between the provinces would make a difference in both operating cash flow and net income. It would also make a difference to the taxes collected by each province.

The operating margin if the market price is used will be 10.59% for the transportation division in Alberta and 3.16% for the refining division in Ontario. This would be the best after-tax choice for Northern Petroleum. The second-best choice would be at the negotiated transfer price, which will leave 8.43% of the operating income in Alberta and transfer 5.26% to Ontario. The least preferred choice from the company's perspective is to use full cost because that leaves only 4.76% of operating income in the provincial jurisdiction with the lowest tax rates (Alberta) and transfers 8.63% to the provincial jurisdiction with the highest tax rates in Canada (Ontario).

Fortunately, the first choice from the company's perspective also ranks first in the transfer price hierarchy of the OECD. The national and provincial governments prefer transfer prices at the market price because it is assured this transfer price is an arm's-length price. In this situation there is no need for Northern Petroleum to approach either tax authority to obtain an **advance transfer price arrangement (APA)**. APAs are a substitute for dispute resolution wherein the company and the tax authority can cooperate to prospectively agree on a transfer price method.[2]

APAs are exceptionally important to sustain good corporate governance. In disputes between the tax authorities and corporations, fines alone can reach billions. This excludes legal expenses and opportunity costs of diverting resources to dispute resolution. Most MNCs will approach the tax authorities in all countries (or provinces) where related-party transfers of intermediate goods will occur. Most tax authorities, including CRA, will negotiate a tax method acceptable to them for some specified future time period. Companies voluntarily undertake APAs, but the agreement is legally binding.

The APA process is costly; however, complex, high-dollar-value related-party transactions should be negotiated in advance because it is exactly these transactions that tax authorities will most likely audit. The opportunity cost of a CRA transfer price audit is very high, especially if the company has failed internally to produce ongoing documentation. All related-party transfers are reportable in the corporate tax return. The maximum late-filing penalty is $10,000, and the maximum failure to file penalty is $12,000 for *each* infraction. Legislation authorizes provinces to levy the same penalties domestically.[3] When companies fail to provide acceptable documentation, a 10% penalty can be added to any transfer-pricing adjustment. The penalty is applied only if the transfer-pricing adjustment exceeds 10% of the gross revenue prior to any transfer-pricing adjustments or $5 million.[4]

Market-Based Transfer Prices

▶ **LO 3**

Assess the market-based transfer price method.

Transferring products or services at market prices generally leads to optimal decisions when three conditions are satisfied: (1) The intermediate market is perfectly competitive, (2) interdependencies of subunits are minimal, and (3) there are no additional costs or benefits to the corporation as a whole in using the market instead of transacting internally. A **perfectly competitive market** exists when there is a homogeneous product with equivalent buying and selling prices and no individual buyers or sellers can affect those prices by their own actions. By using market-based transfer prices in perfectly competitive markets, a company can meet the criteria of goal-congruence, management effort, optimal subunit performance, and (if desired) subunit autonomy.

Reconsider the Northern Petroleum example, assuming that there is a perfectly competitive market for crude oil in the Calgary area and that the market price is $85 per barrel.

---

[2] M. Przysuski, "Advance Pricing Arrangements (APAs) in Canada," *Corporate Business Taxation Monthly*, 6.2 (2004): 11–16.
[3] M. Przysuski, S. Lalapet, and H. Swaneveld, "Transfer Pricing Filing in Canada," *Corporate Business Taxation Monthly*, 6.7 (2005): 25–28.
[4] S.J. Smith and P.L. Kelley, "It's an Art, Not a Science," *CA Magazine*, 138.8 (2005): 44–46.

As a result, the transportation division can sell and the refining division can buy as much crude oil as each wants at $85 per barrel. Northern, however, would like its managers to buy or sell crude oil internally. Think about the decisions that Northern's division managers would make if each had the option to sell or buy crude oil externally.

If the transfer price between Northern's transportation and refining divisions is set below $85, the manager of the transportation division will be motivated to sell all production to outside buyers at $85 per barrel. If the transfer price is set above $85, the manager of the refining division will be motivated to purchase all its crude oil requirements from outside suppliers. A current market value transfer price of $85 could motivate both the transportation and refining division to buy and sell internally.

In perfectly competitive markets, the minimum price the selling division is willing to accept from the buying division is the market price, because the selling division can always sell its output in the external market at that price. The maximum price the buying division is willing to pay to the selling division is the market price, because the buying division can always buy its input in the external market at that price.

Distress Prices

When supply outstrips demand, market prices may drop well below their historical average. If the drop in prices is expected to be temporary, these low market prices are sometimes called *distress prices*. Deciding whether a current market price is a distress price is often difficult. The market prices of several agricultural commodities, such as wheat and oats, have stayed for many years at what observers initially believed were temporary distress levels.

Which transfer-pricing method should be used for judging performance if distress prices prevail? Some companies use the distress prices themselves, but others use long-run average prices, or "normal" market prices. In the short run, the manager of the supplier division should meet the distress price as long as it exceeds the incremental costs of supplying the product or service; if not, the supplying division should stop producing, and the buying division should buy the product or service from an outside supplier. These actions would increase overall companywide operating income. If the long-run average market price is used, forcing the manager to buy internally at a price above the current market price will hurt the buying division's short-run performance and understate its profitability. If, however, prices remain low in the long run, the manager of the supplying division must decide whether to dispose of some manufacturing facilities or shut down and have the buying division purchase the product from outside.

Cost-Based and Negotiated Transfer Prices

Cost-based transfer prices are helpful when market prices are unavailable, inappropriate, or too costly to obtain. For example, the product may be specialized or unique, price lists may not be widely available or the internal product may be different from the products available externally in terms of quality and service.

▶ **LO 4**

Apply relevant costs and tax considerations to evaluate the selection of cost-based and negotiated transfer prices.

Full-Cost Bases

In practice, many companies use transfer prices based on full costs. These prices, however, can lead to suboptimal decisions. Assume that Northern Petroleum makes internal transfers at 105% of full cost. The Sarnia refining division purchases crude oil from a local Sarnia supplier, who delivers the crude oil to the refinery; the freight-on-board (FOB) cost is $85 per barrel. To reduce crude oil costs, the refining division has located an independent producer in Calgary who is willing to sell crude oil at $79 per barrel, delivered to Northern's pipeline in Calgary.

Given Northern's organization structure, the transportation division could purchase the 20,000 barrels of crude oil in Calgary, transport it to Sarnia, and then sell it to the refining division. The pipeline has excess capacity and can ship the 20,000 barrels at its variable costs of $1 per barrel. Will Northern Petroleum incur lower costs by purchasing crude oil from the independent producer in Calgary or by purchasing crude oil from the

Sarnia supplier? Will the refining division show lower crude oil purchasing costs by using oil from the Calgary producer or by using its current Sarnia supplier?

The following analysis shows that operating income of Northern Petroleum as a whole would be maximized by purchasing oil from the independent Calgary producer. The analysis compares the incremental costs in all divisions under the two alternatives:

■ **Alternative 1:** Buy 20,000 barrels from the Sarnia supplier at $85 per barrel.

Total costs to Northern Petroleum = 20,000 × $85 = $1,700,000

■ **Alternative 2:** Buy 20,000 barrels in Calgary at $79 per barrel and transport it to Sarnia at $1 per barrel variable costs or $80 per barrel.

Total costs to Northern Petroleum = 20,000 × $80 = $1,600,000

There is a reduction in total costs to Northern Petroleum of $100,000 by using the independent producer in Calgary ($1,700,000 − $1,600,000).

In turn, suppose the transportation division's transfer price to the refining division is 105% of full cost. The refining division will see its reported division costs increase if the crude oil is purchased from the independent producer in Calgary:

$$\frac{\text{Transfer}}{\text{price}} = 1.05 \times \left(\begin{array}{ccc} \text{Purchase price} & \text{Unit variable cost} & \text{Unit fixed cost} \\ \text{from Calgary} + \text{of transportation} + \text{of transportation} \\ \text{producer} & \text{division} & \text{division} \end{array} \right)$$

$$= 1.05 \times (\$79 + \$1 + \$3) = 1.05 \times \$83 = \$87.15 \text{ per barrel}$$

■ **Alternative 1:** Buy 20,000 barrels from the Sarnia supplier at $85 per barrel.

Total costs to refining division = 20,000 × $85 = $1,700,000 (constant)

■ **Alternative 2:** Buy 20,000 barrels from the transportation division of Northern Petroleum that are purchased from the independent producer in Calgary.

Total costs to refining division = 20,000 × $87.15 = $1,743,000

As a profit centre, the refining division can maximize its short-run division operating income by purchasing from the Sarnia supplier ($1,700,000 versus $1,743,000).

The refining division looks at each barrel that it obtains from the transportation division as a variable cost of $87.15 per barrel; if 10 barrels are transferred, it costs the refining division $871.50; if 100 barrels are transferred, it costs $8,715. In fact, the variable cost per barrel is $80 ($79 to purchase the oil in Calgary plus $1 to transport it to Sarnia). The remaining $7.15 (= $87.15 − $80) per barrel is the transportation division's fixed cost and markup. *The full cost plus a markup transfer-pricing method causes the refining division to regard the fixed cost (and the 5% markup) of the transportation division as a variable cost and leads to goal incongruence.*

A transfer price between the minimum and maximum transfer prices of $80 and $85 respectively will promote goal congruence—both divisions will increase their own reported division operating income by purchasing crude oil from the independent producer in Calgary. In particular, a transfer price based on the full costs of $83 without a markup will achieve goal congruence. The transportation division will show no operating income and will be evaluated as a cost centre. Surveys indicate that managers prefer to use full-cost transfer pricing because it yields relevant costs for long-run decisions and because it facilitates pricing on the basis of full product costs.

Variable Cost Bases

Transferring 20,000 barrels of crude oil from the transportation division to the refining division at the variable cost of $80 per barrel achieves goal congruence, as shown in the preceding section. The refining division would buy from the transportation division because the transportation division's variable cost (which is also the relevant incremental cost for Northern Petroleum as a whole) is less than the $85 price charged by outside suppliers.

At the $80 per barrel transfer price, the transportation division would record an operating loss and the refining division would show large profits because it would be charged only for the variable costs of the transportation division. One approach to addressing this problem is to have the refining division make a lump-sum transfer payment to cover fixed costs and generate some operating income for the transportation division while the transportation division continues to make transfers at variable cost. The fixed payment is the price the refining division pays for using the capacity of the transportation division. The income earned by each division can then be used to evaluate the performance of each division and its manager.

Prorating the Difference Between Minimum and Maximum Transfer Prices

An alternative cost-based approach is for Northern Petroleum to choose a transfer price that splits the $5 difference between the maximum transfer price the refining division is willing to pay and the minimum transfer price the transportation division wants on some equitable basis. Suppose Northern Petroleum allocates the $5 difference on the basis of the budgeted variable costs incurred by the transportation division and the refining division for a given quantity of crude oil. Using the data in Exhibit 21-2, the variable costs are as follows:

Transportation division's variable costs to transport 100 barrels of crude oil ($1 × 100)	$100
Refining division's variable costs to refine 100 barrels of crude oil and produce 50 barrels of gasoline ($8 × 50)	400
Total variable costs	$500

The transportation division gets to keep $100/$500 × $5 = $1, and the refining division gets to keep $400/$500 × $5 = $4 of the $5 difference. That is, the transfer price between the transportation division and the refining division would be $81 per barrel of crude oil ($79 purchase cost + $1 variable costs + $1 that the transportation division gets to keep). Essentially, this approach is a budgeted variable cost plus transfer price; the "plus" indicates the setting of a transfer price above variable costs.

To decide on the $1 and $4 allocation of the $5 contribution to total corporate operating income per barrel, the divisions must share information about their variable costs. In effect, each division does not operate (at least for this transaction) in a totally decentralized manner. Because most organizations are hybrids of centralization and decentralization anyway, this approach deserves serious consideration when transfers are significant. Note, however, that each division has an incentive to overstate its variable costs to receive a more favourable transfer price.

Negotiated Transfer Prices and MNC Issues

Negotiated transfer prices arise as the outcome of a bargaining process between selling and buying divisions. Consider again the choice of a transfer price between the transportation and refining divisions of Northern Petroleum. The transportation division has excess capacity that it can use to transport oil from Calgary to Sarnia. The transportation division will be willing to "sell" oil to the refining division only if the transfer price equals or exceeds $80 per barrel of crude oil (its variable costs). The refining division will be willing to "buy" crude oil from the transportation division only if the cost equals or is below $85 per barrel (the price at which the refining division can buy crude oil in Sarnia).

Given the transportation division's unused capacity, Northern Petroleum as a whole maximizes operating income if the refining division purchases from the transportation division rather than from the Sarnia market (incremental costs of $80 per barrel versus incremental costs of $85 per barrel). Both divisions would be interested in transacting with each other if the transfer price is set between $80 and $85. For example, a transfer price of $83 per barrel will increase the transportation division's operating income by $83 − $80 = $3 per barrel. It will increase the refining division's operating income by $85 − $83 = $2 per barrel because refining can now "buy" the oil for $83 inside rather than for $85 outside.

Exhibit 21-3 Comparison of Different Transfer-Pricing Methods

Criteria	Market-Based	Cost-Based	Negotiated
Achieves goal congruence	Yes, when markets are competitive	Often, but not always	Yes
Useful for evaluating subunit performance	Yes, when markets are competitive	Difficult unless transfer price exceeds full cost and even then is somewhat arbitrary	Yes, but transfer prices are affected by bargaining strengths of the buying and selling divisions
Motivates management effort	Yes	Yes, when based on budgeted costs; less incentive to control costs if transfers are based on actual costs	Yes
Preserves subunit autonomy	Yes, when markets are competitive	No, because it is rule-based	Yes, because it is based on negotiations between subunits
Other factors	Market may not exist, or markets may be imperfect or in distress	Useful for determining full cost of products and services; easy to implement	Bargaining and negotiations take time and may need to be reviewed repeatedly as conditions change

The key question is where between $80 and $85 the transfer price will be. The answer depends on the bargaining strengths of the two divisions. The transportation division has more information about the price less incremental marketing costs of supplying crude oil to outside refineries, while the refining division has more information about its other available sources of oil. Negotiations become particularly sensitive if Northern evaluates each division's performance on the basis of divisional operating income.

The price negotiated by the two divisions will, in general, have no specific relationship to either costs or market price. But cost and price information are often useful starting points in the negotiation process. Exhibit 21-3 compares the three methods of transfer pricing discussed. The full-cost-based transfer price is the most used and negotiated prices are the least frequently used transfer-pricing method worldwide.

Dual Pricing

There is seldom a single transfer price that simultaneously meets the criteria of promoting goal congruence, motivating management effort, evaluating subunit performance, and preserving subunit autonomy. As a result, some companies choose **dual pricing**, using two separate transfer-pricing methods to price each transfer from one subunit to another. An example of dual pricing arises when the selling division receives a full-cost based price and the buying division pays the market price for the internally transferred products.

Assume Northern Petroleum purchases crude oil in Calgary at $79 per barrel. One way of recording the journal entry for the transfer between the transportation division and the refining division is as follows:

1. Debit the refining division (the buying division) with the market-based transfer price of $85 per barrel of crude oil.

2. Credit the transportation division (the selling division) with the 105%-of-full-cost transfer price of $87.15 per barrel of crude oil.

3. Debit a corporate cost account for the $2.15 (= $87.15 − $85) per barrel difference between the two transfer prices.

The dual-pricing system promotes goal congruence because it makes the refining division no worse off if it purchases the crude oil from the transportation division rather than from the external supplier at $85 per barrel. The transportation division receives a corporate subsidy. In dual pricing, the operating income for Northern Petroleum as a whole is less than the sum of the operating incomes of the divisions.

Dual pricing is not widely used in practice even though it reduces the goal incongruence associated with a pure cost-based transfer-pricing method. One concern with dual pricing is that it leads to problems in computing the taxable income of subunits located in different tax jurisdictions.

A General Guideline for Transfer-Pricing Situations

There exists no pervasive rule for transfer pricing that leads toward optimal decisions for the organization as a whole because the three criteria of goal congruence, management effort, and subunit autonomy must all be considered simultaneously. The following general guideline, however, has proven to be a helpful first step in setting a minimum transfer price in many specific situations:

$$\begin{matrix} \text{Minimum} \\ \text{transfer price} \end{matrix} = \begin{matrix} \text{Additional incremental or outlay costs per unit} \\ \text{incurred up to the point of transfer} \end{matrix} + \begin{matrix} \text{Opportunity costs per unit} \\ \text{to the supplying division} \end{matrix}$$

The term *incremental* or *outlay costs* in this context represents the additional costs that are directly associated with the production and transfer of the products or services. *Opportunity costs* are defined here as the maximum contribution forgone by the supplying division if the products or services are transferred internally. For example, if the supplying division is operating at capacity, the opportunity cost of transferring a unit internally rather than selling it externally is equal to the market price minus variable costs. We distinguish incremental costs from opportunity costs because the accounting system typically records incremental costs but not opportunity costs. We illustrate the general guidelines in some specific situations using data from the production and transportation divisions of Northern Petroleum.

1. **A perfectly competitive market for the intermediate product exists, and the selling division has no unused capacity.** If the market for crude oil in Calgary is perfectly competitive, the transportation division can sell all the crude oil it transports to the external market at $85 per barrel, and it will have no unused capacity.

   The transportation division's incremental cost (as shown in Exhibit 21-1) is either $73 per barrel (purchase cost of $72 per barrel plus variable transportation cost of $1 per barrel) for oil purchased under the long-term contract or $80 per barrel (purchase cost of $79 plus variable transportation cost of $1) for oil purchased at current market prices from the Calgary producer. The transportation division's opportunity cost per barrel of transferring the oil internally is the contribution margin per barrel forgone by not selling the crude oil in the external market: $12 for oil purchased under the long-term contract (market price, $85, minus variable cost, $73) and $5 for oil purchased from the Calgary producer (market price, $85, minus variable cost, $80). In either case,

$$\begin{matrix} \text{Minimum transfer} \\ \text{price per barrel} \end{matrix} = \begin{matrix} \text{Incremental} \\ \text{cost per barrel} \end{matrix} + \begin{matrix} \text{Opportunity} \\ \text{costs per barrel} \end{matrix}$$
$$= \$73 + \$12 = \$85$$
$$\text{or}$$
$$= \$80 + \$5 = \$85$$

   Market-based transfer prices are ideal in perfectly competitive markets when there is no idle capacity.

2. **An intermediate market exists that is not perfectly competitive, and the selling division has unused capacity.** In markets that are not perfectly competitive, capacity utilization can be increased only by decreasing prices. Unused capacity exists because decreasing prices is often not worthwhile—it decreases operating income. If the transportation division has unused capacity, its opportunity cost of transferring the oil

internally is zero because the division does not forgo any external sales or contribution margin from internal transfers. In this case,

$$\begin{array}{c} \text{Minimum} \\ \text{transfer price} \\ \text{per barrel} \end{array} = \begin{array}{c} \text{Incremental} \\ \text{cost per barrel} \end{array} + \begin{array}{c} \text{\$73 per barrel for oil purchased under the} \\ \text{long-term contract or \$80 per barrel for oil} \\ \text{purchased from the Calgary producer} \end{array}$$

Any transfer price above incremental cost but below $85—the price at which the refining division can buy crude oil in Sarnia—motivates the transportation division to transport crude oil to the refining division and the refining division to buy crude oil from the transportation division. In this situation, the company could either use a cost-based transfer price or allow the two divisions to negotiate a transfer price between themselves.

Consider the following situation: Suppose the refining division receives an order to supply specially processed gasoline. The refining division will profit from this order only if the transportation division can supply crude oil at a price not exceeding $82 per barrel. Suppose the incremental cost to purchase and supply crude oil is $80 per barrel. In this case, the transfer price that would benefit both divisions must be greater than $80 but less than $82 (rather than $85).

3. *No market exists for the intermediate product.* This would occur, for example, in the Northern Petroleum case if oil from the production well flows directly into the pipeline and cannot be sold to outside parties.

Here, the opportunity cost of supplying crude oil internally is zero because the inability to sell crude oil externally means no contribution margin is forgone. At the transportation division of Northern Petroleum, the minimum transfer price under the general guideline would be the incremental costs per barrel of either $73 or $80. As in the previous case, any transfer price between the incremental cost and $85 will achieve goal congruence. Knowledge of the incremental cost per barrel of crude oil would be helpful to the refining division for many decisions, such as short-run pricing.

In transfer-pricing situations, opportunity cost is the profit the selling division forgoes by selling internally rather than externally. Assume the selling division has no idle capacity for a particular product and can sell all it produces at $4 per unit. Incremental cost is $1 per unit. If the selling division sells internally, the opportunity cost is $3 per unit (= $4 revenue per unit − $1 incremental cost per unit). In contrast, if the selling division has unused capacity with no alternative use, no profit is forgone by selling internally (opportunity cost is $0).

Multinational Corporation (MNC) Transfer Pricing and Tax Considerations

► **LO 5**

Analyze income tax considerations in multinational transfer pricing.

Now we will consider factors affecting transfer prices among corporate subunits in different countries. Sales between corporate subunits are called sales between **related parties**, in contrast to external sales between a subunit and a nonrelated party termed **arm's-length transactions**. The transfer prices have tax implications and therefore affect the government revenues of each country involved. Tax factors include income taxes, payroll taxes, customs duties, tariffs, sales taxes, value-added taxes, environment-related taxes, and other government levies. We focus on income tax factors as a key consideration in transfer-pricing decisions.

The Income Tax Act of Canada (section 247) sets out the laws regarding transfer pricing. The most recent rules were introduced in 1998 after legislative changes in the United States and the publication of transfer price guidelines by the OECD. The CRA intends to achieve harmonization with OECD and US laws to reduce the costs of tax compliance for multinational corporations. The most important laws limit how companies set transfer prices to one of five methods.

Transfer prices also have tax implications, particularly when products are transferred across country borders. Setting transfer prices is almost always a matter of judgment.

Concepts in Action

India Calls Vodafone on Transfer-Pricing Policy

The mobile phone market is India is lucrative, with companies from all over the world seeking to maintain growth by gaining a foothold in a country where 250 million mobile phones are sold every year. The British company Vodafone Group PLC is the second-largest mobile phone operator, measured by subscribers. In 2007, Vodafone entered the Indian mobile phone market by acquiring Hutchison Whampoa's mobile phone assets. From the inception of the operations in India and continuing to the present, Vodafone established a transfer-pricing mechanism between its Indian subsidiary and Vodafone Mauritius Limited. The Indian government claimed that Vodafone had undervalued assets as part of the transfer-pricing policy and as a result had avoided $1.8 billion in taxes that should be due to the Indian government. Establishing the price one division in a company charges another division in the same company for products and services is often controversial, and governments often intervene to alter the company's price charged, and thereby impact the taxes owed. In the case

of India and Vodafone, the Indian government has created a law that allows it to retroactively assess taxes on transfer-pricing schemes. These cases are often expensive in terms of legal fees and time—such as the case of Microsoft and Denmark, where the dispute over taxes owed has lasted more than a dozen years.

Sources: D. Phelan. 2013. The Indian mobile phone market: An alien world where seven-inch tablets are big sellers, *The Independent* (July 22) (http://www.independent.co.uk/life-style/gadgets-and-tech/features/the-indian-mobile-phone-market-an-alien-world-where-seveninch-tablets-are-big-sellers-8726573.html); "Government seeks to scrap 2 billion tax dispute talks with Vodafone," *The Economic Times*, http://economictimes.indiatimes.com/news/news-by-industry/telecom/government-seeks-to-scrap-2-billion-tax-dispute-talks-with-vodafone/articleshow/30293912.cms; A. Mohan. 2012. Income Tax department can move against Vodafone in transfer pricing dispute, *The Economic Times* (February 12) (http://articles.economictimes.indiatimes.com/2014-02-12/news/47270080_1_shell-india-mauritius-based-group-company-revenue-under-priced-shares); L. Clark. 2005. Microsoft may owe Denmark £660 million in tax, Wired News (March 13) (http://www.wired.co.uk/news/archive/2013-03/05/microsoft-danish-billion-dollar-tax-bill).

At no time, however, should management accountants choose transfer prices that do not adhere to the tax codes of different countries. The time and cost to resolve transfer-pricing disputes can be very high.

Traditional transaction methods include the **comparable uncontrolled price (CUP) method, resale price method (RPM)**, and **cost-plus method (CPM)**. The CUP is analogous to the internal market-based price. The related-party transfer price reported by a corporation is compared to prices for similar transactions among arm's-length (nonrelated) parties and must fall within the middle two quartiles of this range of prices.

The RPM requires that a company calculate the arm's-length resale price. Distributors of finished goods typically use this method when the cost of distribution is low relative to the value of the finished goods (i.e. almost non-value-added). Again the CRA compares the estimated transfer price to a range of prices for similar arm's-length transactions and usually accepts transfer prices in the two mid-quartiles of this range.

The CPM highlights the effect of the transfer price on the pretax income of each subunit. This method permits corporations the greatest discretion and most readily justified transfer price to the CRA because of the quality of information provided by management accounting and control systems.

The transactional profit methods of setting a transfer price are the **profit split method (PSM)** and **transactional net margin method (TNMM)**. The PSM requires understanding the value added by the functions performed by each related party and the resulting allocation of profit and loss to each subunit. The fifth method, TNMM, is based on the return on assets (ROA) of the corporation as a whole and provides maximum discretion for establishing a transfer price.

Consider the Northern Petroleum data in Exhibit 21-2. Assume that Northern operates a transportation division in Mexico that pays Mexican income taxes at 30% of operating income and that both the transportation and refining divisions based in Canada pay income taxes at 20% of operating income. Northern Petroleum would minimize its total income tax payments with the 105% of full costs transfer-pricing method, as shown in the following table:

Transfer-Pricing Method	Operating Income for 100 Barrels of Crude Oil			Income Tax on 100 Barrels of Crude Oil		
	Transportation Division (Mexico) (1)	Refining Division (Canada) (2)	Total (3) = (1) + (2)	Transportation Division (Mexico) (4) = 0.30 × (1)	Refining Division (Canada) (5) = 0.20 × (2)	Total (6) = (4) + (5)
Market price	$900	$300	$1,200	$270	$ 60	$330
105% of full costs	380	820	1,200	114	164	278
Negotiated price	700	500	1,200	210	100	310

Tax considerations raise additional issues that may conflict with other objectives of transfer pricing. Suppose that the market for crude oil in Calgary is perfectly competitive. In this case, the market-based transfer price achieves goal congruence and provides effort incentives. It also helps Northern to evaluate the economic profitability of the transportation division. But it is costly from an income tax standpoint.

Northern Petroleum would favour using 105% of full costs for tax reporting, but tax laws in Canada and Mexico constrain this option. In particular, the Mexican tax authorities are fully aware of Northern Petroleum's incentives to minimize income taxes by reducing the income reported in Mexico. They would challenge any attempts to shift income to the refining division through a low transfer price.

The perfectly competitive market for crude oil in Mexico would probably force Northern Petroleum to use the market price for transfers from the production division to the transportation division. Northern Petroleum might successfully argue that the transfer price should be set below the market price because the production division incurs no marketing and distribution costs when "selling" crude oil to the transportation division. Northern Petroleum could obtain advance approval of the transfer-pricing arrangements from the appropriate tax authorities.

To meet multiple transfer-pricing objectives, a company may choose to keep one set of accounting records for tax reporting and a second set for internal management reporting. The difficulty here is that tax authorities may interpret two sets of books as suggestive of the company manipulating its reported taxable income to avoid tax payments. Additional factors that arise in multinational transfer pricing include tariffs and customs duties levied on imports of products into a country. The issues here are similar to the income tax considerations discussed earlier—companies will have incentives to lower transfer prices for products imported into a country to reduce the tariffs and customs duties that those products will attract. MNC transfer prices are sometimes influenced by restrictions that some countries place on the payment of income or dividends to parties outside their national borders. By increasing the prices of goods or services transferred into divisions in these countries, companies can increase the funds paid out of these countries without appearing to violate income or dividend restrictions.

Pulling It All Together—Problem for Self-Study

(Try to solve this problem before examining the solution that follows.)

Problem

The Pillercat Corporation is a highly decentralized company. Each division manager has full authority for sourcing and selling decisions. The machining division of Pillercat has been the major supplier of the 2,000 crankshafts that the tractor division needs each year.

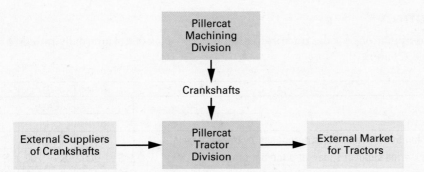

The tractor division, however, has just announced that it plans to purchase all its crankshafts in the forthcoming year from two external suppliers at $200 per crankshaft. The machining division of Pillercat recently increased its price for the forthcoming year to $220 per unit (from $200 per unit in the current year).

Juan Gomez, manager of the machining division, feels that the 10% price increase is fully justified. It results from a higher depreciation charge on some new specialized equipment used to manufacture crankshafts and an increase in labour costs. Gomez wants the president of Pillercat Corporation to direct the tractor division to buy all its crankshafts from the machining division at the price of $220. The additional incremental costs per unit that Pillercat incurs to produce each crankshaft are the machining division's variable costs of $190. Fixed cost per crankshaft in the machining division equals $20.

	A	B
1	Number of crankshafts purchased by tractor division	2,000
2	External supplier's market price per crankshaft	$ 200
3	Variable cost per crankshaft in machining division	$ 190
4	Fixed cost per crankshaft in machining division	$ 20

1. Compute the advantage or disadvantage (in terms of monthly operating income) to ❹ ◀ **Required** the Pillercat Corporation as a whole if the tractor division buys crankshafts internally from the machining division under each of the following cases:
   a. The machining division has no alternative use for the facilities used to manufacture crankshafts.
   b. The machining division can use the facilities for other production operations, which will result in monthly cash operating savings of $29,000.
   c. The machining division has no alternative use for the facilities, and the external supplier drops its price to $185 per crankshaft.
2. As the president of Pillercat, how would you respond to Juan Gomez's request to ❶ order the tractor division to purchase all of its crankshafts from the machining division? Would your response differ according to the scenarios described in parts (a), (b), and (c) of requirement 1? Why?
3. Discuss the tax implications if the machining and tractor divisions were located in ❷ ❸ ❺ different countries. Pillercat management's best transfer price choice would be the current market price or CUP because it conforms with the OECD hierarchy. The managers would be wise to negotiate an advance transfer price arrangement with tax authorities in both countries (APA). If there were no market for the intermediate product, then profit split (PSM) or transactional net margin methods (TNMM) could be negotiated.
4. The best transfer price for performance evaluation may not be the most acceptable to ❶ ❺ tax authorities. In terms of good governance, what option is available to managers?

Solution

1. Computations for the tractor division buying crankshafts internally for cases (a), (b), and (c) are:

	A	B	C	D
1			Case	
2		a	b	c
3	Number of crankshafts purchased by tractor division	2,000	2,000	2,000
4	External supplier's market price per crankshaft	$ 200	$ 200	$ 185
5	Incremental cost per crankshaft in machining division	$ 190	$ 190	$ 190
6	Opportunity costs of the machining division supplying	—	$ 29,000	—
7	crankshafts to the tractor division			
8				
9	Total purchase costs if buying from an external supplier			
10	(2,000 shafts × $200, $200, $185 per shaft)	$400,000	$400,000	$370,000
11	Incremental costs of buying from the machining division			
12	(2,000 shafts × $190 pershaft)	380,000	380,000	380,000
13	Total opportunity costs of the machining division	—	29,000	—
14	Total relevant costs	380,000	$409,000	380,000
15	Annual operating income advantage (disadvantage) to			
16	Pillercat of buying from the machining division	$ 20,000	$ (9,000)	$ (10,000)
17				

Using the general guideline as a first step in setting a transfer price highlights the alternatives:

	A	B	C	D	E	F	G
1		Incremental Cost per		Opportunity Cost			External
2		Unit Incurred to		per Unit to the		Transfer	Market
3	Case	Point of Transfer	+	Supplying Division	=	Price	Price
4	a	$190	+	$ 0	=	$190.00	$200
5	b	$190	+	$14.50[a]	=	$204.50	$200
6	c	$190	+	$ 0	=	$190.00	$185
7							
8	[a]Opportunity cost per unit $=$ Total opportunity costs $\div$ Number of crankshafts $= \$29,000 \div 2,000 = \$14.50$						

The tractor division will maximize monthly operating income of Pillercat Corporation as a whole by purchasing from the machining division in case (a) and by purchasing from the external suppliers in cases (b) and (c).

2. Pillercat Corporation is a highly decentralized company. If no forced transfer were made, the tractor division would use an external supplier, resulting in an optimal decision for the company as a whole in cases (b) and (c) of requirement 1, but not in case (a).

Suppose that in case 1(a), the machining division refuses to meet the price of $200. This decision means that the company will be $20,000 worse off in the short run. Should top management interfere and force a transfer at $200? This interference would undercut the philosophy of decentralization. Many top management teams would not interfere because they would view the $20,000 as an inevitable cost of a suboptimal decision that occasionally occurs under decentralization. But how high must this cost be before the temptation to interfere would be irresistible? $30,000? $40,000?

Any top management interference with lower-level decision making weakens decentralization. Of course, such interference may occasionally be necessary to prevent costly blunders. But recurring interference and constraints simply transform a decentralized organization into a centralized organization.

3. Pillercat management's best transfer price choice would be the current market price or CUP because it conforms with the OECD hierarchy. The managers would be wise to negotiate an advance transfer price arrangement with tax authorities in both countries (APA). If there were no market for the intermediate product, then profit split (PSM) or transactional net margin methods (TNMM) could be negotiated.

4. Assuming that managers do achieve satisfactory standards of good governance, they will have access to relevant information as described in the CPEM and NI 52-109. This implies the presence of coordinated information systems that enable the development of dual accounting records. One management accounting system reports values used for performance evaluation purposes over which tax authorities have no concern. The second reports performance according to methods of transfer pricing acceptable to tax authorities.

Decision Points

The following question-and-answer format summarizes the chapter's learning objectives. Each point presents a key question, and the guidelines are the answer to that question.

Learning Objectives	Guidelines
1. What is a control system, and how should it be designed?	A control system is a means to organize or arrange elements into an orderly structure. Choices of organizational structure are constrained by legislation such as NI 52-109 and NI 58-201 in Canada as well as CRA tax legislation. The goal of control systems is to nurture and sustain good governance.
2. How are transfer-pricing methods ranked?	To ease the compliance burden on MNCs, most countries worldwide have adopted the OECD Hierarchy of Methods for transfer pricing. The principle upon which the ranking is based is the arm's-length principle. The most preferred transfer price is current market price of intermediate products. Other alternatives for internal control include cost-based and negotiated prices.
3. What are the benefits of transferring products at current market price?	Optimal internal management decisions to benefit the entire corporation are made if the intermediate market is perfectly competitive (homogeneous product and prices) and interdependencies among subunits are minimal.
4. How does cost-plus transfer pricing lead to suboptimal internal management decisions?	A transfer price based on full cost plus a markup may lead to suboptimal decisions because it leads the buying division to regard the fixed costs and the markup of the selling division as variable costs. The buying division may then purchase products from an outside vendor expecting savings in variable costs that, in fact, will not occur.
5. What constraints are externally imposed to internal guidelines for determining a minimum transfer?	Transfer prices can reduce income tax payments by recognizing more income in low-tax-rate countries and less income in high-tax-rate countries. However, tax regulations of different countries restrict the transfer prices that companies can choose. Internal guidelines state that the minimum transfer price equals the incremental cost per unit incurred up to the point of transfer plus the opportunity cost per unit to the supplying division resulting from transferring products or services internally.

Terms to Learn

This chapter and the Glossary at the end of the book contain definitions of the following important terms:

advance transfer price arrangement (APA) **(p. 868)**
arm's-length transactions **(p. 874)**
autonomy **(p. 861)**
comparable uncontrolled price (CUP) method **(p. 875)**
cost-plus method (CPM) **(p. 875)**
decentralization **(p. 861)**
dual pricing **(p. 872)**
effort **(p. 861)**

formal management control system **(p. 860)**
goal congruence **(p. 860)**
informal management control system **(p. 860)**
intermediate products **(p. 863)**
management control system **(p. 860)**
motivation **(p. 860)**
Organisation for Economic Co-operation and Development **(p. 864)**

perfectly competitive market **(p. 868)**
profit split method (PSM) **(p. 875)**
related parties **(p. 874)**
resale price method (RPM) **(p. 875)**
subunit **(p. 861)**
transactional net margin method (TNMM) **(p. 875)**
transfer price **(p. 863)**

Assignment Material

MyLab Accounting Make the grade with MyLab Accounting: The Short-Answer Questions, Exercises, and Problems marked with a ⊕ can be found on MyLab Accounting. You can practise them as often as you want, and most feature step-by-step guided instructions to help you find the right answer.

Short-Answer Questions

⊕ **21-1** What is a management control system?
⊕ **21-2** Describe three criteria you would use to evaluate whether a management control system is effective.
⊕ **21-3** What is the relationship among motivation, goal congruence, and effort?
⊕ **21-4** Name three benefits and two costs of decentralization.
⊕ **21-5** "Organizations typically adopt a consistent decentralization or centralization philosophy across all their business functions." Do you agree? Explain.
⊕ **21-6** "Transfer pricing is confined to profit centres." Do you agree? Why?
⊕ **21-7** What are the three general methods for determining transfer prices?
⊕ **21-8** What properties should transfer-pricing systems have?
⊕ **21-9** "All transfer-pricing methods give the same division operating income." Do you agree? Explain.
⊕ **21-10** Under what conditions is a market-based transfer price optimal?
⊕ **21-11** What is one potential limitation of full-cost-based transfer prices?
⊕ **21-12** Give two reasons why a dual-price approach to transfer pricing is not widely used.
⊕ **21-13** "Under the general transfer-pricing guideline, the minimum transfer price will vary depending on whether or not the supplying division has idle capacity." Do you agree? Explain.
⊕ **21-14** Why should managers consider income tax issues when choosing a transfer-pricing method?

Exercises

🌐 **21-15 Terminology.** A number of terms are listed below:

advance transfer price arrangement (APA)	market-based price
comparable uncontrolled price	cost-based
negotiated	cost-plus
cost-plus method (CPM)	dual pricing
goal congruence	profit split method (PSM)
related-party transactions	resale price method (RPM)
tax havens	transactional net margin method (TNMM)

Required

Select the terms from the above list to complete the following sentences.

The CRA constrains global transfer-pricing choices, and provincial tax authorities constrain the interprovincial transfer-pricing choice of management teams. A wise team will undertake an _____ _____ _____ _____ (____) to avoid future tax liabilities. There are two interprovincial transfer-price alternatives when no _____ _____ _____ exists. The alternatives are either _____ _____, which is a cost-plus approach, or _____ transfer prices that fall between a market and cost-plus price. Of course a _____ price may be either full absorption or variable cost-based, and in the transfer the same company may use _____ _____. The transferring division charges at a cost-based price while the receiving division pays at a market-based price. The difference is billed to a common corporate account rather than to the divisions. This method reduces _____ _____ problems between transferring divisions. There are three multinational corporate transfer-price alternatives. The respective tax authorities scrutinize these _____ _____ _____ very carefully to ensure their jurisdictions receive the appropriate tax payments from each party in the transfer. The alternatives are the _____ _____ _____ (CUP), _____ _____ (____), _____ (____), _____ (____), and _____ ___ _____ _____ (___). In addition to negotiating APA with governments, corporations also minimize taxes by establishing legitimate subsidiaries in _____ _____ that share information with other governments.

🌐 **21-16 Evaluating management control systems, balanced scorecard.** Adventure Parks Inc. (API) operates 10 theme parks throughout the United States. The company's slogan is "Name Your Adventure," and its mission is to offer an exciting theme park experience to visitors of all ages. API's corporate strategy supports this mission by stressing the importance of sparkling clean surroundings, efficient crowd management, and, above all, cheerful employees. Of course, improved shareholder value drives this strategy. ◄ LO 1

Required

1. Assume that API uses a balanced scorecard approach (see Chapter 12) to formulating its management control system. List three measures that API might use to evaluate each of the four balanced scorecard perspectives: financial perspective, customer perspective, internal-business-process perspective, and learning-and-growth perspective.
2. How would the management controls related to financial and customer perspectives at API differ between the following three managers: a souvenir shop manager, a park general manager, and the corporation's CEO?

🌐 **21-17 Cost centres, profit centres, decentralization, transfer prices.** Fenster Corporation manufactures windows with wood and metal frames. Fenster has three departments: glass, wood, and metal. The glass department makes the window glass and sends it to either the wood or metal department where the glass is framed. The window is then sold. Upper management sets the production schedules for the three departments and evaluates them on output quantity, cost variances, and product quality. ◄ LO 1

Required

1. Are the three departments cost centres, revenue centres, or profit centres?
2. Are the three departments centralized or decentralized?
3. Can a centralized department be a profit centre? Why or why not?
4. Suppose the upper management of Fenster Corporation decides to let the three departments set their own production schedules, buy and sell products in the external market, and have the wood and metal departments negotiate with the glass department for the glass panes using a transfer price.
   a. Will this change your answers to requirements 1 and 2?
   b. How would you recommend upper management evaluate the three departments if this change is made?

LO 2 ▷
1. a. China to South Korea,
$450 per subunit

🌐 **21-18 Multinational transfer pricing, effect of alternative transfer-pricing methods, global income tax minimization.** User Friendly Computer Inc., with headquarters in Nepean, Ontario, manufactures and sells a premium desktop computer system. User Friendly has three divisions, each of which is located in a different country:

a. China division—manufactures memory devices and keyboards.
b. South Korea division—assembles desktop computers using internally manufactured parts and memory devices and keyboards from the China division.
c. Canada division—packages and distributes desktop computer packages.

Each division is run as a profit centre. The costs for the work done in each division for a single desktop computer system are as follows:

China division	Variable costs = 1,000 yuan
	Fixed costs = 1,800 yuan
South Korea division	Variable costs = 360,000 won
	Fixed costs = 480,000 won
Canada division	Variable costs = CA$100
	Fixed costs = CA$200
Chinese income tax rate on China division's operating income	20%
South Korean income tax rate on South Korea division's operating income	20
Canadian income tax rate on Canada division's operating income	30

Each desktop computer package is sold to retail outlets in Canada for $3,200. Assume that the current foreign exchange rates are

$$8 \text{ yuan } = \text{ CA\$1}$$

$$1,200 \text{ won } = \text{ CA\$1}$$

Both the China and South Korea divisions sell part of their production under a private label. The China division sells the comparable memory/keyboard package used in each User Friendly desktop computer to a Chinese manufacturer for 3,600 yuan. The South Korea division sells the comparable desktop computer package to a South Korean distributor for 1,560,000 won.

Required

1. Calculate the after-tax operating income per unit earned by each division under each of the following transfer-pricing methods: (a) market price, (b) 200% of full cost, and (c) 300% of variable cost. (Income taxes are not included in the computation of the cost-based transfer prices.)
2. Which transfer-pricing method(s) will maximize the after-tax operating income per unit of User Friendly Computer Inc.?

LO 3 ▷
1. Incremental loss $(50) per
100 board feet

🌐 **21-19 Transfer-pricing methods, goal congruence.** British Columbia Lumber has a raw lumber division and a finished lumber division. The variable costs are

- Raw lumber division: $100 per 100 board feet of raw lumber.
- Finished lumber division: $125 per 100 board feet of finished lumber.

Assume that no board feet are lost in processing raw lumber into finished lumber. Raw lumber can be sold at $200 per 100 board feet. Finished lumber can be sold at $275 per 100 board feet.

Required

1. Should British Columbia Lumber process raw lumber into its finished form? Show your calculations.
2. Assume that internal transfers are made at 110% of variable cost. Will each division maximize its division operating-income contribution by adopting the action that is in the best interests of British Columbia Lumber as a whole? Explain.
3. Assume that internal transfers are made at market prices. Will each division maximize its division operating-income contribution by adopting the action that is in the best interests of British Columbia Lumber as a whole? Explain.

⊕ 21-20 Multinational transfer pricing, effect of alternative transfer-pricing methods. Valencia Orange manufactures bottles in its glass Division A, which are then transferred to its packaging Division B. In the upcoming month, 300,000 bottles will be transferred to Division B from Division A, where they are filled and then sold at $7 per bottle. The bottles can be sold from Division A to other bottlers at $5 per bottle. The costs below relate to total manufacturing budgeted costs for the 300,000 bottles.

◀ **LO 4**
1. Division B Operating Income is $360,000

	Division A	Division B
Total variable costs	100,000	90,000
Total fixed costs	230,000	150,000
	330,000	240,000

Required

1. Calculate the operating income for Division B under the market price transfer-pricing method.
2. Calculate the operating income for Division A under the market price transfer-pricing method.
3. What are three benefits of the arrangement between Division A and B?

⊕ 21-21 Multinational transfer pricing, effect of alternative transfer-pricing methods (continuation of Exercise 21-20) Refer to Exercise 21-20. The manager of Valencia Orange has just come back from a transfer-pricing conference where he learned about new methods. Use the following information to answer his questions below:

◀ **LO 4**
1. Division Operating Income is $2,206,500

	Division A	Division B
Total variable costs	100,000	90,000
Total fixed costs	230,000	150,000
	330,000	240,000

1. Calculate the operating income for Division A using 105% of manufacturing cost as the transfer price.
2. Calculate the operating income for Division A using 105% of market value cost as the transfer price.
3. If bonuses are calculated at 5% of operating income, what method will the manager of Division A prefer (market value or 105% of manufacturing cost)?
4. Comment on the 105% of manufacturing costs compared to the $5 market value transfer price. What impacts on behaviours or attitudes might occur within divisions if the company switches from market value to 105% of manufacturing cost?

⊕ 21-22 Effect of alternative transfer-pricing methods on division operating income. (CMA, adapted) Ajax Corporation has two divisions. The mining division makes toldine, which is then transferred to the metals division. The toldine is further processed by the metals division and is sold to customers at a price of $150 per unit. The mining division is currently required by Ajax to transfer its total yearly output of 200,000 units of toldine to the metals division at 110% of full manufacturing cost. Unlimited quantities of toldine can be purchased and sold on the outside market at $90 per unit.

◀ **LO 2**
1. Method A Division Operating Income is $1,800,000

The following table gives the manufacturing cost per unit in the mining and metals divisions for 2017:

	Mining Division	Metals Division
Direct material cost	$12	$ 6
Direct manufacturing labour cost	16	20
Manufacturing overhead cost	32[a]	25[b]
Total manufacturing cost per unit	$60	$51

[a]Manufacturing overhead costs in the mining division are 25% fixed and 75% variable.
[b]Manufacturing overhead costs in the metals division are 60% fixed and 40% variable.

Required

1. Calculate the operating incomes for the mining and metals divisions for the 200,000 units of toldine transferred under the following transfer-pricing methods: (a) market price and (b) 110% of full manufacturing cost.
2. Suppose Ajax rewards each division manager with a bonus, calculated as 1% of division operating income (if positive). What is the amount of bonus that will be paid to each division manager under the transfer-pricing methods in requirement 1? Which transfer-pricing method will each division manager prefer to use?
3. What arguments would Brian Jones, manager of the mining division, make to support the transfer-pricing method that he prefers?

LO 5 ▶
1. Minimum transfer price, $90

🌐 **21-23 Transfer pricing, general guideline, goal congruence.** (CMA, adapted) Quest Motors Inc. operates as a decentralized multidivision company. The tivo division of Quest Motors purchases most of its airbags from the airbag division. The airbag division's incremental cost for manufacturing the airbags is $90 per unit. The airbag division is currently working at 80% of capacity. The current market price of the airbags is $125 per unit.

Required

1. Using the general guideline presented in the chapter, what is the minimum price at which the airbag division would sell airbags to the tivo division?
2. Suppose that Quest Motors requires that whenever divisions with unused capacity sell products internally, they must do so at the incremental cost. Evaluate this transfer-pricing policy using the criteria of goal congruence, evaluating division performance, motivating management effort, and preserving division autonomy.
3. If the two divisions were to negotiate a transfer price, what is the range of possible transfer prices? Evaluate this negotiated transfer-pricing policy using the criteria of goal congruence, evaluating division performance, motivating management effort, and preserving division autonomy.
4. Do you prefer the transfer-pricing policy in requirement 2 or requirement 3? Explain your answer briefly.

LO 4 ▶
1. Fixed Costs = $325/unit

🌐 **21-24 Multinational transfer pricing, effect of alternative transfer-pricing methods, global income tax minimization.** Tech Friendly Computer, Inc., with headquarters in San Francisco, manufactures and sells a desktop computer. Tech Friendly has three divisions, each of which is located in a different country:

a. China division—manufactures memory devices and keyboards
b. South Korea division—assembles desktop computers using locally manufactured parts, along with memory devices and keyboards from the China division
c. U.S. division—packages and distributes desktop computers

Each division is run as a profit centre. The costs for the work done in each division for a single desktop computer are as follows:

China division:	Variable cost = 900 yuan
	Fixed cost = 1,980 yuan
South Korea division:	Variable cost = 350,000 won
	Fixed cost = 470,000 won
U.S. division:	Variable cost = $125
	Fixed cost = $325

- Chinese income tax rate on the China division's operating income: 40%
- South Korean income tax rate on the South Korea division's operating income: 20%
- U.S. income tax rate on the U.S. division's operating income: 30%

Each desktop computer is sold to retail outlets in the United States for $3,800. Assume that the current foreign exchange rates are as follows:

$$9 \text{ yuan} = \$1 \text{ U.S.}$$
$$1{,}000 \text{ won} = \$1 \text{ U.S.}$$

Both the China and the South Korea divisions sell part of their production under a private label. The China division sells the comparable memory/keyboard package used in each Tech Friendly desktop computer to a Chinese manufacturer for 4,500 yuan. The South Korea division sells the comparable desktop computer to a South Korean distributor for 1,340,000 won.

Required

1. Calculate the after-tax operating income per unit earned by each division under the following transfer-pricing methods: (a) market price, (b) 200% of full cost, and (c) 350% of variable cost. (Income taxes are not included in the computation of the cost-based transfer prices.)
2. Which transfer-pricing method(s) will maximize the after-tax operating income per unit of Tech Friendly Computer?

LO 4 ▶
1. Net effect is an increase in import duty and tax payments of $0.04

🌐 **21-25 Multinational transfer pricing, global tax minimization.** The Questron Company manufactures telecommunications equipment at its plant in Scranton, Pennsylvania. The company has marketing divisions throughout the world. A Questron marketing division in Hamburg, Germany, imports 100,000 broadband routers from the United States. The following information is available:

U.S. income tax rate on the U.S. division's operating income	35%
German income tax rate on the German division's operating income	40%
German import duty	15%
Variable manufacturing cost per router	$275
Full manufacturing cost per router	$400
Selling price (net of marketing and distribution costs) in Germany	$575

Suppose the United States and German tax authorities only allow transfer prices that are between the full manufacturing cost per unit of $400 and a market price of $475, based on comparable imports into Germany. The German import duty is charged on the price at which the product is transferred into Germany. Any import duty paid to the German authorities is a deductible expense for calculating German income taxes.

Required

1. Calculate the after-tax operating income earned by the United States and German divisions from transferring 100,000 broadband routers (a) at full manufacturing cost per unit and (b) at market price of comparable imports. (Income taxes are not included in the computation of the cost-based transfer prices.)
2. Which transfer price should the Questron Company select to minimize the total of company import duties and income taxes? Remember that the transfer price must be between the full manufacturing cost per unit of $400 and the market price of $475 of comparable imports into Germany. Explain your reasoning.

🌐 **21-26 Transfer-pricing dispute.** The Goodwin Corporation, manufacturer of tractors and other heavy farm equipment, is organized along decentralized product lines, with each manufacturing division operating as a separate profit centre. Each division manager has been delegated full authority on all decisions involving the sale of that division's output both to outsiders and to other divisions of Goodwin. Division C has in the past always purchased its requirement of a particular tractor-engine component from Division A. However, when informed that Division A is increasing its selling price to $150, Division C's manager decides to purchase the engine component from external suppliers.

Division C can purchase the component for $135 per unit in the open market. Division A insists that, because of the recent installation of some highly specialized equipment and the resulting high depreciation charges, it will not be able to earn an adequate return on its investment unless it raises its price. Division A's manager appeals to top management of Goodwin for support in the dispute with Division C and supplies the following operating data:

◀ **LO 3, 5**
1. Net cost (benefit) of purchasing from an external supplier, $30,000

C's annual purchases of the tractor-engine component	2,000 units
A's variable cost per unit of the tractor-engine component	$ 120
A's fixed cost per unit of the tractor-engine component	$ 20

Required

1. Assume that there are no alternative uses for internal facilities of Division A. Determine whether the company as a whole will benefit if Division C purchases the component from external suppliers for $135 per unit. What should the transfer price for the component be set at so that division managers acting in their own divisions' best interests take actions that are in the best interest of the company as a whole?
2. Assume that internal facilities of Division A would not otherwise be idle. By not producing the 2,000 units for Division C, Division A's equipment and other facilities would be used for other production operations that would result in annual cash-operating savings of $18,000. Should Division C purchase from external suppliers? Show your computations.
3. Assume that there are no alternative uses for Division A's internal facilities and that the price from outsiders drops $20. Should Division C purchase from external suppliers? What should the transfer price for the component be set at so that division managers acting in their own divisions' best interests take actions that are in the best interest of the company as a whole?

🌐 **21-27 Transfer-pricing problem** (continuation of Exercise 21-26). Refer to Exercise 21-26. Assume that Division A can sell the 2,000 units to other customers at $155 per unit, with variable marketing cost of $5 per unit.

◀ **LO 3**
1. Contribution margin from selling units to other customers, $30,000

Required

Determine whether Goodwin will benefit if Division C purchases the 2,000 units from external suppliers at $135 per unit. Show your computations.

LO 5 ▶

1. Minimum transfer price per screen, $115

🌐 **21-28 General guideline, transfer pricing.** Clover Inc. manufactures and sells television sets. Its assembly division (AD) buys television screens from the screen division (SD) and assembles the TV sets. The SD, which is operating at capacity, incurs an incremental manufacturing cost of $80 per screen. The SD can sell all its output to the outside market at a price of $120 per screen, after incurring a variable marketing and distribution cost of $5 per screen. If the AD purchases screens from outside suppliers at a price of $120 per screen, it will incur a variable purchasing cost of $3 per screen. Clover's division managers can act autonomously to maximize their own division's operating income.

Required

1. What is the minimum transfer price at which the SD manager would be willing to sell screens to the AD?
2. What is the maximum transfer price at which the AD manager would be willing to purchase screens from the SD?
3. Now suppose that the SD can sell only 80% of its output capacity of 10,000 screens per month on the open market. Capacity cannot be reduced in the short run. The AD can assemble and sell more than 10,000 sets per month.
   a. What is the minimum transfer price at which the SD manager would be willing to sell screens to the AD?
   b. From the point of view of Clover's management, how much of the SD output should be transferred to the AD?
   c. What transfer-pricing policy will achieve the outcome desired in requirement 3b?

LO 5 ▶

1. Contribution margin per unit, $30

🌐 **21-29 Pertinent transfer price.** Europa Inc., has two divisions, A and B, which manufacture expensive bicycles. Division A produces the bicycle frame, and Division B assembles the rest of the bicycle onto the frame. There is a market for both the subassembly and the final product. Each division has been designated as a profit centre. The transfer price for the subassembly has been set at the long-run average market price. The following data are available for each division:

Selling price for final product	$330
Long-run average selling price for intermediate product	200
Incremental cost per unit for completion in Division B	150
Incremental cost per unit in Division A	120

The manager of Division B has made the following calculation:

Selling price for final product		$300
Transferred-in cost per unit (market)	$200	
Incremental cost per unit for completion	150	350
Contribution (loss) on product		$ (50)

Required

1. Should transfers be made to Division B if there is no unused capacity in Division A? Is the market price the correct transfer price? Show your computations.
2. Assume that Division A's maximum capacity for this product is 1,000 units per month and sales to the intermediate market are now 800 units. Should 200 units be transferred to Division B? At what transfer price? Assume that for a variety of reasons, Division A will maintain the $200 selling price indefinitely. That is, Division A is not considering lowering the price to outsiders even if idle capacity exists.
3. Suppose Division A quoted a transfer price of $150 for up to 200 units. What would be the contribution to the company as a whole if a transfer were made? As manager of Division B, would you be inclined to buy at $150? Explain.

LO 4 ▶

1. Opportunity cost per unit to the supplying division by transferring internally, $55

🌐 **21-30 Pricing in imperfect markets** (continuation of Exercise 21-29). Refer to Exercise 21-29.

Required

1. Suppose the manager of Division A has the option of (a) cutting the external price to $195, with the certainty that sales will rise to 1,000 units or (b) maintaining the external price of $200 for the 800 units and transferring the 200 units to Division B at a price that would produce the same operating income for Division A. What transfer price would produce the same operating income for Division A? Is that price consistent with that recommended by the general guideline in the chapter so that the resulting decision would be desirable for the company as a whole?

2. Suppose that if the selling price for the intermediate product were dropped to $195, sales to external parties could be increased to 900 units. Division B wants to acquire as many as 200 units if the transfer price is acceptable. For simplicity, assume that there is no external market for the final 100 units of Division A's capacity.

   a. Using the general guideline, what is (are) the minimum transfer price(s) that should lead to the correct economic decision? Ignore performance-evaluation considerations.

   b. Compare the total contributions under the alternatives to show why the transfer price(s) recommended lead(s) to the optimal economic decision.

Problems

🌐 **21-31 Effect of alternative transfer-pricing methods on division operating income.** Crango Products is a cranberry cooperative that operates two divisions: a harvesting division and a processing division. Currently, all of Harvesting's output is converted into cranberry juice by the processing division, and the juice is sold to large beverage companies that produce cranberry juice blends. The processing division has a yield of 1,900 litres of juice per 1,000 kilograms of cranberries. Cost and market price data for the two divisions are as follows:

◀ **LO 2**

2.a. Harvesting division operating income is $139,998

	A	B	C	D	E
1	**Harvesting Division**			**Processing Division**	
2	Variable costs per kilogram of cranberries	$0.2205		Variable processing cost per litre of juice produced	$0.05263 per litre
3	Fixed cost per kilogram of cranberries	0.5511		Fixed costs per litre of juice produced	0.1053 per litre
4	Selling price per kilogram of cranberries	1.3228		Selling price per litre of juice	0.55263 per litre

Required

1. Compute Crango's operating income from harvesting 181,440 kilograms of cranberries during June 2018 and processing them into juice.

2. Crango rewards its division managers with a bonus equal to 5% of operating income. Compute the bonus earned by each division manager in June 2018 for each of the following transfer-pricing methods:

   a. 200% of full cost

   b. Market price

3. Which transfer-pricing method will each division manager prefer? How might Crango resolve any conflicts that may arise on the issue of transfer pricing?

🌐 **21-32 Goal-congruence problems with cost-plus transfer-pricing methods, dual-pricing system** (continuation of Problem 21-31). Assume that Pat Borges, CEO of Crango, has mandated a transfer price equal to 200% of full cost. Now she decides to decentralize some management decisions and sends around a memo that states: "Effective immediately, each division of Crango is free to make its own decisions regarding the purchase of direct materials and the sale of finished products."

◀ **LO 2**

2. Harvesting division 200% full costs operating income, $139,998

Required

1. Give an example of a goal-congruence problem that will arise if Crango continues to use a transfer price of 200% of full cost and Borges's decentralization policy is adopted.

2. Borges feels that a dual transfer-pricing policy will improve goal congruence. She suggests that transfers out of the harvesting division be made at 200% of full cost and transfers into the processing division be made at market price. Compute the operating income of each division under this dual transfer-pricing method when 181,440 kilograms of cranberries are harvested during June 2018 and processed into juice.

3. Why is the sum of the division operating incomes computed in requirement 2 different from Crango's operating income from harvesting and processing 181,440 kilograms of cranberries?

4. Suggest two problems that may arise if Crango implements the dual transfer prices described in requirement 2.

🌐 **21-33 Multinational transfer pricing, global tax minimization.** Supergrow, Inc., based in Des Moines, Iowa, sells high-end fertilizers. Supergrow has two divisions:

◀ **LO 1, 2, 3, 4, 5**

- North Italy mining division, which mines potash in northern Italy
- U.S. processing division, which uses potash in manufacturing top-grade fertilizer

The processing division's yield is 50%: It takes 2 tons of raw potash to produce 1 ton of top-grade fertilizer. Although all of the mining division's output of 12,000 tons of potash is sent for processing in the

United States, there is also an active market for potash in Italy. The foreign exchange rate is 0.80 Euro = $1 U.S. The following information is known about the two divisions:

	A	B	C	D	F	G
1	**North Italy Mining Division**					
2	Variable cost per ton of raw potash				72	EURO
3	Fixed cost per ton of raw potash				112	EURO
4	Market price per ton of raw potash				296	EURO
5	Tax rate				30%	
6						
7	**U.S. Processing Division**					
8	Variable cost per ton of fertilizer				48	U.S. dollars
9	Fixed cost per ton of fertilizer				120	U.S. dollars
10	Market price per ton of fertilizer				1,150	U.S. dollars
11	Tax rate				35%	

Required

1. Compute the annual pretax operating income, in U.S. dollars, of each division under the following transfer-pricing methods: (a) 150% of full cost and (b) market price.
2. Compute the after-tax operating income, in U.S. dollars, for each division under the transfer-pricing methods in requirement 1. (Income taxes are not included in the computation of cost-based transfer price, and Supergrow does not pay U.S. income tax on income already taxed in Italy.)
3. If the two division managers are compensated based on after-tax division operating income, which transfer-pricing method will each prefer? Which transfer-pricing method will maximize the total after-tax operating income of Supergrow?
4. In addition to tax minimization, what other factors might Supergrow consider in choosing a transfer-pricing method?

LO 4, 5 ▶   ● **21-34 Pertinent transfer price, perfect and imperfect markets.** Wheely, Inc., has two divisions, A and B, that manufacture expensive bicycles. Division A produces the bicycle frame, and division B assembles the rest of the bicycle onto the frame. There is a market for both the subassembly and the final product. Each division has been designated as a profit centre. The transfer price for the subassembly has been set at the long-run average market price. The following data are available for each division:

Selling price for final product	$360
Long-run average selling price for intermediate product	275
Incremental cost per unit for completion in division B	120
Incremental cost per unit in division A	90

The manager of division B has made the following calculation:

Selling price for final product		$360
Transferred-in cost per unit (market)	$275	
Incremental cost per unit for completion	120	395
Contribution (loss) on product		$ (35)

Required

1. Should transfers be made to division B if there is no unused capacity in division A? Is the market price the correct transfer price? Show your computations.
2. Assume that division A's maximum capacity for this product is 1,200 units per month and sales to the intermediate market are now 900 units. Should 300 units be transferred to division B? At what transfer price? Assume that for a variety of reasons, division A will maintain the $275 selling price indefinitely. That is, division A is not considering lowering the price to outsiders even if idle capacity exists.
3. Suppose division A quoted a transfer price of $240 for up to 300 units. What would be the contribution to the company as a whole if a transfer were made? As manager of division B, would you be inclined to buy at $240? Explain.

4. Suppose the manager of division A has the option of (a) cutting the external price to $270, with the certainty that sales will rise to 1,200 units, or (b) maintaining the external price of $275 for the 900 units and transferring the 300 units to division B at a price that would produce the same operating income for division A. What transfer price would produce the same operating income for division A? Is that price consistent with that recommended by the general guideline in the chapter so that the resulting decision would be desirable for the company as a whole?

21-35 Transfer pricing, goal congruence, ethics. Sustainable Industries manufactures cardboard containers (boxes) made from recycled paper products. The company operates two divisions, paper recycling and box manufacturing, as decentralized entities. The recycling division is free to sell recycled paper to outside buyers, and the box manufacturing division is free to purchase recycled paper from other sources. Currently, however, the recycling division sells all of its output to the manufacturing division, and the manufacturing division does not purchase materials from outside suppliers.

◄ **LO 2, 5**

The recycled paper is transferred from the recycling division to the manufacturing division at 110% of full cost. The recycling division purchases recyclable paper products for $0.075 per pound. The recycling division uses 100 pounds of recyclable paper products to produce one roll of recycled paper. The division's other variable costs equal $6.35 per roll, and fixed costs at a monthly production level of 10,000 rolls are $2.15 per roll. During the most recent month, 10,000 rolls of recycled paper were transferred between the two divisions. The recycling division's capacity is 15,000 rolls.

With the increase in demand for sustainably made products, the manufacturing division expects to use 12,000 rolls of paper next month. Ecofree Corporation has offered to sell 2,000 rolls of recycled paper next month to the manufacturing division for $17.00 per roll.

Required

1. Compute the transfer price per roll of recycled paper. If each division is considered a profit centre, would the manufacturing manager choose to purchase 2,000 rolls next month from Ecofree Corporation?
2. Is the purchase in the best interest of Sustainable Industries? Show your calculations. What is the cause of this goal incongruence?
3. The manufacturing division manager suggests that $17.00 is now the market price for recycled paper rolls and that this should be the new transfer price. Sustainable's corporate management tends to agree. The paper recycling manager is suspicious. Ecofree's prices have always been much higher than $17.00 per roll. Why the sudden price cut? After further investigation by the recycling division manager, it is revealed that the $17.00 per roll price was a one-time-only offer made to the manufacturing division due to excess inventory at Ecofree. Future orders would be priced at $18.50 per roll. Comment on the validity of the $17.00 per roll market price and the ethics of the manufacturing manager. Would changing the transfer price to $17.00 matter to Sustainable Industries?

🌐 **21-36 Transfer pricing, perfect and imperfect markets.** Letang Company has three divisions (R, S, and T), organized as decentralized profit centres. Division R produces the basic chemical Ranbax (in multiples of 1,000 pounds) and transfers it to Divisions S and T. Division S processes Ranbax into the final product Syntex, and Division T processes Ranbax into the final product Termix. No material is lost during processing.

◄ **LO 1, 5**

Division R has no fixed costs. The variable cost per pound of Ranbax is $0.18. Division R has a capacity limit of 10,000 pounds. Divisions S and T have capacity limits of 4,000 and 6,000 pounds, respectively. Divisions S and T sell their final product in separate markets. The company keeps no inventories of any kind.

The *cumulative* net revenues (i.e., total revenues − total processing costs) for divisions S and T at various output levels are summarized below.

Division S				
Pounds of Ranbax processed in S	1,000	2,000	3,000	4,000
Total net revenues ($) from sale of Syntex	$ 500	$ 850	$1,100	$1,200

Division T					
Pounds of Ranbax processed in T	1,000	2,000	3,000	4,000	5,000	6,000
Total net revenues ($) from sale of Termix	$ 600	$1,200	$1,800	$2,100	$2,250	$2,350

Required

1. Suppose there is no external market for Ranbax. What quantity of Ranbax should the Letang Company produce to maximize overall income? How should this quantity be allocated between the two processing divisions?
2. What range of transfer prices will motivate Divisions S and T to demand the quantities that maximize overall income (as determined in requirement 1), as well as motivate Division R to produce the sum of those quantities?

3. Suppose that Division R can sell any quantity of Ranbax in a perfectly competitive market for $0.33 a pound. To maximize Letang's income, how many pounds of Ranbax should Division R transfer to Divisions S and T, and how much should it sell in the external market?

4. What range of transfer prices will result in Divisions R, S, and T taking the actions determined as optimal in requirement 3? Explain your answer.

LO 3 ▶ **21-37 Transfer pricing, goal congruence.** The Croydon Division of CC Industries supplies the Hauser Division with 100,000 units per month of an infrared LED that Hauser uses in a remote control device it sells. The transfer price of the LED is $8, which is the market price. However, Croydon does not operate at or near capacity. The variable cost to Croydon of the LED is $4.80, while Hauser incurs variable costs (excluding the transfer price) of $12 for each remote control. Hauser's selling price is $32.

Hauser's manager is considering a promotional campaign. The market research department of Hauser has developed the following estimates of additional monthly volume associated with additional monthly promotional expenses.

Additional monthly promotional expenses:	$80,000	$120,000	$160,000
Additional monthly volume (units)	10,000	15,000	18,000

Required

1. What level of additional promotional expenses would the Hauser division manager choose?
2. As the manager of the Croydon division, what level of additional promotional expenses would you like to see the Hauser division manager select?
3. As the president of CC Industries, what level of spending would you like the Hauser division manager to select?
4. What is the maximum transfer price that would induce the Hauser division to spend the optimal additional promotional expense from the standpoint of the firm as a whole?

LO 5 ▶ **21-38 International transfer pricing, taxes, goal congruence.** Castor, a division of Gemini Corporation, is located in the United States. Its effective income tax rate is 30%. Another division of Gemini, Pollux, is located in Canada, where the income tax rate is 40%. Pollux manufactures, among other things, an intermediate product for Castor called IP-2014. Pollux operates at capacity and makes 15,000 units of IP-2014 for Castor each period, at a variable cost of $56 per unit. Assume that there are no outside customers for IP-2014. Because the IP-2014 must be shipped from Canada to the United States, it costs Pollux an additional $8 per unit to ship the IP-2014 to Castor. There are no direct fixed costs for IP-2014. Pollux also manufactures other products.

A product similar to IP-2014 that Castor could use as a substitute is available in the United States for $77 per unit.

Required

1. What is the minimum and maximum transfer price that would be acceptable to Castor and Pollux for IP-2014, and why?
2. What transfer price would minimize income taxes for Gemini Corporation as a whole? Would Castor and Pollux want to be evaluated on operating income using this transfer price?
3. Suppose Gemini uses the transfer price from requirement 2 and each division is evaluated on its own after-tax division operating income. Now suppose Pollux has an opportunity to sell 8,000 units of IP-2014 to an outside customer for $62 each. Pollux will not incur shipping costs because the customer is nearby and offers to pay for shipping. Assume that if Pollux accepts the special order, Castor will have to buy 8,000 units of the substitute product in the United States at $77 per unit.
   a. Will accepting the special order maximize after-tax operating income for Gemini Corporation as a whole?
   b. Will Castor want Pollux to accept this special order? Why or why not?
   c. Will Pollux want to accept this special order? Explain.
   d. Suppose Gemini Corporation wants to operate in a decentralized manner. What transfer price should Gemini set for IP-2014 so that each division acting in its own best interest takes actions with respect to the special order that are in the best interests of Gemini Corporation as a whole?

Collaborative Learning Cases

LO 1, 5 ▶
1. Incremental costs of supplying 10,000 CD players to assembly division, $230,000

21-39 Transfer pricing, goal congruence. The Orsilo Corporation makes and sells 10,000 multisystem music players each year. Its assembly division purchases components from other divisions of Orsilo or from external suppliers and assembles the multisystem music players. In particular, the assembly division can purchase the CD player from the compact disc division of Orsilo or from Johnson Corporation. Johnson agrees to meet all of Orsilo's quality requirements and is currently negotiating with the assembly division to supply 10,000 CD players at a price between $38 and $45 per CD player.

A critical component of the CD player is the head mechanism that reads the disc. To ensure the quality of its multisystem music players, Orsilo requires that if Johnson wins the contract to supply CD players, it must purchase the head mechanism from Orsilo's compact disc division for $20 each.

The compact disc division can manufacture at most 12,000 CD players annually. It also manufactures as many additional head mechanisms as can be sold. The incremental cost of manufacturing the head mechanism is $15 per unit. The incremental cost of manufacturing a CD player (including the cost of the head mechanism) is $25 per unit, and any number of CD players can be sold for $35 each in the external market.

Required

1. What are the incremental costs minus revenues from sales to external buyers for the company as a whole if the compact disc division transfers 10,000 CD players to the assembly division and sells the remaining 2,000 CD players on the external market?
2. What are the incremental costs minus revenues from sales to external buyers for the company as a whole if the compact disc division sells 12,000 CD players on the external market and the assembly division accepts Johnson's offer at (a) $38 per CD player or (b) $45 per CD player?
3. What is the minimum transfer price per CD player at which the compact disc division would be willing to transfer 10,000 CD players to the assembly division?
4. Suppose that the transfer price is set to the minimum computed in requirement 3 plus $1, and the division managers at Orsilo are free to make their own profit-maximizing sourcing and selling decisions. Now, Johnson offers 10,000 CD players for $40.50 each.
   a. What decisions will the managers of the compact disc division and assembly division make?
   b. Are these decisions optimal for Orsilo as a whole?
   c. Based on this exercise, at what price would you recommend the transfer price be set?

21-40 Goal-congruence, taxes, different market conditions. TECA Halifax makes kids' bicycles. The frames division makes and paints the frames and supplies them to the assembly division, where the bicycles are assembled. TECA is a successful and profitable corporation that attributes much of its success to its decentralized operating style. Each division manager is compensated on the basis of division operating income.

◀ **LO 1, 2, 3, 4, 5**
1. Contribution margin from new frame, $272

The assembly division currently acquires all its frames from the frames division. The assembly division manager could purchase similar frames in the market for $480.

The frames division is currently operating at 80% of its capacity of 4,000 frames (units) and has the following particulars:

Direct materials ($150 per unit × 3,200 units)	$480,000
Direct manufacturing labour ($60 per unit × 3,200 units)	192,000
Variable manufacturing overhead costs ($30 per unit × 3,200 units)	96,000
Fixed manufacturing overhead costs	724,000

All the frames division's 3,200 units are currently transferred to the assembly division. No frames are sold in the outside market.

The frames division has just received an order for 2,000 units at $450 per frame that would utilize half the capacity of the plant. The order has to be either taken in full or rejected totally. The order is for a slightly different frame than what the frames division currently makes but takes the same amount of manufacturing time. To produce the new frame would require direct materials per unit of $100, direct manufacturing labour per unit of $48, and variable manufacturing overhead costs per unit of $30.

Instructions

Form groups of two or three students to complete the following requirements.

Required

1. From the viewpoint of TECA Halifax as a whole, should the frames division accept the order for the 2,000 units?
2. What range of transfer prices result in achieving the actions determined to be optimal in requirement 1, if division managers act in a decentralized manner?
3. The manager of the assembly division has proposed a transfer price for the frames equal to the full cost of the frames including an allocation of overhead costs. The frames division allocates overhead costs to engines on the basis of the total capacity of the plant used to manufacture the frames.
   a. Calculate the transfer price for the frames transferred to the assembly division under this arrangement.
   b. Do you think that the transfer price calculated in requirement 3a will result in achieving the actions determined to be optimal in requirement 1, if division managers act in a decentralized manner?
   c. Comment in general on one advantage and one disadvantage of using full costs of the producing division as the basis for setting transfer prices.

4. Now consider the effect of income taxes.

    a. Suppose the assembly division is located in a country that imposes a 10% tax on income earned within its boundaries, while the frames division is located in a country that imposes no tax on income earned within its boundaries. What transfer price would be chosen by TECA to minimize tax payments for the corporation as a whole? Assume that only transfer prices that are greater than or equal to full manufacturing costs and less than or equal to the market price of "substantially similar" frames are acceptable to the taxing authorities.

    b. Suppose that TECA announces the transfer price computed in requirement 4a to price all transfers between the frames and assembly divisions. Each division manager then acts autonomously to maximize division operating income. Will division managers acting in a decentralized manner achieve the actions determined to be optimal in requirement 1?

5. Consider your responses to requirements 1 to 4 and assume the frames division will continue to have opportunities for outside business as described in requirement 1. What transfer-pricing policy would you recommend TECA use and why? Would you continue to evaluate division performance on the basis of division operating incomes?

TRY IT! ▶ **SOLUTION**

Try It 21–1

The Raw lumber division generates $225 in revenue less $100 (division variable costs) = $125 in operating income for selling raw or finished lumber.

    The finished lumber division only sells finished lumber, and the operating income is $375 (revenue) − $225 (transferred in costs) − $125 (division variable costs) = $25.

    It is more profitable for the raw lumber division to sell directly to market and not transfer to the finished lumber division.

Multinational Performance Measurement and Compensation

22

▶ Learning Objectives

1. Analyze and evaluate alternative measures of financial performance.

2. Evaluate current-cost and historical-cost asset measurement methods.

3. Analyze the technical difficulties that arise when comparing the performance of divisions operating in different countries.

4. Evaluate the behavioural effects of salaries and incentives in compensation arrangements.

5. Apply strategic concepts to analyze the four levers of control, and evaluate their usefulness.

Qualitative and Nonfinancial Measures Are Relevant

BCE, Canada's largest telecommunications service provider, reported performance results in its 2015 annual report. BCE's goal is to "be recognized by customers as Canada's leading communications company."[1] To achieve this, BCE outlined six strategic imperatives:

- Accelerate wireless growth.
- Leverage wireline momentum.
- Expand media leadership.
- Invest in broadband networks and service.
- Achieve a competitive cost structure.
- Improve customer service.

The 2015 report then presented information that supported the achievement of these imperatives:

- Wireless customer revenue increased from 7.8% per average user.
- Smartphone usage grew faster than any peer company.
- BCE's new venture, Fibe network, connects to 2.2 million homes.
- CTV (a BCE enterprise) maintained the status as the most-watched conventional network for the 14th straight year.
- Bell will invest a further $3 billion in the Fibe network.
- Operating costs were reduced by $100 million, and call centre volume was down by 11%.
- Bell reported a 98% on-time rating for its service calls and a 92% customer satisfaction rating.

▶ CPA Competencies

This chapter covers material outlined in **Section 3: Management Accounting** of the CPA Competency Map. The Learning Objectives in this chapter have been aligned with the CPA Competency Map to ensure the best coverage possible.

3.5.1 Performs sensitivity analysis

3.5.2 Evaluates sustainable profit maximization and capacity management performance

3.6.1 Evaluates performance using accepted frameworks

3.6.2 Evaluates performance of responsibility centres

3.6.3 Evaluates root causes of performance issues

3.4.1 Evaluates sources and drivers of revenue growth

---

[1] BCE, 2015 Annual Report. BCE Inc. (p. 8).

All of these financial and nonfinancial measures were used to evaluate and calculate senior management's executive compensation package. This combination of financial and nonfinancial measures supports both short-term and long-term planning and decision making. It is possibly as a result of this broad-based approach to motivation and compensation that BCE is one of the most successful firms in this highly competitive industry.

This chapter examines technical, governance, and behavioural issues in designing and implementing appropriate financial and nonfinancial performance measures. Performance measures should be a central component of a management accounting control system (MACS). To be effective, however, MACS must motivate not only internal goal congruence but also external governance requirements.

Performance measurement of managers is used in decisions about their salaries, bonuses, future assignments, and career advancement. Moreover, the very act of measuring their performance can motivate managers to strive for the goals used in their evaluation and ignore achieving other equally important goals. At a higher level of analysis, performance measurement of an organization's subunits is a prerequisite for allocating resources within that organization.

Financial and Nonfinancial Performance Measures

► **LO 1**

Analyze and evaluate alternative measures of financial performance.

The information used in a MACS can be financial or nonfinancial (see Chapter 13 and Chapter 21). Many common financial performance measures, such as operating income, rely on internal financial and accounting information. Increasingly complex governance legislation, however, means companies must supplement internal financial with nonfinancial measures (for example, manufacturing lead time) and external nonfinancial information (such as customer satisfaction). In addition, companies often benchmark (see Chapter 7 Appendix) their financial and nonfinancial measures against other companies that are regarded as "best performers."

Corporations adopting a *balanced scorecard* (BSC)[2] approach to performance measurement have progressed to include risk measures. Incorporating risk is most often in the form of probable financial outcomes. Enterprise risk planning software includes automated collection of hundreds of possible financial and nonfinancial measures of performance. The advantage of enterprise risk planning software over a BSC is that more refined data discloses important interdependencies. There is less chance that either subunits or individuals will be unfairly rewarded or penalized for performance that depends on outcomes of other subunits or individuals.

Some performance measures, such as the number of new patents developed, are structural changes to intellectual capital, which have a long-run time horizon. It is sensible to provide a form of deferred compensation to individuals responsible for ensuring that expected benefits are realized. Other measures, such as direct materials efficiency variances, overhead spending variances, and yield, have a short-run time horizon. In this situation, immediate cash or noncash compensation elements are sensible. We will focus on the most widely used performance measures covering an intermediate to long-run time horizon.

Governance and Compensation Decisions

In recent years, corporate governance and compensation decisions have come under increasing scrutiny. When the financial meltdown of 2007–2009 threatened global economic prosperity, employees who had lost their jobs (because companies declared bankruptcy) reacted with anger to the news of executive salary, bonus, and severance payments (from those same bankrupt companies) that amounted to millions of dollars. In some countries, compensation policies appear to have systematically enriched a handful of

---

[2] R.S. Kaplan and D.P. Norton, *The Strategy-Focused Organization: How Balanced Scorecard Companies Thrive in the New Business Environment* (Boston: Harvard Business School Press, 2001); and R.S. Kaplan and D.P. Norton, *Strategy Maps: Converting Intangible Assets into Tangible Outcomes* (Boston: Harvard Business School Press, 2004).

executive millionaires at the expense of other corporate stakeholders. The situation in Canada may be in contrast to that belief. A recent Canadian study shows that for 81% of the S&P/TSX 60 companies, there was a significant (positive) correlation between CEO pay increases and total shareholder returns over the 2004–2011 time frame.[3]

Various global stock exchanges have proposed sweeping changes to corporate governance to require independence of the board of directors (BOD), the compensation committee, and the procedures of the committee. In the United States, the major governance legislation is the **Sarbanes-Oxley Act (SOX)**, which became law in 2002, primarily in response to the Enron scandal. This enhanced governance legislation is not without its costs. In the early years, the cost of compliance with SOX was estimated to average approximately US$4.3 million per firm and had been reported as high as US$40 million. More recent research shows a much lower compliance cost (less than US$1 million) for most firms.[4] This may reflect the fact that the improved control and reporting requirements of SOX have become so integral to most firms' operations that it is difficult to distinguish the extra (SOX-mandated) costs from normal audit costs.

In Canada, **Bill 198 (sometimes commonly referred to as C-SOX)** accomplishes much the same objectives as US SOX. Canadian publicly traded companies are also required to comply with CPA accounting and control standards, Toronto Stock Exchange (TSX) requirements for firms listed on the exchange, and Canadian Securities Administrators (CSA) rules for public issuers of shares. Interestingly, most large Canadian companies also abide by US SOX requirements because their shares are listed on a US stock exchange (in addition to being listed on the TSX).

Some recent developments regarding corporate governance include a new internal control framework issued in 2013 by the Committee on Sponsoring Organizations of the Treadway Commission (COSO). This framework is used by most Canadian and US companies to evaluate their internal control. In Canada, the CSA's Multilateral Instrument 52-109 (Certificate of Disclosure in Issuer's Annual and Interim Filings) includes control regulations that must be attested to each year by the CEO/CFO of the firm. The federal government continues its efforts to harmonize securities oversight across Canada. Instead of one security regulator (i.e., Securities and Exchange Commission) like in the United States, Canada has 13 regulators. In 2013, the federal government, joined by Ontario and BC, announced the formation of the Cooperative Capital Markets Regulators (CCMR). The federal government hopes that all the 13 regulators will join this group but it remains to be seen if Alberta and Quebec will become part of the cooperative.

Governance oversight agencies, such as the CSA, and private shareholder activist groups, such as the Canadian Coalition for Good Governance (CCGG) and Institutional Shareholder Services Inc. (ISS), have intensified their scrutiny of corporate performance and compensation policies. At the global level, partially in response to the increasing presence of multinational corporations (MNC), agencies such as the Organisation for Economic Co-operation and Development (OECD) have established global treaties and guidelines for corporate governance indices (CGI), enabling investors to review the stringency of governance practices required in different countries.[5] The more stringent the practices and the higher the rate of successful enforcement, the lower the risk to the investor.

Shareholders and government agencies have also turned their attention to the specifics of executive and BOD compensation policies. Once a subject that was rarely discussed in public and often with the air of an "old boys' club," compensation transparency is now widely considered to be essential to good governance practices. In the United States, the 2011 Dodd-Frank Wall Street Reform and Consumer Protection Act ushered in a new era of mandated "**say on pay**" shareholder voting.

---

[3] Clarkson Centre for Board Effectiveness, "Pay For Performance Observations S&P/TSX Composite Index—2011," Rotman School of Management, University of Toronto, http://cm-www.rotman.utoronto.ca/FacultyAndResearch/ResearchCentres/ClarksonCentreforBoardEffectiveness/-//-/media/Files/Programs-and-Areas/Institutes/Clarkson/Pay%20for%20Performance%20Observations%202011%20-%20Tony%20-%20CCBE%20July%202012.pdf.

[4] Protiviti, "Building Value in Your SOX Compliance Program," http://www.protiviti.com/en-US/Documents/Surveys/2013-SOX-Compliance-Survey-Protiviti.pdf.

[5] C. Strenger, "The Corporate Governance Scorecard: A Tool for the Implementation of Corporate Governance," *Corporate Governance* (January 2004): 11–15.

Both the UK and Switzerland have adopted similar, mandatory shareholder "say-on-pay" votes. Switzerland went so far as to eliminate bonuses to executives who were joining or leaving a firm. In Canada, "say on pay" shareholder voting is still voluntary for publicly traded companies, but perhaps this is because there does not seem to be the same disparity between corporate performance and executive pay. Currently, according to the Institute for Governance of Private and Public Organizations, 80% of the largest Canadian companies have adopted the practice voluntarily or as a result of pressure from investors.[6] Amendments in 2011 to the CSA's Form 51-102F6 Statement of Executive Compensation require issuing firms to include explicit disclosure in their *Compensation Discussion and Analysis (CD&A)*, which is filed as part of the firm's annual Management Proxy Circular.

Form 51-102F6 outlines specific disclosure requirements for the CD&A around executive compensation. It includes elements such as performance metrics, components of compensation packages, value of compensation, risks associated with incentives, and how compensation packages are determined by the board.

The CSA and Canada Revenue Agency (CRA) continue to discuss new legislation and recommendations. The provincial Ontario Securities Commission (OSC), TSX, and private watchdogs such as the Institute on Corporate Directors (ICD) Blue Ribbon Panel on the Governance of Executive Compensation in Canada have also weighed in, making recommendations to improve decisions made by boards of directors. The ICD recommends that, among other things, the practice of **malus**, or clawback, of previously awarded compensation be instituted when performance has been poor, along with full disclosure of any severance compensation, often referred to as a "golden parachute."

There are now many stakeholders involved in what used to be a purely internal, corporate decision on performance and executive compensation, as illustrated in Exhibit 22-1.

Along with discussion about governance and compensation policies, firms must define the performance measurement(s) needed to evaluate managers, executives, and the BOD.

Exhibit 22-1 Constraints on Board of Directors' (BOD) Performance Measurement Decisions

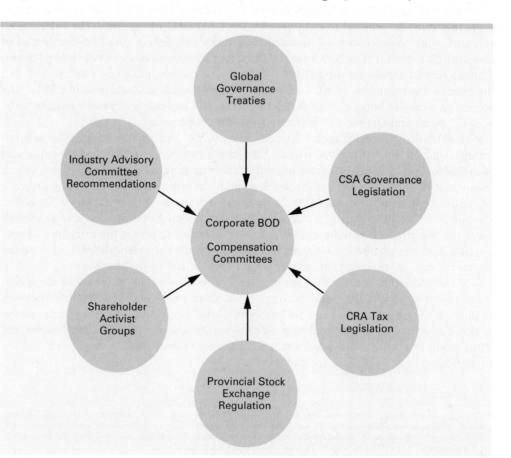

[6] Y. Allaire and F. Daughin. 2016. Making say-on-pay vote binding: A good idea? *Igapp* (September 13) (https://igopp.org/en/say-on-pay-binding-good-idea-2).

Deciding on a performance measure is a complex decision process wherein each decision informs and is interdependent with others. There are very few direct causal relationships in a business, but the relationship between corporate performance measurements and executive compensation is one prominent example.

The corporate management team must decide what performance measurement(s) will be used as the basis for executive and other compensation. This question of what metrics (measurement tools) to choose is one of the most difficult ones faced by senior management and BODs. That is because the efforts of the executive and the officers of the company are not readily observed. In addition, executive effort can be overwhelmed by changes in external factors over which they have no control. This means that the need for best practices (i.e., metrics that are clearly linked to executive performance) is apparent, but the implementation (i.e., choosing the actual metrics) is often difficult because of the lack of clear causal relationships between executive effort and corporate performance.

One commonly used form of corporate compensation avoids the whole question of what metric to use. It uses the same metric that most shareholders feel is most important: stock price. This form of executive (and BOD) compensation is the award of stock and/or stock options. Depending on how the award is structured, it can provide both short- and medium-term rewards. But many factors outside of the executive's control could generate a short-term increase or decrease in share price, independent of the executive's performance.

For example, if external factors caused an increase in the share price, there would be a bonus, even though the executive didn't deserve it. Conversely, the externalities could cause a decrease in the share price, which might result in no bonus or worse, malus (that is, a clawback) of previous bonuses, even though the executive's performance may have been superior (albeit during bad economic times).

Conflict also exists between recommended best governance practices to focus on short-term over long-term performance measures. The nature of investment is to obtain return over the lifetime of the investments made in excess of the cost of the investments. But this entails risk because the future cannot be known. Pay for performance measures in the best interests of shareholders would, logically, include long-term achievement and deferred compensation.

Deferred compensation could include the award of restricted stock options that executives would forfeit should they fail to meet the performance criteria within the specified time period. In theory, the executive who owns the right to purchase shares in the long term will work hard to improve the price of the shares. A complete discussion of this is beyond the scope of this text, in part due to the impact of the Canadian Income Tax Act (ITA) on this discussion, and also due to the fact that this area of the ITA is constantly changing. For example, while stock options were once very popular forms of executive compensation (restricted or not), they have fallen into disfavour in Canada due to their tax treatment and complexity. Instead, another form of compensation called restricted stock units (RSUs) is becoming popular.

From the management team's perspective, there is a set of interdependent decisions to be made in an ever changing legislative environment. Each decision will influence those before and those made after it. The decisions are by no means sequential and the team must often retrace previous decisions before implementation of a compensation policy and selection of performance measures can be finalized. By and large, despite the availability of nonfinancial performance measures and the principles of BSC, compensation remains determined by accounting measures. A typical series of decisions could be

- *Decide which accounting performance measures are best aligned with the executive team's financial goals.* For example, does operating income, net income, return on investment (ROI), or revenue best measure a subunit's financial performance?

- *Decide on the time horizons of each performance measure, short or long term, strategic or operating.* For example, should performance measures such as ROI be calculated for one year or for a multiyear horizon?

- *Decide how to define the components of performance measure.* For example, should assets be defined as total assets or net assets (total assets minus total liabilities)?

Concepts in Action

BP Shareholders Fight to Reject CEO's Pay Package

Barrick Gold Corporation

At the end of the first quarter of 2016, British Petroleum (BP) recorded its worst annual loss in history—£4.5 billion (nearly C\$8 billion). At the same time, the CEO of BP, Bob Dudley, was to be awarded a record compensation package totaling £14 million. At annual meetings, companies such as BP include on the agenda shareholder voting for important issues such as executive compensation. Disclosures for BP's annual meeting included a formal notice and the Management Proxy Circular disclosing relevant information on voting matters.

Royal London Asset Management, an investment firm that owns nearly 1% of BP, took the position that Dudley's pay package (which represented a 20% raise from the previous year) was unreasonable, stating, "We consider the pay of the CEO to be simply too high, and particularly so in a year when the company suffered a record loss in 2015. Even so his pay went up by 20%. Part of the reason for the high pay was the excessively complex remuneration scheme." The argument suggested the complicated performance scheme made it easier to "game" the ratings system and ensure a healthy bonus despite weakening corporate performance.

Sources: Copyright Guardian News & Media Ltd 2017.

- *Decide on the appropriate measurement method.* For example, should assets be measured at historical cost, current cost, or present value?
- *Decide on the criteria—the target against which to gauge the level of performance.* For example, should all subunits have as a target the same required ROI?
- *Decide on the timing of feedback.* For example, should performance reports be sent to top management daily, weekly, or monthly?
- *Decide on the elements of the compensation package.* For example, the percentage of fixed and variable salary, share awards, option grants, pension, medical benefits, and perquisites such as personal accommodation and travel may all be elements of executive compensation.

Accounting Performance Measures

Four measures are commonly used to evaluate the financial performance of organization subunits. These performance measures all use financial accounting information:

- Return on investment (ROI)
- Residual income (RI)
- Economic value added (EVA)
- Return on sales (ROS)

We illustrate these measures using the example of Hospitality Inns, which owns and operates three motels located in Saskatoon, Saskatchewan; Brandon, Manitoba; and

Exhibit 22-2 Annual Financial Data for Hospitality Inns for 2018

	A	B	C	D	E
1		Saskatoon	Brandon	Hull	Total
2		(1)	(2)	(3)	(4) = (1) + (2) + (3)
3	Motel revenue	$1,200,000	$1,400,000	$3,185,000	$5,785,000
4	Motel variable costs	310,000	375,000	995,000	1,680,000
5	Motel fixed costs	650,000	725,000	1,680,000	3,055,000
6	Motel operating income	$ 240,000	$ 300,000	$ 510,000	1,050,000
7	Interest costs on long-term debt at 10%				450,000
8	Income before income taxes				600,000
9	Income tax at 30%				180,000
10	Net income				$ 420,000
11	Net book values at the end of 2018:				
12	Current assets	$ 400,000	$ 500,000	$ 600,000	$1,500,000
13	Long-term assets	600,000	1,500,000	2,400,000	4,500,000
14	Total assets	$1,000,000	$2,000,000	$3,000,000	$6,000,000
15	Current liabilities	$ 50,000	$ 150,000	$ 300,000	$ 500,000
16	Long-term debt	—	—	—	4,500,000
17	Shareholders' equity	—	—	—	1,000,000
18	Total liabilities and shareholders' equity				$6,000,000

Hull, Quebec. Exhibit 22-2 summarizes data for each of the three motels for the most recent year (2018). At present, Hospitality Inns does not allocate to the three separate motels the total long-term debt of the company.

Exhibit 22-2 indicates that the Hull motel generates the highest operating income, $510,000. The Brandon motel generates $300,000; the Saskatoon motel, $240,000. But does this mean that the Hull motel is the most "successful"? Actually, the comparison of operating income ignores potential differences in the size of the investments in the different motels. An investment is a long-term cash allocation decision intended to realize returns (see Chapter 20). The question is how large the return should be, given the resources that were used to earn it.

Return on Investment

Return on investment (ROI) is a performance measure that uses readily available financial accounting information. It takes accounting income (as measured by the income statement) and divides it by the firm's investment in assets (as measured by the balance sheet):

$$\text{Return on investment} = \frac{\text{Income}}{\text{Investment}}$$

The two components can be further broken down into their more basic parts to help understand how the various aspects of the income statement and balance sheet impact the ROI results. They are

$$\frac{\text{Income}}{\text{Investment}} = \frac{\text{Revenue}}{\text{Investment}} \times \frac{\text{Income}}{\text{Revenue}}$$

The two separate elements can be further "deconstructed" as follows:

1. Income ÷ Revenue (also known as return on sales (ROS), or profit margin) tells how much of each revenue dollar becomes income, with the goal being to get as

much income per revenue dollar as possible. Firms can choose a number of different "income" measures for the numerator portion of the equation (e.g., income from operations, income before discontinued operations and taxes, net income, etc.). Obviously, the choice of which "income" figure to use will impact the ROI results.

2. Revenue ÷ Investment (also known as investment turnover or asset turnover) tells how many revenue dollars are generated by each dollar of investment in assets. The goal is to make each investment dollar "work harder" to generate more revenues. Similar to the income discussion above, the choice of which assets to include (e.g., total assets, property/plant/equipment, cost amount vs. depreciated amount, assets minus current liabilities, etc.) can have a dramatic impact on the ROI measurement.

ROI is the most popular approach to incorporating the investment base into a management performance measure. ROI appeals conceptually because it blends all the major ingredients of profitability (revenues, costs, and investments) into a single number. This approach is also known as the *DuPont method of profitability analysis*.[7] Once calculated, an ROI for one opportunity can be compared to the rates of return for other opportunities, either inside or outside the company. However, like any single performance measure, ROI should be used cautiously and in conjunction with other performance measures.

ROI is also called the accounting rate of return (ARR) or the accrual accounting rate of return (AARR). Since accrual accounting measures are present in both the income and investment sections of the measurement, care needs to be taken when there are changes in the accounting standards or accounting policy choices. Either situation could change the ROI calculation, even though the underlying operations or effectiveness of the firm remains the same. Similarly, the choice of which balance sheet asset amount to use could have an impact on the ROI—that is

- end-of-year amounts or
- average-for-the-year calculation, or
- start-of-the-year figures.

Since none of these choices is specified by accounting standards (unlike EPS calculations, which are carefully defined by ASPE and IFRS), care must always be taken when comparing ROI figures calculated by different analysts or companies.

Consider the ROI of each of the three Hospitality motels in Exhibit 22-2. For our calculations, we are using the operating income of each motel for the numerator and total assets of each motel for the denominator.

Motel	Operating Income	÷	Total Assets	=	ROI
Saskatoon	$240,000	÷	$1,000,000	=	24%
Brandon	300,000	÷	2,000,000	=	15
Hull	510,000	÷	3,000,000	=	17

Using these ROI figures, the Saskatoon motel appears to make the best use of its total assets.

Hospitality Inns can increase ROI by either increasing revenues or decreasing costs, since both of these actions will increase the ROI numerator. Similarly, a decrease in the amount invested (which would decrease the ROI denominator) would also increase the ROI. Assume that top management at Hospitality Inns adopts a 30% target ROI for the Saskatoon motel. How can this return be achieved?

---

[7] The DuPont method was originally developed around 1920 by the DuPont Powder Company. The model was used by top management at DuPont for planning and investment purposes. It can be significantly expanded to more detailed levels of analysis and can also be adapted to a return on equity (ROE) model.

The DuPont method shows how changes in specific components (i.e., income, revenue, or investments) can help the firm to reach its target ROI. The current situation and three possible approaches to achieving a 30% ROI are illustrated below.

	Operating Income (1)	Revenue (2)	Total Assets (3)	Operating Income ÷ Revenue (4) = (1) ÷ (2)	×	Revenue ÷ Total Assets (5) = (2) ÷ (3)	=	Operating Income ÷ Total Assets (6) = (1) ÷ (3)
Current Situation	$240,000	$1,200,000	$1,000,000	0.20	×	1.2	=	24%
Alternatives								
A. Decrease assets (e.g., receivables). Revenue and operating income per dollar of revenue remain constant.	$240,000	$1,200,000	$ 800,000	0.20	×	1.5	=	30%
B. Increase revenues (e.g., sell more rooms). Assets and operating income *per dollar* of revenue remain constant.	$300,000	$1,500,000	$1,000,000	0.20	×	1.5	=	30%
C. Decrease costs (e.g., efficient maintenance) to increase operating income per dollar of revenue; assets remain constant.	$300,000	$1,200,000	$1,000,000	0.25	×	1.2	=	30%

ROI highlights the benefits that managers can obtain by reducing their investments in current or fixed assets. Most managers are conscious of the need to boost revenues or to control costs but pay less attention to reducing their investment base. Reducing investments means decreasing idle cash, managing credit judiciously, determining proper inventory levels, and spending carefully on fixed assets.

Operating income or earnings before interest and taxes (EBIT) is a measure of how well managers have deployed assets to generate an operating return. Incurring interest is not a result of any operating decisions made from day to day but rather a strategic decision made by the CFO and the team in the finance subunit. The expanded DuPont measure of ROI does contain a specific ratio to measure the effectiveness and efficiency of financial management. Tax is also the responsibility of the CFO and the management team in finance, not the operating managers. The expanded DuPont measure of ROI contains another specific ratio to measure the effectiveness and efficiency of tax management.

To use net income (after-tax earnings) in the numerator of an ROI measure could misstate by a material amount the actual operating return generated by the operating investments. This is why the operating income (before interest and taxes) is more appropriate than either earnings before tax or net income.

Residual Income

Residual income (RI) is income minus a required dollar return on the investment:[8]

Residual income = Income − (Required rate of return × Investment)

The required rate of return (RRR) multiplied by investment is also called the **imputed cost** of the investment. Imputed costs are costs recognized in particular situations that are not regularly recognized by accrual accounting procedures. An imputed cost is not recognized in accounting records because it is not an incremental cost but instead represents the return forgone by Hospitality Inns as a result of tying up cash in various investments of similar risk. The RRR that management should use to calculate residual income is the company's **weighted-average cost of capital (WACC)**. WACC equals the after-tax average cost of all the long-term funds used.

Conceptually, it would be better to use the cost of capital based on each subunit's risk level. For example, an oil-exploration division would warrant a higher required rate of return than an oil-refining division because the risk of failing to find oil is far higher than the risks of refining oil already being produced. Generally, the cost of capital based on each subunit's risk level is not externally available.

---

[8] Just as in the case of ROI, companies using RI vary in the way they define income (for example, operating income, pretax income, or net income) and investment (for example, total assets or total assets minus current liabilities).

Sustainability in Action

Analysis of Operating Income Uncovers Strategies to Improve Profitability and Sustainability

Best Buy had long enacted a successful strategy of aggressive "big box" store expansion. However, by 2012 an analysis of the company's operating income revealed strategic challenges. Though revenue was growing, operating income fell by 50% from 2008 to 2012. Meanwhile, same-store sales were declining, and selling, general, and administrative expenses were rising.

The reason: E-commerce initiatives were eroding Best Buy's traditional performance. While the company pursued strategic differentiation through customer experience and add-on services, many consumers were drawn to the low prices of Amazon and other online retailers to buy flat-screen televisions, computers, and digital cameras.

To turn the company around, Best Buy announced plans to reduce costs and prices by (1) closing some existing "big box" stores and opening smaller stores focused on selling smartphones, including Samsung mini-shops inside 1,400 locations; (2) further expanding its online presence—and introducing a price-match guarantee—to compete better with Amazon. Best Buy's focus on more sustainable strategies, with smaller physical footprints allowed Best Buy to maintain its market leading position by adding new approaches to customer care and product delivery. Where the operational analysis had previously shown weakness, Best Buy's new strategy was pointing to success.

Sources: K. Kelleher. 2013. Best Buy: Not Your Standard Corporate Comeback, *Fortune* (June 12).

In our example, we will assume that each motel faces similar risks. Hospitality Inns defines residual income for each motel as motel operating income minus a required rate of return of 12% of the total assets of the motel:

Motel	Operating Income	−	(Required Rate of Return	×	Investment)	=	Residual Income
Saskatoon	$240,000	−	(12%	×	$1,000,000)	=	$120,000
Brandon	$300,000	−	(12%	×	$2,000,000)	=	$ 60,000
Hull	$510,000	−	(12%	×	$3,000,000)	=	$150,000

Given the 12% RRR, the Hull motel is performing best in terms of residual income. Generally, residual income is more likely than ROI to induce goal congruence.

Some firms favour the residual-income approach because managers will concentrate on maximizing an absolute amount (dollars of residual income) rather than a percentage (ROI). The objective of maximizing residual income assumes that as long as a division earns a rate in excess of the RRR, that specific division should expand. In this regard, the RI measurement is superior to ROI. Having divisional managers focus on maximizing ROI (in contrast to maximizing RI) may lead them to reject projects that, from the viewpoint of the organization as a whole, should be accepted. However, from their subunit perspective, they may decide to reject a project because its ROI is lower than the average ROI for their unit (which would lower their unit's average ROI and might negatively impact their bonus). This, despite the fact that the project ROI may be above the firm's required rate of return. This is known as the "underinvestment" problem.

To illustrate, assume that Hospitality's RRR is 12%. Assume also that an expansion of the Saskatoon motel will increase its operating income by $160,000 and increase its total assets by $800,000. The ROI for the expansion is 20% (= $160,000 ÷ $800,000), which makes it attractive to Hospitality Inns as a whole. By making this expansion, however, the Saskatoon manager will see that motel's total ROI decrease:

$$\text{Pre-expansion ROI} = \frac{\$240,000}{\$1,000,000} = 24\%$$

$$\text{Post-expansion ROI} = \frac{(\$240,000 + \$160,000)}{(\$1,000,000 + \$800,000)} = \frac{\$400,000}{\$1,800,000} = 22.2\%$$

The annual bonus paid to the Saskatoon manager may decrease if ROI is a key component in the bonus calculation and the expansion option is selected. In contrast, if the annual bonus is a function of residual income, the Saskatoon manager will view the expansion favourably:

$$\text{Pre-expansion residual income} = \$240,000 - (12 \times \$1,000,000) = \$120,000$$

$$\text{Post-expansion residual income} = \$400,000 - (12 \times \$1,800,000) = \$184,000$$

Goal congruence is more likely to be promoted by using residual income rather than ROI as a measure of the division manager's performance.

Economic Value Added

Economic value added (EVA) is a specific type of residual income calculation that attracted considerable attention during the dot-com boom of the late 1990s.[9] The difference between this and other accounting performance measures is that this measure does not use a reported ASPE/IFRS accrual in the numerator. EVA substitutes the following numbers in the residual-income calculations: (1) adjusted income equal to after-tax operating income, (2) a required rate of return equal to the weighted-average cost of capital, and (3) adjusted investment equal to total assets minus current liabilities.[10] We use the Hospitality Inns data in Exhibit 22-2 to illustrate EVA.

$$\begin{matrix} \text{Economic} \\ \text{value added} \\ \text{(EVA)} \end{matrix} = \begin{matrix} \text{Adjusted after-tax} \\ \text{operating income} \end{matrix} - \left[\begin{matrix} \text{Weighted-average} \\ \text{cost of capital} \end{matrix} \times \left(\begin{matrix} \text{Adjusted total} \\ \text{assets} \end{matrix} - \begin{matrix} \text{Current} \\ \text{liabilities} \end{matrix} \right) \right]$$

The key calculation is the weighted-average cost of capital (WACC). Hospitality Inns has two sources of long-term funds—long-term debt with a market and book value of $4.5 million issued at an interest rate of 10%, and equity capital that has a market value of $3 million (and a book value of $1 million).[11] Because interest costs are tax-deductible, the after-tax cost of debt financing equals $0.10 (1 - \text{tax rate}) = 0.10 \times (1 - 0.30) = 0.10 \times 0.70 = 0.07$, or 7%. The cost of equity capital is the opportunity cost to investors of not investing their capital in another investment that is similar in risk to Hospitality Inns. Suppose that Hospitality's cost of equity capital is 15%.[12] The WACC computation, which uses market values of debt and equity, is as follows:

$$\begin{aligned} \text{WACC} &= \frac{(0.07 \times \$4,500,000) + (0.15 \times \$3,000,000)}{\$4,500,000 + \$3,000,000} \\ &= \frac{(\$315,000 + \$450,000)}{\$7,500,000} = \frac{\$765,000}{\$7,500,000} \\ &= 0.102 \text{ or } 10.2\% \end{aligned}$$

---

[9] O'Byrne and D. Young, *EVA and Value-Based Management: A Practical Guide to Implementation* (New York: McGraw-Hill, 2000); J. Stein, J. Shiely, and I. Ross, *The EVA Challenge: Implementing Value Added Change in an Organization* (New York: John Wiley and Sons, 2001).

[10] When implementing EVA, companies make several adjustments to the operating income and asset numbers reported under generally accepted accounting principles. For example, when calculating EVA, costs such as R&D, restructuring costs, and leases that have long-run benefits are recorded as assets (which are then depreciated), rather than as current operating costs. The goal of these adjustments is to obtain a better representation of the economic assets, particularly intangible assets, used to earn income. Of course, the specific adjustments applicable to a company will depend on its individual circumstances.

[11] The market value of Hospitality Inns's equity exceeds book value because book value, based on historical cost, does not measure the current value of the company's assets, and because various intangible assets, such as the company's brand name, are not shown at current value in the balance sheet under ASPE/IFRS.

[12] For details on calculating cost of equity capital adjusted for risk, see J. Van Horne, *Financial Management and Policy*, 12th ed. (Upper Saddle River, NJ: Prentice Hall, 2002).

The company applies the same WACC to all its motels, since it is assumed that each motel faces similar risks.

Total assets minus current liabilities (see Exhibit 22-2) can also be computed as

$$\text{Total assets} - \text{Current liabilities} = \text{Long-term assets} + (\text{Current assets} - \text{Current liabilities})$$
$$= \text{Long-term assets} + \text{Working capital}$$

After-tax motel operating income is

$$\frac{\text{Motel operating}}{\text{income}} \times (1 - \text{Tax rate}) = \frac{\text{Motel operating}}{\text{income}} \times (1 - 0.30) = \frac{\text{Motel operating}}{\text{income}} \times 0.70$$

EVA calculations for Hospitality Inns are as follows:

Motel	After-Tax Operating Income	−	Weighted-Average Cost of Capital	×	Total Assets	−	Current Liabilities	=	EVA
Saskatoon	($240,000 × 0.70)	−	[10.2%	×	($1,000,000	−	$ 50,000)]	=	$71,100
Brandon	($300,000 × 0.70)	−	[10.2%	×	($2,000,000	−	$150,000)]	=	$21,300
Hull	($510,000 × 0.70)	−	[10.2%	×	($3,000,000	−	$300,000)]	=	$81,600

The Hull motel has the highest EVA. EVA, like residual income, charges managers for the cost of their investments in long-term assets and working capital. Value is created only if after-tax operating income exceeds the cost of investing the capital.

To improve EVA, managers have three basic choices:

■ Earn *more operating income* using the same amount of capital.

■ Earn the same amount of operating income using *less capital*.

■ Invest in a *different project* that has a better return.

Return on Sales

The income-to-revenue (sales) ratio—often called **return on sales (ROS)** or profit margin—is a frequently used financial performance measure. ROS is one component of ROI in the DuPont method of profitability analysis. To calculate the ROS of each of Hospitality's motels, we use operating income divided by revenues. The ROS for each motel is:

Motel	Operating Income	÷	Revenues	=	ROS
Saskatoon	$240,000	÷	$1,200,000	=	20.00%
Brandon	300,000	÷	1,400,000	=	21.43
Hull	510,000	÷	3,185,000	=	16.01

The Brandon motel has the highest ROS, whereas its performance is rated worse than the other motels using performance measures such as ROI, RI, and EVA. However, similar to the other measurement methods discussed, there are problems with assessing management's performance solely based on this tool. That is because subunit managers who are assessed primarily by ROS may be tempted to add assets to their unit that will help to generate more sales (e.g., increased lines of credit for account receivable customers, increased inventory selection, etc.). This would increase their sales, which would, all other things being equal, increase their ROS. This is known as the "overinvestment" problem. Some firms address this shortcoming by adding a shadow charge for financing receivables and inventories or by instituting specific policies that limit the levels of receivables and inventories.

That being said, in markets where revenue growth is limited, ROS may be the most meaningful indicator of a subunit's performance.

Comparing Performance Measures

The following table summarizes the performance and ranking of each motel under each of the four performance measures:

Motel	ROI	Rank	Residual Income	Rank	EVA	Rank	ROS	Rank
Saskatoon	24%	1	$120,000	2	$71,100	2	20.00%	2
Brandon	15	3	60,000	3	21,300	3	21.43	1
Hull	17	2	150,000	1	81,600	1	16.01	3

Note that the methods yield different types of metrics (measurements) and three unique rankings for the hotels (in our example, RI and EVA had the same rankings because essentially the same income and investment figures were used for both calculations). The basic pros and cons of each method can be summarized as follows.

Method	Pros	Cons
Return on investment	■ Can be calculated with readily available financial statement information ■ Widely used and accepted as an internal and external evaluation tool	■ Subject to manipulation depending on which numbers are chosen for "income" and "investment" ■ May cause "underinvestment" ■ May lead managers to reject projects that are below current ROI levels for the firm, but should still be accepted because they are above the cost of capital ■ Ignores cost of capital
Residual income	■ Takes cost of capital into account ■ Focuses on absolute (dollar amount) returns instead of relative (percentage amount) returns ■ More likely to lead to unit goal congruence with overall corporate objectives	■ Subject to manipulation depending on which numbers are chosen for "income" and "investment" ■ Cost of capital needs to be available/calculated ■ More complex than ROI or ROS
Economic value added	■ Takes cost of capital into account ■ Focuses on absolute (dollar amount) returns instead of relative (percentage amount) returns ■ Adjusts financial accounting data, which may better reflect the performance of knowledge-based firms	■ Subject to manipulation depending on what "adjustments" are made to the accrual accounting figures ■ Cost of capital needs to be available/calculated ■ Most complex and least understood method ■ Not widely used for comparison purposes
Return on sales	■ Can be calculated with readily available financial statement information ■ Easy to understand ■ May be appropriate in situations where sales growth is constrained ■ Focuses on how well costs are managed compared to sales	■ Ignores the cost of capital ■ Ignores the amount of assets needed to earn the return ■ May cause managers to "overinvest" in assets

None of the methods discussed is uniquely superior to the others because each evaluates a different aspect of performance:

- ROS measures how effectively costs are managed.
- ROI measures which investment yields the highest return (measured as a percentage).
- RI and EVA measure how much "extra" return (in dollar amounts) is generated after the cost of capital is considered.
- EVA takes into account the limitations that financial accounting standards impose on the calculation of income and measurement of assets.

Generally, most companies use multiple financial measures to evaluate performance.

Selecting the Time Horizon

Another consideration in designing accounting-based performance measures is choosing the time horizon of the measures. In our example, the ROI, RI, EVA, and ROS calculations represent the results for a single time period, a year. Managers could take actions that cause short-run increases in these measures but are in conflict with the long-run interests of the organization. For example, managers could curtail R&D and plant maintenance in the last three months of a fiscal year as a way to achieve a target level of annual operating income. For this reason, many companies evaluate subunits on the basis of ROI, RI, EVA, and ROS over multiple years.

The time horizon concern can also be addressed through the use of other management performance measurement systems (such as the BSC) that include forward-looking, nonfinancial measures in addition to more traditional lagging (backward-looking) measures such as ROI and RI.

Another reason for evaluating subunits over a multiyear time horizon is that the benefits of actions taken in the current period may not show up in short-run performance measures such as the current year's ROI or RI. For example, the investment in a new motel may adversely affect ROI and RI in the short-run but benefit ROIs and RIs in the long-run.

A multiyear analysis highlights another advantage of the RI measure. The net present value of all the cash flows over the life of an investment equals the net present value of RIs.[13] This means that if managers use net present value analysis to make investment-decisions, then they could use multiyear RI to evaluate if managers' performances achieve the original forecasts.

Another way that companies motivate managers to take a long-run perspective is by compensating them on changes in the market price of the company's shares (in addition to using multiyear accounting-based performance measures). Why does this approach help to extend managers' time horizons? Because finance theory tells us that share prices rapidly incorporate the expected future period effects of current decisions.

Defining "Investment"

We use the different definitions of investment that companies use to illustrate the second phase of designing accounting-based performance measures. Definitions include the following:

- *Total assets available.* Includes all business assets, regardless of their particular purpose.

- *Total assets employed.* Defined as total assets available minus idle assets and minus assets purchased for future expansion. For example, if the Hull motel in Exhibit 22-2 has unused land set aside for potential expansion, the total assets employed by the motel would exclude the cost of that land.

- *Working capital (current assets minus current liabilities) plus long-term assets.* This definition excludes that portion of current assets financed by short-term creditors (which generally has zero financing cost associated with it).

---

[13] We are grateful to S. Reichelstein for pointing this out. To see this equivalence, suppose a $400,000 investment in the Brandon motel increases operating income by $70,000 per year as follows: Increase in operating cash flows of $150,000 each year for five years minus depreciation of $80,000 per year ($400,000 ÷ 5), assuming straight-line depreciation and zero terminal disposal price equals annual operating income of $70,000. Depreciation reduces the investment amount by $80,000 each year. Assuming a required rate of return of 12%, net present values of cash flows and residual incomes are as follows:

Year	0	1	2	3	4	5	Net Present Value
(1) Cash flow	−$400,000	$150,000	$150,000	$150,000	$150,000	$150,000	
(2) Present value of $1 discounted at 12%	1	0.89286	0.79719	0.71178	0.63552	0.56743	
(3) Present value: (1) × (2)	−$400,000	$133,929	$119,578	$106,767	$ 95,328	$ 85,115	$140,717
(4) Operating income		$ 70,000	$ 70,000	$ 70,000	$ 70,000	$ 70,000	
(5) Assets at start of year		$400,000	$320,000	$240,000	$160,000	$ 80,000	
(6) Capital charge: (5) × 12%		$ 48,000	$ 38,400	$ 28,800	$ 19,200	$ 9,600	
(7) Residual income: (4) − (6)		$ 22,000	$ 31,600	$ 41,200	$ 50,800	$ 60,400	
(8) Present value of RI: (7) × (2)		$ 19,643	$ 25,191	$ 29,325	$ 32,284	$ 34,273	$140,716

■ *Shareholders' equity.* Use of this definition for each individual motel in Exhibit 22-2 requires allocation of the long-term liabilities of Hospitality Inns to the three motels, which would then be deducted from the total assets of each motel.

Most companies that employ ROI, residual income, or EVA for performance measurement use either total assets available or working capital plus long-term assets as the definition of investment. However, when top management directs a division manager to carry extra assets, total assets *employed* can be more informative than total assets *available*. The most common rationale for using working capital plus long-term assets is that the division manager often influences decisions on the amount of short-term debt of the division.

Evaluating Performance Measurement Alternatives

Another issue that must be addressed when deciding which performance measure to use is the question of what accrual accounting measure is the best indicator of performance. When considering the investment component of the ROI, RI, and EVA metrics, should historic cost or current costs be used? Significant differences result, depending on which is chosen. The following example uses the Hospitality Inns data to demonstrate the impact of this choice.

▶ **LO 2**

Evaluate current-cost and historical-cost asset measurement methods.

Current Cost

Current cost is the cost of purchasing an asset today identical to the one currently held. It is the cost of purchasing the services provided by that asset if an identical asset cannot currently be purchased. Of course, measuring assets at current costs will result in different ROIs compared to the ROIs calculated based on historical costs.

We illustrate the current-cost ROI calculations using the Hospitality Inns example (see Exhibit 22-2) and then compare current- and historical-cost-based ROIs. Assume the following information about the long-term assets of each motel:

	Saskatoon	Brandon	Hull
Age of facility (at end of 2018)	8 years	4 years	2 years
Gross book value of long-term assets	$1,400,000	$2,100,000	$2,800,000
Accumulated depreciation (straight-line)	800,000	600,000	400,000
Net book value (at end of 2018)	$ 600,000	$1,500,000	$2,400,000
Depreciation expense for 2018	$ 100,000	$ 150,000	$ 200,000

Hospitality Inns assumes a 14-year estimated useful life, assumes no terminal disposal price for the physical facilities, and calculates depreciation on a straight-line basis.

An index of construction costs for the eight-year period that Hospitality Inns has been operating (year 0 = 100) is as follows:

Year	1	2	3	4	5	6	7	8
Construction cost index	110	122	136	144	152	160	174	180

Earlier in this chapter we computed an ROI of 24% for Saskatoon, 15% for Brandon, and 17% for Hull. One possible explanation for the high ROI of Saskatoon is that this motel's long-term assets are expressed in terms of year 0 construction price levels (eight years ago) and that the long-term assets for the Brandon and Hull motels are expressed in terms of the higher, more recent construction price levels, which depress ROIs for these motels.

Exhibit 22-3 illustrates a step-by-step approach for incorporating current-cost estimates for long-term assets and depreciation into the ROI calculation. The aim is to approximate what it would cost today to obtain assets that would produce the same expected operating income as the subunits currently earn. (Similar adjustments to represent current costs of capital employed and depreciation can also be made in the residual

Exhibit 22-3 ROI for Hospitality Inns: Computed Using Current-Cost Estimates as of the End of Year 8 for Depreciation and Long-Term Assets

Step 1: Restate long-term assets from gross book value at historical cost to gross book value at current cost as of the end of 2018:

Motel	Gross Book Value of Long-Term Assets at Historical Cost	×	Construction Cost Index in 2018	÷	Construction Cost Index in Construction Year	=	Gross Book Value of Long-Term Assets at Current Cost at End of 2018
Saskatoon	$1,400,000	×	(180	÷	100)	=	$2,520,000
Brandon	2,100,000	×	(180	÷	144)	=	2,625,000
Hull	2,800,000	×	(180	÷	160)	=	3,150,000

Step 2: Derive net book value of long-term assets at current cost as of the end of 2018. (Assume estimated useful life of each motel is 14 years.)

Motel	Gross Book Value of Long-Term Assets at Current Cost at End of 2018	×	Estimated Remaining Useful Life	÷	Estimated Total Useful Life	=	Net Book Value of Long-Term Assets at Current Cost at End of 2018
Saskatoon	$2,520,000	×	(6	÷	14)	=	$1,080,000
Brandon	2,625,000	×	(10	÷	14)	=	1,875,000
Hull	3,150,000	×	(12	÷	14)	=	2,700,000

Step 3: Calculate the current cost of total assets at the end of year 8. (Assume the current assets of each motel are expressed in year 8 dollars.)

Motel	Current Assets at End of 2018 (from Exhibit 22-2)	+	Long-Term Assets Derived in Step 2 (above)	=	Current Cost of Total Assets at End of 2018
Saskatoon	$400,000	+	$1,080,000	=	$1,480,000
Brandon	500,000	+	1,875,000	=	2,375,000
Hull	600,000	+	2,700,000	=	3,300,000

Step 4: Calculate current-cost depreciation expense in 2018 dollars.

Motel	Gross Book Value of Long-Term Assets at Current Cost at End of 2018	÷	Estimated Total Useful Life	=	Current Cost of Depreciation Expense in 2018 Dollars
Saskatoon	$2,520,000	÷	14	=	$180,000
Brandon	2,625,000	÷	14	=	187,500
Hull	3,150,000	÷	14	=	225,000

Step 5: Calculate year 8 operating income using year 8 current cost depreciation.

Motel	Historical Cost Operating Income	−	Current Cost of Depreciation Expense in 2018 Dollars	−	Historical Cost Depreciation Expense	=	Operating Income for 2018 Using Current Cost Depreciation Expense in 2018 Dollars
Saskatoon	$240,000	−	($180,000	−	$100,000)	=	$160,000
Brandon	300,000	−	(187,500	−	150,000)	=	262,500
Hull	510,000	−	(225,000	−	200,000)	=	485,000

Step 6: Calculate ROI using current cost estimates for long-term assets and depreciation expense.

Motel	Operating Income for 2018 Using Current Cost Depreciation Expense in 2018 Dollars	÷	Current Cost of Total Assets at End of 2018	=	ROI Using Current Cost Estimate
Saskatoon	$160,000	÷	$1,480,000	=	10.81%
Brandon	262,500	÷	2,375,000	=	11.05
Hull	485,000	÷	3,300,000	=	14.70

income and EVA calculations.) The current-cost adjustment dramatically reduces the ROI of the Saskatoon motel:

	Historical-Cost ROI	Current-Cost ROI
Saskatoon	24%	10.81%
Brandon	15	11.05
Hull	17	14.70

Adjusting for current costs removes the differences in the investment base caused solely by differences in construction price levels. Consequently, compared to historical-cost ROI, current-cost ROI is a better measure of the current economic returns from the investment. For example, current-cost ROI indicates that taking into account current construction price levels, investing in a new motel in Saskatoon will result in an ROI closer to 10.8% than to 24%. If Hospitality Inns were to invest in a new motel today, investing in one like the Hull motel offers the best ROI.

A drawback of the current-cost method is that obtaining current-cost estimates for some assets can be difficult because the estimate requires a company to consider technological advances when determining the current cost of assets needed to earn today's operating income.[14]

Long-Term Assets: Gross or Net Book Value?

Because historical-cost investment measures are used often in practice, there has been much discussion about the relative merits of using gross book value (original cost) or net book value (original cost minus accumulated depreciation). Using the data in Exhibit 22-2, the ROI calculations using net book values and gross book values of plant and equipment are as follows:

	Operating Income (from Exhibit 22-2)	Net Book Value of Total Assets (from Exhibit 22-2)	Accumulated Depreciation	Gross Book Value of Total Assets	2018 ROI Using Net Book Value of Total Assets	2018 ROI Using Gross Book Value of Total Assets
	(1)	(2)	(3)	(4) = (2) + (3)	(5) = (1) ÷ (2)	(6) = (1) ÷ (4)
Saskatoon	$240,000	$1,000,000	$800,000	$1,800,000	24%	13.33%
Brandon	300,000	2,000,000	600,000	2,600,000	15	11.54
Hull	510,000	3,000,000	400,000	3,400,000	17	15.00

Using the gross book value, the ROI of the older Saskatoon motel (13.33%) is lower than that of the newer Hull motel (15%). Those who favour using gross book value claim that it enables more accurate comparisons across subunits. The proponents of using net book value as a base maintain that it is less confusing because (1) it is consistent with the total assets shown on the conventional balance sheet and (2) it is consistent with net income computations that include deductions for depreciation. Surveys of company practice report net book value to be the dominant asset measure used by companies in their internal performance evaluations. When using net book value, the declining denominator increases ROI as an asset ages, all other things being equal. A counter to that criticism of using net book value is that aging assets require more repairs and maintenance which will result in a lower operating income, thus offsetting the declining net asset base. Evaluating managers based on assets at net book value rather than gross book value increases incentives for retaining old property, plant, and equipment. This creates another "underinvestment" problem (in contrast to the potential "overinvestment" problem with ROS). Because older assets valued at net book value inflate ROI (particularly if investment is defined as net book value rather than gross book value), top management can compensate for this problem by setting higher target ROIs for divisions with older assets.

---

[14] When a specific cost index (such as the construction cost index) is not available, companies use a general index (such as the consumer price index) to approximate current costs.

Selecting Performance Goals

We next consider the selection of criteria or goals. Recall that book value accounting measures are often inadequate for evaluating economic returns on old investments and sometimes create disincentives for new expansion. Despite these problems, book value ROIs can be used to evaluate current performance by adjusting target ROIs. Consider our Hospitality Inns example. The key is to recognize that the motels were built at different times, which in turn means they were built at different levels of the construction cost index. Top management could adjust the targets accordingly, perhaps setting Saskatoon's ROI at 26%, Brandon's at 18%, and Hull's at 19%.

Nevertheless, the alternative of comparing actual to target performance is frequently overlooked in the literature. The budget, then, should be carefully negotiated with full knowledge of book value measurement bias. *The desirability of tailoring a budget to a particular subunit and a particular accounting system cannot be overemphasized.* For example, many problems of asset valuation and income measurement (whether based on book value or current cost) can be satisfactorily solved if top management gets everybody to focus on what is attainable in the forthcoming budget period—regardless of whether the financial measures are based on book value or some other measure, such as current costs.

Selecting the Level of Relevance—The Timing of Feedback

The final decision needed to create an effective performance measurement system is the timing of feedback. Timing of feedback depends largely on how critical the information is for the success of the organization, the specific level of management that is receiving the feedback, and the sophistication of the organization's information technology. For example, motel managers responsible for room sales will want information on the number of rooms sold each day on a daily or, at most, weekly basis. A large percentage of motel costs are fixed costs, so achieving high room sales and taking quick action to reverse any declining sales trends are critical to the financial success of each motel. Senior management, on the other hand, in their oversight role may look at information about room sales only on a monthly basis.

Performance Measurement in Multinational Companies

▶ LO 3

Analyze the technical difficulties that arise when comparing the performance of divisions operating in different countries.

Comparing the performance of divisions of a company operating in different countries creates additional difficulties:[15]

- The economic, legal, political, social, and cultural environments differ significantly across countries.

- Governments in some countries limit selling prices and impose controls on a company's products. For example, developing countries in Asia, Latin America, and Eastern Europe impose tariffs and duties to restrict the import of certain goods.

- Availability of materials and skilled labour—as well as costs of materials, labour, and infrastructure (power, transportation, and communication)—may also differ significantly across countries.

- Divisions operating in different countries keep score of their performance in different currencies. Issues of inflation and fluctuations in foreign currency exchange rates then become important.

The following discussion focuses on the last issue.

---

[15] M.Z. Iqbal, T. Melcher, and A. Elmallah, *International Accounting—A Global Perspective* (Cincinnati: Southwestern ITP, 2002).

Calculating the Foreign Division's ROI in the Foreign Currency

Suppose Hospitality Inns notices that many of its Canadian customers also travel to Cancún, Mexico. Hoping to capitalize on its great reputation and large number of repeat customers, it decides to invest in a Mexican property in Cancún. The investment consists mainly of the cost of the land, buildings, and furnishings. Internally, Hospitality Inns refers to the project as Hospitality Inn–Mexico–Cancún, or HIMC for short. The following hypothetical information is available:

- The exchange rate at the time of Hospitality's investment on December 31, 2017, is 3 pesos = $1.
- During 2018, the Mexican peso suffers a steady and steep decline in value.
- The exchange rate on December 31, 2018, is 6 pesos = $1.
- The average exchange rate during 2018 is [(3 + 6) ÷ 2] = 4.5 pesos = $1.
- The investment (total assets) in the Cancún motel = 9,000,000 pesos.
- The operating income of the Cancún motel in 2018 = 1,800,000 pesos.

What is the historical-cost-based ROI for the Cancún motel in 2018? Some specific questions arise. Should we calculate the ROI in pesos or in dollars? If we calculate the ROI in dollars, what exchange rate should we use? How does the ROI of Hospitality Inns–Mexico–Cancún (HIMC) compare with the ROI of Hospitality Inns-Hull (HIH), which is also a relatively new motel of roughly the same size?

$$\text{HIMCs ROI (calculated using pesos)} = \frac{\text{Operating income}}{\text{Total assets}} = \frac{1,800,000 \text{ pesos}}{9,000,000 \text{ pesos}} = 20\%$$

HIMC's ROI of 20% is higher than HIH's ROI of 17% (computed earlier in this chapter). Does this mean that HIMC outperformed HIH on the ROI criterion? Not necessarily, because HIMC operates in a very different economic environment than does HIH.

In this example, the peso has declined steeply in value relative to the dollar in 2018. Research studies show that the peso's decline is correlated with correspondingly higher inflation in Mexico relative to Canada.[16] A consequence of the higher inflation in Mexico is that HIMC will charge higher prices for its motel rooms, which will increase HIMC's operating income and lead to a higher ROI. Inflation clouds the real economic returns on an asset and makes ROI calculated on historical cost of assets unrealistically high, because had there been no inflation, HIMC's room rates and hence operating income would have been much lower. Differences in inflation rates between the two countries make a direct comparison of HIMC's peso-denominated ROI with HIH's dollar-denominated ROI misleading.

Calculating the Foreign Division's ROI in Canadian Dollars

One way to achieve a more meaningful comparison of historical-cost-based ROIs is to restate HIMC's performance in dollars. But what exchange rate(s) should be used to make the comparison meaningful? Assume operating income was earned evenly throughout 2018. We use the average exchange rate of 4.5 pesos = $1 to convert the operating income from pesos to dollars: 1,800,000 pesos ÷ 4.5 = $400,000. The effect of dividing the operating income in pesos by the higher pesos-to-dollars exchange rate is that any increase in operating income in pesos as a result of inflation is undone when converting back to dollars.

At what rate should we convert HIMC's total assets of 9,000,000 pesos? At the exchange rate prevailing when the assets were acquired on December 31, 2017, namely 3 pesos = $1, because HIMC's book value of assets is recorded at the December 31, 2017,

---

[16] W. Beaver and M. Wolfson, "Foreign Currency Translation Gains and Losses: What Effect Do They Have and What Do They Mean?" *Financial Analysts Journal* (March–April 1984); F.D.S. Choi, "Resolving the Inflation/Currency Translation Dilemma," *Management International Review*, Vol. 34, Special Issue, 1994; H. Louis, "The Value Relevance of the Foreign Translation Adjustment," *The Accounting Review* (October 2003).

cost and is not revalued as a result of inflation in Mexico in 2018. Since the book value of assets is unaffected by subsequent inflation, so should be the exchange rate used to convert it into dollars. Total assets would be converted to 9,000,000 pesos ÷ 3 = $3,000,000. Then,

$$\text{HIMCs ROI (calculated using dollars)} = \frac{\text{Operating income}}{\text{Total assets}} = \frac{\$400,000}{\$3,000,000} = 13.33\%$$

These adjustments make the historical-cost-based ROIs of the two motels comparable because they negate the effects of any differences in inflation rates between the two countries. HIMC's ROI of 13.33% is less than HIH's ROI of 17%.

Residual income calculated in pesos suffers from the same problems as ROI calculated using pesos. Instead, calculating HIMC's residual income in dollars adjusts for changes in exchange rates and facilitates comparisons with Hospitality's other motels:

$$\text{HIMC's residual income} = \$400,000 - (12\% \times \$3,000,000)$$
$$= \$400,000 - \$360,000$$
$$= \$40,000$$

This is also less than HIH's residual income of $150,000. In interpreting HIMC's and HIH's ROI and residual income, note that they are historical-cost-based calculations. They do, however, involve relatively new motels.

TRY IT! 22.1

Aviatto Inc. has sales of $1,318 million, an operating income of $492 million, and $683 million dollars in assets.

1. Compute the ROI.
2. Compute the residual income assuming a required return of 25%.

Levels of Analysis Differ Between Managers and Subunits[17]

The performance evaluation of a manager should be distinguished from the performance evaluation of an organization subunit, such as a division of a company. For example, historical-cost-based ROIs for a particular division can be used to evaluate a manager's performance relative to a budget or over time, even though historical-cost ROIs may be unsatisfactory for evaluating economic returns earned by the subunit. But using historical-cost ROIs to compare the performance of managers of different subunits can be misleading.

In the Hospitality Inns example, Hospitality Inns-Hull's (HIH's) ROI of 17% exceeds Hospitality Inns-Mexico-Cancún's (HIMC's) ROI of 13.33% after adjusting for the higher inflation in Mexico. The ROIs may give some indication of the economic returns from each motel but do not mean that the manager of HIH performed better than the manager of HIMC. The reason is that, among other factors, HIMC's ROI may have been adversely affected relative to HIH's ROI because of externalities beyond the HIMC manager's control, such as legal, political, and government regulations as well as economic conditions in Mexico.

Consider another example. Companies often put the most skillful division manager in charge of the weakest division in an attempt to change its fortunes. Such an effort may take years to bear fruit. Furthermore, the manager's efforts may result merely in bringing the division up to a minimum acceptable ROI. The division may continue to be a poor profit performer in comparison with other divisions, but it would be a mistake to conclude from the poor performance of the division that the manager is necessarily performing poorly.

What dictates the intensity of the incentives? That is, how large should the incentive component be relative to salary? A key question is: How well does the performance measure capture the manager's ability to influence the desired results? Measures of

---

[17] The presentations here draw (in part) on teaching notes prepared by S. Huddart, N. Melumad, and S. Reichelstein.

performance that are superior change significantly with the manager's performance and not very much with changes in factors that are beyond the manager's control. We presented the reason for using operating margin instead of either pretax or net margin when measuring ROI.

Superior performance measures motivate the manager but limit the manager's exposure to uncontrollable risk and hence reduce the cost of providing incentives to get the manager to accept the incentive program. When possible, owners use performance evaluation measures that are closely linked to managers' efforts. Managers are evaluated based on factors that they can affect, even if they are not completely controllable. For example, salespeople often earn commissions based on the amount of sales revenues they generate. Salespeople can affect the amount of sales they generate by working harder, but they cannot control other factors (such as the economy and competitors' products) that also affect the amount of their sales.

Continuing with our Hospitality Inns example, suppose that the chain is owned by Sally Fonda. Fonda, as the sole shareholder, has the challenge of designing a compensation package for each of her hotel managers. Roger Brett manages the Hospitality Inns-Saskatoon (HIS) motel. Suppose Brett has no authority to determine investments. Further, suppose revenue is determined largely by external factors such as the local economy. Brett's actions influence only costs. Using RI as a performance measure in these circumstances subjects Brett's bonus to excessive risk, because two components of the performance measure (investments and revenues) are unrelated to his actions. The management accountant might suggest that, to create stronger incentives, Fonda consider using a different performance measure for Brett—perhaps HIS's costs—that more closely captures Brett's effort. Note that in this case, RI may be a perfectly good measure of the economic viability of the HIS submit, but it is not a good measure of Brett's performance.

The salary component of compensation should be large when performance measures sensitive to a manager's effort are unavailable (as in the case of some corporate staff and government officials). This is not to say, however, that incentives are completely absent; promotions and salary increases do depend on some overall measure of performance, but the incentives are less direct. Employers give stronger incentives when superior measures of performance are available to them and when monitoring the employee's effort is very difficult (real estate agencies, for example, reward employees mainly on commissions on houses sold).

In evaluating Brett, Fonda could use measures from multiple perspectives of the BSC because nonfinancial measures on the BSC—employee satisfaction and the time taken for check-in, cleaning rooms, and providing room service—are more sensitive to Brett's actions. Financial measures such as RI are less sensitive to Brett's actions because they are affected by external factors such as local economic conditions that are beyond Brett's control.

Another reason for using nonfinancial measures in the BSC is that these measures follow Hospitality Inns's strategy and are drivers of future performance. Evaluating managers on these nonfinancial measures motivates them to take actions that will sustain long-run performance. Therefore, evaluating performance in all four perspectives of the BSC promotes both short- and long-run actions. Surveys show that division managers' compensation plans usually include a mix of salary, bonus, and long-term compensation tied to earnings and share price of the company. The goal is to balance division and companywide, as well as short-term and long-term, incentives.

If managers are evaluated on a single performance measure, they will treat other critical success factors as secondary to that single measure. For example, managers might curtail advertising and maintenance to increase the current year's ROI. This is why performance evaluation needs to be based on a variety of critical success factors such as those included in the BSC.

Benchmarks and Relative Performance Evaluation

Owners can also use benchmarks to evaluate performance. Benchmarks representing best practice may be available inside or outside the overall organization. In our Hospitality Inns example, benchmarks could be other similar motels, either within or outside the Hospitality Inns chain. Suppose Brett does have authority over revenues, costs, and investments.

In evaluating Brett's performance, Fonda would want to use as a benchmark a motel of a similar size that is influenced by the same uncontrollable factors—for example, location, demographic trends, and economic conditions—that affect HIS. *Differences* in performances of the two motels occur only because of differences in the two managers' performances, not because of random factors. Thus, benchmarking, also called *relative performance evaluation*, "filters out" the effects of the common noncontrollable factors.

Can the performance of two managers responsible for running similar operations *within* a company be benchmarked against one another? Yes, but one problem is that the use of these benchmarks may reduce incentives for these managers to help one another. That is, a manager's performance-evaluation measure improves either by doing a better job or by making the other manager look bad. Failing to work together as a team is, usually, not in the best interests of the organization as a whole. In this case, using external benchmarks for performance evaluation would probably lead to better goal congruence.

Executive Performance Measures and Compensation

► **LO 4**

Evaluate the behavioural effects of salaries and incentives in compensation arrangements.

The performance evaluation of managers and employees often affects their compensation. Compensation arrangements run the range from a flat salary with no direct performance-based bonus (as in the case of government officials) to rewards based only on performance (as in the case of employees of real estate agencies). Most often, however, a manager's total compensation includes some combination of salary and a performance-based bonus. An important consideration in designing compensation arrangements is the tradeoff between creating incentives and imposing risk.

People who become entrepreneurs (owners) are generally more risk-tolerant than those who decide to work for others (managers). The reason is that an entrepreneur has no guaranteed ROI. Entrepreneurs assume that, all other things being equal, their reward is linked to their effort—the harder they work, the higher the reward. What the entrepreneur receives is the residual after all contracted obligations have been paid.

Managers or employees, on the other hand, prefer the security of a salary and are willing to accept a lower but certain return for their hard work. Unfortunately, effort is no guarantee because uncontrollable factors also affect return. Whether or not compensation is well designed depends in large part on how well the performance measures reflect the manager's efforts. For example, Barrick Gold's shareholders complained when the recently appointed co-chair of the board, John Thornton, earned $17 million in 2012 while the company's shares plummeted 50%.

It is more cost-efficient for owners to bear risk than managers, because managers demand a premium (extra compensation) for bearing risk. For risk-averse managers, an incentive is required to take the same level of risk as would an entrepreneurial owner. The objective of many compensation plans is to provide managers with incentives to work hard while minimizing the risk placed on them. We will illustrate this tradeoff (creating incentives vs. imposing risks) in the context of our Hospitality Inns example.

Assume that Fonda (owner of the Hospitality Inns chain) uses RI to measure performance. To achieve good results, as measured by RI, Fonda would like Brett (manager of the Saskatoon inn) to control costs, provide prompt and courteous service, and reduce receivables. But even if Brett does all those things, good results are by no means guaranteed. HIS's RI is affected by many factors outside Fonda's and Brett's control, such as a recession in the Saskatoon economy, or weather that might negatively affect HIS. Alternatively, noncontrollable factors might have a positive influence on HIS's RI. These are known as windfull gains or losses. Either way, noncontrollable factors make HIS's profitability uncertain and risky.

Fonda (the owner) is an entrepreneur who does not mind bearing risk, but Brett does not like being subject to risk; that is why he chose to be an employee rather than an owner. One way of insuring Brett against risk is to pay Brett a flat salary, regardless of the actual amount of residual income attained. All the risk would then be borne by Fonda. There is a problem here, however, because the effort that Brett puts in is difficult to monitor.

The absence of performance-based compensation provides Brett with no incentive to work harder or undertake any extra physical or mental effort beyond the minimum necessary to retain his job or to uphold his own personal values.

Moral hazard[18] describes contexts in which, once risk is shared, the individual fails to make as much effort to avoid harm as when risk is not shared. Effort is generally not observable in employees in management because it is primarily mental, not physical. Assume that managers prefer to exert less effort (or report biased measures of effort) than the effort (or unbiased measures) desired by the owner because the employee's effort (or reported measures) cannot be accurately monitored and enforced. In employment contracting with managers, what the owner wants is performance measures highly correlated with effort. The finer the measures, the more completely will variation in those measures explain variation in effort.

Paying no salary and rewarding Brett *only* on the basis of some performance measure—RI, in our example—raises different concerns. Brett would now be motivated to strive to increase RI because his rewards would increase with increases in RI. But compensating Brett on RI also subjects Brett to risk because HIS's RI depends not only on Brett's effort, but also on external factors such as inflation or other changes in the economy over which Brett has no control. More succinctly, Brett's management effort may be overwhelmed by good or bad luck associated with these changes in externalities.

To compensate Brett, who is risk averse, for taking on the consequences of uncontrollable risk, Fonda must pay Brett some extra compensation within the structure of the RI-based arrangement. Thus, using performance-based incentives will cost Fonda more money, *on average*, than paying Brett a flat salary. "On average" is appropriate because Fonda's compensation payment to Brett will vary with RI outcomes. The motivation for having some salary and some performance-based bonus in compensation arrangements is to balance the benefits of incentives against the extra costs of imposing uncontrollable risk on the manager.

Fonda could also consider using a BSC approach. With this approach, Brett would be compensated for satisfactory performance measured across multiple criteria, in contrast to the single measurement of only using RI. This means that if, due to an uncontrollable factor, performance decreases according to one measure it may increase on another and Brett will be spreading his risk of financial loss over several measures. As a manager, moreover, Brett performs many business functions in the value chain. While the functions may be interdependent, if he excels at them all he should be rewarded more than another manager who excels at only a few. From Fonda's perspective, greater reliance can be placed on a performance report where several measures converge to report the same level of performance.

Team-Based Compensation Arrangements

Many manufacturing, marketing, and design problems require employees with multiple skills, experiences, and judgments to pool their talents. In these situations, a team of employees achieves better results than employees acting on their own.[19]

Team-based incentive compensation encourages employees to work together to achieve common goals. This approach encourages cooperation among interdependent subunits. Individual-based incentive compensation rewards employees for their own performance, consistent with responsibility accounting. This approach encourages competition to excel and be the best. A mix of both types of incentives encourages employees to maximize their own performance while working together in the best interest of the company as a whole.

Whether team-based compensation is desirable depends, to a great extent, on the culture and management style of a particular organization. One criticism of teams is that

---

[18] The term *moral hazard* originated in insurance contracts to represent situations in which insurance coverage, which relieves the owner of assets of part of the risks of loss and/or damage, caused insured parties to take less care of their properties than they would if they bore the full costs of replacement and/or repair. One response to moral hazard in insurance contracts is the system of deductibles (that is, the insured pays for damages up to a specified amount). Therefore, in the event that the insured item is damaged, the owner still bears some of the cost burden. Insurance companies believe that this shared risk makes the owner of the asset more careful, or risk-averse, with the insured asset.

[19] J. Katzenbach and D. Smith, *The Wisdom of Teams* (Boston: The Harvard Business School Press, 1993).

individual incentives to excel are dampened, harming overall performance. This problem becomes more acute when effort cannot be monitored. Unproductive team members contribute less than the effort expected (shirk); nevertheless, they share equally in the team's reward. Shirking is a pervasive problem and you have probably experienced shirking at least once when you have worked with teams of students to obtain shared marks for output.

Executive Compensation Arrangements

The principles of performance evaluation also apply to executive compensation plans at the total-organization level. Executive compensation plans are typically based on both financial and nonfinancial performance measures and consist of a mix of (1) base salary; (2) annual incentives (for example, cash bonus based on yearly net income); (3) long-term incentives (for example, stock options based on achieving a specified return or share price by the end of a five-year period); and (4) fringe benefits (for example, life insurance, an office with a view, or a personal secretary).[20] Designers of executive compensation plans emphasize three factors: achievement of organizational goals, administrative ease, and the likelihood that affected managers will perceive the plan as fair.

Well-designed plans use a compensation mix that carefully balances risk and short- and long-term incentives. For example, evaluating performance on the basis of annual ROI would sharpen an executive's short-term focus. Using a rolling-average ROI and stock option plans over, say, five years would motivate the executive to take a long-term view as well. Stock options give executives and employees the right to buy company shares at a specified price (called the exercise price).

Often stock option plans have a "vesting" period, which is a period of time before the executive gains control over the option. Suppose that on September 16, 2018, Canadian Pacific Railway (CPR) granted its CEO (as part of her compensation package) the option to buy 200,000 shares of the company at an *exercise price* of $175 for a five-year period, any time *after* September 16, 2019 (vesting date). Therefore, 2018 to 2019 represents a four-year vesting period. The option would allow the CEO to buy company shares (directly from the company) at the exercise price, regardless of the market price of the share at that time (i.e., any time after September 16, 2019). Obviously, the executive would want the (future) market price of the share to be greater than the exercise price, thus making a capital gain possible. The compensation theory is that the executive will make decisions in the current period (when she earns the options by meeting certain performance targets) and in future periods that will cause the company's shares to increase to a price above the exercise price.

Continuing with our CPR example, remember that the exercise price of the options was $175 per share. The market price of a share on September 16, 2018 (the granting date), was $150. Thus, when the option was granted, it wasn't "in the money" because the exercise price was more than the current market price. If, over the next four years the company's share price increases to, say, $200, the option would be "in the money" on September 16, 2019 (the vesting date), and the executive would probably exercise the option to buy the shares at the $175 price. If the executive then turned around and sold the shares, she would make a capital gain of $5 million (= ($200 − $175) × 200,000 shares). Alternatively, given that the options (in this situation) are good for a five-year period after September 16, 2019, the executive might decide to wait to see if share prices might go even higher before exercising the option. If, on the other hand, the company's performance over the four-year vesting period is poor, the share price might never reach the $200 exercise price, in which case the executive would probably not use the options (Why buy a share using the $200 option if you can buy a share for less at the market price?), in which case, this part of the executive's compensation package is worth nothing.

There are many different permutations and combinations as to how stock option plans can be structured, but this example gives a basic outline of how they can work to motivate senior managers to consider the longer-term consequences of their current decisions.

---

[20] *The Wall Street Journal*/Mercer Human Resource Consulting, *2003 CEO Compensation Survey and Trends* (May, 2004).

The financial accounting treatment for options and the recognition and timing of their expense (to the firm) is dealt with in a variety of fashions, depending on the accounting standards being followed (e.g., U.S. GAAP, IFRS, etc.) and the specifics of the situation. Most intermediate financial accounting textbooks cover this topic in some detail.

Strategy and Levers of Control[21]

Given the management accounting focus of this text, this chapter has emphasized the role of quantitative financial and nonfinancial performance evaluation measures that companies use to implement their strategies. These measures—such as ROI, RI, EVA, ROS, customer satisfaction, and employee satisfaction—monitor critical performance factors that help managers gauge progress toward attaining the company's strategic goals. Because these measures help diagnose whether a company is performing to expectations, they are collectively called **diagnostic control systems**.

► **LO 5**

Apply strategic concepts to analyze the four levers of control, and evaluate their usefulness.

Companies motivate managers to achieve these goals by holding managers accountable for and by rewarding them for meeting these goals. Recently, however, it has become clear that sometimes one consequence of the pressure to perform is that managers materially misstate financial measures in order to obscure actual performance (e.g., Enron, Nortel, Parmalat, WorldCom). This pressure to perform (as measured by the diagnostic control system) can be balanced by using the other "levers of control" available to the firm. In total, there are four control levers:

- Diagnostic control system
- Boundary system
- Belief system
- Interactive control system

Boundary systems describe standards of behaviour and codes of conduct expected of all employees, especially actions that are off-limits. Ethical behaviour on the part of managers is paramount. In particular, numbers that subunit managers report should be free of overstated assets, understated liabilities, fictitious revenues, and understated costs.

The broad scope of Canadian legislation on corporate governance includes the requirement that the CEO accept full responsibility for any material misstatement of financial information. Under Sarbanes-Oxley, companies must publish their codes of ethics and conduct as part of the material audited for their annual report. Regulations are one set of boundary systems that mandate specific actions.

Belief systems articulate the mission, purpose, and core values of a company. They describe the accepted norms and patterns of behaviour expected of all managers and employees with respect to each other, shareholders, customers, and communities. A great example of one company's approach to describing its belief system is Johnson & Johnson's credo,[22] which specifically mentions the follow groups:

- Doctors, nurses and patients [J&J's customers]
- Employees
- Communities where J&J operates and the world community
- Stockholders

Johnson & Johnson's credo is intended to inspire managers and employees to do their best. Values and culture generate organizational commitment, pride, and belonging and are an important source of **intrinsic motivation**, which is the desire to achieve self-satisfaction from good performance regardless of external rewards such as bonuses or promotion.

Codes of business conduct signal appropriate and inappropriate individual behaviour. The following are specific excerpts from the Vancouver City Savings Credit Union

---

[21] For a more detailed discussion see R. Simons, "Control in an Age of Empowerment," *Harvard Business Review* (March–April 1995).

[22] Johnson & Johnson website, http://www.jnj.com/about-jnj/jnj-credo.

(Vancity) Group Code of Conduct for Employees, which all new employees must learn and sign (and re-sign annually):

■ You are required to be aware of the laws and regulations relating to the business that the Vancity Group conducts and specifically for the areas in which you work. No employee is ever expected to commit or condone an illegal act or instruct others to do so on behalf of Vancity Group.

■ You must ensure that your conduct in and outside of the workplace does not tarnish or negatively impact Vancity's reputation in the community.

■ Unethical business solicitation and/or acceptance activity is forbidden. You cannot accept cash payments of any sort at any time.

■ You are expected to act in accordance with the Vancity Group Respect in the Workplace Policy. Any breach of this and related may result in disciplinary measures up to and including dismissal.[23]

Division managers often cite enormous pressure from top management "to make the budget" as excuses or rationalizations for not adhering to ethical accounting policies and procedures. A healthy amount of motivational pressure is desirable, as long as both the "tone from the top" and the codes of conduct communicate the absolute need for all managers to behave ethically at all times. Managers should train employees to behave ethically, and promptly and severely reprimand unethical conduct, regardless of the benefits that might accrue to the company from unethical actions.

Many organizations also set explicit boundaries precluding actions that harm the environment. Environmental violations (such as water and air pollution) carry heavy fines and are offences punishable by imprisonment under Canadian laws and those of other countries. But in many companies, environmental responsibilities extend beyond legal requirements. There are also many international indices of environmental performance, such as the Dow Jones Sustainability Index in the United States or Corporate Knights in Canada. Some companies, such as TransCanada Corporation (a Canadian natural gas transportation company) and Unilever Group (a US manufacturer of consumer products) believe that a high ranking in these indices is sufficiently important to positively affect share price, and they announce their rankings on the internet and in formal press releases.

Socially responsible companies, such as Tim Hortons, also report specific performance measures to affirm their commitment to human rights and fair pricing. Many existing sets of global principles, such as the **Sullivan Principles**, can be used to compare corporate performance in the area of social responsibility.

Interactive control systems are formal information systems that managers use to focus organization attention and learning on key strategic issues. An excessive focus on diagnostic control systems and critical performance variables can cause an organization to ignore emerging threats and opportunities—changes in technology, customer preferences, regulations, and industry competition that can undercut a business.

Interactive control systems track strategic uncertainties that businesses face, such as the emergence of online shopping in the case of traditional retailers like The Bay and Sears, airline deregulation in the case of Air Canada and WestJet, and the shift in customer preferences for mini- and microcomputers in the case of IBM. The result is ongoing discussion and debate about assumptions and action plans. New strategies emerge from the dialogue and debate surrounding the interactive process. Interactive control systems force busy managers to step back from the actions needed to manage the business today and to shift their focus forward to positioning the organization for the opportunities and threats of tomorrow.

Measuring and rewarding managers for achieving critical performance variables is an important driver of corporate performance. But these diagnostic control systems must be counterbalanced by the other levers of control—boundary systems, belief systems, and interactive control systems—to ensure that proper business ethics, inspirational values, and attention to future threats and opportunities are not sacrificed to achieve business results.

23 Excerpt from Vancity Group Code of Conduct for employees. Copyright © 2013. Used by permission of Vancity Group.

Concepts in Action—Governance

Courage—Boundaries and Beliefs

The managers of for-profit corporations face intense pressures. Not the least of these are the contractual requirements to achieve performance measures such as those specified in long-term debt covenants and compensation contracts and the more informal requirements in operating and capital budgets. Banks and bondholders are not charitable institutions, and the intent of covenants is to alert creditors of possible risk to their investment. These covenants are often based on ratios derived from accrual accounting such as times interest earned, operating cash flow, and debt to equity.

What can be the harm in, say, calling a supplier and asking for a few days' delay in sending an invoice to prevent reporting the additional expense in a quarterly statement of earnings if it avoids contravening a times interest earned ratio and gives the corporation another 90 days to recover? It would postpone recognizing the expense on the actual operating performance report as well and avoid a negative variance. If the cause of the shortfall is uncontrollable, surely the company's owners

and managers should not be penalized by a contract rigidity, especially if the only issue is one of timing.

This type of reasoning leads to earnings management, whereby managers use their discretion to bias both internal and external performance reports. The ethical problem is clear—it is the professional duty of accountants to present unbiased reports—but their managers, who may not be accountants, are not bound to the same ethical standard. The logical problem is also clear—if uncontrollable factors have caused the shortfall in revenue over expenses, how can managers be assured time will fix the problem? They cannot be sure, nor can accountants avoid their professional duty to act in the best interests of the public, not the corporate managers. Where boundary systems fail, professional belief systems can prevail.[a]

---

[a] For a full discussion of earnings management refer to Chapter 11 of W.R. Scott, Financial Accounting Theory 6th edition (Toronto: Prentice Hall, 2012).

Pulling It All Together—Problem for Self-Study

(Try to solve this problem before examining the solution that follows.)

Problem

Budgeted data of the baseball manufacturing division of Home Run Sports for the year-end, February 28, 2017, are as follows:

Current assets	$ 400,000
Long-term assets	600,000
Total assets	$ 1,000,000
Production output	200,000 baseballs
Target ROI (operating income ÷ total assets)	30%
Fixed costs	$ 400,000
Variable costs	$ 4 per baseball

1. Compute the minimum unit selling price necessary to achieve the 30% target ROI, assuming ROI is based on total assets. ◀ **Required**
2. Using the selling price from requirement 1, separate the target ROI into its two components using the DuPont method.
3. Pamela Stephenson, division manager, receives 5% of the residual income of the baseball manufacturing division as a bonus. Compute her bonus for the year-end, February 28, 2017, using the selling price from requirement 1. Home Run Sports uses a 12% required rate of return on total division assets when computing division residual income.

④ 4. What behavioural issues arise from compensation contracts based on a single performance measure?

⑤ 5. If Pamela recommends an investment in new equipment, and for reasons beyond her control revenue is not realized but she has the opportunity to postpone recognition of expenses until the next reporting period, what levers of control can reduce the likelihood she will do so?

Solution

1.　　　Target operating income = 30% of $1,000,000

　　　　　　　= $300,000

Let P = Selling price

Sales − Variable costs − Fixed-costs = Operating income

$200,000P − (200,000 \times \$4) − \$400,000 = \$300,000$

$200,000P = \$300,000 + \$800,000 + \$400,000 = \$1,500,000$

$P = \$7.50$

Proof:		
	Sales, 200,000 × $7.50	$1,500,000
	Variable costs, 200,000 × $4	800,000
	Contribution margin	700,000
	Fixed costs	400,000
	Operating income	$ 300,000

2.　　$\dfrac{\text{Revenues}}{\text{Investment}} \times \dfrac{\text{Income}}{\text{Revenues}} = \dfrac{\text{Income}}{\text{Investment}}$

　　$\dfrac{\$1,500,000}{\$1,000,000} \times \dfrac{\$300,000}{\$1,500,000} = \dfrac{\$300,000}{\$1,000,000}$

　　　　1.5　×　0.2　=　0.30 or 30%

3. Residual income = Operating income − Required return on investment

　　　= $300,000 − (0.12 × $1,000,000)

　　　= $300,000 − $120,000

　　　= $180,000

Stephenson's bonus is $9,000 (5% of $180,000).

4. This bonus is a cash bonus based on short-term operations. Should Pamela have the opportunity to invest in more efficient equipment, the investment will reduce ROI in the short term in two ways. First, the operating costs will increase before the revenues are realized because there is a lag between production and sales. Operating income will decrease and it is possible revenue will also decrease. Investment will increase, and in combination with reduced revenue and income it is unlikely that the 30% ROI will be achieved. If Pamela cares about her bonus, she will not invest.

5. If Pamela is a professional accountant, the belief system embodied in the professional ethical code is one lever of control to constrain the likelihood she will manage earnings. If she is not, then a public statement of the corporate code of ethics, its core values, and the tone at the top from examples set by top management, can also constrain her.

Decision Points

The following question-and-answer format summarizes the chapter's learning objectives. Each point presents a key question, and the guidelines are the answer to that question.

Learning Objectives	Guidelines
1. What financial and nonfinancial measures do companies use to evaluate performance?	Financial measures such as ROI, RI, and EVA measure aspects of both manager performance and organization-subunit performance. In many cases, financial measures are supplemented with nonfinancial measures of performance, such as customer satisfaction ratings, number of defects, and productivity.
2. What is the current cost of an asset?	The current cost of an asset is the cost now of purchasing an asset identical to the one currently held. Historical-cost measurement methods consider the original cost of the asset net of accumulated depreciation.
3. What difficulties arise when comparing the performance of divisions in different countries?	Comparing the performance of divisions operating in different countries is difficult because of legal, political, social, economic, and currency differences. ROI calculations for subunits operating in different countries need to be adjusted for differences in inflation between the two countries and changes in exchange rates.
4. How do salaries and incentives work together in compensation arrangements?	Organizations create incentives by rewarding managers on the basis of performance. But managers may face risks because random factors beyond the managers' control may also affect performance. Owners choose a mix of salary and incentive compensation to trade off the incentive benefit against the cost of imposing risk.
5. What are the levers of control, and why does a company need to implement them?	The four levers of control are diagnostic control systems, boundary systems, belief systems, and interactive control systems. Implementing the four levers of control helps a company simultaneously strive for performance, behave ethically, inspire employees, and respond to strategic threats and opportunities.

Terms to Learn

This chapter and the Glossary at the end of the book contain definitions of the following important terms:

belief systems (**p. 917**)
Bill 198 (C-SOX) (**p. 895**)
boundary systems (**p. 917**)
current cost (**p. 907**)
diagnostic control systems (**p. 917**)
economic value added (EVA) (**p. 903**)
imputed cost (**p. 901**)

interactive control systems (**p. 918**)
intrinsic motivation (**p. 917**)
malus (**p. 896**)
moral hazard (**p. 915**)
residual income (RI) (**p. 901**)
return on investment (ROI) (**p. 899**)
return on sales (ROS) (**p. 904**)

Sarbanes-Oxley Act (SOX) (**p. 895**)
say on pay (**p. 895**)
Sullivan Principles (**p. 918**)
weighted-average cost of capital (WACC) (**p. 901**)

Assignment Material

MyLab Accounting Make the grade with MyLab Accounting: The Short-Answer Questions, Exercises, and Problems marked with a ⊕ can be found on MyLab Accounting. You can practise them as often as you want, and most feature step-by-step guided instructions to help you find the right answer.

Short-Answer Questions

22-1 Give two examples of financial performance measures and two examples of nonfinancial performance measures.

22-2 What are the six steps in designing an accounting-based performance measure?

22-3 What factors affecting ROI does the DuPont method highlight?

22-4 "Residual income is not identical to ROI, although both measures incorporate income and investment into their computations." Do you agree? Explain.

22-5 Describe economic value added.

22-6 Give three definitions of investment used in practice when computing ROI.

22-7 Distinguish among measuring assets based on present value, current cost, and historical cost.

22-8 What special problems arise when evaluating performance in multinational companies?

22-9 Why is it important to distinguish between the performance of a manager and the performance of the organization subunit for which the manager is responsible? Give examples.

22-10 Describe moral hazard.

22-11 Explain the management accountant's role in helping organizations design stronger incentive systems for their employees.

22-12 Explain the role of benchmarking in evaluating managers.

22-13 Explain the incentive problems that can arise when employees have to perform multiple tasks as part of their jobs.

22-14 Describe each of the levers of control and their interrelation with strategy.

Exercises

22-15 Terminology. A number of terms are listed below:

belief systems	boundary systems
economic value added (EVA)	imputed cost of investment
interactivity	intrinsic motivation
malus	return on investment (ROI)
say on pay	social responsibility
weighted-average cost of capital (WACC)	

Required

Select the terms from the above list to complete the following sentences.

Governance, or the management stewardship of assets management does not own, according to laws and regulations is more closely scrutinized than before. Legal reform in the United States now mandates a shareholder vote on any executive compensation packages, referred to as a _____ ___ ___. While we are very familiar with executive bonus, a new clawback of previous compensation, or a _____, is becoming a feature of compensation. One important performance measure that could determine a bonus or malus is the accounting _____ __ _____ (___), calculated by dividing the net income by the investment made. Another measure is the RRR, also called the _____ ___ ___ _____, which represents a return forgone from tying up cash in existing investments. A third measure is the _____ _____ _____ (___), which is calculated by subtracting the total assets minus current liabilities multiplied by the _____ _____ ___ __ _____ (___) from the after-tax operating income. But executive performance is not the only factor or even the most important factor affecting corporate profitability, excellent governance, and corporate _____ _____. Good management control systems will separate the effects of good luck from good management on performance. Additional considerations when designing a good management control system include _____ _____, _____ _____, _____ _____, and _____.

2. Revenue company C, $ 10,000,000

22-16 ROI, comparisons of three companies. ROI is often expressed as follows:

$$\frac{\text{Income}}{\text{Investment}} = \frac{\text{Income}}{\text{Revenue}} \times \frac{\text{Revenue}}{\text{Investment}}$$

Required

1. What advantages are there in the breakdown of the computation into two separate components?
2. Fill in the following blanks:

	Companies in Same Industry		
	A	**B**	**C**
Revenue	$1,000,000	$500,000	?
Income	$ 100,000	$ 50,000	?
Investment	$ 500,000	?	$5,000,000
Income as a percentage of revenue	?	?	0.5%
Investment turnover	?	?	2
ROI	?	1%	?

After filling in the blanks, comment on the relative performance of these companies as thoroughly as the data permit.

🌐 **22-17 Analysis of return on invested assets, comparison of two divisions, DuPont method.** Learning World Inc. has two divisions: Test Preparation and Language Arts. Results (in millions) for the past three years are partially displayed here:

◀ **LO 1**

	A	B	C	D	E	F	G
1		**Operating Income**	**Operating Revenue**	**Total Assets**	**Operating Income/ Operating Revenue**	**Operating Revenue/ Total Assets**	**Operating Income/ Total Assets**
2	Test Preparation Division						
3	2016	$ 680	$ 7,960	$1,920	?	?	?
4	2017	840	?	?	10%	?	42%
5	2018	1,160	?	?	11%	5	?
6	Language Arts Department						
7	2016	$ 620	$ 2,360	$1,280	?	?	?
8	2017	?	3,000	1,800	22%	?	?
9	2018	?	?	2,340	?	2	25%
10	Learning World Inc.						
11	2016	$1,300	$10,320	$3,200	?	?	?
12	2017	?	?	?	?	?	?
13	2018	?	?	?	?	?	?

Required

1. Complete the table by filling in the blanks.
2. Use the DuPont method of profitability analysis to explain changes in the operating-income-to-total-assets ratios over the 2016 through 2018 period for each division and for Learning World as a whole. Comment on the results.

🌐 **22-18 ROI and RI.** The Outdoor Sports Company produces a wide variety of outdoor sports equipment. Its newest division, Golf Technology, manufactures and sells a single product: AccuDriver, a golf club that uses global positioning satellite technology to improve the accuracy of golfers' shots. The demand for Accu-Driver is relatively insensitive to price changes. The following data are available for Golf Technology, which is an investment centre for Outdoor Sports:

◀ **LO 1**
1. ROI, 6.25%

Total annual fixed costs	$30,000,000
Variable cost per AccuDriver	$ 400
Number of AccuDrivers sold each year	150,000
Average operating assets invested in the division	$48,000,000

Required

1. Compute Golf Technology's ROI if the selling price of AccuDrivers is $720 per club.
2. If management requires an ROI of at least 25% from the division, what is the minimum selling price that the Golf Technology Division should charge per AccuDriver club?
3. Assume that Outdoor Sports judges the performance of its investment centres on the basis of RI rather than ROI. What is the minimum selling price that Golf Technology should charge per AccuDriver if the company's required rate of return is 20%?

LO 1 ▶
1. ROI, 16.0%

🌐 **22-19 ROI and RI with manufacturing costs.** Ohms Motor Company makes electric cars and has only two products, the Simplegreen and the Superiorgreen. To produce the Simplegreen, Ohms Motor employed assets of $13,500,000 at the beginning of the period and $13,400,000 of assets at the end of the period. Other costs to manufacture the Simplegreen include

Direct materials	$3,000 per unit
Setup	1,300 per setup-hour
Production	415 per machine-hour

General administration and selling costs total $7,340,000 for the period. In the current period, Ohms Motor produced 10,000 Simplegreen cars using 6,000 setup-hours and 175,200 machine-hours. Ohms Motor sold these cars for $12,000 each. The company bases its ROI on average invested capital.

Required

1. Assuming that Ohms Motor defines investment as average assets during the period, what is the ROI for the Simplegreen division?
2. Calculate the RI for the Simplegreen if Ohms Motor has a required rate of return of 12% on investments.

LO 4 ▶
1. ROI in Year 5 is 10.91%

🌐 **22-20 Goal incongruence and ROI.** McCall Corporation manufactures furniture in several divisions, including the patio furniture division. The manager of the patio furniture division plans to retire in two years. The manager receives a bonus based on the division's ROI, which is currently 10%.

One of the machines that the patio furniture division uses to manufacture the furniture is rather old, and the manager must decide whether to replace it. The new machine would cost $50,000 and would last 10 years. It would have no salvage value. The old machine is fully depreciated and has no trade-in value. McCall uses straight-line depreciation for all assets. The new machine, being new and more efficient, would save the company $8,000 per year in cash operating costs. The only difference between cash flow and net income is depreciation. The internal rate of return of the project is approximately 10%. McCall Corporation's weighted-average cost of capital is 4%. McCall is not subject to any income taxes.

Required

1. Should McCall Corporation replace the machine? Why or why not?
2. Assume that "investment" is defined as average net long-term assets after depreciation. Compute the project's ROI for each of its first five years. If the patio furniture manager is interested in maximizing his bonus, would he replace the machine before he retires? Why or why not?
3. What can McCall do to entice the manager to replace the machine before retiring?

LO 1 ▶
2. ROI end of t1, 7.02%

🌐 **22-21 Goal-incongruence and ROI.** YardScapes Corporation manufactures furniture in several divisions, including the Patio Furniture division. The manager of the Patio Furniture division plans to retire in two years. The manager receives a bonus based on the division's ROI, which is currently 11%.

One of the machines that the Patio Furniture division uses to manufacture the furniture is rather old, and the manager must decide whether to replace it. The new machine would cost $30,000 and would last 10 years. It would have no salvage value. The old machine is fully depreciated and has no trade-in value. YardScapes uses straight-line depreciation for all assets. The new machine, being new and more efficient, would save the company $5,000 per year in cash operating costs. The only difference between cash flow and net income is depreciation. The internal rate of return of the project is approximately 11%. YardScapes Corporation's weighted-average cost of capital is 6%. YardScapes is not subject to any income taxes.

Required

1. Should YardScapes Corporation replace the machine? Why or why not?
2. Assume that "investment" is defined as average net long-term assets after depreciation. Compute the project's ROI for each of Year 1 to Year 5. If the Patio Furniture manager is interested in maximizing his bonus, would he replace the machine before he retires? Why or why not?
3. What can YardScapes do to entice the manager to replace the machine before retiring?

LO 3 ▶
1. ROI New Car Division, 7.5%

🌐 **22-22 ROI, RI, EVA.** Civic Auto Company operates a New Car Division (that sells high-performance sports cars) and a Parts Division (that sells performance improvement parts for family cars). Some division financial measures for 2018 are as follows:

	A	B	C
1		**New Car Division**	**Performance Parts Division**
2	Total assets	$33,000,000	$28,500,000
3	Current liabilities	$ 6,600,000	$ 8,400,000
4	Operating income	$ 2,475,000	$ 2,565,000
5	Required rate of return	12%	12%

Required

1. Calculate ROI for each division using operating income as a measure of income and total assets as a measure of investment.
2. Calculate RI for each division using operating income as a measure of income and total assets minus current liabilities as a measure of investment.
3. William Abraham, the New Car Division manager, argues that the Performance Parts Division has "loaded up on a lot of short-term debt" to boost its RI. Calculate an alternative RI for each division that is not sensitive to the amount of short-term debt taken on by the Performance Parts Division. Comment on the result.
4. Civic Auto Company, whose tax rate is 40%, has two sources of funds: long-term debt with a market value of $18,000,000 at an interest rate of 10%, and equity capital with a market value of $12,000,000 and a cost of equity of 15%. Applying the same weighted-average cost of capital (WACC) to each division, calculate EVA for each division.
5. Use your preceding calculations to comment on the relative performance of each division.

⊕ **22-23 ROI, RI, measurement of assets.** Bailey Corporation recently announced a bonus plan to be awarded to the manager of the most profitable division. The three division managers are to choose whether ROI or RI will be used to measure profitability. In addition, they must decide whether investment will be measured using gross book value or net book value of assets. Bailey defines income as operating income and investment as total assets. The following information is available for the year just ended:

◀ **LO 2**
Radnor ROI using gross book value, 11.84%

Division	Gross Book Value of Assets	Accumulated Depreciation	Operating Income
Radnor	$1,200,000	$645,000	$142,050
Easttown	1,140,000	615,000	137,550
Marion	750,000	420,000	92,100

Bailey uses a required rate of return of 10% on investment to calculate RI.

Required

Each division manager has selected a method of bonus calculation that ranks his or her division number one. Identify the method for calculating profitability that each manager selected, supporting your answer with appropriate calculations. Comment on the strengths and weaknesses of the methods chosen by each manager.

⊕ **22-24 Multinational performance measurement, ROI, RI.** The Grandlund Corporation manufactures similar products in Canada and Norway. The Canadian and Norwegian operations are organized as decentralized divisions. The following information is available for 2019; ROI is calculated as operating income divided by total assets:

◀ **LO 3**
1. a. Operating income, $1,200,000

	Canadian Division	Norwegian Division
Operating income	?	8,100,000 kroner
Total assets	$8,000,000	52,500,000 kroner
ROI	15%	?

Both investments were made on December 31, 2018. The exchange rate at the time of Grandlund's investment in Norway on December 31, 2018, was 6 kroner = $1. During 2019, the Norwegian krone increased steadily in value so that the exchange rate on December 31, 2019, is 7 kroner = $1. The average exchange rate during 2019 is [(6 + 7)/2] = 6.5 kroner = $1.

Required

1. **a.** Calculate the Canadian division's operating income for 2019.
   b. Calculate the Norwegian division's ROI for 2019 in kroner.

2. Top management wants to know which division earned a better ROI in 2019. What would you tell them? Explain your answer.

3. Which division do you think had the better RI performance? Explain your answer. The required rate of return on investment (calculated in Canadian dollars) is 12%.

LO 2 ▷
1. ROI Clothing = 25%

🌐 **22-25 ROI, RI, EVA, and performance evaluation.** Lucy Manufacturing makes fashion products and competes on the basis of quality and leading-edge designs. The company has $3,200,000 invested in assets in its clothing manufacturing division. After-tax operating income from sales of clothing this year is $800,000. The cosmetics division has $7,500,000 invested in assets and an after-tax operating income this year of $1,800,000. Income for the clothing division has grown steadily over the past few years. The weighted-average cost of capital for Lucy is 11%. The CEO of Lucy has told the manager of each division that the division that "performs best" this year will get a bonus.

Required

1. Calculate the ROI and residual income for each division of Lucy Manufacturing, and briefly explain which manager will get the bonus. What are the advantages and disadvantages of each measure?

2. The CEO of Lucy Manufacturing has recently heard of another measure similar to residual income called EVA. The CEO has the accountant calculate EVA adjusted incomes of clothing and cosmetics and finds that the adjusted after-tax operating incomes are $938,000 and $1,147,200, respectively. Also, the clothing division has $520,000 of current liabilities, while the cosmetics division has only $330,000 of current liabilities. Using the preceding information, calculate EVA and discuss which division manager will get the bonus.

3. What nonfinancial measures could Lucy use to evaluate divisional performances?

LO 4 ▷

🌐 **22-26 Risk sharing, incentives, benchmarking, multiple tasks.** The Dexter division of AMCO sells car batteries. AMCO's corporate management gives Dexter management considerable operating and investment autonomy in running the division. AMCO is considering how it should compensate Jim Marks, the general manager of the Dexter division. Proposal 1 calls for paying Marks a fixed salary. Proposal 2 calls for paying Marks no salary and compensating him only on the basis of the division's ROI, calculated based on operating income before any bonus payments. Proposal 3 calls for paying Marks some salary and some bonus based on ROI. Assume that Marks does not like bearing risk.

Required

1. Evaluate the three proposals, specifying the advantages and disadvantages of each.

2. Suppose that AMCO competes against Tiara Industries in the car battery business. Tiara is approximately the same size as the Dexter division and operates in a business environment that is similar to Dexter's. The top management of AMCO is considering evaluating Marks on the basis of Dexter's ROI minus Tiara's ROI. Marks complains that this approach is unfair because the performance of another company, over which he has no control, is included in his performance-evaluation measure. Is Marks's complaint valid? Why or why not?

3. Now suppose that Marks has no authority for making capital-investment decisions. Corporate management makes these decisions. Is ROI a good performance measure to use to evaluate Marks? Is ROI a good measure to evaluate the economic viability of the Dexter division? Explain.

4. Dexter's salespeople are responsible for selling and providing customer service and support. Sales are easy to measure. Although customer service is important to Dexter in the long run, it has not yet implemented customer-service measures. Marks wants to compensate his sales force only on the basis of sales commissions paid for each unit of product sold. He cites two advantages to this plan: (a) It creates strong incentives for the sales force to work hard, and (b) the company pays salespeople only when the company itself is earning revenues. Do you like his plan? Why or why not?

LO 1 ▷
1. RI, $193,800

🌐 **22-27 Residual income and EVA, timing issues.** Brasskey (BK) Company makes doorbells. It has a weighted-average cost of capital of 8%, and total assets of $5,690,000. BK has current liabilities of $700,000. Its operating income for the year was $649,000. BK does not have to pay any income taxes. One of the expenses for accounting purposes was a $100,000 advertising campaign. The entire amount was deducted this year, although the BK CEO believes the beneficial effects of this advertising will last four years.

Required

1. Calculate residual income, assuming BK defines investment as total assets.

2. Calculate EVA for the year. Adjust both the assets and operating income for advertising assuming that for the purposes of economic value added the advertising is capitalized and depreciated on a straight-line basis over four years.

3. Discuss the difference between the outcomes of requirements 1 and 2, and which measure is preferred.

⊕ **22-28 ROI performance measures based on historical cost and current cost.** Nature's Elixir Corporation operates three divisions that process and bottle natural fruit juices. The historical-cost accounting system reports the following information for 2018:

◄ LO 2
1. ROI Kiwi, 19.13%

	Passion Fruit Division	Kiwi Fruit Division	Mango Fruit Division
Revenues	$1,000,000	$1,400,000	$2,200,000
Operating costs (excluding plant depreciation)	600,000	760,000	1,200,000
Plant depreciation	140,000	200,000	240,000
Operating income	$ 260,000	$ 440,000	$ 760,000
Current assets	$ 400,000	$ 500,000	$ 600,000
Long-term assets—plant	280,000	1,800,000	2,640,000
Total assets	$ 680,000	$2,300,000	$3,240,000

Nature's Elixir estimates the useful life of each plant to be 12 years, with no terminal disposal value. The straight-line depreciation method is used. At the end of 2018, the Passion Fruit plant is 10 years old, the Kiwi Fruit plant is 3 years old, and the Mango Fruit plant is 1 year old. An index of construction costs over the 10-year period that Nature's Elixir has been operating (2008 year-end = 100) is

2008	2015	2017	2018
100	136	160	170

Given the high turnover of current assets, management believes that the historical-cost and current-cost measures of current assets are approximately the same.

Required

1. Compute the ROI ratio (operating income to total assets) of each division using historical-cost measures. Comment on the results.
2. Use the approach in Exhibit 22-3 to compute the ROI of each division, incorporating current-cost estimates as of 2018 for depreciation expense and long-term assets. Comment on the results.
3. What advantages might arise from using current-cost asset measures as compared with historical-cost measures for evaluating the performance of the managers of the three divisions?

⊕ **22-29 Executive compensation, balanced scorecard.** Mercantile Bank recently introduced a new bonus plan for its business unit executives. The company believes that current profitability and customer satisfaction levels are equally important to the bank's long-term success. As a result, the new plan awards a bonus equal to 1% of salary for each 1% increase in business unit net income or 1% increase in the business unit's customer satisfaction index. For example, increasing net income from $3 million to $3.3 million (or 10% from its initial value) leads to a bonus of 10% of salary, while increasing the business unit's customer satisfaction index from 70 to 73.5 (or 5% from its initial value) leads to a bonus of 5% of salary. There is no bonus penalty when net income or customer satisfaction declines. In 2018 and 2019, Mercantile Bank's three business units reported the following performance results:

◄ LO 3
1. Change in Net Income Credit Cards = (1.44%)

	Retail Banking		Business Banking		Credit Cards	
	2018	2019	2018	2019	2018	2019
Net income	$3,600,000	$3,912,000	$3,800,000	$3,940,000	$3,550,000	$3,499,000
Customer satisfaction	73	75.48	68	75.9	67	78.88

Required

1. Compute the bonus as a percent of salary earned by each business unit executive in 2019.
2. What factors might explain the differences between improvement rates for net income and those for customer satisfaction in the three units? Are increases in customer satisfaction likely to result in increased net income right away?
3. Mercantile Bank's board of directors is concerned that the 2019 bonus awards may not actually reflect the executives' overall performance. In particular, the bank is concerned that executives can earn large bonuses by doing well on one performance dimension but underperforming on the other. What changes can it make to the bonus plan to prevent this from happening in the future? Explain briefly.

LO 3 ▶

1. Change in Net Income in
NZ is $660,937

🌐 **22-30 Multinational firms, differing risk, comparison of profit, ROI, and RI.** Zeiss Multinational, Inc., has divisions in the Canada, Germany, and New Zealand. The Canadian division is the oldest and most established of the three and has a cost of capital of 6.5%. The German division was started 3 years ago when the exchange rate for the euro was 1 euro = $1.40. The German division is a large and powerful division of Zeiss, Inc., with a cost of capital of 10%. The New Zealand division was started this year, when the exchange rate was 1 New Zealand Dollar (NZD) = $0.75. Its cost of capital is 13%. Average exchange rates for the current year are 1 euro = $1.50 and 1 NZD = $0.60. Other information for the three divisions includes:

	Canada	Germany	New Zealand
Long-term assets	$24,214,700	11,897,321 euros	7,343,744 NZD
Operating revenues	$23,362,940	6,250,000 euros	5,718,750 NZD
Operating expenses	$18,520,000	4,200,000 euros	4,250,000 NZD
Income-tax rate	40%	35%	25%

Required

1. Translate the German and New Zealand information into dollars to make the divisions comparable. Find the after-tax operating income for each division and compare the profits.
2. Calculate ROI using after-tax operating income. Compare among divisions.
3. Use after-tax operating income and the individual cost of capital of each division to calculate residual income and compare.
4. Redo requirement 2 using pretax operating income instead of net income. Why is there a big difference, and what does it mean for performance evaluation?

LO 3 ▶

1a. US Division ROI is 13.75%

🌐 **22-31 Multinational performance measurement, ROI, RI.** The Mountainside Corporation manufactures similar products in the United States and Norway. The U.S. and Norwegian operations are organized as decentralized divisions. The following information is available for 2019; ROI is calculated as operating income divided by total assets:

	U.S. Division	Norwegian Division
Operating income	?	7,560,000 kroner
Total assets	$8,000,000	54,000,000 kroner
ROI	13.75%	?

Both investments were made on December 31, 2018. The exchange rate at the time of Mountainside's investment in Norway on December 31, 2018, was 6 kroner = $1. During 2019, the Norwegian kroner decreased steadily in value so that the exchange rate on December 31, 2019, is 8 kroner = $1. The average exchange rate during 2019 is [(6 + 8) ÷ 2] = 7 kroner = $1.

Required

1. **a.** Calculate the U.S. division's operating income for 2019.
   b. Calculate the Norwegian division's ROI for 2019 in kroner.
2. Top management wants to know which division earned a better ROI in 2019. What would you tell them? Explain your answer.
3. Which division do you think had the better RI performance? Explain your answer. The required rate of return on investment (calculated in U.S. dollars) is 13%.

Problems

LO 2 ▶

2. ROI 2018 with proposal,
22.2%

🌐 **22-32 ROI, RI, DuPont method, investment decisions, balanced scorecard.** Green News Group has two major divisions: Print and Internet. Summary financial data (in millions) for 2017 and 2018 are as follows:

	A	B	C	D	E	F	G	H	I
1		Operating Income			Revenue			Total Assets	
2		2017	2018		2017	2018		2017	2018
3	Print	$3,780	$4,620		$18,900	$19,320		$18,480	$20,580
4	Internet	546	672		25,200	26,880		11,340	12,600

The two division managers' annual bonuses are based on division ROI (defined as operating income divided by total assets). If a division reports an increase in ROI from the previous year, its management is automatically eligible for a bonus; however, the management of a division reporting a decline in ROI has to present an explanation to the Green News Group board and is unlikely to get any bonus.

Carol Mays, manager of the Print Division, is considering a proposal to invest $800 million in a new computerized news reporting and printing system. It is estimated that the new system's state-of-the-art graphics and ability to quickly incorporate late-breaking news into papers will increase 2019 division operating income by $120 million. Green News Group uses a 15% required rate of return on investment for each division.

Required

1. Use the DuPont method of profitability analysis to explain differences in 2018 ROIs between the two divisions. Use 2018 total assets as the investment base.
2. Why might Mays be less than enthusiastic about accepting the investment proposal for the new system, despite her belief in the benefits of the new technology?
3. Murdoch Turner, CEO of Green News Group, is considering a proposal to base division executive compensation on division RI.
   a. Compute the 2018 RI of each division.
   b. Would adoption of an RI measure reduce Mays's reluctance to adopt the new computerized system investment proposal?
4. Turner is concerned that the focus on annual ROI could have an adverse long-run effect on Green News Group's customers. What other measurements, if any, do you recommend that Turner use? Explain briefly.

⊕ **22-33 Division managers' compensation** (continuation of Problem 22-32). Murdoch Turner seeks your advice on revising the existing bonus plan for division managers of Green News Group. Assume division managers do not like bearing risk. Turner is considering three ideas:

◀ **LO 4**

■ Make each division manager's compensation depend on division RI.
■ Make each division manager's compensation depend on companywide RI.
■ Use benchmarking, and compensate division managers on the basis of their division's RI minus the RI of the other division.

Required

1. Evaluate the three ideas Turner has put forth using performance-evaluation concepts described in this chapter. Indicate the positive and negative features of each proposal.
2. Turner is concerned that the pressure for short-run performance may cause managers to cut corners. What systems might Turner introduce to avoid this problem? Explain briefly.
3. Turner is also concerned that the pressure for short-run performance might cause managers to ignore emerging threats and opportunities. What system might Turner introduce to prevent this problem? Explain briefly.

⊕ **22-34 ROI, RI, DuPont method, investment decisions, balanced scorecard.** News Report Group has two major divisions: Print and Internet. Summary financial data (in millions) for 2018 and 2019 are as follows:

◀ **LO 4**

A	B	C	D	E	F	G	H	I
	Operating Income			**Revenues**			**Total Assets**	
	2018	2019		2018	2019		2018	2019
Print	$3,720	$4,500		$18,700	$22,500		$18,200	$25,000
Internet	525	690		25,000	23,000		11,150	10,000

The two division managers' annual bonuses are based on division ROI (defined as operating income divided by total assets). If a division reports an increase in ROI from the previous year, its management is automatically eligible for a bonus; however, the management of a division reporting a decline in ROI has to present an explanation to the News Report Group board and is unlikely to get any bonus.

Carol Mays, manager of the Print division, is considering a proposal to invest $2,580 million in a new computerized news reporting and printing system. It is estimated that the new system's state-of-the-art graphics and ability to quickly incorporate late-breaking news into papers will increase 2020 division operating income by $360 million. News Report Group uses a 10% required rate of return on investment for each division.

Required

1. Use the DuPont method of profitability analysis to explain differences in 2019 ROIs between the two divisions. Use 2019 total assets as the investment base.

2. Why might Mays be less than enthusiastic about accepting the investment proposal for the new system despite her belief in the benefits of the new technology?

3. John Mendenhall, CEO of News Report Group, is considering a proposal to base division executive compensation on division RI.

    a. Compute the 2019 RI of each division.

    b. Would adoption of an RI measure reduce Mays' reluctance to adopt the new computerized system investment proposal?

4. Mendenhall is concerned that the focus on annual ROI could have an adverse long-run effect on News Report Group's customers. What other measurements, if any, do you recommend that Mendenhall use? Explain briefly.

LO 4 ▶ ⊕ **22-35 Division managers' compensation, levers of control** (continuation of 22-34). John Mendenhall seeks your advice on revising the existing bonus plan for division managers of News Report Group. Assume division managers do not like bearing risk. Mendenhall is considering three ideas:

■ Make each division manager's compensation depend on division RI.

■ Make each division manager's compensation depend on company-wide RI.

■ Use benchmarking and compensate division managers on the basis of their division's RI minus the RI of the other division.

Required

1. Evaluate the three ideas Mendenhall has put forth using performance-evaluation concepts described in this chapter. Indicate the positive and negative features of each proposal.

2. Mendenhall is concerned that the pressure for short-run performance may cause managers to cut corners. What systems might Mendenhall introduce to avoid this problem? Explain briefly.

3. Mendenhall is also concerned that the pressure for short-run performance might cause managers to ignore emerging threats and opportunities. What system might Mendenhall introduce to prevent this problem? Explain briefly.

LO 4 ▶ ⊕ **22-36 Residual income and EVA; timing issues.** Doorharmony Company makes doorbells. It has a weighted-average cost of capital of 5% and total assets of $5,900,000. Doorharmony has current liabilities of $750,000. Its operating income for the year was $690,000. Doorharmony does not have to pay any income taxes. One of the expenses for accounting purposes was a $120,000 advertising campaign. The entire amount was deducted this year, although the Doorharmony CEO believes the beneficial effects of this advertising will last 4 years.

Required

1. Calculate residual income, assuming Doorharmony defines investment as total assets.

2. Calculate EVA for the year. Adjust both the assets and operating income for advertising assuming that for the purposes of economic value added the advertising is capitalized and amortized on a straight-line basis over 4 years.

3. Discuss the difference between the outcomes of requirements 1 and 2 and which measure is preferred.

LO 2 ▶ ⊕ **22-37 ROI performance measures based on historical cost and current cost.** Nature's Juice Corporation operates three divisions that process and bottle natural fruit juices. The historical-cost accounting system reports the following information for 2019:

	Passion Fruit Division	Kiwi Fruit Division	Mango Fruit Division
Revenues	$1,300,000	$1,800,000	$2,400,000
Operating costs (excluding plant depreciation)	550,000	1,050,000	900,000
Plant depreciation	270,000	175,000	290,000
Operating income	$ 480,000	$ 575,000	$1,210,000
Current assets	$ 425,000	$ 600,000	$ 700,000
Long-term assets—plant	540,000	1,575,000	3,190,000
Total assets	$ 965,000	$2,175,000	$3,890,000

Nature's Juice estimates the useful life of each plant to be 12 years, with no terminal disposal value. The straight-line depreciation method is used. At the end of 2019, the passion fruit plant is 10 years old, the kiwi fruit plant is 3 years old, and the mango fruit plant is 1 year old. An index of construction costs over the 10-year period that Nature's Juice has been operating (2016 year-end =100) is as follows:

2016	2017	2018	2019
100	120	185	200

Given the high turnover of current assets, management believes that the historical-cost and current-cost measures of current assets are approximately the same.

Required

1. Compute the ROI ratio (operating income to total assets) of each division using historical-cost measures. Comment on the results.
2. Use the approach in Exhibit 22-3 (page 908) to compute the ROI of each division, incorporating current-cost estimates as of 2019 for depreciation expense and long-term assets. Comment on the results.
3. What advantages might arise from using current-cost asset measures as compared with historical-cost measures for evaluating the performance of the managers of the three divisions?

🌐 **22-38 Evaluate accrual measures.** Mineral Waters Ltd. operates three divisions that process and bottle sparkling mineral water. The historical-cost accounting system reports the following data for 2018:

◀ **LO 2**
1. ROI Calistoga, 38.24%

	Calistoga Division	Alpine Springs Division	Rocky Mountains Division
Revenues	$600,000	$ 840,000	$1,320,000
Operating costs (excluding depreciation)	360,000	456,000	720,000
Plant depreciation	84,000	120,000	144,000
Operating income	$156,000	$ 264,000	$ 456,000
Current assets	$240,000	$ 300,000	$ 360,000
Fixed assets—plant	168,000	1,080,000	1,584,000
Total assets	$408,000	$1,380,000	$1,944,000

Mineral Waters estimates the useful life of each plant to be 12 years with a zero terminal disposal price. The straight-line depreciation method is used. At the end of 2018, the Calistoga plant is 10 years old, the Alpine Springs plant is 3 years old, and the Rocky Mountains plant is 1 year old.

An index of construction costs of plants for mineral water production for the 10-year period that Mineral Waters has been operating (2008 year-end = 100) is

2008	2012	2015	2017	2018
100	125	135	140	150

Given the high turnover of current assets, management believes that the historical-cost and current-cost measures of current assets are approximately the same.

Required

1. Compute the ROI (operating income to total assets) ratio of each division using historical-cost measures. Comment on the results.
2. Use the approach in Exhibit 22-3 to compute the ROI of each division, incorporating current-cost estimates as of 2018 for depreciation and fixed assets. Comment on the results.
3. What advantages might arise from using current-cost asset measures as compared with historical-cost measures for evaluating the performance of the managers of the three divisions?

22-39 Financial and nonfinancial performance measures, goal congruence. (CMA, adapted) Precision Equipment specializes in the manufacture of medical equipment, a field that has become increasingly competitive. Approximately 2 years ago, Pedro Mendez, president of Precision, decided to revise the bonus plan (based, at the time, entirely on operating income) to encourage division managers to focus on areas that were important to customers and that added value without increasing cost. In addition to a profitability incentive, the revised plan includes incentives for reduced rework costs, reduced sales returns, and on-time deliveries. The company calculates and rewards bonuses semiannually on the following basis: A base bonus is calculated at 2% of operating income; this amount is then adjusted as:

◀ **LO 4**

a. (i) Reduced by excess of rework costs over and above 2% of operating income
   (ii) No adjustment if rework costs are less than or equal to 2% of operating income
b. (i) Increased by $4,000 if more than 98% of deliveries are on time and by $1,500 if 96–98% of deliveries are on time
   (ii) No adjustment if on-time deliveries are below 96%
c. (i) Increased by $2,500 if sales returns are less than or equal to 1.5% of sales
   (ii) Decreased by 50% of excess of sales returns over 1.5% of sales

Note: If the calculation of the bonus results in a negative amount for a particular period, the manager simply receives no bonus, and the negative amount is not carried forward to the next period.

Results for Precision's Central division and Western division for 2018, the first year under the new bonus plan, follow. In 2017, under the old bonus plan, the Central division manager earned a bonus of $20,295 and the Western division manager a bonus of $15,830.

	Central Division		Western Division	
	Jan. 1, 2018, to June 30, 2017	**July 1, 2018, to Dec. 31, 2018**	**Jan. 1, 2018, to June 30, 2018**	**July 1, 2018, to Dec. 31, 2018**
Revenues	$3,150,000	$3,300,000	$2,137,500	$2,175,000
Operating income	$ 346,500	$ 330,000	$ 256,500	$ 304,500
On-time delivery	95.4%	97.3%	98.2%	94.6%
Rework costs	$ 8,625	$ 8,250	$ 4,500	$ 6,000
Sales returns	$ 63,000	$ 52,500	$ 33,560	$ 31,875

Required

1. Why did Mendez need to introduce these new performance measures? That is, why does Mendez need to use these performance measures in addition to the operating-income numbers for the period?
2. Calculate the bonus earned by each manager for each 6-month period and for 2018.
3. What effect did the change in the bonus plan have on each manager's behaviour? Did the new bonus plan achieve what Mendez wanted? What changes, if any, would you make to the new bonus plan?

LO 4 ▶

22-40 ROI, measurement alternatives for performance measures. Appleton's owns and operates a variety of casual dining restaurants in three cities: St. Louis, Memphis, and New Orleans. Each geographic market is considered a separate division. The St. Louis division includes four restaurants, each built in early 2009. The Memphis division consists of three restaurants, each built in January 2013. The New Orleans division is the newest, consisting of three restaurants built 4 years ago. Division managers at Appleton's are evaluated on the basis of ROI. The following information refers to the three divisions at the end of 2018:

	Home	Insert	Page Layout	Formulas	Data	Review	View
	A				B	C	D	E
1					St. Louis	Memphis	New Orleans	Total
2	Division revenues				$17,336,000	$12,050,000	$10,890,000	$40,276,000
3	Division expenses				15,890,000	11,042,000	9,958,000	36,890,000
4	Division operating income				1,446,000	1,008,000	932,000	3,386,000
5	Gross book value of long-term assets				9,000,000	7,500,000	8,100,000	24,600,000
6	Accumulated depreciation				6,600,000	3,500,000	2,160,000	12,260,000
7	Current assets				1,999,600	1,536,400	1,649,200	5,185,200
8	Depreciation expense				600,000	500,000	540,000	1,640,000
9	Construction cost index for year of construction				100	110	118	

Required

1. Calculate ROI for each division using net book value of total assets.
2. Using the technique in Exhibit 22-3, compute ROI using current-cost estimates for long-term assets and depreciation expense. The construction cost index for 2018 is 122. Estimated useful life of operational assets is 15 years.
3. How does the choice of long-term asset valuation affect management decisions regarding new capital investments? Why might this choice be more significant to the St. Louis division manager than to the New Orleans division manager?

LO 2 ▶

🌐 **22-41 Historical-cost and current-cost ROI measures.** Corners Ltd. owns and manages three convenience stores. The following information has been collected for the year 2018:

	Jane and Rutherford	Major Mackenzie and Keele	Weston and Langstaff
Operating income	$ 28,000	$ 33,000	$15,000
Historical cost of investment	$ 50,000	$100,000	$30,000
Current cost of investment	$120,000	$135,000	$80,000
Age of store	5	2	4

Required

1. Compute the ROI for each store, where investment is measured at (a) historical cost and (b) current cost.
2. How would you judge the performance of each store?

🌐 **22-42 ROI, RI, decision making.** The following data refer to the successful Munger division of Buffett, Inc. Munger makes and sells high-end cordless drills. The drills sell for $80 each, and Munger expects sales of 300,000 units in 2019. Munger's annual fixed costs are $4 million. The variable cost per drill is $48.

◄ **LO 4**

Buffett evaluates Munger based on residual income. The total investment attributed to Munger is $16 million, and Buffett has a required rate of return on investment of 20%.

Ignore taxes and depreciation expense. Answer each of the following parts *independently*, unless otherwise stated.

Required

1. What is the expected residual income in 2019?
2. Munger receives an external special order for 100,000 units at $60 each. If the order is accepted, Munger will have to incur incremental fixed costs of $850,000 and invest an additional $2 million in various assets.

   What is the effect on Munger's residual income of accepting the order?
3. One of the components Munger manufactures for its drill has a variable cost of $4. An outside vendor has offered to supply the 300,000 units required at a cost of $5.25 per unit. If the component is purchased outside, fixed costs will decline by $200,000 and assets with a book value of $760,000 will be sold at book value.

   Will Munger decide to make or buy the component? Explain your answer.
4. One of Munger's regular customers asks for a special drill made of tempered steel. The customer requires 15,000 drills. Munger estimates its variable cost for these special units at $54 apiece. Munger will also have to undertake new investment of $1,500,000 to produce the drills.

   What is the minimum selling price that will make the deal acceptable to Munger?
5. Assume the same facts as in requirement 4. Also suppose that the customer has offered $82 for each special drill. In addition, the customer has indicated that its purchases of the existing product will drop by 6,000 units.
   a. What is the net change in Munger's residual income from taking the offer, relative to its planned 2019 situation?
   b. At what drop in unit sales of the regular drill would Munger be indifferent to the offer?

22-43 Ethics, levers of control. Best Moulding is a large manufacturer of wood picture frame moulding. The company operates distribution centres in Dallas and Philadelphia. The distribution centres cut frames to size (called "chops") and ship them to custom picture framers. Because of the exacting standards and natural flaws of wood picture frame moulding, the company typically produces a large amount of waste in cutting chops. In recent years, the company's average yield has been 78% of length moulding. The remaining 22% is sent to a wood recycler. Best's performance-evaluation system pays its distribution centre managers substantial bonuses if the company achieves annual budgeted profit numbers. In the last quarter of 2019, Stuart Brown, Best's controller, noted a significant increase in yield percentage of the Dallas distribution centre, from 76% to 87%. This increase resulted in a 6% increase in the centre's profits.

◄ **LO 4**

During a recent trip to the Dallas centre, Brown wandered into the moulding warehouse. He noticed that much of the scrap moulding was being returned to the inventory bins rather than being placed in the discard pile. Upon further inspection, he determined that the moulding was in fact unusable. When he asked one of the workers, he was told that the centre's manager had directed workers to stop scrapping all but the very shortest pieces. This practice resulted in the centre overreporting both yield and ending inventory. The overstatement of Dallas inventory will have a significant impact on Best's financial statements.

Required

1. What should Brown do? You may want to refer to the *IMA Statement of Ethical Professional Practice,* page 18.
2. Which lever of control is Best emphasizing? What changes, if any, should be made?

22-44 RI, EVA, measurement alternatives, goal congruence. Refresh Resorts, Inc., operates health spas in Key West, Florida; Phoenix, Arizona; and Carmel, California. The Key West spa was the company's first and opened in 2003. The Phoenix spa opened in 2006, and the Carmel spa opened in 2016.

◄ **LO 2**

Refresh Resorts has previously evaluated divisions based on RI, but the company is considering changing to an EVA approach. All spas are assumed to face similar risks. Data for 2019 are:

	A	B	C	D	E
		Key West	**Phoenix**	**Carmel**	**Total**
2	Revenues	$4,100,000	$4,380,000	$3,230,000	$11,710,000
3	Variable costs	1,600,000	1,630,000	955,000	4,185,000
4	Fixed costs	1,280,000	1,560,000	980,000	3,820,000
5	Operating income	1,220,000	1,190,000	1,295,000	3,705,000
6	Interest costs on long-term debt at 8%	368,000	416,000	440,000	1,224,000
7	Income before taxes	852,000	774,000	855,000	2,481,000
8	Net income after 35% taxes	553,800	503,100	555,750	1,612,650
9					
10	Net book value at 2019 year-end:				
11	Current assets	$1,280,000	$ 850,000	$ 600,000	$ 2,730,000
12	Long-term assets	4,875,000	5,462,000	6,835,000	17,172,000
13	Total assets	6,155,000	6,312,000	7,435,000	19,902,000
14					
15	Current liabilities	330,000	265,000	84,000	679,000
16	Long-term debt	4,600,000	5,200,000	5,500,000	15,300,000
17	Stockholders' equity	1,225,000	847,000	1,851,000	3,923,000
18	Total liabilities and stockholders' equity	6,155,000	6,312,000	7,435,000	19,902,000
19					
20	Market value of debt	$4,600,000	$5,200,000	$5,500,000	$15,300,000
21	Market value of equity	2,400,000	2,660,000	2,590,000	7,650,000
22	Cost of equity capital				14%
23	Required rate of return				11%
24	Accumulated depreciation on long-term assets	$2,200,000	$1,510,000	$ 220,000	

Required

1. Calculate RI for each of the spas based on operating income and using total assets as the measure of investment. Suppose that the Key West spa is considering adding a new group of saunas from Finland that will cost $225,000. The saunas are expected to bring in operating income of $22,000. What effect would this project have on the RI of the Key West spa? Based on RI, would the Key West manager accept or reject this project? Why? Without resorting to calculations, would the other managers accept or reject the project? Why?

2. Why might Refresh Resorts want to use EVA instead of RI for evaluating the performance of the three spas?

3. Refer back to the original data. Calculate the WACC for Refresh Resorts.

4. Refer back to the original data. Calculate EVA for each of the spas, using net book value of long-term assets. Calculate EVA again, this time using gross book value of long-term assets. Comment on the differences between the two methods.

5. How does the selection of asset measurement method affect goal congruence?

Collaborative Learning Cases

LO 1, 2, 4 ▶
1. ROS, 15%

22-45 ROI, RI, division manager's compensation, nonfinancial measures. In 2018, the Mandarin Division of Key Products Corporation generated an operating income of $3,000,000 from $20,000,000 of sales revenues and using assets worth $15,000,000.

Mandarin managers are evaluated and rewarded on the basis of ROI defined as operating income divided by total assets. Key Products Corporation expects its divisions to increase ROI each year.

The year 2019 appears to be a difficult year for Mandarin. Mandarin Division had planned new investments to improve quality but, in view of poor economic conditions, has postponed the investment. ROI for 2018 was certain to decrease had Mandarin made the investment. Management is now considering ways to meet its target ROI of 22% for next year. It anticipates revenue to be steady at $20,000,000 in 2018.

Instructions

Form groups of two or more students to complete the following requirements:

1. Calculate Mandarin Division return on sales (ROS) and ROI for 2018.
2. **a.** By how much would Mandarin have to cut costs in 2019 to achieve its target ROI of 22% in 2019, assuming no change in total assets between 2018 and 2019?
   b. By how much would Mandarin have to decrease total assets in 2019 to achieve its target ROI of 22% in 2019, assuming no change in operating income between 2018 and 2019?
3. Calculate Mandarin's RI in 2018 assuming a required rate of return on investment of 18%.
4. Mandarin wants to increase RI by 30% in 2019. Assuming it could cut costs by $30,000 in 2019, by how much would Mandarin have to decrease total assets in 2019?
5. Key Products Corporation is concerned that the focus on cost cutting and asset sales will have an adverse long-run effect on Mandarin's customers. Yet Key Products Corporation wants Mandarin to meet its financial goals. What other measurements, if any, do you recommend that Key Products use? Explain briefly.

22-46 ROI, RI, division manager's compensation, nonfinancial measures. (CGA, adapted) Home Appliance (HA) builds coffeemakers and battery-powered small tools. For a long time, HA held a reputation for strong, durable, and reliable appliances. This reputation began to decline, however, when increased competition forced HA to cut costs, and this was handled poorly. For a moderate period following the cost cutting, as long as it was able to take advantage of its reputation, HA's sales remained relatively steady. This effect then all but disappeared. The loss of reputation, coupled with increased overseas competition, caused HA's sales to plummet sharply.

◀ **LO 1, 4**
Total bonus Electronic Circuits, $75,000

On January 1, 2017, HA began a massive effort directed toward rewarding for quality. In the two years that followed, sales failed to go up, but remained steady at around $10 million per year. A significant amount of money was spent on testing equipment, increasing inspection, setting up a statistical process control system, reworking or throwing out defective items, and paying incentives. The results of the effort are presented in the following table:

Quality Costs as a % of Sales for the Years Ended:	2016	2017	2018
External failure costs	8.20	2.40	1.15
Internal failure costs	2.80	4.00	3.40
Appraisal costs	2.00	3.20	3.39
Prevention costs	1.20	2.60	2.79
Total quality costs	14.20	12.20	10.73

Also on January 1, 2017, HA organized into three divisions: electronic circuits, coffeemakers, and battery-powered small tools. Electronic circuits were used by the other two divisions, and 100% of its production was transferred at full cost plus an 8% markup (this is the standard practice in the electronic components industry) to coffeemakers and battery-powered small tools. All rejections made by coffeemakers and small tools were treated in the quality control system as internal failures, but most of the time they were not reported simply because electronic circuits replaced them immediately in the production lines.

Each division had a bonus pool with 50% based on quality performance and 50% based on financial performance. The 50% based on financial performance is equal to 20% of the divisional residual income (the minimum required rate of return is the ROI of the worst-performing division). The 50% based on quality performance is calculated as: (Internal Failures as % of sales − External Failures as % of sales) × HA's net profit.

Given the results of last year, the manager of the coffeemaker division asked the top managers to review the current compensation system, because he was having the feeling that his division had been subsidizing those "lazy" fellows of electronic circuits. He supported his claim with the following:

2018	Electronic Circuits	Coffeemakers	Battery-Powered Small Tools
Net profit	$ 500,000	$ 700,000	$ 660,000
Investment	$2,500,000	$7,000,000	$6,000,000
External failures	0% of sales	1.2% of sales	2.4% of sales
Internal failures	5% of sales	2% of sales	3.2% of sales
Appraisal costs	0% of sales	5.2% of sales	3.1% of sales
Prevention costs	1% of sales	7% of sales	4.2% of sales

Instructions

Form groups of two or more students to complete the following requirement.

Calculate the bonus paid to each division. Explain to the upper management if the money is being spent effectively and if the claims of the divisional manager are correct.

TRY IT!

SOLUTION

Try It 22–1

1. ROI = Operating income/Total assets = $492/$683 = 72%
2. Residual income = Operating income − (Target rate of return × Total assets)
   = $492 million − (25% × $683 million) = $321.25 million

Appendix A

NOTES ON COMPOUND INTEREST AND INTEREST TABLES

Interest is the cost of using money. It is the rental charge for funds, just as renting a building and equipment entails a rental charge. When the funds are used for a period of time, it is necessary to recognize interest as a cost of using the borrowed ("rented") funds. This requirement applies even if the funds represent ownership capital and if interest does not entail an outlay of cash. Why must interest be considered? Because the selection of one alternative automatically commits a given amount of funds that could otherwise be invested in some other alternative.

Interest is generally important, even when short-term projects are under consideration. Interest looms correspondingly larger when long-run plans are studied. The rate of interest has significant enough impact to influence decisions regarding borrowing and investing funds. For example, $100,000 invested now and compounded annually for 10 years at 8% will accumulate to $215,900; at 20%, the $100,000 will accumulate to $619,200.

Interest Tables

Many computer programs and pocket calculators are available that handle computations involving the time value of money. You may also turn to the following four basic tables to compute interest.

Table 1—Future Amount of $1

Table 1 shows how much $1 invested now will accumulate in a given number of periods at a given compounded interest rate per period. Consider investing $1,000 now for 3 years at 8% compound interest. A tabular presentation of how this $1,000 would accumulate to $1,259.70 follows:

Year	Interest per Year	Cumulative Interest Called Compound Interest	Total at End of Year
0	$ —	$ —	$1,000.00
1	80.00 (0.08 × $1,000)	80.00	1,080.00
2	86.40 (0.08 × $1,080)	166.40	1,166.40
3	93.30 (0.08 × $1,166.40)	259.70	1,259.70

This tabular presentation is a series of computations that could appear as follows, where S is the future amount and the subscripts 1, 2, and 3 indicate the number of time periods.

$$S_1 = \$1,000(1.08)^1$$
$$S_2 = \$1,000(1.08)^2$$
$$S_3 = \$1,000(1.08)^3$$

The formula for the "amount of 1," often called the "future value of $1" or "future amount of $1," can be written

$$S = P(1 + r)^n$$
$$S = \$1,000(1 + 0.08)^3 = \$1,259.70$$

where S is the future value amount; P is the present value, $1,000 in this case; r is the rate of interest; and n is the number of time periods.

Table 2—Present Value of $1

In the previous example, if $1,000 compounded at 8% per year will accumulate to $1,259.70 in 3 years, then $1,000 must be the present value of $1,259.70 due at the end of 3 years. The formula for the present value can be derived by reversing the process of *accumulation* (finding the future amount) that we just finished.

If

$$S = P(1 + r)^n$$

then

$$P = \frac{S}{(1 + r)^n}$$

$$P = \frac{\$1,259.70}{(1.08)^3} = \$1,000$$

Table 3—Amount of Annuity of $1

An (ordinary) *annuity* is a series of equal payments (receipts) to be paid (or received) at the end of successive periods of equal length. Assume that $1,000 is invested at the end of each of 3 years at 8%:

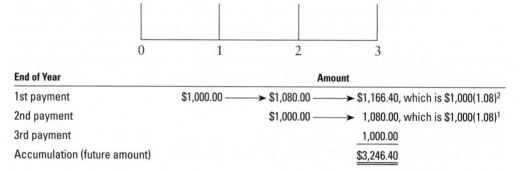

End of Year			Amount
1st payment	$1,000.00 ⟶	$1,080.00 ⟶	$1,166.40, which is $1,000(1.08)²
2nd payment		$1,000.00 ⟶	1,080.00, which is $1,000(1.08)¹
3rd payment			1,000.00
Accumulation (future amount)			$3,246.40

The general formula for the amount of an ordinary annuity of $1 is:

$$S_n = \frac{(1 + r)^n - 1}{r}$$

Table 4—Present Value of an Ordinary Annuity of $1

Using the same example as for Table 3, we can show how the formula of P_n, *the present value of an ordinary annuity*, is developed.

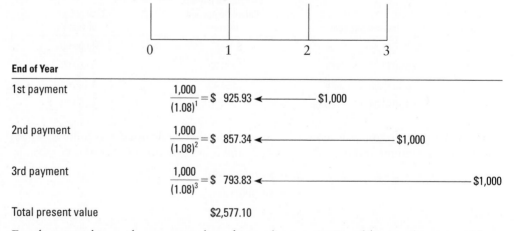

End of Year		
1st payment	$\frac{1,000}{(1.08)^1} = \$\ 925.93 \longleftarrow \$1,000$	
2nd payment	$\frac{1,000}{(1.08)^2} = \$\ 857.34 \longleftarrow \$1,000$	
3rd payment	$\frac{1,000}{(1.08)^3} = \$\ 793.83 \longleftarrow \$1,000$	
Total present value	$2,577.10	

For the general case, the present value of an ordinary annuity of $1 may be expressed as:

$$P_n = \frac{1}{r}\left[1 - \frac{1}{(1 + r)^n}\right]$$

The tables for annuities are not essential. With Tables 1 and 2, compound interest and compound discount can readily be computed. It is simply a matter of dividing either of these by the rate to get values equivalent to those shown in Tables 3 and 4.

Table 1

Compound Amount of $1 (The Future Value of $1)

$S = P(1 - r)^n$. In this table $P = \$1$.

Periods	2%	4%	6%	8%	10%	12%	14%	16%	18%	20%	22%	24%	26%	28%	30%	32%	40%	Periods
1	1.020	1.040	1.060	1.080	1.100	1.120	1.140	1.160	1.180	1.200	1.220	1.240	1.260	1.280	1.300	1.320	1.400	1
2	1.040	1.082	1.124	1.166	1.210	1.254	1.300	1.346	1.392	1.440	1.488	1.538	1.588	1.638	1.690	1.742	1.960	2
3	1.061	1.125	1.191	1.260	1.331	1.405	1.482	1.561	1.643	1.728	1.816	1.907	2.000	2.097	2.197	2.300	2.744	3
4	1.082	1.170	1.262	1.360	1.464	1.574	1.689	1.811	1.939	2.074	2.215	2.364	2.520	2.684	2.856	3.036	3.842	4
5	1.104	1.217	1.338	1.469	1.611	1.762	1.925	2.100	2.288	2.488	2.703	2.932	3.176	3.436	3.713	4.007	5.378	5
6	1.126	1.265	1.419	1.587	1.772	1.974	2.195	2.436	2.700	2.986	3.297	3.635	4.002	4.398	4.827	5.290	7.530	6
7	1.149	1.316	1.504	1.714	1.949	2.211	2.502	2.826	3.185	3.583	4.023	4.508	5.042	5.629	6.275	6.983	10.541	7
8	1.172	1.369	1.594	1.851	2.144	2.476	2.853	3.278	3.759	4.300	4.908	5.590	6.353	7.206	8.157	9.217	14.758	8
9	1.195	1.423	1.689	1.999	2.358	2.773	3.252	3.803	4.435	5.160	5.987	6.931	8.005	9.223	10.604	12.166	20.661	9
10	1.219	1.480	1.791	2.159	2.594	3.106	3.707	4.411	5.234	6.192	7.305	8.594	10.086	11.806	13.786	16.060	28.925	10
11	1.243	1.539	1.898	2.332	2.853	3.479	4.226	5.117	6.176	7.430	8.912	10.657	12.708	15.112	17.922	21.199	40.496	11
12	1.268	1.601	2.012	2.518	3.138	3.896	4.818	5.936	7.288	8.916	10.872	13.215	16.012	19.343	23.298	27.983	56.694	12
13	1.294	1.665	2.133	2.720	3.452	4.363	5.492	6.886	8.599	10.699	13.264	16.386	20.175	24.759	30.288	36.937	79.371	13
14	1.319	1.732	2.261	2.937	3.797	4.887	6.261	7.988	10.147	12.839	16.182	20.319	25.421	31.691	39.374	48.757	111.120	14
15	1.346	1.801	2.397	3.172	4.177	5.474	7.138	9.266	11.974	15.407	19.742	25.196	32.030	40.565	51.186	64.359	155.568	15
16	1.373	1.873	2.540	3.426	4.595	6.130	8.137	10.748	14.129	18.488	24.086	31.243	40.358	51.923	66.542	84.954	217.795	16
17	1.400	1.948	2.693	3.700	5.054	6.866	9.276	12.468	16.672	22.186	29.384	38.741	50.851	66.461	86.504	112.139	304.913	17
18	1.428	2.026	2.854	3.996	5.560	7.690	10.575	14.463	19.673	26.623	35.849	48.039	64.072	85.071	112.455	148.024	426.879	18
19	1.457	2.107	3.026	4.316	6.116	8.613	12.056	16.777	23.214	31.948	43.736	59.568	80.731	108.890	146.192	195.391	597.630	19
20	1.486	2.191	3.207	4.661	6.727	9.646	13.743	19.461	27.393	38.338	53.358	73.864	101.721	139.380	190.050	257.916	836.683	20
21	1.516	2.279	3.400	5.034	7.400	10.804	15.668	22.574	32.324	46.005	65.096	91.592	128.169	178.406	247.065	340.449	1171.356	21
22	1.546	2.370	3.604	5.437	8.140	12.100	17.861	26.186	38.142	55.206	79.418	113.574	161.492	228.360	321.184	449.393	1639.898	22
23	1.577	2.465	3.820	5.871	8.954	13.552	20.362	30.376	45.008	66.247	96.889	140.831	203.480	292.300	417.539	593.199	2295.857	23
24	1.608	2.563	4.049	6.341	9.850	15.179	23.212	35.236	53.109	79.497	118.205	174.631	256.385	374.144	542.801	783.023	3214.200	24
25	1.641	2.666	4.292	6.848	10.835	17.000	26.462	40.874	62.669	95.396	144.210	216.542	323.045	478.905	705.641	1033.590	4499.880	25
26	1.673	2.772	4.549	7.396	11.918	19.040	30.167	47.414	73.949	114.475	175.936	268.512	407.037	612.998	917.333	1364.339	6299.831	26
27	1.707	2.883	4.822	7.988	13.110	21.325	34.390	55.000	87.260	137.371	214.642	332.955	512.867	784.638	1192.533	1800.927	8819.764	27
28	1.741	2.999	5.112	8.627	14.421	23.884	39.204	63.800	102.967	164.845	261.864	412.864	646.212	1004.336	1550.293	2377.224	12347.670	28
29	1.776	3.119	5.418	9.317	15.863	26.750	44.693	74.009	121.501	197.814	319.474	511.952	814.228	1285.550	2015.381	3137.935	17286.737	29
30	1.811	3.243	5.743	10.063	17.449	29.960	50.950	85.850	143.371	237.376	389.758	634.820	1025.927	1645.505	2619.996	4142.075	24201.432	30
35	2.000	3.946	7.686	14.785	28.102	52.800	98.100	180.314	327.997	590.668	1053.402	1861.054	3258.135	5653.911	9727.860	16599.217	130161.112	35
40	2.208	4.801	10.286	21.725	45.259	93.051	188.884	378.721	750.378	1469.772	2847.038	5455.913	10347.175	19426.689	36118.865	66520.767	700037.697	40

Table 2
Present Value of $1

$$P = \frac{S}{(1 + r)^n}$$ In this table $S = \$1$.

Periods	2%	4%	6%	8%	10%	12%	14%	16%	18%	20%	22%	24%	26%	28%	30%	32%	40%	Periods
1	0.980	0.962	0.943	0.926	0.909	0.893	0.877	0.862	0.847	0.833	0.820	0.806	0.794	0.781	0.769	0.758	0.714	1
2	0.961	0.925	0.890	0.857	0.826	0.797	0.769	0.743	0.718	0.694	0.672	0.650	0.630	0.610	0.592	0.574	0.510	2
3	0.942	0.889	0.840	0.794	0.751	0.712	0.675	0.641	0.609	0.579	0.551	0.524	0.500	0.477	0.455	0.435	0.364	3
4	0.924	0.855	0.792	0.735	0.683	0.636	0.592	0.552	0.516	0.482	0.451	0.423	0.397	0.373	0.350	0.329	0.260	4
5	0.906	0.822	0.747	0.681	0.621	0.567	0.519	0.476	0.437	0.402	0.370	0.341	0.315	0.291	0.269	0.250	0.186	5
6	0.888	0.790	0.705	0.630	0.564	0.507	0.456	0.410	0.370	0.335	0.303	0.275	0.250	0.227	0.207	0.189	0.133	6
7	0.871	0.760	0.665	0.583	0.513	0.452	0.400	0.354	0.314	0.279	0.249	0.222	0.198	0.178	0.159	0.143	0.095	7
8	0.853	0.731	0.627	0.540	0.467	0.404	0.351	0.305	0.266	0.233	0.204	0.179	0.157	0.139	0.123	0.108	0.068	8
9	0.837	0.703	0.592	0.500	0.424	0.361	0.308	0.263	0.225	0.194	0.167	0.144	0.125	0.108	0.094	0.082	0.048	9
10	0.820	0.676	0.558	0.463	0.386	0.322	0.270	0.227	0.191	0.162	0.137	0.116	0.099	0.085	0.073	0.062	0.035	10
11	0.804	0.650	0.527	0.429	0.350	0.287	0.237	0.195	0.162	0.135	0.112	0.094	0.079	0.066	0.056	0.047	0.025	11
12	0.788	0.625	0.497	0.397	0.319	0.257	0.208	0.168	0.137	0.112	0.092	0.076	0.062	0.052	0.043	0.036	0.018	12
13	0.773	0.601	0.469	0.368	0.290	0.229	0.182	0.145	0.116	0.093	0.075	0.061	0.050	0.040	0.033	0.027	0.013	13
14	0.758	0.577	0.442	0.340	0.263	0.205	0.160	0.125	0.099	0.078	0.062	0.049	0.039	0.032	0.025	0.021	0.009	14
15	0.743	0.555	0.417	0.315	0.239	0.183	0.140	0.108	0.084	0.065	0.051	0.040	0.031	0.025	0.020	0.016	0.006	15
16	0.728	0.534	0.394	0.292	0.218	0.163	0.123	0.093	0.071	0.054	0.042	0.032	0.025	0.019	0.015	0.012	0.005	16
17	0.714	0.513	0.371	0.270	0.198	0.146	0.108	0.080	0.060	0.045	0.034	0.026	0.020	0.015	0.012	0.009	0.003	17
18	0.700	0.494	0.350	0.250	0.180	0.130	0.095	0.069	0.051	0.038	0.028	0.021	0.016	0.012	0.009	0.007	0.002	18
19	0.686	0.475	0.331	0.232	0.164	0.116	0.083	0.060	0.043	0.031	0.023	0.017	0.012	0.009	0.007	0.005	0.002	19
20	0.673	0.456	0.312	0.215	0.149	0.104	0.073	0.051	0.037	0.026	0.019	0.014	0.010	0.007	0.005	0.004	0.001	20
21	0.660	0.439	0.294	0.199	0.135	0.093	0.064	0.044	0.031	0.022	0.015	0.011	0.008	0.006	0.004	0.003	0.001	21
22	0.647	0.422	0.278	0.184	0.123	0.083	0.056	0.038	0.026	0.018	0.013	0.009	0.006	0.004	0.003	0.002	0.001	22
23	0.634	0.406	0.262	0.170	0.112	0.074	0.049	0.033	0.022	0.015	0.010	0.007	0.005	0.003	0.002	0.002	0.000	23
24	0.622	0.390	0.247	0.158	0.102	0.066	0.043	0.028	0.019	0.013	0.008	0.006	0.004	0.003	0.002	0.001	0.000	24
25	0.610	0.375	0.233	0.146	0.092	0.059	0.038	0.024	0.016	0.010	0.007	0.005	0.003	0.002	0.001	0.001	0.000	25
26	0.598	0.361	0.220	0.135	0.084	0.053	0.033	0.021	0.014	0.009	0.006	0.004	0.002	0.002	0.001	0.001	0.000	26
27	0.586	0.347	0.207	0.125	0.076	0.047	0.029	0.018	0.011	0.007	0.005	0.003	0.002	0.001	0.001	0.001	0.000	27
28	0.574	0.333	0.196	0.116	0.069	0.042	0.026	0.016	0.010	0.006	0.004	0.002	0.002	0.001	0.001	0.000	0.000	28
29	0.563	0.321	0.185	0.107	0.063	0.037	0.022	0.014	0.008	0.005	0.003	0.002	0.001	0.001	0.000	0.000	0.000	29
30	0.552	0.308	0.174	0.099	0.057	0.033	0.020	0.012	0.007	0.004	0.003	0.002	0.001	0.001	0.000	0.000	0.000	30
35	0.500	0.253	0.130	0.068	0.036	0.019	0.010	0.006	0.003	0.002	0.001	0.001	0.000	0.000	0.000	0.000	0.000	35
40	0.453	0.208	0.097	0.046	0.022	0.011	0.005	0.003	0.001	0.001	0.000	0.000	0.000	0.000	0.000	0.000	0.000	40

Table 3
Compound Amount of Annuity of $1 in Arrears* (Future Value of Annuity)

$$S_n = \frac{(1 + r)^n - 1}{r}$$

Periods	2%	4%	6%	8%	10%	12%	14%	16%	18%	20%	22%	24%	26%	28%	30%	32%	40%	Periods
1	1.000	1.000	1.000	1.000	1.000	1.000	1.000	1.000	1.000	1.000	1.000	1.000	1.000	1.000	1.000	1.000	1.000	1
2	2.020	2.040	2.060	2.080	2.100	2.120	2.140	2.160	2.180	2.200	2.220	2.240	2.260	2.280	2.300	2.320	2.400	2
3	3.060	3.122	3.184	3.246	3.310	3.374	3.440	3.506	3.572	3.640	3.708	3.778	3.848	3.918	3.990	4.062	4.360	3
4	4.122	4.246	4.375	4.506	4.641	4.779	4.921	5.066	5.215	5.368	5.524	5.684	5.848	6.016	6.187	6.362	7.104	4
5	5.204	5.416	5.637	5.867	6.105	6.353	6.610	6.877	7.154	7.442	7.740	8.048	8.368	8.700	9.043	9.398	10.946	5
6	6.308	6.633	6.975	7.336	7.716	8.115	8.536	8.977	9.442	9.930	10.442	10.980	11.544	12.136	12.756	13.406	16.324	6
7	7.434	7.898	8.394	8.923	9.487	10.089	10.730	11.414	12.142	12.916	13.740	14.615	15.546	16.534	17.583	18.696	23.853	7
8	8.583	9.214	9.897	10.637	11.436	12.300	13.233	14.240	15.327	16.499	17.762	19.123	20.588	22.163	23.858	25.678	34.395	8
9	9.755	10.583	11.491	12.488	13.579	14.776	16.085	17.519	19.086	20.799	22.670	24.712	26.940	29.369	32.015	34.895	49.153	9
10	10.950	12.006	13.181	14.487	15.937	17.549	19.337	21.321	23.521	25.959	28.657	31.643	34.945	38.593	42.619	47.062	69.814	10
11	12.169	13.486	14.972	16.645	18.531	20.655	23.045	25.733	28.755	32.150	35.962	40.238	45.031	50.398	56.405	63.122	98.739	11
12	13.412	15.026	16.870	18.977	21.384	24.133	27.271	30.850	34.931	39.581	44.874	50.895	57.739	65.510	74.327	84.320	139.235	12
13	14.680	16.627	18.882	21.495	24.523	28.029	32.089	36.786	42.219	48.497	55.746	64.110	73.751	84.853	97.625	112.303	195.929	13
14	15.974	18.292	21.015	24.215	27.975	32.393	37.581	43.672	50.818	59.196	69.010	80.496	93.926	109.612	127.913	149.240	275.300	14
15	17.293	20.024	23.276	27.152	31.772	37.280	43.842	51.660	60.965	72.035	85.192	100.815	119.347	141.303	167.286	197.997	386.420	15
16	18.639	21.825	25.673	30.324	35.950	42.753	50.980	60.925	72.939	87.442	104.935	126.011	151.377	181.868	218.472	262.356	541.988	16
17	20.012	23.698	28.213	33.750	40.545	48.884	59.118	71.673	87.068	105.931	129.020	157.253	191.735	233.791	285.014	347.309	759.784	17
18	21.412	25.645	30.906	37.450	45.599	55.750	68.394	84.141	103.740	128.117	158.405	195.994	242.585	300.252	371.518	459.449	1064.697	18
19	22.841	27.671	33.760	41.446	51.159	63.440	78.969	98.603	123.414	154.740	194.254	244.033	306.658	385.323	483.973	607.472	1491.576	19
20	24.297	29.778	36.786	45.762	57.275	72.052	91.025	115.380	146.628	186.688	237.989	303.601	387.389	494.213	630.165	802.863	2089.206	20
21	25.783	31.969	39.993	50.423	64.002	81.699	104.768	134.841	174.021	225.026	291.347	377.465	489.110	633.593	820.215	1060.779	2925.889	21
22	27.299	34.248	43.392	55.457	71.403	92.503	120.436	157.415	206.345	271.031	356.443	469.056	617.278	811.999	1067.280	1401.229	4097.245	22
23	28.845	36.618	46.996	60.893	79.543	104.603	138.297	183.601	244.487	326.237	435.861	582.630	778.771	1040.358	1388.464	1850.622	5737.142	23
24	30.422	39.083	50.816	66.765	88.497	118.155	158.659	213.978	289.494	392.484	532.750	723.461	982.251	1332.659	1806.003	2443.821	8032.999	24
25	32.030	41.646	54.865	73.106	98.347	133.334	181.871	249.214	342.603	471.981	650.955	898.092	1238.636	1706.803	2348.803	3226.844	11247.199	25
26	33.671	44.312	59.156	79.954	109.182	150.334	208.333	290.088	405.272	567.377	795.165	1114.634	1561.682	2185.708	3054.444	4260.434	15747.079	26
27	35.344	47.084	63.706	87.351	121.100	169.374	238.499	337.502	479.221	681.853	971.102	1383.146	1968.719	2798.706	3971.778	5624.772	22046.910	27
28	37.051	49.968	68.528	95.339	134.210	190.699	272.889	392.503	586.481	819.223	1185.744	1716.101	2481.586	3583.344	5164.311	7425.699	30366.674	28
29	38.792	52.966	73.640	103.966	148.631	214.583	312.094	456.303	669.447	984.068	1447.608	2128.965	3127.798	4587.680	6714.604	9802.923	43214.343	29
30	40.568	56.085	79.058	113.283	164.494	241.333	356.787	530.312	790.948	1181.882	1767.081	2640.916	3942.026	5873.231	8729.985	12940.859	60501.081	30
35	49.994	73.652	111.435	172.317	271.024	431.663	693.573	1120.713	1816.652	2948.341	4783.645	7750.225	12527.442	20188.966	32422.868	51869.427	325400.279	35
40	60.402	95.026	154.762	259.057	442.593	767.091	1342.025	2360.757	4163.213	7343.858	12936.535	22728.803	39792.982	69377.460	120392.883	207874.272	1750091.741	40

*Payments (or Receipts) at the end of each period.

Table 4
Present Value of Annuity $1 in Arrears*

$$p_n = \frac{1}{r}\left[1 - \frac{1}{(1+r)^n}\right]$$

Periods	2%	4%	6%	8%	10%	12%	14%	16%	18%	20%	22%	24%	26%	28%	30%	32%	40%	Periods
1	0.980	0.962	0.943	0.926	0.909	0.893	0.877	0.862	0.847	0.833	0.820	0.806	0.794	0.781	0.769	0.758	0.714	1
2	1.942	1.886	1.833	1.783	1.736	1.690	1.647	1.605	1.566	1.528	1.492	1.457	1.424	1.392	1.361	1.331	1.224	2
3	2.884	2.775	2.673	2.577	2.487	2.402	2.322	2.246	2.174	2.106	2.042	1.981	1.923	1.868	1.816	1.766	1.589	3
4	3.808	3.630	3.465	3.312	3.170	3.037	2.914	2.798	2.690	2.589	2.494	2.404	2.320	2.241	2.166	2.096	1.849	4
5	4.713	4.452	4.212	3.993	3.791	3.605	3.433	3.274	3.127	2.991	2.864	2.745	2.635	2.532	2.436	2.345	2.035	5
6	5.601	5.242	4.917	4.623	4.355	4.111	3.889	3.685	3.498	3.326	3.167	3.020	2.885	2.759	2.643	2.534	2.168	6
7	6.472	6.002	5.582	5.206	4.868	4.564	4.288	4.039	3.812	3.605	3.416	3.242	3.083	2.937	2.802	2.677	2.263	7
8	7.325	6.733	6.210	5.747	5.335	4.968	4.639	4.344	4.078	3.837	3.619	3.421	3.241	3.076	2.925	2.786	2.331	8
9	8.162	7.435	6.802	6.247	5.759	5.328	4.946	4.607	4.303	4.031	3.786	3.566	3.366	3.184	3.019	2.868	2.379	9
10	8.983	8.111	7.360	6.710	6.145	5.650	5.216	4.833	4.494	4.192	3.923	3.682	3.465	3.269	3.092	2.930	2.414	10
11	9.787	8.760	7.887	7.139	6.495	5.938	5.453	5.029	4.656	4.327	4.035	3.776	3.543	3.335	3.147	2.978	2.438	11
12	10.575	9.385	8.384	7.536	6.814	6.194	5.660	5.197	4.793	4.439	4.127	3.851	3.606	3.387	3.190	3.013	2.456	12
13	11.348	9.986	8.853	7.904	7.103	6.424	5.842	5.342	4.910	4.533	4.203	3.912	3.656	3.427	3.223	3.040	2.469	13
14	12.106	10.563	9.295	8.244	7.367	6.628	6.002	5.468	5.008	4.611	4.265	3.962	3.695	3.459	3.249	3.061	2.478	14
15	12.849	11.118	9.712	8.559	7.606	6.811	6.142	5.575	5.092	4.675	4.315	4.001	3.726	3.483	3.268	3.076	2.484	15
16	13.578	11.652	10.106	8.851	7.824	6.974	6.265	5.668	5.162	4.730	4.357	4.033	3.751	3.503	3.283	3.088	2.489	16
17	14.292	12.166	10.477	9.122	8.022	7.120	6.373	5.749	5.222	4.775	4.391	4.059	3.771	3.518	3.295	3.097	2.492	17
18	14.992	12.659	10.828	9.372	8.201	7.250	6.467	5.818	5.273	4.812	4.419	4.080	3.786	3.529	3.304	3.104	2.494	18
19	15.678	13.134	11.158	9.604	8.365	7.366	6.550	5.877	5.316	4.843	4.442	4.097	3.799	3.539	3.311	3.109	2.496	19
20	16.351	13.590	11.470	9.818	8.514	7.469	6.623	5.929	5.353	4.870	4.460	4.110	3.808	3.546	3.316	3.113	2.497	20
21	17.011	14.029	11.764	10.017	8.649	7.562	6.687	5.973	5.384	4.891	4.476	4.121	3.816	3.551	3.320	3.116	2.498	21
22	17.658	14.451	12.042	10.201	8.772	7.645	6.743	6.011	5.410	4.909	4.488	4.130	3.822	3.556	3.323	3.118	2.498	22
23	18.292	14.857	12.303	10.371	8.883	7.718	6.792	6.044	5.432	4.925	4.499	4.137	3.827	3.559	3.325	3.120	2.499	23
24	18.914	15.247	12.550	10.529	8.985	7.784	6.835	6.073	5.451	4.937	4.507	4.143	3.831	3.562	3.327	3.121	2.499	24
25	19.523	15.622	12.783	10.675	9.077	7.843	6.873	6.097	5.467	4.948	4.514	4.147	3.834	3.564	3.329	3.122	2.499	25
26	20.121	15.983	13.003	10.810	9.161	7.896	6.906	6.118	5.480	4.956	4.520	4.151	3.837	3.566	3.330	3.123	2.500	26
27	20.707	16.330	13.211	10.935	9.237	7.943	6.935	6.136	5.492	4.964	4.524	4.154	3.839	3.567	3.331	3.123	2.500	27
28	21.281	16.663	13.406	11.051	9.307	7.984	6.961	6.152	5.502	4.970	4.528	4.157	3.840	3.568	3.331	3.124	2.500	28
29	21.844	16.984	13.591	11.158	9.370	8.022	6.983	6.166	5.510	4.975	4.531	4.159	3.841	3.569	3.332	3.124	2.500	29
30	22.396	17.292	13.765	11.258	9.427	8.055	7.003	6.177	5.517	4.979	4.534	4.160	3.842	3.569	3.332	3.124	2.500	30
35	24.999	18.665	14.498	11.655	9.644	8.176	7.070	6.215	5.539	4.992	4.541	4.164	3.845	3.571	3.333	3.125	2.500	35
40	27.355	19.793	15.046	11.925	9.779	8.244	7.105	6.233	5.548	4.997	4.544	4.166	3.846	3.571	3.333	3.125	2.500	40

*Payments (or Receipts) at the end of each period.

Glossary

Abnormal spoilage Spoilage that would not arise under efficient operating conditions; it is not inherent in a particular production process.

Absorption costing Also known as *full absorption costing*, this is a method of inventory valuation in which inventory "absorbs" both variable and fixed manufacturing costs as inventoriable costs, but all nonmanufacturing costs are classified as period costs.

Account analysis method Cost accounts are classified in the ledger as variable, fixed, or mixed with respect to the cost driver.

Accounting rate of return Also known as *accrual accounting rate of return (AARR)*, or *return on investment (ROI)*; an accounting measure of income divided by an accounting measure of investment.

Accrual accounting rate of return (AARR) Also known as *accounting rate of return*, or *return on investment (ROI)*; an accounting measure of income divided by an accounting measure of investment.

Activity An event, task, or unit of work with a specified purpose.

Activity-based budgeting (ABB) A strategy to identify and control costs that focuses on the cost of activities necessary to produce and sell products and services.

Activity-based costing (ABC) A refined costing system that focuses on activities as the fundamental cost objects.

Activity-based management (ABM) A cost leadership strategy to eliminate non-value-added activities, which are those activities failing to add value for which customers will pay.

Activity cost driver In activity-based costing (ABC) systems, these are cost allocation bases.

Activity cost pool The dollar value of the cost of activities at a specified level.

Activity cost rate The activity cost pool divided by the total quantity consumed of the activity cost driver.

Activity level The cost object that specifies the scope of changes in cost, which may cause a change in the cost of single units, batches, and entire products.

Actual cost Cost incurred (a historical or past cost), as distinguished from a budgeted or forecasted cost.

Actual costing Tracing direct costs to each job by multiplying each actual unit direct cost rate by the quantity of the direct input used.

Actual indirect cost allocation rate The average cost per unit of shared resources used by all types of jobs calculated by dividing the actual MOH cost pool by the actual total quantity of the cost allocation base.

Adjacencies Opportunities to expand to markets related to the core business.

Adjusted allocation rate approach This approach restates all overhead entries in the general ledger and subsidiary ledgers using actual cost rates rather than budgeted cost rates.

Adjusted cost base (ACB) The cost of a property plus any expenses to acquire it.

Advance transfer price arrangement (APA) A substitute for dispute resolution wherein the company and the tax authority can cooperate to prospectively agree on a transfer price method.

Agility The ability for a service company to excel simultaneously in quality, delivery time, customization, and cost in a coordinated way.

Allowable cost A cost that the contract parties agree to include in the costs to be reimbursed.

Appraisal costs Costs incurred to detect which of the individual units of products do not conform to specifications.

Arm's-length principle A transfer price should be the same as it would be if the two subunits were independent companies.

Arm's-length transactions Transactions between a corporate subunit and a nonrelated party.

Artificial costs Also called *complete reciprocated costs*; the actual costs incurred by a support department plus a part of the costs of the other support departments that provide service to it.

Autocorrelation A type of systematic dependence that arises when the current value of X depends upon the value of X either immediately prior (lagged) to it or immediately after (leading) it in time.

Autonomy The degree of freedom to make decisions; the greater the freedom, the greater the autonomy.

Average cost Also called a *unit cost*, average cost is calculated by dividing the total prime cost pool by physical units consumed.

Average waiting time The average amount of time that an order will wait in line before it is set up and processed.

Backflush costing A costing system that omits recording some or all journal entries relating to the cycle from purchase of direct materials to the sale of finished goods.

Balanced scorecard (BSC) A document that translates an organization's mission and strategy into a comprehensive set of performance measures that provide the framework for implementing its strategy.

Batch-level costs Resources sacrificed on activities that are related to a group of units.

Belief systems An articulation of the mission, purpose, and core values of a company.

Behavioural considerations Considerations that motivate managers and other employees to aim for the goals of the organization.

Benchmark The best possible performance achieved anywhere in any industry using a similar process.

Benchmarking reports Reports based on the costs of other companies that can be developed for many activities and products.

BEP in revenue See *Breakeven point (BEP), revenue*.

BEP in volume See *Breakeven point (BEP), volume*.

Bill 198 (C-SOX) Canadian corporate governance legislation that accomplishes much the same objectives as the U.S. Sarbanes-Oxley Act (SOX) (see *Sarbanes-Oxley Act (SOX)*).

Board of directors The independent group who hold the external auditors, CEO, CFO, and COO accountable for both the quality of financial information and organizational outcomes.

Book value The original acquisition cost of a long-term asset minus accumulated depreciation.

Bottleneck An operation where the work required to be performed approaches or exceeds the available capacity.

Boundary systems An articulation of standards of behaviour and codes of conduct expected of all employees, especially actions that are off-limits.

Breakeven point (BEP) Quantity of output at which total revenues and total costs are equal; that is, where the operating income is zero.

Breakeven point (BEP), revenue Level of sales in dollars at which total revenues and total costs are equal; that is, where the operating income is zero.

Breakeven point (BEP), volume Level of sales in units at which total revenues and total costs are equal; that is, where the operating income is zero.

Budget A quantitative expression for a set time period of a proposed (future) plan of action by management.

Budget constraints The combination of limitations on non-financial and financial resources within a company's management control.

Budgetary slack The practice of underestimating budgeted revenues (or overestimating budgeted costs) to make budgeted targets easier to achieve.

Budgeted cost Predicted or forecasted cost (future cost) as distinguished from an actual or historical cost.

Budgeted indirect-cost rate For each cost pool, the budgeted annual indirect costs divided by the budgeted annual quantity of the cost-allocation base.

Budgeting cycle The process of budgeting: planning performance, providing a frame of reference, investigating variations from plans, and adjusting plans as necessary.

Business function costs The sum of all the costs (variable costs and fixed costs) in a particular business function in the value chain.

Byproducts A product that has a low sales value compared with the sales value of the main or joint product(s).

Capacity The quantity of outputs that can be produced from long-term resources available to the company.

Capacity cost The cost of maintaining a certain plant capacity—a fixed overhead cost. It is often a cost pool grouping all fixed overhead costs.

Capital budgeting The process of collating information in a familiar pro forma financial accounting format.

Capital intensive companies Companies with a high percentage of fixed costs in their cost structure.

Capital cost allowance (CCA) The legally required income tax counterpart to annual depreciation expense in financial reporting.

Capital gain Arises when the selling price of a capital property exceeds the total ACB plus sales' expenses.

Capital loss Arises when the selling price of a capital property is less than the total ACB plus sales' expenses.

Carrying costs These costs arise when a business holds inventories of goods for sale.

Cash budget A schedule of expected cash receipts and disbursements.

Cash cycle Also known as a *self-liquidating cycle, working capital cycle,* or *operating cycle*; the movement of cash to inventories, to receivables, and back to cash.

Cause-and-effect diagram A diagram that identifies potential causes of failures or defects.

Chief executive officer (CEO) This person is independent of and legally accountable to the board of directors for all organizational outcomes.

Chief financial officer (CFO) Also called the *finance director,* this is the senior officer empowered with overseeing the financial operations of an organization.

Chief operating officer (COO) This person is accountable to the CEO for all operating results.

Coefficient *a* Coefficient *a* represents the fixed cost component in the linear cost function $Y = a + bX$, which is constant and unavoidable even if the value of X is 0. b is the coefficient of the slope, or rate of change in y (or Y) when X changes by 1 unit.

Coefficient of determination r^2 Measures the percentage of variation in an outcome variable explained by one or more predictor variables.

Collusive pricing Companies in an industry conspire in their pricing and output decisions to achieve a price above the competitive price.

Combined-variance analysis Also called *three-variance analysis*; combines variable-cost and fixed-cost variances when reporting overhead cost variances.

Common costs Costs of operating a facility, operation, activity, or like cost object that are shared by two or more users.

Comparable uncontrolled price (CUP) method A transfer price that is analogous to the internal market-based price.

Composite unit A hypothetical unit with weights based on the mix of individual units.

Conference method Develops cost estimates based on analysis and opinions gathered from various departments of an organization.

Confidence level The probability that the conclusion based on the student *t*-statistic is wrong.

Conformance quality The performance of a product or service according to design and production specifications.

Constant A factor that does not vary.

Constant gross margin percentage of NRV method The gross margin (based on the overall gross margin percentage) and separable costs deducted from the final sales value of units produced for each product. The residual amount for each product is its allocation of joint costs.

Constraint (as a limiting factor) A factor or operation that limits production or causes a bottleneck.

Constraint (of an LP problem) In linear programming techniques, a mathematical inequality or equality that must be satisfied by the variables in a mathematical model.

Continuous improvement A strategy whereby a budgeted cost is successively reduced over succeeding time periods.

Contribution statement of comprehensive income Income statement that groups line items by cost-behaviour pattern to highlight the contribution margin.

Contribution margin (CM) Revenues minus all costs of the output (a product or service) that vary with respect to the number of output units.

Contribution margin per unit The difference between selling price and variable cost per unit.

Contribution margin percentage Contribution margin per unit divided by unit selling price, or total contribution margin divided by total revenue.

Contribution margin ratio The contribution margin per unit divided by the selling price per unit. Also called *contribution margin percentage*.

Control Coordinated action that companies take to implement their planning decisions, evaluate actual against expected performance, and provide timely feedback on current results.

Control chart Graphs a time series of successive observations of a particular step, procedure, or operation taken at regular time intervals. In addition to actual results, the expected range of specified results is also presented.

Controllability The degree of authority that a specific manager has over costs, revenues, or other items in question.

Controllable cost Any cost that is primarily subject to the authorization of a specific manager of a specific responsibility centre for a specific time span.

Controller The financial executive primarily responsible for both management accounting and financial accounting.

Conversion costs Any manufacturing costs (may include direct labour) other than direct material costs.

Core (operating) division (department, production department) This core division or department, also called an *operating division*, or, in manufacturing companies, a *production division or department*, adds value that is observable by a customer to a product or service.

Corporate governance Mandatory compliance with existing laws, regulations, and standards.

Corporate social responsibility (CSR) The voluntary integration by companies of social and environmental concerns into their business operation.

Correlation (or *covariance*) Identifies two events that systematically vary together.

Cost Resource sacrificed or forgone to achieve a specific objective.

Cost accounting Measures, analyzes, and reports financial and nonfinancial information relating to the costs of acquiring or using resources in an organization. It provides information for both management accounting and financial accounting.

Cost accumulation The collection (accumulation) of actual cost data in an organized way.

Cost allocation (or *cost application*) A method to attribute or assign relevant indirect costs to each job.

Cost allocation base (or *cost application base*) An input factor that systematically links some proportion of each indirect cost pool to each job or cost object.

Cost allocation rate A unit average cost of an input common to all jobs. It is the result of dividing a cost pool by its cost-allocation base.

Cost application (or *cost allocation*) A method to attribute or assign relevant indirect costs to each job.

Cost application base A synonym for *cost allocation base*.

Cost assignment The multiplication of the cost-allocation rate by the specific quantity of inputs in the denominator that is consumed by the specific job.

Cost–benefit approach Promotes decision making in which the perceived net benefits from spending corporate resources should exceed their perceived expected costs.

Cost centre A responsibility centre for which managers are accountable for costs only, not revenue lost or gained.

Cost cross-subsidization (or *cross-subsidization*) A result that arises when at least one miscosted product results in miscosting at least one other product in the organization.

Cost driver A variable, such as the level of activity or volume, that causally affects costs over a given time span.

Cost function A mathematical description of how a cost changes with changes in the level of an activity relating to that cost.

Cost hierarchy The name given to the management-accounting logic used to separate one indirect cost pool into one of four possible cost pools according to the level at which activities contribute to producing output.

Cost incurrence Costs are incurred when a resource is sacrificed or consumed.

Cost leadership An organization's ability to achieve low costs relative to competitors through productivity and efficiency improvements, elimination of waste, and tight cost control.

Cost management The approaches and activities of managers who undertake both short-run and long-run planning and control decisions to increase value to customers and to achieve organizational goals.

Cost object Anything for which it is desirable to measure the costs.

Cost of capital The required rate of return, which is the minimum acceptable annual rate of return on an investment; also called the *discount rate*, *hurdle rate*, or *opportunity cost of capital*.

Costs of goods manufactured (COGM) Cost of goods brought to completion, whether they were started before or during the current accounting period.

Costs of goods sold (COGS) The accumulation of all costs incurred to manufacture the finished products that have been sold during a specific time period.

Costs of quality (COQ) Costs incurred to prevent or rectify the production of a low-quality product.

Costs of sales (COS) The accumulated purchase costs for merchandise sold by merchandising companies.

Cost-plus method (CPM) A method of determining a transfer price that highlights the effect of the transfer price on the pre-tax income of each subunit.

Cost-plus pricing Pricing in which the gross margin equals a certain percentage of the price.

Cost pools The accumulation of relevant costs from general ledger accounts.

Cost smoothing A costing system that spreads the costs of conversion and inputs uniformly.

Cost tracing The method of assigning direct costs to a distinct cost object.

Cost–volume–profit (CVP) analysis Examines the behaviour of total revenues, total costs, and operating income as changes occur in the output level, selling price, variable costs per unit, or fixed costs; a single revenue driver and a single cost driver are used in this analysis.

Critical value A benchmark value for the student *t*-statistic such that if the calculated value of *t* for the values of the coefficients *a*, and *b* exceed the critical value, then at a specificconfidence level, the values of *a* and *b* are not due to chance.

Cross-sectional data Data that has been systematically collected simultaneously at many different locations.

Cross-subsidization (or *cost cross-subsidization*) The situation that, when a simple average method is used, one output, batch, or product will be undercosted and at least one output, batch, or product will be overcosted.

Cumulative average-time learning model Depicts a relationship such that the cumulative average time per unit declines by a constant percentage each time the cumulative quantity of units produced doubles.

Cumulative eligible capital (CEC) This pool is the balance of the eligible capital property remaining after deducting CECA.

Cumulative eligible capital amount (CECA) The annual CRA deduction permitted on intangible assets, calculated at 7% on a declining-balance basis.

Current cost The cost of purchasing an asset today identical to the one currently held.

Curvilinear cost function Depicts in arithmetic notation a non-linear relationship between consumption of a resource and a cost. When the data points are joined they form a curve.

Cushion Excess capacity.

Customer life-cycle costing Costing that focuses on the external customer's costs to acquire, maintain, and dispose of the product or services.

Customer perspective This perspective identifies the targeted market segments and measures the company's success in these segments.

Customer preference map A graphical analysis with various desirable attributes that customers perceive as adding value to a product on one axis, and ratings of those attributes on the other axis.

Customer profitability analysis The reporting and analysis of customer revenues and customer costs.

Customer-response time The amount of time between when a customer places an order for a product or requests a service and when the product or service is delivered to the customer.

Customer service Providing after-sale support to customers.

Decentralization A strategic response made by organizations that enables individual discretion. Primarily useful to organizations that face great uncertainties in their diverse environments, require detailed local knowledge for performing various jobs, and have few interdependencies among subunits.

Decision model A formal method of making a choice that often involves both quantitative and qualitative analyses.

Degree of operating leverage Contribution margin divided by operating income.

Degrees of freedom, df A way to properly classify a critical value for each sample size.

Delivery time How long it takes to deliver a completed order to a customer.

Denominator-level variance A production-volume or output-level variance equal to the difference between budgeted fixed overhead and the assigned fixed overhead for the actual quantity of outputs.

Dependent variable The cost to be predicted and managed in cost function estimation.

Design of products, services, or processes The detailed planning and engineering of products, services, or processes.

Designed-in costs (or *locked-in costs*) Costs that have not yet been incurred but that will be incurred in the future on the basis of decisions that have already been made.

Diagnostic control systems Measures that help diagnose whether a company is performing to expectations.

Differential approach This approach analyzes only relevant cash flows—those future cash outflows and inflows that differ between alternatives.

Differential cost (or *net relevant cost*) The difference in total cost between two alternatives.

Differential revenue The difference between the total revenue of two or more alternatives.

Direct allocation method This cost allocation method applies each support division's costs directly to the operating divisions.

Direct costing Inaccurately describes the inventory costing (valuation) method we call *variable costing*.

Direct costs Costs related to a particular cost object that can be traced to that object in an economically feasible way.

Direct labour (DL) cost The compensation of all period labour that can be traced to a cost object in an economically feasible way but are *not* part of cost of goods sold.

Direct machine-hour costs The quantity of machine-hours used when a product is manufactured.

Direct manufacturing labour (DML) cost The compensation of all manufacturing labour that can be traced to a cost object (work in process and then finished goods) in an economically feasible way.

Direct materials (DM) cost Acquisition costs of all materials that eventually become part of the cost object (work in process and then finished goods), and that can be traced to the cost object in an economically feasible way.

Direct materials inventory Materials in stock and awaiting use in the manufacturing process.

Direct materials mix variance The difference between two amounts: (1) the budgeted cost for the actual mix of the total quantity of direct materials used, and (2) the budgeted cost of the budgeted mix of the actual total quantity of direct materials used.

Direct materials yield variance The difference between two amounts: (1) the budgeted cost of direct materials based on the actual total quantity of all direct materials inputs used, and (2) the flexible-budget cost of direct materials based on the budgeted total quantity of direct materials inputs for the actual output, holding the budgeted input mix constant.

Direct method (also called the *direct allocation method*) Allocates each support department's costs directly to the operating departments.

Discontinuous cost function Arises when, within the relevant range of production inputs, the graph of total costs with a single resource consumed does not form a straight line with a constant slope (also called *step fixed cost*).

Discount rate Also known as *hurdle rate, (opportunity) cost of capital*, or *required rate of return (RRR)*; the minimum acceptable rate of return on an investment.

Discounted cash flow (DCF) Two methods are net present value (NPV) and internal rate of return (IRR).

Discretionary costs These costs arise from periodic (usually yearly) decisions regarding the maximum amount to be incurred; they have no clearly measurable cause-and-effect relationship between output and resources used.

Distribution Delivering products or services to customers.

Downside risk (also called *upside potential risk/return, cost/benefit*) Used to make resource allocations such that the expected benefits exceed the expected costs.

Downsizing (or *rightsizing*) An integrated approach to configure processes, products, and people to match costs to the activities needed to be performed to operate efficiently and effectively in the present and future.

Downstream cost Costs incurred after production.

Downward demand spiral A progressive reduction in sales and production that leads to an increase in the fixed overhead rate. As sales decrease, the realized quantity in the denominator of any fixed overhead cost rate decreases but the fixed cost pool is constant. Diminishing sales must bear higher costs per unit, which leads to diminishing sales.

Dual pricing Using two separate transfer pricing methods to price each interdivision transaction.

Dual-rate method This method first classifies costs in the cost pool into two pools (typically into a variable-cost pool and a fixed-cost pool), and each pool has a different allocation rate or base.

Dumping A non-Canadian company sells goods in Canada at a price below the market value in the home country or receives a government subsidy and this action materially injures or threatens to materially injure an industry in Canada.

Dysfunctional decision making Also known as *goal-incongruent decision making*, or *suboptimal decision making*; arises when a decision's benefit to one subunit is more than offset by the costs or loss of benefits to the organization as a whole.

Economic order quantity (EOQ) A decision model that calculates the optimal quantity of inventory to order.

Economic plausibility The cost drivers X_i under consideration as predictor variables are actually consumed when the indirect costs are incurred.

Economic substance The financial outcome of the all the different types of business transactions that happened in a specified time period.

Economic value added (EVA) A calculation that substitutes the following numbers in the residual-income calculations: (1) income equal to after-tax operating income, (2) a required rate of return equal to the weighted-average cost of capital, and (3) investment equal to total assets minus current liabilities.

Economies of scale Given a specific fixed cost of capacity, the greater the volume of output in the relevant range, the lower the unitized fixed cost of any one output.

Economies of scope These economies are achieved if a company designs different products that can be produced using the same equipment and plant.

Effectiveness The degree to which a predetermined objective or target is met.

Efficiency The relative amount of inputs used to achieve a given level of output.

Efficiency variance The difference between the actual quantity of input used and the budgeted quantity of input that should have been used multiplied by the budgeted input price.

Effort Exertion toward a goal. Effort goes beyond physical exertion, such as a worker producing at a faster rate, to include all conscientious actions (physical and mental).

Eligible capital expenditure The acquisition cost of an intangible asset.

Eligible capital property 75% of the acquisition cost of an intangible asset.

Engineered costs These costs arise specifically from a clear cause-and-effect relationship between output (or cost driver) and the (direct or indirect) resources used to produce that output.

Enterprise resource planning (ERP) system System that improves internal business process flows of information enabling effective inventory cost control.

Enterprise risk management (ERM) Aligns strategy with risk management and evaluates how management initiatives have improved the overall risk profile of the company.

Equivalent units (EU) Derived amount of output units that (a) takes the quantity of each input (factor of production) in units completed and in incomplete units of work in process and (b) converts the quantity of input into the amount of completed output units that could be produced with that quantity of input.

Estimated net realizable value (NRV) method A method that allocates joint costs on the basis of the *relative estimated net realizable value* (expected final sales value in the ordinary course of business minus the expected separable costs of production and marketing of the total production of the period).

Ethical guidelines Guidelines that help members of a profession reason through an appropriate response to an ethical issue.

Ethics Agreed-upon standards of honesty and fairness that apply to everyone in all their dealings with one another.

Excess present value index (or *profitability index*) The total present value of future net cash inflows of a project divided by the total present value of the net initial investment.

Expected monetary value The sum of the weighted outcomes as measured in monetary terms.

Expected value The sum of multiplying each cash inflow, a_i, by the probability or $\sum_{a=1}^{i} E(a) = \sum (p_i) \times a_i$.

Experience curve A cost function that shows how full product costs per unit (including manufacturing, marketing, distribution, and so on) decrease as total quantity produced increases.

Explanatory power A change in the quantity of an activity cost driver will explain the change in cost of a distinct type of output.

External failure costs Costs incurred to detect a nonconforming product after it is shipped to customers.

Facility-sustaining costs The cost of activities that cannot be traced to individual products or services but support the organization as a whole.

Favourable (F) variance A favourable variance results when actual operating income exceeds the budgeted amount.

Finance director (or *chief financial officer*) The senior officer empowered with overseeing the financial operations of an organization.

Financial accounting Measures and records business transactions and provides financial statements that are based on generally accepted accounting principles. It focuses on reporting to external parties such as investors and banks.

Financial budgets That part of the master budget that comprises the capital budget, cash budget, budgeted balance sheet, and budgeted statement of cash flows.

Financial perspective This perspective highlights achievement of financially strategic goals.

Fineness A characteristic of reliable information that enables users of that information to better predict how one factor will change with a change in another factor.

Finished goods inventory Unsold finished goods.

First-in, first-out (FIFO) process-costing method A method of process costing that assigns the cost of the previous accounting period's equivalent units in beginning work-in-process inventory to the first units completed and transferred out of the process, and assigns the cost of equivalent units worked on during the current period first to complete beginning inventory, next to start and complete new units, and finally to units in ending work-in-process inventory.

Fixed cost A cost that remains unchanged in total for a particular time period despite wide changes in the related level of total activity or volume.

Fixed overhead rate variance The difference between the budgeted fixed manufacturing overhead cost minus the actual fixed manufacturing overhead cost.

Flexible budget A budget that is adjusted in accordance with ensuing changes in either actual output or actual revenue and cost drivers.

Flexible-budget variance The difference between the actual (realized) results and the flexible-budget (pro forma) amount for the actual levels of the revenue and cost drivers.

Formal management control system Includes explicit rules, procedures, performance measures, and incentive plans that guide the behaviour of its managers and other employees.

Full absorption costing A method of inventory valuation in which inventory "absorbs" both variable and fixed manufacturing costs as inventoriable costs, but all nonmanufacturing costs are classified as period costs.

Full product costing Recovering all the costs generated by all business functions in the value chain.

Full product costs The sum of all the costs in all the business functions in the value chain (R&D, design, production, marketing, distribution, and customer service).

Goal congruence Exists when individuals and groups work towards the publicly declared organization goals.

Goal-incongruent decision making Also known as *dysfunctional decision making*, or *suboptimal decision making*; arises when a decision's benefit to one subunit is more than offset by the costs or loss of benefits to the organization as a whole.

Goodness of fit The term statisticians use to describe the proportion of change in an outcome variable Y that is explained by a predictor variable X. r^2 is the statistic or measure of goodness of fit.

Gross margin Revenue minus cost of goods sold (or cost of sales); Rev—COGS (or COS).

Gross margin percentage (GM%) The result obtained from dividing the gross margin by the total revenue.

Gross profit percentage See *operating margin percentage*.

Half-year rule Assumes that all net additions are purchased in the middle of the year, and thus only one-half of the stated CCA rate is allowed in the first year.

Heterogeneous cost pool A mix of different types of costs caused by different cost drivers that may contain both variable and fixed costs.

High–low method Uses only the highest and lowest observed values of the common input within the relevant range. The line connecting these two points becomes the estimated cost function.

Human capital The value added by people with skill and experience gained from working together.

Hurdle rate Also known as *discount rate, (opportunity) cost of capital*, or *required rate of return (RRR)*; the minimum acceptable rate of return on an investment.

Hybrid-costing system Costing system that blends characteristics from both job-costing systems and process-costing systems.

Idle time Wages paid for unproductive time caused by lack of orders, machine breakdowns, material shortages, poor scheduling, and the like that interrupt production.

Imputed costs Costs recognized in particular situations that are not regularly recognized by accrual accounting procedures.

Incremental cost allocation method This method ranks the individual cost objects and then uses this ranking to allocate costs among those cost objects.

Incremental cost Also known as *out-of-pocket costs*, or *outlay costs*; additional costs made to obtain either additional resources or sales.

Incremental revenue Any additional total revenue from one alternative.

Incremental revenue-allocation method A method that ranks the individual products in a bundle and then uses this ranking to allocate the bundled revenues to these individual products. The first-ranked product is termed the *primary product* in the bundle.

Incremental unit-time learning model The incremental unit time (the time needed to produce the last unit) declines by a constant percentage each time the cumulative quantity of units produced doubles.

Independent variable The factor used to predict the dependent variable.

Indirect costs Costs related to a particular cost object that cannot be traced to that object in an economically feasible way.

Indirect cost allocation rate The result of dividing an indirect cost pool by the quantity of resources in the indirect cost-allocation base. It is the estimated unit or average cost of indirect inputs.

Industrial engineering method This work measurement begins with an analysis of the relationship between quantities of physical inputs and physical outputs.

Inflation The decline in the general purchasing power of the monetary unit.

Informal management control system Includes shared values, loyalties, and mutual commitments among members of the organization; company culture; and the unwritten norms about acceptable behaviour for managers and other employees.

Infrastructure costs These costs arise from having property, plant, and equipment and a functioning organization.

Input-efficiency variance The difference between the actual quantity of input used and the budgeted quantity of input that should have been used multiplied by the budgeted input price.

Input mix The determination of the *standard* combination and proportion of very similar direct material inputs that may be substituted for one another.

Input price variance The difference between the actual price and the budgeted price multiplied by the actual quantity of input in question.

Insource To produce goods or provide services within the organization.

Inspection point Stage of the production process at which products are examined to determine whether they are acceptable or unacceptable units. In the situation of process costing, spoilage is typically assumed to occur at the stage of completion where inspection takes place.

Intellectual capital This comprises human, structural, and relational capital.

Interactive control systems Formal information systems that managers use to focus organization attention and learning on key strategic issues.

Intermediate products Unfinished products transferred from one subunit to another subunit of the same organization in a multi-stage production process.

Internal-business-process perspective This perspective requires analysis of how to improve internal operations, which implicates the entire value chain of business functions.

Internal failure costs Costs incurred to detect a nonconforming product before it is shipped to customers.

Internal rate of return (IRR) The discount rate at which the present value of expected cash inflows from a project equals the present value of expected cash outflows of the project (also called *time-adjusted rate of return*).

International financial centres Countries with very low income tax rates that have tax treaties with Canada.

Intrinsic motivation The desire to achieve self-satisfaction from good performance regardless of external rewards such as bonuses or promotion.

Inventoriable costs All costs of a product that are considered as assets in the balance sheet when they are incurred and that become cost of goods sold only when the product is sold.

Inventory management The planning, coordinating, and control activities related to the flow of inventory into, through, and from the organization.

Invested capital Total assets plus current assets required to fund a specific project.

Investment centre A responsibility centre for which managers are accountable for investments, revenues, and costs.

Investment decision Also known as *investment program*, or *investment project*; a long-term cash allocation decision.

Investment program Also known as *investment*, or *investment project*; a long-term cash allocation decision.

Investment project Also known as *investment*, or *investment program*; a long-term cash allocation decision.

Job A distinct output unit or set of units.

Job-cost record (or *job-cost sheet*) The document where the costs for a job are recorded and accumulated. Jobs usually require some type of direct materials input.

Job-cost sheet See *job-cost record.*

Job-costing system A system where costs are assigned to a distinct unit, or set of units, of a product or service called a job.

Joint costs The costs of a production process that yields multiple main products simultaneously.

Joint products Products that have relatively high sales value but are not separately identifiable as individual products until the splitoff point.

Just-in-time (JIT) production (or *lean production*) A demand-pull system in which each component in a production line is produced immediately as the next step in the production line needs the component.

Just-in-time (JIT) purchasing A strategy to purchase goods or materials such that a delivery immediately precedes demand or use.

Kaizen budgeting Budgeting to implement a strategy of systematic elimination of waste in every business process.

Key performance factor Interdependent BSC factors most relevant to implementing a strategy successfully. Also called *key success factors (KSF)*.

Key success factors Strategic factors that require close attention and control to assure an organization will survive and thrive.

Labour intensive Labour costs are a significant proportion of total costs.

Labour-time sheet A source document recording the type of labour, quantity of time, unit labour rate, and total cost of labour for each job.

Lagged relationship The cost driver activity occurred the time period $(t-1)$ before the costs were recorded in the cost pool.

Leading relationship Costs were prepaid or incurred the time period before the cost driver activity occurred in the time period $(t+1)$.

Lean accounting A costing method that supports creating value for customers by costing the value streams, as distinguished from individual products or departments, thereby eliminating waste in the accounting process.

Lean production (or *JIT production*) A demand-pull system in which each component in a production line is produced immediately as the next step in the production line needs the component.

Learning Arises from examining actual performance and systematically exploring how to make better informed predictions, decisions, and plans in the future.

Learning and growth perspective A field of study on the identification, development, retention, and valuation of intellectual capital, which comprises human, structural, and relational capital.

Learning curve A curvilinear mathematical production function that shows how the ratio of quantity produced increases at a faster rate than the rate at which the time spent in activities of production decreases (Q_t output $÷ Q_t$ DLH).

Life-cycle budgeting A form of budgeting that requires that managers estimate full product costs across the entire value chain of business functions.

Life-cycle costing This process tracks and accumulates the actual costs attributable to each product from start to finish.

Life-cycle pricing Cradle-to-grave pricing that includes the environmental costs of production, reclamation, recycling, and reuse of materials.

Line management Managers (for example, in production, marketing, or distribution) who are directly responsible for attaining the goals of the organization.

Linear cost function Can be depicted on a graph as a straight line of the equation $y = a + bX$.

Linear programming An *optimization technique* used to maximize total contribution margin (the objective function) given multiple constraints.

Locked-in costs (or *designed-in costs*) Costs that have not yet been incurred but that will be incurred in the future on the basis of decisions that have already been made.

Main product One product with a high sales value relative to the other products that a single process yields.

Make/buy decision The decision whether to insource or outsource a business service or product.

Malus The clawback of previously awarded compensation from an executive because of poor performance.

Management accountants Accountants who measure, analyze, and report financial and nonfinancial information to internal managers.

Management accounting Measures, analyzes, and reports financial and nonfinancial information that helps managers make decisions to fulfill the goals of an organization. It focuses on internal reporting.

Management accounting control system (MACS) A system that provides relevant information as a basis for assurance of effective control.

Management by exception The practice of focusing management attention on areas not operating as expected (such as a cost overrun on a project) and giving less attention to areas operating as expected.

Management control system A means of gathering and using information to aid and coordinate the planning and control decisions throughout an organization and to guide the behaviour of its managers and other employees.

Management information system (MIS) Sometimes called a data warehouse, these databases consist of small, detailed bits of information that can be used for several purposes.

Manufacturing cells A grouping of all the different types of equipment used to make a given product.

Manufacturing cycle efficiency (MCE) The ratio of value-added manufacturing cycle time divided by the total manufacturing cycle time.

Manufacturing cycle time The sum of waiting time plus production cycle time.

Manufacturing lead time The sum of waiting time plus manufacturing time for the order.

Manufacturing overhead (MOH) See *indirect costs*.

Manufacturing overhead allocated The amount of manufacturing overhead costs allocated to distinct types of jobs based on the budgeted rate multiplied by the actual quantity of the allocation base used. Also called *manufacturing overhead applied*.

Manufacturing overhead applied See *manufacturing overhead allocated*.

Manufacturing-sector companies Companies that purchase materials and components and convert them into various finished goods.

Margin of safety The excess of forecasted or budgeted revenues over the breakeven revenues.

Marginal income tax rate The tax rate paid on additional amounts of pretax income.

Market-share variance The difference between two amounts: (1) the budgeted amount based on actual market size in units, *actual market share*, and budgeted contribution margin per composite unit for the budgeted mix, and (2) the budgeted amount based on actual market size in units, *budgeted market share*, and budgeted contribution margin per composite unit for the budgeted mix.

Market-size contribution margin variance The difference between two amounts: (1) the budgeted amount based on *actual market size in units*, budgeted market share, and budgeted contribution margin per composite unit for budgeted mix, and (2) the static budget amount based on the *budgeted market size in units*, budgeted market share, and budgeted contribution margin per composite unit for budgeted mix.

Marketing Promoting and selling products or services to customers or prospective customers.

Master budget Summarizes the financial projections of all the organization's individual schedules and subunit budgets required to produce an operating budget.

Master-budget capacity The level of output that will satisfy customer demand for a single budget cycle and complies with Canada Revenue Agency (CRA) for tax purposes.

Materials requirements planning (MRP) A demand push-through system that manufactures finished goods for inventory on the basis of demand forecasts.

Materials-requisition record A source document recording the job for which materials are needed.

Matrix A way of succinctly communicating relevant information in rows and columns.

Merchandising-sector companies Companies that purchase and then sell tangible products without changing their basic form.

Mix variance A measurement of the variance of actual from expected input mix.

Mixed cost A cost pool that comprises both variable and fixed costs.

Moral hazard Describes contexts in which, once risk is shared, the individual fails to make as much effort to avoid harm as when risk was not shared.

Motivation The desire to attain a selected goal (the goal-congruence aspect) combined with the resulting drive or pursuit towards that goal (the effort aspect).

Multicollinearity When two or more predictor variables are highly correlated with each other.

Multiple regression The technique used to measure the strength of relationships among at least two predictor variables and the outcome variable.

Net addition Arises when the purchase price of new equipment exceeds proceeds of disposition of the old equipment.

Net income margin (or *net profit margin*) An alternative technical term for *net* income.

Net income margin percentage Net income divided by revenue.

Net present value (NPV) A method that calculates the expected net monetary gain or loss from a project by discounting all expected future cash inflows and outflows to the present point in time, using the required rate of return.

Net relevant cost (or *differential cost*) The difference in total cost between two alternatives.

Nominal approach An internally consistent approach to incorporating inflation that predicts cash inflows and outflows in nominal (or, stated) monetary units *and* uses a nominal rate as the required rate of return.

Nominal rate of return The rate of return required to cover investment risk and the anticipated decline, due to inflation, in the general purchasing power of the cash that the investment generates.

Nonfinancial budgets Budgets that report on both the timing and quantity of resources required to achieve predicted financial results.

Nonlinear cost function Arises when, within the relevant range of production inputs, the graph of total costs with a single cost driver does not form a straight line.

Non-productive idle capacity A capacity level that incorporates downtime for setups.

Non-value-added activities Activities that fail to contribute to the customer's value proposition.

Non-value-added cost A cost that, if eliminated, would not reduce the value customers obtain from using the product or service.

Normal capacity The level of output that will satisfy average customer demand over a specified time period and complies with GAAP.

Normal costing The use of standard or predetermined or budgeted indirect cost-allocation rates to assign overhead costs but actual direct cost rates to assign direct costs.

Normal spoilage Spoilage inherent in a particular production process that arises even under efficient operating conditions; often a locked-in cost.

Objective function The objective or goal to be maximized expressed by a linear program.

Off-limits idle capacity A capacity level that accounts for unavoidable operating interruptions such as scheduled maintenance time, shutdowns for holidays, safety inspections, and so on.

On-time performance Situations in which the product or service is actually delivered at the time it is scheduled to be delivered.

Operating budget (or *pro forma net income statement*) When the income statement refers to the future and not the past, it is an *operating budget*, also referred to as a *pro forma net income statement*. The operating budget presents the results of operations in many value-chain business functions prior to financing and taxes.

Operating cycle Also known as a *self-liquidating cycle*, *working capital cycle*, or *cash cycle*; the movement of cash to inventories, to receivables, and back to cash.

Operating (core) division (department, production department) This core division or department, also called in manufacturing companies, a *production division or department*, adds value that is observable by a customer to a product or service.

Operating leverage The effects that different fixed costs (FC) have on changes in operating income (OI) as changes occur in the quantity (Q) available and sold, and hence either the unit or total contribution margin.

Operating margin Total revenues from operations minus total costs from operations (excluding interest and income tax expenses) including inventoriable and period costs.

Operating margin percentage (or *gross profit percentage*) The result obtained from dividing the operating income by the total revenue.

Operation A standardized method or technique that is performed repetitively, often on different materials, resulting in different finished goods. Operations are usually conducted within departments.

Operations The activities that convert various resources into a product or service ready for sale.

Opportunity cost The contribution to income that is forgone (rejected) by not using a limited resource in its next-best alternative use.

Opportunity cost of capital Also known as *discount rate*, *hurdle rate*, or *required rate of return (RRR)*; the minimum acceptable rate of return on an investment.

Optimization technique A way to find the best answer using a mathematical model.

Order delivery time The time it takes distribution to pick up the order from manufacturing and deliver it to the customer.

Order receipt time The time it takes the marketing department to send engineering and other specifications to the manufacturing department.

Ordering costs The costs to prepare and issue a purchase order.

Ordinary least squares (OLS) linear regression A method that computes a formal measure of goodness of fit, called the *coefficient of determination*.

Organic revenue growth Growth obtained without mergers or acquisitions.

Organisation for economic co-operation and development An organization that promotes policies that will improve the economic and social well-being of people around the world.

Organizational structure An arrangement of centres of responsibility within an entity.

Out-of-pocket costs Also known as *incremental costs*, or *outlay costs*; additional costs made to obtain either additional resources or sales.

Outcome variable Any value (*Y*), that increases and decreases after a change in the value of another factor (*X*).

Outcomes Refer to the company and are uncertain if they are possible-but-unidentified consequences from different combinations of actions and events.

Outlay costs Also known as *incremental costs*, or *out-of-pocket costs*; additional costs made to obtain either additional resources or sales.

Outliers Actual observations outside the specified limits that are ordinarily regarded as nonrandom and worth investigating.

Output-level overcosting A unit, batch, or product consumes a relatively low level of input materials and conversion activities but is reported to have a relatively high total cost.

Output-level overhead variance A production-volume or denominator-level variance equal to the difference between budgeted fixed overhead and the assigned fixed overhead for the actual quantity of outputs.

Output-level undercosting A unit, batch, or product consumes a relatively high level of input materials and conversion activities but is reported to have a relatively low total cost.

Output unit-level costs Costs that arise when activities contribute to the cost of each unit of a product or service.

Outsource The process of purchasing goods and services from outside vendors rather than producing the same goods or providing the same services within the organization.

Overallocated indirect costs Also known as *overapplied indirect costs* or *overabsorbed indirect costs*; costs that occur when the allocated amount of indirect costs in an accounting period is greater than the actual (incurred) amount in that period.

Overtime premium The wage rate paid to workers for any labour in excess of their straight-time wage rates.

P-value The probability that, regardless of the statistical significance of the *t*-Stat, we are wrong to conclude that either *a* or *b* are not random.

Padding The practice of underestimating budgeted revenues (or overestimating budgeted costs) to make budgeted targets easier to achieve.

Paralysis by analysis A phrase that describes situations where managers delay making a decision because they decide to wait for more information.

Pareto diagram (frequency chart) This diagram indicates how frequently each type of failure (defect) occurs.

Pareto principle Expresses materiality in a straightforward way—for many events, 80% of effects arise from 20% of the causes.

Partial productivity This most frequently used productivity measure compares the quantity of output produced with the quantity of an individual input used.

Payback method A method that measures the time it will take to recoup, in the form of net cash inflows, the net initial investment in a project.

Peak-load pricing The practice of charging a higher price for the same product or service when demand approaches physical capacity limits.

Peanut-butter costing A costing system that spreads the costs of conversion and inputs uniformly.

Perfectly competitive market Exists when there is a homogeneous product with equivalent buying and selling prices and no individual buyers or sellers can affect those prices by their own actions.

Period costs All costs incurred to generate revenue during a specific time period except the costs of manufacturing accumulated as cost of goods sold.

Perverse incentive Rewards inappropriate management behaviour to present the appearance of cost-effective performance instead of to achieve actual cost-effective performance.

Physical measure method This method allocates joint costs on the basis of their relative proportions at the splitoff point, using a common physical measure such as weight or volume of the total production of each product.

Physical units The units present at any given point in time in a production process.

Planning Selecting organizational goals, predicting results under various ways of achieving those goals, deciding how to attain the desired goals, and communicating the goals and how to attain them to the entire organization.

Practical capacity The amount of output possible if idle time for maintenance, safety inspections, and holidays is scheduled.

Predatory pricing A company sells products at unreasonably low prices that either tend to substantially lessen competition or were designed to have that effect.

Predictor variable(s) *X* Measured first for changes then associated changes are measured for the outcome variable *Y*.

Prevention costs Costs incurred to preclude the production of products that do not conform to specifications.

Previous department costs Costs incurred in previous departments that are carried forward as the product's costs when it moves to a subsequent process in the production cycle (also called *transferred-in costs*).

Price discounting The reduction of selling prices below listed levels to encourage an increase in purchases by customers.

Price discrimination The practice of charging some customers a higher price than is charged to other customers.

Prime costs May include only direct materials, or may include all direct manufacturing costs including direct labour.

Pro forma statements Budgeted, forecasted, or estimated financial statements.

Probability Likelihood an actual or realized value, event or outcome will differ from an expected or budgeted value, event, or outcome.

Process-costing system A system where costs are assigned to masses of similar units produced during a specific time period.

Product Any output that has a positive sales value (or an output used internally that enables an organization to avoid incurring costs).

Product bundle A combination of two or more different products, two or more different services, or products combined with services.

Product cost Sum of the costs assigned to a product for a specific purpose.

Product-cost cross-subsidization When a cost is uniformly spread (broadly averaged) across multiple products without recognizing the amount of resources consumed by each product.

Product differentiation A company's ability to offer products or services perceived by its customers as being superior and unique relative to those of its competitors.

Product life cycle From the viewpoint of the producer, the product life cycle spans the time from initial R&D to the time at which support to customers is withdrawn.

Product overcosting A product consumes a low level of resources but is reported to have a high cost per unit.

Product-sustaining costs (or *service-sustaining costs*) Resources sacrificed on activities undertaken to support product lines, not batches of product lines or units of product.

Product undercosting A product consumes a high level of resources but is reported to have a low cost per unit.

Production Acquiring, coordinating, and assembling resources to produce a product or deliver a service.

Production denominator level (or *production denominator volume*) A measure of capacity. The denominator can be one of four choices.

Production (core, operating) division (department, production department) This core division or department, also called an *operating division*, or, in manufacturing companies, a *production department*, adds value that is observable by a customer to a product or service.

Production-volume variance A denominator-level or output-level variance equal to the difference between budgeted fixed overhead and the assigned fixed overhead for the actual quantity of outputs.

Productivity Measurement of the relationship between actual inputs used (both quantities and costs) and actual outputs produced.

Professional codes of conduct Codes that specify how the professions must behave in professional practice.

Profit centre A responsibility centre for which managers are accountable for revenues and costs and have some authority over others who decide upon key factors affecting both revenue and cost.

Profit split method (PSM) A transactional profit method of setting a transfer price that requires understanding the value added by the functions performed by each related party and the resulting allocation of profit and loss to each subunit.

Profitability index (or *excess present value index*) The total present value of future net cash inflows of a project divided by the total present value of the net initial investment.

Proration An allocation method that uses the percentages of manufacturing overhead allocated based on normal costing to allocate the underallocation or overallocation among the relevant accounts.

Purchase order lead time The time between the placement of an order and its delivery.

Purchasing costs The acquisition costs of goods acquired from suppliers including freight in, the transportation costs.

Qualitative factors Outcomes that cannot be measured in numerical terms.

Quality of design Measures how closely the characteristics of products or services match the needs and wants of customers.

Quantitative factors Outcomes that are measured in numerical terms.

r^2 (or *coefficient of determination r^2*) Measures the percentage of variation in an outcome variable explained by one or more predictor variables.

Rate of return (ROR) The ratio of the predicted cost inflow minus outflow divided by the total outflow for the investment.

Rate variance The difference between the actual price and the budgeted price multiplied by the actual quantity of input in question.

Real approach An internally consistent method of incorporating inflation into the NPV method that predicts cash inflows and outflows in real monetary units *and* uses a real rate as the required rate of return.

Real rate of return The rate of return required to cover only investment risk.

Recapture of CCA If, upon sale of the last of a specific asset class, the calculation results in a negative UCC balance, CRA deems this a *recapture of CCA* and it is taxed as normal business income for the calendar year of the transaction.

Receipt time How long it takes the marketing department to specify to the manufacturing department the exact requirements in the customer's order.

Reciprocal allocation method Allocates costs by explicitly including the mutual services provided among all support departments.

Reciprocated cost This is also known as an artificial cost pool for each support services division. It identifies the output from an intermediate step used in Excel Solver and in Excel matrix calculations to eventually calculate the results of reciprocal cost allocation.

Redesigning The fundamental rethinking and redesign of business processes to achieve improvements in critical measures such as cost, quality, speed, and customer satisfaction. Also called *reengineering*.

Reengineering The fundamental rethinking and redesign of business processes to achieve improvements in critical measures of performance such as cost, quality, service, speed, and customer satisfaction.

Refined costing system A costing system that improves the measure of non-uniformity in the use of an organization's shared resources.

Regression analysis A statistical method that measures the average amount of change in the dependent variable associated with a unit change in one or more independent variables.

Related parties Corporate subunits conducting sales activity between one another.

Relevant costs Forecast future costs that *differ* because of a decision.

Relevant range Band of normal activity level or volume in which there is a specific relationship between the level of activity or volume and the cost in question.

Relevant revenues Forecast future revenues that *differ* because of a decision.

Reorder point The quantity level of the inventory on hand that triggers a new order.

Required rate of return (RRR) Also known as *discount rate*, *hurdle rate*, or *(opportunity) cost of capital*; the minimum acceptable rate of return on an investment.

Resale price method (RPM) This transaction method requires a company calculate the arm's-length resale price.

Research and development (R&D) Generating and experimenting with ideas related to new products, services, or processes.

Residual income (RI) Income minus a required dollar return on the investment.

Residual term Also called the *disturbance* or the *error* term. The residual is calculated as $e = Y - y$ and graphically it appears as the vertical deviation of the actual data point (X, Y) from the estimated data point (X, y).

Responsibility accounting A system that measures the plans (by budgets) and actions (by actual results) of each responsibility centre.

Responsibility centre A part, segment, or subunit of an organization whose manager is accountable for a specified set of activities.

Return on investment (ROI) Also known as *accounting rate of return*, or *accrual accounting rate of return (AARR)*; an accounting measure of income divided by an accounting measure of investment.

Return on sales (ROS) The income-to-revenue (sales) ratio and a frequently used financial performance measure.

Revenue allocation Allocation that occurs when revenues must be assigned to distinct types of sales, but it is not economically feasible to trace the revenue (which would result in a more accurate assignment of revenues to products).

Revenue centre A responsibility centre for which managers are accountable for revenues only, not costs incurred to generate the revenues.

Revenue driver Any factor that affects revenues.

Rework Unacceptable units of production that are subsequently reworked into good units and sold.

Rightsizing (or *downsizing*) An integrated approach to configure processes, products, and people to match costs to the activities needed to be performed to operate efficiently and effectively in the present and future.

Risk The probability that actual future results will differ from budgeted or expected results. Risk is uncertainty quantified as a probability.

Risk aversion Low risk tolerance.

Risk loving High risk tolerance.

Risk neutral The decision maker will feel as much pain at losing a dollar as joy at gaining a dollar.

Risk tolerance The risk of loss measured in percent that a person or team is willing to take.

Risk-weights Probabilities of a particular outcome occurring; that is, the probability of receiving a financial payout from pursuing a specific course of action.

Rolling budget A budget or plan that is always available for a specified future period by adding a month, quarter, or year in the future as the month, quarter, or year just ended is dropped.

Safety stock Inventory held at all times regardless of inventory ordered using EOQ.

Sales mix The relative contribution of quantities of products or services that constitutes total revenues.

Sales-mix contribution margin variance The difference between two amounts: (1) the budgeted amount for the actual sales mix and (2) the budgeted amount for the budgeted sales mix.

Sales-quantity variance The difference between two amounts: (1) the budgeted contribution margin based on actual units sold of all products and the budgeted mix, and (2) the contribution margin in the static budget (which is based on the budgeted units to be sold of all products and the budgeted mix).

Sales value at splitoff method This method allocates joint costs on the basis of the relative sales value at the splitoff point of the total production in the accounting period for each product.

Sales-volume variance The difference between the flexible-budget amount and the static-budget amount; unit selling prices, unit variable costs, and fixed costs are held constant.

Sarbanes-Oxley Act (SOX) A law that took effect in the United States in 2002 and that is the U.S. equivalent of Canada's Bill 198 (C-SOX).

Say on pay A requirement that shareholders vote for or against executive compensation packages.

Scaleability Adding one computer chip to another in a single circuit to increase the speed and power of the device.

Scrap Outputs that have minimal sales value, or, residual material left over when making a product. Some outputs can have a negative revenue when their disposal costs are considered.

Self-liquidating cycle Also known as a working *capital cycle*, *cash cycle*, or *operating cycle*; the movement of cash to inventories, to receivables, and back to cash.

Semivariable cost A cost that has both fixed and variable elements; also called a *mixed cost*.

Sensitivity analysis Uses percentage changes to understand what changes cause the largest effect on profit.

Separable costs Costs incurred beyond the splitoff point that can be assigned to one or more individual products.

Sequential method Often called the *step-down* or *step allocation method*; allows for *partial* recognition of the services rendered by support departments to other support departments.

Sequential tracking Any product costing method in which the accounting system entries occur in the same order as actual purchases and production (also called *synchronous tracking*).

Service department A support department providing services that assist other internal departments in the company.

Service-sector companies Companies that provide services (intangible products)—for example, legal advice or audits—to their customers.

Service-sustaining costs Resources sacrificed on activities undertaken to support service lines, not batches of service lines or units of service.

Shrinkage costs Costs that arise from theft, embezzlement, misclassifications, and clerical errors.

Simple regression An analysis of the relationship between alternative cost drivers X_i, and the total indirect cost pool y, one at a time.

Single-rate method Pools all costs in one cost pool and allocates them to cost objects using the same rate per unit of the single allocation base.

Slope coefficient b Represents the rate of change in total variable cost Y, when the variable cost driver X changes by one unit.

Source document An original record, such as a time sheet for an employee where the hours worked per job are recorded as well as the cost per hour.

Specification analysis The testing of the assumptions of regression analysis.

Splitoff point The juncture in the process when one or more products in a joint cost setting become separately identifiable.

Spoilage Units of production that do not meet the specifications required by customers for good units and that are discarded or sold at reduced prices. Partially completed or fully completed units of output may be spoiled.

Spurious correlation A repetitive but useless coincidence.

Staff management Staff, such as management accountants and human resources managers, who provide advice and assistance to line management.

Stand-alone cost-allocation method Uses information pertaining to each cost object as a separate operating entity to determine the cost-allocation weights.

Stand-alone revenue-allocation method An allocation method that uses product-specific information pertaining to products in the bundle to determine the weights used to allocate the bundled revenues to those individual products. The term *stand-alone* refers to the product as a separate (nonsuite) item.

Standard A carefully determined price, cost, or quantity used for judging performance; frequently refers to amounts estimated from either engineering or time-motion studies. Standard and budgeted amounts are often interchangeable for the purpose of calculating variance.

Standard cost A carefully predetermined cost. Standard costs can relate to units of inputs or units of outputs.

Standard-costing method A predetermined average cost per input or a predetermined average total input cost per unit of output.

Standard error of the estimated coefficient An indicator of how much the estimated value, b, is likely to be affected by random factors. The t-value of the b coefficient measures how large the value of the estimated coefficient is relative to its standard error.

Standard error of the regression The variance of the residuals, used as a measure of the goodness of fit and how well the predicted values match actual observations.

Standard input A carefully predetermined quantity of inputs (such as kilograms of materials or hours of labour time) required for one unit of output.

Static budget A budget that is based on one level of output; it is not adjusted or altered after it is set, regardless of ensuing changes in either actual output or actual revenue and cost drivers.

Step allocation method See *step-down method*.

Step cost function A nonlinear cost function in which the cost remains the same over various ranges of the level of activity, but the cost increases by discrete amounts—that is, increases in steps—as the level of activity increases from one range to the next.

Step-down method Sometimes called the *step allocation method*, or *sequential method*; allows for *partial* recognition of the services rendered by support departments to other support departments.

Step fixed (discontinuous) cost function (or *discontinuous cost function*) Arises when, within the relevant range of production inputs, the graph of total costs with a single resource consumed does not form a straight line with a constant slope.

Step variable cost function A function in which the cost is constant over various ranges of the predictor variable, but the cost increases by discrete amounts (that is, in steps) as the range of the predictor variable changes from one set of values to another set of values.

Stockout costs Costs that occur when a company runs out of an item for which there is customer demand.

Strategic analysis Evaluation of how well an organization has combined its own capabilities with the competitive environment to progress towards its future.

Strategic management Cost management that focuses on strategic issues.

Strategy Specifies how an organization matches its own capabilities with the opportunities in the marketplace to accomplish its objectives.

Strategy map A diagram that describes how an organization creates value by connecting strategic objectives in explicit cause-and-effect relationships with each other in the financial, customer, internal business process, and learning and growth perspectives.

Stretch goals Goals that challenge managers to achieve excellent performance rather than maintain the status quo.

Student's t (or *t-Stat, test of statistical significance*) The ratio of how large the estimated value of the coefficient a or b is relative to its standard error.

Suboptimal decision making Also known as *dysfunctional decision making*, or *goal-incongruent decision making*; arises when a decision's benefit to one subunit is more than offset by the costs or loss of benefits to the organization as a whole.

Substitutable inputs Inputs for which the manufacturer can readily replace one with the other.

Subunit Any part of an organization.

Sullivan principles A set of principles that can be used to compare corporate performance in the area of social responsibility.

Sunk costs Past costs that cannot be changed, no matter what action is taken.

Super-variable costing (or *throughput costing*) A costing method that treats all costs except variable direct materials as period costs that are expensed when they are incurred. Only variable direct materials costs are inventoriable.

Supply chain An integrated system of suppliers, subcontractors, manufacturers, distributors, and retailers collaborating with the purpose of adding value to the output for the customer.

Supply-chain strategy A strategy that transforms external suppliers into internal partners with the buyer.

Support department Departments which do not work directly on a product or service, but are necessary for the organization's operations.

Synchronous tracking Any product costing method in which the accounting system entries occur in the same order as actual purchases and production. Also called *sequential tracking*.

t-Stat (or *Student's t, test of statistical significance*) The ratio of how large the estimated value of the coefficient *a* or *b* is relative to its standard error.

Target cost per unit The estimated long-run cost per unit of a product (or service) that, when sold at the target price, enables the company to achieve the target operating income per unit.

Target margin percentage Determined by management teams based on the target price. Then the costs must be such that the target price minus costs equals the target margin percentage.

Target operating income per unit The operating income that a company wants to earn on each unit of a product (or service) sold.

Target price The estimated price for a product or service that potential customers will pay.

Target pricing Pricing based on what customers are willing to pay.

Target rate of return on investment (ROI) The target operating income that an organization must earn divided by invested capital.

Tax havens Countries that have no tax agreements with Canada and share no information, which will increase the costs of any tax audit for the company.

Tax shield formula An efficient way to calculate the present value of the tax savings as a result of deducting CCA.

Technical considerations Considerations that help managers make wise economic decisions by providing them with costs in the appropriate format and at the preferred frequency.

Terminal loss When the last property in a specific asset class is sold but the calculation results in a positive UCC balance for the asset class, the remainder is called a *terminal loss*.

Test of statistical significance (also known as *t-Stat* or *student's t*) The ratio of how large the estimated value of the coefficient *a* or *b* is relative to its standard error.

Theoretical capacity The amount of output theoretically possible if there were never any delays or interruptions; a 24/7/365 quantity.

Theory of constraints (TOC) This theory describes methods to maximize operating income when faced with some bottleneck and some nonbottleneck operations.

Throughput costing (or *super-variable costing*) A costing method that treats all costs except variable direct materials as period costs that are expensed when they are incurred. Only variable direct materials costs are inventoriable.

Time-adjusted rate of return The discount rate at which the present value of expected cash inflows from a project equals the present value of expected cash outflows of the project (also called *internal rate of return (IRR)*).

Time driver Any factor where change in the factor causes a change in the speed with which an activity is undertaken.

Time-series data The collection of historical data over a long time horizon about the same process.

Time value of money A dollar (or any other monetary unit) received today is worth more than a dollar received at any future time.

Total factor productivity (TFP) The ratio of the quantity of output produced to the costs of all inputs used, where the inputs are combined on the basis of current period prices.

Total-project approach Calculates the present value of *all* future cash inflows and outflows under each alternative separately.

Toxic waste Process byproducts that are potentially harmful and that have negative revenue when the costs of remediation and reclamation are considered.

Traditional costing Also known as *cost smoothing*, or *peanut butter costing*; a costing system that spreads the costs of conversion and inputs uniformly.

Transactional net margin method (TNMM) A transactional profit method of setting a transfer price that is based on the return on assets (ROA) of the corporation as a whole and provides maximum discretion for establishing a transfer price.

Transfer price The price one subunit of an organization charges for a product (tangible or intangible) or service supplied to another subunit of the same organization.

Transferred-in costs Costs incurred in previous departments that are carried forward as the product's costs when it moves to a subsequent process in the production cycle. (Also called *previous department costs.*)

Trigger point A stage in the cycle going from purchase of direct materials (Stage A) to sale of finished goods (Stage D) at which journal entries are made in the accounting system.

Triple bottom line This type of reporting is a formal response to the Global Reporting Initiative (GRI) and augments standard financial reports with specific environmental and social sustainability reports.

Unamortized capital cost (UCC) The balance of a capital expenditure after the allowable CCA has been deducted.

Underallocated indirect costs (or *underapplied indirect costs, underabsorbed indirect costs*) Costs that occur when the allocated amount of indirect costs in an accounting period is less than the actual (incurred) amount in that period.

Unfavourable (U) variance A variance that results in an actual operating income that is less than the budgeted amount.

Unit cost Also called the *average cost*, it is calculated by dividing the total prime cost pool by physical units consumed.

Unused capacity The amount of productive capacity available over and above the productive capacity employed to meet consumer demand in the current period.

Upside potential Also called *downside risk, risk/return, cost/benefit;* used to make resource allocations such that the expected benefits exceed the expected costs.

Upstream costs Costs incurred prior to production.

Usage variance The difference between the actual quantity of input used and the budgeted quantity of input that should have been used multiplied by the budgeted input price.

Value-added activities Activities that contribute directly to the customer's value proposition.

Value-added cost A cost that, if eliminated, would reduce the value customers obtain from using the product or service.

Value analysis With the purpose of reducing costs, an analysis that focuses on the product design stage, where there is the greatest opportunity to change design, materials, and manufacturing processes.

Value chain The sequence of business functions in which customer usefulness is added to products or services.

Value engineering An analysis of the entire value chain of all business functions to determine where non-value-added costs can be eliminated.

Value leadership A strategy of developing and sustaining the unique characteristics of a product or service for which consumers will pay because there is a price inelasticity of demand.

Value proposition A distinct benefit for which customers will pay.

Value streams All the value-added activities needed to design, manufacture, and deliver a given product or product line to customers.

Variable cost A cost that changes in total in proportion to changes in the related level of total activity or volume.

Variable costing A method of inventory valuation in which only *variable manufacturing* costs are included as inventoriable costs. All fixed and all nonmanufacturing costs are classified as period costs expensed during the specific time period they are incurred.

Variable overhead efficiency variance A measure of the efficiency with which the cost allocation base is used.

Variable overhead rate variance The difference between actual variable overhead cost per unit of the cost allocation base and budgeted variable overhead cost per unit of the cost allocation base.

Variance The difference between actual (realized) and budgeted (pro forma) results.

Variance analysis An exceptions-based approach to management.

Vertical integration A company that incorporates as much of the value chain as possible within itself is vertically integrated.

Volume Amount of product or measure of capacity.

Weighted-average cost of capital (WACC) Equals the after-tax average cost of all the long-term funds used.

Weighted-average (WA) process-costing method Method of process costing that assigns the equivalent-unit cost of the work done to date (regardless of the accounting period in which it was done) to equivalent units completed and transferred out of the process and to equivalent units in ending work-in-process inventory.

Work-in-process (WIP) inventory Goods partially worked on but not yet completed. Also called *work in progress*.

Work in progress Goods partially worked on but not yet completed. Also called *work-in-process inventory*.

Work-measurement method This *industrial engineering* method begins with an analysis of the relationship between quantities of physical inputs and physical outputs.

Working capital cycle Also known as a *self-liquidating cycle*, *cash cycle*, or *operating cycle*; the movement of cash to inventories, to receivables, and back to cash.

Yield The proportion of output obtained from a specified quantity of input.

Yield variance A measurement of the variance of the actual from expected yield of outputs obtained from expected quantity of inputs.

Zero-sum game A game in which what one gains the other loses.

Name Index

Note: Page numbers followed by *n* or *e* represent footnotes or exhibits respectively.

Subject Index

Prepare, Apply, and Confirm

- **Enhanced eText**—The Pearson eText gives students access to their textbook anytime, anywhere. In addition to note-taking, highlighting, and bookmarking, the Pearson eText offers interactive and sharing features. Instructors can share their comments or highlights, and students can add their own, creating a tight community of learners in any class.

- Keep students engaged in learning on their own time, while helping them achieve greater conceptual understanding of course material through videos and opportunities to Try It!.

- **Dynamic Study Modules**—With a focus on key topics, these modules work by continuously assessing student performance and activity in real time and, using data and analytics, provide personalized content to reinforce concepts that target each student's particular strengths and weakness.

- **Hallmark Features**—Personalized Learning Aids, like Help Me Solve This, and instant feedback are available for further practice and mastery when students need the help most!